Lecture Notes in Computer Science 16501

Founding Editors

Gerhard Goos
Juris Hartmanis

Editorial Board Members

Elisa Bertino, USA
Wen Gao, China
Bernhard Steffen, Germany
Moti Yung, USA

Advanced Research in Computing and Software Science

Subline of Lecture Notes in Computer Science

Subline Series Editors

Giorgio Ausiello, *University of Rome 'La Sapienza', Italy*
Vladimiro Sassone, *University of Southampton, UK*

Subline Advisory Board

Susanne Albers, *TU Munich, Germany*
Benjamin C. Pierce, *University of Pennsylvania, USA*
Bernhard Steffen, *University of Dortmund, Germany*
Deng Xiaotie, *Peking University, Beijing, China*
Jeannette M. Wing, *Microsoft Research, Redmond, WA, USA*

More information about this series at https://link.springer.com/bookseries/558

Robbert Krebbers

Editor

Programming Languages and Systems

35th European Symposium on Programming, ESOP 2026
Held as Part of the International Joint Conferences
on Theory and Practice of Software, ETAPS 2026
Turin, Italy, April 11–16, 2026
Proceedings, Part I

 Springer

Editor
Robbert Krebbers 
Radboud University Nijmegen
Nijmegen, The Netherlands

ISSN 0302-9743   ISSN 1611-3349 (electronic)
Lecture Notes in Computer Science
ISBN 978-3-032-22719-5   ISBN 978-3-032-22720-1 (eBook)
https://doi.org/10.1007/978-3-032-22720-1

ETAPS Foreword

Welcome to the 29th edition of ETAPS, which took place as an on-site event in Turin, Italy during April 11–16, 2026!

ETAPS 2026 was the 29th instance of the International Joint Conferences on Theory and Practice of Software (ETAPS). ETAPS is an annual federated conference established in 1998, and consists of four main conferences: ESOP, FASE, FoSSaCS, and TACAS. Each conference has its own Program Committee (PC) and its own Steering Committee (SC). The ETAPS main conferences cover various aspects of software systems, ranging from theoretical computer science to foundations of programming languages, tools and algorithms for system analysis, and formal approaches to software engineering. Organizing these conferences in a coherent, highly synchronized conference programme enables researchers to participate in an exciting event, having the possibility to meet many colleagues working in different directions in the field, and to easily attend talks of different conferences. In addition to its four main conferences, ETAPS 2026 also hosted fifteen satellite workshops and two colocated events, which together further attracted many researchers from all over the globe.

ETAPS 2026 received 456 submissions in total, 138 of which were accepted, yielding an overall acceptance rate of 30%. Out of the 138 accepted papers, 16 papers were selected as ETAPS distinguished papers. I thank all the authors of submitted papers for their interest in ETAPS, all the reviewers for their reviewing efforts, the PC members for their contributions, and in particular the PC (co-)chairs for their hard work in running this entire intensive process in a constructive, objective and timely manner. I congratulate all authors of the ETAPS 2026 accepted papers!

ETAPS 2026 featured the unifying invited keynotes by

- Monika Henzinger (Institute of Science and Technology Austria, Austria), delivering a talk about "Guarding Privacy Over Time: Challenges and Solutions in Continuous Data Observation",
- Einar Broch Johnsen (University of Oslo, Norway), discussing "Formal Methods Meet Digital Twins: Challenges and Opportunities".

ETAPS 2026 hosted the invited keynote speakers

- Christel Baier (Technische Universität Dresden, Germany) for FoSSaCS, presenting "Verification of Infinite-horizon Properties of Dynamic Bayesian Networks",
- Guy Van den Broeck (University of California, Los Angeles, USA) for TACAS, introducing "Symbolic Reasoning in the Age of Large Language Models".

The ETAPS 2026 invited tutorials were provided by

- Mieke Massink (CNR-ISTI Pisa, Italy) on "Model Checking in Space with Applications to Medical Image Analysis",
- Leonardo de Moura (Amazon Web Services, USA) surveying "The Lean Programming Language and Theorem Prover".

The ETAPS 2026 programme also featured a lively Ask-Me-Anything session, interactive tool demos, a Diversity, Equity, and Inclusion session, SV-Comp and Test-Comp community building events, and the ETAPS industry day. The goal of the ETAPS industry day is to bring industrial practitioners into the heart of the research community and to catalyze the interaction between industry and academia. The ETAPS 2026 industry day was organized by Giorgio Audrito (University of Turin, Italy), Sean Kauffman (Queen's University, Kingston, Canada), and Nikolai Kosmatov (Thales Research and Technology, Palaiseau, France).

ETAPS 2026 was organized by the Department of Computer Science of the University of Turin, which is the center for coordinating research, teaching, dissemination and technological transfer in computer science in Turin, Italy. The department covers both methodological and application oriented aspects of computer science, and performs research in several interdisciplinary areas. This is reflected in the collaborations with other research centers and companies in many scientific areas and in its participation in national, European and international projects.

ETAPS 2026 was further supported by the following associations and societies: ETAPS e. V. (the ETAPS Association), EATCS (European Association for Theoretical Computer Science), EAPLS (European Association for Programming Languages and Systems), and EASST (European Association of Software Science and Technology).

The ETAPS Steering Committee consists of an Executive Board, and representatives of the individual ETAPS conferences, as well as representatives of EATCS, EAPLS, and EASST. The Executive Board consists of Laura Kovács (TU Wien, chair), Andrzej Wąsowski (IT University of Copenhagen, vice-chair), Thomas Noll (RWTH Aachen, treasurer), Arnd Hartmanns (University of Twente, artifact evaluation coordinator), Barbara König (University of Duisburg-Essen, proceedings coordination), Caterina Urban (Inria, PhD activities), Elizabeth Polgreen (University of Edinburgh, social media), Jan Kofroň (Charles University Prague, organisational support, website), Jan Křetínský (Masaryk University Brno and TU Munich, diversity & inclusion), and Marieke Huisman (University of Twente, blog, awards). Further members of the ETAPS Steering Committee committee are: Robbert Krebbers (Radboud University Nijmegen), Azalea Raad (Imperial College London), Luís Caires (Tecnico ULisboa), Elvira Albert (Universidad Complutense de Madrid), Corina Păsăreanu (Carnegie Mellon University), Erika Ábrahám (RWTH Aachen), Marsha Chechik (University of Toronto), Marie-Christine Jakobs (LMU Munich), Nathalie Bertrand (Inria Rennes), Stefan Milius (Friedrich-Alexander Universität Erlangen-Nürnberg), Alexandra Silva (Cornell University), Joël Ouaknine (MPI-SWS Saarbrücken), Andrzej Murawski (University of Oxford), Sebastian Junges (Radboud University Nijmegen), Guy Katz (The Hebrew University of Jerusalem), Christian Schilling (Aalborg University), Naijun Zhan (Peking University), Joost-Pieter Katoen (RWTH Aachen and University of Twente), Dirk Beyer (LMU Munich), Fabrice Kordon (Sorbonne University Paris), Laure Petrucci (Université Paris 13), Peter Y.A. Ryan (University of Luxembourg), Claudio Menghi (University of Bergamo and McMaster University Hamilton), Mark Lawford (McMaster University Hamilton), Maurice ter Beek (CNR-ISTI Pisa), Ferruccio Damiani (University of Turin), Kim Guldstrand Larsen (Aalborg University), Bernhard Beckert (KIT Karlsruhe), Mattias Ulbrich (KIT Karlsruhe), Reiko Heckel (University of Leicester), Vladimiro Sassone

(University of Southampton), Anton Wijs (Eindhoven University of Technology), and Nikolai Kosmatov (Thales Research and Technology, Palaiseau).

The ETAPS 2026 local organization team consisted of Maurice ter Beek (CNR-ISTI Pisa, general co-chair), Ferruccio Damiani (University of Turin, general co-chair), Barbara Boni (Synesthesia Turin, local organization chair), Vincenzo Ciancia (CNR-ISTI Pisa, satellite events co-chair), Luca Paolini (University of Turin, satellite events co-chair), Maria Tacconi (Synesthesia Turin, satellite events co-chair and publicity co-chair), Francesco Brocero (Synesthesia Turin, web co-chair and volunteers co-chair), José Proença (University of Porto, web co-chair), Gianluca Torta (University of Turin, publicity co-chair and local proceedings co-chair), Lucy James (Synesthesia Turin, sponsor chair), Giovanna Broccia (CNR-ISTI Pisa, local proceedings co-chair), Giorgio Audrito (University of Turin, volunteers co-chair), Riccardo Sieve (UiO Oslo, volunteers co-chair), and Reiner Hähnle (TU Darmstadt, wine chair).

I would like to take this opportunity to thank all authors, keynote speakers, invited tutorial speakers, and attendees. Special thanks goes to the organizers of the ETAPS 2026 satellite workshops and colocated events. ETAPS 2026 is grateful for the generous support of Amazon Web Services, AccessiWay, Camera di Commercio Industria Artigianato e Agricoltura di Torino, the Department of Computer Science of the University of Turin, Springer Nature, and Turismo Torino e provincia Convention Bureau. I thank our general co-chairs Maurice ter Beek (CNR-ISTI Pisa) and Ferruccio Damiani (University of Turin), who made it all happen in Turin, and their local organization team for their enormous efforts to make ETAPS 2026 a fantastic event. I am especially grateful to Barbara Boni, Maria Tacconi, and Lucy James (Synesthesia Turin) for handling the organizational process in a smooth and reliable way. Last but not least, a big thanks to Jan Kofroň for all his help as an ETAPS Fellow and providing online presence support for the ETAPS conferences and the ETAPS Association.

I hope you all enjoyed ETAPS 2026!

April 2026

Laura Kovács
ETAPS SC Chair, President of the ETAPS
Association

Preface

These proceedings volumes contain papers that were presented at the 35th European Symposium on Programming (ESOP 2026), held April 14–16 in Turin, Italy. ESOP is part of the International Joint Conferences on Theory and Practice of Software (ETAPS) and promotes the specification, design, analysis and implementation of programming languages and systems.

In total, these two volumes contain 31 contributed papers and 1 invited paper. Following recent editions of ESOP, ESOP 2026 had three submission categories: research papers, fresh perspectives, and experience reports. Of the 31 papers, these volumes contain 29 research papers and 2 experience reports. For the second time in its history, ESOP had two submission and evaluation rounds. The submission deadline of the first round was in June 2025, while the submission deadline of the second round was in October 2025. The first round attracted 38 submissions, of which 6 (16%) were immediately accepted, 23 (60%) were immediately rejected, and 9 (24%) were invited to submit a revised version in the second round. For submissions that were invited to submit a revision, the program committee proposed concrete suggestions for improvement, and the revised submissions in the second round were reviewed by the same set of reviewers. The second round attracted 65 submissions, of which 9 were revisions from the first round, and 56 were entirely new submissions. Submissions in the second round were either immediately accepted or immediately rejected. Of the revisions submitted to the second round, 7 were accepted (78%) and 2 were rejected (22%). Of the new submissions submitted to the second round, 18 were accepted (32%) and 38 (68%) were rejected. In total, out of 94 unique submissions, 31 were accepted, yielding an acceptance rate of 33%.

Submissions were reviewed in a double-blind fashion, with author identities only revealed to reviewers on definite paper acceptance. Submissions were typically reviewed by 3 program committee members. For some submissions, external reviewers provided their expertise and insights through additional reviews. In total, every submission received at least 3 reviews, and in some cases 4 or 5 reviews. In both submission rounds, authors were allowed to submit an author response before the program committee discussed and selected the papers asynchronously using the HotCRP system. Submissions for which the PC chair had a conflict of interest were kindly handled by Ilya Sergey.

Similar to prior years, ESOP 2026 employed an artifact evaluation process. Of the 31 accepted papers, 17 elected to make their artifacts available on archival websites. The artifact committee awarded the badge "Functional" to 6 of these papers and the badges "Functional and Reusable" to 10 of these papers.

My sincere thanks go to all who worked together for ESOP 2026 and its proceedings. Foremost, I wish to thank the authors, who provided the technical content of the conference. The program committee and external reviewers deserve particular thanks for their efforts in providing detailed reviews and participating in the discussions, and the artifact evaluation committee for reviewing the accompanying artifacts. I thank Michael Sammler as the representative for ESOP among the artifact evaluation committee co-chairs. Finally, I would like to thank the ETAPS steering committee and its chair Laura Kovács, the proceedings coordinator Barbara König, the local proceedings chairs Gianluca Torta and Giovanna Broccia, and the webmaster Jan Kofroň for their assistance in the organization of ESOP as a part of the entire ETAPS meeting. Finally, thanks are due to the members of the ESOP steering committee and, in particular, Luís Caires (SC chair) and Viktor Vafeiadis (PC chair 2025) for their advice and guidance.

April 2026

Robbert Krebbers
ESOP 2026 PC Chair

Organization

Program Committee Chair

Robbert Krebbers — Radboud University Nijmegen, Netherlands

Program Committee

Alasdair Armstrong	University of Cambridge, UK
Aslan Askarov	Aarhus University, Denmark
Mohamed Faouzi Atig	Uppsala University, Sweden
Andrej Bauer	University of Ljubljana, Slovenia
Veronique Benzaken	LMF Université Paris-Saclay, France
Małgorzata Biernacka	University of Wrocław, Poland
Liang-Ting Chen	Academia Sinica, Taiwan
Raphaëlle Crubillé	Aix Marseille Univ, CNRS, LIS, France
Deepak D'Souza	Indian Institute of Science, India
Ankush Das	Boston University, USA
Farzaneh Derakhshan	Illinois Institute of Technology, USA
Emanuele D'Osualdo	University of Konstanz, Germany
Paulo Emílio de Vilhena	Imperial College London, UK
Francesco Gavazzo	University of Padua, Italy
Justin Hsu	Cornell University, USA
Ambrus Kaposi	Eötvös Loránd University, Hungary
Sven Keidel	TU Darmstadt, Germany
Ori Lahav	Tel Aviv University, Israel
Christoph Matheja	University of Oldenburg, Germany and DTU Compute, Denmark
Andreia Mordido	LASIGE, University of Lisbon, Portugal
Christopher Pulte	University of Cambridge, UK
Jorge A. Pérez	University of Groningen, Netherlands
Ryosuke Sato	Tokyo University of Agriculture and Technology, Japan
Ilya Sergey	National University of Singapore, Singapore
Kathrin Stark	Heriot-Watt University, UK
Bernardo Toninho	NOVA FCT and NOVA LINCS, Portugal
Jana Wagemaker	Radboud University Nijmegen, Netherlands
John Wickerson	Imperial College London, UK
Fabio Zanasi	University College London, UK

ESOP/FASE/FoSSaCS Joint Artifact Evaluation Committee Chairs

Michael Sammler	ISTA, Austria
Yannic Noller	Ruhr University Bochum, Germany
Guillermo Alberto Perez	University of Antwerp, Belgium

ESOP/FASE/FoSSaCS Joint Artifact Evaluation Committee

Mohammad Afzal	TCS Research and IIT Bombay, India
Flavio Ascari	University of Konstanz, Germany
Aren A. Babikian	University of Toronto, Canada
Alexander Bai	New York University, USA
David Boetius	University of Konstanz, Germany
Michaël Cadilhac	DePaul University, USA
Ronaldo Canizales	Colorado State University, USA
William Eiers	Stevens Institute of Technology, USA
Kasper Engelen	University of Antwerp, Belgium
Máté Földiák	Linköping University, Sweden
Alvin George	IISc Bangalore, India
Holly Hendry	University of York, UK
Martin Kristjansen	Aalborg University, Denmark
Andrea Laretto	Tallinn University of Technology, Estonia
Megan Maton	University of Sheffield, UK
Logan Murphy	University of Toronto, Canada
Olek Osikowicz	University of Sheffield, UK
Jan-Paul Ramos-Dávila	Boston University, USA
Wojciech Rozowski	Lean FRO, USA
Chia Sabah	University of Leicester, UK
William Scarbro	Colorado State University, USA
Hitarth Singh	Hong Kong University of Science and Technology, Hong Kong
Steffan Sølvsten	Aarhus University, Denmark
Stephan Spengler	Uppsala University, Sweden
Gaëtan Staquet	École Centrale Nantes, France
Abhishek U	IISc, India
Alexandra van der Spuy	Stellenbosch University, South Africa
Szumi Xie	Eötvös Loránd University, Hungary
Ekaterina Zhuchko	Tallinn University of Technology, Estonia

ESOP Steering Committee

Luís Caires (Chair)	Instituto Superior Técnico, Universidade de Lisboa, Portugal
Robbert Krebbers	Radboud University Nijmegen, Netherlands
Brigitte Pientka	McGill University, Canada
Azalea Raad	Imperial College London, UK
Viktor Vafeiadis	MPI-SWS, Germany
Stephanie Weirich	University of Pennsylvania, USA
Nobuko Yoshida	University of Oxford, UK

Additional Reviewers

Flavio Ascari
Lara Bargmann
Albert Benvenistea
Elie Bermot
Victor Blanchi
Richard Bubel
Tej Chajed
James Cheney
Claudio Sacerdoti Coen
Pierre-Evariste Dagand
Ryan Doenges
Vorashil Farzaliyev
Roberto Giacobazzi
Peter Habermehl
Jan Hoffmann
Johannes Hostert
Jules Jacobs
Swen Jacobs
Matan Kalp
Maja H. Kirkeby
Aleks Kissinger
Quang Loc Le
Leo Lobski
Raz Lotan

Kenji Maillard
Vaibhav Mehta
Magnus Myreen
Max New
Jennifer Paykin
Daniel Pelsmaeker
Roberto Pettinau
Frank Pfenning
Robin Piedeleu
Nicolò Pizzo
Francois Pottier
Damien Pous
Enguerrand Prebet
Ralph Sarkis
Rahul Sharma
Stephen F. Siegel
Zachary Tatlock
Mateo Torres-Ruiz
David Trabish
Renaud Vilmart
Uwe Waldmann
Mingsheng Ying
Vladimir Zamdzhiev

Contents

Formal Methods meet Digital Twins: Challenges and Opportunities 1
Einar Broch Johnsen, Eduard Kamburjan, Andrea Pferscher,
and Silvia Lizeth Tapia Tarifa

Contextual Metaprogramming for Session Types 13
Pedro Ângelo, Atsushi Igarashi, Yuito Murase, and Vasco T. Vasconcelos

Specifying and Verifying RDMA Synchronisation 42
Guillaume Ambal, Max Stupple, Brijesh Dongol, and Azalea Raad

In Cantor Space No One Can Hear You Stream 72
Martin Baillon, Assia Mahboubi, and Pierre-Marie Pédrot

Deciding not to Decide: Sound and Complete Effect Inference
in the Presence of Higher-Rank Polymorphism 104
Patrycja Balik, Szymon Jędras, and Piotr Polesiuk

Recursive Logical Relations for Intuitionistic Linear Logic Session Types 135
Stephanie Balzer, Farzaneh Derakhshan, Robert Harper, and Yue Yao

Code Generation via Meta-programming in Dependently Typed Proof
Assistants 166
Mathis Bouverot-Dupuis and Yannick Forster

Linear Effects, Exceptions, and Resource Safety: A Curry-Howard
Correspondence for Destructors 190
Sidney Congard, Guillaume Munch-Maccagnoni, and Rémi Douence

Rely-Guarantee Is Coinductive – A Proof-Centered Investigation
of Inductively Approximated Coinduction – 220
John Derrick, Chelsea Edmonds, Andrei Popescu, and Jamie Wright

Reduction for Structured Concurrent Programs 252
Namratha Gangamreddypalli, Constantin Enea, and Shaz Qadeer

Specification-Driven Generation of Summaries for Symbolic Execution 283
Rafael Gonçalves, Frederico Ramos, Pedro Adão,
and José Fragoso Santos

Generating Functions Meet Occupation Measures: Invariant Synthesis
for Probabilistic Loops 314
  *Darion Haase, Kevin Batz, Adrian Gallus, Benjamin Lucien Kaminski,
  Joost-Pieter Katoen, Lutz Klinkenberg, and Tobias Winkler*

A Program Logic for Under-approximating Worst-case Resource Usage 344
  Ziyue Jin and Di Wang

Causal-Broadcast Memory 373
  Amir Karniel and Ori Lahav

A Category-Theoretic Framework for Dependent Effect Systems 401
  Satoshi Kura, Marco Gaboardi, Taro Sekiyama, and Hiroshi Unno

Validating Quantum State Preparation Programs 432
  *Liyi Li, Anshu Sharma, Zoukarneini Difaizi Tagba, Sean Frett,
  and Alex Potanin*

The Memorist Tale: Every Thunk Every Cost All At Once 463
  Xing Li, Yao Li, Peter Schachte, and Christine Rizkallah

Author Index 493

Formal Methods meet Digital Twins: Challenges and Opportunities

Einar Broch Johnsen[1], Eduard Kamburjan[2,1],
Andrea Pferscher[1], and Silvia Lizeth Tapia Tarifa[1]

[1] University of Oslo, Oslo, Norway
`{einarj,andreapf,sltarifa}@uio.no`
[2] IT University of Copenhagen, Copenhagen, Denmark
`eduard.kamburjan@itu.dk`

Abstract. The advent of digital twins gives us an opportunity to reflect on the relationship between models and modelled systems. We may think of digital twins not merely as models, but as systems for model management, integration, and composition. In fact, digital twins are model-centric systems that maintain a two-way connection between an ecosystem of models and the modelled system, realised through streams of observations and streams of interventions. This connection introduces agility as the digital twin can typically both adapt its models on-the-fly to changes in a modelled system and influence the modelled system's behaviour. In this paper, we discuss key concepts of digital twins from a formal methods perspective and suggest opportunities and challenges for formal methods in digital twin systems. In particular, we consider how formal techniques can be integral to the digital twin, both in terms of digital twin technology and in terms of digital twin models, as well as notions of correctness for the digital twin itself.

1   Introduction

Today, digital twins (DTs) are subject to a fair amount of hype[1] for their potential to improve efficiency and mitigate failure in a broad range of systems, during system operation. DTs are a key concept in Industry 4.0 [10,54]; applications of DTs are found across engineering disciplines, based on the idea of creating an increasingly accurate "virtual replica" of a cyber-physical system to predict behaviour by means of sophisticated simulation techniques and a closed feedback loop to the actual system (e.g., [15]). DTs are now increasingly found in application domains beyond engineering, including medicine [42], healthcare [55], energy [44], manufacturing [6,40], transportation [11], and software systems [1].

DTs are useful to explain unexpected incidents, for short-term decision-making and for long-term strategic planning. To this aim, a DT can have the ability to deliver different analytical services, including *historical* analysis (what

---

[1] https://www.weforum.org/stories/2024/06/digital-twins-and-industrial-clusters-are-about-to-change-the-face-of-manufacturing/

© The Author(s) 2026
R. Krebbers (Ed.): ESOP 2026, LNCS 16501, pp. 1–12, 2026.
https://doi.org/10.1007/978-3-032-22720-1_1

happened in the past), *descriptive* analysis (what just happened), *predictive* analysis (what do we expect to happen next), *prescriptive/proactive* analysis (strategic planning, what can we do to change the expected behaviour), and *reactive* analysis (provide an immediate response for what to do now).

DTs realise these services by enabling a target system and its models to interact at runtime; e.g., models in the DT and observations from the real system work together to drive analytical services. Conceptually, DTs represent a shift from model-based to model-centric system design, and hence from a correctness-preserving perspective on system construction to a correctness-adapting perspective on system maintenance. The models and our ability to automatically analyse them, are integral to the target system, rather than a means to develop this target system. Consequently, the lifetime of a DT matches the lifetime of the actual system: we may need the ability to automatically adapt our models when these need better alignment with observed data from the actual system, and to analyse new or adapted models on-the-fly.

Formal methods are different techniques to mathematically specify and verify system behaviour, in which systems are modelled as mathematically defined structures [5, 60, 61]; these methods are interesting for the strength of the guarantees they can provide, allowing the presence (or absence) of a particular behaviour to be mathematically proven for the given model. Thus, formal methods are complementary to testing- or simulation-based analysis techniques [20]. Formal methods can be applied at different stages of system design. In terms of industrial applications, formal methods have traditionally been used for safety-critical applications, but there is an increasing uptake in other domains [5, 16].

In this paper, we argue that DTs may be of significant interest to developers of formal methods and that DTs give us an opportunity to revisit how we think formal models may be developed and used. We consider two perspectives on how formal methods and DTs can come together: how formal methods can be used as components in DTs (Sect. 3) and how formal methods can be used to analyse DTs (Sect. 4). For each perspective, we outline some open research challenges related to DTs and formal methods in a broad sense, and hint at how we have started to approach these challenges in our own work.

2   What are Digital Twins?

DTs are virtual information constructs that capture the structure, context, and behaviour of the system they are twinning, are dynamically updated with data from the actual system, have predictive capability, and inform decisions that realise value, according to a recent definition by the National Academy for Science, Engineering and Medicine (NASEM) [46]. This notion of a DT puts less weight on bidirectionality (i.e., the reactive control of a cyber-physical system) and emphasises the tight integration between a model and the modelled system to provide services for, e.g., analysis, diagnosis, prediction, fault detection and strategic planning [43].

An essential aspect of a DT is its *life cycle*: DTs are intended to be long-lived systems. Often, the DT predates the target system as a design or construction artefact that is later transformed into an operational tool, and may persist also after the actual system has ceased to operate. It closely mimics the life cycle of the actual system; specifically, this means that it needs to adapt its models to changes in its environment, which can include both the actual system and the requirements to the actual system. In fact, the user requirements to the DT may also change over the lifetime of the DT [43]; i.e., the *purpose* of the DT is likely to evolve over time. This way, the DT becomes a self-adaptive system for advanced model management, generating and adjusting its models and determining the analyses to be performed using these models on-the-fly.

A self-adaptive system typically consists of a managed and a managing layer, often organised as a MAPE-K feedback loop [58], in which *m*onitor-, *a*nalyse-, *p*lan- and *e*xecute-components interact with a *k*nowledge base. The knowledge base is often used to provide a context for the MAPE-components, capturing, e.g., historical data, domain knowledge and requirements. While the DT can be seen as a managing layer for its target system, self-adaptation within the DT can be addressed by adding an additional layer of self-adaptation to capture how the twin itself evolves over time [29], see Fig. 1. Remark that the knowledge base may include so-called *runtime models* [9] that blur the distinction between software development and execution [4], enabling introspection in support of the self-adaptation process.

The purpose of *behavioural self-adaptation* in Layer 1 is to control how the current models of the DT capture the behaviour of the actual system (thus addressing the so-called real-to-sim or reality gap, e.g. [7, 56, 62]) and make adjustments to the actual system if needed. In the feedback loop of Layer 1, the monitor collects data from the sensors connected to the actual system, the analyser assesses whether these observations of the actual system comply with requirements, the planner determines whether changes to the actual system are needed and the executor manipulates the actuators to influence the behaviour of the actual system.

The purpose of *structural self-adaptation* in Layer 2 is to control how the DT captures the structure and context of the actual system. In the feedback loop of Layer 2, the analyser determines that the requirements to the actual system have changed, that the targeted behaviour is different and that the means to achieve this behaviour are no longer the same, leading to changes in the components of Layer 1 of the DT, including its models.

3   Formal Methods in Digital Twins

Let us first consider how formal methods can be integrated in the analysis services of the DT. One important aspect of this integration, is that we are dealing with an *open environment*: we do not assume that the models perfectly reflect the actual system. Instead, analysis inside the DT is data-driven; i.e., the model configuration at a given point in time depends on the stream of observations

4   E. B. Johnsen et al.

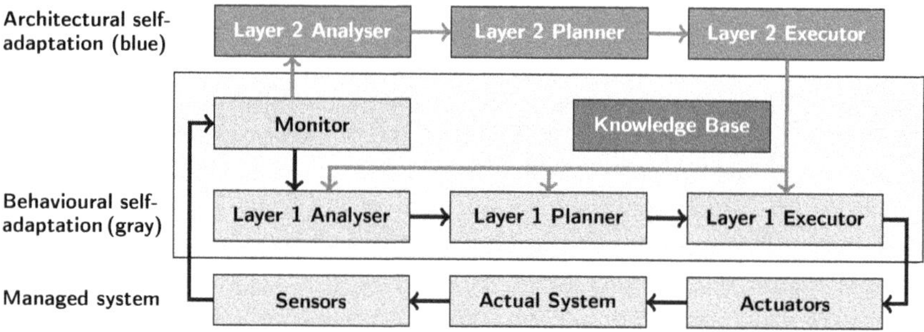

Fig. 1. A two-layered self-adaptive DT architecture with MAPE-K feedback loops for behavioural (Layer 1, gray) and architectural (Layer 2, blue) self-adaptation.

that the twin receives from the actual system. Hence, our methods need to support the dynamic configuration and composition of models reflecting the current structure and observed state of the actual system. The DT needs a strategy for how that should be done, depending on the analysis service it delivers.

Challenge 1 *How can formal models be dynamically configured and composed?*

We can understand a DT as a model management system that, driven by streams of observations of the actual system, uses contextual information to decide how to configure its models to deliver analysis services. We can build on the experiences from model management systems for *consistency* [52], and consider formal methods from this perspective as well. If we assume that the contextual information is captured in its knowledge base, we can see the DT as a model orchestrator that can compose different models. Simulation models can be orchestrated using co-simulation algorithms [17], and dynamically deployed [19]. Similar workflows may be conceived to configure and compose heterogeneous formal models, and their corresponding analyses. For example, BedreFlyt [35,51] is a DT for hospital ward planning that uses incoming patient data as its stream of observations from the ward and information about treatments stored in the knowledge base to dynamically configure and deploy an actor-model in ABS [28], which outputs a stream of resource requirements reflecting day-to-day bed bay needs for the patients in the ward. These are, together with constraints on bed bay capacity in the ward derived from the knowledge base, used to dynamically configure a stream of optimisation problems, which are given to Z3 [8]. The twin's output is a stream of bed bay allocations that can be given to the ward's admitting nurse. This way, the twin combines several formal methods.

Challenge 2 *How can formal methods help in automatically adapting digital twin models to life cycle changes in the target system?*

We all know how challenging it can be to manually create adequate formal models [60]. Already for standardised communication protocols, ambiguities allow for different behaviours, which may require different model representations;

this suggests that incremental approaches are needed in an open world setting in which not all behaviours are known in advance [41]. Manually modelling all these different representations would be tedious and error-prone. Here, one interesting direction is to explore model learning [53], a technique to automatically generate finite state models from system traces, to automatically generate and test models in the model ecosystem of DTs [47,57]. However, for bilateral synchronisation between the DTs and real system, the underlying models must reflect the behaviour of the actual system. One way to address this problem can be to use techniques from probabilistic model checking [3] to support the model management process of the DT in selecting models based on the current environment [38].

Challenge 3 *How can formal methods enhance a digital twin by providing advanced behavioural insights into its target system?*

Formal methods can provide worst-case analyses as well as statistical guarantees not readily available with symbolic or mechanistic models. Given that the actual system is not fully understood, or that it operates in an uncontrolled environment, it seems interesting to not only analyse these streams using expressive runtime verification techniques [39], but also to investigate the generation of such analysis problems on-the-fly, driven by the stream of observations from the actual system. As a step in this direction, we have explored the use of model checking techniques over sliding window segments of event streams to analyse how properties of learnt models evolve over time [36,37]. Another interesting research direction is to use formal specifications to define input scenarios amenable to a hypothetical (what-if) analysis; e.g., in the BedreFlyt DT, we have used this kind of techniques to analyse average case and worst-case resource usage for bed-bay allocation in a hospital ward [35].

4   Formal Methods for Digital Twins

Let us next consider formal methods for the overall DT architecture and focus on the DT's need to be dynamically updated, driven by data from the actual system, i.e., its self-adaptive capabilities. Early work on formal methods to model and analyse self-adaptive systems was surveyed by Weyns et al. [59], who reports a "remarkably low" number of papers on this topic. By structuring the configuration space of the self-adaptive system, self-adaptation has connections to variability and especially to dynamic software product lines [18, 21] in the sense that they provide a means to reconfigure the system between different configurations. While software product lines have been formalised using, e.g., featured transition systems [13], formal methods for dynamic software product lines have received less attention [49]. However, tools such as ProFeat [12], which supports family-based model-checking with a feature controller that can activate and deactivate features in the configuration space, have been used to formally model and analyse self-adaptive systems (e.g., [48]).

Early work on the modelling and analysis of MAPE-K feedback loops essentially treated the knowledge base as a shared memory between processes [2,23].

However, in DTs the knowledge base tends to capture domain knowledge as a static context, for example using knowledge graphs [22]. In this setting, we may understand the knowledge base of a self-adaptive system such as a DT as a system invariant; i.e., a set of properties that should hold for the system in quiescent states during execution. However, the knowledge base of a DT can be rather complex, especially if it includes contextual information such as domain knowledge.

Challenge 4 *How can formal methods improve guarantees for the expected behaviour and services of a digital twin?*

While *consistency* between different models and components is a common research topic in DT research [45], the notion of *correctness*, especially functional correctness, has not been investigated in depth. We take the view that correctness for DTs needs to relate the twin's configuration and behaviour to that of the actual system. However, we cannot generally assume that the actual system is fully understood; instead it is observed through its sensor readings and interpreted in the context of the domain knowledge. If we assume that the knowledge base is formally represented as a set of logical formulae, correctness can be expressed as a relation between the DT's Layer 1 and the knowledge base. Seen as an invariant, the knowledge base should have the current state of the DT's Layer 1 as a model. In our work, we have approached this problem through *semantic lifting* [32], a technique to integrate the runtime state of a DT in a knowledge base [33]. By providing a specific structure to the knowledge base and to the operations used for self-adaptation, both correctness and quiescent states can then be formally expressed (see, e.g., [50]).

Challenge 5 *How can we reason about systems that interact with external knowledge bases?*

In fact, little work has been done on assessing the behaviour of software that interacts with external knowledge. We have opened a line of work on testing such software, using mutations over knowledge graphs to evaluate the robustness of the software using the knowledge and identifying the assumptions over the structure of the graph that are crucial for the software [25–27]. In a similar vein, we have shown how fuzzing techniques can be used to find bugs in software for interacting with knowledge graphs [24], such as logical reasoners. One may think of these assumptions as an interface between the software and the external knowledge, and we have introduced a verification system that integrates information from the knowledge base directly into a Hoare logic [30]. Complementing this line of work, Dubslaff et al. have developed an approach to incorporate domain knowledge in the form of ontologies into model checking [14].

Challenge 6 *How can we provide programmatic support for self-adaptation with external knowledge bases?*

While most work on self-adaptive systems fall into the "systems" category of computer science research, it is interesting to see if more programmatic support can be provided for developing DTs and related software. We have explored this problem by proposing *semantically reflected programs* in SMOL [31,32]. SMOL is a programming language specially constructed for programs that interact with an external knowledge base. The runtime states of SMOL can be automatically integrated in this knowledge base, to support introspection: programs can query the knowledge base about how their runtime state relates to external knowledge, and make runtime decisions based on that. In this way, SMOL is designed to support DTs that use external knowledge bases [34,35]. The integration of mechanisms for dynamic reclassification of objects in SMOL provides programmatic support for type-safe self-adaptation [50].

5   Conclusion

This paper argues why the emergence of DTs should be of interest to the formal methods community. We claim that DTs give us an opportunity to revisit the relationship between models and modelled systems, and explore how data-driven and self-adaptive aspects of DTs require a dynamic way of developing and composing models to perform on-the-fly analyses. The paper considers both the use of formal methods to deliver analysis services inside a DT and the use of formal methods to analyse the DT itself, and suggests a number of interesting, open challenges for model development, composition and integration in the context of DTs. These challenges touch upon model heterogeneity, correctness for self-adaptive systems such as DTs and interaction with external knowledge such as formalised domain expertise. Admittedly, we are barely scratching the surface by indicating these specific challenges, with a focus on methodology, at the intersection of formal methods and DTs. We have concretised each challenge by indicating a direction of research in our own work. We believe there is a huge potential here that deserves more attention from the formal methods community.

References

1. Ahlgren, J., Bojarczuk, K., Drossopoulou, S., Dvortsova, I., George, J., Gucevska, N., Harman, M., Lomeli, M., Lucas, S.M.M., Meijer, E., Omohundro, S., Rojas, R., Sapora, S., Zhou, N.: Facebook's cyber-cyber and cyber-physical digital twins. In: Proc. Evaluation and Assessment in Software Engineering (EASE 2021). pp. 1–9. ACM (2021). https://doi.org/10.1145/3463274.3463275
2. Arcaini, P., Riccobene, E., Scandurra, P.: Modeling and analyzing MAPE-K feedback loops for self-adaptation. In: Inverardi, P., Schmerl, B.R. (eds.) Proc. 10th Intl. Symp. on Software Engineering for Adaptive and Self-Managing Systems (SEAMS 2015). pp. 13–23. IEEE Computer Society (2015). https://doi.org/10.1109/SEAMS.2015.10
3. Baier, C., de Alfaro, L., Forejt, V., Kwiatkowska, M.: Model checking probabilistic systems. In: Handbook of Model Checking, pp. 963–999. Springer (2018). https://doi.org/10.1007/978-3-319-10575-8_28
4. Baresi, L., Ghezzi, C.: The disappearing boundary between development-time and run-time. In: Proc. Workshop on Future of Software Engineering Research, (FoSER 2010). pp. 17–22. ACM (2010). https://doi.org/10.1145/1882362.1882367

5. ter Beek, M.H., Chapman, R., Cleaveland, R., Garavel, H., Gu, R., ter Horst, I., Keiren, J.J.A., Lecomte, T., Leuschel, M., Rozier, K.Y., Sampaio, A., Seceleanu, C., Thomas, M., Willemse, T.A.C., Zhang, L.: Formal Methods in Industry. Formal Aspects Comput. **37**(1), 7:1–7:38 (2025). https://doi.org/10.1145/3689374

6. Billey, A., Wuest, T.: Energy digital twins in smart manufacturing systems: A case study. Robotics Comput. Integr. Manuf. **88**, 102729 (2024). https://doi.org/10.1016/J.RCIM.2024.102729

7. Birchler, C., Khatiri, S., Rani, P., Kehrer, T., Panichella, S.: A roadmap for simulation-based testing of autonomous cyber-physical systems: Challenges and future direction. ACM Trans. Softw. Eng. Methodol. **34**(5), 152:1–152:9 (2025). https://doi.org/10.1145/3711906

8. Bjørner, N.S., Phan, A., Fleckenstein, L.: νz - an optimizing SMT solver. In: Proc. TACAS 2015. LNCS, vol. 9035, pp. 194–199. Springer (2015). https://doi.org/10.1007/978-3-662-46681-0_14

9. Blair, G.S., Bencomo, N., France, R.B.: Models@ run.time. Computer **42**(10), 22–27 (2009). https://doi.org/10.1109/MC.2009.326

10. Braun, S., Dalibor, M., Jansen, N., Jarke, M., Koren, I., Quix, C., Rumpe, B., Wimmer, M., Wortmann, A.: Engineering digital twins and digital shadows as key enablers for industry 4.0. In: Digital Transformation - Core Technologies and Emerging Topics from a Computer Science Perspective, pp. 3–31. Springer (2022). https://doi.org/10.1007/978-3-662-65004-2_1

11. Chang, X., Zhang, R., Mao, J., Fu, Y.: Digital twins in transportation infrastructure: An investigation of the key enabling technologies, applications, and challenges. IEEE Trans. Intell. Transp. Syst. **25**(7), 6449–6471 (2024). https://doi.org/10.1109/TITS.2024.3401716

12. Chrszon, P., Dubslaff, C., Klüppelholz, S., Baier, C.: ProFeat: Feature-Oriented Engineering for Family-Based Probabilistic Model Checking. Formal Aspects Comput. **30**(1), 45–75 (2018). https://doi.org/10.1007/s00165-017-0432-4

13. Classen, A., Cordy, M., Schobbens, P.Y., Heymans, P., Legay, A., Raskin, J.F.: Featured Transition Systems: Foundations for Verifying Variability-Intensive Systems and Their Application to LTL Model Checking. IEEE Transaction on Software Engineering **39**(8), 1069–1089 (2013). https://doi.org/10.1109/TSE.2012.86

14. Dubslaff, C., Koopmann, P., Turhan, A.: Enhancing probabilistic model checking with ontologies. Formal Aspects Comput. **33**(6), 885–921 (2021). https://doi.org/10.1007/S00165-021-00549-0

15. Fitzgerald, J., Gomes, C., Larsen, P.G. (eds.): The Engineering of Digital Twins. Springer (2024). https://doi.org/10.1007/978-3-031-66719-0

16. Gleirscher, M., Marmsoler, D.: Formal Methods in Dependable Systems Engineering: A Survey of Professionals from Europe and North America. Empir. Softw. Eng. **25**(6), 4473–4546 (2020). https://doi.org/10.1007/s10664-020-09836-5

17. Gomes, C., Thule, C., Broman, D., Larsen, P.G., Vangheluwe, H.: Co-simulation: A survey. ACM Comput. Surv. **51**(3), 49:1–49:33 (2018). https://doi.org/10.1145/3179993

18. Hallsteinsen, S., Hinchey, M., Park, S., Schmid, K.: Dynamic Software Product Lines. In: Systems and Software Variability Management: Concepts, Tools and Experiences, pp. 253–260. Springer (2013). https://doi.org/10.1007/978-3-642-36583-6_16

19. Hansen, S.T., Kamburjan, E., Kazemi, Z.: Monitoring reconfigurable simulation scenarios in co-simulated digital twins. In: Proc. 12th Intl. Symp. on Leveraging Applications of Formal Methods, Verification and Validation. Application Areas

(ISoLA 2024). LNCS, vol. 15223, pp. 47–61. Springer (2024). `https://doi.org/10.1007/978-3-031-75390-9_4`

20. Hierons, R.M., Bogdanov, K., Bowen, J.P., Cleaveland, R., Derrick, J., Dick, J., Gheorghe, M., Harman, M., Kapoor, K., Krause, P.J., Lüttgen, G., Simons, A.J.H., Vilkomir, S.A., Woodward, M.R., Zedan, H.: Using formal specifications to support testing. ACM Comput. Surv. **41**(2), 9:1–9:76 (2009). `https://doi.org/10.1145/1459352.1459354`

21. Hinchey, M., Park, S., Schmid, K.: Building Dynamic Software Product Lines. IEEE Computer **45**(10), 22–26 (2012). `https://doi.org/10.1109/MC.2012.332`

22. Hogan, A., et al.: Knowledge graphs. ACM Comput. Surv. **54**(4) (Jul 2021). `https://doi.org/10.1145/3447772`

23. de la Iglesia, D.G., Weyns, D.: MAPE-K formal templates to rigorously design behaviors for self-adaptive systems. ACM Trans. Auton. Adapt. Syst. **10**(3), 15:1–15:31 (2015). `https://doi.org/10.1145/2724719`

24. John, T., Johnsen, E.B., Kamburjan, E., Steinhöfel, D.: Language-based testing for knowledge graphs. In: Proc. 22nd European Semantic Web Conf. (ESWC 2025). LNCS, vol. 15719, pp. 24–46. Springer (2025). `https://doi.org/10.1007/978-3-031-94578-6_2`

25. John, T., Kamburjan, E., Johnsen, E.B.: Mutation-based integration testing of knowledge graph applications. In: Proc. 35th Intl. Symp. on Software Reliability Engineering (ISSRE 2024). pp. 475–486. IEEE (2024). `https://doi.org/10.1109/ISSRE62328.2024.00052`

26. John, T., Kamburjan, E., Johnsen, E.B.: Mutation-based testing of knowledge graphs. Empir. Softw. Eng. (2026), to appear.

27. John, T., Kamburjan, E., Johnsen, E.B.: RDFMutate: Mutation-based generation of knowledge graphs. In: Proc. 24th Intl. Semantic Web Conf. (ISWC 2025). LNCS, vol. 16141, pp. 295–312. Springer (2026). `https://doi.org/10.1007/978-3-032-09530-5_17`

28. Johnsen, E.B., Hähnle, R., Schäfer, J., Schlatte, R., Steffen, M.: ABS: A core language for abstract behavioral specification. In: Proc. FMCO. LNCS, vol. 6957, pp. 142–164. Springer (2010). `https://doi.org/10.1007/978-3-642-25271-6_8`

29. Kamburjan, E., Bencomo, N., Tapia Tarifa, S.L., Johnsen, E.B.: Declarative life-cycle management in digital twins. In: Proc. 1st Intl. Conf. on Engineering Digital Twins (EDTconf 2024). pp. 353—363. MODELS Companion'24, ACM (2024). `https://doi.org/10.1145/3652620.3688248`

30. Kamburjan, E., Gurov, D.: Multi-perspective correctness of programs. In: Proc. 22nd Intl. Colloquium on Theoretical Aspects of Computing (ICTAC 2025). LNCS, vol. 16237, pp. 69–86. Springer (2025). `https://doi.org/10.1007/978-3-032-11176-0_6`

31. Kamburjan, E., Klungre, V.N., Qu, Y., Schlatte, R., Kostylev, E.V., Giese, M., Johnsen, E.B.: Semantically reflected programs. CoRR **abs/2509.03318** (2025). `https://doi.org/10.48550/ARXIV.2509.03318`

32. Kamburjan, E., Klungre, V.N., Schlatte, R., Johnsen, E.B., Giese, M.: Programming and debugging with semantically lifted states. In: Proc. 18th Extended Semantic Web Conference (ESWC 2021). LNCS, vol. 12731, pp. 126–142. Springer (2021). `https://doi.org/10.1007/978-3-030-77385-4_8`

33. Kamburjan, E., Pferscher, A., Schlatte, R., Sieve, R., Tapia Tarifa, S.L., Johnsen, E.B.: Semantic reflection and digital twins: A comprehensive overview. In: The Combined Power of Research, Education, and Dissemination: Essays Dedicated to Tiziana Margaria on the Occasion of Her 60th Birthday, LNCS, vol. 15240, pp. 129 145. Springer (2025). `https://doi.org/10.1007/978-3-031-73887-6_11`

34. Kamburjan, E., Sieve, R., Baramashetru, C.P., Amato, M., Barmina, G., Occhipinti, E., Johnsen, E.B.: GreenhouseDT: An exemplar for digital twins. In: Proc. 19th Intl. Symp. on Software Eng. for Adaptive and Self-Managing Systems (SEAMS 2024). pp. 175–181. ACM (2024). https://doi.org/10.1145/3643915.3644108
35. Kløvstad, Å.A.A., Kobialka, P., Sieve, R., Pferscher, A., Slaughter, L., Tapia Tarifa, S.L., Johnsen, E.B.: What-if scenarios for the BedreFlyt digital twin. In: Principles of formal quantitative analysis — Essays dedicated to Christel Baier on the occasion of her 60th birthday. p. 360–381. LNCS, Springer (2026). https://doi.org/10.1007/978-3-031-97439-7_18
36. Kobialka, P., Pferscher, A., Bergersen, G.R., Johnsen, E.B., Tapia Tarifa, S.L.: Stochastic games for user journeys. In: Proc. 26th Intl. Symp. on Formal Methods (FM 2024). LNCS, vol. 14934, pp. 167–186. Springer (2024). https://doi.org/10.1007/978-3-031-71177-0_12
37. Kobialka, P., Tapia Tarifa, S.L., Bergersen, G.R., Johnsen, E.B.: User journey games: automating user-centric analysis. Softw. Syst. Model. **23**(3), 605–624 (2024). https://doi.org/10.1007/S10270-024-01148-2
38. Korn, M.: Formal-Methods Support for Runtime Adaptation in Self-Adaptive Systems. Ph.D. thesis, Dresden University of Technology, Germany (2025)
39. Kristensen, M.H., Bonizzi, A., Gomes, C., Hansen, S.T., Martin, C.I.I., Iven, H., Kamburjan, E., Larsen, P.G., Leucker, M., Talasila, P., Tang, V.T., Tonetta, S., Vosteen, L.B., Wright, T.: Runtime verification of autonomous systems utilizing digital twins as a service. In: Proc. Intl. Conf. on Autonomic Computing and Self-Organizing Systems (ACSOS 2024). pp. 121–127. IEEE (2024). https://doi.org/10.1109/ACSOS-C63493.2024.00042
40. Kritzinger, W., Karner, M., Traar, G., Henjes, J., Sihn, W.: Digital twin in manufacturing: A categorical literature review and classification. IFAC-PapersOnLine **51**(11), 1016–1022 (2018). https://doi.org/10.1016/j.ifacol.2018.08.474
41. Kruger, L., Kobialka, P., Pferscher, A., Johnsen, E.B., Junges, S., Rot, J.: Incremental fingerprinting in an open world. In: Proc. CSF 2026. IEEE (2026). https://doi.org/10.48550/arXiv.2601.21680, to appear.
42. Laubenbacher, R., Mehrad, B., Shmulevich, I., Trayanova, N.: Digital twins in medicine. Nat Comput Sci **4**, 184–191 (2024). https://doi.org/10.1038/s43588-024-00607-6
43. Michael, J., et al.: Model-driven engineering for digital twins: Opportunities and challenges. Syst. Eng. **28**(5), 659–670 (2025). https://doi.org/10.1002/SYS.21815
44. Michalec, O.: Models vs infrastructures? on the role of digital twins' hype in anticipating the governance of the UK energy industry. Environmental Science & Policy **168**, 104041 (2025). https://doi.org/10.1016/j.envsci.2025.104041
45. Muctadir, H.M., Kamburjan, E., Cleophas, L., van den Brand, M.: A consistency management framework for digital twin models. Journal of Systems and Software **234**, 112750 (2026). https://doi.org/10.1016/j.jss.2025.112750
46. National Academies of Sciences, Engineering, and Medicine (NASEM): Foundational Research Gaps and Future Directions for Digital Twins. The National Academies Press (2024). https://doi.org/10.17226/26894
47. Pferscher, A., Wunderling, B., Aichernig, B.K., Muskardin, E.: Mining digital twins of a VPN server. In: Proc. Workshop on Applications of Formal Methods and Digital Twins. CEUR Workshop Proc. vol. 3507. CEUR-WS.org (2023), https://ceur-ws.org/Vol-3507/paper6.pdf

48. Päßler, J., ter Beek, M.H., Damiani, F., Dubslaff, C., Johnsen, E.B., Tapia Tarifa, S.L.: Feature-oriented modelling and analysis of a self-adaptive robotic system. Formal Aspects Comput. **37**(4), 1–39 (2025). https://doi.org/10.1145/3709159
49. Päßler, J., ter Beek, M.H., Damiani, F., Johnsen, E.B., Tapia Tarifa, S.L.: Analysing self-adaptive systems as software product lines. Journal of Systems and Software **222**, 112324 (2025). https://doi.org/10.1016/j.jss.2024.112324
50. Sieve, R., Kamburjan, E., Damiani, F., Johnsen, E.B.: Declarative dynamic object reclassification. In: Proc. ECOOP 2025. LIPIcs, vol. 333, pp. 29:1–29:31. Schloss Dagstuhl - Leibniz-Zentrum für Informatik (2025). https://doi.org/10.4230/LIPICS.ECOOP.2025.29
51. Sieve, R., Kobialka, P., Slaughter, L., Schlatte, R., Johnsen, E.B., Tapia Tarifa, S.L.: BedreFlyt: Improving patient flows through hospital wards with digital twins. In: Proc. First Intl. Workshop on Autonomous Systems Quality Assurance and Prediction with Digital Twins (ASQAP 2025). EPTCS, vol. 418, pp. 1–15. Open Publishing Association (2025). https://doi.org/10.4204/EPTCS.418.1
52. Torres, W., van den Brand, M.G.J., Serebrenik, A.: A systematic literature review of cross-domain model consistency checking by model management tools. Softw. Syst. Model. **20**(3), 897–916 (2021). https://doi.org/10.1007/S10270-020-00834-1
53. Vaandrager, F.W.: Model learning. Commun. ACM **60**(2), 86–95 (2017). https://doi.org/10.1145/2967606
54. Vachálek, J., Bartalský, L., Rovný, O., Šišmišová, D., Morháč, M., Lokšík, M.: The digital twin of an industrial production line within the Industry 4.0 concept. In: Proc. 21st Intl. Conf. on Process Control (PC 2017). pp. 258–262 (2017). https://doi.org/10.1109/PC.2017.7976223
55. Vallée, A.: Digital twin for healthcare systems. Frontiers in Digital Health **5**, 1253050 (Sep 2023). https://doi.org/10.3389/fdgth.2023.1253050
56. Wagenmaker, A., Huang, K., Ke, L., Jamieson, K.G., Gupta, A.: Overcoming the sim-to-real gap: Leveraging simulation to learn to explore for real-world RL. In: Proc. NeuRIPS 2024 (2024), http://papers.nips.cc/paper_files/paper/2024/hash/8fa068ffe59817175d176bd75641fe16-Abstract-Conference.html
57. Wallner, F., Aichernig, B.K., Burghard, C.: It's not a feature, it's a bug: Fault-tolerant model mining from noisy data. In: Proc. ICSE 2024. pp. 29:1–29:13. ACM (2024). https://doi.org/10.1145/3597503.3623346
58. Weyns, D.: An Introduction to Self-Adaptive Systems: A Contemporary Software Engineering Perspective. Wiley-IEEE Computer Society Pr (2021). https://doi.org/10.1002/9781119574910
59. Weyns, D., Iftikhar, M.U., de la Iglesia, D.G., Ahmad, T.: A survey of formal methods in self-adaptive systems. In: Proc. Fifth Intl. C* Conf. on Computer Science & Software Engineering (C3S2E 2012). pp. 67–79. ACM (2012). https://doi.org/10.1145/2347583.2347592
60. Wing, J.M.: A specifier's introduction to formal methods. Computer **23**(9), 8–24 (1990). https://doi.org/10.1109/2.58215
61. Woodcock, J., Larsen, P.G., Bicarregui, J., Fitzgerald, J.: Formal methods: Practice and experience. ACM Comput. Surv. **41**(4), 19:1–19:36 (2009). https://doi.org/10.1145/1592434.1592436
62. Zhao, W., Queralta, J.P., Westerlund, T.: Sim-to-real transfer in deep reinforcement learning for robotics: a survey. In: Proc. Symposium Series on Computational Intelligence (SSCI 2020). pp. 737–744. IEEE (2020). https://doi.org/10.1109/SSCI47803.2020.9308468

Contextual Metaprogramming for Session Types

Pedro Ângelo[1] , Atsushi Igarashi[2] , Yuito Murase[2] , and Vasco T. Vasconcelos[1]

[1] LASIGE, Faculdade de Ciências da Universidade de Lisboa, Portugal
`{pjangelo,vmvasconcelos}@ciencias.ulisboa.pt`
[2] Kyoto University, Kyoto, Japan
`{murase@fos.,igarashi@}kuis.kyoto-u.ac.jp`

Abstract. We propose the integration of staged metaprogramming into a session-typed message passing functional language. We build on a model of contextual modal type theory with multi-level contexts, where contextual values, closing arbitrary terms over a series of variables, may be boxed and transmitted in messages. Once received, one such value may then be unboxed and locally applied before being run. To motivate this integration, we present examples of real-world use cases, for which our system would be suitable, such as servers preparing and shipping code on demand via session typed messages. We present a type system that distinguishes linear (used exactly once) from unrestricted (used an unbounded number of times) resources, and further define a type checker, suitable for a concrete implementation. We show type preservation, a progress result for sequential computations and absence of runtime errors for the concurrent runtime environment, as well as the correctness of the type checker.

1 Introduction

This paper brings together two established paradigms in programming languages: metaprogramming and session types. Metaprogramming is about generating and evaluating code fragments as first-class values [13,46,32,57,24]. As metaprogramming inherently risks generating ill-formed code fragments, typing disciplines to ensure the safety of generated code and its evaluation have been extensively studied. We show a simple example of a function genTimes in the style of *contextual metaprogramming* [22,30]. This function takes an integer n and returns a code fragment that takes the product of n copies of x.

```
genTimes : Int → [ Int ⊢ Int ]
genTimes 0 = box (y. 1)
genTimes n = let box u = genTimes (n − 1) in box (x. x * u[x])
```

For example, when called with argument 3, the resulting code fragment is represented by a *box* **box** (x. x * x * x * 1), consisting of a list of free variables (x in this case) and the content (x * x * x * 1). We distinguish two cases. If the function is called with 0, it returns a code fragment containing number 1. Otherwise, the function first calls genTimes (n − 1) to generate a smaller code fragment,

R. Krebbers (Ed.): ESOP 2026, LNCS 16501, pp. 13–41, 2026.
https://doi.org/10.1007/978-3-032-22720-1_2

then uses **let box** to bind its content to the *meta-variable* u. Then u[x] expands its content, where its free variables are substituted with x; hence, **box** (x. x ∗ u[x]) results in a code fragment that multiplies x by itself n times. The type for code fragments reflects the structure of boxes: the *contextual type* [**Int** ⊢ **Int**] represents a code fragment that is typed as integer under a typing context consisting of single integer variable. In this way, contextual types ensure safety of metaprogramming by capturing explicit context information in their code types.

On an orthogonal axis, session types have been advocated as a means to discipline concurrent computations, by accurately describing protocols for the channels used to exchange messages between processes [2,16,18,19,47,48,52]. For example, a channel to which one can iteratively send integers is described by the following session type:

```
type Stream = ⊕{More: !Int.Stream, Done: Close}
```

The writer chooses between selecting More values or selecting Done. In the former case, the writer sends an integer value (!**Int**) and "goes back to the beginning" (Stream); in the latter case the writer must close the channel (**Close**). Then, we can write a program that sends integer 5 a given number of times:

```
sendFives : Int → Stream → unit
sendFives 0 x = close (select Done x)
sendFives n x = sendFives (n−1) (send 5 (select More x))
```

The function takes a number n and channel x, and writes on channel x number 5 n times. When n is 0, the function selects the Done option and then closes the channel. The **select** Done function returns a continuation channel, in this case, ready to be closed. Otherwise, the function selects the More option, writes 5 on the continuation channel, and calls itself recursively. Session types statically track the state of channels, ensuring that function sendFives consumes a given channel of type Stream.

The integration of session types with metaprogramming allows one to set up code-producing servers that run in parallel with the rest of the program and provide code on demand, exchanged via typed channels. Linearity is central to session types, but current metaprogramming models lack support for such a feature. We extend a simple model of contextual modal type theory with support for session types, to obtain a call-by-value linear lambda calculus with multi-level contexts.

Our development is based on Davies and Pfenning [13], where we use a box modality to distinguish generated code. We further allow code to refer to variables in a context, described by contextual types, along the lines of Nanevski et al. [30]. Mœbius, by Jang et al. [22], further adds to modal contextual type theory the provision for pattern matching on code, for generating polymorphic code, and for generating code that depends on other code fragments. We forgo the first two directions, and base our development on the last. We propose a multilevel contextual modal linear lambda calculus with support for session types, where in particular the composition of code fragments avoids creating extraneous administrative redexes due to boxing and unboxing. An alternative starting point would have been the Fitch- or Kripke-style formulation, providing for the Lisp quote/unquote, where typing contexts are viewed as stacks modeling the different stages of computation [11,28,51]. It seemed to us that the let-box approach would simplify the extension to the linear setting and to session types.

It is worth emphasizing that our contribution is not merely to combine contextual metaprogramming and session types. In order to integrate the two, we needed to introduce (message passing) concurrency and a linear type system capable of handling both (recursive) linear and unrestricted resources. This extension forms one of the key technical contributions of this work.

The rest of the paper is structured as follows. In Section 2 we motivate our proposal by means of examples. Section 3 introduces terms, processes, term evaluation and process reduction. Section 4 describes types and a type assignment system. Section 6 introduces type checking. Section 7 reviews related work. Section 8 concludes the paper and points directions for future work.

2   Motivation

This section informally introduces the language proposed in this paper through several examples. We start by presenting a small program in which processes send and receive code fragments over channels and execute them, illustrating the basic ideas of the language's syntax and type system. We then discuss how the language can model various real-world use cases that involve transmitting code fragments via channels.

The first example specializes function sendFives. We use the Stream type described in Section 1. Function genSendFives below accepts an integer value and returns a code fragment. The code fragment requires a channel endpoint (of type Stream) and, when executed, produces a unit value; its type is written [Stream ⊢ Unit], which is called a *box type*. We proceed by pattern-matching on the integer parameter.

```
genSendFives  :  Int  →  [Stream ⊢ Unit]
genSendFives 0 = box (y. close (select Done y))
genSendFives n = let box u = genSendFives (n − 1)
                 in box (x. u[send 5 (select More x)])
```

When all values have been sent on the stream (when n is 0), all it remains is to **select** Done and then close the channel. The **box** term generates code under a variable environment (an evaluation context), in this case containing variable y alone, denoting the channel endpoint. The code fragment y. **close** (**select** Done y) enclosed inside **box** is called a *contextual value*.

When there are values left to be sent (when n is different from 0), we recursively compute code to send n−1 values, unbox it storing the resulting contextual value (say z.**close** (**select** Done z)) in u, and then prepare code to send the n-th value. The use of the let-box bound variable u, which is given a *contextual type* Stream ⊢ Unit (without square brackets [ ]), always takes the form u[e], where e is a term of type Stream, and results in a term of type Unit obtained by substituting e (without being evaluated) for z. The part [e] is called an *explicit* *substitution*. In this example, term u[**send** 5 (**select** More x)] applies u of type Stream ⊢ **Unit** to term **send** 5 (**select** More x) of type Stream. If u is the contextual value z.**close** (**select** Done z), then **box** x.u[**send** 5 (**select** More x)] evaluates to **box** x. **close** (**select** Done (**send** 5 (**select** More x))), a piece of code that sends number 5 on channel x and then closes the channel.

The main difference between a contextual type such as Stream ⊢ **Unit** and the corresponding box type ([Stream ⊢ **Unit**]) is that the latter kind of types represents *first-class* code values—one can pass it to another function or store into a data structure—whereas the former kind are second-class—a variable of type Stream ⊢ **Unit** may only be used with an explicit substitution to compose another piece of code. See work on contextual modal type theory (e.g., [30]) for more details.

We may now compute and run code to send a fixed number of integer values.

```
send4Fives  :  Stream  →  Unit
send4Fives  c  =  let  box  u  =  genSendFives  4  in  u[c]
```

Term genSendFives 4 is a boxed code fragment (a term) of type [Stream ⊢ **Unit**]. Then, u is an unboxed code fragment (a contextual value) of contextual type Stream ⊢ **Unit**. We provide the contextual value with an explicit substitution [c]. The whole **let** term then amounts to running the code

```
close (select Done (send 5 (select More (...send 5 (select
    More c)...)))))
```

without calling function sendFives or using recursion in any other form.

The next example transmits code on channels. Imagine a server preparing code on behalf of clients. The server uses a channel to interact with its clients: it first receives a number n, then replies with code to send n fives, and finally waits for the channel to be closed. The type of the communication channel is as follows.

```
type  Builder  =  ?Int .![Stream ⊢ Unit]. Wait
```

The server receives n on a given channel and computes the code using a call to genSendFives. It then waits for the channel to be closed.

```
serveFives  :  Builder  →  Unit
serveFives  c  =
  let  (n,c)  =  receive  c  in  wait  (send  (genSendFives  n)  c)
```

On the other end of the channel sits a client: it sends a number (4 in this case), receives the code (of type [Stream ⊢ **Unit**]), closes the channel and evaluates the code received.

```
sendFives'  :  Dual  Builder  →  Stream  →  Unit
sendFives'  c  d  =
  let  (code,c)  =  receive  (send  4  c)  in  close  c  ;
  let  box  u  =  code  in  u[d]
```

The **Dual** operator on session types provides a view of the other end of the channel. In this case, **Dual** Builder is the type !**Int** .?[Stream ⊢ **Unit**].**Close**, where

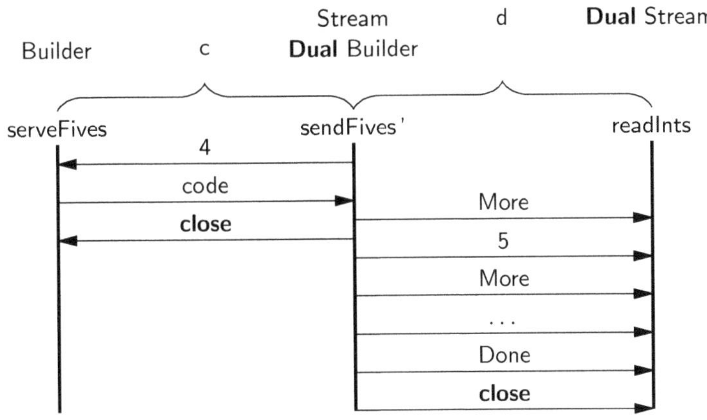

Fig. 1. Message sequence chart for the SendFives example

! is turned into ? and **Wait** is turned into **Close** (and conversely in both cases). Notice that code is a boxed code fragment of type [Stream ⊢ **Unit**], hence u is the corresponding code fragment (of type Stream ⊢ **Unit**) and u[d] runs the code on channel d.

To complete the example we need a function for reading streams, that is, a consumer of type **Dual Stream** →**Unit**. Function readInts reads and discards all integer values on the stream and then waits for the stream to be closed. Here we proceed by pattern matching on the label received on the channel.

```
readInts  :  Dual Stream  →  Unit
readInts  (Done c) =  wait c
readInts  (More c) =  let  (_, c) =  receive  c  in  readInts  c
```

Finally, the main thread forks two threads—one running serveFives, the other to collect the integer values (readInts)—and continues with sendFives'. We take advantage of a primitive function, forkWith that expects a suspended computation (a thunk), creates a new channel, forks the thunk on one end of the channel, and returns the other end of the channel for further interaction.

```
main  :  Unit
main =
   let  c = forkWith  (λ_.serveFives)  in  —  c  :  Dual  Builder
   let  d = forkWith  (λ_.readInts)  in    —  d  :  Stream
   sendFives ' c d
```

The interaction among the three processes is depicted in Fig. 1, where the code fragment produced by function serveFives and transmitted to sendFives' is

```
box (c.close (select Done (send 5 (select More (...( select
   More c)...)))))
```

Contextual metaprogramming for session types runs on the top of a linear type system: each resource is classified as *linear* (used exactly once) or *unrestricted* (used an unbounded number of times, including zero). Channel endpoints are always linear so that protocols may not encounter unexpected interactions. Functions may be linear or unrestricted. All the functions we have seen so far are unrestricted because they do not capture free linear values. The recursive functions (sendFives for example) are necessarily unrestricted, for they are discarded at the end of recursion. Some other values could be classified as linear if so desired. One such example is function serveFives which is used exactly once in function main. We annotate arrows with ω for unrestricted and 1 for linear. In examples, we often omit the ω label. Function serveFives could as well be of type Builder $\rightarrow_1$ **Unit**.

Boxed code fragments are always unrestricted, so that they may be used as many times as needed. Below are examples where a code fragment (denoted by u and of type Stream ⊢ Stream) that sends 5 on a given channel is duplicated (first example) or discarded (second example).

```
sendTwice  :  Stream  →  Unit
sendTwice  =  let  box  u  =  box  (y.  send  5  (select  More  y))
              in  λx. close  (select  Done  (u[u[x]]))
sendNone   :  Stream  →  Unit
sendNone   =  let  box  u  =  box  (y.  send  5  (select  More  y))
              in  λx. close  (select  Done  x)
```

In the first case, two 5 messages are sent on channel x and then the channel is closed; in the second, the only interaction on the channel is to close it.

The sendFives example is somewhat artificial and serves mainly to illustrate the basic idea of combining session types with metaprogramming. Nevertheless, this combination naturally appears in various forms in real-world programs, which we now discuss.

Distributed computing. In distributed systems, the computational power of several networked machines, which need not be in the same geographical location or network, is harnessed towards the completion of a shared goal. To distribute tasks between nodes, messages, containing code to be executed, are dispatched across the network. Commercial implementations such as Apache Spark [59] and Hadoop [55], follow the *MapReduce* programming model [14], inspired by functional programming. A related concept is that of *volunteer computing*, where volunteers (e.g., personal laptops) donate their idle processing power to solve large-scale problems. Boinc [7], targeting scientific projects with intensive computational needs, is one such example: volunteers subscribe to receive tasks as code, compute it and then return the result.

Consider the following protocol, structuring the communication between the central server and a volunteer, in the context of a prime search computational effort, such as PrimeGrid [37].

```
type  PrimeTask  =  &{  Task:  ![Int  ⊢  Bool].PrimeTask,
                        Test:  !Int.?Bool.PrimeTask,
                        Done:  Wait  }
```

The server offers three alternatives to subscribed volunteers. The first alternative is Task, which will provide the volunteer with a task to be performed. The task itself is specified as the box type [Int ⊢ Bool]. The task is then sent to the volunteer (![Int ⊢ Bool]), and then the protocol continues from the beginning (PrimeTask). Afterwards, the volunteer can donate its idle computational resources by selecting Test. The server sends a number (!Int), which we will call the *prime candidate*, to be tested, and then expects a result, i.e., either **True** or **False** in return (?Bool), which the volunteer stores. The interaction again goes back to the beginning. The server provides a third alternative, Done, allowing the volunteer to stop contributing, subsequently waiting for the volunteer to close the connection (**Wait**).

Assuming a testPrime function of type [Int ⊢ Bool], i.e., code that accepts the splicing in of a number and returns either **True** or **False**, we write the server as follows:

```
server  :  [Int]  →  [Bool]  →  PrimeTask  →  [Int]
server  cs  res  (Task s) =
   let  s = send  testPrime  in  server  cs  res  s
server  (c:cs)  res  (Test s) =
   let  s = send  c  in
   let  (result ,  s) = receive  s  in
   server  cs  (res ++ [result])  s
server  _  res  (Done s) = wait  s  ;  res
```

A volunteer, when connected to the server, selects between these three options. By selecting Task and then received the code, the volunteer stores it for later use. By selecting Test, the volunteer receives the prime candidate and runs the test by splicing the candidate into the code. The result is then sent to the server. The volunteer may repeat this action as many times as he wishes, thus donating more processing time. Finally, when the volunteer no longer wishes to contribute, he can just select Done and close the connection.

```
volunteer  :  Dual  PrimeTask  →  Unit
volunteer  v  =
   let  v = select  Task  v  in
   let  (primeTest ,  v) = receive  v  in
   let  v = select  Test  v  in
   let  (cand ,  v) = receive  v  in
   let  box  t = primeTest  in  send  (t[cand])  v  in
   let  v = select  Test  v  in
   let  (cand ,  v) = receive  v  in
   let  box  t = primeTest  in  send  (t[cand])  v  in

   . . .

   let  v = select  Done  v  in  close  v
```

When running our main program, the interaction unfolds as depicted in Fig. 2.

```
main  :  [Bool]
main = let  s = forkWith  (λ_.volunteer)  in —  s  :  Dual
       PrimeTask
       server  [7..]  s
```

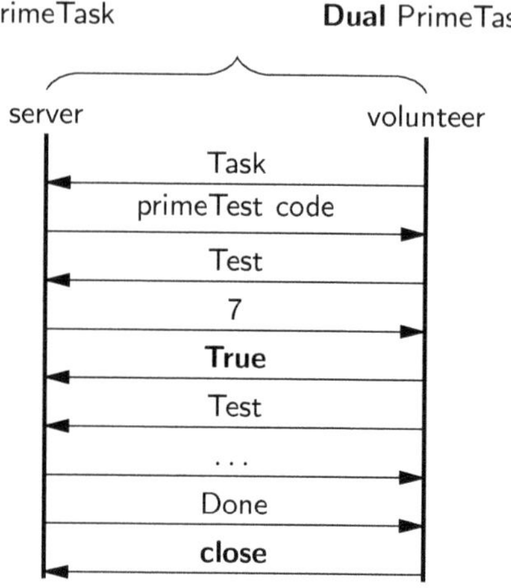

Fig. 2. Message sequence chart for the PrimeTask example

However, during the course of the interaction, the primality test algorithm can be improved. Hence, the volunteer can regularly poll for updated code, by selecting Task again.

```
volunteer  :  Dual PrimeTask  →  Unit
volunteer  v  =
   . . .
   let  v = select  Task  v  in
   let  (primeTest ,  v)  =  receive  v  in
   . . .
```

In this example, session types are used to govern the communication aspect of task assignment, whereas staged metaprogramming models sending code via messages.

Computation offloading consists in transferring computationally intensive tasks from resource-constrained devices (drones, IoT devices, smartphones) to more powerful remote servers. The main advantage lies in circumventing the shortcomings of these devices, particularly low storage capacity, low processing power and low battery life, enabling greater efficiency and decreased energy consumption on the device, as witnessed by Clonecloud [10]. The advantages of this concept become highly relevant in the context of high-throughput networks, since the overhead costs regarding the communication aspect are lessened. Our contribution relates closely with the concept of computation offloading, where session types broker the offloading of tasks, described as code via box types, as in the type below.

```
type  ComputeServer  =  &{ Compute :?[ ⊢ Int ] . ! Int . ComputeServer
```

$$, \; \mathsf{Done:Wait} \;\}$$

Code generation service. Template metaprogramming, as proposed by Sheard and Peyton Jones [43] for Haskell, allows one to write metaprograms that can produce other programs, such as those capable of manipulating arbitrary-sized data structures. For example, in Haskell, it is possible to write metaprograms such as fstN, which produces functions to extract the first element of an arbitrary-sized tuple, or zipN, which produces n-ary zip functions. Consider the protocol for a server offering code generating services:

```
type CodeGenerator = &{
    Fst3:  ![ ⊢  (a,b,c)  →  a ]. CodeGenerator ,
    Fst4:  ![ ⊢  (a,b,c,d)  →  a ]. CodeGenerator ,

    . . .

    Zip3:  ![ ⊢  [a]  →  [b]  →  [c]  →  [(a,b,c)]]. CodeGenerator

    . . .

    Done:  Close}
```

The server provides clients with functions to manipulate data structures of arbitrary size. To satisfy a request, the server evaluates the specified template metaprogram, splicing in the size of the data structure, and sending the result to the client. By only storing the function templates, and deriving the instances, i.e., by running the metaprograms, the server's storage requirements remain low as the service is scaled with more function instances it offers. While this example is still not feasible, it serves to illustrate the advantages of our contribution.

Other use cases. Multi-tier programming languages, such as Hop.js [42], Ocsigen/Eliom [5], Meteor.js [25] and Unison [49], allow a single program to describe the functionality of the different tiers of an application, e.g., client, server and database tier, in one unifying language. Session types allow to structure and verify client-server interactions, while providing type-safety properties compatible with multi-tier programming. ScalaLoci [41] and Ur/Web [50] are languages which relate to multi-staged programming, but lack explicit communication models. These would benefit from session types, e.g., to ensure correctness across computation stages.

HTMX [20], Next.js [31] and React Server Components [38] are web frameworks featuring pre-rendering strategies, where the server pre-renders parts of the UI and sends them to the client, while also allowing server components, i.e., code that only runs in servers. Session types allow to verify the correctness of UI update flows, while staged metaprogramming helps establish the theoretical basis behind the pre-rendering strategies.

3 Terms, processes and operational semantics

We build our language on the syntactic categories of variables, x, y, z and of labels l. We write $\overline{X}$ for a sequence of objects $X_1 \cdots X_n$ with $n \geq 0$. The empty sequence (when $n = 0$) is denoted by ε. The syntax of terms is in Fig. 3. It includes channel related primitives: close for closing a channel, wait for waiting

22   Pedro Ângelo, Atsushi Igarashi, Yuito Murase, and Vasco T. Vasconcelos

Constant c ::= close | wait | send | receive | select l | new | fork | fix | unit
Contextual value ρ, σ ::= $\overline{x}.M$
Value v, u ::= $c \mid x[\varepsilon] \mid \lambda x.M \mid (v, v) \mid$ box $\sigma \mid$ send v
Term M, N ::= $v \mid x[\overline{\sigma}] \mid M\,M \mid (M, M) \mid$ let $(x, x) = M$ in $M \mid$
                                     let box $x = M$ in $M \mid$ match M with $\{l \to M_l\}^{l \in L}$
Process P, Q ::= $\langle M \rangle \mid P \parallel Q \mid (\nu xx)P$
Evaluation context E ::= $[] \mid E\,M \mid v\,E \mid (E, M) \mid (v, E) \mid$ let $(x, x) = E$ in $M \mid$
                                     match E with $\{l \to M_l\}^{l \in L} \mid$ let box $x = E$ in M

Fig. 3. Terms and processes

for a channel to be closed, send to write a given value on a channel, receive to read a value from a channel, select l for sending label l on a given channel and new for creating a channel. fork creates a new thread, fix is the call-by-value fixed point combinator. unit is the only value of its type, and can be thought as a placeholder for other primitive values, such as integer or boolean values found in examples.

Further terms include constants, modal variables (playing the dual role of term variables and of channel endpoints), lambda abstraction and application, pair introduction and elimination, box introduction and elimination, a match term to branch according to the label l selected. The examples in Section 2 use forkWith, a convenient function that puts together channel creation and process spawning:

```
forkWith f = let (x,y) = new () in fork (λ_.f y) ; x
```

To objects of the form $\overline{x}.M$ we call *contextual values*. They denote code fragments M parameterized by the variables in sequence $\overline{x}$. A *contextual term variable* $x[\overline{\sigma}]$ applies the code fragment described by x to contextual values $\overline{\sigma}$. The box σ term turns a code fragment denoted by a contextual value σ into a term; the let box $x = M$ in N term eliminates the box in M and binds x to it, to be used in N. The let-box term allows code to be spliced into another code fragment (N), by eliminating the box in M and binding the result. When $\overline{x}$ is the empty sequence we sometimes write M in place of the contextual value $\varepsilon.M$. Similarly, when $\overline{\sigma}$ is the empty sequence we sometimes write x instead of the contextual term variable $x[\varepsilon]$. Channel endpoints are always expressed as terms $x[\varepsilon]$, which are included in values.

The *bindings* in the language are the following. Variable x is bound in M in terms $\lambda x.M$ and let box $x = N$ in M; variables x and y are bound in M in term let $(x, y) = N$ in M; the variables in $\overline{x}$ are bound in M in contextual value $\overline{x}.M$. The set of bound and free variables in terms (free M) are defined accordingly. We follow the variable convention whereby all bound variables are chosen to be different from the free variables, in all contexts [6,34].

R-BETA
$(\lambda x.M)\,v \to \{\varepsilon.v/x\}M$

R-SPLIT
$\text{let }(x,y) = (u,v)\text{ in }M \to \{\varepsilon.u/x\}\{\varepsilon.v/y\}M$

R-LETBOX
$\text{let box }x = \text{box}\,\sigma\text{ in }M \to \{\sigma/x\}M$

R-FIX
$\text{fix}\,v \to v\,(\lambda x.(\text{fix}\,v)\,x)$

R-CTX
$$\frac{M \to N}{E[M] \to E[N]}$$

Fig. 4. Term evaluation $\boxed{M \to M}$

Substitution is defined accordingly, from the bindings in the language, while taking advantage of the variable convention. Substitution is rather conventional except for the fact that the term language includes applied modal variables $x[\overline{\sigma}]$ rather than ordinary variables x. We denote by $\{\sigma/x\}M$ the term obtained by replacing the free occurrences of variable x by the contextual value σ in term M, and similarly for $\{\sigma/x\}\rho$. The rules are as follows:

$$\{\overline{z}.M/x\}(x[\overline{\rho}]) = \{\{\overline{z}.M/x\}\overline{\rho}/\overline{z}\}M \qquad \{\sigma/x\}(y[\overline{\rho}]) = y[\{\sigma/x\}\overline{\rho}] \quad \text{if } x \neq y$$

$$\{\sigma/x\}(\overline{y}.M) = \overline{y}.\{\sigma/x\}M$$

Multiple substitution $\{\overline{\rho}/\overline{z}\}M$ is defined only when $\overline{\rho}$ and $\overline{z}$ are sequences of the same length. We require that variables in $\overline{z}$ are pairwise distinct and not free outside M, hence the substitution of the various variables in $\overline{z}$ can be performed in sequence. Substitution on applied variables, $\{\overline{z}.M/x\}(x[\overline{\rho}])$, triggers further substitution for $\overline{z}$ in M. For example, $\{z_1, z_2.\text{send }z_1\,z_2/x\}(x[y, 42]) = \{y/z_1\}\{42/z_2\}(\text{send }z_1\,z_2) = \text{send}\,y\,42$. Substitution on the remaining term constructors is a homomorphism; for example $\{\sigma/x\}(\text{box}\,\rho) = \text{box}\,(\{\sigma/x\}\rho)$ and $\{\sigma/x\}(\text{let box }y = M\text{ in }N) = \text{let box }y = \{\sigma/x\}M\text{ in }\{\sigma/x\}N$. Since substitution for an applied variable triggers another, well-definedness is not trivial. We show that substitution is well defined for typable terms (provided that a few additional side conditions are met).

If terms provide for the sequential part of the language, *processes* deal with concurrency and are used as a runtime only. Programmers write terms M that are run on an initial thread $\langle M \rangle$ that may eventually fork new threads and create new communication channels. Process $P \parallel Q$ denotes the parallel composition of two processes. Process $(\nu xy)P$ introduces in process P a communication channel described by its two endpoints x and y. Our development is quite standard in the literature [16].

Evaluation on terms is given by the relation $M \to N$, defined by the rules in Fig. 4. It includes function application (R-BETA), the elimination of a pair of values (u, v) and their binding to variables x and y in M (R-SPLIT). Notice that substitution is defined for contextual values only, hence we lift value u to $\varepsilon.u$, and similarly for v. Rule R-LETBOX unboxes a boxed code fragment σ, binds it to x to be used in M. Rule R-FIX unfolds the call by value fixed point constructor fix [27]. Finally, rule R-CTX evaluates terms under evaluation contexts, the syntax

$$P \equiv \langle \mathsf{unit} \rangle \parallel P \qquad P \parallel Q \equiv Q \parallel P \qquad (P_1 \parallel P_2) \parallel P_3 \equiv P_1 \parallel (P_2 \parallel P_3)$$

$$(\nu xy)P \parallel Q \equiv (\nu xy)(P \parallel Q) \qquad\qquad (\nu xy)P \equiv (\nu yx)P$$

$$(\nu xy)(\nu zw)P \equiv (\nu zw)(\nu xy)P$$

Fig. 5. Structural congruence $\boxed{P \equiv Q}$

of which is in Fig. 3. These are the standard call-by-value evaluation contexts. Notice we do not allow reduction inside boxes just as we do not allow reduction under λ.

Reduction on processes is given by the relation $P \to Q$, defined by the rules in Fig. 6. Note that we overload the symbol $\to$ to denote reduction on both terms and processes, and the intended meaning is clear from the context, namely by inspecting the operands. As customary in the π-calculus, reduction builds on a further relation—structural congruence $P \equiv Q$—that provides for the syntactic rearrangement of processes, while preparing these for reduction [26].

Structural congruence is the least congruence relation generated by the axioms in Fig. 5. The first axiom posits thread $\langle \mathsf{unit} \rangle$ as the neutral element of parallel composition. The next two axioms tell that parallel composition is commutative and associative. Law $(\nu xy)P \parallel Q \equiv (\nu xy)(P \parallel Q)$ is called scope extrusion and allows the scope of a ν-binder to expand to a new process Q or to retract from it, as needed. Further axioms allow exchanging the order of the two endpoints of a channel, and exchanging the order of ν-binders. In scope extrusion, because of the variable convention, the condition 'x, y not free in Q' is redundant: x and y occur bound in $(\nu xy)P$ and therefore cannot occur free in Q.

We now describe the reduction rules. Rule R-Exp lifts term evaluation to process reduction. Rule R-Fork creates a new thread. Value v is supposed to be a suspended computation (a thunk), so that v unit runs the computation. The hole in the context in the original thread is filled with unit: all communication between the two threads must be accomplished via message passing on channels free in v. Rule R-New creates a new channel denoted by its two endpoints x and y. The hole in the thread is filled with a pair (x, y) so that the thread may manipulate the channel.

The next three rules manipulate channels via their endpoints x, y. For ease of reading we abbreviate contextual term value $x[\varepsilon]$ to x, and similarly for y. Rule R-Close closes a channel: one thread must be closing one endpoint, the other waiting for the channel to be closed. The ν-binder is eliminated since the channel cannot be further used. Rule R-Com exchanges a value between a **send** and a **receive** thread. The result of sending is the endpoint itself, x; the result of receiving is a pair composed of the value exchanged and the endpoint y. The two threads may then continue exchanging values on these endpoints. Rule R-

R-Exp
$$\frac{M \to N}{\langle M \rangle \to \langle N \rangle}$$

R-Fork
$$\langle E[\mathsf{fork}\, v] \rangle \to \langle E[\mathsf{unit}] \rangle \parallel \langle v\, \mathsf{unit} \rangle$$

R-New
$$\langle E[\mathsf{new}] \rangle \to (\nu xy)\langle E[(x,y)] \rangle$$

R-Close
$$(\nu xy)(\langle E[\mathsf{close}\, x] \rangle \parallel \langle F[\mathsf{wait}\, y] \rangle) \to \langle E[\mathsf{unit}] \rangle \parallel \langle F[\mathsf{unit}] \rangle$$

R-Com
$$(\nu xy)(\langle E[\mathsf{send}\, v\, x] \rangle \parallel \langle F[\mathsf{receive}\, y] \rangle) \to (\nu xy)\langle E[x] \rangle \parallel \langle F[(v,y)] \rangle$$

R-Branch
$$(\nu xy)(\langle E[\mathsf{select}\, l'\, x] \rangle \parallel \langle F[\mathsf{match}\, y\, \mathsf{with}\, \{l \to M_l\}^{l \in L}] \rangle) \to (\nu xy)(\langle E[x] \rangle \parallel \langle F[M_{l'}\, y] \rangle)$$

R-Par
$$\frac{P \to P'}{P \parallel Q \to P' \parallel Q}$$

R-Res
$$\frac{P \to Q}{(\nu xy)P \to (\nu xy)Q}$$

R-Struct
$$\frac{P \equiv P' \qquad P' \to Q' \qquad Q' \equiv Q}{P \to Q}$$

Fig. 6. Process reduction $\boxed{P \to P}$

Multiplicity	m	$::=$	$1 \mid \omega$
Type	T, U	$::=$	$\mathsf{Unit} \mid T \to_m T \mid T \times T \mid \Box\tau^{n+1} \mid S$
Session type	R, S	$::=$	$\mathsf{Close} \mid \mathsf{Wait} \mid {!}T.S \mid {?}T.S \mid \oplus\{l\colon S_l\}^{l \in L} \mid \&\{l\colon S_l\}^{l \in L} \mid a \mid \mu a.S$
Contextual type τ^n		$::=$	$\overline{\tau} \vdash^n T$
Typing context	Γ, Δ	$::=$	$\varepsilon \mid \Gamma, x\colon \tau$

Fig. 7. Types

Branch exercises the choice of a branch in a match process. The label selected
on a thread (l') chooses branch $M_{l'}$ on the other thread. The result of selection
is the endpoint itself, as in send; the result of match is $M_{l'}$, which is supposed to
be a function, applied to endpoint y. Similarly to R-Com, the two threads may
continue interacting on channel xy. Finally, the last three rules allow reduction
under parallel composition and ν-binders, and incorporate structural congruence
in reduction.

4   Types and typing assignment

This section introduces the notion of type and a type assignment system to terms
and to processes.

We build the language of types on the syntactic category of *type references*,
a, b. We further use letters k, n to denote natural numbers, and may call them
levels. The syntax of *types* is in Fig. 7. *Multiplicities m*, include 1 denoting a

$$\text{Close} \perp \text{Wait} \qquad \text{Wait} \perp \text{Close} \qquad \frac{S \perp R}{!T.S \perp ?T.R} \qquad \frac{S \perp R}{?T.S \perp !T.R}$$

$$\frac{R \perp S\{\mu a.S/a\}}{R \perp \mu a.S} \qquad \frac{R\{\mu a.R/a\} \perp S}{\mu a.R \perp S} \qquad \frac{S_l \perp R_l \quad \forall l \in L}{\oplus\{l : S_l\}^{l \in L} \perp \&\{l : R_l\}^{l \in L}}$$

$$\frac{S_l \perp R_l \quad \forall l \in L}{\&\{l : S_l\}^{l \in L} \perp \oplus\{l : R_l\}^{l \in L}}$$

Fig. 8. Type duality (coinductive) $\boxed{S \perp S}$

linear resource—a resource that must be used exactly once—and ω describing an *unrestricted* resource—a resource that may be used an unbounded number of times, including zero.

Type Unit (for constant unit) can be thought as a placeholder for other base types, such as those for integer or boolean values. Further types include those for linear and unrestricted functions, $T \to_1 U$ and $T \to_\omega U$, that for linear pairs, $T \times U$ (for simplicity we do not consider unrestricted pairs), and for box types $\Box\tau$, that is, code fragments characterised by contextual types τ. The grammar for contextual types is indexed by levels; when levels are not important we omit them and abbreviate contextual types to τ.

Session types describe communication channel endpoints. Types Close and Wait are for channels ready, or waiting, to be closed, respectively. Type $!T.S$ and $?T.S$ are for channels that send, or receive, values of type T and continue as S, respectively. Type $\oplus\{l: S_l\}^{l \in L}$ is for channels that may select one branch $k \in L$ and proceed as S_k (internal choice). Its dual, $\&\{l: S_l\}^{l \in L}$, is for channels that offer a menu of labelled choices (external choice). Recursive session types are built from type references a and recursion $\mu a.S$. We take an *equi-recursive* approach to types, not distinguishing a recursive type from its unfolding [1,34].

The notion of *duality* in session types is captured by relation $R \perp S$, in Fig. 8. Types Wait and Close; input and output; and internal and external choice are dual to each other. Recursive types are unfolded. The definition is coinductive, so that we accept possible infinite derivations. We refer to Gay et al. for details [15].

Box types are of the form $\bar{\tau} \vdash^n T$, where $\bar{\tau}$ denotes a possible empty sequence of contextual types. Such a type represents a code fragment M of type T, parameterised by a sequence of variables $\bar{x}$ of contextual types $\bar{\tau}$, together called contexts [22,28]. Ordinary (modal) variables are typed at level 0. The context of an ordinary variable is always empty, which justifies writing T for the contextual type $\varepsilon \vdash^0 T$. Furthermore, in a type $\bar{\tau} \vdash^{n+1} T$, we require all contextual types in $\bar{\tau}$ to be of levels smaller than or equal to n. The types in $\bar{\tau}$ characterise the parameters $\bar{x}$ of the contextual value $\bar{x}.M$ and thus must be typed at levels smaller than that of the of value itself. We capture these intuitions with a family

$$\frac{T\,\omega}{(\varepsilon \vdash^0 T)\,\omega} \qquad (\overline{\tau} \vdash^{n+1} T)\,\omega \qquad \mathsf{Unit}\,\omega \qquad (T \to_\omega U)\,\omega \qquad (\Box\tau)\,\omega$$

Fig. 9. Unrestricted types $\boxed{T\,\omega}$ $\boxed{\tau\,\omega}$

of type formation predicates, $T\ \mathrm{ctype}^n$, defined by the rules below.

$$(\varepsilon \vdash^0 T)\ \mathrm{ctype}^0 \qquad \frac{\overline{\tau}\ \mathrm{ctype}^n}{(\overline{\tau} \vdash^{n+1} T)\ \mathrm{ctype}^{n+1}} \qquad \frac{\tau\ \mathrm{ctype}^n}{\tau\ \mathrm{ctype}^{n+1}}$$

Henceforth we assume that all contextual types τ are well formed, that is, that $\tau\ \mathrm{ctype}^n$ holds for some n. For example, object $(\mathsf{Wait} \vdash^1 U) \vdash^1 T$ cannot be deemed a well formed type. This formulation adheres to the development of Mœbius and its kinding system [22].

Finally, the *box type* $\Box\tau^{n+1}$ represents a code fragment of contextual type τ. Boxed code fragments are typed at levels starting at 1.

Types denote resources that may be used exactly once or else an unbounded number of types. The ω predicate is true of types and contextual types whose values can be used an unbounded number of times. The definition is in Fig. 9. Contextual types of level 1 or above are all unrestricted, whereas those of level 0 are unrestricted only when the type T of the code in unrestricted. Level 0 represents ordinary code (of type T) and hence $\varepsilon \vdash^0 T$ is unrestricted if T is. On the other hand, levels higher than 0 represent boxed code fragments that can be duplicated or discarded at will, hence they are all of unrestricted nature. For types, Unit, unrestricted arrows $T \to_\omega U$ and box types $\Box\tau$ are the only unrestricted types. The rules in Fig. 9 are algorithmic. The ω predicate is thus decidable, which allows us to talk of its negation. A contextual type τ that is not unrestricted is called linear. The corresponding predicate is denoted $\tau\,1$. Two further predicates describe upper and lower bounds to the levels of contextual types. The predicate $< k$ is true of contextual types $\overline{\tau} \vdash^n T$ such that $n < k$. The predicate $\geq k$ is true of contextual types $\overline{\tau} \vdash^n T$ such that $n \geq k$.

Typing contexts Γ, Δ bind variables x to contextual types τ. We assume no variable is bound twice in the same context and take typing contexts up to the *exchange* of individual entries. The remaining two substructural rules— contraction and weakening—are handled by context split (described below) and by allowing contexts with unrestricted types in axioms. The four predicates are then lifted to typing contexts in the standard way. For example $\Gamma\,\omega$ is true of contexts $x_1 : \tau_1, \ldots, x_k : \tau_k$ such that $\tau_1\,\omega, \ldots, \tau_k\,\omega$. Intuitively, $\Gamma < n$ is true of a context Γ suitable for the *local variables* in a code fragment of level n, whereas $\Gamma \geq n$ is true of a context suitable for the *outer variables*. Notice that there is no context Γ for which $\Gamma < 0$ holds, with the exception of the empty context ε. On the other hand, $\Gamma^{\geq 0}$ is a tautology.

$$\text{typeof}(\mathsf{close}) = \mathsf{Close} \to_\omega \mathsf{Unit}$$
$$\text{typeof}(\mathsf{wait}) = \mathsf{Wait} \to_\omega \mathsf{Unit}$$
$$\text{typeof}(\mathsf{send}) = T \to_\omega \,!T.S \to_1 S$$
$$\text{typeof}(\mathsf{receive}) = ?T.S \to_\omega T \times S$$
$$\text{typeof}(\mathsf{select}\,k) = \oplus\{l : S_l\}^{l \in L} \to_\omega S_k, \text{with } k \in L$$
$$\text{typeof}(\mathsf{new}) = \mathsf{Unit} \to_\omega R \times S, \text{with } R \perp S$$
$$\text{typeof}(\mathsf{fork}) = (\mathsf{Unit} \to_1 \mathsf{Unit}) \to_\omega \mathsf{Unit}$$
$$\text{typeof}(\mathsf{fix}) = ((T \to_\omega T) \to_\omega (T \to_\omega T)) \to_\omega (T \to_\omega T)$$
$$\text{typeof}(\mathsf{unit}) = \mathsf{Unit}$$

Fig. 10. Type schemes for constants $\boxed{\text{typeof}(c) = T}$

We use notation τ^ω to denote a contextual type τ for which $\tau\,\omega$ holds, and similarly for τ^1. For contexts, we use notation Γ^ω to denote a context Γ for which $\Gamma\,\omega$ holds, and similarly for $\Gamma^{<n}$ and $\Gamma^{\geq n}$.

The *types for constants* are described by the type schemes in Fig. 10. Those for session types are taken mostly from Gay and Vasconcelos [16]. Constants close and wait close different ends of a channel and return Unit. Constant send accepts a value and a channel on which to send the value and returns the continuation channel; the second arrow is linear for T may denote a linear value. Constant receive accepts a channel and returns a pair composed of the value read and the continuation channel. Constant select k accepts an external choice type selects branch k, returning the appropriate continuation. Constant new denotes a suspended computation that, when invoked (with unit), returns a pair of channel endpoints of dual types. Constant fork receives a suspended computation, spawns a new thread to run the computation and returns Unit. Finally the type of fix is that of the call-by-value lambda calculus fixed-point combinator; all arrows are unrestricted for the argument function may be used an unbounded number of times (in each recursive call), including zero (in the base case), and fix itself can be used an unbounded number of times.

There will be times when the type system must merge typing contexts coming from different subderivations into a single context. *Context split* (read bottom-up) does the job. The rules are in Fig. 11 and taken verbatim from Walker [54]: linear types go left or right (but not in both directions); unrestricted types are copied into both contexts.

Typing judgements are of the form $\Gamma \vdash M : T$, stating that term M has type T under typing context Γ. The rules for the judgements, which we describe below, are in Fig. 12.

Contextual terms are closures of the form $\overline{x}.M$, closing term M over a sequence of variables $\overline{x}$. Such a contextual term is given a contextual type $\overline{\tau} \vdash^n T$ when T is of type M under the hypothesis that the variables in $\overline{x}$ are of the types

$$\varepsilon = \varepsilon \circ \varepsilon \qquad \frac{\Gamma = \Gamma_1 \circ \Gamma_2}{\Gamma, x : \tau^1 = (\Gamma_1, x : \tau^1) \circ \Gamma_2} \qquad \frac{\Gamma = \Gamma_1 \circ \Gamma_2}{\Gamma, x : \tau^1 = \Gamma_1 \circ (\Gamma_2, x : \tau^1)}$$

$$\frac{\Gamma = \Gamma_1 \circ \Gamma_2}{\Gamma, x : \tau^\omega = (\Gamma_1, x : \tau^\omega) \circ (\Gamma_2, x : \tau^\omega)}$$

Fig. 11. Context split $\boxed{\Gamma = \Gamma \circ \Gamma}$

T-Const
$$\Gamma^\omega \vdash c : \mathrm{typeof}(c)$$

T-Var
$$\frac{\overline{\Gamma} \vdash \overline{\sigma} : \overline{\tau}}{(\Delta^\omega, x : (\overline{\tau} \vdash^n T)) \circ \overline{\Gamma} \vdash x[\overline{\sigma}] : T}$$

T-LinFunI
$$\frac{\Gamma, x : (\varepsilon \vdash^0 T) \vdash M : U}{\Gamma \vdash \lambda x.M : T \to_1 U}$$

T-UnFunI
$$\frac{\Gamma^\omega, x : (\varepsilon \vdash^0 T) \vdash M : U}{\Gamma^\omega \vdash \lambda x.M : T \to_\omega U}$$

T-FunE
$$\frac{\Gamma \vdash M : T \to_m U \qquad \Delta \vdash N : T}{\Gamma \circ \Delta \vdash M\,N : U}$$

T-PairI
$$\frac{\Gamma \vdash M : T \qquad \Delta \vdash N : U}{\Gamma \circ \Delta \vdash (M, N) : T \times U}$$

T-PairE
$$\frac{\Gamma \vdash M : T \times U \qquad \Delta, x : (\varepsilon \vdash^0 T), y : (\varepsilon \vdash^0 U) \vdash N : V}{\Gamma \circ \Delta \vdash \mathsf{let}\ (x, y) = M\ \mathsf{in}\ N : V}$$

T-Ctx
$$\frac{\Gamma^{\geq n}, \overline{x : \tau}^{<n} \vdash M : T}{\Gamma^{\geq n} \vdash \overline{x}.M : (\overline{\tau} \vdash^n T)}$$

T-BoxI
$$\frac{\Gamma^\omega \vdash \sigma : \tau}{\Gamma^\omega, \Delta^\omega \vdash \mathsf{box}\ \sigma : \Box\tau}$$

T-BoxE
$$\frac{\Gamma \vdash M : \Box\tau \qquad \Delta, x : \tau \vdash N : T}{\Gamma \circ \Delta \vdash \mathsf{let}\ \mathsf{box}\ x = M\ \mathsf{in}\ N : T}$$

T-Match
$$\frac{\Gamma \vdash M : \&\{l : S_l\}^{l \in L} \qquad \Delta \vdash N_l : S_l \to_1 T \quad (\forall l \in L)}{\Gamma \circ \Delta \vdash \mathsf{match}\ M\ \mathsf{with}\ \{l : N_l\}^{l \in L} : T}$$

Fig. 12. Term formation $\boxed{\Gamma \vdash M : T}$

in $\overline{\tau}$ (rule T-Ctx). Intuitively, the free variables of M are split in two groups: local and outer. The local variables, $\overline{x}$, are distinguished in the contextual term $\overline{x}.M$ and typed under context $\overline{x : \tau}^{<n}$ where n is an upper bound of the levels k_i assigned to each local variable x_i in $\overline{x}$. The level of each local variable is arbitrary, as long as it is smaller than n. Outer variables are typed under context $\Gamma^{\geq n}$. Natural number n thus denotes the level at which the code fragment $\overline{x}.M$ is typed. In general, a contextual term can be typed at different levels. All resources (variables) in the context in the conclusion, as well as resources $\overline{x}$ are consumed in the derivation of M.

Modal variables are of the form $x[\sigma_1 \cdots \sigma_k]$, denoting a contextual term applied to contextual values $\sigma_1 \cdots \sigma_k$. To type each σ_i we need a separate context Γ_i. The type of x must be a contextual type of the form $\tau_1 \cdots \tau_k \vdash^n T$ and each contextual term σ_i must be of type τ_i. Since x may occur free in any of σ_i, we use context split to allow the entry $x \colon (\tau_1 \cdots \tau_k \vdash^n T)$ to occur in each Γ_i. In this case, the contextual type must be unrestricted.

In rule T-VAR, the lengths of all sequences—$\overline{\Gamma}$, $\overline{\sigma}$ and $\overline{\tau}$—must coincide. When the sequences are empty, the rule becomes the conventional axiom for variables. In fact rule T-VAR is the natural generalization of the axiom in Walker's linear λ-calculus [54], obtained by writing type $\varepsilon \vdash^n T$ in the context as T, and writing modal variable $x[\varepsilon]$ as x, thus $\Delta^\omega, x \colon (\varepsilon \vdash^n T) \vdash x[\varepsilon] : T$ abbreviates to $\Delta^\omega, x \colon T \vdash x : T$. The axiom justifies the presence of the unrestricted context Δ in the conclusion of T-VAR.

We briefly pause the presentation of the type system to address substitution. The *substitution principle* in the presence of linear typing is tricky because substitution can duplicate or discard terms [16,54]. In addition, we have to take levels of types into account. The resulting substitution principle can be stated as follows.

$$
\text{SUBS} \\
\frac{\Gamma \vdash \sigma : \tau^n \qquad \Delta, x \colon \tau^n \vdash M : T \qquad (\tau\, 1 \text{ or } \Gamma\, \omega) \qquad (\Gamma \geq n)}{\Gamma \circ \Delta \vdash \{\sigma/x\}M : T}
$$

We write $\Gamma \circ \Delta$ to denote the context Θ such that $\Theta = \Gamma \circ \Delta$. When we do so, we assume that the context split operation is defined. The first side condition, $\tau^n\, 1$ or $\Gamma\, \omega$, prevents free variables of linear types in σ from being duplicated or discarded by substitution $\{\sigma/x\}M$: if τ^n is linear, then no duplication or discarding occurs and, if $\Gamma\, \omega$, then free variables are safe to be duplicated or discarded. The second side condition, $\Gamma \geq n$, means that the levels of free variables in σ have to be equal to or greater than the level of σ.

If $n = 0$, that is when x is an ordinary variable, the condition $\Gamma \geq n$ trivially holds. Although the second formula in the condition does not hold in general, we can show that it holds for values (that is, when $\sigma = \varepsilon.v$ for some v). We can thus obtain the conventional (call-by-value) substitution principle:

$$
\frac{\Gamma \vdash \varepsilon.v : (\varepsilon \vdash^0 U) \qquad \Delta, x \colon (\varepsilon \vdash^0 U) \vdash M : T}{\Gamma \circ \Delta \vdash \{\varepsilon.v/x\}M : T} \quad \text{abbreviated to} \quad \frac{\Gamma \vdash v : U \qquad \Delta, x \colon U \vdash M : T}{\Gamma \circ \Delta \vdash \{v/x\}M : T}
$$

Returning to the type system, we address the conventional typing rules for *λ-abstraction and application* in the linear lambda calculus. The rules are those of Walker [54] with the necessary adaptation of the introduction rules to account for contexts featuring contextual types. There are two introduction rules, one for the linear, the other for the unrestricted arrow. In either case, the λ-bound variable x is local to M, hence of level 0. We record this fact by assigning x a type of the form $\varepsilon \vdash^0 T$. For the unrestricted arrow we require an unrestricted context, given that the context contains entries for the free variables in term $\lambda x.M$ and this, being unrestricted, may be duplicated or discarded.

The *box introduction and elimination* rules are as follows. In rule T-BoxI, the type of the box is the type $\Box\tau$ if the contextual term σ has contextual type τ. The context for the box elimination rule, T-BoxE, is split into two: one part (Γ) to type M, the other (Δ) to type N. Term M must denote a boxed code fragment, hence the type of M must be $\Box\tau$. Term N is typed under context Δ extended with an entry for x.

Linear type systems with a context split operator perform all the required weakening at the leaves of derivations. Hence all axioms expect a Γ^ω context to discard unrestricted variables. This is the case of rules T-Const and T-Var (with $\overline{\sigma}$ empty), and is all we need in most cases. But, when typing a box, we need weakening for a different reason: to discard unrestricted resources of small level (of levels smaller than that necessary to type the code fragment inside the box). Context Δ^ω plays this role; we expect this context to contain all unrestricted entries of levels below n. Linear resources cannot be discarded in any case.

Rule T-BoxI is perfectly aligned with preceding work [13,22,29], where level control is checked at box introduction. A derived rule, composed of T-Ctx followed by T-BoxI, coincides with the box introduction rule of Mœbius [22]:

$$\frac{\Gamma^\omega, \overline{x : \tau}^{<n} \vdash M : T \qquad (\Gamma^\omega \geq n)}{\Gamma^\omega, \Delta^\omega \vdash \mathsf{box}\,(\overline{x}.M) : \Box(\overline{\tau} \vdash^n T)}$$

5 Main results

This section discusses local soundness and completeness for the different type constructors, as well as the type safety result for the process language.

To ensure the introduction and elimination rules form a valid type constructor, the local soundness and completeness conditions must be shown for that type constructor [13,33]. Local soundness states that no extra information is gained by applying an introduction rule directly followed by an elimination rule. Hence, this detour should not be required to complete a derivation, since the same judgement can be reached without it. Its dual, local completeness, states that we can recover all the information present before applying an elimination rule, by simply applying an introduction rule. Local soundness materialises the reduction rules, while local completeness materialises the expansion rules, and the proof of local soundness implies type preservation for the reduction rule.

We start by studying the rules for the introduction and elimination of the arrow type. For *local soundness* we have:

$$\frac{\dfrac{\Gamma, x : (\varepsilon \vdash^0 T) \vdash M : U}{\Gamma \vdash \lambda x.M : T \to_\omega U}\ \text{T-LinFunI} \qquad \dfrac{}{\Delta \vdash v : T}\ \text{T-FunE}}{\Gamma \circ \Delta \vdash (\lambda x.M)\,v : U} \qquad \Rightarrow$$

$$\frac{\dfrac{\Delta \vdash v : T}{\Delta \vdash \varepsilon.v : (\varepsilon \vdash^0 T)}\ \text{T-Ctx} \qquad \Gamma, x : (\varepsilon \vdash^0 T) \vdash M : U}{\Gamma \circ \Delta \vdash \{\varepsilon.v/x\}M : U}\ \text{Subs}$$

The case for $\to_\omega$, that is for rule T-UNFUNI against T-FUNE, is similar and can be obtained by adding the ω restriction to context Γ.

For *local completeness*, assume that x is not free in M and let τ be the contextual type $\varepsilon \vdash^0 T$. We must distinguish four cases, according to when Γ and/or T are unrestricted or linear. We start with the case when both Γ and T are linear. Then, τ is linear and $\Gamma, x\colon \tau = \Gamma \circ x\colon \tau$, which justifies the instance of rule T-FUNE below.

$$\Gamma \vdash M : T \to_1 U \quad \Rightarrow$$

$$\cfrac{\cfrac{\Gamma \vdash M : T \to_1 U \qquad \cfrac{}{x\colon \tau \vdash x[\varepsilon] : T}\ \text{T-VAR}}{\Gamma, x\colon \tau \vdash M\,x[\varepsilon] : U}\ \text{T-FUNE}}{\Gamma \vdash \lambda x.(M\,x[\varepsilon]) : T \to_1 U}\ \text{T-LINFUNI}$$

When T is unrestricted, then so is τ and we have $\Gamma, x\colon \tau = (\Gamma, x\colon \tau) \circ x\colon \tau$. We use weakening to add $x\colon \tau$ to the context of M. We show the case when Γ is also unrestricted; the two remaining cases are similar.

$$\Gamma^\omega \vdash M : T \to_\omega U \quad \Rightarrow$$

$$\cfrac{\cfrac{\cfrac{\Gamma^\omega \vdash M : T \to_\omega U}{\Gamma^\omega, x\colon \tau \vdash M : T \to_\omega U}\ \text{WEAK} \qquad \cfrac{}{x\colon \tau \vdash x[\varepsilon] : T}\ \text{T-VAR}}{\Gamma^\omega, x\colon \tau \vdash M\,x[\varepsilon] : U}\ \text{T-FUNE}}{\Gamma^\omega \vdash \lambda x.(M\,x[\varepsilon]) : T \to_\omega U}\ \text{T-UNFUNI}$$

We now address the rules for box introduction and elimination. For *local soundness* we have the following derivations, where rule WEAK introduces unrestricted entries in the context.

$$\cfrac{\cfrac{\cdots \quad \cfrac{\Gamma^\omega \geq n}{\Gamma^\omega \vdash \sigma : \tau^n}\ \text{T-CTX}}{\Gamma^\omega, \Delta^\omega \vdash \mathsf{box}\,\sigma : \Box\tau^n}\ \text{T-BoxI} \qquad \Theta, x\colon \tau^n \vdash N : T}{(\Gamma^\omega, \Delta^\omega) \circ \Theta \vdash \mathsf{let\ box}\ x = \mathsf{box}\,\sigma\ \mathsf{in}\ N : T}\ \text{T-BoxE} \qquad \Rightarrow$$

$$\cfrac{\cfrac{\Gamma^\omega \vdash \sigma : \tau^n}{\Gamma^\omega, \Delta^\omega \vdash \sigma : \tau^n}\ \text{WEAK} \qquad \Theta, x\colon \tau^n \vdash M : T \qquad (\Gamma^\omega \geq n)}{(\Gamma^\omega, \Delta^\omega) \circ \Theta \vdash \{\sigma/x\}N : T}\ \text{SUBS}$$

For *local completeness* we first define eta expansion for contextual types, written as $\eta(x, \tau)$ by the following rules, where variables in $\overline{y}$ are taken freshly.

$$\eta(x, \varepsilon \vdash^0 T) = \varepsilon.x[\epsilon] \qquad\qquad \eta(x, \overline{\tau} \vdash^{n+1} T) = \overline{y}.x[\overline{\eta(y, \tau)}]$$

Eta expansion $\eta(x, \tau)$ is defined at any contextual type τ because the level of τ strictly decreases at each step. We can confirm that the following lemma holds; the proof is by induction on the level of τ.

$$\dfrac{\text{R-Exp}\quad \Gamma \vdash M : \mathsf{Unit}}{\Gamma \vdash \langle M \rangle} \qquad \dfrac{\text{P-Par}\quad \Gamma \vdash P \qquad \Delta \vdash Q}{\Gamma \circ \Delta \vdash P \parallel Q} \qquad \dfrac{\text{P-Res}\quad \Gamma, x \colon (\varepsilon \vdash^0 R), y \colon (\varepsilon \vdash^0 S) \vdash P \qquad R \perp S}{\Gamma \vdash (\nu x y) P}$$

Fig. 13. Process formation $\boxed{\Gamma \vdash P}$

Lemma 1. $x : \tau \vdash \eta(x, \tau) : \tau.$

We now witness local completeness. Let Δ be the unrestricted part of Γ. Then $\Gamma = \Gamma \circ \Delta$. Let $\overline{\rho}$ be the sequence of contextual types, whose level is lower than n, and τ be the contextual type $\overline{\rho} \vdash^n T$. We have $(\overline{x : \rho})^{<n}$ and $(u : \tau)^{\geq n}$. Furthermore, we can see the context $(u : \tau)^{\geq n}$ is unrestricted because $n > 0$ is required by the well-formedness condition of $\Box \tau$. We then have:

$$\Gamma \vdash M : \Box \tau \quad \Rightarrow$$

$$\dfrac{\Gamma \vdash M : \Box \tau \qquad \dfrac{\dfrac{\dfrac{\dfrac{\dfrac{\quad}{\overline{x : \rho} \vdash \overline{\eta(x, \rho) : \rho}}\;\text{Lemma 1}}{\overline{x : \rho} \circ u : \tau \vdash u[\overline{\eta(x, \rho)}] : T}\;\text{T-Var}}{u : \tau \vdash \overline{x}.u[\overline{\eta(x, \rho)}] : \tau}\;\text{T-Ctx}}{\Delta, u : \tau \vdash \mathsf{box}\,(\overline{x}.u[\overline{\eta(x, \rho)}]) : \Box \tau}\;\text{T-BoxI}}{\Gamma \circ \Delta \vdash \mathsf{let\ box}\ u = M\ \mathsf{in\ box}\,(\overline{x}.u[\overline{\eta(x, \rho)}]) : \Box \tau}\;\text{T-BoxE}$$

The second part of this section addresses type safety. Even if programmers are not supposed to write processes directly, we still need to type them in order to state and prove the type safety result for the process language. The rules, in Fig. 13, are straightforward and taken from Vasconcelos [52] and Thiemann et al. [2,48]. In a thread $\langle M \rangle$, term M must be of Unit type. Given that the result of the evaluation is discarded, any unrestricted type would do. The parallel composition splits the context in the conclusion and uses one part for each process. Scope restriction introduces entries for each of the two channel ends. These must be of dual types.

We show a conventional safety property for the term language based on *preservation* and *progress*—Theorems 1 and 2—following Pierce [34]. In the case of progress we take into consideration terms that may be (temporarily) stuck waiting for a communication on a channel.

Theorem 1 (Preservation).

1. *If* $M \to N$ *and* $\Gamma \vdash M : T$, *then* $\Gamma \vdash N : T$.
2. *If* $\Gamma \vdash P$ *and* $P \to Q$, *then* $\Gamma \vdash Q$.

Progress is usually stated for closed terms. Because channel endpoints are also variables, we must take into account terms with free endpoints, that is variables of a session type. We say that a context Γ *contains session types only,* and write Γ^S when Γ is of the form $x_1 : \varepsilon \vdash^0 S_1, \dots, x_n : \varepsilon \vdash^0 S_n.$

Theorem 2 (Progress for evaluation). *Let $\Gamma^S \vdash M : T$. Then,*

1. *M is a value, or*
2. *$M \to N$, for some N, or*
3. *M is of the form $E[N]$, for some E, with N of one of the following forms:* close x, wait x, send $v\ x$, receive x, select $l\ x$, match x with $\{l \to N_l\}^{l \in L}$, new v *or* fork v.

The process language does not enjoy progress due to possible occurrences of deadlocks. Safety for the process language is based on *preservation* and *absence of runtime errors*—Theorems 1 and 3—following Honda et al. [19]. In order to address the absence of runtime errors for the process language, we start with a few definitions. The *subject* of a term M is variable x (denoting a channel endpoint) in the following cases and undefined in all other cases.

$$\text{close}\ x \qquad \text{wait}\ x \qquad \text{send}\ v\ x \qquad \text{receive}\ x \qquad \text{select}\ k\ x$$

$$\text{match}\ x\ \text{with}\ \{l \to N_l\}^{l \in L}$$

A process $(\nu xy)(\langle E[M] \rangle \parallel \langle F[N] \rangle)$ is a *redex* if

- M is close x and N is wait y,
- M is send $v\ x$ and N is receive y,
- M is select $l'\ x$ and N is match y with $\{l \to N_l\}^{l \in L}$ and $l' \in L$.

or conversely for processes $(\nu xy)(\langle F[N] \rangle \parallel \langle E[M] \rangle)$. This definition corresponds to the axioms R-Close, R-Com and R-Branch in the operational semantics (Fig. 6). Saying that P is a redex is equivalent to say that P reduces by one of these rules.

Finally a process P is a *runtime error* if it is structural congruent to a process of the form $(\nu x_1 y_1) \cdots (\nu x_n y_n)(P_1 \parallel \cdots \parallel P_m)$ and there are i, j, k such that the subject of P_i is x_k, the subject of P_j is y_k but $(\nu x_k y_k)(P_i \parallel P_j)$ is not a redex.

Theorem 3 (Absence of immediate errors). *If $\vdash P$ then P is not a runtime error.*

6   Algorithmic type checking

The typing rules of Fig. 12 are not algorithmic. Two problems arise: guessing the right context split (a non-deterministic procedure) and guessing the types (and levels) of λ-abstractions and contextual values' bound variables. For the former, we refactor the typing rules so they return the unused part of the incoming context [54]. For the latter, we work with an explicitly typed term language: we now write c^τ to resolve the polymorphism of constants, $\lambda_m x : T.M$ to introduce the type of bound variable x, and $(\overline{x : \tau})^n.M$ to introduce the contextual types and the level of the contextual value.

We introduce a new type synthesis judgement $\Gamma_{\text{in}} \vdash M_{\text{in}} \Rightarrow T_{\text{out}} \mid \Delta_{\text{out}}$, where context Γ and term M are considered inputs and type T and context Δ

$$\text{A-Const} \qquad \Gamma \vdash c^\tau \Rightarrow \tau \mid \Gamma$$

$$\text{A-UnVar} \qquad \frac{\Gamma_1, x \colon (\overline{\tau} \vdash^n T) \vdash \sigma_1 \Rightarrow \tau_1 \mid \Gamma_2 \qquad \Gamma_2 \vdash \sigma_2 \Rightarrow \tau_2 \mid \Gamma_3 \ \ldots \ \Gamma_k \vdash \sigma_n \Rightarrow \tau_n \mid \Gamma_{k+1}}{\Gamma_1, x \colon (\overline{\tau} \vdash^n T)^\omega \vdash x[\sigma_1, \ldots, \sigma_k] \Rightarrow T \mid \Gamma_{k+1}}$$

$$\text{A-LinVar} \qquad \frac{\Gamma_1 \vdash \sigma_1 \Rightarrow \tau_1 \mid \Gamma_2 \ \ldots \ \Gamma_k \vdash \sigma_k \Rightarrow \tau_k \mid \Gamma_{k+1}}{\Gamma_1, x \colon (\overline{\tau} \vdash^n T) \vdash x[\sigma_1, \ldots, \sigma_k] \Rightarrow T \mid \Gamma_{k+1}}$$

$$\text{A-LinFunI} \qquad \frac{\Gamma, x \colon (\varepsilon \vdash^0 T) \vdash M \Rightarrow U \mid \Delta}{\Gamma \vdash \lambda_1 x \colon T.M \Rightarrow T \to_1 U \mid \Delta \div x}$$

$$\text{A-UnFunI} \qquad \frac{\Gamma, x \colon (\varepsilon \vdash^0 T) \vdash M \Rightarrow U \mid \Delta \qquad \Delta \div x = \Gamma}{\Gamma \vdash \lambda_\omega x \colon T.M \Rightarrow T \to_\omega U \mid \Gamma}$$

$$\text{A-FunE} \qquad \frac{\Gamma_1 \vdash M \Rightarrow T \to_m U \mid \Gamma_2 \qquad \Gamma_2 \vdash N \Rightarrow T \mid \Gamma_3}{\Gamma_1 \vdash M\,N \Rightarrow U \mid \Gamma_3}$$

$$\text{A-PairI} \qquad \frac{\Gamma_1 \vdash M \Rightarrow T \mid \Gamma_2 \qquad \Gamma_2 \vdash N \Rightarrow U \mid \Gamma_3}{\Gamma_1 \vdash (M, N) \Rightarrow T \times U \mid \Gamma_3}$$

$$\text{A-PairE} \qquad \frac{\Gamma_1 \vdash M \Rightarrow T \times U \mid \Gamma_2 \qquad \Gamma_2, x \colon (\varepsilon \vdash^0 T), y \colon (\varepsilon \vdash^0 U) \vdash N \Rightarrow V \mid \Gamma_3}{\Gamma_1 \vdash \mathsf{let}\ (x, y) = M \ \mathsf{in}\ N \Rightarrow V \mid \Gamma_3 \div x \div y}$$

$$\text{A-BoxI} \qquad \frac{\Gamma \vdash \sigma \Rightarrow \tau \mid \Gamma}{\Gamma \vdash \mathsf{box}\,\sigma \Rightarrow \Box\tau \mid \Gamma}$$

$$\text{A-BoxE} \qquad \frac{\Gamma_1 \vdash M \Rightarrow \Box\tau \mid \Gamma_2 \qquad \Gamma_2, x \colon \tau \vdash N \Rightarrow T \mid \Gamma_3}{\Gamma_1 \vdash \mathsf{let\ box}\ x = M \ \mathsf{in}\ N \Rightarrow T \mid \Gamma_3 \div x}$$

$$\text{A-Match} \qquad \frac{\Gamma_1 \vdash M \Rightarrow \&\{l : S_l\}^{l \in L} \mid \Gamma_2 \qquad \Gamma_2 \vdash N_l \Rightarrow S_l \to_1 T \mid \Gamma_3 \quad (\forall l \in L)}{\Gamma_1 \vdash \mathsf{match}\ M \ \mathsf{with}\ \{l : N_l\}^{l \in L} \Rightarrow T \mid \Gamma_3}$$

$$\text{A-Ctx} \qquad \frac{\Gamma_1 \overset{n}{\rightsquigarrow} \Gamma_3^{\geq n}, \Gamma_4^{<n} \qquad \Gamma_2 < n \qquad \Gamma_2, \Gamma_3 \vdash M \Rightarrow T \mid \Delta}{\Gamma_1 \vdash (\Gamma_2^n.M) \Rightarrow (\overline{\tau} \vdash^n T) \mid \Delta \div \overline{x}, \Gamma_4}$$

Fig. 14. Algorithmic type checking $\boxed{\Gamma \vdash M \Rightarrow T \mid \Delta}$

are considered outputs. The rules are in Fig. 14. Some rules make use of *context difference*, $\Gamma \div x = \Delta$, an operation that ensures the binding for x is removed from Γ, in case the type bound is unrestricted, or it doesn't even occur, in case the type is linear. We let operator $\div$ be left-associative.

$$\frac{x \colon \tau \notin \Gamma}{\Gamma \div x = \Gamma} \qquad\qquad \frac{}{(\Gamma, x \colon \tau^\omega, \Delta) \div x = \Gamma, \Delta}$$

The typing rules A-UnVar, A-LinVar, A-BoxI, A-BoxE and A-Ctx are novel, the remaining are inspired by Almeida et al. [2]. In rules A-Const, A-UnFunI and A-BoxI, the input and output contexts are the same, meaning no linear variables may be consumed. Rules A-LinFunI, A-UnFunI, A-PairE, A-BoxE and A-Ctx ensure that bound variables do not escape their scope. In rule A-CTX, we must split the context $(\Gamma \stackrel{n}{\leadsto} \Delta)$ according to the level n, using only the outer fragment to type the subexpression, mimicking rule T-CTX. The remaining rules are easy to understand.

If we denote by $M^\bullet$ an annotated term (as those in Fig. 14), we can easily define an erasure function, $\text{erase}(M^\bullet)$ by induction on the structure of $M^\bullet$. Then we have the following result.

Theorem 4 (Algorithmic correctness).

1. *If* $\Gamma \vdash M^\bullet \Rightarrow T \mid \Delta$ *and* Δ^ω, *then* $\Gamma \vdash \text{erase}(M^\bullet) : T$.
2. *If* $\Gamma \vdash M : T$, *then there is a* $M^\bullet$ *s.t.* $M = \text{erase}(M^\bullet)$, *and* $\Gamma \vdash M^\bullet \Rightarrow T \mid \Delta$ *and* Δ^ω.

7   Related work

Our approach to staged metaprogramming is based on contextual modal types. The logical basis for this approach goes back to modal logic S4 [13,36], where a type $\Box T$ stands for a closed code fragment that evaluates to a value with type T. Box types are then generalized by introducing contexts, such as $\Box(\overline{T_1} \vdash T_2)$, allowing free variables in a code fragment by listing their types in the box type. These types are called contextual modal types [29,30]. To avoid confusion with contextual types, we call them box types in this paper. Mœbius [22] further generalizes contextual modal types to hold contexts with different levels, allowing wider variety of metaprogramming. There seems to be two styles when it comes to formalizing contextual modal types: one is a dual-context style [13,29,30] where box values are deconstructed with let-box syntax and meta-variables, and the other is Kripke-style or Fitch-style [11,13,28,51] where box values are deconstructed with an unquote term. In this classification, Mœbius [22] can be considered a calculus in dual-context style, but further generalized to allow multi-level contexts.

Temporal types [12] could be another alternative approach for metaprogramming, which is adopted by MetaML and many staged programming languages [24,45,46,57]. Temporal type systems, however, are known to be unsound in the presence of computational effects [23,39,46], whereas channel-based communication is inherently effectful. We therefore preferred contextual modal type–based systems such as Mœbius, which are compatible with session types.

Intensional analysis [21,32], i.e., the ability to perform pattern matching on code fragments, is a desirable feature with which to improve our work. Despite the original formulation of Mœbius also supporting intensional analysis, extending it to support linear types can be a non-trivial problem. Supporting polymorphism is another potential extension. Mœbius supports generating code that depends on polymorphic types, which should be feasible in our type system. Murase et al. proposed polymorphic contexts [28] that can abstract several parts of a context by context variables. Such extension could also be useful in our type system, but it is not clear if we can extend our Mœbius-based type system, given that polymorphic contexts as defined by Murase et al. [28] are designed for a Fitch-style formulation.

Session types were introduced by Honda et al. [18,19,47] in the 1990s. The types we employ—input/output and internal/external choice—are from these early works. The types for channels ready to be closed are from Caires et al. [8,9]. The early works on session types were built on the π-calculus; session types for functional programming were later suggested by Gay and Vasconcelos [16]. The idea of using different identifiers to denote the two ends of a same communication channel is by Vasconcelos [52]. The only works integrating linear type systems and multi-stage programming that we are aware of are those proposed by Georges et al. [17], Sano et al. [40], and Ângelo et al. [4]. Here we provide for concurrency, recursive types, linear and unrestricted types, session types, and a programming model encompassing a single (functional) programming language.

An alternative starting point would have been a linear logic inspired language, providing for deadlock freedom, as proposed by Caires, Pfenning, Wadler [8,53]. However, enforcing the absence of deadlocks along the ideas of the aforementioned works would impose significant syntactic restrictions, which we prefer to avoid in favour of a more flexible design.

Although our proposal may appear similar to FuSes, by Sano et al. [40], i.e., both integrate contextual modal types with session types, they pursue very different design goals. Our work aims to model a real programming language (such as JavaScript) that supports both concurrent programming and metaprogramming, which motivates our integration of GV [16] (for session-typed functional and concurrent programming) and Mœbius [22] (for metaprogramming). In contrast, FuSes seeks to provide a novel paradigm for integrating concurrent and functional programming, employing contextual types to separate a functional layer from a session-typed process' layer. Note that linearity is addressed only at the process level. In this sense, FuSes should be compared to GV rather than to our proposal (as also noted in [40]).

Even if inspired in linear logic, FuSes, as our system, offers no guarantees of deadlock freedom. Furthermore even if the process layer can exchange recursive functional code in messages, it can't splice the result into code without resorting to the functional level. Our proposal, on the other hand offers a much more streamlined programming experience with all the programming happening at the functional level. Hence, our calculus can naturally express programs such as sendFives or volunteer programming, whereas FuSes does not permit a direct description of such programs. Again, this distinction arises from the difference in design goals and does not necessarily imply that one approach is superior or inferior to the other. FuSes, however, offers code analysis and pattern matching, topics that we decided to leave to future work.

Another relevant line of work concerns the uniformisation of the metatheory of substructural type systems, with the explicit goal of facilitating their mechanisation. Wood and Atkey [56] present a general framework for reasoning about and expressing linear type systems, more specifically those commonly referred to in the literature as *resource-aware* or *quantitative*, thus making their mechanisation more straightforward. Zackon et al. [58] pursue a similar goal, focusing instead on encoding contexts as resource vectors (CARVe), which allows an uniform treatment of various substructural logics, be it affine, linear or others. The major advantage of these works lies in the uniformisation of the formalisation of such systems, albeit at the cost of more involved rules and machinery. In our work, we strive for clarity and, above all, succinctness and simplicity of the type system itself. These goals would be harder to attain had we employed such generic frameworks as the basis for our machinery, rather than the more classic approach based on splitting contexts.

8   Conclusion and future work

We show the merits of enhancing a session type system with staged meta-programming, allowing protocols that exchange code. Such an extension requires the integration of staged meta-programming into a linear type system (on top of which session types are defined), accounting for the main technical challenge. We also show our system can be implemented in a practical way, by providing type checking rules, as well as correctness results. We further plan on improving the system's expressivity, both on the way protocols are defined and on how code is created and used. One could aim at two orthogonal extensions. The first is polymorphism: both for session types [2] and for staged meta-programming [22]. The second is the incorporation of context-free session types, allowing programming with the sequential composition of types [35,44]. These extensions would lead to more general and reusable code and protocols.

Acknowledgements We thank Chuta Sano for his insightful comments. This work was partly supported by JSPS Invitational Short-Term Fellowships for Research in Japan. It was further supported by the FCT through project Reliable and Expressive Concurrent Systems through Advanced Session Types ref. 2023.13752.PEX (https://doi.org/10.54499/2023.13752.PEX), and the LASIGE Research Unit, ref. UID/00408/2025 (https://doi.org/10.54499/UID/00408/2025), and by the LIACC Research Unit (10.54499/UIDB/00027/2020 and 10.54499/UIDP/00027/2020). A full version of this paper, with extra proofs, is available elsewhere [3].

References

1. Abadi, M., Fiore, M.P.: Syntactic considerations on recursive types. In: LICS. pp. 242–252. IEEE Computer Society (1996). https://doi.org/10.1109/LICS.1996.561324
2. Almeida, B., Mordido, A., Thiemann, P., Vasconcelos, V.T.: Polymorphic lambda calculus with context-free session types. Inf. Comput. **289**(Part), 104948 (2022). https://doi.org/10.1016/J.IC.2022.104948
3. Ângelo, P., Igarashi, A., Murase, Y., Vasconcelos, V.T.: Contextual metaprogramming for session types. CoRR **abs/2601.15180** (2026). https://doi.org/10.48550/arXiv.2601.15180

4. Ângelo, P., Igarashi, A., Vasconcelos, V.T.: Linear contextual metaprogramming and session types. In: PLACES. EPTCS, vol. 401, pp. 1–10 (2024). https://doi.org/10.4204/EPTCS.401.1
5. Balat, V.: Ocsigen: typing web interaction with objective caml. In: Workshop on ML. pp. 84–94. ACM (2006). https://doi.org/10.1145/1159876.1159889
6. Barendregt, H.P.: The lambda calculus - its syntax and semantics, Studies in logic and the foundations of mathematics, vol. 103. North-Holland (1985)
7. Boinc. https://boinc.berkeley.edu/, accessed: 2025-04-09
8. Caires, L., Pfenning, F.: Session types as intuitionistic linear propositions. In: Proceedings of CONCUR. LNCS, vol. 6269, pp. 222–236. Springer (2010). https://doi.org/10.1007/978-3-642-15375-4_16
9. Caires, L., Pfenning, F., Toninho, B.: Linear logic propositions as session types. Math. Struct. Comput. Sci. **26**(3), 367–423 (2016). https://doi.org/10.1017/S0960129514000218
10. Chun, B., Ihm, S., Maniatis, P., Naik, M., Patti, A.: Clonecloud: elastic execution between mobile device and cloud. In: EuroSys. pp. 301–314. ACM (2011). https://doi.org/10.1145/1966445.1966473
11. Clouston, R.: Fitch-style modal lambda calculi. In: FOSSACS. LNCS, vol. 10803, pp. 258–275. Springer (2018). https://doi.org/10.1007/978-3-319-89366-2_14
12. Davies, R.: A temporal logic approach to binding-time analysis. J. ACM **64**(1), 1:1–1:45 (2017). https://doi.org/10.1145/3011069
13. Davies, R., Pfenning, F.: A modal analysis of staged computation. J. ACM **48**(3), 555–604 (2001). https://doi.org/10.1145/382780.382785
14. Dean, J., Ghemawat, S.: MapReduce: simplified data processing on large clusters. Commun. ACM **51**(1), 107–113 (2008). https://doi.org/10.1145/1327452.1327492
15. Gay, S.J., Thiemann, P., Vasconcelos, V.T.: Duality of session types: The final cut. In: PLACES. EPTCS, vol. 314, pp. 23–33 (2020). https://doi.org/10.4204/EPTCS.314.3
16. Gay, S.J., Vasconcelos, V.T.: Linear type theory for asynchronous session types. J. Funct. Program. **20**(1), 19–50 (2010). https://doi.org/10.1017/S0956796809990268
17. Georges, A.L., Murawska, A., Otis, S., Pientka, B.: LINCX: A linear logical framework with first-class contexts. In: ESOP. LNCS, vol. 10201, pp. 530–555. Springer (2017). https://doi.org/10.1007/978-3-662-54434-1_20
18. Honda, K.: Types for dyadic interaction. In: CONCUR. LNCS, vol. 715, pp. 509–523. Springer (1993). https://doi.org/10.1007/3-540-57208-2_35
19. Honda, K., Vasconcelos, V.T., Kubo, M.: Language primitives and type discipline for structured communication-based programming. In: ESOP. LNCS, vol. 1381, pp. 122–138. Springer (1998). https://doi.org/10.1007/BFb0053567
20. HTMX. https://htmx.org/, accessed: 2025-02-22
21. Hu, J.Z.S., Pientka, B.: Layered modal type theory - where meta-programming meets intensional analysis. In: ESOP. LNCS, vol. 14576, pp. 52–82. Springer (2024). https://doi.org/10.1007/978-3-031-57262-3_3
22. Jang, J., Gélineau, S., Monnier, S., Pientka, B.: Mœbius: metaprogramming using contextual types: the stage where system F can pattern match on itself. Proc. ACM Program. Lang. **6**(POPL), 1–27 (2022). https://doi.org/10.1145/3498700
23. Kameyama, Y., Kiselyov, O., Shan, C.: Shifting the stage - staging with delimited control. J. Funct. Program. **21**(6), 617–662 (2011). https://doi.org/10.1017/S0956796811000256
24. Kiselyov, O.: MetaOCaml theory and implementation. CoRR **abs/2309.08207** (2023). https://doi.org/10.48550/ARXIV.2309.08207

25. Meteor.js. https://www.meteor.com/, accessed: 2025-04-09
26. Milner, R.: Functions as processes. Math. Struct. Comput. Sci. **2**(2), 119–141 (1992). https://doi.org/10.1017/S0960129500001407
27. Mitchell, J.C.: Foundations for programming languages. Foundation of computing series, MIT Press (1996)
28. Murase, Y., Nishiwaki, Y., Igarashi, A.: Contextual modal type theory with polymorphic contexts. In: ESOP. LNCS, vol. 13990, pp. 281–308. Springer (2023). https://doi.org/10.1007/978-3-031-30044-8_11
29. Nanevski, A., Pfenning, F.: Staged computation with names and necessity. J. Funct. Program. **15**(5), 893–939 (2005). https://doi.org/10.1017/S095679680500568X
30. Nanevski, A., Pfenning, F., Pientka, B.: Contextual modal type theory. ACM Trans. Comput. Log. **9**(3), 23:1–23:49 (2008). https://doi.org/10.1145/1352582.1352591
31. Next.js. https://nextjs.org/, accessed: 2025-04-09
32. Parreaux, L., Voizard, A., Shaikhha, A., Koch, C.E.: Unifying analytic and statically-typed quasiquotes. Proc. ACM Program. Lang. **2**(POPL), 13:1–13:33 (2018). https://doi.org/10.1145/3158101
33. Pfenning, F., Davies, R.: A judgmental reconstruction of modal logic. Math. Struct. Comput. Sci. **11**(4), 511–540 (2001). https://doi.org/10.1017/S0960129501003322
34. Pierce, B.C.: Types and programming languages. MIT Press (2002)
35. Poças, D., Costa, D., Mordido, A., Vasconcelos, V.T.: System f^μ ømega with context-free session types. In: ESOP. LNCS, vol. 13990, pp. 392–420. Springer (2023). https://doi.org/10.1007/978-3-031-30044-8_15
36. Prawitz, D.: Natural deduction. Almquist & Wiksell, Stockholm, Sweden (1965)
37. Primegrid. https://www.primegrid.com/, accessed: 2025-04-09
38. React server components. https://react.dev/reference/rsc/server-components, accessed: 2025-04-09
39. Rhiger, M.: Staged computation with staged lexical scope. In: ESOP. LNCS, vol. 7211, pp. 559–578. Springer (2012). https://doi.org/10.1007/978-3-642-28869-2_28
40. Sano, C., Garg, D., Kavanagh, R., Pientka, B., Toninho, B.: Fusing session-typed concurrent programming into functional programming. Proc. ACM Program. Lang. **9**(ICFP) (Aug 2025). https://doi.org/10.1145/3747519, https://doi.org/10.1145/3747519
41. Scala-loci. https://scala-loci.github.io/, accessed: 2025-04-09
42. Serrano, M., Prunet, V.: A glimpse of hopjs. In: ICPF. pp. 180–192. ACM (2016). https://doi.org/10.1145/2951913.2951916
43. Sheard, T., Jones, S.P.: Template meta-programming for haskell. In: Workshop on Haskell. pp. 1–16. ACM (2002). https://doi.org/10.1145/581690.581691
44. Silva, G., Mordido, A., Vasconcelos, V.T.: Subtyping context-free session types. In: CONCUR. LIPIcs, vol. 279, pp. 11:1–11:19. Schloss Dagstuhl - Leibniz-Zentrum für Informatik (2023). https://doi.org/10.4230/LIPICS.CONCUR.2023.11
45. Stucki, N., Brachthäuser, J.I., Odersky, M.: Multi-stage programming with generative and analytical macros. In: GPCE. pp. 110–122. ACM (2021). https://doi.org/10.1145/3486609.3487203
46. Taha, W., Nielsen, M.F.: Environment classifiers. In: POPL. pp. 26–37. ACM (2003). https://doi.org/10.1145/604131.604134
47. Takeuchi, K., Honda, K., Kubo, M.: An interaction-based language and its typing system. In: PARLE. LNCS, vol. 817, pp. 398–413. Springer (1994). https://doi.org/10.1007/3-540-58184-7_118

48. Thiemann, P., Vasconcelos, V.T.: Context-free session types. In: ICFP. pp. 462–475. ACM (2016). https://doi.org/10.1145/2951913.2951926
49. Unison. https://www.unison-lang.org/, accessed: 2025-04-09
50. Ur/Web. https://github.com/urweb/urweb, accessed: 2025-04-09
51. Valliappan, N., Ruch, F., Tom'e Corti nas, C.: Normalization for Fitch-style modal calculi. Proc. ACM Program. Lang. **6**(ICFP), 772–798 (2022). https://doi.org/10.1145/3547649
52. Vasconcelos, V.T.: Fundamentals of session types. Inf. Comput. **217**, 52–70 (2012). https://doi.org/10.1016/J.IC.2012.05.002
53. Wadler, P.: Propositions as sessions. J. Funct. Program. **24**(2-3), 384–418 (2014)
54. Walker, D.: Advanced Topics in Types and Programming Languages, chap. Substructural Type Systems, pp. 3–44. The MIT Press (2005)
55. White, T.: Hadoop - The Definitive Guide: Storage and Analysis at Internet Scale (4. ed., revised & updated). O'Reilly (2015)
56. Wood, J., Atkey, R.: A framework for substructural type systems. In: ESOP. LNCS, vol. 13240, pp. 376–402. Springer (2022). https://doi.org/10.1007/978-3-030-99336-8_14
57. Xie, N., White, L., Nicole, O., Yallop, J.: Macocaml: Staging composable and compilable macros. Proc. ACM Program. Lang. **7**(ICFP), 604–648 (2023). https://doi.org/10.1145/3607851
58. Zackon, D., Sano, C., Momigliano, A., Pientka, B.: Split decisions: Explicit contexts for substructural languages. In: CPP. pp. 257–271. ACM (2025). https://doi.org/10.1145/3703595.3705888
59. Zaharia, M., Chowdhury, M., Franklin, M.J., Shenker, S., Stoica, I.: Spark: Cluster computing with working sets. In: HotCloud'10. USENIX Association (2010)

Specifying and Verifying RDMA Synchronisation

Guillaume Ambal[1] , Max Stupple ,
Brijesh Dongol[2] , and Azalea Raad[1]

[1] Imperial College London, London, UK
{g.ambal,max.stupple21,azalea.raad}@imperial.ac.uk
[2] University of Surrey, Guildford, UK
b.dongol@surrey.ac.uk

Abstract. Remote direct memory access (RDMA) allows a machine
to directly read from and write to the memory of remote machine, enabling high-throughput, low-latency data transfer. Ensuring correctness
of RDMA programs has only recently become possible with the formalisation of RDMA^{TSO} semantics (describing the behaviour of RDMA networking over a TSO CPU). However, this semantics currently lacks a
formalisation of remote synchronisation, meaning that the implementations of common abstractions such as locks cannot be verified. In this
paper, we close this gap by presenting $\text{RDMA}^{\text{TSO}}_{\text{RMW}}$, the first semantics for
remote 'read-modify-write' (RMW) instructions over TSO. It turns out
that remote RMW operations are weak and only ensure atomicity against
other remote RMWs. We therefore build a set of composable synchroni-
sation abstractions starting with the $\text{RDMA}^{\text{WAIT}}_{\text{RMW}}$ library. Underpinned by
$\text{RDMA}^{\text{WAIT}}_{\text{RMW}}$, we then specify, implement and verify three classes of remote
locks that are suitable for different scenarios. Additionally, we develop
the notion of a strong RDMA model, $\text{RDMA}^{\text{SC}}_{\text{RMW}}$, which is akin to sequential consistency in shared memory architectures. Our libraries are built
to be compatible with an existing set of high-performance libraries called
LOCO, which ensures compositionality and verifiability.

Keywords: RDMA · Distributed computing · Declarative semantics ·
Verification

1 Introduction

Remote Direct Memory Access (RDMA), as implemented by RoCE and Infiniband, is a high-performance networking technology that enables low-latency
wire-speed data transmission. Specifically, a n R DMA d evice c an d irectly read
and write from the memory of a remote (network) *node* (machine), bypassing the
remote CPU and operating system. RDMA technology has been used in high-
performance computing applications (including supercomputers) since the early
2000s, and is being branched out to support a much wider range of applications,
ranging from production-grade data centres [26, 33, 35] to distributed AI training [18]. Thus, there is currently a push towards developing programmer-friendly
libraries to improve the reliability and robustness of such applications.

© The Author(s) 2026
R. Krebbers (Ed.): ESOP 2026, LNCS 16501, pp. 42–71, 2026.
https://doi.org/10.1007/978-3-032-22720-1_3

To enable rigorous development and verification, there is ongoing work aimed at formalising the semantics of RDMA architectures, primarily the RDMA memory model. Dan et al [14] proposed an early model, called coreRMA, which was used to formalise the behaviours of remote read/write operations, assuming a sequentially consistent CPU. Ambal et al [3] have presented a more realistic RDMA^{TSO} specification, which assumes a total-store-order (TSO) CPU (e.g. as implemented by Intel processors) that (unlike coreRMA) has been validated against real RoCE and Infiniband hardware. RDMA^{TSO} precisely describes the interaction between the CPU and NIC (Network Interface Card) and the reorderings that they allow. Their formalisation comprises both declarative and operational models (which are proved equivalent). However, RDMA^{TSO} only covers a *subset* of RDMA instructions. In particular it only covers local (i.e. CPU-level) 'read-modify-write' (RMW) synchronisation, relegating remote (i.e. RDMA) RMWs to future work. This means that RDMA^{TSO} cannot be used to specify and verify locks and other related high-level mechanisms that require synchronisation at the network level.

In this work, we address this gap and extend the existing efforts with a notion of remote (RDMA) synchronisation. Specifically, we develop the RDMA$^{\mathrm{TSO}}_{\mathrm{RMW}}$ model by extending RDMA^{TSO} to account for remote RMWs. To ensure the fidelity of our extension, we developed RDMA$^{\mathrm{TSO}}_{\mathrm{RMW}}$ by careful inspection of the Infiniband technical manual [22] and in close consultation with engineers at NVIDIA, the largest manufacturer of RDMA products worldwide (after acquiring Mellanox in 2019). We then build a series of synchronisation libraries and prove them correct (as we discuss below). An overview of our development is given in Fig. 1. The full development is available in the arXiv extended version [EV].

Remote RMW instructions are surprisingly *weak* in that they only guarantee a weak form of isolation: remote RMWs are atomic *only* with respect to other remote RMWs and not CPU accesses or remote read and write operations (*cf.* weak transactional isolation [9,11,17,29,30]). We provide a set of litmus tests that exemplify these behaviours in two- and three-node configurations. A second challenge is that (like RDMA^{TSO}) RDMA$^{\mathrm{TSO}}_{\mathrm{RMW}}$ is *not* compositional: the semantics of a certain remote operation, `Poll`, directly depends on the *exact number of remote operations* in the program up to that point! As such, one cannot specify the behaviour of `Poll` *modularly* (in isolation).

To address both issues, we build on the *Library of Composable Objects* (LOCO) framework [4, 21], which is a modular set of objects for constructing RDMA libraries. We start at the lowest level of LOCO, called RDMA^{WAIT}, which is a compositional analogue of RDMA^{TSO} (i.e. also does not support remote RMWs). As shown in Fig. 1, the RDMA^{WAIT} library itself is implemented using RDMA^{TSO}.

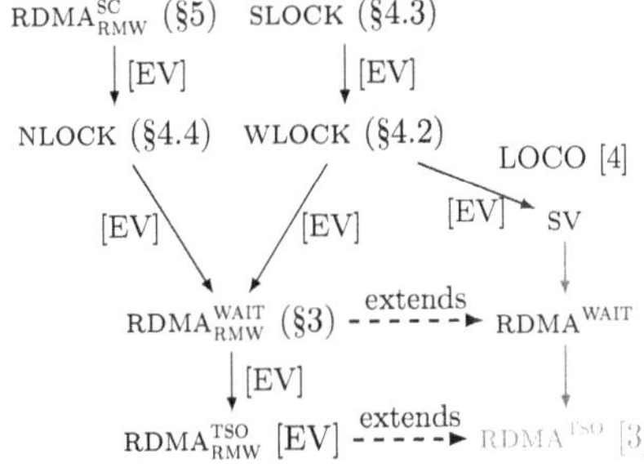

Fig. 1: Development overview

Importantly, $\text{RDMA}^{\text{WAIT}}$ abstracts RDMA^{TSO} by replacing its non-modular operation (`Poll`) with a modular analogue (`Wait`, see §2.1). As such, unlike RDMA^{TSO}, $\text{RDMA}^{\text{WAIT}}$ is *modular* and can be *composed* with other LOCO libraries (thanks to its `Wait` operation). Accordingly, we develop $\text{RDMA}^{\text{WAIT}}_{\text{RMW}}$ by extending $\text{RDMA}^{\text{WAIT}}$ with RMW operations. Specifically, in $\text{RDMA}^{\text{WAIT}}_{\text{RMW}}$ we specify two remote RMWs: `RCAS` (remote compare-and-swap) and `RFAA` (remote fetch-and-add). In doing so, we also ensure that our extensions are compatible with $\text{RDMA}^{\text{WAIT}}$ and the modular design of LOCO, thus guaranteeing that $\text{RDMA}^{\text{WAIT}}_{\text{RMW}}$ is also modular and can be composed with other LOCO libraries.

We next use $\text{RDMA}^{\text{WAIT}}_{\text{RMW}}$ to develop several RDMA libraries (Fig. 1). First, we combine $\text{RDMA}^{\text{WAIT}}_{\text{RMW}}$ with the *shared variable* (SV) library (that provides a mechanism for broadcasting to many nodes) of LOCO to develop three lock libraries with varying synchronisation guarantees (§4), each offering a different trade-off between intuitive behaviours and efficiency. Second, we develop an RDMA library with strong *sequential consistency* (SC) [24] semantics (§5).

Our first lock library is a *weak lock*, WLOCK, that provides *mutual exclusion* across multiple threads over the network, but does not provide any ordering guarantees on RDMA instructions enclosed within critical sections. Nevertheless, it is possible to recover such strong ordering guarantees on RDMA operations within a WLOCK critical section by inserting a *global fence* immediately before the lock is released. To capture this, we thus develop a *strong lock*, SLOCK, that guarantees the desired strong guarantees by executing a global fence before releasing the lock. The most novel aspect of our library is the notion of a *node lock*, NLOCK, that takes a node n as a parameter, and only guarantees synchronisation on RDMA operations specific to n, while operations within a critical section acting on a different node $n' \neq n$ are left unsynchronised.

Interestingly, we show that it is possible to build a novel, strong model for RDMA using NLOCK. Specifically, we develop the $\text{RDMA}^{\text{SC}}_{\text{RMW}}$ library, which, unlike $\text{RDMA}^{\text{WAIT}}$, provides support for strong isolation of remote RMW instructions, with strong synchronisation akin to SC.[3]

For each library L in our development (Fig. 1), we 1) *formally specify L*; 2) develop a *reference implementation* of L using lower-level libraries; and 3) *prove* our implementation is *correct* against its specification. For (1) and (3), we use MOWGLI [4], a declarative framework previously used to verify a subset of LOCO (those *without* RMWs). MOWGLI is a compositional framework for specification and verification of very weak libraries where program order is not preserved (e.g. RDMA programs). However, previous definitions [4] are not sufficient to specify remote RMWs out of the box, and we extend them with the features needed (§3).

Contributions. Our core contributions are as follows. **(1)** We develop the *first formal semantics of remote RMWs* through the $\text{RDMA}^{\text{TSO}}_{\text{RMW}}$ and $\text{RDMA}^{\text{WAIT}}_{\text{RMW}}$ models by carefully inspecting the (informal) technical specification [22]. Our models have further been validated by NVIDIA engineers. **(2)** We extend the definitions of MOWGLI to support RMW operations, and use it to develop *several*

---

[3] In related work, Ambal et al. [5] write RDMA^{SC} for an RDMA model where the underlying CPU is SC (instead of TSO). This is unrelated to $\text{RDMA}^{\text{SC}}_{\text{RMW}}$.

programmer-friendly and composable RDMA libraries. Specifically, we specify, implement and verify *three lock libraries* offering varying degrees of synchronisation guarantees and efficiency; and **(3)** we develop a novel, strong RDMA model, $\text{RDMA}_{\text{RMW}}^{\text{SC}}$, ensuring strong isolation of RDMA instructions with strong synchronisation guarantees of SC.

Outline. The remainder of this article is organised as follows. In §2 we discuss the necessary background and present an intuitive overview of our contributions. In §3 we describe how we extend the MOWGLI framework and present our $\text{RDMA}_{\text{RMW}}^{\text{WAIT}}$ model. In §4 we present our three lock libraries (including their specification, implementation, and verification), which we build on top of $\text{RDMA}_{\text{RMW}}^{\text{WAIT}}$. In §5 we specify, implement, and verify our $\text{RDMA}_{\text{RMW}}^{\text{SC}}$ library (simulating SC in RDMA programs). Finally, we discuss related work in §6.

2   Background and Overview

We present an intuitive account of our contributions via a series of litmus tests. We begin with a summary of necessary background (§2.1 and §2.2). We discuss the behaviour of remote RMW ('read-modify-write') synchronisation, culminating in our formal $\text{RDMA}_{\text{RMW}}^{\text{WAIT}}$ model (§2.3). We then describe our RDMA libraries (§2.4), including locks and a library for sequential consistency we build from it.

Terminology and Litmus Test Notation. Throughout this article, we present small examples (litmus tests) to highlight particular behaviours. A single vertical bar (e.g. in Fig. 8a) separates threads on the *same* (network) node, while a double vertical bar (e.g. in Fig. 2a) separates *distinct* nodes. For each annotated outcome, ✓ denotes that the outcome is *allowed* by the semantics, while ✗ states that the outcome is *disallowed*. To distinguish local and remote (memory) locations, we write x^n for a location on a remote node n, and write x for a location on the current local node. We number nodes from left to right, starting at 1. The statement on the top line of each column denotes where locations reside as well as their initial values; e.g. $x = 0$ and $z = 0$ on top of Fig. 2a denote that x and z respectively reside on nodes 1 and 2 with initial value 0. When a thread on local node n issues a remote operation to be executed on remote node n', we denote this by stating that the operation is by n *towards* n'.

2.1   Background: RDMA^{TSO}, $\text{RDMA}^{\text{WAIT}}$, and LOCO

The RDMA^{TSO} **Model.** Ambal et al. [3] developed RDMA^{TSO}, the first formal model of RDMA programs where the underlying CPUs are assumed to follow the x86-TSO memory model [27]. RDMA^{TSO} formalises the semantics of *RDMA Writes* (referred to as *puts*), *RDMA Reads* (referred to as *gets*) and *polling* instructions, executed by the *network interface card* (NIC). A put operation towards n, written $x^n := y$, reads from local location y (referred to as a *NIC local read*) and writes to remote location x on node n (a *NIC remote write*). Similarly, a get operation towards n, written $y := x^n$ reads from remote location

Fig. 2 (Polling on RDMA^{TSO})

(a)
$x=0$	$z=0$
$z^2 := x$ $\texttt{Poll}(2)$ $x := 1$	

(b)
$x=0$	$z=0$
$z^2 := x$ $z^2 := x$ $\texttt{Poll}(2)$ $x := 1$	

(c)
$x=0$	$z=0$
$z^2 := x$ $z^2 := x$ $\texttt{Poll}(2)$ $\texttt{Poll}(2)$ $x := 1$	

(a) $z = 0$ ✓ $z = 1$ ✗

(b) $z = 0$ ✓ $z = 1$ ✓

(c) $z = 0$ ✓ $z = 1$ ✗

Fig. 2: Polling on RDMA^{TSO}

Fig. 3 (Waiting on $\text{RDMA}^{\text{WAIT}}$)

(a)
$x=0$	$z=0$
$z^2 :=^d x$ $\texttt{Wait}(d)$ $x := 1$	

(b)
$x=0$	$z=0$
$z^2 :=^e x$ $z^2 :=^d x$ $\texttt{Wait}(d)$ $x := 1$	

(a) $z = 0$ ✓ $z = 1$ ✗

(b) $z = 0$ ✓ $z = 1$ ✗

Fig. 3: Waiting on $\text{RDMA}^{\text{WAIT}}$

x (a *NIC remote read*) and writes to local location y (a *NIC local write*). The RDMA^{TSO} semantics is unintuitive as remote operations are executed by NIC *independently* from later CPU operations, *as if* run in parallel to them. For instance, the program $z^2 := x; x := 1$ (comprising a put towards node 2, followed by a standard CPU store) can result in z containing value 1 as follows: 1) CPU offloads the put instruction to the NIC; 2) CPU executes $x := 1$; 3) NIC executes the put, fetching the *new* value 1 of x and updating the remote location z in node 2 to this new value. To prevent this weak behaviour, a programmer can *poll* the remote instruction (towards node 2) by executing $\texttt{Poll}(2)$, as shown in Fig. 2a: this blocks the CPU until the NIC confirms that the put has been executed, thereby preventing the above scenario.

The polling system on RDMA hardware (and thus RDMA^{TSO}) is highly brittle in that it synchronises with the *earliest* (in program order) unpolled remote operation. For instance, in Fig. 2b the single poll only acknowledges the first put, and the second put can be arbitrarily delayed, once again enabling the outcome $z = 1$. Preventing unintended weak behaviours therefore often relies on *counting* remote operations and polling them accordingly; e.g. in this case we must use two polls to prevent the weak outcome, as in Fig. 2c.

The $\text{RDMA}^{\text{WAIT}}$ Model. The non-local semantics of polls does not lend itself to compositional programming and verification. That is, the polling semantics depends on the *exact number* of earlier remote operations towards the same node. To address this, recent work developed LOCO [4] as an RDMA library for composable objects with a more abstract completion system that ensures modularity and compositionality through a *waiting* instruction that is analogous to polling but is compositional. Specifically, in LOCO each remote operation is associated with a *work identifier*, $d \in \text{Wid}$, and the wait operation $\texttt{Wait}(d)$ ensures the acknowledgement of all previous operations with this identifier (multiple remote operations may have the same identifier). This is illustrated in Figs. 3a and 3b (obtained from Figs. 2a and 2b by replacing polls with waits), where $z^2 :=^d x$ denotes a put (as before) with work id d. Unlike previously in Fig. 2b, adding an earlier put in Fig. 3b (with different work id e) towards the same remote node does not alter the behaviour of $\texttt{Wait}(d)$. Since, in this case, the ordering between the two puts is also preserved, the weak outcome $z=1$ remains prohibited.

$y = 0$	$x = 0$
$x^2 :=^d 1$ $\texttt{Wait}(d)$ $a := y$	$y^1 :=^e 1$ $\texttt{Wait}(e)$ $b := x$

$$(a, b) = (0, 0) \checkmark$$

Fig. 4: Store buffering

SVar $x = 0$	
	$z = 0$
$z^2 := 1$ $x :=_{\mathrm{sv}} 1$ $\texttt{Bcast}_{\mathrm{sv}}(x)$	$a :=_{\mathrm{sv}} x$ $b := z$

(a) $(a, b) = (1, 0)$ ✗

SVar $x = 0$		
	$y, z = 0, 0$	
$z^2 := 1$ $x :=_{\mathrm{sv}} 1$ $\texttt{Bcast}_{\mathrm{sv}}(x)$	$a := y$ $b := z$	$c :=_{\mathrm{sv}} x$ $y^2 := 1$

(b) $(a, b, c) = (1, 0, 1) \checkmark$

Fig. 5: Shared variable examples

From a reordering perspective, RDMA^{WAIT} is still quite permissive. For example, because a remote NIC sends an acknowledgement for a put as soon as it is received (but before the put takes effect in memory), RDMA^{WAIT} permits the store-buffering behaviour in Fig. 4. Therefore, using RDMA^{WAIT}, LOCO additionally implements a *global-fence operation* towards a node n, written $\texttt{GFence}(\{n\})$, that blocks until all previous remote operations towards n are *fully* completed (see §4.1). Replacing $\texttt{Wait}(d)$ and $\texttt{Wait}(e)$ in Fig. 4 respectively with fences $\texttt{GFence}(\{2\})$ and $\texttt{GFence}(\{1\})$ would prevent the store-buffering behaviour.

2.2 Background: MOWGLI

To support compositional specification and verification, Ambal et al. have developed the MOWGLI framework [4]. They have specified the RDMA^{WAIT} formal model (obtained from RDMA^{TSO} by replacing the $\texttt{poll}$ instruction with $\texttt{Wait}$) in MOWGLI and subsequently used it as a foundation for developing and verifying a suite of RDMA libraries. The principal one is a *shared variable* (SV) library (see §4.1), where each node possesses a local copy of each variable x. The methods include store ($x :=_{\mathrm{sv}} v$) and load ($a :=_{\mathrm{sv}} x$) operations to access the local copy, as well as a broadcast ($\texttt{Bcast}_{\mathrm{sv}}(x)$) operation to forward the local value to other nodes.

Specification. MOWGLI [4] is a declarative framework for modularly specifying and verifying libraries in the context of (very) weak concurrency models. Unlike other declarative frameworks in the literature [28, 32], MOWGLI can handle the behaviours allowed by RDMA programs. The key novelty in MOWGLI enabling this is the use of a fixed set of *stamps*, $\mathsf{Stamp} = \{a_1, \ldots\}$, and the *stamp-order* relation, $\mathsf{sto} \subseteq \mathsf{Stamp} \times \mathsf{Stamp}$, defined as a subset of the program order that is *preserved*. This then allows one to define weak libraries where the program order is not fully preserved, as is the case in RDMA.

We present the stamps and their ordering in Fig. 9 (assuming that the underlying CPUs follow the TSO model). Intuitively, each stamp denotes a behaviour category, such as a CPU write ($\texttt{aCW}$), a CPU read ($\texttt{aCR}$), a NIC remote read ($\texttt{aNRR}_n$) or write ($\texttt{aNRW}_n$) towards n, or a NIC local read ($\texttt{aNLR}_n$) or write ($\texttt{aNLW}_n$) towards n. Compared to [4], we also introduce a new stamp $\texttt{aNAR}_n$ to represent the ordering guarantees of remote RMWs (see §2.3).

This stamp mechanism addresses two problems. The first is the reordering of methods of different libraries. As libraries are defined *independently*, the exact

48   G. Ambal et al.

interaction between pairs of methods of different libraries cannot be explicit. Instead, libraries can associate their method calls with generic behaviour categories (stamps), so that their interactions can be implicitly deduced. For instance, in Fig. 5a, $z^2 := 1$ and $b := z$ are part of $\mathrm{RDMA}^{\mathrm{WAIT}}_{\mathrm{RMW}}$, while $\mathtt{Bcast}_{\mathrm{SV}}(x)$ and $a :=_{\mathrm{SV}} x$ are part of the SV library. To determine if the outcome $(a, b) = (1, 0)$ is allowed, we need to check if $z^2 := 1$ and $\mathtt{Bcast}_{\mathrm{SV}}(x)$ can be reordered on node 1, and if $a :=_{\mathrm{SV}} x$ and $b := z$ can be reordered on node 2. The semantics of the two libraries (§3 and [EV]) ensure that $z^2 := 1$ and $\mathtt{Bcast}_{\mathrm{SV}}(x)$ behave as remote writes towards node 2 (stamp $\mathtt{aNRW}_2$) and that $a :=_{\mathrm{SV}} x$ and $b := z$ behave as CPU reads (stamp $\mathtt{aCR}$). This enforces their respective program orders as $\langle z^2 := 1, \mathtt{aNRW}_2 \rangle \xrightarrow{\mathrm{ppo}} \langle \mathtt{Bcast}_{\mathrm{SV}}(x), \mathtt{aNRW}_2 \rangle$ and $\langle a :=_{\mathrm{SV}} x, \mathtt{aCR} \rangle \xrightarrow{\mathrm{ppo}} \langle b := z, \mathtt{aCR} \rangle$, where ppo is the *preserved program order*, i.e. they cannot be reordered. Moreover, if $a = 1$, then we have the *happens-before* (hb) relation $\langle \mathtt{Bcast}_{\mathrm{SV}}(x), \mathtt{aNRW}_2 \rangle \xrightarrow{\mathrm{hb}} \langle a :=_{\mathrm{SV}} x, \mathtt{aCR} \rangle$, and as $\mathrm{ppo} \subseteq \mathrm{hb}$, by transitivity we have $\langle z^2 := 1, \mathtt{aNRW}_2 \rangle \xrightarrow{\mathrm{hb}} \langle b := z, \mathtt{aCR} \rangle$, i.e. the weak outcome $(a, b) = (1, 0)$ is prohibited.

The second problem stamps address is the *partial* execution of methods. A method call may have multiple visible effects, and observing one does not necessarily imply that others are also observed. In Fig. 5b the shared variable x is read by the *third* node, which then sends a message to node 2 (through $y^2 := 1$). As such, when $(a, c) = (1, 1)$, we have a $\xrightarrow{\mathrm{hb}}$ chain from $\mathtt{Bcast}_{\mathrm{SV}}(x)$ to $b := z$ and may naturally expect $b = 1$. However, this is *not* the case. Specifically, as per the semantics of SV, $\mathtt{Bcast}_{\mathrm{SV}}(x)$ is associated with (at least) two stamps, $\mathtt{aNRW}_2$ (remote write towards node 2) and $\mathtt{aNRW}_3$ (remote write towards node 3), where the latter is observed but is *not* ordered with the earlier $z^2 := 1$ operation (as they are toward different nodes). That is, we have the hb orders $\langle z^2 := 1, \mathtt{aNRW}_2 \rangle \xrightarrow{\mathrm{ppo} \subseteq \mathrm{hb}} \langle \mathtt{Bcast}_{\mathrm{SV}}(x), \mathtt{aNRW}_2 \rangle$ (as in example Fig. 5a) and $\langle \mathtt{Bcast}_{\mathrm{SV}}(x), \mathtt{aNRW}_3 \rangle \xrightarrow{\mathrm{hb}} \langle b := z, \mathtt{aCR} \rangle$, and when put together they do *not* imply $\langle z^2 := 1, \mathtt{aNRW}_2 \rangle \xrightarrow{\mathrm{hb}} \langle b := z, \mathtt{aCR} \rangle$, allowing the weak outcome $b = 0$. In other words, $z^2 := 1$ and $\mathtt{Bcast}_{\mathrm{SV}}(x)$ can be *partially* reordered: although their respective updates (on z and x) towards node 2 stay ordered, the update on x towards *other* nodes (i.e. node 3) may take place before $z^2 := 1$ is executed. A pair formed by a method call and a stamp is called a subevent. Associating a method call with multiple stamps generates multiple subevents and allows us to express such nuances.

Implementation and Soundness. Within the MOWGLI framework, Ambal et al. [4] also formalise the notion of a *library implementation* and what it means for an implementation I to be *sound* against its specification, i.e. that the behaviours of the implementation are contained in those of its specification. To enable proving implementation soundness *compositionally*, they establish a *local soundness* theorem. Specifically, to show that an implementation I of library L is correct, one must show that for *all* client programs P with calls to L (where P may in general contain calls to libraries other than L), replacing the calls to L with their corresponding (inlined) implementation yields the same outcomes. Intuitively, as the only calls being replaced (inlined) are those of L, the

	$x = 0$
RCAS $(a, x^2, 0, 2)$	$x := 1$

(a) $x = 2$ ✓

		$x = 0$
RCAS $(a, x^3, 0, 2)$	$x^3 := 1$	

(b) $x = 2$ ✓

		$x = 0$
RCAS $(a, x^3, 0, 2)$	RFAA $(b, x^3, 1)$	

(c) $x = 2$ ✗

Fig. 6: Examples showcasing the limited atomicity of remote RMW operations

calls to libraries other than L should not affect the outcome. That is, it should be sufficient to show that the implementation is *locally sound* by considering client programs that only constitute calls to L. Ambal et al. then prove that local soundness implies soundness: if I is a locally sound implementation of L (i.e. for all client programs that only comprise calls to L), then I is a sound implementation of L (i.e. for all client programs).

As we discuss below, we use MOWGLI to specify several RDMA libraries and verify their implementations, as shown in Fig. 1.

2.3 Remote Read-Modify-Write Operations

CPU Read-Modify-Writes. Read-modify-writes (RMW) are a category of synchronisation operations that simultaneously read the value v of a location and update (modify-write) it in place. Examples of common RMWs include the compare-and-swap, $CAS(x, v_1, v_2)$, instruction (it reads the current value v of x and updates it to v_2 if $v = v_1$ and otherwise leaves it unchanged); and the fetch-and-add, $FAA(x, v)$, instruction (it increments the value of x by v unconditionally). Both operations return the old value of x. These operations are useful for ensuring inter-thread synchronisation and are often used to implement strong synchronisation mechanisms such as locks (mutexes).

CPU RMWs behave *atomically*: their 'read' and 'modify-write' phases cannot be interleaved by concurrent instructions. As such, RMWs are commonly referred to as 'atomic operations'. This is illustrated in the example across where the outcome $x = 2$ is

$x = 0$	
$a := CAS(x, 0, 2)$	$x := 1$
$x = 2$ ✗	

disallowed. If the right thread executes first, then x is updated to 1 and subsequently the CAS fails. If the left thread executes first, then the right thread overwrites x to 1.

Remote RMWs. The RDMA hardware specification [22] optionally supports two remote RMW instructions, referred to as 'atomics[4]': $RCAS(a, x, v_1, v_2)$, analogous to $a := CAS(x, v_1, v_2)$ on CPUs, and $RFAA(a, x, v)$, analogous to $a := FAA(x, v)$ on CPUs, where x is a remote location in both cases.

Unlike CPU RMWs, remote RMWs do *not* always behave atomically: their 'read' and 'modify-write' phases may be interleaved by other CPU or (remote)

---

[4] Although RMWs are commonly referred to as 'atomics' in the RDMA specification, they do *not* always behave atomically.

put/get instructions. This is illustrated in the examples of Figs. 6a and 6b, executing a remote CAS in parallel with a CPU store (Fig. 6a) and a put (Fig. 6b), where the remote CAS can first read 0 from x, be interleaved with the concurrent CPU store/put writing 1 to x, and then update x to 2.

This weakness is due to an inherent hardware limitation. Atomicity is possible on CPUs because a CPU core can: 1) request exclusive access to a cache line; 2) read the cache line; 3) write to the cache line; 4) release the cache line. During periods of exclusive access, other components (e.g. other CPU cores or the NIC) cannot access the cache line in-between the 'read' and 'modify-write'. This, however, is not feasible over RDMA since NICs cannot lock a cache line; they can only submit read and write operations to their PCIe root complex. As such, it is not possible to block accesses by other components (e.g. the CPU) interleaving between the NIC's 'read' and the 'modify-write'.

Nevertheless, remote RMWs do behave atomically with respect to other remote RMWs. For instance, as shown in Fig. 6c, a remote FAA cannot interleave between the 'read' and 'modify-write' phases of a remote CAS.

In practice, one can ensure atomicity of accesses to a location x by ensuring x is *only* ever accessed through remote RMWs. As such, it is common for RDMA programs to access *local* locations (i.e. those residing on their node) through remote RMWs (via loop-back). To provide atomicity between remote RMWs and other operations, we require software solutions, as supported by $\text{RDMA}^{\text{SC}}_{\text{RMW}}$.

Extending RDMA^{TSO} **with RMWs.** The RDMA^{TSO} and $\text{RDMA}^{\text{WAIT}}$ models do not include the semantics of remote RMWs; we close this gap in this work. Specifically, starting from RDMA^{TSO} [3], we formulate $\text{RDMA}^{\text{TSO}}_{\text{RMW}}$ both declaratively and operationally and prove the two characterisations are equivalent (see [EV]).

Our main reference for modelling the semantics of remote RMWs is the Infiniband technical specification [22]. However, as the specification is often ambiguous, we developed our model in close collaboration with NVIDIA experts specialising in RDMA hardware who confirmed the expected behaviours of RMWs and that our model captures them faithfully.

Compared to RDMA^{TSO}, our $\text{RDMA}^{\text{TSO}}_{\text{RMW}}$ declarative model brings two important changes. The first is a new relation, the '*remote-atomic-order*' rao, capturing the mutual exclusion of remote RMWs. We require a total order rao_n on remote RMWs towards each node n, such that $\text{rao}_n \subseteq \text{hb}$ (i.e. it induces synchronisation). The second is a new stamp, aNAR_n (the 'NIC atomic read'), encoding the new ordering guarantees of the read phase of a remote RMW (see Fig. 9). Recall that a `Get` performs a NIC remote read (stamp aNRR_n) followed by a NIC local write (aNLW_n), while a `Put` performs a NIC local read (aNLR_n) followed by a NIC remote write (aNRW_n). Analogously, a remote RMW, e.g. $\text{RFAA}(x, y, v)$, performs (up to) three NIC accesses: 1) it remotely reads y (aNAR_n); 2) remotely updates y (aNRW_n); and 3) locally writes (the return value) to x (aNLW_n).

Note that the stamp aNAR_n is required because a remote read stamp (aNRR_n) is insufficient for modelling the stronger ordering guarantees of the 'read' phase of an RMW. We show an example of this in Figs. 7a and 7b. The (remote) read phase of a `Get` (aNRR_n) may be delayed (reordered) after a later remote

	$x,y = 0,0$
$a := x^2$	$b := y$
$y^2 := 1$	$x := 1$

(a) $(a,b) = (1,1)$ ✓

	$x,y = 0,0$
$\mathtt{RCAS}(a, x^2, 8, 9)$	$b := y$
$y^2 := 1$	$x := 1$

(b) $(a,b) = (1,1)$ ✗

$y = 0$	$x = 0$
$\mathtt{RFAA}(\_, x^2, 1)$	$\mathtt{RFAA}(\_, y^1, 1)$
$\mathtt{Poll}(2)$	$\mathtt{Poll}(1)$
$a := y$	$b := x$

(c) $(a,b) = (0,0)$ ✓

Fig. 7: Examples of remote RMW behaviours and how they compare from $\mathtt{Puts}$.

write ($\mathtt{aNRW}_n$ of a $\mathtt{Put}$ or RMW). As such, the weak 'load-buffering' behaviour in Fig. 7a is allowed. By contrast, the read phase of a remote RMW ($\mathtt{aNAR}_n$) cannot be delayed, and thus the analogous behaviour is prohibited in Fig. 7b.

Finally, the example in Fig. 7c shows that the remote write ('modify') phase ($\mathtt{aNRW}_n$) of an RMW behaves similarly to that of a $\mathtt{Put}$. In particular, a poll does *not* enforce the full completion of the remote write and thus the weak 'store-buffering' behaviour presented is allowed, similarly to Fig. 4.

Supporting Modularity with $\mathrm{RDMA}_{\mathrm{RMW}}^{\mathrm{WAIT}}$. As $\mathrm{RDMA}_{\mathrm{RMW}}^{\mathrm{TSO}}$ is not modular, we develop $\mathrm{RDMA}_{\mathrm{RMW}}^{\mathrm{WAIT}}$ by adapting $\mathrm{RDMA}^{\mathrm{WAIT}}$ [4,21]. We then implement $\mathrm{RDMA}_{\mathrm{RMW}}^{\mathrm{WAIT}}$ using $\mathrm{RDMA}_{\mathrm{RMW}}^{\mathrm{TSO}}$ and prove that it is correct ([EV]) against its specification.

2.4 Modular RDMA Synchronisation Libraries

We now implement RDMA libraries *modularly* and specify and verify them using MOWGLI. A key use case of our remote RMWs is for implementing network-wide locks that ensure mutual exclusion of critical sections. A lock library provides two main operations, $\mathtt{Acq}(l)$ and $\mathtt{Rel}(l)$, for acquiring and releasing a lock l, respectively. When specifying such a network lock, there are several choices for defining its semantics as there are trade-offs between the guarantees (strength) of a lock and the efficiency of its implementation.

Fig. 8 presents several variants of an example where two threads use a lock l to access locations x and y in a critical section (the first thread writing to x and y and the last thread reading from x and y). As the locks are expected to ensure atomicity of the critical sections (enclosed within the lock acquisition and release blocks), the expected outcomes are either $a = b = 0$ or $a = b = 1$, i.e. not $a \neq b$. However, ensuring this strong guarantee for locks is not straightforward over RDMA. Specifically, while ensuring mutual exclusion is necessary for prohibiting the weak $a \neq b$ behaviour, it is not sufficient. We must additionally ensure that the operations enclosed in a critical section are *completed* before the end of the critical section (and hence are not *reordered* past the lock release). However, as we demonstrated above, meeting these latter constraints are not always straightforward due to the weak ordering guarantees on remote operations.

Weak Lock Library. The weakest network lock that we consider ensures mutual exclusion *only*, but does not prohibit the enclosed operations from being reordered. As shown in Fig. 8a, when the operations enclosed in a critical section are CPU loads and stores, the weak outcome $a \neq b$ is prohibited. By contrast,

$x, y = 0, 0$	
$\texttt{Acq}_{\text{WL}}(l)$ $x := 1$ $y := 1$ $\texttt{Rel}_{\text{WL}}(l)$	$\texttt{Acq}_{\text{WL}}(l)$ $a := x$ $b := y$ $\texttt{Rel}_{\text{WL}}(l)$

(a) $a \neq b$ ✗

	$x, y = 0, 0$
$\texttt{Acq}_{\text{WL}}(l)$ $x^2 := 1$ $y^2 := 1$ $\texttt{Rel}_{\text{WL}}(l)$	$\texttt{Acq}_{\text{WL}}(l)$ $a := x$ $b := y$ $\texttt{Rel}_{\text{WL}}(l)$

(b) $a \neq b$ ✓

	$x, y = 0, 0$
$x^2 := 1$ $y^2 := 1$ $\texttt{GFence}(\{2\})$	$a := x$ $b := y$

(c) $a \neq b$ ✓

	$x, y = 0, 0$
$\texttt{Acq}_{\text{WL}}(l)$ $x^2 := 1$ $y^2 := 1$ $\texttt{GFence}(\{2\})$ $\texttt{Rel}_{\text{WL}}(l)$	$\texttt{Acq}_{\text{WL}}(l)$ $a := x$ $b := y$ $\texttt{Rel}_{\text{WL}}(l)$

(d) $a \neq b$ ✗

$x = 0$	$y = 0$
$\texttt{Acq}_{\text{SL}}(l)$ $y^2 := 1$ $x := 1$ $\texttt{Rel}_{\text{SL}}(l)$	$\texttt{Acq}_{\text{SL}}(l)$ $a := x^1$ $b := y$ $\texttt{Rel}_{\text{SL}}(l)$

(e) $a \neq b$ ✗

	$x, y = 0, 0$ NLOCK l	
$\texttt{Acq}_{\text{NL}}(l^2)$ $x^2 := 1$ $y^2 := 1$ $\texttt{Rel}_{\text{NL}}(l^2)$		$\texttt{Acq}_{\text{NL}}(l^2)$ $a := x^2$ $b := y^2$ $\texttt{Rel}_{\text{NL}}(l^2)$

(f) $a \neq b$ ✗

Fig. 8: Examples of weak, strong, and node lock behaviours

as shown in Fig. 8b, when the enclosed operations are over RDMA (two $\texttt{Puts}$ in Fig. 8b), then a weak lock is insufficient and we may observe $a \neq b$. This is because the remote operations may not complete before the critical section ends.

Thus, we require an operation akin to a global fence (see §2.1) to ensure that these remote operations are completed. Note that as shown in Fig. 8c, the global fence in isolation (without the protection provided by a weak lock) is also insufficient for prohibiting the weak behaviour as it only provides intra-thread synchronisation (and does not ensure mutual exclusion). However, as shown in Fig. 8d, if we combine a weak lock with a global fence, we can attain the desired strong guarantees and prohibit $a \neq b$.

Strong Lock Library. The weak lock library discussed above is efficient and gives programmers full control over synchronisation. However, if not used correctly, without the relevant global fences, its guarantees are not as strong as one may expect. That is, in designing the weak lock library, we opted for better performance over the strength of guarantees. We next develop a *strong* lock library that achieves the desired strong guarantees (without the need for additional synchronisation via fences). Specifically, on releasing a strong lock *all* earlier operations are guaranteed to have *fully* completed.

This is illustrated in Fig. 8e, where the outcome $a \neq b$ is once again prohibited. However, the strong guarantees of strong locks come at the cost of their implementation efficiency. Intuitively, an implementation of a strong lock release issues a global fence towards *every* node on the network to ensure that there are no pending remote operations. This is in contrast to a weak lock release implementation that issues no fence by default, and developers have full control over fencing the relevant nodes.

Node Lock Library. As a midway between the efficient weak locks, requiring manual synchronisation, and the inefficient strong locks, we develop the concept of (more fine-grained) *node* locks. Intuitively, as shown in Fig. 8f, a node lock

l is associated with a specific node n (node 2 in Fig. 8f) and provides strong guarantees only for locations on n.

A node lock is stronger than a weak lock: as shown in Fig. 8f the weak behaviour $a \neq b$ is prohibited without the need for additional synchronisation. Moreover, a node lock is weaker than a strong lock in two ways. First, it only provides guarantees for operations towards *one* node. For instance, consider a variant of the example in Fig. 8f where the lock l is associated with node 1 (instead of 2); the outcome $a \neq b$ would once again be allowed. Second, it does *not* provide any intra-thread ordering guarantees in that releasing a node lock does not guarantee that previous operations (even towards the associated node) have completed. For instance, in the program $\mathtt{Acq}_{\mathrm{NL}}(l^2); z^2 := x; \mathtt{Rel}_{\mathrm{NL}}(l^2); x := 1$ the outcome $z = 1$ is *allowed*: $z^2 := x$ and the lock release may not have fully completed before the CPU runs the subsequent $x := 1$ store; i.e., while $z^2 := x$ cannot be reordered past $\mathtt{Rel}_{\mathrm{NL}}(l^2)$, the $x := 1$ can be reordered *before* both of them. More concretely, our implementation of $\mathtt{Rel}_{\mathrm{NL}}$ (§4.4) comprises RDMA operations that can be delayed after later CPU operations.

Nevertheless, as a common usage of a lock is to protect a specific object that is likely to reside on a single node, this level of guarantee is sufficient for many applications, while enabling efficient implementations.

The $\mathrm{RDMA}_{\mathrm{RMW}}^{\mathrm{SC}}$ Library. Lastly, to simplify RDMA programming, we specify and implement the $\mathrm{RDMA}_{\mathrm{RMW}}^{\mathrm{SC}}$ library that fully abstracts away the notion of nodes and provides strong *sequentially consistent* (SC) [24] semantics via four (per-location) instructions, $\mathtt{Write}_{\mathrm{SC}}$, $\mathtt{Read}_{\mathrm{SC}}$, $\mathtt{CAS}_{\mathrm{SC}}$, and $\mathtt{FAA}_{\mathrm{SC}}$ analogous to stores, loads, and RMWs on CPUs with strong SC semantics. Our implementation uses node locks to wrap RDMA operations and ensure they become visible in the order they are submitted. Indeed, as we discuss later in §5, we can use the same approach to implement *any concurrent data structure* over RDMA, and show that it is correct in that it is *linearisable* [20].

3 Extending $\mathrm{RDMA}^{\mathrm{WAIT}}$ to $\mathrm{RDMA}_{\mathrm{RMW}}^{\mathrm{WAIT}}$

We present $\mathrm{RDMA}_{\mathrm{RMW}}^{\mathrm{WAIT}}$ *model*, an extension of $\mathrm{RDMA}^{\mathrm{WAIT}}$ [4] with remote RMW instructions. Our definitions naturally extend those of $\mathrm{RDMA}^{\mathrm{WAIT}}$. To underline the distinction between the two, we have highlighted our extensions from $\mathrm{RDMA}^{\mathrm{WAIT}}$ to $\mathrm{RDMA}_{\mathrm{RMW}}^{\mathrm{WAIT}}$. We specify $\mathrm{RDMA}_{\mathrm{RMW}}^{\mathrm{WAIT}}$ in MOWGLI [4], yielding a *modular* semantics that enables *compositional* reasoning. In particular, as we show below, since LOCO libraries can be freely composed together, this allows us to use the *locality* result of MOWGLI to verify each library modularly (in isolation). We proceed with an account of MOWGLI preliminaries (§3.1) and present $\mathrm{RDMA}_{\mathrm{RMW}}^{\mathrm{WAIT}}$ in §3.2.

3.1 The MOWGLI Framework Preliminaries

MOWGLI assumes a type Val of values and a type Loc $\subseteq$ Val of locations. We also assume two sets for threads $t \in$ Tid and nodes $n \in$ Node, where each thread t is associated with a node $\mathbf{n}(t)$. Recall from §2.2 that MOWGLI can be instantiated

54   G. Ambal et al.

Later (in Program Order) Stamp

Earlier \ sto		single					families						
		1	2	3	4	5	6	7	8	9	10	11	12
		aCR	aCW	aCAS	aMF	aWT	aNLR$_n$	aNRW$_n$	aNAR$_n$	aNRR$_n$	aNLW$_n$	aRF$_n$	aGF$_n$
single	A	aCR	✓	✓	✓	✓	✓	✓	✓	✓	✓	✓	✓	✓
	B	aCW	✗	✓	✓	✓	✗	✓	✓	✓	✓	✓	✓	✓
	C	aCAS	✓	✓	✓	✓	✓	✓	✓	✓	✓	✓	✓	✓
	D	aMF	✓	✓	✓	✓	✓	✓	✓	✓	✓	✓	✓	✓
	E	aWT	✓	✓	✓	✓	✓	✓	✓	✓	✓	✓	✓	✓
families	F	aNLR$_n$	✗	✗	✗	✗	✗	SN	SN	SN	SN	SN	SN	SN
	G	aNRW$_n$	✗	✗	✗	✗	✗	✗	SN	SN	SN	SN	✗	SN
	H	aNAR$_n$	✗	✗	✗	✗	✗	✗	SN	SN	SN	SN	SN	SN
	I	aNRR$_n$	✗	✗	✗	✗	✗	✗	✗	✗	✗	SN	SN	SN
	J	aNLW$_n$	✗	✗	✗	✗	✗	✗	✗	✗	✗	SN	✗	SN
	K	aRF$_n$	✗	✗	✗	✗	✗	SN	SN	SN	SN	SN	SN	SN
	L	aGF$_n$	✓	✓	✓	✓	✓	✓	✓	✓	✓	✓	✓	✓

Fig. 9: The sto order in $\mathrm{RDMA}^{\mathrm{WAIT}}$ and $\mathrm{RDMA}^{\mathrm{WAIT}}_{\mathrm{RMW}}$, where highlighted cells denote our extensions from $\mathrm{RDMA}^{\mathrm{WAIT}}$ to $\mathrm{RDMA}^{\mathrm{WAIT}}_{\mathrm{RMW}}$. The ✓ denotes that the (program-order-related) stamps are *ordered*; the ✗ denotes that the stamps are *not ordered*; the SN denotes the stamps are ordered iff they are associated with the *same node*.

with a set of *stamps* Stamp and a relation sto $\subseteq$ Stamp $\times$ Stamp. In the case of $\mathrm{RDMA}^{\mathrm{WAIT}}$ and $\mathrm{RDMA}^{\mathrm{WAIT}}_{\mathrm{RMW}}$, the stamps and their associated sto are as presented in Fig. 9. Note that certain stamps, e.g. aNLR$_n$, are associated with a node n, and each induce a *family* of stamps, e.g. aNLR $\triangleq \bigcup_{n \in \mathsf{Node}} \{\mathrm{aNLR}_n\}$. The highlighted sections (row H and column 8) denote our extensions from $\mathrm{RDMA}^{\mathrm{WAIT}}$ to $\mathrm{RDMA}^{\mathrm{WAIT}}_{\mathrm{RMW}}$ and are associated with the new stamp family aNAR used to specify RMWs (see §2.2). The ✓ (e.g. in cell A2) denotes that the corresponding stamps (e.g. aCR and aCW) are *ordered*. This means that the program order between relevent subevents (pair of a function call and a stamp, see Def. 1) is *preserved* and thus their effects are observed in order. Conversely, ✗ denotes that the stamps are *not ordered* (they may be reordered) and thus the effects of subevents with these stamps may be observed *out of order*. The SN denotes the stamps are ordered if and only if they are associated with the *same node*.

Libraries. Intuitively, a library L specification identifies its associated *methods* as well as the semantics of these methods. A *method call* is of the form $m(\widetilde{v})$, where m denotes the method name and $\widetilde{v}$ denote its arguments. Ambal et al. capture the method semantics in MOWGLI by identifying the set of *executions* that are *L-consistent* in that they uphold the guarantees promised by L. To this end, they associate L with a set $\mathcal{C}$ of *L-consistent executions*. A *library* is then formally defined as a triple $L = \langle M, \mathtt{loc}, \mathcal{C} \rangle$, where M is its set of *method names* (e.g. `Write` or `Put`); loc associates each method call with its set of accessed locations (within the method call arguments); and $\mathcal{C}$ is its set of *L-consistent executions*. (MOWGLI further requires $\mathcal{C}$ to adhere to some basic properties to ensure modularity [4], which we elide here.) We use the prefix 'L.' to project the components of a library L, e.g. $L.M$.

Events and Executions. In the literature of declarative models, traces of a program are represented as a set of *executions*. An execution is a graph comprising: 1) a set of *events* (graph nodes), where each event is associated with the execution of a method call; and 2) a number of relations on events (graph edges). For instance, if thread t executes a $\texttt{Read}(x)$ and reads value v, the corresponding event is of the form $\langle t, \iota, \langle \texttt{Read}, (x), v \rangle \rangle$, where ι denotes its (unique) event identifier. Identifiers serve to distinguish calls to the same method (with same arguments and output) by the same thread in an execution. For an event $\texttt{e}$, we write $\texttt{t(e)}$ and $\texttt{m(e)}$ to extract its thread and method name, respectively.

Definition 1 (Events and Executions). *An event is a tuple $\langle t, \iota, \langle m, \widetilde{v}, v' \rangle \rangle$, where $t \in \textsf{Tid}$ denotes the executing thread, ι is the (unique) event identifier, m denotes the method being executed, $\widetilde{v} \in \textsf{Val}^*$ is the method input (arguments) and $v' \in \textsf{Val}$ is its output (return value, which may be unit ()). An execution $\mathcal{G}$ is a tuple $\langle E, \textsf{po}, \texttt{stmp}, \textsf{so}, \textsf{hb} \rangle$ where:*

- *E is the set of events;*
- *$\textsf{po} \subseteq E \times E$ is the (strict) program order, total for each thread;*
- *$\texttt{stmp} : E \to \mathcal{P}(\textsf{Stamp})$ associates each event with a non-empty set of stamps and induces a set of subevents, $\textsf{SEvent} \triangleq \{\langle \texttt{e}, a \rangle \mid \texttt{e} \in E \wedge a \in \texttt{stmp}(\texttt{e})\}$;*
- *$\textsf{so} \subseteq \textsf{SEvent} \times \textsf{SEvent}$ is the synchronisation order, representing the intra-library dependencies exported by each library;*
- *$\textsf{hb} \subseteq \textsf{SEvent} \times \textsf{SEvent}$ is the happens-before order, a strict partial order such that $\textsf{so} \cup \textsf{ppo} \subseteq \textsf{hb}$, where $\textsf{ppo} \subseteq \textsf{SEvent} \times \textsf{SEvent}$ denotes the preserved program order capturing inter-library dependencies and is defined as follows:*

$$\textsf{ppo} \triangleq \{\langle \langle \texttt{e}_1, a_1 \rangle, \langle \texttt{e}_2, a_2 \rangle \rangle \mid \langle \texttt{e}_1, \texttt{e}_2 \rangle \in \textsf{po} \wedge a_i \in \texttt{stmp}(\texttt{e}_i) \wedge \langle a_1, a_2 \rangle \in \textsf{sto}\}$$

Notations. Given a set A and a relation $\textsf{r} \subseteq A \times A$, we write $\textsf{r}^+$ for the transitive closure of $\textsf{r}$; $\textsf{r}^*$ for its reflexive transitive closure; $\textsf{r}^{-1}$ for the inverse of $\textsf{r}$; and $[A]$ for the identity relation on A, i.e. $\{\langle a, a \rangle \mid a \in A\}$. We write $\textsf{r}_1 ; \textsf{r}_2$ for the relational composition of $\textsf{r}_1$ and $\textsf{r}_2$: $\{\langle a, b \rangle \mid \exists c. \langle a, c \rangle \in \textsf{r}_1 \wedge \langle c, b \rangle \in \textsf{r}_2\}$. We write $A|_c$ to restrict A with condition c. For instance, given a set of events E, we define $E|_L \triangleq \{\texttt{e} \in E \mid \texttt{m(e)} \in L.M\}$, $E|_t \triangleq \{\texttt{e} \in E \mid \texttt{t(e)} = t\}$, and we write $E|_d$ for the set of events in E with work identifier d. We define $E_x \triangleq \{\texttt{e} \in E \mid x \in \texttt{loc(e)}\}$. Similarly, we define $\textsf{r}|_c \triangleq [A|_c] ; \textsf{r} ; [A|_c]$ (e.g. $\textsf{po}|_t$) and $\textsf{r}_x \triangleq [E_x] ; \textsf{r} ; [E_x]$ (e.g. $\textsf{po}_x$). Given a subset $A' \subseteq A$, we define $\textsf{r}|_{A'} \triangleq [A'] ; \textsf{r} ; [A']$. When $\textsf{r}$ is a strict partial order, we write $\textsf{r}|_{\textsf{imm}}$ for its immediate edges, i.e. $\textsf{r} \setminus (\textsf{r} ; \textsf{r})$.

Given execution $\mathcal{G} = \langle E, \textsf{po}, \texttt{stmp}, \textsf{so}, \textsf{hb} \rangle$, we write $\mathcal{G}|_L$ for $\langle E|_L, \textsf{po}|_L, \texttt{stmp}|_L, \textsf{so}|_L, \textsf{hb}|_L \rangle$, where $\texttt{stmp}|_L$ denotes the function obtained by restricting the domain of $\texttt{stmp}$ (i.e. E) to $E|_L$. We use the prefix '$\mathcal{G}$.' to project the components of $\mathcal{G}$ (e.g. $\mathcal{G}.\textsf{po}$), including its derived ones (e.g. $\mathcal{G}.\textsf{SEvent}$). Given a stamp a, we write $\mathcal{G}.a$ for $\{\texttt{s} \in \mathcal{G}.\textsf{SEvent} \mid \texttt{s} = \langle \_, a \rangle\}$; analogously for a stamp family, e.g. $\mathcal{G}.\textsf{aNRR}$. We define the set of *read subevents* as $\mathcal{G}.\mathcal{R} \triangleq \mathcal{G}.\textsf{aCR} \cup \mathcal{G}.\textsf{aCAS} \cup \mathcal{G}.\textsf{aNLR} \cup \mathcal{G}.\textsf{aNAR} \cup \mathcal{G}.\textsf{aNRR}$, and *write subevents* as $\mathcal{G}.\mathcal{W} \triangleq \mathcal{G}.\textsf{aCW} \cup \mathcal{G}.\textsf{aCAS} \cup \mathcal{G}.\textsf{aNLW} \cup \mathcal{G}.\textsf{aNRW}$. Given a set of subevents A, we define $A_x \triangleq \{ s \in A \mid \mathtt{loc}(s) = \{x\} \}$; e.g. $\mathcal{G}.\mathcal{W}_x$ is the set of write subevents on x. When the choice of $\mathcal{G}$ is clear, we omit '$\mathcal{G}.$', e.g. we simply write $\mathcal{W}$ for $\mathcal{G}.\mathcal{W}$ and $[\mathtt{aCW}]$ for $[\mathcal{G}.\mathtt{aCW}]$.

Consistency. An execution is *consistent* against a set of libraries Λ iff 1) $\mathcal{G}|_L$ is L-consistent for each $L \in \Lambda$; 2) its events and their synchronisation are those of the libraries in Λ; and 3) its happens-before relation is irreflexive. Note that the first condition ensures *modularity* as each library can specify independently the visible behaviours of its functions (stamps), its allowed outcomes (consistency) and the synchronisation (guarantees) it offers ($\mathtt{so}$).

Definition 2 (Consistency). *Let Λ be a set of libraries where $L_1.M \cap L_2.M = \emptyset$ for distinct L_1, L_2. An execution $\mathcal{G} = \langle E, \mathtt{po}, \mathtt{stmp}, \mathtt{so}, \mathtt{hb} \rangle$ is Λ-consistent iff:*

- *For all $L \in \Lambda$: $\mathcal{G}|_L \in L.\mathcal{C}$ (i.e. $\mathcal{G}$ is L-consistent for each $L \in \Lambda$);*
- *$E = \bigcup_{L \in \Lambda} E|_L$ and $\mathtt{so} = \bigcup_{L \in \Lambda} \mathtt{so}|_L$; and*
- *$\mathtt{hb}$ is irreflexive (i.e. $\mathtt{hb}$ is a strict partial order).*

3.2   The Declarative $\text{RDMA}_{\text{RMW}}^{\text{WAIT}}$ Model

We present $\text{RDMA}_{\text{RMW}}^{\text{WAIT}}$ as an extension of $\text{RDMA}^{\text{WAIT}}$ [4] with remote RMWs. Our definitions naturally extend those of $\text{RDMA}^{\text{WAIT}}$. To underline the distinction between the two, we have highlighted our extensions from $\text{RDMA}^{\text{WAIT}}$ to $\text{RDMA}_{\text{RMW}}^{\text{WAIT}}$.

The $\text{RDMA}_{\text{RMW}}^{\text{WAIT}}$ Methods. $\text{RDMA}_{\text{RMW}}^{\text{WAIT}}$ methods extend those of $\text{RDMA}^{\text{WAIT}}$ with remote RMWs as defined by the following grammar, where $\text{RDMA}^{\text{WAIT}}$ methods comprise local (CPU) operations on TSO machines and remote operations.

$$m(\widetilde{v}) ::= \mathtt{Write}(x, v) \mid \mathtt{Read}(x) \mid \mathtt{CAS}(x, v_1, v_2) \mid \mathtt{Mfence}() \quad // \ \text{RDMA}^{\text{WAIT}}: \text{Local}$$
$$\mid \mathtt{Get}(x, y, d) \mid \mathtt{Put}(x, y, d) \mid \mathtt{Wait}(d) \mid \mathtt{Rfence}(n) \quad // \ \text{RDMA}^{\text{WAIT}}: \text{Remote}$$
$$\mid \mathtt{RCAS}(x, y, v_1, v_2, d) \mid \mathtt{RFAA}(x, y, v, d) \qquad // \ \text{Remote RMWs}$$

The remote operations comprise $\mathtt{Get}$, $\mathtt{Put}$, $\mathtt{Wait}$ (as described in §2.1), and $\mathtt{Rfence}$ instructions. Note that for readability in our examples we write $x :=^d y^n$ (resp. $x^n :=^d y$) for $\mathtt{Get}(x, y, d)$ (resp. $\mathtt{Put}(x, y, d)$). Similarly, we write $x := v$ (resp. $a := x$) for $\mathtt{Write}(x, v)$ (resp. $\mathtt{let}\, a = \mathtt{Read}(x)\,\mathtt{in}\, \ldots$). The $\mathtt{Rfence}(n)$ denotes a *remote fence* that strongly orders all operations towards n without blocking the (local) CPU. That is, given a (sequential) program of the form $C; \mathtt{Rfence}(n); C'$, all remote operations towards n in C are ordered before those in C'. The $\mathtt{RCAS}(x, y, v_1, v_2, d)$ is the remote analogue of writing $\mathtt{let}\, v = \mathtt{CAS}(y, v_1, v_2)\,\mathtt{in}\,\mathtt{Write}(x, v)$ with work identifier d, where the RMW is run on remote location y and the result is written to local location x. Similarly, $\mathtt{RFAA}(x, y, v, d)$ increments (remote) y by v and writes its old value to x.

Well-addressed $\text{RDMA}_{\text{RMW}}^{\text{WAIT}}$ Executions. We assume each location x is associated with exactly one node denoted by $\mathbf{n}(x)$. We write $\mathbf{n}(t)$ to denote the node on which t is run. An execution $\mathcal{G}$ is *well-addressed* iff it comprises method calls (in $\mathcal{G}.E$) with appropriate local locations when expected; e.g. for each $\mathtt{Write}(x, \_)$ or $\mathtt{Put}(\_, x, \_)$ call by thread t in $\mathcal{G}$, $\mathbf{n}(x) = \mathbf{n}(t)$. We define $\mathtt{loc}$ for $\text{RDMA}_{\text{RMW}}^{\text{WAIT}}$ as expected; e.g. $\mathtt{loc}(\mathtt{Write}(x, \_)) = \{x\}$, $\mathtt{loc}(\mathtt{Put}(x, y, \_)) = \{x, y\}$ and $\mathtt{loc}(\mathtt{Mfence}) = \emptyset$.

Well-stamped $\text{RDMA}_{\text{RMW}}^{\text{WAIT}}$ **Executions.** An execution $\mathcal{G}$ is *well-stamped* if for all $\mathsf{e} = \langle \_, \_, \langle m, (\widetilde{v}), v' \rangle \rangle \in \mathcal{G}.E$: $\mathcal{G}.\mathtt{stmp}(\mathsf{e}) \in \mathtt{stmp}_{\text{RW}}(m(\widetilde{v}), v')$, with $\mathtt{stmp}_{\text{RW}}$ defined as follows. Note that depending on whether RCAS calls succeed, they may have multiple valid sets of stamps; as such, the $\mathtt{stmp}_{\text{RW}}$ function returns a set of stamp sets (set of set of stamps), though in all cases but for RCAS this set is a singleton.

$$
\mathtt{stmp}_{\text{RW}}(\mathtt{CAS}(x, v_1, \_), v_2) \triangleq \begin{cases} \{\{\mathtt{aMF}, \mathtt{aCR}\}\} & \text{if } v_1 \neq v_2 \\ \{\{\mathtt{aCAS}\}\} & \text{if } v_1 = v_2 \end{cases} \qquad \mathtt{stmp}_{\text{RW}}(\mathtt{Write}(x, v), \_) \triangleq \{\{\mathtt{aCW}\}\}
$$

$$
\mathtt{stmp}_{\text{RW}}(\mathtt{Get}(x, y^n, \_), \_) \triangleq \{\{\mathtt{aNRR}_n, \mathtt{aNLW}_n\}\} \qquad \mathtt{stmp}_{\text{RW}}(\mathtt{Read}(x), \_) \triangleq \{\{\mathtt{aCR}\}\}
$$

$$
\mathtt{stmp}_{\text{RW}}(\mathtt{Put}(x^n, y, \_), \_) \triangleq \{\{\mathtt{aNLR}_n, \mathtt{aNRW}_n\}\} \qquad \mathtt{stmp}_{\text{RW}}(\mathtt{Mfence}(), \_) \triangleq \{\{\mathtt{aMF}\}\}
$$

$$
\mathtt{stmp}_{\text{RW}}(\mathtt{RFAA}(x, y^n, \_, \_), \_) \triangleq \{\{\mathtt{aNAR}_n, \mathtt{aNRW}_n, \mathtt{aNLW}_n\}\} \qquad \mathtt{stmp}_{\text{RW}}(\mathtt{Wait}(d), \_) \triangleq \{\{\mathtt{aWT}\}\}
$$

$$
\mathtt{stmp}_{\text{RW}}(\mathtt{RCAS}(x, y^n, \_, \_, \_), \_) \triangleq \{\{\mathtt{aNAR}_n, \mathtt{aNLW}_n\}, \{\mathtt{aNAR}_n, \mathtt{aNRW}_n, \mathtt{aNLW}_n\}\} \qquad \mathtt{stmp}_{\text{RW}}(\mathtt{Rfence}(n), \_) \triangleq \{\{\mathtt{aRF}_n\}\}
$$

A successful remote RMW has three stamps for reading the remote location, modifying it, and writing it to the local location, while a failed RCAS does not modify the remote location. Recall that the remote read of a remote RMW yields stamp $\mathtt{aNAR}_n$, which offers more guarantees than the stamp $\mathtt{aNRR}_n$ of Gets.

We extend the location function ($\mathtt{loc}$, defined above for $\text{RDMA}_{\text{RMW}}^{\text{WAIT}}$) to subevents. For method calls corresponding to *local operations* (with one or zero locations) their subevents have the same locations. The subevents of Get, Put, RCAS, and RFAA are associated with the relevant location as expected. For instance, if $\mathsf{e} = \langle \_, \_, \langle \mathtt{Get}, (x, y, d), \_ \rangle \rangle$ (with subevents $\mathtt{aNRR}_n$ and $\mathtt{aNLW}_n$), then $\mathtt{loc}(\langle \mathsf{e}, \mathtt{aNRR}_n \rangle) = \{y\}$ and $\mathtt{loc}(\langle \mathsf{e}, \mathtt{aNLW}_n \rangle) = \{x\}$; whereas if $\mathsf{e} = \langle \_, \_, \langle \mathtt{RFAA}, (x, y, v, d), \_ \rangle \rangle$, then $\mathtt{loc}(\langle \mathsf{e}, \mathtt{aNAR}_n \rangle) = \{y\}$, $\mathtt{loc}(\langle \mathsf{e}, \mathtt{aNRW}_n \rangle) = \{y\}$ and $\mathtt{loc}(\langle \mathsf{e}, \mathtt{aNLW}_n \rangle) = \{x\}$.

Well-formed $\text{RDMA}_{\text{RMW}}^{\text{WAIT}}$ **Executions.** We shortly define the notion of $\text{RDMA}_{\text{RMW}}^{\text{WAIT}}$-consistency for an execution $\mathcal{G}$. To do this, we need a few auxiliary functions and relations as follows. We assume functions $\mathsf{v}_{\text{R}} : \mathcal{G}.\mathcal{R} \to \mathsf{Val}$ and $\mathsf{v}_{\text{W}} : \mathcal{G}.\mathcal{W} \to \mathsf{Val}$, which associate each read (resp. write) subevent with the value returned (resp. written). We define the '*reads-from*' relation, $\mathsf{rf} \subseteq \mathcal{G}.\mathcal{W} \times \mathcal{G}.\mathcal{R}$, on subevents of the same location with matching values (formalised below); the '*modification-order*' relation, $\mathsf{mo} \subseteq \mathcal{G}.\mathcal{W} \times \mathcal{G}.\mathcal{W}$, describing a (total) order in which writes reach the memory; and the '*NIC flush order*', nfo, capturing the PCIe guarantee that NIC reads flush previous NIC writes. For remote RMWs, we define the '*remote-atomic-order*', rao, describing the (total) order in which (remote read parts of) remote RMWs towards each node are executed. A tuple $\langle \mathsf{v}_{\text{R}}, \mathsf{v}_{\text{W}}, \mathsf{rf}, \mathsf{mo}, \mathsf{nfo}, \mathsf{rao} \rangle$ is *well-formed* if the following hold for all $\mathsf{e}, v, v', v_1, v_2, \mathsf{s}_1, \mathsf{s}_2, n, x, y$.

- If e is of the form $\langle \mathtt{Read}, \_, v \rangle$ or $\langle \mathtt{CAS}, \_, v \rangle$, then $\mathsf{v}_{\text{R}}(\mathsf{e}) = v$.
- If e is of the form $\langle \mathtt{Write}, (\_, v), \_ \rangle$ or $\langle \mathtt{CAS}, (\_, v', v), v' \rangle$, then $\mathsf{v}_{\text{W}}(\mathsf{e}) = v$
- If $\mathsf{s}_1 = \langle \mathsf{e}, \mathtt{aNLR}_n \rangle \wedge \mathsf{s}_2 = \langle \mathsf{e}, \mathtt{aNRW}_n \rangle$, then $\mathsf{v}_{\text{R}}(\mathsf{s}_1) = \mathsf{v}_{\text{W}}(\mathsf{s}_2)$; *mutatis mutandis* for $\mathsf{s}_1 = \langle \mathsf{e}, \mathtt{aNRR}_n \rangle, \mathsf{s}_2 = \langle \mathsf{e}, \mathtt{aNLW}_n \rangle$ and $\mathsf{s}_1 = \langle \mathsf{e}, \mathtt{aNAR}_n \rangle, \mathsf{s}_2 = \langle \mathsf{e}, \mathtt{aNLW}_n \rangle$.
- $\langle \mathsf{s}_1, \mathsf{s}_2 \rangle \in \mathsf{rf} \Rightarrow \mathtt{loc}(\mathsf{s}_1) = \mathtt{loc}(\mathsf{s}_2) \wedge \mathsf{v}_{\text{W}}(\mathsf{s}_1) = \mathsf{v}_{\text{R}}(\mathsf{s}_2)$.
- rf^{-1} is a function, i.e. every read is related to at most one write. If a read is not related to a write, it returns zero: $\mathsf{s}_2 \notin \mathtt{img}(\mathsf{rf}) \Rightarrow \mathsf{v}_{\text{R}}(\mathsf{s}_2) = 0$.
- $\mathsf{mo} \triangleq \bigcup_{x \in \mathsf{Loc}} \mathsf{mo}_x$, where each mo_x is a strict total order on $\mathcal{G}.\mathcal{W}_x$.
- if $\langle \mathsf{s}_1, \mathsf{s}_2 \rangle \in (\mathtt{aNLR}_n \times \mathtt{aNLW}_n) \cup ((\mathtt{aNRR}_n \cup \mathtt{aNAR}_n) \times \mathtt{aNRW}_n)$ and $\mathsf{t}(\mathsf{s}_1) = \mathsf{t}(\mathsf{s}_2)$ then $\langle \mathsf{s}_1, \mathsf{s}_2 \rangle \in \mathsf{nfo} \cup \mathsf{nfo}^{-1}$.

- RCAS succeeds iff it reads the expected value, in which case it overwrites with the given value. That is, given $\mathsf{e} = \langle \_, \_, \langle \mathrm{RCAS}, (x, y, v_1, v_2, \_), \_ \rangle \rangle$:
  if $\mathtt{stmp}(\mathsf{e}) = \{\mathtt{aNAR}_{\mathtt{n}(y)}, \mathtt{aNLW}_{\mathtt{n}(y)}\}$, then $\mathrm{v_R}(\langle \mathsf{e}, \mathtt{aNAR}_{\mathtt{n}(y)} \rangle) \neq v_1$; and
  if $\mathtt{stmp}(\mathsf{e}) = \{\mathtt{aNAR}_{\mathtt{n}(y)}, \mathtt{aNRW}_{\mathtt{n}(y)}, \mathtt{aNLW}_{\mathtt{n}(y)}\}$, then $\mathrm{v_R}(\langle \mathsf{e}, \mathtt{aNAR}_{\mathtt{n}(y)} \rangle) = v_1$ and $\mathrm{v_W}(\langle \mathsf{e}, \mathtt{aNRW}_{\mathtt{n}(y)} \rangle) = v_2$.
- If $\mathsf{e} = \langle \_, \_, \langle \mathrm{RFAA}, (x, y, v, \_), \_ \rangle \rangle$, then $\mathrm{v_W}(\langle \mathsf{e}, \mathtt{aNRW}_{\mathtt{n}(y)} \rangle) = \mathrm{v_R}(\langle \mathsf{e}, \mathtt{aNAR}_{\mathtt{n}(y)} \rangle) + v$.
- $\mathsf{rao} \triangleq \bigcup_{n \in \mathsf{Node}} \mathsf{rao}_n$, where rao_n is a strict total order on the set of subevents
  $\{\langle \mathsf{e}, \mathtt{aNAR}_n \rangle \mid \mathsf{e} = \langle \_, \_, \langle m, (x, y, \ldots), \_ \rangle \rangle \wedge m \in \{\mathrm{RFAA}, \mathrm{RCAS}\} \wedge \mathtt{n}(y) = n\}$

We distinguish the point subevents *start* executing (point of 'issue') from when they *complete*. We define the *issued-before* relation, ib, to record dependencies between the starts of subevents, while so records dependencies between their ends. Note that ib and so are incomparable: $\langle \mathsf{s}_1, \mathsf{s}_2 \rangle \in \mathsf{ib}$ does *not* imply $\langle \mathsf{s}_1, \mathsf{s}_2 \rangle \in \mathsf{so}$ and vice versa. We define *instantaneous subevents*, $\mathcal{G}.\mathtt{Inst} \triangleq \mathcal{G}.\mathsf{SEvent} \backslash (\mathcal{G}.\mathsf{aCW} \cup \mathcal{G}.\mathsf{aNLW} \cup \mathcal{G}.\mathsf{aNRW})$, as those that start and end at the same time.

Given an execution $\mathcal{G}$ and well-formed $\langle \mathrm{v_R}, \mathrm{v_W}, \mathsf{rf}, \mathsf{mo}, \mathsf{nfo}, \mathsf{rao} \rangle$, we further define the following relations that will help us define ib and so for $\mathrm{RDMA}_{\mathrm{RMW}}^{\mathrm{WAIT}}$:

$$\mathsf{rb} \triangleq \left\{ \langle r, w \rangle \in \mathcal{G}.\mathcal{R} \times \mathcal{G}.\mathcal{W} \;\middle|\; \begin{array}{l} (\langle r, w \rangle \in (\mathsf{rf}^{-1}; \mathsf{mo}) \vee r \notin \mathsf{img}(\mathsf{rf})) \\ \wedge\ \mathtt{loc}(r) = \mathtt{loc}(w) \end{array} \right\} \backslash [\mathcal{G}.\mathsf{SEvent}]$$

$$\mathsf{rb_i} \triangleq [\mathsf{aCR}]; ((\mathsf{po} \cup \mathsf{po}^{-1}) \cap \mathsf{rb}); [\mathsf{aCW}] \qquad \mathsf{pfg} \triangleq \{\langle \langle \mathsf{e}_1, \mathtt{aNLW}_n \rangle, \langle \mathsf{e}_2, \mathtt{aWT} \rangle \rangle \mid \exists d. \langle \mathsf{e}_1, \mathsf{e}_2 \rangle \in \mathsf{po}|_d\}$$

$$\mathsf{rf_i} \triangleq [\mathsf{aCW}]; (\mathsf{po} \cap \mathsf{rf}); [\mathsf{aCR}] \qquad \mathsf{rf_e} \triangleq \mathsf{rf} \backslash \mathsf{rf_i} \qquad \mathsf{pfp} \triangleq \{\langle \langle \mathsf{e}_1, \mathtt{aNRW}_n \rangle, \langle \mathsf{e}_2, \mathtt{aWT} \rangle \rangle \mid \exists d. \langle \mathsf{e}_1, \mathsf{e}_2 \rangle \in \mathsf{po}|_d\}$$

$$\mathsf{iso} \triangleq \{\langle \langle \mathsf{e}, \mathtt{aMF} \rangle, \langle \mathsf{e}, \mathtt{aCR} \rangle \rangle \mid \mathtt{m}(\mathsf{e}) = \mathtt{CAS}\}$$
$$\cup \{\langle \langle \mathsf{e}, \mathtt{aNRR}_n \rangle, \langle \mathsf{e}, \mathtt{aNLW}_n \rangle \rangle \mid \mathtt{m}(\mathsf{e}) = \mathtt{Get}\} \cup \{\langle \langle \mathsf{e}, \mathtt{aNLR}_n \rangle, \langle \mathsf{e}, \mathtt{aNRW}_n \rangle \rangle \mid \mathtt{m}(\mathsf{e}) = \mathtt{Put}\}$$
$$\cup \{\langle \langle \mathsf{e}, \mathtt{aNAR}_n \rangle, \langle \mathsf{e}, \mathtt{aNLW}_n \rangle \rangle \mid \mathtt{m}(\mathsf{e}) \in \{\mathrm{RCAS}, \mathrm{RFAA}\}\}$$
$$\cup \{\langle \langle \mathsf{e}, \mathtt{aNAR}_n \rangle, \langle \mathsf{e}, \mathtt{aNRW}_n \rangle \rangle \mid \mathtt{m}(\mathsf{e}) \in \{\mathrm{RCAS}, \mathrm{RFAA}\} \wedge \mathtt{aNRW}_n \in \mathtt{stmp}(\mathsf{e})\}$$

The rb denotes the '*reads-before*' relation: given a read r that reads from a write w_r, i.e. $\langle w_r, r \rangle \in \mathsf{rf}$, then rb relates r to all writes w (on the same location) that are mo-*later* than w_r. The *internal* rb relation, $\mathsf{rb_i}$, restricts rb to CPU reads and writes on the same thread; similarly for $\mathsf{rf_i}$ (internal rf). The *external* rf, $\mathsf{rf_e}$, is defined as rf edges that are not internal. The pfg (resp. pfp) relation captures the synchronisation between the local write subevent of a Get or remote RMW (resp. remote write subevent of a Put or remote RMW) and a later Wait with the same work identifier. As we describe shortly, while both are included in ib, only pfg is included in so as waiting for a Put (or remote RMW) does not guarantee that the NIC remote write has completed. The '*internal synchronisation order*', iso, captures ordering between subevents of the same event and ensures that a failing CPU CAS performs a memory fence before reading; RDMA operations (Get, Put, and remote RMW) read before copying the value; and a successful remote RMW reads before updating the remote value.

Finally, we define ib as follows and it includes a superset ippo of ppo. Specifically, while a later CPU read might finish before an earlier CPU write or wait (cells B1 and B5, in Fig. 9), they start (are issued) in order; and while a remote fence does not guarantee previous NIC writes have completed (cells G11 and J11, in Fig. 9), it guarantees they have at least started.

$$\mathsf{ib} \triangleq (\mathsf{ippo} \cup \mathsf{iso} \cup \mathsf{rf} \cup \mathsf{pfg} \cup \mathsf{pfp} \cup \mathsf{nfo} \cup \mathsf{rb_i})^+$$

with $\mathsf{ippo} \triangleq \mathsf{ppo} \cup ([\mathtt{aCW}]; \mathsf{po}; [\mathtt{aCR} \cup \mathtt{aWT}]) \cup \bigcup_{n \in \mathsf{Node}}([\mathtt{aNRW}_n \cup \mathtt{aNLW}_n]; \mathsf{po}; [\mathtt{aRF}_n])$

We next define *consistency* for $\mathrm{RDMA}_{\mathrm{RMW}}^{\mathrm{WAIT}}$. We require that ib and so be irreflexive (the latter is implied by irreflexivity of hb in Def. 2 as $\mathsf{so} \subseteq \mathsf{hb}$ (Def. 1)).

Definition 3 ($\mathrm{RDMA}_{\mathrm{RMW}}^{\mathrm{WAIT}}$-consistency). *An execution* $\mathcal{G} = \langle E, \mathsf{po}, \mathsf{stmp}, \mathsf{so}, \mathsf{hb} \rangle$ *is* $\mathrm{RDMA}_{\mathrm{RMW}}^{\mathrm{WAIT}}$-*consistent iff it is well-addressed, well-stamped, and there exists a well-formed tuple* $\langle \mathsf{v_R}, \mathsf{v_W}, \mathsf{rf}, \mathsf{mo}, \mathsf{nfo}, \mathsf{rao} \rangle$ *such that:*

1) ib *is irreflexive; and*
2) $\mathsf{so} = \mathsf{iso} \cup \mathsf{rf_e} \cup \mathsf{pfg} \cup \mathsf{nfo} \cup \mathsf{rb} \cup \mathsf{mo} \cup \mathsf{rao} \cup ([\mathtt{aNRW}]; \mathsf{iso}^{-1}; \mathsf{rao}) \cup ([\mathtt{Inst}]; \mathsf{ib}).$

As described above, rao captures the order in which remote read parts of remote RMWs towards a node is executed. The extension $([\mathtt{aNRW}]; \mathsf{iso}^{-1}; \mathsf{rao})$ ensures that remote RMWs towards the same node do not overlap: if a remote RMW succeeds, then its remote write completes before the next RMW can read.

4 Specifying and Verifying RDMA Lock Libraries

We use the $\mathrm{RDMA}_{\mathrm{RMW}}^{\mathrm{WAIT}}$ library to *specify, implement, and verify* three RDMA lock libraries. As discussed in §2.4, designing an RDMA lock presents a trade-off between strong, intuitive behaviours and efficient implementations. As such, after introducing the required preliminaries (§4.1), we develop a weak (WLOCK), strong (SLOCK), and node (NLOCK) lock library.

4.1 Preliminaries

Well-formed Locks. A lock library typically provides two methods $\mathtt{Acq}(x)$ and $\mathtt{Rel}(x)$ for acquiring and releasing a (network-shared) lock x, ensuring mutual exclusion; i.e. two threads cannot hold the lock on x simultaneously. We assume the existence of a *location function* $\mathtt{loc}$ such that $\mathtt{loc}(\mathtt{Acq}(x)) = \mathtt{loc}(\mathtt{Rel}(x)) = \{x\}$. We further assume that locks are used in a *well-formed* fashion: a thread only acquires (resp. releases) lock x if it has not (resp. has) already acquired x. We formalise this in Def. 4 below, requiring that each $\mathtt{Acq}(x)$ (resp. $\mathtt{Rel}(x)$) is followed (resp. preceded) by $\mathtt{Rel}(x)$ (resp. $\mathtt{Acq}(x)$) in program order.

Definition 4. *An execution* $\langle E, \mathsf{po}, \_, \_, \_ \rangle$ *is* lock-well-formed *iff for all* x:

1) for all $\mathsf{e}_a \in E_x$ *there exists an* $\mathsf{e}_r \in E_x$ *such that* $\langle \mathsf{e}_a, \mathsf{e}_r \rangle \in \mathsf{po}_x|_{imm}$; *and*
2) for all $\mathsf{e}_r \in E_x$ *there exists an* $\mathsf{e}_a \in E_x$ *such that* $\langle \mathsf{e}_a, \mathsf{e}_r \rangle \in \mathsf{po}_x|_{imm}$

where $\mathsf{e}_a, \mathsf{e}_r$ *are acquire and release events:* $\mathtt{m}(\mathsf{e}_a) = \mathtt{Acq}$ *and* $\mathtt{m}(\mathsf{e}_r) = \mathtt{Rel}$.

Library guarantees only hold for programs that adhere to this well-formedness requirement. For those that do not, *any* behaviour is allowed.

Background: SV Library. Ambal et al. [4] use $\mathrm{RDMA}^{\mathrm{WAIT}}$ to define higher-level libraries such as a *shared-variable* library (SV) where each node maintains its own *copy* for each location x. A thread then accesses (reads/writes) its own local copies, and can broadcast its local value to other nodes. The SV library comprises these methods: $M = \{\text{Write}_\text{SV}, \text{Read}_\text{SV}, \text{Bcast}_\text{SV}, \text{Wait}_\text{SV}, \text{GFence}\}$. The $\text{Write}_\text{SV}(x, v)$ (resp. $\text{Read}_\text{SV}(x)$) writes (resp. reads) value v to the local copy of x on the current node. The $\text{Bcast}_\text{SV}(x, d, \{n_1, \ldots, n_k\})$ broadcasts the local value of x and overwrites x on nodes $n_1, \ldots, n_k$, which may include the local node itself (where d is the work id). The $\text{Wait}_\text{SV}(d)$ waits for previous broadcasts of the thread associated with work id $d \in \text{Wid}$. Finally, the global fence $\text{GFence}(\{n_1, \ldots, n_k\})$ ensures every previous operation of the thread towards nodes $n_1, \ldots, n_k$ is fully completed. We repeat the formal semantics of SV in the extended version [EV]. In the remainder of this article we use SV to implement several libraries.

4.2 The Weak Lock Library

We present our WLOCK library, which only guarantees *mutual exclusion*, without any guarantees on the completion order of submitted RDMA operations.

The WLOCK Specification. The stamps for WLOCK are defined through the stmp_WL function as follows. That is, acquiring a weak lock behaves as a memory fence (stamp aMF) on TSO, while releasing it behaves merely as a write (aCW).

$$\text{stmp}_\text{WL}(\langle t, \_, \langle \text{Acq}_\text{WL}, (x), () \rangle \rangle) \triangleq \{\text{aMF}\} \qquad \text{stmp}_\text{WL}(\langle t, \_, \langle \text{Rel}_\text{WL}, (x), () \rangle \rangle) \triangleq \{\text{aCW}\}$$

As we formulate in Def. 5 below (the second condition), WLOCK provides synchronisation between lock releases and acquisitions of each lock.

Definition 5 (WLOCK-consistency). *A lock-well-formed execution* $\mathcal{G} = \langle E, \text{po}, \text{stmp}, \text{so}, \text{hb} \rangle$ *is* WLOCK-consistent *iff:*

1) $\text{stmp} = \text{stmp}_\text{WL}$ *(where* stmp_WL *is as defined above); and*
2) $\text{so} = \bigcup_x \{\langle\langle \text{e}_1, \text{aCW}\rangle, \langle \text{e}_2, \text{aMF}\rangle\rangle \mid \langle \text{e}_1, \text{e}_2\rangle \in (\text{po}_x|_{imm})^{-1}; \text{lo}_x\}$, *where* lo_x *is a total order on acquisition events on* x, *i.e. on* $\{\text{e} \in E_x \mid \text{m}(\text{e}) = \text{Acq}_\text{WL}\}$.

Given a release event e_1 on x (in a lock-well-formed execution), the $(\text{po}_x|_{imm})^{-1}$ component identifies an acquire event e_3 that is the latest corresponding acquire event on x preceding e_1 (in po). As such, so induces synchronisation between e_1 and all later (in lo_x) acquisition events e_2. Note that lo_x is also indirectly included in hb, since the acquire and release operations stay in order.

The release stamp (aCW) does not synchronise with previous RDMA-specific stamps (bottom-left part of Fig. 9). As such, reacquiring a lock does not guarantee that previous RDMA operations submitted with the lock are completed.

The WLOCK (Distributed) Implementation. We present our WLOCK implementation in Fig. 10 (via the I_WL function), inspired by the well-known ticket lock implementation. For each lock location x, we create a ticket dispenser x_a (on some arbitrary node) that records the value of the next *available* ticket, thread-local locations (p_x^t for each $t \in \text{Tid} = \{1, \ldots, T\}$) to track the ticket allocated to t (i.e. its turn), and shared variables x_t (for each $t \in \text{Tid}$) to signal releasing the lock.

$$I_{\text{WL}}(t, \text{Acq}_{\text{WL}}, (x)) \triangleq$$
$$\quad \text{RFAA}(p_x^t, x_a, 1, d); \ \text{Wait}(d);$$
$$\quad \text{let } v = \text{Read}(p_x^t) \text{ in}$$
$$\quad \text{loop } \{ \text{if } \text{Read}_{\text{SV}}(x_1) = v \text{ then break else}$$
$$\quad\quad \ldots$$
$$\quad\quad \text{if } \text{Read}_{\text{SV}}(x_T) = v \text{ then break } \}$$

$$I_{\text{WL}}(t, \text{Rel}_{\text{WL}}, (x)) \triangleq$$
$$\quad \text{let } v = \text{Read}(p_x^t) \text{ in}$$
$$\quad \text{Write}_{\text{SV}}(x_t, v + 1);$$
$$\quad \text{Bcast}_{\text{SV}}(x_t, \_, \text{Node} \setminus \{\text{n}(t)\})$$

Fig. 10: The WLOCK implementation using $\text{RDMA}_{\text{RMW}}^{\text{WAIT}}$ and SV libraries.

To release the lock on x, thread t writes the *next* turn, i.e. $v+1$ when t holds ticket v (obtained by reading p_x^t), to its release location x_t and subsequently broadcasts it to all nodes other than itself ($\text{n}(t)$). To acquire the lock on x, thread t calls a fetch-and-add on x_a to fetch the next available ticket (i.e. its turn) in p_x^t and increments x_a. It then records its turn in v and repeatedly examines the release location $x_{t'}$ of each thread $t' \in \{1, \ldots, T\}$ until one has value v, indicating that its turn has come and thus t holds the lock. Note that t' may be t itself, i.e. $t = t'$, if it was the last thread to release the lock.

At the cost of more network messages (through broadcasts), our implementation provides lower latency than centralised systems (e.g. in Fig. 13) as messages are transmitted directly from the thread releasing the lock to the next thread acquiring the lock. We next prove (Theorem 1) that our implementation is correct against the WLOCK specification with the full proof given in the extended version [EV].

Theorem 1. *The implementation I_{WL} is sound.*

4.3   The Strong Lock Library

We present our strong lock library SLOCK that, as well as ensuring mutual exclusion of critical sections, additionally guarantees that *all* earlier operations have *fully* completed on releasing a strong lock. We present several examples of the 'message-passing' behaviour in Fig. 11 contrasting the behaviour of weak and strong locks when interacting with Gets and whether the weak outcome $a \neq b$ is allowed. In particular, we may observe $a \neq b$ when using a weak lock (Fig. 11a) and this can be prohibited by explicitly waiting (using $\text{Wait}(d)$) on the completion of the Gets before releasing the weak lock (Fig. 11b). By contrast, when using a strong lock we no longer need to wait for their completion as this is guaranteed by the strong lock release (Fig. 11c).

The SLOCK Specification. The SLOCK stamps are defined (via stmp_{SL}) as:

$$\text{stmp}_{\text{SL}}(\langle t, \_, \langle \text{Acq}_{\text{SL}}, (x), () \rangle \rangle) \triangleq \{\text{aMF}\} \quad \text{stmp}_{\text{SL}}(\langle t, \_, \langle \text{Rel}_{\text{SL}}, (x), () \rangle \rangle) \triangleq \bigcup_{n \in \text{Node}} \{\text{aGF}_n\}$$

As with WLOCK, acquiring a strong lock behaves as a memory fence (aMF), while releasing it behaves as a global fence (aGF), ensuring that all previous remote operations are completed.

$x, y = 0, 0$	
$\texttt{Acq}_{\text{WL}}(l)$ $x := 1$ $y := 1$ $\texttt{Rel}_{\text{WL}}(l)$	$\texttt{Acq}_{\text{WL}}(l)$ $a := x^1$ $b := y^1$ $\texttt{Rel}_{\text{WL}}(l)$

(a) $a \neq b$ ✓

$x, y = 0, 0$	
$\texttt{Acq}_{\text{WL}}(l)$ $x := 1$ $y := 1$ $\texttt{Rel}_{\text{WL}}(l)$	$\texttt{Acq}_{\text{WL}}(l)$ $a :=^d x^1$ $b :=^d y^1$ $\texttt{Wait}(d)$ $\texttt{Rel}_{\text{WL}}(l)$

(b) $a \neq b$ ✗

$x, y = 0, 0$	
$\texttt{Acq}_{\text{SL}}(l)$ $x := 1$ $y := 1$ $\texttt{Rel}_{\text{SL}}(l)$	$\texttt{Acq}_{\text{SL}}(l)$ $a := x^1$ $b := y^1$ $\texttt{Rel}_{\text{SL}}(l)$

(c) $a \neq b$ ✗

Fig. 11: Weak versus strong locks when interacting with $\texttt{Get}$ instructions.

Definition 6 (SLOCK-**consistency**). *A lock-well-formed execution* $\mathcal{G} = \langle E, \textsf{po}, \textsf{stmp}, \textsf{so}, \textsf{hb} \rangle$ *is* SLOCK-*consistent iff:*

1) $\textsf{stmp} = \textsf{stmp}_{\text{SL}}$ *(where* $\textsf{stmp}_{\text{SL}}$ *is defined above); and*
2) $\textsf{so} = \bigcup_{x \in \textsf{Loc}, n \in \textsf{Node}} \left\{ \langle \langle \textsf{e}_1, \texttt{aGF}_n \rangle, \langle \textsf{e}_2, \texttt{aMF} \rangle \rangle \mid \langle \textsf{e}_1, \textsf{e}_2 \rangle \in (\textsf{po}_x|_{imm})^{-1}; \textsf{lo}_x \right\}$, *where* $\textsf{lo}_x$ *is a total order on* $\{ \textsf{e} \in E_x \mid \textsf{m}(\textsf{e}) = \texttt{Acq}_{\text{SL}} \}$.

Strong Lock Implementation. We implement SLOCK (via I_{SL}) simply by combining the weak locks and global fences (from the SV library) as follows:

$$I_{\text{SL}}(t, \texttt{Acq}_{\text{SL}}, (x)) \triangleq \texttt{Acq}_{\text{WL}}(x) \qquad I_{\text{SL}}(t, \texttt{Rel}_{\text{SL}}, (x)) \triangleq \texttt{GFence}(\textsf{Node}); \texttt{Rel}_{\text{WL}}(x)$$

Finally, we prove (Theorem 2) that our implementation is sound against the SLOCK specification with the full proof given in the extended version [EV].

Theorem 2. *The implementation* I_{SL} *is sound.*

4.4   The Node Lock Library

A common use case of locks is to protect an object (set of locations) on a specific node. In such cases, neither weak nor strong locks are suitable as they either incur a high programmer burden (weak locks) or a high performance overhead (strong locks). To address this, we develop *node locks*, NLOCK, a novel lock library that provides synchronisation on a specific node. Given a node lock x on node n, we write $\textsf{n}(x)$ for n. A node lock x ensures that on re-acquiring it all previous remote operations (within a critical section of x) towards n are observable.

The NLOCK **Specification.** The NLOCK stamps are defined (via $\textsf{stmp}_{\text{NL}}$) as:

$$\textsf{stmp}_{\text{NL}}(\langle t, \_, \langle \texttt{Acq}_{\text{NL}}, (x), () \rangle \rangle) \triangleq \{\texttt{aMF}\} \qquad \textsf{stmp}_{\text{NL}}(\langle t, \_, \langle \texttt{Rel}_{\text{NL}}, (x), () \rangle \rangle) \triangleq \{\texttt{aRF}_{\textsf{n}(x)}, \texttt{aNRW}_{\textsf{n}(x)}\}$$

Note that unlike WLOCK, the NLOCK releases use $\texttt{aRF}_n$ and $\texttt{aNRW}_n$ stamps to synchronise with previous remote operations towards n (i.e. those with stamps $\texttt{aNAR}_n$, $\texttt{aNRR}_n$, and $\texttt{aNRW}_n$). Importantly, note that unlike in SLOCK, the release *should not* include a global fence stamp ($\texttt{aGF}_n$) as that would be too strong. By using $\texttt{aRF}_n$ and $\texttt{aNRW}_n$, we ensure that previous operations towards n are completed only when the lock is *later re-acquired*, and they may not have yet completed on release. This means that, when appropriate, using a node lock is more efficient than combining a weak lock with a global fence.

(a)

	$x = 0$	$y = 0$
$\texttt{Acq}_{\text{SL}}(l)$ $x^2 := 1$ $\texttt{Rel}_{\text{SL}}(l)$ $y^3 := 1$		$a := y$ $b := x^2$

(a) $(a, b) = (1, 0)$ ✗

(b)

	$x = 0$ NLOCK l	$y = 0$
$\texttt{Acq}_{\text{NL}}(l^2)$ $x^2 := 1$ $\texttt{Rel}_{\text{NL}}(l^2)$ $y^3 := 1$		$a := y$ $b := x^2$

(b) $(a, b) = (1, 0)$ ✓

(c)

	$x = 0$ NLOCK l	$y = 0$	$z = 0$
$\texttt{Acq}_{\text{NL}}(l^2)$ $x^2 := 1$ $z^4 := 1$ $\texttt{Rel}_{\text{NL}}(l^2)$ $y^3 := 1$		$a := y$ $\texttt{Acq}_{\text{NL}}(l^2)$ $b := x^2$ $c := z^4$ $\texttt{Rel}_{\text{NL}}(l^2)$	

(c) $(a, b, c) = (1, 0, \_)$ ✗
$(a, b, c) = (1, \_, 0)$ ✓

Fig. 12: Strong (left) versus node (middle and right) locks examples.

To understand the difference between strong and node locks, consider the examples in Figs. 12a and 12b, where the $x^2 := 1$ $\texttt{Put}$ by node 1 is enclosed *within* a lock, while the $b := x^2$ $\texttt{Get}$ by node 3 is *without* a lock. In Fig. 12a, $\texttt{Rel}_{\text{SL}}(l)$ ensures that the earlier $x^2 := 1$ has completed. As such, $a = 1$ implies that $y^3 := 1$ has been executed and that x (in node 2) has been modified, ensuring $b = 1$. By contrast, the $\texttt{Rel}_{\text{NL}}(l^2)$ in Fig. 12b does not wait for $x^2 := 1$ to complete, i.e. $x^2 := 1$ may complete after $y^3 := 1$. We can prevent this by enclosing $b := x^2$ within the node lock, as shown in Fig. 12c. Specifically, $y^3 := 1$ in Fig. 12c may still complete before earlier remote operations. However, $a = 1$ implies that $y^3 := 1$ is executed, and that thread 1 has at least acquired the lock. As such, when thread 3 acquires the lock via $\texttt{Acq}_{\text{NL}}(l)$, it synchronises with $\texttt{Rel}_{\text{NL}}(l)$ in thread 1 and ensures that $x^2 := 1$ is completed on lock acquisition. Note that the node lock l protects the accesses towards locations on *node 2 only*. Thus, in Fig. 12c, it only guarantees that $x^2 := 1$ is completed but not necessarily $z^4 := 1$ (towards node 4), and thus $(a, c)=(1, 0)$ is an allowed outcome. By contrast, Fig. 8f in the overview showcases the lock guarantees: as x and y both reside on node 2, the lock ensures that their accesses by threads 1 and 3 are mutually exclusive, i.e. $a \neq b$ is disallowed. Specifically, if thread 1 acquires l first, x and y are modified before being read by thread 3, i.e. $a=b=1$. Conversely, if thread 3 acquires l first, x and y are read before being modified by thread 1, i.e. $a=b=0$.

Definition 7 (NLOCK-consistency). *A lock-well-formed execution $\mathcal{G} = \langle E, \textsf{po},$ $\textsf{stmp}, \textsf{so}, \textsf{hb} \rangle$ is NLOCK-consistent iff:*

1) $\textsf{stmp} = \textsf{stmp}_{\text{NL}}$ (where $\textsf{stmp}_{\text{NL}}$ is as defined above); and
2) $\textsf{so} = \big\{ \langle \langle \text{e}, \texttt{aRF}_{\text{n}(\text{loc}(\text{e}))} \rangle, \langle \text{e}, \texttt{aNRW}_{\text{n}(\text{loc}(\text{e}))} \rangle \rangle \mid \textsf{m}(\text{e}) = \texttt{Rel}_{\text{NL}} \big\}$
$\bigcup_{x \in \textsf{Loc}} \big\{ \langle \langle \text{e}_1, \texttt{aNRW}_{\text{n}(\text{loc}(\text{e}_1))} \rangle, \langle \text{e}_2, \texttt{aMF} \rangle \rangle \mid \langle \text{e}_1, \text{e}_2 \rangle \in (\textsf{po}_x|_{imm})^{-1}; \textsf{lo}_x \big\}$
where $\textsf{lo}_x$ is a total order on $\{ \text{e} \in E_x \mid \textsf{m}(\text{e}) = \texttt{Acq}_{\text{NL}} \}$.

The NLOCK Implementation. We implement NLOCK as a centralised ticket lock using remote RMWs (Fig. 13). For each (node) lock x associated with node $\text{n}(x)$, we create two remote locations x_a and x_r on $\text{n}(x)$. As before, x_a is the ticket dispenser and records the next available ticket. The x_r tracks the release counter and indicates which ticket currently holds the lock. Each thread also uses a local location p_x^t to hold the result of remote operations.

Acquiring the lock on x calls a fetch-and-add on x_a to fetch the next available ticket in p_x^t and increments x_a. It then records the ticket value in v and repeatedly examines x_r until it has value v, indicating that its turn has come and thus t holds the lock. Finally, it increments its ticket value in p_x^t in preparation for later releasing the lock; i.e. p_x^t now records the ticket whose turn is next. As such, releasing the lock simply updates x_r to p_x^t using a `Put` rather than an RMW; this is because only the lock holder can write to x_r. Note that the preceding `Rfence` en-

$$I_{\mathrm{NL}}(t, \mathrm{Acq}_{\mathrm{NL}}, (x)) \triangleq$$
$$\quad \mathrm{RFAA}(p_x^t, x_a, 1, d); \mathrm{Wait}(d);$$
$$\quad \mathtt{let}\, v = \mathrm{Read}(p_x^t)\, \mathtt{in}$$
$$\quad \mathtt{loop}\ \{$$
$$\quad\quad \mathrm{Get}(p_x^t, x_r, d); \mathrm{Wait}(d);$$
$$\quad\quad \mathtt{if}\ \mathrm{Read}(p_x^t) = v\ \mathtt{then}\ \mathtt{break}\ \};$$
$$\quad \mathrm{Write}(p_x^t, v + 1)$$

$$I_{\mathrm{NL}}(t, \mathrm{Rel}_{\mathrm{NL}}, (x)) \triangleq$$
$$\quad \mathrm{Rfence}(\mathrm{n}(x));$$
$$\quad \mathrm{Put}(x_r, p_x^t, \_)$$

Fig. 13: Node lock implementation (I_{NL}) using RDMA$_{\mathrm{RMW}}^{\mathrm{WAIT}}$

sures that earlier `Get` operations towards $\mathrm{n}(x)$ have completed before the lock is released. We prove (Theorem 3) that our implementation is correct against the NLOCK specification with the full proof given in the extended version [EV].

Theorem 3. *The implementation I_{NL} is sound.*

5 The RDMA$_{\mathrm{RMW}}^{\mathrm{SC}}$ Library

We specify (§5.1), implement, and verify (§5.2) the RDMA$_{\mathrm{RMW}}^{\mathrm{SC}}$ library that provides *intuitive* read, write, and RMW operations with the strong semantics of *sequential consistency* (SC) [24]. That is, as with SC, the instructions in each thread under RDMA$_{\mathrm{RMW}}^{\mathrm{SC}}$ are always observed in (program) order. Moreover, unlike in RDMA$_{\mathrm{RMW}}^{\mathrm{WAIT}}$ or the lock libraries in §4, the users do not need to specify whether a location is local or remote and which node it resides on. For instance, a user can simply call $\mathrm{Write}_{\mathrm{SC}}(\mathtt{x}, v)$ to write (with SC semantics) to location $\mathtt{x}$, regardless of whether $\mathtt{x}$ is local (on the current node) or remote. As such, we use the **typewriter** font and write $\mathtt{x}$ to denote an abstract RDMA$_{\mathrm{RMW}}^{\mathrm{SC}}$ location whose underlying memory address may be local (i.e. $\mathtt{x}=x$) or on a remote node n (i.e. $\mathtt{x}=x^n$).

5.1 The RDMA$_{\mathrm{RMW}}^{\mathrm{SC}}$ Specification

The RDMA$_{\mathrm{RMW}}^{\mathrm{SC}}$ Methods. The RDMA$_{\mathrm{RMW}}^{\mathrm{SC}}$ library has four methods: $\mathrm{Read}_{\mathrm{SC}}(\mathtt{x})$, to read from $\mathtt{x}$; $\mathrm{Write}_{\mathrm{SC}}(\mathtt{x}, v)$ to write v to $\mathtt{x}$; $\mathrm{CAS}_{\mathrm{SC}}(\mathtt{x}, v_1, v_2)$, a compare-and-swap on $\mathtt{x}$; and $\mathrm{FAA}_{\mathrm{SC}}(\mathtt{x}, v)$, a fetch-and-add on $\mathtt{x}$. We define loc as expected, i.e. $\mathrm{loc}(\mathrm{Write}_{\mathrm{SC}}(\mathtt{x}, v)) = \mathrm{loc}(\mathrm{Read}_{\mathrm{SC}}(\mathtt{x})) = \mathrm{loc}(\mathrm{CAS}_{\mathrm{SC}}(\mathtt{x}, v_1, v_2)) = \mathrm{loc}(\mathrm{FAA}_{\mathrm{SC}}(\mathtt{x}, v)) = \{\mathtt{x}\}$. We extend po and loc to subevents as expected.

Well-formedness. Given an RDMA$_{\mathrm{RMW}}^{\mathrm{SC}}$ execution $\mathcal{G}$, we define the sets of read subevents ($\mathcal{R}$) to comprise all subevents except writes and the set of write subevents ($\mathcal{W}$) to include all subevents except reads and failed RMWs.

$$\mathcal{R} \triangleq \{\langle \mathtt{e}, \mathrm{aMF} \rangle \mid \mathtt{e} \in \mathcal{G}.E \setminus \{\langle \_, \_, \langle \mathrm{Write}_{\mathrm{SC}}, \_, \_ \rangle \rangle\}\}$$

$$\begin{array}{|l|} \hline I_{\text{SC}}(t, \texttt{Write}_{\text{SC}}, (\texttt{x}, v)) \triangleq \\ \quad \texttt{Acq}_{\text{NL}}(l_{\texttt{x}}); \\ \quad \texttt{Write}(p_{\texttt{x}}^t, v); \\ \quad \texttt{Put}(x, p_{\texttt{x}}^t, \_); \\ \quad \texttt{Rel}_{\text{NL}}(l_{\texttt{x}}) \\ \hline \end{array} \quad \begin{array}{|l|} \hline I_{\text{SC}}(t, \texttt{Read}_{\text{SC}}, (\texttt{x})) \triangleq \\ \quad \texttt{Acq}_{\text{NL}}(l_{\texttt{x}}); \\ \quad \texttt{Get}(r_t, x, d); \\ \quad \texttt{Rel}_{\text{NL}}(l_{\texttt{x}}); \\ \quad \texttt{Wait}(d); \\ \quad \texttt{Read}(r_t) \\ \hline \end{array} \quad \begin{array}{|l|} \hline I_{\text{SC}}(t, \texttt{CAS}_{\text{SC}}, (\texttt{x}, v_1, v_2)) \triangleq \\ \quad \texttt{Acq}_{\text{NL}}(l_{\texttt{x}}); \\ \quad \texttt{RCAS}(r_t, x, v_1, v_2, d); \\ \quad \texttt{Rel}_{\text{NL}}(l_{\texttt{x}}); \\ \quad \texttt{Wait}(d); \\ \quad \texttt{Read}(r_t) \\ \hline \end{array} \quad \begin{array}{|l|} \hline I_{\text{SC}}(t, \texttt{FAA}_{\text{SC}}, (\texttt{x}, v)) \triangleq \\ \quad \texttt{Acq}_{\text{NL}}(l_{\texttt{x}}); \\ \quad \texttt{RFAA}(r_t, x, v, d); \\ \quad \texttt{Rel}_{\text{NL}}(l_{\texttt{x}}); \\ \quad \texttt{Wait}(d); \\ \quad \texttt{Read}(r_t) \\ \hline \end{array}$$

Fig. 14: The implementation of $\text{RDMA}_{\text{RMW}}^{\text{SC}}$ (through the I_{SC} function)

$$\mathcal{W} \triangleq \{\langle \mathsf{e}, \texttt{aMF}\rangle \mid \mathsf{e} \in \mathcal{G}.E \setminus \{\langle \_, \_, \langle \texttt{Read}_{\text{SC}}, \_, \_\rangle\rangle\} \setminus \{\langle \_, \_, \langle \texttt{CAS}_{\text{SC}}, (\_, v, \_), v'\rangle\rangle \mid v \neq v'\}\}$$

As before, a tuple $\langle \mathsf{v_R}, \mathsf{v_W}, \mathsf{rf}, \mathsf{mo}\rangle$ is *well-formed* if the following holds:

- $\mathsf{v_R}/\mathsf{v_W}$ map each read/write subevent to the value read/written:

$$\mathsf{v_R}(\langle\langle \_, \_, \langle \_, \_, v\rangle\rangle, \_\rangle) \triangleq v \qquad \mathsf{v_W}(\langle\langle \_, \_, \langle \texttt{CAS}_{\text{SC}}, (\_, v_1, v_2), v_1\rangle\rangle, \_\rangle) \triangleq v_2$$

$$\mathsf{v_W}(\langle\langle \_, \_, \langle \texttt{Write}_{\text{SC}}, (\_, v), \_\rangle\rangle, \_\rangle) \triangleq v \qquad \mathsf{v_W}(\langle\langle \_, \_, \langle \texttt{FAA}_{\text{SC}}, (\_, v), v'\rangle\rangle, \_\rangle) \triangleq v + v'$$

- rf and mo satisfy the same constraints as well-formedness of $\text{RDMA}_{\text{RMW}}^{\text{WAIT}}$ (§3.2).

We next define $\text{RDMA}_{\text{RMW}}^{\text{SC}}$-consistency, which requires that 1) each event be associated with (single) stamp $\texttt{aMF}$; and 2) $\mathsf{so} = \mathsf{po} \cup \mathsf{rf} \cup \mathsf{mo} \cup \mathsf{rb}$. The former ensures that $\text{RDMA}_{\text{RMW}}^{\text{SC}}$ calls remain ordered with respect to other non-RDMA operations. The latter captures the standard notion of happens-before in SC [28].

Definition 8 ($\text{RDMA}_{\text{RMW}}^{\text{SC}}$-**consistency**). *Execution* $\mathcal{G}$ *is* $\text{RDMA}_{\text{RMW}}^{\text{SC}}$-*consistent if:*

1) $\forall \mathsf{e} \in E.\ \texttt{stmp}(e) = \{\texttt{aMF}\}$, *and*
2) there exists a well-formed $\langle \mathsf{v_R}, \mathsf{v_W}, \mathsf{rf}, \mathsf{mo}\rangle$ *such that* $\mathcal{G}.\mathsf{so} = \mathcal{G}.\mathsf{po} \cup \mathsf{rf} \cup \mathsf{mo} \cup \mathsf{rb}$, *where* rb *is defined as in §3.2.*

5.2 The $\text{RDMA}_{\text{RMW}}^{\text{SC}}$ Implementation

We implement $\text{RDMA}_{\text{RMW}}^{\text{SC}}$ using node locks and $\text{RDMA}_{\text{RMW}}^{\text{WAIT}}$ operations, as shown in Fig. 14. For each $\text{RDMA}_{\text{RMW}}^{\text{SC}}$ location $\texttt{x}$, we create an $\text{RDMA}_{\text{RMW}}^{\text{WAIT}}$ location x on some arbitrary node. We assume each thread t has access to a private location r_t for recording the remote data it reads, and a private location $p_{\texttt{x}}^t$ for recording the value to be put to a remote location (i.e. the second argument of a $\texttt{Put}$)[5]. Moreover, each location $\texttt{x}$ is associated with a node lock $l_{\texttt{x}}$ hosted on the same node as x. We implement $\text{RDMA}_{\text{RMW}}^{\text{SC}}$ writes, reads, and RMWs respectively using $\texttt{Put}$, $\texttt{Get}$, and remote RMWs of $\text{RDMA}_{\text{RMW}}^{\text{WAIT}}$ while holding the $l_{\texttt{x}}$ lock.

Note that the $\texttt{Write}_{\text{SC}}(\texttt{x}, v)$ implementation does not wait for $\texttt{Put}(x, p_{\texttt{x}}^t, \_)$ to complete. As such, when running $\texttt{Write}_{\text{SC}}(\texttt{x}, 1); \texttt{Write}_{\text{SC}}(\texttt{y}, 1)$ in Fig. 15a with $\mathsf{n}(x) \neq \mathsf{n}(y)$, location y may be modified before x. However, this out-of-order completion is *not observable*, i.e. the (non-SC) outcome $(a, b) = (1, 0)$ is disallowed,

---

[5] In practice, we can use a $\texttt{Put}$ with 'inlined data' and forgo temporary location $p_{\texttt{x}}^t$.

x, y = 0, 0	
$\texttt{Write}_{\text{SC}}(\text{x}, 1)$	$a := \texttt{Read}_{\text{SC}}(\text{y})$
$\texttt{Write}_{\text{SC}}(\text{y}, 1)$	$b := \texttt{Read}_{\text{SC}}(\text{x})$

(a) $(a, b) = (1, 0)$ ✗

x, y = 0, 0	
$\texttt{Write}_{\text{SC}}(\text{x}, 1)$	$\texttt{Write}_{\text{SC}}(\text{y}, 1)$
$a := \texttt{Read}_{\text{SC}}(\text{y})$	$b := \texttt{Read}_{\text{SC}}(\text{x})$

(b) $(a, b) = (0, 0)$ ✗

x = 0	
$\texttt{CAS}_{\text{SC}}(\text{x}, 0, 2)$	$\texttt{Write}_{\text{SC}}(\text{x}, 1)$

(c) x = 2 ✗

x = 0		
	z = 0	
$z^2 := 1$	$a := \texttt{Read}_{\text{SC}}(\text{x})$	
$\texttt{Write}_{\text{SC}}(\text{x}, 1)$	$b := z$	

(d) $(a, b) = (1, 0)$ ✓

x = 0		
	z = 0	
$\texttt{Write}_{\text{SC}}(\text{x}, 1)$	$a := z^1$	
$z := 1$	$b := \texttt{Read}_{\text{SC}}(\text{x})$	

(e) $(a, b) = (1, 0)$ ✓

Fig. 15: $\text{RDMA}_{\text{RMW}}^{\text{SC}}$ examples

because re-acquiring a node lock makes all previous operations towards its node visible (see §4.4). Specifically, $a{=}1$ implies that $\texttt{Put}(x, p_{\text{x}}^t, \_)$ has been issued. As the implementation of $\texttt{Read}_{\text{SC}}(\text{x})$ acquires l_{x}, this enforces $\texttt{Put}(x, p_{\text{x}}^t, \_)$ to become visible; i.e. $\texttt{Read}_{\text{SC}}(\text{x})$ reads 1 and $(a, b){=}(1, 0)$ is disallowed.

In contrast to $\texttt{Write}_{\text{SC}}(\text{x}, v)$, the implementations of the other three operations must wait (via $\texttt{Wait}(d)$) for their remote operations to complete prior to reading the result via $\texttt{Read}(r_t)$ to ensure they observe the correct value. For instance, were we to remove $\texttt{Wait}(d)$ in the implementation of $\texttt{Read}_{\text{SC}}(\text{x})$, the $\texttt{Read}(r_t)$ could read a stale value from r_t *before* $\texttt{Get}(r_t, x, d)$ completes and updates r_t. Nevertheless, it is sufficient to wait for the remote operation to complete *after* releasing the lock. That is, it is possible for another thread to acquire l_{x} (and modify x) before $\texttt{Get}(r_t, x, d)$ completes; however, the semantics of NLOCK ensures that $\texttt{Get}(r_t, x, d)$ reads the old value into r_t.

The $\text{RDMA}_{\text{RMW}}^{\text{SC}}$ library, when used in isolation (without calls to e.g. $\text{RDMA}_{\text{RMW}}^{\text{WAIT}}$), ensures SC behaviour. As such, the weak behaviours of 'message-passing' in Fig. 15a and 'store-buffering' in Fig. 15b are disallowed. Moreover, $\text{RDMA}_{\text{RMW}}^{\text{SC}}$ RMW operations are strongly isolated with $\text{RDMA}_{\text{RMW}}^{\text{SC}}$ reads and writes; e.g. outcome x=2 is disallowed in Fig. 15c. This is in contrast to remote RMWs of $\text{RDMA}_{\text{RMW}}^{\text{WAIT}}$, where outcome $x{=}2$ is allowed in Fig. 6b. However, $\text{RDMA}_{\text{RMW}}^{\text{SC}}$ operations does not ensure that earlier remote operations by *other libraries* are completed, and thus outcome $(a, b){=}(1, 0)$ is allowed in both Figs. 15d and 15e.

More generally, we can use this strategy to *linearise* [20] accesses to any sequential data structure D by wrapping each call to D inside a node lock. This allows us to port existing sequential data structures to RDMA settings with minimal effort. Finally, we prove (Theorem 4) that our implementation is correct against the $\text{RDMA}_{\text{RMW}}^{\text{SC}}$ specification with the full proof given in the extended version [EV].

Theorem 4. *The implementation I_{SC} is sound.*

6 Related Work

RDMA Semantics. The coreRMA model [14] is an early attempt at formalising remote memory accesses, but this semantics does not match the RDMA technical specification. This gap is addressed by RDMA^{TSO} [3], which formalises the actual RDMA semantics over TSO, but the formalisation did not cover remote RMWs. A later model, RDMA^{SC} [5], explored the semantics from RDMA^{TSO} [3] but over an SC CPU alongside programming strategies to efficiently prevent weak behaviours. RDMA^{SC} is unrelated to our work, including $\text{RDMA}^{\text{SC}}_{\text{RMW}}$.

RDMA-Based Distributed Systems. Besides LOCO [4, 21], prior work has covered a range of distributed systems, e.g. consensus protocols [1], databases [2, 25], stand-alone data structures [10,15]. However, unlike LOCO (and our work), these are bespoke systems rather than a programming methodology or library.

Verification. Our proofs for the soundness of library implementations have followed the declarative style [4, 28, 32]. For $\text{RDMA}^{\text{TSO}}_{\text{RMW}}$ (like RDMA^{TSO}), we also provide an operational model (see [EV]) which could ultimately form a basis for a program logic (e.g., [8, 23]), ultimately enabling operational abstractions and proofs of refinement [13, 31]. We consider such extensions to be future work.

RDMA Locks. There are several implementations of network locks using RDMA operations, including centralised lock managers [12], decentralised algorithms [34], asymmetric implementations to favour local accesses [7], and technology-agnostic designs that are more general than RDMA [16]. Other stated objectives of these implementations can include fairness, starvation freedom, low latency, load balancing, scalability, contention mitigation, fault tolerance [19], etc.

However, none of these existing implementations have been formally verified (since $\text{RDMA}^{\text{TSO}}_{\text{RMW}}$ is the first formal semantics of remote RMWs). These works, at most, have offered intuitive explanations to support the correctness of their approach. Moreover, these implementations lack an explicit description of the interaction guarantees between locks and other RDMA operations, which as we have seen can be subtle. In most cases, programmers are made responsible to ensure relevant operations are completed before releasing the lock, thus aligning with the weak lock semantics that we have presented.

Acknowledgements. Ambal is supported by the EPSRC grant EP/X037029/1. Raad is supported by a UKRI fellowship MR/V024299/1, by the EPSRC grant EP/X037029/1, and by VeTSS. Dongol is supported by EPSRC grants EP/Y036 425/1, EP/X037142/1, EP/V038915/1, and EP/X015149/1; and Royal Society grant IES\R1\221226; and VeTSS.

References

1. Aguilera, M.K., Ben-David, N., Guerraoui, R., Marathe, V.J., Xygkis, A., Zablotchi, I.: Microsecond consensus for microsecond applications. In: 14th USENIX Symposium on Operating Systems Design and Implementation (OSDI

20). pp. 599–616. USENIX Association (Nov 2020), https://www.usenix.org/conference/osdi20/presentation/aguilera
2. Alquraan, A., Udayashankar, S., Marathe, V., Wong, B., Al-Kiswany, S.: Lolkv: the logless, line the logless, linearizable, rdma-based key-value storage system arizable, rdma-based key-value storage system. In: Proceedings of the 21st USENIX Symposium on Networked Systems Design and Implementation. NSDI'24, USENIX Association, USA (2024)
3. Ambal, G., Dongol, B., Eran, H., Klimis, V., Lahav, O., Raad, A.: Semantics of remote direct memory access: Operational and declarative models of RDMA on TSO architectures. Proc. ACM Program. Lang. **8**(OOPSLA2), 1982–2009 (2024). https://doi.org/10.1145/3689781, https://doi.org/10.1145/3689781
4. Ambal, G., Hodgkins, G., Madler, M., Chockler, G., Dongol, B., Izraelevitz, J., Raad, A., Vafeiadis, V.: A verified high-performance composable object library for remote direct memory access. Proc. ACM Program. Lang. **10**(POPL) (Jan 2026). https://doi.org/10.1145/3776713, https://doi.org/10.1145/3776713
5. Ambal, G., Lahav, O., Raad, A.: Sufficient conditions for robustness of RDMA programs. In: Vafeiadis, V. (ed.) Programming Languages and Systems - 34th European Symposium on Programming, ESOP 2025, Held as Part of the International Joint Conferences on Theory and Practice of Software, ETAPS 2025, Hamilton, ON, Canada, May 3-8, 2025, Proceedings, Part I. Lecture Notes in Computer Science, vol. 15694, pp. 56–87. Springer (2025). https://doi.org/10.1007/978-3-031-91118-7_3, https://doi.org/10.1007/978-3-031-91118-7_3
6. Ambal, G., Stupple, M., Dongol, B., Raad, A.: Specifying and verifying rdma synchronisation (extended version) (2026), https://arxiv.org/abs/2601.14642
7. Baran, A., Nelson-Slivon, J., Tseng, L., Palmieri, R.: Alock: Asymmetric lock primitive for rdma systems. In: Proceedings of the 36th ACM Symposium on Parallelism in Algorithms and Architectures. p. 15–26. SPAA '24, Association for Computing Machinery, New York, NY, USA (2024). https://doi.org/10.1145/3626183.3659977, https://doi.org/10.1145/3626183.3659977
8. Bila, E.V., Dongol, B., Lahav, O., Raad, A., Wickerson, J.: View-based owicki-gries reasoning for persistent x86-tso. In: Sergey, I. (ed.) Programming Languages and Systems. pp. 234–261. Springer International Publishing, Cham (2022)
9. Blundell, C., Lewis, E.C., Martin, M.M.: Subtleties of transactional memory atomicity semantics. IEEE Computer Architecture Letters **5**(2), 17–17 (2006). https://doi.org/10.1109/L-CA.2006.18
10. Brock, B., Buluç, A., Yelick, K.: Bcl: A cross-platform distributed data structures library. In: Proceedings of the 48th International Conference on Parallel Processing. ICPP '19, Association for Computing Machinery, New York, NY, USA (2019). https://doi.org/10.1145/3337821.3337912, https://doi.org/10.1145/3337821.3337912
11. Chong, N., Sorensen, T., Wickerson, J.: The semantics of transactions and weak memory in x86, power, arm, and C++. In: Foster, J.S., Grossman, D. (eds.) Proceedings of the 39th ACM SIGPLAN Conference on Programming Language Design and Implementation, PLDI 2018, Philadelphia, PA, USA, June 18-22, 2018. pp. 211–225. ACM (2018). https://doi.org/10.1145/3192366.3192373, https://doi.org/10.1145/3192366.3192373
12. Chung, Y., Zamanian, E.: Using RDMA for lock management. CoRR **abs/1507.03274** (2015), http://arxiv.org/abs/1507.03274
13. Dalvandi, S., Dongol, B.: Implementing and verifying release-acquire transactional memory in C11. Proc. ACM Program. Lang. **6**(OOPSLA2), 1817–1844 (2022). https://doi.org/10.1145/3563352, https://doi.org/10.1145/3563352

14. Dan, A.M., Lam, P., Hoefler, T., Vechev, M.: Modeling and analysis of remote memory access programming. SIGPLAN Not. **51**(10), 129–144 (oct 2016). https://doi.org/10.1145/3022671.2984033, `https://doi.org/10.1145/3022671.2984033`
15. Devarajan, H., Kougkas, A., Bateman, K., Sun, X.H.: Hcl: Distributing parallel data structures in extreme scales. In: 2020 IEEE International Conference on Cluster Computing (CLUSTER). pp. 248–258 (2020). https://doi.org/10.1109/CLUSTER49012.2020.00035
16. Devulapalli, A., Wyckoff, P.: Distributed queue-based locking using advanced network features. In: 34th International Conference on Parallel Processing (ICPP 2005), 14-17 June 2005, Oslo, Norway. pp. 408–415. IEEE Computer Society (2005). https://doi.org/10.1109/ICPP.2005.34, `https://doi.org/10.1109/ICPP.2005.34`
17. Dongol, B., Jagadeesan, R., Riely, J.: Transactions in relaxed memory architectures. Proc. ACM Program. Lang. **2**(POPL), 18:1–18:29 (2018). https://doi.org/10.1145/3158106, `https://doi.org/10.1145/3158106`
18. Gangidi, A., Miao, R., Zheng, S., Bondu, S.J., Goes, G., Morsy, H., Puri, R., Riftadi, M., Shetty, A.J., Yang, J., et al.: Rdma over ethernet for distributed training at meta scale. In: Proceedings of the ACM SIGCOMM 2024 Conference. pp. 57–70 (2024)
19. Gao, J., Wang, Q., Shu, J.: Shiftlock: Mitigate one-sided RDMA lock contention via handover. In: Gunawi, H.S., Tarasov, V. (eds.) 23rd USENIX Conference on File and Storage Technologies, FAST 2025, Santa Clara, CA, February 25-27, 2025. pp. 355–372. USENIX Association (2025), `https://www.usenix.org/conference/fast25/presentation/gao`
20. Herlihy, M., Wing, J.M.: Linearizability: A correctness condition for concurrent objects. ACM Trans. Program. Lang. Syst. **12**(3), 463–492 (1990). https://doi.org/10.1145/78969.78972, `https://doi.org/10.1145/78969.78972`
21. Hodgkins, G., Madler, M., Izraelevitz, J.: Loco: Rethinking objects for network memory (2025), `https://arxiv.org/abs/2503.19270`
22. IBTA: Infiniband architecture specification volume 1 release 1.6. `https://www.infinibandta.org/ibta-specification/` (2022)
23. Lahav, O., Dongol, B., Wehrheim, H.: Rely-guarantee reasoning for causally consistent shared memory. In: Enea, C., Lal, A. (eds.) Computer Aided Verification - 35th International Conference, CAV 2023, Paris, France, July 17-22, 2023, Proceedings, Part I. Lecture Notes in Computer Science, vol. 13964, pp. 206–229. Springer (2023). https://doi.org/10.1007/978-3-031-37706-8_11, `https://doi.org/10.1007/978-3-031-37706-8_11`
24. Lamport, L.: How to make a multiprocessor computer that correctly executes multiprocess programs. IEEE Trans. Computers **28**(9), 690–691 (Sep 1979). https://doi.org/10.1109/TC.1979.1675439, `http://dx.doi.org/10.1109/TC.1979.1675439`
25. Li, P., Hua, Y., Zuo, P., Chen, Z., Sheng, J.: ROLEX: A scalable RDMA-oriented learned Key-Value store for disaggregated memory systems. In: 21st USENIX Conference on File and Storage Technologies (FAST 23). pp. 99–114. USENIX Association, Santa Clara, CA (Feb 2023), `https://www.usenix.org/conference/fast23/presentation/li-pengfei`
26. Lu, Y., Chen, G., Li, B., Tan, K., Xiong, Y., Cheng, P., Zhang, J., Chen, E., Moscibroda, T.: {Multi-Path} transport for {RDMA} in datacenters. In: 15th USENIX symposium on networked systems design and implementation (NSDI 18). pp. 357–371 (2018)

27. Owens, S., Sarkar, S., Sewell, P.: A better x86 memory model: x86-tso. In: Berghofer, S., Nipkow, T., Urban, C., Wenzel, M. (eds.) Theorem Proving in Higher Order Logics, 22nd International Conference, TPHOLs 2009, Munich, Germany, August 17-20, 2009. Proceedings. Lecture Notes in Computer Science, vol. 5674, pp. 391–407. Springer (2009). https://doi.org/10.1007/978-3-642-03359-9_27, https://doi.org/10.1007/978-3-642-03359-9_27

28. Raad, A., Doko, M., Rozic, L., Lahav, O., Vafeiadis, V.: On library correctness under weak memory consistency: specifying and verifying concurrent libraries under declarative consistency models. Proc. ACM Program. Lang. **3**(POPL), 68:1–68:31 (2019). https://doi.org/10.1145/3290381, https://doi.org/10.1145/3290381

29. Raad, A., Lahav, O., Vafeiadis, V.: On parallel snapshot isolation and release/acquire consistency. In: Ahmed, A. (ed.) Programming Languages and Systems. pp. 940–967. Springer International Publishing, Cham (2018)

30. Raad, A., Lahav, O., Vafeiadis, V.: On the semantics of snapshot isolation. In: Enea, C., Piskac, R. (eds.) Verification, Model Checking, and Abstract Interpretation. pp. 1–23. Springer International Publishing, Cham (2019)

31. Singh, A.K., Lahav, O.: An operational approach to library abstraction under relaxed memory concurrency. Proc. ACM Program. Lang. **7**(POPL), 1542–1572 (2023). https://doi.org/10.1145/3571246, https://doi.org/10.1145/3571246

32. Stefanesco, L., Raad, A., Vafeiadis, V.: Specifying and verifying persistent libraries. In: Weirich, S. (ed.) Programming Languages and Systems - 33rd European Symposium on Programming, ESOP 2024, Held as Part of the European Joint Conferences on Theory and Practice of Software, ETAPS 2024, Luxembourg City, Luxembourg, April 6-11, 2024, Proceedings, Part II. Lecture Notes in Computer Science, vol. 14577, pp. 185–211. Springer (2024). https://doi.org/10.1007/978-3-031-57267-8_8, https://doi.org/10.1007/978-3-031-57267-8_8

33. Wang, Z., Luo, L., Ning, Q., Zeng, C., Li, W., Wan, X., Xie, P., Feng, T., Cheng, K., Geng, X., et al.: {SRNIC}: A scalable architecture for {RDMA}{NICs}. In: 20th USENIX Symposium on Networked Systems Design and Implementation (NSDI 23). pp. 1–14 (2023)

34. Yoon, D.Y., Chowdhury, M., Mozafari, B.: Distributed lock management with RDMA: decentralization without starvation. In: Das, G., Jermaine, C.M., Bernstein, P.A. (eds.) Proceedings of the 2018 International Conference on Management of Data, SIGMOD Conference 2018, Houston, TX, USA, June 10-15, 2018. pp. 1571–1586. ACM (2018). https://doi.org/10.1145/3183713.3196890, https://doi.org/10.1145/3183713.3196890

35. Zhu, Y., Eran, H., Firestone, D., Guo, C., Lipshteyn, M., Liron, Y., Padhye, J., Raindel, S., Yahia, M.H., Zhang, M.: Congestion control for large-scale rdma deployments. ACM SIGCOMM Computer Communication Review **45**(4), 523–536 (2015)

In Cantor Space No One Can Hear You Stream

Martin Baillon[1], Assia Mahboubi[1,2], and Pierre-Marie Pédrot[1]

[1] INRIA
[2] Vrije Universiteit Amsterdam

Abstract. We revisit the famous notion of sheaves through the lens of type theory and side-effects. Using the language of MLTT, we show that they inductively approximate idealized functional objects as decision trees, realizing a generalized form of continuity. We materialize this intuition in MLTT^f, a case-study sheaf extension of MLTT with a Cohen real and leverage it to show uniform continuity of all MLTT functionals of type $(\mathbb{N} \to \mathbb{B}) \to \mathbb{N}$. The latter results were mechanized in Rocq.

Keywords: type theory, continuity, sheaves, logical relation

1 Introduction

In classical general topology, a family $(O_i)_{i \in I}$ is an *open cover* of a space X if $X = \bigcup_{i \in I} O_i$ and X is *compact* if any potentially infinite open cover of X contains a finite cover. Sub-families of an open cover can be seen as approximations of the underlying space X, and compactness can be viewed as an abstract interface for a complete finitary description of X. Implementing this interface typically involves some form of choice principle, with various degrees of effectiveness.

Classical examples of compact spaces include the unit interval $[0, 1]$ for the usual topology on $\mathbb{R}$, and arbitrary products of compact spaces, for the product topology — a result known as Tychonoff's theorem. Equivalent to the axiom of choice in its full generality, this theorem has far-reaching consequences. For instance, it ensures the compactness of the space of functions $\{0, 1\}^{\mathbb{N}}$, called the *Cantor space* and denoted $\mathbb{N} \to \mathbb{B}$, as this space is the countable product of a discrete set. Tychonoff's theorem also proves that an arbitrary theory in propositional logic has a model as soon as any finite subset thereof has a model. This property also holds for first-order logic, and this generalization is equivalent to the Boolean prime ideal theorem, a weak form of the axiom of choice.

Modern classical topology gradually generalized the intuitions acquired on the study of concrete metric spaces, i.e. spaces with an underlying set of elements that can be equipped with a notion of distance, to more a abstract, point-free understanding of topology as relations between open sets. In particular, Serre's introduction of *sheaves* into algebraic geometry [60] brought a general machinery previously pertaining to topological algebra for deducing global properties from local ones. As of today, topos theory has promoted the study of sheaves as a field of its own, with applications in geometry, number theory or logic. Forcing is one such notorious application of sheaves in logic. It generalizes compactness as a

© The Author(s) 2026
R. Krebbers (Ed.): ESOP 2026, LNCS 16501, pp. 72–103, 2026.
https://doi.org/10.1007/978-3-032-22720-1_4

tool for building models of set theory, in particular for proving independence results like that of the axiom of choice or the continuum hypothesis [47].

About at the same time, different schools of constructive mathematics strived to avoid non-effective forms of choice principles in analysis, typically for implementing the compactness interface, thus eliminating the "convenient fictions" of classical topology. Brouwer's fan theorem is actually the effective, equivalent wording of the compactness of the Cantor space. Formal, point-free topology was later introduced by Martin-Löf and Sambin as a foundation of constructive topology, see e.g. Palmgren's survey on the foundations of homotopy theory [50]. Brouwer also investigated the *meaning* of defining a function on a domain such as the Cantor space, or on the Baire space of functions $\mathbb{N} \to \mathbb{N}$. Notably, Brouwer's continuity principle states that *any* function $F : (\mathbb{N} \to \mathbb{N}) \to \mathbb{N}$, defined on the Baire space, can only rely on finitely many values of its input to compute its output, otherwise said, F is *continuous*. This principle should also hold for any $F : (\mathbb{N} \to \mathbb{B}) \to \mathbb{N}$ by subtyping. Moreover, compactness of the Cantor space actually makes this finite collection of values *independent* from the considered input. This property is called *uniform continuity* of F and the collection of such values, a modulus of continuity. Note that Brouwer's continuity principle is outright wrong in a classical setting, as the later actually even allows for defining the nowhere continuous function on the Baire space that tests whether its input is the decimal representation of a rational number in $[0, 1[$. Brouwer's principle however holds for definable functions in certain systems, notably Gödel's System T [65], by careful inspection of computation trees for recursive functionals.

Brouwer's heterodox convictions have not pervaded his contemporary mathematical community. They however found echoes in the subsequent unfolding of theoretical computer science, whose central notion of algorithm is at odds with the classical mathematical notion of functions. For instance, the encoding of recursive functions by means of inductive trees has been rediscovered in several areas, from Kleene trees [45] to game semantics, and constructive analysis and topology underpin the foundations of programming languages for safe cyber-physical systems [61].

Maybe even more surprisingly, as a second validation of Brouwer's approach, intuitionistic logic ended up becoming one of the two pillars of the Curry-Howard correspondence, which identifies intuitionistic proofs with functional programs. It turned out to be an incredibly valuable tool to understand logic. More than just allowing to interpret proofs computationally, the correspondence can be followed along several axes. Some logical interpretations can be seen as program transformations, a process called indirect style. This contrasts with the so-called direct style approach, where originally non-provable axioms can be realized through new computational behaviours called *side-effects*. The most famous instance of such a relationship is undoubtedly the interpretation of classical logic, which identifies in indirect style the double-negation translation with continuation-passing style, and corresponds in direct style to the implementation of Peirce's law via the `callcc` operator inspired by the Scheme programming language [40].

In terms of expressivity, the apex of this correspondence is Martin-Löf type theory (MLTT), a system which makes no formal difference between proofs and programs. Both objects are represented by the very same structure of terms, and computation is built into the system thanks to dependent types. Since MLTT is a close cousin to topos theory, it is natural to wonder about the computational interpretation of sheaves. What effect do they perform? We unravel that they interpret programs as *decision trees* capturing a generalized notion of continuity.

The first contribution of this paper is MLTT$^\mathsf{F}$, a direct style extension of MLTT to a prototypical sheaf construction known as *Cohen real* [23,24]. We use it to construct a syntactic model of MLTT via a logical relation à la Abel [2], and a mechanized version thereof in Rocq. We show that this model entails the uniform continuity of all MLTT functionals of type $(\mathbb{N} \to \mathbb{B}) \to \mathbb{N}$. We argue this is a first step towards a more general understanding of sheaf type theories.

The description of the later contribution actually comes after a perhaps unusually expanded section devoted to motivating and situating the later sheaf model in the diverse landscape of related work. For this purpose, we string together observations and definitions that, albeit not novel, are scattered across different domains and explained in different languages. We advocate for the use of MLTT as a unifying device providing a clear and high-level description of the objects, stripped from encodings or low-level considerations. This unified perspective is the second contribution of this paper. One source of inspiration is the original formulation by Escardó of Brouwer trees as a simple inductive type, and its clever use to prove continuity of System T functionals [31] that was generalized to a weak variant of MLTT by Baillon et al. [12] Escardó's technique of effectful forcing indeed can be seen as an analogue to sheaf-theoretic forcing techniques, transposed to the realm of type theory. Another important source is Rijke, Schulman and Spitters' article [59] which describes a generalization of sheaves called *localization* in the context of homotopy type theory, yet without emphasis on computation. Coquand et al. also gave a very similar account [25]. A good chunk of the computational behaviour of sheaves have been explained in the setting of Beth-style realizability in a long series of papers by Rahli et al., the most recent being [18], but the importance of the tree-like nature is not recognized. Finally, the series of work by Coquand and collaborators on dynamical methods [20] help us bridge the gap between our type-theoretical point of view and the more common mathematical usage of sheaf-like interpretations.

This paper is thus organized in two parts. The first part consists of Section 2, which discusses the use of sheaves for building models of type theory. We present sheaves in indirect style synthetically in the language of MLTT, getting rid of the presheaf middleman. This allows to pinpoint where the tree-like nature of sheaves arises and to relate them to other constructions from programming language theory. Furthermore, it also highlights an extremely specific property of the side-effects they provide which distinguishes them from more traditional effects.

The second part is devoted to the definition of MLTT$^\mathsf{F}$ and to the study of its metatheoretical properties. The theory itself is defined in Section 3 and we describe a complete realizability model for it in Section 4. We use this model to derive our main result, i.e. that MLTT functionals on the Cantor space are uniformly continuous and thus cannot observe the potential infinity of their argument. Therefore, in Cantor space, no one can hear you stream. Hyperlinks point to relevant parts of the Rocq mechanization of this model.

2   Sheaves

This section argues that sheaves constitute a very nice kind of side-effect, much better behaved than double-negation interpretations. We defend our case by untangling their traditional definition from the notion of presheaves and rephrasing it directly in MLTT. By expressing them synthetically, we revisit various well-known results with a computational point of view.

2.1   Sheaves and Presheaves

We first recall here the usual presentation of sheaves in a set-theoretical but otherwise underspecified metatheory. For a more comprehensive overview, we refer to the MacLane and Moerdijk's reference book [47]. Let us fix a category $\mathbb{P}$. For any of its objects p, q, written $p, q \in \mathbb{P}$, we denote $\mathbb{P}(q, p)$ the class of morphisms with source q and target p. A sieve on $p \in \mathbb{P}$ is a set of morphisms with target p that is closed under precomposition. We write $\mathfrak{S}_p$ for the set of sieves on p and $\Sigma q \in \mathbb{P}.\, \mathbb{P}(q, p)$ for the full sieve on p, as we rather see a point in a sieve on p as a pair (q, α) of an object $q \in \mathbb{P}$ and a morphism $\alpha \in \mathbb{P}(q, p)$.

Definition 1. *A Grothendieck topology $\mathfrak{T}$ on $\mathbb{P}$ is a $\mathbb{P}$-indexed family of collection of sieves, i.e. $\mathfrak{T}_p \subseteq \mathfrak{S}_p$ for all $p \in \mathbb{P}$, that enjoys the following properties.*

1. *If $P \in \mathfrak{T}_p$ and $\alpha \in \mathbb{P}(q, p)$ then $\alpha^* P \in \mathfrak{T}_q$ where $\alpha^* P$ is the pullback of P.*
2. *The full sieve on p belongs to $\mathfrak{T}_p$.*
3. *If $P \in \mathfrak{T}_p$, $Q \in \mathfrak{S}_p$ and $P \subseteq \bigcup_{q \in \mathbb{P}} \{(q, \alpha) \mid \alpha^* Q \in \mathfrak{T}_q\}$ then $Q \in \mathfrak{T}_p$.*

Grothendieck topologies provide an abstract generalization of the notion of an open cover and an element $\mathfrak{T}_p$ of a Grothendieck topology $\mathfrak{T}$ is thus often called a covering. Axiom 2. states that the trivial covering is a covering and Axiom 3. that a covering of coverings is still a covering. We fix a topology $\mathfrak{T}$ in the rest of this section. Recall that the category of *presheaves over* $\mathbb{P}$ is defined as $\mathbf{Psh}(\mathbb{P}) := \mathbb{P}^{\mathrm{op}} \to \mathbf{Set}$ and that it forms a topos [47].

Definition 2. *Let A be a presheaf and $P \in \mathfrak{S}_p$. A compatible family of A on P is a family of elements $x_{q,\alpha} \in A_q$ for every $(q, \alpha) \in P$ that satisfies the equation $A[\beta](x_{q,\alpha}) = x_{r,\beta \circ \alpha}$ for all $(q, \alpha) \in P$ and $\beta \in \mathbb{P}(r, q)$.*

Definition 3. *A presheaf A is a $\mathfrak{T}$-sheaf whenever for every $P \in \mathfrak{T}_p$ and every compatible family x of A on P there exists a unique element $\hat{x} \in A_p$ s.t. $A[\alpha](\hat{x}) = x_{q,\alpha}$ for all $(q, \alpha) \in P$.*

Theorem 1. *The full subcategory $\mathbf{Sh}(\mathbb{P}, \mathfrak{T})$ of $\mathfrak{T}$-sheaves is a topos. Furthermore, the inclusion $\mathbf{Sh}(\mathbb{P}, \mathfrak{T}) \subseteq \mathbf{PSh}(\mathbb{P})$ has a left adjoint called sheafification.*

Sheaf toposes are such a commonplace notion and a historical artifact that they have a name of their own. They are called *Grothendieck toposes*.

Let us step back for a second to assess what a topos is from a type-theoretic point of view. A topos is a kind of type theory, or to be more correct a *model* of certain type theory. This type theory is dubbed the *internal language* of a topos. Fully describing it would lead us to too far, but let us sketch it here briefly. When compared to MLTT, the type theory arising from a topos is weird, being both stronger and weaker. It is stronger because it features an impredicative universe Prop of proof-irrelevant propositions, bringing it closer to CIC. It also inherits extensionality principles from **Set**, including equality reflection, thus making it an *extensional* type theory. As a consequence, it validates function extensionality (`funext`) and uniqueness of identity proofs (UIP). In addition, it also validates propositional extensionality (`propext`). Finally, it interprets quotients together with a strong form of unique choice. On the weaker side, the usual formulation of toposes lacks proper universes Type and hence does not feature in general a true notion of large elimination, where types can be constructed by pattern-matching on terms. Instead, thanks to Prop, they only allow for *propositions* being constructed by case-analysis. This is expressive enough to side-step the lack of expressivity of pure type systems such as the Calculus of Constructions, which cannot prove $0 \neq 1$, but is still far from the rich setting of MLTT.

2.2   Sheaves without Presheaves

The notions exposed above can in fact be rephrased in a purely internal way, a phenomenon that was already observed early on. Indeed, since $\mathbf{Psh}(\mathbb{P})$ is a topos, as we explained above it hosts a rich logical system by itself. Assuming Grothendieck universes in the host set theory, we can even show that it also features actual universes in the internal language, making it a model of MLTT. As a result, everything we write in MLTT can be interpreted straightforwardly into $\mathbf{Psh}(\mathbb{P})$. In this section, we will work in PshTT, an ambient type theory extending MLTT that is voluntarily kept underspecified. Its intended semantics is given by presheaf models, so PshTT will provide us in particular with a small universe of definitional proof-irrelevant propositions Prop [35]. We will liberally and silently rely on the aforementioned extensionality principles that hold there. Note that we will refrain from relying on equality reflection though, so some flavour of observational type theory would be enough to capture PshTT [7].

The goal of this section is to replay all the set-theoretic definitions from Section 2.1 directly in PshTT so that the type-theoretic definition will coincide with the set-theoretic one when interpreted into a presheaf model. This endeavour is not really novel, but our insistence to use dependent type theory will unravel a few properties that are not so obvious when using e.g. first-order based internal languages. Much closer to our approach is the Rijke, Shulman and Spitters' significant work on modalities in HoTT [59] which tackles amongst others a more generic construction known as localization. Sheafification is a degenerate form of localization, so our definitions are a simplification of theirs. Yet the fact it is much simpler also emphasizes computational properties that are not apparent in their article. Without further ado, let us now describe sheaves synthetically.

Definition 4. *A Lawvere-Tierney topology is a term* $\mathsf{T} : \mathsf{Prop} \to \mathsf{Prop}$ *together with two terms* $\eta_\mathsf{T} : \Pi(P : \mathsf{Prop}). P \to \mathsf{T}\ P$ *and* $\gg\!=_\mathsf{T} : \Pi(P\,Q : \mathsf{Prop}). \mathsf{T}\ P \to (P \to \mathsf{T}\ Q) \to \mathsf{T}\ Q.$

It is reasonably easy to observe that a Lawvere-Tierney topology in the presheaf model is exactly a Grothendieck topology. The family of sieves $\mathfrak{T}$ together with condition 1. correspond to the term T itself, condition 3. corresponds to $\gg\!=_\mathsf{T}$ and 2. is internally a proof of $\mathsf{T}\ \top$, which is equivalent to η_T up to propositional extensionality. Through this presentation, it is immediate that T is just a monad on Prop. All equations hold trivially as Prop is proof-irrelevant in PshTT.

Definition 5. *A type* $A : \mathsf{Type}$ *is a* T*-sheaf if it is equipped with two terms*

- $\digamma_A : \Pi(P : \mathsf{Prop}). \mathsf{T}\ P \to (P \to A) \to A$;
- $e_A : \Pi(P : \mathsf{Prop})\,(p : \mathsf{T}\ P)\,(x : A). \digamma_A\ P\ p\ (\lambda(q : P).x) =_A x.$

Again, we can read back the historical presentation in the internal statement, namely $\digamma_A$ gives the existence of glueing and e_A corresponds to its uniqueness.

Sheafification is somewhat horrendous when performed analytically, as one has to pay a lot of attention to low-level details. There also exists an internal way to define it from topos theory called Grothendieck's $-^+$ construction [47], which is similar to an impredicative encoding. Such encodings suffer from a lot of issues in type theory [51], and the $-^+$ construction is no exception. Fortunately for us we can define sheafification in a direct way assuming our ambient type theory to be expressive enough. It is indeed a free functor, so it can be described very easily as a quotient inductive type [6] (QIT).

Definition 6. *We define sheafification as the* QIT^3 $\mathcal{S}$ *in Figure 1.*

Here, the internal approach really shines. Assuming that our internal notion of sheaves is indeed the right one, there is nothing to show about the interpretation of $\mathcal{S}$ through a presheaf model. By construction, it is the free sheaf arising from some type. Obviously, the hard part is that one has to show that QITs exist in presheaf models. Albeit technical, this is actually doable as QITs can be encoded in extensional type theory using basic inductive and quotient types [43,33], and presheaf models provide all of this material.

Lemma 1. $\mathcal{S}$ *defines a monad on* Type *with the obvious combinators.*

It is worth recalling some abstract properties of sheaves in this synthetic setting. We have function extensionality at hand, so all usual categorical definitions work as expected. We swear to the reader that this is the only place in this paper where we insist so much on categorical notions. First, let us state the obvious.

---

[3] For completeness, we also write the recursor equation for the quotient constructor as if it were a higher inductive type (HIT) [66]. For QITs, this equation holds trivially.

```
Inductive 𝒮 (A : Type) : Type :=
| η𝒮 : A → 𝒮 A
| F𝒮 : Π(P : Prop). T P → (P → 𝒮 A) → 𝒮 A
| e𝒮 : Π(P : Prop) (p : T P) (x : 𝒮 A). F𝒮 P p (λ(q : P). x) =𝒮 A x.

𝒮rec : Π(A : Type) (R : 𝒮 A → Type) (rη : Π(x : A). R (η𝒮 x))
         (rF : ΠP (p : T P) (k : P → 𝒮 A) (r : Π(p : P). R (k p)). R (F𝒮 P p k))
         (re : ΠP (p : T P) (x : 𝒮 A) (r : R x).
           (e𝒮 P p x) # rF P p (λ(q : P). x) (λ(q : P). r) = r).
         Π(s : 𝒮 A). R s
```

$$
\begin{aligned}
\mathcal{S}_{\text{rec}}\ A\ R\ r_\eta\ r_F\ r_e\ (\eta_\mathcal{S}\ x) &\equiv r_\eta\ x \\
\mathcal{S}_{\text{rec}}\ A\ R\ r_\eta\ r_F\ r_e\ (F_\mathcal{S}\ P\ p\ k) &\equiv r_F\ P\ p\ k\ (\lambda(p : P).\mathcal{S}_{\text{rec}}\ A\ R\ r_\eta\ r_F\ r_e\ (k\ p)) \\
\mathrm{ap}\ (\mathcal{S}_{\text{rec}}\ A\ R\ r_\eta\ r_F\ r_e)\ (e_\mathcal{S}\ P\ p\ x) &\equiv r_e\ P\ p\ x\ (\mathcal{S}_{\text{rec}}\ A\ R\ r_\eta\ r_F\ r_e\ x)
\end{aligned}
$$

Fig. 1. Sheafification and its associated recursor

Lemma 2. *A type A is a* T*-sheaf exactly when it is an $\mathcal{S}$-algebra. Moreover, being a* T*-sheaf is a mere proposition in the* HoTT *sense.*

The latter property makes the monad $\mathcal{S}$ idempotent, which has a lot of far-reaching consequences. One of them is that any function $f : A \to B$ between two sheaves becomes an algebra morphism. This will be important in what follows.

2.3   Oracles as Logical Operating Systems

Before further studying sheaves as computational objects, we first generalize the notion of topology to an extreme without losing their fundamental properties. This little shift of perspective will make the relationship of sheafification with well-known computational objects unmistakable.

Definition 7. *A logical operating system (LOS) is given by two terms* I : Type *and* O : I → Prop.

The name might seem mysterious at first, but it will become clear soon. The types I and O stand respectively for *input* and *output*. We will now define a slight variant of sheafification from the previous section relying on a LOS (I, O) rather than a topology. We reuse the same notations for uniformity.

Definition 8. *From now on, we will redefine the type $\mathcal{S}$ from Definition 6 as*

```
Inductive 𝒮 (A : Type) : Type :=
| η𝒮 : A → 𝒮 A
| F𝒮 : Π(i : I). (O i → 𝒮 A) → 𝒮 A
| e𝒮 : Π(i : I) (x : 𝒮 A). F𝒮 i (λ(o : O i). x) =𝒮 A x.
```

Any T : Prop → Prop gives rise to a LOS by setting I := $\Sigma(P : $ Prop$).$ T P and O $(P, p) := P$. Through this encoding the above definition of $\mathcal{S}$ is isomorphic to the one from Section 2.2. We can similarly define sheafness w.r.t. a LOS.

Definition 9. *A type $A : \mathsf{Type}$ is an (I, O)-sheaf if it is equipped with two terms*

- $\digamma_A : \Pi(i : \mathsf{I}).\,(\mathsf{O}\ i \to A) \to A$;
- $e_A : \Pi(i : \mathsf{I})\,(x : A).\,\digamma_A\ i\ (\lambda(o : \mathsf{O}\ i).\,x) =_A x.$

Note that we actually do not need the monadic closure properties on T for $\mathcal{S}$ to behave well, they are freely added by the QIT. The reason it is a requirement in the historical presentation is mostly because the $\mathcal{S}$ type constructor is traditionally defined via an impredicative encoding that requires collapsing together all $\digamma$ constructors. Indeed, using **propext** and the quotient $e_{\mathcal{S}}$ one can replace two subsequent calls to $\digamma$ first on $P : \mathsf{Prop}$ and then on $Q : P \to \mathsf{Prop}$ by one call on $\exists p : P.\,Q\ p$ thanks to the monadic structure. All calls are compacted this way by recursion on the list of questions, where the nullary case is given by $\top : \mathsf{Prop}$ and η_T.

We call (I, O) an *operating system* because it morally corresponds to the abstract interface for *system calls* (syscalls). That is, a term $i : \mathsf{I}$ codes for a syscall number with its arguments while $\mathsf{O}\ i$ is the return type of this call. For some sheaf A, the term $\digamma_A$ provides a handler that is not unlike the actual low-level implementation of operating systems where syscalls are implemented using some form of delimited continuations [44], i.e. objects of type $\mathsf{O}\ i \to A$.

As a matter of fact, this observation has been put to practical use with *interaction trees* [68] which are a way to encode a vast range of I/O effects in type theory. There are several variants of interaction trees, but they all share a striking similarity with our $\mathcal{S}$ type. The most basic kind is defined as the type

$$\begin{aligned}
&(\mathsf{Co})\mathsf{Inductive}\ \mathcal{T}\ (A : \mathsf{Type}) : \mathsf{Type} := \\
&\mid \eta_\mathcal{T} : A \to \mathcal{T}\ A \\
&\mid \digamma_\mathcal{T} : \Pi(i : \mathsf{I}).\,(\mathsf{O}\ i \to \mathcal{T}\ A) \to \mathcal{T}\ A
\end{aligned}$$

for some $\mathsf{I} : \mathsf{Type}$ and $\mathsf{O} : \mathsf{I} \to \mathsf{Type}$. The major differences with $\mathcal{S}$ are the following. First $\mathcal{T}$ is usually coinductive rather than inductive, but the only reason for that is it is also meant to encode non-terminating programs. One could use an inductive variant if they did not care about potential non-termination. Second, the output type O is proof-relevant, as users care about return values of their syscalls. Finally, and perhaps more importantly, there is no quotient in sight, as the order of operations matters critically in an I/O world.

The two latter points are the fundamental reason why in our setting we talk about a *logical* operating system. With sheaves, there is no way to extract proof-relevant content out of a syscall by virtue of O returning propositions, and furthermore the quotient prevents one to observe not only the order of syscalls but also their multiplicity and even useless calls.

Lemma 3. *For any sheaf A, we can prove the following equalities in PshTT:*

$$\begin{aligned}
i : \mathsf{I}, x : A &\vdash \digamma_A\ i\ (\lambda(o : \mathsf{O}\ i).\,x) = x \\
i : \mathsf{I}, j : \mathsf{I}, x : \mathsf{O}\ i \to \mathsf{O}\ j \to A \vdash\ &\digamma_A\ i\ (\lambda(o_i : \mathsf{O}\ i).\,\digamma_A\ j\ (\lambda(o_j : \mathsf{O}\ j).\,x\ o_i\ o_j)) = \\
&\quad \digamma_A\ j\ (\lambda(o_j : \mathsf{O}\ j).\,\digamma_A\ i\ (\lambda(o_i : \mathsf{O}\ i).\,x\ o_i\ o_j))
\end{aligned}$$

This is actually quite surprising when considering (I, O) as introducing side-effects. Somehow, sheaves provide a kind of *unobservable* side-effect in the sense of [54]. There are new normal forms represented by uninterpreted calls to the oracle via $\mathsf{F}_\mathcal{S}$, but they cannot be exploited internally because of the quotient. We defer a proper discussion of this phenomenon to Section 2.4.

The relationship between operating systems and forcing was already observed by Krivine and Miquel in classical realizability [49]. It is part of the folklore of the French school of type theory, although there is little published material on the topic, except maybe vulgarization [55]. Regardless, set-theoretic forcing can be seen as a specific case of sheafification for the double negation monad [47]. It is interesting to observe that Miquel's computational interpretation is state-like rather than tree-like. The deep reason for this is that Miquel's paper only models F_ω, which lacks dependent elimination. Therefore, it can be re-explained as the composition of the double-negation translation with the presheaf translation, which is strictly weaker than $\neg\neg$-sheaves.

2.4 Sheaves in Homotopy Type Theory

An interesting question is the type of type theory that one can obtain from our synthetic sheaf interpretation. More precisely, we will be looking at syntactic models, i.e. models defined as mere syntactic translations between theories that interpret conversion in the source as conversion in the target. We know that usual sheaves result in a Grothendieck topos, but as mentioned this is hardwiring extensionality both in the source and in the target. What if we want to get an intensional theory instead? It turns out that synthetic sheaves go quite a long way. We sketch the syntactic-synthetic sheaf model in this section. Once again, this is a simplification and a reformulation of the localization paper [59].

Infrastructure Following the category-with-family (CwF) setting, we will be translating contexts into contexts, types into synthetic sheaves, i.e.

$$\mathsf{Typ}^\mathcal{S}(\Gamma) := \Sigma[A] : \mathsf{Typ}(\Gamma). \, \mathsf{isSh}\,[A]$$

and terms as terms of the underlying type. Above $\mathsf{isSh}\,A$ is the data for A from Definition 9. We assume a target CwF that is rich enough, i.e. basically a model of PshTT. This construction preserves strictness of substitution from the target, since this is just a subuniverse model as in [59]. We write terms and types in the target directly using the MLTT syntax and consciously confuse the target theory with the ambient type theory, effectively working in the standard CwF. In particular, $\mathsf{Typ}^\mathcal{S}$ can be conflated with the record type $\mathsf{Type}^\mathcal{S}$ defined below.

$$\mathsf{Type}^\mathcal{S} := \left\{ \begin{array}{l} \mathtt{el} : \mathsf{Type}; \\ \mathsf{F} : \Pi(i:\mathsf{I}). \, (\mathsf{O}\,i \to \mathtt{el}) \to \mathtt{el}; \\ e : \Pi(i:\mathsf{I})\,(x:A). \, \mathsf{F}\,i\,(\lambda(o:\mathsf{O}\,i). \, x) = x; \end{array} \right\}$$

For readability, we will implicitly use the $\mathtt{el}$ projection to cast a $\mathsf{Type}^\mathcal{S}$ to a Type and identify $[\cdot]$ with $\mathtt{el}$.

Π-types The first meaningful type former one usually consider in dependent type theory is the dependent product. Assuming `funext` in the target, one can straightforwardly show that Π-types are inherited from it, i.e. with a bit of abuse of notation, we pick $[\Pi(x:A).B] := \Pi(x:[A]).[B]$. Indeed, $\mathsf{isSh}\,([\Pi(x:A).B])$ holds as soon as we have $\Pi(x:[A]).\mathsf{isSh}\,[B]$, the algebra structure being given pointwise as in any call-by-name model. There is really no more to say about it.

Inductive types Inductive types are much more fascinating. A Grothendieck topos readily interprets inductive types, so they should have a syntactic equivalent. By relying on QITs in the synthetic approach, it becomes crystal clear. Essentially, we just take the original inductive type $\mathcal{I}$ and freely adjoin it the $\digamma_\mathcal{I}$ and $e_\mathcal{I}$ constructors. This construction scales to all inductive types, but we concentrate on $\mathbb{N}$ as a running example, where $[\mathbb{N}]$ boils down to the QIT below.

$$
\begin{aligned}
&\mathtt{Inductive}\ \mathbb{N}^\mathcal{S}\ : \mathsf{Type} := \\
&\mid \mathsf{O}_\mathcal{S} : \mathbb{N}^\mathcal{S} \\
&\mid \mathsf{S}_\mathcal{S} : \mathbb{N}^\mathcal{S} \to \mathbb{N}^\mathcal{S} \\
&\mid \digamma_\mathbb{N} : \Pi(i:\mathsf{I}).(\mathsf{O}\ i \to \mathbb{N}^\mathcal{S}) \to \mathbb{N}^\mathcal{S} \\
&\mid e_\mathbb{N} : \Pi(i:\mathsf{I})\,(x:\mathbb{N}^\mathcal{S}).\digamma_\mathbb{N}\ i\ (\lambda(o:\mathsf{O}\ i).x) =_{\mathbb{N}^\mathcal{S}} x.
\end{aligned}
$$

While defining the type and its constructors is not very exciting, it turns out that the eliminator packs a little bit of magic. To implement the dependent eliminator, we need a term in the target

$$
\mathbb{N}^\mathcal{S}_{\mathrm{rec}} : \Pi(P:\mathbb{N}^\mathcal{S} \to \mathsf{Type}^\mathcal{S})\,(p_\mathsf{O} : P\ \mathsf{O}_\mathcal{S})\,(p_\mathsf{S} : \Pi(n:\mathbb{N}^\mathcal{S}).P\ n \to P\ (\mathsf{S}_\mathcal{S}\ n))\,(n:\mathbb{N}^\mathcal{S}).P\ n
$$

satisfying the usual conversion rules. The latter constraints leaves virtually no leeway for the constructors $\mathsf{O}^\mathcal{S}$ and $\mathsf{S}^\mathcal{S}$. But precisely, at this point we are facing a puzzling situation: we are only given branches for the $\mathsf{O}_\mathcal{S}$ and $\mathsf{S}_\mathcal{S}$ constructors, as the source eliminator only knows about those ones. How can we fill in the two remaining branches for $\digamma_\mathbb{N}$ and $e_\mathbb{N}$? In fact, we can, by defining $\mathbb{N}^\mathcal{S}_{\mathrm{rec}}$ as follows.

$$
\begin{aligned}
&\mathbb{N}^\mathcal{S}_{\mathrm{rec}} : \Pi(P:\mathbb{N}^\mathcal{S} \to \mathsf{Type}^\mathcal{S})\,(p_\mathsf{O} : P\ \mathsf{O}_\mathcal{S})\,(p_\mathsf{S} : \Pi n.\,P\ n \to P\ (\mathsf{S}_\mathcal{S}\ n))\,(n:\mathbb{N}^\mathcal{S}).P\ n \\
&\mathbb{N}^\mathcal{S}_{\mathrm{rec}}\ P\ p_\mathsf{O}\ p_\mathsf{S}\ \mathsf{O}_\mathcal{S} \qquad := \ p_\mathsf{O} \\
&\mathbb{N}^\mathcal{S}_{\mathrm{rec}}\ P\ p_\mathsf{O}\ p_\mathsf{S}\ (\mathsf{S}_\mathcal{S}\ n) \quad := \ p_\mathsf{S}\ n\ (\mathbb{N}^\mathcal{S}_{\mathrm{rec}}\ P\ p_\mathsf{O}\ p_\mathsf{S}\ n) \\
&\mathbb{N}^\mathcal{S}_{\mathrm{rec}}\ P\ p_\mathsf{O}\ p_\mathsf{S}\ (\digamma_\mathbb{N}\ i\ k) \quad := \ (P\ (\digamma_\mathbb{N}\ i\ k)).\digamma\ i\ (\lambda(o:\mathsf{O}\ i).(e_\mathbb{N}\ i\ (k\ o))^{-1}\ \# \\
&\qquad\qquad\qquad\qquad\qquad\qquad\qquad (\mathbb{N}^\mathcal{S}_{\mathrm{rec}}\ P\ p_\mathsf{O}\ p_\mathsf{S}\ (k\ o))) \\
&\mathbb{N}^\mathcal{S}_{\mathrm{rec}}\ P\ p_\mathsf{O}\ p_\mathsf{S}\ (e_\mathbb{N}\ i\ x) \quad := \ \ldots
\end{aligned}
$$

We explain here how to derive the missing branches from the material that is available. We believe that this is an enlightening point that needs to be given a strong emphasis, as it differs radically with other settings where adding side-effects break dependent elimination [53]. As in the effectful case, we use the algebra structure on P to propagate the effect of $\digamma_\mathbb{N}$ to the surrounding context, i.e. $\digamma_\mathbb{N}$ behaves as a kind of call-by-name exception. Yet, we crucially have to use $e_\mathbb{N}$ to rectify the type of the returned term. In the above definition,

$$
i : \mathsf{I}, k : \mathsf{O}\ i \to \mathbb{N}^\mathcal{S}, o : \mathsf{O}\ i \vdash \mathbb{N}^\mathcal{S}_{\mathrm{rec}}\ P\ p_\mathsf{O}\ p_\mathsf{S}\ (k\ o) : P\ (k\ o)
$$

but we actually want to return a term of type P ($\mathsf{F_N}\ i\ k$). With most monads, these two types are not isomorphic, and we have to restrict the recursor to predicates P enjoying additional linearity properties, namely they must be definitional algebra morphisms, i.e. commuting with F up to conversion [5,4]. Thankfully, with sheaves the additional quotient $e_\mathbb{N}$ is enough to derive a proof

$$i : \mathsf{I}, k : \mathsf{O}\ i \to \mathbb{N}^\mathcal{S}, o : \mathsf{O}\ i \vdash e_\mathbb{N}\ i\ (k\ o) : {}_{\mathsf{F_N}}\ i\ (\lambda(q : \mathsf{O}\ i).\,k\ o) = k\ o$$

but as we consider Prop to contain strict propositions, we also have

$$i : \mathsf{I}, k : \mathsf{O}\ i \to \mathbb{N}^\mathcal{S}, o : \mathsf{O}\ i \vdash (\lambda(q : \mathsf{O}\ i).\,k\ o) \equiv k : \mathsf{O}\ i \to \mathbb{N}^\mathcal{S}$$

hence in the end we do get a proof of $\mathsf{F_N}\ i\ k = k\ o$ out of $e_\mathbb{N}$ by conversion.

The branch for the quotient constructor $e_\mathbb{N}$ requires a proof of its own, although this is a proof-irrelevant equality so the exact term does not matter as long as it exists, which is an easy consequence of the quotient preservation of P.

At the risk of sounding repetitive, the validity of dependent elimination is quite surprising given that we have additional constructors for our translated inductive types, a landmark of side-effects. What saves us really is that the quotient prevents one to exploit these effects in a computational way. At a more abstract level, one usually needs to restrict dependent elimination to some form of linear predicates when throwing in effects in a dependent type theory, as observed in [53]. Yet, $\mathcal{S}$ is an idempotent monad, which magically makes all morphisms linear, hence full dependent elimination becomes valid again. To be really fair, this line of reasoning only holds when reasoning extensionally enough, something which is easy in a categorical setting but much less so in MLTT. The fact that synthetic sheaves can be presented in a very computational way through QITs is critical for this trick to go through in type theory.

Universes The last big ingredient that is still missing from our model to properly model MLTT is the existence of universes. Here the story becomes way more blurry, and the literature is somewhat confusing. Sheaf models are the archetypical instance of a topos, so they do provide us with a small impredicative universe of propositions Prop. We can easily reflect it in our translation. We do not give the full details, but basically by using **propext** it is easy to show that

$$[\mathsf{Prop}]\quad :=\quad \Sigma(P : \mathsf{Prop}).\,\Pi(i : \mathsf{I}).\,(\mathsf{O}\ i \to P) \to P$$

is a sheaf by taking

$$\mathsf{F_{Prop}}\ (i : \mathsf{I})\ (k : \mathsf{O}\ i \to [\mathsf{Prop}]) : [\mathsf{Prop}]\quad :=\quad (\Pi(o : \mathsf{O}\ i).\,(k\ o).1,\quad \dots\quad).$$

If we try to replicate the same technique with Type, the intuitive equivalent is to show that $\mathsf{Type}^\mathcal{S}$ is indeed a sheaf. Except that in general, it is not. The reason is that the use of **propext** for Prop does not scale to Type. One would have to find a term $\mathsf{F_{Type}}\ (i : \mathsf{I})\ (k : \mathsf{O}\ i \to \mathsf{Type}^\mathcal{S}) : \mathsf{Type}^\mathcal{S}$. We are quite constrained in what we can put here because of the quotient condition. Just like for Prop, the natural candidate for the `el` component of this operation is $\Pi(i : \mathsf{I}).\,(k\ o).\mathtt{el}$. If we do this, we have a problem though: we cannot prove that the quotient is preserved! Indeed, we have to show

$$A : \mathsf{Type}^{\mathcal{S}}, i : \mathsf{I} \vdash \_ : (\Pi(o : \mathsf{O}\ i).\,A.\mathtt{el}) = A.\mathtt{el}$$

but the best we can hope for is an *isomorphism* $(\Pi(o : \mathsf{O}\ i).\,A.\mathtt{el}) \cong A.\mathtt{el}$ by the sheafness of A. This is sufficient for Prop as isomophism implies logical equivalence and thus equality, but this does not carry to proof-relevant types.

This is a very well-known problem that led to the introduction of *stacks* [10], which are essentially sheaves where the quotient based on propositional equality is replaced by a tower of proof-relevant relations, resulting in some kind of ω-groupoid. This kind of endeavour is unfortunately way beyond our syntactic approach, as it would morally entail reimplementing a cubical model [16]. Without stacks, the universe of sheaves is only a weak universe [64], which is not enough for our purposes. As argued in [63], there is some misunderstanding in the literature about the availability of strict universes in run-of-the-mill sheaves. For the sake of completeness, we recall here two ways to get them.

The first solution is to blindly replace PshTT with HoTT in everything we did previously. There is nothing specific to be done, apart maybe for replacing Prop with some predicative variant of strict propositions in case one does not want to buy into resizing axioms. All other constructions are carried just the same, except that we silently interpret equality as a univalent one, and thus in particular the QITs we wrote before are now implicitly HITs — this is but a mere point of view, the syntax remains unchanged. The surprising part is that by doing so, we do not have to suffer with stacks: the universe of sheaves effortlessly becomes a sheaf by what seems to be sheer magic. Indeed, in the strict setting, there is no way to turn the isomorphism $(\Pi(o : \mathsf{O}\ i).\,A.\mathtt{el}) \cong A.\mathtt{el}$ into an equality. But in a univalent theory, this isomorphism is actually an *equivalence*, and hence by univalence gives rise to the equality sought after. Once again, this is the path taken by [59], although in our opinion they do not insist enough on this miraculous phenomenon.

The other way is to replace an open universe of sheaves by a closed one, that is, using some inductive-recursive encoding and replacing sheaves by their code. We believe that this is the approach taken by [39], although they build directly this object from first principles in a very non-constructive way. For this to be applied to our syntactic setting, we would need a first-class notion of *quotient inductive recursive types* (QIRT) in PshTT. To be clear, we have no idea whether general QIRTs can be shown to exist in some models or if we can encode it away using some variant of small induction recursion [41,37] or realignment types. Nonetheless we sketch what they would look like to give a short, intuitive albeit arguably too approximate explanation of the definition from [39]. The QIRT of sheaf codes is described by an inductive definition $\mathcal{U}^{\mathcal{S}}$ of codes together with a recursive function $\mathtt{El}^{\mathcal{S}} : \mathcal{U}^{\mathcal{S}} \to \mathsf{Type}^{\mathcal{S}}$ additionally satisfying the sheaf quotient condition by fiat, thanks to a quotient constructor similar to $e_{\mathcal{S}}$ in $\mathcal{U}^{\mathcal{S}}$. It is not clear exactly how this would compute, let alone be properly defined. We refer to the exploratory work of Kaposi [42] and leave this to future study.

2.5 Computational Content of Sheaves

We want to highlight now a fact that is less well-known about sheaves that has important consequences when thinking about computation. This fact is absent from the historical definition of sheaves, and a bit hidden in the HoTT presentation [59], but our inductive description of sheafification makes it extremely clear. In a nutshell, sheaves are actually about approximating idealized infinite objects through finite approximations. This viewpoint is a staple of some constructivist schools under the name of *dynamical methods* [20]. In particular, Coquand, Lombardi and co-authors have conducted a systematic research program exploring how these methods unveil the effective content of classical proofs [20,26,46]. Yet, it does not seem to have percolated that much in the world of the proof-as-program correspondence. We seize the opportunity to expose clearly here this technique. Let (I, O) be a LOS in the remainder of this section.

It is a truism that ultimately, when performing computations, one only cares about the value of some concrete datatypes. In first-order logic, this is often conflated with the requirement that Σ_0^1 formulae enjoy a witness property, while in type theory, we typically expect closed terms $\vdash M : \mathbb{N}$ to evaluate to some concrete natural number. Such a property is traditionally called *canonicity*, and can be defined more generally for all closed terms of an inductive type.

We now easily see that our sheafified theory enjoys a weaker form of canonicity inherited from the ambient theory by inspecting the translation from Section 2.4. For each inductive $\mathcal{I}$, we have two additional constructors $\digamma_{\mathcal{I}}$ and $e_{\mathcal{I}}$, where the latter is only used to build equalities. Our weaker canonicity thus says that a value in the model is a *finite* chain of $\digamma_{\mathcal{I}}$ ending with an actual constructor.

We argue that this is a generalization of the fact that in MLTT, if Γ is a consistent, purely negative context, terms $\Gamma \vdash M : \mathbb{N}$ still enjoy canonicity [22]. With sheaves, O needs not be purely negative, but the price to pay is that we have to keep an explicit list of calls to the $\digamma$ constructors. It is still better than just adding opaque axioms to the theory, since these terms bubble up to toplevel.

Note that weak canonicity also applies in particular to the empty type, which has no actual constructor. Hence the sheaf theory is consistent exactly when O is finitely consistent, i.e. the inductive type $F := \digamma_F : \Pi(i : \mathsf{I}). (\mathsf{O}\, i \to F) \to F$ is empty. This is highly remininiscent of both the compactness lemma of first-order logic and Herbrand's theorem. Thus, sheafification is manifestly about finiteness. But what is the infinite thing it approximates? With our presentation, it becomes straightforward.

Definition 10. *An omniscient oracle is a function* $\alpha : \Pi(i : \mathsf{I}).\mathsf{O}\, i.$

Assuming an omniscient oracle α, one can evaluate a term $M : \mathcal{S}\, A$ into an actual value of A through the `eval` function defined recursively as

$$\begin{aligned}
&\texttt{eval} : (\Pi(i : \mathsf{I}).\mathsf{O}\, i) \to \mathcal{S}\, A \to A \\
&\texttt{eval}\ \alpha\ (\eta_{\mathcal{S}}\, x) := x \\
&\texttt{eval}\ \alpha\ (\digamma_{\mathcal{S}}\, i\, k) := \texttt{eval}\ \alpha\ (k\, (\alpha\, i))
\end{aligned}$$

where the quotient preservation is left implicit but can be easily proved.

We see the term α as the embodiment of the infinite, able to answer all questions. It is an idealized object that may not necessarily exist in a constructive setting. By contrast, due to its inductive nature, a term $M : \mathcal{S}\,A$ can only ask a finite number of questions via $F_{\mathcal{S}}$. The `eval` function mediates between the finite and the infinite, giving a relativized meaning to an object that does only depend on a finite approximation of an idealized abstraction. Working in a sheaf type theory progagates this identification at all types.

This pattern is a commonplace in constructive mathematics, yet we are not aware of any reference where it is explicitly explained through the inductive quality of sheafification. To name a few classic instances of this viewpoint, let us cite the algebraic closure, the ultrafilter theorem, etc. More generally, in first-order logic all these objects can be axiomatized through the notion of geometric theories, i.e. sets of geometric formulae of the shape

$$\boldsymbol{x} \mid \alpha_1(\boldsymbol{x}), \ldots \alpha_n(\boldsymbol{x}) \vdash \bigvee_{i \in I} \exists \boldsymbol{y}_i.\, \beta_1(\boldsymbol{x}, \boldsymbol{y}_i) \wedge \ldots \wedge \beta_{m_i}(\boldsymbol{x}, \boldsymbol{y}_i)$$

where the α, β predicates are atomic. Assuming a single-axiom theory, the I type corresponds to the input $\boldsymbol{x}$ s.t. $\alpha_i(\boldsymbol{x})$ for all $1 \leq i \leq n$ and O is the big disjunction in the conclusion, which depends on the input $\boldsymbol{x}$. This generalizes to arbitrary sets of axioms by taking I to be the product of the corresponding input types.

The relationship between geometric formulae and finite approximations was already observed by Coquand [21], who gives a model of first-order geometric theories where proofs of Σ_0^1 formulae are interpreted as inductive decision trees.

3   A Case Study of Type-Theoretical Forcing: MLTT^{F}

3.1   General Motivation

The second part of this article discusses how sheaves shall earn a first-class status in type theory. The critical point here is to be able to *compute* directly in the sheaf theory. Note that we mean it in a strong sense, i.e. the objective here is actually to obtain an extension of MLTT that can be equipped with an algorithmic reduction generating normal forms.

To the reader, it may seem like the synthetic approach we have been advocating in the previous section is already a satisfying answer. Assuming univalence in the target and following [59], we sketched that one can recover such a syntactic model. Unfortunately, this is only part of the story.

A first drawback is the reliance on univalence. It brings in some technicalities, as it is usually available through some cubical theory. Moreover, it hardwires a lot of additional logical baggage that one may not desire to expose. For better or for worse, traditional sheaves are developped in an anti-univalent setting. The more neutral the foundations we define sheaves in, the more users they will reach.

One could argue that minimalism is no virtue in itself, and that type theorists should bite the univalent bullet already. This is fair enough, but there is another roadblock. Traditional sheaf models are the composition of a synthetic sheaf model with a presheaf model. The latter corresponds to a monotonic reader effect, i.e. morally a new kind of context, where the base category gives access to modalities restricting the current state. See e.g. [38] for a type-theoretic account.

In this setting, it is virtually always the case that the LOS (I, O) is made of *exotic* types, i.e. types defined through non-standard modalities of the presheaf model that cannot be written directly in MLTT. As mentioned, it is typical for O to be some kind of disjunction capturing a geometric formula. Yet, these disjunctions are not arbitrary propositions: there is a one-to-one mapping between atomic exotic formulae and principal sieves from the underlying base category. What we mean is that, in traditional sheaf models, there is a universe of propositions $_F\mathsf{Prop} \subsetneq \mathsf{Prop}$ that contains all principal sieves and is closed under e.g. finite meets and joins, but is still at the same time *definitionally* proof-irrelevant and enjoys unique choice. We believe that this is an amazing feature of these models. In general, if one wants to keep decidability of type-checking, one has to choose between definitional irrelevance or unique choice. Sheaf models resolve this tension by giving both for propositions that arise a finite way from the base category. More generally, even without taking these type-theoretic considerations into account, all serious uses of sheaves are constructed above a presheaf model. Thus there seems to be both foundational and empirical evidence that we want to revisit the traditional setting by composing synthetic sheaves with presheaves in a type-theoretic world.

And this is where we hit a wall. On the one hand, we have a sheaf model requiring univalence. On the other hand, we do have a syntactic model which interprets a theory equivalent to presheaves [52]... but this model requires and propagates definitional UIP! As a result, we simply cannot plug one into the other. A syntactic model of univalent presheaves seems completely out of reach, so there is no clear way out of this conundrum via the syntactic route.

Note that the failed approach above tries to define a syntactic presheaf model over a base category $\mathbf{C}$ *internal* to a homotopic type theory, whose precise model does not matter but should be computational. This is subtly but fundamentally different from the sheaf models from Coquand et al. [25]. While they also rely on univalence and use the same synthetic encoding of sheaves, their presheaves are defined externally in an unspecified metatheory. Said otherwise, their models are built out of presheaves $\square \times \mathfrak{C} \to \mathbf{Set}$ where $\square$ is some cube category and $\mathfrak{C}$ an *external* base category. Unfortunately, there is no hope to recover a decent computational content out of usual presheaves [52], so this is a no-go.

We need a more semantic approach. We want to define a type theory capturing the internal language of Grothendieck toposes that keeps all the great properties of MLTT. The task is daunting, given the variety of sheaf models. As an initial step, we will focus in this paper on the simplest non-trivial case of sheafification we could think of, namely the addition of a Cohen real to MLTT, that is to say, an uninterpreted variable $\alpha : \mathbb{N} \to \mathbb{B}$ that is approximated by partial functions of finite support. A close variant of this theory was first sketched by Coquand and Jaber in [23,24]. Up to unique choice, Cohen reals correspond to the geometric theory with one atom $\alpha : \mathbb{N} \to \mathbb{B} \to \mathsf{Prop}$ and the two axioms

$$n : \mathbb{N} \mid \cdot \vdash \alpha\, n\, \mathsf{tt} \vee \alpha\, n\, \mathsf{ff} \qquad \text{and} \qquad n : \mathbb{N} \mid \alpha\, n\, \mathsf{tt}, \alpha\, n\, \mathsf{ff} \vdash \bot.$$

This theory enjoys some remarkable properties: it is infinite and the branching is at the same time non-trivial, finite and disjoint. In terms of LOS, the first property means our type I is infinite, and thus our idealized object as well. This is the whole point of forcing. The other properties constrain the O predicate. Being non-trivial means that we get trees instead of lists in the semantics, and finiteness will maintain decidability properties. Finally, disjointness makes the whole setting much more tractable at the cost of some degeneracy. Semantically, this means that the decision diagram is not a directed acyclic graph but a proper tree. Because of this, we can completely ignore issues with unique choice and replace the functional predicate α with an actual function. Disjoint branching is very specific to Cohen reals, and makes our model a lot simpler, syntactically and semantically.

3.2   Continuity

As specific as it may seem, adding a single Cohen real to a type theory can already bring in interesting metatheoretical results about MLTT. In some way that we already laid down in Section 2.5, the very purpose of sheafification is to provide generalized continuity results. It is thus tempting to hope that the archetypical continuity property shall follow from a simple form of sheaves. As there are several non-equivalent notions of continuity [11], we need some paraphernalia to formally explain what we mean by this word. Escardó introduced a close relative to interaction trees called *dialogue trees* [31], which is just the type

$$\begin{aligned}
&\texttt{Inductive } \mathfrak{D}\ (A : \mathsf{Type}) : \mathsf{Type} := \\
&\mid \eta_{\mathfrak{D}} : A \to \mathfrak{D}\, A \qquad\qquad\qquad \text{with} \qquad \mathsf{I} : \mathsf{Type} \text{ and } \mathsf{O} : \mathsf{I} \to \mathsf{Type}. \\
&\mid \mathsf{F}_{\mathfrak{D}} : \Pi(i : \mathsf{I}). (\mathsf{O}\, i \to \mathfrak{D}\, A) \to \mathfrak{D}\, A
\end{aligned}$$

As explained in Section 2.3, similarity to sheaves is not coincidental. The main difference between $\mathfrak{D}$ and $\mathcal{S}$ is that $\mathfrak{D}$ lacks any kind of quotient, and furthermore that its O type is proof-relevant. Just like for $\mathcal{S}$, we can define an evaluation function $\texttt{eval}_{\mathfrak{D}} : (\Pi(i : \mathsf{I}).\mathsf{O}\, i) \to \mathfrak{D}\, A \to A$ which can be used to define a rather strong notion of *continuity* for functionals.

Definition 11. *A function* $F : (\Pi(i : \mathsf{I}).\mathsf{O}\, i) \to A$ *is dialogue-continuous, written* $\mathcal{C}_{\mathfrak{D}}\, F$, *if there is* $d : \mathfrak{D}\, A$ *s.t.* $\Pi(\alpha : \Pi(i : \mathsf{I}).\mathsf{O}\, i).F\, \alpha = \texttt{eval}\, \alpha\, d$.

This notion is strong because it implies a specific sequentialization of calls to the higher-order argument, an intensional property not present in the traditional view of continuity as a dependency on a finite prefix of the input. Taking specific instances of (I, O), one can recover well-known notions of continuity. Notably, for $\mathsf{I} := \mathbb{N}$ and $\mathsf{O}\, i := \mathbb{B}$, this definition is equivalent to uniform continuity over the

Cantor space $\mathbb{N} \to \mathbb{B}$. For $\mathsf{I} := \mathbb{N}$ and $\mathsf{O}\ i := \mathbb{N}$, it implies pointwise continuity over the Baire space $\mathbb{N} \to \mathbb{N}$, but is weaker than uniform continuity. As uniform continuity over the Baire space is very strong, Fujiwara and Kawai [34] argue that dialogue continuity is the proper way to extend uniform continuity from the Cantor to the Baire space. Moreover, note that this generalization to arbitrary (I, O) types is reminiscent of Brede and Herbelin's *generalized bar induction* [15].

Using the fact $\mathfrak{D}$ is a monad, Escardó gave a proof that System T enjoys dialogue continuity for the Baire space in an external way via what amounts to a syntactic effectful model [22]. Here, the argument $\mathbb{N} \to \mathbb{N}$ is handled as an oracle in the sheaf way by interpreting System T into the call-by-value embedding of $\mathfrak{D}$. This result was extended by Sterling to Brouwer sequences [62]. Finally, Baillon et al. generalized Escardó's result to dependent type theory [12]. Their model interprets universes but lacks full dependent elimination. Indeed, oracle calls are added freely via a $\digamma$ constructor, introducing an observable effect which forces them to restrict the interpreted theory to Baclofen Type Theory [53].

Escardó and Xu also studied more semantic approaches to the same kind of questions [69,29] veering towards sheaves. Due to the semantic nature of these works, it is hard to recover actual computation from their results.

There was an important series of papers around this topic from the PER community, Rahli being in the intersection of all of their authors [58,56,57,19,17,18]. These papers consider various forms of continuity in realizability models of MLTT à la NuPRL, with some built-in form of computation, and where the metatheory is actually Rocq. By loyalty to the Brouwerian tradition, they are advertized as Beth models, but they really are sheaf models, since they are proof-relevant. Note that in their approach, the models are by design open, as there is no inductive definition of well-typedness in sight: everything is defined in a semantics that only cares about closed terms. Completeness is in particular a non-object, and there is no hope to get a decidable type-checking algorithm for their non-theory. While we boast no obsession for Brouwerian choice sequences, we believe the intuitions developed in this community to be valuable, and that it is enlightening to revisit these historical artifacts with a modern type-theoretic point of view.

In the remainder of this paper, we leverage recent developments in the mechanization of models of normalization by evaluation [2,3]. Our goal is twofold. First, we define and study $\mathsf{MLTT}^{\mathsf{f}}$, the most elementary sheaf extension of MLTT with a single Cohen real. Given the complexity of the objects at play, we formalize our results in the Rocq proof assistant. Then, as a byproduct, we derive a constructive proof of continuity for MLTT functionals over the Cantor space.

3.3   MLTT^{f}

It is now time to enter the real matter. We define in this section $\mathsf{MLTT}^{\mathsf{f}}$, a variant of MLTT extended with a formal oracle $\alpha : \mathbb{N} \to \mathbb{B}$, together with a local state of forcing conditions $\ell \in \mathfrak{L}$ that represent finite knowledge about α. Note that $\mathfrak{L}$ is a type in the metatheory, not in $\mathsf{MLTT}^{\mathsf{f}}$. Since we will often switch from one to the other, we will try to write $\mathsf{MLTT}^{\mathsf{f}}$ objects in a normal font and metatheoretical ones in a fraktur font. To further insist, we will use set-theoretical notations for the metatheory, though it is technically the type theory of Rocq.

In the mechanization we set $\mathfrak{L} := \mathsf{list}\,(\mathfrak{N} \times \mathfrak{B})$, where list, $\mathfrak{N}$ and $\mathfrak{B}$ respectively are metatheoretical lists, natural numbers and booleans. We will write $[]$ for the empty list and $::$ for the cons operator. Despite use of lists, conditions should rather be thought of as finite sets, and all operations will preserve the implict reordering quotient. In particular, $\mathfrak{L}$ enjoys the reverse inclusion order

$$\ell' \preceq \ell \quad := \quad \Pi(\mathfrak{n} \in \mathfrak{N})\,(\mathfrak{b} \in \mathfrak{B}).\,(\mathfrak{n}, \mathfrak{b}) \ltimes \ell \to (\mathfrak{n}, \mathfrak{b}) \ltimes \ell'$$

where $\ltimes$ is any reasonable definition of list membership. When $\ell' \preceq \ell$, we view ℓ' as more *precise* than ℓ, insofar as it contains more information. Finally, given $\ell \in \mathfrak{L}$, we will write $\mathsf{dom}(\ell) \in \mathsf{list}\,\mathfrak{N}$ for the list of the first projections of ℓ.

MLTT^F follows the usual presentation of dependent type theory with five kind of judgments, i.e. context, type and term well-formedness together with type and term conversion. The only difference with MLTT here is that we annotate all judgments with forcing conditions, leading to the judgment shapes below.

well-formed context	$\vdash \ell \mid \Gamma$		
well-formed type	$\ell \mid \Gamma \vdash A$	well-formed term	$\ell \mid \Gamma \vdash M : A$
convertible types	$\ell \mid \Gamma \vdash A \equiv B$	convertible terms	$\ell \mid \Gamma \vdash M \equiv N : A$

Let us mention we only ever consider forcing conditions satisfying a well-formedness predicate, checking that all bindings in ℓ appear at most once. This ensures that conditions indeed code for finite approximations of functions. Formal definition of this predicate can be found 🔗 here.

Typing and conversion rules for MLTT^F are an extension of the rules for MLTT, with negative Π and Σ-types with definitional η-rules, natural numbers, booleans, empty and identity types, and one universe. We refer the interested reader to 🔗 the mechanization for a complete description of the theory.

$$\textsc{(Oracle)}\ \frac{\ell \mid \Gamma \vdash M : \mathbb{N}}{\ell \mid \Gamma \vdash \alpha\,M : \mathbb{B}} \qquad \frac{\vdash \ell \mid \Gamma \qquad (\mathfrak{n}, \mathfrak{b}) \ltimes \ell}{\ell \mid \Gamma \vdash \alpha\,\bar{\mathfrak{n}} \equiv \bar{\mathfrak{b}} : \mathbb{B}}\ \textsc{(Eval)}$$

$$\frac{(\mathfrak{n}, \mathsf{tt}) :: \ell \mid \Gamma \vdash \mathcal{J} \qquad (\mathfrak{n}, \mathsf{ff}) :: \ell \mid \Gamma \vdash \mathcal{J} \qquad \mathfrak{n} \not\ltimes \mathsf{dom}(\ell)}{\ell \mid \Gamma \vdash \mathcal{J}}\ \textsc{(Split)}$$

Fig. 2. New rules for MLTT^F

We only describe the additional rules handling the oracle and forcing conditions in Figure 2. The $\textsc{Oracle}$ rule states that α is a function in the Cantor space. We define α as a unary term former but abuse the application notation. This is for technical reasons and we can retrieve a proper function by η-expansion. The $\textsc{Eval}$ rule states that the state of knowledge ℓ can be reflected into conversion for α itself. As forcing conditions $(\mathfrak{n}, \mathfrak{b}) \ltimes \ell$ live in the meta-theory, we rely on injections $\bar{n} : \mathbb{N}$ and $\bar{b} : \mathbb{B}$ as terms of MLTT^f. Finally, sheafness of MLTT^f is embodied in the SPLIT rule scheme, available for any judgment $\mathcal{J}$ of our theory. It allows extending the local knowledge about α by making a case analysis on its value at some concrete input $\mathfrak{n}$. We have to be ready to handle either value, but note that the judgment is the same in both premises. This does not prevent performing pattern-matching on $\alpha\,\bar{\mathfrak{n}}$ further down the term, but forces the SPLIT rule to separate local extension of knowledge from its analysis. A typical use of this rule is to derive a restricted η-rule for α, as it allows e.g. proving

$$\ell \mid \Gamma \vdash \texttt{if } \alpha\,\bar{\mathfrak{n}} \texttt{ then tt else ff} \equiv \alpha\,\bar{\mathfrak{n}} : \mathbb{B}$$

for some concrete $\mathfrak{n} \in \mathfrak{N}$ where the $\texttt{if} - \texttt{then} - \texttt{else}$ is syntactic sugar for the boolean recursor.

3.4 Canonicity

As explained in Section 2.5, in sheaf models usual canonicity results do not stand. This carries over to MLTT^f as it is not the case that a closed term $[] \mid \cdot \vdash M : \mathbb{N}$ reduces to a value, since M may depend on α. We instead get a *weak canonicity* result, i.e. canonicity up to an inductive tree of splits. To make this formal, we first define the metatheoretic type $\mathfrak{D}$ of dialogue trees parameterized by ℓ.

```
Inductive 𝔇 (ℓ : list (𝔑 × 𝔅)) : Type :=
| η𝔇 : 𝔇 ℓ
| F𝔇 : Π(n : 𝔑). n ∉ dom(ℓ) → (Π(b : 𝔅). 𝔇 ((n, b) :: ℓ)) → 𝔇 ℓ
```

Intuitively, $d : \mathfrak{D}\,\ell$ describes a tree of questions that are left unanswered by ℓ. We then define $d \lhd \ell'$, a predicate capturing that there is a path from ℓ to ℓ' in d. Both $\mathfrak{D}$ and $d \lhd \ell'$ are formally defined 🖝 here.

$$\frac{}{\eta_{\mathfrak{D}}\,\ell \lhd \ell} \qquad \frac{k\ \text{tt} \lhd \ell}{F_{\mathfrak{D}}\,\mathfrak{n}\,\mathfrak{n}_\varepsilon\,k \lhd (\mathfrak{n}, \text{tt}) :: \ell} \qquad \frac{k\ \text{ff} \lhd \ell}{F_{\mathfrak{D}}\,\mathfrak{n}\,\mathfrak{n}_\varepsilon\,k \lhd (\mathfrak{n}, \text{ff}) :: \ell}$$

The last thing we need before stating the weak canonicity theorem is a notion of weak-head reduction for MLTT^f. We define it as an extension of the usual rules for MLTT, adding specific rules to handle α. Contrarily to MLTT, reduction rules are annotated with a state of knowledge ℓ which is used in the new rules for α. We only state these ones and 🖝 refer to the mechanization for further details.

$$\frac{(\mathfrak{n}, \mathfrak{b}) \bowtie \ell}{\alpha\,\bar{\mathfrak{n}} \rightsquigarrow_\ell \bar{\mathfrak{b}}} \qquad \frac{M \rightsquigarrow_\ell M' \qquad k \in \mathfrak{N}}{\alpha\,(\mathsf{S}^k\,M) \rightsquigarrow_\ell \alpha\,(\mathsf{S}^k\,M')}$$

The first rule is the counterpart to the EVAL conversion rule. It reflects in the reduction the current state of knowledge about α. The second rule is a congruence rule for α, which allows reducing its argument as long as it may still evaluate to a closed integer. This rule introduces a tiny amount of deep reduction, since it can fire under an arbitrary amount of successor nodes.

In a pure setting like MLTT, there are exactly two kinds of normal forms: values and neutrals. Values are terms which start with a introduction rule, e.g. $S\ M$ or $\lambda x : A.\ M$. Meanwhile, neutrals are terms whose head is an elimination blocked on a variable. In MLTT^f, due to the oracle, we get a third kind of normal form, which we call α-*neutrals*. An α-neutral at world ℓ is a term stuck on $\alpha\ \overline{\mathfrak{n}}$ in head position with $\mathfrak{n} \not\in (\mathsf{dom}\ \ell)$. Moving to a more informative $\ell' \preceq \ell$ may unlock further computation. It will correspond to a node in the split tree of a normal form, and the model will ensure that α-neutrals can be eventually unblocked.

We will also consider hereditary reduction to a deep normal form $M \Downarrow_\ell N$, which is defined in a standard way. We are now ready to state weak canonicity for MLTT^f. Proving it is one of the goals of Section 4. It will be the cornerstone to the proof that all MLTT-definable functionals are continuous.

Theorem 2 (Weak canonicity). *For any closed term* $[]\ |\ \cdot \vdash M : \mathbb{N}$ *of* MLTT^f,

$$\Sigma(d \in \mathfrak{D}\ []).\ \Pi(\ell \in \mathfrak{L}).\ d \lhd \ell \longrightarrow \Sigma(\mathfrak{n} \in \mathfrak{N}).\ M \Downarrow_\ell^* \overline{\mathfrak{n}}.$$

3.5   Continuity

We will assume in this section that Theorem 2 holds, and will use it to prove that MLTT functionals of type $(\mathbb{N} \to \mathbb{B}) \to \mathbb{N}$ are continuous. First, we need to agree about what we actually mean by that, i.e. what the statement really says and how internal it is. We focus first on the latter.

Assuming some formal definition of continuity, we have various levels in which it can be reflected in MLTT. We single out three specific points on this continuum, that we will call *external* continuity, the continuity *rule* and the continuity *principle*. External continuity is an exclusively metatheoretical property, i.e. "for any closed term F, we have $\mathfrak{C}\ F$" where $\mathfrak{C}$ is a predicate in the metatheory. This is the only one one can state when the object language is not expressive enough. A recent paper by Escardó et al [30] internalizes an encoding of a dialogue tree in System T but cannot *internally say* that it is a witness of dialogue continuity. Here, MLTT, can express any reasonable notion of continuity as an internal property $\vdash C : ((\mathbb{N} \to \mathbb{B}) \to \mathbb{N}) \to \mathsf{Type}$. So we can ask for the continuity principle, a term Φ_C that proves continuity uniformly, i.e. $\vdash \Phi_C : \Pi(f : (\mathbb{N} \to \mathbb{B}) \to \mathbb{N}).C\ f$. Being the strongest of the three, it is also the trickiest. Baillon et al. [11] provide a large range of continuity definitions, but even with one of the weakest, namely *modulus continuity*, Escardó and Xu [32] show that the continuity principle on the Baire space is inconsistent in MLTT. For the Cantor type, their counter-example does not hold however, so hope remains.

Finally, the continuity rule states that $\vdash F : (\mathbb{N} \to \mathbb{B}) \to \mathbb{N}$ implies the existence of some term $\vdash \{F\}^C : C\ F$. It allows reflecting the continuity proof in MLTT itself, but in a non-uniform way. Here, the operation $\{F\}^C$ is defined in the metatheory, typically via some external induction on the syntax of F which must be a *closed* term. Clearly, the continuity principle implies the continuity rule, but the inverse is not true in general. Moreover, with some mild assumptions on the object theory, the continuity rule often implies its external variant.

We will focus on the continuity rule, taking uniform continuity as definition. It is easier to state and equivalent to dialogue continuity on the Cantor space.

Definition 12. $F : (\mathbb{N} \to \mathbb{B}) \to \mathbb{N}$ *is uniformly continuous, written* $\mathcal{C}\ F$, *if*

$$\Sigma(n : \mathbb{N}).\ \Pi(\alpha\,\beta : \mathbb{N} \to \mathbb{B}).\ \alpha \approx_n \beta \to F\ \alpha = F\ \beta$$

where $\approx_n$ *is defined as pointwise equality on the n-th first integers.*

Theorem 3 (Uniform continuity rule). *For any* $\vdash_{\mathsf{MLTT}} F : (\mathbb{N} \to \mathbb{B}) \to \mathbb{N}$, *there exists a closed term* $\vdash_{\mathsf{MLTT}} \{F\}^{\mathcal{C}} : \mathcal{C}\ F$.

Proof. Let us assume such a F. By inclusion $[]\ |\ \cdot \vdash_{\mathsf{MLTT}^{\mathsf{f}}} F\ \tilde{\alpha} : \mathbb{N}$, where $\tilde{\alpha} := \lambda n.\ \alpha\ n$. By Theorem 2, there is a finite set $\mathfrak{F}$ of forcing conditions s.t. for each $\ell \in \mathfrak{F}$, $F\ \tilde{\alpha} \Downarrow_\ell \overline{n}_\ell$ for some $n_\ell \in \mathfrak{N}$. We can replay this reduction in MLTT by substituting α with any MLTT term α_0 that is compatible on ℓ reduction-wise. In particular for any such α_0:

$$\vdash_{\mathsf{MLTT}} \mathtt{refl}\ \mathbb{N}\ \overline{n}_\ell : F\ \alpha_0 = \overline{n}_\ell. \tag{1}$$

For any $\mathfrak{p} \in \mathfrak{N}$, there is $\vdash_{\mathsf{MLTT}} \mathtt{set}_\mathfrak{p} : (\mathbb{N} \to \mathbb{B}) \to \mathbb{B}^\mathfrak{p} \to \mathbb{N} \to \mathbb{B}$ defined by finite case analysis s.t. for $0 \le \mathfrak{i} < \mathfrak{p}$, $\mathtt{set}_\mathfrak{p}\ M\ B_0\ \ldots\ B_{\mathfrak{p}-1}\ \overline{\mathfrak{i}} \rightsquigarrow^*_{\mathsf{MLTT}} B_\mathfrak{i}$ and for $\mathfrak{p} \le \mathfrak{i}$, $\vdash_{\mathsf{MLTT}} \mathtt{set}_\mathfrak{p}\ M\ B_0\ \ldots\ B_{\mathfrak{p}-1}\ \overline{\mathfrak{i}} \equiv M\ \overline{\mathfrak{i}}$.

Since $\mathfrak{F}$ is a covering, there is $\mathfrak{m} \in \mathfrak{N}$ and $\vdash_{\mathsf{MLTT}} \Phi : \mathbb{B}^\mathfrak{m} \to \mathbb{N}$ together with a proof $\vdash_{\mathsf{MLTT}} \_ : \Pi\alpha\,(b_0\ \ldots\ b_{\mathfrak{m}-1} : \mathbb{B}).\ F\ (\mathtt{set}_\mathfrak{m}\ \alpha\ b_0\ \ldots\ b_{\mathfrak{m}-1}) = \Phi\ b_0\ \ldots\ b_{\mathfrak{m}-1}$ where Φ is defined out of $\{n_\ell\}_{\ell \in \mathfrak{F}}$, and the proof is carried by destructing all b_i variables and concluding by Eq. (1). By reasoning internally, we easily get a proof

$$\vdash_{\mathsf{MLTT}} \_ : \Pi(\alpha\,\beta : \mathbb{N} \to \mathbb{B}).\ \alpha \approx_{\overline{\mathfrak{m}}} \beta \to$$
$$F\ (\mathtt{set}_\mathfrak{m}\ \alpha\ (\alpha\ 0)\ \ldots\ (\alpha\ \overline{\mathfrak{m}-1})) = F\ (\mathtt{set}_\mathfrak{m}\ \beta\ (\beta\ 0)\ \ldots\ (\beta\ \overline{\mathfrak{m}-1}))$$

To conclude we need to show that F is extensional enough to behave the same on α and its $\mathtt{set}_\mathfrak{m}$ expansion. But this is a consequence of *parametricity* [13], which shows that for any closed term $\vdash_{\mathsf{MLTT}} M : (\mathbb{N} \to \mathbb{B}) \to \mathbb{N}$ we have a proof $\vdash_{\mathsf{MLTT}} \_ : \Pi(f\,g : \mathbb{N} \to \mathbb{B}).\ (\Pi(n : \mathbb{N}).\ f\ n = g\ n) \to M\ f = M\ g$.

4   A syntactic model of **MLTT** in **MLTT**^{f}

This section is dedicated to the description of both the theoretical and practical aspects of our MLTT^{f} model. Such models are fairly technical, so we will try to stay high-level and will refer to the mechanization for the nitty-gritty details.

4.1   A Mechanized Logical Relation

Our model of MLTT^{f} can be aptly described as a logical relation. Here, we use this syntagm in a restricted and idiosyncratic sense to describe a specific kind of model whose earliest representative is probably Girard's strong normalization model of System F [36] and whose canonical example is Abel et al. model of MLTT [2].

We recall here the salient features of this flavour of models. First, the semantics of terms is described by recursion on some syntactic description of types. In presence of dependent types, we thus have to resort to some form of induction-recursion to define at the same time types inductively and terms recursively from types. Semantically, well-typedness of a term $\Vdash M \in A$ is typically defined through reduction to a weak-head normal form whose shape is constrained by A. Hence, these models qualify as realizability models. Then, when caring about the equational theory, which is the case when the source has a conversion rule and thus in MLTT, it is customary to consider a binary PER presentation $\Vdash M \equiv N \in A$ of the unary variant $\Vdash M \in A$. Finally, in these models all semantic relations are presheaves over the category of contexts and weakenings. This latter point is a departure from most common forms of realizability, and singles out the critical notion of *neutral terms*, i.e. normal forms stuck on a variable. It also makes it possible for the model to be complete with respect to the syntax, which allows proving valuable results such as decidability of type-checking.

Our model follows Abel's approach and the Rocq port [3] of the original Agda implementation. The major difference with Abel's complete model of MLTT is that we morally introduce side-effects in the semantics via a splitting monad similarly to [18]. All properties now live up to a finite tree of extensions of the current forcing conditions, i.e. our semantic interpretations are sheaves for the ℓ contexts. We refer to the Adjedj et al. paper [3] for the infrastructure, and we will focus on the major differences with the original model instead.

4.2 Reducibility

Abel-style models are built in two steps. The first step is called *reducibility* and is the actual model construction. The second step is called *validity* and consists in closing reducibility under substitution. In usual realizability models this part is often implicit in the soundness proof. We will concentrate on MLTT^f reducibility and will only allude to validity, as the latter is not specific to our model.

A model is typically defined through (small) induction-recursion. To each type $\Gamma \vdash A$, one associates an inductively defined reducibility statement $\Gamma \Vdash A$. Then type convertibility, term typedness and term convertibility are defined by recursion on a proof of $\Gamma \Vdash A$. In our setting, things get more subtle. We indeed start by ▧ inductively defining what we call *strong reducibility* $\ell \mid \Gamma \Vdash^s A$. Then, given a proof $\mathfrak{H}_A \in \ell \mid \Gamma \Vdash^s A$, we define three reducibility relations at this type:

- strong reducible type convertibility $\ell \mid \Gamma \Vdash^s A \equiv B \mathbin{/} \mathfrak{H}_A$;
- strong reducible typedness $\ell \mid \Gamma \Vdash^s M : A \mathbin{/} \mathfrak{H}_A$;
- strong reducible term convertibility $\ell \mid \Gamma \Vdash^s M \equiv N : A \mathbin{/} \mathfrak{H}_A$.

The intuition is that strongly reducible types and terms reduce to a value *now*, at the current forcing condition ℓ. Then, to account for sheafification, we

94   M. Baillon et al.

derive what we call *split* or *weak* reducibility relations, which will be the ones that indeed interpret MLTT^f judgments. Split reducibility ⚑ is defined as the closure of strong reducibility under what amounts to the splitting monad in the presheaf model over ℓ contexts. The idea is that split reducible types and terms will *eventually* reduce to a value in every branch, once enough splits are performed. With $\mathfrak{H}_A \in \ell \mid \Gamma \Vdash^\mathsf{f} A$, it is formally defined as

$$\ell \mid \Gamma \Vdash^\mathsf{f} A \quad := \Sigma(d \in \mathfrak{D}\,\ell).\,\Pi\{\ell' \in \mathfrak{L}\}.\,d \vartriangleleft \ell' \to \ell' \mid \Gamma \Vdash^\mathsf{s} A$$
$$\ell \mid \Gamma \Vdash^\mathsf{f} \mathcal{J} \mathbin{/} \mathfrak{H}_A := \Sigma(d \in \mathfrak{D}\,\ell).\,\Pi\{\ell' \in \mathfrak{L}\}\,(d_\varepsilon \in \mathfrak{H}_A.\pi_1 \vartriangleleft \ell').\,\ell' \mid \Gamma \Vdash^\mathsf{s} \mathcal{J} \mathbin{/} (\mathfrak{H}_A.\pi_2\,d_\varepsilon)$$

The standard notion of syntactic neutrals from MLTT needs to be tweaked w.r.t. the new reduction rules. In addition to terms stuck on variables, we need to account for a call to the oracle stuck on a finite amount of S on top of a neutral. We give an excerpt of old cases together with the single new case below.

$$\dfrac{}{\mathsf{whne}\ x} \qquad \dfrac{\mathsf{whne}\ n}{\mathsf{whne}\ (n\ M)} \qquad \dfrac{\mathsf{whne}\ n}{\mathsf{whne}\ (\mathbb{N}_{\mathsf{rec}}\ P\ P_0\ P_\mathsf{S}\ n)} \quad \cdots \quad \dfrac{\mathsf{whne}\ n \qquad k \in \mathfrak{N}}{\mathsf{whne}\ (\alpha\ (S^k\ n))}$$

We sketch a few representative cases of strong reducibility. Due to the wealth of side-conditions in the definitions, writing it in full in print would not fit on the page, so we only present the core data. Importantly, all definitions contain syntactic well-formedness conditions ensuring completeness w.r.t. the syntax, but we skip these annotations here. Similarly, for readability we concentrate on the unary predicates but all these definitions also pack in the heterogeneous PER variant. We abuse notations and implicit arguments quite a bit. We write $\rho \in \Delta \subseteq \Gamma$ for weakenings and $M[\sigma]$ both for term substitution and weakening.

In Figure 3, we give reducibility for Π-types, the proverbial negative type. With this level of abstraction, it is clear that our metatheoretical semantics is call-by-value, even though the object theory enjoys a call-by-name equational theory. Barring the flurry of technical annotations needed to preserve completeness, the semantics is the one one would have expected from an effectful model. Most importantly, the codomain of Π-types is not strong but split reducible, since applying a function may perform side-effects, unlocking additional splits.

In Figure 4, we sketch reducibility of the typical positive type, namely $\mathbb{N}$. Contrarily to negative types, the relation is defined inductively, each constructor being mapped to an inductive case. Since we have first-class variables, we also need to freely add all well-typed neutrals. This was not visible in the term reducibility for Π-types because neutrals are closed by head application.

In semantic models, the hard part is to justify universes. As argued in Section 2.4, this is even a showstopper in traditional sheaf models. We have no such trouble, because types are directly interpreted by their code. The infrastructure is hard to erect for MLTT, which is why we have to use induction-recursion, but once this is done sheafification poses no further trouble. We model the universe as a ⚑ positive type whose constructors are the type formers of the theory, and this is about it. No need for stacks, univalence or QIRTs. *It just works.*

We quickly review some important properties of the model. The first one, which we already advertized, is that the model is complete w.r.t. the syntax.

$$\ell \mid \Gamma \Vdash^{\mathsf{s}}_{\Pi} A := \left\{ \begin{array}{l} \_ \ \in A \leadsto^{*}_{\ell} \Pi(x:F).\,G; \\ \mathfrak{H}_F \in \Pi\{\Delta\,\ell'\}\,(\rho \in \Delta \subseteq \Gamma).\,\ell' \preceq \ell \to \ell' \mid \Delta \Vdash^{\mathsf{s}} F[\rho]; \\ \mathfrak{H}_G \in \Pi\{\Delta\,\ell'\,a\}\,(\rho \in \Delta \subseteq \Gamma)\,(\tau \in \ell' \preceq \ell). \\ \quad \ell' \mid \Delta \Vdash^{\mathsf{s}} a : F[\rho] \ / \ (\mathfrak{H}_F\ \rho\ \tau) \to \ell' \mid \Delta \Vdash^{\mathsf{f}} G[a,\rho]; \ldots \end{array} \right\}$$

$$\ell \mid \Gamma \Vdash^{\mathsf{s}}_{\Pi} M : A \ / \ \mathfrak{H}_A := \left\{ \begin{array}{l} \_ \ \in M \leadsto^{*}_{\ell} V; \\ \mathsf{app} \in \Pi\{\Delta\,\ell'\,a\}\,(\rho \in \Delta \subseteq \Gamma)\,(\tau \in \ell' \preceq \ell). \\ \quad \Pi(\mathfrak{a} \in \ell' \mid \Delta \Vdash^{\mathsf{s}} a : F[\rho] \ / \ (\mathfrak{H}_F\ \rho\ \tau)). \\ \quad \ell' \mid \Delta \Vdash^{\mathsf{f}} V[\rho]\ a : G[a,\rho] \ / \ (\mathfrak{H}_G\ \rho\ \tau\ \mathfrak{a}); \ldots \end{array} \right\}$$

Fig. 3. Strong 🐦 type reducibility and 🐦 term reducibility for Π-types

$$\ell \mid \Gamma \Vdash^{\mathsf{s}}_{\mathbb{N}} A \quad := \quad \{\ \_ \in A \leadsto^{*}_{\ell} \mathbb{N};\ \ldots\ \}$$

$$\frac{M \leadsto^{*}_{\ell} 0 \qquad \ldots}{\ell \mid \Gamma \Vdash^{\mathsf{s}}_{\mathbb{N}} M : A \ / \ \mathfrak{H}_A} \qquad \frac{M \leadsto^{*}_{\ell} n \qquad \mathsf{whne}\ n \qquad \ldots}{\ell \mid \Gamma \Vdash^{\mathsf{s}}_{\mathbb{N}} M : A \ / \ \mathfrak{H}_A}$$

$$\frac{M \leadsto^{*}_{\ell} \mathsf{S}\ N \qquad \ell \mid \Gamma \Vdash^{\mathsf{s}}_{\mathbb{N}} N : A \ / \ \mathfrak{H}_A \qquad \ldots}{\ell \mid \Gamma \Vdash^{\mathsf{s}}_{\mathbb{N}} M : A \ / \ \mathfrak{H}_A}$$

Fig. 4. Strong 🐦 type reducibility and 🐦 term reducibility for natural numbers

Theorem 4 (🐦 Completeness). *If $\ell \mid \Gamma \Vdash^{\mathsf{f}} \mathcal{J}$ then $\ell \mid \Gamma \vdash \mathcal{J}$.*

The second theorem is a critical semantic property of reducibility. In a nutshell, for all reducibility predicates, everything behaves as if type well-formedness were a mere proposition. That is, no matter the exact proof used to build the predicate, all proofs lead to logically equivalent relations.

Theorem 5 (🐦 Irrelevance). *If $\mathfrak{H}_A, \mathfrak{H}'_A \in \ell \mid \Gamma \Vdash^{\mathsf{f}} A$ and $\ell \mid \Gamma \Vdash^{\mathsf{f}} \mathcal{J} \ / \ \mathfrak{H}_A$ then $\ell \mid \Gamma \Vdash^{\mathsf{f}} \mathcal{J} \ / \ \mathfrak{H}'_A$.*

We cannot insist enough on the importance of this property. Without it, we would face coherence hell, and would have to resort to overly abstract categorical contraptions à la synthetic Tait computability [63] to obtain our model. Unfortunately, such approaches are totally unapplicable to a proof assistant such as Rocq, and we would have to buy into a much more expressive foundation that is not even implemented yet. Thanks to irrelevance, we can pretend that everything is propositional and hide coherence issues under a nice, practical abstraction.

Finally, we provide some sanity checks about the intended semantics of our model. In particular, our predicates behave respectively as presheaves over contexts and as sheaves for the topology induced by the splitting operation.

Theorem 6 (Intended semantics). *Reducibility is closed under 🐦 weakenings, 🐦 splits and 🐦 neutrals.*

4.3 Validity and Soundness

To prove soundness of our model, we need to generalize reducibility a bit, a standard technique for MLTT models [2]. Note that forcing contexts $\ell \in \mathfrak{L}$ only get a degenerate form of substitutions through reverse inclusions of forcing conditions. Hence, when defining validity, closure by forcing context substitutions is trivial.

Definition 13 (Validity). *We define semantic validity $\Vdash^{\vee}$ for all our syntactic classes as usual by closing reducibility by all well-typed substitutions.*

We now have all the tools to state and prove the main result of our model, of which Theorem 2 is an immediate corollary.

Theorem 7 (Fundamental lemma). *If $\ell \mid \Gamma \vdash \mathcal{J}$ then $\ell \mid \Gamma \Vdash^{\vee} \mathcal{J}$.*

Proof. We only focus on changes w.r.t. the proof for MLTT, i.e. the rules from Figure 2. The SPLIT rule is literally baked in the model as per Theorem 6, leaving us with EVAL and ORACLE. We focus on ORACLE as it subsumes the other. We have to prove that $\alpha\ M$ is split-reducible at type $\mathbb{B}$. By induction hypothesis, the argument $M : \mathbb{N}$ is a split reducible integer. Binding it, we can assume that M is a strongly reducible integer. By definition of $\Vdash^{s}_{\mathbb{N}}$, we have two cases. Either M hereditarily reduces to a proper integer $\bar{n}$, or to a term of the form $\mathsf{S}^{k}\ n$ for some neutral n. In the first case we can split on $\bar{n}$ to conclude by reduction to a concrete $\bar{b}$. In the second case, the whole expression is a neutral, hence reducible.

5   Conclusion

The different approaches to building models discussed in this paper can be framed along three axes: *realizability, open terms* and *sheafness*. Figure 5 illustrates this classification by placing some representative models of MLTT from the literature on a cube. The realizability axis opposes computation-free models to models based on reduction. The open term axis contrasts semantics defined with respect to closed terms only to models with a first-class notion of variable, i.e. which are presheaves on contexts. Finally, the sheafness axis delineates models of "pure" MLTT, with the usual notion of canonicity, from those where side-effects in the semantics weaken canonicity. To the best of our knowledge, our model is the only mechanized MLTT model that features all these properties.

As mentioned in Section 3.5, we believe that adding the continuity principle to MLTT^{F} is within grasp. All the necessary building blocks are already there, we just need a local context of oracles rather than a single global one, and add term that exploits the weak canonicity theorem in an internal way. Similarly, we have not formally proved decidability of type-checking for MLTT^{F} yet, but we expect it to be a minor variation on the already mechanized proof for MLTT.

A more difficult task would be to define a variant of MLTT^{F} for more general Grothendieck topologies. As explained in Section 3.1, branching for Cohen reals is both finite and disjoint. Finiteness is a must-have if we want to keep decidability of type-checking, but the disjointness condition is very restrictive. Studying a type-theoretic interpretation of the algebraic closure of a field, for which Coquand and Manaa have provided a suitable site model in a intuitionistic

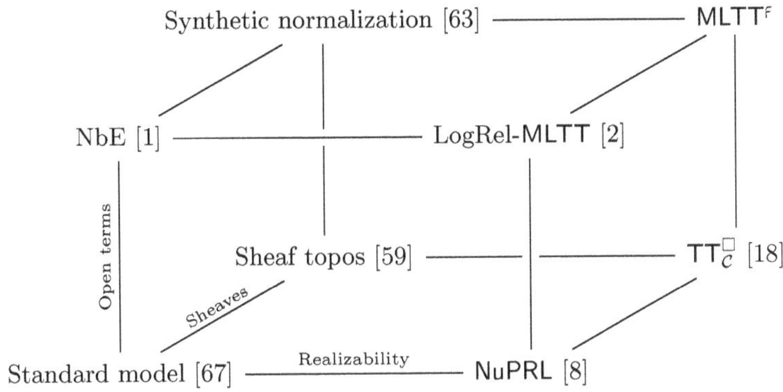

Fig. 5. The Model Cube

higher-order logic [48], would be a first step towards less elementary models. The Zariski topos [14] is another interesting and historically significant candidate.

More generally, recent works on dynamical methods in constructive mathematics, as mentioned in Section 2.5, provide potentially interesting type-theoretic models. Some of these results are quite spectacular. For instance, rephrasing classical local-global principles in algebraic geometry unveiled a simplification and generalization of previous proofs of Serre's conjecture (Quillen-Suslin's theorem) in commutative algebra [46]. Dynamical methods are actually about turning the oracle-based algorithm suggested by a classical proof into a branching process, e.g. some dialogue tree. Originally formulated in a categorical framework based on sketches [28], dynamical methods have also found significant appplications in computer algebra, e.g. for computing with algebraic numbers [27], transseries [9], etc. We thus believe in the interest of revisiting Coquand, Lombardi et al.'s research program, coined *hidden constructions in abstract algebra* in a series of papers, through the type-theoretic perspective advocated in the present paper.

Acknowledgments This project has received funding from the European Research Council (ERC) under the European Union's Horizon 2020 research and innovation programme (grant agreement No. 101001995.

References

1. Abel, A., Aehlig, K., Dybjer, P.: Normalization by evaluation for martin-löf type theory with one universe. In: Fiore, M. (ed.) Proceedings of the 23rd Conference on the Mathematical Foundations of Programming Semantics, MFPS 2007, New Orleans, LA, USA, April 11-14, 2007. Electronic Notes in Theoretical Computer Science, vol. 173, pp. 17–39. Elsevier (2007). https://doi.org/10.1016/J.ENTCS.2007.02.025, https://doi.org/10.1016/j.entcs.2007.02.025

2. Abel, A., Öhman, J., Vezzosi, A.: Decidability of conversion for type theory in type theory. Proc. ACM Program. Lang. **2**(POPL) (dec 2017). https://doi.org/10.1145/3158111, https://doi.org/10.1145/3158111

3. Adjedj, A., Lennon-Bertrand, M., Maillard, K., Pédrot, P., Pujet, L.: Martin-löf à la coq. In: Timany, A., Traytel, D., Pientka, B., Blazy, S. (eds.) Proceedings of the 13th ACM SIGPLAN International Conference on Certified Programs and Proofs, CPP 2024, London, UK, January 15-16, 2024. pp. 230–245. ACM (2024). https://doi.org/10.1145/3636501.3636951, https://doi.org/10.1145/3636501.3636951

4. Ahman, D.: Handling fibred algebraic effects. Proc. ACM Program. Lang. 2(POPL), 7:1–7:29 (2018). https://doi.org/10.1145/3158095, https://doi.org/10.1145/3158095

5. Ahman, D., Ghani, N., Plotkin, G.D.: Dependent types and fibred computational effects. In: Jacobs, B., Löding, C. (eds.) Foundations of Software Science and Computation Structures - 19th International Conference, FOSSACS 2016, Held as Part of the European Joint Conferences on Theory and Practice of Software, ETAPS 2016, Eindhoven, The Netherlands, April 2-8, 2016, Proceedings. Lecture Notes in Computer Science, vol. 9634, pp. 36–54. Springer (2016). https://doi.org/10.1007/978-3-662-49630-5_3, https://doi.org/10.1007/978-3-662-49630-5_3

6. Altenkirch, T., Capriotti, P., Dijkstra, G., Kraus, N., Forsberg, F.N.: Quotient inductive-inductive types. In: Baier, C., Lago, U.D. (eds.) Foundations of Software Science and Computation Structures - 21st International Conference, FOSSACS 2018, Held as Part of the European Joint Conferences on Theory and Practice of Software, ETAPS 2018, Thessaloniki, Greece, April 14-20, 2018, Proceedings. Lecture Notes in Computer Science, vol. 10803, pp. 293–310. Springer (2018). https://doi.org/10.1007/978-3-319-89366-2_16, https://doi.org/10.1007/978-3-319-89366-2_16

7. Altenkirch, T., McBride, C., Swierstra, W.: Observational equality, now! In: Stump, A., Xi, H. (eds.) Proceedings of the ACM Workshop Programming Languages meets Program Verification, PLPV 2007, Freiburg, Germany, October 5, 2007. pp. 57–68. ACM (2007). https://doi.org/10.1145/1292597.1292608, https://doi.org/10.1145/1292597.1292608

8. Anand, A., Rahli, V.: Towards a formally verified proof assistant. In: Klein, G., Gamboa, R. (eds.) Interactive Theorem Proving - 5th International Conference, ITP 2014, Held as Part of the Vienna Summer of Logic, VSL 2014, Vienna, Austria, July 14-17, 2014. Proceedings. Lecture Notes in Computer Science, vol. 8558, pp. 27–44. Springer (2014). https://doi.org/10.1007/978-3-319-08970-6_3, https://doi.org/10.1007/978-3-319-08970-6_3

9. Aschenbrenner, M., Dries, L.v.d., Hoeven, J.v.d.: Asymptotic Differential Algebra and Model Theory of Transseries. No. 195 in Annals of Mathematics studies, Princeton University Press (2017), http://arxiv.org/abs/1509.02588

10. Authors, T.S.P.: Stacks project, https://stacks.math.columbia.edu/

11. Baillon, M., Forster, Y., Mahboubi, A., Pédrot, P.M., Piquerez, M.: A Zoo of Continuity Properties in Constructive Type Theory. In: Fernández, M. (ed.) 10th International Conference on Formal Structures for Computation and Deduction (FSCD 2025). Leibniz International Proceedings in Informatics (LIPIcs), vol. 337, pp. 9:1–9:20. Schloss Dagstuhl – Leibniz-Zentrum für Informatik, Dagstuhl, Germany (2025). https://doi.org/10.4230/LIPIcs.FSCD.2025.9, https://drops.dagstuhl.de/entities/document/10.4230/LIPIcs.FSCD.2025.9

12. Baillon, M., Mahboubi, A., Pédrot, P.: Gardening with the pythia A model of continuity in a dependent setting. In: Manea, F., Simpson, A. (eds.) 30th EACSL Annual Conference on Computer Science Logic, CSL 2022, February 14-19, 2022, Göttingen, Germany (Virtual Conference). LIPIcs, vol. 216, pp. 5:1–5:18. Schloss

Dagstuhl - Leibniz-Zentrum für Informatik (2022). `https://doi.org/10.4230/LIPICS.CSL.2022.5`, `https://doi.org/10.4230/LIPIcs.CSL.2022.5`

13. Bernardy, J., Lasson, M.: Realizability and parametricity in pure type systems. In: Hofmann, M. (ed.) Foundations of Software Science and Computational Structures - 14th International Conference, FOSSACS 2011, Held as Part of the Joint European Conferences on Theory and Practice of Software, ETAPS 2011, Saarbrücken, Germany, March 26-April 3, 2011. Proceedings. Lecture Notes in Computer Science, vol. 6604, pp. 108–122. Springer (2011). `https://doi.org/10.1007/978-3-642-19805-2_8`, `https://doi.org/10.1007/978-3-642-19805-2_8`

14. Blechschmidt, I.: Using the internal language of toposes in algebraic geometry. Ph.D. thesis, Augsburg University (2017), `https://rawgit.com/iblech/internal-methods/master/notes.pdf`

15. Brede, N., Herbelin, H.: On the logical structure of choice and bar induction principles. In: 36th Annual ACM/IEEE Symposium on Logic in Computer Science, LICS 2021, Rome, Italy, June 29 - July 2, 2021. pp. 1–13. IEEE (2021). `https://doi.org/10.1109/LICS52264.2021.9470523`, `https://doi.org/10.1109/LICS52264.2021.9470523`

16. Cavallo, E., Mörtberg, A., Swan, A.W.: Unifying cubical models of univalent type theory. In: Fernández, M., Muscholl, A. (eds.) 28th EACSL Annual Conference on Computer Science Logic, CSL 2020, January 13-16, 2020, Barcelona, Spain. LIPIcs, vol. 152, pp. 14:1–14:17. Schloss Dagstuhl - Leibniz-Zentrum für Informatik (2020). `https://doi.org/10.4230/LIPICS.CSL.2020.14`, `https://doi.org/10.4230/LIPIcs.CSL.2020.14`

17. Cohen, L., Rahli, V.: Realizing continuity using stateful computations. In: Klin, B., Pimentel, E. (eds.) 31st EACSL Annual Conference on Computer Science Logic, CSL 2023, February 13-16, 2023, Warsaw, Poland. LIPIcs, vol. 252, pp. 15:1–15:18. Schloss Dagstuhl - Leibniz-Zentrum für Informatik (2023). `https://doi.org/10.4230/LIPICS.CSL.2023.15`, `https://doi.org/10.4230/LIPIcs.CSL.2023.15`

18. Cohen, L., Rahli, V.: $TT_C^{\square}$: A family of extensional type theories with effectful realizers of continuity. Logical Methods in Computer Science **Volume 20, Issue 2**, 18 (Jun 2024). `https://doi.org/10.46298/lmcs-20(2:18)2024`, `https://lmcs.episciences.org/11666`

19. Cohen, L., da Rocha Paiva, B., Rahli, V., Tosun, A.: Inductive continuity via Brouwer trees. In: Leroux, J., Lombardy, S., Peleg, D. (eds.) 48th International Symposium on Mathematical Foundations of Computer Science, MFCS 2023, August 28 to September 1, 2023, Bordeaux, France. LIPIcs, vol. 272, pp. 37:1–37:16. Schloss Dagstuhl - Leibniz-Zentrum für Informatik (2023). `https://doi.org/10.4230/LIPICS.MFCS.2023.37`, `https://doi.org/10.4230/LIPIcs.MFCS.2023.37`

20. Coquand, T.: Dynamical method in algebra: A survey. In: Mayer, M.C., Pirri, F. (eds.) Automated Reasoning with Analytic Tableaux and Related Methods, International Conference, TABLEAUX 2003, Rome, Italy, September 9-12, 2003. Proceedings. Lecture Notes in Computer Science, vol. 2796, p. 2. Springer (2003). `https://doi.org/10.1007/978-3-540-45206-5_2`, `https://doi.org/10.1007/978-3-540-45206-5_2`

21. Coquand, T.: A completeness proof for geometrical logic. Logic, Methodology and Philosophy of Sciences (2005)

22. Coquand, T., Danielsson, N.A., Escardó, M.H., Norell, U., Xu, C.: Negative consistent axioms can be postulated without loss of canonicity (2013), `https://martinescardo.github.io/papers/negative-axioms.pdf`

23. Coquand, T., Jaber, G.: A note on forcing and type theory. Fundam. Informaticae **100**(1-4), 43–52 (2010). `https://doi.org/10.3233/FI-2010-262`, `https://doi.org/10.3233/FI-2010-262`

24. Coquand, T., Jaber, G.: A computational interpretation of forcing in type theory. In: Dybjer, P., Lindström, S., Palmgren, E., Sundholm, G. (eds.) Epistemology versus Ontology - Essays on the Philosophy and Foundations of Mathematics in Honour of Per Martin-Löf, Logic, Epistemology, and the Unity of Science, vol. 27, pp. 203–213. Springer (2012). `https://doi.org/10.1007/978-94-007-4435-6_10`, `https://doi.org/10.1007/978-94-007-4435-6_10`

25. Coquand, T., Ruch, F., Sattler, C.: Constructive sheaf models of type theory. Math. Struct. Comput. Sci. **31**(9), 979–1002 (2021). `https://doi.org/10.1017/S0960129521000359`, `https://doi.org/10.1017/S0960129521000359`

26. Coste, M., Lombardi, H., Roy, M.: Dynamical method in algebra: effective nullstellensätze. Ann. Pure Appl. Log. **111**(3), 203–256 (2001). `https://doi.org/10.1016/S0168-0072(01)00026-4`, `https://doi.org/10.1016/S0168-0072(01)00026-4`

27. Dora, J.D., Dicrescenzo, C., Duval, D.: About a new method for computing in algebraic number fields. In: European Conference on Computer Algebra (2). Lecture Notes in Computer Science, vol. 204, pp. 289–290. Springer (1985)

28. Duval, D., Reynaud, J.C.: Sketches and computation – ii: dynamic evaluation and applications. Mathematical Structures in Computer Science **4**(2), 239–271 (1994). `https://doi.org/10.1017/S096012950000044X`

29. Escardó, M., Xu, C.: A constructive manifestation of the Kleene-Kreisel continuous functionals. Ann. Pure Appl. Log. **167**(9), 770–793 (2016). `https://doi.org/10.1016/J.APAL.2016.04.011`, `https://doi.org/10.1016/j.apal.2016.04.011`

30. Escardó, M.H., da Rocha Paiva, B., Rahli, V., Tosun, A.: Internal effectful forcing in system T. In: Fernández, M. (ed.) 10th International Conference on Formal Structures for Computation and Deduction, FSCD 2025, July 14-20, 2025, Birmingham, UK. LIPIcs, vol. 337, pp. 19:1–19:17. Schloss Dagstuhl - Leibniz-Zentrum für Informatik (2025). `https://doi.org/10.4230/LIPICS.FSCD.2025.19`, `https://doi.org/10.4230/LIPIcs.FSCD.2025.19`

31. Escardó, M.H.: Continuity of Gödel's System T definable functionals via effectful forcing. Proceedings of the Twenty-ninth Conference on the Mathematical Foundations of Programming Semantics, MFPS 2013, New Orleans, LA, USA, June 23-25, 2013 (2013). `https://doi.org/10.1016/j.entcs.2013.09.010`, `https://doi.org/10.1016/j.entcs.2013.09.010`

32. Escardó, M.H., Xu, C.: The inconsistency of a brouwerian continuity principle with the Curry-Howard interpretation. 13th International Conference on Typed Lambda Calculi and Applications, TLCA 2015, July 1-3, 2015, Warsaw, Poland (2015). `https://doi.org/10.4230/LIPIcs.TLCA.2015.153`, `https://doi.org/10.4230/LIPIcs.TLCA.2015.153`

33. Fiore, M.P., Pitts, A.M., Steenkamp, S.C.: Quotients, inductive types, and quotient inductive types. Log. Methods Comput. Sci. **18**(2) (2022). `https://doi.org/10.46298/LMCS-18(2:15)2022`, `https://doi.org/10.46298/lmcs-18(2:15)2022`

34. Fujiwara, M., Kawai, T.: Equivalence of bar induction and bar recursion for continuous functions with continuous moduli. Ann. Pure Appl. Log. **170**(8), 867–890 (2019). `https://doi.org/10.1016/J.APAL.2019.04.001`, `https://doi.org/10.1016/j.apal.2019.04.001`

35. Gilbert, G., Cockx, J., Sozeau, M., Tabareau, N.: Definitional proof-irrelevance without K. Proc. ACM Program. Lang. **3**(POPL), 3:1–3:28 (2019). `https://doi.org/10.1145/3290316`, `https://doi.org/10.1145/3290316`

36. Girard, J.Y., Taylor, P., Lafont, Y.: Proofs and Types. Cambridge University Press, Cambridge (1989), http://www.worldcat.org/isbn/0521371813
37. Gratzer, D.: An inductive-recursive universe generic for small families. CoRR **abs/2202.05529** (2022), https://arxiv.org/abs/2202.05529
38. Gratzer, D., Kavvos, G.A., Nuyts, A., Birkedal, L.: Multimodal dependent type theory. In: Hermanns, H., Zhang, L., Kobayashi, N., Miller, D. (eds.) LICS '20: 35th Annual ACM/IEEE Symposium on Logic in Computer Science, Saarbrücken, Germany, July 8-11, 2020. pp. 492–506. ACM (2020). https://doi.org/10.1145/3373718.3394736, https://doi.org/10.1145/3373718.3394736
39. Gratzer, D., Shulman, M., Sterling, J.: Strict universes for grothendieck topoi. CoRR **abs/2202.12012** (2022), https://arxiv.org/abs/2202.12012
40. Griffin, T.: A formulae-as-types notion of control. In: Allen, F.E. (ed.) Conference Record of the Seventeenth Annual ACM Symposium on Principles of Programming Languages, San Francisco, California, USA, January 1990. pp. 47–58. ACM Press (1990). https://doi.org/10.1145/96709.96714, https://doi.org/10.1145/96709.96714
41. Hancock, P.G., McBride, C., Ghani, N., Malatesta, L., Altenkirch, T.: Small induction recursion. In: Hasegawa, M. (ed.) Typed Lambda Calculi and Applications, 11th International Conference, TLCA 2013, Eindhoven, The Netherlands, June 26-28, 2013. Proceedings. Lecture Notes in Computer Science, vol. 7941, pp. 156–172. Springer (2013). https://doi.org/10.1007/978-3-642-38946-7_13, https://doi.org/10.1007/978-3-642-38946-7_13
42. Kaposi, A.: Towards quotient inductive-inductive-recursive types. In: 29th International Conference on Types for Proofs and Programs, TYPES 2023. pp. 124–126 (2023), https://types2023.webs.upv.es/TYPES2023.pdf
43. Kaposi, A., Kovács, A., Altenkirch, T.: Constructing quotient inductive-inductive types. Proc. ACM Program. Lang. **3**(POPL), 2:1–2:24 (2019). https://doi.org/10.1145/3290315, https://doi.org/10.1145/3290315
44. Kiselyov, O., Shan, C.: Delimited continuations in operating systems. In: Kokinov, B.N., Richardson, D.C., Roth-Berghofer, T., Vieu, L. (eds.) Modeling and Using Context, 6th International and Interdisciplinary Conference, CONTEXT 2007, Roskilde, Denmark, August 20-24, 2007, Proceedings. Lecture Notes in Computer Science, vol. 4635, pp. 291–302. Springer (2007). https://doi.org/10.1007/978-3-540-74255-5_22, https://doi.org/10.1007/978-3-540-74255-5_22
45. Kleene, S.C.: Recursive Functionals and Quantifiers of Finite Types I. Transactions of the American Mathematical Society **91**(1), 1 (Apr 1959). https://doi.org/10.2307/1993145, https://www.jstor.org/stable/1993145?origin=crossref
46. Lombardi, H., Quitté, C., Yengui, I.: Hidden constructions in abstract algebra. VI. The theorem of Maroscia and Brewer & Costa. J. Pure Appl. Algebra **212**(7), 1575–1582 (2008). https://doi.org/10.1016/j.jpaa.2007.10.009, https://doi.org/10.1016/j.jpaa.2007.10.009
47. Mac Lane, S., Moerdijk, I.: Sheaves in Geometry and Logic a First Introduction to Topos Theory. Springer New York, New York, NY (1992), http://link.springer.com/book/10.1007/978-1-4612-0927-0
48. Mannaa, B., Coquand, T.: A sheaf model of the algebraic closure. In: CL&C. EPTCS, vol. 164, pp. 18–32 (2014)
49. Miquel, A.: Forcing as a program transformation. In: Proceedings of the 26th Annual IEEE Symposium on Logic in Computer Science, LICS 2011, June 21-24, 2011, Toronto, Ontario, Canada. pp. 197–206. IEEE Computer Society (2011). https://doi.org/10.1109/LICS.2011.47, https://doi.org/10.1109/LICS.2011.47

50. Palmgren, E.: From intuitionistic to point-free topology: on the foundation of homotopy theory. In: Logicism, intuitionism, and formalism, Synth. Libr., vol. 341, pp. 237–253. Springer, Dordrecht (2009). `https://doi.org/10.1007/978-1-4020-8926-8_12`, `https://doi.org/10.1007/978-1-4020-8926-8_12`

51. Paulin-Mohring, C.: Définitions Inductives en Théorie des Types. Accreditation to supervise research, Université Claude Bernard - Lyon I (Dec 1996), `https://theses.hal.science/tel-00431817`

52. Pédrot, P.: Russian constructivism in a prefascist theory. In: Hermanns, H., Zhang, L., Kobayashi, N., Miller, D. (eds.) LICS '20: 35th Annual ACM/IEEE Symposium on Logic in Computer Science, Saarbrücken, Germany, July 8-11, 2020. pp. 782–794. ACM (2020). `https://doi.org/10.1145/3373718.3394740`, `https://doi.org/10.1145/3373718.3394740`

53. Pédrot, P., Tabareau, N.: An effectful way to eliminate addiction to dependence. In: 32nd Annual ACM/IEEE Symposium on Logic in Computer Science, LICS 2017, Reykjavik, Iceland, June 20-23, 2017. pp. 1–12. IEEE Computer Society (2017). `https://doi.org/10.1109/LICS.2017.8005113`, `https://doi.org/10.1109/LICS.2017.8005113`

54. Pédrot, P., Tabareau, N.: The fire triangle: how to mix substitution, dependent elimination, and effects. Proc. ACM Program. Lang. **4**(POPL), 58:1–58:28 (2020). `https://doi.org/10.1145/3371126`, `https://doi.org/10.1145/3371126`

55. Poirier, H.: La vraie nature de l'intelligence. Science & Vie **1013**, 38–57 (February 2002)

56. Rahli, V., Bickford, M.: Validating brouwer's continuity principle for numbers using named exceptions. Math. Struct. Comput. Sci. **28**(6), 942–990 (2018). `https://doi.org/10.1017/S0960129517000172`, `https://doi.org/10.1017/S0960129517000172`

57. Rahli, V., Bickford, M., Cohen, L., Constable, R.L.: Bar induction is compatible with constructive type theory. J. ACM **66**(2), 13:1–13:35 (2019). `https://doi.org/10.1145/3305261`, `https://doi.org/10.1145/3305261`

58. Rahli, V., Bickford, M., Constable, R.L.: Bar induction: The good, the bad, and the ugly. In: 32nd Annual ACM/IEEE Symposium on Logic in Computer Science, LICS 2017, Reykjavik, Iceland, June 20-23, 2017. pp. 1–12. IEEE Computer Society (2017). `https://doi.org/10.1109/LICS.2017.8005074`, `https://doi.org/10.1109/LICS.2017.8005074`

59. Rijke, E., Shulman, M., Spitters, B.: Modalities in homotopy type theory. Log. Methods Comput. Sci. **16**(1) (2020). `https://doi.org/10.23638/LMCS-16(1:2)2020`, `https://doi.org/10.23638/LMCS-16(1:2)2020`

60. Serre, J.P.: Faisceaux algébriques cohérents. Ann. of Math. (2) **61**, 197–278 (1955). `https://doi.org/10.2307/1969915`, `https://doi.org/10.2307/1969915`

61. Sherman, B., Sciarappa, L., Chlipala, A., Carbin, M.: Computable decision making on the reals and other spaces: via partiality and nondeterminism. In: LICS. pp. 859–868. ACM (2018)

62. Sterling, J.: Higher order functions and brouwer's thesis. J. Funct. Program. **31**, e11 (2021). `https://doi.org/10.1017/S0956796821000095`, `https://doi.org/10.1017/S0956796821000095`

63. Sterling, J.: First Steps in Synthetic Tait Computability: The Objective Metatheory of Cubical Type Theory. Ph.D. thesis, Carnegie Mellon University, USA (2022). `https://doi.org/10.1184/R1/19632681.V1`, `https://doi.org/10.1184/r1/19632681.v1`

64. Streicher, T.: Universes in toposes. In: Crosilla, L., Schuster, P.M. (eds.) From sets and types to topology and analysis - Towards practicable foundations for constructive mathematics, Oxford logic guides, vol. 48. Oxford University Press (2005)
65. Troelstra, A., van Dalen, D.: Constructivism in Mathematics An Introduction, vol. 121. Elsevier (1988)
66. Univalent Foundations Program, T.: Homotopy Type Theory: Univalent Foundations of Mathematics. `https://homotopytypetheory.org/book`, Institute for Advanced Study (2013)
67. Werner, B.: Une Théorie des Constructions Inductives. Ph.D. thesis, Paris Diderot University, France (1994), `https://tel.archives-ouvertes.fr/tel-00196524`
68. Xia, L., Zakowski, Y., He, P., Hur, C., Malecha, G., Pierce, B.C., Zdancewic, S.: Interaction trees: representing recursive and impure programs in coq. Proc. ACM Program. Lang. 4(POPL), 51:1–51:32 (2020). `https://doi.org/10.1145/3371119`, `https://doi.org/10.1145/3371119`
69. Xu, C., Escardó, M.H.: A constructive model of uniform continuity. In: Hasegawa, M. (ed.) Typed Lambda Calculi and Applications, 11th International Conference, TLCA 2013, Eindhoven, The Netherlands, June 26-28, 2013. Proceedings. Lecture Notes in Computer Science, vol. 7941, pp. 236–249. Springer (2013). `https://doi.org/10.1007/978-3-642-38946-7_18`, `https://doi.org/10.1007/978-3-642-38946-7_18`

Deciding not to Decide
Sound and Complete Effect Inference in the Presence of Higher-Rank Polymorphism

Patrycja Balik, Szymon Jędras, and Piotr Polesiuk

University of Wrocław
{pbalik,sjedras,ppolesiuk}@cs.uni.wroc.pl

Abstract. Type-and-effect systems help the programmer to organize data and computational effects in a program. While for traditional type systems expressive variants with sophisticated inference algorithms have been developed and widely used in programming languages, type-and-effect systems did not yet gain widespread adoption. One reason for this is that type-and-effect systems are more complex and the existing inference algorithms make compromises between expressiveness, intuitiveness, and decidability. In this work, we present an effect inference algorithm for a type-and-effect system with subtyping, expressive higher-rank poly-morphism, and intuitive set-like semantics of effects. In order to deal with scoping issues of higher-rank polymorphism, we delay solving of effect constraints by transforming them into formulae of propositional logic. We prove soundness and completeness of our algorithm with re-spect to a declarative type-and-effect system. All the presented results have been formalized in the Rocq proof assistant, and the algorithm has been successfully used in the implementation of the Fram programming language.

Keywords: Type-and-effect systems · Higher-rank polymorphism · Effect reconstruction · Constraints · Algebraic type scheme.

1 Introduction

Type-and-effect systems [33,54] permit tracking information not just about the data in a program, but also the allowed behavior of computations. This informa-tion is especially important in languages with advanced control mechanisms, such as those featuring algebraic effect handlers [51]. Ideally, a programmer-facing type-and-effect system should be ergonomic, expressive, and intuitive.

In terms of ergonomics, one obstacle is that effect information tends to be quite large. Fortunately, this can be remedied with effect reconstruction, where the effect information omitted by the programmer can be automatically inferred. As for expressiveness, a usable effect system almost certainly needs a form of effect polymorphism. Finally, intuitiveness requires that the representation of effects

© The Author(s) 2026
R. Krebbers (Ed.): ESOP 2026, LNCS 16501, pp. 104–134, 2026.
https://doi.org/10.1007/978-3-032-22720-1_5

matches the user's understanding of effect information. Many effect systems described in the literature [33,54,43,67,15,39,9] represent this information as a set of possible behaviors. This design choice leads to both an elegant theory and intuitive semantics of types with effects for the programmer, but is not always easy to implement in practice.

A common approach is to use effect rows [36,29,34,30,60] to approximate sets of effects. Effect rows can be thought of as a list of behaviors, potentially terminated by a polymorphic row variable. This technique can be easily combined with the Hindley-Milner algorithm, which is the gold standard for type reconstruction, and grants some additional expressiveness in the form of ML-polymorphism. The key advantage of using rows is that unification is decidable and unitary [61,53], making the resulting reconstruction algorithm decidable. Moreover, since it is a fairly lightweight addition to the Hindley-Milner algorithm, it composes well with other extensions.

One such extension is rank-N polymorphism, which has been observed by Xie *et al.* [65] to be very useful in the context of algebraic effects. For example, consider a higher-order function that opens a file for the duration of a computation received as its argument. A naive approach could yield us the type $\forall \beta.$`Filepath` $\rightarrow$ (`File` $\rightarrow_{\mathtt{IO} \cdot \beta}$ `Unit`) $\rightarrow_{\mathtt{IO} \cdot \beta}$ `Unit`. The effect $\mathtt{IO} \cdot \beta$ associated with the argument and the entire function says that input/output effects can be performed, as well as any effects described by the polymorphic variable β. However, this type does not guarantee that the file handle will not be used after it is closed. For example, the argument could store the handle in some data structure for later use. Taking inspiration from Haskell's ST monad [64] and the work of Xie *et al.*, we can use rank-2 polymorphism to restrict the scope of the handle, by rewriting the type as $\forall \beta.$`Filepath` $\rightarrow$ ($\forall \alpha.$`File` $\alpha \rightarrow_{\alpha \cdot \beta}$ `Unit`) $\rightarrow_{\mathtt{IO} \cdot \beta}$ `Unit`. This time, the argument is polymorphic in the effect α, which is associated with a particular file handle. Since all operations on `File` α have the effect α, they cannot be used outside this function.

The considered example glosses over a certain difficulty with using effect rows. We attempt to perform a concatenation of the variables α and β, but a row cannot contain two row variables. One way of salvaging the ability to express this is to make α of a different kind (of atomic effects, which are elements of effect rows). However, if we do that, the unification of rows stops being unitary, somewhat compromising type and effect reconstruction. Therefore, while effect rows and rank-N polymorphism are easy to combine in a single language, the end result is not as expressive as one could expect.

The authors of the Flix programming language [38] chose a different approach. Effects in Flix are set-like, with operations like union, intersection and difference available as effect constructors. Such a system is highly expressive, and admits a decidable inference algorithm via boolean unification [39]. However, Flix does not currently support any form of higher-rank polymorphism.

Effect inference for set-like effects was thoroughly studied in the context of static analysis [55,58,42,44,22,46]. Notably, Talpin and Jouvelot [54] proposed an algorithm that transforms the problem of effect inference into a corresponding problem of satisfying subeffect constraints, which, for set-like effects, behave like set inclusion. Following Jouvelot and Gifford [33], their algorithm implements a variant of ML-polymorphism with algebraic type schemes of the form $\forall \alpha_1 \ldots \alpha_n. [\Omega]\ \tau$, which store a set of constraints Ω together with universally quantified variables $\alpha_1 \ldots \alpha_n$. This allows for solving constraints involving polymorphic variables to be delayed to the point at which the scheme is instantiated. Another interesting observation made in this area by Nielson and Nielson [45] is that subtyping induced by subeffecting does not affect the shape of types. They propose a two-stage approach to type-and-effect inference, where effects are reconstructed once the type shapes are already known from the previous phase. Unfortunately, solutions introduced in this path of research were designed for static analysis internal to the compiler, and not exposed to the user directly. As a result, they had no need to support rank-N polymorphism, which requires programmer-provided annotations.

In this paper, we present a sound and complete effect reconstruction algorithm that needs minimal annotations to aid ergonomics, supports higher-rank polymorphism for expressiveness, and enjoys an intuitive set-like representation of effects. Though none of the previously existing solutions fully satisfy these requirements, we base our work on the results originating in the area of static analysis. Our algorithm is based on the work of Talpin and Jouvelot with its algebraic type schemes, modified to use the two-stage approach. The main difficulty arose from extending these techniques to support rank-N polymorphism.

Widespread implementations of rank-N polymorphism tend to require some annotations to regain decidability of inference. In those algorithms, whenever higher-rank polymorphism is required, the annotations include, at the very least, both the polymorphic variable *binding*, as well as each *bound occurrence*. In contrast, our algorithm allows for rank-N effect polymorphism where only the quantifiers have to be indicated, while the bound occurrences can be inferred. This means that the annotation of the argument in the scheme can be simplified from $\forall \alpha. (\_ \rightarrow_\alpha \_) \rightarrow_\alpha \_$ to just $\forall \alpha. \_$. As most programmers are not used to programming with effect systems at all, requiring minimal amount of programmer-supplied effect information is fairly important for encouraging greater adoption.

Designing an algorithm that supports the explosive mixture of subeffecting and rank-N polymorphism with such minimal effect annotations is challenging due to issues related to ubiquitous variable binding and a lack of the principal type property in our setting. As an example, suppose that we have a function f known to be of type $(\texttt{Int} \rightarrow_{\texttt{IO}} \texttt{Int}) \rightarrow_{\texttt{DB}} \texttt{Int}$. Now, consider the following function definition.

```
let g (h : ∀α. Int →_ Int) = h (f h)
```

Two possible different types for the function g are $(\forall \alpha.\ \texttt{Int} \rightarrow_\alpha \texttt{Int}) \rightarrow_{\texttt{DB}} \texttt{Int}$ or $(\forall \alpha.\ \texttt{Int} \rightarrow_{\texttt{IO}} \texttt{Int}) \rightarrow_{\texttt{IO·DB}} \texttt{Int}$, but neither is more general than the other. Indeed, no principal type exists for g at all.

When further definitions using g are added, it may turn out that only one of these solutions is valid for the complete program. Unfortunately, as we are processing the annotation for h, that information is not available, and we do not even know whether the wildcard contains α or not. While algebraic type schemes provide a mechanism to delay the solving of some constraints, it is not enough to delay decisions involving higher-rank polymorphic variables, since they are confined to a smaller scope than the entire scheme of a let-bound identifier.

In our solution to this problem we introduce two new mechanisms. First, we introduce effect guards to delay the decision whether a locally-bound variable should appear in a given effect. Second, when leaving the scope of a quantified variable, we transform constraints involving this variable into formulae, which do not contain effect variables, and can therefore be solved later.

Our contributions can be summarized as follows.

- In Section 3 we propose a sound and complete algorithm for effect inference in the presence of higher-rank polymorphism. Our algorithm works even if we replace rank-N with the more general System F polymorphism.
- In Section 4 we show that the problem of effect inference is decidable even when algebraic type schemes are replaced by simple type schemes without subeffect constraints.
- As the considered problem is prone to subtle variable scoping issues, we have taken care to formalize all the presented results in the Rocq proof assistant[1]. In Section 5 we briefly describe the design decisions we made in our development.
- We have successfully implemented the algorithm as a part[2] of Fram—a realistic programming language with algebraic effects [25]. In Section 6 we summarize the insights that enable such a practical implementation.

The considered type system and proposed algorithm are quite large, so we focus on the most important ideas in the main body of the paper. The full definitions can be found in the technical report [4].

2   Simplified Setting

Before we present a full algorithm, let us start with a simpler problem of effect inference in a language with ML-style effect polymorphism, but without any form of rank-N polymorphism. In this section we present a variation of a well-established solution based on the early work of Talpin and Jouvelot [54] that lays down the foundation for our algorithm presented in the later sections. The algorithm presented in this section differs from the original formulation, as it has been adjusted to better fit our setting and adapted to the two-stage approach proposed by Nielson and Nielson [45].

2.1   Syntax

The syntax of the simplified calculus is presented in Figure 1. The calculus is a standard lambda calculus extended with the standard polymorphic let-binding.

---

[1] https://doi.org/10.5281/zenodo.18197463
[2] https://github.com/fram-lang/dbl/releases/tag/esop26

$$e ::= x \mid \lambda x : T.e \mid e\,e \mid \texttt{let}\ x = e\ \texttt{in}\ e \qquad\qquad \text{(expressions)}$$

$$T ::= \alpha^\mathsf{T} \mid T \to_E T \qquad\qquad \text{(syntactic types)}$$

$$E ::= \alpha^\mathsf{E} \mid \iota \mid E \cdot E \mid \_ \qquad\qquad \text{(syntactic effects)}$$

$$\tau ::= \alpha^\mathsf{T} \mid \tau \to_\varepsilon \tau \qquad\qquad \text{(types)}$$

$$\varepsilon ::= \alpha^\mathsf{E} \mid \iota \mid \varepsilon \cdot \varepsilon \qquad\qquad \text{(effects)}$$

$$\Omega ::= \overline{\varepsilon <: \varepsilon} \qquad\qquad \text{(sets of constraints)}$$

$$\sigma ::= \forall \Delta^\mathsf{E}.\,[\Omega]\,\tau \qquad\qquad \text{(type schemes)}$$

Fig. 1. The syntax of the simplified calculus.

Lambda abstractions are annotated with *syntactic types*, which are built from type variables (α^T) and arrows ($T_1 \to_E T_2$) annotated with *syntactic effects* (E), which in turn are built from effect variables (α^E), the pure effect (ι), joins ($E_1 \cdot E_2$), and wildcards (_). We use the same metavariables α, β, γ for both type and effect variables, but we distinguish them by a kind annotation. By convention, we omit the kind annotation when it is clear from the context.

Since syntactic effects contain wildcards, we introduce separate syntactic categories of (internal) types and effects used by the type system, with a similar grammar, except without wildcards. Moreover, we consider two internal effects equal if they can be proven equivalent using the laws of an idempotent, commutative monoid with join ($\cdot$) as the monoidal operation, and the pure effect (ι) as the neutral element. This guarantees a set-like semantics of effects. The syntax of constraints and type schemes will be described later in this section.

2.2   Scopes and Substitutions

We have found that in the presence of higher-rank polymorphism, algorithms as well as their metatheories are prone to errors related to variable binding, such as variable escape or variable capture. Therefore, in the technical presentation of this paper as well as in the accompanying formalization we are very precise about the scopes of variables. To do so, we use the functorial approach to representing syntax [24]. This is crucial for our Rocq formalization. While in the paper we take a more traditional approach, some issues should be explained in the paper.

First, each syntactic category is in fact a family of sets of terms indexed by sets of variables that are allowed to occur free. For instance, the set of types is in fact a family of sets $\{\mathsf{Type}(A, B)\}_{A,B}$ indexed by a set A of possibly free effect variables, and a set B of possibly free type variables. In order to avoid escaping variables, each time when we write a term (*e.g.*, a type), there is an explicit or implicit object that "binds" these possibly free variables. For example, in case of a typing relation, these variables are bound by the typing environment.

A *substitution* is a function (or tuple of functions) from *all* potentially free variables to the substituted terms. In the case of types, a substitution θ is a pair

Effect Matching

$$\boxed{\Delta \vdash E \sim \varepsilon}$$

$$\frac{}{\Delta \vdash \alpha^{\mathsf{E}} \sim \alpha^{\mathsf{E}}} \qquad \frac{}{\Delta \vdash \iota \sim \iota} \qquad \frac{\Delta \vdash E_1 \sim \varepsilon_1 \qquad \Delta \vdash E_2 \sim \varepsilon_2}{\Delta \vdash E_1 \cdot E_2 \sim \varepsilon_1 \cdot \varepsilon_2} \qquad \frac{}{\Delta \vdash \_ \sim \varepsilon}$$

Type Matching

$$\boxed{\Delta \vdash T \sim \tau}$$

$$\frac{}{\Delta \vdash \alpha^{\mathsf{T}} \sim \alpha^{\mathsf{T}}} \qquad \frac{\Delta \vdash T_1 \sim \tau_1 \qquad \Delta \vdash T_2 \sim \tau_2 \qquad \Delta \vdash E \sim \varepsilon}{\Delta \vdash T_1 \to_E T_2 \sim \tau_1 \to_\varepsilon \tau_2}$$

Fig. 2. Type and effect matching.

of functions $\theta_e \colon A_1 \to \mathsf{Effect}(A_2)$ and $\theta_t \colon B_1 \to \mathsf{Type}(A_2, B_2)$ that substitute for effect variables and type variables respectively. Note that the effects and types returned by θ_e and θ_t are themselves indexed by new sets of potentially free variables A_2 and B_2, which need not be related to the domains of the functions, A_1 and B_1, in any way. We write $\theta^* \tau$ for a capture-avoiding simultaneous substitution for all free variables in τ according to θ.

When we use a term, for instance $\tau \in \mathsf{Type}(A, B)$, in a context where more variables are available, *e.g.*, as an element of $\mathsf{Type}(X \uplus A, B)$, we have to apply a substitution $\iota_2 \colon A \to X \uplus A$ that injects the old variables into a larger set. While in the formalization we keep this precise, in the paper we omit obvious projections, injections, and permutations to reduce noise. Similarly, we omit identity-like parts of substitutions whenever we substitute only for a subset of the available variables. For instance, when substituting ε for α in $\tau \in \mathsf{Type}(\{\alpha\} \uplus A, B)$, we write $\{\alpha \mapsto \varepsilon\}^* \tau$, which resembles the standard notation for substitution[3].

2.3   Declarative Type System

Here we present a type-and-effect system, which serves as a specification for the effect inference algorithm presented later in this section. We call this system *declarative*, because it doesn't need to be algorithmic (we allow non-syntax directed rules, and guessing data which are not part of the input), but it should be simple and intuitive. We start from some auxiliary relations. Due to space constraints, we omit most of the obvious rules, and focus on presenting the main ideas and the most notable rules. We refer the reader to technical report [4] for the full definition of the system.

Type and effect matching. A programmer may omit some effect annotations using wildcard syntactic effects. The declarative system "guesses" the internal effects that should appear in place of these wildcards. We accomplish this with the

---

[3] We decided to use this bind-like notation $(\{\alpha \mapsto \varepsilon\}^* \tau)$ instead of the standard notation $(\tau\{\alpha \mapsto \varepsilon\})$ in order to keep the notation consistent.

effect matching relation $\Delta \vdash E \sim \varepsilon$ defined in Figure 2. The relation uses a type environment (Δ), which keeps track of the available type and effect variables in the current scope, and says that the syntactic effect E matches the internal effect ε. As mentioned in Section 2.2, we implicitly assume that both syntactic and internal effects are well-formed in Δ. For instance, in the first rule we implicitly assume that $\alpha^{\mathsf{E}} \in \Delta$, but we omit such premises to avoid clutter.

The definition of effect matching consists of three obvious structural rules, and the last rule saying that a wildcard can be matched by any (well-formed) effect. On top of this relation we define *type matching*. Since we assume that the types were inferred in the previous phase, the definition of this relation consists of structural rules only.

Constraints, subeffecting, and subtyping. The key feature of the presented type system is that it allows for abstracting over subeffecting constraints of the form $\varepsilon_1 <: \varepsilon_2$. Therefore, the *subeffecting relation* (with the judgement of the form $\Delta; \Omega \vdash \varepsilon_1 <: \varepsilon_2$) uses another environment Ω which is a set of abstracted subeffecting constraints. For a fixed Δ and Ω, the subeffecting relation $\Delta; \Omega \vdash \varepsilon_1 <: \varepsilon_2$ is defined as the least preorder on effects containing Ω, with $\cdot$ as the semilattice join, and ι as the least element. The full definition can be found in the Appendix. Using this relation we can also define the constraint set entailment relation $\Delta; \Omega \vdash \Omega'$ by ensuring that subeffecting holds for every constraint in Ω'. Moreover, subeffecting induces subtyping in the standard way: the definition of $\Delta; \Omega \vdash \tau_1 <: \tau_2$ consists of the standard structural rules with contravariant left-hand-side of the arrow type.

Type schemes. As observed by Jouvelot and Gifford, a reasonable effect reconstruction algorithm may be unable to solve generated constraints while examining a let-binding [33]. To address this problem, they propose *algebraic type schemes* to be attached to let-bound variables. In their approach a type scheme abstracts constraints that cannot be solved yet, and requires that these constraints are satisfied at the place of the scheme instantiation.

As the last ingredient of the syntax presented in Figure 1 our type schemes follow this path. A type scheme $\forall \Delta^{\mathsf{E}}. [\Omega]\, \tau$ abstracts a set of effect variables Δ^{E} and remembers a set of subeffecting constraints Ω that may use variables bound in Δ^{E}. We write just τ when both Δ^{E} and Ω are empty. Since we assume a two-stage approach to type-and-effect inference, type schemes do not bind type variables: type polymorphism can be handled in the previous phase, and expressed using rank-N polymorphism introduced in Section 3.

Typing relation. The definition of the typing relation is given in Figure 3. In the variable rule, the scheme assigned to a variable is immediately instantiated with any substitution θ that satisfies the constraints attached to the scheme. In the λ-abstraction rule, the variable is annotated with a syntactic type T, so the actual (monomorphic) type τ_1 assigned to the variable must match the annotation. As usual for type-and-effect systems, the λ-abstraction is pure, but the effect of the body is remembered in the arrow type. The application rule is

Typing $\boxed{\Delta;\Omega;\Gamma \vdash e : \tau \; / \; \varepsilon}$

$$\frac{\Gamma(x) = \forall\Delta'.\,[\Omega']\,\tau \qquad \Delta;\Omega \vdash \theta^*\Omega'}{\Delta;\Omega;\Gamma \vdash x : \theta^*\tau \; / \; \iota} \qquad \frac{\Delta \vdash T \sim \tau_1 \qquad \Delta;\Omega;\Gamma, x : \tau_1 \vdash e : \tau_2 \; / \; \varepsilon}{\Delta;\Omega;\Gamma \vdash \lambda x : T.\,e : \tau_1 \rightarrow_\varepsilon \tau_2 \; / \; \iota}$$

$$\frac{\Delta;\Omega;\Gamma \vdash e_1 : \tau_2 \rightarrow_\varepsilon \tau_1 \; / \; \varepsilon \qquad \Delta;\Omega;\Gamma \vdash e_2 : \tau_2 \; / \; \varepsilon}{\Delta;\Omega;\Gamma \vdash e_1\, e_2 : \tau_1 \; / \; \varepsilon}$$

$$\frac{\begin{array}{c}\Delta, \Delta_g^{\mathsf{E}};\Omega, \Omega_g;\Gamma \vdash e_1 : \tau_1 \; / \; \iota \\ \Delta;\Omega;\Gamma, x : \forall\Delta_g^{\mathsf{E}}.\,[\Omega_g]\,\tau_1 \vdash e_2 : \tau_2 \; / \; \varepsilon\end{array}}{\Delta;\Omega;\Gamma \vdash \mathtt{let}\ x = e_1\ \mathtt{in}\ e_2 : \tau_2 \; / \; \varepsilon} \qquad \frac{\begin{array}{c}\Delta;\Omega;\Gamma \vdash e : \tau \; / \; \varepsilon \\ \Delta;\Omega \vdash \tau <: \tau' \\ \Delta;\Omega \vdash \varepsilon <: \varepsilon'\end{array}}{\Delta;\Omega;\Gamma \vdash e : \tau' \; / \; \varepsilon'}$$

Fig. 3. Typing relation.

standard. The let-rule resembles the one known from ML-style polymorphism, but deserves additional explanation. First, it allows to implicitly abstract over some effect variables Δ_g^{E} and constraints Ω_g in the first expression. Moreover, while it allows polymorphic definitions, it enforces *purity restriction* [3] in order to ensure that the type system is sound. The last rule is the standard subsumption rule, which allows to change the type and effect of an expression to a supertype and supereffect.

It can be shown that the presented type system is sound wrt the standard operational semantics (not presented here) using the standard methods of logical relations [2,8] or progress and preservation [63,35]. However, these results lie outside the scope of this paper, and therefore we focus our attention on the algorithmic effect inference.

2.4   Algorithmic Effect Inference

The effect inference algorithm proposed by Talpin and Jouvelot [54] is a modification of the well-known Hindley-Milner algorithm $\mathcal{W}$ [40]. In the algorithm $\mathcal{W}$ unknown types are represented by unification variables, which may be instantiated by the unification procedure. Similarly, the presented algorithm uses unification variables to represent unknown effects, and such variables may be instantiated by solving subeffecting constraints. While for convenience in our implementation we use a separate syntactic category for unification variables, in the presentation in this paper, as well as in the formalization, we use regular effect variables for that purpose, but we explicitly keep track which variables were generated.

To be more precise, when the algorithm examines some term defined over the set of effect variables Δ, it returns a tuple $(\Delta_g; \ldots)$ whose other elements are defined over the set of effect variables $\Delta \uplus \Delta_g$. Let us start with some auxiliary functions, which correspond to the auxiliary relations of the declarative system.

```
tr_effect(α) = (∅; α)            tr_effect(E₁ · E₂) =
tr_effect(ι) = (∅; ι)               let (Δ₁; ε₁) = tr_effect(E₁) in
tr_effect(_) =                      let (Δ₂; ε₂) = tr_effect(E₂) in
  fresh α in ({α}; α)               (Δ₁ ⊎ Δ₂; ε₁ · ε₂)
```

Fig. 4. Translation of syntactic effects.

Type and effect matching. Effect matching is realized by the function that translates a syntactic effect to the internal representation and is given in Figure 4. The function is defined by structural recursion on syntactic effects, and returns a tuple containing generated effect variables and translated effects. Most cases are straightforward and just replace each syntactic effect construct with its corresponding internal effect construct. The only interesting case is for wildcards, where the function "guesses" the effect that should be returned. This "guessing" is realized by generating a fresh variable, similarly to how type guessing is implemented in the original algorithm $\mathcal{W}$.

Using effect matching, we define the function `tr_type`, which translates types. The definition consists of structural cases only, so we omit it in our presentation. Precise definition of this, as well as other functions can be found in the technical report [4].

Constraints, subeffecting, and subtyping. Subtyping is realized by a function `subtype` that collects subeffecting constraints that need to be satisfied in order to make the relevant subtyping judgment hold. For arrow types this function is defined as follows.

```
subtype(τ′₁ →_{ε₁} τ₁; τ′₂ →_{ε₂} τ₂) =
  let Ω₁ = subtype(τ′₂; τ′₁) in
  let Ω₂ = subtype(τ₁; τ₂) in
  Ω₁ ∪ Ω₂ ∪ {ε₁ <: ε₂}
```

Since there are no effect binders in types, the other cases are straightforward and omitted in the presentation.

The algorithm. Now we are in a position to present the sound and complete effect inference algorithm for the simplified problem of this section. The algorithm is presented in Figure 5. The function `infer` takes the typing environment and an expression and returns tuple of the form $(\Delta; \tau; \varepsilon; \Omega)$ containing a set of generated variables that may appear in other components of the tuple: inferred type, effect, and the set of constraints that should be satisfied to make the typing judgement hold. The function is defined by a structural recursion on the expression.

In the variable case, its scheme $(\forall \Delta_1. [\Omega_1] \tau)$ is instantiated with fresh effect variables. Since variables introduced by opening a binder are always fresh by convention, it is enough to return the set Δ_1 as the generated variables, together

```
infer($\Gamma$; $x$) =
  let ($\forall\Delta_1.[\Omega_1]\,\tau$) = $\Gamma(x)$ in
  ($\Delta_1$; $\tau$; $\iota$; $\Omega_1$)

infer($\Gamma$; $\lambda x : T.e$) =
  let ($\Delta_1$; $\tau_1$) = tr_type($T$) in
  let ($\Delta_2$; $\tau_2$; $\varepsilon$; $\Omega$) = infer($\Gamma, x : \tau_1$; $e$) in
  ($\Delta_1 \uplus \Delta_2$; $\tau_1 \to_\varepsilon \tau_2$; $\iota$; $\Omega$)

infer($\Gamma$; $e_1\,e_2$) =
  let ($\Delta_1$; $\tau_1$; $\varepsilon_1$; $\Omega_1$) = infer($\Gamma$; $e_1$) in
  match $\tau_1$ with
  | $\tau_a \to_\varepsilon \tau_v$ =>
    let ($\Delta_2$; $\tau_2$; $\varepsilon_2$; $\Omega_2$) = infer($\Gamma$; $e_2$) in
    let $\Omega_s$ = subtype($\tau_2$; $\tau_a$) in
    ($\Delta_1 \uplus \Delta_2$; $\tau_v$; $\varepsilon_1 \cdot \varepsilon_2 \cdot \varepsilon$; $\Omega_1 \cup \Omega_2 \cup \Omega_s$)
  | _ => fail

infer($\Gamma$; let $x$ = $e_1$ in $e_2$) =
  let ($\Delta_1$; $\tau_1$; $\varepsilon_1$; $\Omega_1$) = infer($\Gamma$; $e_1$) in
  infer($\Gamma, x : \forall\Delta_1.[\Omega_1 \cup \{\varepsilon_1 <: \iota\}]\,\tau_1$; $e_2$)
```

Fig. 5. The effect inference algorithm for the simplified problem.

with the type τ and the pure effect. In the declarative system, the constraints Ω_1 needs to be satisfied, so the algorithm includes Ω_1 in the returned tuple.

The type annotation for the λ-abstraction argument needs to be translated to the internal representation and this process may generate new variables (Δ_1). The recursive call to the body is performed in the context where these variables are available and may also generate new variables (Δ_2). Both sets Δ_1 and Δ_2 are combined in the final result. The case for function application is standard and as usual for systems with subtyping, allows expressions of smaller type in the argument position. Note that thanks to two-stage approach, subtype-checking generates only subeffecting constraints. These constraints can be propagated in the result tuple, instead of solving them immediately.

Now we focus on the let-binding case that introduces effect polymorphism into the language. For the simplified calculus it is surprisingly simple: all variables and constraints generated during the first recursive call are abstracted and put into the algebraic type scheme. The constraint set in the scheme is extended with $\varepsilon_1 <: \iota$ in order to ensure that the expression e_1 is pure.

Remark 1. In the presented algorithm, we generalize all the variables generated during type-checking of the body of the let-binding. This differs from the original presentation of Talpin-Jouvelot algorithm as well as classical Hindley-Milner algorithm, where only the variables that do not escape through the environment are generalized. We can do so, because (a) our algorithm doesn't return any substitution and (b) all generated constraints can be included in the type scheme, so generated variables have no means to escape through the environment. In the algorithm presented in the next section, the condition (b) will be no longer true, so an additional step of constraint factorization will be required. Interestingly, the classical Hindley-Milner algorithm can be presented in the style of the algorithm from this section with an additional step of factorizing substitution into its kernel and additional renaming. However, the details are outside the scope of this paper.

The presented algorithm is sound and complete with respect to the declarative type system, which can be stated formally by the following two theorems.

Theorem 1 (Soundness). *For an expression e defined over the set of type variables Δ, if $\mathtt{infer}(\Gamma; e) = (\Delta'; \tau; \varepsilon; \Omega)$, then $\Delta, \Delta'; \Omega; \Gamma \vdash e : \tau \mathbin{/} \varepsilon$.*

Theorem 2 (Completeness). *If $\Delta; \Omega; \Gamma \vdash e : \tau \mathbin{/} \varepsilon$, then $\mathtt{infer}(\Gamma; e) = (\Delta'; \tau'; \varepsilon'; \Omega')$ for some Δ', τ', ε', and Ω'. Moreover, there exists a substitution θ that maps effect variables from Δ' to effects over Δ, such that $\Delta; \Omega \vdash \theta^* \Omega'$, $\Delta; \Omega \vdash \theta^* \tau' <: \tau$, and $\Delta; \Omega \vdash \theta^* \varepsilon' <: \varepsilon$.*

3   Effect Inference with Higher-Rank Polymorphism

A major increase in difficulty arises when we introduce two changes into the underlying type system: higher-rank polymorphism announced in the introduction, and restriction of constraints that can be included in type schemes. Both changes are motivated by practical reasons.

Higher-rank polymorphism. Usually, practical type systems with type reconstruction restrict the expressiveness of parametric polymorphism. For instance, the Hindley-Milner type system allows only polymorphic types in the prenex form, and its more liberal extension to rank-N, distinguishes between monomorphic types and polymorphic type schemes, and allows polymorphic variables to be instantiated with monomorphic types only. Since we use two-stage approach, we assume that the types are already inferred, so decisions on particular restrictions are left to the designer of the underlying type system (without effects). Such decisions seem to be orthogonal to the problem of effect inference, so for simplicity we extend the system with a general form of polymorphism in the style of System F. We extend the grammar of expressions, syntactic types, and types as follows.

$$
\begin{aligned}
e &::= \ldots \mid \Lambda\alpha^{\mathsf{T}}.e \mid \Lambda\alpha^{\mathsf{E}}.e \mid e\,[T] \mid e\,[E] &&\text{(expressions)}\\
T &::= \ldots \mid \forall\alpha^{\mathsf{T}}.T \mid \forall\alpha^{\mathsf{E}}.T &&\text{(syntactic types)}\\
\tau &::= \ldots \mid \forall\alpha^{\mathsf{T}}.\tau \mid \forall\alpha^{\mathsf{E}}.\tau &&\text{(types)}
\end{aligned}
$$

Type Matching $\boxed{\Delta \vdash T \sim \tau}$

$$\frac{\Delta, \alpha^{\mathsf{T}} \vdash T \sim \tau}{\Delta \vdash \forall \alpha^{\mathsf{T}}.T \sim \forall \alpha^{\mathsf{T}}.\tau} \qquad \frac{\Delta, \alpha^{\mathsf{E}} \vdash T \sim \tau}{\Delta \vdash \forall \alpha^{\mathsf{E}}.T \sim \forall \alpha^{\mathsf{E}}.\tau}$$

Subtyping $\boxed{\Delta; \Omega \vdash \tau <: \tau}$

$$\frac{\Delta, \alpha^{\mathsf{T}}; \Omega \vdash \tau_1 <: \tau_2}{\Delta; \Omega \vdash \forall \alpha^{\mathsf{T}}.\tau_1 <: \forall \alpha^{\mathsf{T}}.\tau_2} \qquad \frac{\Delta, \alpha^{\mathsf{E}}; \Omega \vdash \tau_1 <: \tau_2}{\Delta; \Omega \vdash \forall \alpha^{\mathsf{E}}.\tau_1 <: \forall \alpha^{\mathsf{E}}.\tau_2}$$

Typing $\boxed{\Delta; \Gamma; \Omega \vdash e : \tau \,/\, \varepsilon}$

$$\frac{\Delta, \alpha^{\mathsf{T}}; \Omega; \Gamma \vdash e : \tau \,/\, \iota}{\Delta; \Omega; \Gamma \vdash \Lambda \alpha^{\mathsf{T}}.e : \forall \alpha^{\mathsf{T}}.\tau \,/\, \iota} \qquad \frac{\Delta, \alpha^{\mathsf{E}}; \Omega; \Gamma \vdash e : \tau \,/\, \iota}{\Delta; \Omega; \Gamma \vdash \Lambda \alpha^{\mathsf{E}}.e : \forall \alpha^{\mathsf{E}}.\tau \,/\, \iota}$$

$$\frac{\Delta; \Omega; \Gamma \vdash e : \forall \alpha^{\mathsf{T}}.\tau \,/\, \varepsilon \quad \Delta \vdash T \sim \tau'}{\Delta; \Omega; \Gamma \vdash e \,[T] : \{\alpha \mapsto \tau'\}^* \tau \,/\, \varepsilon} \qquad \frac{\Delta; \Omega; \Gamma \vdash e : \forall \alpha^{\mathsf{E}}.\tau \,/\, \varepsilon \quad \Delta \vdash E \sim \varepsilon'}{\Delta; \Omega; \Gamma \vdash e \,[E] : \{\alpha \mapsto \varepsilon'\}^* \tau \,/\, \varepsilon}$$

Fig. 6. New inference rules for explicit polymorphism.

Types and syntactic types are extended with polymorphic quantifiers, that can abstract both type and effect variables. Places where such polymorphic type is introduced or eliminated are explicitly marked in the syntax of expressions by a type or effect λ-abstraction and application. The type application ($e \,[T]$) contains syntactic type, as it contains complete information inferred by a previous type-inference phase and additionally may contain effects provided by the user. Similarly, in the effect application ($e \,[E]$), the syntactic effect may be just a wildcard, but it can be also more precise.

The new constructs come with new inference rules presented in Figure 6. The new matching and subtyping rules are structural, but since they extend the type environment (Δ) in the premise, their presence has serious consequence: wildcards under the quantifier $\forall \alpha^{\mathsf{E}}.T$ can be matched with effects containing α^{E}. The new typing rules are mostly standard, with a minor exception that in the application rules the matching relation is used in order to translate syntactic representation of type or effect to the internal one.

Type schemes revisited. The algebraic type schemes ($\forall \Delta.\,[\Omega]\,\tau$) from the previous section allowed abstracting any set of constraints Ω. While this decision led to a simple, sound, and complete effect inference algorithm, the obtained system is impractical and counter-intuitive. The main reason is that the type scheme may abstract contradictory constraints, *e.g.*, $\mathrm{IO} <: \iota$, delaying reporting programming errors to unexpected moments. As an extreme case, a mistake in a library function may be reported to the user of the library, but not to the developer.

In order to avoid such strange behavior, we should restrict somehow the constraints that can be included in a type scheme. Such a restriction should (a) disallow contradictory constraints and (b) be intuitive to the programmer. One could say that the Holy Grail would be disallowing constraints at all, and using type schemes of the form $\forall \Delta.\, \tau$ like in the classical Hindley-Milner type system. In Section 4 we show that with such a restriction we can still obtain a sound and complete algorithm, but the price we pay seems to be unacceptable.

In this section we propose another restriction. We allow only constraints in the form of upper-bounds of effect variables bound by the scheme. Formally, the scope-aware definition of valid type scheme is the following.

$$\mathsf{UB}_\Delta(\Delta') \triangleq \{\alpha <: \varepsilon \mid \alpha \in \Delta' \wedge \varepsilon \in \mathsf{Effect}(\Delta \uplus \Delta')\}$$

$$\mathsf{ValidScheme}(\Delta) \triangleq \{\forall \Delta'.\, [\Omega]\, \tau \mid \forall (\varepsilon_1 <: \varepsilon_2) \in \Omega.\, (\varepsilon_1 <: \varepsilon_2) \in \mathsf{UB}_\Delta(\Delta')\}$$

For the purpose of this section we assume that the type schemes assigned to let-bound variables are valid.

Upper-bound constraints are never contradictory, because they are trivially satisfied when we substitute pure effects for variables bound by the scheme. Moreover, type schemes with upper-bound constraints can give a quite precise information about function behavior, as in the following example.

Example 1. Assume we have a function `callLater : (Unit` $\to_{\mathtt{IO}}$ `Unit)` $\to_{\mathtt{DB}}$ `Unit` that registers the given function is some data structure (effect `DB`) for calling it later, where the effect `IO` is available. Consider the following function.

```
let callNowOrLater now f =
  if now then f ()
  else callLater f
```

It can accept a function with the `IO` effect, but there is nothing wrong in passing a pure function. In the latter case, the call to `callNowOrLater` would not perform the `IO` effect, so there is no need to pollute its effect with `IO`. It can be achieved by assigning the type scheme

$$\forall \alpha.\, [\alpha <: \mathtt{IO}]\ \mathtt{Bool} \to (\mathtt{Unit} \to_\alpha \mathtt{Unit}) \to_{\alpha \cdot \mathtt{DB}} \mathtt{Unit}.$$

Such a general type scheme cannot be expressed in the type system without constraints.

3.1   Effect Guards

Before presenting the algorithm we will try to grab some intuitions that will help us understand the problem we face. Let us go back to one of the motivating examples, when the user provided a syntactic type annotation $T \triangleq \forall \alpha^{\mathsf{E}}.\, \beta \to\!\_\, \beta.$

While translating it to the internal representation, a reasonable algorithm would generate a fresh variable γ in place of the wildcard. However, problems arise when it comes to leave the scope of the quantifier. The syntactic type T is matched by both $\forall\alpha^{\mathsf{E}}.\ \beta \to_\gamma \beta$ and $\forall\alpha^{\mathsf{E}}.\ \beta \to_{\gamma\cdot\alpha} \beta$, but neither of them is more general than another. The algorithm should decide if it should include α in the effect matched with the wildcard. The idea behind our algorithm is to delay such decisions by conditionally including bound variable in places where it can appear. To do so, we extend the grammar of effects used by the algorithm by the construct $\varepsilon?\varphi$ called *effect guard*, where φ is a formula of propositional logic.

$$\varphi ::= p \mid \top \mid \bot \mid \varphi \wedge \varphi \mid \varphi \vee \varphi \mid \varphi \Rightarrow \varphi \qquad \text{(formulae)}$$
$$\varepsilon ::= \ldots \mid \varepsilon?\varphi \qquad \text{(effects)}$$

The grammar of effects used by the declarative type system remains unchanged. Intuitively, the effect $\varepsilon?\varphi$ means ε when the formula φ is satisfied, and ι otherwise. With this new construct, the most general type that can be matched with T would be $\forall\alpha^{\mathsf{E}}.\ \beta \to_{\gamma\cdot(\alpha?p)} \beta$, where p is a fresh propositional variable.

As we extend the syntax of effects, for the purpose of the metatheory of the algorithm we define a version of a declarative type system that takes into account the extended grammar of effects. For a given valuation ρ of propositional variables we define matching, subeffecting, subtyping, and typing relations (all denoted with $\vdash_\rho$) all defined by the rules analogous to the original declarative system, with the following three subeffecting rules that handle additional effect guard construct.

$$\frac{\rho \not\models \varphi}{\Delta;\Omega \vdash_\rho \varepsilon_1?\varphi <: \varepsilon_2} \qquad \frac{\Delta;\Omega \vdash_\rho \varepsilon_1 <: \varepsilon_2}{\Delta;\Omega \vdash_\rho \varepsilon_1?\varphi <: \varepsilon_2} \qquad \frac{\rho \models \varphi \qquad \Delta;\Omega \vdash_\rho \varepsilon_1 <: \varepsilon_2}{\Delta;\Omega \vdash_\rho \varepsilon_1 <: \varepsilon_2?\varphi}$$

The first rule says that guarded effect is pure, when the formula is false. The second and the third rule say that guard can be discarded if the formula is true. Note that in the second rule, there is no premise $\rho \models \varphi$ for simplicity: the conclusion always holds when the formula is false, by the first rule.

In order to motivate the second ingredient of our solution, let us consider when the type $\forall\alpha^{\mathsf{E}}.\ \beta \to_{\alpha?\varphi_1} \beta$ is a subtype of $\forall\alpha^{\mathsf{E}}.\ \beta \to_{\alpha?\varphi_2} \beta$. The algorithm from Section 2 simply collects subeffecting constraints that are required the subtyping to hold. In this case we cannot simply return the constraint $\alpha?\varphi_1 <: \alpha?\varphi_2$, because α would escape its scope. However, we can observe that this constraint is satisfied for each effect substituted for α if and only if the implication $\varphi_1 \Rightarrow \varphi_2$ is true. We can see this implication as another form of constraint, which does not contain effect variables, and can be propagated outside the quantifier.

For a systematic method of generating formula when leaving the scope of the effect variable, we define the operation of extracting formulae guarding this variable in an effect. The definition is given in Figure 7. It simply builds the formula that is true when the effect variable is present in the effect. We extend this definition to (finite) sets of constraints, by taking a conjunction of implications.

$$(\alpha^{\mathsf{E}})[\alpha^{\mathsf{E}}] \triangleq \top \qquad\qquad (\beta^{\mathsf{E}})[\alpha^{\mathsf{E}}] \triangleq \bot \quad (\alpha^{\mathsf{E}} \neq \beta^{\mathsf{E}})$$

$$(\iota)[\alpha^{\mathsf{E}}] \triangleq \bot \qquad\qquad (\varepsilon_1 \cdot \varepsilon_2)[\alpha^{\mathsf{E}}] \triangleq \varepsilon_1[\alpha^{\mathsf{E}}] \vee \varepsilon_2[\alpha^{\mathsf{E}}]$$

$$(\varepsilon?\varphi)[\alpha^{\mathsf{E}}] \triangleq \varepsilon[\alpha^{\mathsf{E}}] \wedge \varphi \qquad \Omega[\alpha^{\mathsf{E}}] \triangleq \bigwedge_{(\varepsilon_1 <: \varepsilon_2) \in \Omega} \left(\varepsilon_1[\alpha^{\mathsf{E}}] \Rightarrow \varepsilon_2[\alpha^{\mathsf{E}}] \right)$$

Fig. 7. Extracting formulae from effects.

3.2   Algorithmic Effect Inference

Once we have intuitive understanding of required tools we proceed to presenting the algorithm. In the presentation we focus mostly on effect polymorphism, because—as we have seen above—scope leaving requires special attention. On the other hand, type polymorphism doesn't pose similar problems, so we omit it in the presentation. However, we refer the interested reader to the technical report [4] for the details of the whole construction.

Type matching. As we observed, the key idea of our algorithm is to delay some decisions by introducing predicates of propositional logic. Therefore, some functions, like `tr_type` generate fresh propositional variables when dealing with problematic effect binders. Similarly to effect variables, we explicitly keep track which propositional variables were generated by the algorithm, so now, the `tr_type` function returns triples of the form $(P;\ \Delta;\ \tau)$, where P is the set of generated propositional variables, while the meaning of other components remains unchanged. For most cases, the set of generated propositional variables is a union of sets generated by subexpressions (and empty when there are no subexpressions). The only interesting case is the following case for effect-polymorphic types.

```
tr_type (∀αᴱ.T)  =
   let (P;  Δ;  τ) = tr_type (T) in
   fresh Pₛ = {p_β | β ∈ Δ} in
   fresh Δ' = {γ_β | β ∈ Δ} in
   (P ⊎ Pₛ;  Δ';  ∀αᴱ.{β ∈ Δ ↦ γ_β · α?p_β}*τ)
```

When leaving the scope of variable α, the algorithm should decide for each effect matched by a wildcard if it should contain α. Such effects are represented by effect variables from Δ, so the algorithm delay the decision, by extending each effect containing $\beta \in \Delta$ by $\alpha?p$. The fresh propositional variable p represents the decision: if it is true, α is included in the effect, otherwise $\alpha?p$ is pure. This procedure should be done for each effect variable in Δ separately, so we generate a fresh p_β for each $\beta \in \Delta$.

Example 2. Consider the type annotation $\forall\alpha^{\mathsf{E}}.\texttt{Int} \rightarrow_{\_} \texttt{Int}$. This annotation can stand for many different types, such as $\forall\alpha^{\mathsf{E}}.\texttt{Int} \rightarrow_{\texttt{IO}} \texttt{Int}$ or $\forall\alpha^{\mathsf{E}}.\texttt{Int} \rightarrow_\alpha \texttt{Int}$. The `tr_type` function returns $\forall\alpha^{\mathsf{E}}.\texttt{Int} \rightarrow_{\gamma\cdot\alpha?p} \texttt{Int}$, which can be instantiated to:

- $\forall\alpha^{\mathsf{E}}.\texttt{Int} \rightarrow_{\texttt{IO}} \texttt{Int}$ by substituting $\texttt{IO}$ for γ and valuating p to false,

$- \ \forall \alpha^{\mathsf{E}}.\, \mathtt{Int} \rightarrow_{\alpha} \mathtt{Int}$ by substituting ι for γ and valuating p to true.

Remark 2. This trick works well for the problem of effect inference, because of flat, set-like structure of effects: any effect ε containing variable α is equivalent to $\varepsilon' \cdot \alpha$ for some ε' that doesn't contain α. Similar property doesn't hold for types that have more rigid structure, so we don't see how our method could be applied for the problem of type inference.

Subtyping. The `subtype` function collects constraints that should be satisfied in order for a given subtyping judgement to hold. But now, the constraints are represented in two forms: set of subeffecting constraints Ω and propositional-logic formula φ. Therefore, the `subtype` function now returns a pair of the form $(\Omega,\ \varphi)$. As before, the only interesting case concerns the effect-polymorphic quantifier.

```
subtype (∀αᴱ.τ;  ∀αᴱ.τ′)  =
   let (Ω,  φ) = subtype(τ,  τ′) in
   ({α ↦ ι}*Ω;  φ ∧ Ω[α])
```

Again after returning from the recursive call, we need to prevent the variable α from escaping its scope while preserving the meaning of collected constraints. First, we remove variable α from constraints set Ω, by substituting pure effect for α. The information lost by this step is restored in the form of formula $\Omega[\alpha]$.

Example 3. Consider passing a value of type $\forall \alpha^{\mathsf{E}}.\, \mathtt{Int} \rightarrow_{\gamma \cdot \alpha?p} \mathtt{Int}$ to a higher-order function expecting an argument of type $\forall \alpha^{\mathsf{E}}.\, \mathtt{Int} \rightarrow_{\mathtt{IO}} \mathtt{Int}$. To type-check this call, we need to call `subtype` on these two types, which returns a single constraint $\gamma <: \mathtt{IO}$ and a formula $p \Rightarrow \bot$. The constraint and formula can be satisfied by substituting $\mathtt{IO}$ for γ and valuating p to false.

Constraint Separation. The other technical challenge in designing the algorithm comes from restricting constraints that can appear in type schemes. When examining a let-expression, the algorithm should divide constraints from the first subexpressions into two sets: one that can be included in the type scheme, and one that should be propagated upwards. With the syntax of effects not extended with guards this task is easy. Any constraint set can be normalized to the set of constraints of the form $\alpha <: \varepsilon$ [44], and from such constraints we can select those that describe upper-bounds for generalized effect variables.

In the case of the extended syntax we can proceed similarly, if we slightly relax the upper-bound condition. First, observe that any constraint set can be normalized to set of constraints of the form $\alpha?\varphi <: \varepsilon$ (for details, we refer the reader to the technical report). Then, for the purposes of the algorithm we allow such constraints to appear in a type scheme if α is a variable bound by the scheme. For fixed valuation ρ of propositional variables, such a relaxation doesn't influence on the expressive power of type schemes: if $\rho \models \varphi$ then the constraint $\alpha?\varphi <: \varepsilon$ is equivalent to $\alpha <: \varepsilon$, otherwise it is trivially satisfied.

Now, we can define function that separates constraints as follows.

```
infer(Γ; Λα^E.e) =
  let (P_1; Δ_1; τ; ε; Ω_1; φ_1) = infer(Γ; e) in
  fresh P_s = {p_β | β ∈ Δ_1} in
  fresh Δ'_1 = {γ_β | β ∈ Δ_1} in
  let θ = {β ∈ Δ_1 ↦ γ_β · α?p_β} in
  let Ω'_1 = θ*(Ω_1 ∪ {ε <: ι}) in
  (P_1 ⊎ P_s; Δ'_1; ∀α^E.θ*τ; ι; {α ↦ ι}*Ω'_1; φ_1 ∧ Ω'_1[α])


infer(Γ; e[E]) =
  let (P_1; Δ_1; τ_1; ε_1; Ω_1; φ_1) = infer(Γ; e) in
  match τ_1 with
  | ∀α^E.τ =>
     let (Δ_2; ε_2) = tr_effect(E) in
     (P_1; Δ_1 ⊎ Δ_2; {α ↦ ε_2}*τ; ε_1; Ω_1; φ_1)
  | _ => fail


infer(Γ; let x = e_1 in e_2) =
  let (P_1; Δ_1; τ_1; ε_1; Ω_1; φ_1) = infer(Γ; e_1) in
  fresh Δ'_1 = {β_α | α ∈ Δ_1} in
  fresh Δ_g = {γ_α | α ∈ Δ_1} in
  let θ = {α ∈ Δ_1 ↦ β_α · γ_α} in
  let (Ω_g, Ω_p) = separate(Δ_g; θ*(Ω_1 ∪ {ε_1 <: ι})) in
  let (P_2; Δ_2; τ_2; ε_2; Ω_2; φ_2) = infer(Γ, x : ∀Δ_g.[Ω_g] θ*τ_1; e_2) in
  (P_1 ⊎ P_2; Δ'_1 ⊎ Δ_2; τ_2; ε_2; Ω_p ∪ Ω_2; φ_1 ∧ φ_2)
```

Fig. 8. Selected cases of the effect inference algorithm.

```
separate(Δ_g; Ω) =
  let Ω_n = normalize(Ω) in
  let Ω_g = {γ?φ <: ε | (γ?φ <: ε) ∈ Ω_n ∧ γ ∈ Δ_g} in
  let Ω_p = {β?φ <: {γ ∈ Δ_g ↦ ι}*ε | (β?φ <: ε) ∈ Ω_n ∧ β ∉ Δ_g} in
  (Ω_g; Ω_p)
```

The function takes the set of variables Δ_g that will be generalized in the scheme, and divides the set of constraints Ω into the set Ω_g that will be included in the type scheme, and the set Ω_p of remaining constraints. The `normalize` function normalizes constraints to the form described above. Additionally, we substitute pure effects for variables from Δ_g in Ω_p, because Ω_p will be used outside the scope of Δ_g. By doing so, we don't lose any information: all normalized constraints that non-trivially used variables from Δ_g are included in Ω_g.

The algorithm. Now we proceed to discussing the main function `infer` of the reconstruction algorithm. As before, the function takes the environment Γ and the examined expression, but the returned tuple $(P;\ \Delta;\ \tau;\ \varepsilon;\ \Omega;\ \varphi)$ contains two new components: a set P of generated propositional variables, and a formula φ that can be seen as a kind of constraint. Adding these components to the algorithm of Section 2 is straightforward, so we focus on the cases presented in Figure 8, that require deeper explanation. The full algorithm can be found in the technical report [4].

The effect abstraction $\Lambda\alpha^{\mathsf{E}}.\,e$ introduces a new effect variable α, so a special care should be taken when the algorithm leaves the scope of α. First, for each variable $\beta \in \Delta_1$, the algorithm should decide if β should be instantiated with an effect containing α or not. We do so the same way as we have seen in the `tr_type` function: by substituting $\gamma \cdot \alpha?p$ for β, where p is a fresh propositional variable representing the decision. Moreover, we should transform constraints Ω_1' to the equivalent form that doesn't contain variable α. We proceed as we have seen in the `subtype` function: by substituting pure effect $\{\alpha \mapsto \iota\}^*\Omega_1'$, and recovering lost information in the form of the formula $\Omega_1'[\alpha]$.

The effect application $e\ [E]$ doesn't pose any problems. In this case, the algorithm makes sure that the type of the expression e is an effect-polymorphic quantifier $\forall\alpha^{\mathsf{E}}.\,\tau$, and just substitutes for α the result of translating syntactic effect E into the internal representation.

For the let-expression, the idea is simple: infer type τ_1 of the first expression, generalize all generated variables in τ_1 together with constraints, and continue with the second expression. However two additional steps are required: in the first step called *variable splitting*, each variable α from Δ_1 is split into join of two variables β_α and γ_α. The former is propagated as one of generated variables, while the latter is generalized in the polymorphic scheme. In the second step, using the `separate` function constraints are separated into generalizable constraints Ω_g in the relaxed upper-bound form, and remaining constraints Ω_p that are propagated upwards. The purpose of the second step was already explained, when the `separate` was described.

The purpose of variable splitting is to avoid too restrictive constraints produced by the second step. Intuitively, a variable $\alpha \in \Delta_1$ stands for some unknown yet effect. This effect can contain some variables generalized in the scheme (γ_α), as well as other effects defined outside the let-expression. The latter are unknown yet, so they are represented by a variable β_α.

Example 4. To show that variable splitting is needed, consider a set $\{\mathtt{IO} <: \alpha\}$ containing single constraint, where α was generated during the type inference. Without variable splitting, the `separate` function would return a pair $(\varnothing;\ \{\mathtt{IO} <: \iota\})$, where propagated constraints are obviously contradictory. On the other hand, with variable splitting we obtain a pair $(\varnothing;\ \{\mathtt{IO} <: \beta_\alpha\})$ which preserves the original meaning of the input set.

Soundness and Completeness. The presented algorithm is sound and complete with respect to the declarative system from the beginning of the section.

Theorem 3 (Soundness). *If* $\mathtt{infer}(\Gamma;\ e) = (P;\ \Delta';\ \tau;\ \varepsilon;\ \Omega;\ \varphi)$ *for an expression e defined over Δ, then $\Delta, \Delta'; \Omega; \Gamma \vdash_\rho e : \tau \ / \ \varepsilon$ for each valuation ρ satisfying formula φ.*

The Soundness Theorem is stated as precisely as possible, therefore it uses the auxiliary typing relation defined in Section 3.1 for the extended syntax. However, knowing the valuation ρ we can simplify all guarded effects and return to the original syntax used by the declarative system.

Corollary 1. *If* $\mathtt{infer}(\Gamma;\ e) = (P;\ \Delta';\ \tau;\ \varepsilon;\ \Omega;\ \varphi)$ *for expression e defined over Δ, then for each valuation ρ satisfying formula φ there exist τ', ε', and Ω' such that $\Delta, \Delta'; \Omega'; \Gamma \vdash e : \tau' \ / \ \varepsilon'$ and $\Delta, \Delta'; \Omega \vdash_\rho \Omega'$.*

The statement of the completeness says that the algorithm finds the most general solution, *i.e.*, that every derivation of the typing relation must be an instance of the one found by the algorithm.

Theorem 4 (Completeness). *If $\Delta; \Omega; \Gamma \vdash e : \tau \ / \ \varepsilon$, then* $\mathtt{infer}(\Delta;\ e) = (P';\ \Delta';\ \tau';\ \varepsilon';\ \Omega';\ \varphi)$ *for some P', Δ', τ', ε', Ω', and φ. Moreover, there exists substitution θ that maps variables from P' and Δ' to formulae and effects, respectively, defined over Δ, such that $\theta^*\varphi$ is a tautology, $\Delta; \Omega \vdash \theta^*\Omega'$, $\Delta; \Omega \vdash \theta^*\tau' <: \tau$, and $\Delta; \Omega \vdash \theta^*\varepsilon' <: \varepsilon$.*

3.3   Solving Toplevel Constraints

The algorithm transforms the problem of effect inference to a constraint-solving problem. At the end, we get constraints of two kinds: subeffecting constraints Ω and a formula φ. We can solve these constraints in two steps.

1. Since we strictly avoid effect variables escaping their scopes, effect constraints in Ω can contain only top-level effect variables. We can pretend that all top-level effect variables are bound at the beginning of the program, so we leave their scope as we proceeded in the effect-abstraction case. We transform the set Ω into formula $\varphi_\Omega \overset{\triangle}{=} \bigwedge_{\alpha \in \Delta} \Omega[\alpha]$, where Δ is a set of top-level effects. Note that the scope leaving procedure produces also constraints $\{\alpha \in \Omega \mapsto \iota\}^*\Omega$, but since there are no variables in them, they are trivially satisfied.
2. The remaining work to do is to satisfy the formula $\varphi \wedge \varphi_\Omega$. This is a formula of propositional logic, so we can find a satisfying valuation using *e.g.*, SAT solver.

4   Type System Without Constraints

Algebraic type schemes are useful for designing a reconstruction algorithm due to their ability to abstract some constraints. However, a natural question arises whether it is possible to develop a similar algorithm for a type system where type schemes have the following simpler form.

$$\sigma ::= \forall \Delta. \tau$$

In this section, we consider such a system, and positively answer this question. Since now there is no way of abstracting constraints, the typing, subtyping, and subeffecting judgements don't contain the constraint environment (Ω). Here, we present only the two most notable inference rules of the modified declarative system, as the others remain unchanged (except removing unnecessary constraint environment). These rules resemble polymorphic instantiation and generalization in the standard declarative formulation of the Hindley-Milner type system [40].

$$\frac{\Gamma(x) = \forall\Delta'.\tau}{\Delta; \Gamma \vdash x : \theta^*\tau \;/\; \iota} \qquad \frac{\Delta, \Delta'; \Gamma \vdash e_1 : \tau_1 \;/\; \iota \qquad \Delta; \Gamma, x : \forall\Delta'.\tau_1 \vdash e_2 : \tau_2 \;/\; \varepsilon}{\Delta; \Gamma \vdash \texttt{let } x = e_1 \texttt{ in } e_2 : \tau_2 \;/\; \varepsilon}$$

Interestingly, the problem of effect inference in this system is still decidable. However, the price we pay is that the algorithm generates a huge number of variables, which makes it impractical for real-world programs. Before we go into the details, we start with the two examples that illustrate that the problem is not as simple as it may seem at first glance.

Example 5. Since the let-binding ($\texttt{let } x = e_1 \texttt{ in } e_2$) introduces new effect variables, it might be tempting to abstract a single variable for each effect variable generated during the effect inference of e_1 and leave the scope similarly to the effect-abstraction case from the previous section. The let-binding case in the algorithm would then look like this:

```
infer (Γ; let x = e₁ in e₂) =
   let (P₁; Δ₁; τ₁; ε₁; Ω₁; φ₁) = infer (Γ; e₁) in
   fresh Δ'₁ = {βα | α ∈ Δ₁} in
   fresh Δg = {γα | α ∈ Δ₁} in
   fresh P'₁ = {pα | α ∈ Δ₁} in
   let θ = {α ∈ Δ₁ ↦ βα · γα?pα} in
   let Ω'₁ = θ*(Ω₁ ∪ {ε₁ <: ι}) in
   let (P₂; Δ₂; τ₂; ε₂; Ω₂; φ₂) = infer (Γ, x : ∀Δg.θ*τ₁; e₂) in
   (P₁ ⊎ P'₁ ⊎ P₂; Δ'₁ ⊎ Δ₂; τ₂; ε₂; {γα ↦ ι}*Ω'₁ ∪ Ω₂; φ₁ ∧ φ₂ ∧ ⋀γ∈Δg Ω'₁[γ]).
```

This approach gives us a sound algorithm, but it is not complete. Suppose that the algorithm on expression e_1 returns the tuple

$$(P_1; \{\alpha_1, \alpha_2\}; \tau_1(\alpha_1, \alpha_2); \iota; \{\alpha_1 <: \alpha_2, \alpha_2 <: \alpha_1\}; \varphi_1),$$

where $\tau_1(\alpha_1, \alpha_2)$ is a type where α_1 and α_2 occur in invariant positions. Since the generated constraints state that α_1 and α_2 are equal, to obtain completeness the algorithm should assign to variable x a scheme equivalent to $\forall\alpha.\tau_1(\alpha, \alpha)$. However, the assigned scheme is

$$\forall\gamma_{\alpha_1}, \gamma_{\alpha_2}.\tau_1(\beta_{\alpha_1} \cdot \gamma_{\alpha_1}?p_{\alpha_1}, \beta_{\alpha_2} \cdot \gamma_{\alpha_2}?p_{\alpha_2}),$$

and the returned formula contains conjuncts $\theta(\alpha_1)[\gamma_{\alpha_i}] \Rightarrow \theta(\alpha_2)[\gamma_{\alpha_i}]$ for $i = 1, 2$, each of which simplifies to $(\beta_{\alpha_1} \cdot \gamma_{\alpha_1}?p_{\alpha_1})[\gamma_{\alpha_i}] \Rightarrow (\beta_{\alpha_2} \cdot \gamma_{\alpha_2}?p_{\alpha_2})[\gamma_{\alpha_i}]$, and further to $p_{\alpha_1} \Rightarrow \bot$ and $p_{\alpha_2} \Rightarrow \bot$. The obtained scheme is not polymorphic at all, so such a naive algorithm is not complete.

From the above example we see that the algorithm should take into account the fact that generated effect variables are not necessarily independent. We can achieve this by allowing any combination of generalized variables (γ) to be substituted for the generated effect variables (α). The change is relatively simple: we substitute for α a join of all the effect variables from Δ_g, guarded by fresh propositional variables. The rest of the algorithm remains unchanged.

```
infer(Γ; let x = e₁ in e₂) =

    . . .

    fresh Δ_g =  ... in
    fresh P'₁ = {p_{α,γ} | α ∈ Δ₁ ∧ γ ∈ Δ_g} in
    let θ = α ∈ Δ₁ ↦ β_α · ⊙_{γ∈Δ_g} γ?p_{α,γ}  in

    . . .
```

Since we take any combination of variables from Δ_g, the size of Δ_g doesn't have to be the same as the size of Δ_1. The question is how many variables we need to generate in Δ_g to obtain a complete algorithm. The next example shows that sometimes we need to generate strictly more variables than the size of Δ_1.

Example 6. Assume that the size of Δ_g is equal to the size of Δ_1. The above algorithm is sound, but still not complete. To expose its shortcomings, suppose that the algorithm called on the subexpression e_1 of the let-binding `let x = e₁ in e₂` returns

$$(P_1; \{\alpha_0, \alpha_1, \alpha_2\}; \ \tau_1(\alpha_0, \alpha_1, \alpha_2); \ \iota; \ \{\alpha_0 <: \alpha_1 \cdot \alpha_2\}; \ \varphi_1),$$

where variables α_0, α_1, and α_2 occur on invariant position in $\tau_1(\alpha_0, \alpha_1, \alpha_2)$. Moreover, suppose that e_2 is typable only if both

$$\tau_p \stackrel{\triangle}{=} \tau_1(\iota, \iota, \iota) \qquad \tau_i \stackrel{\triangle}{=} \tau_1(A_1 \cdot A_2, A_1 \cdot B_1, A_2 \cdot B_2)$$

are valid instantiations of a type scheme assigned to x (where A_1, A_2, B_1, B_2 are some pairwise different effect constants). The type-scheme assigned to x by the algorithm would be

$$\sigma \stackrel{\triangle}{=} \forall \gamma_0, \gamma_1, \gamma_2.\, \tau_1(\beta_{\alpha_0} \cdot \gamma_0?p_{0,0} \cdot \gamma_1?p_{0,1} \cdot \gamma_2?p_{0,2},$$
$$\beta_{\alpha_1} \cdot \gamma_0?p_{1,0} \cdot \gamma_1?p_{1,1} \cdot \gamma_2?p_{1,2},$$
$$\beta_{\alpha_2} \cdot \gamma_0?p_{2,0} \cdot \gamma_1?p_{2,1} \cdot \gamma_2?p_{2,2})$$

and the formula generated from the constraint $\alpha_0 <: \alpha_1 \cdot \alpha_2$ contains a conjunction of the following subformulae.

$$p_{0,0} \Rightarrow p_{1,0} \lor p_{2,0} \qquad p_{0,1} \Rightarrow p_{1,1} \lor p_{2,1} \qquad p_{0,2} \Rightarrow p_{1,2} \lor p_{2,2}$$

An inquisitive reader may verify that there is no valuation of propositional variables that satisfies the above formulae and allows τ_p and τ_i to be valid instantiations of σ. On the other hand, the expression is typable in the declarative type system if x gets the type scheme

$$\sigma' \stackrel{\triangle}{=} \forall \gamma_0, \gamma_1, \gamma_2, \gamma_3.\, \tau_1(\gamma_0 \cdot \gamma_1, \gamma_0 \cdot \gamma_2, \gamma_1 \cdot \gamma_3).$$

The above example shows that when the size of Δ_g is the same as Δ_1 the algorithm is still not complete. However, it gives us hope that if we were able to find an upper-bound for the number of generalized variables used by the declarative system (in this example four is enough), completeness could be regained. Observe that in a type scheme $\forall \alpha_1, \ldots, \alpha_n . \tau$ if $n > 2^{|\tau|}$, where $|\tau|$ is the number of arrows in τ, then there are two variables α_i and α_j that always appear together in τ. We could equate them and get the equivalent scheme $\forall \alpha_1, \ldots \alpha_{i-1}, \alpha_{i+1}, \alpha_n . \{\alpha_i \mapsto \alpha_j\}^* \tau$.

Example 7. A type scheme $\forall \beta, \gamma . \alpha \rightarrow_{\beta \cdot \gamma} \alpha$ is equivalent to $\forall \beta . \alpha \rightarrow_\beta \alpha$, *i.e.*, they have the same instantiations.

Moreover, $|\tau|$ does not depend on effects (and is invariant with respect to effect substitutions), therefore it is known after the type reconstruction phase! With this intuition in mind, we can construct an algorithm that is sound and complete with respect to the declarative system and uses $2^{|\tau|}$ as a mentioned upper-bound. In sake of brevity, we present only the let-case.

```
infer(Γ; let x = e₁ in e₂) =
  let (P₁; Δ₁; τ₁; ε₁; Ω₁; φ₁) = infer(Γ; e₁) in
  fresh Δ₁' = {βₐ | α ∈ Δ₁} in
  fresh Δ_g = {γᵢ | i ∈ 1,...,2^|τ₁|} in
  fresh P₁' = {pₐ,ᵧ | α ∈ Δ₁ ∧ γ ∈ Δ_g} in
  let θ = {α ∈ Δ₁ ↦ βₐ · •_{γ∈Δ_g} γ?pₐ,ᵧ} in
  let Ω₁' = θ*(Ω₁ ∪ {ε₁ <: ι}) in
  let (P₂; Δ₂; τ₂; ε₂; Ω₂; φ₂) = infer(Γ,x : ∀Δ_g.θ*τ₁; e₂) in
  (P₁ ⊎ P₁' ⊎ P₂ ; Δ₁' ⊎ Δ₂ ; τ₂; ε₂; {γₐ ↦ ι}*Ω₁' ∪ Ω₂; φ₁ ∧ φ₂ ∧ ⋀_{γ∈Δ_g} Ω₁'[γ]).
```

Theorem 5 (Soundness). *Suppose that* $\mathtt{infer}(\Gamma; e) = (P; \Delta'; \tau; \varepsilon; \Omega; \varphi)$ *for an expression e defined over Δ and θ is a substitution mapping P and Δ, Δ' to terms over Δ''. Then $\Delta'' \vdash_\rho \theta^* \Omega$ implies $\Delta''; \theta^* \Omega; \theta^* \Gamma \vdash_\rho e : \theta^* \tau \mid \theta^* \varepsilon$ for each valuation ρ satisfying formula $\theta^* \varphi$.*

Theorem 6 (Completeness). *If $\Delta; \Gamma \vdash e : \tau \mid \varepsilon$, then $\mathtt{infer}(\Delta; e) = (P'; \Delta'; \tau'; \varepsilon'; \Omega'; \varphi)$ for some $P', \Delta', \tau', \varepsilon', \Omega'$, and φ. Moreover, there exists substitution θ that maps variables from P' and Δ' to formulae and effects, respectively, defined over Δ, such that $\theta^* \varphi$ is a tautology, $\Delta \vdash \theta^* \Omega'$, $\Delta \vdash \theta^* \tau' <: \tau$, and $\Delta \vdash \theta^* \varepsilon' <: \varepsilon$.*

5 Formalization

The metatheory of effect inference in presence of general polymorphism is particularly prone to errors related to variable bindings. In order to avoid such mistakes, we formalized all the presented results using Rocq proof assistant. The key issue in such a formalization is the representation of variable binding. We decided to use a functorial approach [24] a.k.a. nested datatypes approach [10]. However, the algorithm strongly relies on the finiteness of the generated sets, so parametrizing syntax with arbitrary types instead of finite sets, like in the original nested datatype approach does not work well.

At the beginning we tried to use Binding library [52] designed for a functorial approach, because of its flexibility in the representation of sets of potentially free variables. We parametrized the syntax with a cartesian product of finite sets with a disjoint union as one of the constructors. However, Binding heavily uses type classes mechanism that didn't work well when multiple instantiations of the same class were used in a single formalization. Therefore, we ended up with a functorial approach reimplemented from scratch.

6   Implementation and Practical Considerations

Looking at the algorithm presented in this work, it might not be immediately obvious whether it is viable in practice. In the following, we will share some insights we have gained from implementing it in our Fram programming language.

Higher kinds. While our implementation includes arrow kinds $\kappa_1 \to \kappa_2$, it has the restriction that the effect kind cannot appear on the right-hand side of an arrow. Due to this, type-level application cannot appear in effects, and so effects remain simple sets of variables. As we have not found any use cases for effects depending on types or effects in our language, we consider this limitation to be acceptable.

Constraint simplification. The constraints generated by the algorithm can be quite large if left as-is. In turn, the schemes inferred for let-definitions run the risk of containing huge constraint sets, which are unwieldy for the programmer to read and inefficient for the implementation to satisfy at each use site of such a definition. Fortunately, in practice, constraints can often be significantly simplified, or completely eliminated, with a collection of straightforward heuristics, for example similar to those in [44].

Checking formula satisfiability. After running our algorithm and eliminating the resulting subeffect constraints, we are left with a propositional-logic formula which needs to be satisfied in order to consider the effect inference successful. Though of course the SAT problem is well-known to be NP-complete, in practice we found that the formulae generated by the algorithm are easy to solve. In the current implementation, we use a hand-written SAT solver that exploits certain properties of the formulae to attain a reasonable runtime, but since many optimized SAT solvers are available, a ready-made solution is also an option.

REPL and incremental solving. When running the interpreter in REPL mode, it is necessary to check the satisfiability of the produced formula for each expression and definition given by the programmer to catch any errors. However, unlike when operating on complete programs, the values of propositional variables cannot be fixed too eagerly, as future input can make some valuations invalid, while other satisfying valuations remain. The simplest implementation can check whether any satisfying valuation exists after each input, but not set the values of any propositional variables. Unfortunately, that results in checking an ever-larger formula every time, which could be a problem for long-running REPL sessions. As an optimization, in our implementation we fix the values of propositional variables as soon as possible if there is only one satisfying valuation for them.

7   Related Work

Effect inference in presence of higher-rank polymorphism. Jouvelot and Gifford [33] presented an algorithm of effect inference in their FX programming language [37,27]. Their algorithm collects effect equivalence constraints and attaches them to algebraic type schemes. Their language supports explicit higher-rank polymorphism and allows omitting type annotation in λ-abstractions, but doesn't support subtyping and wildcards under effect quantifiers. This is the only work that we are aware of that tackles the problem of effect reconstruction in a setup similar to ours. Jouvelot and Gifford claimed that their algorithm is sound and complete. However, it turned out that they had a subtle bug related to variable binding that made their theorems untrue with no simple fix in sight [6,32].

Effect inference as a static analysis. After the original work on effect inference by Jouvelot and Gifford, the research community's attention shifted in the direction of static analysis. Talpin and Jouvelot [54] used the technique of algebraic type schemes to perform effect and region inference. Because the region inference is more like a static analysis transparent to the user, considering explicit higher-rank polymorphism doesn't make much sense, so they focused on ML-style polymorphism only, making their work free of the aforementioned bug. This work started a long line of research on effect based static analysis [55,58,42,56,12,44,22,57,46,28,20]. Nielson and Nielson [43] observed that subtyping doesn't influence shape of types, and concluded that this allows for a two-stage approach. Amtoft et al. [1] and Birkedal and Tofte [11] attacked the problem of effect inference where type schemes don't contain constraints. However, their systems don't admit general polymorphism, and we don't see how their solutions may scale to our system.

Effect inference in surface type systems. The interest in type-and-effect systems as a facility exposed to the programmer has experienced a resurgence alongside the research on algebraic effects [50,51,34,64,7,29,8,67,15,9,65,38,60]. However, the idea is much older, and the previously discussed work by Jouvelot and Gifford [33] fits into this category. Surprisingly, later research in this area does not build on that work, and most of it opts for inference based on row reconstruction [61,53].

The idea to use row polymorphism for effects first appeared in Links [36]. The advantage of this approach is that since row unification is decidable, it is easy to extend the standard Hindley-Milner algorithm with effect rows while maintaining completeness of the inference. Effect rows are essentially lists of behaviors, possibly ending with a row variable. There is a lot of work on effect rows [36,29,34,30,60] with slightly different approaches and design decisions. From our perspective, the main disadvantage of effect rows is that they are conceptually more complex than sets, and also less intuitive. Additionally, some expressiveness is lost by not being able to use multiple polymorphic variables within a row.

Two notable exceptions with effect sets rather than rows include the Flix [38] and Effekt [15] languages. In Flix, effects are sets with all the usual boolean operations such as union, intersection and difference. As a result, effect inference can be implemented using boolean unification [39]. We note the common thread between our solution and the approach used by Flix: both reduce inference to solving boolean algebra problems of some kind, in our case satisfying propositional formulae, and in the case of Flix performing boolean unification on sets. We found the rich grammar of effects in Flix a bit too complicated for our needs, as we sought to present the programmer with effects with just the union operation. Effekt takes an entirely different approach by replacing parametric effect polymorphism with contextual polymorphism. In summary, this view of polymorphism means that effects do not need to contain polymorphic variables at all, and in turn effects can be represented as sets without complicating effect inference. This simplicity comes with a trade-off: functions in Effekt are second-class.

Type inference in System F. Full type reconstruction of System F is known to be undecidable [62], however algorithms to reconstruct types in presence of partial annotation have been developed for some time. Starting with Pierce *et al.* [49], bidirectional approach to this problem became a standard. Here community split into two paths. One dedicated to the problem of type checking in System F with explicit type application [18,21,19,14] The other decided to loosen the type system, and adopted rank-N polymorphism [47,48].

Formalization of type reconstruction. Surprisingly, type reconstruction algorithms were rarely formalized using proof assistants for a long time. In the early works [41,17,59,26] a concrete or nominal approach to variable binding was used, and the scopes of variables were managed manually with relatively large overhead. The situation has changed when Dunfield and Krishnaswami [18] proposed a framework for type reconstruction algorithms where scopes of unification variables are tracked via ordered contexts. They didn't formalized their work in a proof assistant, but following their approach many advanced algorithms related to subtyping were formalized in Abella [69,70,68,16], Coq/Rocq [13,31], and Agda [66]. Our result also explicitly keeps track of variable scopes, but instead of using ordered contexts, we rely on functorial syntax. Recently, Fan *et al.* [23] presented a different approach to formalizing scopes using levels, which is closer to modern implementations of type reconstruction algorithms.

8 Conclusion and Future Work

In this paper we have proposed an effect reconstruction algorithm with set-like semantics of effects and support for higher-rank polymorphism. The algorithm requires only minimal annotations from the programmer. Our algorithm utilizes effect guards and extracts propositional formulae from subeffecting constraints in order to correctly manage the scopes of effect variables. We have proven our algorithm to be both sound and complete with respect to the declarative type-and-effect system. We have also shown that it is feasible to implement in practice by adding it to a realistic programming language with algebraic effects.

This study opens a number of avenues for further research. One concerns the algorithm without constraints in schemes presented in Section 4. Our upper bound for the number of variables needed to preserve the algorithm's completeness is $2^{|\tau|}$. However this estimation does not take into account the number of constraints associated with the variables present in the type. It is easy to see that in the case where there are no such constraints, there is no need to create any fresh variables. This observation suggests that a better upper bound exists, which gives the hope for a practical implementation.

In the opposite direction, we can imagine allowing the programmer to provide algebraic type schemes in rank-N annotations. For example, this would enable types like $\forall \alpha. (\forall \beta. [\beta <: \alpha] \; \mathtt{Int} \rightarrow_\_ \mathtt{Int}) \rightarrow_\_ \mathtt{Int}$. We believe it will be possible to have sound and complete algorithm in such a setting, but foresee difficulties associated with calculating the transitive closure of subeffecting constraints.

Acknowledgements. We would like to thank Wojciech Jasiński for his participation in the early stages of this project, and Pierre Jouvelot for the valuable discussions about his and our work on this topic. Finally, we would like to express our gratitude to Dariusz Biernacki, Witold Charatonik, Bartłomiej Królikowski, Maciej Piróg, Filip Sieczkowski, and the Anonymous Reviewers for their insightful comments that helped improve the presentation of this work.

Data Availability Statement. The Rocq formalization of the results presented in this paper is available via Zenodo [5]. Both the Rocq sources and a Docker image containing the Rocq version used to type-check the proofs can be downloaded from there. The implementation of the inference algorithm described in Section 3, using the implementation techniques from Section 6, is a part of Fram's interpreter, DBL, and can be accessed as a tagged release on GitHub: https://github.com/fram-lang/dbl/releases/tag/esop26.

References

1. Amtoft, T., Nielson, F., Nielson, H.R.: Type and behaviour reconstruction for higher-order concurrent programs. J. Funct. Program. **7**(3), 321–347 (1997), https://doi.org/10.1017/s0956796897002700

2. Appel, A.W., Melliès, P., Richards, C.D., Vouillon, J.: A very modal model of a modern, major, general type system. In: Hofmann, M., Felleisen, M. (eds.) Proceedings of the 34th ACM SIGPLAN-SIGACT Symposium on Principles of Programming Languages, POPL 2007, Nice, France, January 17–19, 2007. pp. 109–122. ACM (2007), https://doi.org/10.1145/1190216.1190235

3. Asai, K., Kameyama, Y.: Polymorphic delimited continuations. In: Shao, Z. (ed.) Programming Languages and Systems, 5th Asian Symposium, APLAS 2007, Singapore, November 29–December 1, 2007, Proceedings. Lecture Notes in Computer Science, vol. 4807, pp. 239–254. Springer (2007), https://doi.org/10.1007/978-3-540-76637-7_16

4. Balik, P., Jędras, S., Polesiuk, P.: Deciding not to decide: Full definitions of the declarative type system and the effect inference algorithm. Tech. rep. (2026), https://github.com/fram-lang/fram-papers/releases/download/esop26/esop26-appendix.pdf

5. Balik, P., Jędras, S., Polesiuk, P.: Formalization for article "Deciding not to Decide: Sound and Complete Effect Inference in the Presence of Higher-Rank Polymorphism" (Jan 2026), https://doi.org/10.5281/zenodo.18197463

6. Balik, P., Jędras, S., Polesiuk, P.: Remarks on algebraic reconstruction of types and effects (2026), https://arxiv.org/abs/2601.15455

7. Bauer, A., Pretnar, M.: Programming with algebraic effects and handlers. J. Log. Algebr. Methods Program. **84**(1), 108–123 (2015), https://doi.org/10.1016/j.jlamp.2014.02.001

8. Biernacki, D., Piróg, M., Polesiuk, P., Sieczkowski, F.: Handle with care: relational interpretation of algebraic effects and handlers. Proc. ACM Program. Lang. **2**(POPL), 8:1–8:30 (2018), https://doi.org/10.1145/3158096

9. Biernacki, D., Piróg, M., Polesiuk, P., Sieczkowski, F.: Binders by day, labels by night: effect instances via lexically scoped handlers. PACMPL **4**(POPL), 48:1–48:29 (2020), https://doi.org/10.1145/3371116

10. Bird, R.S., Meertens, L.G.L.T.: Nested datatypes. In: Jeuring, J. (ed.) Mathematics of Program Construction, MPC'98, Marstrand, Sweden, June 15–17, 1998, Proceedings. Lecture Notes in Computer Science, vol. 1422, pp. 52–67. Springer (1998), https://doi.org/10.1007/BFb0054285

11. Birkedal, L., Tofte, M.: A constraint-based region inference algorithm. Theor. Comput. Sci. **258**(1–2), 299–392 (2001), https://doi.org/10.1016/S0304-3975(00)00025-6

12. Birkedal, L., Tofte, M., Vejlstrup, M.: From region inference to von Neumann machines via region representation inference. In: Boehm, H., Jr., G.L.S. (eds.) Conference Record of POPL'96: The 23rd ACM SIGPLAN-SIGACT Symposium on Principles of Programming Languages, Papers Presented at the Symposium, St. Petersburg Beach, Florida, USA, January 21–24, 1996. pp. 171–183. ACM Press (1996), https://doi.org/10.1145/237721.237771

13. Bosman, R., Karachalias, G., Schrijvers, T.: No unification variable left behind: Fully grounding type inference for the HDM system. In: Naumowicz, A., Thiemann, R. (eds.) 14th International Conference on Interactive Theorem Proving, ITP 2023, July 31 to August 4, 2023, Białystok, Poland. LIPIcs, vol. 268, pp. 8:1–8:18. Schloss Dagstuhl - Leibniz-Zentrum für Informatik (2023), https://doi.org/10.4230/LIPIcs.ITP.2023.8

14. Botlan, D.L., Rémy, D.: ML^{F}: raising ML to the power of system F. In: Runciman, C., Shivers, O. (eds.) Proceedings of the Eighth ACM SIGPLAN International Conference on Functional Programming, ICFP 2003, Uppsala, Sweden, August 25-29, 2003. pp. 27–38. ACM (2003), https://doi.org/10.1145/944705.944709

15. Brachthäuser, J.I., Schuster, P., Ostermann, K.: Effects as capabilities: effect handlers and lightweight effect polymorphism. PACMPL **4**(OOPSLA), 126:1–126:30 (2020), https://doi.org/10.1145/3428194

16. Cui, C., Jiang, S., d. S. Oliveira, B.C.: Greedy implicit bounded quantification. Proc. ACM Program. Lang. **7**(OOPSLA2), 2083–2111 (2023), https://doi.org/10.1145/3622871

17. Dubois, C., Ménissier-Morain, V.: Certification of a type inference tool for ML: Damas-Milner within Coq. J. Autom. Reason. **23**(3–4), 319–346 (1999), https://doi.org/10.1023/A:1006285817788

18. Dunfield, J., Krishnaswami, N.R.: Complete and easy bidirectional typechecking for higher-rank polymorphism. In: Morrisett, G., Uustalu, T. (eds.) ACM SIGPLAN International Conference on Functional Programming, ICFP'13, Boston, MA, USA — September 25 – 27, 2013. pp. 429–442. ACM (2013), https://doi.org/10.1145/2500365.2500582

19. Dunfield, J., Krishnaswami, N.R.: Sound and complete bidirectional typechecking for higher-rank polymorphism with existentials and indexed types. Proc. ACM Program. Lang. **3**(POPL), 9:1–9:28 (2019), https://doi.org/10.1145/3290322

20. Elsman, M.: Explicit effects and effect constraints in ReML. Proc. ACM Program. Lang. **8**(POPL), 2370–2394 (2024), https://doi.org/10.1145/3632921

21. Emrich, F., Lindley, S., Stolarek, J., Cheney, J., Coates, J.: FreezeML: complete and easy type inference for first-class polymorphism. In: Donaldson, A.F., Torlak, E. (eds.) Proceedings of the 41st ACM SIGPLAN International Conference on Programming Language Design and Implementation, PLDI 2020, London, UK, June 15-20, 2020. pp. 423–437. ACM (2020), https://doi.org/10.1145/3385412.3386003

22. Fähndrich, M., Aiken, A.: Program analysis using mixed term and set constraints. In: Hentenryck, P.V. (ed.) Static Analysis, 4th International Symposium, SAS '97, Paris, France, September 8-10, 1997, Proceedings. Lecture Notes in Computer Science, vol. 1302, pp. 114–126. Springer (1997), https://doi.org/10.1007/BFb0032737

23. Fan, A., Xu, H., Xie, N.: Practical type inference with levels. Proc. ACM Program. Lang. **9**(PLDI), 2180–2203 (2025), https://doi.org/10.1145/3729338

24. Fiore, M.P., Plotkin, G.D., Turi, D.: Abstract syntax and variable binding. In: 14th Annual IEEE Symposium on Logic in Computer Science, Trento, Italy, July 2–5, 1999. pp. 193–202. IEEE Computer Society (1999), https://doi.org/10.1109/LICS.1999.782615

25. The Fram programming language, https://fram-lang.org

26. Garrigue, J.: A certified implementation of ML with structural polymorphism. In: Ueda, K. (ed.) Programming Languages and Systems — 8th Asian Symposium, APLAS 2010, Shanghai, China, November 28 – December 1, 2010. Proceedings. Lecture Notes in Computer Science, vol. 6461, pp. 360–375. Springer (2010), https://doi.org/10.1007/978-3-642-17164-2_25

27. Gifford, D.K., Jouvelot, P., Sheldon, M.A., O'Toole, J.W.: Report on the FX-91 programming language (1992)

28. Helsen, S., Thiemann, P.: Polymorphic specialization for ML. ACM Trans. Program. Lang. Syst. **26**(4), 652–701 (2004), https://doi.org/10.1145/1011508.1011510

29. Hillerström, D., Lindley, S.: Liberating effects with rows and handlers. In: Chapman, J., Swierstra, W. (eds.) Proceedings of the 1st International Workshop on Type-Driven Development, TyDe@ICFP 2016, Nara, Japan, September 18, 2016. pp. 15–27. ACM (2016), https://doi.org/10.1145/2976022.2976033

30. Ikemori, K., Cong, Y., Masuhara, H., Leijen, D.: Sound and complete type inference for closed effect rows. In: Swierstra, W., Wu, N. (eds.) Trends in Functional

Programming — 23rd International Symposium, TFP 2022, Virtual Event, March 17–18, 2022, Revised Selected Papers. Lecture Notes in Computer Science, vol. 13401, pp. 144–168. Springer (2022), https://doi.org/10.1007/978-3-031-21314-4_8

31. Jiang, S., Cui, C., d. S. Oliveira, B.C.: Bidirectional higher-rank polymorphism with intersection and union types. Proc. ACM Program. Lang. **9**(POPL), 2118–2148 (2025), https://doi.org/10.1145/3704907

32. Jouvelot, P.: Personal communication

33. Jouvelot, P., Gifford, D.K.: Algebraic reconstruction of types and effects. In: Wise, D.S. (ed.) Conference Record of the Eighteenth Annual ACM Symposium on Principles of Programming Languages, Orlando, Florida, USA, January 21–23, 1991. pp. 303–310. ACM Press (1991), https://doi.org/10.1145/99583.99623

34. Leijen, D.: Koka: Programming with row polymorphic effect types. In: Levy, P.B., Krishnaswami, N. (eds.) Proceedings of 5th Workshop on Mathematically Structured Functional Programming, MSFP@ETAPS 2014, Grenoble, France, April 12, 2014. EPTCS, vol. 153, pp. 100–126 (2014), https://doi.org/10.4204/EPTCS.153.8

35. Leijen, D.: Type directed compilation of row-typed algebraic effects. In: Castagna, G., Gordon, A.D. (eds.) Proceedings of the 44th ACM SIGPLAN Symposium on Principles of Programming Languages, POPL 2017, Paris, France, January 18–20, 2017. pp. 486–499. ACM (2017), https://doi.org/10.1145/3009837.3009872

36. Lindley, S., Cheney, J.: Row-based effect types for database integration. In: Pierce, B.C. (ed.) Proceedings of the 8th ACM SIGPLAN Workshop on Types in Languages Design and Implementation, TLDI 2012, Philadelphia, PA, USA, Saturday, January 28, 2012. pp. 91–102. ACM (2012), https://doi.org/10.1145/2103786.2103798

37. Lucassen, J.M., Gifford, D.K.: Polymorphic effect systems. In: Ferrante, J., Mager, P. (eds.) Conference Record of the Fifteenth Annual ACM Symposium on Principles of Programming Languages, San Diego, California, USA, January 10–13, 1988. pp. 47–57. ACM Press (1988), https://doi.org/10.1145/73560.73564

38. Madsen, M.: The principles of the Flix programming language. In: Scholliers, C., Singer, J. (eds.) Proceedings of the 2022 ACM SIGPLAN International Symposium on New Ideas, New Paradigms, and Reflections on Programming and Software, Onward! 2022, Auckland, New Zealand, December 8–10, 2022. pp. 112–127. ACM (2022), https://doi.org/10.1145/3563835.3567661

39. Madsen, M., van de Pol, J.: Polymorphic types and effects with boolean unification. Proc. ACM Program. Lang. **4**(OOPSLA), 154:1–154:29 (2020), https://doi.org/10.1145/3428222

40. Milner, R.: A theory of type polymorphism in programming. J. Comput. Syst. Sci. **17**(3), 348–375 (1978), https://doi.org/10.1016/0022-0000(78)90014-4

41. Naraschewski, W., Nipkow, T.: Type inference verified: Algorithm W in Isabelle/HOL. J. Autom. Reason. **23**(3-4), 299–318 (1999), https://doi.org/10.1023/A:1006277616879

42. Nielson, F., Nielson, H.R.: Constraints for polymorphic behaviours of concurrent ML. In: Jouannaud, J. (ed.) Constraints in Computational Logics, First International Conference, CCL'94, Munich, Germany, September 7–9, 1994. Lecture Notes in Computer Science, vol. 845, pp. 73–88. Springer (1994), https://doi.org/10.1007/BFb0016845

43. Nielson, F., Nielson, H.R.: Type and effect systems. In: Correct System Design: Recent Insights and Advances, pp. 114–136. Springer (2000)

44. Nielson, F., Nielson, H.R., Amtoft, T.: Polymorphic subtyping for effect analysis: The algorithm. In: Dam, M. (ed.) Analysis and Verification of Multiple-Agent Languages, 5th LOMAPS Workshop, Stockholm, Sweden, June 24–26, 1996, Selected

Papers. Lecture Notes in Computer Science, vol. 1192, pp. 207–243. Springer (1996), https://doi.org/10.1007/3-540-62503-8_10

45. Nielson, F., Nielson, H.R., Hankin, C.: Principles of program analysis. Springer (1999), https://doi.org/10.1007/978-3-662-03811-6

46. Nielson, H.R., Amtoft, T., Nielson, F.: Behaviour analysis and safety conditions: A case study in CML. In: Astesiano, E. (ed.) Fundamental Approaches to Software Engineering, 1st Internationsl Conference, FASE'98, Held as Part of the European Joint Conferences on the Theory and Practice of Software, ETAPS'98, Lisbon, Portugal, March 28 – April 4, 1998, Proceedings. Lecture Notes in Computer Science, vol. 1382, pp. 255–269. Springer (1998), https://doi.org/10.1007/BFb0053595

47. Odersky, M., Läufer, K.: Putting type annotations to work. In: Boehm, H., Jr., G.L.S. (eds.) Conference Record of POPL'96: The 23rd ACM SIGPLAN-SIGACT Symposium on Principles of Programming Languages, Papers Presented at the Symposium, St. Petersburg Beach, Florida, USA, January 21–24, 1996. pp. 54–67. ACM Press (1996), https://doi.org/10.1145/237721.237729

48. Peyton Jones, S., Vytiniotis, D., Weirich, S., Shields, M.: Practical type inference for arbitrary-rank types. JFP **17**(1), 1–82 (2007), https://doi.org/10.1017/S0956796806006034

49. Pierce, B.C., Turner, D.N.: Local type inference. ACM Trans. Program. Lang. Syst. **22**(1), 1–44 (2000), https://doi.org/10.1145/345099.345100

50. Plotkin, G.D., Power, A.J.: Computational effects and operations: An overview. In: Escardó, M., Jung, A. (eds.) Proceedings of the Workshop on Domains VI 2002, Birmingham, UK, September 16–19, 2002. Electronic Notes in Theoretical Computer Science, vol. 73, pp. 149–163. Elsevier (2002), https://doi.org/10.1016/j.entcs.2004.08.008

51. Plotkin, G.D., Pretnar, M.: Handling algebraic effects. Log. Methods Comput. Sci. **9**(4) (2013), https://doi.org/10.2168/LMCS-9(4:23)2013

52. Polesiuk, P., Sieczkowski, F.: Functorial syntax for all. In: CoqPL 2024, London, United Kingdom, January 20, 2024 (2024)

53. Rémy, D.: Type inference for records in natural extension of ML, p. 67–95. MIT Press, Cambridge, MA, USA (1994)

54. Talpin, J., Jouvelot, P.: Polymorphic type, region and effect inference. J. Funct. Program. **2**(3), 245–271 (1992), https://doi.org/10.1017/S0956796800000393

55. Talpin, J., Jouvelot, P.: The type and effect discipline. Inf. Comput. **111**(2), 245–296 (1994), https://doi.org/10.1006/inco.1994.1046

56. Tang, Y.M.: Control-Flow Analysis by Effect Systems and Abstract Interpretation. Ph.D. thesis, PhD thesis, Ecoles des Mines de Paris (1994)

57. Tofte, M., Birkedal, L.: A region inference algorithm. ACM Trans. Program. Lang. Syst. **20**(4), 724–767 (1998), https://doi.org/10.1145/291891.291894

58. Tofte, M., Talpin, J.: Implementation of the typed call-by-value lambda-calculus using a stack of regions. In: Boehm, H., Lang, B., Yellin, D.M. (eds.) Conference Record of POPL'94: 21st ACM SIGPLAN-SIGACT Symposium on Principles of Programming Languages, Portland, Oregon, USA, January 17–21, 1994. pp. 188–201. ACM Press (1994), https://doi.org/10.1145/174675.177855

59. Urban, C., Nipkow, T.: Nominal verification of algorithm W, p. 363–382. Cambridge University Press (2009)

60. de Vilhena, P.E., Pottier, F.: A type system for effect handlers and dynamic labels. In: Wies, T. (ed.) Programming Languages and Systems — 32nd European Symposium on Programming, ESOP 2023, Held as Part of the European Joint Conferences on Theory and Practice of Software, ETAPS 2023, Paris, France,

April 22–27, 2023, Proceedings. Lecture Notes in Computer Science, vol. 13990, pp. 225–252. Springer (2023), https://doi.org/10.1007/978-3-031-30044-8_9

61. Wand, M.: Complete type inference for simple objects. In: Proceedings of the Symposium on Logic in Computer Science (LICS '87), Ithaca, New York, USA, June 22–25, 1987. pp. 37–44. IEEE Computer Society (1987)

62. Wells, J.B.: Typability and type checking in system F are equivalent and undecidable. Ann. Pure Appl. Log. **98**(1–3), 111–156 (1999), https://doi.org/10.1016/S0168-0072(98)00047-5

63. Wright, A.K., Felleisen, M.: A syntactic approach to type soundness. Inf. Comput. **115**(1), 38–94 (1994), https://doi.org/10.1006/inco.1994.1093

64. Wu, N., Schrijvers, T., Hinze, R.: Effect handlers in scope. In: Swierstra, W. (ed.) Proceedings of the 2014 ACM SIGPLAN symposium on Haskell, Gothenburg, Sweden, September 4–5, 2014. pp. 1–12. ACM (2014), https://doi.org/10.1145/2633357.2633358

65. Xie, N., Cong, Y., Ikemori, K., Leijen, D.: First-class names for effect handlers. Proc. ACM Program. Lang. **6**(OOPSLA2), 30–59 (2022), https://doi.org/10.1145/3563289

66. Xue, X., d. S. Oliveira, B.C.: Contextual typing. Proc. ACM Program. Lang. **8**(ICFP), 880–908 (2024), https://doi.org/10.1145/3674655

67. Zhang, Y., Myers, A.C.: Abstraction-safe effect handlers via tunneling. PACMPL **3**(POPL), 5:1–5:29 (2019), https://doi.org/10.1145/3290318

68. Zhao, J., d. S. Oliveira, B.C.: Elementary type inference. In: Ali, K., Vitek, J. (eds.) 36th European Conference on Object-Oriented Programming, ECOOP 2022, June 6–10, 2022, Berlin, Germany. LIPIcs, vol. 222, pp. 2:1–2:28. Schloss Dagstuhl - Leibniz-Zentrum für Informatik (2022), https://doi.org/10.4230/LIPIcs.ECOOP.2022.2

69. Zhao, J., d. S. Oliveira, B.C., Schrijvers, T.: Formalization of a polymorphic subtyping algorithm. In: Avigad, J., Mahboubi, A. (eds.) Interactive Theorem Proving — 9th International Conference, ITP 2018, Held as Part of the Federated Logic Conference, FloC 2018, Oxford, UK, July 9–12, 2018, Proceedings. Lecture Notes in Computer Science, vol. 10895, pp. 604–622. Springer (2018), https://doi.org/10.1007/978-3-319-94821-8_36

70. Zhao, J., d. S. Oliveira, B.C., Schrijvers, T.: A mechanical formalization of higher-ranked polymorphic type inference. Proc. ACM Program. Lang. **3**(ICFP), 112:1–112:29 (2019), https://doi.org/10.1145/3341716

Recursive Logical Relations for Intuitionistic Linear Logic Session Types[*]

Stephanie Balzer[1], Farzaneh Derakhshan[2], Robert Harper[1], and Yue Yao[1]

[1] Carnegie Mellon University, `{balzers,rwh,yueyao}@cs.cmu.edu`
[2] Illinois Institute of Technology, `fderakhshan@illinoistech.edu`

Abstract. Program *equivalence* is the heart of reasoning about and proving properties of programs. To assert noninterference, for example, a program is shown to be equivalent to itself up to the confidentiality level of an observer. A powerful enabler for such proofs are *logical relations*, which, guided by the type structure, prescribe when two programs are indistinguishable. Logical relations enjoy ample exploration in functional languages, including languages with general recursion and a higher-order store—yet logical relations for session types only exist for terminating languages. This paper scales logical relations to *general recursive* session types. It develops a logical relation for *progress-sensitive equivalence* for *intuitionistic linear logic session types*, tackling the challenges non-termination and concurrency pose. In particular, the relation only equates a diverging program with another diverging one and accounts for nondeterminism of scheduling. The logical relation has two distinguishing characteristics: it is (i) indexed with an *intuitionistic linear sequent*, validating *cut reductions* and affording *biorthogonal closure*, and (ii) bound by an *observation index*, stratifying the logical relation in the presence of recursion. Biorthogonal closure validates the logical relation, proving that the induced equivalence is *sound and complete* with regard to closure of weak bisimilarity under parallel composition. Soundness guarantees that the equivalence has enough discriminatory power, completeness ensures that it is maximally permissive. The logical relation is then put to test on the example of noninterference.

Keywords: Logical relations · Biorthogonality · Step-indexing · Intuitionistic linear logic session types · Progress-sensitive noninterference.

1 Introduction

Whether two programs are *equivalent* is at the heart of many program verification problems, such as proofs of parametricity, compiler correctness, and noninterference. This paper develops a *logical relation* to reason about program equivalence of *session-typed processes* and proves soundness and completeness of the relation via a *biorthogonality* argument.

---

[*] The first two authors have equal contributions.

© The Author(s) 2026
R. Krebbers (Ed.): ESOP 2026, LNCS 16501, pp. 135–165, 2026.
https://doi.org/10.1007/978-3-032-22720-1_6

Message-passing concurrency. Rooted in process calculi [28, 44, 45], message-passing concurrency enjoys widespread adoption, including languages such as Erlang, Go, and Rust. A program in this setting amounts to a number of *processes* connected by *channels*, which compute by exchanging *messages* along these channels. Messages can even amount to channels themselves, giving rise to so-called *higher-order* channels, as present in the π-calculus [46,57]. This feature is equally empowering as daunting because it changes the process topology dynamically. Originally untyped, the π-caluclus [46] has gradually been enriched with types [57] to prescribe the kinds of messages that can be exchanged over a channel. More advanced type systems [33, 34, 36, 37] additionally assert correctness properties, such as deadlock freedom and data race freedom.

To prescribe not only the types of exchanged messages but also the *protocol* underlying the exchange, *session types* [29, 30] were introduced. Session types rely on a *linear* treatment of channels to model the state transitions induced by a protocol. This foundation manifests in a correspondence between linear logic and the session-typed π-calculus [12,66], resulting in two families of session type languages: *intuitionistic linear logic session types (ILLST)* [12, 13, 63, 64] and *classical linear logic session types (CLLST)* [38, 40, 41, 66]. Due to their logical foundation well-typed ILLST/CLLST processes not only are protocol-compliant (a.k.a., preservation), but also free of data races and deadlocks (a.k.a., progress).

This paper studies logical relations for ILLST-typed processes. ILLST reject linear negation and distinguish the *provider* from the *client* side of a channel. Run-time configurations of processes thus give raise to a *rooted tree*, with a *child* node as the provider and the *parent* node as the client.

Program equivalence. Today's predominant techniques for reasoning about program equivalence of stateful programs are Kripke logical relations (KLRs) [3, 21, 31, 48, 52, 61] and bisimulations [39, 56, 59, 60]. KLRs tend to be used for sequential, ML-like languages, bisimulations for concurrent process calculi. KLRs are phrased by structural induction on types, bisimulations by coinduction. Hur et al. [32] note that KLRs and bisimulations have mutually disjoint strengths and weaknesses. Whereas KLRS naturally support higher-order features, but struggle with recursive types, bisimulations naturally support recursion, but struggle with higher-order features. To support recursive types KLRs employ step-indexing [1, 2, 4], complicating proofs with step arithmetic [10] and challenging transitivity of the logical relation [32].

This paper scales logical relations to session-typed concurrency in the presence of *general recursive types*, contributing a *recursive session logical relation (RSLR)* for intuitionistic linear logic session types (ILLST). In contrast to KLRs, which index the logical relation with the type of the considered expression, RSLRs index the logical relation with an *intuitionistic linear sequent*, denoting the types of the free channels along which the considered process configuration exchanges messages with the outside world. The usual term interpretation clause

$$(e_1; e_2) \in \mathcal{E}[\![\tau]\!] \text{ iff } \ldots$$

for expressions e_1 and e_2 and a type τ in KLRs thus takes the form

$$(\mathcal{D}_1; \mathcal{D}_2) \in \mathcal{E}[\![\Delta \Vdash A]\!] \text{ iff } \ldots$$

in RSLRs, for configurations $\mathcal{D}_1$ and $\mathcal{D}_1$ with the types of free channels denoted by the sequent $\Delta \Vdash A$. This generalization is necessitated by the underlying computational model (message-passing concurrency) and the goal to accommodate various program verification problems, including noninterference. The use of a sequent as an index makes explicit the *duality* of session types, allowing a type to be associated with two interpretations: as a *provider* of a session of that type and a *client*. For example, as a provider of a session $\&\{left{:}A, right{:}B\}$, two related configurations may *assume* to receive related messages, i.e., either they both receive *left* or *right*. As a client of such a session, conversely, related configurations must *assert* to either both send *left* or *right*. The latter condition, crucial for establishing noninterference, is lost when only indexing the logical relation with one type (i.e., the type of the provider). Duality is also central to enforcing a *resource* semantics for channels. For example, as a provider of a session $A \otimes B$, promising to send a channel of type A, related configurations must give up access to the sent channel, whereas a client of such a session will become its owner. Thanks to the validity of semantic cut (Lem. 2), the usual, single-type-index interpretation falls out for free as a special case.

To accommodate general recursive types, RSLRs use an *observation index* to stratify the logical relation. An observation index m is associated with the free channels in $(\mathcal{D}_1; \mathcal{D}_2) \in \mathcal{E}[\![\Delta \Vdash A]\!]^m$ and bounds the number of messages that $\mathcal{D}_1$ and $\mathcal{D}_2$ exchange along those channels. The index is thus associated with an *externally observable* event, symmetrically bounding both configurations. In contrast KLRs employ a step index [2,4,20], which is tied to the internal computation or unfolding steps of one of the two terms, making the relation asymmetric.

We establish several metatheoretic properties of RSLRs. In particular, we show that RSLRs entail an *equivalence relation*, whose proof of transitivity (Lem. 5) benefits from the extensionality of the observation index. Given the possibility of divergence, the equivalence is *progress-sensitive* [26] in that it equates a divergent program only with another diverging one. We also show that RSLRs are *sound and complete* (Thm. 1) with regard to closure of weak *bisimilarity* under parallel composition, using a *biorthogonality* argument à la Pitts [51]. The *duality* of session types establishes a natural connection to biorthogonality. To put the RSLR to test, we employ it to verify *progress-sensitive noninterference*.

Contributions. In summary, this paper makes the following contributions:

- *Recursive session logical relation (RSLR)*, a binary logical relation for *progress-sensitive equivalence* of ILLST processes with general recursion, featuring an *intuitionistic linear sequent* and *observation index*, to capture duality and to support general recursion without compromising extensionality, resp.
- Closure of the RSLR under parallel composition, a.k.a., *semantic cut* (Lem. 2).
- RSLR induces an *equivalence relation*, including *transitivity* (Lem. 5).
- Soundness and completeness of the RSLR with regard to *weak asynchronous bisimilarity*, a.k.a., *adequacy* (Lem. 6).

- Biorthogonal ($\top\top$-) closure of the induced equivalence relation (Thm. 1), guaranteeing that the equivalence has enough discriminatory power (soundness), while being maximally permissive (completeness).
- Small case study applying the RSLR to *progress-sensitive noninterference*.

Technical report. The complete formalization and all proofs are available in [5].

2   Background

This section familiarizes with intuitionistic linear logic session types (ILLST).

ILLST type system. Our development is based on a variant of ILLST languages [12, 13, 63, 64] that supports general recursive types [6, 64]. We refer to this language as SESSION.

SESSION's connectives are drawn from intuitionistic linear logic and obey the following grammar

$$A, B ::= \oplus\{\ell{:}A_\ell\}_{\ell\in L} \mid \&\{\ell{:}A_\ell\}_{\ell\in L} \mid A \otimes B \mid A \multimap B \mid 1 \mid Y,$$

where L ranges over finite, non-empty sets of labels denoted by ℓ and k, the primitive values in SESSION. Type variable Y is a fixed point whose definition $Y = A$ is collected in a global signature Σ. General recursive types are supported through this definition mechanism. They must be *contractive* [23], demanding a message exchange before recurring, and *equi-recursive* [16], avoiding explicit (un)fold messages and relating types up to their unfolding.

Process terms are typed using the *intuitionistic sequent*

$$\Omega \vdash_\Sigma P :: x{:}A$$

to be read as *"process P provides a session of type A along channel variable x, given the typing of sessions offered along channel variables in Ω and given the type and process definitions in Σ"*. Ω is a *linear* context, consisting of assumptions $y_i{:}B_i$, indicating for each channel variable y_i its session type B_i. The signature Σ contains global type and process definitions and facilitates recursive type and process definitions. Bound channel variables are substituted with channels that are created at run-time upon process spawning. When the distinction is clear from the context we refer to either as "channels" for brevity.

ILLST rejects linear negation, allowing the singleton right-hand side of the sequent to be interpreted as the type of the *providing* process, which, conversely, is the *client* of the sessions in Ω. Channels can thus be typed with the type of the providing process, rather than typing the two channel endpoints dually, as done in classical linear logic session types (CLLST) [40, 41, 66]. To express the *duality* in behavior the ILLST type system is given as *sequent calculus*, comprising both a *right* and a *left* rule per connective. Right rules define a communication from the point of view of the provider, left rules from the point of view of the client.

Fig. 1 summarizes the typing rules. Cut reduction in the sequent calculus invites a computational, bottom-up reading of the rules, where the type of the conclusion denotes the protocol state of the provider before the message exchange and the type of the premise the protocol state after the message exchange. The polarity of type moreover determines the direction of communication: for positive connectives, the provider sends and the client receives, for negative connectives, the provider receives and the client sends. We review each rule in turn next.

$$\frac{\Omega \vdash_\Sigma P :: x{:}A_k \qquad k \in L}{\Omega \vdash_\Sigma x.k; P :: x{:} \oplus \{\ell{:}A_\ell\}_{\ell \in L}} \oplus R$$

$$\frac{\Omega, x{:}A_k \vdash_\Sigma Q_k :: y{:}C \quad \forall k \in L}{\Omega, x{:} \oplus \{\ell : A_\ell\}_{\ell \in L} \vdash_\Sigma \mathbf{case}\, x(\ell \Rightarrow Q_\ell)_{\ell \in L} :: y{:}C} \oplus L$$

$$\frac{\Omega \vdash_\Sigma Q_k :: x{:}A_k \qquad \forall k \in L}{\Omega \vdash_\Sigma \mathbf{case}\, x(\ell \Rightarrow Q_\ell)_{\ell \in I} :: x{:}\&\{\ell : A_\ell\}_{\ell \in L}} \&R \qquad \frac{\Omega, x{:}A_k \vdash_\Sigma P :: y{:}C \qquad k \in L}{\Omega, x{:}\&\{\ell : A_\ell\}_{\ell \in I} \vdash_\Sigma x.k; P :: y{:}C} \&L$$

$$\frac{\Omega \vdash_\Sigma P :: x{:}B}{\Omega, z{:}A \vdash_\Sigma \mathbf{send}\, z\, x; P :: x{:}A \otimes B} \otimes R \qquad \frac{\Omega, z{:}A, x{:}B \vdash_\Sigma P :: y{:}C}{\Omega, x{:}A \otimes B \vdash_\Sigma z \leftarrow \mathbf{recv}\, x; P :: y{:}C} \otimes L$$

$$\frac{\Omega, z{:}A \vdash_\Sigma P :: x{:}B}{\Omega \vdash_\Sigma z \leftarrow \mathbf{recv}\, x; P :: x{:}A \multimap B} \multimap R \qquad \frac{\Omega, x{:}B \vdash_\Sigma P :: y{:}C}{\Omega, z{:}A, x{:}A \multimap B \vdash_\Sigma \mathbf{send}\, z\, x; P :: y{:}C} \multimap L$$

$$\frac{}{\cdot \vdash_\Sigma \mathbf{close}\, x :: x : 1} 1R \qquad \frac{\Omega \vdash_\Sigma Q :: y : C}{\Omega, x : 1 \vdash_\Sigma \mathbf{wait}\, x; Q :: y : C} 1L$$

$$\frac{\Omega_1' \vdash X = P :: x'{:}A \in \Sigma \qquad \Omega_1, x{:}A \Vdash \gamma :: \Omega_1', x'{:}A \qquad \Omega_2, x{:}A \vdash_\Sigma Q :: y{:}C}{\Omega_1, \Omega_2 \vdash_\Sigma (x \leftarrow X[\gamma] \leftarrow \Omega_1); Q :: y{:}C} \textsc{Spawn}$$

$$\frac{\begin{array}{c} z'{:}C \vdash F_Y = \mathtt{Fwd}_{C, y' \leftarrow z'} :: y'{:}C \in \Sigma \\ Y = C \in \Sigma \qquad z{:}C, y{:}C \Vdash \gamma :: z'{:}C, y'{:}C \end{array}}{z{:}Y \vdash_\Sigma F_Y[\gamma] :: y{:}C} \textsc{D:Fwd}$$

$$\frac{Y = A \in \Sigma \qquad \Omega \vdash_\Sigma P :: x{:}A}{\Omega \vdash_\Sigma P :: x{:}Y} \textsc{TVar}_R \qquad \frac{Y = A \in \Sigma \qquad \Omega, x{:}A \vdash_\Sigma P :: z{:}C}{\Omega, x{:}Y \vdash_\Sigma P :: z{:}C} \textsc{TVar}_L$$

$$\frac{}{\Vdash_\Sigma (\cdot)\, \mathbf{sig}} \Sigma_1 \qquad \frac{\Vdash_\Sigma A\, \mathbf{contr} \qquad \Vdash_\Sigma \Sigma'\, \mathbf{sig}}{\Vdash_\Sigma Y = A, \Sigma'\, \mathbf{sig}} \Sigma_2 \qquad \frac{\Omega \vdash_\Sigma P :: x{:}A \qquad \Vdash_\Sigma \Sigma'\, \mathbf{sig}}{\Vdash_\Sigma \Omega \vdash_\Sigma X = P :: x{:}A, \Sigma'\, \mathbf{sig}} \Sigma_3$$

Fig. 1: Process term typing rules and signature checking rules of SESSION.

The additive connectives $\oplus\{\ell{:}A_\ell\}_{\ell \in L}$ and $\&\{\ell{:}A_\ell\}_{\ell \in L}$ denote *labelled choices* of sessions A_ℓ, where the labels ℓ range over the finite, non-empty set L. The two connectives differ in who sends a label and thus makes a choice. For $\oplus\{\ell{:}A_\ell\}_{\ell\in L}$, the provider chooses, for $\&\{\ell{:}A_\ell\}_{\ell\in L}$, the client chooses, giving the connectives the names *internal choice* and *external choice*, resp. The duality of behavior of a provider and client is conveyed by the process terms of the right and left rules, resp. For example, a provider of an internal choice (rule $\oplus R$) executes the process term $x.k; P$ to send the label k along its providing channel x, after which it will continue with P of type A_k. Conversely, a client of an internal choice (rule $\oplus L$) executes the process term $\mathbf{case}\, x(\ell \Rightarrow Q_\ell)_{\ell\in L}$ to receive any label $k \in L$ along x, after which it will continue with the chosen branch Q_k of type A_k.

The multiplicative connectives $A \otimes B$ (tensor) and $A \multimap B$ (lolli) allow channels themselves to be sent over channels, changing the process topology at run-time. These connectives endow SESSION with *higher-order channels*, making channels first-class values. Again, the two connectives differ in who sends a channel: for $A \otimes B$, the provider sends, for $A \multimap B$, the client sends. Due to linearity, absence of weakening specifically, the sender loses access to the sent channel in its continuation; as can be seen in the premises of rules $\otimes R$ and $\multimap L$. We use $\leftarrow$ to denote variable binding. For example, the process term $z \leftarrow \mathbf{recv}\, x; P$ in the conclusion of rule $\otimes L$ binds the received channel to y, with scope P.

The unit of $\otimes$, 1, allows a process to terminate. Here, the provider sends a close message, $\mathbf{close}\, x$, along its providing channel x (rule $1R$), awaited by the client. Due to absence of weakening, rule $1R$ demands that the typing context Ω be empty, ensuring that no channels become orphans. Consequently, the client continuation Q loses access to x after receipt of the close message (rule $1L$).

Rule SPAWN types a process that spawns another process using the process definition X. The invocation $x \leftarrow X[\gamma] \leftarrow \Omega_1$ binds the newly spawned process to x and gives it the argument channels Ω_1. After the invocation, the process continues with executing Q, now with $x{:}A$ in its context. For the invocation to succeed, a corresponding process definition $\Omega_1' \vdash X = P :: x'{:}A$ must exist in the signature Σ. The definition associates a name X with the process term P and indicates the names and types of argument channels Ω_1' and the name and type of the providing channel $x'{:}A$. To account for the difference in variable names, the programmer must provide a corresponding mapping $\Omega_1, x{:}A \Vdash \gamma :: \Omega_1', x'{:}A$ as part of the invocation, assigning to each variable in the definition $\Omega_1', x'{:}A$ a corresponding variable of the same type in the invocation $\Omega_1, x{:}A$.

Rule D:FWD allows a process to delegate requests to its singleton child z by passing any messages received along y to z and vice versa. The rule uses a forwarder definition $z'{:}C \vdash F_Y = \mathtt{Fwd}_{C,y'\leftarrow z'} :: y'{:}C$, for the type definition $Y = C$, both to be present in the signature Σ. A corresponding forwarder $\mathtt{Fwd}_{C,y'\leftarrow z'}$ of type C is defined by structural induction on the type of every user-provided type definition, amounting to an *identity expansion*, and can be automatically generated. In combination with rule D:FWD, we get a coinductive definition (see [5] for details). The programmer can use the syntactic sugar $y \leftarrow z$ instead, which can be expanded into the corresponding forwarder.

Rules TVAR$_R$ and TVAR$_L$ allow us to unfold type definitions. The rules insist that a corresponding definition exists in the global signature $Y = A \in \Sigma$.

Rules Σ_1, Σ_2, and Σ_3 type check the signature itself. Rule Σ_2 type checks type definitions, requiring the type be contractive ($\Vdash_\Sigma A$ **contr**) and thus not a type variable itself [23]. Rule Σ_3 type checks the body P of a process definition X, whose existence is assumed when spawning the process in rule SPAWN.

We illustrate the typing rules on a simple PIN-based authentication example, shown in Fig. 2. Fig. 2 introduces two recursive type definitions, pin and ver, as well as two process definitions, Verifier and Pin. A verifier expects to receive a PIN channel from its client, which it validates. If validation is successful, the verifier sends the message *succ*, otherwise the message *fail* to the client. In either case, the verifier also returns the PIN channel. The PIN itself is encoded as an internal choice of labels tok_i, with one being the correct security token.

$$\mathsf{ver} = \mathsf{pin} \multimap \oplus\{succ{:}\mathsf{pin} \otimes \mathsf{ver}, fail{:}\mathsf{pin} \otimes \mathsf{ver}\} \qquad \mathsf{pin} = \oplus\{tok_1{:}\mathsf{pin}, \dots, tok_n{:}\mathsf{pin}\}$$

$$\cdot \vdash \mathsf{Verifier} :: x{:}\mathsf{ver} = (\; u \leftarrow \mathbf{recv}\, x \quad // \quad u{:}\mathsf{pin} \vdash x{:} \oplus \{succ : \mathsf{pin} \otimes \mathsf{ver}, fail{:}\mathsf{pin} \otimes \mathsf{ver}\}$$

$$\mathbf{case}\, u\, (tok_j \Rightarrow x.succ;\, \mathbf{send}\, u\, x;\, x \leftarrow \mathsf{Verifier} \leftarrow \cdot$$

$$|\; tok_{i \neq j} \Rightarrow x.fail;\, \mathbf{send}\, u\, x;\, x \leftarrow \mathsf{Verifier} \leftarrow \cdot))$$

$$\cdot \vdash \mathsf{Pin} :: u{:}\mathsf{pin} = (u.tok_j;\, u \leftarrow \mathsf{Pin} \leftarrow \cdot)$$

Fig. 2: Example: PIN-based authentication.

ILLST configuration typing At runtime, SESSION programs become configurations of processes, forming *rooted trees* and obeying the following grammar:

$$\mathcal{C}, \mathcal{D}, \mathcal{F}, \mathcal{T} ::= \mathbf{proc}(x_\alpha, \hat{\delta}(P))\, \mathcal{C} \mid \mathbf{msg}(M)\, \mathcal{C} \mid \cdot$$
$$M \qquad ::= x_\alpha.k \mid \mathbf{send}\, z_\beta\, x_\alpha \mid \mathbf{close}\, y_\alpha$$

Configurations consist of a set of processes of the form $\mathbf{proc}(y_\alpha, \hat{\delta}(P))$ and a set of messages of the form $\mathbf{msg}(M)$. Every spawn results in a process $\mathbf{proc}(y_\alpha, \hat{\delta}(P))$, every send in a message $\mathbf{msg}(M)$, making SESSION's dynamics asynchronous. The metavariable y_α in $\mathbf{proc}(y_\alpha, \hat{\delta}(P))$ denotes the process' providing channel and the metavariable P the process' source code. Run-time channels y_α can be distinguished from channel variables y by their generation subscript α, whose meaning we clarify in § 2. The substitution δ maps variables to channels; $\hat{\delta}(P)$ yields the term with all free channel variables substituted by channels.

The configuration typing rules of SESSION are given in Fig. 3, using the judgment $\Delta_0 \Vdash \mathcal{C} :: \Delta$. We allow configurations to have *free channels*, which amount to Δ_0 and Δ for the given judgment. The channels in Δ comprise the channels for which there exist providing processes in the configuration $\mathcal{C}$, the channels in Δ_0 comprise the channels for which there exist client processes in the configuration $\mathcal{C}$. It may be surprising that we refer to these channels as free, given that they occur in $\mathcal{C}$. Would linearity not imply that they occur "exactly once", and thus must be bound? It is more fruitful to think of channels as shared resources, like memory locations, *shared* among processes. ILLST then ensures that at most two processes, a provider and a client, share a channel at any point in time, where each "owns" one endpoint of (i.e., a reference to) the channel. The careful accounting of "resources" is visible in the configuration typing rules. For example, rule **proc** insists that for all the channel endpoints used by process $\mathbf{proc}(x_\alpha, \hat{\delta}(P))$ there exists either a provider in the sub-configuration $\mathcal{C}$, making the channel bound, or the endpoint is free and occurs in Δ_0'.

$$\frac{}{x_\alpha{:}A \Vdash \cdot :: x_\alpha{:}A}\ \mathbf{emp}_1 \qquad \frac{}{\cdot \Vdash \cdot :: \cdot}\ \mathbf{emp}_2 \qquad \frac{\Delta_0 \Vdash \mathcal{C} :: \Delta \qquad \Delta_0' \Vdash \mathcal{C}_1 :: x_\alpha{:}A}{\Delta_0, \Delta_0' \Vdash \mathcal{C}\, \mathcal{C}_1 :: \Delta, x_\alpha{:}A}\ \mathbf{comp}$$

$$\frac{\Delta_0 \Vdash \mathcal{C} :: \Delta \qquad \Delta_0', \Delta, x_\alpha{:}A \vdash \delta :: \Omega_0', \Omega, x{:}A \qquad \Omega_0', \Omega \vdash_\Sigma P :: x{:}A}{\Delta_0, \Delta_0' \Vdash \mathcal{C}\, \mathbf{proc}(x_\alpha, \hat{\delta}(P)) :: x_\alpha{:}A}\ \mathbf{proc}$$

$$\frac{\Delta_0 \Vdash \mathcal{C} :: \Delta \qquad \Delta_0', \Delta \vdash M :: x_\alpha{:}A}{\Delta_0, \Delta_0' \Vdash \mathcal{C}\, \mathbf{msg}(M) :: x_\alpha{:}A}\ \mathbf{msg}$$

$$\frac{k \in L}{y_{\alpha+1}{:}A_k \vdash y_\alpha.k :: y_\alpha{:} \oplus \{\ell{:}A_\ell\}_{\ell\in L}}\ \mathbf{m}_{\oplus R} \qquad \frac{k \in L}{x_\alpha{:}\&\{\ell : A_\ell\}_{\ell\in I} \vdash x_\alpha.k :: x_{\alpha+1}{:}A_k}\ \mathbf{m}_{\&L}$$

$$\frac{}{z_\beta{:}A, y_{\alpha+1}{:}B \vdash \mathbf{send}\, z_\beta\, y_\alpha :: y_\alpha{:}A \otimes B}\ \mathbf{m}_{\otimes R}$$

$$\frac{}{z_\beta{:}A, x_\alpha{:}A \multimap B \vdash \mathbf{send}\, z_\beta\, x_\alpha :: x_{\alpha+1}{:}B}\ \mathbf{m}_{\multimap L} \qquad \frac{}{\cdot \vdash \mathbf{close}\, y_\alpha :: y_\alpha{:}1}\ \mathbf{m}_{1R}$$

Fig. 3: Configuration typing rules of SESSION.

ILLST asynchronous dynamics SESSION's asynchronous dynamics is given in Fig. 4. It is phrased as multiset rewriting rules [14]. Multiset rewriting rules express the dynamics as state transitions between configurations $C \mapsto C'$ and are *local* in that they only mention the parts of a configuration they rewrite.

Being *asynchronous*, the dynamics implements sends by spawning off a message $\mathbf{msg}(M)$ that carries the sent message M. In rule $\otimes_{\mathsf{snd}}$, for example, the provider $\mathbf{proc}(y_\alpha, \mathbf{send}\, x_\beta\, y_\alpha; P)$ generates the message $\mathbf{msg}(\mathbf{send}\, x_\beta\, y_\alpha)$, indicating that the channel x_β is sent over channel y_α. In rule $\otimes_{\mathsf{rcv}}$, the client then consumes the message when receiving the channel. To preserve the invariant stipulated by typing that at most two processes share a channel at any point in time, a new providing channel must be generated for the continuation of the provider. This new channel must be linked to the old providing channel, otherwise proper sequencing of messages would be violated.

An elegant way to achieve proper sequencing are *channel generations*. Rather than creating an entirely fresh channel name for each send, we keep the name of a channel constant but increment its generation, provided as a subscript to the channel name. For example, the provider $\mathbf{proc}(y_\alpha, \mathbf{send}\, x_\beta\, y_\alpha; P)$ in rule $\otimes_{\mathsf{snd}}$ steps to its continuation $\mathbf{proc}(y_{\alpha+1}, [y_{\alpha+1}/y_\alpha]P)$, creating a new generation $\alpha + 1$ of its providing channel y_α. The receiving client process $\mathbf{proc}(u_\eta, w \leftarrow \mathbf{recv}\, y_\alpha; P)$ will then increment the channel generation of the carrier channel y_α upon receipt in its continuation $\mathbf{proc}(u_\eta, [x_\beta/w][y_{\alpha+1}/y_\alpha]P)$ (see rule $\otimes_{\mathsf{rcv}}$). Like bound variables, bound channels are subject to α-variance and capture-avoiding substitution, as usual [57], with the understanding that only the name y of a channel y_α can be renamed, but not its generation.

$$
\begin{array}{lll}
\textsc{Spawn} & \mathbf{proc}(y_\alpha, (x \leftarrow X[\gamma] \leftarrow \Delta_1); Q) \;\mapsto & (\Omega_1' \vdash X = P :: x' : B \in \Sigma) \\
& \quad \mathbf{proc}(x_0, \hat{\gamma}([x_0/x]P))\, \mathbf{proc}(y_\alpha, [x_0/x]Q) & (\Omega_1' \Vdash \gamma : \Delta_1,\; x_0\, \mathit{fresh}) \\[4pt]
\textsc{d:fwd} & \mathbf{proc}(y_\alpha, F_Y[\gamma]) \;\mapsto & (x' : C \vdash F_Y = \mathtt{Fwd}_{C, y' \leftarrow x'} :: y' : C \in \Sigma) \\
& \quad \mathbf{proc}(y_\alpha, \mathtt{Fwd}_{C, y_\alpha \leftarrow x_\beta}) & (x', y' \Vdash \gamma : x_\beta, y_\alpha) \\[4pt]
1_{\mathsf{snd}} & \mathbf{proc}(y_\alpha, \mathbf{close}\, y_\alpha) \;\mapsto\; \mathbf{msg}(\mathbf{close}\, y_\alpha) \\[4pt]
1_{\mathsf{rcv}} & \mathbf{msg}(\mathbf{close}\, y_\alpha)\, \mathbf{proc}(x_\beta, \mathbf{wait}\, y_\alpha; Q) \;\mapsto\; \mathbf{proc}(x_\beta, Q) \\[4pt]
\oplus_{\mathsf{snd}} & \mathbf{proc}(y_\alpha, y_\alpha.k; P) \;\mapsto\; \mathbf{proc}(y_{\alpha+1}, [y_{\alpha+1}/y_\alpha]P)\, \mathbf{msg}(y_\alpha.k) \\[4pt]
\oplus_{\mathsf{rcv}} & \mathbf{msg}(y_\alpha.k)\, \mathbf{proc}(u_\eta, \mathbf{case}\, y_\alpha (\ell \Rightarrow P_\ell)_{\ell \in L}) \;\mapsto\; \mathbf{proc}(u_\eta, [y_{\alpha+1}/y_\alpha]P_k) \\[4pt]
\&_{\mathsf{snd}} & \mathbf{proc}(y_\alpha, x_\beta.k; P) \;\mapsto\; \mathbf{msg}(x_\beta.k)\, \mathbf{proc}(y_\alpha, [x_{\beta+1}/x_\beta]P) \\[4pt]
\&_{\mathsf{rcv}} & \mathbf{proc}(y_\alpha, \mathbf{case}\, y_\alpha (\ell \Rightarrow P_\ell)_{\ell \in L})\, \mathbf{msg}(y_\alpha.k) \;\mapsto\; \mathbf{proc}(y_{\alpha+1}, [y_{\alpha+1}/y_\alpha]P_k) \\[4pt]
\otimes_{\mathsf{snd}} & \mathbf{proc}(y_\alpha, \mathbf{send}\, x_\beta\, y_\alpha; P) \;\mapsto\; \mathbf{proc}(y_{\alpha+1}, [y_{\alpha+1}/y_\alpha]P)\, \mathbf{msg}(\mathbf{send}\, x_\beta\, y_\alpha) \\[4pt]
\otimes_{\mathsf{rcv}} & \mathbf{msg}(\mathbf{send}\, x_\beta\, y_\alpha)\, \mathbf{proc}(u_\eta, w \leftarrow \mathbf{recv}\, y_\alpha; P) \;\mapsto\; \mathbf{proc}(u_\eta, [x_\beta/w][y_{\alpha+1}/y_\alpha]P) \\[4pt]
\multimap_{\mathsf{snd}} & \mathbf{proc}(y_\alpha, \mathbf{send}\, x_\beta\, u_\eta; P) \;\mapsto\; \mathbf{msg}(\mathbf{send}\, x_\beta\, u_\eta)\, \mathbf{proc}(y_\alpha, [u_{\gamma+1}/u_\gamma]P) \\[4pt]
\multimap_{\mathsf{rcv}} & \mathbf{proc}(y_\alpha, w \leftarrow \mathbf{recv}\, y_\alpha; P)\, \mathbf{msg}(\mathbf{send}\, x_\beta\, y_\alpha) \;\mapsto\; \mathbf{proc}(y_{\alpha+1}, [x_\beta/w][y_{\alpha+1}/y_\alpha]P)
\end{array}
$$

Fig. 4: Asynchronous dynamics of SESSION.

3 Recursive session logical relation (RSLR)

This section develops a logical relation for ILLST with general recursive types (§ 3.1) and shows that the logical relation is closed under parallel composition (§ 3.2), amounts to an equivalence relation (§ 3.3), and adequate, i.e., a weak asynchronous bisimilarity (§ 3.4). The logical relation is shown to have enough discriminatory power (soundness), while being maximally permissive (completeness) via a biorthogonality argument (Thm. 1).

3.1 Logical relation

Logical relations have been developed for session types [11, 17–19, 27, 49, 50, 54], both in unary and binary forms, but *without* considering general recursion. We contribute a logical relation for ILLST with support of *general recursive types*. In devising the resulting *recursive session logical relation (RSLR)*, we had to tackle the following challenges:

- *Well-foundedness:* Recursive types mandate use of a measure like step-indexing or later modalities [2,4,20] to keep the logical relation well-founded. Our logical relation makes use of a more *extensional* notion, an *observation index*, which bounds the number of messages exchanged with the outside world along the free channels of a configuration. The observation index facilitates proofs of various results shown in this section.
- *Non-termination:* In the presence of general recursive types, divergence is a possible outcome. Our logical relation is *progress-sensitive* [26] with regard to divergence; it equates a divergent program only with another diverging one.
- *Nondeterminism:* Although ILLST are confluent, processes run *concurrently*. As a result, the logical relation has to account for the relatedness of messages that may not be sent in the same order due to nondeterministic scheduling.

A logical relation for message-passing concurrency. It may be helpful to pause a moment and ask what a logical relation for session-typed processes should amount to. Logical relations for functional languages relate terms by defining their equality at their type when evaluated to values. This can be phrased in terms of two mutually recursive relations, a value interpretation $\mathcal{V}[\![\tau]\!]$ and a term interpretation $\mathcal{E}[\![\tau]\!]$, defined by structural induction on the type τ. The former defines equality of values by inducting over a type, with values at ground type forming the base cases, and the latter steps the terms until they reach a value, demanding that these must be related by the value interpretation. In imperative languages, logical relations are enriched with Kripke possible worlds to model dynamically evolving shapes of storage [3,21,31,48,52,61].

To answer our question, it is helpful to remind ourselves that logical relations are a means to prove observational equivalence [47], which equates two programs, if the same observations can be made about them. In a pure functional setting, the observables are the values to which the terms evaluate. In an imperative setting, the observables can additionally comprise the values of locations in the store. The observables in a message-passing concurrent setting are the messages that a configuration of processes exchanges with the outside world.

A logical relation for session-typed processes thus relates pairs of process configurations $(\mathcal{D}_1; \mathcal{D}_2)$, such that $\Delta \Vdash \mathcal{D}_1 :: x_\alpha{:}A$ and $\Delta \Vdash \mathcal{D}_2 :: x_\alpha{:}A$, demanding that the same messages can be observed along the free channels Δ and $x_\alpha{:}A$. Fig. 5 shows the resulting logical relation for well-typed process configurations in SESSION, which is indexed with an *intuitionistic linear sequent* $\Delta \Vdash A$, comprising the free channels. We find it convenient to distinguish a value interpretation $\mathcal{V}$ from a term interpretation $\mathcal{E}$. As expected, the term interpretation steps the configurations until they reach a "value". But what does it mean for a configuration to be a value in a message-passing concurrent setting? It means that a configuration is *ready to send* or *receive* along any of the free channels in $\Delta \cup \{x_\alpha{:}A\}$. For any such channel, the term interpretation invokes the value interpretation, which demands that the exchanged messages be related, and then invokes the term interpretation for the configurations resulting after the message exchange. The mutually recursive relations are defined by clauses of the form

$$(\mathcal{D}_1; \mathcal{D}_2) \in \mathcal{V}[\![\Delta \Vdash A]\!] \quad \text{iff} \quad \ldots (\mathcal{D}_1'; \mathcal{D}_2') \in \mathcal{E}[\![\Delta' \Vdash A']\!].$$

In a terminating setting, the relations are defined *multiset induction over the structure of types of the free channels* [17] such that $\Delta' \Vdash A' < \Delta \Vdash A$. To support general recursive types, we will augment the relations with an observation index, as discussed shortly, yielding an inductive definition.

The sequent $\Delta \Vdash A$ singles out the typing A of the providing free channel of the configurations $\mathcal{D}_1$ and $\mathcal{D}_2$. If the providing free channel is not observable, we write $\_$. We use the metavariable K to stand for either $x_\alpha{:}A$ or simply $\_$. The ability to mark some free channels as unobservable becomes important when we apply the logical relation to noninterference in § 4.

The transition from the value to the term interpretation amounts to an *observation* of a message exchange along a free channel in $\Delta \Vdash K$. The exchange will advance the protocol state of the concerned process, and as a result transition the sequent to $\Delta' \Vdash K'$, describing the post-state of the configurations $(\mathcal{D}_1'; \mathcal{D}_2')$ after the message exchange. The logical relation comprises two value interpretation clauses for each connective, one for the communications occurring on the *right* along K, and one for those occurring on the *left* along Δ.

Assume and assert—a pas de deux. A key characteristic of logical relations is *extensionality*. In a functional context this means that relatedness has to be shown for values of types in positive positions, but values of types in negative positions can be assumed to be related. This idea translates equally to a message-passing concurrent setting, embodied by the logical relation shown in Fig. 5 as:

- *Positive* types: *assert* sending of related messages when communicating on the *right*; *assume* receipt of related messages when communicating on the *left*.
- *Negative* types: *assume* receipt of related messages when communicating on the *right*; *assert* sending of related messages when communicating on the *left*.

At base types (1, $\oplus$, and $\&$), relatedness of messages means that the same messages are being exchanged. For example, clause (2) in Fig. 5 for $\oplus$-right asserts existence of messages $\mathbf{msg}(y_\alpha.k_1)$ and $\mathbf{msg}(y_\alpha.k_2)$ in $\mathcal{D}_1$ and $\mathcal{D}_2$, resp., such that $k_1 = k_2$. Conversely, clause (3) in Fig. 5 for $\&$-right assumes receipt of messages $\mathbf{msg}(y_\alpha.k_1)$ and $\mathbf{msg}(y_\alpha.k_2)$ to be added to $\mathcal{D}_1$ and $\mathcal{D}_2$ in the post-states, resp., such that $k_1 = k_2$, for arbitrary k_1 and k_2.

For higher-order types ($\otimes$ and $\multimap$) relatedness means that future observations to be made along the exchanged channels must be related. For example, clause (10) in Fig. 5 for $\multimap$-left asserts existence of a message $\mathbf{msg}(\mathbf{send}\,x_\beta\,y_\alpha)$ and of subtrees $\mathcal{T}_1$ and $\mathcal{T}_2$ in $\mathcal{D}_1$ and $\mathcal{D}_2$, resp. The subtrees $\mathcal{T}_1$ and $\mathcal{T}_2$ are rooted at the sent channel x_β and will be transferred (and thus lost) together with the sent channel. The clause comprises two invocations of the term relation, $(\mathcal{T}_1; \mathcal{T}_2) \in \mathcal{E}[\![\Delta' \Vdash x_\beta{:}A]\!]$, asserting that future observations to be made along the sent channel x_β are related, and $(\mathcal{D}_1''; \mathcal{D}_2'') \in \mathcal{E}[\![\Delta'', y_{\alpha+1}{:}B \Vdash K]\!]$, asserting that

$(1)\ (\mathcal{D}_1; \mathcal{D}_2) \in \mathcal{V}[\![\cdot \Vdash y_\alpha{:}1]\!]^{m+1}_{\cdot;y_\alpha}$ iff $\mathcal{D}_1 = \mathbf{msg}(\mathbf{close}\ y_\alpha)$ and $\mathcal{D}_2 = \mathbf{msg}(\mathbf{close}\ y_\alpha)$

$(2)\ (\mathcal{D}_1; \mathcal{D}_2) \in$ iff $\exists k_1, k_2 \in I.k_1 = k_2$ and
$\quad \mathcal{V}[\![\Delta \Vdash y_\alpha{:} \oplus \{\ell{:}A_\ell\}_{\ell \in I}]\!]^{m+1}_{\cdot;y_\alpha}$ $\quad \mathcal{D}_1 = \mathcal{D}_1'\mathbf{msg}(y_\alpha.k_1)$ and
$\quad\quad \mathcal{D}_2 = \mathcal{D}_2'\mathbf{msg}(y_\alpha.k_2)$ and
$\quad\quad (\mathcal{D}_1'; \mathcal{D}_2') \in \mathcal{E}[\![\Delta \Vdash y_{\alpha+1}{:}A_{k_1}]\!]^m$

$(3)\ (\mathcal{D}_1; \mathcal{D}_2) \in$ iff $\forall k_1, k_2 \in I.$ if $k_1 = k_2$ then
$\quad \mathcal{V}[\![\Delta \Vdash y_\alpha{:}\&\{\ell{:}A_\ell\}_{\ell \in I}]\!]^{m+1}_{y_\alpha;\cdot}$ $\quad (\mathcal{D}_1\mathbf{msg}(y_\alpha.k_1); \mathcal{D}_2\mathbf{msg}(y_\alpha.k_2)) \in$
$\quad\quad \mathcal{E}[\![\Delta \Vdash y_{\alpha+1}{:}A_{k_1}]\!]^m$

$(4)\ (\mathcal{D}_1; \mathcal{D}_2) \in$ iff $\exists x_\beta$ s.t.
$\quad \mathcal{V}[\![\Delta', \Delta'' \Vdash y_\alpha{:}A \otimes B]\!]^{m+1}_{\cdot;y_\alpha}$ $\quad \mathcal{D}_1 = \mathcal{D}_1'\mathcal{T}_1\mathbf{msg}(\mathbf{send}\ x_\beta\ y_\alpha)$ and
$\quad\quad \mathcal{D}_2 = \mathcal{D}_2'\mathcal{T}_2\mathbf{msg}(\mathbf{send}\ x_\beta\ y_\alpha)$ and
$\quad\quad (\mathcal{T}_1; \mathcal{T}_2) \in \mathcal{E}[\![\Delta'' \Vdash x_\beta{:}A]\!]^m$ and
$\quad\quad (\mathcal{D}_1'; \mathcal{D}_2') \in \mathcal{E}[\![\Delta' \Vdash y_{\alpha+1}{:}B]\!]^m$

$(5)\ (\mathcal{D}_1; \mathcal{D}_2) \in$ iff $\forall x_\beta \notin dom(\Delta, y_\alpha{:}A \multimap B).$
$\quad \mathcal{V}[\![\Delta \Vdash y_\alpha{:}A \multimap B]\!]^{m+1}_{y_\alpha;\cdot}$ $\quad (\mathcal{D}_1\mathbf{msg}(\mathbf{send}\ x_\beta\ y_\alpha); \mathcal{D}_2\mathbf{msg}(\mathbf{send}\ x_\beta\ y_\alpha)) \in$
$\quad\quad \mathcal{E}[\![\Delta, x_\beta{:}A \Vdash y_{\alpha+1}{:}B]\!]^m$

$(6)\ (\mathcal{D}_1; \mathcal{D}_2) \in \mathcal{V}[\![\Delta, y_\alpha{:}1 \Vdash K]\!]^{m+1}_{y_\alpha;\cdot}$ iff $(\mathbf{msg}(\mathbf{close}\ y_\alpha)\mathcal{D}_1; \mathbf{msg}(\mathbf{close}\ y_\alpha)\mathcal{D}_2) \in$
$\quad\quad \mathcal{E}[\![\Delta \Vdash K]\!]^m$

$(7)\ (\mathcal{D}_1; \mathcal{D}_2) \in$ iff $\forall k_1, k_2 \in I.$if $k_1 = k_2$ then
$\quad \mathcal{V}[\![\Delta, y_\alpha : \oplus\{\ell{:}A_\ell\}_{\ell \in I} \Vdash K]\!]^{m+1}_{y_\alpha;\cdot}$ $\quad (\mathbf{msg}(y_\alpha.k_1)\mathcal{D}_1; \mathbf{msg}(y_\alpha.k_2)\mathcal{D}_2) \in$
$\quad\quad \mathcal{E}[\![\Delta, y_{\alpha+1}{:}A_{k_1} \Vdash K]\!]^m$

$(8)\ (\mathcal{D}_1; \mathcal{D}_2) \in$ iff $\exists k_1, k_2 \in I.k_1 = k_2$ and
$\quad \mathcal{V}[\![\Delta, y_\alpha{:}\&\{\ell{:}A_\ell\}_{\ell \in I} \Vdash K]\!]^{m+1}_{\cdot;y_\alpha}$ $\quad \mathcal{D}_1 = \mathbf{msg}(y_\alpha.k_1)\mathcal{D}_1'$ and
$\quad\quad \mathcal{D}_2 = \mathbf{msg}(y_\alpha.k_2)\mathcal{D}_2'$ and
$\quad\quad (\mathcal{D}_1'; \mathcal{D}_2') \in \mathcal{E}[\![\Delta, y_{\alpha+1}{:}A_{k_1} \Vdash K]\!]^m$

$(9)\ (\mathcal{D}_1; \mathcal{D}_2) \in$ iff $\forall x_\beta \notin dom(\Delta, y_\alpha{:}A \otimes B, K).$
$\quad \mathcal{V}[\![\Delta, y_\alpha{:}A \otimes B \Vdash K]\!]^{m+1}_{y_\alpha;\cdot}$ $\quad (\mathbf{msg}(\mathbf{send} x_\beta\ y_\alpha)\mathcal{D}_1; \mathbf{msg}(\mathbf{send} x_\beta\ y_\alpha)\mathcal{D}_2) \in$
$\quad\quad \mathcal{E}[\![\Delta, x_\beta{:}A, y_{\alpha+1}{:}B \Vdash K]\!]^m$

$(10)\ (\mathcal{D}_1; \mathcal{D}_2) \in$ iff $\exists x_\beta$ s.t.
$\quad \mathcal{V}[\![\Delta', \Delta'', y_\alpha{:}A \multimap B \Vdash K]\!]^{m+1}_{\cdot;y_\alpha}$ $\quad \mathcal{D}_1 = \mathcal{T}_1\mathbf{msg}(\mathbf{send} x_\beta\ y_\alpha)\ \mathcal{D}_1''$ and
$\quad\quad \mathcal{D}_2 = \mathcal{T}_2\mathbf{msg}(\mathbf{send} x_\beta\ y_\alpha)\ \mathcal{D}_2''$ and
$\quad\quad (\mathcal{T}_1; \mathcal{T}_2) \in \mathcal{E}[\![\Delta' \Vdash x_\beta{:}A]\!]^m$ and
$\quad\quad (\mathcal{D}_1''; \mathcal{D}_2'') \in \mathcal{E}[\![\Delta'', y_{\alpha+1}{:}B \Vdash K]\!]^m$

$(11)\ (\mathcal{D}_1; \mathcal{D}_2) \in \mathcal{E}[\![\Delta \Vdash K]\!]^{m+1}$ iff $(\mathcal{D}_1; \mathcal{D}_2) \in \mathsf{Tree}(\Delta \Vdash K)$ and
$\quad \forall \Upsilon_1, \Theta_1, \mathcal{D}_1'.$ if $\mathcal{D}_1 \mapsto^{*\Upsilon_1;\Theta_1} \mathcal{D}_1'$ then
$\quad \exists \Upsilon_2, \mathcal{D}_2'$ such that $\mathcal{D}_2 \mapsto^{*\Upsilon_2} \mathcal{D}_2'$, and $\Upsilon_1 \subseteq \Upsilon_2$ and
$\quad \forall y_\alpha \in \mathbf{Out}(\Delta \Vdash K).$
$\quad\quad$ if $y_\alpha \in \Upsilon_1.$ then $(\mathcal{D}_1'; \mathcal{D}_2') \in \mathcal{V}[\![\Delta \Vdash K]\!]^{m+1}_{\cdot;y_\alpha}$ and
$\quad \forall y_\alpha \in \mathbf{In}(\Delta \Vdash K).$
$\quad\quad$ if $y_\alpha \in \Theta_1.$ then $(\mathcal{D}_1'; \mathcal{D}_2') \in \mathcal{V}[\![\Delta \Vdash K]\!]^{m+1}_{y_\alpha;\cdot}$

$(12)\ (\mathcal{D}_1; \mathcal{D}_2) \in \mathcal{E}[\![\Delta \Vdash K]\!]^0$ iff $(\mathcal{D}_1; \mathcal{D}_2) \in \mathsf{Tree}(\Delta \Vdash K)$

Fig. 5: Recursive session logical relation (RSLR) for ILLST. (Clauses (1)-(10) are only defined for well-typed configurations, a condition we elided for concision.)

the continuations $\mathcal{D}_1''$ and $\mathcal{D}_2''$ are related. [3] The channel endpoint x_β is existentially quantified and occurs either bound or free in both $\mathcal{D}_1$ and $\mathcal{D}_2$. Conversely, clause (5) in Fig. 5 for $\multimap$-right assumes receipt of a message $\mathbf{msg}(\mathbf{send}\,x_\beta\,y_\alpha)$ that carries a universally quantified free channel x_β, different from the free channels available in the pre-state ($\forall x_\beta \notin dom(\Delta, y_\alpha{:}A \multimap B)$). The sequent is enlarged with the received channel x_β for the invocation of the term relation $(\mathcal{D}_1\,\mathbf{msg}(\mathbf{send}\,x_\beta\,y_\alpha); \mathcal{D}_2\,\mathbf{msg}(\mathbf{send}\,x_\beta\,y_\alpha)) \in \mathcal{E}[\![\Delta, x_\beta{:}A \Vdash y_{\alpha+1}{:}B]\!]$.

The *duality* of ILLST, established by "cutting" the left and right rule of a connective, translates equally to our logical relation, allowing us to compose related configurations in parallel, such that the assumptions made by one pair of configurations are discharged by the other. We prove this result in §3.2 and exploit it connect our development to biorthogonality in §3.5.

Syntactic well-typedness. The value and term interpretations of our logical relation relate pairs of process configurations only if both are syntactically well-typed. The predicate $(\mathcal{D}_1; \mathcal{D}_2) \in \mathsf{Tree}(\Delta \Vdash K)$ stipulates this requirement and is defined as $\mathcal{D}_1 \in \mathsf{Tree}(\Delta \Vdash K)$ and $\mathcal{D}_2 \in \mathsf{Tree}(\Delta \Vdash K)$, with $\mathcal{D}_i \in \mathsf{Tree}(\Delta \Vdash K)$ defined as $\Delta \Vdash \mathcal{D}_i :: K$ (see [5] for details). For concision, we elide appeals to the $\mathsf{Tree}()$ predicate in the value interpretation (clauses (1)-(10) in Fig. 5). Syntactic typing ensures that configurations form *rooted trees*, a property our proof of semantic cut (Lem. 2 in §3.2) relies upon.

Well-foundedness. In the presence of general recursive types, it is no longer sound to define the logical relation by multiset induction over the structure of types in its sequent $\Delta \Vdash K$. To restore well-foundedness a measure like step-indexing [2, 4] can be employed. Step-indexing is typically tied to the number of type unfolding or computation steps by which one of the two programs is bound. A more natural and symmetric measure for our setting is the number of *observations* that can be made along the free channels $\Delta \Vdash K$ of the logical relation. We thus bound the value and term interpretation of our logical relation by this number and attach the resulting *observation index* as the superscript m to the sequent $\Delta \Vdash K$, yielding clauses of the form

$$(\mathcal{D}_1; \mathcal{D}_2) \in \mathcal{V}[\![\Delta \Vdash K]\!]^{m+1} \text{ iff } \ldots (\mathcal{D}_1'; \mathcal{D}_2') \in \mathcal{E}[\![\Delta' \Vdash K']\!]^m$$

The observation index gets decremented whenever the value interpretation "observes" a message exchange. If $m = 0$, well-typed configurations are trivially related, as expressed by clause (12) in Fig. 5.

Non-termination and nondeterminism. It is now time to take a closer look at the definition of the term interpretation of our logical relation. Its definition is challenged by the possibility of divergence and nondeterminism of scheduling. For the former, a progress-sensitive statement of equivalence demands that the

---

[3] We will momentarily explain the superscript and subscripts of these invocations.

relation relates a divergent program only with another diverging one. For the latter, the term interpretation has to account for the possibility that two configurations may not *simultaneously* be ready to send or receive along a free channel in $\Delta \Vdash K$. To address these challenges, the term interpretation is phrased as follows (we are repeating clause (11) in Fig. 5):

$$(\mathcal{D}_1; \mathcal{D}_2) \in \mathcal{E}[\![\Delta \Vdash K]\!]^{m+1} \text{ iff}$$
$$(\mathcal{D}_1; \mathcal{D}_2) \in \mathsf{Tree}(\Delta \Vdash K) \text{ and } \forall \Upsilon_1, \Theta_1, \mathcal{D}_1'. \text{if } \mathcal{D}_1 \mapsto^{*\Upsilon_1;\Theta_1} \mathcal{D}_1' \text{ then}$$
$$\exists \Upsilon_2, \mathcal{D}_2' \text{ such that } \mathcal{D}_2 \mapsto^{*\Upsilon_2} \mathcal{D}_2' \text{ and } \Upsilon_1 \subseteq \Upsilon_2 \text{ and}$$
$$\forall y_\alpha \in \mathbf{Out}(\Delta \Vdash K). \text{ if } y_\alpha \in \Upsilon_1. \text{ then } (\mathcal{D}_1'; \mathcal{D}_2') \in \mathcal{V}[\![\Delta \Vdash K]\!]^{m+1}_{\cdot;y_\alpha}$$
$$\text{and } \forall y_\alpha \in \mathbf{In}(\Delta \Vdash K). \text{if } y_\alpha \in \Theta_1. \text{ then } (\mathcal{D}_1'; \mathcal{D}_2') \in \mathcal{V}[\![\Delta \Vdash K]\!]^{m+1}_{y_\alpha;\cdot}$$

The term interpretation uses the transition $\mathcal{D}_1 \mapsto^{*\Upsilon_1;\Theta_1} \mathcal{D}_1'$, amounting to the iterated application of the rewriting rules defined in Fig. 4. The star expresses that zero to multiple steps can be taken. The superscript Υ_1 denotes the set of channels in $\Delta \Vdash K$ for which there exist messages in $\mathcal{D}_1'$ to be sent along these channels. The superscript Θ_1 denotes set of channels in $\Delta \Vdash K$ for which there exist processes in $\mathcal{D}_1'$ waiting to receive along these channels.

To ensure progress-sensitivity, the term interpretation asserts, that, whenever $\mathcal{D}_1$ can step, so can $\mathcal{D}_2$. This correspondence is expressed by the condition $\Upsilon_1 \subseteq \Upsilon_2$, ensuring that the messages ready to be sent to the outside world in $\mathcal{D}_2'$ are at least the ones ready to be sent in $\mathcal{D}_1'$. An analogous condition for incoming messages is omitted due to asynchrony of the dynamics where the receipt of a message is not observable. The existentially quantified $\mathcal{D}_2'$ is justified by nondeterminism of scheduling, allowing the term interpretation to choose an appropriate way of stepping $\mathcal{D}_2$ to catch up with $\mathcal{D}_1'$.

The set $\mathbf{Out}(\Delta \Vdash K)$ includes all channels whose types in Δ, K indicate a send. This includes channels in Υ_1 for which the messages are ready to be sent. Similarly, the set $\mathbf{In}(\Delta \Vdash K)$ includes all channels whose types in Δ, K indicate a receive, including those in Θ_1 for which the processes are ready to receive.

To resolve the issue of simultaneity, the term interpretation makes use of two *focus* channels ranging over the sets Υ_1 and Θ_1. These are added as a subscript $\_;\_$ to the value interpretation, where $\cdot;y_\alpha$ indicates that $y_\alpha \in \Upsilon_1$ and $y_\alpha;\cdot$ that $y_\alpha \in \Theta_1$. The term interpretation invokes the value interpretation for all the channels in Υ_1 and Θ_1, thus ensuring that any messages ready to be sent in $\mathcal{D}_1'$ and $\mathcal{D}_2'$ and any processes waiting to receive in $\mathcal{D}_1'$ will be "observed" by the value interpretation. Non-productive configurations are trivially accommodated by the term interpretation, by allowing the sets Υ_1 and Θ_1 to be empty.

Example. We revisit the Verifier example (Fig. 2) to showcase the design of our logical relation. Consider the configuration $\mathcal{D} = \mathbf{proc}(x_0, [x_0/x]\mathsf{Verifier})$, in which the channel x_0 instantiates the channel variable x in the Verifier process. We outline the first few steps required to establish that $\mathcal{D}$ is self-related at observation index 3, i.e., $(\mathcal{D}; \mathcal{D}) \in \mathcal{E}[\![\cdot \Vdash x_0{:}\mathsf{ver}]\!]^3$. By Fig. 4, we observe that $\mathcal{D}$ cannot take any internal steps, that no outgoing message exists in the configuration, and that the only channel on which $\mathcal{D}$ is ready to receive is x_0. Hence, the only possible transition for $\mathcal{D}$ is $\mathcal{D} \mapsto^0_{\emptyset;\{x_0\}} \mathcal{D}$. It follows that the only value relation invoked by this term interpretation is $(\mathcal{D};\mathcal{D}) \in \mathcal{V}[\![\cdot \Vdash x_0{:}\mathsf{ver}]\!]^3_{x_0;\cdot}$, which we can rewrite as $(\mathcal{D};\mathcal{D}) \in \mathcal{V}[\![\cdot \Vdash x_0{:}\mathsf{pin} \multimap \oplus\{succ{:}\mathsf{pin}\otimes\mathsf{ver}, fail{:}\mathsf{pin}\otimes\mathsf{ver}\}]\!]^3_{x_0;\cdot}$ by unfolding the type ver; the latter now matches clause (5) in Fig. 5. To establish this value relation, it remains to show that for an arbitrary $u_\beta \neq x_\alpha$, we can derive $(\mathcal{D}\mathbf{msg}(\mathbf{send}\, u_\beta\, x_0); \mathcal{D}\mathbf{msg}(\mathbf{send}\, u_\beta\, x_0)) \in \mathcal{E}[\![u_\beta{:}\mathsf{pin} \Vdash x_0{:} \oplus \{succ{:}\mathsf{pin} \otimes \mathsf{ver}, fail{:}\mathsf{pin} \otimes \mathsf{ver}\}]\!]^2$, which again invokes the term interpretation via clause (11). The remaining steps follow similarly.

A reader may wonder why the logical relation seems oblivious to recursive type unfoldings. This is because the relation is indexed by the number of external observations and is therefore invariant under such unfoldings. In particular, for the example above, $(\mathcal{D};\mathcal{D}) \in \mathcal{E}[\![\Delta \Vdash x_0{:}\mathsf{ver}]\!]^3$ and $(\mathcal{D};\mathcal{D}) \in \mathcal{E}[\![\Delta \Vdash x_0{:}\mathsf{pin} \multimap \oplus\{succ{:}\mathsf{pin} \otimes \mathsf{ver}, fail{:}\mathsf{pin} \otimes \mathsf{ver}\}]\!]^3$, are equivalent: the value interpretation with focus on channel x_0 is only triggered when the process is waiting to receive a message along x_0. After consumption of the message, the recursive invocation of the term interpretation in clause (5) will then happen at index 2.

3.2   Semantic cut: closure under parallel composition

The use of an observation index rather than a step index by the RSLR is fundamental in proving various metatheoretic properties in the remainder of this section. It allows us to keep the observation index *constant* in the term interpretation, while stepping the configurations internally, permitting disagreement in the number of internal messages exchanged. As a result, internal steps cannot depend on the observation index, facilitating proof of the following lemma:

Lemma 1 (Moving existential over universal quantifier).
If

$$\forall m. \forall \Upsilon_1, \Theta_1, \mathcal{D}'_1.\ \text{if}\ \mathcal{D}_1 \mapsto^{*r_1;\Theta_1} \mathcal{D}'_1,\ \text{then}$$
$$\exists \Upsilon_2, \mathcal{D}'_2\ \text{such that}\ \mathcal{D}_2 \mapsto^{*r_2} \mathcal{D}'_2\ \text{and}\ \Upsilon_1 \subseteq \Upsilon_2\ \text{and}$$
$$\forall x_\alpha \in \mathbf{Out}(\Delta \Vdash K).\ \text{if}\ x_\alpha \in \Upsilon_1.\ \text{then}$$
$$(\mathcal{D}'_1; \mathcal{D}'_2) \in \mathcal{V}[\![\Delta \Vdash K]\!]^{m+1}_{\cdot;x_\alpha}\ \text{and}$$
$$\forall x_\alpha \in \mathbf{In}(\Delta \Vdash K).\text{if}\ x_\alpha \in \Theta_1.\ \text{then}$$
$$(\mathcal{D}'_1; \mathcal{D}'_2) \in \mathcal{V}[\![\Delta \Vdash K]\!]^{m+1}_{x_\alpha;\cdot},$$

then

$$\forall \Upsilon_1, \Theta_1, \mathcal{D}'_1.\text{if}\ \mathcal{D}_1 \mapsto^{*r_1;\Theta_1} \mathcal{D}'_1,\ \text{then}$$
$$\exists \Upsilon_2, \mathcal{D}'_2\ \text{such that}\ \mathcal{D}_2 \mapsto^{*r_2} \mathcal{D}'_2\ \text{and}\ \Upsilon_1 \subseteq \Upsilon_2\ \text{and}$$
$$\forall x_\alpha \in \mathbf{Out}(\Delta \Vdash K).\ \text{if}\ x_\alpha \in \Upsilon_1.\ \text{then}$$
$$\forall m.\ (\mathcal{D}'_1; \mathcal{D}'_2) \in \mathcal{V}[\![\Delta \Vdash K]\!]^{m+1}_{\cdot;x_\alpha}\ \text{and}$$
$$\forall x_\alpha \in \mathbf{In}(\Delta \Vdash K).\text{if}\ x_\alpha \in \Theta_1.\ \text{then}$$
$$\forall m.\ (\mathcal{D}'_1; \mathcal{D}'_2) \in \mathcal{V}[\![\Delta \Vdash K]\!]^{m+1}_{x_\alpha;\cdot}.$$

Proof. The full proof is available in [5]. The proof relies on confluence and backwards closure.

With this lemma in hand, we can now prove that the logical relation is closed under parallel composition.

Lemma 2 (Semantic cut). $\forall m. (\mathcal{D}_1; \mathcal{D}_2) \in \mathcal{E}[\![\Delta, u_\alpha{:}T \Vdash K]\!]^m$ *iff for all* $\mathcal{T}_1$ *and* $\mathcal{T}_2$ *if* $\forall m. (\mathcal{T}_1; \mathcal{T}_2) \in \mathcal{E}[\![\Delta' \Vdash u_\alpha{:}T]\!]^m$ *then* $\forall k. (\mathcal{T}_1\mathcal{D}_1; \mathcal{T}_2\mathcal{D}_2) \in \mathcal{E}[\![\Delta', \Delta \Vdash K]\!]^k$.

Proof. The full proof is available in [5]. The proof relies on Lem. 1.

The semantic cut lemma is analogous to the syntactic cut-elimination theorem, with T serving as the analog of the cut formula. Consider the left-to-right direction. For internal steps in $\mathcal{T}_1\mathcal{D}_1$ invoked by the term interpretation that do not involve the channel $u_\alpha : T$, we can perform corresponding internal steps in $\mathcal{T}_1$ or $\mathcal{D}_1$. Using the fact that $\mathcal{T}_1$ and $\mathcal{D}_1$ are related to $\mathcal{T}_2$ and $\mathcal{D}_2$, resp., we can construct the next step(s) of $\mathcal{T}_2\mathcal{D}_2$ as required by the term interpretation. For internal steps in $\mathcal{T}_1\mathcal{D}_1$ along the channel $u_\alpha : T$, we use the fact that $\mathcal{T}_1$ is ready to send a message along u_α and $\mathcal{D}_1$ is ready to receive along u_α (or vice versa). Here, we take advantage of the duality in the value interpretation for the provider and client of each connective to show that the assertions made by the sender are sufficient to establish the assumptions of the receiver. With this, we invoke the definition of value interpretations to transition to a new term interpretation involving subformula(s) of type T in the sequent and apply the inductive hypothesis. This step is analogous to internal cut reductions in the cut-elimination proof. For any communication in $\mathcal{T}_1\mathcal{D}_1$ along its external channel, we use the fact that either $\mathcal{T}_1$ or $\mathcal{D}_1$ can perform the same communication. Using their respective value interpretations and the inductive hypothesis, we establish the value interpretation for $\mathcal{T}_1\mathcal{D}_1$ and $\mathcal{T}_2\mathcal{D}_2$. This step corresponds to external cut reductions in the cut-elimination proof.

3.3   Logical equivalence

To prove that the RSLR induces an equivalence relation, we introduce the notation $\Delta \Vdash \mathcal{D}_1 :: K \equiv \Delta \Vdash \mathcal{D}_2 :: K$, defined below, where $(\mathcal{C}_1; \mathcal{C}_2) \in \mathsf{Forest}(\Delta' \Vdash \Delta)$ stands for $\Delta' \Vdash \mathcal{C}_1 :: \Delta$ and $\Delta' \Vdash \mathcal{C}_2 :: \Delta$:

Definition 1 (Logical equivalence).
- *We define the relation* $\Delta \Vdash \mathcal{D}_1 :: K \equiv \Delta \Vdash \mathcal{D}_2 :: K$ *as* $(\mathcal{D}_1; \mathcal{D}_2) \in \mathsf{Tree}(\Delta \Vdash K)$ *and* $\forall m. (\mathcal{D}_1; \mathcal{D}_2) \in \mathcal{E}[\![\Delta \Vdash K]\!]^m$ *and* $\forall m.(\mathcal{D}_2; \mathcal{D}_1) \in \mathcal{E}[\![\Delta \Vdash K]\!]^m$.
- *We define the relation* $\Delta \dashv \mathcal{C}_1[\,]\mathcal{F}_1 \dashv K \equiv \Delta \dashv \mathcal{C}_2[\,]\mathcal{F}_2 \dashv K$ *as (i)* $\exists K'$ *such that* $K \Vdash \mathcal{F}_1 :: K' \equiv K \Vdash \mathcal{F}_2 :: K'$ *and (ii)* $\exists \Delta'$ *such that* $(\mathcal{C}_1; \mathcal{C}_2) \in \mathsf{Forest}(\Delta' \Vdash \Delta)$ *and* $\forall \mathcal{T}_1 \in \mathcal{C}_1$, *and* $\forall \mathcal{T}_2 \in \mathcal{C}_2$ *with* $(\mathcal{T}_1; \mathcal{T}_2) \in \mathsf{Tree}(\Delta'_1 \Vdash K'')$, *we have* $\Delta'_1 \Vdash \mathcal{T}_1 :: K'' \equiv \Delta'_1 \Vdash \mathcal{T}_2 :: K''$.

Next, we show that the relation $\equiv$ is reflexive, symmetric, and transitive.

Lemma 3 (Reflexivity). *For all configurations* $\Delta \Vdash \mathcal{D} :: x_\alpha{:}T$, *we have* $(\Delta \Vdash \mathcal{D} :: x_\alpha{:}T) \equiv (\Delta \Vdash \mathcal{D} :: x_\alpha{:}T)$.

Proof. The full proof is available in [5].

Lemma 4 (Symmetry). *For all configurations* $\mathcal{D}_1$ *and* $\mathcal{D}_2$, *we have* $(\Delta \Vdash \mathcal{D}_1 :: x_\alpha{:}T) \equiv (\Delta \Vdash \mathcal{D}_2 :: x_\alpha{:}T)$, *iff* $(\Delta \Vdash \mathcal{D}_2 :: x_\alpha{:}T) \equiv (\Delta \Vdash \mathcal{D}_1 :: x_\alpha{:}T)$,

Proof. The proof is straightforward by Def. 1.

Lemma 5 (Transitivity). *For all configurations $\mathcal{D}_1$, $\mathcal{D}_2$, and $\mathcal{D}_3$, we have*

$$\text{if } (\Delta \Vdash \mathcal{D}_1 :: x_\alpha{:}T) \equiv (\Delta \Vdash \mathcal{D}_2 :: x_\alpha{:}T), \text{ and}$$
$$(\Delta \Vdash \mathcal{D}_2 :: x_\alpha{:}T) \equiv (\Delta \Vdash \mathcal{D}_3 :: x_\alpha{:}T)$$
$$\text{then } (\Delta \Vdash \mathcal{D}_1 :: x_\alpha{:}T) \equiv (\Delta \Vdash \mathcal{D}_3 :: x_\alpha{:}T).$$

Proof. The full proof is available in [5].

3.4   Adequacy

To show that the RSLR is adequate, we prove that configurations related by the logical relation are bisimilar and vice versa. To facilitate this proof, we first give the definition of weak *asynchronous bisimilarity* [57] (Def. 2). The definition relies on a standard labeled transition system displayed in Fig. 6, which rephrases our dynamics in Fig. 4. We define *weak* transitions as

(1) $\Rightarrow$ is the reflexive and transitive closure of $\overset{\tau}{\rightarrow}$,

(2) $\overset{\alpha}{\Rightarrow}$ is $\Rightarrow\overset{\alpha}{\rightarrow}$.

Definition 2 (Weak asynchronous bisimilarity). *Asynchronous bisimilarity, written $\mathcal{D}_1 \approx_{\mathsf{a}} \mathcal{D}_2$, is the largest symmetric relation such that whenever $\mathcal{D}_1 \approx_{\mathsf{a}} \mathcal{D}_2$, we have*

$-(\tau - \mathsf{step})$ *if* $\mathcal{D}_1 \overset{\tau}{\rightarrow} \mathcal{D}_1'$ *then* $\exists \mathcal{D}_2'.\, \mathcal{D}_2 \overset{\tau}{\Rightarrow} \mathcal{D}_2'$ *and* $\mathcal{D}_1' \approx_{\mathsf{a}} \mathcal{D}_2'$,

$-(\mathsf{output})$ *if* $\mathcal{D}_1 \overset{\overline{x_\alpha\, q}}{\rightarrow} \mathcal{D}_1'$ *then* $\exists \mathcal{D}_2'.\, \mathcal{D}_2 \overset{\overline{x_\alpha\, q}}{\Rightarrow} \mathcal{D}_2'$ *and* $\mathcal{D}_1' \approx_{\mathsf{a}} \mathcal{D}_2'$.

$-(\mathsf{left\,input})$ *for all* $q \notin \mathsf{fn}(\mathcal{D}_1)$, *if* $\mathcal{D}_1 \overset{\mathbf{L}\, x_\alpha\, q}{\longrightarrow} \mathcal{D}_1'$ *then* $\exists \mathcal{D}_2'.\, \mathcal{D}_2 \overset{\tau}{\Rightarrow} \mathcal{D}_2'$ *and* $\mathcal{D}_1' \approx_{\mathsf{a}}$

$\mathbf{msg}(x_\alpha.q)\mathcal{D}_2'$,

$-(\mathsf{right\,input})$ *for all* $q \notin \mathsf{fn}(\mathcal{D}_1)$, *if* $\mathcal{D}_1 \overset{\mathbf{R}\, x_\alpha\, q}{\longrightarrow} \mathcal{D}_1'$ *then* $\exists \mathcal{D}_2'.\, \mathcal{D}_2 \overset{\tau}{\Rightarrow} \mathcal{D}_2'$ *and*

$\mathcal{D}_1' \approx_{\mathsf{a}} \mathcal{D}_2' \mathbf{msg}(x_\alpha.q)$.

where $\mathbf{msg}(x_\alpha.q)$ *is defined as* $\mathbf{msg}(\mathbf{close}\, x_\alpha)$ *if* $q = \mathbf{close}$, $\mathbf{msg}(x_\alpha.k)$ *if* $q = k$, *and* $\mathbf{msg}(\mathbf{send}\, z_\delta\, x_\alpha)$ *if* $q = z_\delta$. *Here,* $\mathsf{fn}(\mathcal{D}_1)$ *is the set of free channels in the configuration* $\mathcal{D}_1$.

Our adequacy theorem (Lem. 6) shows that RSLRs are sound and complete with regard to asynchronous bisimilarity.

Lemma 6 (Adequacy). *For all* $(\mathcal{D}_1; \mathcal{D}_2) \in \mathsf{Tree}(\Delta \Vdash K)$, *we have* $\mathcal{D}_1 \approx_{\mathsf{a}} \mathcal{D}_2$ *iff* $\forall m.(\mathcal{D}_1; \mathcal{D}_2) \in \mathcal{E}[\![\Delta \Vdash K]\!]^m$ *and* $\forall m.(\mathcal{D}_2; \mathcal{D}_1) \in \mathcal{E}[\![\Delta \Vdash K]\!]^m$.

Proof. The full proof is available in [5].

Internal transition $\xrightarrow{\tau}$ *defined as:*

$\mathcal{D}_1 \xrightarrow{\tau} \mathcal{D}_1'$ iff $\mathcal{D}_1 \mapsto \mathcal{D}_1'$

Actions $\xrightarrow{\overline{y_\alpha}\,q}$, $\xrightarrow{\mathbf{L}\,y_\alpha\,q}$ *and* $\xrightarrow{\mathbf{R}\,y_\alpha\,q}$ *defined as below when* $y \in \mathbf{fn}(\mathcal{D}_1)$:

(1) $\mathcal{D}_1\,\mathbf{msg}(\mathbf{close}\,y_\alpha)\,\mathcal{D}_2$ $\qquad\qquad\xrightarrow{\overline{y_\alpha}\,\mathbf{close}}$
$\mathcal{D}_1\mathcal{D}_2$

(2) $\mathcal{D}_1\,\mathbf{msg}(y_\alpha.k)\mathcal{D}_2$ $\qquad\qquad\xrightarrow{\overline{y_\alpha}\,k}$
$\mathcal{D}_1\mathcal{D}_2$

(3) $\mathcal{D}_1\,\mathbf{msg}(\mathbf{send}\,x_\beta\,y_\alpha)\mathcal{D}_2$ $\qquad\qquad\xrightarrow{\overline{y_\alpha}\,x_\beta}$
$\mathcal{D}_1\mathcal{D}_2$

(4) $\mathcal{D}_1\mathbf{proc}(z_\delta,\mathbf{wait}\,y_\alpha;P)\mathcal{D}_2$ $\qquad\xrightarrow{\mathbf{L}\,y_\alpha\,\mathbf{close}}$
$\mathbf{msg}(\mathbf{close}\,y_\alpha)\,\mathcal{D}_1\mathbf{proc}(z_\delta,\mathbf{wait}\,y_\alpha;P)\,\mathcal{D}_2$

(5) $\mathcal{D}_1\mathbf{proc}(z_\delta,\mathbf{case}\,y_\alpha\,(\ell \Rightarrow P_\ell)_{\ell \in I})\,\mathcal{D}_2$ $\qquad\xrightarrow{\mathbf{L}\,y_\alpha\,k}$
$\mathbf{msg}(y_\alpha.k)\mathcal{D}_1\mathbf{proc}(z_\delta,\mathbf{case}\,y_\alpha\,(\ell \Rightarrow P_\ell)_{\ell \in I})\mathcal{D}_2$

(6) $\mathcal{D}_1\,\mathbf{proc}(z_\delta,w \leftarrow \mathbf{recv}\,y_\alpha)\mathcal{D}_2$ $\qquad\xrightarrow{\mathbf{L}\,y_\alpha\,x_\beta}$
$\mathbf{msg}(\mathbf{send}\,x_\beta\,y_\alpha)\mathcal{D}_1\,\mathbf{proc}(z_\delta,w \leftarrow \mathbf{recv}\,y_\alpha)\,\mathcal{D}_2$

(7) $\mathcal{D}_1\,\mathbf{proc}(y_\alpha,\mathbf{case}\,y_\alpha\,(\ell \Rightarrow P_\ell)_{\ell \in I})\mathcal{D}_2$ $\qquad\xrightarrow{\mathbf{R}\,y_\alpha\,k}$
$\mathcal{D}_1\,\mathbf{proc}(y_\alpha,\mathbf{case}\,y_\alpha\,(\ell \Rightarrow P_\ell)_{\ell \in I})\,\mathcal{D}_2\mathbf{msg}(y_\alpha.k)$

(8) $\mathcal{D}_1\mathbf{proc}(y_\alpha,w \leftarrow \mathbf{recv}\,y_\alpha)\,\mathcal{D}_2$ $\qquad\xrightarrow{\mathbf{R}\,y_\alpha\,x_\beta}$
$\mathcal{D}_1\mathbf{proc}(y_\alpha,w \leftarrow \mathbf{recv}\,y_\alpha)\mathcal{D}_2\,\mathbf{msg}(\mathbf{send}\,x_\beta\,y_\alpha)$

Fig. 6: Labeled transition system for SESSION.

3.5   Biorthogonality

Our main result, biorthogonal closure of $\equiv$ (Thm. 1), relies upon various definitions, including an *orthogonality* operation $\top$ [9, 43, 51] (Def. 5), which we give next. We follow the development of Pitts [51].

We first define the program relations $PRel(\Delta \Vdash K)$ and environment relations $ERel(\Delta \Vdash K)$ (Def. 4), reliant upon a session-typed environment (Def. 3):

Definition 3 (Session-typed environment). *A session-typed environment with the sequent* $\Delta \Vdash K$, *is of the form* $\mathcal{C}[\,]\mathcal{F}$, *such that for some* Δ' *and* K', *we have* $\Delta' \Vdash \mathcal{C} :: \Delta$ *and* $K \Vdash \mathcal{F} :: K'$.

Definition 4 (Program- and environment- relations). *A session program-relation is a binary relation between session-typed programs, i.e., open configurations of the form* $\Delta \Vdash \mathcal{D} :: K$. *Given the sequent* $\Delta \Vdash K$, *we write* $PRel(\Delta \Vdash K)$ *for the set of all program relations that relate programs* $\Delta \Vdash \mathcal{D} :: K$.

A session environment-relation is a binary relation between session-typed environments. Given the sequent $\Delta \Vdash K$, we write $ERel(\Delta \Vdash K)$ for the set of all environment relations that relate environments $\mathcal{C}[\ ]\mathcal{F}$ with the sequent $\Delta \Vdash K$.

We can now define the orthogonality operation $\top$ [43, 51].

Definition 5 (The $(\_)^{\top}$ operation). *Given sequent $\Delta \Vdash K$ and program relation $r \in PRel(\Delta \Vdash K)$, we define $r^{\top} \in ERel(\Delta \Vdash K)$ by*

$$(\mathcal{C}_1[\ ]\mathcal{F}_1, \mathcal{C}_2[\ ]\mathcal{F}_2) \in r^{\top} \text{ iff}$$
$$\forall(\mathcal{D}_1, \mathcal{D}_2) \in r.(\mathcal{C}_1\mathcal{D}_1\mathcal{F}_1 \approx_a \mathcal{C}_2\mathcal{D}_2\mathcal{F}_2),$$

and given $s \in ERel(\Delta \Vdash K)$, we define $s^{\top} \in PRel(\Delta \Vdash K)$ by

$$(\mathcal{D}_1, \mathcal{D}_2) \in s^{\top} \text{ iff}$$
$$\forall(\mathcal{C}_1[\ ]\mathcal{F}_1, \mathcal{C}_2[\ ]\mathcal{F}_2) \in s.(\mathcal{C}_1\mathcal{D}_1\mathcal{F}_1 \approx_a \mathcal{C}_2\mathcal{D}_2\mathcal{F}_2).$$

By definition, the $\top$ operation is inflationary and idempotent [51].

Finally, we state our main result that the logical equivalence relation $\equiv$ induced by our RSLR (Def. 1) is sound and complete with regard to closure of weak bisimilarity under parallel composition.

Theorem 1 ($\top\top$-closure). *Consider $(\mathcal{D}_1, \mathcal{D}_2) \in \mathsf{Tree}(\Delta \Vdash K)$, we have*

$$(\Delta \Vdash \mathcal{D}_1 :: K) \equiv (\Delta \Vdash \mathcal{D}_2 :: K) \textbf{ iff}$$
$$\forall \mathcal{C}_1, \mathcal{C}_2, \mathcal{F}_1, \mathcal{F}_2. \text{ if } (\Delta \dashv \mathcal{C}_1[\ ]\mathcal{F}_1 \dashv K) \equiv (\Delta \dashv \mathcal{C}_2[\ ]\mathcal{F}_2 \dashv K)$$
$$\text{then } \mathcal{C}_1\mathcal{D}_1\mathcal{F}_1 \approx_a \mathcal{C}_2\mathcal{D}_2\mathcal{F}_2.$$

Proof. The full proof is available in [5].

The main purpose of Thm. 1 is to validate the logical equivalence induced by our logical relation, ensuring that it has enough discriminatory power (soundness) while being maximally permissive (completeness). To do that, Thm. 1 uses biorthogonal closure. As detailed in [51], to prove that a relation r is $\top\top$-closed, i.e., $r = r^{\top\top}$, it is enough to show that for some witness relation s, we have $r = s^{\top}$. Thm. 1 instantiates the program-relation r and environment-relation s (Def. 5) with the logical equivalences (Def. 1) induced by our logical relation: it defines $(\mathcal{D}_1, \mathcal{D}_2) \in r$ as the program relation $(\Delta \Vdash \mathcal{D}_1 :: K) \equiv (\Delta \Vdash \mathcal{D}_2 :: K)$, and shows that if we define the witness relation $(\mathcal{C}_1[\ ]\mathcal{F}_1, \mathcal{C}_2[\ ]\mathcal{F}_2) \in s$ as the environment relation $(\Delta \dashv \mathcal{C}_1[\ ]\mathcal{F}_1 \dashv K) \equiv (\Delta \dashv \mathcal{C}_2[\ ]\mathcal{F}_2 \dashv K)$, then we can prove $r = s^{\top}$. In particular, the theorem proves that related programs cannot be discriminated by related environments ($r \subseteq s^{\top}$) and that programs that cannot be discriminated by related environments are related ($s^{\top} \subseteq r$). Thm. 1 is stated in terms of the definitions of the relations r and s, and Dcf. 5, i.e., the left side is equivalent to $(\mathcal{D}_1, \mathcal{D}_2) \in r$, by the definition of r, and the right side is equivalent to $(\mathcal{D}_1, \mathcal{D}_2) \in s^{\top}$ by Def. 5 and s.

Thm. 1 thus establishes that our logical relation is compositional and extensional (behavioral). It shows that our logical relation includes exactly the programs whose compositions with related environments are observationally equivalent. Soundness ensures that related environments are not very strong and do not have too much discriminatory power with respect to the observable behavior – related environments cannot distinguish between the related programs. Completeness guarantees that related environments are not very weak and have enough discriminatory power – if related environments cannot distinguish between two programs, the programs are indeed related. This aligns with the assert-assume pas de deux described in § 3.1, ensuring that the assumptions made by related programs are exactly those asserted by the related environments and the assertions of the programs are exactly those assumed by the environments.

4   Noninterference

This section applies the RSLR to noninterference, phrased as an equivalence up to the secrecy level ξ of an observer, $\equiv_{\xi}^{\Psi_0}$, given a security lattice Ψ_0 (§ 4.2). The section then illustrates the up-to equivalence $\equiv_{\xi}^{\Psi_0}$ on an example (§ 4.3) and concludes with its metatheoretic properties (§ 4.4), including $\top\top$-closure.

4.1   Attacker model

Our attacker model is parametric in the secrecy level $\xi \in \Psi_0$ of an attacker and a program P, given prior annotation of the free channels of P with secrecy levels $c \in \Psi_0$. It assumes

– that the attacker knows the source code of P;
– that the attacker can only observe the messages sent along the free channels of P with secrecy level $c \sqsubseteq \xi$;
– that an attacker cannot measure the passing of time;
– that an attacker is oblivious of channel names;
– a nondeterministic scheduler.

4.2   Up-to equivalence

To prove noninterference, we introduce an *equivalence relation up to* the secrecy level ξ of an observer, $\equiv_{\xi}^{\Psi_0}$, defined in Def. 8 below. This relation is reminiscent of logical equivalence $\equiv$ (Def. 1), but expects free channels to be annotated with secrecy levels and allows ignoring those channels with secrecy level $\sqsubseteq \xi$.

We first define two auxiliary notions: *(i)* downward projections on context of free channels $\Gamma \Downarrow \xi$ and on the providing free channel $x_\alpha{:}T[c] \Downarrow \xi$ (Def. 6), as well as *(ii)* the predicates **H-Provider**$^\xi$ and **H-Client**$^\xi$ (Def. 7). Since channels are now annotated with secrecy levels, we use the metavariables Γ and K^s to range over the linear typing context and providing channel, resp.

Definition 6 (Typing context projections). *Downward projection on security linear contexts Γ and providing channels K^s is defined as follows:*

$$\Gamma, x_\alpha{:}T[c] \Downarrow \xi \overset{\text{def}}{=} \Gamma \Downarrow \xi, x_\alpha{:}T[c] \quad \text{if } c \sqsubseteq \xi$$
$$\Gamma, x_\alpha{:}T[c] \Downarrow \xi \overset{\text{def}}{=} \Gamma \Downarrow \xi \qquad\qquad \text{if } c \not\sqsubseteq \xi$$
$$\cdot \Downarrow \xi \overset{\text{def}}{=} \cdot$$
$$x_\alpha{:}T[c] \Downarrow \xi \overset{\text{def}}{=} x_\alpha{:}T[c] \qquad\quad \text{if } c \sqsubseteq \xi$$
$$x_\alpha{:}T[c] \Downarrow \xi \overset{\text{def}}{=} \_{:}1[\top] \qquad\quad \text{if } c \not\sqsubseteq \xi$$

The projections are used to keep only the free channels that are observable to an attacker. We close the nonobservable channels off by composing the configuration with high-confidentiality clients (**H-Client**$^\xi$) and providers (**H-Provider**$^\xi$), which may differ for each configuration. These high-confidentiality clients and providers are connected to the configurations through nonobservable channels, making the messages they exchange with the configurations nonobservable to the attacker as well.

Definition 7 (High provider and High client).

$$\cdot \in \textbf{H-Provider}^\xi(\cdot)$$

$$\mathcal{B} \in \textbf{H-Provider}^\xi(\Gamma, x_\alpha{:}A[c]) \qquad \text{iff}$$
$$\textbf{either } c \not\sqsubseteq \xi \text{ and } \mathcal{B} = \mathcal{B}'\mathcal{T} \text{ and } \mathcal{B}' \in \textbf{H-Provider}^\xi(\Gamma) \text{ and}$$
$$\mathcal{T} \in \mathsf{Tree}(\cdot \Vdash x_\alpha{:}A),$$
$$\textbf{or } c \sqsubseteq \xi \text{ and } \mathcal{B} \in \textbf{H-Provider}^\xi(\Gamma)$$

$$\mathcal{T} \in \textbf{H-Client}^\xi(x_\alpha{:}A[c]) \qquad \text{iff}$$
$$\textbf{either } c \not\sqsubseteq \xi \text{ and } \mathcal{T} \in \mathsf{Tree}(x_\alpha{:}A \Vdash \_ : 1), \textbf{ or}$$
$$\textbf{or } c \sqsubseteq \xi \text{ and } \mathcal{B} = \cdot$$

Finally, we can state the relation $\equiv_\xi^{\Psi_0}$. Like $\equiv$ (Def. 1), $\equiv_\xi^{\Psi_0}$ is phrased in terms of the term interpretation of the RSLR, but restricts observations to those free channels that are observable. The remaining free channels will be composed in parallel with arbitrary ILLST-typed configurations.

Definition 8 (Logical equivalence up to observer level). *We define the relation* $(\Gamma_1 \Vdash \mathcal{D}_1 :: x_\alpha{:}A_1[c_1]) \equiv_\xi^{\Psi_0} (\Gamma_2 \Vdash \mathcal{D}_2 :: y_\beta{:}A_2[c_2])$ *as*

$$\mathcal{D}_1 \in \mathsf{Tree}(|\Gamma_1| \Vdash x_\alpha{:}A_1) \text{ and } \mathcal{D}_2 \in \mathsf{Tree}(|\Gamma_2| \Vdash y_\beta{:}A_2) \text{ and}$$
$$\Gamma_1 {\Downarrow} \xi = \Gamma_2 {\Downarrow} \xi = \Gamma \text{ and } x_\alpha{:}A_1[c_1]{\Downarrow}\xi = y_\beta{:}A_2[c_2]{\Downarrow}\xi = K^s \text{ and}$$
$$\forall \mathcal{B}_1 \in \textbf{H-Provider}^\xi(\Gamma_1). \forall \mathcal{B}_2 \in \textbf{H-Provider}^\xi(\Gamma_2).$$
$$\forall \mathcal{T}_1 \in \textbf{H-Client}^\xi(x_\alpha{:}A_1[c_1]). \forall \mathcal{T}_2 \in \textbf{H-Client}^\xi(y_\beta{:}A_2[c_2]).$$
$$\forall m. (\mathcal{B}_1\mathcal{D}_1\mathcal{T}_1, \mathcal{B}_2\mathcal{D}_2\mathcal{T}_2) \in \mathcal{E}[\![|\Gamma| \Vdash |K^s|]\!]^m, \text{ and}$$
$$\forall m. (\mathcal{B}_2\mathcal{D}_2\mathcal{T}_2, \mathcal{B}_1\mathcal{D}_1\mathcal{T}_1) \in \mathcal{E}[\![|\Gamma| \Vdash |K^s|]\!]^m.$$

Def. 8 makes use of an erasure operation $|\_|$ to drop the secrecy annotations, to match the sequent of the logical relation whose free channels lack secrecy annotations. As a result, $\equiv_\xi^{\Psi_0}$ can be used for configurations that type check using an information flow control (IFC) type system as well as "plain-vanilla" ILLST-typed configurations, facilitating *semantic typing* [15,42,62] for progress-sensitive noninterference (PSNI).

4.3   Case study: progress-sensitive noninterference (PSNI)

To illustrate $\equiv_\xi^{\Psi_0}$, we instantiate it on a simplistic example, in the spirit of an insecure version of the Verifier encountered earlier (Fig. 2), shown below. Assuming that our security lattice (Ψ_0) is **guest** $\sqsubseteq$ **alice**, and that the attacker level is **guest**, the below process leaks to an attacker y whether authentication was successful or not by either sending the label s or f, resp.

$$\mathsf{pin} = \&\{tok_1{:}1, tok_2{:}1\} \qquad \mathsf{bit} = \&\{zero{:}1, one{:}1\}$$

$$y{:}\mathsf{bit}[\mathbf{guest}] \vdash \mathsf{X} :: x{:}\mathsf{pin}[\mathbf{alice}] = (\mathbf{case}\, x\, (tok_1 \Rightarrow y.zero; \mathbf{wait}\, y;\, \mathbf{close}\, x$$
$$\mid tok_2 \Rightarrow y.one; \mathbf{wait}\, y;\, \mathbf{close}\, x))$$

To prove that this process is secure, we would have to show that for any substitution that instantiates free variables x and y with free channels x_α and y_β

$$y_\beta : \mathsf{bit}[\mathbf{guest}] \Vdash \mathbf{proc}(x_\alpha, \mathsf{X}) :: x_\alpha{:}\mathsf{pin}[\mathbf{alice}] \quad \equiv_{\mathbf{guest}}^{\Psi_0}$$
$$y_\beta : \mathsf{bit}[\mathbf{guest}] \Vdash \mathbf{proc}(x_\alpha, \mathsf{X}) :: x_\alpha{:}\mathsf{pin}[\mathbf{alice}]$$

We compose the process with the following high-secrecy clients $\mathcal{T}_1$ and $\mathcal{T}_2$, sending different tokens along the high-secrecy channel $x_\alpha{:}\mathsf{pin}[\mathbf{alice}]$,

$$\mathcal{T}_1 = \mathbf{proc}(z_\eta, x_\alpha.tok_1; \mathbf{wait}\, x_\alpha; \mathbf{close}\, z_\eta)$$
$$\mathcal{T}_2 = \mathbf{proc}(z_\eta, x_\alpha.tok_2; \mathbf{wait}\, x_\alpha; \mathbf{close}\, z_\eta),$$

leaving us left to show that for all m:

$$(\mathbf{proc}(x_\alpha, \mathsf{X})\, \mathbf{proc}(z_\eta, x_\alpha.tok_1; \mathbf{wait}\, x_\alpha; \mathbf{close}\, z_\eta);$$
$$\mathbf{proc}(x_\alpha, \mathsf{X})\, \mathbf{proc}(z_\eta, x_\alpha.tok_2; \mathbf{wait}\, x_\alpha; \mathbf{close}\, z_\eta)) \in \mathcal{E}[\![y_\beta{:}\mathsf{bit} \vdash \_\,{:}1]\!]^m$$

Obviously this does not hold true, confirming that process X is insecure. Consider a variant of X that sends the bit *zero* in either case. This variant would be accepted by our logical relation, as it should because it is secure.

Alternatively, we could employ an *information flow control (IFC)* type system [55, 58, 65] to verify whether process X is secure. Such type systems label observables (e.g., output, locations, channels) with secrecy levels drawn from a given security lattice Ψ_0 to prevent "flows from high to low". Next, we sketch such an IFC type system as a refinement of **SESSION**. The full refinement type system is included in [5]. It is based on existing work [17, 18], and thus we only summarize its main characteristics and discuss the typing rules relevant for the example.

To type process terms, we use the judgment

$$\Psi; \Gamma \vdash_\Sigma P@c :: x : A[d].$$

The new elements, compared to **SESSION**'s judgment (see § 2), is the security lattice Ψ and the possible worlds annotations @c and [d] [8], to denote a process' running secrecy and maximal secrecy, resp. Γ is a linear typing context, like Δ, but where types now have maximal secrecy annotations. The idea is that a process' *maximal secrecy* indicates the maximal level of secret information the process may ever obtain, whereas a process' *running secrecy* denotes the highest level of secret information the process has obtained so far.

To constrain the propagation of information, the following invariants are presupposed on the typing judgment $\Psi; \Gamma \vdash_\Sigma P@c :: x : A[d]$

(i) $\forall y{:}B[d'] \in \Gamma. \Psi \Vdash d' \sqsubseteq d$

(ii) $\Psi \Vdash c \sqsubseteq d$

ensuring that the maximal secrecy of a child node is capped by the maximal secrecy of its parent and that the running secrecy of a process is less than or equal to its maximal secrecy, resp. Additionally, the type system ensures that

1. no channel of high secrecy is sent along one with lower secrecy; and
2. a process does not send any message along a low-secrecy channel after receipt of high secrecy information.

The first condition prevents direct flows and is enforced by requiring that the maximal secrecy level of a carrier channel and the channels sent over it match. The second condition is met by ensuring that a process' running secrecy is a sound approximation of the level of secret information a process has obtained so far. To this end, the type system increases the running secrecy of a process upon receipt to *at least* the maximal secrecy of the sending process and, correspondingly, guards sends by making sure that the running secrecy of the sending process is *at most* the maximal secrecy of the receiving process.

This working can be seen in the typing rules for external choice:

$$\frac{\Psi; \Gamma \vdash_\Sigma Q_k@c :: y{:}A_k[c] \qquad \forall k \in L}{\Psi; \Gamma \vdash_\Sigma (\mathbf{case}\, y^c(\ell \Rightarrow Q_\ell)_{\ell \in I})@d_1 :: y{:}\&\{\ell : A_\ell\}_{\ell \in L}[c]} \,\&R$$

$$\frac{\Psi \Vdash d_1 \sqsubseteq c \qquad \Psi; \Gamma, x{:}A_k[c] \vdash_\Sigma P@d_1 :: y{:}C[c'] \qquad k \in L}{\Psi; \Gamma, x{:}\&\{\ell : A_\ell\}_{\ell \in I}[c] \vdash_\Sigma (x^c.k; P)@d_1 :: y{:}C[c']} \,\&L$$

The right rule increases the provider's running secrecy from d_1 to its maximal secrecy c after receipt of the label k. The left rule guards the send by the premise $\Psi \Vdash d_1 \sqsubseteq c$, demanding that the provider's running secrecy d_1 is less than or equal to the maximal secrecy c of the recipient. It is precisely this guard that prevents process X to type check using the refinement IFC type system. This guard also prevents the variant of X, which sends the bit *zero* in either case, to type check, which is accepted by our logical relation. This outcome is expected because type systems have the benefit of automatic verification, foregoing completeness. Our logical relation thus amounts to a *semantic* logical relation [15, 42, 62] for PSNI, as it only requires configurations to be ILLST-typed, but not IFC-typed. The fact that IFC-typed processes are non-interfering is proved as the *fundamental theorem* of the logical relation, see [5].

4.4   Metatheoretic properties of up-to equivalence

Unsurprisingly, $\equiv_\xi^{\Psi_0}$ has analogous properties to $\equiv$, except for reflexivity, which only holds for IFC-typed configurations, as demonstrated by our X process in

§ 4.3. We provide a selection of the most important properties of $\equiv^{\Psi_0}_\xi$, the complete listing is given in [5].

Definition 9 (Bisimulation with secrecy annotated sequent). *For $\mathcal{D}_1 \in$ Tree($|\Gamma_1| \Vdash x_\alpha{:}A_1$), $\mathcal{D}_2 \in$ Tree($|\Gamma_2| \Vdash y_\beta{:}A_2$) we define $\Gamma_1 \Vdash \mathcal{D}_1 :: x_\alpha{:}A_1[c_1] \approx^\xi_{\mathsf{a}} \Gamma_2 \Vdash \mathcal{D}_2 :: y_\beta{:}A_2[c_2]$ as*

$$\Gamma_1 \Downarrow \xi = \Gamma_2, \Downarrow \xi \ \text{ and } \ y_\beta{:}A_2[c_2] \Downarrow \xi = x_\alpha{:}A_1[c_1] \Downarrow \xi \ \text{ and}$$
$$\forall \mathcal{B}_1 \in \mathsf{H\text{-}Provider}^\xi(\Gamma_1).\forall \mathcal{B}_2 \in \mathsf{H\text{-}Provider}^\xi(\Gamma_2).$$
$$\forall \mathcal{T}_1 \in \mathsf{H\text{-}CLient}^\xi(x_\alpha{:}A_1[c_1]).\ \forall \mathcal{T}_2 \in \mathsf{H\text{-}Client}^\xi(y_\beta{:}A_2[c_2]).$$
$$\mathcal{B}_1 \mathcal{D}_1 \mathcal{T}_1 \approx_{\mathsf{a}} \mathcal{B}_2 \mathcal{D}_2 \mathcal{T}_2.$$

Lemma 7 (Adequacy). *For all $\mathcal{D}_1 \in$ Tree($|\Gamma_1| \Vdash x_\alpha{:}A_1$) and $\mathcal{D}_2 \in$ Tree($|\Gamma_2| \Vdash y_\beta{:}A_2$), we have $(\Gamma_1 \Vdash \mathcal{D}_1 :: x_\alpha{:}A_1[c_1]) \equiv^{\Psi_0}_\xi (\Gamma_2 \Vdash \mathcal{D}_2 :: y_\beta{:}A_2[c_2])$ iff $(\Gamma_1 \Vdash \mathcal{D}_1 :: x_\alpha{:}A_1[c_1]) \approx^\xi_{\mathsf{a}} (\Gamma_2 \Vdash \mathcal{D}_2 :: y_\beta{:}A_2[c_2])$.*

Proof. The full proof is available in [5].

Theorem 2 ($\top\top$-closure). *Consider $\mathcal{D}_1 \in$ Tree($|\Gamma_1| \Vdash |x_\alpha{:}A_1[c_1]|$) and $\mathcal{D}_2 \in$ Tree($|\Gamma_2| \Vdash |y_\beta{:}A_2[c_2]|$) and a given observer level $\xi \in \Psi_0$. We have*

$$(\Gamma_1 \Vdash \mathcal{D}_1 :: x_\alpha{:}A_1[c_1]) \equiv^\xi_{\Psi_0} (\Gamma_2 \Vdash \mathcal{D}_2 :: y_\beta{:}A_2[c_2]) \ \textbf{iff}$$

$$\forall \mathcal{C}_1, \mathcal{C}_2, \mathcal{F}_1, \mathcal{F}_2.$$
$$\text{if } (\Gamma_1 \dashv \mathcal{C}_1[\ ]\mathcal{F}_1 \dashv x_\alpha{:}A_1[c_1]) \equiv^\xi_{\Psi_0} (\Gamma_2 \dashv \mathcal{C}_2[\ ]\mathcal{F}_2 \dashv y_\beta{:}A_2[c_2])$$
$$\text{then } \forall \mathcal{B}_1 \in \mathsf{H\text{-}Provider}^\xi(\Gamma_1).\forall \mathcal{B}_2 \in \mathsf{H\text{-}Provider}^\xi(\Gamma_2).$$
$$\forall \mathcal{T}_1 \in \mathsf{H\text{-}CLient}^\xi(x_\alpha{:}A_1[c_1]).\ \forall \mathcal{T}_2 \in \mathsf{H\text{-}Client}^\xi(y_\beta{:}A_2[c_2]).$$
$$\mathcal{B}_1 \mathcal{C}_1 \mathcal{D}_1 \mathcal{F}_1 \mathcal{T}_1 \approx_{\mathsf{a}} \mathcal{B}_2 \mathcal{C}_2 \mathcal{D}_2 \mathcal{F}_2 \mathcal{T}_2$$

Proof. The full proof is available in [5].

Completeness ensures that the logical relation relates all secure programs, while IFC type systems, by nature, reject infinitely many secure programs. Our logical relation thus becomes generally applicable. For example, we may conceive a more permissive IFC refinement type system that accepts more secure programs. All we would have to do in this case is prove the fundamental theorem for that new refinement type system, guaranteeing that well-typed programs are self-related by our logical relation and thus non-interfering. We conclude this section by noting that all the results presented here are corollaries of the results in Section 3.

5   Related work and discussion

Logical relations for session types. The application of logical relations to session types has focused predominantly on unary logical relations for proving termination [19,49,50,54], except for a binary logical relation for parametricity [11] and noninterference [17,18,27]. Our RSLR shares its foundation in linear logic with this line of work, but contributes significantly through its support of general recursive types.

Caires et al. [11] show parametricity for a terminating language and restrict observations to the single offering channel of a configuration, i.e., observations are only made at the root. Thanks to the validity of semantic cut, a single-type-indexed logical relation, such as the authors', falls out as a special case of our RSLR. However, more fine-grained program equivalences, such as noninterference, demand distinguishing the two roles a process configuration may assume. To the best of our understanding, our account of duality ultimately also enabled biorthogonal closure to prove the logical equivalence sound and complete.

Among prior work on logical relations for ILLST, the work by Derakhshan et al. [17] is most closely related to ours. The authors contribute an IFC session type system and develop a logical relation to show noninterference. The refinement type system that we use in our case study (§ 4.3) is based on that IFC system, extended with secrecy-polymorphic processes [18]. Besides the authors' confinement to a terminating language, sidestepping the intricacies of non-termination and nondeterminism, the authors' metatheoretic results are significantly more limited than ours. In particular, the logical relation is dependent on IFC typing, and thus only amounts to a *syntactic* logical relation for noninterference. Moreover, their development lacks metatheoretic results about the entailed program equivalence, i.e., that it is sound with respect to bisimilarity. There are several nuances in the design of our logical relation that enable us to show such results in a more general setting, which also allows for non-termination: Unlike [17], which only considers closed configurations, i.e., it cannot relate two programs without their clients and providers, our logical relation is defined over open configurations and thus allows for connection to biorthogonality. Furthermore, our term interpretation carefully uses the universal and existential quantifiers and thus enables the proof of transitivity for the logical relation, which is not proven in [17]. Our logical relation also handles non-termination via focus channels and the observation index. These features enable defining the logical relation for equivalence in a general context, proving that it is both sound and complete with respect to asynchronous bisimilarity by establishing a connection to biorthogonality, and then instantiating it in various settings, such as noninterference.

Also noteworthy is the work by Rocha and Caires [53, 54]. The authors contribute CLASS, a calculus based on classical linear logic session types enriched with memory cells, acting as mutexes to share affine data between processes. Unlike more liberal support of sharing [6–8], the authors adopt the propositions-as-types paradigm to ensure deadlock freedom and strong normalization. These guarantees are realized by stratifying resources into nested hierarchies. Interesting in relation to our work, is CLASS' metatheory: to prove strong normalization, the authors develop a unary logical relation, defined to be $\top\top$-closed reliant on Girard's orthogonality [24]. Besides being binary to express program equivalence and admitting open configurations, our logical relation is not defined to be $\top\top$-closed, but the logical equivalence induced by our relation shown to be $\top\top$-closed (Thm. 1). As discussed in § 3.5, the proof of admissibility of $\top\top$ closure serves a validation of the equivalence, guaranteeing that its discriminatory power is strong enough (soundness) while being maximally permissive (completeness).

Relationship to logical relations for stateful languages. Logical relations have been scaled to accommodate state using Kripke logical relations (KLRs) [52]. KLRs are indexed by a *possible world* W, providing a semantic model of the heap. Invariants can then be imposed that must be preserved by any future worlds W'. KRLs can be combined with step indexing [2, 4] to address circularity arising from higher-order stores [3, 21, 22] and to express state transition systems. For example, Gregersen et al. [25] use the KLR supported in Iris [35] to prove noninterference for a functional language with a higher-order store, recursive types, and impredicative polymorphism. The authors also adopt semantic typing [15, 42, 62], admitting syntactically ill-typed programs, if shown to inhabit the logical relation. Besides the difference in language, the authors consider termination-*insensitive* noninterference, whereas we consider progress-*sensitive* noninterference. Like KLRs, our RSLR is situated in a stateful setting because channels, like locations, are subject to concurrent mutation. However, our RSLR is rooted in ILLST, which guarantees race freedom, stratifies the store (the configuration of processes), and prescribes state transitions. When squinting one's eyes, the sequent $\Delta \Vdash K$ of the logical relation seems reminiscent of a possible world, since it provides the semantic typing of the free channels. However, linearity would not comport well with the usual monotonicity requirement of logical relations. We would like to investigate this connection as future work.

6   Concluding remarks

We have contributed a recursive session logical relation (RSLR) for progress-sensitive equivalence of programs. The RSLR is rooted in intuitionistic linear logic session types, inheriting from it a strong foundation in linear logic, ensuring that channel endpoints are treated as resources. A novel aspect of the RSLR is its use of an *observation index* to keep the logical relation well-defined in the presence of general recursive types. This shift, from a step index / unfolding index associated with *internal* computation steps to an index only associated with *external* observations, facilitates statement and proof of metatheoretic properties of the logical relation: closure under parallel composition, soundness and completeness with regard to weak asynchronous bisimilarity, and biorthogonal closure of the logical equivalence relation induced by the RSLR. A biorthogonality argument arises naturally from the duality inherent to session types. In future work, we would like to explore these connections more deeply, possibly connecting to Kripke logical relations and game semantics.

Acknowledgments. This material is based upon work supported by the Air Force Office of Scientific Research under Award No. FA9550-21-1-0385 (Tristan Nguyen, program manager) and upon work supported by the National Science Foundation under Grant No. 2442461. Any opinions, findings, and conclusions or recommendations expressed in this material are those of the author(s) and do not necessarily reflect the views of the U.S. Department of Defense or the National Science Foundation.

References

1. Ahmed, A.: Semantics of Types for Mutable State. Ph.D. thesis, Princeton University (2004)
2. Ahmed, A.: Step-indexed syntactic logical relations for recursive and quantified types. In: 15th European Symposium on Programming (ESOP). Lecture Notes in Computer Science, vol. 3924, pp. 69–83. Springer (2006). https://doi.org/10.1007/11693024_6
3. Ahmed, A., Dreyer, D., Rossberg, A.: State-dependent representation independence. In: 36th ACM SIGPLAN-SIGACT Symposium on Principles of Programming Languages (POPL). pp. 340–353. ACM (2009). https://doi.org/10.1145/1480881.1480925
4. Appel, A.W., McAllester, D.A.: An indexed model of recursive types for foundational proof-carrying code. ACM Transactions on Programming Languages and Systems (TOPLAS) **23**(5), 657–683 (2001). https://doi.org/10.1145/504709.504712
5. Balzer, S., Derakhshan, F., Harper, R., Yao, Y.: Logical relations for session-typed concurrency. CoRR **abs/2309.00192** (2026). https://doi.org/10.48550/ARXIV.2309.00192
6. Balzer, S., Pfenning, F.: Manifest sharing with session types. Proceedings of the ACM on Programming Languages **1**(ICFP), 37:1–37:29 (2017). https://doi.org/10.1145/3110281
7. Balzer, S., Pfenning, F., Toninho, B.: A universal session type for untyped asynchronous communication. In: 29th International Conference on Concurrency Theory (CONCUR). LIPIcs, vol. 118, pp. 30:1–30:18. Schloss Dagstuhl - Leibniz-Zentrum für Informatik (2018). https://doi.org/10.4230/LIPICS.CONCUR.2018.30
8. Balzer, S., Toninho, B., Pfenning, F.: Manifest deadlock-freedom for shared session types. In: 28th European Symposium on Programming (ESOP). Lecture Notes in Computer Science, vol. 11423, pp. 611–639. Springer (2019). https://doi.org/10.1007/978-3-030-17184-1_22
9. Benton, N., Hur, C.: Biorthogonality, step-indexing and compiler correctness. In: 14th ACM SIGPLAN International Conference on Functional Programming (ICFP). pp. 97–108. ACM (2009). https://doi.org/10.1145/1596550.1596567
10. Benton, N., Hur, C.: Step-indexing: The good, the bad and the ugly. In: Modelling, Controlling and Reasoning About State. Dagstuhl Seminar Proceedings, vol. 10351, pp. 1–9. Schloss Dagstuhl - Leibniz-Zentrum für Informatik, Germany (2010), http://drops.dagstuhl.de/opus/volltexte/2010/2808/
11. Caires, L., Pérez, J.A., Pfenning, F., Toninho, B.: Behavioral polymorphism and parametricity in session-based communication. In: 22nd European Symposium on Programming (ESOP). pp. 330–349 (2013). https://doi.org/10.1007/978-3-642-37036-6_19
12. Caires, L., Pfenning, F.: Session types as intuitionistic linear propositions. In: 21th International Conference onf Concurrency Theory (CONCUR). Lecture Notes in Computer Science, vol. 6269, pp. 222–236. Springer (2010). https://doi.org/10.1007/978-3-642-15375-4_16
13. Caires, L., Pfenning, F., Toninho, B.: Linear logic propositions as session types. Mathematical Structures in Computer Science **26**(3), 367–423 (2016). https://doi.org/10.1017/S0960129514000218

14. Cervesato, I., Scedrov, A.: Relating state-based and process-based concurrency through linear logic. Information and Computation **207**(10), 1044–1077 (2009). `https://doi.org/10.1016/j.ic.2008.11.006`
15. Constable, R.L., Allen, S.F., Bromley, M., Cleaveland, R., Cremer, J.F., Harper, R., Howe, D.J., Knoblock, T.B., Mendler, N.P., Panangaden, P., Sasaki, J.T., Smith, S.F.: Implementing Mathematics with the Nuprl Proof Development System. Prentice Hall (1986), `http://dl.acm.org/citation.cfm?id=10510`
16. Crary, K., Harper, R., Puri, S.: What is a recursive module? In: ACM SIGPLAN Conference on Programming Language Design and Implementation (PLDI). pp. 50–63. ACM (1999). `https://doi.org/10.1145/301618.301641`
17. Derakhshan, F., Balzer, S., Jia, L.: Session logical relations for noninterference. In: 36th Annual ACM/IEEE Symposium on Logic in Computer Science (LICS). pp. 1–14. IEEE Computer Society (2021). `https://doi.org/10.1109/LICS52264.2021.9470654`
18. Derakhshan, F., Balzer, S., Yao, Y.: Regrading policies for flexible information flow control in session-typed concurrency. In: 38th European Conference on Object-Oriented Programming (ECOOP). LIPIcs, vol. 313, pp. 11:1–11:29. Schloss Dagstuhl - Leibniz-Zentrum für Informatik (2024). `https://doi.org/10.4230/LIPICS.ECOOP.2024.11`
19. DeYoung, H., Pfenning, F., Pruiksma, K.: Semi-axiomatic sequent calculus. In: 5th International Conference on Formal Structures for Computation and Deduction (FSCD). LIPIcs, vol. 167, pp. 29:1–29:22. Schloss Dagstuhl - Leibniz-Zentrum für Informatik (2020). `https://doi.org/10.4230/LIPIcs.FSCD.2020.29`
20. Dreyer, D., Ahmed, A., Birkedal, L.: Logical step-indexed logical relations. In: 24th Annual IEEE Symposium on Logic in Computer Science (LICS). pp. 71–80. IEEE Computer Society (2009). `https://doi.org/10.1109/LICS.2009.34`
21. Dreyer, D., Neis, G., Birkedal, L.: The impact of higher-order state and control effects on local relational reasoning. In: 15th ACM SIGPLAN International Conference on Functional Programming (ICFP). pp. 143–156. ACM (2010). `https://doi.org/10.1145/1863543.1863566`
22. Dreyer, D., Neis, G., Birkedal, L.: The impact of higher-order state and control effects on local relational reasoning. Journal of Functional Programming **22**(4-5), 477–528 (2012). `https://doi.org/10.1017/S095679681200024X`
23. Gay, S.J., Hole, M.: Subtyping for session types in the pi calculus. Acta Informatica **42**(2-3), 191–225 (2005). `https://doi.org/10.1007/s00236-005-0177-z`
24. Girard, J.: Linear logic. Theoretical Computer Science **50**, 1–102 (1987). `https://doi.org/10.1016/0304-3975(87)90045-4`
25. Gregersen, S.O., Bay, J., Timany, A., Birkedal, L.: Mechanized logical relations for termination-insensitive noninterference. Proceedings of the ACM on Programming Languages **5**(POPL), 1–29 (2021). `https://doi.org/10.1145/3434291`
26. Heidin, D., Sabelfeld, A.: A perspective on information-flow control. Tech. rep., Marktoberdorf (2011)
27. van den Heuvel, B., Derakhshan, F., Balzer, S.: Information flow control in cyclic process networks. In: 38th European Conference on Object-Oriented Programming (ECOOP). LIPIcs, vol. 313, pp. 40:1–40:30. Schloss Dagstuhl - Leibniz-Zentrum für Informatik (2024). `https://doi.org/10.4230/LIPICS.ECOOP.2024.40`
28. Hoare, C.A.R.: Communicating Sequential Processes. Prentice-Hall (1985)
29. Honda, K.: Types for dyadic interaction. In: 4th International Conference on Concurrency Theory (CONCUR). Lecture Notes in Computer Science, vol. 715, pp. 509–523. Springer (1993). `https://doi.org/10.1007/3-540-57208-2_35`

30. Honda, K., Vasconcelos, V.T., Kubo, M.: Language primitives and type discipline for structured communication-based programming. In: 7th European Symposium on Programming (ESOP). Lecture Notes in Computer Science, vol. 1381, pp. 122–138. Springer (1998). https://doi.org/10.1007/BFb0053567
31. Hur, C., Dreyer, D.: A kripke logical relation between ML and assembly. In: 38th ACM SIGPLAN-SIGACT Symposium on Principles of Programming Languages (POPL). pp. 133–146. ACM (2011). https://doi.org/10.1145/1926385.1926402
32. Hur, C., Dreyer, D., Neis, G., Vafeiadis, V.: The marriage of bisimulations and kripke logical relations. In: 39th ACM SIGPLAN-SIGACT Symposium on Principles of Programming Languages (POPL). pp. 59–72. ACM (2012). https://doi.org/10.1145/2103656.2103666
33. Igarashi, A., Kobayashi, N.: A generic type system for the pi-calculus. In: 8th ACM SIGPLAN-SIGACT Symposium on Principles of Programming Languages (POPL). pp. 128–141 (2001). https://doi.org/10.1145/360204.360215
34. Igarashi, A., Kobayashi, N.: A generic type system for the pi-calculus. Theoretical Computer Science **311**(1-3), 121–163 (2004). https://doi.org/10.1016/S0304-3975(03)00325-6
35. Jung, R., Krebbers, R., Jourdan, J., Bizjak, A., Birkedal, L., Dreyer, D.: Iris from the ground up: A modular foundation for higher-order concurrent separation logic. Journal of Functional Programming **28**, e20 (2018). https://doi.org/10.1017/S0956796818000151
36. Kobayashi, N.: A partially deadlock-free typed process calculus. In: 12th Annual IEEE Symposium on Logic in Computer Science (LICS). pp. 128–139. IEEE Computer Society (1997). https://doi.org/10.1109/LICS.1997.614941
37. Kobayashi, N.: A new type system for deadlock-free processes. In: 17th International Conference on Concurrency Theory (CONCUR). LNCS, vol. 4137, pp. 233–247 (2006). https://doi.org/10.1007/11817949_16
38. Kokke, W., Montesi, F., Peressotti, M.: Better late than never: A fully-abstract semantics for classical processes. Proceedings of the ACM on Programming Languages **3**(POPL), 24:1–24:29 (2019). https://doi.org/10.1145/3290337
39. Koutavas, V., Wand, M.: Small bisimulations for reasoning about higher-order imperative programs. In: 33rd ACM SIGPLAN-SIGACT Symposium on Principles of Programming Languages (POPL). pp. 141–152. ACM (2006). https://doi.org/10.1145/1111037.1111050
40. Lindley, S., Morris, J.G.: A semantics for propositions as sessions. In: 24th European Symposium on Programming (ESOP). Lecture Notes in Computer Science, vol. 9032, pp. 560–584. Springer (2015). https://doi.org/10.1007/978-3-662-46669-8_23
41. Lindley, S., Morris, J.G.: Talking bananas: Structural recursion for session types. In: 21st ACM SIGPLAN International Conference on Functional Programming (ICFP). pp. 434–447. ACM (2016). https://doi.org/10.1145/2951913.2951921
42. Martin-Löf, P.: Constructive mathematics and computer programming. In: Logic, Methodology and Philosophy of Science VI, Studies in Logic and the Foundations of Mathematics, vol. 104, pp. 153–175. Elsevier (1982). https://doi.org/https://doi.org/10.1016/S0049-237X(09)70189-2
43. Melliès, P., Vouillon, J.: Recursive polymorphic types and parametricity in an operational framework. In: 20th Annual IEEE Symposium on Logic in Computer Science (LICS). pp. 82–91. IEEE Computer Society (2005). https://doi.org/10.1109/LICS.2005.42
44. Milner, R.: A Calculus of Communicating Systems, Lecture Notes in Computer Science, vol. 92. Springer (1980). https://doi.org/10.1007/3-540-10235-3

45. Milner, R.: Communication and Concurrency. PHI Series in Computer Science, Prentice Hall (1989)
46. Milner, R.: Communicating and Mobile Systems: the π-calculus. Cambridge University Press (1999)
47. Morris, J.H.: Lambda-Calculus Models of Programming Languages. Ph.D. thesis, Massachusetts Institute of Technology (1968)
48. Neis, G., Dreyer, D., Rossberg, A.: Non-parametric parametricity. Journal of Functional Programming **21**(4-5), 497–562 (2011). https://doi.org/10.1017/S0956796811000165
49. Pérez, J.A., Caires, L., Pfenning, F., Toninho, B.: Linear logical relations for session-based concurrency. In: 21st European Symposium on Programming (ESOP). Lecture Notes in Computer Science, vol. 7211, pp. 539–558. Springer (2012). https://doi.org/10.1007/978-3-642-28869-2_27
50. Pérez, J.A., Caires, L., Pfenning, F., Toninho, B.: Linear logical relations and observational equivalences for session-based concurrency. Information and Computation **239**, 254–302 (2014). https://doi.org/10.1016/j.ic.2014.08.001
51. Pitts, A.M.: Parametric polymorphism and operational equivalence. Mathematical Structures in Computer Science **10**(3), 321–359 (2000), http://journals.cambridge.org/action/displayAbstract?aid=44651
52. Pitts, A.M., Stark, I.: Operational reasoning for functions with local state. Higher Order Operational Techniques in Semantics (HOOTS) pp. 227–273 (1998)
53. Rocha, P.: CLASS: A Logical Foundation for Typeful Programming with Shared State. Ph.D. thesis, NOVA University Lisbon (2022)
54. Rocha, P., Caires, L.: Safe session-based concurrency with shared linear state. In: 32nd European Symposium on Programming (ESOP). Lecture Notes in Computer Science, vol. 13990, pp. 421–450. Springer (2023). https://doi.org/10.1007/978-3-031-30044-8_16
55. Sabelfeld, A., Myers, A.C.: Language-based information-flow security. IEEE Journal of Selected Areas in Communications **21**(1), 5–19 (2003). https://doi.org/10.1109/JSAC.2002.806121
56. Sangiorgi, D., Kobayashi, N., Sumii, E.: Environmental bisimulations for higher-order languages. In: 22nd Annual IEEE Symposium on Logic in Computer Science (LICS). pp. 293–302. IEEE Computer Society (2007). https://doi.org/10.1109/LICS.2007.17
57. Sangiorgi, D., Walker, D.: The π-calculus: a Theory of Mobile Processes. Cambridge University Press (2001)
58. Smith, G., Volpano, D.M.: Secure information flow in a multi-threaded imperative language. In: 25th ACM SIGPLAN-SIGACT Symposium on Principles of Programming Languages (POPL). pp. 355–364. ACM (1998). https://doi.org/10.1145/268946.268975
59. Støvring, K., Lassen, S.B.: A complete, co-inductive syntactic theory of sequential control and state. In: 34th ACM SIGPLAN-SIGACT Symposium on Principles of Programming Languages (POPL). pp. 161–172. ACM (2007). https://doi.org/10.1145/1190216.1190244
60. Sumii, E., Pierce, B.C.: A bisimulation for type abstraction and recursion. Journal of the ACM **54**(5), 26 (2007). https://doi.org/10.1145/1284320.1284325
61. Thamsborg, J., Birkedal, L.: A kripke logical relation for effect-based program transformations. In: 16th ACM SIGPLAN International Conference on Functional Programming (ICFP). pp. 445–456. ACM (2011). https://doi.org/10.1145/2034773.2034831

62. Timany, A., Krebbers, R., Dreyer, D., Birkedal, L.: A logical approach to type soundness. Journal of the ACM (JACM) **71**(6), 40:1–40:75 (2024). https://doi.org/10.1145/3676954
63. Toninho, B.: A Logical Foundation for Session-Based Concurrent Computation. Ph.D. thesis, Carnegie Mellon University and New University of Lisbon (2015)
64. Toninho, B., Caires, L., Pfenning, F.: Higher-order processes, functions, and sessions: A monadic integration. In: 22nd European Symposium on Programming (ESOP). Lecture Notes in Computer Science, vol. 7792, pp. 350–369. Springer (2013). https://doi.org/10.1007/978-3-642-37036-6_20
65. Volpano, D.M., Irvine, C.E., Smith, G.: A sound type system for secure flow analysis. Journal of Computer Security **4**(2/3), 167–188 (1996). https://doi.org/10.3233/JCS-1996-42-304
66. Wadler, P.: Propositions as sessions. In: ACM SIGPLAN International Conference on Functional Programming (ICFP). pp. 273–286. ACM (2012). https://doi.org/10.1145/2364527.2364568

Code Generation via Meta-programming in Dependently Typed Proof Assistants

Mathis Bouverot-Dupuis[1,2] ⋆,
Yannick Forster[1]

[1] Inria Paris `{mathis.bouverot-dupuis,yannick.forster}@inria.fr`
[2] ENS Paris

Abstract. Dependently typed proof assistants offer powerful meta-programming features, which allow users to implement proof automation or compile-time code generation. This paper surveys meta-programming frameworks in Rocq, Agda, and Lean, with seven implementations of a running example: deriving instances for the `Functor` typeclass. This example is fairly simple, but realistic enough to highlight recurring difficulties with meta-programming: conceptual limitations of frameworks such as term representation – and in particular binder representation –, meta-language expressiveness, and verifiability, as well as current limitations such as API completeness, learning curve, and prover state management, which could in principle be remedied. We conclude with insights regarding features an ideal meta-programming framework should provide.

1 Introduction

All proof assistants support user-extensible tactics and code generation through meta-programming frameworks. Meta-programs are programs that produce or manipulate other programs as data. They can in particular be used to generate boilerplate code, i.e. code that can be mechanically derived from definitions, thereby increasing the productivity of proof assistant users. Common examples are induction principles [79, 48], equality deciders [79, 38], finiteness proofs [25], countability proofs [25], or substitution functions for syntax [77]. Naturally, the default meta-programming language of a proof assistant is its implementation language, and several proof assistants even come with multiple independent meta-programming frameworks. However, we can observe that meta-programming is not widespread on the example of boilerplate generation tools which often fall into one of the following: Either proof assistants come with built-in boilerplate generation support (such as induction principles or typeclass instances) which is widely used. Or tools for generating boilerplate are developed, but not adopted by the community [79, 38, 16]. Lastly, many papers remark that automatic boilerplate generation would be feasible and interesting, but do not carry it out [83, 85, 34, 30]. Furthermore, subcommunities often seem to be split into silos regarding frameworks and we are not aware of scientific comparative work between different frameworks and proof assistants. The notable exception is Dubois de Prisque's PhD thesis [27], using several meta-programming frameworks in Rocq, but not coming with one central example implemented in different frameworks and focusing solely on Rocq.

⋆ Corresponding author: mathis.bouverot-dupuis@inria.fr

R. Krebbers (Ed.): ESOP 2026, LNCS 16501, pp. 166–189, 2026.
https://doi.org/10.1007/978-3-032-22720-1_7

An additional barrier to adoption is that most frameworks are organically grown and documentation is not accessible to non-experts: pros and cons are often implicitly known by developers but not readily accessible. In fact, the situation is so chaotic that, at times, in order to generate boilerplate code authors create ad hoc meta-programming facilities from scratch [77, 51, 78, 39] instead of taking advantage of existing meta-programming facilities.

On the other hand, the vast choice of meta-programming frameworks also hints that we are at a point where enough evidence is available to evaluate the state of the art and suggest future developments. In this paper, we focus on three major dependently typed proof assistants based on the Calculus of Inductive Constructions (CIC) [21, 65]: Rocq [80], Agda [62, 63], and Lean 4 [56]. We survey their respective meta-programming frameworks: Rocq OCaml plugins (§ 3), MetaRocq [5, 75] (§ 4), Agda's Reflection A PI [84] (§ 5), L ean 4's meta-programming API (§ 6)[3], and Elpi [31, 79] (§ 7). In the extended version [12], we furthermore survey Ltac2 [71] and explain a novel approach to use Rocq's OCaml API with locally nameless syntax. This means that we focus on systems which are designed as proof assistants with consistent meta-theory, rather than dependently typed programming languages, and focus on those with conceptual similarity and shared foundations. In particular, we do not consider Idris [13, 14], HOL-based systems, or LF-based systems, but discuss them in § 8.

We evaluate the different m eta-programming f rameworks o n a s imple yet realistic example: automatically deriving instances of the `Functor` typeclass for a simple family of inductives, covering, amongst many other types, options, lists, and trees. For Rocq we e.g. want to generate the following for the list type:

```
Fixpoint map {A B : Type} (f : A -> B) (l : list A) : list B :=
  match l with [] => [] | x :: l => f x :: map f l end.
```

Our implementations support non-mutual, non-indexed, possibly nested inductives with a single parameter. The only exception is the Lean implementation which does not support recursive (and thus nested) inductives, the reasons of which are explained in section § 6.

Many tasks involving automatic boilerplate generation follow the same model as this example: take an inductive as input and produce a term as output. We choose this example because it is simple enough for code to be readable and explainable, yet complex enough to expose issues that arise in more realistic meta-programs, and makes use of common meta-programming features such as typeclass search or the ability to extend the global environment.

Our evaluation criteria are split into *conceptual* criteria, which are inherent to the approach used by the meta-programming framework, and *current* criteria, which are incidental characteristics of the framework and could be changed in the future. *Conceptual* criteria include the expressiveness of the meta-language (especially access to printing, exceptions, non-termination, and mutable state), term representation used (especially of binders), and verifiability of meta-programs. Since this is an experience report, we also comment on learning curve: the author(s) of examples in this paper had no previous contact to most

---

[3] There is no publication on meta-programming in Lean 4 yet, just a collaborative book draft [66]. Lean 3's meta-programming was surveyed by Ebner et al. [32].

meta-programming frameworks, excluding Ltac2 and OCaml Rocq plugins. *Current* criteria include API completeness, management of the prover state (such as the global environment or unification state), and the presence of term quotation.

We do not consider performance issues in this paper: most inductive to term meta-programs run in an order of magnitude of seconds, and only have to be run once per inductive definition. In practice, developments rarely contain many inductive type definitions or very large inductive type definitions. Thus, we deem performance less critical than the aspects discussed here. Performance issues are critical when implementing proof automation (such as tactics) or more complex meta-programs such as unification algorithms or type checkers (for instance Rocq's verified kernel in MetaRocq [76] or Lean's kernel in Lean4Lean [15]), which are out of scope for this paper. We also do not consider actual verification of meta-programs, as it is not achievable in most of the frameworks we consider as of today, but still comment on verifiability when relevant.

This paper is the first evaluation of the state of the art in meta-programming and lays the foundations for future projects regarding meta-programming. Our perspective is of course subjective, and the perspective of an *average user* of the discussed frameworks. One of the authors is a developer of MetaRocq, and the other author had some amount of experience with meta-programming in Lean, Ltac2, and OCaml plugins prior to this survey.

Consequently, insights in this paper might be well-known or even folklore for experts in the field and developers of frameworks. However, as far as we are aware, none of these insights have ever been written down transparently, and they are thus inaccessible for users of meta-programming frameworks.

Of all the aspects we discuss, variable binding techniques are certainly the one which has been discussed the most densely in related work. However, these techniques have mainly been discussed from the perspective of doing meta-theoretic proofs [9, 1], and not from the perspective of meta-programming. We thus think that our report complements these insights. We would not go as far as saying that we have identified a meta-programming challenge akin to the POPLmark challenge for formalisation, but our report can certainly be seen as a first step.

Contributions.

1. A comprehensive survey of the six meta-programming frameworks in Rocq, Agda, and Lean, from the point of view of users rather than experts
2. An overview of their pros and cons.
3. A simple but realistic tool with different implementations for automatically deriving instances of the `Functor` typeclass.
4. Suggestions for the development of future frameworks. Our paper can also be seen as a first step towards a suggested Rosetta Stone project for meta-programming in Rocq, which is stalled [link anonymised].

This paper has an extended version on HAL [12], containing two additional sections surveying Ltac2 and OCaml plugins using a locally nameless approach, as well as several appendices containing code for the various implementations.

2   Preliminaries

Meta-programs crucially rely on the features provided by the *elaborator* of the proof assistant, such as unification, type checking or inference, and typeclass resolution. They also need to manipulate the *state* of a proof assistant, consisting of the *global environment* (stores global definitions and inductives), *local environment* (local variables, and in the case of Rocq also section variables and hypotheses), and *evar-map* (unification variables). This manipulation can be implicit, or explicit by threading the three components through programs.

How binders are represented is a key question for meta-programs. De Bruijn indices and the locally nameless approach were both introduced by de Bruijn in his seminal paper [26] and are used in the implementations of Rocq, Agda, and Lean and consequently in the associated meta-programming frameworks. The notable exception is Coq-Elpi, which uses higher-order abstract syntax (HOAS) [67]. We give examples of the representations in the respective sections.

Our example is the generation of instances of the following Functor typeclass:

```
Class Functor (F : Type -> Type) : Type :=
  { fmap {A B} : (A -> B) -> F A -> F B }.
```

We have already shown the instance for `list` in the introduction. Our implementation also handles more complex types, for instance using nesting:

```
Inductive tree (A : Type) : Type :=
| Leaf : tree A
| Node : A -> list (tree A) -> tree A.


Fixpoint fmap {A B : Type} (f : A -> B) (t : tree A) : tree B :=
  match t with Leaf => Leaf
             | Node x ts => Node (f x) (List.map (fmap f) ts) end.
```

In general, inductives can be non-recursive (e.g. `bool`, `option`), recursive (`nat`, `list`), have parameters (`option`, `list`), or have indices (`vector`). We support as input inductive types with a single (uniform) parameter and no indices. We do not support mutual recursion for simplicity. For simplicity, the code samples shown in the paper do not handle recursive inductives: the complete implementations do handle the general case, apart from the one in Lean, see § 6.

In the case of `Node` in the example above, we applied `f` to the first argument `x`, and `List.map (fmap f)` to the second argument `ts`. In general, there are various ways to disambiguate what function to apply. The canonical way is to do type-based disambiguation. An alternative is to use typeclass inference of the proof assistant, which is what we do in our implementation.

For instance, we define the second branch as `Node (fmap f x) (fmap f ts)` in the example above, and let typeclass resolution determine which functor we are mapping over. To be able to do so, we need to use the identity functor for `x` and for `ts` the composition of the `list` and `tree` functors.

Consequently, we globally declare:

```
Instance fid : Functor (fun T => T).
Instance fcomp (F G : Type -> Type) `(Functor F) `(Functor G) :
  Functor (fun T => G (F T)).
```

Naively using the typeclass-based approach may fail in the case of recursive inductives such as `tree` or `list`. For instance in the `tree` example, typeclass resolution will fail to find a `Functor` instance for `fmap f ts` (because there is no instance of `Functor tree` in scope). We can solve this issue by using a local typeclass instance. In the case of `tree`:

```
Fixpoint fmap {A B : Type} (f : A -> B) (t : tree A) : tree B :=
  let _ := Build_Functor tree fmap in
  match t with Leaf => Leaf
             | Node x ts => Node (fmap f x) (fmap f ts) end.
```

Typeclass resolution will now consider the local instance `_ : Functor tree` when elaborating `fmap f ts`. Note that this stretches the limits of what the termination checker is capable of accepting: we had to disable Agda's termination checker, and in the case of Rocq we had to help the guard checker by normalizing `fmap` before adding it to the global environment.

We do not expect alternative approaches to this problem to alter the conclusions of this experience report.

3   OCaml Plugin

As Rocq is implemented in OCaml, writing an OCaml plugin is historically the most common way of meta-programming [64, 72, 29, 24], see the extended version [12, Appendix A] for the code.

Pros – Conceptual	P1 - Plugins have access to full implementation.
Pros – Current	P2 - OCaml is a mature programming language.
Cons – Conceptual	C1 - De Bruijn index arithmetic is difficult.
	C2 - No term quotations.
Cons – Current	C3 - OCaml plugins are hard to set up.
	C4 - Cluttered meta-programming API.
	C5 - Explicit state management.

P1 - Conceptual OCaml plugins allow users to directly access all of Rocq's implementation. Meta-programs manipulate the kernel representation of terms:

```
type EConstr.t =
| tRel (idx : int)                         (** Local variable. *)
| tApp (f : EConstr.t) (l : EConstr.t list)  (** Application. *)
| ...
```

For instance the function `build_fmap` in our code simply returns a term corresponding to the mapping function over the given inductive:

```
let build_fmap env sigma ind : evar_map * EConstr.t = ...
```

The evar-map `sigma` is updated and returned alongside the resulting term. Meta-programs have access to all the functionality provided by Rocq, including term manipulation functions, unification, and the tactic engine. Such direct access guarantees that the API is complete: users can leverage every customisable aspect of the proof assistant, including features not commonly found in other meta-programming languages, such as the ability to extend the parser. Moreover, it ensures the API stays up to date with the latest Rocq features: when new features (e.g. universe polymorphism) are added to Rocq, one typically has to wait some time before the various Rocq meta-languages add support for them.

P2 - Current OCaml is a general-purpose programming language used in many applications besides Rocq meta-programming and thus enjoys a large ecosystem of packages, as well as robust and well-maintained tools (such as a language server, a code formatter, an optimising compiler, a package manager, etc), which is not the case for Rocq's other meta-languages.

C1 - Conceptual OCaml plugins directly manipulate the kernel representation of terms, which uses de Bruijn indices for variables. For instance the term $\lambda f.\lambda x.\lambda y.f\ x\ y$ is represented as $\lambda.\lambda.\lambda.3\ 2\ 1$. De Bruijn indices require a significant amount of experience to manipulate correctly: writing explicit indices and lifting terms was a major source of errors when getting started, e.g.

```
let sigma, arg' = build_arg env sigma
  ( lift_inputs (i+1) inp) ( mkRel 1 )
  ( Vars.lift 1 @@ EConstr.of_constr @@ get_type decl)
in loop env sigma (i+1) ( lift (ca.cs_nargs-i-1) arg' :: acc) decls
```

C2 - Conceptual Most meta-languages provide a high-level method to build terms using *term quotations*, which is a lightweight mechanism allowing one to turn user syntax terms into the internal representation used by the meta-language. Plugins do not provide any quotation mechanism: building terms is thus rather verbose and tedious. In the absence of term quotations, one has to provide fully qualified kernel names, pass all implicit arguments to functions, provide typeclass instances by hand (or manually create unification variables to stand in for unknown instances), and explicitly instantiate all universe polymorphic constants and inductives.

C3 - Current Integrating a plugin into a build system currently requires significant overhead, even when using the modern **dune** build system for Rocq: one has to include plugin-specific dune stanzas as well as several other build-specific files. This is in stark contrast with most other meta-languages.

C4 - Current The plugin API is cluttered, thus hard to use for non-experts. It provides code to accomplish common meta-programming tasks but finding the right function often requires reading their *implementation* (i.e. reading *.ml* files in addition to *.mli* files), or asking the Rocq developers for help. Fortunately the developers are easy to reach (via online forums) and eager to provide help.

C5 - Current Finally, plugins provide no good solution for managing the prover state: the environment and evar-map are explicitly passed as arguments to and returned from most functions. For instance, here is the code which builds the outer lambda abstractions of `fmap`:

```
lambda env sigma "a" ta @@ fun env ->
lambda env sigma "b" tb @@ fun env ->
lambda env sigma "f" (arr (mkRel 2) (mkRel 1)) @@ fun env ->
lambda env sigma "x" (apply_ind env ind @@ mkRel 3) @@ fun env ->
  (sigma, ...)
```

Here `lambda env sigma "x" T k` builds a lambda abstraction with a binder named x and of type T; the continuation k takes in the new environment (updated with a binding for x) and returns the body of the lambda abstraction alongside the updated evar-map. The resulting code is verbose and obfuscates the core logic.

4   MetaRocq

The MetaRocq project [5, 75] is a fully verified re-implementation of Rocq's kernel in Rocq, and also includes a meta-programming API in one of its subprojects. The bare-bones meta-programming framework has been used in [23, 48, 35, 76, 36, 7, 27, 4, 6]. The extended version [12, Appendix C] shows the Rocq code for the MetaRocq plugin.

Pros – Conceptual	P1 - Users already know Rocq.
	P2 - Meta-programs can be formally verified.
Pros – Current	P3 - Significant parts are formally verified.
Cons – Conceptual	C1 - De Bruijn index arithmetic is difficult.
	C2 - Lack of abstractions to handle effects.
Cons – Current	C3 - Explicit state management.
	C4 - Missing high-level meta-programming features.
	C5 - Performance issues in some cases.

P1 - Conceptual An appealing aspect of MetaRocq is the ability to perform meta-programming directly using the host language Rocq, flattening the learning curve significantly. To this end, the AST of terms is *reified* in Rocq:

```
Inductive term :=
| tRel : nat -> term
| tApp : term -> list term -> term
| ...
```

Rocq's kernel is re-implemented in Rocq, thus standard functions such as reduction, conversion, and type checking are readily available:

```
(** Conversion checking, implemented in Rocq. *)
Definition eq_term : term -> term -> bool.
```

For higher-level APIs (e.g. extending the global environment), MetaRocq comes with a monad `TemplateMonad` with bindings to Rocq's actual OCaml implementation:

```
(** Declare a new constant. Simply a wrapper around OCaml code. *)
Axiom tmMkDefinition : constant_entry -> TemplateMonad unit.
```

Such monadic programs can be run using the `MetaRocq Run` command.

P2 - Conceptual In addition to useful meta-programming features, MetaRocq includes an extensive formalisation of Rocq's type theory, with proofs of key results of theoretical interest such as subject reduction. It is possible to formally verify meta-programs by leveraging Rocq's theorem proving features in combination with the numerous lemmas already present in MetaRocq. Note however that there is no specification for the operations which use the template monad: verifying meta-programs which use high-level features such as unification or type inference is still an active research area.

P3 - Current Many of the functions provided by MetaRocq are formally verified with respect to Rocq's type theory, providing strong correctness guarantees. This is used to build a certified extraction procedure by Forster, Sozeau, and Tabareau [35]. Formal verification is very appealing considering the complexity inherent to proof assistants; note however that verified implementations often do not benefit from the same optimisations and clever heuristics (for instance reduction using explicit substitutions or abstract machines) as the equivalent code in Rocq's OCaml implementation.

C1 - Conceptual MetaRocq implements binders using de Bruijn indices, which have the same drawbacks we explained in § 3.

C2 - Conceptual Rocq does not provide abstractions to handle effects s uch as printing, raising exceptions, or writing non-terminating functions, so writing non-trivial programs quickly becomes tedious. Herbelin's `reduction-effects` plugin [41] allows to print values, but is currently only suitable for debugging. Moreover, writing partial or possibly non-terminating programs is impractical: Common solutions include disabling the guard checker or using step-indexing.

MetaRocq relies crucially on *monads* to handle effects, most notably the template monad, which is in our experience a notable friction point: monadic programs in Rocq are difficult to debug, as programming errors often cause implicit argument resolution to fail, leading to obscure error messages. There does not seem to be a consensus on how to implement monads in Rocq: a promising attempt is the Monae library [73] which formalises monads in the style of Rocq's Mathematical-Components library using the Hierarchy Builder tool [19]. MetaRocq packages its own monad library following a simpler design called *semi-bundled* typeclasses. The latter approach is used successfully in languages such as Haskell and in Lean's mathematical library [55], but its current implementation in MetaRocq is unsatisfactory.

C3 - Current State management in MetaRocq is explicit: the global environment and local context have to be threaded manually, and this issue will only worsen as more state (such as the evar-map) is added. Rocq being a pure language, the obvious solution is to use monads to hide the state.

C4 - Current MetaRocq's high-level API lacks many crucial features. Indeed, MetaRocq only re-implements Rocq's kernel: higher-level features such as unification or typeclass resolution have to be exposed via bindings to Rocq's actual OCaml implementation. Many of these bindings are either missing or incomplete. For instance, unification is entirely missing, and defining new constants does not currently support universe polymorphism.

C5 - Current Performance of MetaRocq programs which use the template monad can be quite poor: we noticed slowdowns of up to two orders of magnitude. Obtaining reasonable performance required writing our program in two layers. The inner layer `build_fmap` does not make use of the template monad. All effects (e.g. declaring the new typeclass instance) are pushed to the outer layer `derive_functor`:

```
(** Inner layer: build the mapping function for a given inductive. *)
Definition build_fmap : inductive -> term.
```

```
(** Outer layer: wrap build_fmap with pre- and post-processing. *)
Definition derive_functor {A} : A -> TemplateMonad unit.
```

This approach does not scale: in a more realistic meta-program, `build_fmap` might need to perform unification or typeclass resolution, which requires using the template monad.

5   Agda

Meta-programming in Agda is similar to MetaRocq: Meta-programs are directly written in Agda, using the *Reflection* API [84], and interact with the elaborator and kernel via the `TC` monad. The extended version [12, Appendix D] shows the code for the Agda plugin.

Pros – Conceptual	P1 - Users already know Agda.
Pros – Current	P2 - Implicit state management using monads.

Cons – Conceptual	C1 - De Bruijn index arithmetic is difficult.
	C2 - Restrictive term representation.
Cons – Current	C3 - Type-class search is hard to control.
	C4 - Performance issues in some cases.

P1 - Conceptual Agda meta-programs are simply Agda programs with a return type in the type checking monad (`TC`): this has the benefit that users do not need to learn a new programming language. MetaRocq uses the same approach based around a monad – the MetaRocq equivalent of the type checking monad is the template monad – however in Agda's case the type checking monad also contains the prover state, whereas in MetaRocq the state is threaded explicitly.

P2 - Current The prover state is contained in the type checking monad. It is accessed through primitives provided by the type checking monad, e.g.:

```
-- Get the definition of a constant.
getDefinition : Name -> TC Definition
-- Extend the current context with a variable.
extendContext : {a} {A : Set a} -> String -> Arg Type -> TC A -> TC A
```

We found monadic programming in Agda to be lightweight and enjoyable, thanks to the extensive library agda-stdlib-classes [20] based on typeclasses.

C1 - Conceptual Agda implements binders in terms using de Bruijn indices, which have the same drawbacks we explained in § 3. Additionally, we note that the API to manipulate the local (de Bruijn) context is currently awkward to use: for instance some functions expect the context in reverse order (last to first), and some expect it in normal order (first to last).

C2 - Conceptual The internal representation of terms is quite restrictive. First, `let` bindings (as well as `where` clauses) are not represented in the abstract syntax, but are instead inlined during type checking: meta-programs cannot make use of such features when building terms. Second, terms are represented in spine form (the head of an application cannot be a lambda abstraction), making it difficult to build some terms. Implementing substitution on this representation of terms is quite delicate, and in fact there is no substitution function available in the meta-programming API (some third-party libraries [61] implement substitution).

C3 - Current Type-class resolution is difficult to use when meta-programming. First, although Agda has the concept of local typeclass instances, using local instances via the meta-programming API is not directly supported and requires awkward workarounds. Second, Agda's implementation of typeclass search is quite weak when compared to Rocq and Lean: support for overlapping instances and backtracking search is relatively recent, and recursive instances can still cause typeclass resolution to loop. This is because instance search is implemented using a depth-first search. In our case a crucial typeclass instance (for the composition of functors) is recursive: we had to cap instance search at a very low depth to get acceptable type checking times. This workaround would not scale to real-world applications, and in our case means that our Agda example does not support deeply nested inductives.

C4 - Current Performance of meta-programs in the type checking monad can be poor: we noticed significant slowdowns compared to equivalent pure code on small examples, but providing larger benchmarks is outside our scope.

6 Lean

The elaborator of Lean 4 (including parsing, unification, type inference, and typeclass resolution) is implemented in Lean itself [57], and self-hosting the kernel is subject to active research (see the Lean4Lean project [15]). Meta-programs are simply Lean programs which have access to the Lean implementation. Lean's meta-programming features are used in many projects [50, 10, 49, 59], notably its mathematical library [55], and most of the implementation of Lean's elaborator can be considered meta-programming. The extended version [12, Appendix E] shows the Lean code.

Pros – Conceptual	P1 - Users already know Lean.
	P2 - Access to complete Lean implementation.
	P3 - Locally nameless binder representation.
Pros – Current	P4 - Implicit state management using monads.
Cons – Conceptual	C1 - Restricted term representation.
Cons – Current	

P1 - Conceptual Meta-programming is done directly in Lean: this has the benefit of relieving the user from learning a new domain-specific language, but goes much further, as explained in the next paragraph.

P2 - Conceptual Meta-programs can access the entire API of the Lean implementation. This has benefits for the developers, which do not need to manually expose bindings to every useful API function, and allows users to seamlessly access parts of the implementation which would typically not be part of a meta-programming language, e.g. related to the *concrete* syntax of terms, such as the parser. We also note that support for instrumenting the parser to implement various notations, macros, and embedded DSLs is particularly good. In fact Lean macros are so powerful that they allow some form of basic meta-programming, although we did not make use of such functionality during this study. We refer the reader to the work by Ullrich [81] for an overview of Lean macros.

P3 - Conceptual Local variables are internally represented using locally nameless: free variables use names, while bound variables use de Bruijn indices. For instance the term $\lambda x.\lambda y.f\ x\ y$, which has one free variable f and two bound variables x and y, is represented as $\lambda.\lambda.\lambda.f\ 2\ 1$. The user is responsible for maintaining the invariant that free variables are named and bound variables use indices. For instance in our code:

```
-- Build the function `fmap` as `fun A B f x => body`
def buildFmap ind : MetaM Expr := do
  -- The body contains free (i.e. named) variables.
  let body := ...
  -- Replace names with indices and add lambda abstractions.
  mkLambdaFVars #[A, B, f, x] body
```

Overall there is no need to directly manipulate de Bruijn indices, and we found locally nameless to be pleasant to use.

P4 - Current Lean is a pure language, and modifying prover state is done using monads: this provides the lightweight programming experience of implicit state, while keeping some level of control over which effects can be performed. A meta-program in `CoreM` can access the global environment but may not assign metavariables, while a meta-program in `MetaM` has access to the global environment, local context, and metavariables. We note that Lean has excellent support for monadic programming, as described by Ullrich and de Moura [82].

C1 - Conceptual Lean's abstract term syntax has no first-class fixpoints or case expressions (as for instance in Rocq): instead, concrete syntax fixpoints and case expressions are compiled to primitive recursors, which are represented as global constants with special reduction rules. For instance a case expression on an `option` is represented as an application of the `` `option.casesOn`` primitive recursor.

Benefits include having a simpler meta theory and no need for a guard checker in the kernel. However, we perceived this as a severe limitation. In practice recursors for nested inductives quickly become unwieldy. Because the fixpoint and pattern matching compiler only accepts concrete syntax, it cannot be used by meta-programs which work on abstract syntax.

Generating concrete syntax (instead of abstract syntax) solves this particular issue with fixpoints and case expressions, but concrete syntax is very difficult to manipulate, and most functions in the Lean meta-programming API (such as unification or type inference) do not work with concrete syntax. Due to these difficulties, our Lean implementation does not support recursive inductives (e.g. lists or trees).

7   Elpi

Elpi is a logic programming language based on λProlog [58] which can be used as a meta-programming language for Rocq [74, 27, 22, 18, 79, 38, 54]. Elpi is notably used to implement Hierarchy Builder [19], a type checker and elaborator for the Calculus of Inductive Constructions [40], and a typeclass resolution algorithm for Rocq [33]. The extended version [12, Appendix G] shows the Elpi code.

Pros – Conceptual	P1 - Higher-order abstract syntax.
Pros – Current	P2 - Powerful quoting and unquoting mechanism.
Cons – Conceptual	C1 - Paradigm shift (logic programming).
Cons – Current	C2 - Limited representations for structured data.

P1 - Conceptual A key feature of Elpi is the abstract syntax it uses for Rocq terms, and in particular for binders, called higher-order abstract syntax (HOAS) and due to Pfenning and Elliott [67]. The syntax of Rocq terms is encoded in a data-type `term`, of which we show a few constructors:

```
type app     list term -> term.
type fun     name -> term -> (term -> term) -> term.
```

Application nodes are represented using `app`, lambda abstractions using `fun`. There is no constructor for variables. The last argument of `fun` is the body of the lambda abstraction, an elpi function of type `term -> term`: Rocq variables correspond to Elpi variables. For instance the Rocq function `fun x : nat => x` is encoded in Elpi as `fun `x` (global (indt «nat»)) (x\ x)`, where `x\ x` is the Elpi identity function.

Meta-programming in Elpi does not require dealing with de Bruijn arithmetic, and the type checker helps catch scope issues when building terms. Overall we found HOAS easy to use.

We note that HOAS relies crucially on the logic programming aspects of Elpi. HOAS is incompatible with dependently typed proof assistants due to the strict positivity condition on inductives, and even in languages such as OCaml in which it is possible to define a HOAS term grammar, it is unclear how to define basic term manipulations (such as counting the number of variables) [17, Section. 2.1]. We did not investigate parametric higher-order abstract syntax [17].

P2 - Current Elpi offers a powerful quotation mechanism to build the AST of Rocq terms with Rocq user syntax. Quotations are inserted using braces:

```
pred build-fmap i:inductive, o:term.
build-fmap I {{fun A B (f : A -> B) (x : lp:(FI A)) => lp:(M A B f x)}}
```

Anti-quotations `lp:(...)` insert elpi code inside quotations. Most importantly, quotations and anti-quotations allow open terms. This is not the case in most meta-languages which support quoting (Lean being a notable exception). Moreover, Rocq unification variables correspond almost one to one with Elpi unification variables, allowing meta-programs to trigger Rocq's unification simply by using Elpi's built-in unification.

C1 - Conceptual Elpi is a logic programming language, which is a paradigm shift compared to dependently-typed proof assistants. An Elpi program is composed of predicates, which relate input(s) to output(s):

```
pred build-fmap i:inductive, o:term.
build-fmap I F :- ...
```

The program above declares the predicate `build-fmap` with one input `I` (the inductive we are mapping over) and one output `F` (the term `fmap` we are building). The second line adds a rule with conclusion `build-fmap I F`, which describes how to build the term `F` given `I`. A consequence of this paradigm shift is that Elpi comes with a steep learning curve.

C2 - Current On the language level, Elpi provides limited options for representing structured data. There are no ML-style records; in fact it is common for Elpi functions to have more than half a dozen input and output parameters, e.g.:

```
pred build-branch i:inductive, i:term, i:term, i:term, i:term,
                  i:term, i:list term, i:list term, o:term.
```

Only open sums are available: constructors can be added at any point in the program. Open sums enable clever programming tricks, but the lack of closed sums prevents statically checking whether a function handles all input cases.

8   Related Work

Dubois de Prisque [27] compares Ltac1, Ltac2, MetaRocq, and Elpi as meta-programming languages in tutorial style through different examples. The methodology differs from ours in that the choice of frameworks is restricted to a single proof assistant (Rocq), and we focus on a single example which - while realistic enough to highlight many issues - yields implementations simple enough to be understood by non-experts. The conclusions of Dubois de Prisque are that Ltac1 lacks a clear semantics and static typing, and tactics not being allowed to have side effects and return a value leads to ubiquitous, hard-to-read CPS translations. Ltac2 solves many of the issues of Ltac1, but manipulating the low-level term representation is difficult (many things were even impossible at the time the thesis was written). MetaRocq allows to manipulate the low-level term representation, and might allow formally proving correctness of the meta-programs. However, de Bruijn arithmetic and the lack of proper abstractions for effects (in particular mutable state and non-terminating functions) is criticised. For Elpi, Dubois de Prisque lauds the benefits of HOAS and remarks that term quotations are beneficial. However, HOAS seems to be difficult for term-to-term transformations when the structure of the output is very different from the input. Writing tactics was reported as tedious, which however could be a problem related to how Elpi represents the proof context, i.e. might not be conceptual.

HOL-based proof assistants come with meta-programming support in their host language. HOL4 and HOL light might offer the most natural experience, since proving happens just in an OCaml session. Isabelle allows meta-programming in Standard ML. Beluga is a proof assistant for the mechanisation of meta-theory based on contextual modal type theory. There is a lot of ongoing work on how to make quotation native in contextual modal type theory and thus allow certifiable meta-programming [43, 68, 44, 46, 45, 42]. The concerns of this setting are somewhat orthogonal to ours: they try to understand the foundations of meta-programming by extending type theory, whereas we focus on power and usability of frameworks that are built on top of type theory.

9 Conclusion

	OCaml	MetaRocq	Agda	Lean	Ltac2	Elpi
De Bruijn indices	✕	✕	✕		✕	
Restricted term AST			✕	✕		
No quasi-quotations	✕	✕	✕		✕	
Explicit prover state handling	✕	✕				
Cannot verify meta-programs	✕	✕	✕	✕	✕	✕

Conceptual issues with each meta-programming framework.

	OCaml	MetaRocq	Agda	Lean	Ltac2	Elpi
Need to learn a new language	✕				✕	✕
Incomplete API		✕	✕		✕	✕
Lack of learning resources	✕	✕				
Lack of documentation	✕	✕	✕	✕	✕	✕

Current issues with each meta-programming framework.

Conceptual. *Binder representation* was a recurring issue in this paper. Meta-programs involve manipulating terms as data, and as such it must be easy to construct and inspect the structure of terms, including binders. In particular, we note that our de Bruijn-based implementations use arithmetic on indices, which leads to frequent mistakes and bugs. The locally nameless representation simplifies writing correct code, but comes with minor efficiency considerations. Finding the best representation for meta-programming is still an open problem.

Term representation is crucial, which became especially apparent for the example in Lean 4, where the need to fall back on primitive recursors prevented us from implementing a plugin with the same features as in the other systems (our implementation does not support recursive types such as lists). Term representation was also an issue in Agda, because the abstract syntax does not contain let-bindings and terms can only be beta-normal. Thus, a meta-programming framework must either expose a sufficiently expressive term representation, or a high-level API to build terms if the representation of kernel terms is too low-level.

Term quotations allow one to use user syntax directly when constructing and pattern matching on terms, thereby removing the need to spell out low-level details such as fully qualified constant names, implicit arguments, typeclass instances, or universe levels. Additionally, term quotations allow some amount of type checking at compile time (such as scope analysis) which allows one to catch errors earlier. Quasiquotations (i.e. the ability to nest anti-quotations and quotations) and the ability to quote open terms are especially useful, but are currently only supported in Lean and Elpi.

State is inherent to meta-programs, which can read and modify the global environment, local environment, and unification state. A good meta-programming framework must more generally provide good abstractions to deal with various kinds of effects, such as printing, exceptions, non-termination, and (prover) state. Lean and Agda handle printing using an IO monad and generally provide good libraries, while Rocq only provides ad hoc printing using the `reduction-effects` plugin [41] and does not have a satisfactory monad library (see § 4).

Verifiability is a desirable property of frameworks. Ideally formal verification of meta-programs should be possible. Verification is not so attractive for users of meta-programs because properties such as well-typedness can be checked a posteriori by the kernel, but implementors of meta-programs might be interested in (partial) correctness guarantees. Indeed, formal specifications can partly replace documentation – which is lacking for all considered frameworks anyway – and can help in writing correct meta-programs, which is far from an easy task considering the complexity of the underlying systems.

Current. *The learning curve* of a meta-programming framework is crucial, and writing meta-programs in a different language than that of the underlying proof assistant leads to a steeper curve. Learning Elpi was especially challenging due to the paradigm shift to logical programming.

Many meta-programming frameworks provide an *incomplete meta-programming API*, missing crucial features such as the ability to define new constants dynamically (Ltac2, Agda), bindings to high-level algorithms such as unification and type inference (MetaRocq), or support for e.g. mutual inductives (Elpi).

A proper meta-programming language requires adequate tooling, such as a language server, a documentation generator, an optimising compiler or efficient interpreter, and a good integration with the proof assistant's build system. Most of these tools come for free when the meta-language is the proof assistant itself or an already established programming language (such as OCaml), but require significant engineering work in the case of a DSL (e.g. Elpi or Ltac2).

Finally, we note that documentation is lacking for all considered frameworks, and some frameworks even lack basic learning resources.

Precise performance considerations are outside the scope of this paper, although we did comment on performance when relevant. We argue that meta-programming should prioritise usability over performance when possible. Performance is however important when considering tactic programming or more complex meta-programs such as unification algorithms and type checkers.

Summary Conceptually, two promising meta-programming approaches emerge: directly in the proof assistant or using a domain-specific language (DSL).

The first option, while of course relieving users from learning a new programming language, also provides crucial benefits to the quality of the tooling and libraries available for meta-programming. Moreover, this option allows users to verify their meta-programs. Verifying meta-programs requires both a specification of the basic meta-programming operations provided by the framework, and adequate means to use these basic specifications in order to derive guarantees about complex meta-programs. We note that one cannot realistically expect to prove that the meta-programming framework fulfills its specification, as this would amount to proving the correctness of the entire elaborator and kernel of the underlying proof assistant. A more realistic approach is to interface with two implementations of the elaborator and kernel: a naive but verified implementation à la MetaRocq [76], and an efficient but unverified implementation.

The second option does not allow certifying meta-programs, but enables using domain-specific programming language features. Elpi is an example of such a DSL: logic programming is a valuable tool for working with syntax and binders.

In both cases, one needs a feature-complete meta-programming API, which stays up to date with the evolution of the proof assistant. For implementors of a meta-programming framework, *bootstrapping* the proof assistant gives a feature-complete API for free, but requires significant work a priori (for instance Lean 4's elaborator is bootstrapped). An alternate approach, which MetaRocq and Agda follow, is to do meta-programming directly in the proof assistant, without bootstrapping. Interfacing with the elaborator is done using a meta-programming monad, which from a user's point of view is very similar to bootstrapping.

10   Future Work

A natural direction for future work is to extend this study to other systems. On the side of dependently-typed programming languages, Idris 2 seems to come with a built-in plugin for deriving functor instances [3], which is however more general than our plugin, since it covers all types that can be proved functorial. In this paper, we focused on proof assistants rather than programming languages. Regarding proof assistants, it would be interesting to extend the study to systems from the HOL family, as well as to Beluga [69], Abella [37], or Dedukti [8]. We believe that insights will be largely orthogonal though, since both the underlying theory and the implementation methods differ vastly.

We also want to study *term-to-term* transformations, where we expect most of our results to carry over, although Dubois de Prisque remarks that HOAS can cause issues for these transformations [27]. Surveying tactic frameworks might also provide valuable insights. There are however far fewer tactic- than meta-programming frameworks: a survey would amount to comparing proof assistants.

An orthogonal direction is to extend one of the implementations into a standalone tool, and derive **Functor** instances for more general types, following the ideas of Laurent, Lennon-Bertrand, and Maillard [47].

A central direction for future work is to develop a meta-programming framework based on our insights, potentially in parallel for different proof assistants. We believe that a key insight is that meta-programs are inherently effectful programs, which have access both to generic effects such as failure and non-termination, and to domain-specific effects such as the ability to read and modify the global environment, local context and evar-map. We also argue that, considering the complexity of the underlying systems, verifying meta-programs is of great interest for implementors of meta-programs. These ideas hint at the possibility of using powerful verification techniques to ease reasoning about meta-programs: following the line of work on Dijkstra monads [2, 52, 53] one can use specialised program logics tailored to domain-specific effects, and in particular separation logic to handle the evar-map, building on ideas from Nigron and Dagand [60] and Vistrup, Sammler, and Jung [86]. The line of work on algebraic effects [70, 28] and the Andromeda proof assistant [11] is also very relevant.

Bibliography

[1] Andreas Abel, Guillaume Allais, Aliya Hameer, Brigitte Pientka, Alberto Momigliano, Steven Schäfer, and Kathrin Stark. POPLMark Reloaded: Mechanizing proofs by logical relations. *J. Funct. Program.*, 29, 2019.

[2] Danel Ahman, Cătălin Hriţcu, Kenji Maillard, Guido Martínez, Gordon Plotkin, Jonathan Protzenko, Aseem Rastogi, and Nikhil Swamy. Dijkstra monads for free. In *Proceedings of the 44th ACM SIGPLAN Symposium on Principles of Programming Languages*, POPL '17, page 515–529, New York, NY, USA, 2017. Association for Computing Machinery.

[3] Guillaume Allais and André Videla. Deriving for functor instances in idris 2 (idris 2 standard library).

[4] Abhishek Anand, Andrew W. Appel, Greg Morrisett, Zoe Paraskevopoulou, Randy Pollack, Olivier Savary Bélanger, Matthieu Sozeau, and Matthew Z. Weaver. Certicoq : A verified compiler for coq. 2016.

[5] Abhishek Anand, Simon Boulier, Cyril Cohen, Matthieu Sozeau, and Nicolas Tabareau. Towards certified meta-programming with typed template-coq. In *ITP 2018*, pages 20–39, 2018.

[6] Abhishek Anand, Anvay Grover, John Li, Greg Morrisett, Randy Pollack, Olivier Savary Belanger, Matthew Weaver, Andrew Appel, Yannick Forster, Joomy Korkut, Zoe Paraskevopoulou, Kathrin Stark, and Matthieu Sozeau. Certicoq: A verified compiler for coq (github repository). accessed Feb 18th 2025, 2025.

[7] Danil Annenkov, Jakob Botsch Nielsen, and Bas Spitters. Concert: a smart contract certification framework in coq. In Jasmin Blanchette and Catalin Hritcu, editors, *Proceedings of the 9th ACM SIGPLAN International Conference on Certified Programs and Proofs, CPP 2020, New Orleans, LA, USA, January 20-21, 2020*, pages 215–228. ACM, 2020.

[8] Ali Assaf, Guillaume Burel, Raphaël Cauderlier, David Delahaye, Gilles Dowek, Catherine Dubois, Frédéric Gilbert, Pierre Halmagrand, Olivier Hermant, and Ronan Saillard. Dedukti: a logical framework based on the $\lambda\Pi$-calculus modulo theory. *CoRR*, abs/2311.07185, 2023.

[9] Brian E. Aydemir, Aaron Bohannon, Matthew Fairbairn, J. Nathan Foster, Benjamin C. Pierce, Peter Sewell, Dimitrios Vytiniotis, Geoffrey Washburn, Stephanie Weirich, and Steve Zdancewic. Mechanized metatheory for the masses: The POPLMark challenge. In Joe Hurd and Tom Melham, editors, *Theorem Proving in Higher Order Logics*, pages 50–65, Berlin & Heidelberg, 2005. Springer.

[10] Anne Baanen. A lean tactic for normalising ring expressions with exponents (short paper). In Nicolas Peltier and Viorica Sofronie-Stokkermans, editors, *Automated Reasoning*, pages 21–27, Cham, 2020. Springer International Publishing.

[11] Andrej Bauer, Gaëtan Gilbert, Philipp G. Haselwarter, Matija Pretnar, and Christopher A. Stone. Design and Implementation of the Andromeda

Proof Assistant. In Silvia Ghilezan, Herman Geuvers, and Jelena Ivetic, editors, *22nd International Conference on Types for Proofs and Programs (TYPES 2016)*, volume 97 of *Leibniz International Proceedings in Informatics (LIPIcs)*, pages 5:1–5:31, Dagstuhl, Germany, 2018. Schloss Dagstuhl – Leibniz-Zentrum für Informatik.

[12] Mathis Bouverot-Dupuis and Yannick Forster. Code Generation via Meta-programming in Dependently Typed Proof Assistants (extended version). working paper or preprint, January 2026.

[13] Edwin C. Brady. Idris, a general-purpose dependently typed programming language: Design and implementation. *J. Funct. Program.*, 23(5):552–593, 2013.

[14] Edwin C. Brady. Idris 2: Quantitative type theory in practice. In Anders Møller and Manu Sridharan, editors, *35th European Conference on Object-Oriented Programming, ECOOP 2021, July 11-17, 2021, Aarhus, Denmark (Virtual Conference)*, volume 194 of *LIPIcs*, pages 9:1–9:26. Schloss Dagstuhl - Leibniz-Zentrum für Informatik, 2021.

[15] Mario Carneiro. Lean4lean: Towards a verified typechecker for lean, in lean, 2024.

[16] Tej Chajed. Record updates in coq. In *CoqPL 2021: The Seventh International Workshop on Coq for Programming Languages*, 2021. Extended Abstract.

[17] Adam Chlipala. Parametric higher-order abstract syntax for mechanized semantics. *SIGPLAN Not.*, 43(9):143–156, September 2008.

[18] Cyril Cohen, Enzo Crance, and Assia Mahboubi. Trocq: Proof transfer for free, with or without univalence. *CoRR*, abs/2310.14022, 2023.

[19] Cyril Cohen, Kazuhiko Sakaguchi, and Enrico Tassi. Hierarchy builder: Algebraic hierarchies made easy in coq with elpi (system description). In Zena M. Ariola, editor, *5th International Conference on Formal Structures for Computation and Deduction, FSCD 2020, June 29-July 6, 2020, Paris, France (Virtual Conference)*, volume 167 of *LIPIcs*, pages 34:1–34:21. Schloss Dagstuhl - Leibniz-Zentrum für Informatik, 2020.

[20] Agda Community. agda-stdlib-classes.

[21] Thierry Coquand and Gérard P Huet. The calculus of constructions. *Information and Computation*, 76(2/3):95–120, 1988.

[22] Enzo Crance. *Méta-programmation pour le transfert de preuve en théorie des types dépendants*. Theses, Nantes Université, December 2023.

[23] Adrian Dapprich. Autosubst metacoq, 2021.

[24] Adrian Dapprich. Generating infrastructural code for terms with binders using metacoq, 2021. Bachelor's thesis, Saarland University.

[25] Arthur Azevedo de Amorim. Deriving instances with dependent types. In *Proceedings of the Sixth International Workshop on Coq for Programming Languages (CoqPL 2020)*, 2020.

[26] N.G de Bruijn. Lambda calculus notation with nameless dummies, a tool for automatic formula manipulation, with application to the church-rosser theorem. *Indagationes Mathematicae (Proceedings)*, 75(5):381–392, 1972.

[27] Louise Dubois de Prisque. *Prétraitement compositionnel en Coq. (Compositional preprocessing in Coq)*. PhD thesis, University of Paris-Saclay, France, 2024.

[28] Paulo Emílio de Vilhena and François Pottier. A separation logic for effect handlers. *Proc. ACM Program. Lang.*, 5(POPL), January 2021.

[29] Pablo Donato, Pierre-Yves Strub, and Benjamin Werner. A drag-and-drop proof tactic. In Andrei Popescu and Steve Zdancewic, editors, *CPP '22: 11th ACM SIGPLAN International Conference on Certified Programs and Proofs, Philadelphia, PA, USA, January 17 - 18, 2022*, pages 197–209. ACM, 2022.

[30] Catherine Dubois, Nicolas Magaud, and Alain Giorgetti. Pragmatic isomorphism proofs between coq representations: Application to lambda-term families. In Delia Kesner and Pierre-Marie Pédrot, editors, *28th International Conference on Types for Proofs and Programs, TYPES 2022, June 20-25, 2022, LS2N, University of Nantes, France*, volume 269 of *LIPIcs*, pages 11:1–11:19. Schloss Dagstuhl - Leibniz-Zentrum für Informatik, 2022.

[31] Cvetan Dunchev, Ferruccio Guidi, Claudio Sacerdoti Coen, and Enrico Tassi. ELPI: fast, embeddable, λprolog interpreter. In Martin Davis, Ansgar Fehnker, Annabelle McIver, and Andrei Voronkov, editors, *Logic for Programming, Artificial Intelligence, and Reasoning - 20th International Conference, LPAR-20 2015, Suva, Fiji, November 24-28, 2015, Proceedings*, volume 9450 of *Lecture Notes in Computer Science*, pages 460–468. Springer, 2015.

[32] Gabriel Ebner, Sebastian Ullrich, Jared Roesch, Jeremy Avigad, and Leonardo de Moura. A metaprogramming framework for formal verification. *Proc. ACM Program. Lang.*, 1(ICFP), August 2017.

[33] Davide Fissore and Enrico Tassi. A new Type-Class solver for Coq in Elpi. In *The Coq Workshop 2023*, Bialystok, Poland, July 2023.

[34] João Paulo Pizani Flor, Wouter Swierstra, and Yorick Sijsling. Pi-ware: Hardware description and verification in agda. In Tarmo Uustalu, editor, *21st International Conference on Types for Proofs and Programs, TYPES 2015, May 18-21, 2015, Tallinn, Estonia*, volume 69 of *LIPIcs*, pages 9:1–9:27. Schloss Dagstuhl - Leibniz-Zentrum für Informatik, 2015.

[35] Yannick Forster, Matthieu Sozeau, and Nicolas Tabareau. Verified extraction from coq to ocaml. *Proc. ACM Program. Lang.*, 8(PLDI), June 2024.

[36] Yannick Forster and Kathrin Stark. Coq à la carte: a practical approach to modular syntax with binders. In Jasmin Blanchette and Catalin Hritcu, editors, *Proceedings of the 9th ACM SIGPLAN International Conference on Certified Programs and Proofs, CPP 2020, New Orleans, LA, USA, January 20-21, 2020*, pages 186–200. ACM, 2020.

[37] Andrew Gacek. The abella interactive theorem prover (system description). In *Proceedings of the 4th International Joint Conference on Automated Reasoning (IJCAR)*, pages 154–161. Springer, 2008.

[38] Benjamin Grégoire, Jean-Christophe Léchenet, and Enrico Tassi. Practical and sound equality tests, automatically – Deriving eqType instances for Jasmin's data types with Coq-Elpi. In *CPP 2023: Proceedings of the*

12th ACM SIGPLAN International Conference on Certified Programs and Proofs, CPP 2023: Proceedings of the 12th ACM SIGPLAN International Conference on Certified Programs and Proofs, pages 167–181, Boston MA USA, France, January 2023. ACM.

[39] Jason Gross, Théo Zimmermann, Miraya Poddar-Agrawal, and Adam Chlipala. Automatic test-case reduction in proof assistants: A case study in coq. In June Andronick and Leonardo de Moura, editors, *13th International Conference on Interactive Theorem Proving, ITP 2022, August 7-10, 2022, Haifa, Israel*, volume 237 of *LIPIcs*, pages 18:1–18:18. Schloss Dagstuhl - Leibniz-Zentrum für Informatik, 2022.

[40] Ferruccio Guidi, Claudio Sacerdoti Coen, and Enrico Tassi. Implementing Type Theory in Higher Order Constraint Logic Programming. *Mathematical Structures in Computer Science*, 29(8):1125–1150, March 2019.

[41] Hugo Herbelin. reduction-effects.

[42] Jason Z. S. Hu and Brigitte Pientka. A layered approach to intensional analysis in type theory. *ACM Trans. Program. Lang. Syst.*, 46(4):15:1–15:43, 2024.

[43] Jason Z. S. Hu and Brigitte Pientka. Layered modal type theory - where meta-programming meets intensional analysis. In Stephanie Weirich, editor, *Programming Languages and Systems - 33rd European Symposium on Programming, ESOP 2024, Held as Part of the European Joint Conferences on Theory and Practice of Software, ETAPS 2024, Luxembourg City, Luxembourg, April 6-11, 2024, Proceedings, Part I*, volume 14576 of *Lecture Notes in Computer Science*, pages 52–82. Springer, 2024.

[44] Jason Z. S. Hu and Brigitte Pientka. A dependent type theory for meta-programming with intensional analysis. *Proc. ACM Program. Lang.*, 9(POPL):416–445, 2025.

[45] Jason Z. S. Hu, Brigitte Pientka, and Ulrich Schöpp. A category theoretic view of contextual types: From simple types to dependent types. *ACM Trans. Comput. Log.*, 23(4):25:1–25:36, 2022.

[46] Junyoung Jang, Samuel Gélineau, Stefan Monnier, and Brigitte Pientka. Mœbius: metaprogramming using contextual types: the stage where system f can pattern match on itself. *Proc. ACM Program. Lang.*, 6(POPL):1–27, 2022.

[47] Théo Laurent, Meven Lennon-Bertrand, and Kenji Maillard. Definitional functoriality for dependent (Sub)Types. In *Lecture Notes in Computer Science*, pages 302–331. 2024.

[48] Bohdan Liesnikov, Marcel Ullrich, and Yannick Forster. Generating induction principles and subterm relations for inductive types using metacoq. *CoRR*, abs/2006.15135, 2020.

[49] Jannis Limperg. A novice-friendly induction tactic for lean. In *Proceedings of the 10th ACM SIGPLAN International Conference on Certified Programs and Proofs*, CPP 2021, page 199–211, New York, NY, USA, 2021. Association for Computing Machinery.

[50] Jannis Limperg and Asta Halkjær From. Aesop: White-box best-first proof search for lean. In *Proceedings of the 12th ACM SIGPLAN International*

Conference on Certified Programs and Proofs, CPP 2023, page 253–266, New York, NY, USA, 2023. Association for Computing Machinery.

[51] Nicolas Magaud. Towards automatic transformations of coq proof scripts. In Pedro Quaresma and Zoltán Kovács, editors, *Proceedings 14th International Conference on Automated Deduction in Geometry, ADG 2023, Belgrade, Serbia, 20-22th September 2023*, volume 398 of *EPTCS*, pages 4–10, 2023.

[52] Kenji Maillard, Danel Ahman, Robert Atkey, Guido Martínez, Cătălin Hriţcu, Exequiel Rivas, and Éric Tanter. Dijkstra monads for all. *Proc. ACM Program. Lang.*, 3(ICFP), July 2019.

[53] Kenji Maillard, Cătălin Hriţcu, Exequiel Rivas, and Antoine Van Muylder. The next 700 relational program logics. *Proc. ACM Program. Lang.*, 4(POPL), December 2019.

[54] Matteo Manighetti, Dale Miller, and Alberto Momigliano. Two Applications of Logic Programming to Coq. In Ugo de'Liguoro, Stefano Berardi, and Thorsten Altenkirch, editors, *26th International Conference on Types for Proofs and Programs (TYPES 2020)*, volume 188 of *Leibniz International Proceedings in Informatics (LIPIcs)*, pages 10:1–10:19, Dagstuhl, Germany, 2021. Schloss Dagstuhl – Leibniz-Zentrum für Informatik.

[55] The mathlib Community. The lean mathematical library. In *Proceedings of the 9th ACM SIGPLAN International Conference on Certified Programs and Proofs*, CPP 2020, page 367–381, New York, NY, USA, 2020. Association for Computing Machinery.

[56] Leonardo de Moura and Sebastian Ullrich. The lean 4 theorem prover and programming language. In *Lecture Notes in Computer Science*, pages 625–635. 2021.

[57] Leonardo de Moura and Sebastian Ullrich. The lean 4 theorem prover and programming language. In André Platzer and Geoff Sutcliffe, editors, *Automated Deduction – CADE 28*, pages 625–635, Cham, 2021. Springer International Publishing.

[58] Gopalan Nadathur and Dale Miller. An overview of lambda prolog. Technical report, USA, 1988.

[59] Wojciech Nawrocki, Edward W. Ayers, and Gabriel Ebner. An extensible user interface for lean 4. In Adam Naumowicz and René Thiemann, editors, *14th International Conference on Interactive Theorem Proving, ITP 2023, July 31 to August 4, 2023, Białystok, Poland*, volume 268 of *LIPIcs*, pages 24:1–24:20. Schloss Dagstuhl - Leibniz-Zentrum für Informatik, 2023.

[60] Pierre Nigron and Pierre-Évariste Dagand. Reaching for the Star: Tale of a Monad in Coq. In *Leibniz International Proceedings in Informatics (LIPIcs)*, volume 193 of *Leibniz International Proceedings in Informatics (LIPIcs)*, pages 29:1–29:19, Rome, Italy, June 2021. Schloss Dagstuhl.

[61] Ulf Norell. agda-prelude: Programming library for agda.

[62] Ulf Norell. *Towards a practical programming language based on dependent type theory*, volume 32. Chalmers University of Technology, 2007.

[63] Ulf Norell, Nils Anders Danielsson, Jesper Cockx, and Andreas Abel. Agda wiki. `http://wiki.portal.chalmers.se/agda/pmwiki.php`.

[64] Zoe Paraskevopoulou, Aaron Eline, and Leonidas Lampropoulos. Computing correctly with inductive relations. In Ranjit Jhala and Isil Dillig, editors, *PLDI '22: 43rd ACM SIGPLAN International Conference on Programming Language Design and Implementation, San Diego, CA, USA, June 13 - 17, 2022*, pages 966–980. ACM, 2022.

[65] Christine Paulin-Mohring. Inductive definitions in the system Coq rules and properties. In *International Conference on Typed Lambda Calculi and Applications*, pages 328–345. Springer, 1993.

[66] Arthur Paulino, D Testa, E Ayers, H Böving, J Limperg, S Gadgil, and S Bhat. Metaprogramming in lean 4. *Online Book. https://github. com/arthurpaulino/lean4-metaprogramming-book*, 2024.

[67] F. Pfenning and C. Elliott. Higher-order abstract syntax. *SIGPLAN Not.*, 23(7):199–208, June 1988.

[68] Brigitte Pientka. A type-theoretic framework for certified metaprogramming (invited talk extended abstract). In Guillaume Allais and Yanhong Annie Liu, editors, *Proceedings of the 2025 ACM SIGPLAN International Workshop on Partial Evaluation and Program Manipulation, PEPM 2025, Denver, CO, USA, 21 January 2025*, pages 10–11. ACM, 2025.

[69] Brigitte Pientka and Joshua Dunfield. Beluga: A framework for programming and reasoning with contextual data. In *Proceedings of the 10th International Symposium on Functional and Logic Programming (FLOPS)*, pages 1–17. Springer, 2010.

[70] Gordon D. Plotkin and Matija Pretnar. Handling algebraic effects. *Log. Methods Comput. Sci.*, 9, 2013.

[71] Pierre-Marie Pédrot. Ltac2: Tactical warfare. In *The 5th International Workshop on Coq for Programming Languages (CoqPL 2019)*, 2019. Talk at CoqPL 2019, affiliated with POPL 2019.

[72] Talia Ringer. *Proof Repair*. PhD thesis, University of Washington, USA, 2021.

[73] Ayumu Saito and Reynald Affeldt. Towards a practical library for monadic equational reasoning in coq. In Ekaterina Komendantskaya, editor, *Mathematics of Program Construction*, pages 151–177, Cham, 2022. Springer International Publishing.

[74] Kazuhiko Sakaguchi. Reflexive tactics for algebra, revisited. In June Andronick and Leonardo de Moura, editors, *13th International Conference on Interactive Theorem Proving, ITP 2022, August 7-10, 2022, Haifa, Israel*, volume 237 of *LIPIcs*, pages 29:1–29:22. Schloss Dagstuhl - Leibniz-Zentrum für Informatik, 2022.

[75] Matthieu Sozeau, Abhishek Anand, Simon Boulier, Cyril Cohen, Yannick Forster, Fabian Kunze, Gregory Malecha, Nicolas Tabareau, and Théo Winterhalter. The MetaCoq Project. *Journal of Automated Reasoning*, February 2020.

[76] Matthieu Sozeau, Simon Boulier, Yannick Forster, Nicolas Tabareau, and Théo Winterhalter. Coq coq correct! verification of type checking and erasure for coq, in coq. *Proc. ACM Program. Lang.*, 4(POPL), December 2019.

[77] Kathrin Stark, Steven Schäfer, and Jonas Kaiser. Autosubst 2: reasoning with multi-sorted de bruijn terms and vector substitutions. In Assia Mahboubi and Magnus O. Myreen, editors, *Proceedings of the 8th ACM SIGPLAN International Conference on Certified Programs and Proofs, CPP 2019, Cascais, Portugal, January 14-15, 2019*, pages 166–180. ACM, 2019.

[78] Carst Tankink, Herman Geuvers, James McKinna, and Freek Wiedijk. Proviola: A tool for proof re-animation. *CoRR*, abs/1005.2672, 2010.

[79] Enrico Tassi. Deriving Proved Equality Tests in Coq-Elpi: Stronger Induction Principles for Containers in Coq. In John Harrison, John O'Leary, and Andrew Tolmach, editors, *10th International Conference on Interactive Theorem Proving (ITP 2019)*, volume 141 of *Leibniz International Proceedings in Informatics (LIPIcs)*, pages 29:1–29:18, Dagstuhl, Germany, 2019. Schloss Dagstuhl – Leibniz-Zentrum für Informatik.

[80] The Coq Development Team. The coq proof assistant, September 2024.

[81] Sebastian Ullrich and Leonardo de Moura. Beyond notations: Hygienic macro expansion for theorem proving languages. In *Automated Reasoning: 10th International Joint Conference, IJCAR 2020, Paris, France, July 1–4, 2020, Proceedings, Part II*, page 167–182, Berlin, Heidelberg, 2020. Springer-Verlag.

[82] Sebastian Ullrich and Leonardo de Moura. 'do' unchained: embracing local imperativity in a purely functional language (functional pearl). *Proc. ACM Program. Lang.*, 6(ICFP), August 2022.

[83] Cas van der Rest and Wouter Swierstra. A completely unique account of enumeration. *Proc. ACM Program. Lang.*, 6(ICFP):411–437, 2022.

[84] Paul van der Walt and Wouter Swierstra. Engineering proof by reflection in agda. In *International Symposium on Implementation and Application of Functional Languages*, 2012.

[85] Marcell van Geest and Wouter Swierstra. Generic packet descriptions: verified parsing and pretty printing of low-level data. In Sam Lindley and Brent A. Yorgey, editors, *Proceedings of the 2nd ACM SIGPLAN International Workshop on Type-Driven Development, TyDe@ICFP 2017, Oxford, UK, September 3, 2017*, pages 30–40. ACM, 2017.

[86] Max Vistrup, Michael Sammler, and Ralf Jung. Program logics à la carte. *Proc. ACM Program. Lang.*, 9(POPL), January 2025.

Linear Effects, Exceptions, and Resource Safety
A Curry-Howard Correspondence for Destructors

Sidney Congard[1,2], Guillaume Munch-Maccagnoni[1], and Rémi Douence[2]

[1] INRIA, LS2N CNRS, Nantes, France
[2] IMT Atlantique, Nantes, France

Abstract. We analyse the problem of combining linearity, effects, and exceptions, in abstract models of programming languages, as the issue of providing some kind of strength for a monad $T(- \oplus E)$ in a linear setting. We consider in particular for T the *allocation monad*, which we introduce to model and study resource-safety properties. We apply these results to a series of two linear effectful calculi for which we establish their resource-safety properties. The first calculus is a linear (optionally ordered) call-by-push-value language with two allocation effects **new** and **delete**. The resource-safety properties follow from the linear and ordered character of the typing rules.

We then integrate exceptions with linearity and effects by adjoining default destruction actions to types, as inspired by C++/Rust destructors. We see destructors as objects $\delta : A \to TI$ in the slice category over TI. This construction gives rise to a second calculus, the *resource call-by-push-value*, featuring exceptions and destructors, and whose weakening and exchange rules perform side-effects. It is therefore affine at the level of types but ordered at the level of derivations. As in C++ and Rust, a "move" operation—the side-effecting exchange rule—is necessary for releasing resources in random order, as opposed to LIFO order.

1 Introduction

The application of monads to study effects in programming languages [38, 39, 15, 49, 46, 31, 30], as well as the application of linearity to study resource-sensitive aspects of computation [19, 29, 3, 14, 33, 5, 26], are well-established. However, the combination of effects and resources, despite receiving some attention [50, 22, 23, 51, 36, 37, 11], has much less developed theory and case studies.

In order to understand why the combination of effects and resources poses new challenges, it is useful to remind that a monad T modelling computational effects is given by an endofunctor on a cartesian category $\mathscr{C}$, together with families of maps

$$\eta_A : A \to TA \qquad \text{and} \qquad \mu_A : TTA \to TA \tag{1}$$

natural in $A \in \mathscr{C}$ and satisfying monoid-like laws, and together with a family of maps called *strength*

$$\sigma_{\Gamma,A} : \Gamma \times TA \to T(\Gamma \times A) \tag{2}$$

natural in $\Gamma \in \mathscr{C}$ and $A \in \mathscr{C}$ and satisfying four laws stating the compatibility

R. Krebbers (Ed.): ESOP 2026, LNCS 16501, pp.190–219, 2026.
https://doi.org/10.1007/978-3-032-22720-1_8

with η, μ and with the monoidal structure induced by $\times$ and 1. The general principle is that two typed expressions of type $\Gamma \vdash A$ and $\Gamma, A \vdash B$ are allowed to compose as follows:

$$\Gamma \vdash t : A \quad \text{and} \quad \Gamma, x : A \vdash u : B \quad \Longrightarrow \quad \Gamma \vdash \text{let } x = t \text{ in } u : B \qquad (3)$$

which reflects in their interpretation as morphisms in the Kleisli category of T

$$[\![t]\!] : \Gamma \to TA \qquad \text{and} \qquad [\![u]\!] : \Gamma \times A \to TB$$

through the ability to select x in u where the strength plays an essential role:

$$[\![\text{let } x = [\,] \text{ in } u]\!] : \Gamma \times TA \xrightarrow{\sigma_{\Gamma,A}} T(\Gamma \times A) \xrightarrow{T[\![u]\!]} TTB \xrightarrow{\mu_B} TB . \qquad (4)$$

It is also useful to remind that the application of linearity to model resource-sensitive phenomena of data and computation requires to move from a cartesian category $(\mathscr{C}, \times, 1)$ to a symmetric monoidal category $(\mathscr{C}, \otimes, I)$. This modification gives control over duplication and erasure (corresponding to contraction and weakening in logic) since the maps

$$A \to A \otimes A \qquad \text{and} \qquad A \to I \qquad (5)$$

are no longer available for a general A. The linear logic viewpoint nevertheless subsumes the cartesian viewpoint using a resource modality "!". Such a resource modality is a comonad such that its Eilenberg-Moore category $\mathscr{C}^!$, whose objects are coalgebras $(A, \tau : A \to !A)$, has a symmetric monoidal structure that coincides with the symmetric monoidal structure of $\mathscr{C}$ in terms of the underlying objects, and such that this symmetric monoidal structure on $\mathscr{C}^!$ is cartesian [34, 35]. Concretely, duplication and erasure (5) are available whenever A is given with a map $\tau : A \to !A$ satisfying two laws of compatibility with the comonad structure. More rarely—but importantly in our story—the symmetric monoidal structure is sometimes replaced by a monoidal structure, which amounts to providing control over the exchange rule in logic since the symmetry

$$A \otimes B \to B \otimes A \qquad (6)$$

is no longer available unconditionally. The corresponding logics are called *ordered* instead of linear. But again, the exchange rule can be reintroduced selectively with a resource modality [21]. Ordered logic can be useful to model the order in the release of resources [47, 48, 58], as we will see again in this paper.

1.1 Linear effects

In this context, it is tempting to define a notion of *linear computational effect* to be given again by a monad (T, η, μ) (1) on $\mathscr{C}$ and a strength now given as a family of maps

$$\sigma_{\Gamma,A} : \Gamma \otimes TA \to T(\Gamma \otimes A) \qquad (7)$$

natural in Γ and A and satisfying the same four laws. It is also called a *left strength* when the monoidal structure $\otimes$ is non-symmetric. An example of such a strong monad is the linear state monad $S \multimap (- \otimes S)$ for any $S \in \mathscr{C}$ in any symmetric monoidal closed category $\mathscr{C}$. This transposition to the linear context of computational effects is well-behaved and works similarly to (non-linear) monadic effects [49, 22].

Unfortunately, important examples of effects in models of linear logic do not have a strength (7) in such a restrictive sense, such as the control effects modelled by the following monads in models of linear logic [8, 22, 23]:

- the monad "?" of *linearly-defined continuations* (but not *linearly-used*) $?A \overset{\text{def}}{=} !(A \multimap \bot) \multimap \bot$, whose effect corresponds to call/cc-style control operators;
- for any object E, the exception monad $\mathcal{E} \overset{\text{def}}{=} (- \oplus E)$, which is used to model error types and exceptions with $\oplus$ the categorical coproduct—the focus of this paper.

At this point, it is instructive to go back to the computational intuition behind the strength with the interpretation of the monadic binding (4, where $\times$ is now replaced by $\otimes$). We can see that the parameter Γ in (7) represents the context of variables in the rest of the computation (let $x = [\ ]$ in u) at the location where an effect is performed. But control effects have this particularity that they can change how many times the rest is computed, so we cannot guarantee that variables in Γ are not duplicated nor erased.

1.2   Strength with respect to a resource modality

In fact, starting from this intuition we can suggest a relaxed notion of strength, something like (7) where Γ is assumed to possess a coalgebra structure $\tau : \Gamma \to !\Gamma$, so that it can be erased. It so happens [8, 22, 23] that the monad ? of linearly-defined continuations and the exception monad $\mathcal{E}$ each do have a *(left) strength with respect to $U^!$*, where $U^! : \mathscr{C}^! \to \mathscr{C}$ is the forgetful functor of the category of coalgebras,[3] defined as a family of maps

$$\sigma_{\Gamma,A} : U^!\Gamma \otimes TA \to T(U^!\Gamma \otimes A) \tag{8}$$

natural in $\Gamma \in \mathscr{C}^!$ and $A \in \mathscr{C}$ and satisfying again four laws of compatibility with η, μ and with the monoidal structures of $\mathscr{C}$ and $\mathscr{C}^!$. If we look concretely at the strength with respect to $U^!$ of the exception monad $\mathcal{E}$, we see that it consists for each $A \in \mathscr{C}$ and $\Gamma \in \mathscr{C}^!$ of two maps

$$U^!\Gamma \otimes A \to (U^!\Gamma \otimes A) \oplus E \qquad \text{and} \qquad U^!\Gamma \otimes E \to (U^!\Gamma \otimes A) \oplus E \tag{9}$$

corresponding respectively to the *normal case* and the *exceptional case* describing the propagation of the exception, whose copairing must be subject to the mentioned naturality and coherence conditions. The normal case is given by the

---

[3] The cited authors actually consider this notion for the Kleisli adjoint resolution of !, but it can be defined similarly for any adjoint resolution, and even any strong monoidal functor U.

left inclusion whereas the exceptional case is obtained from $U^! \Gamma \otimes E \to E$, which follows from the erasure (5) given the hypothesis that the monoidal structure on $\mathscr{C}^!$ is cartesian. We are now ready to make an important observation: for the purpose of deriving a strength (8) we could consider other resource modalities than !; for instance the hypothesis that $\mathscr{C}^!$ is semi-cartesian suffices (the monoidal unit of $\mathscr{C}^!$ being a terminal object). This amounts to replacing ! in (8) with an affine resource modality that permits erasure but not duplication in (5).

Now that we have described a relaxed notion of strength for the monad of linearly-defined continuations and the exception monad in a linear context, we have to mention how restrictive a strength (8) seems to be in light of the interpretation of composition (3). The notion of strength with respect to ! amounts to precluding any linear variable from appearing in the monadic binding (4), in other words linear variables can only appear in Γ if it can be ensured that no control effect is performed. This models a restrictive approach in which linearity and control effects are exclusive with one another (see section 6).

1.3   Destructors

It is now clear that linearity and control effects do not mix well, or so it seems. Our goal is to show how linearity and exceptions can actually be mixed in more important situations than it seems, with a technique that we explain abstractly but that has been discovered from practical consideration in the context of resource management by the designers of the C++ programming language [28, 52, 24]. (We are deferring the more historical discussion to section 6.)

The starting point for describing this important discovery is to assume a linear model of computation as above given by a symmetric monoidal closed category $\mathscr{C}$ together with a given notion of linear effect, that is, a given monad T on $\mathscr{C}$ with a strength (7). As we have explained, this is a notion of linear model with linear effect which has previously been studied [49, 22, 36]; in particular a concrete model of computation is given by a *linear call-by-push-value* (linear CBPV) calculus [11] that will provide the basis of a first linear calculus we study.

In this model, we are interested in integrating exceptions. Assuming $\mathscr{C}$ has finite coproducts and that tensor products distribute over the coproducts, this means that we want to combine the monad T and the exception monad $\mathcal{E}$ into a strong monad $T\mathcal{E}$. Remember that as a general principle of the exception monad, $T\mathcal{E}$ has a monad structure arising from a distributive law of monads $\mathcal{E}T \to T\mathcal{E}$. However we meet again the obstacle that $\mathcal{E}$ does not have a strength in general, so we cannot obtain a strength for $T\mathcal{E}$ by composition.

But it might still be the case that $T\mathcal{E}$ has some kind of strength. This amounts to finding for all $A \in \mathscr{C}$ something like

$$\Gamma \otimes T(A \oplus E) \to T((\Gamma \otimes A) \oplus E) \tag{10}$$

for which, given that T is strong, it suffices to find maps

$$\Gamma \otimes A \to T((\Gamma \otimes A) \oplus E) \qquad \text{and} \qquad \Gamma \otimes E \to T((\Gamma \otimes A) \oplus E)$$

subject to some conditions. The one on the left-hand side—the normal return—is obtained in a straightforward manner by inclusion and unit of T. For the one on the right-hand side—the exceptional return—observe that the difference with (9) is the presence of T on the right-hand side. This second type suggests that Γ has to be erasable, but that erasure is allowed to perform effects in T. Indeed, observe that the second map above can be derived if Γ is provided with some map $\Gamma \to TI$. We call such an erasure map that performs an effect a *destructor*, by analogy with C++ destructors.

1.4   The monoidal category of destructors

The desire to find a strength for $T\mathcal{E}$ therefore suggests to consider for Γ in (10) an object with a given destructor $\delta : \Gamma \to TI$, that is to say an object in the slice category $\mathcal{C}_{/TI}$. Recall that it is the category whose objects are arbitrary pairs $(A \in \mathcal{C}, \delta : A \to TI)$, and whose morphisms are morphisms in $\mathcal{C}$ that preserve the second component δ. The slice category $\mathcal{C}_{/TI}$ enjoys a series of nice properties, the most striking one being that it gives rise to a resource modality on $\mathcal{C}$ [10]. Indeed:

- $\mathcal{C}_{/TI}$ has a monoidal structure arising from the monoid structure on TI:

$$TI \otimes TI \xrightarrow{\sigma_{TI,I}} T(TI \otimes I) \xrightarrow{\cong} TTI \xrightarrow{\mu} TI$$

  The monoidal unit is given by $(I, \eta_I : I \to TI)$ and, for $(A, \delta_A : A \to TI)$ and $(B, \delta_B : B \to TI)$, the tensor product is given by:

$$(A \otimes B, \delta_{A \otimes B} : A \otimes B \xrightarrow{\delta_A \otimes \delta_B} TI \otimes TI \to TI)\,.$$

  In words, $A \otimes B$ has a canonical destructor which releases B and A, as we will see in the reverse order of allocation.
- We also observe that there is a strong monoidal functor $U : \mathcal{C}_{/TI} \to \mathcal{C}$, that sends the monoidal structure of $\mathcal{C}_{/TI}$ to the one of $\mathcal{C}$ (strictly so).
- If we assume that $\mathcal{C}$ has finite products that we note $(\&, \top)$, then U has a right adjoint $G : \mathcal{C} \to \mathcal{C}_{/TI}$ sending objects $A \in \mathcal{C}$ to

$$(A \& TI, \pi_2 : A \& TI \to TI) \in \mathcal{C}_{/TI} \tag{11}$$

  and morphisms $f : A \to B$ to $f \& TI$. In particular if we note $\mathcal{D} \overset{\text{def}}{=} UG$ the comonad on $\mathcal{C}$ associated to the adjunction, one has $\mathcal{D} = (- \& TI)$ as our resource modality.
- The latter adjunction is comonadic: $\mathcal{C}_{/TI} \simeq \mathcal{C}^{\mathcal{D}}$. This can be observed from the fact that a coalgebra $(A, \tau : A \to \mathcal{D}A)$ for $\mathcal{D}$ boils down to an object A provided with a morphism $A \to TI$ in $\mathcal{C}$ without any other condition.

This setup was advocated as a starting point to study C++ destructors in [10].

  At this stage we find it useful to sum up the assumptions on $\mathcal{C}$: a distributive symmetric monoidal category with finite products and a chosen strong monad T. In particular any model of linear logic or intuitionistic linear logic is suitable (where T can be any linear state monad, for instance). We have just established that in those models, $\mathcal{D} = (- \& TI)$ has the structure of a resource modality whose Eilenberg-Moore category is (equivalent to) $\mathscr{C}_{/TI}$.

It is a nice exercise to check that this setup indeed gives a strength for the composite monad $T\mathcal{E}$ with respect to $U : \mathscr{C}_{/TI} \to \mathscr{C}$, more precisely:

Theorem 1. *Let $E \in \mathscr{C}$, $\mathcal{E}$ the exception monad $- \oplus E$, and $T\mathcal{E}$ the monad obtained arising from the distributive law of monads $\mathcal{E}T \to T\mathcal{E}$. Then the monad $T\mathcal{E}$ underlies a strong monad on the $\mathscr{C}^+$-category $(\mathscr{C}_{/TI}, *)$, in the terminology of Melliès [36], where $*$ is the pseudo-action defined with $-_1 * -_2 \overset{\mathrm{def}}{=} (U-_1) \otimes -_2$.*

Now, unlike usual resource modalities that add duplication and/or erasure (5), $\mathscr{C}_{/TI}$ *is in general not cartesian nor even semi-cartesian. In fact, its monoidal structure is not even symmetric* (unless T is commutative). Indeed, $\delta_{A \otimes B}$ and $\delta_{B \otimes A}$ can in general be distinguished by the order in which the effects of δ_A and δ_B are performed.

Nevertheless, just as linear models with a resource modality "!" give rise to an intuitionistic model by the Girard translations [19], one can build an *ordered CBPV* model whose (positive) objects are those of $\mathscr{C}_{/TI}$, as an instance of a general principle generalising the Girard translation [36, 11] applied to the resource modality $\mathcal{D}$. This motivates the study of a second calculus after the first one, whose (positive) types are supplied with a destructor and whose effects include those of T and exceptions.

1.5 Modelling resources with the allocation monad

In this new context, notice that everything is linear in the sense that we did not make use of a resource modality "!". We set out to show how *resource-safety* properties are thus ensured by construction. *Resource management* in programming aims to ensure the correct allocation, use, and release of *resources*, which are transient values denoting the validity of some state (a memory allocation, a lock, or typically resources from the operating system). The need for correct resource management in programming further complicates the problems with mixing linearity and control: indeed, a need to handle errors arises from the possibility that resource acquisition can fail, whereas a need for linearity arises from the fact that the resources must be released in a timely fashion and no more than once.

We introduce the *allocation monad* as a way to model resource management and state and establish resource-safety properties. The allocation monad will play the role of T in the slice category $\mathscr{C}_{/TI}$. We first assume given an atomic type R of resources and ask for two effectful operations:

- **new** $: I \multimap R \oplus I$ acquires a resource, or fails if there are no resources available. Later on, it will also be given with type $I \multimap R$ when the failure can be represented with an exception;
- **delete** $: R \multimap I$ releases the given resource without fail.

Notice that no operation is given for interacting with resources: we are only interested in observing resource-safety properties of the program state arising from the (correct) use of **new** and **delete**. Notice also that we represent failure with an explicit use of the exception monad $\mathcal{E} = (- \oplus E)$ for $E \stackrel{\text{def}}{=} I$ as an error type. But using an error type explicitly is not a solution to the lack of exceptions since we can expect similar obstacles to programming to arise from the lack of general strength for $\mathcal{E}$ (see discussion in section 6).

To implement those effectful operations, we then define the allocation monad as the linear state monad on the type $[R]$ of lists of R:

$$T A \stackrel{\text{def}}{=} [R] \multimap A \otimes [R]$$

As an instance of the linear state monad, it is strong. The morphism **new** : $I \to T(R \oplus I)$ is defined by popping an element from the list, or returning the error I if the list is empty. The morphism **delete** : $R \to TI$ is defined by pushing the resource onto the list; this is guaranteed to never fail.

Observe that an effectful, closed program of type A in this setup corresponds to a morphism $I \to ([R] \multimap A \otimes [R])$. Its execution consists of supplying an initial list of available resources (*free-list*). Now if the type A is purely positive and does not contain the type R, we expect that *a correct linear program will have as final free-list the same list as given initially, up to a permutation*. We can understand this as a resource-safety property: only resources acquired from the initial free-list have been released, all resources have eventually been released including in case of error; no resource has been released twice.

Moreover, assuming now an ordered rather than linear setting, that is without symmetry (6), we expect that *the final free-list is* identical *to the initial free-list*. This reflects the observation that without symmetry, resources are managed in a last-in-first-out (LIFO) order. Ordered logics often have two forms of closures operating on opposite sides $B \circ\!\!-\ A$ and $A \multimap B$, but as we will see this ordered resource-safety property is only true when one does not have $A \multimap B$; hence we only have $B \circ\!\!-\ A$ in this paper for the ordered logics (which still coincides with $A \multimap B$ when adding symmetry).

1.6   Outline and contributions

We have just explained abstractly how to mix linearity and exceptions, and we introduced the *allocation monad* modelling an idealised global "free-list" allocator, with the purpose of studying resource-safety properties. In **Section 2** we define a *linear CBPV* calculus $\mathcal{L}$ which has an *ordered* fragment by removing its exchange rule (6), hence named $\mathcal{O}$. This calculus features allocation effects (**new**, **delete**), together with a simple type system and a small-step operational semantics. We establish elementary properties of $\mathcal{L}$ and $\mathcal{O}$ relating typing to reduction. Then, in **Section 3** we define and prove *resource-safety properties* based on the allocation monad.

In **Section 4** we present the *resource CBPV*, an extension of the ordered language, through a calculus $\mathcal{O}_{\mathcal{E},\textbf{move}}$. It is a linear CBPV language with allocation effects and exceptions, in which every positive type has a chosen effectful erasure map (**drop**), and in which allocation failure results in an exception. Its exchange rule does a side-effect, as it changes the observable execution order of destructors; we also consider its ordered fragment $\mathcal{O}_{\mathcal{E}}$. We define the semantics of $\mathcal{O}_{\mathcal{E},\mathbf{move}}$ by a translation into $\mathcal{L}$ that preserves the ordered fragment.

$$
\begin{array}{ccc}
\mathcal{O}_{\mathcal{E}} & \xrightarrow{\ [\![-]\!]\ } & \mathcal{O} \\
\cap & & \cap \\
\mathcal{O}_{\mathcal{E},\mathbf{move}} & \xrightarrow{\ [\![-]\!]\ } & \mathcal{L}
\end{array}
$$

$\mathcal{O}_{\mathcal{E},\mathbf{move}}$ and $\mathcal{O}_{\mathcal{E}}$ inherit the resource-safety properties of $\mathcal{L}$ and $\mathcal{O}$, respectively.

Then, in **Section 5** we define a presheaf model for $\mathcal{O}$, which models an ordered logic with a destructor for all types, without being a model of affine logic in a traditional sense. Lastly, in **Section 6**, we conclude with a discussion placing the results in the context of the theory of programming languages.

A version with more details is available as doi:10.48550/arXiv.2510.23517.

2   An ordered effectful calculus of allocations

In this section, we describe a calculus with allocation effects **new**, **delete**, and with an ordered type system ($\mathcal{O}$) which optionally can be upgraded to linear ($\mathcal{L}$). We provide a common small-step operational semantics modelling this concrete effect. Our starting point is a simplified version of the linear CBPV calculus [11]: for simplicity we consider a calculus given in natural deduction, as opposed to sequent calculus, as we do not investigate the reductions and conversions on open terms. Starting from the linear CBPV calculus, this amounts to considering the derivation of natural deduction rules in the sequent calculus of [11], which directly gives an operational semantics in the form of typed abstract machines in head reduction. It is then adapted to the allocation effect by adding a list of resources, the free-list, to every machine configuration.

Ordered logic refines linear logic by removing the exchange rule, due to which the order of formulae in the antecedent matters for provability. As in Walker [58], we consider a sequencing (composition) rule restricted as follows:

$$
\frac{\Gamma, A \vdash B \qquad \Delta \vdash A}{\Gamma, \Delta \vdash B}\ \text{let}
$$

Unlike [48, 58], we consider left functions:

$$
\frac{A, \Gamma \vdash B}{\Gamma \vdash B \multimap A}\ \multimap_i
\qquad\qquad
\frac{\Gamma \vdash A \qquad \Delta \vdash B \multimap A}{\Gamma, \Delta \vdash B}\ \multimap_e
$$

instead of right functions whose rules are symmetric. The notation for left functions might seem unusual but one can think of the notation for an exponential object B^A, and it is justified by the isomorphism $(C \multimap B) \multimap A \cong C \multimap (B \otimes A)$. We will justify the choice of left vs. right functions in section 3.

CBPV will play an important role for the translation in section 4, and is also interesting in its own right since its treatment of the arrow type is useful to comprehend the multiplicity of closure types in the present of first-class resources

$$\frac{}{x:A \vdash x:A}\ \text{var} \qquad \frac{\Gamma \vdash t:A \qquad \sigma \in \Sigma(\Gamma,\Gamma')}{\Gamma' \vdash t[\sigma]:A}\ \text{struct}$$

$$\frac{}{\vdash \mathbf{new}:(R \oplus 1) \multimap 1}\ \text{new} \qquad \frac{}{\vdash \mathbf{delete}:1 \multimap R}\ \text{delete}$$

$$\frac{\Delta \vdash t:A_\varepsilon \qquad \Gamma,x:A \vdash u:B_{\varepsilon'}}{\Gamma,\Delta \vdash (\mathsf{let}\ x^\varepsilon = t\ \mathsf{in}\ u)^{\varepsilon'}:B}\ \text{let}$$

$$\frac{}{\vdash ():1}\ 1_i \qquad \frac{\Delta \vdash v:1 \qquad \Gamma,\Gamma' \vdash t:A_\varepsilon}{\Gamma,\Delta,\Gamma' \vdash \delta(v,().t)^\varepsilon:A}\ 1_e$$

$$\frac{\Gamma \vdash v:A \qquad \Delta \vdash w:B}{\Gamma,\Delta \vdash (v,w):A \otimes B}\ \otimes_i \qquad \frac{\Gamma \vdash v:A}{\Gamma \vdash \iota_1 v:A \oplus B}\ \oplus_{i1} \qquad \frac{\Gamma \vdash v:B}{\Gamma \vdash \iota_2 v:A \oplus B}\ \oplus_{i2}$$

$$\frac{\Delta \vdash v:A \otimes B \qquad \Gamma,x:A,y:B,\Gamma' \vdash t:C_\varepsilon}{\Gamma,\Delta,\Gamma' \vdash \delta(v,(x,y).t)^\varepsilon:C}\ \otimes_e$$

$$\frac{\Delta \vdash v:A \oplus B \qquad \Gamma,x:A,\Gamma' \vdash t:C_\varepsilon \qquad \Gamma,y:B,\Gamma' \vdash u:C}{\Gamma,\Delta,\Gamma' \vdash \delta(v,x.t,y.u)^\varepsilon:C}\ \oplus_e$$

$$\frac{x:A,\Gamma \vdash t:B}{\Gamma \vdash \lambda x.t:B \multimap A}\ \multimap_i \qquad \frac{\Gamma \vdash w:A \qquad \Delta \vdash v:B_\varepsilon \multimap A}{\Gamma,\Delta \vdash (vw)^\varepsilon:B}\ \multimap_e$$

$$\frac{\Gamma \vdash t:A \qquad \Gamma \vdash u:B}{\Gamma \vdash \langle t,u \rangle:A \& B}\ \&_i \qquad \frac{\Gamma \vdash v:A_\varepsilon \& B}{\Gamma \vdash (\pi_1 v)^\varepsilon:A}\ \&_{e1} \qquad \frac{\Gamma \vdash v:A \& B_\varepsilon}{\Gamma \vdash (\pi_2 v)^\varepsilon:B}\ \&_{e2}$$

Fig. 1. Typing rules for $\mathcal{L}$

(as we will discuss in section 6). Concretely, connectives and types are classified into two kinds, positive and negative, which require different evaluation strategies. Notably, the type R of allocated resources is positive.

$$\text{Types } A,B : \begin{cases} \text{Positive types} & P,Q ::= R \mid 1 \mid A \otimes B \mid A \oplus B \\ \text{Negative types} & N,M ::= B \multimap A \mid A \& B \end{cases}$$

Expressions of positive type evaluate eagerly, whereas expressions of negative type evaluate lazily. We introduce the notation $\varepsilon ::= + \mid -$ for polarities.

2.1 Grammar of terms

We define *expressions* and *values* with the following grammars:

$$\begin{aligned}
\text{Expressions } t,u ::=\ & v \mid (\mathsf{let}\ x^+ = t\ \mathsf{in}\ u)^+ \mid (\mathsf{let}\ x^- = v\ \mathsf{in}\ u)^+ \mid \delta(v,(x,y).t)^+ \mid \\
& \delta(v,().t)^+ \mid \delta(v,x.t,y.u)^+ \mid (vw)^+ \mid (\pi_1 v)^+ \mid (\pi_2 v)^+ \\
\text{Values } v,w ::=\ & (\mathsf{let}\ x^+ = t\ \mathsf{in}\ v)^- \mid (\mathsf{let}\ x^- = v\ \mathsf{in}\ w)^- \mid \delta(v,(x,y).w)^- \mid \\
& \delta(v,().w)^- \mid \delta(v,x.w,y.w')^- \mid (vw)^- \mid (\pi_1 v)^- \mid (\pi_2 v)^- \mid \\
& x \mid \mathbf{new} \mid \mathbf{delete} \mid (v,w) \mid () \mid \iota_1 v \mid \iota_2 v \mid \lambda x.t \mid \langle t,u \rangle \mid r_{n \in \mathbb{N}}
\end{aligned}$$

Our untyped expressions do not have typing annotations. Instead, expressions corresponding to elimination rules and let bindings have polarity annotations, which is the minimal amount of information determined by the type that we need to know the evaluation strategy.

Values are substitutable expressions: they are made of variables, all negative expressions (as they follow the call-by-name evaluation strategy) and positive expressions that have the shape of values in call-by-value. Positive values are eliminated with pattern matching: we note these with a dedicated δ eliminators for units, strict pairs and sums. Negative value eliminators follow the usual notation from lambda-calculus: lazy pair projections and function applications.

2.2 Typing rules

We define in fig. 1 typing rules for $\mathcal{L}$. Type polarity annotations in subscript A_ε assert that A has polarity ε. Contexts Γ, Δ are lists of typed variables. $\Sigma(\Gamma, \Gamma')$ is the set of maps from Γ to Γ' made of permutations and renamings. The term $t[\sigma]$ appearing in the *struct*(ural) rule denotes t where all variables have been substituted according to σ; in effect (struct) contains the unrestricted exchange rule. For $\mathcal{O}$ we simply restrict σ to be order-preserving.

Polarity annotations of expressions are inferred from the type polarities in typing rules. Hence, we will leave them implicit for typed expressions. The following notations allow to define and type expressions without restrictions with respect to values, by picking an arbitrary order to evaluate expressions. Such expressions may not always be well-typed in $\mathcal{O}$, since let bindings can only bind the right-most variable.

$$\iota_i t^* \overset{\text{def}}{=} \text{let } x = t \text{ in } \iota_i x \qquad\qquad \delta^*(t, (x, y).u) \overset{\text{def}}{=} \text{let } z = t \text{ in } \delta(z, (x, y).u)$$

$$(t, u)^* \overset{\text{def}}{=} \text{let } x = t \text{ in let } y = u \text{ in}(x, y) \quad \delta^*(t, x.u, y.u') \overset{\text{def}}{=} \text{let } z = t \text{ in } \delta(z, x.u, y.u')$$

$$(vt)^* \overset{\text{def}}{=} \text{let } x = t \text{ in } vx \qquad\qquad\qquad t; u \overset{\text{def}}{=} \text{let } x = t \text{ in } \delta(x, ().u)$$

As an example, we can define in $\mathcal{O}$ the following program that allocates then frees two resources. Upon allocation failure of s, it is forced to free r before returning:

$$\vdash \delta^*\big(\mathbf{new}\,(), r.\delta^*\big(\mathbf{new}\,(), s.(\mathbf{delete}\,s; \mathbf{delete}\,r), i.(i; \mathbf{delete}\,r)\big), i.i\big) : 1 \qquad (12)$$

2.3 Purely-positive types without resources

An important notion that we will need is that of *purely-positive types without resources* defined as follows:

$$W ::= 1 \mid W \otimes W' \mid W \oplus W' \qquad (13)$$

These types are in particular *central*: they commute for $\otimes$ with any other types, naturally so. We indeed can define by induction values

$$\text{swap}_W^A : W \otimes A \multimap A \otimes W$$

(corresponding to natural isomorphisms in the semantics of section 5). These types also happen to be discardable ($1 \multimap A$) and copyable ($A \otimes A \multimap A$) but we only rely on centrality in what follows.

$$\langle(\text{let } x^- = v \text{ in } t)^\varepsilon \,|\, s \,|\, l\rangle^\varepsilon \rightsquigarrow \langle t[v/x] \,|\, s \,|\, l\rangle^\varepsilon$$

$$\langle(\text{let } x^+ = t \text{ in } u)^\varepsilon \,|\, s \,|\, l\rangle^\varepsilon \rightsquigarrow \langle t \,|\, (x^+.u)^\varepsilon \cdot s \,|\, l\rangle^+ \qquad \langle v \,|\, (x^+.t)^\varepsilon \cdot s \,|\, l\rangle^+ \rightsquigarrow \langle t[v/x] \,|\, s \,|\, l\rangle^\varepsilon$$

$$\langle(vw)^\varepsilon \,|\, s \,|\, l\rangle^\varepsilon \rightsquigarrow \langle v \,|\, w^\varepsilon \cdot s \,|\, l\rangle^- \qquad \langle\lambda x.t \,|\, v^\varepsilon \cdot s \,|\, l\rangle^- \rightsquigarrow \langle t[v/x] \,|\, s \,|\, l\rangle^\varepsilon$$

$$\langle(\pi_i v)^\varepsilon \,|\, s \,|\, l\rangle^\varepsilon \rightsquigarrow \langle v \,|\, \pi_i^\varepsilon \cdot s \,|\, l\rangle^- \qquad \langle\langle t_1, t_2\rangle \,|\, \pi_i^\varepsilon \cdot s \,|\, l\rangle^- \rightsquigarrow \langle t_i \,|\, s \,|\, l\rangle^\varepsilon$$

$$\langle\delta((v,w),(x,y).t)^\varepsilon \,|\, s \,|\, l\rangle^\varepsilon \rightsquigarrow \langle t[v/x, w/y] \,|\, s \,|\, l\rangle^\varepsilon \qquad \langle\mathbf{new} \,|\, () \cdot s \,|\, \text{Nil}\rangle^- \rightsquigarrow \langle\iota_2() \,|\, s \,|\, \text{Nil}\rangle^+$$

$$\langle\delta((),().t)^\varepsilon \,|\, s \,|\, l\rangle^\varepsilon \rightsquigarrow \langle t \,|\, s \,|\, l\rangle^\varepsilon \qquad \langle\mathbf{new} \,|\, () \cdot s \,|\, r_n :: l\rangle^- \rightsquigarrow \langle\iota_1 r_n \,|\, s \,|\, l\rangle^+$$

$$\langle\delta(\iota_i v, x_1.t_1, x_2.t_2)^\varepsilon \,|\, s \,|\, l\rangle^\varepsilon \rightsquigarrow \langle t_i[v/x_i] \,|\, s \,|\, l\rangle^\varepsilon \qquad \langle\mathbf{delete} \,|\, r_n \cdot s \,|\, l\rangle^- \rightsquigarrow \langle() \,|\, s \,|\, r_n :: l\rangle^+$$

Fig. 2. Reduction rules

2.4 Operational semantics

We define in fig. 2 a small-step operational semantics for untyped expressions with an abstract machine. We begin by defining a stack that stores the arguments of delayed operations along with their polarity: indices of lazy pair projections, arguments of function applications and continuations of let bindings of positive values. Finally, a command consists of an expression, a stack, a free-list of resources interpreting the allocation monad and the current polarity.

$$\text{Stacks } s ::= \star \mid v^\varepsilon \cdot s \mid \pi_i^\varepsilon \cdot s \mid (x^+.u)^\varepsilon \cdot s$$
$$\text{Lists } l ::= \text{Nil} \mid r_{n \in \mathbb{N}} :: l$$
$$\text{Commands } c ::= \langle t \mid s \mid l\rangle^\varepsilon$$

We now define reduction rules: let bindings of negative expressions perform the substitution them immediately, following call-by-name reduction, while let bindings of positive expressions push their continuation on the stack to first reduce the expression to a value. All rules that push arguments on the stack come with their dual rule that consumes the argument on the stack. Pattern-matching rules can reduce immediately as only values can be bound. Finally, rules for constants **new** and **delete** are the only ones that manipulate the free-list of resources.

If we interpret our previous program $p = (12)$ with the list of resources $r_0 :: r_1 :: l$, we obtain in particular the following reduction steps:

$$\langle p \mid \star \mid r_0 :: r_1 :: l\rangle^+$$

$$\rightsquigarrow^* \left\langle \iota_1 r_1 \,\middle|\, \left(x^+.\delta(x, s.(\mathbf{delete}\, s; \mathbf{delete}\, r_0), i.(i; \mathbf{delete}\, r_0))\right) \cdot \star \,\middle|\, l\right\rangle^+$$

$$\rightsquigarrow^* \langle() \mid \star \mid r_0 :: r_1 :: l\rangle^+$$

2.5 Properties

We now study properties of $\mathcal{L}$. First, we establish standard properties such as confluence (through determinism), subject reduction and progress.

$$\frac{}{\star : A \vdash_p A} \qquad \frac{s : B_\varepsilon \vdash_p C \qquad \vdash_p v : A}{v^\varepsilon \cdot s : B \multimap A \vdash_p C} \qquad \frac{s : B_\varepsilon \vdash_p C \qquad x : A \vdash_p t : B}{(x^+.t)^\varepsilon \cdot s : A \vdash_p C}$$

$$\frac{s : A_\varepsilon \vdash_p C}{\pi_1^\varepsilon \cdot s : A \mathbin{\&} B \vdash_p C} \qquad \frac{s : B_\varepsilon \vdash_p C}{\pi_2^\varepsilon \cdot s : A \mathbin{\&} B \vdash_p C}$$

Fig. 3. Stack typing rules

Proposition 2. *The reduction rules are deterministic: at most one reduction rule can be applied to any command.*

We define typing judgements for expressions $\vdash_p t : A$ by extending all typing rules given in section 2.2 with the following axiom scheme for resources: $\vdash_p r_n : R$, to type resources that occur in commands through a program execution. We then extend those judgements in fig. 3 for closed stacks $s : A \vdash_p B$ which follow sequent calculus rules. Finally, we extend judgements to commands $c : A$, which consist of pairs of judgements $\vdash_p t : B_\varepsilon$ and $s : B \vdash_p A$ for $c = \langle t \mid s \mid l \rangle^\varepsilon : A$. We prove the following substitution lemma by induction on the derivation of t:

Lemma 3 (Substitution lemma (SL)). *If $\vdash_p v : A$ and $\Gamma, x : A, \Gamma' \vdash_p t : B$, then $\Gamma, \Gamma' \vdash_p t[v/x] : B$.*

Theorem 4 (Subject reduction). *The reduction rules preserve typing judgements: for any $c_1 : A$ and c_2, $c_1 \rightsquigarrow c_2$ implies $c_2 : A$. This also holds in the ordered fragment, i.e. for $\vdash_p$ without the exchange rule.*

We define final values $v_t ::= () \mid (v, w) \mid \iota_i v \mid r_n \mid \langle t, u \rangle \mid \lambda x.t \mid \mathbf{new} \mid \mathbf{delete}$. They include in particular all values v such that $\vdash_p v : A_+$.

Theorem 5 (Progress). *A well-typed command reduces if and only if it is not of the shape $\langle v_t \mid \star \mid l \rangle^\varepsilon$. This also holds in $\mathcal{O}$.*

Together, subject reduction and progress ensures that any well-typed expression $\vdash_p t : A$ reduces either indefinitely[4] or to a final command $\langle v_t \mid \star \mid l \rangle$ with $\vdash_p v_t : A$.

3   Resource-safety properties

In this section, we prove a resource-safety property for $\mathcal{L}$ pertaining to its linear character. This property is stated for *complete programs*: closed expressions that return a purely positive type without resource, executed in an empty context. We show that for such a program t, the execution starting with any free-list leaves it unchanged upon return, up to a permutation σ:

$$\langle t \mid \star \mid l \rangle \rightsquigarrow^* \langle v \mid \star \mid l' \rangle \qquad \implies \qquad \exists \sigma, l' = \sigma(l)$$

---

[4] Although we do not have non-terminating features, our proof by progress & subject reduction does not rely on termination.

The property is indeed about resource safety as it provides several good properties expected in programs that manipulate resources:

- all allocated resources are released by the end of the program,
- only previously-allocated resources are released,
- no resource has been released twice (i.e. no "use after free", in this limited context where the only way to use a resource is to release it),
- these properties remain true in case of an error during the program execution, including an allocation error.

We start by describing a stronger property for $\mathcal{O}$: in the ordered language, the final free-list is identical to the initial one ($\sigma = \mathrm{id}$). This corresponds to the expected property with ordered type systems that resources are freed in a LIFO order [58, §1.4]. We also provide a counter-example showing that we cannot include right functions in $\mathcal{O}$ without breaking the LIFO property.

3.1 Ordered case

Let W a purely positive type without resource and $\vdash t : W$ a closed typed expression of $\mathcal{O}$ (i.e. without exchange rule).

Proposition 6. *For any value v and lists of resources l, l', if*

$$\langle t \mid \star \mid l \rangle \leadsto^* \langle v \mid \star \mid l' \rangle$$

then $l' = l$.

To prove this property, we will define the list of resources $LR(t)$ of a term t by tracking resources in contexts of typing rules, and show that such lists are invariant by reduction. In order to reason about resources in case of substitutions, $LR(t[v/x])$ must be definable in terms of $LR(t)$ and $LR(v)$, hence their concatenation. To ensure this (see lemma 8), we restrict contexts to have the shape $\Theta \stackrel{\mathrm{def}}{=} \Gamma; L; \Delta$ with L the list of resources, Γ, Δ contexts of variables and x to be the right-most variable in Γ or the left-most variable in Δ.

Given $+\!\!+$ the concatenation operation for lists, $\Theta = \Gamma_\Theta; L_\Theta; \Delta_\Theta$ and $\Theta' = \Gamma_{\Theta'}; L_{\Theta'}; \Delta_{\Theta'}$, the expression $\Theta @ \Theta'$ asserts that we are in one of the three following cases to define the concatenation of both contexts:

- $L_\Theta = []$, then $\Theta @ \Theta' \stackrel{\mathrm{def}}{=} \Gamma_\Theta, \Delta_\Theta, \Gamma_{\Theta'}; L_{\Theta'}; \Delta_{\Theta'}$.
- $L_{\Theta'} = []$, then $\Theta @ \Theta' \stackrel{\mathrm{def}}{=} \Gamma_\Theta; L_\Theta; \Delta_\Theta, \Gamma_{\Theta'}, \Delta_{\Theta'}$.
- $\Delta_\Theta = \Gamma_{\Theta'} = \emptyset$, then $\Theta @ \Theta' \stackrel{\mathrm{def}}{=} \Gamma_\Theta; L_\Theta +\!\!+ L_{\Theta'}; \Delta_{\Theta'}$.

We can now type terms with resources with the judgement $\vdash_o$ indexed by such contexts, which enrich the previous typing judgements with information to track their resources (in fig. 4, where types are omitted for brevity). Given an ordered expression $\Gamma; L; \Delta \vdash_o t$, we define its list of resources $LR(t) \stackrel{\mathrm{def}}{=} L$. For $\Theta = \Gamma; L; \Delta$, we define the notations $\Theta, x \stackrel{\mathrm{def}}{=} \Gamma; L; \Delta, x$ and $x, \Theta \stackrel{\mathrm{def}}{=} x, \Gamma; L; \Delta$.

Lemma 7. *If $\Gamma \vdash t : A$, then $\Gamma; ; \vdash_o t : A$.*

$$\dfrac{}{;[\,];x \vdash_o x} \qquad \dfrac{}{;[\,];\vdash_o ()} \qquad \dfrac{}{;[\,];\vdash_o \textbf{new}} \qquad \dfrac{}{;[\,];\vdash_o \textbf{delete}} \qquad \dfrac{}{;[r_n];\vdash_o r_n}$$

$$\dfrac{\Gamma;[\,];x,\Delta \vdash_o x}{\Gamma,x;[\,];\Delta \vdash_o x} \qquad\qquad \dfrac{\Gamma,x;[\,];\Delta \vdash_o x}{\Gamma;[\,];x,\Delta \vdash_o x}$$

$$\dfrac{\Theta \vdash_o v}{\Theta \vdash_o \iota_i v} \qquad \dfrac{\Theta \vdash_o v}{\Theta \vdash_o \pi_i v} \qquad \dfrac{\Theta \vdash_o t \quad \Theta \vdash_o u}{\Theta \vdash_o \langle t,u\rangle} \qquad \dfrac{x,\Theta \vdash_o t}{\Theta \vdash_o \lambda x.t}$$

$$\dfrac{\Theta \vdash_o v \quad \Theta' \vdash_o w}{\Theta @ \Theta' \vdash_o (v,w)} \qquad\qquad \dfrac{\Theta,x \vdash_o u \quad \Theta' \vdash_o t}{\Theta @ \Theta' \vdash_o \text{let } x = t \text{ in } u}$$

$$\dfrac{\Theta,x,y @ \Theta'' \vdash_o t \quad \Theta' \vdash_o v}{\Theta @ \Theta' @ \Theta'' \vdash_o \delta(v,(x,y).t)} \qquad\qquad \dfrac{\Theta @ \Theta'' \vdash_o t \quad \Theta' \vdash_o v}{\Theta @ \Theta' @ \Theta'' \vdash_o \delta(v,().t)}$$

$$\dfrac{\Theta,x @ \Theta'' \vdash_o t \quad \Theta,y @ \Theta'' \vdash_o u \quad \Theta' \vdash_o v}{\Theta @ \Theta' @ \Theta'' \vdash_o \delta(v,x.t,y.u)} \qquad \dfrac{\Theta \vdash_o w \quad \Theta' \vdash_o v}{\Theta @ \Theta' \vdash_o vw}$$

Fig. 4. Typing rules of ordered expressions with resources (types omitted)

$$\dfrac{}{[\,] \vdash_o^S \star} \qquad\qquad \dfrac{;L_v;\vdash_o v \quad L_s \vdash_o^S s}{L_s + L_v \vdash_o^S v \cdot s}$$

$$\dfrac{;L_t;x \vdash_o t \quad L_s \vdash_o^S s}{L_s + L_t \vdash_o^S (x^+.t)\cdot s} \qquad\qquad \dfrac{;L_t;\vdash_o t \quad L_s \vdash_o^S s}{L_s + L_t + l \vdash_o^C \langle t \mid s \mid l\rangle}$$

Fig. 5. Typing rules of ordered stacks and commands with resources (types omitted)

We can then accept substitutions of expressions that preserve well-formed contexts. The following left and right substitution lemmas cover substitutions encountered in the operational semantics.

Lemma 8. (Left SL) *If* $;L_t;\vdash_o t$ *and* $\Gamma,x;L_u;\Delta \vdash_o u$, *then* $\Gamma;L_t + L_u;\Delta \vdash_o u[t/x]$. (Right SL) *If* $;L_t;\vdash_o t$ *and* $\Gamma;L_u;x,\Delta \vdash_o u$, *then* $\Gamma;L_u + L_t;\Delta \vdash_o u[t/x]$.

We then extend $\vdash_o$ for stacks and commands, with only resources in their contexts. Resources from stacks remain to the left of resources from expressions in the context of commands:

Theorem 9. *Reducing an ordered command results in an ordered command with the same list of resources, i.e. for all c_1,c_2,M such that $L \vdash_o^C c_1$ and $c_1 \rightsquigarrow c_2$ one has $L \vdash_o^C c_2$.*

We can now prove proposition 6:

Proof (proposition 6). For any expression with a purely-positive type without resource $\vdash t : W$ in $\mathcal{O}$, by subject reduction and progress we have that $\langle t \mid \star \mid l\rangle$ either reduces indefinitely, or there exists a final value $\vdash v_t : W$ such that $\langle t \mid \star \mid l\rangle \rightsquigarrow^* \langle v \mid \star \mid l'\rangle$. We then prove by induction on derivations that typed expressions without structural rules are ordered: they do not include resources, so concatenated contexts are always well-formed. So both t and v are ordered and without resources. Since reduction rules preserve the list of resources, we have $l = l'$.

3.2 A counter-example for right functions

We only have left functions in $\mathcal{O}$, that is, abstractions binding the leftmost variable together with the matching elimination rule from ordered logic. We provide the following counter-example to the resource-safety property with right functions. We underline the right function abstractions and applications.

$$p \stackrel{\text{def}}{=} \delta^* \left(\mathbf{new}(), r.\delta^* \left(\mathbf{new}(), s.(\underline{t_r}s), i.(\mathbf{delete}\, r; i) \right), i.i \right)$$

$$\text{where } t_r = \left(\text{let } i = \mathbf{delete}\, r \text{ in } \delta(i, ().\underline{\lambda x}.\, \mathbf{delete}\, x) \right)^{-} \qquad (14)$$

This example does not belong to $\mathcal{O}$ as it uses the right function $t_r : R \multimap 1$ and its application $\underline{t_r}s$.

$$
\cfrac{
  \times \quad
  \cfrac{
    \cfrac{\overline{x : R \vdash \mathbf{delete}\, x : 1}}{\vdash \lambda x.\, \mathbf{delete}\, x : R \multimap 1}\, {\scriptstyle\multimap_e} \;\; {\scriptstyle\multimap_i\ (\text{not in } \mathcal{O})}
  }{
    i : 1 \vdash \delta(i, ().\underline{\lambda x}.\, \mathbf{delete}\, x) : R \multimap 1
  }\, {\scriptstyle 1_e}
}{
  \cfrac{
    \cfrac{\overline{r : R \vdash \mathbf{delete}\, r : 1}}{r : R \vdash \text{let } i = \mathbf{delete}\, r \text{ in } \delta(i, ().\underline{\lambda x}.\, \mathbf{delete}\, x) : R \multimap 1}\, {\scriptstyle\multimap_e \; \text{let}}
  }{
    \cfrac{\times \quad \cfrac{r : R \vdash t_r : R \multimap 1 \qquad\qquad s : R \vdash s : R}{r : R, s : R \vdash \underline{t_r}s : 1}\, {\scriptstyle\multimap_e\ (\text{not in } \mathcal{O})}}{}
  }\, {\scriptstyle =}
}
$$

As we can see from the typing derivation, the context is ordered as r, s, which is the converse of what we would have obtained with a left function. Subsequently, we can then calculate that two resources r_0 and r_1 are reordered during the execution as follows (with the obvious reductions rules for the right abstraction and application):

$$\langle p \mid \star \mid r_0 :: r_1 :: l \rangle \rightsquigarrow^* \langle () \mid \star \mid r_1 :: r_0 :: l \rangle$$

This contradicts the LIFO property for $\mathcal{O}$.

3.3 Non-ordered case

If we consider expressions $\vdash t : W$ in $\mathcal{L}$, that is by adding the exchange rule, they have a weaker property:

Theorem 10. *For all v, l, l' such that $\langle t \mid \star \mid l \rangle \rightsquigarrow^* \langle v \mid \star \mid l' \rangle$, there exists a permutation σ of lists of resources such that $l' = \sigma(l)$.*

This is proved similarly to proposition 6, by forgetting the order of variables and resources in the predicate $\Gamma; L; \Delta \vdash_o t$. This simplifies context concatenation by removing preconditions and requires a single substitution lemma.

4   The resource call-by-push-value

We now introduce a resource CBPV: an ordered variant of CBPV with an allocation effect **new**, exceptions, a chosen effectful destructor **drop** at all types, and a **move** operation that implements a side-effecting exchange rule.

Formally, we define a calculus $\mathcal{O}_{\mathcal{E},\mathbf{move}}$ which extends $\mathcal{O}$. Its semantics is given by translation into $\mathcal{L}$: exceptions are propagated as errors, removing variables from the context with their associated destructor. Hence, $\mathcal{L}$ serves as a meta-language in which the ambient allocation monad remains implicit, and which gives resource-safety properties for $\mathcal{O}_{\mathcal{E},\mathbf{move}}$. In addition, by removing **move**, we obtain a calculus $\mathcal{O}_{\mathcal{E}}$ whose translation falls into $\mathcal{O}$.

As a starting point, we picture the situation described in section 1.4:

$$
\mathscr{C}_{/TI} \underset{F^{\mathcal{D}}}{\overset{U^{\mathcal{D}}}{\rightleftarrows}} \perp (a) \quad \mathscr{C} \underset{U^{T\mathcal{E}}}{\overset{F^{T\mathcal{E}}}{\rightleftarrows}} \perp (b) \quad \mathscr{C}^{T\mathcal{E}} \tag{15}
$$

where $\mathcal{D} = - \,\&\, TI$ provides, for an arbitrary linear type, the free type with destructor (given by its second projection).

When trying to add exceptions to a general notion of effect given by a strong monad T, one would look at the adjunction (b), which, assuming $T\mathcal{E}$ strong, gives rise to a linear CBPV model [11], with positive types interpreted in $\mathscr{C}$ and negative types interpreted in $\mathscr{C}^{T\mathcal{E}}$. It is unnatural, though, to assume that $T\mathcal{E}$ is strong. In order to recover a strength for $T\mathcal{E}$, we want to restrict the positive types to the linear types that are provided with a chosen destructor, by looking at the monoidal adjunction (a) above. When starting from an adjunction model, composing with a monoidal adjunction on the left yields another adjunction model, a construction which generalises the Girard translations [42, 11, §5.3]. This suggests that we look at the adjoint situation $\uparrow \dashv \downarrow : \mathscr{C}^{T\mathcal{E}} \to \mathscr{C}_{/TI}$ obtained by composition: $\uparrow \overset{\text{def}}{=} F^{T\mathcal{E}}U^{\mathcal{D}}$ and $\downarrow \overset{\text{def}}{=} F^{\mathcal{D}}U^{T\mathcal{E}}$. Note that in terms of underlying types, one has $\uparrow A = T(A \oplus E)$ and $\downarrow A = A \,\&\, TI$.

We cannot apply the results of [11] directly, which only deals with the situation where the monoidal categories are symmetric and the monad is strong. Instead, we do this construction by hand, which we give as a translation of the resource CBPV into $\mathcal{O}$ and $\mathcal{L}$. Within this more focused approach, we refine the Girard translation from [11, §5.3] with ordered sequents, and with the consideration of a strength of $T\mathcal{E}$ with respect to $U^{\mathcal{D}}$, which is necessary for having antecedents with several variables in the first place.

Another important difference is that we are translating direct-style calculi into direct-style calculi: the monad T is, already, the ambient monad for side-effects in $\mathcal{O}$ and $\mathcal{L}$. As it turns out, we can still adapt the translation to work in this way. Note that the type $\downarrow A = A \,\&\, TI$ is $A \,\&\, 1$ in $\mathcal{O}$, and that the type $\uparrow A = T(A \oplus E)$ describes effectful computations of type $A \oplus E$ in $\mathcal{O}$. In what follows, we make use of $\Downarrow A \overset{\text{def}}{=} A \,\&\, 1$ and $\Uparrow A \overset{\text{def}}{=} A \oplus E$.

$$\frac{}{x : A \vdash x : A} \ \text{var} \qquad \frac{\Delta \vdash t : A \qquad \Gamma, x : A \vdash u : B}{\Gamma, \Delta \vdash \text{let } x = t \text{ in } u : B} \ \text{let}$$

$$\frac{}{\vdash \mathbf{drop}_A : 1 \multimap A} \ \text{drop}_A \qquad \frac{\Gamma, \Gamma', x : A \vdash t : C}{\Gamma, x : A, \Gamma' \vdash \mathbf{move}(x) \text{ in } t : C} \ \text{move}$$

$$\frac{}{\vdash \mathbf{new} : R \multimap 1} \ \text{new} \qquad \frac{}{\vdash \mathbf{raise} : A \multimap E} \ \text{raise}$$

$$\frac{\Delta \vdash t : P \qquad \Gamma, x : P \vdash u : A \qquad \Gamma, e : E \vdash u' : A}{\Gamma, \Delta \vdash \mathbf{try}\, x \Leftarrow t \text{ in } u \,\mathbf{unless}\, e \Rightarrow u' : A} \ \text{try}$$

$$\frac{\Gamma \vdash v : A \qquad \Delta \vdash w : B}{\Gamma, \Delta \vdash (v, w) : A \otimes B} \ \otimes_i \qquad \frac{\Delta \vdash v : A \otimes B \qquad \Gamma, x : A, y : B, \Gamma' \vdash t : C}{\Gamma, \Delta, \Gamma' \vdash \delta(v, (x, y).t) : C} \ \otimes_e$$

$$\frac{}{\vdash () : 1} \ 1_i \qquad \frac{\Delta \vdash v : 1 \qquad \Gamma, \Gamma' \vdash t : A}{\Gamma, \Delta, \Gamma' \vdash \delta(v, ().t) : A} \ 1_e$$

$$\frac{\Gamma \vdash v : A}{\Gamma \vdash \iota_1 v : A \oplus B} \ \oplus_{i1} \qquad \frac{\Gamma \vdash v : B}{\Gamma \vdash \iota_2 v : A \oplus B} \ \oplus_{i2}$$

$$\frac{\Delta \vdash v : A \oplus B \qquad \Gamma, x : A, \Gamma' \vdash t : C \qquad \Gamma, y : B, \Gamma' \vdash u : C}{\Gamma, \Delta, \Gamma' \vdash \delta(v, x.t, y.u) : C} \ \oplus_e$$

$$\frac{x : A, \Gamma \vdash t : B}{\Gamma \vdash \lambda x.t : B \multimap A} \ \multimap_i \qquad \frac{\Gamma \vdash w : A \qquad \Delta \vdash v : B \multimap A}{\Gamma, \Delta \vdash vw : B} \ \multimap_e$$

$$\frac{\Gamma \vdash t : A \qquad \Gamma \vdash u : B}{\Gamma \vdash \langle t, u \rangle : A \,\&\, B} \ \&_i \qquad \frac{\Gamma \vdash v : A \,\&\, B}{\Gamma \vdash \pi_1 v : A} \ \&_{e1} \qquad \frac{\Gamma \vdash v : A \,\&\, B}{\Gamma \vdash \pi_2 v : B} \ \&_{e2}$$

New and changed rules are in **bold**.

Fig. 6. Typing rules for $\mathcal{O}_{\mathcal{E}, \text{move}}$

4.1 Expressions and types

The grammar of terms of $\mathcal{O}_{\mathcal{E}, \text{move}}$ extends that for $\mathcal{O}$, with the following terms:

- "**new**", now of type $1 \multimap R$, which raises an exception in case of allocation error.
- "**drop**$_A$", a function of type $1 \multimap A$ that releases the resources contained in its argument.
- "**move**(x) in t", an expression that places x on top of the stack in t.
- "**raise**", a value that inhabits any type with a given exception.
- "**try** $x \Leftarrow t$ in u **unless** $e \Rightarrow u'$", an expression that catches exceptions occurring in t based on [4].

We call $\mathcal{O}_{\mathcal{E}}$ the fragment of $\mathcal{O}_{\mathcal{E}, \text{move}}$ without **move**. Also, from now on we leave polarity annotations implicit because they can always be inferred from the type.

The grammar of types is unchanged:

$$\text{Types } A, B : \begin{cases} \text{Positive types} & P, Q ::= R \mid 1 \mid A \otimes B \mid A \oplus B \\ \text{Negative types} & N, M ::= B \multimap A \mid A \,\&\, B \end{cases}$$

However, the interpretation of types is changed, since each positive type is assigned a chosen destructor.

The calculus is parameterised by a type of exceptions E. In $\mathcal{O}_{\mathcal{E}}$, exceptions must not exchange resources during stack unwinding, so we add the constraint that E *is a purely-positive type without resource*. We also assume given some closed value $\vdash$ Alloc_failure $: E$, which is the exception raised whenever an allocation fails. (For instance, $E = 1$ and Alloc_failure $= ()$.) We will rely on terms swap_W^A in $\mathcal{O}_{\mathcal{E}}$ defined as in $\mathcal{O}$ (section 2.3).

4.2   Move as an effectful exchange rule

As explained in section 1.4, the category $\mathscr{C}_{/TI}$ in the situation (15) depicted above is not symmetric in general. However, when $\mathscr{C}$ is symmetric, there is nevertheless an effectful map $A \otimes B \to B \otimes A$, as found in the following hom-set:

$$\mathscr{C}_{/TI}(A \otimes B, F^{\mathcal{D}}U^{\mathcal{D}}(B \otimes A)) \cong \mathscr{C}(U^{\mathcal{D}}A \otimes U^{\mathcal{D}}B, U^{\mathcal{D}}B \otimes U^{\mathcal{D}}A)$$

This is reflected in $\mathcal{O}_{\mathcal{E},\mathbf{move}}$ with the operation **move** which exchanges variables. It is not presented as a structural rule in the traditional way: it indeed performs an effect and does not commute with other rules. In the following example, two terms allocate three resources and then frees them in reverse order. They would be identified if **move** was treated as a structural rule in the usual manner (e.g. as in $\mathcal{L}$), but they behave differently:

<table>
<tr><td>let $r = \mathbf{new}()$ in</td><td>let $r = \mathbf{new}()$ in</td></tr>
<tr><td>let $s = \mathbf{new}()$ in</td><td>let $s = \mathbf{new}()$ in $\mathbf{move}(r)$ in</td></tr>
<tr><td>let $t = \mathbf{new}()$ in</td><td>let $t = \mathbf{new}()$ in</td></tr>
<tr><td>$\mathbf{drop}_R\, t; \mathbf{drop}_R\, s; \mathbf{drop}_R\, r$</td><td>$\mathbf{drop}_R\, t; \mathbf{move}(s)$ in $\mathbf{drop}_R\, s; \mathbf{drop}_R\, r$</td></tr>
</table>

Both terms allocate three resources then frees them in reverse order. If the allocation of t fails, then the raised exception will free the first two resources in a different order, which can be observed with the evaluation context $\mid \star \mid [r_0, r_1] \rangle$: the final free-lists are respectively $[r_0, r_1]$ and $[r_1, r_0]$.

For this reason, **move** cannot give rise to a *contextual isomorphism* [32] between $A \otimes B$ and $B \otimes A$ for arbitrary A and B, that is, which would allow us to replace $A \otimes B$ with $B \otimes A$ in arbitrary context without changing the meaning. Since a contextual isomorphism just requires inverses and purity (thunkability) [32], **move** must be effectful in any reasonable interpretation.

4.3   Translation into $\mathcal{L}$

Each type A has a positive interpretation A^+ equipped with a destructor written drop_A and a negative interpretation A^-.

$$1^+ \stackrel{\mathrm{def}}{=} 1 \qquad\qquad \mathrm{drop}_1 \stackrel{\mathrm{def}}{=} \lambda v.v$$
$$R^+ \stackrel{\mathrm{def}}{=} R \qquad\qquad \mathrm{drop}_R \stackrel{\mathrm{def}}{=} \lambda r.\, \mathbf{delete}\, r$$

$$(A \otimes B)^+ \stackrel{\text{def}}{=} A^+ \otimes B^+$$
$$(A \oplus B)^+ \stackrel{\text{def}}{=} A^+ \oplus B^+$$
$$N^+ \stackrel{\text{def}}{=} \Downarrow N^-$$
$$(B \multimapinv A)^- \stackrel{\text{def}}{=} B^- \multimapinv A^+$$
$$(A \& B)^- \stackrel{\text{def}}{=} A^- \& B^-$$
$$P^- \stackrel{\text{def}}{=} \Uparrow P^+$$

$$\text{drop}_{(A \otimes B)} \stackrel{\text{def}}{=} \lambda p.\delta(p, (a, b).\, \text{drop}_B\, b;\, \text{drop}_A\, a)$$
$$\text{drop}_{(A \oplus B)} \stackrel{\text{def}}{=} \lambda s.\delta(s, a.\, \text{drop}_A\, a, b.\, \text{drop}_B\, b)$$
$$\text{drop}_N \stackrel{\text{def}}{=} \lambda a.\pi_2 a$$

$$\star^+ \stackrel{\text{def}}{=} \star$$
$$(\Gamma, x : A)^+ \stackrel{\text{def}}{=} \Gamma^+, x : A^+$$

Note that for any purely positive type (hence also E), we have $W^+ = W$. We define three expressions which we use in the translation:

- $\Gamma^+ \vdash \text{drop\_ctx}_\Gamma : 1$ by induction on Γ, which drops each variable from right to left.

$$\text{drop\_ctx}_\star \stackrel{\text{def}}{=} ()$$
$$\text{drop\_ctx}_{\Gamma, x:A} \stackrel{\text{def}}{=} \text{drop}_A\, x;\, \text{drop\_ctx}_\Gamma$$

- $\Gamma^+, e : E \vdash \text{unwind}_\Gamma(e) : E$ by induction on Γ, which drops the context and returns e.

$$\text{unwind}_\star(e) \stackrel{\text{def}}{=} e$$
$$\text{unwind}_{\Gamma, x:A}(e) \stackrel{\text{def}}{=} \text{let } p = \text{swap}_E^A(x, e) \text{ in } \delta(p, (e, x).\, \text{drop}_A\, x;\, \text{unwind}_\Gamma(e))$$

- $\Gamma^+, e : E \vdash \text{raise}_\Gamma^A(e) : A^-$ by induction on A, which drops the context and inhabits A^- with e.

$$\text{raise}_\Gamma^{C \multimapinv B}(e) \stackrel{\text{def}}{=} \lambda b.\, \text{raise}_{b:B, \Gamma}^{C}(e)$$
$$\text{raise}_\Gamma^{B \,\&\, C}(e) \stackrel{\text{def}}{=} \langle \text{raise}_\Gamma^{B}(e), \text{raise}_\Gamma^{C}(e) \rangle$$
$$\text{raise}_\Gamma^{P}(e) \stackrel{\text{def}}{=} \text{let } e' = \text{unwind}_\Gamma(e) \text{ in } \iota_2 e'$$

We then translate $\mathcal{O}_{\mathcal{E}, \text{move}}$ derivations with two functions noted $[\![-]\!]$ defined by mutual induction on derivations of the two kinds of judgements:

- $\mathcal{O}_{\mathcal{E}, \text{move}}$ values of type $\Gamma \vdash A$ are translated to $\mathcal{L}$ values of type $\Gamma^+ \vdash A^+$.
- $\mathcal{O}_{\mathcal{E}, \text{move}}$ expressions of type $\Gamma \vdash A$ are translated to $\mathcal{L}$ expressions of type $\Gamma^+ \vdash \Downarrow A^-$.

We add explicit coercions to treat positive values as expressions with the notation $\text{coerc}(v)$. The monad strength for $T\mathcal{E}$ can be observed when translating let bindings of expressions, where the context of the continuation is dropped in case of an error.

$$ax : [\![x \vdash x : A]\!] \stackrel{\text{def}}{=} x$$
$$\textbf{drop} : [\![\vdash \textbf{drop} : 1 \multimapinv A]\!] \stackrel{\text{def}}{=} \langle \text{drop}_A, () \rangle$$
$$\text{coerc} : [\![\Gamma \vdash \text{coerc}(v) : P]\!] \stackrel{\text{def}}{=} \langle \iota_1 [\![v]\!], \text{drop\_ctx}_\Gamma \rangle$$

$$\mathbf{move} : [\![\Gamma, x : A, \Delta \vdash \mathbf{move}(x)\,\mathrm{in}\,t : C]\!] \stackrel{\mathrm{def}}{=} [\![t]\!]$$

$$\mathbf{new} : [\![\vdash \mathbf{new} : R \multimap 1]\!] \stackrel{\mathrm{def}}{=} \mathrm{let}\,x = \mathbf{new}()\,\mathrm{in}\,\delta\big(x, r.\iota_1 r, i.(i; \iota_2\,\mathrm{Alloc\_failure})\big)$$

$$\mathrm{let}_v : [\![\Gamma, \Delta \vdash \mathrm{let}\,x = (v : A)\,\mathrm{in}\,t : B]\!] \stackrel{\mathrm{def}}{=} \mathrm{let}\,x = [\![v]\!]\,\mathrm{in}[\![t]\!]$$

$$\mathrm{let}_t : [\![\Gamma, \Delta \vdash \mathrm{let}\,x = (t : P)\,\mathrm{in}\,u : A]\!]$$
$$\stackrel{\mathrm{def}}{=} \mathrm{let}\,s = \pi_1[\![t]\!]\,\mathrm{in}\,\delta\big(s, x.[\![u]\!], e.\,\mathrm{raise}_\Gamma^{A\,\&\,I}(e)\big)$$

$$\mathbf{raise} : [\![\vdash \mathbf{raise} : A \multimap E]\!] \stackrel{\mathrm{def}}{=} \langle \lambda e.\,\mathrm{raise}_\star^A(e), ()\rangle$$

$$\mathbf{try} : [\![\Gamma, \Delta \vdash \mathbf{try}\,x \Leftarrow (t : P)\,\mathrm{in}\,u\,\mathbf{unless}\,e \Rightarrow u' : B]\!]$$
$$\stackrel{\mathrm{def}}{=} \mathrm{let}\,s = \pi_1[\![t]\!]\,\mathrm{in}\,\delta(s, x.[\![u]\!], e.[\![u']\!])$$

$$\otimes_i : [\![\Gamma, \Delta \vdash (v, w) : A \otimes B]\!] \stackrel{\mathrm{def}}{=} ([\![v]\!], [\![w]\!])$$

$$\otimes_e : [\![\Gamma, \Delta, \Gamma' \vdash \delta(v, (x, y).t) : C]\!] \stackrel{\mathrm{def}}{=} \delta([\![v]\!], (x, y).[\![t]\!])$$

$$1_i : [\![\vdash () : 1]\!] \stackrel{\mathrm{def}}{=} ()$$

$$1_e : [\![\Gamma, \Delta, \Gamma' \vdash \delta(v, ().t) : C]\!] \stackrel{\mathrm{def}}{=} \delta([\![v]\!], ().[\![t]\!])$$

$$\oplus_{i1} : [\![\Gamma \vdash \iota_1 v : A \oplus B]\!] \stackrel{\mathrm{def}}{=} \iota_1[\![v]\!]$$

$$\oplus_{i2} : [\![\Gamma \vdash \iota_2 v : A \oplus B]\!] \stackrel{\mathrm{def}}{=} \iota_2[\![v]\!]$$

$$\oplus_e : [\![\Gamma, \Delta, \Gamma' \vdash \delta(v, x.t, y.u) : C]\!] \stackrel{\mathrm{def}}{=} \delta([\![v]\!], x.[\![t]\!], y.[\![u]\!])$$

$$\multimap_i : [\![\Gamma \vdash \lambda x.t : B \multimap A]\!] \stackrel{\mathrm{def}}{=} \langle \lambda x.\pi_1[\![t]\!], \mathrm{drop\_ctx}_\Gamma\rangle$$

$$\multimap_e : [\![\Gamma, \Delta \vdash vw : B]\!] \stackrel{\mathrm{def}}{=} \langle (\pi_1[\![v]\!])[\![w]\!], \mathrm{drop\_ctx}_{\Gamma, \Delta}\rangle$$

$$\&_i : [\![\Gamma \vdash \langle t, u\rangle : A \,\&\, B]\!] \stackrel{\mathrm{def}}{=} \langle\langle \pi_1[\![t]\!], \pi_1[\![u]\!]\rangle, \mathrm{drop\_ctx}_\Gamma\rangle$$

$$\&_{e1} : [\![\Gamma \vdash \pi_1 v : A]\!] \stackrel{\mathrm{def}}{=} \langle \pi_1\pi_1[\![v]\!], \mathrm{drop\_ctx}_\Gamma\rangle$$

$$\&_{e2} : [\![\Gamma \vdash \pi_2 v : B]\!] \stackrel{\mathrm{def}}{=} \langle \pi_2\pi_1[\![v]\!], \mathrm{drop\_ctx}_\Gamma\rangle$$

Note that expressions $t : P$ have a second component that is immediately discarded, and they are evaluated eagerly. Hence, they are essentially expressions of type $A \oplus E$. The operational semantics of an affine value v is that of $[\![v]\!]$, and the operational semantics of an affine expression t is that of $\pi_1[\![t]\!]$.

Theorem 11. *For any expression t of $\mathcal{O}_{\mathcal{E}, \mathbf{move}}$ with a purely-positive type without resource W, if $\langle \pi_1[\![t]\!] \mid \star \mid l\rangle \rightsquigarrow^* \langle v \mid \star \mid l'\rangle$ then $l' = \sigma(l)$ for some permutation σ. Moreover, if the expression does not contain "$\mathbf{move}$", then $l' = l$.*

Proof. The translation defined below is well-typed, and use $\mathcal{L}$ structural rules only for **move**, so the $\mathcal{O}_{\mathcal{E}}$ fragment is translated in $\mathcal{O}$. Because purely-positive types without resources are translated as themselves, $\Downarrow W^- = (W \oplus E) \,\&\, I$, hence $\pi_1[\![t]\!]$ is a linear expression of type $W \oplus E$. By hypothesis E is purely-positive without resource, and so $W \oplus E$ is as well. Hence, the resource-safety property of $\mathcal{L}$ apply to $\pi_1[\![t]\!]$, as well as that of $\mathcal{O}$ if t is in $\mathcal{O}_{\mathcal{E}}$. Those are precisely the properties we needed to prove.

5   A presheaf model of $\mathcal{O}$

The ordered calculus $\mathcal{O}$ shows some peculiarities compared to usual formulations of ordered logic: it has a left arrow and no right arrow, and a right let binding without left let binding. We find it illustrative to give a simple concrete model showing that these peculiarities are natural and arise by construction upon consideration of the strengths for the allocation monad.

We interpret the calculus $\mathcal{O}$ in the presheaf category $\mathscr{C} \stackrel{\text{def}}{=} \mathcal{S}et^{[\mathbf{R}]}$, with $[\mathbf{R}]$ the set of lists of natural numbers considered as a discrete category. We note $+\!\!+$ the non-symmetric monoidal product on $[\mathbf{R}]$ obtained by concatenating two lists of resources. Its Day convolution [12] lifts it to a non-symmetric monoidal product in $\mathscr{C}$ with a right closed and left closed structure, corresponding to the multiplicative fragment. We define $R \in \mathcal{S}et^{[\mathbf{R}]}$ to be the indicator function for singleton lists. As a presheaf category, $\mathscr{C}$ has products and coproducts. The initial algebra of $1 \oplus (R \otimes -)$ interpreting lists of resources is the terminal object $\top$. Concretely, we have the following constructions in $\mathscr{C}$:

- The monoidal product $(A \otimes B)(l) \stackrel{\text{def}}{=} \sum_{(l_1, l_2) \in [R]^2 \wedge (l_1 +\!\!+ l_2 = l)} A(l_1) \times B(l_2)$.
- The unit $1([]) \stackrel{\text{def}}{=} \{()\}, 1(l) \stackrel{\text{def}}{=} \emptyset$ is the indicator function for the empty list.
- The right arrow $(A \multimap B)(l_1) \stackrel{\text{def}}{=} \prod_{l_2 \in [R]} A(l_2) \to B(l_1 +\!\!+ l_2)$.
- The left arrow $(B \circ\!\!- A)(l_2) \stackrel{\text{def}}{=} \prod_{l_1 \in [R]} A(l_1) \to B(l_1 +\!\!+ l_2)$.
- The type of resources $R([n]) \stackrel{\text{def}}{=} \{n\}, R(l) \stackrel{\text{def}}{=} \emptyset$.
- The type of lists of resources $[R](l) \stackrel{\text{def}}{=} \{l\}$.
- The product $(A \& B)(l) \stackrel{\text{def}}{=} A(l) \times B(l)$.
- The coproduct $(A \oplus B)(l) \stackrel{\text{def}}{=} A(l) + B(l)$.

We exploit the fact that the canonical adjunction

$$F \stackrel{\text{def}}{=} (- \otimes [R]) \dashv G \stackrel{\text{def}}{=} [R] \multimap -$$

for the allocation monad is made of endofunctors such that

$$A \otimes FB \simeq F(A \otimes B) \tag{16}$$

to interpret positive and negative terms in the same category: this allows us to adapt the model theory of [11] while avoiding the formalism of enriched categories.

We now have all the ingredients to interpret the calculus $\mathcal{O}$. We interpret expressions typed with $\Gamma; [r_1 \cdots r_n]; \Delta \vdash_o A$ as (oblique) morphisms in $\mathscr{C}(F(\Gamma \otimes R^n \otimes \Delta), A)$, following [11] which we adapt to the ordered case.

Interpreting the left function and the right let binding uses the isomorphism (16) as a left strength. We cannot interpret a right function or left let-binding for $\mathcal{O}$, as it would require an isomorphism $FA \otimes B \simeq F(A \otimes B)$ which swaps the ambient list of resources with B. This corresponds to the re-ordering of resources by the incorrect term t_r (14).

Lemma 12 (Substitution lemma). *For all $\Theta'' \vdash_o v : A$ and $\Theta, x : A @ \Theta' \vdash_o t : B$, one has $[\![t[v/x]]\!] = (id_{\Theta^+} \otimes [\![v]\!] \otimes id_{\Theta'^+}); [\![t]\!]$*

Theorem 13 (Soundness of the interpretation). *For all L, c, c' such that $L \vdash_o c$ and $L \vdash_o c'$, if $c \rightsquigarrow c'$ then $[\![c]\!] = [\![c']\!]$.*

5.1   Exceptions and destructors

Exceptions need to be chosen among central objects in order to define a strength for the exception monad. We ask for objects that commute with all other objects A in a coherent way. Those are the objects in the *Drinfeld centre* of $\mathscr{C}$ (as defined e.g. in [41, §3]).

Proposition 14. *Given an object E, the three following properties are equivalent:*

- *E is in the Drinfeld centre of $\mathscr{C}$.*
- *E is resource-free: for all non-empty list l, $E(l) = \emptyset$.*
- *E has a trivial destructor: there is a morphism $\mathscr{C}(E, I)$.*

By induction, central types in $\mathcal{O}$ are resource-free, therefore they belong to the Drinfeld centre of $\mathscr{C}$.

Proposition 15. *Every object in $\mathscr{C}$ has a (unique) destructor, but $\mathscr{C}$ is not a model of affine logic in the sense of having an isomorphism $I \simeq \top$ (cf. [9, §3.2]).*

Proof. Recall that $[R] = \top$ is the terminal object. Destructors for A are objects in $(A, \delta) \in \mathscr{C}/TI$; i.e. $\delta \in \mathscr{C}(A, TI) \simeq \mathscr{C}(A, [R] \multimap [R]) \simeq \mathscr{C}(A \otimes \top, \top)$ and no other condition. By the universal property of $\top$ there exists a unique such morphism. On the other hand, only central objects have a trivial destructor $\mathscr{C}(A, I)$, which is not the case for $[R] = \top$.

Given that any Γ has a unique destructor, one has $\mathscr{C}/TI \cong \mathscr{C}$. In particular, the monad $T\mathcal{E}$ is left strong.

Proposition 16. *Let E a central object. The monad $T\mathcal{E}$ where $\mathcal{E} = (- \oplus E)$ has a left strength $\Gamma \otimes T\mathcal{E}A \to T\mathcal{E}(\Gamma \otimes A)$.*

Thus, this gives a model of an affine logic in the sense of the calculus with destructors $\mathcal{O}_\mathcal{E}$, but we do not have a model of affine logic in the usual sense of semi-cartesian monoidal categories. Even if we consider that the monoidal unit I is indeed terminal in the Kleisli category of T, the destructors are not thunkable for T, a common requirement for morphisms interpreting structural rules in premonoidal categories (see e.g. Führmann [17]). This is another way of observing the fact that weakening performs a side effect.

We might wonder how we could extend this model to ones of $\mathcal{L}$ and $\mathcal{O}_{\mathcal{E},\text{move}}$. This amounts to somehow regaining the symmetry of the monoidal product to interpret the exchange rule. One way to do that would be to quotient our base category $[\mathbf{R}]$ to obtain multisets. However, T would become commutative and so $\mathscr{C}/TI$ would be symmetric; intuitively the model does not observe the order of destruction. Instead, adding permutations as isomorphisms in $[\mathbf{R}]$ would result in a presheaf model on a setoid in which T is not commutative; intuitively the model tracks in the interpretation of terms their action on the free-list of resources. As we cannot re-use our trick with endofunctors to avoid the presheaf-enriched formalism, we leave this as future work.

6   Discussion and perspectives

After this formal development, we find it useful to place our results in the context of the theory and practice of programming languages.

6.1   Integrating linear types and error handling

We modelled a global allocator with a linear state monad to study notions of resource-safety for linear calculi: for instance, every allocated resource in $\mathcal{L}$ and $\mathcal{O}_{\mathcal{E},\text{move}}$ is freed exactly once, even in case of errors during the execution of the program. This result strengthens when the exchange rule (6) is not used: in $\mathcal{O}$ and $\mathcal{O}_{\mathcal{E}}$, the resources are released in a LIFO order. A relationship between ordered logic and stack-like allocation was proposed previously [47, 48, 58, 45]. In this context, our results suggest to consider a variant of ordered logic that only has one arrow type and whose composition (let) is restricted to the opposite side of abstraction (λ)—where in particular λ cannot express let. The modelling of the exchange rule with a side-effecting "move" operation is also novel.

Conceptually close to stack allocation, LISP's higher-order combinator `unwind-protect` that executes a clean-up function upon normal or exceptional return of its argument (like its variants found in modern academic programming languages such as OCaml and Haskell) has the same constraint of deallocation in LIFO order.

"Linear types," on the other hand, promised to let us manipulate resources as first-class values (see [2, 1] among others). However, extensive practical experiments with linear types stumbled (among other) on the problematic interaction of linearity with error handling, another important aspect with resources that are acquired in a program. For instance, Cyclone, a source of inspiration for the Rust language, permitted resource leaks in the name of *"flexibility and usability"* [53, §3.5] (necessitating back-up collection mechanisms). The practical experiment of Tov and Pucella [57, 55], another milestone in exploring practical aspects of linear type systems, also mentioned the issue of combining linearity and control effects, which became the motivation for their *"practical"* linear type system to be affine.

Tov and Pucella [56], separately, seeking to lift the limitation of the affine system for manipulating resources as first-class values, proposed a type system that offers both linearity and control effects (e.g. checked exceptions), by typing effects in addition to linearity. Essentially, effects are constrained when linear variables are in scope (or conversely), matching the restrictive approach we described in section 1.2 corresponding to the notion of strength with respect to an affine or an unrestricted resource modality (8). It should be noted that this system [56], unlike the previous experiment [57], is mainly justified by its mathematical properties; how useful such a system is, in practice, remains unclear.[5]

---

[5] As Tov themselves explains: *"One question that remains, however, concerns the pragmatics of checked exceptions in a higher-order language such as Alms, where*

Lastly, *affine session types* [40] do mix linearity and cancellation in a sense similar to ours. They guarantee a safety property (absence of deadlock) after an exception (cancellation) arises, by communicating cancellation across channels.

Our analysis from the introduction applies equally to explicit error handling with an error monad, as illustrated with the language $\mathcal{L}$. Indeed, manual error handling encounters similar obstacles arising from the lack of unrestricted monadic strength for the error monad. Concretely, for each location where one would like to use a monadic binding (4), one needs to implement by hand a repetitive description of whichever clean-up functions should be called in case of error propagation—a well-known and tedious problem in C, which gave rise to specific programming patterns involving `goto`.

By 2012, these limitations of linear types with respect to the handling of errors and exceptions, arising from practical considerations, might seem well-established in the literature. However, more recent works on linear type systems purporting to implement practical first-class resources in academic programming languages [6, 44] do not explore nor mention these obstacles. In the case of [6], a section describing limitations arising from Haskell exceptions indeed appears in an earlier version with a different title [7], but is absent from the published peer-reviewed version.

With the resource CBPV, we set out to model some aspects of C++ resources with destructors and move operations. Compared to the works cited previously, C++ realised, much earlier [52], a shift in viewpoint whereby clean-up functions are deduced from the types, whilst it also later pioneered "move semantics" [24] for treating resources as first-class values. As we have seen, interpreting resource types in the slice category over some TI, i.e. as types provided with some chosen effectful weakening map $A \to TI$, suffices to provide a notion of strength for the exception (or error) monad. Concretely this means that we can both program with an error monad, and give a meaning to exceptions as a side-effect. One surprising aspect of the resource CBPV is that it combines facets of all three of affine, linear and ordered logics:

affine	in terms of types and available control effects
linear	in terms of first-class values and resource-safety properties
ordered	in terms of proof-relevant semantics and type isomorphisms

Given that the logical expressiveness is that of affine logic (including the exchange rule), without sacrificing the linear character of values (which are correctly released), we do not have to choose between linearity and control effects. This perspective suggests that it should be possible to adapt practical works on affine typing (in the lineage of [57]) in order to integrate first-class resources in functional programming languages [43].

---

latent exception effects are likely to appear on many function arrows. Weighing the cost against the benefit, I have decided that adding linear types to Alms is not worth the complexity of a programmer-visible effect system." [55, p. 238]

6.2 A model of C++/Rust-style resource management and its interpretation

The resource CBPV is a very idealised model of C++/Rust-style resource management situated at the intersection of linear logic and the theory of effects. Various models of ownership in Rust—more practical and less idealised—have been developed to prove safety and functional properties of Rust programs, such as with separation logic [27], a dedicated functional logic [13], or by translation into a purely functional language [25]. These recent works, explicitly, do not model exceptions with destructor calls, and they do not develop a specific understanding of destructors in relationship with linearity.

To our knowledge, our model is the first to reproduce various phenomena seen with C++/Rust's resource management such as: the propagation of errors involving the release of resources in scope as part of monadic binding; destructors having to never fail; resources being first-class values that can be passed, returned, or stored in algebraic data types and closures, and for which "moving" resources (identified with an exchange rule in logic, albeit performing a side-effect) is responsible for altering the order of destruction; and indeed closures themselves being resources. In fact, in the presence of both resource modalities ! and $\mathcal{D}$, different positive types of closures, derived from $\multimap$, coexist ($!(A \multimap B)$ and $\mathcal{D}(A \multimap B)$), distinguished by the restrictions on the typing context in accordance with the resource modality (e.g. copyable or resource-like)—a distinction between several types of closures that can also be seen in C++ and Rust.

One very interesting aspect of the resource CBPV is that exchange and weakening are interpreted by morphisms that perform effects. For instance, $A \otimes B$ and $B \otimes A$ are not contextually isomorphic in the language with destructors because they can be distinguished observationally from the order in which the destructors of A and B are executed. So we can have a logical equivalence in the form of inverse morphisms:

$$A \otimes B \rightleftarrows B \otimes A \tag{17}$$

without the two types being isomorphic. This is because a *contextual* notion of isomorphism (allowing to substitute equals by equals) also requires the two inverse maps (17) to be pure [32]. This radically departs from symmetric premonoidal categories [49].

We usually see the Curry-Howard correspondence at work when algebraic and logical structures inspire new programming language features. Could the concept of destructors have appeared out of theoretical consideration or practical experiments starting from linear logic? As it turns out, the interpretation of resource types with destructors as ordered logic formulae almost arose on several occasions, such as when Baker suggested that C++ constructors and destructors could fit within his linear language, in rarely-cited essays that anticipated C++ move semantics [2, 1], and when Gan, Tov and Morrisett approached substructural types using type classes `dup` and `drop` [18]. But we find it remarkable that the Curry-Howard correspondence actually worked this time in the converse direction, with C++ destructors and move semantics arising from practical consideration over more than 20 years [28, 52, 24], and with the use of the slice category in this context being prompted by empirically-observed phenomena with C++ resources [10].

6.3   Conclusion and future work

Our hope is that this newfound understanding of resources in programming will be inspire improvements to programming languages and designs for better ones. It could also help proving more properties of programs with formal methods, such as methods based on translations into pure functional programs. Indeed, the functional correctness of some Rust programs can depend on the resource-safety properties enforced by the language, for instance when they use the typestate programming pattern or when they are made fault-tolerant.

The Curry-Howard correspondence is sometimes stated as a more technical result relating logic, categorical structures and programming language models, as in the Curry-Howard-Lambek correspondence for linear CBPV [11] which the present work is based on. Though not essential to the results of this paper, it is now clear that extending the Curry-Howard-Lambek correspondence to ordered CBPV would be useful as a meta-theory to study resources. Removing the symmetry in monoidal categories and the exchange rule in logic can create technical issues—we have made some progress already by understanding that λ and let bindings work on opposite sides, and that being merely left-closed or right-closed but not both is already interesting and useful.

Lastly, much remains to be understood in an idealised and principled manner within this framework, the most obvious ones being:

- **Copyable types** Linear languages, including with C++ and Rust, mix in practice resource types and unconstrained types. The interaction of the resource modality arising from the slice construction with the resource modality ! which controls freely copyable and erasable types, should therefore be explored. Interesting questions also arise from the necessity of kind polymorphism in such languages.
- **Borrowing** We have modelled resources that can only be allocated and deallocated, which lets us observe the effect of deallocations on the final state of the program. More questions arise when resources can be used between their allocation and their deallocation. Operations that do not consume the resource can be implemented by returning it [2, 1]. Borrowing [20, 16], inspired by regions [54], and refined into unique borrowing in Rust, was introduced as a more usable and expressive alternative to this linear threading of values. As we already mentioned, various works account for borrowing using different approaches [27, 13, 25], but it remains to be seen whether and how borrowing may be derived in a principled way from a concept of linearity (ownership) arising from destructors.

References

1. Baker, H.G.: "Use-Once" Variables and Linear Objects - Storage Management, Reflection and Multi-Threading. SIGPLAN Notices **30**(1), 45–52 (1995). https://doi.org/10.1145/199818.199860
2. Baker, H.G.: Linear logic and permutation stacks - the Forth shall be first. SIGARCH Computer Architecture News **22**(1), 34–43 (1994). https://doi.org/10.1145/181993.181999
3. Baker, H.G.: Lively linear lisp: "Look ma, no garbage!" ACM Sigplan notices **27**(8), 89–98 (1992)
4. Benton, N., Kennedy, A.: Exceptional syntax. Journal of Functional Programming **11**, 395–410 (2001). https://doi.org/10.1017/S0956796801004099
5. Berdine, J., O'Hearn, P.W., Reddy, U.S., Thielecke, H.: Linearly used continuations. In: Proceedings of the Third ACM SIGPLAN Workshop on Continuations (CW'01), pp. 47–54 (2000)
6. Bernardy, J., Boespflug, M., Newton, R.R., Peyton Jones, S., Spiwack, A.: Linear Haskell: practical linearity in a higher-order polymorphic language. PACMPL **2**(POPL), 5:1–5:29 (2018). https://doi.org/10.1145/3158093
7. Bernardy, J., Boespflug, M., Newton, R.R., Peyton Jones, S., Spiwack, A.: Retrofitting Linear Types (In submission), (2017). https://www.microsoft.com/en-us/research/wp-content/uploads/2017/03/haskell-linear-submitted.pdf.
8. Blute, R., Cockett, J., Seely, R.: ! and ?-Storage as tensorial strength. Mathematical Structures in Computer Science **6**(4), 313–351 (1996)
9. Braüner, T.: A model of intuitionistic affine logic from stable domain theory. In: International Colloquium on Automata, Languages, and Programming, pp. 340–351 (1994)
10. Combette, G., Munch-Maccagnoni, G.: A resource modality for RAII (abstract). In: LOLA 2018: Workshop on Syntax and Semantics of Low-Level Languages (2018). https://hal.inria.fr/hal-01806634
11. Curien, P.-L., Fiore, M., Munch-Maccagnoni, G.: A Theory of Effects and Resources: Adjunction Models and Polarised Calculi. In: Proc. POPL (2016). https://doi.org/10.1145/2837614.2837652
12. Day, B.: On closed categories of functors. In: MacLane, S., Applegate, H., Barr, M., Day, B., Dubuc, E., Phreilambud, Pultr, A., Street, R., Tierney, M., Swierczkowski, S. (eds.) Reports of the Midwest Category Seminar IV, pp. 1–38. Springer Berlin Heidelberg, Berlin, Heidelberg (1970)
13. Denis, X., Jourdan, J.-H., Marché, C.: Creusot: a Foundry for the Deductive Verification of Rust Programs. In: ICFEM 2022 - 23th International Conference on Formal Engineering Methods. LNCS, Springer, Heidelberg (2022). https://inria.hal.science/hal-03737878
14. Filinski, A.: Linear Continuations. In: Proc. POPL, pp. 27–38 (1992)
15. Filinski, A.: Representing Monads. In: Proc. POPL, pp. 446–457. ACM Press (1994)
16. Fluet, M., Morrisett, G., Ahmed, A.J.: Linear Regions Are All You Need. In: Sestoft, P. (ed.) Programming Languages and Systems, 15th European Symposium on Programming, ESOP 2006, Held as Part of the Joint European Conferences on Theory and Practice of Software, ETAPS 2006, Vienna, Austria, March 27-28, 2006, Proceedings. LNCS, vol. 3924, pp. 7–21. Springer, Heidelberg (2006). https://doi.org/10.1007/11693024_2
17. Führmann, C.: Direct Models for the Computational Lambda Calculus. Electr. Notes Theor. Comput. Sci. **20**, 245–292 (1999)

18. Gan, E., Tov, J.A., Morrisett, G.: Type Classes for Lightweight Substructural Types. In: Alves, S., Cervesato, I. (eds.) Proceedings Third International Workshop on Linearity, LINEARITY 2014, Vienna, Austria, 13th July, 2014. EPTCS, pp. 34–48 (2014). https://doi.org/10.4204/EPTCS.176.4
19. Girard, J.-Y.: Linear Logic. Theoretical Computer Science **50**, 1–102 (1987)
20. Grossman, D., Morrisett, J.G., Jim, T., Hicks, M.W., Wang, Y., Cheney, J.: Region-Based Memory Management in Cyclone. In: Knoop, J., Hendren, L.J. (eds.) Proceedings of the 2002 ACM SIGPLAN Conference on Programming Language Design and Implementation (PLDI), Berlin, Germany, June 17-19, 2002, pp. 282–293. ACM (2002). https://doi.org/10.1145/512529.512563
21. Hasegawa, M.: Linear Exponential Comonads without Symmetry. In: Fourth International Workshop on Linearity (2016). http://arxiv.org/abs/1701.04919
22. Hasegawa, M.: Linearly Used Effects: Monadic and CPS Transformations into the Linear Lambda Calculus. In: Hu, Z., Rodríguez-Artalejo, M. (eds.) Functional and Logic Programming, 6th International Symposium, FLOPS 2002, Aizu, Japan, September 15-17, 2002, Proceedings. LNCS, vol. 2441, pp. 167–182. Springer, Heidelberg (2002). https://doi.org/10.1007/3-540-45788-7_10
23. Hasegawa, M.: Semantics of linear continuation-passing in call-by-name. In: International Symposium on Functional and Logic Programming, pp. 229–243 (2004)
24. Hinnant, H.E., Dimov, P., Abrahams, D.: A Proposal to Add Move Semantics Support to the C++ Language, (2002). http://www.open-std.org/jtc1/sc22/wg21/docs/papers/2002/n1377.htm
25. Ho, S., Protzenko, J.: Aeneas: Rust Verification by Functional Translation. Proc. ACM Program. Lang. **6**(ICFP) (2022). https://doi.org/10.1145/3547647
26. Hofmann, M.: A Type System for Bounded Space and Functional In-Place Update. Nord. J. Comput. **7**(4), 258–289 (2000)
27. Jung, R., Jourdan, J., Krebbers, R., Dreyer, D.: RustBelt: securing the foundations of the rust programming language. PACMPL **2**(POPL), 66:1–66:34 (2018). https://doi.org/10.1145/3158154
28. Koenig, A., Stroustrup, B.: Exception Handling for C++. In: Proceedings of the C++ Conference. San Francisco, CA, USA, April 1990, pp. 149–176 (1990)
29. Lafont, Y.: The linear abstract machine. Theoretical computer science **59**(1-2), 157–180 (1988)
30. Levy, P.B.: Call-By-Push-Value: A Functional/Imperative Synthesis (Semantics Structures in Computation, V. 2). Kluwer Academic Publishers, USA (2004)
31. Levy, P.B.: Call-by-Push-Value: A Subsuming Paradigm. In: Proc. TLCA '99, pp. 228–242 (1999)
32. Levy, P.B.: Contextual isomorphisms. In: Proceedings of the 44th ACM SIGPLAN Symposium on Principles of Programming Languages, pp. 400–414 (2017)
33. Maraist, J., Odersky, M., Turner, D.N., Wadler, P.: Call-by-Name, Call-by-Value, Call-by-Need, and the Linear Lambda Calculus. In: Proc. MFPS '95 (1994)
34. Melliès, P.-A.: "Categorical models of linear logic revisited". working paper or preprint.
35. Melliès, P.-A.: "Categorical semantics of linear logic". In: vol. 27. Panoramas et Synthèses. Société Mathématique de France, 2009. Chap. 1, pp. 15–215.
36. Melliès, P.-A.: "Parametric monads and enriched adjunctions". Draft.
37. Møgelberg, R.E., Staton, S.: Linear usage of state. Log. Methods Comput. Sci. **10**(1) (2014). https://doi.org/10.2168/LMCS-10(1:17)2014

38. Moggi, E.: Computational lambda-calculus and monads. In: Proceedings of the Fourth Annual IEEE Symposium on Logic in Computer Science (LICS 1989), pp. 14–23. IEEE Computer Society Press, Pacific Grove, CA, USA (1989)

39. Moggi, E.: Notions of computation and monads. Information and Computation **93**(1), 55–92 (1991). https://doi.org/10.1016/0890-5401(91)90052-4

40. Mostrous, D., Vasconcelos, V.T.: Affine Sessions. Logical Methods in Computer Science, Volume 14, Issue 4 (November 15, 2018) lmcs:4973 (2018). https://doi.org/10.23638/LMCS-14(4:14)2018. arXiv: 1809.02781v2 [cs.LO]

41. Müger, M.: From subfactors to categories and topology II: The quantum double of tensor categories and subfactors. Journal of Pure and Applied Algebra **180**(1), 159–219 (2003). https://doi.org/10.1016/S0022-4049(02)00248-7

42. Munch-Maccagnoni, G.: Note on models of polarised intuitionistic logic. Tech. rep., INRIA (2017). https://hal.inria.fr/hal-01540760

43. Munch-Maccagnoni, G.: Resource Polymorphism, (2018). https://doi.org/10.48550/arXiv.1803.02796.

44. Orchard, D., Liepelt, V.-B., Eades III, H.: Quantitative program reasoning with graded modal types. Proc. ACM Program. Lang. **3**(ICFP) (2019). https://doi.org/10.1145/3341714

45. Pfenning, F., Simmons, R.J.: Substructural Operational Semantics as Ordered Logic Programming. In: Proceedings of the 24th Annual IEEE Symposium on Logic in Computer Science, LICS 2009, 11-14 August 2009, Los Angeles, CA, USA, pp. 101–110. IEEE Computer Society (2009). https://doi.org/10.1109/LICS.2009.8

46. Plotkin, G., Power, J.: "Notions of Computation Determine Monads". In: Foundations of Software Science and Computation Structures. Springer Berlin Heidelberg, 2002, pp. 342–356. ISBN: 9783540459316. https://doi.org/10.1007/3-540-45931-6_24.

47. Polakow, J.: Ordered Linear Logic and Applications. PhD thesis, Carnegie Mellon University (2001).

48. Polakow, J., Yi, K.: Proving Syntactic Properties of Exceptions in an Ordered Logical Framework. In: Kuchen, H., Ueda, K. (eds.) Functional and Logic Programming, 5th International Symposium, FLOPS 2001, Tokyo, Japan, March 7-9, 2001, Proceedings. LNCS, vol. 2024, pp. 61–77. Springer, Heidelberg (2001). https://doi.org/10.1007/3-540-44716-4_4

49. Power, A.J., Robinson, E.: Premonoidal categories and notions of computation. Mathematical Structures in Computer Science **5**(7), 453–468 (1997)

50. Power, J.: Premonoidal categories as categories with algebraic structure. Theoretical Computer Science **278**(1), 303–321 (2002). https://doi.org/10.1016/S0304-3975(00)00340-6

51. Selinger, P., Valiron, B.: A linear-non-linear model for a computational call-by-value lambda calculus. Lecture Notes in Computer Science **4962**, 81–96 (2008)

52. Stroustrup, B.: A History of C++: 1979–1991. In: The Second ACM SIGPLAN Conference on History of Programming Languages. HOPL-II, pp. 271–297. Association for Computing Machinery, Cambridge, Massachusetts, USA (1993). https://doi.org/10.1145/154766.155375

53. Swamy, N., Hicks, M., Morrisett, G., Grossman, D., Jim, T.: Safe manual memory management in Cyclone. Science of Computer Programming **62**(2), 122–144 (2006)

54. Tofte, M., Talpin, J.-P.: Region-based memory management. Information and computation **132**(2), 109–176 (1997)

55. Tov, J.A.: Practical Programming with Substructural Types. PhD thesis, Northeastern University (2012).

56. Tov, J.A., Pucella, R.: A Theory of Substructural Types and Control. In: Proceedings of the 2011 ACM International Conference on Object Oriented Programming Systems Languages and Applications. OOPSLA '11, pp. 625–642. ACM, Portland, Oregon, USA (2011). https://doi.org/10.1145/2048066.2048115
57. Tov, J.A., Pucella, R.: Practical affine types. In: Ball, T., Sagiv, M. (eds.) Proceedings of the 38th ACM SIGPLAN-SIGACT Symposium on Principles of Programming Languages, POPL 2011, Austin, TX, USA, January 26-28, 2011, pp. 447–458. ACM (2011). https://doi.org/10.1145/1926385.1926436
58. Walker, D.: Substructural type systems. In: Advanced Topics in Types and Programming Languages. Ed. by B.C. Pierce, pp. 3–44. The MIT Press (2005)

Rely-Guarantee Is Coinductive
– A Proof-Centered Investigation of Inductively Approximated Coinduction –

John Derrick, Chelsea Edmonds, Andrei Popescu, Jamie Wright

School of Computer Science, University of Sheffield

Abstract. We make the case that the foundation for Rely-Guarantee reasoning can be fruitfully delivered by a coinductive semantics. Using insight from an Isabelle formalization, via a proof analysis we show that the coinductive semantics tends to simplify the proof development; in particular it enables more direct proofs for the soundness of the Rely-Guarantee rules. The comparison between inductive and coinductive proofs also suggests inductive counterparts of coinductive "up-to" enhancements. On the way, we fill a gap in the literature, by showing that three previously defined inductive semantics for Rely-Guarantee are equivalent. Underlying our transformation of an inductive into a coinductive semantics is the notion of inductively approximating a coinductive predicate—which, deployed in the opposite direction (from coinduction to induction), is a standard technical tool for approximating process algebra bisimilarities. On the spectrum between the abstract fixpoint theorems and concrete instances, we formalize effective format-based criteria that enable sound approximation.

1 Introduction

The coinduction definition and proof method, which is the categorical dual of induction, has recently emerged as a powerful methodology for specifying and reasoning about systems. Roughly speaking, while induction is most suitable for describing finitary syntax and behavior, coinduction excels in the compact description of infinite system behavior [55,36,25,31,53,42,68].

The Rely-Guarantee method (§2) for the compositional verification of concurrent programs, introduced by Jones at the beginning of the 1980s [28,29], has had a major intellectual and practical influence on formal verification [23]. Several verification tools have incorporated ideas from Rely-Guarantee [46,17], whose application success has been further boosted by their combination with ideas from Separation Logic [47,54,26] which started with the work of Vafeiadis and Parkinson [64,62] on the "marriage" between the two logics.

Here we advocate another useful marriage, namely basing Rely-Guarantee on a coinductive foundation, instead of (or in addition to) its traditional inductive foundation (§3). While the first rigorous semantics for Rely-Guarantee, introduced by Xu et al. [69], employs a heavy inductive definition on interactive computation traces, in subsequent developments this account was simplified to use rely-directed reachability relations [12], and then further simplified to use counting-based

© The Author(s) 2026
R. Krebbers (Ed.): ESOP 2026, LNCS 16501, pp. 220–251, 2026.
https://doi.org/10.1007/978-3-032-22720-1_9

inductive safety predicates [64,62,63]—allowing for increasingly simpler and more transparent proofs of soundness for the Rely-Guarantee rules (§3.1).

Placing ourselves at the end of this simplification spectrum, we further push its boundaries: We show that an induction-to-coinduction shift in foundation can be performed by amending the counting-based semantics (§3.2). We argue that the coinductive semantics is the lightest and in some sense the most natural, and caters for the most direct (though admittedly less elementary) proofs of rule soundness. Furthermore, we formally prove all four semantics to be equivalent.

Then we engage in a proof-centered exploration of what makes the above shift possible: the sound inductive approximation of coinductive predicates, emerging from the properties of fixpoints in lattices via the Knaster-Tarski and Kleene theorems (§4). From our concrete analysis of inductive versus coinductive proofs of soundness for the Rely-Guarantee rules, we extract patterns of proof connections between inductive and coinductive predicates (§5). These allow us to explain the inductive-to-coinductive simplification in general terms, revealing the coinductive proof as the *core* of the inductive one (§5.1). Going deeper on the connection between coinduction and its approximating induction, we identify the inductive counterparts of coinductive "up-to" enhancements (§5.2).

Further exploring the scope of the inductive approximations of coinduction (§6), we formalize format-based criteria (§6.1, §6.3). These are easier to instantiate and to implement in program verifiers, and also cover the cases of (bi)similarity relations from process algebra (§6.2), and of Rely-Guarantee mixed with Separation Logic (§6.4). Capturing bisimilarities and Rely-Guarantee under a common format is particularly desirable, given that what we propose for Rely-Guarantee (switching from a well-established inductive to a coinductive notion) has been widely applied *in reverse* with bisimilarities, namely using induction to approximate a well-established coinductive notion.

Our findings have been driven by our experience of mechanizing in Isabelle the semantics of Rely-Guarantee while trying to simplify the "formalities" [14]. We take inspiration from, and create bridges between previous developments on Rely-Guarantee semantics, rule systems, and coinduction enhancements (§7).

More details and proofs of the results in this paper are provided in a technical report [15]. The report is identical to the paper, except for an appendix containing additional details and proofs.

Here is a summary of our novel contributions. On Rely-Guarantee, we give (1) the first coinductive semantics, and also (2) the first rigorous (and formal) proof of the equivalence of previously introduced inductive semantics. On inductive approximations for coinduction, we provide (3) a detailed comparison of inductive and coinductive proofs that starts with the Rely-Guarantee case study and extrapolates to general proof connections for least and greatest fixpoints of operators, (4) a novel inductive counterpart of coinductive up-to enhancements, shedding some "elementary" light on these enhancements, and (5) a formalization of general effective criteria that ensure ω-continuity (hence the soundness of the inductive approximations).

$$\frac{s' = \text{evalA } a\ s}{(a, s) \Rightarrow (\text{done}, s')}(\text{Atom}) \qquad\qquad \frac{(c_1, s) \Rightarrow (c_1', s')}{(\text{seq } c_1\ c_2, s) \Rightarrow (\text{seq } c_1'\ c_2, s')}(\text{Seq})$$

$$(\text{seq done } c, s) \Rightarrow (c, s)\quad(\text{Seq-Done})$$

$$\frac{\text{evalT } t\ s}{(\text{if } t\ c_1\ c_2, s) \Rightarrow (c_1, s)}(\text{If-True}) \qquad\qquad \frac{\neg\ \text{evalT } t\ s}{(\text{if } t\ c_1\ c_2, s) \Rightarrow (c_2, s)}(\text{If-False})$$

$$(\text{while } t\ c, s) \Rightarrow (\text{if } t\ (\text{seq } c\ (\text{while } t\ c))\ \text{done},\ s)\quad(\text{While})$$

$$\frac{(c_1, s) \Rightarrow (c_1', s')}{(\text{par } c_1\ c_2, s) \Rightarrow (\text{par } c_1'\ c_2, s')}(\text{Par-L}) \qquad\qquad \frac{(c_2, s) \Rightarrow (c_2', s')}{(\text{par } c_1\ c_2, s) \Rightarrow (\text{par } c_1\ c_2', s')}(\text{Par-R})$$

$$(\text{par done done}, s) \Rightarrow (\text{done}, s)\quad(\text{Par-Done})$$

Fig. 1: Small-step operational semantics

Notations and conventions. Bool denotes the two-element set of booleans, $\{\text{true}, \text{false}\}$. A predicate on a set A is a function of type $A \to$ Bool, and a relation between sets A and B is a function of type $A \to B \to$ Bool. For a predicate $P : A \to$ Bool and $a \in A$, we write $P\ a$ instead of $P\ a = \text{true}$, and read it as "P holds for a"; and similarly for relations. We use "RG" as an abbreviation for "Rely-Guarantee". We will sometimes use gray boxes to draw attention to certain parts of the formulas, often emphasizing changes or additions compared to previous formulas; these boxes do not have any mathematical meaning.

2   The Rely-Guarantee Reasoning Rules

We consider a simple imperative language with parallel composition whose syntax is given by the following grammar (where we have underlined the syntactic categories, Com, Atom and Test, in order to more clearly distinguish them from keywords/terminals such as done and while):

$$\underline{\text{Com}}\ ::=\ \text{done}\ |\ \underline{\text{Atom}}\ |\ \text{seq } \underline{\text{Com}}\ \underline{\text{Com}}\ |\ \text{if } \underline{\text{Test}}\ \underline{\text{Com}}\ \underline{\text{Com}}\ |$$
$$\text{while } \underline{\text{Test}}\ \underline{\text{Com}}\ |\ \text{par } \underline{\text{Com}}\ \underline{\text{Com}}$$

Thus, a command is either done (completed), an atom (atomic command), a sequential composition, an if-branching over a test, a while loop again regulated by a test, or the parallel composition of two commands. We leave the tests and atoms abstract. The small-step semantics, shown in Fig. 1, is quite standard. It indicates how command-state pairs, which we call *configurations*, evolve during a single execution step. Thus, the semantics is a (binary) relation $\Rightarrow$

between configurations. While the syntax is parameterized by the sets Test and Atom of tests and atoms respectively, the semantics is further parameterized by a set State of states, and by functions evalT : Test → State → Bool and evalA : Atom → State → State that evaluate tests and commands in any given state. Thus, given a state s and a test t, evalT t s returns the boolean value obtained by evaluating t in s. Similarly, given an atom a and two states s, s', evalA a s s' says that evaluating a starting in s can produce s'. The while loops proceed by unfolding into a conditional that nests a sequential composition, and parallel composition proceeds via shared-state concurrency.

A *Rely-Guarantee (RG) clause* is a tuple (P, R, G, Q) where P : State → Bool is the *pre-condition*, R : State → State → Bool the *rely-condition*, G : State → State → Bool the *guarantee-condition*, and Q : State → Bool the *post-condition*. We think of a rely-guarantee clause (P, R, G, Q) as making the following statement about a command c: If the execution of c starts in a state satisfying the pre-condition P, and if during the execution the environment is guaranteed to only change the state according to the rely-condition R, then the following hold: (1) each execution step of c will only change the state according to the guarantee-condition G, and (2) if the execution terminates, then the final state will satisfy the post-condition Q. This intuition will be made formal by the rely-guarantee semantics which we will discuss in §3.

Fig. 2 shows a standard RG proof system for reasoning compositionally about programs. It defines the relation ⊢ between commands and RG clauses inductively, i.e., as the smallest relation closed under the given rules. Besides the monotonicity rule (Mono), we have one rule for each language construct.

3   Four Ways of Making Sense of Rely-Guarantee

In this section we revisit three increasingly light inductive semantics for RG (§3.1), establish their equivalence, and propose our coinductive semantics further up on the lightness spectrum (§3.2).

A configuration (c, s) is *final*, written final (c, s), when there is no (c', s') such that $(c, s) \Rightarrow (c', s')$ (equivalently, when $c =$ done).

3.1   Three inductive ways

We next describe the three main semantics previously proposed for RG.

(i) The trace-based semantics of Xu, de Roever and He [69] was the first rigorous semantics proposed for RG. It uses *labeled configurations*, which are triples (l, c, s) such that (c, s) is a configuration and l is an element of the two-element set $\{C, E\}$, where C indicates a command step and E an environment step. An *(interactive computation) trace* is a nonempty list of labeled configurations $[(l^1, c^1, s^1), \ldots, (l^n, c^n, s^n)]$ such that, for all $i \in \{1, \ldots, n-1\}$, $l^{i+1} = C$ implies $(c^i, s^i) \Rightarrow (c^{i+1}, s^{i+1})$, and $l^{i+1} = E$ implies $c^{i+1} = c^i$. We write Trace(c) for the set of traces $[(l^1, c^1, s^1), \ldots, (l^n, c^n, s^n)]$ starting in c, i.e., such that $c^1 = c$.

$$\frac{c \vdash (P', R', G', Q') \quad P \leq P' \quad R \leq R' \quad G' \leq G \quad Q' \leq Q}{c \vdash (P, R, G, Q)}\text{(Mono)}$$

$$\frac{\mathsf{stable}\ Q\ R \quad P \leq Q}{\mathsf{done} \vdash (P, R, G, Q)}\text{(DoneRG)}$$

$$\frac{\mathsf{stable}\ P\ R \quad \mathsf{stable}\ Q\ R}{(\lambda s'.\ \exists s.\ P\ s \wedge \mathsf{evalA}\ a\ s\ s') \leq Q \quad (\lambda s, s'.\ P\ s \wedge \mathsf{evalA}\ a\ s\ s') \leq G}{a \vdash (P, R, G, Q)}\text{(AtomRG)}$$

$$\frac{c_1 \vdash (P, R, G, P') \quad c_2 \vdash (P', R, G, Q) \quad \mathsf{refl}\ G}{\mathsf{seq}\ c_1\ c_2 \vdash (P, R, G, Q)}\text{(SeqRG)}$$

$$\frac{c_1 \vdash (P \sqcap (\mathsf{evalT}\ t), R, G, Q) \quad c_2 \vdash (P \sqcap (\neg\ (\mathsf{evalT}\ t)), R, G, Q)}{\mathsf{stable}\ P\ R \quad \mathsf{refl}\ G}{\mathsf{if}\ t\ c_1\ c_2 \vdash (P, R, G, Q)}\text{(IfRG)}$$

$$\frac{c \vdash (P \sqcap (\mathsf{evalT}\ t), R, G, P) \quad P \sqcap (\neg\ (\mathsf{evalT}\ t)) \leq Q}{\mathsf{stable}\ P\ R \quad \mathsf{stable}\ Q\ R \quad \mathsf{refl}\ G}{\mathsf{while}\ t\ c \vdash (P, R, G, Q)}\text{(WhileRG)}$$

$$\frac{c_1 \vdash (P_1, R_1, G_1, Q_1) \quad c_2 \vdash (P_2, R_2, G_2, Q_2)}{P \leq P_1 \sqcap P_2 \quad R \sqcup G_2 \leq R_1 \quad R \sqcup G_1 \leq R_2}{G_1 \sqcup G_2 \leq G \quad Q_1 \sqcap Q_2 \leq Q \quad \mathsf{refl}\ G}{\mathsf{par}\ c_1\ c_2 \vdash (P, R, G, Q)}\text{(ParRG)}$$

Fig. 2: RG proof system. We write $\mathsf{refl}\ G$ to express that the relation G is reflexive. $\leq$ denotes the standard orders on predicates and relations, e.g., $P \leq P'$ means $\forall s.\ P\ s \longrightarrow P'\ s$, and similarly for relations. $\sqcap$ and $\sqcup$ denote the infimum and supremum in the lattices of predicates and relations, which are component-wise conjunction and disjunction. $\neg\ (\mathsf{evalT}\ t)$ denotes the componentwise negation of $\mathsf{evalT}\ t$, mapping each state s to $\neg\ (\mathsf{evalT}\ t\ s)$. Finally, $\mathsf{stable}\ P\ R$ says the predicate P is stable w.r.t. the relation R, i.e., $\forall s, s'.\ P\ s \wedge R\ s\ s' \longrightarrow P\ s'$.

The *Xu–de–Roever–He satisfaction* of an RG clause by a command, $c \models_{\mathsf{XRH}}$ (P, R, G, Q), is defined as follows: For all t $r = [(l^1, c^1, s^1), \dots, (l^n, c^n, s^n)] \in$ $\mathsf{race}(c)$, if $P \, s^1$ (the pre-condition holds at the beginning of tr) and $\forall i \in$ $\{1, \dots, n-1\}$. $l^{i+1} = \mathsf{E} \longrightarrow R \, s^i \, s^{i+1}$ (the rely-condition holds on all environment steps), then $\forall i \in \{1, \dots, n-1\}$. $l^{i+1} = \mathsf{C} \longrightarrow G \, s^i \, s^{i+1}$ (the guarantee-condition holds on all computation steps) and $Q \, s^n$ (the post-condition holds at the end).

(ii) The reachability-based semantics of Coleman and Jones [12]. For a relation R on configurations, we define $\mathsf{stepRel}_R$ by the rules:

$$\frac{(c, s) \Rightarrow (c', s')}{\mathsf{stepRel}_R \, (c, s) \, (c', s')} \qquad\qquad \frac{R \, s \, s'}{\mathsf{stepRel}_R \, (c, s) \, (c, s')}$$

The reflexive-transitive closure of this relation, $\mathsf{stepRel}_R^* \, (c, s) \, (c', s')$ says that the configuration (c', s') is reachable from (c, s) through a combination of computation steps, and environment steps respecting the rely relation R. The *Coleman–Jones satisfaction* of an RG clause, $c \models_{\mathsf{CJ}} (P, R, G, Q)$, is defined as follows: For all s, c', s' such that $P \, s$ and $\mathsf{stepRel}_R^* \, (c, s) \, (c', s')$, we have that **(1)** $G \, s' \, s''$ for all c'', s'' with $(c', s') \Rightarrow (c'', s'')$, and **(2)** $\mathsf{final} \, (c', s')$ implies $Q \, s'$.

(iii) The counting-based (step-indexed) semantics of Vafeiadis and Parkinson [62,64]. This semantics uses a count of the number of interactive computation steps, and states that any number of such steps is "safe". While RG clauses are quadruples (P, R, G, Q), let us call any triple of the form (R, G, Q) a *reduced RG clause* (where the pre-condition was removed, i.e., retaining only the rely-, guarantee- and post-conditions). The notion of *safety* of a configuration (c, s) with respect to a reduced RG clause (R, G, Q) *within n execution steps*, $\mathsf{safe}_{(R,G,Q)} \, n \, (c, s)$, is defined inductively as shown in Fig. 3. Thus, every command in every state is safe after 0 execution steps, since of course nothing happened yet. For the inductive step, the predicate says that the $(n+1)$-safety of (c, s) (i.e., the safety of executing $n+1$ steps of c from state s) can be concluded from three hypotheses: **(1)** any rely-compliant environment step to s' (i.e., such that $R \, s \, s'$ holds) produces an n-safe configuration (c, s'); **(2)** the post-condition holds (i.e., $Q \, s$) in case (c, s) is final. ( ) any computation step $(c, s) \Rightarrow (c', s')$ produces an n-safe configuration (c', s') along a guarantee-compliant state change (i.e., such that $G \, s \, s'$).

The *Vafeiadis–Parkinson satisfaction* of an RG clause, $c \models_{\mathsf{VP}} (P, R, G, Q)$, is now defined to mean safety for any number of steps, $\forall s \in \mathsf{State}$, $\forall n \in \mathbb{N}$. $P \, s \longrightarrow$ $\mathsf{safe}_{(R,G,Q)} \, n \, (c, s)$.

We can show that these three semantics are all equivalent, and the rules of the standard RG proof system are sound for them.

Thm 1 Consider the following statements:

 (1) $c \models_{\mathsf{XRH}} (P, R, G, Q)$; (2) $c \models_{\mathsf{CJ}} (P, R, G, Q)$;

 (3) $c \models_{\mathsf{VP}} (P, R, G, Q)$; (4) $c \vdash (P, R, G, Q)$.

Then (1), (2) and (3) are equivalent, and (4) implies them. Moreover, the equivalences between (1), (2) and (3) are language-independent, i.e., they still hold if we replace the small-step operational semantics of our language with any sets C and State and relation $\Rightarrow : (\mathsf{C} \times \mathsf{State}) \to (\mathsf{C} \times \mathsf{State}) \to \mathbb{B}$.

226   J. Derrick et al.

$$\mathsf{safe}_{(R,G,Q)}\, 0\, (c,s) \quad \text{(Base)}$$

$$\frac{\begin{array}{l} 1.\ \forall s'.\ R\, s\, s' \longrightarrow \mathsf{safe}_{(R,G,Q)}\, n\, (c,s') \\ 2.\ \mathsf{final}\, (c,s) \longrightarrow Q\, s \\ 3.\ \forall c',s'.\ ((c,s) \Rightarrow (c',s')) \longrightarrow G\, s\, s' \wedge \mathsf{safe}_{(R,G,Q)}\, n\, (c',s') \end{array}}{\mathsf{safe}_{(R,G,Q)}\, (n+1)\, (c,s)}\ \text{(Step)}$$

Fig. 3: The inductive-safety predicate safe

Although equivalent, the three semantics differ in the heaviness of their inductive machinery:

- $\vDash_{\mathsf{XRH}}$ talks about long-distance action, i.e., quantifies over multiple execution steps, via explicit computation traces.
- $\vDash_{\mathsf{CJ}}$ still talks about long-distance action, but keeps the traces implicit, abstracted under the notion of reachability.
- $\vDash_{\mathsf{VP}}$ goes further, abstracting the (long-)distance into a numeric argument n, and only talks about single steps, n to $n+1$.

These differences are reflected in the level of formal bureaucracy involved in the proofs of RG rules soundness (the equivalence "(4) implies (i)" where $i \in \{1,2,3\}$ in Thm. 1). Take for example the soundness of the rule for sequential composition, (SeqRG) in Fig. 2:

- For $\vDash_{\mathsf{XRH}}$, where we need to prove that $c_1 \vDash_{\mathsf{XRH}} (P,R,G,P')$, $c_2 \vDash_{\mathsf{XRH}} (P',R,G,Q)$ and $\mathsf{refl}\, G$ implies $\mathsf{seq}\, c_1\, c_2 \vDash_{\mathsf{XRH}} (P,R,G,Q)$, we require a lemma characterizing traces that start in $\mathsf{seq}\, c_1\, c_2$, stating that such a trace:
  - either is obtained by wrapping $\mathsf{seq}\, \_\, c_2$ around a trace starting in c_1 (i.e., sequentially post-composing c_2 with all the commands of the trace),
  - or consists of a trace obtained by wrapping $\mathsf{seq}\, \_\, c_2$ around a trace starting in c_1 and ending in $\quad$ne, followed by a trace starting in c_2.
- For $\vDash_{\mathsf{CJ}}$ (where we must prove the same as above but with $\vDash_{\mathsf{CJ}}$), we require a lighter inversion lemma for multistep reachability: stating that, if $\mathsf{stepRel}^*_R(\mathsf{seq}\, c_1\, c_2, s)(c',s')$, then
  - either c' has the form $\mathsf{seq}\, c_1'\, c_2$ for some c_1' such that $\mathsf{stepRel}^*_R\, (c_1,s)\, (c_1',s')$,
  - or $\mathsf{stepRel}^*_R\, (c_1,s)\, (\quad\mathsf{ne},s'')$ for some s'', and $\mathsf{stepRel}^*_R\, (c_2,s'')\, (c',s')$.
- Finally, for $\vDash_{\mathsf{VP}}$, we only require the native inversion lemma stemming from the inductive definition of the small-step semantics: stating that, if $(\mathsf{seq}\, c_1\, c_2, s) \Rightarrow (c',s')$, then
  - either c' has the form $\mathsf{seq}\, c_1'\, c_2$ for some c_1' such that $(c_1,s) \Rightarrow (c_1',s')$,
  - or $(c_1,s) \Rightarrow (\quad\mathsf{ne},s'')$ for some s'', and $(c_2,s'') \Rightarrow (c',s')$.

So, proof bureaucracy decreases as we move along the above spectrum: from trace decomposition, to inversion for multi-steps, to inversion for single steps.

2   A f ur h w :   du   ve-s fe   sem   s

Next, we discuss a further simplification from the lightest of the above semantics, the counting-based one of Vafeiadis and Parkinson. Taking advantage of the

$$\frac{\begin{array}{l} 1.\ \forall s'.\ R\,s\,s' \longrightarrow \mathsf{safeC}_{(R,G,Q)}(c,s') \\ 2.\ \mathsf{final}\,(c,s) \longrightarrow Q\,s \\ 3.\ \forall c',s'.\ ((c,s) \Rightarrow (c',s')) \longrightarrow G\,s\,s' \wedge \mathsf{safeC}_{(R,G,Q)}\,(c',s') \end{array}}{\mathsf{safeC}_{(R,G,Q)}\,(c,s)} \quad \text{(StepC)}$$

Fig. 4: The coinductive-safety predicate safeC

implicit (co)iterative nature of coinduction, we remove the explicit counting of the number n of steps from Fig. 3's inductive-safety predicate safe, and retain only the (Step) case. This leads us to the coinductive-safety predicate safeC defined by the rule schema in Fig. 4. The definition is now interpreted not inductively but coinductively [50,49,31], as indicated by a double-line in the rule. The *coinductive satisfaction* of an RG clause by a command, $c \vDash_\mathsf{C} (P,R,G,Q)$, is defined as $\forall s \in \mathsf{State}.\,P\,s \longrightarrow \mathsf{safeC}_{(R,G,Q)}\,(c,s)$ (so similarly to how the counting-based semantics $\vDash_\mathsf{VP}$ is defined from safe).

The coinductive semantics is equivalent to the counting-based one (hence, according to Thm. 1, to all three inductive semantics).

Thm 2 $c \vDash_\mathsf{VP} (P,R,G,Q)$ is equivalent to $c \vDash_\mathsf{C} (P,R,G,Q)$. Moreover, this equivalence is again language-independent (in the sense defined in Thm. 1).

The proof of the theorem relies on a lemma about safe versus safeC.

Lemm The following are equivalent:
(i) $\forall n \in \mathbb{N}.\ \mathsf{safe}_{(R,G,Q)}\,n\,(c,s)$;   (ii) $\mathsf{safeC}_{(R,G,Q)}\,(c,s)$.

The lemma says that a $\mathbb{N}$-indexed family of inductive predicates, $\mathsf{safe}_{(R,G,Q)}$, forms a convergent approximation of a coinductive predicate, $\mathsf{safeC}_{(R,G,Q)}$.

4   d t   Appr x mated I d t ve y   Ge era

Next we recall the abstract phenomenon behind the inductive approximation of coinduction—as background for our proof-based investigation to follow.

Let $(L,\leq)$ be a complete lattice, where we write $\sqcap$ and $\sqcup$ for the binary infima and suprema, and $\sqcap$ and $\bigsqcup$ for infima and suprema of arbitrary families of elements in L. A *decreasing ω-chain* in L is a family $(l_i)_{i\in\mathbb{N}}$ such that $l_i \geq l_{i+1}$ for all $i \in \mathbb{N}$. Let $F : L \to L$ be a monotonic operator. An element $k \in L$ is said to be a *fixpoint* for F if $F\,k = k$, a *pre-fixpoint* for F if $F\,k \leq k$, and a *post-fixpoint* for F if $k \leq F\,k$. We recall the Knaster-Tarski theorem [60]:

Thm If L is a complete lattice and $F : L \to L$ a monotonic operator, then: **(1)** There exists a unique least fixpoint lfp_F for F, which is also the least pre-fixpoint. **(2)** Dually, there exists a unique greatest fixpoint gfp_F for F, which is also the greatest post-fixpoint.

This enables an induction proof principle for lfp_F: to show $\mathsf{lfp}_F \leq k$, it suffices to show that k is a pre-fixpoint. Dually, we have a coinduction proof principle: to show $k \leq \mathsf{gfp}_F$, it suffices to show that k is a post-fixpoint. A small enhancement called *strong (co)induction* includes lfp_F and gfp_F too in the (co)inductive proofs:

r ll r 5 Under the hypotheses of Thm. 4:

(1) $F\left(\mathsf{lfp}_F \sqcap k\right) \le k$ implies $\mathsf{lfp}_F \le k$ for all $k \in L$, and

(2) $k \le F\left(\mathsf{gfp}_F \sqcup k\right)$ implies $k \le \mathsf{gfp}_F$ for all $k \in L$.

Ex mple 6 The inductive definition of $\mathsf{safe}_{(R,G,Q)}$ comes from applying the Knaster-Tarski theorem for least fixpoints. Namely, for (R,G,Q) fixed, $\mathsf{safe}_{(R,G,Q)}$ is the least fixpoint of an operator H on the lattice $\mathbb{N} \to (\mathsf{C} \quad \times \mathsf{State}) \to \mathsf{B}$ l, defined, for each K, n and (c,s), by taking $H\,K\,n\,(c,s)$ to be

$$n = 0 \vee (\exists m.\, n = m + 1 \wedge$$
$$(\mathsf{final}\,(c,s) \longrightarrow Q\,s) \wedge$$
$$(\forall c', s'.\,((c,s) \Rightarrow (c',s'))) \longrightarrow G\,s\,s' \wedge K\,(c',s')\,m) \wedge$$
$$(\forall s'.\,R\,s\,s' \longrightarrow K\,(c,s')\,m))$$

And the coinductive definition of $\mathsf{safeC}_{(R,G,Q)}$ comes from applying Knaster-Tarski for greatest fixpoints: $\mathsf{safeC}_{(R,G,Q)} = \mathsf{gfp}_F$ where the lattice L is $(\mathsf{C} \quad \times \mathsf{State}) \to \mathsf{B}$ l, and $F : L \to L$ is defined by taking $F\,K\,(c,s)$ to be

$$(\mathsf{final}\,(c,s) \longrightarrow Q\,s) \wedge$$
$$(\forall c', s'.\,((c,s) \Rightarrow (c',s'))) \longrightarrow G\,s\,s' \wedge K\,(c',s')) \wedge$$
$$(\forall s'.\,R\,s\,s' \longrightarrow K\,(c,s'))$$

We will denote by $_{(R,G,Q)}$ and $\mathsf{F}_{(R,G,Q)}$ the above particular lattice L and particular operator F underlying the coinductive definition of $\mathsf{safeC}_{(R,G,Q)}$.   □

To capture abstractly the connection between safeC and safe we need a more fine-grained description of greatest fixpoints, via upper approximations. This is offered by Kleene's theorem [13], which we recall next (in the dual form, for greatest fixpoints). We say that $F : L \to L$ is ω-*cocontinuous* if it commutes with the infima of decreasing ω-chains $(a_i)_{i \in \mathbb{N}}$, i.e., $F\left(\sqcap_{i \in \mathbb{N}}\, a_i\right) = \sqcap_{i \in \mathbb{N}}(F\,a_i)$. Note that ω-cocontinuity is a strengthening of monotonicity. We write F^n for the n'th iteration of F, i.e., the composition with itself n times.

Thm 7 (Kleene's Theorem) If L is a complete lattice (or at least a copointed ω-cocomplete lattice) where $\top$ denotes its top element and the operator $F : L \to L$ is ω-cocontinuous, then $\mathsf{gfp}_F = \sqcap_{n \in \mathbb{N}} F^n \top$.

We recall the proof idea for future reference: The ω-cocontinuity of F ensures that $\sqcap_{n \in \mathbb{N}} F^n \top$ is a fixpoint. To show that it is the greatest, let k be a fixpoint. By induction on n it follows that $\forall n.\, k \le F^n\,\top$, i.e., $k \le \sqcap_{n \in \mathbb{N}} F^n\,\top$. In the inductive step, $k \le F^n\,\top$ implies, also using F's monotonicity, that $k = F\,k \le F\,(F^n\,\top) = F^{n+1}\,\top$.   □

For any operator $F : L \to L$, we define its *approximating operator* $F^\sharp : (\mathbb{N} \to L) \to (\mathbb{N} \to L)$ as follows, for all $f : \mathbb{N} \to L$ and $n \in \mathbb{N}$:

$$F^\sharp\,f\,n = \begin{cases} \top, & \text{if } n = 0 \\ F\,(f\,(n-1)) & \text{otherwise} \end{cases}$$

The definition of $F^\sharp$ from F represents the pattern of how $\mathsf{safe}_{(R,G,Q)}$ *could have been* obtained from $\mathsf{safeC}_{(R,G,Q)}$. Indeed, by direct inspection of the definitions, we can see that $\mathsf{safeC}_{(R,G,Q)}$ is $\mathsf{gfp}_{\mathsf{F}_{(R,G,Q)}}$ and $\mathsf{safe}_{(R,G,Q)}$ is $\mathsf{lfp}_{\mathsf{F}^\sharp_{(R,G,Q)}}$ (the least fixpoint of the approximating operator associated to $\mathsf{F}_{(R,G,Q)}$). Lemma 3, connecting $\mathsf{safe}_{(R,G,Q)}$ with $\mathsf{safeC}_{(R,G,Q)}$, is thus an instance of the following consequence of Kleene's theorem:

Thm 8 Assume that L is a complete lattice and $F : L \to L$ is an ω-cocontinuous operator. Then $\mathsf{gfp}_F = \bigsqcap_{n\in\mathbb{N}} \mathsf{lfp}_{F^\sharp} n$.

Thus, our discussed approximation phenomenon is abstractly the coincidence between the greatest fixpoint gfp_F and the infimum of the applications of the approximating operator's fixpoint $\mathsf{lfp}_{F^\sharp} n$; and this coincidence is enabled by the ω-cocontinuity of the underlying operator F.

Pr f Deve pme t Per pe t ve

The above discussion shows that, even though we derived $\mathsf{safeC}_{(R,G,Q)}$ from $\mathsf{safe}_{(R,G,Q)}$, it is more natural to see $\mathsf{safe}_{(R,G,Q)}$ as being derived from $\mathsf{safeC}_{(R,G,Q)}$, since $\mathsf{safeC}_{(R,G,Q)}$ is the simpler of the two. However, one is inductive and the other is coinductive, resulting in different styles of proofs, which we will compare next. We start with a concrete comparison, taking as a case study the soundness of the rule for sequential composition, then we extract general patterns in terms of the abstract operators $F^\sharp$ versus F (§5.1). Then we compare inductive with coinductive enhancements, starting with the soundness proofs of the RG rule for while (susceptible to "up-to" enhancement due to its reliance on other constructs), and again generalizing to abstract operators (§5.2).

5 1 I du ve versus du ve pr fs

Recall from §3.1 that the counting-based semantics is at the lightweight end of the spectrum of semantics for RG, with consequences on the simplicity of the soundness proofs. Next we illustrate how shifting from this to the coinductive semantics (i.e., from $\vDash_{\mathsf{VP}}$ which is based on safe to $\vDash_{\mathsf{C}}$ which is based on safeC), incurs a further degree of proof simplification. We again consider the rule for sequential composition ((SeqRG) in Fig. 2). The proofs of its soundness w.r.t. the counting-based and coinductive semantics are shown in Fig. 5, side by side. We arranged the layout and the notations to emphasize the similarity between their structures. Ignoring the specific formats required for starting (co)induction (i.e., the universal quantification for induction and the existential one for coinduction) and the vacuous base case present for induction only, the two proofs consist of very similar "face-offs" between what we know, labeled (3.i)–(3.iii), and what we must prove, labeled (i)–(iii). The differences, highlighted in gray in the figure, are:

- in the inductive proof, in addition to (3.i)–(3.iii) we also know (and of course need) the inductive hypothesis (IH);
- in the coinductive proof, in the goals (i) and (iii) we have the extra slack offered by a disjunct with the coinductive invariant (via Corollary 5(2)).

Preliminaries

We assume refl G, $c_1 \models_{\mathsf{VP}} (P, R, G, P')$ and $c_2 \models_{\mathsf{VP}} (P', R, G, Q)$ and must show seq $c_1\, c_2 \models_{\mathsf{VP}} (P, R, G, Q)$. Expanding the definition of $\models_{\mathsf{VP}}$ in the first assumption and the conclusion, the goal is reduced to the following, for all s and n:

Preliminaries

We assume refl G, $c_1 \models_{\mathsf{C}} (P, R, G, P')$ and $c_2 \models_{\mathsf{C}} (P', R, G, Q)$ and must show seq $c_1\, c_2 \models_{\mathsf{C}} (P, R, G, Q)$. Expanding the definition of $\models_{\mathsf{C}}$ in the first assumption and the conclusion, the goal is reduced to the following, for all s:

Main part

We assume **(1)** refl G and **(2)** $\forall s', m.\ P'\, s' \longrightarrow \mathsf{safe}_{(R,G,Q)}\, m\, (c_2, s')$, and must prove $\forall c_1, s.\ (\forall m.\ \mathsf{safe}_{(R,G,P')}\, m\, (c_1, s)) \longrightarrow \mathsf{safe}_{(R,G,Q)}\, n\, (\mathsf{seq}\, c_1\, c_2, s)$, which we do by induction on n.

The base case is trivial, since the conclusion $\mathsf{safe}_{(R,G,Q)}\, 0$ is vacuously true.

For the induction step, we assume

$$\textbf{(IH)}\quad \forall c_1, s.\ (\forall m.\ \mathsf{safe}_{(R,G,P')}\, m\, (c_1, s)) \longrightarrow$$
$$\mathsf{safe}_{(R,G,Q)}\, n\, (\mathsf{seq}\, c_1\, c_2, s)$$

and must prove
$$\forall c_1, s.\ (\forall m.\ \mathsf{safe}_{(R,G,P')}\, m\, (c_1, s)) \longrightarrow$$
$$\mathsf{safe}_{(R,G,Q)}\, (n + 1)\, (\mathsf{seq}\, c_1\, c_2, s).$$
To this end, we fix c_1 and s, and assume $\forall m.\ \mathsf{safe}_{(R,G,P')}\, m\, (c_1, s)$, in particular **(3)** $\forall m.\ \mathsf{safe}_{(R,G,P')}\, (m + 1)\, (c_1, s)$, which by the definition of $\mathsf{safe}_{(R,G,P')}$ yields the following:

(3.i) $\forall m.\ \forall s'.\ R\, s\, s' \longrightarrow \mathsf{safe}_{(R,G,P')}\, m\, (c_1, s')$

(3.ii) final $(c_1, s) \longrightarrow P'\, s$

(3.iii) $\forall m.\ \forall c_1', s'.\ ((c_1, s) \Rightarrow (c_1', s')) \longrightarrow$
$G\, s\, s' \wedge \mathsf{safe}_{(R,G,P')}\, m\, (c_1', s')$

We must prove $\mathsf{safe}_{(R,G,Q)}\, (n + 1)\, (\mathsf{seq}\, c_1\, c_2, s)$, which by the definition of $\mathsf{safe}_{(R,G,Q)}$ amounts to:

(i) $\forall s'.\ R\, s\, s' \longrightarrow \mathsf{safe}_{(R,G,Q)}\, n\, (\mathsf{seq}\, c_1\, c_2, s')$

(ii) final $(\mathsf{seq}\, c_1\, c_2, s) \longrightarrow Q\, s$

(iii) $\forall c', s'.\ ((\mathsf{seq}\, c_1\, c_2, s) \Rightarrow (c', s')) \longrightarrow$
$G\, s\, s' \wedge \mathsf{safe}_{(R,G,Q)}\, n\, (c', s')$

Now, (i) follows from (3.i) and (IH) , and (ii) follows by virtue of final $(\mathsf{seq}\, c_1\, c_2, s)$ being false. To prove (iii), fix c' and s' and assume $(\mathsf{seq}\, c_1\, c_2, s) \Rightarrow (c', s')$. We must prove $G\, s\, s' \wedge \mathsf{safe}_{(R,G,Q)}\, n\, (c', s')$. We have two cases:

Case I: $c_1 = \mathsf{done}$. Then $(c', s') = (c_2, s)$, hence $G\, s\, s'$, i.e., $G\, s\, s$, follows from (1). Moreover, since final (c_1, s) holds, from (3.ii) we obtain $P'\, s$, i.e., $P'\, s'$. This together with (2) implies $\mathsf{safe}_{(R,G,Q)}\, n\, (c_2, s')$, i.e., $\mathsf{safe}_{(R,G,Q)}\, n\, (c', s')$.

Case II: $c_1 \neq \mathsf{done}$. Then there exists c_1' such that $(c_1, s) \Rightarrow (c_1', s')$ and $c' = \mathsf{seq}\, c_1'\, c_2$, which together with (3.iii) implies $G\, s\, s'$ (as desired) and $\forall m.\ \mathsf{safe}_{(R,G,P')}\, m\, (c_1', s')$. Using the latter and (IH) , we obtain $\mathsf{safe}_{(R,G,Q)}\, n\, (\mathsf{seq}\, c_1'\, c_2, s')$, i.e., $\mathsf{safe}_{(R,G,Q)}\, n\, (c', s')\ (R, G, Q)$. $\square$

Main part

We assume **(1)** refl G and **(2)** $\forall s'.\ P'\, s' \longrightarrow \mathsf{safeC}_{(R,G,Q)}\, (c_2, s')$, and must prove $(\exists c_1.\ c = \mathsf{seq}\, c_1\, c_2 \wedge \mathsf{safeC}_{(R,G,P')}(c_1, s)) \longrightarrow \mathsf{safeC}_{(R,G,Q)}\, (c, s)$. We prove this by strong coinduction on the definition of $\mathsf{safeC}_{(R,G,Q)}$. Thus, we assume the coinductive invariant $\exists c_1.\ c = \mathsf{seq}\, c_1\, c_2 \wedge \mathsf{safeC}_{(R,G,P')}(c_1, s)$, which amounts to fixing c_1 and assuming $c = \mathsf{seq}\, c_1\, c_2$ and **(3)** $\mathsf{safeC}_{(R,G,P')}\, (c_1, s)$, the latter yielding the following from the definition of $\mathsf{safeC}_{(R,G,P')}$:

(3.i) $\forall s'.\ R\, s\, s' \longrightarrow \mathsf{safeC}_{(R,G,P')}\, (c_1, s')$

(3.ii) final $(c_1, s) \longrightarrow P'\, s$

(3.iii) $\forall c_1', s'.\ ((c_1, s) \Rightarrow (c_1', s')) \longrightarrow$
$G\, s\, s' \wedge \mathsf{safeC}_{(R,G,P')}\, (c_1', s')$

We must show the following:

(i) $\forall s'.\ R\, s\, s' \longrightarrow \mathsf{safeC}_{(R,G,Q)}\, (\mathsf{seq}\, c_1\, c_2, s') \vee$
$(\exists c_1'.\ \mathsf{seq}\, c_1\, c_2 = \mathsf{seq}\, c_1'\, c_2 \wedge \mathsf{safeC}_{(R,G,P')}(c_1', s))$

(ii) final $(\mathsf{seq}\, c_1\, c_2, s) \longrightarrow Q\, s$

(iii) $\forall c', s'.\ ((\mathsf{seq}\, c_1\, c_2, s) \Rightarrow (c', s')) \longrightarrow$
$G\, s\, s' \wedge (\ \mathsf{safeC}_{(R,G,Q)}\, (c', s') \vee$
$(\exists c_1'.\ c' = \mathsf{seq}\, c_1'\, c_2 \wedge \mathsf{safeC}_{(R,G,P')}(c_1', s')))$

Now, (i) follows from (3.i) taking $c_1' = c_1$, and (ii) follows by virtue of final $(\mathsf{seq}\, c_1\, c_2, s)$ being false. To prove (iii), fix c' and s' and assume $(\mathsf{seq}\, c_1\, c_2, s) \Rightarrow (c', s')$. We must prove $G\, s\, s' \wedge (*)$ where $(*)$ is $\mathsf{safeC}_{(R,G,Q)}\, (c', s')) \vee (\exists c_1'.\ c' = \mathsf{seq}\, c_1'\, c_2 \wedge \mathsf{safeC}_{(R,G,P')}(c_1', s'))$. We have two cases:

Case I: $c_1 = \mathsf{done}$. Then $(c', s') = (c_2, s)$, hence $G\, s\, s'$, i.e., $G\, s\, s$, follows from (1). Moreover, since final (c_1, s) holds, from (3.ii) we obtain $P'\, s$, i.e., $P'\, s'$. This together with (2) implies $\mathsf{safeC}_{(R,G,Q)}\, (c_2, s')$, i.e., $\mathsf{safeC}_{(R,G,Q)}\, (c', s')$, the first disjunct of $(*)$.

Case II: $c_1 \neq \mathsf{done}$. Then there exists c_1' such that $(c_1, s) \Rightarrow (c_1', s')$ and $c' = \mathsf{seq}\, c_1'\, c_2$, which with (3.iii) implies $G\, s\, s'$ (as desired) and $\mathsf{safeC}_{(R,G,P')}\, (c_1', s')$. Using the latter together with $c' = \mathsf{seq}\, c_1'\, c_2$, we obtain the second disjunct of $(*)$. $\square$

a F   h   g a   a   F   h   a

Fig. 5: Soundness proofs for the RG seq rule

The coinductive proof is more direct. Indeed, for inferring (i)–(iii) from (3.i)–(3.iii), the inductive version involves a back-and-forth between the premise and the conclusion of the fact to be proved, mediated by the inductive hypothesis. For example, when proving (iii) while in Case II, the inductive argument obtains $\forall m.\ \mathsf{safe}_{(R,G,P')}\ m\ (c_1',s')$ which is fed as premise of the inductive hypothesis to produce the desired $\mathsf{safe}_{(R,G,Q)}\ n\ (\mathsf{seq}\ c_1'\ c_2, s')$. (Note that the premise cannot be decoupled from the fact to be proved inductively, since the state in the premise can change during proof.) By contrast, in the coinductive version one obtains the corresponding fact $\mathsf{safeC}_{(R,G,P')}(c_1',s')$, fed directly to (iii) via the coinductive invariant component.

This conceptual simplification offered by the coinductive semantics can be traced back to the abstract operators F and $F^\sharp$, generalizing $\mathsf{safeC}_{(R,G,Q)}$ and $\mathsf{safe}_{(R,G,Q)}$ to gfp_F and $\mathsf{lfp}_{F^\sharp}$. The nontrivial part of an inductive proof of $k \leq \mathsf{gfp}_F = (\bigsqcap_{n\in\mathbb{N}} \mathsf{lfp}_{F^\sharp}\ n)$, i.e., of $\forall n \in \mathbb{N}.\ k \leq \mathsf{lfp}_{F^\sharp}\ n$, is to show that $k \leq \mathsf{lfp}_{F^\sharp}\ n$ implies $k \leq \mathsf{lfp}_{F^\sharp}(n+1)$. And oftentimes, in particular for the soundness proofs of all RG rules (including the Fig. 5 one), the reason why this implication holds is that $k \leq F(\mathsf{gfp}_F \sqcup k)$—exactly what a proof of $k \leq \mathsf{gfp}_F$ by strong coinduction entails. Indeed, we infer $k \leq \mathsf{lfp}_{F^\sharp}(n+1)$ from $k \leq \mathsf{lfp}_{F^\sharp}\ n$ by plugging $k \leq F(\mathsf{gfp}_F \sqcup k)$ into the following chain of (in)equalities:

$$k \leq F\,(\mathsf{gfp}_F \sqcup k) \ \leq F\,(\mathsf{gfp}_F \sqcup \mathsf{lfp}_{F^\sharp}\ n) = F\,(\mathsf{lfp}_{F^\sharp}\ n) = F^\sharp\ \mathsf{lfp}_{F^\sharp}\ (n{+}1) = \mathsf{lfp}_{F^\sharp}(n{+}1)$$

(where, from left to right: the second inequality and the first equality follow from $k \leq \mathsf{lfp}_{F^\sharp}(n)$, $\mathsf{gfp}_F \leq \mathsf{lfp}_{F^\sharp}(n)$ and the monotonicity of F; the second equality follows from the definition of $F^\sharp$; and the third equality follows form $\mathsf{lfp}_{F^\sharp}$ being a fixpoint of $F^\sharp$). Thus, the coinductive proof corresponds to the core of the inductive proof; and the rest of the proof is boilerplate, essentially repeating the argument for Kleene's theorem (Thm. 7)!

So in our concrete example from Fig. 5, gfp_F is $\mathsf{safeC}_{(R,G,Q)}$, $\mathsf{lfp}_{F^\sharp}$ is $\mathsf{safe}_{(R,G,Q)}$ (so F is $\mathsf{F}_{(R,G,Q)}$), and k is expressed by the coinductive invariant. To see more clearly that our abstract discussion actually matches the concrete Fig. 5 situation, we concretize one notch of the abstract discussion, assuming L is $A \to \mathsf{B}$ l for some set A and $k : A \to \mathsf{B}$ l is existentially quantified over parameters from a set Prm, i.e., $k\,a = (\exists p.\ k'\ p\ a)$ for some $k' : Prm \to A \to \mathsf{B}$ l. Then:

- The inductive version proves $k \leq \mathsf{gfp}_F = \bigsqcap_n \mathsf{lfp}_{F^\sharp}\ n$, i.e., $\forall n, a.\ k\ a \longrightarrow \mathsf{lfp}_{F^\sharp}\ n\ a$, i.e., $\forall n, a, p.\ k'\ p\ a \longrightarrow \mathsf{lfp}_{F^\sharp}\ n\ a$. Hence, the inductive goal is the following: $\forall a, p.\ k'\ p\ a \longrightarrow \mathsf{lfp}_{F^\sharp}\ n\ a$ implies $\forall a, p.\ k'\ p\ a \longrightarrow \mathsf{lfp}_{F^\sharp}(n+1)\ a$.
- The coinductive version proves $k \leq \mathsf{gfp}_F$, i.e., $\forall a.\ k\ a \longrightarrow \mathsf{gfp}_F\ a$, i.e., $\forall a.\ (\exists p.\ k'\ p\ a) \longrightarrow \mathsf{gfp}_F\ a$. Hence, coinductively, the goal is the following: $\exists p.\ k'\ p\ a$ implies $F\,(\mathsf{gfp}_F \sqcup (\exists p.\ k'\ p))\ a$.

In our example from Fig. 5, A is C $\times$ State, Prm is C , and k' is defined by $k'\ c_1\ (c, s) \longleftrightarrow (c = \mathsf{seq}\ c_1\ c_2 \wedge \mathsf{safeC}_{(R,G,P')}(c_1, s))$.

5.2   Inductive versus coinductive theorems

As seen in Fig. 5, the soundness of the RG rule for seq w.r.t. the inductive (counting-based) and coinductive semantics amounts to seq preserving the

	Sa a	E ha
done	$$\dfrac{1\ \ Q\,s \qquad\qquad 2\ \ \text{stable}\,Q\,R}{\forall n.\ \text{safe}_{(R,G,Q)}\ n\ \text{done}}$$	, h j h a g
seq	$$\dfrac{\begin{array}{l}1\ \ \text{refl}\,G \quad 2\ \ \forall m\,.\,\text{safe}_{(R,G,P)}\ m\ (c_1,s)\\ 3\ \ \forall s'.\,P\,s' \longrightarrow \forall n.\,\text{safe}_{(R,G,Q)}\ n\ (c_2,s')\end{array}}{\forall n.\ \text{safe}_{(R,G,Q)}\ n\ (\text{seq}\ c_1\ c_2,s)}$$	$$\begin{array}{l}a\ \ n\ldots\\[2pt]\dfrac{\begin{array}{l}1\ \ \text{refl}\,G \quad 2\ \ \text{safe}_{(R,G,P)}\ n\ (c_1,s)\\ 3\ \ \forall s'.\,P\,s' \longrightarrow \text{safe}_{(R,G,Q)}\ n\ (c_2,s')\end{array}}{\text{safe}_{(R,G,Q)}\ n\ (\text{seq}\ c_1\ c_2,s)}\end{array}$$
if	$$\dfrac{\begin{array}{l}1\ \ \text{refl}\,G\\ 2\ \ \forall s'.\,R^{*}\,s\,s' \longrightarrow\\ (\text{evalT}\ t\ s' \longrightarrow \forall n.\,\text{safe}_{(R,G,Q)}\ n\ (c_1,s'))\,\wedge\\ (\neg\,\text{evalT}\ t\ s' \longrightarrow \forall n.\,\text{safe}_{(R,G,Q)}\ n\ (c_2,s'))\end{array}}{\forall n.\ \text{safe}_{(R,G,Q)}\ n\ (\text{seq}\ c_1\ c_2,s)}$$	$$\begin{array}{l}a\ \ n\ldots\\[2pt]\dfrac{\begin{array}{l}1\ \ \text{refl}\,G\\ 2\ \ \forall s'.\,R^{*}\,s\,s' \longrightarrow\\ (\text{evalT}\ t\ s' \longrightarrow \text{safe}_{(R,G,Q)}\ n\ (c_1,s'))\,\wedge\\ (\neg\,\text{evalT}\ t\ s' \longrightarrow \text{safe}_{(R,G,Q)}\ n\ (c_2,s'))\end{array}}{\text{safe}_{(R,G,Q)}\ n\ (\text{seq}\ c_1\ c_2,s)}\end{array}$$

Fig. 6: Inductive enhancements

safety predicates. The same is true for the other language constructs. For example, Fig. 6(left) shows the safety preservation properties needed for the soundness of the RG rules for   ne, seq and if w.r.t. the inductive semantics.

Now let us look at the soundness proofs for the RG rule of the while construct ((WhileRG) from Fig. 2), which is interesting because its operational semantics relies on other constructs, namely   ne, seq and if. Fig. 9 shows the soundness proofs relative to the two semantics, side by side. In the inductive case, we end up having to prove the implication shown in Fig. 9(a)'s box, which amounts to $\text{safe}_{(R,G,Q)}\ n\ (\text{while}\ t\ c,s)$ implies $\text{safe}_{(R,G,Q)}\ n\ (\text{if}\ t\ (\text{seq}\ c\ (\text{while}\ t\ c))\ \ \text{ne},s)$. Here, safety preservation properties for if, seq and   ne would of course be handy. But the ones from Fig. 6(left) for if and seq, which *were* sufficient for proving the inductive soundness of the rules for these operators, are not strong enough for helping out with the proof for while. This is because now we need to work index-wise with a fixed n. Fortunately, the index-wise versions of these properties, shown in Fig. 6(right), are also provable—for example, we can prove that safety holds for seq $c_1\ c_2$ in the same number of steps n as the assumed safety for c_2. And indeed, as shown in Fig. 9(a) after the box, these stronger, index-wise versions are just what we need to complete the proof for while. In summary, since while depends on other operators, its safety preservation property needed for the soundness of its RG rule required an index-wise enhancement of the safety preservation properties needed for the soundness of these operators. But what is the corresponding phenomenon within the coinductive semantics?

Before answering this question, let us first rephrase and then generalize the preservation properties for inductive safety. All the original preservation

$$U_Q^{\mathsf{done}}\,(c,s) = c = \mathsf{done} \wedge Q\,s$$
$$U_{(R,G,P,c_2)}^{\mathsf{seq}}\,K\,(c,s) = \exists c_1.\,c = \mathsf{seq}\,c_1\,c_2 \wedge \mathsf{safe}_{(R,G,P)}(c_1,s) \wedge$$
$$(\forall s'.\,P\,s' \longrightarrow K\,(c_2,s'))$$
$$U_{(R,t,c_1,c_2)}^{\mathsf{if}}\,(K_1,K_2)\,(c,s) = (c = \mathsf{if}\,t\,c_1\,c_2 \wedge$$
$$\forall s'.\,R^*\,s\,s' \longrightarrow (\mathsf{evalT}\,t\,s' \longrightarrow K_1\,(c_1,s')) \wedge$$
$$(\neg\,\mathsf{evalT}\,t\,s' \longrightarrow K_2\,(c_2,s')))$$

Fig. 7: Operators underlying ne, seq and if (more details in [15, App. D])

properties from Fig. 6(left) can be stated (under side conditions) as

$$U\,\Big(\bigsqcap_n \mathsf{safe}_{R,G,Q}\,n, \ldots, \bigsqcap_n \mathsf{safe}_{R,G,Q}\,n\Big) \leq \bigsqcap_n \mathsf{safe}_{R,G,Q}\,n$$

where U is an m-ary operator on the lattice (R,G,Q) (in our case with $m \in \{0,1,2\}$). Similarly, their index-wise enhancements from Fig. 6(right) can be stated (under the same conditions) as

$$\forall n.\,U(\mathsf{safe}_{R,G,Q}\,n, \ldots, \mathsf{safe}_{R,G,Q}\,n) \leq \mathsf{safe}_{R,G,Q}\,n\,.$$

For example, the operators for ne, seq, if are U_Q^{done}, $U_{(R,G,P,c_2)}^{\mathsf{seq}}$, $U_{(R,t,c_1,c_2)}^{\mathsf{if}}$, shown in Fig. 7; they were extracted from the soundness preservation properties.

So in general, for an ω-cocomplete operator $F : L \to L$ on a complete lattice L, where we have $\mathsf{gfp}_F = \bigsqcap_n \mathsf{lfp}_{F^\sharp}\,n$, a gfp_F-preservation property has the form

$$(*) \qquad U\,(\mathsf{gfp}_F, \ldots, \mathsf{gfp}_F) \leq \mathsf{gfp}_F$$

where $U : L^m \to L$; and an inductive enhancement of it has the form

$$(**) \qquad \forall n.\,U\,(\mathsf{lfp}_{F^\sharp}\,n, \ldots, \mathsf{lfp}_{F^\sharp}\,n) \leq \mathsf{lfp}_{F^\sharp}\,n\,.$$

And indeed, $(**)$ is stronger than $(*)$ if U itself is ω-cocontinuous (which *is* the case with our safety preservation operators).

Next, we will infer the coinductive version of enhancement by analyzing the typical pattern of a proof of the inductive enhancement $(**)$ by induction on n, and (similarly to what we did in §5.1) trying to identify its coinductive core. For the inductive step, assuming $U\,(\mathsf{lfp}_{F^\sharp}\,n, \ldots, \mathsf{lfp}_{F^\sharp}\,n) \leq \mathsf{lfp}_{F^\sharp}\,n$, one typically proves $U\,(\mathsf{lfp}_{F^\sharp}\,(n+1), \ldots, \mathsf{lfp}_{F^\sharp}\,(n+1)) \leq \mathsf{lfp}_{F^\sharp}\,(n+1)$ via reasoning that amounts to the following chain of (in)equalities:

$$U(\mathsf{lfp}_{F^\sharp}(n+1), \ldots, \mathsf{lfp}_{F^\sharp}\,(n+1)) = U(\,F(\mathsf{lfp}_{F^\sharp}n)\,, \ldots,\,F(\mathsf{lfp}_{F^\sharp}n)\,)$$
$$\leq F(\,\mathsf{lfp}_{F^\sharp}n \sqcup U(\,\mathsf{lfp}_{F^\sharp}n\,, \ldots,\,\mathsf{lfp}_{F^\sharp}n\,)) = F(\mathsf{lfp}_{F^\sharp}n) = \mathsf{lfp}_{F^\sharp}(n+1)$$

In concrete cases, the highlighted inequality typically holds regardless of whether we have $F\,(\mathsf{lfp}_{F^\sharp}\,n)$ on the left and $\mathsf{lfp}_{F^\sharp}\,n$ on the right, except for the fact that $F\,(\mathsf{lfp}_{F^\sharp}\,n) \leq \mathsf{lfp}_{F^\sharp}\,n$; in other words, we could equally well prove that

$$(***) \qquad U\,(k_1, \ldots, k_m) \leq F\,((k_1' \sqcup \ldots \sqcup k_m') \sqcup U\,(k_1, \ldots, k_m))$$

whenever $k_i \leq k_i'$ and $k_i \leq F\,k_i'$ for all $i \in \{1, \ldots, m\}$.

Thus, at the core of an inductive enhancement proof, we discovered property $(***)$, which happens to be a variation of a well-known concept. Let us

	Safety preservation needed for coinductive soundness	Enhanced version
ne	$$\dfrac{(1)\ Q\ s \quad (2)\ \text{stable}\ Q\ R}{\text{safeC}_{(R,G,Q)}(\ \text{ne},s)} \quad \text{i.e.,} \quad \dfrac{(1)\ Q\ s \quad (2)\ \text{stable}\ Q\ R}{\mathsf{U}^{\text{done}}_Q \le \text{safeC}_{(R,G,Q)}}$$ proved by strong coinduction in the form: $$\dfrac{(1)\ Q\ s \quad (2)\ \text{stable}\ Q\ R}{\mathsf{U}^{\text{done}}_Q(c,s) \le \mathsf{F}_{(R,G,Q)}(\text{safe}_{(R,G,Q)} \sqcup \mathsf{U}^{\text{done}}_Q)}$$	No enhancement needed for 0-ary operators such as $\mathsf{U}^{\text{done}}_Q$.
seq	$$\dfrac{(1)\ \text{refl}\ G \quad (2)\ \text{safeC}_{(R,G,P)}(c_1,s) \quad (3)\ \forall s'.\ P\ s' \longrightarrow \text{safeC}_{(R,G,Q)}(c_2,s')}{\text{safeC}_{(R,G,Q)}(\text{seq}\ c_1\ c_2,s)}$$ i.e., $$\dfrac{(1)\ \text{refl}\ G}{\mathsf{U}^{\text{seq}}_{(R,G,P,c_2)}\text{safeC}_{(R,G,Q)} \le \text{safeC}_{(R,G,Q)}}$$ proved by strong coinduction in the form: $$\dfrac{(1)\ \text{refl}\ G}{\mathsf{U}^{\text{seq}}_{(R,G,P,c_2)}\ \text{safeC}_{(R,G,Q)} \le \mathsf{F}_{(R,G,Q)}(\text{safe}_{(R,G,Q)} \sqcup \mathsf{U}^{\text{seq}}_{(R,G,P,c_2)}\ \text{safeC}_{(R,G,Q)})}$$	$$\dfrac{(1)\ \text{refl}\ G \qquad K \le K' \qquad K \le \mathsf{F}_{(R,G,Q)}\ K'}{\mathsf{U}^{\text{seq}}_{(R,G,P,c_2)}\ K \le \mathsf{F}_{(R,G,Q)}(\ K' \sqcup \mathsf{U}^{\text{seq}}_{(R,G,P,c_2)}\ K')}$$
if	$$\dfrac{\begin{array}{c}(1)\ \text{refl}\ G \\ (2)\ \forall s'.\ R^*\ s\ s' \longrightarrow (\text{eval}\ t\ s' \longrightarrow \text{safeC}_{(R,G,Q)}(c_1,s')) \wedge (\neg\ \text{eval}\ t\ s' \longrightarrow \text{safeC}_{(R,G,Q)}(c_2,s'))\end{array}}{\text{safeC}_{(R,G,Q)}(\text{if}\ t\ c_1\ c_2,s)}$$ i.e., $$\dfrac{(1)\ \text{refl}\ G}{\mathsf{U}^{\text{if}}_{(R,t,c_1,c_2)}(\text{safeC}_{(R,G,Q)},\text{safeC}_{(R,G,Q)}) \le \text{safeC}_{(R,G,Q)}}$$ proved by strong coinduction in the form: $$\dfrac{(1)\ \text{refl}\ G}{\mathsf{U}^{\text{if}}_{(R,t,c_1,c_2)}(\text{safeC}_{(R,G,Q)},\text{safeC}_{(R,G,Q)}) \le \mathsf{F}_{(R,G,Q)}(\text{safe}_{(R,G,Q)} \sqcup \mathsf{U}^{\text{if}}_{(R,t,c_1,c_2)}(\text{safeC}_{(R,G,Q)},\text{safeC}_{(R,G,Q)}))}$$	$$\dfrac{\begin{array}{c}(1)\ \text{refl}\ G \\ K_1 \le K_1' \qquad K_1 \le \mathsf{F}_{(R,G,Q)}\ K_1' \\ K_2 \le K_2' \qquad K_2 \le \mathsf{F}_{(R,G,Q)}\ K_2'\end{array}}{\mathsf{U}^{\text{if}}_{(R,t,c_1,c_2)}(\ K_1,\ K_2\ ) \le \mathsf{F}_{(R,G,Q)}(\ K_1' \sqcup K_2' \sqcup \mathsf{U}^{\text{if}}_{(R,t,c_1,c_2)}(\ K_1',\ K_2'\ ))}$$

Fig. 8: Coinductive enhancements

call an operator $U : L^m \to L$ *weakly F-respectful* if it satisfies (***); and *F-respectful* if it satisfies (***) even without the $\sqcup$ part, i.e., with conclusion $U(k_1, \ldots, k_m) \leq F(U(k'_1, \ldots, k'_m))$. Unary respectful operators were studied by Sangiorgi and Pous [56,51], who proved that they enable *up-to enhancements* of coinduction. This generalizes to weakly respectful m-ary operators:

Thm 9 If $F : L \to L$ is a monotonic operator on a complete lattice and $U : L^m \to L$ is monotonic and weakly F-respectful, then the following *up-to-U coinduction* principle holds: Given $k_1, \ldots, k_m \in L$, for proving $k_i \leq \mathsf{gf}_F$ for all $i \in \{1, \ldots, m\}$, it suffices to prove $k_i \leq F(U(k_1, \ldots, k_m))$ for all $i \in \{1, \ldots, m\}$.

Assuming $m = 1$, the principle allows inferring $k \leq \mathsf{gf}_F$ from $k \leq F(U\,k)$, which generalizes the Knaster-Tarski coinduction principle: taking $U = 1_L$ we obtain ordinary coinduction, and taking $U = \lambda k.\ \mathsf{gf}_F \sqcup k$ we obtain strong coinduction; overall, it offers more flexibility in a coinductive proof, since $U\,k$ is usually larger than k. The class of (weakly) respectful operators contains many useful basic operators such as the projections. It is closed under composition, in that $V \circ (U_1, \ldots, U_n)$ is (weakly) respectful whenever V and $U_1, \ldots, U_n$ are, and suprema, in that $U_1 \sqcup U_2$ is (weakly) respectful whenever U_1 and U_2 are. Thus, we can obtain coinductive enhancements by quite freely combining weakly respectful operators.

Back to our concrete situation, Fig. 8(right) shows the conditions under which the operators $\mathsf{U}^{\mathsf{eq}}_{(R,G,P,c_2)}$ and $\mathsf{U}^{\mathsf{if}}_{(R,t,c_1,c_2)}$ are weakly respectful. Indeed, the (conditional) weak respectfulness of these operators represent the coinductive enhancements we are after. Moreover, the gray highlighting in Fig. 8 shows how the weak respectfulness properties (from the right) can be regarded as a generalization of the coinductive goal arising when proving the corresponding safety preservation property (from the left). For example, in the case of sequential composition, Fig. 8(left) indicates that the safety preservation for $\mathsf{s}\ \mathsf{q}$, rephrased as $\mathsf{U}^{\mathsf{eq}}_{(R,G,P,c_2)}\mathsf{saf}\ \mathsf{C}_{(R,G,Q)} \leq \mathsf{saf}\ \mathsf{C}_{(R,G,Q)}$, is proved by strong coinduction, thus the goal takes the form

(****) $\mathsf{U}^{\mathsf{eq}}_{(R,G,P,c_2)}\mathsf{saf}\ \mathsf{C}_{(R,G,Q)} \leq \mathsf{F}_{(R,G,Q)}(\mathsf{saf}_{(R,G,Q)} \sqcup \mathsf{U}^{\mathsf{eq}}_{(R,G,P,c_2)}\mathsf{saf}\ \mathsf{C}_{(R,G,Q)}).$

And Fig. 8(right) generalizes this to weak respectfulness, by replacing in (****) the left occurrence of $\mathsf{saf}_{(R,G,Q)}$ with K and the right one with K'. Moreover, here as well as for all the other constructs, the proof of weak respectfulness can be generalized in a completely systematic way from that of the original preservation property (****): In Fig. 5(b)'s coinductive proof of (****), by writing $\mathsf{saf}_{(R,G,Q)}$ and respectively $\mathsf{saf}'_{(R,G,Q)}$ for the occurrences of $\mathsf{saf}_{(R,G,Q)}$ stemming from the left and respectively right of (****), we see that the only properties of this predicate needed in the proof are $\mathsf{saf}_{(R,G,Q)} \leq \mathsf{saf}'_{(R,G,Q)}$ and $\mathsf{saf}_{(R,G,Q)} \leq \mathsf{F}_{(R,G,Q)}\mathsf{saf}'_{(R,G,Q)}$—meaning we can replace $\mathsf{saf}_{(R,G,Q)}$ and $\mathsf{saf}'_{(R,G,Q)}$ with arbitrary K and K' such that $K \leq K'$ and $K \leq \mathsf{F}_{(R,G,Q)}K'$, yielding a proof of weak respectfulness.

We now come to the coinductive proof of the soundness preservation for whil. Fixing R, G, Q, t, c, we take advantage of the coinductive enhancements for s q and if, and combine them in an operator W that follows the operational semantics of whil , namely

$$W = 1_{\mathsf{L}_{(R,G,Q)}} \sqcup (\mathsf{U}^{\mathsf{if}}_{(R,t,\ \mathsf{eq}\ c\ (\mathsf{while}\ t\ c),\mathsf{done})} \circ (\mathsf{U}^{\mathsf{eq}}_{(R,G,P,\mathsf{while}\ t\ c)}, \lambda K.\ \mathsf{U}^{\mathsf{done}}_Q)) .$$

Combining the weak $\mathsf{F}_{(R,G,Q)}$-respectfulness properties of $U^{\mathsf{done}}_{\_}$, $U^{\mathsf{if}}_{\_}$ and $U^{\ \mathsf{eq}}_{\_}$ from Fig. 8(right), we obtain that W is weakly respectful whenever r fl G, s abl $Q R$ and s abl $P R$.

The proof by up-to-W coinduction is shown in Fig. 9(b). Comparing it to the inductive proof from Fig. 9(a), similar comments to those in §5.1 apply about the coinductive proof being more direct. As for the enhancement dimension, the benefit of using the inductive hypothesis on the larger term if t (s q c (whil t c))   n is now achieved by using the coinductive invariant up-to W, i.e., applying W to it in the coinductive goals (4.i) and (4.iii). Admittedly, the more elementary nature of the inductive enhancements can be an advantage. Moreover, the coinductive proof requires anticipation on how the semantics will unfold, to decide which (weakly) respectful operator to use, whereas the inductive proof proceeds analytically, decomposing the goal and using the properties on a need basis—but this can be achieved with the coinductive enhancements too, via the companion (which is also the largest respectful operator) [25,52].

To summarize the enhancement situation abstractly: For operators $F : L \to L$ and $U : L^m \to L$, assume that we were able to prove that U preserves F's greatest fixpoint, i.e., $U\ (\mathsf{gf}\ _F, \dots, \mathsf{gf}\ _F) \le \mathsf{gf}\ _F$,

either inductively, by showing $\forall n.\ U\ (\sqcap_m \mathsf{lf}\ _{F\sharp} m) \le \mathsf{lf}\ _{F\sharp} n$,

or coinductively, by showing $U\ (\mathsf{gf}\ _F, \dots, \mathsf{gf}\ _F) \le F\ (U\ (\mathsf{gf}\ _F, \dots, \mathsf{gf}\ _F))$.

Then the enhancements proceed as follows:

for induction, by showing the finer property $\forall n.\ U\ (\mathsf{lf}\ _{F\sharp} n, \dots, \mathsf{lf}\ _{F\sharp} n) \le \mathsf{lf}\ _{F\sharp} n$, which we will refer to as *F-approximation-preservation*;

for coinduction, by showing the finer property that U is weakly F-respectful.

In concrete cases such as our safety preservation properties, for both induction and coinduction the proof of the finer property can be obtained by systematically generalizing the proof of the original one. The two enhancement types are connected as follows.

Thm 10   Assume L is a complete lattice and $F : L \to L$ and $U : L^m \to L$ are monotonic. Then the following hold:
(1) If U is weakly F-respectful, then it is also F-approximation-preserving.
(2) If F is ω-cocontinuous and U is F-approximation-preserving, then up-to-U coinduction is a sound proof method (in the sense of Thm. 9).

Point (1) of the above theorem says that what traditionally makes coinductive enhancements possible, namely (weak) respectfulness, is stronger than what we have identified as making inductive enhancements possible, namely the approximation-preserving property. And point (2) says that what makes the inductive enhancements possible, although a weaker property, still makes the coinductive ones possible.

Preliminaries

We assume **(1)** $P \sqcap (\neg\,(\mathsf{evalT}\ t)) \le Q\ \wedge$ table $P\ R\ \wedge$ table $Q\ R\ \wedge$ refl G. We must prove that $c \vDash_{\mathsf{VP}} (P\sqcap(\mathsf{evalT}\ t), R, G, P)$ implies while $t\ c \vDash_{\mathsf{VP}} (P, R, G, Q)$. Expanding the definition of $\vDash_{\mathsf{VP}}$, this reduces to:

Main part

Assuming **(2)** $\forall m, s'.\ P\ s'\ \wedge\ \mathsf{evalT}\ t\ s'\ \longrightarrow$ $\mathsf{afe}_{(R,G,P)}\ m\ (c, s')$, we must prove $\forall n, s.\ P\ s \longrightarrow$ $\mathsf{afe}_{(R,G,Q)}\ n\ (\text{while}\ t\ c, s)$, which we do by induction on n. The base case is again trivial.

For the inductive step, we assume **(IH)** $\forall s.\ P\ s\ \longrightarrow\ \mathsf{afe}_{(R,G,Q)}\ n\ (\text{while}\ t\ c, s)$ and must prove $\forall s.\ P\ s\ \longrightarrow\ \mathsf{afe}_{(R,G,Q)}\ (n + 1)\ (\text{while}\ t\ c, s)$. To this end, we fix s, assume **(3)** $P\ s$, and must prove **(4)** $\mathsf{afe}_{(R,G,Q)}\ (n + 1)\ (\text{while}\ t\ c, s)$, which by the definition of $\mathsf{afe}_{(R,G,Q)}$ amounts to:

(4.i) $\forall s'.\ R\ s\ s' \longrightarrow\ \mathsf{afe}_{(R,G,Q)}\ n\ (\text{while}\ t\ c, s')$

(4.ii) final $(\text{while}\ t\ c, s) \longrightarrow Q\ s$

(4.iii) $\forall d', s'.\ ((\text{while}\ t\ c, s) \Rightarrow (d', s')) \longrightarrow$ $G\ s\ s' \wedge\ \mathsf{afe}_{(R,G,Q)}\ n\ (d', s')$,

of which the last, thanks to the fact that by the semantics of while its hypothesis means $s = s' \wedge$ $d' = \text{if}\ t\ (\ \text{eq}\ c\ (\text{while}\ t\ c))\ \text{done}$, reduces to $G\ s\ s \wedge$ $\mathsf{afe}_{(R,G,Q)}\ n\ (\text{if}\ t\ (\ \text{eq}\ c\ (\text{while}\ t\ c))\ \text{done}, s)$, which, since $G\ s\ s$ follows from (1), further reduces to

(4.iii') $\mathsf{afe}_{(R,G,Q)}\ n\ (\text{if}\ t\ (\ \text{eq}\ c\ (\text{while}\ t\ c))\ \text{done}, s)$

Now, from (1), (3) and (IH), we obtain (4.i); and (4.ii) holds because its hypothesis is vacuously false.

> Remains to prove (4.iii'), using (IH) and (3)...

Thanks to enhanced preservation for if, (4.iii') reduces to:

- refl G, which holds by (1);
- Fixing s', assuming **(5)** $R^*\ s\ s'$, and:
  - Assuming $\neg\ \mathsf{evalT}\ t\ s'$ and showing $\mathsf{afe}_{(R,G,Q)}\ n\ (\text{done}, s')$, which follows from (1), (3), (5) and the preservation for done.
  - Assuming **(6)** $\mathsf{evalT}\ t\ s'$ and showing $\mathsf{afe}_{(R,G,Q)}\ n\ (\ \text{eq}\ c\ (\text{while}\ t\ c), s')$, which, thanks to the enhanced preservation for eq, reduces to:
    * (again) refl G, holding by (1);
    * $\forall m.\ \mathsf{afe}_{(R,G,P)}\ m\ (c, s')$, following from (2), (3), (6);
    * $\forall s.\ P\ s\ \longrightarrow\ \mathsf{afe}_{(R,G,Q)}\ n\ (\text{while}\ t\ c, s)$, i.e., (IH). $\qquad\square$

a For the counting-based semantics

Preliminaries

We assume **(1)** $P \sqcap (\neg\,(\mathsf{evalT}\ t)) \le Q\ \wedge$ table $P\ R\ \wedge$ table $Q\ R\ \wedge$ refl G. We must prove that $c \vDash_{\mathsf{C}} (P\sqcap(\mathsf{evalT}\ t), R, G, P)$ implies while $t\ c \vDash_{\mathsf{C}} (P, R, G, Q)$. Expanding the definition of $\vDash_{\mathsf{C}}$, this reduces to:

Main part

Assuming **(2)** $\forall s'.\ P\ s'\ \wedge\ \mathsf{evalT}\ t\ s'\ \longrightarrow$ $\mathsf{afeC}_{(R,G,P)}\ (c, s')$, we must prove $\forall s.\ P\ s \longrightarrow$ $\mathsf{afeC}_{(R,G,Q)}\ (\text{while}\ t\ c, s)$. To this end, we fix s, c, t, d, assume $P\ s$ and $d = \text{while}\ t\ c$, and must prove $\mathsf{afe}_{(R,G,Q)}\ (d, s)$, which we do by up-to-$W$ coinduction, since W is indeed $F_{(R,G,Q)}$-respectful thanks to (1).

Thus, we assume **(3)** $P\ s$ and $d = \text{while}\ t\ c$, and must show **(4)** $\mathsf{F}_{(R,G,Q)}(W\ (\lambda(d, s).\ P\ s \wedge d = \text{while}\ t\ c))\ (d, s)$, which amounts to:

(4.i) $\forall s'.\ R\ s\ s' \longrightarrow\ W\ (\lambda(d, s).\ P\ s\ \wedge\ d = \text{while}\ t\ c))\ (d, s)$, which, taking the left disjoint in W, reduces to

(4.i') $\forall s'.\ R\ s\ s' \longrightarrow P\ s' \wedge d = \text{while}\ t\ c$, i.e., $\forall s'.\ R\ s\ s' \longrightarrow P\ s'$

(4.ii) final $(d, s) \longrightarrow Q\ s$, i.e., final $(\text{while}\ t\ c, s) \longrightarrow Q\ s$

(4.iii) $\forall d', s'.\ ((d, s) \Rightarrow (d', s')) \longrightarrow$ $G\ s\ s' \wedge\ W\ (\lambda(d, s).\ P\ s\ \wedge\ d = \text{while}\ t\ c))\ (d', s')$, which, taking the right disjoint in W, reduces to

(4.iii') $\forall d', s'.\ ((d, s) \Rightarrow (d', s')) \longrightarrow$
  (a) $G\ s\ s' \wedge d' = \text{if}\ t\ (\ \text{eq}\ c\ (\text{while}\ t\ c))\ \text{done}\ \wedge$
  (b) $(\forall s'.\ R^*\ s\ s' \wedge \mathsf{evalT}\ t\ s'\ \longrightarrow$ $\mathsf{afe}_{(R,G,P)}(c, s'))\ \wedge$
  (c) $(\forall s'.\ R^*\ s\ s' \wedge \neg\,\mathsf{evalT}\ t\ s'\ \longrightarrow\ Q\ s')\ \wedge$
  (d) $(\forall s'.\ P\ s'\ \longrightarrow\ P\ s' \wedge d = \text{while}\ t\ c)$

Now, from (1) and (3), we obtain (4.i'); and (4.ii) holds because its hypothesis is vacuously false.

Finally, using $d = \text{while}\ t\ c$ and the semantics of while, the hypothesis of (4.iii') means $s = s' \wedge d' = \text{if}\ t\ (\ \text{eq}\ c\ (\text{while}\ t\ c))\ \text{done}$, which makes (a) true thanks to (1). Moreover:

- (b) is true thanks to (1), (2) and (3),
- (c) is true thanks to (1) and (3),
- (d) is trivially true (since $d = \text{while}\ t\ c$). $\qquad\square$

b For the coinductive semantics

Fig. 9: Proofs of soundness of the RG rule for whil : for the (inductive) counting-based and coinductive semantics.

6   The Coinduction Approximated Inductively Landscape

Next we look at the scope of coinduction approximated inductively in finer granularity. While so far we only looked at the concrete instances of RG safety operators and a very abstract generalization to operators on lattices, here we will explore a spectrum between these two extremes.

6 1   Th r   s s m forma

Thm. 8 captures the general phenomenon behind coinduction approximated inductively, but does not give us a good intuition on its more concrete scope, notably on how it applies to (co)inductive definitions described by sets of rules [2]. To address this, we slightly lower the generality, by focusing on lattices of predicates on a set A, namely $L = (A \to \mathsf{B} \quad \mathsf{I})$ with order defined again by component-wise implication ($K \leq K'$ iff $\forall\, a \in A\,.\, K\ a\ -\to K'a$), and operators given by sets of rules on A, i.e., subsets $Rl \subseteq \mathcal{P}(A) \times A$. So a $rule$ on A will be a pair (B, a) where $B \subseteq A$ and $a \in A$; we think of B as the set of the rule's $hypotheses$ and of a as the rule's $conclusion$. The associated operator $\mathsf{F}_{Rl} : (A \to \mathsf{B} \quad \mathsf{I}) \to (A \to \mathsf{B} \quad \mathsf{I})$ is defined by applying the rules, namely $\mathsf{F}_{Rl}\ K\ a = (\exists B.\ (B, a) \in Rl \wedge (\forall b \in B.\ K\ b))$. Thus, the notion of a predicate $K : A \to \mathsf{B} \quad \mathsf{I}$ being closed under the rules, namely $\forall (B, a) \in Rl.\ (\forall b \in B.\ K\ b) \longrightarrow K\ a$, is the same as K being a pre-fixpoint of F_{Rl}, i.e., $\mathsf{F}_{Rl} K \leq K$. And the notion of K being consistent with (i.e., backwards closed under) the rules, namely $\forall (B, a) \in Rl.\ K\ a \longrightarrow (\forall b \in B.\ K\ b)$, is the same as K being a post-fixpoint of F_{Rl}, i.e. $K \leq \mathsf{F}_{Rl} K$. For the least and greatest fixpoints of rule-system operator F_{Rl}, we will write lf_{Rl} for $\mathsf{lf}_{\mathsf{F}_{Rl}}$ and gf_{Rl} for $\mathsf{gf}_{\mathsf{F}_{Rl}}$.

A first practical observation is that the inductive approximation can be performed intensionally, at the level of rules. Given a set of rules Rl on A, we define $Rl^{\sharp}$, called the $approximation\ rules\ of\ Rl$, as a set of rules on $\quad \times A$, namely $\{(\varnothing, (0, a)) \mid a \in A\} \cup \bigcup_{n\in} \{(\{n\} \times B, (n + 1, a)) \mid (B, a) \in Rl\}$. Thus, $Rl^{\sharp}$ consists of rules over the same set A but enriched with numeric levels (indexes), i.e., over $\quad \times A$. Specifically, it consists of two kinds of rules: (1) any element a of A at level 0 (i.e., paired with 0) becomes an axiom (rule without premises) of the form $(\varnothing, (0, a))$; (2) any rule (B, a) from Rl becomes a rule $(\{n\} \times B, (n + 1, a)))$ in $Rl^{\sharp}$, i.e., adding levels and making sure that the level decreases from $n + 1$ to n when applying the rule backwards. Then $\mathsf{F}_{Rl^{\sharp}}$ and $(\mathsf{F}_{Rl})^{\sharp}$ are the same (modulo currying), which shifts the discussion from the semantic realm of operators to the (usually) syntactic realm of rules:

L mma 11   Given $Rl \subseteq \mathcal{P}(A) \times A$ and $K : \quad \to A \to \mathsf{B} \quad \mathsf{I}$, we have that $\mathsf{F}_{Rl^{\sharp}}\ K = (\mathsf{F}_{Rl})^{\sharp}\ (\lambda n, a.\ K(n, a))$.

And our motivating example predicates are indeed given by rule systems:

Examp   1   Both $\mathsf{F}_{(R,G,Q)}$ and $\mathsf{F}^{\sharp}_{(R,G,Q)}$ are rule-system based. Namely, we have that $\mathsf{F}_{(R,G,Q)} = \mathsf{F}_{Rl_{(R,G,Q)}}$ and $\mathsf{F}^{\sharp}_{(R,G,Q)} = (\mathsf{F}_{Rl_{(R,G,Q)}})^{\sharp} = \mathsf{F}_{(Rl_{(R,G,Q)})^{\sharp}}$, and therefore saf $\mathsf{C}_{(R,G,Q)}$ = gf $_{Rl_{(R,G,Q)}}$ and saf $_{(R,G,Q)}$ = lf $_{(Rl_{(R,G,Q)})^\sharp}$, where $Rl_{(R,G,Q)}$ is the set of pairs $(B, (c,s))$ such that $B = \{(c',s') \mid ((c,s) \Rightarrow (c',s'))\} \cup \{(c,s') \mid R\ s\ s'\}$ and $(\mathsf{final}\,(c,s) \longrightarrow Q\ s) \wedge (\forall c',s'. ((c,s) \Rightarrow (c',s')) \longrightarrow G\ s\ s')$ holds.

We are ready to describe a more effective criterion for sound approximation. We call a set of rules $Rl \subseteq \mathcal{P}(A) \times A$ *backwards-finite* provided that each $a \in A$ has only a finite number of rules that backwards-apply to it, namely $\forall a \in A$, fini $\{B \subseteq A \mid (B,a) \in Rl\}$. This is a sufficient condition for ω-cocontinuity.

Prop 13 If $Rl \subseteq \mathcal{P}(A) \times A$ is backwards-finite, then F_{Rl} is ω-cocontinuous.

This, together with Lemma 11 and Thm. 8, give us:

Thm 1   Assume that $Rl \subseteq \mathcal{P}(A) \times A$ is backwards-finite. Then, for any $a \in A$, we have that gf $_{Rl}\,a$ if and only if $\forall n \in$. lf $_{Rl^\sharp}\,(n,a)$.

Thus, Thm. 14 is a more concrete depiction of the root cause for the inductive approximation soundness: the backwards finiteness of the defining rules.

6   Approx ma ons of   s m ar

The rule system format has limitations. Notably, it fails to cover the prominent instances of coinduction approximated inductively that occur in the theory of (bi)simulations and (bi)similarity going back to Park and Milner [48,40]—where bisimilarity is first defined coinductively, after which an inductive counterpart is introduced as a technical tool (e.g., for proving logical completeness [24] or domain-theoretic properties [1]). The problem is that the many notions of bisimilarity [40,20,19] cannot be defined via rule systems due to their quantification format. Indeed, the operators underlying rule systems are essentially defined using $\exists\forall$ quantification ("there exists a matching rule such that for all its hypotheses ..."), whereas bisimilarities typically have a $\forall\exists$ format ("for all transitions there exists a matching transition ...").

Furthermore, bisimilarities for systems with names and substitutions, such as late bisimilarity for the π-calculus [41,58], even have a $\forall\exists\forall$ format ("for all input transitions there exists a matching transition such that, for all instantiations of the generic name from the transition..."), as shown in the next example.

Examp   15 We assume an Ac-labeled transition system $\mathcal{L} = (\ \mathsf{a}\ ,\mathsf{Ac}\ ,\Rightarrow)$ with $\Rightarrow\ \subseteq\ \mathsf{a}\ \times\mathsf{Ac}\times\ \mathsf{a}$ such that there is a set N of (channel) names and a renaming operation $\_[\_/\_] : \ \mathsf{a}\ \times\mathsf{N}\ \times\mathsf{N}\ \rightarrow\ \mathsf{a}$. The elements $s \in\ \mathsf{a}$ are called processes, and we think of $s[u/v]$ as the process obtained by the capture-free renaming of u to v. Moreover, we assume a subset $\mathsf{IAc} \subseteq \mathsf{Ac}$ of *input actions*, where each input actions has the form $u(v)$ for $u,v \in \mathsf{N}$. Now, a *(strong) late bisimulation* is a symmetric relation K on a such that, for all

s_1, s_2, if $K\, s_1\, s_2$ then the following holds:

$$(\ \forall\, a, s_1'.\ a \in \mathsf{Ac} \setminus \mathsf{IAc} \ \wedge s_1 \xrightarrow{a} s_1' \ \longrightarrow \ \exists\, s_2'.\, s_2 \xrightarrow{a} s_2' \wedge K\, s_1'\, s_2') \wedge$$
$$(\ \forall\, u, v, s_1'.\ u, v \in \mathsf{N} \ \ \wedge s_1 \xrightarrow{u(v)} s_1' \ \longrightarrow \qquad (*)$$
$$\exists\, s_2'.\, s_2 \xrightarrow{u(v)} s_2' \wedge (\ \forall\, w \in \mathsf{N} \ .K\, (s_1'[w/v])\, (s_2'[w/v]))$$

The *late bisimilarity* is the largest late bisimulation, i.e., greatest fixpoint of the operator F on relations defined as $F\, K\, (s_1, s_2) \longleftrightarrow K\, (s_2, s_1) \wedge (*)$.

6 3   An a rna ng q an fi r forma

As we discuss next, what makes bisimilarity-defining operators ω-cocontinuous, hence bisimilarities inductively approximable, is the finiteness of the space for existential quantification. Obeying this, any quantifier alternation can be allowed.

We model this by the following predicate. Given a set A and a set of sets Π, of whose elements $P \in \Pi$ we think of as sets of parameters, we define the *existentially-finite alternating quantifier format* predicate al r $: ((A \to \mathsf{B} \quad |) \to (A \to \mathsf{B} \quad |)) \to \mathsf{B} \quad |$, (thus, a predicate on operators in $A \to \mathsf{B} \quad |$) inductively:

$$\frac{K' : A \to \mathsf{Bool}}{\mathsf{alter}\,(\lambda K.\, K')}(\mathsf{Const}) \qquad\qquad \frac{f : A \to A}{\mathsf{alter}\,(\lambda K.\, K \circ f)}(\mathsf{Comp})$$

$$\frac{\begin{array}{c} F : P \to (A \to \mathsf{Bool}) \to (A \to \mathsf{Bool}) \qquad T : P \to (A \to \mathsf{Bool}) \\ P \in \Pi \qquad\qquad \forall p \in P.\ \mathsf{alter}\,(F\,p) \end{array}}{\mathsf{alter}\,(\lambda\, K, a.\ \forall p \in P.\ T\,p\,a \to F\,p\,K\,a)}(\mathsf{Forall})$$

$$\frac{\begin{array}{c} F : P \to (A \to \mathsf{Bool}) \to (A \to \mathsf{Bool}) \qquad T : P \to (A \to \mathsf{Bool}) \\ \forall a.\ \mathsf{finite}\,\{p \mid T\,p\,a\} \qquad P \in \Pi \qquad \forall p \in P.\ \mathsf{alter}\,(F\,p) \end{array}}{\mathsf{alter}\,(\lambda\, K, a.\ \exists p \in P.\ T\,p\,a \wedge F\,p\,K\,a)}(\mathsf{Exists})$$

Thus, al r F says that the operator F (on predicates on A) is obtained by starting with operators that either are constant or just compose their argument predicates with a function on A, and applying (in any order) a sequence of universal and existential quantifiers over parameters, relative to predicates T connecting parameters with the elements of A. Highlighted in the case of existential quantification is that this takes place within a finite space, i.e., the relativization predicate T has finite extension.

The inductive rules defining the al r predicate validate (as being in the "alternating quantifier" format) operators on predicates on a given set A; so these operators map predicates in $A \to \mathsf{B} \quad |$ to predicates in $A \to \mathsf{B} \quad |$. Namely, the rules first validate operators that are constant (the (C ns) rule) or just compose their input predicate with a function (the (C) rule). Moreover, the rules (F rall) and (Exis s) validate operators that are obtained from previously validated ones by means of universal or existential quantification over the parameters in some set P, with the additional requirement that existential quantification acts in a finite space. For example, the rule (F rall) says: If, for a given set P of parameters (belonging to the fixed set of sets Π), we have a P-parameterized operator F (i.e., a function F from P to operators on predicates) and a P-parameterized predicate T (i.e., a function T from P to predicates) such that $F\,p$ has already been validated (i.e., al r $(F\,p)$ holds) for all parameters $p \in P$, then we can validate the operator on predicates that takes any predicate K to the universal quantification of $F \_ K$ over P relativized according to T; namely, when applied to any $a \in A$, this returned predicate says that, for all $p \in P$, $T\,p\,a$ implies $F\,p\,K\,a$.

In the inductive definition of al r, we work with a fixed set of sets Π from which we choose our sets of parameters used for quantification (as opposed to considering arbitrary sets of parameters) in order to make sure that al r is well-defined, i.e., does not rely on large collections. In fact, al r depends on A and Π, and we write al $r_{A,\Pi}$ when we want to emphasize this dependency.

Note that al r acts on operators on predicates (and not just on predicates) because this is what we are after: identifying operators on predicates that are, by their quantifier format, guaranteed to be ω-continuous (and thus enable the converging inductive approximation of their greatest fixpoints). And indeed, all the operators validated by al r are guaranteed to be ω-cocontinuous:

Thm 16 If al $r_{A,\Pi}\,F$ holds, then F is ω-cocontinuous; in particular, for any $a \in A$, we have that gf $_F\,a$ if and only if $\forall n \in$ .If $_{F^{\sharp}}\,n\,a$.

This criterion, which generalizes the rule system format, captures the image-finiteness condition for bisimilarity approximations. Moreover, since al r is also closed under conjunction and disjunction (as a particular case of closure under quantification), we can obtain operators satisfying al r by freely combining positive logical operators, as long as the existentials are finite. In particular, the criterion applies to Example 15, since the π-calculus yields an image-finite labeled transition system. (Note that the additional nested universal quantification in Example 15 takes place in an infinite space (since N is usually infinite), but universal quantification is not constrained by the format.) It also generalizes a syntactic criterion implemented in the Dafny program verifier [32] by Leino and Moskal [33]. Their formulation refers to the syntax of predicates definable in Dafny, and involves a syntactic check on a predicate's negation normal form, namely that existential quantification happens over finite types. But their proof (in a technical report cited from [33]) already contains the general apparatus in terms of ω-continuity that we use here.

6   G n r   G S para on Log

We now go back to our starting topic, RG reasoning. The counting-based semantics for RG, which served as our motivating example, is actually a trimmed down version of a semantics for a combination of RG with Separation Logic [62,64,63].

GenRGSep has a process algebra syntax. What is relevant here is that there is a set of actions Ac (ranged over by α) which contains a special silent action τ. Moreover, the states s are pairs (s_1, s_2) where s_1 is the local part of the state s_2 is the part shared with the environment (hence subject to change according

$$\mathsf{safeSep}_{(R,G,Q)}\ 0\ (c, s\ , s\ )\quad \text{(Base)}$$

$$
\begin{aligned}
&1.\ \forall s',\alpha.\ R\ s\ s'\ \longrightarrow\ \mathsf{safeSep}_{(R,G,Q)}\ n\ (c, s\ , s')\\
&2.\ \mathsf{final}\ (c, s\ , s\ )\ \longrightarrow\ Q\ (s\ , s\ )\\
&3.\ \forall c', t\ , s', s', \alpha.\ \alpha \neq \tau \wedge s\ \leq t\ \wedge\\
&\qquad\qquad (c, t\ , s\ ) \overset{\alpha}{\Rightarrow} (c', s', s')\ \longrightarrow\ G\ s\ s'\\
&4.\ (c, s\ , s\ ) \overset{\alpha}{\Rightarrow} (c', s', s')\ \longrightarrow\ \mathsf{safeSep}_{(R,G,Q)}\ n\ (c, s', s')\\
&5.\ ((c, t\ + u\ , s\ ) \overset{\alpha}{\Rightarrow} (c', s', s'))\ \longrightarrow\\
&\qquad (\exists t'.\ t'\ \#\ u\ \wedge s' = t'\ + u\ \wedge (\alpha = \tau\ \longrightarrow\ t' = t\ ) \wedge\\
&\qquad\quad \mathsf{safeSep}_{(R,G,Q)}\ n\ (c, t', s'))
\end{aligned}
$$

$$\rule{10cm}{0.4pt}\ \text{(Step)}$$

$$\mathsf{safeSep}_{(R,G,Q)}\ (n+1)\ (c, s\ , s\ )$$

Fig. 10: The inductive counting-based predicate saf . Its coinductive counterpart saf C is obtained (like before) by removing the items highlighted and interpreting the (Step) rule coinductively.

to the rely relation R). Differently from RG, the execution steps in GenRGSep are labelled by actions, so they have the form $(c, s_1, s_2) \overset{\alpha}{\Rightarrow} (c', s_1', s_2')$. Moreover, local states form *permission algebras* [11], where $+$ denotes the partial semi-group operator and $\#$ denotes the definedness predicate for this operator. We think of $s\ \#\ t$ as saying that s and t are non-overlapping (or consistently overlapping) and of $s + t$ as putting together two such non-overlapping components.

The formulation of safety for GenRGSep, predicate saf , is shown in Fig. 10. The base case and the inductive hypotheses for the post- and rely-conditions (hypotheses 1 and 2) are essentially the same as those for the RG predicate saf (Fig. 3), but factoring in the distinction between the local and environment-exposed parts of the state. On the other hand, the hypotheses involving steps taken by the command (hypotheses 3–5) are more complex, quantifying universally over extensions of the local state ($s_1 \leq t_2$ in hypothesis 4) and existentially over non-overlapping partitions of the local state ($t_1'\ \#\ u_1$ in the frame-safety hypothesis 5). Details on the rationale for these are provided in [27].

Because hypothesis 5 introduces nested existential quantification (over the component t_1'), this case does not fall under the rule-system format (Thm. 14). However, since all quantification (including the nested one) takes place in a finite space, Thm. 16 applies and produces a coinductive semantics based on a coinductive counterpart saf C of saf , which is provably equivalent to the inductive semantics—via corresponding versions of Lemma 3 and Thm. 2:

L mma 17 We have that $\forall n \in\ .\ \mathsf{saf}\quad {}_{(R,G,Q)} n\ (c, s_1, s_2)$ holds if and only if saf $\mathsf{C}_{(R,G,Q)}(c, s_1, s_2)$ holds.

Thus, considering the inductive and coinductive satisfaction relations for GenRGSep, $\vDash_{\mathsf{Sep,VP}} (P, R, G, Q)$ and $c \vDash_{\mathsf{Sep,C}}$, defined from saf and saf C just like for RG, we obtain:

Thm 18 We have that $c \vDash_{\mathsf{Sep,VP}} (P, R, G, Q)$ if and only if $c \vDash_{\mathsf{Sep,C}} (P, R, G, Q)$.

S mmar Below is the hierarchy of the results we discussed pertaining to coinduction approximated inductively, with arrows representing instantiation. ω-cocontinuity is at the top, followed by the existentially-finite alternating quantifier format. The latter is an essential bridge in this hierarchy, because (1) it is an effective criterion, (2) it unifies rule systems and (bi)similarities, and (3) it accommodates systems with nested quantification such as GenRGSep.

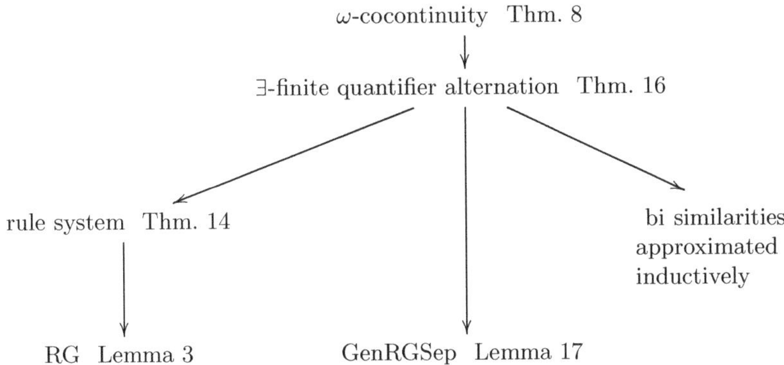

7   Conclusions and Related Work

Isa   -s ppor   xp ora ons The starting point of this work was the goal of formalizing in Isabelle different semantics for Rely-Guarantee and proving them equivalent. The coinductive semantics came from the realization that safety w.r.t. any number of steps in the counting-based semantics is an instance of Kleene-style convergence. Isabelle was instrumental in our proof-mining-like explorations of this realization, which we have described in §5. The Isabelle scripts formalizing this paper's results are provided as supplementary material [14], and details on the formalization are included in our extended technical report [15].

Forma s man s for   -G aran Nieto [46] formalized the trace-based semantics in Isabelle; Coleman and Jones [12] developed the reachability based semantics informally, and listed the comparison with Nieto's formal semantics as future work. Vafeiadis and Parkinson [62,64,63] informally, then Jackson et al. formally in Isabelle [27] developed the counting-based semantics for Separation Logic extensions. In particular, Vafeiadis's account from [63], including the more direct soundness proof, was the explicit inspiration for the Jackson et al. paper. We seem to be the first to provide a coinductive semantics of RG, and also to prove the equivalence between previous semantics.

We mostly focused on a simple while language and the basic RG logic, but the coinductive transformation we applied to RG also fits richer languages and logics, as we have illustrated with GenRGSep. Moreover, we focused on Hoare-style RG definitions, rather than algebraic or refinement approaches, which also have a rich literature [6,7,22]. Several RG semantics variations are

244   J. Derrick et al.

reviewed by Van Staden [59] who, taking a trace-based view, classifies them based on whether the guarantee and rely conditions are decoupled.

Co n ng-fr n v an o n v a o n s of Hoar og s man s The idea of defining the partial correctness semantics coinductively has been explored by Wickerson [66,67] in the context of Hoare logic. He proves that a counting-free coinductive semantics for the partial correctness of Hoare triples is equivalent to the standard one. He also proves that the same counting-free definition, but interpreted *inductively* rather than coinductively, yields exactly *total* correctness. His approach to total correctness seems extendable from Hoare logic to Rely-Guarantee. It would be interesting to study how well this compares with the indexed semantics on rule soundness proofs.

s s ms an forma s Aczel introduced rule systems in his study of inductive definitions [2], considering coinductive definitions only briefly via duality with induction. He singled out deterministic rule systems (where each item can be the conclusion of at most one rule), because these enable defining the least fixpoint by (possibly transfinite) well-founded recursion; deterministic systems are particular cases of backwards-finite rule systems, so they would also ensure ω-cocontinuity. Aczel, and previously Moschovakis [43], were interested in abstract inductive definitions for studying recursively enumerable sets and Gödel encodings. In their theory, inductive predicates specified by positive logic formats play a central role—our alternating quantifier format (generalizing the one implemented in Dafny) is a refinement of the positive logic format. While, in process algebra, formats for operational semantics rules ensuring desirable properties of (bi)similarity have been studied extensively [44], we seem to be the first to look at the formats of the (bi)similarity definitions themselves.

Co n on approx ma n v Approximating coinduction by induction is useful for implementing coinduction in theorem provers that initially only support induction. We already mentioned Danfy's coinduction, certified by the Leino-Moskal syntactic criterion. More recently, Mastorou et al. [38] implemented coinduction in Liquid Haskell [65], also relying on inductive approximations. So far their examples do not involve existential quantification, but in general ensuring the relevance of inductive reasoning for the coinductive counterparts will seem to require a criterion similar to Dafny's. Alternatively, if a prover supports transfinite recursion (as is already partially the case with Dafny [34]), then any coinductive predicate can be approximated inductively (without restriction), via a generalization of Kleene's theorem [15, App. C].

While we focused on (co)inductive predicates, similar phenomena occur with datatypes versus codatatypes and recursion versus corecursion. Barr showed that a codatatype can be regarded as a Cauchy completion of a datatype [8,9], and this enables defining functions on codatatypes as convergent approximations of recursive definitions. Matthews [39], and Di Gianantonio and Miculan [18] have built definitional frameworks around these ideas using order-theoretic approximation structures, implemented in Isabelle and Coq respectively.

Usually in the literature (e.g., process algebra bisimilarities, and the aforementioned implementations of coinduction in verifiers) one starts with the goal of capturing coinductive definitions, and then thinks of how to represent / approximate these inductively. By contrast, here we started with a well-established definition of Rely-Guarantee semantics based on step-indexing, and argued for its "coinductivization". This approach can be applied more generally to step-indexed logical relations [4,3,35], where the numeric index counts the number of steps for which a certain desirable property (such as typing, or in our case RG contract compliance) is guaranteed not to be falsified. Indeed, Nakano's "later" modality [45] used in reasoning with step-based logical relations [16,5] corresponds to our approximating operators $F^\sharp$, and Löb's rule [10] for this modality corresponds to inductive reasoning over approximations; and the approximations are here coinductively sound thanks to the finite branching (and in fact often the determinism) of the transition relation. It would be interesting to explore the connection between Löb's rule and coinduction up-to along the lines of our discussion in §5.2. However, such a coinductive abstraction for step-indexed logical relations would fail as soon as the indexing involves not only numbers (of execution steps) but also other "world" data such as resources *that are mutually dependent* with these numbers—as is the case, for example, when reasoning in higher-order separation logic frameworks such as Iris [30,61].

(Co) n v nhan m n s Notwithstanding the prominently up-to feature of the whil construct, the literature on verification based on coinduction up-to did not seem to handle while programs directly like we do, although imperative features were shown to be in the scope of the technique (e.g., [37]).

Our established connection between up-to enhancements of coinduction and corresponding index-wise enhancements of the greatest fixpoint's inductive approximations recommends approximation-preserving operators as a potentially interesting class of operators that are sound for coinduction up-to, which are both compositional and extremely lightweight. In future work, we will study their interaction with parameterized coinduction [25] and second-order reasoning [52] when restricted to ω-cocontinuous operators. Sangiorgi [57] considered a different type of inductive-coinductive connection, adapting up-to techniques to behavioral relations, where coinduction becomes structural induction over the observation contexts. A similar connection has been studied by Goguen and Malcolm in the context of hidden algebra [21].

A know gm n We thank the three anonymous reviewers for their careful reading of the paper and for their insightful comments and suggestions, which helped identify a number of technical typos at key points and improve the overall presentation. Due to space limitations, some suggestions (notably a deeper exploration of the Hoare logic fragment) could not be developed in full; we plan to do so in an extended version to be submitted to a journal. We also thank Rob van Glabbeek for pointing us to his survey papers that systematise the variety of bisimilarity relations used in process algebra. This work was supported by the EPSRC grant EP/X015114/1, "Safe and secure COncurrent programming for adVancEd aRchiTectures (COVERT)". The authors are listed alphabetically, regardless of individual contributions or seniority.

References

1. Abramsky, S. A domain equation for bisimulation. Inf. Comput. 92 2 , 161–218 1991 , https://doi.org/10.1006/inco.1991.9999
2. Aczel, P. An introduction to inductive definitions. In Barwise, J. ed. Handbook of Mathematical Logic, Studies in Logic and the Foundations of Mathematics, vol. 90, pp. 739–782. Elsevier 1977 , https://www.sciencedirect.com/science/article/pii/S0049237X08711200
3. Ahmed, A. Step-indexed syntactic logical relations for recursive and quantified types. In European Symposium on Programming ESOP . Lecture Notes in Computer Science, vol. 3924, pp. 69–83. Springer 2006 , https://doi.org/10.1007/11693024_6
4. Appel, A.W., McAllester, D.A. An indexed model of recursive types for foundational proof-carrying code. ACM Trans. Program. Lang. Syst. 23 5 , 657–683 2001 , https://doi.org/10.1145/504709.504712
5. Appel, A.W., Melliès, P., Richards, C.D., Vouillon, J. A very modal model of a modern, major, general type system. In Hofmann, M., Felleisen, M. eds. Proceedings of the 34th ACM SIGPLAN-SIGACT Symposium on Principles of Programming Languages, POPL 2007, Nice, France, January 17-19, 2007. pp. 109–122. ACM 2007 , https://doi.org/10.1145/1190216.1190235
6. Armstrong, A., Gomes, V.B.F., Struth, G. Algebraic principles for rely-guarantee style concurrency verification tools. In Jones, C., Pihlajasaari, P., Sun, J. eds. FM 2014 Formal Methods. pp. 78–93. Springer International Publishing, Cham 2014
7. Armstrong, A., Gomes, V.B.F., Struth, G. Algebras for program correctness in isabelle/hol. In Höfner, P., Jipsen, P., Kahl, W., Müller, M.E. eds. Relational and Algebraic Methods in Computer Science - 14th International Conference, RAMiCS 2014, Marienstatt, Germany, April 28-May 1, 2014. Proceedings. Lecture Notes in Computer Science, vol. 8428, pp. 49–64. Springer 2014 , https://doi.org/10.1007/978-3-319-06251-8_4
8. Barr, M. Terminal coalgebras in well-founded set theory. Theor. Comput. Sci. 114 2 , 299–315 1993 , https://doi.org/10.1016/0304-3975(93)90076-6
9. Barr, M. Additions and corrections to "terminal coalgebras in well-founded set theory". Theor. Comput. Sci. 124 1 , 189–192 1994 , https://doi.org/10.1016/0304-3975(94)90060-4
10. Boolos, G.S. The Logic of Provability. Cambridge University Press, Cambridge and New York 1993 , https //www.cambridge.org/core/books/logic-of-provability/F1549530F91505462083CE2FEB6444AA
11. Calcagno, C., O'Hearn, P.W., Yang, H. Local action and abstract separation logic. In 22nd IEEE Symposium on Logic in Computer Science LICS 2007 , 10-12 July 2007, Wroclaw, Poland, Proceedings. pp. 366–378. IEEE Computer Society 2007 , https://doi.org/10.1109/LICS.2007.30
12. Coleman, J.W., Jones, C.B. A structural proof of the soundness of rely/guarantee rules. J. Log. Comput. 17 4 , 807–841 2007 , https://doi.org/10.1093/logcom/exm030
13. Cousot, P., Cousot, R. Constructive versions of Tarski's fixed point theorems. Pacific Journal of Mathematics 82 1 , 43 – 57 1979
14. Derrick, J., Edmonds, C., Popescu, A., Wright, J. Formal Isabelle development associated with this paper. https://zenodo.org/records/18319366 2026

15. Derrick, J., Edmonds, C., Popescu, A., Wright, J. Rely-Guarantee Is Coinductive A Proof-Centered Investigation of Inductively Approximated Coinduction. Extended Technical Report. `https://www.andreipopescu.uk/TechReports/ESOP2026/TR_RelyGuarantee_is_Coinductive.pdf` 2026
16. Dreyer, D., Ahmed, A., Birkedal, L. Logical step-indexed logical relations. Log. Methods Comput. Sci. 7 2 2011 , `https://doi.org/10.2168/LMCS-7(2:16)2011`
17. Gavran, I., Niksic, F., Kanade, A., Majumdar, R., Vafeiadis, V. Rely/guarantee reasoning for asynchronous programs. In Aceto, L., de Frutos-Escrig, D. eds. 26th International Conference on Concurrency Theory, CONCUR 2015, Madrid, Spain, September 1.4, 2015. LIPIcs, vol. 42, pp. 483–496. Schloss Dagstuhl - Leibniz-Zentrum für Informatik 2015 , `https://doi.org/10.4230/LIPIcs.CONCUR.2015.483`
18. Gianantonio, P.D., Miculan, M. A unifying approach to recursive and co-recursive definitions. In Geuvers, H., Wiedijk, F. eds. Types for Proofs and Programs, Second International Workshop, TYPES 2002, Berg en Dal, The Netherlands, April 24-28, 2002, Selected Papers. Lecture Notes in Computer Science, vol. 2646, pp. 148–161. Springer 2002 , `https://doi.org/10.1007/3-540-39185-1_9`
19. van Glabbeek, R.J. The linear time - branching time spectrum II. In Best, E. ed. CONCUR '93, 4th International Conference on Concurrency Theory, Hildesheim, Germany, August 23-26, 1993, Proceedings. Lecture Notes in Computer Science, vol. 715, pp. 66–81. Springer 1993 , `https://doi.org/10.1007/3-540-57208-2_6`
20. van Glabbeek, R.J. The linear time - branching time spectrum I. In Bergstra, J.A., Ponse, A., Smolka, S.A. eds. Handbook of Process Algebra, pp. 3–99. North-Holland / Elsevier 2001 , `https://doi.org/10.1016/b978-044482830-9/50019-9`
21. Goguen, J.A., Malcolm, G. Hidden coinduction behavioural correctness proofs for objects. Math. Struct. Comput. Sci. 9 3 , 287–319 1999 , `http://journals.cambridge.org/action/displayAbstract?aid=44821`
22. Hayes, I.J. Generalised rely-guarantee concurrency an algebraic foundation. Form. Asp. Comput. 28 6 , 1057–1078 Nov 2016 , `https://doi.org/10.1007/s00165-016-0384-0`
23. Hayes, I.J., Jones, C.B. A guide to rely/guarantee thinking. In Bowen, J.P., Liu, Z., Zhang, Z. eds. Engineering Trustworthy Software Systems - Third International School, SETSS 2017, Chongqing, China, April 17-22, 2017, Tutorial Lectures. Lecture Notes in Computer Science, vol. 11174, pp. 1–38. Springer 2017 , `https://doi.org/10.1007/978-3-030-02928-9_1`
24. Hennessy, M., Milner, R. Algebraic laws for nondeterminism and concurrency. J. ACM 32 1 , 137–161 1985 , `https://doi.org/10.1145/2455.2460`
25. Hur, C., Neis, G., Dreyer, D., Vafeiadis, V. The power of parameterization in coinductive proof. In Giacobazzi, R., Cousot, R. eds. The 40th Annual ACM SIGPLAN-SIGACT Symposium on Principles of Programming Languages, POPL '13, Rome, Italy - January 23 - 25, 2013. pp. 193–206. ACM 2013 , `https://doi.org/10.1145/2429069.2429093`
26. Ishtiaq, S.S., O'Hearn, P.W. BI as an assertion language for mutable data structures. In Hankin, C., Schmidt, D. eds. Conference Record of POPL 2001 The 28th ACM SIGPLAN-SIGACT Symposium on Principles of Programming Languages, London, UK, January 17-19, 2001. pp. 14–26. ACM 2001 , `https://doi.org/10.1145/360204.375719`
27. Jackson, V., Murray, T., Rizkallah, C. A generalised union of rely-guarantee and separation logic using permission algebras. In Bertot, Y., Kutsia, T., Norrish, M.

eds. 15th International Conference on Interactive Theorem Proving, ITP 2024, September 9-14, 2024, Tbilisi, Georgia. LIPIcs, vol. 309, pp. 23 1–23 16. Schloss Dagstuhl - Leibniz-Zentrum für Informatik 2024 , `https://doi.org/10.4230/LIPIcs.ITP.2024.23`

28. Jones, C.B. Development Methods for Computer Programs including a Notion of Interference. Ph.D. thesis, Oxford University Jun 1981 , `http://www.cs.ox.ac.uk/files/9025/PRG-25.pdf`, printed as Programming Research Group, Technical Monograph 25

29. Jones, C.B. Specification and design of parallel programs. In Mason, R.E.A. ed. Information Processing 83, Proceedings of the IFIP 9th World Computer Congress, Paris, France, September 19-23, 1983. pp. 321–332. North-Holland/IFIP 1983

30. Jung, R., Swasey, D., Sieczkowski, F., Svendsen, K., Turon, A., Birkedal, L., Dreyer, D. Iris Monoids and invariants as an orthogonal basis for concurrent reasoning. In Rajamani, S.K., Walker, D. eds. Proceedings of the 42nd Annual ACM SIGPLAN-SIGACT Symposium on Principles of Programming Languages, POPL 2015, Mumbai, India, January 15-17, 2015. pp. 637–650. ACM 2015 , `https://doi.org/10.1145/2676726.2676980`

31. Kozen, D., Silva, A. Practical coinduction. Math. Struct. Comput. Sci. 27 7 , 1132–1152 2017 , `https://doi.org/10.1017/S0960129515000493`

32. Leino, K.R.M. Dafny An automatic program verifier for functional correctness. In Clarke, E.M., Voronkov, A. eds. Logic for Programming, Artificial Intelligence, and Reasoning - 16th International Conference, LPAR-16, Dakar, Senegal, April 25-May 1, 2010, Revised Selected Papers. Lecture Notes in Computer Science, vol. 6355, pp. 348–370. Springer 2010 , `https://doi.org/10.1007/978-3-642-17511-4_20`

33. Leino, K.R.M., Moskal, M. Co-induction simply - automatic co-inductive proofs in a program verifier. In Jones, C.B., Pihlajasaari, P., Sun, J. eds. FM 2014 Formal Methods - 19th International Symposium, Singapore, May 12-16, 2014. Proceedings. Lecture Notes in Computer Science, vol. 8442, pp. 382–398. Springer 2014 , `https://doi.org/10.1007/978-3-319-06410-9_27`

34. Leino, K.R.M., Tristan, J.B. Dafny power user Working with coinduction, extreme predicates, and ordinals 2023 , technical report. `https://leino.science/papers/krml285.html`

35. Leroy, X. Step carefully Step-indexing techniques. Lecture Notes, Collège de France Jan 2019 , `https://xavierleroy.org/CdF/2018-2019/8.pdf`

36. Leroy, X., Grall, H. Coinductive big-step operational semantics. Inf. Comput. 207 2 , 284–304 2009 , `https://doi.org/10.1016/j.ic.2007.12.004`

37. Madiot, J., Pous, D., Sangiorgi, D. Modular coinduction up-to for higher-order languages via first-order transition systems. Log. Methods Comput. Sci. 17 3 2021 , `https://doi.org/10.46298/lmcs-17(3:25)2021`

38. Mastorou, L., Papaspyrou, N., Vazou, N. Coinduction inductively mechanizing coinductive proofs in liquid haskell. In Polikarpova, N. ed. Haskell '22 15th ACM SIGPLAN International Haskell Symposium, Ljubljana, Slovenia, September 15 - 16, 2022. pp. 1–12. ACM 2022 , `https://doi.org/10.1145/3546189.3549922`

39. Matthews, J. Recursive function definition over coinductive types. In Bertot, Y., Dowek, G., Hirschowitz, A., Paulin-Mohring, C., Théry, L. eds. Theorem Proving in Higher Order Logics, 12th International Conference, TPHOLs'99, Nice, France, September, 1999, Proceedings. Lecture Notes in Computer Science, vol. 1690, pp. 73–90. Springer 1999 , `https://doi.org/10.1007/3-540-48256-3_6`

40. Milner, R. Communication and concurrency. Prentice Hall 1989
41. Milner, R., Parrow, J., Walker, D. A calculus of mobile processes, II. Inf. Comput. 100 1 , 41–77 1992 , https://doi.org/10.1016/0890-5401(92)90009-5
42. Momigliano, A., Pientka, B., Thibodeau, D. A case study in programming coinductive proofs Howe's method. Math. Struct. Comput. Sci. 29 8 , 1309–1343 2019 , https://doi.org/10.1017/S0960129518000415
43. Moschovakis, Y.N. Elementary induction on abstract structures Studies in logic and the foundations of mathematics . American Elsevier Pub. Co 1974
44. Mousavi, M.R., Reniers, M.A., Groote, J.F. SOS formats and meta-theory 20 years after. Theor. Comput. Sci. 373 3 , 238–272 2007 , https://doi.org/10.1016/j.tcs.2006.12.019
45. Nakano, H. A modality for recursion. In 15th Annual IEEE Symposium on Logic in Computer Science, Santa Barbara, California, USA, June 26-29, 2000. pp. 255–266. IEEE Computer Society 2000 , https://doi.org/10.1109/LICS.2000.855774
46. Nieto, L.P. The Rely-Guarantee method in Isabelle/HOL. In Degano, P. ed. Programming Languages and Systems, 12th European Symposium on Programming, ESOP 2003, Held as Part of the Joint European Conferences on Theory and Practice of Software, ETAPS 2003, Warsaw, Poland, April 7-11, 2003, Proceedings. Lecture Notes in Computer Science, vol. 2618, pp. 348–362. Springer 2003 , https://doi.org/10.1007/3-540-36575-3_24
47. O'Hearn, P.W., Reynolds, J.C., Yang, H. Local reasoning about programs that alter data structures. In Fribourg, L. ed. Computer Science Logic, 15th International Workshop, CSL 2001. 10th Annual Conference of the EACSL, Paris, France, September 10-13, 2001, Proceedings. Lecture Notes in Computer Science, vol. 2142, pp. 1–19. Springer 2001 , https://doi.org/10.1007/3-540-44802-0_1
48. Park, D.M.R. Concurrency and automata on infinite sequences. In Deussen, P. ed. Theoretical Computer Science, 5th GI-Conference, Karlsruhe, Germany, March 23-25, 1981, Proceedings. Lecture Notes in Computer Science, vol. 104, pp. 167–183. Springer 1981 , https://doi.org/10.1007/BFb0017309
49. Paulson, L.C. A fixedpoint approach to implementing co inductive definitions. In Bundy, A. ed. Automated Deduction - CADE-12, 12th International Conference on Automated Deduction, Nancy, France, June 26 - July 1, 1994, Proceedings. Lecture Notes in Computer Science, vol. 814, pp. 148–161. Springer 1994 , https://doi.org/10.1007/3-540-58156-1_11
50. Pierce, B.C. Types and Programming Languages. MIT Press 2002
51. Pous, D. Complete lattices and up-to techniques. In Shao, Z. ed. Programming Languages and Systems, 5th Asian Symposium, APLAS 2007, Singapore, November 29-December 1, 2007, Proceedings. Lecture Notes in Computer Science, vol. 4807, pp. 351–366. Springer 2007 , https://doi.org/10.1007/978-3-540-76637-7_24
52. Pous, D. Coinduction all the way up. In Grohe, M., Koskinen, E., Shankar, N. eds. Proceedings of the 31st Annual ACM/IEEE Symposium on Logic in Computer Science, LICS '16, New York, NY, USA, July 5-8, 2016. pp. 307–316. ACM 2016 , https://doi.org/10.1145/2933575.2934564
53. Pous, D. Coinduction Automata, formal proof, companions invited paper . In Roggenbach, M., Sokolova, A. eds. 8th Conference on Algebra and Coalgebra in Computer Science, CALCO 2019, June 3-6, 2019, London, United Kingdom. LIPIcs, vol. 139, pp. 4 1–4 4. Schloss Dagstuhl - Leibniz-Zentrum für Informatik 2019 , https://doi.org/10.4230/LIPIcs.CALCO.2019.4

54. Reynolds, J.C. Separation logic A logic for shared mutable data structures. In 17th IEEE Symposium on Logic in Computer Science LICS 2002 , 22-25 July 2002, Copenhagen, Denmark, Proceedings. pp. 55–74. IEEE Computer Society 2002 , https://doi.org/10.1109/LICS.2002.1029817
55. Rutten, J.J.M.M. Universal coalgebra a theory of systems. Theor. Comput. Sci. 249 1 , 3–80 2000 , https://doi.org/10.1016/S0304-3975(00)00056-6
56. Sangiorgi, D. On the proof method for bisimulation extended abstract . In Wiedermann, J., Hájek, P. eds. Mathematical Foundations of Computer Science 1995, 20th International Symposium, MFCS'95, Prague, Czech Republic, August 28 - September 1, 1995, Proceedings. Lecture Notes in Computer Science, vol. 969, pp. 479–488. Springer 1995 , https://doi.org/10.1007/3-540-60246-1_153
57. Sangiorgi, D. An abstract account of up-to techniques for inductive behavioural relations. In Margaria, T., Steffen, B. eds. Leveraging Applications of Formal Methods, Verification and Validation. REoCAS Colloquium in Honor of Rocco De Nicola - 12th International Symposium, ISoLA 2024, Crete, Greece, October 27-31, 2024, Proceedings, Part I. Lecture Notes in Computer Science, vol. 15219, pp. 62–74. Springer 2024 , https://doi.org/10.1007/978-3-031-73709-1_5
58. Sangiorgi, D., Walker, D. The Pi-Calculus - a theory of mobile processes. Cambridge University Press 2001
59. van Staden, S. On rely-guarantee reasoning. In Hinze, R., Voigtländer, J. eds. Mathematics of Program Construction - 12th International Conference, MPC 2015, Königswinter, Germany, June 29 - July 1, 2015. Proceedings. Lecture Notes in Computer Science, vol. 9129, pp. 30–49. Springer 2015 , https://doi.org/10.1007/978-3-319-19797-5_2
60. Tarski, A. A lattice-theoretical fixpoint theorem and its applications. Pacific Journal of Mathematics 5, 285–309 1955 , https://api.semanticscholar.org/CorpusID:13651629
61. Timany, A., Krebbers, R., Dreyer, D., Birkedal, L. A logical approach to type soundness. J. ACM 71 6 , 40 1–40 75 2024 , https://doi.org/10.1145/3676954
62. Vafeiadis, V. Modular fine-grained concurrency verification. Tech. Rep. UCAM-CL-TR-726, University of Cambridge, Computer Laboratory Jul 2008 , https://www.cl.cam.ac.uk/techreports/UCAM-CL-TR-726.pdf
63. Vafeiadis, V. Concurrent separation logic and operational semantics. In Mislove, M.W., Ouaknine, J. eds. Twenty-seventh Conference on the Mathematical Foundations of Programming Semantics, MFPS 2011, Pittsburgh, PA, USA, May 25-28, 2011. Electronic Notes in Theoretical Computer Science, vol. 276, pp. 335–351. Elsevier 2011 , https://doi.org/10.1016/j.entcs.2011.09.029
64. Vafeiadis, V., Parkinson, M.J. A marriage of rely/guarantee and separation logic. In Caires, L., Vasconcelos, V.T. eds. CONCUR 2007 - Concurrency Theory, 18th International Conference, CONCUR 2007, Lisbon, Portugal, September 3-8, 2007, Proceedings. Lecture Notes in Computer Science, vol. 4703, pp. 256–271. Springer 2007 , https://doi.org/10.1007/978-3-540-74407-8_18
65. Vazou, N., Seidel, E., Vytiniotis, D., Peyton Jones, S., Jhala, R. Liquid types. In Proceedings of the 41st ACM SIGPLAN-SIGACT Symposium on Principles of Programming Languages. pp. 159–170. ACM 2014
66. Wickerson, J. Partial and total correctness as greatest and least fixed points. https://johnwickerson.github.io/papers/Partial_Total_Correctness_As_Fixed_Points.pdf 2009 , Unpublished technical note.
67. Wickerson, J. Partial and total correctness as greatest and least fixed points. https://johnwickerson.wordpress.com/2009/11/25/partialtotal/ 2009 , Blog post.

68. Xia, L., Zakowski, Y., He, P., Hur, C., Malecha, G., Pierce, B.C., Zdancewic, S.
Interaction trees representing recursive and impure programs in coq. Proc. ACM
Program. Lang. 4 POPL , 51 1–51 32 2020 , https://doi.org/10.1145/3371119
69. Xu, Q., de Roever, W.P., He, J. The rely-guarantee method for verifying shared
variable concurrent programs. Formal Aspects Comput. 9 2 , 149–174 1997 ,
https://doi.org/10.1007/BF01211617

Reduction for Structured Concurrent Programs

Namratha Gangamreddypalli[1], Constantin Enea[1], and Shaz Qadeer[2]

[1] LIX, Ecole Polytechnique, CNRS and Institut Polytechnique de Paris, France
{namratha, cenea}@lix.polytechnique.fr
[2] Microsoft

Abstract. Commutativity reasoning based on Lipton's movers is a powerful technique for verification of concurrent programs. The idea is to define a program transformation that preserves a subset of the initial set of interleavings, which is sound modulo reorderings of commutative actions. Scaling commutativity reasoning to routinely-used features in software systems, such as procedures and parallel composition, remains a significant challenge.

In this work, we introduce a novel reduction technique for structured concurrent programs that unifies two key advances. First, we present a reduction strategy that soundly replaces parallel composition with sequential composition. Second, we generalize Lipton's reduction to support atomic sections containing (potentially recursive) procedure calls. Crucially, these two foundational strategies can be composed arbitrarily, greatly expanding the scope and flexibility of reduction-based reasoning. We implemented this technique in Civl and demonstrated its effectiveness on a number of challenging case studies, including a snapshot object, a fault-tolerant and linearizable register, the FLASH cache coherence protocol, and a non-trivial variant of Two-Phase Commit.

1   Introduction

Commutativity reasoning is a powerful technique for verification of concurrent programs. This method derives from the observation that certain pairs of concurrently-executing statements can be reordered without affecting program behavior, i.e., such statements commute. Interleavings (i.e., concurrent execution sequences) that differ only in the ordering of commuting statements are considered equivalent. As a result, it is sufficient to verify the correctness of a single representative interleaving from each equivalence class. These techniques are also called *reduction* techniques because they reduce reasoning to a smaller set of representative interleavings.

In static verification of concurrent programs, a standard method to exploit commutativity reasoning is to capture the reduced program via a syntactic transformation of the original program. The proof of correctness is then done on the transformed program and the reduction argument is used to carry over the results of the verification to the original program. Lipton [35] introduced atomic sections as a simple method to capture such a transformation. Since then, atomic

R. Krebbers (Ed.): ESOP 2026, LNCS 16501, pp. 252–282, 2026.
https://doi.org/10.1007/978-3-032-22720-1_10

sections have been used extensively to specify non-interference in and simplify reasoning about concurrent programs [19,17,11,23,15].

In this paper, we focus on the application of commutativity reasoning towards deductive verification of concurrent programs. Applying commutativity reasoning to real-world programs is challenging. Software systems routinely use procedures for code structuring and scaling software engineering. Concurrent systems, in addition, are performance oriented and often launch multiple tasks in parallel, collecting results as the tasks complete. These features, procedures and dynamic concurrency, are not adequately addressed by existing approaches. Lipton [35] only addresses the problem of concurrent programs with bounded threads and atomic sections of bounded size. QED [11] and Civl [23] handle atomic sections containing loops, but do not handle procedure calls (unless they are inlined beforehand) or parallel composition. Kragl et al. [30] present a program transformation that synchronizes asynchronous procedure calls by demonstrating that the called procedure can be summarized as a single atomic action that commutes to the left of any other program action (a so-called left mover). While asynchronous calls can be viewed as a restricted form of parallel composition, this model is not general enough for our purposes (see Section 9).

We introduce a novel reduction technique for structured concurrent programs that unifies two key advances. First, we present a reduction strategy that soundly replaces parallel composition with sequential composition, addressing a dimension orthogonal to atomic section introduction explored in prior work. Second, we generalize Lipton's reduction to support atomic sections containing (potentially recursive) procedure calls. Crucially, these two foundational strategies can be composed arbitrarily, greatly expanding the scope and flexibility of reduction-based reasoning.

Our reduction technique is based on a concept of *movers* or commuting statements [35,11,23]. The soundness of atomic section introduction relies on demonstrating that it consists of a sequence of *right* movers, followed by an arbitrary statement, and then a sequence of *left* movers. Right movers are statements that commute to the right of any other statement in the program, while left movers commute to the left; this terminology imagines time flowing from left to right. Importantly, mover classification is relative to the set of actions under consideration: whether a statement is a right or left mover depends on how it interacts with the other actions in the program. This straightforward intuition for movers is deceptive; precise definitions are non-trivial since they must account for statements that may fail or are non-deterministic.

To handle structured code, we extend the notion of movers to procedures through a type system [19] that analyzes their bodies. This enables the sound introduction of atomic sections that may include recursive procedure calls (as before, soundness relies on ensuring a well-structured sequencing of right and left movers). For example, if the body of a procedure Q consists solely of right mover statements–including nested procedure calls, which are recursively typed–then Q is classified as a right mover procedure. An analogous classification applies to left mover procedures, with the additional requirement that they must terminate when executed in isolation. This termination condition ensures the preservation of failure behaviors: a non-terminating procedure could otherwise unsoundly eliminate potential failures. Notably, although we are reasoning about concurrency, this condition relies solely on the behavior of the procedure when executed in isolation, a surprising and useful aspect of our framework.

The second key contribution of our technique is the ability to soundly transform a parallel construct, where an arbitrary number of threads are spawned and joined immediately afterward, into a sequential composition of their respective code blocks. This transformation again builds on the notion of movers and is achieved through an iterative process that sequences left-mover code blocks first and right-mover code blocks last.

The two contributions of our technique are integrated within a unified framework that supports arbitrary sequential and parallel composition of procedures. Furthermore, the two contributions work in tandem: transforming parallel constructs may yield left or right mover procedures which may further enable the introduction of atomic sections. Our technique is formalized in a core programming language, where the two reduction principles are invoked via specific keywords, and a type system guarantees their correct and sound composition. We note that our notion of movers is more general than that used in Civl; that is, certain statements commute under our definition but not under Civl's. Moreover, our work provides the first formal proof of the soundness of Civl's reduction theory. This proof played a key role in identifying the most general form of commutativity sufficient to ensure soundness (Section 4).

The soundness of this reduction framework is based on non-trivial arguments. For instance, reductions are defined at code level, which means that even a single reduction can apply an unbounded number of times in an execution (where the same procedure is called multiple times). This requires defining a non-trivial strategy for reordering steps in an execution wrt their commutativity properties. Also, the side conditions for using left or right movers are asymmetric, which may seem counterintuitive. For instance, in parallel reduction, right movers are not allowed to fail, and left mover procedures, when run without interference, are required to terminate—the latter is notable because it concerns sequential executions, even though it is applied to concurrent programs. Furthermore, the restriction that right movers must be non-failing applies only to parallel reduction and not to sequential reduction.

We have implemented our technique as an extension to Civl, preserving compatibility with its existing features. To assess its effectiveness, we applied our implementation to a series of challenging case studies: a parallel implementation of a snapshot object [3], the ABD register [4] which simulates shared memory over message passing, the FLASH cache coherence protocol [32], and a non-trivial variant of the Two-Phase Commit protocol. These examples span diverse domains, including concurrent objects, distributed protocols, and hardware cache coherence, demonstrating the broad applicability of our approach. In particular, the first two case studies are concurrent objects for which we prove that they are linearizable [24]. Proving linearizability for these objects is known to be chal-

```
procedure scan() returns (snapshot: [int]StampVal) {
  var r1: [int]StampVal;
  var r2: [int]StampVal;
  while (true) {
    (call r1[1] := read(1)) par
    (call r1[2] := read(2));
    (call r2[1] := read(1)) par
    (call r2[2] := read(2));
    if (r1 == r2) {
      snapshot := r1;
      return;
    }
  }
}
```

```
datatype StampVal {
  StampVal(ts: int, value: Value)
}

var mem: [int]StampVal;

action read (i: int) returns (v:
    StampVal) {
  v := mem[i];
}

action write(i: int, v: Value) {
  mem[i] := StampVal(mem[i]->ts +
      1, v);
}

action scan_spec() returns
    (snapshot: [int]StampVal) {
  assume (snapshot := mem);
}
```

Fig. 1: A snapshot object. The scan procedure carries out two consecutive collects, meaning it reads the entire memory in parallel twice. If both collects yield identical results, the procedure returns. Otherwise, it restarts.

lenging, because it can not be done via so-called fixed linearization points, i.e., the effect of a method invocation cannot be mapped to the execution of a fixed statement in the body of the method, and it requires prophecy variables[1].

Reduction was indispensable for our case studies, each of which involves fine-grained access to shared state by an unbounded number and dynamically-created concurrent tasks. The previous version of Civl could not handle these case studies because reduction was applicable only to sequential code fragments consisting solely of actions (and no procedure calls) and had no notion of parallel reduction. We are not aware of any other proof technique based on reduction that can handle our case studies. Without reduction, proofs based purely on inductive invariants would be substantially more complex: the required invariants would be large and difficult to formulate.

2   Overview

We demonstrate our reduction proof technique on an implementation of a concurrent *snapshot* object [3] that provides two methods: `write(i,v)` that writes value `v` to memory cell `i`, and `scan()` which returns a snapshot of the entire memory. We assume that the memory is represented using an array. These methods can be called concurrently from an arbitrary number of threads. We first describe the implementation and the specification we are trying to prove, and then detail the application of our reduction proof technique.

2.1   A Concurrent Snapshot Object

Implementation. Figure 1 lists the code of the snapshot object (`scan_spec` is explained later). Each memory cell holds a timestamped value (a value along with an integer timestamp). For simplicity, we consider a memory with just two cells. The arbitrary-size case is considered in Section 2.4.

The code uses a programming language with regular procedure calls and parallel composition, where each access to the shared memory is encapsulated

```
procedure scan() returns (snapshot: [int]StampVal) {
  var r1: [int]StampVal;
  var r2: [int]StampVal;
  while (true) {
    seq-reduce {
      par-reduce {
        (call r1[1] := read_f(1)) par
        (call r1[2] := read_f(2))
      }
      par-reduce {
        (call r2[1] := read_s(1)) par
        (call r2[2] := read_s(2))
      }
      if (r1 == r2) {
        snapshot := r1;
        return;
      }
    }
  }
}
```

```
right action read_f(i: int) returns
          (out: StampVal) {
  var k: int;
  var v: Value;
  if (*) {
    assume k < mem[i]->ts;
    out := StampVal(v, k);
  } else {
    out := mem[i];
  }
}

left action read_s(i: int) returns
          (out: StampVal) {
  var k: int;
  var v: Value;
  if (*) {
    assume k > mem[i]->ts;
    out := StampVal(v, k);
  } else {
    out := mem[i];}
}
```

Fig. 2: An abstraction `scan`. Compared to the original, the two memory reads call the abstracted actions `read_f` and `read_s`, resp. In these actions, $*$ is non-deterministic choice and local variables are initially assigned arbitrary values. The annotations `seq-reduce` and `par-reduce` are related to our reduction technique.

into a so-called *action*. Actions are assumed to execute atomically in a single indivisible step. In this case, we have two actions, `read(i)` reads the i-th memory cell, and `write(i,v)` updates the i-th memory cell with value v and a timestamp incremented by 1 from its current timestamp.

The procedure `scan` consists of a "spin" loop that exits when two consecutive reads of the entire memory yield identical results. A read of the memory is parallelized, each memory cell is read in a different thread. This is written using the `par` keyword in between the two calls to the action `read` (actions are called in the same way as procedures). The meaning of s `par` s' for two statements s and s' is that s and s' are executed in two different threads which are joined before executing the next statement. This ensures that the two reads of the entire memory do not overlap in time. For an expert reader, this corresponds to the fork-join model.

The procedure `write(i,v)` is omitted; it simply calls the homonymous action.

Specification: Linearizability. Our goal is to show that this object is *linearizable*, i.e., each concurrent invocation of `scan` or `write` seems to take effect instantaneously at some point between the call and the return. That is, each concurrent execution of multiple invocations corresponds to a *linearization*—a valid sequence of those invocations where every `scan` returns the memory state resulting from all preceding `write` operations.

The aforementioned sequential semantics of `scan` is defined by the action `scan_spec` in Figure 1, which assumes that the return value equals some instantaneous read of the memory (recall that actions execute in a single indivisible step). Linearizability can be reduced to showing that `scan` is a refinement of `scan_spec`, in a sense that will be made precise later. Note that `scan_spec` may block and this is sound because linearizability does not imply any notion of progress by itself.

Linearizability Proof. The work of Attiya et al.[5] shows that any "unreduced" linearizability proof requires prophecy variables, where an "unreduced" proof is one that attempts to establish a linearization for every possible execution of any number of invocations. Linearizability is equivalent to a standard notion of *trace inclusion* between the concurrent object and an atomic (sequential) specification where every invocation performs a single indivisible step. Traces are sequences of call and return events storing input and return values. Trace inclusion is known to be equivalent to the existence of a composition of a forward and backward simulation relations [37]. Attiya et al. [5] show that there exists no forward simulation from this snapshot object to the corresponding atomic (sequential) specification, which implies the need for using backward simulations (a forward simulation corresponds to a proof using so-called fixed linearization points). Backward simulations are known to correspond to using prophecy variables in a deductive verification context [1,37].

Next, we present a proof using our reduction technique which avoids the use of notoriously challenging prophecy variables. After a step of abstraction, the reads will become movers and they can be reordered to form an atomic section which is a "direct" refinement of `scan_spec`.

This goes beyond previous reduction techniques since the `scan` implementation nests parallel composition and sequential composition of statements.

2.2   Using Abstraction to Enable Reduction

The actions `read` and `write` do not commute for obvious reasons. To enable reduction, we introduce two abstractions of `read`: a right-mover abstraction `read_f` and a left-mover abstraction `read_s`, which are listed on the right of Figure 2. In general, an abstraction of an action over-approximates its effect on the global state and the set of possible return values.

A `read` abstraction commutes to the right of a write if it can return a value with an older timestamp than the one in memory, meaning any value it returns before the write remains valid afterward. We introduce this behavior via a non-deterministic choice: `read_f` can either return the timestamped value in memory, or an arbitrary timestamped value provided that the timestamp is strictly smaller than the timestamp in memory. The left mover abstraction `read_s` is very similar except that the returned timestamp in the "arbitrary" case should be strictly higher than the timestamp in memory. We note that designing such abstractions requires creativity, as in any other deductive proof system. The advantage here is that they lead to more ergonomic proofs—both more succinct and less tedious. Moreover, soundness of mover abstractions is a local property, as it concerns only pairs of actions, and the induced reduction significantly simplifies subsequent reasoning.

Figure 2 lists an abstraction of the `scan` procedure which calls the abstract actions `read_f` and `read_s` during the first and second read of the memory, resp. The occurrences of `seq-reduce` and `par-reduce` are explained below and should be ignored for now. This is a sound abstraction in the sense that any concurrent execution of the original snapshot implementation is also possible when `scan` is replaced by this abstract version. Soundness is a straightforward consequence of the fact that `read_f` and `read_s` over-approximate the behavior of `read`.

In the following, we show that this abstraction of `scan` is a refinement of the atomic action `scan_spec`, which concludes the linearizability proof.

2.3   Reducing Parallel Statements

We prove that it is sound to treat all reads in the abstract `scan` from Figure 2 as executing atomically, without interference from other threads. The first reduction step removes the use of parallel composition, represented by the annotation `par-reduce`. The first occurrence of `par-reduce` relies on `read_f(2)` being a right mover and thus,

$$\text{(call r1[1] := read\_f(1)) par (call r1[2] := read\_f(2))}$$

can be rewritten to

$$\text{call r1[1] := read\_f(1); call r1[2] := read\_f(2)}$$

where the parallel composition `par` has been replaced by sequential composition `;`. This fixes an order between the two actions, but interference is still allowed in between the two calls (i.e., after `read_f(1)` completes but before `read_f(2)` starts).

Indeed, for any interleaving where `read_f(2)` executes before `read_f(1)`, the right moverness of `read_f(2)` implies that it can be soundly swapped to the right of all actions that execute until `read_f(1)` and `read_f(1)` itself (here, soundness means preserving the final state and all return values of actions or procedures).

Dually, the second occurrence of `par-reduce` relies on `read_s(1)` being a left mover in order to reduce the parallel composition `par` to sequential composition.

The result of reducing the two parallel statements is shown on the left, in Figure 3. For simplicity, we write just the loop iteration. The sequence of reads is now a sequence of right movers followed by a sequence of left movers and we can use Lipton's reduction in order to rewrite it as an atomic section (the conditional and the assignments that follow the reads are accessing local variables and can be reordered in any direction, to the left in this case). Invoking this reduction principle is done via the keyword `seq-reduce`. The final reduced form of `scan` will group all reads and the if conditional inside an atomic section, marked using the keyword `atomic`. It is now quite straightforward to show that `scan` refines the atomic action `scan_spec`:

```
seq-reduce { // -> atomic {
  call r1[1] := read_f(1);
    // right
  call r1[2] := read_f(2);
    // right
  call r2[1] := read_s(1);
    // left
  call r2[2] := read_s(2);
    // left
  if (r1 == r2) {
    snapshot := r1;
    return;
  }
}
```

Fig. 3: A reduced loop iteration.

- every iteration where the conditional fails has no effect on the return value,
- if the conditional succeeds, then for every cell, the timestamps returned by `read_f` and `read_s` are identical. This indicates that both reads accessed the current memory state, and the values were not chosen arbitrarily. Specifically, if `read_f` had returned a timestamp smaller than the one in memory,

```
procedure scan() returns (snapshot:
    [int]StampVal){
  var r1: [int]StampVal;
  var r2: [int]StampVal;
  while (true) {
    seq-reduce {
      call r1 := collect_f(n); // right
      call r2 := collect_s(n); // left
      if (r1 == r2) {
        snapshot := r1;
        return;
      }
    }
  }
}
```

```
right procedure collect_f(n: int)
      returns (r: [int]StampVal) {
  var out: StampVal;
  if (n == 0) { return; }
  else {
    par-reduce {
      (call r := collect_f(n-1)) par
      (call out := read_f(n))
    }
    r[n] := out;}
}

left procedure collect_s(n: int) returns
      (r: [int]StampVal) {
  var out: StampVal;
  if (n == 0) { return; }
  else {
    par-reduce {
      (call out := read_s(n)) par
      (call r := collect_s(n-1))
    }
    r[n] := out;}
}
```

Fig. 4: Applying reduction on an abstraction of the **scan** procedure for an unbounded size memory.

then **read_s** could not have returned the same timestamp, as it only returns timestamps strictly greater than those currently in memory (which increase monotonically). The action **read_s** cannot return a timestamp greater than the one in memory for similar reasons.

2.4   The Unbounded Memory Case: Reductions for Structured Code

Figure 4 lists a reduction proof for an extension of the previous **scan** implementation to an unbounded size memory. Memory reads are performed inside two recursive procedures **collect_f** and **collect_s** which use the corresponding **read_f** and **read_s** actions to read memory cells.

Notably, this demonstrates an extension of Lipton's reduction to structured programs, code that contains procedure calls. For compositionality, we introduce a moverness type for procedures, and use that moverness type in a similar way to Lipton's reduction. After a parallel reduction step (explained below), **collect_f** and **collect_s** are typed as right and left procedures, respectively. This enables a reduction step that yields an atomic section encompassing an entire iteration of the outer **scan** loop, as in the previous case.

The parallel reductions are now performed inside each of the two recursive procedures, and rely on similar arguments as above (the moverness of the **read_f** and **read_s** actions). After this reduction step, they contain no more parallel composition, and since all the actions they perform have the same moverness type, this type can be exported at the procedure level. The left moverness case requires that the procedure terminates *when executed in isolation*, which is obvious here because the parameter decreases and it is bounded below by 0.

Once both reduction steps have been applied, proving that the **scan** procedure is a refinement of **scan_spec** is similar to the bounded case presented above.

Formalizing the correctness of this reduction technique, which handles both structured code and parallel composition, is non-trivial. The next section in-

$$A \in \mathit{ActionName} \quad Q \in \mathit{ProcName} \quad X \in \mathit{ActionName} \cup \mathit{ProcName}$$

$$
\begin{aligned}
\mathit{Val} &\ni \text{☣} \\
v \in \mathit{Var} &= \mathit{GVar} \cup \mathit{LVar} \\
g \in \mathit{GStore} &= \mathit{GVar} \to \mathit{Val} \\
\ell \in \mathit{LStore} &= \mathit{LVar} \rightharpoonup \mathit{Val} \\
\sigma \in \mathit{Store} &= \mathit{Var} \rightharpoonup \mathit{Val} \\
\rho \in \mathit{Gate} &= 2^{\mathit{Store}} \\
\tau \in \mathit{Trans} &= 2^{\mathit{Store} \times \mathit{Store}} \\
\iota, o \in \mathit{IOMap} &= \mathit{LVar} \rightharpoonup \mathit{LVar} \\
x \in \mathit{LVar} & \\
I, O \in 2^{\mathit{LVar}} & \\
M \in \mathit{MoverType} &= \{B, R, L, N, \top\} \\
F \in \{\mathit{true}, \mathit{false}\} &
\end{aligned}
$$

$$
\begin{aligned}
s \in \mathit{Stmt} ::=\ & \texttt{skip} \mid \texttt{if } x\ s\ s \\
& \mid\ s\,;s \mid s\ \texttt{par}\ s \\
& \mid\ \texttt{call }(X, \iota, o) \\
& \mid\ \texttt{atomic } s \\
& \mid\ \texttt{par-reduce } s\ \texttt{par}\ s \\
& \mid\ \texttt{seq-reduce } s \\
\mathit{Action} ::=\ & (I, O, \rho, \tau, M, F) \\
\mathit{ProcSig} ::=\ & (I, O, M, F) \\
\mathit{as} \in\ & \mathit{ActionName} \to \mathit{Action} \\
\mathit{ps} \in\ & \mathit{ProcName} \to \mathit{ProcSig} \\
\mathcal{P} \in \mathit{Prog} =\ & \mathit{ProcName} \to \mathit{Stmt}
\end{aligned}
$$

Fig. 5: RedPL: Syntax

troduces a simple yet expressive programming language used to reason about correctness in the following sections.

3 RedPL: Syntax and Semantics

In this section we present our core programming language RedPL to formalize our approach to reduction. Our language is inspired by RefPL [31]. Figure 5 summarizes the syntax of RedPL.

Variables and stores. We assume there is a fixed set of *global variables* GVar and a fixed set of *local variables* LVar such that GVar and LVar are disjoint. The set of *variables* Var is the union of GVar and LVar. A *store* σ is a partial map from variables to *values*. We write $\sigma' \subseteq \sigma$ if σ is an extension of σ', $\sigma|_V$ for the restriction of σ to V, $\sigma - V$ for $\sigma|_{\mathrm{dom}(\sigma) \setminus V}$, $\sigma[\sigma']$ for the store that is like σ' on $\mathrm{dom}(\sigma')$ and otherwise like σ, and $g \cdot \ell$ for the combination of *global store* g and *local store* ℓ.

Actions. RedPL models uninterrupted execution by a thread using atomic actions [11,30]. We assume there is a fixed set of actions with names from the set *ActionName*. All accesses to global variables are confined to actions. The action map *as* maps each $A \in \mathit{ActionName}$ to a tuple $as(A) = (I, O, \rho, \tau, M, F)$. The set of input variables I and the set of output variables O are each a subset of LVar. The gate ρ is a set of stores such that $\mathrm{dom}(\ell) = I$ for each $g \cdot \ell \in \rho$. The transition relation τ is a relation over stores such that $\mathrm{dom}(\ell) = I$ and $\mathrm{dom}(\ell') = O$ for each $(g \cdot \ell, g' \cdot \ell') \in \tau$. Executing the action from a store σ that does not satisfy the gate (i.e., $\sigma \notin \rho$) fails the execution. Otherwise, every transition (σ, σ') in τ describes a possible atomic state transition from σ (over $\mathit{GVar} \cup I$) to σ' (over $\mathit{GVar} \cup O$). The mover type M of the action is a member of the set *MoverType* [19]; it captures succinctly the nature of commutativity of this action compared to other actions defined by *as*. The failure type F is a Boolean value that indicates whether it is possible for this action to fail. If $F = \mathit{false}$, then the gate must include all possible stores over $\mathit{GVar} \cup I$.

Our formalization does not provide concrete syntax for the bodies of atomic actions, instead choosing to model them abstractly using a symbolic transition system. Our modeling approach is general and allows actions to be arbitrary and potentially failing computations over global, input, and output variables. Specifically, actions can model a variety of statements—asserts, assumes, (nondeterministic) assignments, choice, and sequencing.

Procedures. RedPL models preemptible concurrent execution using procedures. We assume there is a fixed set of procedures with names from the set *ProcName* which is disjoint from *ActionName*. We split the specification of procedures into two maps—the signature ps and the program $\mathcal{P}$. An important aspect of our formalization is to transform procedure bodies while keeping their signature fixed. Splitting the specification of procedure behavior into the signature map and the program aids our formalization.

The signature map ps maps each $Q \in ProcName$ to a tuple (I, O, M, F). The set of input variables I and the set of output variables O are each a subset of *LVar*. When Q is called, its local store gets a binding for each variable in *LVar*. The mover type M is a member of the set *MoverType*. The failure type F is a Boolean indicating whether it is possible for the execution of the procedure to fail. Our type checker, described later, checks the consistency of M and F against the body of the procedure.

The program $\mathcal{P}$ maps each $Q \in ProcName$ to a statement s that is executed when Q is called. The primitive statement `skip` does nothing; it serves as a marker in the formal operational semantics explained later. The statement `if` x s_1 s_2 looks up the value of x in the local store and continues to execute s_1 if the value is *true* or s_2 if the value is *false*. The statement $s_1 \,;\, s_2$ executes s_1 followed by s_2. The statement s_1 `par` s_2 executes both s_1 and s_2 in parallel.

The statement `ca` (X, ι, o) calls either an action or a procedure. Parameter passing is expressed using an *input map* ι from I to *LVar*, and an injective *output map* o from O to *LVar*. For both ι and o, the domain is callee's formals and the range is caller's actuals. Input variables are immutable, since they are not mapped to by output maps and the variables of a procedure are not modified anywhere else. An action call is the only way to access global variables or to modify either the global or the local store.

The statement `at mic` s executes s with preemptions disabled, i.e., the statement s is executed to completion before any other concurrent execution is scheduled. The statement `par-reduce` s_1 `par` s_2 expresses the programmer intention to reduce the parallel computation s_1 `par` s_2 to the sequential computation $s_1 \,;\, s_2$. The statement `seq-reduce` s expresses the programmer intention to reduce the statement s to `at mic` s. A statement s is *atomic-free* if s does not have any occurrences of `at mic`. A statement s is *reduce-free* if s does not have any occurrences of `seq-reduce` or `par-reduce`. A program $\mathcal{P}$ is *atomic-free* if $\mathcal{P}(Q)$ is atomic-free for all $Q \in \mathrm{dom}(\mathcal{P})$.

Although RedPL does not have explicit support for loops and nondeterministic choice, both can be modeled. We can model a loop using a recursive procedure. We can model nondeterministic choice using the conditional statement `if` x s s after assigning a nondeterministically chosen value to the local variable x (via an action).

$$f ::= (\ell, SC[s])$$
$$t ::= \mathsf{Lf}\ f \mid \mathsf{Nd}\ f\ \bar{t}$$
$$\mathcal{T} ::= \{t, \ldots, t\}$$
$$c ::= (g, \mathcal{T}) \mid \maltese$$

$$SC ::= \bullet_s \mid SC\,;s \mid \mathbf{in\text{-}atomic}\ SC$$
$$\mid \mathbf{in\text{-}seq\text{-}reduce}\ SC$$
$$TC ::= \bullet_t \mid \mathsf{Nd}\ f\ \bar{t}TC\bar{t}$$
$$PC ::= \{TC\} \uplus \mathcal{T}$$
$$LC ::= PC[\mathsf{Lf}\ (\bullet_\ell, SC)]$$

(proc call) $(g, PC[\mathsf{Lf}\ (\ell, SC[\mathtt{call}\ (Q, \iota, o)])]) \rightarrow$
$\qquad (g, PC[\mathsf{Nd}\ (\ell, SC[\mathtt{call}\ (Q, \iota, o)])\ \mathsf{Lf}\ (\{v \mapsto \mbox{\Biohazard} \mid v \in LVar\}[\ell \circ \iota], \mathcal{P}(Q))])$

(return) $(g, PC[\mathsf{Nd}\ (\ell, SC[\mathtt{call}\ (Q, \iota, o)])\ \mathsf{Lf}\ (Q, \ell', \mathtt{skip})]) \rightarrow$
$\qquad (g, PC[\mathsf{Lf}\ (\ell[\ell' \circ o^{-1}], SC[\mathtt{skip}])])$

(fork) $(g, PC[\mathsf{Lf}\ (\ell, SC[s_1\ \mathbf{par}\ s_2])]) \rightarrow$
$\qquad (g, PC[\mathsf{Nd}\ (\ell, SC[s_1\ \mathbf{par}\ s_2])\ \mathsf{Lf}\ (\ell, s_1)\ \mathsf{Lf}\ (\ell, s_2)])$

(join) $(g, PC[\mathsf{Nd}\ (\ell, SC[s_1\ \mathbf{par}\ s_2])\ \mathsf{Lf}\ (\ell_1, \mathtt{skip})\ \mathsf{Lf}\ (\ell_2, \mathtt{skip})]) \rightarrow$
$\qquad (g, PC[\mathsf{Lf}\ (\ell[\ell_1|_{mod(s_1)}][\ell_2|_{mod(s_2)}], SC[\mathtt{skip}])])$

(action call) $\dfrac{as(A) = (\_, \_, \rho, \tau) \quad (g \cdot (\ell \circ \iota), g' \cdot \hat{\ell}) \in \rho \circ \tau \quad \ell' = \ell[\hat{\ell} \circ o^{-1}]}{(g, LC[\ell][\mathtt{call}\ (A, \iota, o)]) \rightarrow (g', LC[\ell'][\mathtt{skip}])}$

(action fail) $\dfrac{as(A) = (\_, \_, \rho, \_, \_, \_) \quad g \cdot (\ell \circ \iota) \notin \rho}{(g, LC[\ell][\mathtt{call}\ (A, \iota, o)]) \rightarrow \maltese}$
$\qquad$
(branch) $s' = \begin{cases} s_1 & \ell[x] = true \\ s_2 & \ell[x] = false \end{cases}$
$\qquad\qquad \dfrac{}{(g, LC[\ell][\mathbf{if}\ x\ s_1\ s_2]) \rightarrow (g, LC[\ell][s'])}$

(skip) $(g, LC[\ell][\mathtt{skip}\,;s]) \rightarrow (g, LC[\ell][s])$
$\qquad$
(stop) $(g, \{\mathsf{Lf}\ (\_, \mathtt{skip})\} \uplus \mathcal{T}) \rightarrow (g, \mathcal{T})$

(atomic enter) $(g, LC[\ell][\mathbf{atomic}\ s]) \rightarrow (g, LC[\ell][\mathbf{in\text{-}atomic}\ s])$

(atomic exit) $(g, LC[\ell][\mathbf{in\text{-}atomic\ skip}]) \rightarrow (g, LC[\ell][\mathtt{skip}])$

(par-reduce enter) $(g, PC[\mathsf{Lf}\ (\ell, SC[\mathbf{par\text{-}reduce}\ s_1\ \mathbf{par}\ s_2])]) \rightarrow$
$\qquad (g, PC[\mathsf{Nd}\ (\ell, SC[\mathbf{par\text{-}reduce}\ s_1\ \mathbf{par}\ s_2])\ \mathsf{Lf}\ (\ell, s_1)\ \mathsf{Lf}\ (\ell, s_2)])$

(par-reduce exit) $(g, PC[\mathsf{Nd}\ (\ell, SC[\mathbf{par\text{-}reduce}\ s_1\ \mathbf{par}\ s_2])\ \mathsf{Lf}\ (\ell_1, \mathtt{skip})\ \mathsf{Lf}\ (\ell_2, \mathtt{skip})]) \rightarrow$
$\qquad (g, PC[\mathsf{Lf}\ (\ell[\ell_1|_{mod(s_1)}][\ell_2|_{mod(s_2)}], SC[\mathtt{skip}])])$

(seq-reduce enter) $(g, LC[\ell][\mathbf{seq\text{-}reduce}\ s]) \rightarrow (g, LC[\ell][\mathbf{in\text{-}seq\text{-}reduce}\ s])$

(seq-reduce exit) $(g, LC[\ell][\mathbf{in\text{-}seq\text{-}reduce\ skip}]) \rightarrow (g, LC[\ell][\mathtt{skip}])$

Fig. 6: RedPL: Operational semantics for program $\mathcal{P}$

3.1 Semantics

Figure 6 presents the operational semantics of RedPL as a transition relation $\to$ over *configurations*. Each configuration is either a failure $\lightning$ or a pair $(g, \mathcal{T})$ comprising a global store g and a finite multiset $\mathcal{T}$ of threads. Each thread is a tree (which generalizes a call stack); new leaf nodes (Lf) are created via the call and **par** statements. Both of these statements block the caller in an internal node Nd until the leaf nodes are finished. Each tree node contains a *frame* (ℓ, s), where ℓ is the local store and s is the remaining statement to execute.

In the definition of $\to$ we use several evaluation contexts that have a unique hole $\bullet$ which marks the evaluation position; filling the hole is denoted by $\cdot[\cdot]$. SC is the statement context, which is a statement with a hole $\bullet$. $SC[s]$ is a statement with s in evaluation position. In addition to a hole $\bullet$, there are three other statement contexts. The context $SC\,;s$ finishes evaluating SC before moving on to s. The context in-at mic SC is introduced when in-at mic is entered. The context in-seq-reduce SC is introduced when in-seq-reduce is entered. PC is a multiset of thread trees with a hole $\bullet$ in one of the trees. We have additional conditions on this multiset PC: (1) Trees that do not contain a hole $\bullet$ do not have the in-at mic statement in them. (2) If t is the tree with the hole $\bullet$, and if there is any in-at mic statement in t, then it must be on the unique path from root of t to the hole. These conditions ensure that an atomic statement executes without interference. The hole in a PC may be filled with an arbitrary tree. LC is a specialization of PC in which the hole is filled with a leaf with holes inside it for a local store and the next statement to be executed.

$$
\begin{aligned}
mod(\texttt{skip}) &= \varnothing \\
mod(\texttt{call}\ (X, \iota, o)) &= \mathrm{img}(o) \\
mod(s_1\,;s_2) &= mod(s_1) \cup mod(s_2) \\
mod(s_1\ \texttt{par}\ s_2) &= mod(s_1) \cup mod(s_2) \\
mod(\texttt{atomic}\ s) &= mod(s) \\
mod(\texttt{par-reduce}\ s_1\ \texttt{par}\ s_2) &= mod(s_1) \cup mod(s_2) \\
mod(\texttt{seq-reduce}\ s) &= mod(s) \\
mod(\texttt{if}\ x\ s_1\ s_2) &= mod(s_1) \cup mod(s_2)
\end{aligned}
$$

Fig. 7: The *mod* function

Figure 6 provides the semantics for a fixed program $\mathcal{P}$ organized as a collection of rules, one for each kind of statement in the hole. The rule **(proc call)** for executing call (Q, ι, o) from a context with local store ℓ creates a new leaf and initializes its frame with a local store where the input variables of Q get their values from $\ell \circ \iota$ ($\circ$ means function or relation composition) and the rest of the variables are initialized to the default value $\circledast$. The rule **(return)** for returning from a call updates the caller's local store with the values in the callee's local store using the output map o.

The rule **(fork)** for executing $s_1\ \texttt{par}\ s_2$ creates two leaf nodes for executing s_1 and s_2, each node getting a copy of the local store of the parent. The parent is blocked until both children nodes have finished executing. Then, the modified variables from each child node are written back to the parent's local store in the rule **(join)**. The type checker for RedPL (described in Section 5) checks that the local variables modified by s_1 are not accessed by s_2 and vice-versa. This check ensures that the updates to the local store of the parent from the local stores of the children nodes are conflict-free. The *mod* function, shown in Figure 7, approximates the set of local variables that are modified by a statement.

Atomic actions execute directly in the context of the caller. If the current store does not satisfy the gate of an executed action, the execution stops in the *failure configuration* $\lightning$ (rule **(action fail)**). Otherwise, the execution takes a step according to the transition relation of the action (rule **(action call)**). We refer to transitions in which an atomic action executes as an *action* transition, and all other transitions as *local* transitions. For any action transition t_A of an action A called with input mapping ι_A from a leaf node with local store ℓ in the frame, we define the input parameter binding of the transition as $in\text{-}bind(t_A) = \ell \circ \iota_A$.

Rule **(branch)** executes a conditional statement. Rule **(skip)** moves the evaluation context forward. Rule **(stop)** removes a finished tree from the multiset of trees. Rule **(atomic enter)** enters an atomic section and rule **(atomic exit)** exits it. Rules **(par-reduce enter)** and **(par-reduce exit)** are similar to **(fork)** and **(join)**, respectively. Rules **(seq-reduce enter)** and **(seq-reduce exit)** enter and exit a `seq-reduce` block.

4 Commutativity of Atomic Actions

We present basic concepts that will be used towards the end of this section to define a well-formed action map. Intuitively, an action map as is well-formed if the mover type of each atomic action is correct w.r.t. the entire pool of atomic actions in as. For the next few definitions, we fix two actions $X = (I_X, O_X, \rho_X, \tau_X, \text{-}, \text{-})$ and $Y = (I_Y, O_Y, \rho_Y, \tau_Y, \text{-}, \text{-})$,

Weakest liberal precondition The weakest liberal precondition $wlp(X, \rho_Y)$ is the set of all triples (g, ℓ_X, ℓ_Y) such that X does not fail in $g \cdot \ell_X$ and executing X from $g \cdot \ell_X$ always leads to a global store g' where gate of Y holds on $g' \cdot \ell_Y$.

$$wlp(X, \rho_Y) = \{(g, \ell_X, \ell_Y) \mid g \cdot \ell_X \in \rho_X \wedge$$
$$(\forall g', \ell_X' : (g \cdot \ell_X, g' \cdot \ell_X') \in \tau_X \implies g' \cdot \ell_Y \in \rho_Y)\}$$

A consequence of this definition is that if a state satisfies the gate of X but not $wlp(X, \rho_Y)$, then there is a way to execute X and get to a state where gate of Y does not hold. This consequence, noted formally below, is used heavily in the proof of soundness of our reduction theorem.

$$\forall g, \ell_X, \ell_Y : g \cdot \ell_X \in \rho_X \wedge (g, \ell_X, \ell_Y) \notin wlp(X, \rho_Y) \implies$$
$$\exists \hat{g}, \hat{\ell} : (g \cdot \ell_X, \hat{g} \cdot \hat{\ell}) \in \tau_X \wedge \hat{g} \cdot \ell_Y \notin \rho_Y$$

Commutes We say X commutes with Y, denoted by $commutes(X, Y)$, if executing X followed by Y leads to a state that is also possible by executing Y before X.

$$\forall g, g', \bar{g}, \ell_X, \ell_Y, \ell_X', \ell_Y' : (g, \ell_X, \ell_Y) \in wlp(X, \rho_Y) \wedge (g, \ell_Y, \ell_X) \in wlp(Y, \rho_X)$$
$$\wedge (g \cdot \ell_X, \bar{g} \cdot \ell_X') \in (\rho_X \circ \tau_X) \wedge (\bar{g} \cdot \ell_Y, g' \cdot \ell_Y') \in (\rho_Y \circ \tau_Y)$$
$$\implies \exists \hat{g} : (g \cdot \ell_Y, \hat{g} \cdot \ell_Y') \in (\rho_Y \circ \tau_Y) \wedge (\hat{g} \cdot \ell_X, g' \cdot \ell_X') \in (\rho_X \circ \tau_X)$$

Success preservation We say X *preserves the success* of Y, denoted by $preserves\text{-}success(X, Y)$, if whenever gate of Y and gate of X hold from a state, then any transition of X leads to a state that also satisfies gate of Y.

$$\forall g, \ell_X, \ell_Y : g \cdot \ell_X \in \rho_X \wedge g \cdot \ell_Y \in \rho_Y \implies (g, \ell_X, \ell_Y) \in wlp(X, \rho_Y)$$

Failure preservation We say X *preserves the failure* of Y, denoted by *preserves-failure*(X, Y), if whenever X does not fail from a state but Y does, there exists a transition of X from that state that leads to the failure of Y. Equivalently, if X does not fail from a state and cannot make a transition that leads to the failure of Y, then Y does not fail from that state.

$$\forall g, \ell_X, \ell_Y : (g, \ell_X, \ell_Y) \in wlp(X, \rho_Y) \implies g \cdot \ell_Y \in \rho_Y$$

Well-formed action map. We have 5 types: right-mover ($\mathbf{R}$), left-mover ($\mathbf{L}$), both-mover ($\mathbf{B}$), non-mover ($\mathbf{N}$), top ($\top$). These types form a lattice under a partial order defined as: $\mathbf{B} \sqsubseteq a \sqsubseteq \mathbf{N} \sqsubseteq \top$ where $a \in \{\mathbf{R}, \mathbf{L}\}$. Let the join operator for this partial order be denoted by $\sqcup$. An action map *as* is *well-formed* if for all action $A \in ActionName$, if $as(A) = (I_A, O_A, \rho_A, \tau_A, M_A, F_A)$, then the following conditions are satisfied:

1. $M_A \neq \top$.
2. If $M_A \sqsubseteq \mathbf{L}$, then for all $X \in ActionName$:

        (**L1**)   *preserves-success*(X, A)
        (**L2**)   *preserves-failure*(A, X)
        (**L3**)   *commutes*(X, A)

3. If $M_A \sqsubseteq \mathbf{R}$, then for all $X \in ActionName$:

        (**R1**)   *preserves-success*(A, X)
        (**R2**)   *commutes*(A, X)

4. If $F_A = false$, then $\rho_A = \{ g \cdot \ell_A \mid g \in GStore \wedge \ell_A \in LStore \wedge \mathrm{dom}(\ell_A) = I_A \}$.

There are important differences between our conditions for a well-formed action map and those in prior work on Civl [28]. Our conditions are weaker and we were able to identify these in the process of writing the proof for the soundness of our reduction techniques (Theorem 1).

First, our definition of *commutes*(X, Y) is weaker. The corresponding condition for Civl only assumes ρ_X and ρ_Y in the initial state while verifying that X and Y can be reordered. In contrast, our condition makes the stronger assumption $wlp(X, \rho_Y)$ and $wlp(Y, \rho_X)$ in the initial state. Intuitively, our check requires reordering X and Y only for those initial states from which it is impossible to fail for any ordering of X and Y. The following example illustrates this difference. Let S be a shared set, and define actions A and B by $A(j) : S := S \setminus \{j\}$, $B(i) : \texttt{assert } i \in S$ where the assertion is the gate of B. Under our commutativity condition, A is a right mover and B is a left mover, but this does not hold under Civl's original condition.

Second, Civl performs two separate checks, backward preservation and non-blocking, for left movers. Backward preservation requires a left mover A to demonstrate for every action X that if ρ_X holds after a step of A then ρ_X also holds before the step. The nonblocking check requires A to either fail or take a step from every initial state. Instead, we have a single failure preservation check that requires less of A than the combination of backward preservation and nonblocking requirements. Intuitively, our check requires A to take a step only when trying to preserve a failure of the action X. For example, if X does not have any failing behavior, failure preservation would hold trivially, but nonblocking check for A could still be nontrivial.

5   Types for Reduction

In this section, we exploit mover types of atomic actions to check that the application of `par-reduce` and `seq-reduce` in a program are applicable to achieve sound reduction. We achieve this goal by defining two helper functions on statements—*may-fail* and *mover-type*. The function *may-fail* propagates the failure types of actions to statements by using a conservative static analysis. The function *mover-type* lifts mover types of actions to statements using an effect system [19]. Together, these functions allow us to define a well-typed program which implies that applications of reduction in the program are valid.

Failure typing for statements We compute $may\text{-}fail(s)$ for any statement s by conservatively propagating the failure types of atomic actions.

$$may\text{-}fail(\texttt{skip}) = \mathit{false}$$
$$may\text{-}fail(\texttt{call}\ (A, \iota, o)) = may\text{-}fail(A)$$
$$may\text{-}fail(\texttt{call}\ (Q, \iota, o)) = may\text{-}fail(Q)$$
$$may\text{-}fail(s_1\,;s_2) = may\text{-}fail(s_1) \vee may\text{-}fail(s_2)$$
$$may\text{-}fail(s_1\ \texttt{par}\ s_2) = may\text{-}fail(s_1) \vee may\text{-}fail(s_2)$$
$$may\text{-}fail(\texttt{atomic}\ s) = may\text{-}fail(s)$$
$$may\text{-}fail(\texttt{par-reduce}\ s_1\ \texttt{par}\ s_2) = may\text{-}fail(s_1) \vee may\text{-}fail(s_2)$$
$$may\text{-}fail(\texttt{seq-reduce}\ s) = may\text{-}fail(s)$$
$$may\text{-}fail(\texttt{if}\ x\ s_1\ s_2) = may\text{-}fail(s_1) \vee may\text{-}fail(s_2)$$

Fig. 8: The *may-fail* function.

Mover typing for statements Given a well-formed action map *as* and a procedure signature map *ps*, we define *mover-type* function, which assigns a mover type to a statement. To define this function, we first define the sequential composition of mover types in the table below. Using this table, we can define *mover-type* recursively as follows:

$$mover\text{-}type(\texttt{skip}) = \mathbf{B}$$
$$mover\text{-}type(s_1\ \texttt{par}\ s_2) = \top$$
$$mover\text{-}type(\texttt{call}\ (A, \iota, o)) = mover\text{-}type(A)$$
$$mover\text{-}type(\texttt{call}\ (Q, \iota, o)) = mover\text{-}type(Q)$$
$$mover\text{-}type(\texttt{atomic}\ s) = mover\text{-}type(s)$$
$$mover\text{-}type(\texttt{seq-reduce}\ s) = mover\text{-}type(s)$$
$$mover\text{-}type(\texttt{par-reduce}\ s_1\ \texttt{par}\ s_2) = mover\text{-}type(s_1; s_2)$$
$$mover\text{-}type(s_1\,;s_2) = mover\text{-}type(s_1); mover\text{-}type(s_2)$$
$$mover\text{-}type(\texttt{if}\ x\ s_1\ s_2) = mover\text{-}type(s_1) \sqcup mover\text{-}type(s_2)$$

;	B	L	R	N	$\top$
B	B	L	R	N	$\top$
R	R	N	R	N	$\top$
L	L	L	$\top$	$\top$	$\top$
N	N	N	$\top$	$\top$	$\top$
$\top$	$\top$	$\top$	$\top$	$\top$	$\top$

Fig. 9: The *mover-type* function.

For example, consider the following seq-reduce statement from the example in the overview. The mover type assigned to the seq-reduce block will be $\mathbf{N}$.

```
seq-reduce {
    par-reduce {(call r1[1] := read_f(1)) par (call r1[2] := read_f(2))};
    par-reduce {(call r2[1] := read_s(1)) par (call r2[2] := read_s(2))};
}
```

Each call to **read_f** within the first par-reduce has $\mathbf{R}$ type. The par-reduce statement then gets the mover type of $\mathbf{R}; \mathbf{R} = \mathbf{R}$ from the table. Similarly, the second par-reduce contains calls to **read_s**, which are each $\mathbf{L}$, and the par-reduce statement gets the mover type of $\mathbf{L}; \mathbf{L} = \mathbf{L}$. Now, the statement inside seq-reduce composes the two par-reduce blocks sequentially: the first has type $\mathbf{R}$, and the second has type $\mathbf{L}$. The sequential composition $\mathbf{R}; \mathbf{L}$ results in an $\mathbf{N}$ type, which is then assigned to the entire seq-reduce block.

The rules above imply that if s is nested inside s' and $mover\text{-}type(s) = \top$ then $mover\text{-}type(s') = \top$. Since $mover\text{-}type(s_1 \text{ par } s_2) = \top$, if $s_1 \text{ par } s_2$ is nested inside a statement s, then $mover\text{-}type(s) = \top$. We will return to this observation when we discuss the rules for well-typed programs below.

Well-typed programs We define a predicate $well\text{-}typed(s, l)$ where $s \in Stmt$ and $l \in 2^{LVar}$. The predicate $well\text{-}typed(s, l)$ is checking two aspects of a statement. First, it checks that s only accesses the local variables it is allowed to. This check is relevant because if s contains a nested occurrence of two statements s_1 and s_2 executing in parallel, then local variables modified by these two statements must be disjoint from each other. In fact, we check a stronger, yet simpler to check, property that local variables modified by s_1 are neither read nor written by s_2, and vice-versa. This requirement is used only to simplify the formalization. One could consider fresh copies of local variables instead (note that the number of arms in a parallel construct is constant). In our implementation, the arms of the par construct can only be procedure calls, so this restriction just translates to requiring their input and output parameters to be disjoint, which is both natural and easy to check. Second, we check that applications of **par-reduce** and **seq-reduce** have the appropriate mover and failure types on their target statements. This part of the check uses the previously defined functions $mover\text{-}type$ and $may\text{-}fail$.

$$
\begin{aligned}
well\text{-}typed(\texttt{skip}, l) &= true \\
well\text{-}typed(\texttt{atomic } s, l) &= well\text{-}typed(s, l) \\
well\text{-}typed(\texttt{call } (X, \iota, o), l) &= \text{img}(\iota) \subseteq l \wedge \text{img}(o) \subseteq l \\
well\text{-}typed(\texttt{if } x\ s_1\ s_2, l) &= well\text{-}typed(s_1, l) \wedge well\text{-}typed(s_2, l) \wedge x \in l \\
well\text{-}typed(s_1\ ; s_2, l) &= well\text{-}typed(s_1, l) \wedge well\text{-}typed(s_2, l) \\
well\text{-}typed(s_1\ \texttt{par}\ s_2, l) &= well\text{-}typed(s_1, l - mod(s_2)) \wedge \\
&\quad well\text{-}typed(s_2, l - mod(s_1)) \\
well\text{-}typed(\texttt{seq-reduce } s, l) &= well\text{-}typed(s, l) \wedge mover\text{-}type(s) \sqsubseteq \mathbf{N} \\
well\text{-}typed(\texttt{par-reduce } s_1\ \texttt{par}\ s_2, l) &= well\text{-}typed(s_1, l - mod(s_2)) \wedge \\
&\quad well\text{-}typed(s_2, l - mod(s_1)) \wedge \\
&\quad (mover\text{-}type(s_1) \sqsubseteq \mathbf{L} \vee \\
&\quad\quad mover\text{-}type(s_2) \sqsubseteq \mathbf{R} \wedge \neg may\text{-}fail(s_2))
\end{aligned}
$$

Fig. 10: The well-typed function

Most rules in the definition above are straightforward. We take a closer look at the rules for parallel and sequential reduction, focusing on the mover-related checks. **par-reduce** s_1 **par** s_2 checks that one of two cases apply: either s_1 is a left mover or s_2 is a right mover and must not fail. Intuitively, in both cases, all the code in s_1 may be commuted before all the code in s_2. For instance, here is an example illustrating why the right mover statement s_2 is not allowed to fail. Let $\mathbf{x}$ be a shared integer variable, and let **read** and **inc** be actions, where **read** is a right-mover that first asserts $\mathbf{x} > \mathbf{0}$ (this corresponds to its gate) and then

```
var x: int;                                          procedure Q {
                                                       par-reduce {
right action read() returns (out: int) {                 call inc() par (call read())
  assert x > 0;                                        }
  assume out <= x;                                   }
}
action inc() {                                       procedure Q' {
  x := x + 1;                                          call inc();
}                                                      call read();
                                                     }
```

Fig. 11: Example illustrating need for right movers do not fail condition

reads the value of x (exactly or less), and inc is a non-mover that increments x by 1 (it is not a left-mover because it does not satisfy failure preservation, and it is not a right-mover because it does not commute to the right of a read). Let Q be a procedure in the original program P, and assume that it gets reduced to Q' in the reduced program P' by an application of par-reduce (as shown in the snippet above). Assuming an initial state where x = 0, P can fail (if read executes first) but P' has no execution that fails (since inc always executes before read). This is problematic since the reduction "hides" failures which goes against sound reasoning. Hence we require that right movers do not fail. This is what the helper function *may-fail* checks.

seq-reduce s checks that *mover-type*$(s) \sqsubseteq \mathbf{N}$ which implies that any execution through s is of a form $\mathbf{R}^* \cdot \mathbf{N}? \cdot \mathbf{L}^*$, and therefore s can be converted to an atomic section [19]. In this case, the statement s must not have any unreduced parallel statement (whose mover type is $\top$) nested inside it. But it is possible for s to have a reduced parallel statement (whose mover type could be different from $\top$) nested inside it. This flexibility is important in practice and is particularly useful for our case studies described in Section 8.

A program $\mathcal{P}$ is *well-typed* if for all $Q \in \mathrm{dom}(\mathcal{P})$, if $ps(Q) = (\_, \_, M, F)$ then the following hold: (1) *well-typed*$(\mathcal{P}(Q), LVar)$, (2) *mover-type*$(\mathcal{P}(Q)) \sqsubseteq M$, and (3) *may-fail*$(\mathcal{P}(Q)) \Rightarrow F$. The well-typed predicate is computed separately for each procedure Q in the program using the signatures of all procedures and actions called by Q. First, the body of Q is checked to be well-typed w.r.t. the set of all local variables. Second, the mover type of the body of Q must be stronger than the annotated mover type M of Q. This check ensures that the type checking of procedures that call Q will succeed even if Q was inlined at the call site. In essence, this means that the mover type of any procedure is valid regardless of the specific execution taken in completing a call to that procedure. Third, the failure type of Q is checked to be a conservative approximation of the failure type of the body of Q. We use the notion of well-typed programs in Section 6 to state the soundness theorem of our reduction technique.

6   Reduction for **RedPL** Programs

In this section, we give a meaning to the seq-reduce and par-reduce annotations in RedPL programs, and state the related soundness theorem. Soundness is stated in terms of a *refinement* relation between programs that we define hereafter.

A configuration $(g, \mathcal{T})$ is *initial* if it contains an arbitrary number of threads that are about to execute a well-typed statement, i.e., for all $t \in \mathcal{T}$, there exist ℓ and s such that $t = Lf(\ell, s)$, *well-typed*$(s, LVar)$, and s is atomic-free and reduce-free. A configuration $(g, \mathcal{T})$ is *final* if $\mathcal{T} = \varnothing$, i.e., all threads have finished executing successfully. The failure configuration $\frac{1}{2}$ is also final.

Given two well-typed programs $\mathcal{P}$ and $\mathcal{P}'$, we say $\mathcal{P}$ refines $\mathcal{P}'$ (denoted $\mathcal{P} \preccurlyeq \mathcal{P}'$) if the following two properties hold for all initial configurations $(g, \mathcal{T})$:
(1) If there is an execution of $\mathcal{P}$ that fails from the initial configuration $(g, \mathcal{T})$, then there also is an execution of $\mathcal{P}'$ that fails from the same initial configuration:

$$(g, \mathcal{T}) \xrightarrow{\mathcal{P}}{}^* \tfrac{1}{2} \implies (g, \mathcal{T}) \xrightarrow{\mathcal{P}'}{}^* \tfrac{1}{2}$$

(2) If there exists an execution of $\mathcal{P}$ starting from the initial configuration $(g, \mathcal{T})$ that reaches the final configuration $(g', \varnothing)$, then there also exists an execution of $\mathcal{P}'$ from the same initial configuration, that either reaches the same final configuration or results in a failure:

$$(g, \mathcal{T}) \xrightarrow{\mathcal{P}}{}^* (g', \varnothing) \implies (g, \mathcal{T}) \xrightarrow{\mathcal{P}'}{}^* (g', \varnothing) \vee (g, \mathcal{T}) \xrightarrow{\mathcal{P}'}{}^* \tfrac{1}{2}$$

The refines relation is transitive, i.e., if $\mathcal{P}_1 \preccurlyeq \mathcal{P}_2$ and $\mathcal{P}_2 \preccurlyeq \mathcal{P}_3$, then $\mathcal{P}_1 \preccurlyeq \mathcal{P}_3$.

The notation $s[s_2/s_1]$ denotes the result of replacing all occurrences of statement s_1 with statement s_2 inside the statement s. Similarly, the notation $\mathcal{P}[s_2/s_1]$ denotes a new program in which, for every procedure Q, all occurrences of s_1 in the body of Q, as defined in $\mathcal{P}$, are replaced with s_2:

$$\mathcal{P}[s_2/s_1] = \{Q \mapsto \mathcal{P}(Q)[s_2/s_1] \mid Q \in ProcName\}$$

A statement s is *terminating* in program $\mathcal{P}$ if $\mathcal{P}$ does not have any infinite executions from any configuration $(g, \mathsf{Lf}(\ell, s))$ such that *well-typed*$(s, LVar)$. A well-typed program $\mathcal{P}$ is *terminating* if for all $Q \in \mathrm{dom}(\mathcal{P})$ such that *mover-type*$(Q) \sqsubseteq \mathbf{L}$, we have $\mathcal{P}(Q)$ is terminating in $\mathcal{P}$.

Theorem 1. *Let $\mathcal{P}_s$ be an atomic-free and well-typed program. Let*

$$\mathcal{P}_i = \mathcal{P}_s[s_1 \,; s_2 \,/\, \mathtt{par\text{-}reduce}\ s_1 \ \mathtt{par}\ s_2]$$
$$\mathcal{P}_r = \mathcal{P}_i[\mathtt{atomic}\ s \,/\, \mathtt{seq\text{-}reduce}\ s]$$

Then, the programs $\mathcal{P}_i$ and $\mathcal{P}_r$ are well-typed. Furthermore, if $\mathcal{P}_i$ is terminating, then: (1) $\mathcal{P}_s \preccurlyeq \mathcal{P}_i$, and (2) $\mathcal{P}_i \preccurlyeq \mathcal{P}_r$. Therefore, $\mathcal{P}_s \preccurlyeq \mathcal{P}_r$.

[Proof Sketch] First, we establish that $\mathcal{P}_s \preccurlyeq \mathcal{P}_i$, thereby showing that it is sound to sequentialize the concurrent behavior inside $\mathtt{par\text{-}reduce}$. We prove refinement properties (1) and (2) separately. The top-level strategy is to rewrite an execution of $\mathcal{P}_s$ into an execution of $\mathcal{P}_i$ such that, for each application of the $\mathtt{par\text{-}reduce}$ rule, the statement s_1 executes before s_2, using an induction on the number of unreduced $\mathtt{par\text{-}reduce}$ applications. Note that $\mathcal{P}_i$ eliminates all occurrences of $\mathtt{par\text{-}reduce}$, including those nested inside $\mathtt{seq\text{-}reduce}$. As a consequence, there is no parallelism within any $\mathtt{seq\text{-}reduce}$ application.

Second, we establish that $\mathcal{P}_i \preccurlyeq \mathcal{P}_r$, thereby showing that it is sound to define atomic sections for all code blocks inside $\mathtt{seq\text{-}reduce}$. This step also proceeds by induction on the number of unreduced $\mathtt{seq\text{-}reduce}$ applications. We show this by rewriting an execution of $\mathcal{P}_i$ into an execution of $\mathcal{P}_r$ in which each code block inside $\mathtt{seq\text{-}reduce}$ is of the form $\mathbf{R^*N?L^*}$.

See the full version of the paper[20] for more details.

7   Implementation

We have implemented our proof rule in Civl [29] verifier for layered concurrent programs [28]. Our implementation covers every aspect of our formalization except for the side conditions on termination of left-mover procedures and absence of failures in right-mover statements. For the examples reported in Section 8, the verification of these side conditions was done manually.

Civl is an extension of the Boogie verifier [7] for sequential programs. Similar to Boogie, the implementation of Civl is broadly split into a type checker and a verification-condition generator. The type checker handles basic type analysis and checks in addition that layer annotations on variables, yield invariants, actions, and procedures are consistent with each other. It also checks that the mover type of each procedure is consistent with the mover type inferred from the body of the procedure. The verification-condition generator in Civl eliminates all concurrency features from the input program and produces a collection of sequential procedures annotated with specfications. These sequential procedures encode checks related to mover types of atomic actions, refinement checks for each procedure, and noninterference checks related to yield invariants. The sequential procedures are processed by the standard Boogie flow that converts each procedure to a logical constraint and checks it using an SMT solver.

Our implementation modifies and extends Civl as follows. First, we modified the verification conditions generated for checking mover types of actions according to the rules laid out for well-formed action map in Section 4. The revised rules are more general and therefore applicable in more scenarios. The revised failure preservation check for left movers provide an easier mental model while debugging unsuccessful proofs.

Second, we added mover types to procedures and implemented the checking of these types against procedure bodies, as described in Section 5. Our type checker also accounts for mover types of procedures in determining the degree of program transformation allowed between successive program layers. The ability to reduce programs in a fully nested manner, as described in Section 6, is important to enable a single layer to perform a large chunk of the proof, thus reducing the proof overhead of layers. We allow procedures annotated with mover types to be summarized using preconditions and postconditions. Atomic code fragments with calls to such procedures can now be analyzed without inlining these procedures. Our implementation also handles loops directly in the same manner as recursive procedures.

Finally, we allow parallel calls to be reduced using the parallel reduction technique introduced in this paper. We provide parallel execution of procedure calls rather than parallel execution of statements. This design choice simplified parameter passing between the caller and the callees. The modified local variable analysis described in this paper is unnecessary and replaced by a simple check that the output variables used across all arms of a parallel call are all distinct from each other. Our implementation includes, in the same framework, the proof rule for synchronizing asynchronous calls reported earlier [30].

Our formalization of RedPL in Section 3 makes explicit every application of `par-reduce` and `seq-reduce` in the source program. These annotations are not explicitly declared in a Civl program; instead, our type checker automatically infers information equivalent to them.

8   Evaluation

We evaluate the implementation described above on a diverse set of challenging case studies: a parallelized snapshot object (Section 2), the classic message-passing simulation of shared memory by Attiya, Bar-Noy, and Dolev [4] (ABD), an implementation of the FLASH cache coherence protocol [32], and a version of the Two-Phase Commit protocol. These implementations naturally decompose into procedures and make significant use of dynamic thread creation. Message passing is modeled in the style of RPC: broadcasting and waiting for responses is expressed as a parallel composition of procedure calls, each modifying the receiver's state and returning an acknowledgment.

Example	#LOC Total	#LOC Impl & Spec	Time sec
Snapshot	119	82	0.4
ABD	389	206	1.4
Coherence	608	401	5
2PC	146	111	1.8

Fig. 12: Evaluation metrics.

The evaluation shows that each case study involves substantial nesting of parallel and sequential reductions, leveraging both left and right mover types. This approach helps avoid the need for complex invariants that would otherwise arise from fine-grained interleavings. As common in Civl, the proofs are decomposed into a sequence of refinement steps, some of these steps being "abstraction" steps that are not related to reduction (they introduce non-deterministic abstractions or ghost variables). Also, these proofs rely on using the other features of Civl, e.g., inductive invariants and permission-based reasoning. The latter is particularly useful to enable commutativity reasoning. Many times, commutativity between actions is implied by the distinctness of (some of) their inputs and this is encoded using permissions.

Figure 12 presents quantitative metrics from our evaluation. We report the total lines of code for each proof, along with a separate count for the implementation and specification components. We also report that the wall-clock time required for executing each proof. The ratio of proof annotation lines to the combined lines of implementation and specification ranges from 0.31 (for Two-Phase Commit) to 0.88 (for ABD). Also, all these proofs can be completed in few seconds. In addition, the Civl repository contains approximately 50 further examples, including larger benchmarks (on the order of hundreds to thousands of lines) where the seq-reduce rule applies. We focused on the four case studies in the paper because they incorporate both seq-reduce and par-reduce, and therefore most clearly illustrate the interaction and use of the two rules.

In the following, we give more details about each case study, except for the snapshot object that we already described in Section 2. We present the implementation and the specification we prove, and the use of reduction. The proof files are available in the supplementary material.

8.1 The ABD register

```
type TimeStamp // a set with a total order and a
    lower bound
TS: TimeStamp // global timestamp used to order
    operations
value_store: Map TimeStamp Value
procedure ReadClient(pid) returns (val) {
  old_ts := Begin(pid)
  ts, val := Read(pid, old_ts)
  End(pid, ts);
}
procedure WriteClient(pid, val) {
  old_ts := Begin(pid)
  ts := Write(pid, old_ts)
  End(pid, ts);
}
```

```
action Begin(pid) returns (ts) {
  ts = TS;
}
action Read(pid, old_ts) returns
    (ts, val) {
  assume old_ts <= ts
  assume ts in value_store
  val := value_store[ts]
}
action Write(pid, val) returns (ts) {
  assume old_ts < ts
  assume ts not in value_store
  value_store[ts] := val
}
action End(pid, ts) {
  TS := max(TS, ts)
}
```

Fig. 13: A linearizable specification for ABD. The `TS` global variable models a clock which is read when operations start and advances when they end.

The ABD algorithm implements a read-write register (shared memory) on top of message passing. It provides two operations `Read` and `Write` on a register that is replicated across n replicas for fault tolerance. Less than half of the replicas can crash. The operations are invoked in parallel by a collection of clients.

Each replica stores a timestamped value (timestamp, value) where timestamp comes from a totally ordered set with a lower bound (e.g., natural numbers). Both `Read` and `Write` operations have two phases: the `QueryPhase` and the `UpdatePhase`. In the `QueryPhase`, they send `Query` messages to all replicas in parallel, wait for a quorum (at least half) of replies, and retrieve the reply (`t`, `v`) with the maximum timestamp `t` among the responses. Then they enter the `UpdatePhase`, where they send `Update` messages to all replicas. The `Read` operation sends an `Update(t, v)` message, while the `Write` operation sends an `Update(t+1, v')` where v' is the new value to be written. They both wait for a quorum of acknowledgements before returning. When receiving an `Update(t, v)` message, a replica updates its store to (`t`, `v`) if t is greater than its current timestamp, and replies with an acknowledgment regardless of whether it updates. Upon receiving a `Query` message, it replies with its current copy.

Specification: Linearizability. Our goal is to prove that this register implementation is linearizable, which we reduce to a refinement check. To capture the condition that each operation appears to take effect atomically between its call and return, we instrument operations to read a global clock at the start, which advances when they end. This clock is aligned with ABD timestamps: each `Read` returns a value with a timestamp greater than or equal to the clock at invocation, and each `Write` writes a value with a timestamp strictly greater than the clock at invocation. At the end of an operation, the clock advances as the timestamp read/written by that operation. The resulting specification is shown in Figure 13, where `ReadClient` and `WriteClient` wrap the respective operations with `Begin` and `End` actions for clock access. Each method contains a single "internal" step (a call to the action `Read` or `Write`), reflecting the requirement that they take effect instantaneously. The map `value_store`, updated by `Write` and accessed by `Read`, ensures that reads return previously written values.

```
right procedure {:layer 3} QueryPhase(i: int,        procedure Read(pid: ProcessId, old_ts:
    old_ts: TimeStamp)                                   TimeStamp) returns (ts:
 returns (max_ts: TimeStamp, max_value: Value) {        TimeStamp, value: Value) {
 ...                                                   ...
 par-reduce {                                          seq-reduce {
   call max_ts, max_value :=                             call ts, value :=
     QueryPhase(i + 1, old_ts)                             QueryPhase(0, old_ts);    // right
   par call ts, value :=                                 call UpdatePhase(0, ts, value); //
     Query(i, old_ts)  // right                           left
 }                                                     }
 if (less_than(max_ts, ts)) {                        }
   max_ts := ts; max_value := value;
 }
}
```

Fig. 14: <code>QueryPhase</code> and <code>Read</code> procedures.

We prove that the "concrete" versions of `ReadClient` and `WriteClient` where the calls to the actions `Read` or `Write` are replaced by calls to the homonymous ABD procedures are a refinement of the abstract specification in Figure 13.

Applying reduction. The goal is to apply reduction to show that the ABD procedures `Read` and `Write` can be rewritten to execute within a *single* atomic section, which is then shown to refine the abstract `Read` and `Write` actions in Figure 13. To achieve this, we introduce an abstraction of the `Query` handler which is a right mover, which in turn ensures that the `Update` handler becomes a left mover. This abstraction enables parallel reductions in both the `QueryPhase` and `UpdatePhase`; for example, in the `QueryPhase` shown below, it allows the recursive procedure to be reduced by sequentializing all `Query` handlers (which initially happened in parallel). This sequentialization, in turn, enables a sequential reduction within the `Read` and `Write` procedures—illustrated below for `Read`—since the `Query` handlers (right movers) are followed by `Update` handlers (left movers).

The abstraction of `Query` allows it to return a timestamp lower than the current replica timestamp. However, it cannot return any arbitrarily low timestamp—it should be greater than or equal to the clock timestamp `old_ts` obtained in `Begin`. This reduction eliminates the need for an inductive invariant that tracks relationships between read and write operations across different stages of their query or update phases.

8.2   Cache coherence

We implement the FLASH cache coherence protocol [32] which is a directory-based MESI cache coherence protocol. The protocol manages consistency across multiple caches in a shared memory multiprocessor system using a centralized directory.

Figure 15 shows our model for the memory (`mem`), directory (`dir`) and a set of caches (`cache`). The memory is indexed by memory addresses (`MemAddr`), while each cache uses local cache addresses (`CacheAddr`) for indexing. Because the memory address space is larger than the cache address space, a hash function maps each memory address to a cache address, allowing multiple memory addresses to correspond to the same cache address. Each cache stores data in cache lines, which contain a memory address, a value, and a state (`Modified`, `Exclusive`, `Shared`, `Invalid`). The directory tracks the status of each memory address across all caches. If a memory address is held in the Modified or Exclusive state by a cache, the directory records this as `Owner(i)`, where `i` is the ID of

```
type MemAddr; type CacheAddr;          // Implementation state
function Hash(MemAddr): CacheAddr;     var {:layer 0,2} mem: [MemAddr]Value;
datatype State                         var {:layer 0,2} dir:
  {Modified(), Exclusive(), Shared(), Invalid()}       [MemAddr]DirState;
datatype CacheLine                     var {:layer 0,2} cache:
  {CacheLine(ma: MemAddr, value: Value, state:       [CacheId][CacheAddr]CacheLine;
    State)}                            // Specification state
datatype DirState                      var {:layer 1,3} absMem:
  {Owner(i: CacheId), Sharers(iset: Set CacheId)}       [MemAddr]Value;
```

Fig. 15: State representation for cache coherence protocol

```
procedure dir_read_exc_req(i: CacheId, ma: MemAddr)
{
  ... // variable initialization        left procedure invalidate_sharers
  seq-reduce {                          (ma: MemAddr, victims: Set CacheId)
    call dirState := dir_req_begin(ma); // right     {
    if (dirState is Owner) {              ...
      call value := cache_invalidate_exc     if (victims == Set_Empty()) {
                  (dirState->i, ma, Invalid())       return;
      // non-mover                          }
      call write_mem(ma, value); // both mover     victim := Choice(victims->val);
    }                                      victims' := Set_Remove(victims,
    else {                                     victim);
      call dp := invalidate_sharers(ma,     par-reduce { // left
      dirState->iset); // left              call
      call value := read_mem(ma); // both mover         cache_invalidate_shd(victim,
    }                                          ma, Invalid())
    call cache_read_resp(i, ma, value, Exclusive());     par call invalidate_sharers(ma,
      // left                                  victims')
    call dir_req_end(ma, Owner(i)); // left     }
  }                                      }
}
```

Fig. 16: Reduction applied at directory for exclusive state request

the owning cache. Otherwise, the directory records it as **Sharers(iset)**, where **iset** is the set of cache IDs having the memory address in Shared state.

We implement 5 top-level operations on the cache:

- **cache_read** and **cache_write** which read and write a cache entry, respectively.
- **cache_evict_req** initiates eviction of a cache line.
- **cache_read_shd_req** and **cache_read_exc_req** initiate bringing a memory address into the cache in Shared and Exclusive mode, respectively.

We now detail the operation of **cache_read_exc_req** and the interactions between cache and directory. The cache initiates an exclusive request to the directory via **dir_read_exc_req** shown in Figure 16. If the directory state for the requested memory address is **Owner**, it sends an invalidate request to the owner by calling **cache_invalidate_exc**. The owner is then expected to change its state to **Invalid** and send the data back to the directory, which writes it to memory by calling **write_mem**. If the directory state is **Sharers**, it sends invalidate requests in parallel to all caches in the sharers list by invoking **cache_invalidate_shd**. The directory then reads the memory by calling **read_mem** and sends the response back to the orginal cache via **cache_read_resp**, and ending the request by calling **dir_req_end**.

Specification. We introduce an abstract memory, **absMem**. The goal is to show that the **cache_write** and **cache_read** operations are refinement of atomic actions that directly read and write from **absMem**. We hide directory and all cache operations that interact with it. This specification naturally captures the cache coherence property.

Applying reduction. After introducing the ghost variable `absMem` used in the specification, we define a number of abstractions of actions used in the implementation that become movers. The memory operations `read_mem` and `write_mem` are made both movers, the shared invalidate request `cache_invalidate_shd` is made a left mover, the response to a read request at a cache `cache_read_resp` is made a left mover, the actions `dir_req_begin` and `dir_req_end` for reading and updating the directory state are made right and left movers, respectively. These movers enable reduction at many sites in the implementation. In particular, they enable parallel reduction in the invalidate loop (`invalidate_sharers`) to sequentialize them, and subsequently, a sequential reduction on the entire body of the procedure `dir_read_exc_req` for bringing a memory address into the cache in Exclusive mode. This is made precise in Figure 16.

The reduction helps a refinement proof to hide the directory and all the caches so that the read and write operations at cache are refinements of the atomic operations over `absMem`.

8.3   Two-phase Commit (2PC)

Two-phase Commit is a classic distributed protocol used to implement concurrent transactions. A number of *coordinator* processes make a number of *replicas* agree on an order between concurrent transactions. Each transaction is associated with a start time and an end time, and it is submitted to a single coordinator. Two transactions conflict if their time intervals overlap. The goal is to ensure that all committed transactions are not conflicting pairwise.

A coordinator runs in two phases. In the vote phase, it sends vote requests to all replicas which reply with `YES` or `NO` (accept or not a transaction). A replica stores the set of pending transactions (which are not yet committed or aborted) for which it already voted `YES` in a so-called *locked set*, and it answers `YES` iff the incoming vote request concerns a transaction that does not conflict with some transaction in the locked set. In the finalize phase, if all replies are `YES`, the coordinator sends a commit request and otherwise, an abort request. If a replica receives an abort request, it removes the transaction from the locked set.

Specification. We add a ghost variable, `committed_transactions`, which keeps track of all transactions that have been committed. Before adding a transaction to this set (in the coordinator's code), we assert that it does not conflict with any previously committed transaction.

Applying reduction. To enable reduction, we abstract the vote request handler to allow it to non-deterministically respond with `NO` without modifying the state. This abstraction makes the vote request handler a right mover, while the abort request handler becomes a left mover. The commit request handler is a both mover, since it does not change the state. To illustrate, consider two successive vote requests handled by the same replica (requests at different replicas commute, as they access disjoint state). If the transactions conflict, one handler might return `YES` and the other `NO`. Without the abstraction, reordering these handlers isn't sound: if the second executes first, it might respond `YES`, which breaks commutativity. However, with the abstraction, the second handler can non-deterministically return NO, allowing the reordered execution where the first still responds YES. Similar reasoning applies to other combinations of handlers.

As in previous cases, the abstraction enables a combination of parallel reduction and sequential reduction. The parallel reduction is used to sequentialize the two phases, as exemplified below for the vote requests, and then, the sequentialization enables showing that the whole computation for a transaction can be executed within an atomic section.

```
right procedure vote_all(xid: TransactionId, i:        procedure TPC(xid: TransactionId) {
    ReplicaId)                                              ...
  returns (votes: [ReplicaId]Vote) {                       seq-reduce {
  ...                                                         call votes := vote_all(xid, n);
  if (1 <= i) {                                               // right
    vr = VoteRequest(xid, i);                                 // locally calculate decision
    par-reduce {                                                 based on votes
     (call votes := vote_all(xid, i-1))                       call finalize_all(decision,
     par (call out := vote(vr)); } // right                      xid); // left
    }                                                        }
    votes[i] := out;                                         ...
}}                                                         }
```

Fig. 17: <code>vote_all</code> and <code>TPC</code> procedures.

9   Related Work

We review works concerning the use of commutativity reasoning in proving correctness of concurrent or distributed systems.

Commutativity reasoning in deductive verification. Lipton's reduction theory [35] introduced the concept of *movers* to define a program transformation that creates bounded-size atomic blocks. This work assumes a simple programming language without procedure calls and a fixed number of threads. QED [11] expanded the scope of Lipton's theory by introducing iterated application of reduction and abstraction over atomic actions. Also, atomic sections are allowed to contain loops but no procedure calls or dynamic thread creation. Civl [23] builds upon the foundation of QED, adding invariants [38,25], refinement layers and permission-based reasoning via a linear type system [28], and pending asyncs [30,27]. Pending asyncs can be viewed as threads restricted to executing a single atomic step and which cannot be joined. They are used to summarize asynchronous procedure calls and define a reduction scheme where asynchronous procedure calls are transformed to synchronous ones [30]. This reduction scheme is based on proving that the asynchronously called procedure can be summarized to a left-mover pending async. This idea has been extended to sequentializing an asynchronous program that creates an unbounded number of pending asyncs via an induction principle [27]. In this work, we introduce more flexible reduction schemes that improve scalability. These schemes support greater compositionality by allowing atomic sections to include both sequential and parallel procedure calls. Additionally, they expand the capabilities of reduction by enabling both left- and right-mover-based commutative reorderings.

Anchor [15] applies reduction to a low-level object-oriented language, where mover annotations are assigned to read and write accesses to object fields. It introduces a type system that enables proving the atomicity of entire procedures, which builds on Lipton's reduction. In contrast, our work is set in a more abstract language, supports compositional reduction reasoning about procedures, and accounts for parallel composition. [16] investigates the integration of reduction with rely-guarantee reasoning, which falls outside the scope of this work.

CSPEC [8] takes an approach similar to Civl but mechanizes all metatheory within the Rocq theorem prover [39] for flexibility and sound extensibility. Armada [36] also has flexible and mechanized metatheory whose usefulness is demonstrated by implementing a variety of program transformations, including those catering to fine-grained concurrency and weak memory models. Iron-Fleet [22] embeds TLA-style state-machine modeling [33] into the Dafny verifier [34] to refine high-level distributed systems specifications into low-level executable implementations. Their proofs embed reduction reasoning into Dafny in a rather ad-hoc manner.

Movers have also been used to define an equivalence-preserving transformation that eliminates buffers in message-passing programs [6,40]. These works define a restricted class of programs and prove that reasoning about the set of *rendezvous* executions of these programs, where messages are delivered instantaneously, is complete, i.e., any other execution is equivalent to a rendezvous execution, up to reordering of mover actions. For instance, [40] introduces some number of heuristics which are based on syntax in order to reduce a given program. Those heuristics do not apply to our case studies, and it is hard to imagine an extension where they would become applicable. For instance, reduction is sometimes enabled by abstracting actions (message handlers) and this cannot be handled via syntactical arguments. Two-phase commit (2PC) is a canonical benchmark in this line of work and has been verified many times in a variety of systems, including automated ones[10,40]. In our 2PC, replicas use nontrivial logic to determine their votes, which is not the case for the versions used in these systems. In those previous works, replicas vote *Yes* or *No* nondeterministically, which significantly simplifies the correctness argument: all message handlers are left movers without requiring any abstraction [30]. In contrast, in our version of 2PC, some message handlers are right movers and some are left movers, after devising appropriate abstractions.

Commutativity reasoning in algorithmic verification. In the context of algorithmic verification, commutativity reasoning manifests in the so-called partial-order reduction techniques [21,18,2,26] which mostly concern finite-state systems or executions of bounded length.

In the context of automated proof synthesis for infinite-state programs, most existing work focuses on programs with a bounded number of threads [9,12,13]. The work in [14] proposes an instrumentation scheme for parameterized programs, where an unbounded number of threads execute the same code. This scheme enables the representation of sound reductions in such settings. Additionally, they formalize a notion of reduction usefulness, suggesting that a suitable reduction can lead to proofs requiring fewer or simpler ghost variables.

Acknowledgments. This work is partially partially supported by the French National Research Agency (project SCEPROOF).

10   Data Availability Statement

The implementation and all artifacts required to reproduce the results of this paper are publicly available. The source code of the Civl extension and the underlying Boogie infrastructure can be obtained from

https://github.com/boogie-org/boogie/tree/master/Source

The examples and benchmarks used in the evaluation are available in the Civl test suite at

https://github.com/boogie-org/boogie/tree/master/Test/civl

The experiments rely on the versions of Boogie and Z3 retrieved by the build scripts in the repository. These scripts contain the exact commands used to run the benchmarks and to produce the results reported in the paper. Reproduction can therefore be achieved by checking out the repository and following the documented build and evaluation instructions.

References

1. Martín Abadi and Leslie Lamport. The Existence of Refinement Mappings. *Theor. Comput. Sci.*, 82(2):253–284, 1991. `doi:10.1016/0304-3975(91)90224-P`.
2. Parosh Aziz Abdulla, Stavros Aronis, Bengt Jonsson, and Konstantinos Sagonas. Optimal dynamic partial order reduction. In Suresh Jagannathan and Peter Sewell, editors, *The 41st Annual ACM SIGPLAN-SIGACT Symposium on Principles of Programming Languages, POPL '14, San Diego, CA, USA, January 20-21, 2014*, pages 373–384. ACM, 2014. `doi:10.1145/2535838.2535845`.
3. Yehuda Afek, Hagit Attiya, Danny Dolev, Eli Gafni, Michael Merritt, and Nir Shavit. Atomic Snapshots of Shared Memory. *J. ACM*, 40(4):873–890, 1993. `doi:10.1145/153724.153741`.
4. Hagit Attiya, Amotz Bar-Noy, and Danny Dolev. Sharing Memory Robustly in Message-Passing Systems. *J. ACM*, 42(1):124–142, 1995. `doi:10.1145/200836.200869`.
5. Hagit Attiya and Constantin Enea. Putting Strong Linearizability in Context: Preserving Hyperproperties in Programs that Use Concurrent Objects. In Jukka Suomela, editor, *33rd International Symposium on Distributed Computing, DISC 2019, October 14-18, 2019, Budapest, Hungary*, volume 146 of *LIPIcs*, pages 2:1–2:17. Schloss Dagstuhl - Leibniz-Zentrum für Informatik, 2019. URL: https://doi.org/10.4230/LIPIcs.DISC.2019.2, `doi:10.4230/LIPICS.DISC.2019.2`.
6. Alexander Bakst, Klaus von Gleissenthall, Rami Gökhan Kici, and Ranjit Jhala. Verifying distributed programs via canonical sequentialization. *Proc. ACM Program. Lang.*, 1(OOPSLA):110:1–110:27, 2017. `doi:10.1145/3133934`.
7. Michael Barnett, Bor-Yuh Evan Chang, Robert DeLine, Bart Jacobs, and K. Rustan M. Leino. Boogie: A Modular Reusable Verifier for Object-Oriented Programs. In Frank S. de Boer, Marcello M. Bonsangue, Susanne Graf, and Willem P. de Roever, editors, *Formal Methods for Components and Objects, 4th International Symposium, FMCO 2005, Amsterdam, The Netherlands, November 1-4, 2005, Revised Lectures*, volume 4111 of *Lecture Notes in Computer Science*, pages 364–387. Springer, 2005. `doi:10.1007/11804192_17`.

8. Tej Chajed, M. Frans Kaashoek, Butler W. Lampson, and Nickolai Zeldovich. Verifying concurrent software using movers in CSPEC. In Andrea C. Arpaci-Dusseau and Geoff Voelker, editors, *13th USENIX Symposium on Operating Systems Design and Implementation, OSDI 2018, Carlsbad, CA, USA, October 8-10, 2018*, pages 306–322. USENIX Association, 2018. URL: https://www.usenix.org/conference/osdi18/presentation/chajed.

9. Duc-Hiep Chu and Joxan Jaffar. A Framework to Synergize Partial Order Reduction with State Interpolation. In Eran Yahav, editor, *Hardware and Software: Verification and Testing - 10th International Haifa Verification Conference, HVC 2014, Haifa, Israel, November 18-20, 2014. Proceedings*, volume 8855 of *Lecture Notes in Computer Science*, pages 171–187. Springer, 2014. `doi: 10.1007/978-3-319-13338-6_14`.

10. Cezara Drăgoi, Thomas A. Henzinger, and Damien Zufferey. PSync: a partially synchronous language for fault-tolerant distributed algorithms. *SIGPLAN Not.*, 51(1):400–415, January 2016. `doi:10.1145/2914770.2837650`.

11. Tayfun Elmas, Shaz Qadeer, and Serdar Tasiran. A calculus of atomic actions. In Zhong Shao and Benjamin C. Pierce, editors, *Proceedings of the 36th ACM SIGPLAN-SIGACT Symposium on Principles of Programming Languages, POPL 2009, Savannah, GA, USA, January 21-23, 2009*, pages 2–15. ACM, 2009. `doi: 10.1145/1480881.1480885`.

12. Azadeh Farzan, Dominik Klumpp, and Andreas Podelski. Sound sequentialization for concurrent program verification. In Ranjit Jhala and Isil Dillig, editors, *PLDI '22: 43rd ACM SIGPLAN International Conference on Programming Language Design and Implementation, San Diego, CA, USA, June 13 - 17, 2022*, pages 506–521. ACM, 2022. `doi:10.1145/3519939.3523727`.

13. Azadeh Farzan, Dominik Klumpp, and Andreas Podelski. Stratified Commutativity in Verification Algorithms for Concurrent Programs. *Proc. ACM Program. Lang.*, 7(POPL):1426–1453, 2023. `doi:10.1145/3571242`.

14. Azadeh Farzan, Dominik Klumpp, and Andreas Podelski. Commutativity Simplifies Proofs of Parameterized Programs. *Proc. ACM Program. Lang.*, 8(POPL):2485–2513, 2024. `doi:10.1145/3632925`.

15. Cormac Flanagan and Stephen N. Freund. The Anchor verifier for blocking and non-blocking concurrent software. *Proc. ACM Program. Lang.*, 4(OOPSLA):156:1–156:29, 2020. `doi:10.1145/3428224`.

16. Cormac Flanagan and Stephen N. Freund. Mover Logic: A Concurrent Program Logic for Reduction and Rely-Guarantee Reasoning. In Jonathan Aldrich and Guido Salvaneschi, editors, *38th European Conference on Object-Oriented Programming, ECOOP 2024, September 16-20, 2024, Vienna, Austria*, volume 313 of *LIPIcs*, pages 16:1–16:29. Schloss Dagstuhl - Leibniz-Zentrum für Informatik, 2024. URL: https://doi.org/10.4230/LIPIcs.ECOOP.2024.16, `doi:10.4230/LIPICS.ECOOP.2024.16`.

17. Cormac Flanagan, Stephen N. Freund, and Shaz Qadeer. Exploiting Purity for Atomicity. *IEEE Trans. Software Eng.*, 31(4):275–291, 2005. `doi:10.1109/TSE.2005.47`.

18. Cormac Flanagan and Patrice Godefroid. Dynamic partial-order reduction for model checking software. In Jens Palsberg and Martín Abadi, editors, *Proceedings of the 32nd ACM SIGPLAN-SIGACT Symposium on Principles of Programming Languages, POPL 2005, Long Beach, California, USA, January 12-14, 2005*, pages 110–121. ACM, 2005. `doi:10.1145/1040305.1040315`.

19. Cormac Flanagan and Shaz Qadeer. A type and effect system for atomicity. In Ron Cytron and Rajiv Gupta, editors, *Proceedings of the ACM SIGPLAN 2003 Conference on Programming Language Design and Implementation 2003, San Diego, California, USA, June 9-11, 2003*, pages 338–349. ACM, 2003. `doi:10.1145/781131.781169`.

20. Namratha Gangamreddypalli, Constantin Enea, and Shaz Qadeer. Reduction for Structured Concurrent Programs, 2026. URL: https://arxiv.org/abs/2601.13341, `arXiv:2601.13341`.

21. Patrice Godefroid. *Partial-Order Methods for the Verification of Concurrent Systems - An Approach to the State-Explosion Problem*, volume 1032 of *Lecture Notes in Computer Science*. Springer, 1996. `doi:10.1007/3-540-60761-7`.

22. Chris Hawblitzel, Jon Howell, Manos Kapritsos, Jacob R. Lorch, Bryan Parno, Michael Lowell Roberts, Srinath T. V. Setty, and Brian Zill. IronFleet: proving practical distributed systems correct. In Ethan L. Miller and Steven Hand, editors, *Proceedings of the 25th Symposium on Operating Systems Principles, SOSP 2015, Monterey, CA, USA, October 4-7, 2015*, pages 1–17. ACM, 2015. `doi:10.1145/2815400.2815428`.

23. Chris Hawblitzel, Erez Petrank, Shaz Qadeer, and Serdar Tasiran. Automated and Modular Refinement Reasoning for Concurrent Programs. In Daniel Kroening and Corina S. Pasareanu, editors, *Computer Aided Verification - 27th International Conference, CAV 2015, San Francisco, CA, USA, July 18-24, 2015, Proceedings, Part II*, volume 9207 of *Lecture Notes in Computer Science*, pages 449–465. Springer, 2015. `doi:10.1007/978-3-319-21668-3_26`.

24. Maurice Herlihy and Jeannette M. Wing. Linearizability: A Correctness Condition for Concurrent Objects. *ACM Trans. Program. Lang. Syst.*, 12(3):463–492, 1990. `doi:10.1145/78969.78972`.

25. Cliff B. Jones. Specification and Design of (Parallel) Programs. In R. E. A. Mason, editor, *Information Processing 83, Proceedings of the IFIP 9th World Computer Congress, Paris, France, September 19-23, 1983*, pages 321–332. North-Holland/IFIP, 1983.

26. Michalis Kokologiannakis, Iason Marmanis, Vladimir Gladstein, and Viktor Vafeiadis. Truly stateless, optimal dynamic partial order reduction. *Proc. ACM Program. Lang.*, 6(POPL):1–28, 2022. `doi:10.1145/3498711`.

27. Bernhard Kragl, Constantin Enea, Thomas A. Henzinger, Suha Orhun Mutluergil, and Shaz Qadeer. Inductive sequentialization of asynchronous programs. In Alastair F. Donaldson and Emina Torlak, editors, *Proceedings of the 41st ACM SIGPLAN International Conference on Programming Language Design and Implementation, PLDI 2020, London, UK, June 15-20, 2020*, pages 227–242. ACM, 2020. `doi:10.1145/3385412.3385980`.

28. Bernhard Kragl and Shaz Qadeer. Layered Concurrent Programs. In Hana Chockler and Georg Weissenbacher, editors, *Computer Aided Verification - 30th International Conference, CAV 2018, Held as Part of the Federated Logic Conference, FloC 2018, Oxford, UK, July 14-17, 2018, Proceedings, Part I*, volume 10981 of *Lecture Notes in Computer Science*, pages 79–102. Springer, 2018. `doi:10.1007/978-3-319-96145-3_5`.

29. Bernhard Kragl and Shaz Qadeer. The Civl verifier. In *Formal Methods in Computer Aided Design, FMCAD 2021, New Haven, CT, USA, October 19-22, 2021*, pages 143–152. IEEE, 2021. URL: https://doi.org/10.34727/2021/isbn.978-3-85448-046-4_23, `doi:10.34727/2021/ISBN.978-3-85448-046-4_23`.

30. Bernhard Kragl, Shaz Qadeer, and Thomas A. Henzinger. Synchronizing the Asynchronous. In Sven Schewe and Lijun Zhang, editors, *29th International Conference on Concurrency Theory, CONCUR 2018, September 4-7, 2018, Beijing, China*, volume 118 of *LIPIcs*, pages 21:1–21:17. Schloss Dagstuhl - Leibniz-Zentrum für Informatik, 2018. URL: https://doi.org/10.4230/LIPIcs.CONCUR.2018.21, `doi:10.4230/LIPICS.CONCUR.2018.21`.

31. Bernhard Kragl, Shaz Qadeer, and Thomas A. Henzinger. Refinement for Structured Concurrent Programs. In Shuvendu K. Lahiri and Chao Wang, editors, *Computer Aided Verification - 32nd International Conference, CAV 2020, Los Angeles, CA, USA, July 21-24, 2020, Proceedings, Part I*, volume 12224 of *Lecture Notes in Computer Science*, pages 275–298. Springer, 2020. `doi:10.1007/978-3-030-53288-8_14`.

32. Jeffrey Kuskin, David Ofelt, Mark A. Heinrich, John Heinlein, Richard Simoni, Kourosh Gharachorloo, John Chapin, David Nakahira, Joel Baxter, Mark Horowitz, Anoop Gupta, Mendel Rosenblum, and John L. Hennessy. The Stanford FLASH Multiprocessor. In David A. Patterson, editor, *Proceedings of the 21st Annual International Symposium on Computer Architecture. Chicago, IL, USA, April 1994*, pages 302–313. IEEE Computer Society, 1994. `doi:10.1109/ISCA.1994.288140`.

33. Leslie Lamport. *Specifying Systems, The TLA+ Language and Tools for Hardware and Software Engineers*. Addison-Wesley, 2002. URL: http://research.microsoft.com/users/lamport/tla/book.html.

34. K. Rustan M. Leino. Dafny: An Automatic Program Verifier for Functional Correctness. In Edmund M. Clarke and Andrei Voronkov, editors, *Logic for Programming, Artificial Intelligence, and Reasoning - 16th International Conference, LPAR-16, Dakar, Senegal, April 25-May 1, 2010, Revised Selected Papers*, volume 6355 of *Lecture Notes in Computer Science*, pages 348–370. Springer, 2010. `doi:10.1007/978-3-642-17511-4_20`.

35. Richard J. Lipton. Reduction: A Method of Proving Properties of Parallel Programs. *Commun. ACM*, 18(12):717–721, 1975. `doi:10.1145/361227.361234`.

36. Jacob R. Lorch, Yixuan Chen, Manos Kapritsos, Bryan Parno, Shaz Qadeer, Upamanyu Sharma, James R. Wilcox, and Xueyuan Zhao. Armada: low-effort verification of high-performance concurrent programs. In Alastair F. Donaldson and Emina Torlak, editors, *Proceedings of the 41st ACM SIGPLAN International Conference on Programming Language Design and Implementation, PLDI 2020, London, UK, June 15-20, 2020*, pages 197–210. ACM, 2020. `doi:10.1145/3385412.3385971`.

37. Nancy A. Lynch and Frits W. Vaandrager. Forward and Backward Simulations: I. Untimed Systems. *Inf. Comput.*, 121(2):214–233, 1995. URL: https://doi.org/10.1006/inco.1995.1134, `doi:10.1006/INCO.1995.1134`.

38. Susan S. Owicki and David Gries. Verifying Properties of Parallel Programs: An Axiomatic Approach. *Commun. ACM*, 19(5):279–285, 1976. `doi:10.1145/360051.360224`.

39. The Coq Development Team. The Coq Proof Assistant, version 8.11.0, 2020. `doi:10.5281/zenodo.3744225`.

40. Klaus von Gleissenthall, Rami Gökhan Kici, Alexander Bakst, Deian Stefan, and Ranjit Jhala. Pretend synchrony: synchronous verification of asynchronous distributed programs. *Proc. ACM Program. Lang.*, 3(POPL):59:1–59:30, 2019. `doi:10.1145/3290372`.

Specification-Driven Generation of Summaries for Symbolic Execution

Rafael Gonçalves[1,2,3] (✉) , Frederico Ramos[2,3] , Pedro Adão[2,4] ,
and José Fragoso Santos[2,3]

[1]Carnegie Mellon University, Pittsburgh, PA, USA
`rgoncalv@andrew.cmu.edu`
[2]Instituto Superior Técnico, Universidade de Lisboa, Lisbon, Portugal
`{frederico.ramos,pedro.adao,jose.fragoso}@tecnico.ulisboa.pt`
[3]INESC-ID, Lisbon, Portugal
[4]Instituto de Telecomunicações, Aveiro, Portugal

Abstract. Symbolic execution is a popular program analysis technique that has been successfully used for bug-finding and bounded verification in various modern programming languages. Despite its popularity, however, symbolic execution suffers from two main limitations when applied to real-world code: interactions with the runtime environment and path explosion. Symbolic summaries are the standard solution to tackle these challenges. Yet, the development of summaries remains to this day a manual task that is known to be highly error-prone. To address this, we propose SUMGEN, a new tool for automatically generating correct-by-construction summaries from function specifications. With SUMGEN, we were able to generate a total of 131 summaries for 47 LIBC functions, demonstrating the effectiveness of our methodology in producing correct summaries for real-world, highly complex code.

Keywords: Symbolic Execution, Symbolic Summaries, Summary Generation, Separation Logic.

1 Introduction

Symbolic execution (SE) [8,35] is a program analysis technique that bridges the gap between program testing and verification. It has been used for bug detection and bounded verification in multiple programming languages, such as C [9,59], JavaScript [18,19,37], and WebAssembly [43,44]. By allowing the execution of programs with symbolic inputs instead of concrete ones, SE engines are able to explore all execution paths of a given program up to a bound. The idea is to maintain for each execution path a *symbolic state* with: **(i)** a *symbolic store and heap* holding the contents of the variable store and heap memory of the program along that path; and **(ii)** a first order formula, called *path condition*, describing the constraints on the symbolic inputs that led the execution towards that path. SE engines rely on SMT solvers such as Z3 [45] or cvc5 [5] to check the feasibility of explored paths as well as the validity of any assertions provided by the developers.

R. Krebbers (Ed.): ESOP 2026, LNCS 16501, pp. 283–313, 2026.
https://doi.org/10.1007/978-3-032-22720-1_11

Despite its widespread use, symbolic execution suffers from two main limitations when applied to real-world code: interactions with the runtime environment and path explosion [3]. A common solution employed by modern SE engines to tackle these challenges is to use *symbolic summaries* [9,12,15,44,55,59] to model both external functions and internal functions with a high degree of branching. A symbolic summary is an operational model of a function that simulates its behavior by interacting directly with the underlying symbolic state. In general, summaries extend the current path condition with constraints that capture the behavior of their corresponding functions without having to actually symbolically execute them. By acting directly on the symbolic state, summaries are an effective mechanism to both model the execution of external functions, whose code is not available for analysis, and contain the number of explored paths by avoiding unnecessary branching [3,54].

Modern summaries, however, are typically handwritten, often in a tool-specific manner and without being verified. This manual approach is far from ideal, as it is highly error-prone and can introduce subtle bugs that are difficult to detect. Such bugs can undermine the soundness and/or completeness guarantees of the tools that rely on these summaries, potentially leading to the incorrect exclusion of valid execution paths [54]. The consequences can be dire; for instance, *angr* [59], a state-of-the-art binary analysis tool, may fail to identify vulnerable paths due to its reliance on buggy summaries, resulting in missed vulnerabilities. Furthermore, this issue is widespread; Ramos et al. [54] automatically analyzed 37 summaries sourced from three popular SE engines (*angr* [59], *Binsec* [15] and *Manticore* [44]), and detected bugs in 24 of those. The significant percentage of summaries with bugs clearly shows that the manual approach to writing summaries is inadequate. Instead, symbolic summaries should be generated using automated methods.

To fill this gap, we propose a new methodology for automatically generating symbolic summaries from function specifications. The declarative nature of specifications makes the behaviors they model much easier to understand compared to those captured by summaries, which are often procedural, lengthy, and dependent on complex symbolic formulas. We advocate the philosophy that tool developers should focus on writing specifications for the library functions they wish to support, rather than writing highly complex summaries that lack any correctness guarantees. Examples of LIBC function specifications are available [2,21,47,48] and can be adapted for this purpose.

Prior work on program synthesis has mostly relied on SMT solvers to drive code generation [16,33,51]. This paper examines a different approach; namely, that we can represent the specifications themselves in a format that directly translates into executable code, bypassing the need for an SMT solver-guided search. To this end, we introduce *matching trees*, which coalesce the various cases of a specification into a single tree-like data structure. Matching trees are the cornerstone of our methodology, as they provide a convenient format for the internal representation of assertions. While approaches similar to matching trees have been used for frame inference calculation in Separation Logic engines [17,19,39,40], we are the first to employ them to drive code synthesis. Moreover, while we use them here to generate symbolic summaries, matching trees can also be applied to produce other forms of executable code, including regular programs.

We implement our methodology in SUMGEN, a new tool for the automatic generation of summaries for modern SE engines. To produce a summary, SUM-GEN constructs a matching tree from the corresponding specification, which it then leverages to: **(i)** resolve the existential bindings in the function's precondition; and **(ii)** use the computed bindings to update the symbolic state according to the function's postcondition. SUMGEN produces code in an intermediate language, allowing for summaries to be generated for multiple tools. Currently, we support the generation of summaries in C and Python, respectively using the symbolic reflection API proposed by Ramos et al. [54] and the internal API of *angr* [59]. Extending SUMGEN with support for other backends is straightforward (*cf.* §3). To evaluate SUMGEN, we used it to generate 131 symbolic summaries for 47 LIBC functions. Our evaluation shows that these summaries are both correct by construction, easier to obtain, and as performant as handcrafted summaries.

In short, we make the following contributions:

- A methodology for generating summaries from function specifications (§3);
- SUMGEN, a tool for automatically generating symbolic summaries in C and Python (§3);
- A library of 131 summaries modeling 47 LIBC functions, shown to be correct, easier to obtain, and as performant as handcrafted summaries (§5).

2   Motivation and Overview

In this section, we present our motivation and approach for summary generation. We begin by discussing summary support in state-of-the-art tools (§2.1) and the challenges posed by buggy summaries (§2.2), and then give a high-level overview of SUMGEN (§2.3).

2.1   Summaries in State-of-the-Art Tools

To motivate our approach, we survey summary support for LIBC functions in nine state-of-the-art symbolic execution tools: *angr* [59], *Binsec* [15], *Divine* [4], *Klee* [9], *Manticore* [44], *otter* [55], *PySymEmu* [42], *S2E* [12], and *Symbiotic* [10]. We have excluded tools that do not include any LIBC summary or that are not open source. We focus on LIBC functions because they are widespread, foundational to many C programs, and have a significant security impact, making robust summaries essential for effectively detecting vulnerabilities. Furthermore, their well-defined behaviors and specifications make them amenable to precise modeling for symbolic execution. The results of our survey are shown in Figure 1.

The first notable observation is that symbolic summaries are pervasive in modern symbolic execution tools. Figure 1a shows, for each selected tool, the

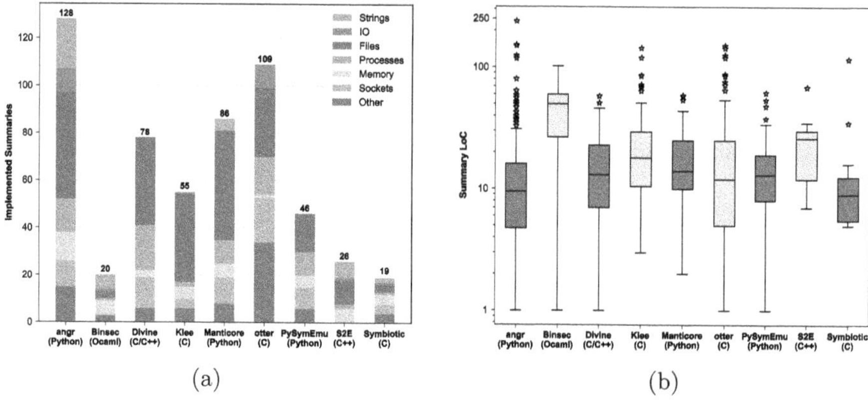

Fig. 1. Tool statistics: (a) number of implemented summaries, and (b) complexity of summaries.

total number of supported LIBC summaries and the programming language in which those summaries are implemented. We divide LIBC summaries into seven categories: string manipulation, I/O, file handling, process management, memory, sockets, and other system calls (*e.g.*, time and sysinfo). All tools implement multiple summaries from different categories; for instance, the three tools with the highest support, *angr*, *otter* and *Manticore*, implement 128, 109, and 86 summaries, respectively. In contrast, the tool with the least support, *Symbiotic*, implements 19 summaries from all seven categories.

Another notable observation is the significant variation in summary complexity. The box plot given in Figure 1b shows, for each of the tools, the complexity of the implemented summaries in terms of lines of code (LoC). Despite the large variety of summaries, the average number of LoC per summary is relatively stable across different tools, ranging between 10 and 20. This stems from the fact that many summaries are simple stubs (*e.g.*, those in the file handling and I/O categories) rather than fully-fledged models of the corresponding concrete functions. However, the complexity of individual summaries varies greatly; for example, *angr*'s summaries range from 1 to 238 LoC, with a significant number of outliers on the longer end. Large summaries, in particular, present a significant challenge for tool developers, as their reliance on complex handcrafted symbolic formulas makes them highly error-prone. We elaborate on this issue in §2.2 through a motivating example.

2.2 Bugs in Summaries

In the context of symbolic summaries, we define a *bug* as a defect that causes the summary's behavior to deviate from the reference implementation of the function it models in an irregular manner (*cf.* §2.3 for the formal definition). Buggy summaries are a common occurrence in symbolic execution tools. In a study analyzing 37 summaries from *angr* [59], *Binsec* [15] and *Manticore* [44], Ramos

```python
1  def sum_strcmp(s1, s2):
2      min_zero_idx = min(api.find_zero(s1), api.find_zero(s2))
3      ret = s1[min_zero_idx] - s2[min_zero_idx]
4      for i in range(min_zero_idx - 1, -1, -1):
5          c1, c2 = s1[i], s2[i]
6          if api.is_symb(c1) or api.is_symb(c2):
7              ret = api.mk_ite(c1 != c2, c1 - c2, ret)
8          elif c1 != c2:
9              ret = c1 - c2
10     return ret
```

Fig. 2. Buggy strcmp summary in *Manticore*.

et al. [54] found bugs in 24, including in summaries for popular LIBC functions such as strcmp, strcpy and atoi. These bugs are often subtle and linked to corner cases that can cause tools to miss potential vulnerabilities when verifying complex codebases.

Bug in Manticore. In the following, we examine a buggy summary for the LIBC function strcmp sourced from *Manticore* [44]. The strcmp function compares two null-terminated strings, s1 and s2, returning 0 if they are equal or the difference between the first non-matching pair of characters otherwise.

Figure 2 shows a simplified but functionally equivalent implementation of the summary. This version improves clarity by removing unnecessary details and standardizing notation; the original summary is substantially more complex, totaling 24 LoC.[1] Nevertheless, even in this simplified form, the summary remains difficult to debug, as it manipulates complex symbolic formulas and depends on several symbolic reflection primitives [54]: **(i)** find_zero, which returns the index of the *first* byte whose value (concrete or symbolic) is guaranteed to be zero; **(ii)** is_symb, which checks if a variable is symbolic; and **(iii)** mk_ite, which creates an if-then-else (ITE) expression. In addition, arithmetic and logical operators are overloaded to operate on symbolic expressions; for example, the formula c1 != c2 is interpreted as a not-equal constraint between c1 and c2 whenever at least one of them is symbolic.

The summary begins by locating the first byte guaranteed to be zero (line 2) and setting the initial return value to be the difference between the two strings at that position (line 3). It then iterates backwards through the strings, considering two cases at each position: **(1)** if at least one byte is symbolic, it builds an if-then-else expression that evaluates to the difference between the bytes if they differ, or to the previous return value otherwise (line 7); or **(2)** if both bytes are concrete, it updates the return value only if they differ (line 9).

As an example, consider an execution with symbolic strings $s1 \mapsto [\hat{c}_1, \hat{c}_2, `\backslash 0`]$ and $s2 \mapsto [\hat{c}_3, \hat{c}_4, `\backslash 0`]$, where $\hat{c}_1, \ldots, \hat{c}_4$ are unconstrained symbolic bytes. Since

---

[1] https://github.com/trailofbits/manticore/blob/master/manticore/native/models.py#L99

$\hat{c}_1, \ldots, \hat{c}_4$ are unconstrained, the return value is initially set to 0, and the summary subsequently builds a nested if-then-else expression to compare the remaining pairs of symbolic bytes, producing the formula:

$$\mathsf{ITE}(\hat{c}_1 \neq \hat{c}_3, \hat{c}_1 - \hat{c}_3, \mathsf{ITE}(\hat{c}_2 \neq \hat{c}_4, \hat{c}_2 - \hat{c}_4, 0))$$

This summary, however, contains a subtle bug: it overlooks the possibility that intermediate symbolic bytes may be the null terminator. A counterexample is given by constraining $\hat{c}_1, \ldots, \hat{c}_4$ in the formula above such that $\mathsf{s1} \mapsto [\text{'}\backslash 0\text{'}, \text{'}a\text{'}, \text{'}\backslash 0\text{'}]$ and $\mathsf{s2} \mapsto [\text{'}\backslash 0\text{'}, \text{'}b\text{'}, \text{'}\backslash 0\text{'}]$, for which the if-then-else expression incorrectly evaluates to -1, while the strcmp function returns 0.

2.3 Summary Generation

The example given above shows that the manual approach to summary writing is highly error-prone. In contrast, our methodology allows for the automatic generation of correct-by-construction summaries from function specifications. With our approach, rather than writing a potentially buggy summary from scratch, users need only to provide a specification for the target function, and our tool automatically generates a summary that captures its behavior.

Specifications SumGen supports three types of specifications: **(1)** *under-approximating* (UX) specifications [49,53] that model a subset of the paths of the function; **(2)** *over-approximating* (OX) specifications [50,56] that model a superset of the paths of the function; and **(3)** *exact* (EX) specifications [41] that model the same set of paths as the function.

Consider, for example, the strcmp function. To write a specification for strcmp, we first define a predicate $\mathsf{strd}(s1, s2, \delta)$, which asserts that the difference between the values of the first non-matching pair of characters in $s1$ and $s2$ is δ. The predicate $\mathsf{strd}(s1, s2, \delta)$ has two cases: **(1)** $s1$ or $s2$ point to '$\backslash 0$', or to two distinct non-null characters, and δ is the difference between those characters; or **(2)** $s1$ and $s2$ point to equal non-null characters and δ is the difference between $s1 + 1$ and $s2 + 1$. We assume that all character arrays are eventually null-terminated by a concrete '$\backslash 0$'. Put formally:

$$\mathsf{strd}(s1, s2, \delta) \triangleq$$
$$\quad s1 \mapsto c1 \uplus s2 \mapsto c2 \uplus (c1 = \text{'}\backslash 0\text{'} \vee c2 = \text{'}\backslash 0\text{'} \vee c1 \neq c2) \uplus \delta = c1 - c2$$
$$\quad \vee$$
$$\quad s1 \mapsto c1 \uplus s2 \mapsto c2 \uplus (c1 \neq \text{'}\backslash 0\text{'} \wedge c2 \neq \text{'}\backslash 0\text{'} \wedge c1 = c2) \uplus \mathsf{strd}(s1 + 1, s2 + 1, \delta)$$

where $\uplus$ denotes the *overlapping conjunction* [20,31]. The overlapping conjunction $P \uplus Q$ states that the heap may be split into two subheaps, one satisfying P and the other Q, but these subheaps need not be disjoint. Unlike the more traditional separating conjunction $P \star Q$, the overlapping conjunction does not enforce resource non-duplication. This is particularly useful in our setting, as the functions we target may have overlapping arguments, making it counterproductive to enforce strict separation. Given this predicate, we can easily write an exact specification for strcmp:

$$\{\mathrm{strd}(s1, s2, \delta)\}\ \mathsf{int\ strcmp(char * s1, char * s2)}\ \{\mathrm{ret} = \delta\}$$

where ret denotes the return value of the function.

The core challenge in specification-based synthesis lies in how one goes about generating heap-manipulating code from *declarative* specifications such as the one above. Prior work addresses this by encoding specifications as a set of constraints and letting an SMT solver find a program that satisfies them [16,33,51]. We advocate a different approach; namely, that we can leverage matching plans [17,19,39,40] for code synthesis by encoding specifications in a new intermediate representation that we call *matching trees*. A matching tree is a tree-like data structure that coalesces the various cases of a specification/predicate in a format that more closely resembles procedural code. Matching trees are the cornerstone of our methodology; we elaborate on them in §3.1.

From Specifications to Summaries Like specifications, there are three types of symbolic summaries: **(1)** *under-approximating* (UX) summaries that model a subset of the paths of the function; **(2)** *over-approximating* (OX) summaries that model a superset of the paths of the function; and **(3)** *exact* (EX) summaries that model the same set of paths as the function. A summary is considered *buggy* if it is neither UX, OX, nor EX, meaning that it excludes correct paths (*i.e.*, it does not over-approximate) and includes spurious paths (*i.e.*, it does not under-approximate). For example, the *Manticore* summary for strcmp (Figure 2) is buggy because it may produce an ITE expression that evaluates to -1 when $s1 \mapsto$ ['\0', 'a', '\0'] and $s2 \mapsto$ ['\0', 'b', '\0'], excluding a correct path (where the return value should be 0) and including a spurious one (where the return value is -1).

Table 1. Specification types and the summaries they produce.

		Summary		
		UX	OX	EX
	UX	✓	✗	✗
Spec	OX	✗	✓	✗
	EX	✓	✓	✓

SUMGEN supports the generation of the three types of summaries (UX, OX and EX). Which type of summary is more useful depends on the application: UX summaries are generally better suited for bug finding, whereas verification typically relies on OX summaries [49]. Table 1 shows which summary types can be generated from each specification type. Note that not all summary types can be generated from every specification type. For example, attempting to generate an OX summary from a UX specification could lead to both missing correct paths that the UX specification does not cover, and including spurious paths introduced by the OX generation procedure, rendering the summary buggy. Conversely, we cannot obtain a UX summary from an OX specification, nor an EX summary from UX and OX specifications.

```
1   def sum_strcmp(s1, s2):
2       c1, c2 = s1[0], s2[0]
3       if api.is_certain(c1 == '\0' or c2 == '\0' or c1 != c2):
4           return c1 - c2
5       else if api.is_certain(c1 != '\0' and c2 != '\0' and c1 == c2):
6           return sum_strcmp(s1[1:], s2[1:])
7       else:
8           d1 = api.scoped_call(sum_strcmp, [s1, s2], \
9                                c1 == '\0' or c2 == '\0' or c1 != c2)
10          d2 = api.scoped_call(sum_strcmp, [s1, s2], \
11                               c1 != '\0' and c2 != '\0' and c1 == c2)
12          return api.mk_ite(c1 == '\0' or c2 == '\0' or c1 != c2, d1, d2)
```

Fig. 3. Exact SUMGEN summary for strcmp.

Broadly speaking, the task of generating a summary can be understood as producing code that simulates the behavior of the corresponding function. To achieve this, SUMGEN constructs a matching tree from the given specification and compiles it into a program that: **(i)** resolves the existential bindings in the function's precondition; and **(ii)** uses the computed bindings to update the symbolic state according to the function's postcondition. As part of step **(ii)**, the summary computes a symbolic expression denoting the return value of the target function and updates the current path condition with the appropriate constraints on that value.

Figure 3 shows the exact strcmp summary generated by SUMGEN. This summary relies on two new symbolic reflection primitives: **(i)** is_certain, which checks if a given formula provably holds in the current state; and **(ii)** scoped_call, which performs a scoped function call. Scoped calls are central to our approach. In a nutshell, they augment the path condition with some logical constraint and call a function under that scope, restoring the original path condition once the call returns. We delve into the mechanics of scoped calls further in §3.2.

Given the two symbolic strings $s1 \mapsto [\hat{c}_1, \hat{c}_2, `\backslash 0\text{'}]$ and $s2 \mapsto [\hat{c}_3, \hat{c}_4, `\backslash 0\text{'}]$, where $\hat{c}_1, \ldots, \hat{c}_4$ are unconstrained symbolic bytes, this summary produces the formula:

$$\mathsf{ITE}(\hat{c}_1 = `\backslash 0\text{'} \vee \hat{c}_3 = `\backslash 0\text{'} \vee \hat{c}_1 \neq \hat{c}_3, \hat{c}_1 - \hat{c}_3,$$
$$\mathsf{ITE}(\hat{c}_2 = `\backslash 0\text{'} \vee \hat{c}_4 = `\backslash 0\text{'} \vee \hat{c}_2 \neq \hat{c}_4, \hat{c}_2 - \hat{c}_4, 0))$$

In general, SUMGEN summaries can be seen as a disjunction of the various cases of a specification. When the summary knows precisely which case to apply, it computes the return value directly (lines 4 and 6). When it does not, the summary guides execution towards a *default branch* modeling the possible cases of the call (lines 8–12). For instance, if we do not know whether the constraint $c1 = `\backslash 0\text{'} \vee c2 = `\backslash 0\text{'} \vee c1 \neq c2$ or its negation holds, the summary computes the return values d1 and d2 based on each assumption (lines 8–9 and 10–11, respectively) and builds an if-then-else expression that evaluates to d1 if the first constraint holds and to d2 otherwise (line 12). In our example, since $\hat{c}_1, \ldots, \hat{c}_4$ are unconstrained symbolic bytes, the execution is guided towards the default

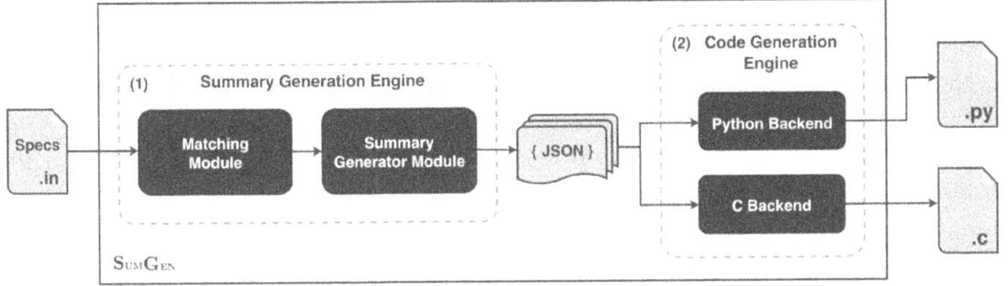

Fig. 4. Architecture of SumGen.

branch, building a nested if-then-else expression that exactly models the possible outcomes of the call to strcmp.

Unlike the strcmp summary implemented by *Manticore*, this summary is correct; in particular, the if-then-else expression derived above correctly evaluates to 0 if both $\hat{c}_1$ and $\hat{c}_3$ are equal to '\0'.

3   Summary Generation

Figure 4 gives a high-level overview of the architecture of SumGen. The implementation consists of two main components: **(1)** a *summary generation engine* implemented in Haskell ($\approx$3.5k LoC) that, given a specification and desired correctness property (UX/OX/EX), generates a summary in our intermediate language; and **(2)** a *code generation engine* implemented in Python ($\approx$700 LoC) that translates the generated summaries into executable code. SumGen is open source [28] and available online as a web application [27].

The summary generation engine consists of two modules: **(i)** the *matching module*, which parses a function specification written in our assertion language together with its associated predicate definitions and constructs the appropriate matching trees (*cf.* §3.1); and **(ii)** the *summary generator module*, which produces symbolic summaries in our intermediate language and outputs their ASTs in JSON format (*cf.* §3.2).

Our choice to produce summaries first in an intermediate language allows for the modularity of the code generation engine, which can be adapted to support multiple backends with minimal development effort. Currently, we support two backends: a C backend, which generates C summaries that use Ramos et al.'s [54] tool-independent symbolic reflection API, and a Python backend, which generates Python summaries that use *angr*'s [59] symbolic API. In order to extend SumGen with support for other languages, one needs only to implement the corresponding backend and add it to the code generation engine.

3.1   Syntax and Matching Trees

SumGen is built on top of a simple assertion language whose syntax is given below. Simple assertions, $p \in \mathcal{SA}$, are either pure assertions (*e.g.*, relational and logical operations over expressions $e \in \mathcal{E}xpr$), directed equalities, cell assertions, or predicate assertions. Directed equalities, $x \ominus e$, differ from regular equalities in that they can be interpreted as an assignment; for example, if x is existentially quantified, the directed equality $x \ominus e$ gives us the binding of x. The cell assertion, $x \mapsto_\tau y$, states that x points to a memory cell holding y with type τ. Predicate assertions are of the form $\alpha(\bar{e}; y)$, where $\bar{e}$ is a list of arguments and y is a special return argument to be used by the generation procedure. Assertions, $P, Q \in \mathcal{A}srt$, are either the empty assertion, a simple assertion, or two assertions conjoined by the overlapping conjunction $P \uplus Q$.

The syntax of assertions

$$\pi \in \Pi \triangleq e_1 \ominus e_2 \mid \pi_1 \wedge \pi_2 \mid \pi_1 \vee \pi_2 \mid \neg\pi \qquad \ominus \in \{>, <, \geq, \leq, =, \neq\}$$

$$p, q \in \mathcal{SA} \triangleq \pi \mid x \ominus e \mid x \mapsto_\tau y \mid \alpha(\bar{e}; y) \qquad P, Q \in \mathcal{A}srt \triangleq \mathsf{emp} \mid p \mid P \uplus Q$$

$$\Phi \in \mathcal{P}red \triangleq \mathsf{pred}\ \alpha(\bar{x}; y)\,\{\bar{P}\} \qquad \Sigma \in \mathcal{S}pec \triangleq \{P\}\,\mathsf{fn}\ f(\bar{x})\,\{Q; y; \pi\}$$

Predicate definitions, $\Phi \in \mathcal{P}red$, are of the form $\mathsf{pred}\ \alpha(\bar{x}; y)\,\{\bar{P}\}$, where α is the predicate name, $\bar{x}$ a list of the formal parameters, y a special return parameter to be used by the generation procedure, and $\bar{P}$ a sequence of assertions, each corresponding to a predicate case (*i.e.*, the full predicate definition is a disjunction of the elements of $\bar{P}$). Specifications, $\Sigma \in \mathcal{S}pec$, are of the form $\{P\}\,\mathsf{fn}\ f(\bar{x})\,\{Q; y; \pi\}$, where P is the precondition, Q the postcondition, y the return variable, and π a set of restrictions on the value of y. A specification is said to be *non-mutating* if it does not modify heap memory (*i.e.*, if the postcondition Q equals the precondition P); otherwise, it is said to be *mutating*. For simplicity, we omit the postcondition in non-mutating specifications, writing them as $\{P\}\,\mathsf{fn}\ f(\bar{x})\,\{y; \pi\}$. Moreover, we assume any variables that appear in an assertion and are not among the formal parameters of the corresponding specification/predicate to be existentially quantified; for instance, in the $\mathsf{strd}(s1, s2; \delta)$ predicate, the variables $c1$ and $c2$ are existentially quantified. Following this syntax, we write the strcmp specification as:

$$\{\mathsf{strd}(s1, s2; \delta)\}\,\mathsf{fn}\ \mathsf{strcmp}(s1, s2)\,\{\delta\}$$

and the predicate $\mathsf{strd}(s1, s2; \delta)$ as:

$$\mathsf{pred}\ \mathsf{strd}(s1, s2; \delta)\,\{$$
$$s1 \mapsto c1 \uplus s2 \mapsto c2 \uplus (c1 = \text{`\textbackslash 0'} \vee c2 = \text{`\textbackslash 0'} \vee c1 \neq c2) \uplus \delta \ominus c1 - c2;$$
$$s1 \mapsto c1 \uplus s2 \mapsto c2 \uplus (c1 \neq \text{`\textbackslash 0'} \wedge c2 \neq \text{`\textbackslash 0'} \wedge c1 = c2) \uplus \mathsf{strd}(s1 + 1, s2 + 1; \delta)$$
$$\}$$

Note that, in the strcmp specification, both Q and π are omitted, as the function is non-mutating and does not place any constraints on the return value (*i.e.*, δ).

SUMGEN implements its *specification parser* on top of *Parsec* [36]. For simplicity, we omit some implementation details; in particular, while most types are implicit in the theory, all types are explicit in practice to support statically typed languages such as C.

Matching Generating a summary requires representing assertions in a format that can be more directly translated into executable code. To this end, we build on matching plans [19,17,40,39] with a new structure called *matching trees*.

In/Out-Parameters. Matching trees leverage *in/out-parameters* [19,46] to describe how the existentially quantified variables of a given specification/predicate can be determined from its formal parameters. Let us consider the case of simple assertions, which may contain any number of variables. Intuitively, an in-parameter of a simple assertion can be understood as a variable that we "know" and an out-parameter as a variable that we can "learn" from the assertion by inspecting the current state. For instance, the cell assertion $s1 \mapsto c1$ appearing in the predicate $\mathrm{strd}(s1, s2; \delta)$ has one in-parameter, $s1$, and one out-parameter, $c1$. Note that, given the value of $s1$ and the current state, we can learn the value of $c1$ by inspecting the contents of $s1$, but the opposite does not hold. The definition also extends to specifications and predicates, where the in-parameters are the formal parameters $\bar{x}$ and the out-parameter is the return variable/parameter y.

Matching Trees. Matching trees describe how the out-parameters of specifications/predicates can be computed from their in-parameters. In short, a *matching tree* is a tree-like data structure that coalesces the various cases of a specification/predicate by representing a disjunction of compound assertions as a single tree of simple assertions. We formalize matching trees in Definition 1.

Definition 1 (Matching Tree). *A matching tree* $t \in \mathcal{MT}$ *is defined as:*

$$t \in \mathcal{MT} \triangleq \bullet \mid \langle p, t' \rangle \mid \langle \pi, t_1, t_2 \rangle$$

The leaf node $\bullet$ is simply emp. The single node $\langle p, t' \rangle$ represents a simple assertion. The double node $\langle \pi, t_1, t_2 \rangle$ represents a condition that discriminates between two disjuncts. In Figure 5, we show a matching tree for the predicate $\mathrm{strd}(s1, s2; \delta)$. Notice the double node labeled $c1 = \text{'}\backslash 0\text{'} \vee c2 = \text{'}\backslash 0\text{'} \vee c1 \neq c2$, which discriminates between the two cases of the predicate, and how we compute the out-parameter δ accordingly.

A matching tree t is said to be *valid* w.r.t. to a set of variables X *iff*, for every node, each of its in-parameters is either an out-parameter of one of its ancestors or an element of X. A matching tree representing a specification/predicate should always be valid w.r.t. the set containing its formal parameters, ensuring that the out-parameters can be computed from the in-parameters. The matching tree we derived for $\mathrm{strd}(s1, s2; \delta)$, for instance, is valid w.r.t. the set $\{s1, s2\}$ containing the in-parameters of the predicate. However, if we were to remove the simple assertion $s1 \mapsto c1$, the tree would no longer

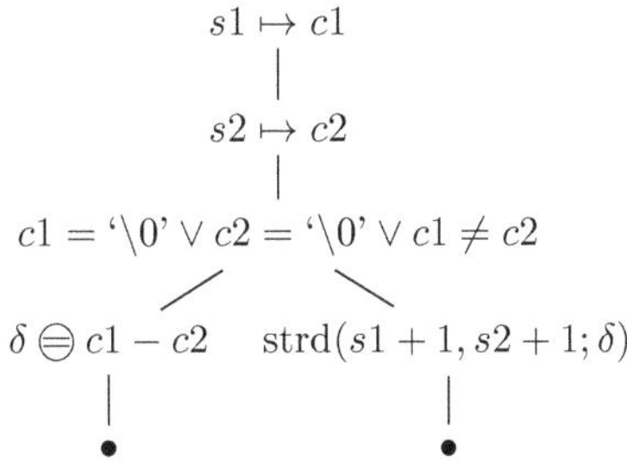

Fig. 5. Matching tree for $\mathrm{strd}(s1, s2; \delta)$.

be valid: in the node labeled $\delta \ominus c1 - c2$, the in-parameter $c1$ would be neither an out-parameter of its ancestors nor an element of $\{s1, s2\}$.

To construct valid matching trees from the given specifications and predicate definitions, SUMGEN implements a *matching module*. At a high level, it performs a search over the space of candidate matching trees and selects one that satisfies the validity constraints defined above.

3.2 Summary Generation

At the center of SUMGEN is a *summary generator module* that compiles matching trees into our intermediate summary language. This language can be easily transpiled to more complex programming languages, provided they expose the symbolic primitives required by our summaries. The syntax is given below.

The syntax of statements

$$e \in \mathcal{E}xpr \triangleq v \in \mathcal{V} \mid x \in \mathcal{X} \mid \ominus e \mid e_1 \oplus e_2 \qquad b \in \mathcal{BE} \triangleq \pi \mid \mathsf{isCertain}(\pi)$$

$$s \in \mathcal{S}tmt \triangleq \mathsf{skip} \mid x \leftarrow (\tau)\, e \mid x \leftarrow (\tau)\, \mathsf{symvar}() \mid x \leftarrow (\tau) * e \mid * e_1 \leftarrow e_2$$

$$\mid * e_1 \overset{\pi}{\leftarrow} e_2 \mid s_1; s_2 \mid \mathsf{assume}\ \pi \mid \mathsf{assert}\ \pi \mid \mathsf{if}\ (b)\ \{s_1\}\ \mathsf{else}\ \{s_2\}$$

$$\mid x \leftarrow (\tau)\, f(\bar{e}) \mid x \leftarrow (\tau)\, f(\bar{e})\ \mathsf{with}\ \pi \mid \mathsf{return}\ e$$

Summary Language Expressions, $e \in \mathcal{E}xpr$, include literals, program variables, and unary and binary operators. Boolean expressions, $b \in \mathcal{BE}$, include pure assertions and isCertain expressions, which check if the given formula provably holds in the current state. Statements, $s \in \mathcal{S}tmt$, include: **(i)** the skip primitive; **(ii)** typed operations: the standard variable assignment, $x \leftarrow (\tau)\, e$, symbolic variable generation, $x \leftarrow (\tau)\, \mathsf{symvar}()$, and the memory read operation, $x \leftarrow (\tau) * e$; **(iii)** the standard and conditional memory update operations, $* e_1 \leftarrow e_2$ and $* e_1 \overset{\pi}{\leftarrow} e_2$; **(iv)** sequenced statements, $s_1; s_2$; **(v)** the assume and assert statements; **(vi)** if-then-else conditionals; **(vii)** non-scoped and scoped function calls, $x \leftarrow (\tau)\, f(\bar{e})$ and $x \leftarrow (\tau)\, f(\bar{e})\ \mathsf{with}\ \pi$; and **(viii)** return statements. Function declarations are of the form $\mathsf{fn}\ f(\bar{x})\ \{s\}$, where f is the function identifier, $\bar{x}$ the list of parameters, and s the function body. With the exception of scoped calls and conditional memory updates, the semantics of our language is standard (*cf.* [54] for a similar one). A scoped call, $x \leftarrow (\tau)\, f(\bar{e})\ \mathsf{with}\ \pi$, augments the path condition with π and calls f under that scope, restoring the original path condition once the call returns. A conditional memory update, $* e_1 \overset{\pi}{\leftarrow} e_2$, stores an ITE expression at address e_1 that evaluates to e_2 if π holds and to its previous content otherwise.

To support SUMGEN summaries, the target runtime must expose a set of symbolic reflection primitives that implement these statements. With the exception of scoped calls, modern SE engines offer most of these primitives by default. Scoped calls can be easily implemented by storing the path condition before the function call, augmenting it with the appropriate constraints, and restoring it afterwards. Additionally, executing a statement in a state that violates its semantic precondition results in an error state. For instance, we do not allow reads/writes that access uninitialized memory or are incorrectly typed.

Specification and Predicate Definition Compilation The goal of the summary generation procedure is to transform the specification of the target function into a symbolic summary. To achieve this, we must also transform predicate definitions into executable code. Below, we give an overview of both procedures; for a more detailed discussion and formalization, see [29].

Specifications. The task of compiling a specification can be understood as producing code that: **(i)** resolves the existential bindings in the function's precondition; and **(ii)** uses the computed bindings to update the symbolic state according to the function's postcondition. We define a *specification compiler* $\mathcal{S}^{\beta}(\Sigma)$, parameterized by a flag $\beta \in \{\mathrm{UX}, \mathrm{OX}, \mathrm{EX}\}$, that, given a specification:

$$\Sigma = \{P\}\ \mathsf{fn}\ f(\bar{x})\ \{Q;\ y;\ \pi\}$$

generates a summary observing the specified correctness property. Informally, $\mathcal{S}^{\beta}(\Sigma)$ proceeds as follows: **(1)** it compiles the matching tree of the precondition P into a statement that computes the existentially quantified variables in P; **(2)** it compiles the matching tree of the postcondition Q into a statement that updates the heap memory according to the semantics of Q; and **(3)** it generates the summary's return value and extends the current path condition with π. Note that the returned expression may either be a fresh symbolic variable constrained by π or the result of a series of operations applied to the variables of the precondition.

Figure 6 shows the generated summary for strcmp. Recall that the precondition of strcmp has a single existentially quantified variable, δ, which denotes the difference between the values of the first non-matching pair of characters in $s1$ and $s2$. To obtain the symbolic value of δ, the summary calls the function $fold^{\beta}_{\mathrm{strd}}$ with the in-parameters of $\mathrm{strd}(s1, s2; \delta)$ (*i.e.*, $s1$ and $s2$) as its arguments. The function $fold^{\beta}_{\mathrm{strd}}$ computes the out-parameter δ by *folding* [11] the predicate $\mathrm{strd}(s1, s2; \delta)$ using its in-parameters. We delve into the specifics of folding/unfolding in our discussion of predicate definition compilation. Note that the summary works for all correctness properties; one needs only to substitute β with the desired property.

```
fn strcmp(s1, s2) {
    δ ← fold^β_strd(s1, s2);
    return δ
}
```

Fig. 6. Full strcmp summary.

Predicate Definitions. SUMGEN uses *fold/unfold reasoning* [11] to handle predicate definitions. In brief, *folding* a predicate computes its out-parameter from its in-parameters, while *unfolding* a predicate updates the resources reachable from its in-parameters using the value of its out-parameter. Hence, predicates in the precondition should be compiled into fold functions that resolve existential bindings in the specification, whereas predicates in the postcondition should be

PURE ASSERTION
$$\mathcal{A}^{\beta}(\pi) \triangleq \text{assert } \pi$$

DIRECTED EQUALITY
$$\mathcal{A}^{\beta}(x \ominus e) \triangleq x \leftarrow e$$

CELL ASSERTION
$$\mathcal{A}^{\beta}(x \mapsto_{\tau} y) \triangleq y \leftarrow (\tau) * x$$

PREDICATE ASSERTION
$$\mathcal{A}^{\beta}(\alpha(\bar{e}; y)) \triangleq y \leftarrow fold_{\alpha}^{\beta}(\bar{e})$$

(a)

LEAF NODE
$$\frac{t = \bullet}{\mathcal{C}_{\Gamma}^{\text{EX}}(t) \triangleq \text{skip}}$$

SINGLE NODE
$$\frac{t = \langle p, t' \rangle}{\mathcal{C}_{\Gamma}^{\text{EX}}(t) \triangleq \mathcal{A}^{\text{EX}}(p); \mathcal{C}_{\Gamma}^{\text{EX}}(t')}$$

DOUBLE NODE
$$\frac{t = \langle \pi, t_1, t_2 \rangle \qquad \Gamma = \alpha(\bar{x}; y)}{\begin{aligned} \mathcal{C}_{\Gamma}^{\text{EX}}(t) \triangleq \; &\text{if } (\text{isCertain}(\pi)) \; \{\mathcal{C}_{\Gamma}^{\text{EX}}(t_1)\} \\ &\text{elif } (\text{isCertain}(\neg\pi)) \; \{\mathcal{C}_{\Gamma}^{\text{EX}}(t_2)\} \\ &\text{else } \{y_1 \leftarrow fold_{\alpha}^{\text{EX}}(\bar{x}) \text{ with } \pi; \\ &\qquad y_2 \leftarrow fold_{\alpha}^{\text{EX}}(\bar{x}) \text{ with } \neg\pi; \\ &\qquad y \leftarrow \text{ITE}(\pi, y_1, y_2)\} \end{aligned}}$$

(b)

Fig. 7. Compilers: (a) simple assertion, $\mathcal{A}^{\beta}$; and (b) exact matching tree, $\mathcal{C}_{\Gamma}^{\text{EX}}$.

compiled into unfold functions that use these bindings to update the symbolic state. In what follows, we focus on the former, noting that the latter is its dual. We expand on unfold compilation when discussing the generation of summaries for mutating functions.

To compile predicates appearing in the precondition, we define a *predicate definition compiler* $\mathcal{P}^{\beta}(\Phi)$, again parameterized by a flag $\beta \in \{\text{UX}, \text{OX}, \text{EX}\}$, that, given a predicate definition:

$$\Phi = \text{pred } \alpha(\bar{x}; y) \{\bar{P}\}$$

generates a fold function observing the specified correctness property. Informally, $\mathcal{P}^{\beta}(\Phi)$ compiles the matching tree derived for the sequence of predicate cases $\bar{P}$ into a statement that computes the predicate's out-parameter from its in-parameters and returns it. The compilation of matching trees is at the core of the summary generation procedure, and depends on which correctness property the generated summary should observe.

Matching Tree Compilation The compilation of matching trees depends on whether we want to generate a UX, OX or EX summary. We define for each case a compilation function (henceforth referred to as *matching tree compiler*) that, given a matching tree t, generates a statement that computes the out-parameters of t. Here, we focus on the exact compiler, and then briefly outline how the under- and over-approximating variants differ from it.

Simple Assertion Compilation. The matching tree compilers make use of an auxiliary compiler $\mathcal{A}^{\beta} : \mathcal{SA} \to \mathcal{Stmt}$, formalized in Figure 7a, which compiles a simple assertion p into a statement that computes the out-parameters of p from its in-parameters. Broadly, $\mathcal{A}^{\beta}$ has four cases:

- **Pure Assertions:** A pure assertion π is compiled to the statement $\text{assert } \pi$ that checks whether π is implied by the current path condition.

- **Directed Equalities:** A directed equality $x \stackrel{\ominus}{=} e$ is compiled to the variable assignment $x \leftarrow e$, which assigns to the out-parameter x the in-expression e.
- **Cell Assertions:** A cell assertion $x \mapsto_\tau y$ is compiled to the statement $y \leftarrow (\tau) * x$, which assigns to the out-parameter y the value pointed to by x.
- **Predicate Assertions:** A predicate assertion $\alpha(\bar{e}; y)$ is compiled to the function call $y \leftarrow \mathit{fold}^\beta_\alpha(\bar{e})$, which assigns to the out-parameter y its corresponding value by folding the predicate α using its in-parameters.

Exact Matching Tree Compilation. We define a compiler $\mathcal{C}^{\mathrm{EX}}_\Gamma : \mathcal{MT} \to \mathcal{Stmt}$, formalized in Figure 7b, which, for some context Γ, transforms a valid matching tree into an EX summary $s \in \mathcal{Stmt}$. The context Γ contains the signature of the target predicate, or $\varnothing$ when compiling a specification. $\mathcal{C}^{\mathrm{EX}}_\Gamma$ has three cases, each corresponding to a matching tree constructor:

- **Leaf Nodes:** The leaf node is simply compiled to the skip instruction.
- **Single Nodes:** A single node $\langle p, t' \rangle$ is compiled by sequencing the compilation of p with that of t'.
- **Double Nodes:** A double node $\langle \pi, t_1, t_2 \rangle$ is compiled to an if-then-else conditional with three outcomes: **(1)** if π is certain, we follow the branch t_1; **(2)** if $\neg\pi$ is certain, we follow t_2; or **(3)** if neither is certain, we follow the *default* (exact) case. In the latter, the function builds an ITE expression capturing the value of the out-parameter y for both cases **(1)** and **(2)**. To this end, it calls itself under a path condition augmented with π, which will guide execution towards the left branch and compute y_1, and under a path condition augmented with $\neg\pi$, which will guide execution towards the right branch and compute y_2. It then assigns to the out-parameter y the expression $\mathsf{ITE}(\pi, y_1, y_2)$ modeling the two branches.

The strcmp summary shown in Figure 3 roughly mirrors the fold function $\mathit{fold}^{\mathrm{EX}}_{\mathrm{strd}}$ generated for the predicate $\mathrm{strd}(s1, s2; \delta)$. Notice how it builds the ITE out-expression in the exact case. For example, given the strings $\mathsf{s1} \mapsto [\hat{c}_1, \text{`\\0'}]$ and $\mathsf{s2} \mapsto [\hat{c}_2, \text{`\\0'}]$ (where $\hat{c}_1, \hat{c}_2$ are unconstrained symbolic characters), the first scoped call yields $\delta_1 = \hat{c}_1 - \hat{c}_2$, as the constraint implies that δ is the difference between the first pair of characters. Conversely, the second scoped call yields $\delta_2 = 0$, since in that case δ is the difference between the second pair of characters. The function then builds the out-expression:

$$\delta = \mathsf{ITE}(\hat{c}_1 = \text{`\\0'} \vee \hat{c}_2 = \text{`\\0'} \vee \hat{c}_1 \neq \hat{c}_2, \hat{c}_1 - \hat{c}_2, 0)$$

which exactly models the two possible values of δ.

Under-Approximating Matching Tree Compilation. The compilation of UX summaries is analogous to the EX case for leaf and single nodes. For double nodes, the compilation differs in the default case: instead of building an ITE expression modeling both branches, one path is chosen as a default path that will never be dropped by the engine. A double node is then compiled to an if-then-else conditional with two outcomes: **(1)** if the non-default case is implied by the path

```
fn fold_strd^UX(s1, s2) {
    c1 ← * s1;
    c2 ← * s2;
    π ← c1 = '\0' ∨ c2 = '\0' ∨ c1 ≠ c2;
    if (isCertain(π)) { δ ← c1 − c2 }
    else {
        assume ¬π;
        δ ← fold_strd^UX(s1 + 1, s2 + 1)
    }; return δ
}
```

```
fn fold_strd^OX(s1, s2) {
    c1 ← * s1;
    c2 ← * s2;
    π ← c1 = '\0' ∨ c2 = '\0' ∨ c1 ≠ c2;
    if (isCertain(π)) { δ ← c1 − c2 }
    elif (isCertain(¬π)) {
        δ ← fold_strd^OX(s1 + 1, s2 + 1)
    } else { δ ← symvar() };
    return δ
}
```

(a)(b)

Fig. 8. Fold functions for $\mathrm{strd}(s1, s2; \delta)$: (a) $fold_{\mathrm{strd}}^{\mathrm{UX}}$ (UX), and (b) $fold_{\mathrm{strd}}^{\mathrm{OX}}$ (OX).

condition, we follow that path; **(2)** otherwise, we assume the constraints of the default case and follow that path.

Figure 8a shows the generated function $fold_{\mathrm{strd}}^{\mathrm{UX}}$. Notice how, unlike its EX counterpart, this function has a default case, $\neg\pi$:

$$\neg(c1 = \text{`}\backslash 0\text{'} \vee c2 = \text{`}\backslash 0\text{'} \vee c1 \neq c2) \equiv c1 \neq \text{`}\backslash 0\text{'} \wedge c2 \neq \text{`}\backslash 0\text{'} \wedge c1 = c2$$

towards which the engine is guided if π is not implied by the path condition. Given the strings $s1 \mapsto [\hat{c}_1, \text{`}\backslash 0\text{'}]$ and $s2 \mapsto [\hat{c}_2, \text{`}\backslash 0\text{'}]$, the fold function now returns $\delta = 0$ and adds $c1 \neq \text{`}\backslash 0\text{'} \wedge c2 \neq \text{`}\backslash 0\text{'} \wedge c1 = c2$ to the path condition, as the default case of the predicate assumes that $\hat{c}_1$ and $\hat{c}_2$ are equal non-null characters.

Over-Approximating Matching Tree Compilation. The compilation of OX summaries is similarly analogous to the EX case for leaf and single nodes. Conversely, a double node $\langle \pi, t_1, t_2 \rangle$ is compiled to an if-then-else conditional with three outcomes: **(1)** if π is certain, we follow the branch t_1; **(2)** if $\neg\pi$ is certain, we follow t_2; or **(3)** if neither is certain, we follow an over-approximating case. In the latter, the summary creates a fresh symbolic variable representing the out-parameter y and constrains it with the simple assertions shared by t_1 and t_2, if any.

Figure 8b shows the generated function $fold_{\mathrm{strd}}^{\mathrm{OX}}$. Notice that, instead of guiding execution towards a default case, the function guides it towards an OX case that generates a new symbolic variable representing the out-parameter. Given the strings $s1 \mapsto [\hat{c}_1, \text{`}\backslash 0\text{'}]$ and $s2 \mapsto [\hat{c}_2, \text{`}\backslash 0\text{'}]$, the fold function now returns a fresh unconstrained symbolic variable δ.

Mutating Summary Generation We give a brief overview of the summary generation procedure for mutating functions by appealing to the example of the LIBC function strcpy. Given two pointers, *dest* and *src*, strcpy copies the string pointed to by *src*, up to and including the first null byte, to the address specified

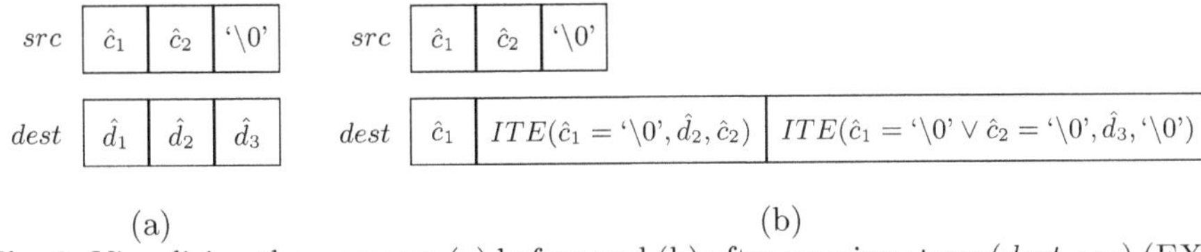

(a)   (b)

Fig. 9. Visualizing the memory: (a) before and (b) after running strcpy($dest, src$) (EX).

by $dest$. We write the strcpy specification as:

$$\{\text{cstr}(src; \sigma) \uplus \text{len}(\sigma; n) \uplus \text{allocd}(dest, n + 1)\}$$
$$\text{fn strcpy}(dest, src)$$
$$\{\text{cstr}(src; \sigma) \uplus \text{cstr}(dest; \sigma); dest\}$$

where: **(i)** $\text{cstr}(s; \sigma)$ states that the string s can be mathematically represented as the list of characters σ; **(ii)** $\text{len}(\sigma; n)$ states that the list σ has length n; and **(iii)** $\text{allocd}(l, n)$ asserts that n consecutive cells are allocated starting at l. The predicate $\text{cstr}(s; \sigma)$ has two cases: **(1)** s points to '\0' and σ is empty; or **(2)** s points to a non-null character c and σ is constructed by prepending c to the list σ' representing the rest of the string. Put formally:

$$\text{pred cstr}(s; \sigma) \, \{ s \mapsto \text{`}\backslash 0\text{'} \uplus \sigma \ominus [\,];$$
$$s \mapsto c \uplus c \neq \text{`}\backslash 0\text{'} \uplus \sigma \ominus c : \sigma' \uplus \text{cstr}(s + 1; \sigma')\}$$

Figure 10 shows the generated summary for strcpy. The summary starts by obtaining the symbolic values of σ and n by calling the fold functions $fold_{\text{cstr}}^{\beta}$ and $fold_{\text{len}}^{\beta}$. It then checks via the SumGen builtin allocd whether there exist n consecutive allocated cells starting at address $dest$. If the check succeeds, the summary calls $unfold_{\text{cstr}}^{\beta}$ with $dest$ and σ as arguments and returns $dest$. The function $unfold_{\text{cstr}}^{\beta}$ updates the memory segment pointed to by $dest$ using the character list

```
fn strcpy(dest, src) {
    σ ← fold_cstr^β(src);
    n ← fold_len^β(σ);
    allocd(dest, n + 1);
    unfold_cstr^β(dest, σ);
    return dest
}
```

Fig. 10. Full strcpy summary.

σ by *unfolding* [11] the predicate $\text{cstr}(s; \sigma)$. Note that the summary does not update the resource src, as it remains unchanged from the precondition.

Figure 9 shows the symbolic memory during an execution of the EX strcpy summary. We assume that a sufficient number of consecutive memory cells (three, in this case) are allocated starting at address $dest$. Figure 9a shows the memory segments pointed to by src and $dest$ before calling the summary, where $\hat{c}_1, \hat{c}_2$ are unconstrained symbolic characters and $\hat{d}_1, \ldots, \hat{d}_3$ are the previous contents of $dest$, symbolic or otherwise. For simplicity, we assume that the path condition is initially set to true.

When executing the EX strcpy summary, the call $fold_{\text{cstr}}^{\text{EX}}(src)$ produces a list given by the symbolic expression:

$$\sigma = \text{ITE}(\hat{c}_1 = \text{`}\backslash 0\text{'}, [\,], \text{ITE}(\hat{c}_2 = \text{`}\backslash 0\text{'}, [\hat{c}_1], [\hat{c}_1, \hat{c}_2]))$$

300   R. Gonçalves, F. Ramos, P. Adão, J. Fragoso Santos

```
1   void vuln1() {
2       char dest[5];
3       char src[20] = "aaaabbbbcccc";
4       strcpy(dest, src);
5   }
```
(a)

```
1   void vuln2() {
2       char src[20] = "aaaabbbbcccc";
3       strcpy(src + 1, src);
4   }
```
(b)

Fig. 11. Issues: (a) out-of-bounds write (incorrect behavior), and (b) overlapping buffers (undefined behavior).

which exactly models the possible values of src. Given the list σ, the call $unfold^{\text{EX}}_{\text{cstr}}(dest, \sigma)$ results in the memory given in Figure 9b. Let us analyze each memory cell from $dest$ at a time. Regardless of the value of $\hat{c}_1$, the *first cell* has content $\hat{c}_1$: if $\hat{c}_1 \neq$ '\0', it is copied to $dest$; if $\hat{c}_1 =$ '\0', the summary stores '\0' at $dest$, making it also equal to $\hat{c}_1$. Next, if $\hat{c}_1 =$ '\0', the content of the *second cell* is left unchanged; otherwise, it is set to $\hat{c}_2$. In the latter case, $\hat{c}_2$ is copied to $dest + 1$ even if $\hat{c}_2 =$ '\0', similarly to what happens in the first cell. Finally, if $\hat{c}_1 =$ '\0' or $\hat{c}_2 =$ '\0', the content of the *third cell* is left unchanged; otherwise, it is set to '\0'. One may easily confirm that the generated output memory is correct by replacing the symbolic characters with concrete values. For instance, executing the summary with $src \mapsto$ ['a', 'b', '\0'] yields $dest \mapsto$ ['a', 'b', '\0'], while executing it with $src \mapsto$ ['a', '\0', '\0'] yields $dest \mapsto$ ['a', '\0', $\hat{d}_3$] and executing it with $src \mapsto$ ['\0', '\0', '\0'] yields $dest \mapsto$ ['\0', $\hat{d}_2$, $\hat{d}_3$].

The compilation of unfold functions is dual to that of fold functions. Whereas in the latter we compile the corresponding matching tree to compute its out-parameter from its in-parameters, in the former we compile it to update the resources reachable from its in-parameters using the value of its out-parameter.

3.3   Usage in Symbolic Execution Tools

We discuss how SUMGEN summaries can be used by symbolic execution tools to analyze C programs. We focus on two main issues: *bugs and incorrect behavior* and *undefined behavior*.

Bugs and Incorrect Behavior One of the main applications of symbolic execution is to find bugs in programs. For example, a symbolic execution engine should detect accesses to unallocated memory, as well as those that are incorrectly typed. To that end, both our specification language and SUMGEN summaries should also capture and prevent incorrect behavior.

Consider, for instance, the C function vuln1 shown in Figure 11a, which copies a larger string src to a smaller buffer dest via the LIBC function strcpy. Since only five bytes are allocated for dest, the copy operation writes past the end of the buffer, resulting in a segmentation fault. Our specification for strcpy disallows this behavior by requiring that the destination buffer be large enough to hold the source string via the predicate $\text{allocd}(l, n)$. As a consequence, the generated summary will also prevent out-of-bounds writes through the SumGen builtin allocd (*cf.* Figure 10, line 4). In this example, dest is only allocated five bytes, while the src string requires at least 13, so the engine will detect that the precondition is violated and report an error.

Undefined Behavior Another common issue in C programs is undefined behavior, which occurs when a program executes operations that are not well-defined by the standard. For example, consider the function vuln2 shown in Figure 11b, which copies a string from src to $src + 1$, causing source and destination buffers to overlap. According to the ISO/IEC 9899:2024 C standard [32], calling strcpy on overlapping buffers results in undefined behavior. The risk is that if a strcpy implementation writes to the destination buffer before reading the full source, it may overwrite data that is yet to be copied and enter an infinite loop. While modern LIBC implementations like *glibc* [23] avoid this by caching the source buffer before writing it to the destination, such behavior is not enforced by the standard. By default, SumGen summaries do not disallow undefined behavior; for instance, our strcpy summary assumes the caching approach. If the developer wishes to exclude such behavior, or enforce a different solution to handle it, they must express this explicitly in the function's precondition.

4   Soundness of Summary Generation

In this section, we establish the soundness of the summary generation procedure. We first define the formal semantics of specifications and symbolic summaries (Definition 2). Essentially, both semantics are defined in terms of sets of tuples of the form (μ_i, ρ, μ_o, v), where μ_i and ρ are the input memory and variable store, μ_o is the output memory, and v is the returned value. Note that we do not take into account the output variable store, as it cannot be accessed by the calling function.

Definition 2 (Formal Semantics of Specifications and Summaries).

SPECIFICATION SEMANTICS
$$[\![\{P\}\, \mathsf{fn}\, f(\bar{x})\, \{Q; y; \pi\}]\!] \triangleq \{(\mu, \rho, \mu', \varepsilon(y)) \mid \mu, \rho, \varepsilon \vDash P \,\wedge\, \mu', \rho, \varepsilon \vDash Q \,\wedge\, \varepsilon \vDash \pi\}$$

SUMMARY SEMANTICS
$$[\![\mathsf{fn}\, f(\bar{x})\, \{s\}]\!] \triangleq \{(\mu, \rho, \mu', \varepsilon(\hat{v})) \mid [\![\hat{\mu}, \hat{\rho}]\!]_\varepsilon = (\mu, \rho) \,\wedge\, [\![\hat{\mu}']\!]_\varepsilon = \mu'$$
$$\wedge\, \langle \hat{\mu}, \hat{\rho}, s \rangle \Downarrow \langle \hat{\mu}', \pi, \hat{v} \rangle \,\wedge\, \varepsilon \vDash \pi\}$$

In the definition, $\mu, \rho, \varepsilon \vDash P$ denotes the satisfiability relation for spatial formulas introduced by Hobor and Villard [31], which differs from the standard Separation Logic satisfiability relation [50,56] in that it accounts for the overlapping conjunction. Essentially, we say that a memory μ, variable store ρ, and logical environment ε satisfy an assertion P if μ exactly matches the resource described by P after replacing program and logical variables with the mappings given by ρ

and ε, respectively. Furthermore, we write: **(i)** $\varepsilon \vDash \pi$ for standard first-order satisfiability; **(ii)** $[\![\hat{\mu}, \hat{\rho}]\!]_\varepsilon = (\mu, \rho)$ to mean that the concrete state (μ, ρ) corresponds to the interpretation of the symbolic state $(\hat{\mu}, \hat{\rho})$ under the logical environment $\varepsilon : \mathcal{X} \rightharpoonup \mathcal{V}$ that maps symbolic variables to concrete values; **(iii)** $[\![\hat{\mu}']\!]_\varepsilon = \mu'$ to mean that the concrete memory μ' corresponds to the interpretation of the symbolic memory $\hat{\mu}'$ under ε; and **(iv)** $\langle \hat{\mu}, \hat{\rho}, s \rangle \Downarrow \langle \hat{\mu}', \pi, \hat{v} \rangle$ to capture the symbolic execution of s that starts in the input state $(\hat{\mu}, \hat{\rho})$ and finishes in an output state with memory $\hat{\mu}'$, path condition π and return value $\hat{v}$. Both semantics are defined using set comprehension style, with variables appearing on the right-hand side of the comprehension but not on the left assumed to be existentially quantified.

Next, we define what it means for a specification/summary to be UX, OX, and EX, using Ξ to range over both specifications and summaries. In a nutshell, a specification/summary is: **(1)** UX if all the return values/memories it models are return values/memories of the corresponding function; **(2)** OX if it models all the return values/memories of the corresponding function; and **(3)** EX if it models all the return values/memories of the corresponding function and only those, *i.e.*, if it is both UX and OX. Definition 3 captures these intuitions. In the definition, we use $\langle \mu, \rho, s \rangle \Downarrow \langle \mu', v \rangle$ to denote the concrete execution that starts in state (μ, ρ) and generates the output memory μ' and return value v.

Definition 3 (Correctness Properties). *Let* $\mathsf{fn}\, f(\bar{x})\,\{s\}$ *be a concrete function. A specification or symbolic summary* Ξ *for* f *is said to be:*

- *UX iff* $\forall \mu, \rho, \mu', v.\, (\mu, \rho, \mu', v) \in [\![\Xi]\!] \implies \langle \mu, \rho, s \rangle \Downarrow \langle \mu', v \rangle.$
- *OX iff* $\forall \mu, \rho, \mu', v.\, \langle \mu, \rho, s \rangle \Downarrow \langle \mu', v \rangle \implies (\mu, \rho, \mu', v) \in [\![\Xi]\!].$
- *EX iff it is both UX and OX.*

Theorem 1 captures the soundness of the summary generation procedure. In a nutshell, it guarantees that: **(i)** $\mathcal{S}^{\mathrm{UX}}$ generates summaries whose semantics is included in that of the given specification; **(ii)** $\mathcal{S}^{\mathrm{OX}}$ generates summaries whose semantics includes that of the given specification; and **(iii)** $\mathcal{S}^{\mathrm{EX}}$ generates summaries whose semantics coincides with that of the given specification.

Theorem 1 (Summary Generation: Soundness). *Suppose that:*

$$\mathcal{S}^\beta(\{P\}\,\mathsf{fn}\, f(\bar{x})\,\{Q; y; \pi\}) = \mathsf{fn}\, f(\bar{x})\,\{s\}$$

Then it holds that:

- *If* $\beta = UX$, *then* $[\![\{P\}\,\mathsf{fn}\, f(\bar{x})\,\{Q; y; \pi\}]\!] \supseteq [\![\mathsf{fn}\, f(\bar{x})\,\{s\}]\!].$
- *If* $\beta = OX$, *then* $[\![\{P\}\,\mathsf{fn}\, f(\bar{x})\,\{Q; y; \pi\}]\!] \subseteq [\![\mathsf{fn}\, f(\bar{x})\,\{s\}]\!].$
- *If* $\beta = EX$, *then* $[\![\{P\}\,\mathsf{fn}\, f(\bar{x})\,\{Q; y; \pi\}]\!] = [\![\mathsf{fn}\, f(\bar{x})\,\{s\}]\!].$

An immediate corollary of the theorem is the set of properties summarized in Table 1, which we state below as a theorem.

Theorem 2 (Correctness of Generated Summaries). *Suppose that:*

$$\mathcal{S}^\beta(\{P\}\,\mathsf{fn}\, f(\bar{x})\,\{Q; y; \pi\}) = \mathsf{fn}\, f(\bar{x})\,\{s\}$$

and $\{P\}\,\mathsf{fn}\, f(\bar{x})\,\{Q; y; \pi\}$ *is a* β-*specification. Then,* $\mathsf{fn}\, f(\bar{x})\,\{s\}$ *is a* β-*summary.*

Table 2. Correctness of generated summaries.

Function Categories			Specifications				Summary Correctness			
			UX	OX	EX	N_{Total}	UX	OX	EX	N_{Total}
Non-Mutating	*Characters*	13	13	13	13	39	13	13	13	39
	I/O	3	2	3	2	7	n/a	n/a	n/a	n/a
	Numbers	5	1	5	1	7	1	4	1	6
	Strings	13	13	13	13	39	13	13	13	39
Mutating	*Memory*	7	7	7	7	21	5	5	5	15
	Strings	6	6	6	6	18	6	6	6	18
Total		47	42	47	42	131	38	41	38	117

5   Evaluation

In this section, we answer the following evaluation questions:

EQ1: Is SUMGEN capable of generating correct UX, OX and EX summaries?
EQ2: How does the complexity of SUMGEN specifications compare to that of handcrafted summaries?
EQ3: How does the performance of SUMGEN summaries compare to that of handcrafted summaries?

5.1   EQ1: Correctness of Generated Summaries

To evaluate the expressivity of our assertion language and the soundness of the subsequent summary generation, we developed: **(i)** a set of 92 specifications encompassing 34 non-mutating LIBC functions from four different categories (*Characters, I/O, Numbers* and *Strings*); and **(ii)** a set of 39 specifications covering 13 mutating LIBC functions from two different categories (*Memory* and *Strings*).

For most of these functions, we defined one specification of each type (UX, OX and EX), generating a total of 131 summaries out of a possible 141. While the theoretical results in §4 guarantee the soundness of our approach, it is still possible to introduce soundness errors at the implementation level. To demonstrate that this does not occur, we used SUMBOUNDVERIFY [54] to check if each generated summary adheres to its specified property. SUMBOUNDVERIFY validates the bounded correctness of a summary by comparing the paths it models with those generated by symbolically executing the corresponding function.

The validation results are shown in Table 2. Out of 131 generated summaries, we were able to confirm the correctness of 117. All 14 non-validated summaries correspond to functions which SUMBOUNDVERIFY does not support, as they step outside the bounds of the engine (*e.g.*, putchar and malloc).

> **Takeaway EQ1:** All SUMGEN-generated summaries supported by SUM-BOUNDVERIFY were successfully validated (117/131).

Table 3. Average LoC of SumGen specifications vs. handcrafted summaries (C/Py).

		Non-Mutating				Mutating		All
		Characters	*I/O*	*Numbers*	*Strings*	*Memory*	*Strings*	
UX	*Specs*	9	9	–	12	14	14	12
	Handcrafted	18 / –	20 / –	– / –	28 / –	21 / –	27 / –	25 / –
OX	*Specs*	9	–	9	11	–	–	10
	Handcrafted	19 / –	– / –	42 / –	17 / –	– / –	– / –	22 / –
EX	*Specs*	9	5	–	10	14	13	11
	Handcrafted	21 / 5	5 / 7	– / –	38 / 126	– / 42	– / 108	28 / 75

5.2   EQ2: Complexity of Specifications vs. Summaries

We assessed the complexity of SumGen specifications, measured in terms of lines of code (LoC), against a baseline of: **(1)** native *angr* [59] summaries implemented in Python; and **(2)** tool-independent summaries developed by Ramos et al. [54] directly in C. We note that the LoC criterion is not exhaustive, and may not always reflect the true complexity of a specification/summary. However, it serves as a quantitative metric to assess the complexity of specifications versus that of summaries, and, in our own experience, provides a good estimate of the required implementation effort.

SumGen allows for the generation of UX, OX and EX summaries. However, our baseline of handcrafted summaries does not provide every kind of summary for all of the analyzed LIBC functions; for instance, *angr* offers a single, usually exact, summary per function. In contrast, we typically generate three summaries, one per correctness property. To address this discrepancy, for this experiment we consider only the functions for which we have both an input specification and a handcrafted summary in C and/or Python.

Results. Table 3 shows the average number of LoC, computed with *cloc* [14], across the six function categories. We group specifications and summaries by correctness property, showing, for each category, the average LoC of our specifications versus that of handcrafted summaries. For the latter, we give in each cell the LoC for both the C and Python summaries.

Results show that, across all correctness properties, SumGen specifications are approximately 56% and 85% shorter than handcrafted summaries implemented in C and Python, respectively. These results are expected, given that specifications are typically simpler than summaries.

> **Takeaway EQ2:** On average, SumGen specifications are 56% shorter than handcrafted C summaries and 85% shorter than handcrafted Python ones.

5.3   EQ3: Performance of Generated Summaries

We measured the execution time and code coverage of generated and handcrafted summaries on two symbolic test suites.

Test Suites. To compare the performance of SUMGEN summaries against that of handcrafted ones in the wild, we evaluated them on a symbolic test suite based on real-world codebases. Popular test suites for symbolic execution such as *TestComp* [6] and *SVComp* [7] make very limited use of LIBC functions, as they were designed to evaluate the core performance of symbolic execution engines rather than support for LIBC. To evaluate SUMGEN summaries, we required a symbolic test suite with emphasis on LIBC usage. We built on the symbolic test suite developed by Ramos et al. [54], based on two open-source C libraries that make heavy use of LIBC functions: **(i)** the *HashMap* [61] library, which offers an implementation of a standard hash table; and **(ii)** the *Dynamic Strings* [57] library, which extends the string handling functionality of LIBC by introducing support for dynamic-size heap-allocated strings. To maximize interactions with LIBC and improve code coverage, we implemented 63 new symbolic tests across the two libraries. In particular, we extended the *HashMap* library from 10 original tests to 20, and the *Dynamic Strings* library from 12 to 65.

Experimental Setup. As the test bed for our experiments, we extended *angr*'s symbolic engine with support for our generated summaries. *angr* [59] is a widely used binary analysis toolkit developed at UC Santa Barbara that has the ability to perform symbolic execution on C-compiled binaries. All tests were run on an Ubuntu server (18.04.5 LTS) with an Intel Xeon E5–2620 CPU and 32 GB of RAM. Each test was allowed to consume a maximum of 16 GB of RAM with a timeout of 1800 seconds (30 minutes).

Results. We ran *angr* on our symbolic test suite using four categories of summaries: **(1)** our generated C summaries (*Generated-C*); **(2)** our generated Python summaries (*Generated-Python*); **(3)** Ramos et al.'s C-implemented summaries (*Handcrafted-C*); and **(4)** *angr*'s native summaries (*Handcrafted-Python*). For reference, we also executed the test suites using concrete implementations of the LIBC functions (*Concrete*), which we sourced from the *glibc* [23] and *libiberty* [22] LIBC implementations. Note that not all test runs include categories **(3)** and **(4)**. The UX and OX runs do not include *Handcrafted-Python* summaries, given that *angr*'s native summaries are all EX. Conversely, Ramos et al.'s mutating summaries are exclusively UX, and so are excluded from the OX and EX runs.

The combined results for the *HashMap* and *Dynamic Strings* libraries are given in Table 4. We show for each summary type: **(i)** the number of tests that failed due to exceeding the memory limit (Memout); **(ii)** the number of tests that failed due to exceeding the time limit (Timeout); **(iii)** the number of tests that executed successfully (Success); **(iv)** the average number of explored paths per test (Avg. N_{Paths}); **(v)** the average execution time per test (Avg. *Time*); and **(vi)** the line coverage achieved using the inputs computed by the symbolic engine, expressed as a percentage of the total number of lines (Total *Cov.*).

Results show that the performance of the generated summaries is comparable to that of their handcrafted counterparts. In the UX case, *Generated-C* summaries perform slightly better than *Handcrafted-C* summaries in terms of

Table 4. Performance of SumGen summaries on the *HashMap* and *DStrings* libraries.

	Summaries		Memout ✗	Timeout ✗	Success ✓	Avg. N_{Paths}	Avg. $Time\,(s)$	Total $Cov.\,(\%)$
UX	*Handcrafted*	C	2	10	73	47	187.75	79%
	Generated	C	2	9	74	65	194.2	81%
		Python	4	7	74	70	121.21	81%
OX	*Generated*	C	40	23	22	226	921.27	65%
		Python	3	55	27	60	887.25	64%
EX	*Handcrafted*	Python	6	1	78	90	104.28	82%
	Generated	C	11	18	56	87	630.36	82%
		Python	10	10	65	78	247.08	82%
Concrete			19	14	52	1.20k	521.85	80%

completed tests (74 vs. 73) and line coverage (81% vs. 79%). In the EX case, results are more mixed: *Generated-Python* summaries underperform compared to *Handcrafted-Python* summaries in completed tests (65 vs. 78), while performing identically in terms of coverage (82% for both). Finally, in the OX case, we have no baseline to compare to. However, we note that the performance of OX summaries is considerably worse than that of its UX and EX counterparts.

The comparison with *angr* warrants a more careful examination. First, as we have previously noted, *angr*'s summaries are often buggy, excluding feasible paths and including spurious ones. This skews the results in their favor, as these summaries may ignore relevant paths without being adequately penalized. Second, *angr*'s summaries are tailored to the specificities of its underlying engine. In contrast, SumGen summaries are designed to be compatible with any symbolic execution tool that implements our symbolic reflection API, and therefore do not exploit the internal details of *angr*'s implementation. Moreover, with our methodology, a developer can easily create native summaries in Python for *angr*, which consistently execute faster than summaries written in C (since C summaries must be interpreted), without needing any knowledge of *angr*'s architecture and implementation details.

> **Takeaway EQ3:** The performance of SumGen summaries is comparable to the performance of handcrafted summaries.

6 Discussion

We discuss the implications of our work, focusing on two main points: the *recommended summary development workflow* and the *limitations of our approach*.

Summary Development Workflow Developers often write summaries without much guidance. SumGen helps streamline summary development by automatically generating summaries from function specifications. However, this approach alone is not foolproof, as writing specifications remains error-prone, particularly for non-experts.

To help avoid mistakes, we recommend using SUMGEN in combination with SUMBOUNDVERIFY [54]. The workflow is straightforward: the developer writes a specification, uses SUMGEN to generate a summary, and then validates it against a reference implementation with SUMBOUNDVERIFY. If the specification is incorrect, the generated summary will also be incorrect, and SUMBOUNDVERIFY will produce a counterexample. Thus, validating the summary also indirectly validates the specification, reducing the need to trust it blindly.

Limitations While general, our approach has both theoretical and practical limitations. First, we assume that all input specifications are well-formed. Second, our theoretical framework is restricted to modeling functions whose behavior can be expressed through a finite number of recursive predicates where out-parameters can be deterministically computed from in-parameters. As a result, we do not support, among others: **(i)** non-deterministic functions; **(ii)** higher-order functions; and **(iii)** concurrency. Additionally, while theoretically allowed by our approach, the current implementation does not support: **(i)** structures; and **(ii)** interactions with the file system.

7 Related Work

Summaries in Symbolic Execution There is a vast body of work on the use of summaries in symbolic execution. Existing approaches can be roughly divided into three main types of summaries: *first-order summaries* [24,30,38], *structured summaries* [19,52] and *operational summaries* [9,12,15,44,54,55,59].

A first-order summary is a simple first-order formula with either limited support for reasoning about heap memory or no support at all. Early work in the area is attributed to Godefroid et al. [1,24,25,26], who leverage *compositionality* by symbolically executing functions in isolation and producing first-order summaries that can later be reused to analyze code that relies on those functions. In contrast, structured summaries are able to reason about the heap. Qiu et al. [52] introduce *memoization trees*, a tree-like data structure that captures the various paths in a function and their respective path conditions, including constraints on the heap memory. Fragoso Santos et al. [19] propose JaVerT 2.0, a compositional symbolic execution tool for JavaScript that allows for the generation of Separation Logic-based specifications, which can be used as function summaries by its symbolic execution engine.

Operational summaries are a loose grouping of summaries developed for the express purpose of usage in symbolic execution tools. Interestingly, despite their widespread use in practice [9,12,15,44,55,59], existing work on operational summaries is sparse. To the best of our knowledge, Ramos ct al. [54] were the first to address their formalization and verification. Their work further includes a symbolic reflection API for the implementation of tool-independent summaries, which SUMGEN supports, and SUMBOUNDVERIFY, which we use to validate our summaries.

Specification-Based Synthesis Prior work in specification-based synthesis includes *test synthesis* [13,18,58], *program synthesis* [33,34,51,60] and *wrapper synthesis* [46]. COSETTE [18] allows for the generation of symbolic tests for JavaScript from Separation Logic specifications. Similarly to our own use of matching trees, COSETTE employs *unification* to find the bindings of existentially quantified variables and generate executable code. SUSLIK [51] is a program syntheziser that works by reducing the problem of deriving heap-manipulating programs to a proof search under Synthetic Separation Logic (SSL) [33,51]. The authors have since extended their work to *cyclic program synthesis* [33], *synthesis certification* [60] and *synthesis in Rust* [16]. SLICK [46] is a runtime checker for Java programs that ensures that the pre- and postconditions of a function are met before and after its execution, respectively. SLICK makes use of a partial ordering of Separation Logic formulas by means of a topological sort similar to matching trees. However, to the best of our knowledge, SUMGEN is the first tool that is able to generate *symbolic summaries* from function specifications.

8   Conclusions

Symbolic summaries are an essential tool for modern symbolic execution engines to tackle the challenges of modeling interactions with the runtime environment and countering path explosion. However, the development of summaries remains to this day a manual task that is known to be highly error-prone. In this paper, we propose a novel methodology for generating correct-by-construction summaries from function specifications, which we realize as the tool SUMGEN. We used SUMGEN to generate a total of 131 summaries for 47 LIBC functions. Our evaluation shows that SUMGEN summaries are not only correct, but also easier to obtain and as performant as their handcrafted counterparts, demonstrating the effectiveness of our methodology in producing symbolic summaries for real-world, highly complex code.

Acknowledgments. We thank the anonymous reviewers for their comments and insightful feedback. This work was supported by national funds through Fundação para a Ciência e a Tecnologia, I.P. (FCT) via a CMU Portugal Dual Degree PhD fellowship (ref. 2024.12581.PRT), as well as projects UID/50021/2025 (DOI: 10.54499/UID/50021/2025), UID/PRR/50021/2025 (DOI: 10.54499/UID/PRR/50021/2025), and WebCAP (ref. 2024.07393.IACDC, DOI: 10.54499/2024.07393.IACDC), and by IAPMEI under grant ref. C6632206063-00466847 (SmartRetail).

Data Availability Statement. SUMGEN, including its source code, benchmarks, and experimental data, is open source [28] and publicly available online as a web application [27].

References

1. Anand, S., Godefroid, P., Tillmann, N.: Demand-driven compositional symbolic execution. In: Ramakrishnan, C.R., Rehof, J. (eds.) Tools and Algorithms for the Construction and Analysis of Systems. pp. 367–381. Springer Berlin Heidelberg, Berlin, Heidelberg (2008)
2. Appel, A.W., Beringer, L., Cao, Q.: Verifiable C, Software Foundations, vol. 5. Electronic textbook (2022), version 1.2.1. http://softwarefoundations.cis.upenn.edu
3. Baldoni, R., Coppa, E., D'elia, D.C., Demetrescu, C., Finocchi, I.: A survey of symbolic execution techniques. ACM Comput. Surv. **51**(3) (May 2018). https://doi.org/10.1145/3182657
4. Baranová, Z., Barnat, J., Kejstová, K., Kučera, T., Lauko, H., Mrázek, J., Ročkai, P., Štill, V.: Model checking of C and C++ with DIVINE 4. In: Automated Technology for Verification and Analysis. pp. 201–207. Springer International Publishing, Cham (2017)
5. Barbosa, H., Barrett, C., Brain, M., Kremer, G., Lachnitt, H., Mann, M., Mohamed, A., Mohamed, M., Niemetz, A., Nötzli, A., Ozdemir, A., Preiner, M., Reynolds, A., Sheng, Y., Tinelli, C., Zohar, Y.: CVC5: A versatile and industrial-strength SMT solver. In: Fisman, D., Rosu, G. (eds.) Tools and Algorithms for the Construction and Analysis of Systems. pp. 415–442. Springer International Publishing, Cham (2022)
6. Beyer, D.: Advances in automatic software testing: Test-Comp 2022. In: Fundamental Approaches to Software Engineering - 25th International Conference, FASE 2022. Lecture Notes in Computer Science, vol. 13241, pp. 321–335. Springer (2022)
7. Beyer, D.: Progress on software verification: SV-COMP 2022. In: Tools and Algorithms for the Construction and Analysis of Systems - 28th International Conference, TACAS 2022. Lecture Notes in Computer Science, vol. 13244, pp. 375–402. Springer (2022)
8. Boyer, R.S., Elspas, B., Levitt, K.N.: SELECT: A formal system for testing and debugging programs by symbolic execution. In: Proceedings of the International Conference on Reliable Software. p. 234–245. Association for Computing Machinery, New York, NY, USA (1975). https://doi.org/10.1145/800027.808445
9. Cadar, C., Dunbar, D., Engler, D.: KLEE: Unassisted and automatic generation of high-coverage tests for complex systems programs. In: Proceedings of the 8th USENIX Conference on Operating Systems Design and Implementation. p. 209–224. OSDI'08, USENIX Association, USA (2008)
10. Chalupa, M., Mihalkovič, V., Řechtáčková, A., Zaoral, L., Strejček, J.: Symbiotic 9: String analysis and backward symbolic execution with loop folding. In: Tools and Algorithms for the Construction and Analysis of Systems. pp. 462–467. Springer International Publishing, Cham (2022)
11. Chin, W.N., David, C., Nguyen, H.H., Qin, S.: Automated verification of shape, size and bag properties via user-defined predicates in separation logic. Science of Computer Programming **77**(9), 1006–1036 (2012). https://doi.org/10.1016/j.scico.2010.07.004, the Programming Languages track at the 24th ACM Symposium on Applied Computing (SAC'09)
12. Chipounov, V., Kuznetsov, V., Candea, G.: The S2E platform: Design, implementation, and applications. ACM Trans. Comput. Syst. **30**(1) (Feb 2012). https://doi.org/10.1145/2110356.2110358

13. Claessen, K., Hughes, J.: QuickCheck: A lightweight tool for random testing of Haskell programs. In: Proceedings of the Fifth ACM SIGPLAN International Conference on Functional Programming. p. 268–279. ICFP '00, Association for Computing Machinery, New York, NY, USA (2000). https://doi.org/10.1145/351240.351266
14. Danial, A.: cloc: v1.92 (Dec 2021). https://doi.org/10.5281/zenodo.5760077
15. David, R., Bardin, S., Ta, T.D., Mounier, L., Feist, J., Potet, M.L., Marion, J.Y.: Binsec/SE: A dynamic symbolic execution toolkit for binary-level analysis. In: 2016 IEEE 23rd International Conference on Software Analysis, Evolution, and Reengineering (SANER). vol. 1, pp. 653–656 (2016). https://doi.org/10.1109/SANER.2016.43
16. Fiala, J., Itzhaky, S., Müller, P., Polikarpova, N., Sergey, I.: Leveraging Rust types for program synthesis. Proc. ACM Program. Lang. **7**(PLDI) (Jun 2023). https://doi.org/10.1145/3591278
17. Fragoso Santos, J., Maksimović, P., Ayoun, S.E., Gardner, P.: Gillian, Part I: A multi-language platform for symbolic execution. In: Proceedings of the 41st ACM SIGPLAN Conference on Programming Language Design and Implementation. p. 927–942. PLDI 2020, Association for Computing Machinery, New York, NY, USA (2020). https://doi.org/10.1145/3385412.3386014
18. Fragoso Santos, J., Maksimović, P., Grohens, T., Dolby, J., Gardner, P.: Symbolic execution for JavaScript. In: Proceedings of the 20th International Symposium on Principles and Practice of Declarative Programming. PPDP '18, Association for Computing Machinery, New York, NY, USA (2018). https://doi.org/10.1145/3236950.3236956
19. Fragoso Santos, J., Maksimović, P., Sampaio, G., Gardner, P.: JaVerT 2.0: Compositional symbolic execution for JavaScript. Proc. ACM Program. Lang. **3**(POPL) (Jan 2019). https://doi.org/10.1145/3290379
20. Gardner, P., Maffeis, S., Smith, G.D.: Towards a program logic for JavaScript. In: Proceedings of the 39th Annual ACM SIGPLAN-SIGACT Symposium on Principles of Programming Languages. p. 31–44. POPL '12, Association for Computing Machinery, New York, NY, USA (2012). https://doi.org/10.1145/2103656.2103663
21. Gardner, P., Ntzik, G., Wright, A.: Local reasoning for the POSIX file system. In: Shao, Z. (ed.) Programming Languages and Systems. pp. 169–188. Springer Berlin Heidelberg, Berlin, Heidelberg (2014)
22. GNU: GNU libiberty (2022), https://gcc.gnu.org/onlinedocs/libiberty/, accessed: January 22, 2026
23. GNU: The GNU C library (2022), https://www.gnu.org/software/libc/, accessed: January 22, 2026
24. Godefroid, P.: Compositional dynamic test generation. SIGPLAN Not. **42**(1), 47–54 (Jan 2007). https://doi.org/10.1145/1190215.1190226
25. Godefroid, P., Luchaup, D.: Automatic partial loop summarization in dynamic test generation. In: Proceedings of the 2011 International Symposium on Software Testing and Analysis. p. 23–33. ISSTA '11, Association for Computing Machinery, New York, NY, USA (2011). https://doi.org/10.1145/2001420.2001424
26. Godefroid, P., Nori, A.V., Rajamani, S.K., Tetali, S.D.: Compositional may-must program analysis: Unleashing the power of alternation. In: Proceedings of the 37th Annual ACM SIGPLAN-SIGACT Symposium on Principles of Programming Languages. p. 43–56. POPL '10, Association for Computing Machinery, New York, NY, USA (2010). https://doi.org/10.1145/1706299.1706307
27. Gonçalves, R., Ramos, F., Adão, P., Fragoso Santos, J.: SUMGEN Web Interface (2025), https://sumsynth.duckdns.org/

28. Gonçalves, R., Ramos, F., Adão, P., Fragoso Santos, J.: Specification-Driven Generation of Summaries for Symbolic Execution (Artifact) (2026). https://doi.org/10.6084/m9.figshare.30992707
29. Gonçalves, R., Ramos, F., Adão, P., Fragoso Santos, J.: Specification-Driven Generation of Summaries for Symbolic Execution (Extended Version) (2026). https://doi.org/10.5281/zenodo.18296457
30. Gopan, D., Reps, T.: Low-level library analysis and summarization. In: Damm, W., Hermanns, H. (eds.) Computer Aided Verification. pp. 68–81. Springer Berlin Heidelberg, Berlin, Heidelberg (2007)
31. Hobor, A., Villard, J.: The ramifications of sharing in data structures. In: Proceedings of the 40th Annual ACM SIGPLAN-SIGACT Symposium on Principles of Programming Languages. p. 523–536. POPL '13, Association for Computing Machinery, New York, NY, USA (2013). https://doi.org/10.1145/2429069.2429131
32. ISO/IEC 9899:2024: Information technology – Programming languages – C. International Standard, International Organization for Standardization and International Electrotechnical Commission, Geneva, CH (Oct 2024)
33. Itzhaky, S., Peleg, H., Polikarpova, N., Rowe, R.N.S., Sergey, I.: Cyclic program synthesis. In: Proceedings of the 42nd ACM SIGPLAN International Conference on Programming Language Design and Implementation. p. 944–959. PLDI 2021, Association for Computing Machinery, New York, NY, USA (2021). https://doi.org/10.1145/3453483.3454087
34. Itzhaky, S., Peleg, H., Polikarpova, N., Rowe, R.N.S., Sergey, I.: Deductive synthesis of programs with pointers: Techniques, challenges, opportunities. In: Silva, A., Leino, K.R.M. (eds.) Computer Aided Verification. pp. 110–134. Springer International Publishing, Cham (2021)
35. King, J.C.: A new approach to program testing. In: Proceedings of the International Conference on Reliable Software. p. 228–233. Association for Computing Machinery, New York, NY, USA (1975). https://doi.org/10.1145/800027.808444
36. Leijen, D., Meijer, E.: Parsec: A practical parser library. Electronic Notes in Theoretical Computer Science $41(1)$, 1–20 (2001)
37. Li, G., Andreasen, E., Ghosh, I.: SymJS: Automatic symbolic testing of JavaScript web applications. In: Proceedings of the 22nd ACM SIGSOFT International Symposium on Foundations of Software Engineering. p. 449–459. FSE 2014, Association for Computing Machinery, New York, NY, USA (2014). https://doi.org/10.1145/2635868.2635913
38. Lin, Y., Miller, T., Søndergaard, H.: Compositional symbolic execution using fine-grained summaries. In: 2015 24th Australasian Software Engineering Conference. pp. 213–222 (2015). https://doi.org/10.1109/ASWEC.2015.32
39. Lööw, A., Nantes-Sobrinho, D., Ayoun, S.E., Maksimović, P., Gardner, P.: Matching plans for frame inference in compositional reasoning. In: Aldrich, J., Salvaneschi, G. (eds.) 38th European Conference on Object-Oriented Programming (ECOOP 2024). Leibniz International Proceedings in Informatics (LIPIcs), vol. 313, pp. 26:1–26:20. Schloss Dagstuhl – Leibniz-Zentrum für Informatik, Dagstuhl, Germany (2024). https://doi.org/10.4230/LIPIcs.ECOOP.2024.26
40. Maksimović, P., Ayoun, S.É., Santos, J.F., Gardner, P.: Gillian, Part II: Real-world verification for JavaScript and C. In: Silva, A., Leino, K.R.M. (eds.) Computer Aided Verification. pp. 827–850. Springer International Publishing, Cham (2021)
41. Maksimović, P., Cronjäger, C., Lööw, A., Sutherland, J., Gardner, P.: Exact separation logic: Towards bridging the gap between verification and bug-finding. In: Ali, K., Salvaneschi, G. (eds.) 37th European Conference on Object-Oriented Programming (ECOOP 2023). Leibniz International Proceedings in Informatics (LIPIcs),

vol. 263, pp. 19:1–19:27. Schloss Dagstuhl – Leibniz-Zentrum für Informatik, Dagstuhl, Germany (2023). https://doi.org/10.4230/LIPIcs.ECOOP.2023.19

42. Manzano, F.A.: Pysymemu, https://github.com/feliam/pysymemu, accessed: January 22, 2026

43. Marques, F., Fragoso Santos, J., Santos, N., Adão, P.: Concolic execution for WebAssembly. In: Ali, K., Vitek, J. (eds.) 36th European Conference on Object-Oriented Programming (ECOOP 2022). Leibniz International Proceedings in Informatics (LIPIcs), vol. 222, pp. 11:1–11:29. Schloss Dagstuhl – Leibniz-Zentrum für Informatik, Dagstuhl, Germany (2022). https://doi.org/10.4230/LIPIcs.ECOOP.2022.11

44. Mossberg, M., Manzano, F., Hennenfent, E., Groce, A., Grieco, G., Feist, J., Brunson, T., Dinaburg, A.: Manticore: A user-friendly symbolic execution framework for binaries and smart contracts. In: 2019 34th IEEE/ACM International Conference on Automated Software Engineering (ASE). pp. 1186–1189 (2019). https://doi.org/10.1109/ASE.2019.00133

45. de Moura, L., Bjørner, N.: Z3: An efficient SMT solver. In: Ramakrishnan, C.R., Rehof, J. (eds.) Tools and Algorithms for the Construction and Analysis of Systems. pp. 337–340. Springer Berlin Heidelberg, Berlin, Heidelberg (2008)

46. Nguyen, H.H., Kuncak, V., Chin, W.N.: Runtime checking for separation logic. In: Logozzo, F., Peled, D.A., Zuck, L.D. (eds.) Verification, Model Checking, and Abstract Interpretation. pp. 203–217. Springer Berlin Heidelberg, Berlin, Heidelberg (2008)

47. Ntzik, G., Gardner, P.: Reasoning about the POSIX file system: local update and global pathnames. In: Proceedings of the 2015 ACM SIGPLAN International Conference on Object-Oriented Programming, Systems, Languages, and Applications. p. 201–220. OOPSLA 2015, Association for Computing Machinery, New York, NY, USA (2015). https://doi.org/10.1145/2814270.2814306

48. Ntzik, G., da Rocha Pinto, P., Sutherland, J., Gardner, P.: A concurrent specification of POSIX file systems. In: Millstein, T. (ed.) 32nd European Conference on Object-Oriented Programming (ECOOP 2018). Leibniz International Proceedings in Informatics (LIPIcs), vol. 109, pp. 4:1–4:28. Schloss Dagstuhl – Leibniz-Zentrum für Informatik, Dagstuhl, Germany (2018). https://doi.org/10.4230/LIPIcs.ECOOP.2018.4

49. O'Hearn, P.W.: Incorrectness logic. Proc. ACM Program. Lang. **4**(POPL) (Dec 2019). https://doi.org/10.1145/3371078

50. O'Hearn, P.W., Reynolds, J.C., Yang, H.: Local reasoning about programs that alter data structures. In: Proceedings of the 15th International Workshop on Computer Science Logic. p. 1–19. CSL '01, Springer-Verlag, Berlin, Heidelberg (2001)

51. Polikarpova, N., Sergey, I.: Structuring the synthesis of heap-manipulating programs. Proc. ACM Program. Lang. **3**(POPL) (Jan 2019). https://doi.org/10.1145/3290385

52. Qiu, R., Yang, G., Pasareanu, C.S., Khurshid, S.: Compositional symbolic execution with memoized replay. In: 2015 IEEE/ACM 37th IEEE International Conference on Software Engineering. vol. 1, pp. 632–642 (2015). https://doi.org/10.1109/ICSE.2015.79

53. Raad, A., Berdine, J., Dang, H.H., Dreyer, D., O'Hearn, P., Villard, J.: Local reasoning about the presence of bugs: Incorrectness separation logic. In: Lahiri, S.K., Wang, C. (eds.) Computer Aided Verification. pp. 225–252. Springer International Publishing, Cham (2020), https://doi.org/10.1007/978-3-030-53291-8_14

54. Ramos, F., Sabino, N., Adão, P., Naumann, D.A., Fragoso Santos, J.: Toward tool-independent summaries for symbolic execution. In: Ali, K., Salvaneschi, G. (eds.) 37th European Conference on Object-Oriented Programming (ECOOP 2023). Leibniz International Proceedings in Informatics (LIPIcs), vol. 263, pp. 24:1–24:29. Schloss Dagstuhl – Leibniz-Zentrum für Informatik, Dagstuhl, Germany (2023). https://doi.org/10.4230/LIPIcs.ECOOP.2023.24
55. Reisner, E., Song, C., Ma, K.K., Foster, J.S., Porter, A.: Using symbolic evaluation to understand behavior in configurable software systems. In: Proceedings of the 32nd ACM/IEEE International Conference on Software Engineering - Volume 1. p. 445–454. ICSE '10, Association for Computing Machinery, New York, NY, USA (2010). https://doi.org/10.1145/1806799.1806864
56. Reynolds, J.: Separation logic: a logic for shared mutable data structures. In: Proceedings 17th Annual IEEE Symposium on Logic in Computer Science. pp. 55–74 (2002). https://doi.org/10.1109/LICS.2002.1029817
57. Sanfilippo, S.: Simple dynamic strings (2015), https://github.com/antirez/sds, accessed: January 22, 2026
58. Seidel, E.L., Vazou, N., Jhala, R.: Type targeted testing. In: Vitek, J. (ed.) Programming Languages and Systems. pp. 812–836. Springer Berlin Heidelberg, Berlin, Heidelberg (2015)
59. Shoshitaishvili, Y., Wang, R., Salls, C., Stephens, N., Polino, M., Dutcher, A., Grosen, J., Feng, S., Hauser, C., Kruegel, C., Vigna, G.: SOK: (State of) The art of war: Offensive techniques in binary analysis. In: 2016 IEEE Symposium on Security and Privacy (SP). pp. 138–157 (2016). https://doi.org/10.1109/SP.2016.17
60. Watanabe, Y., Gopinathan, K., Pîrlea, G., Polikarpova, N., Sergey, I.: Certifying the synthesis of heap-manipulating programs. Proc. ACM Program. Lang. **5**(ICFP) (Aug 2021). https://doi.org/10.1145/3473589
61. Wiedenhöft, R.: C hashmap (2014), https://gist.github.com/Richard-W/9568649, accessed: January 22, 2026

Generating Functions Meet Occupation Measures: Invariant Synthesis for Probabilistic Loops

Darion Haase[(✉)1], Kevin Batz[2,3], Adrian Gallus[4],
Benjamin Lucien Kaminski[5,2], Joost-Pieter Katoen[1],
Lutz Klinkenberg[1], and Tobias Winkler[1]

[1] RWTH Aachen University, Aachen, Germany
{darion.haase, katoen, lutz.klinkenberg,
tobias.winkler}@cs.rwth-aachen.de
[2] University College London, London, United Kingdom
[3] Cornell University, Ithaca, NY, USA
k.batz@ucl.ac.uk
[4] Independent Researcher, Aachen, Germany
adrian.gallus@rwth-aachen.de
[5] Saarland University, Saarbrücken, Germany
kaminski@cs.uni-saarland.de

Abstract. A fundamental computational task in probabilistic programming is to infer a program's output (posterior) distribution from a given initial (prior) distribution. This problem is challenging, especially for expressive languages that feature loops or unbounded recursion. While most of the existing literature focuses on statistical approximation, in this paper we address the problem of mathematically exact inference. To achieve this for programs with loops, we rely on a relatively underexplored type of probabilistic loop invariant, which is linked to a loop's so-called *occupation measure*. The occupation measure associates program states with their expected number of visits, given the initial distribution. Based on this, we derive the notion of an *occupation invariant*. Such invariants are essentially dual to probabilistic martingales, the predominant technique for formal probabilistic loop analysis in the literature. A key feature of occupation invariants is that they can take the initial distribution into account and often yield a proof of positive almost sure termination as a by-product. Finally, we present an automatic, template-based invariant synthesis approach for occupation invariants by encoding them as *generating functions*. The approach is implemented and evaluated on a set of benchmarks.

1 Introduction

Probabilistic programs (PPs) are like ordinary programs with the added ability to flip coins or, more generally, sample values from probability distributions. PPs are ubiquitous in modern computing; they appear, for example, in randomized algorithms [27], random sampling [40], statistical inference routines [10, 20, 8], cognitive science [21], and autonomous systems [41].

© The Author(s) 2026
R. Krebbers (Ed.): ESOP 2026, LNCS 16501, pp. 314–343, 2026.
https://doi.org/10.1007/978-3-032-22720-1_12

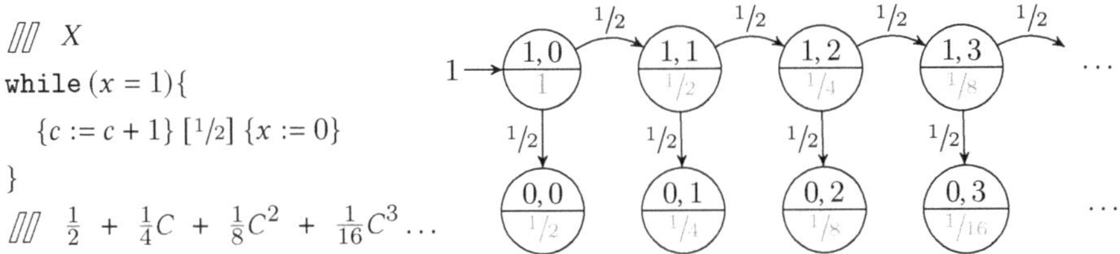

```
/// X
while (x = 1){
   {c := c + 1} [1/2] {x := 0}
}
/// 1/2 + 1/4 C + 1/8 C² + 1/16 C³ ...
```

Fig. 1: **Left:** A probabilistic loop, annotated with initial and final distributions. The annotations use *probability generating functions* (PGFs), where indeterminates represent program variables (e.g., X for x), exponents represent values (variables with value 0 are omitted since $X^0 = 1$; exponent 1 is omitted since $X^1 = X$), and coefficients represent probabilities (coefficient 1 is also omitted) [33]. For example, the PGF X represents the Dirac distribution where, with probability 1, x has value 1 and c has value 0.

Right: Markov chain representation of the program (transitions mimic entire loop iterations). The upper part of each state is the variable valuation x, c. The red numbers constitute the *occupation measure* (expected number of visits).

Probabilistic Programs as Measure Transformers. Intuitively, running a PP on a given input produces a *probability distribution*[6] over possible outputs. Nearly half a century ago, Kozen [36] has cast this intuition into a formal (denotational) program semantics, which associates each program C with a function[7]

$$\mathcal{K}[\![C]\!]: \quad \mathcal{M}(\mathsf{States}) \;\to\; \mathcal{M}(\mathsf{States}) \,.$$

In this paper we restrict to *discrete* measures over a countable state space States. For example, the program in Figure 1 transforms the initial point-mass distribution on state $[x \mapsto 1, c \mapsto 0]$ to a distribution where c is geometrically distributed with parameter $1/2$ (and $x = 0$ with probability 1). Notice that Figure 1 uses *generating function* (GF) notation for distributions. GFs play an important role for our development, which we explain later on page 4.

Our Goal: Inference for Loops — Exact and Automatic. Characterizing a program's exact output distribution is desirable for many applications — yet extremely challenging in general, especially in the presence of loops. The goal of this paper is to push the limits of *exact* and *automatic* loop analysis:

> **Problem statement:** Given a discrete probabilistic loop `while (φ) {C}` with a distribution μ over input states, *automatically* compute an *exact* representation of the output distribution $\mathcal{K}[\![\texttt{while}\,(\phi)\,\{C\}]\!](\mu)$.

---

[6] Or *sub*-distribution, if the program does not terminate with probability 1.

[7] Notice that $\mathcal{K}[\![\cdot]\!]$ operates on general *measures*, including (sub-)probability distributions as a special case.

Two remarks on our problem statement are in order: (1) Due to standard undecidability results for while loops, no complete algorithmic solution exists. We thus provide *heuristics* covering many instances. (2) Since the final distribution may have *infinite support* (as in Figure 1), we employ *closed-form* generating functions as a succinct encoding of probability distributions [33] (details follow).

Automatic Reasoning with Kozen's Definition — Infeasible? Kozen [36] characterizes the semantics of loops by the functional least fixed point equation[8]

$$\mathcal{K}\,[\![\texttt{while}\,(\phi)\,\{C\}]\!] \;=\; \mathcal{K}\,[\![\texttt{while}\,(\phi)\,\{C\}]\!] \,\circ\, \mathcal{K}\,[\![C]\!] \,\circ\, [\![\phi]\!] \;+\; [\![\neg\phi]\!]\,, \quad (\dagger)$$

where $[\![\phi]\!]$ and $[\![\neg\phi]\!]$ *filter* the incoming distribution according to ϕ and $\neg\phi$, respectively. This equation reflects the intuition that a loop is unaffected by unrolling it once. However, there is a discrepancy between $(\dagger)$ and our problem statement: Our goal is to determine $\mathcal{K}\,[\![\texttt{while}\,(\phi)\,\{C\}]\!](\mu)$ for a *given initial distribution μ* — yet $(\dagger)$ does not depend on such a μ. In other words, an approach based on solving $(\dagger)$ *would require to reason about all possible initial distributions simultaneously* (see [33, 13, 34, 32]), whereas we are interested in the solution of the functional equation only at one point, namely at the initial distribution μ.

Occupation Measures to the Rescue. An equivalent but seemingly less well-known[9] characterization of a loop's output distribution is due to Sharir, Pnueli, and Hart [49]. Their technique takes the initial distribution into account and considers the so-called *occupation measure* (e.g., [47]) of the induced stochastic process. The occupation measure associates each program state with its *expected number of visits at the loop header*. To see how occupation measures help determine the final distribution after the loop, the following observations are key:

- For states *satisfying the loop guard*, the number of visits is a random value in $\mathbb{N}\cup\{\infty\}$. (Unlike in deterministic programs, a probabilistic loop can return to the same state multiple times without necessarily entering an infinite cycle.) The *expected* number of visits thus lies in the interval $[0, \infty]$.
- For states *violating the loop guard*, the situation is different: Such states are visited *at most once* at the loop header, since the loop terminates immediately upon entering them. Therefore, the *expected* number of visits to such a terminal state s equals

$$\underbrace{0 \cdot Pr(s \text{ is never reached}) \quad + \quad 1 \cdot Pr(s \text{ is reached once})}_{} \\ + \; 2 \cdot Pr(s \text{ is reached twice}) \; + \; \ldots \quad = \; Pr(s \text{ is reached once})\,.$$

Consequently, the expected number of visits to s is precisely the *probability* of ever reaching s — and thus the probability of the loop terminating in s.

---

[8] The equation may have multiple solutions; as usual, the *least* one w.r.t. a suitable order is of interest (see Section 4.2).

[9] Beyond [49], we are not aware of any other work on occupation measures of PPs.

To summarize, if we denote the occupation measure with OM, then we have

$$\mathcal{K}[\![\texttt{while}\,(\phi)\,\{C\}]\!](\mu) \;=\; [\![\neg\phi]\!](OM)\,; \qquad \text{(as formally proved in Theorem 2)}$$

that is, by *restricting* OM to the states not satisfying the guard ϕ, we obtain the final distribution $\mathcal{K}[\![\texttt{while}\,(\phi)\,\{C\}]\!](\mu)$ of the loop $\texttt{while}\,(\phi)\,\{C\}$.

The occupation measure of our running example program is visualized by means of the program's Markov chain unfolding in Figure 1. The states in the bottom row are the ones not satisfying the loop guard. Observe that their expected visiting times indeed constitute the anticipated geometric distribution.

Reasoning about Loops with Occupation Measures. It can be shown (Theorem 3) that the occupation measure of a loop $\texttt{while}\,(\phi)\,\{C\}$ with initial distribution μ is the least solution OM of the fixed point equation

$$OM \;=\; \mu \;+\; \mathcal{K}[\![C]\!]([\![\phi]\!](OM))\,. \tag{$\ddagger$}$$

Note that, unlike ($\dagger$), this fixed point equation *depends on the initial distribution* μ. Equation ($\ddagger$) suggests the following *guess-and-check* heuristic:

1. Guess a candidate solution M of ($\ddagger$) — think of this as a *loop invariant.*
2. Check whether the candidate M is indeed a solution. If yes, then M is a (pointwise) *upper bound* on the occupation measure OM, and thus — by the argument from above — $\mathcal{K}[\![\texttt{while}\,(\phi)\,\{C\}]\!](\mu) \le [\![\neg\phi]\!](M)$.

We can exploit another key feature of occupation measures: Their total mass equals the loop's *expected runtime*[10] on μ [49]. Therefore, any *finite* measure M satisfying ($\ddagger$) witnesses *positive almost sure termination* (PAST) of the loop on input μ. Since terminating loops preserve the probability mass of their input measure, we can conclude the following: If a finite measure M satisfies ($\ddagger$) and $[\![\neg\phi]\!](M)$ is a probability distribution (i.e., has total mass 1), then the inequality $\mathcal{K}[\![\texttt{while}\,(\phi)\,\{C\}]\!](\mu) \le [\![\neg\phi]\!](M)$ from Step 2 becomes an *exact* equality $\mathcal{K}[\![\texttt{while}\,(\phi)\,\{C\}]\!](\mu) = [\![\neg\phi]\!](M)$. See Theorem 6 for details.

Effective Verification and Synthesis with Closed-form Generating Functions. Steps (1) and (2) in the foregoing paragraph still involve dealing with measures defined on the *infinite* set of program states. This is where GFs shine: For example, the — infinite support — occupation measure of the loop in Figure 1 has as GF

$$OM \;=\; 1X \;+\; \tfrac{1}{2}XC \;+\; \tfrac{1}{4}XC^2 \;+\; \ldots \;\;+\;\; \tfrac{1}{2} \;+\; \tfrac{1}{4}C \;+\; \tfrac{1}{8}C^2 \;+\; \ldots\,,$$

which has the following (rational) *closed form*:

$$=\; \frac{1+2X}{2-C}\,.$$

Under suitable assumptions, it is possible to verify equation ($\ddagger$) algorithmically for candidate measures M represented in such a closed form, that is, to implement Step (2) of the guess-and-check heuristic. Based on this, we furthermore show that Step (1) can be implemented via *template-based synthesis*, using parameterized rational GFs as templates (as detailed in Section 6).

---

[10] We define the expected runtime as the expected number of visits at the loop header.

Contributions. We revisit the relatively unknown utility of occupation measures in probabilistic loop analysis [49] and present the following novel contributions:

1. We show that a loop's occupation measure can be characterized as the least fixed point of a measure transformer defined *compositionally by induction on the program structure* (Theorem 3).
2. We formally relate our semantic perspective to Kozen's semantics [36] (Theorem 2), to occupation measures on operational Markov chains (Theorem 3), and to expected runtimes [30] (Theorem 4).
3. We propose GFs (generating functions) as an effective encoding of occupation measures over program states on nonnegative integer variables (Section 6).
4. We present the first *fully automatic synthesis of occupation measures* (or approximations thereof) based on templates for rational GFs. We evaluate the effectiveness of our algorithm through experiments (Section 7).

Outline. Section 2 introduces preliminaries on measure theory and Markov chains. Section 3 specifies the program syntax; Section 4 develops the denotational semantics and establishes equivalence to Kozen's semantics. Section 5 presents loop invariants based on occupation measures. Section 6 describes symbolic synthesis using rational GFs. Section 7 provides implementation details and experimental results. Section 8 discusses related work, and Section 9 concludes.

2   Preliminaries

$\mathcal{P}(X)$ denotes the powerset of X. $\mathbb{N}$ is the set of natural numbers including 0.

2.1   Measure Theory

We briefly recall necessary notions of measure theory [9].

Definition 1 (σ-Algebra). *Let X be a set. A subset $\Sigma \subseteq \mathcal{P}(X)$ is called a σ-algebra (on X) if (1) $X \in \Sigma$, (2) $A \in \Sigma$ implies $X \setminus A \in \Sigma$, and (3) for all countable sets I, $(A_i)_{i \in I} \in \Sigma^I$ implies $\bigcup_{i \in I} A_i \in \Sigma$.*

The sets that constitute a σ-algebra are called *measurable*. A *measure* assigns a nonnegative real number (or ∞) to each measurable set in a σ-algebra:

Definition 2 (Measure and Distribution). *Let Σ be a σ-algebra on X.*

- *A function $\mu \colon \Sigma \to \mathbb{R}^\infty_{\geq 0}$ is called a* measure *if for all countable families $(A_i)_{i \in I}$ of pairwise disjoint sets in Σ, we have $\mu\left(\bigcup_{i \in I} A_i\right) = \sum_{i \in I} \mu(A_i)$ (implying $\mu(\emptyset) = 0$). We write $|\mu| := \mu(X)$ for the total mass of μ. The set of measures on X is denoted by $\mathcal{M}(X)$ (the σ-algebra will always be clear from the context).*
- *A measure μ is a* probability distribution *if $|\mu| = 1$ and a* sub-probability distribution *if $|\mu| \leq 1$. The sets of probability and sub-probabilty distributions over X are denoted by $\mathcal{D}_{=1}(X)$ and $\mathcal{D}(X)$, respectively.*

Throughout the paper, we often refer to sub-probability distributions simply as *distributions*. If μ and ν are measures on the same σ-algebra, then their pointwise sum $\mu + \nu$ and, for any $c \geq 0$, the pointwise scaled $c \cdot \mu$ are also measures.

A function $f \colon X \to \mathbb{R}_{\geq 0}^{\infty}$, where X is equipped with a σ-algebra Σ, is *measurable* if $f^{-1}((a, \infty]) \in \Sigma$ for all $a \in \mathbb{R}_{\geq 0}$. The *expected value* of f under $\mu \in \mathcal{M}(X)$ is defined as the Lebesgue integral $\mathbb{E}_{\mu}[f] := \int f \, d\mu$. The *Dirac measure* δ_x of an element $x \in X$ and the *indicator function* $\mathbf{1}_A$ of a measurable set $A \in \Sigma$ are

$$\delta_x \colon \Sigma \to \mathbb{R}_{\geq 0}^{\infty} \, , \quad B \mapsto \begin{cases} 1, & \text{if } x \in B, \\ 0, & \text{else;} \end{cases} \quad \text{and} \quad \mathbf{1}_A \colon X \to \mathbb{R}_{\geq 0}^{\infty}, \quad y \mapsto \begin{cases} 1, & \text{if } y \in A, \\ 0, & \text{else.} \end{cases}$$

We often represent a measurable set $A \in \Sigma$ by a predicate ϕ_A on X; in this case, the *Iverson bracket* $[\phi_A]$ denotes the indicator function $\mathbf{1}_A$. We write $[\phi_A] \cdot \mu$ for the measure of μ restricted to A, that is, $([\phi_A] \cdot \mu)(B) := \mu(A \cap B)$ for $B \in \Sigma$.

In this paper, X is usually a *countable* set for which the collection of all subsets $\mathcal{P}(X)$ is a σ-algebra. We thus identify a measure $\mu \in \mathcal{M}(X)$ with a function $X \to \mathbb{R}_{\geq 0}^{\infty}$ by writing $\mu(x) = \mu(\{x\})$ for $x \in X$. In this setting, every function $f \colon X \to \mathbb{R}_{\geq 0}^{\infty}$ is measurable and Lebesgue integrals become countable sums: $\mathbb{E}_{\mu}[f] = \sum_{x \in X} f(x) \cdot \mu(x)$. The set of measures $\mathcal{M}(X)$ is partially ordered by $\mu \leq \nu$ iff $\mu(x) \leq \nu(x)$ for all $x \in X$; this order makes $(\mathcal{M}(X), \leq)$ a *complete lattice* (i.e., every subset of $\mathcal{M}(X)$ has an infimum and a supremum w.r.t. $\leq$).

2.2 Markov Chains

Markov chains model stochastic processes in which transition probabilities depend only on the current state, disregarding any prior history [14].

Definition 3 (Markov Chain). *A* Markov chain *is a pair $C = (S_C, P_C)$ where S_C is a countable set of states, and $P_C \colon S_C \to \mathcal{D}_{=1}(S_C)$ is the transition probability function. We write $P_C[s](t) := P_C(s)(t)$ for $s, t \in S_C$. We omit the subscript C if the Markov chain is clear from the context.*

A Markov chain induces a measure on the set of its infinite paths:

Definition 4 (Infinite Path). *Let C be a Markov chain. An* infinite path *in C is a sequence $\pi = \pi_0 \pi_1 \ldots \in S_C^{\omega}$ with $P_C[\pi_i](\pi_{i+1}) > 0$ for $i \in \mathbb{N}$. Paths_C denotes the (generally uncountable) set of all infinite paths in C.*

For a finite sequence $\bar{\pi} \in S_C^*$, the *cylinder set* $\mathrm{Cyl}(\bar{\pi}) := \{\pi \in \mathsf{Paths}_C \mid \exists \pi' \in \mathsf{Paths}_C \colon \pi = \bar{\pi}\pi'\}$ consists of all infinite paths in C with prefix $\bar{\pi}$. Paths_C is equipped with the σ-algebra generated by all cylinder sets; see [14] for details.

Definition 5 ((Probability) Measure induced by a Markov Chain). *Let C be a Markov chain. Given an initial measure $\iota \in \mathcal{M}(S_C)$, C induces a unique measure Pr_C^{ι} on Paths_C with $\mathsf{Pr}_C^{\iota}(\mathrm{Cyl}(\varepsilon)) := |\iota|$ and, for $\bar{\pi} \in S_C^+$, $\mathsf{Pr}_C^{\iota}(\mathrm{Cyl}(\bar{\pi})) := \iota(\bar{\pi}_0) \cdot \prod_{i=0}^{|\bar{\pi}|-1} P_C[\bar{\pi}_i](\bar{\pi}_{i+1})$.*

Notice that Pr_C^ι in Definition 5 is a probability measure if and only if ι is a probability distribution. Our framework, however, requires defining Pr_C^ι for arbitrary measures $\iota \in \mathcal{M}(S_C)$, including those with mass $|\iota| < 1$ *and* $|\iota| > 1$.

We can now define occupation measures, a key concept of this paper:

Definition 6 (Occupation Measure). *Let C be a Markov chain with initial measure $\iota \in \mathcal{M}(S_C)$. We define the* occupation measure $\mathrm{OM}_C^\iota \in \mathcal{M}(S_C)$ *as* $\mathrm{OM}_C^\iota(s) := \mathbb{E}_{\mathrm{Pr}_C^\iota}\left[\mathrm{occ}_C^s\right]$, *which, for each state $s \in S_C$, gives the expected value of the measurable function* $\mathrm{occ}_C^s \colon \mathsf{Paths}_C \to \mathbb{R}_{\geq 0}^\infty$, $\pi \mapsto \sum_{i \in \mathbb{N}}\left[\pi_i = s\right]$.

Intuitively, occ_C^s counts how many times a state s occurs in a path of C. More general definitions of occupation measures [47] include a stopping time T, which prescribes when to stop counting; in our case, $T = \infty$. For a given initial distribution $\iota \in \mathcal{D}(S_C)$, $\mathrm{OM}_C^\iota(s)$ is the *expected total number of visits* of C to s.

3   Syntax of Probabilistic Programs

In this section, we introduce a discrete *probabilistic guarded command language* (pGCL) à la McIver and Morgan [42]. Let $\mathsf{Vars} \neq \emptyset$ be a finite set of (program) variables ranged over by x, y, etc. A *program state* $s\colon \mathsf{Vars} \to \mathbb{N}$ assigns a natural number $s(x) \in \mathbb{N}$ to every variable $x \in \mathsf{Vars}$. We write $s[x/n]$ for the *updated* state in which $x \in \mathsf{Vars}$ maps to $n \in \mathbb{N}$, and every other variable $x' \neq x$ maps to $s(x')$. We denote the countable set of all program states by $\mathsf{States} := \mathsf{Vars} \to \mathbb{N}$.

Definition 7 (pGCL). *The set of* pGCL-*programs adheres to the grammar:*

$$
\begin{array}{lll}
C \to \texttt{skip} & \mid \texttt{diverge} & \textit{(effectless} \mid \textit{endless loop)} \\
\mid x := E & \mid x :\approx \mu & \textit{(assignment} \mid \textit{prob. assignment)} \\
\mid \{C\}\,[p]\,\{C\} & \mid C\,\mathbin{;}\,C & \textit{(prob. choice} \mid \textit{seq. composition)} \\
\mid \texttt{if}\,(\phi)\,\{C\}\,\texttt{else}\,\{C\} & \mid \texttt{while}\,(\phi)\,\{C\} & \textit{(conditional branch} \mid \textit{while loop)}
\end{array}
$$

where $x \in \mathsf{Vars}$, $E\colon \mathsf{States} \to \mathbb{N}$ is an arithmetic expression, $\mu\colon \mathsf{States} \to \mathcal{D}_{=1}(\mathbb{N})$ is a distribution expression, $p \in [0,1] \cap \mathbb{Q}$, and $\phi \subseteq \mathsf{States}$ is a predicate.

A program C is called *loop-free*, if it contains neither $\texttt{while}$ nor $\texttt{diverge}$ statements. For practical verification purposes, a concrete syntax for the E's, μ's, and ϕ's in Definition 7 will be introduced in Section 6. We do not yet require such a syntax here and thus omit it.

Let us briefly go over each program statement from Definition 7. $\texttt{skip}$ does nothing. $\texttt{diverge}$ is a shorthand for the loop $\texttt{while}\,(\texttt{true})\,\{\texttt{skip}\}$. There are two types of assignment statements: the *deterministic assignment* $x := E$ updates the value of x in the current program state s according to $E(s)$, whereas the *probabilistic* assignment $x :\approx \mu$ samples a value from the probability distribution $\mu(s)$ and assigns the result to x. The probabilistic choice $\{C_1\}\,[p]\,\{C_2\}$ executes C_1 with probability p and C_2 with probability $1 - p$. Finally, $C_1 \mathbin{;} C_2$, $\texttt{if}\,(\phi)\,\{C_1\}\,\texttt{else}\,\{C_2\}$, and $\texttt{while}\,(\phi)\,\{C\}$ are standard sequential composition, conditional branching, and while loops, respectively.

Table 1: Inductive definitions of the posterior measure of program C w.r.t. initial measure g via occupation measures (column $\mathrm{pm}[\![C]\!]\,(g)$) and à la Kozen [36, Semantics 2] (column $\mathcal{K}[\![C]\!]\,(g)$). Notably, the two definitions differ only in the treatment of loops; in particular, for pm, the fixed point variable (v) is of type $\mathcal{M}\,(\mathsf{States})$ whereas for $\mathcal{K}$, the fixed point variable (T) is of type $\mathcal{M}\,(\mathsf{States}) \to \mathcal{M}\,(\mathsf{States})$. In Theorem 2, we show that the definitions are equivalent.

C	$\mathrm{pm}[\![C]\!]\,(g)$	$\mathcal{K}[\![C]\!]\,(g)$
`skip`	g	
`diverge`	0	
$x := E$	$\lambda s.\ \sum_{s'}\ [s'\,[x/E(s')] = s] \cdot g(s')$	
$x :\approx \mu$	$\lambda s.\ \sum_{s'}\ [s'\,[x/s(x)] = s] \cdot \mu(s')(s(x)) \cdot g(s')$	
$\{C_1\}\,[p]\,\{C_2\}$	$\mathrm{pm}[\![C_1]\!]\,(p \cdot g) + \mathrm{pm}[\![C_2]\!]\,((1-p) \cdot g)$	$\mathcal{K}[\![C_1]\!]\,(p \cdot g) + \mathcal{K}[\![C_2]\!]\,((1-p) \cdot g)$
$C_1 \,\fatsemi\, C_2$	$\mathrm{pm}[\![C_2]\!]\,(\mathrm{pm}[\![C_1]\!]\,(g))$	$\mathcal{K}[\![C_2]\!]\,(\mathcal{K}[\![C_1]\!]\,(g))$
`if` $(\phi)\ \{C_1\}$ `else` $\{C_2\}$	$\mathrm{pm}[\![C_1]\!]\,([\phi] \cdot g) + \mathrm{pm}[\![C_2]\!]\,([\neg\phi] \cdot g)$	$\mathcal{K}[\![C_1]\!]\,([\phi] \cdot g) + \mathcal{K}[\![C_2]\!]\,([\neg\phi] \cdot g)$
`while` $(\phi)\ \{C_0\}$	$[\neg\phi] \cdot (\mathrm{lfp}\,v.\ g + \mathrm{pm}[\![C_0]\!]\,([\phi] \cdot v))$	$\left(\mathrm{lfp}\,T.\ \lambda v.\ [\neg\phi] \cdot v + T(\mathcal{K}[\![C_0]\!]\,([\phi] \cdot v))\right)(g)$

4 Semantics of PPs via Occupation Measures

We now introduce our semantics based on occupation measures and relate it to several other well-established semantic concepts for probabilistic programs. More precisely, we introduce our key semantic functional in Section 4.1, establish equivalence to Kozen's semantics in Section 4.2, and relate our semantic functional to operational Markov chains and expected runtimes in Section 4.3.

4.1 Loop Semantics via Occupation Measures

Towards defining our semantic functional, we define arithmetic operations on measures pointwise, i.e., for $\circledcirc \in \{+, \cdot\}$, we let $f \circledcirc g = \lambda s.f(s) \circledcirc g(s)$. Moreover, recall that $[\phi]$ is the Iverson bracket (i.e., the indicator function) of the predicate ϕ. Now consider the following:

Definition 8 (pm). *The function* $\mathrm{pm}[\![C]\!] \colon \mathcal{M}\,(\mathsf{States}) \to \mathcal{M}\,(\mathsf{States})$ *is defined inductively on the structure of C by the rules in Table 1 (middle column). We call* $\mathrm{pm}[\![C]\!]\,(g)$ *the* posterior measure *of C w.r.t. initial measure g.*

If the initial measure g is a probability distribution, the intuition on the posterior measure $\mathrm{pm}[\![C]\!]\,(g)$ is straightforward and as expected:

If g is a probability distribution, then $\mathrm{pm}[\![C]\!]\,(g)$ *is the subprobability[11] distribution of states obtained from executing C on the initial distribution g.*

Let us now go over each rule in the middle column of Table 1. A `skip` statement does not modify the initial measure. Since `diverge` does not terminate in

----

[11] The *leaked* mass $|g| - |\mathrm{pm}[\![C]\!]\,(g)|$ is the probability that C diverges on g.

any state, the posterior measure is constantly 0. For assignments, the mass of the posterior measure in state s is obtained from accumulating the mass of all states s' which, after executing the assignment, become s. For a deterministic assignment $x := E$, these are all states s with $E(s') = s(x)$ and such that s' and s coincide on all other variables. Similarly, for a probabilistic assignment $x :\approx \mu$, the incoming mass $g(s')$ is weighted by the probability of sampling the value $s(x)$ from $\mu(s')$. Sequential composition $C_1 \,\mathring{,}\, C_2$ propagates the measure through C_1 first, and then through C_2. For a conditional branch $\texttt{if } (\phi) \, \{C_1\} \, \texttt{else} \, \{C_2\}$ the measure is restricted to the states satisfying ϕ and the states satisfying $\neg\phi$, and then propagated through C_1 and C_2, respectively. The final result is obtained by adding the measures resulting from executing the two branches.

The posterior measure of a loop $C = \texttt{while } (\phi) \, \{C_0\}$ involves a least fixed point construction. It is this construction where occupation measures come into a play — a fact we formalize and prove in Section 4.3. Let us define some auxiliary notation. Given an initial measure g, we call

$$\Phi_{g,C} : \mathcal{M}\,(\text{States}) \to \mathcal{M}\,(\text{States}), \qquad v \mapsto g + \mathrm{pm}[\![C_0]\!]\,([\phi] \cdot v)$$

the *characteristic function of C w.r.t. g*. Note that $\mathrm{pm}[\![C]\!]\,(g) = [\neg\phi] \cdot (\mathrm{lfp}\, v.\, \Phi_{g,C}(v))$ by definition. If g is a probability distribution, then $(\mathrm{lfp}\, v.\, \Phi_{g,C}(v))(s)$ is the *expected number of times state s is encountered at the loop head when executed on the initial measure g* (as formalized in Theorem 3) — the least fixed point thus denotes an occupation measure. After — so to speak — cutting off all states from $\mathrm{lfp}\, v.\, \Phi_{g,C}(v)$ that satisfy the loop guard, we obtain precisely the (sub-)distribution of final states reached after executing C on g (see Theorem 2).

Example 1. The loop C in Program 1 generates a geometric distribution. In each iteration, the loop body $C_0 = \{c := c + 1\}\,[^1\!/_2]\,\{x := 0\}$ either increments the *counter variable* c with probability $^1\!/_2$, or terminates the loop by setting x to zero. For the initial measure $g = [x = 1 \wedge c = 0]$, we have

---

Program 1 The geometric loop.

```
/// X    /* Initially, x = 1 and c = 0 */
while (x = 1){
    {c := c + 1} [1/2] {x := 0}
}
/// 1/2 + 1/4 C + 1/8 C^2 + ...
```

$$\mathrm{lfp}\, \Phi_{g,C} \;=\; \sum_{k=0}^{\infty} 2^{-k} \cdot [x = 1 \wedge c = k] + \sum_{k=0}^{\infty} 2^{-(k+1)} \cdot [x = 0 \wedge c = k] \,.$$

For every $s \in \text{States}$, the value $(\mathrm{lfp}\, \Phi_{g,C})(s)$ gives the expected number of times s is encountered at the loop header when executing C on g.[12] This is intuitive: any state s with $s(x) \notin \{0, 1\}$ is *never* visited since we execute the loop on $x = 1$ and x can only ever be set to 0. All states with $s(x) \in \{0, 1\}$ are visited at most once. Hence, for such states, $(\mathrm{lfp}\, \Phi_{g,C})(s)$ coincides with the probability of reaching s.

---

[12] We will show how to obtain this fixed point using Theorem 6 in Example 3.

Filtering on $x \neq 1$, we obtain the anticipated geometric distribution:

$$\mathrm{pm}[\![C]\!]\,(g) \;=\; [x \neq 1] \cdot (\mathrm{lfp}\ \Phi_{g,C}) \;=\; \sum_{k=0}^{\infty} 2^{-(k+1)} \cdot [x = 0 \wedge c = k]\ .$$

Notably, despite the fact that g and $\mathrm{pm}[\![C]\!]\,(g)$ are probability distributions, the fixed point is a measure with mass $\left|\mathrm{lfp}\ \Phi_{g,C}\right| = \sum_{k=0}^{\infty} 2^{-k} + \sum_{k=0}^{\infty} 2^{-(k+1)} = 3 > 1$, showing the need to consider arbitrary measures in the definition of pm.

Well-definedness of our least fixed point construction follows from Tarski's theorem [51]: Measures $\mathcal{M}\,(\mathsf{States})$ equipped with the pointwise order $\leq$ are a complete lattice and $\mathrm{pm}[\![C]\!]$ (and thus $\Phi_{g,C}$) is a monotonic function on this lattice. We collect the latter fact and several other properties in the next theorem, which follows from the equivalence to Kozen's semantics (Theorem 2) and [36]:

Theorem 1 (Properties of pm). *Let $C \in \mathrm{pGCL}$. Then:*

1. $\mathrm{pm}[\![C]\!]$ *is* monotonic, *i.e., for all $\mu, v \in \mathcal{M}\,(\mathsf{States})$, we have*

$$\mu \leq v \quad implies \quad \mathrm{pm}[\![C]\!]\,(\mu) \leq \mathrm{pm}[\![C]\!]\,(v)\ .$$

2. $\mathrm{pm}[\![C]\!]$ *is* linear, *i.e., for all $\mu, v \in \mathcal{M}\,(\mathsf{States})$ and all $a \in \mathbb{R}_{\geq 0}^{\infty}$, we have*

$$\mathrm{pm}[\![C]\!]\,(\mu + v) = \mathrm{pm}[\![C]\!]\,(\mu) + \mathrm{pm}[\![C]\!]\,(v) \quad and \quad \mathrm{pm}[\![C]\!]\,(a \cdot \mu) = a \cdot \mathrm{pm}[\![C]\!]\,(\mu)\ .$$

3. $\mathrm{pm}[\![C]\!]$ *is* feasible, *i.e., for all $\mu \in \mathcal{M}\,(\mathsf{States})$, we have $\left|\mathrm{pm}[\![C]\!]\,(\mu)\right| \leq |\mu|$.*
4. $\mathrm{pm}[\![C]\!]$ *preserves distributions, i.e., for all $\mu \in \mathcal{M}\,(\mathsf{States})$, we have*

$$\mu \in \mathcal{D}\,(\mathsf{States}) \quad implies \quad \mathrm{pm}[\![C]\!]\,(\mu) \in \mathcal{D}\,(\mathsf{States})\ .$$

4.2   Equivalence to Kozen's Semantics

For each program C, Kozen's [36] measure transformer semantics $\mathcal{K}\,[\![C]\!]$ is defined inductively on the structure of C by the rules in Table 1 (right column). The definitions of pm and $\mathcal{K}$ are identical *except for the case of loops*. This difference, however, is crucial: Whereas pm's loop characteristic functional is of type $\mathcal{M}\,(\mathsf{States}) \to \mathcal{M}\,(\mathsf{States})$, that is, a measure transformer, Kozen's fixed point functional is of the *higher-order* type

$$\bigl(\mathcal{M}\,(\mathsf{States}) \to \mathcal{M}\,(\mathsf{States})\bigr) \;\to\; \bigl(\mathcal{M}\,(\mathsf{States}) \to \mathcal{M}\,(\mathsf{States})\bigr)\ ,$$

that is, a *measure-transformer transformer*. This is because Kozen's construction does *not take the initial measure g into account*: $\mathrm{lfp}\,T.\,\lambda v.\,[\neg\phi]\cdot v + T(\mathcal{K}\,[\![C_0]\!]\,([\phi] \cdot v))$ is a function of type $\mathcal{M}\,(\mathsf{States}) \to \mathcal{M}\,(\mathsf{States})$ that maps *every* initial measure to the corresponding posterior measure. It is the fact that our functional *does* take the initial measure into account which significantly simplifies invariant-based reasoning and enables our novel template-based invariant synthesis approach. Put simply: whereas Kozen's approach requires to find a higher order object, we can get away with a lower order object.

We now state and prove the main result of this section:

Theorem 2 (Semantic Equivalence). *For all programs C, $\mathrm{pm}[\![C]\!] = \mathcal{K}[\![C]\!]$.*

Hence, our pm transformer based on occupation measures indeed soundly determines the sought-after posterior measures even though the functionals for loops are much simpler than the functionals involved in Kozen's semantics. The rest of this section is devoted to the proof of Theorem 2.

Proof (of Theorem 2). The key idea is to exploit the *Kozen duality* between measure transformers and so-called *expectation transformers* [35]: Given a random variable $f : \mathsf{States} \to \mathbb{R}_{\geq 0}^{\infty}$, denote by

$$\mathbf{wp}[\![C]\!]\,(f) : (\mathsf{States} \to \mathbb{R}_{\geq 0}^{\infty}), \qquad s \mapsto \mathbb{E}_{\mathcal{K}[\![C]\!](1_s)}\,[f]$$

the *weakest pre-expectation of C w.r.t. f*, that is, the function which maps every initial program state s to the expected value of f w.r.t. the distribution of final states $\mathcal{K}[\![C]\!]\,(1_s)$ reached after executing C on s. The Kozen duality states that, for every initial measure μ, we have

$$\mathbb{E}_{\mu}\left[\mathbf{wp}[\![C]\!]\,(f)\right] = \sum_{s} \mathbf{wp}[\![C]\!]\,(f)\,(s) \cdot \mu(s) = \sum_{s} f(s) \cdot \mathcal{K}[\![C]\!]\,(\mu)\,(s) = \mathbb{E}_{\mathcal{K}[\![C]\!](\mu)}\,[f]\,.$$

It immediately follows from [58, Theorem 4.5][13] that pm analogously satisfies

$$\mathbb{E}_{\mu}\left[\mathbf{wp}[\![C]\!]\,(f)\right] = \sum_{s} \mathbf{wp}[\![C]\!]\,(f)\,(s) \cdot \mu(s) = \sum_{s} f(s) \cdot \mathrm{pm}[\![C]\!]\,(\mu)\,(s) = \mathbb{E}_{\mathrm{pm}[\![C]\!](\mu)}\,[f]\,.$$

This yields $\mathbb{E}_{\mathrm{pm}[\![C]\!](\mu)}\,[f] = \mathbb{E}_{\mathcal{K}[\![C]\!](\mu)}\,[f]$ for all $f \in \mathsf{States} \to \mathbb{R}_{\geq 0}^{\infty}$ and all initial measures μ. Define for every state s the random variable $f_s = \lambda s'.\,[s' = s]$. Then

$$\mathrm{pm}[\![C]\!]\,(\mu)\,(s)\; =\; \mathbb{E}_{\mathrm{pm}[\![C]\!](\mu)}\,[f_s]\; =\; \mathbb{E}_{\mathcal{K}[\![C]\!](\mu)}\,[f_s]\; =\; \mathcal{K}[\![C]\!]\,(\mu)\,(s)\,,$$

and thus $\mathrm{pm}[\![C]\!] = \mathcal{K}[\![C]\!]$, which proves Theorem 2. $\qquad\qquad\square$

4.3   Relating Occupation Measures to Expected Runtimes

In this section, we formally show that the least fixed point in the definition of pm for loops[14] is indeed an occupation measure (in a suitably defined Markov chain; see Definition 6); we also relate this measure to the loop's *expected runtime*.

Definition 9 (Big-step Operational Markov Chain). *Let $C = \mathtt{while}\,(\phi)\,\{C_0\}$ be a loop with loop-free body C_0. We define the Markov chain $\mathcal{L}[\![C]\!]$ with states $S_{\mathcal{L}[\![C]\!]} := \mathsf{States} \cup \{\downarrow\}$ and transition probability function*

$$P_{\mathcal{L}[\![C]\!]}(s)\; :=\; \begin{cases} \mathrm{pm}[\![C_0]\!]\,(\delta_s), & \textit{if } s \in \mathsf{States} \textit{ and } s \models \phi, \\ \delta_{\downarrow}, & \textit{else.} \end{cases}$$

---

[13] Zhang et al.'s framework [58] is to be instantiated with the semiring $(\mathbb{R}_{\geq 0}^{\infty}, +, \cdot, 0, 1)$.

[14] We restrict to loop with *loop-free bodies* for simplicity; with loopy bodies, Definition 9 and subsequent theorems would need to handle potential divergence of inner loops.

Every state of $\mathcal{L}[\![C]\!]$ is either a program state or $\downarrow$, the latter indicating termination. For every state s satisfying the loop guard ϕ, the probability of transitioning to some state s' is the probability of reaching s' from s through *one* loop iteration. Every such transition in $\mathcal{L}[\![C]\!]$ thus corresponds to an *entire* loop iteration, hence the term *big-step*. With this perspective, we get:

Theorem 3 (Relation of pm and OM). *For $C = \texttt{while}\,(\phi)\,\{C_0\}$, C_0 loop-free:*

$$\forall \textit{ initial measures } g \in \mathcal{M}\,(\textsf{States}) : \forall s \in \textsf{States:} \quad \left(\mathrm{lfp}\,\Phi_{g,C}\right)(s) = \mathrm{OM}^{g}_{\mathcal{L}[\![C]\!]}(s)\ .$$

Theorem 3 formalizes our claims from Section 4.1: If g is a probability measure, then $\left(\mathrm{lfp}\,\Phi_{g,C}\right)(s)$ is the expected number of times that state s is visited at the loop head when executing C on g.

Let us now relate a loop's occupation measure to its expected runtime. For every loop $C = \texttt{while}\,(\phi)\,\{C_0\}$ with loop-free body C_0, we let

$$\mathbf{ert}[\![C]\!] : \textsf{States} \to \mathbb{R}^{\infty}_{\geq 0}, \quad s \quad \mapsto \quad \begin{array}{c} \textit{expected number of loop guard } \phi \\ \textit{evaluations when executing } C \textit{ on } s \end{array} \ \cdot$$

The function $\mathbf{ert}[\![C]\!]$ can be defined in a weakest pre-condition style by induction on the structure of C; see [30] for details. We obtain the following correspondence:

Theorem 4 (Relation of pm and ert). *For $C = \texttt{while}\,(\phi)\,\{C_0\}$:*

$$\forall \textit{ initial measures } g \in \mathcal{M}\,(\textsf{States}) : \quad \left|\mathrm{lfp}\,\Phi_{g,C}\right| = \sum_{s \in \textsf{States}} \mathbf{ert}[\![C]\!](s) \cdot g(s)\ .$$

In particular, if $g = \delta_s$ is a Dirac measure, the mass of $\mathrm{lfp}\,\Phi_{g,C}$ equals the expected number of guard evaluations when executing C on s. This observation yields a connection to *positive almost sure termination* (PAST) — a property which, by definition, holds for a loop C and initial state s, if $\mathbf{ert}[\![C]\!](s) < \infty$ [30].

Corollary 1. *Let $C = \texttt{while}\,(\phi)\,\{C_0\}$ be a loop with loop-free body C_0 and let $s \in \textsf{States}$. Then C is PAST on s if and only if for $g = \delta_s$, we have $\left|\mathrm{lfp}\,\Phi_{g,C}\right| < \infty$.*

5   Occupation Measure-Based Loop Invariants

In this section, we introduce the notion of *occupation invariant*, which allows determining or upper-bounding a loop's posterior measure and forms the basis of our invariant synthesis approach. Our invariants correspond to [49, p. 306], if one uses (countable) discrete-time Markov chains as the program model.

Definition 10 (Occupation Invariant). *Let $C = \texttt{while}\,(\phi)\,\{C_0\}$ and let $g \in \mathcal{M}\,(\textsf{States})$ be an initial measure. We call a measure $I \in \mathcal{M}\,(\textsf{States})$ an (occupation) superinvariant of C w.r.t. g, if $\Phi_{g,C}(I) \leq I$. If $\Phi_{g,C}(I) = I$, then we call I an (occupation) invariant.*

Note that — as is to be expected from invariant-based reasoning — determining $\Phi_{g,C}(I)$ requires us to reason about a *single guarded loop iteration* only. Superinvariants yields upper bounds on a loop's posterior measure as follows:

Theorem 5. *If I is a superinvariant of $C = \texttt{while}\,(\phi)\,\{C_0\}$ w.r.t. g, then*

$$\mathrm{pm}[\![C]\!]\,(g) \;\le\; [\neg\phi]\cdot I\;.$$

Proof. By Park induction [46], $\Phi_{g,C}(I) \le I$ implies lfp $\nu.\,\Phi_{g,C}(\nu) \le I$. Hence,

$$\begin{aligned}
&\Phi_{g,C}(I) \;\le\; I\\
\text{implies}\quad &\text{lfp } \nu.\,\Phi_{g,C}(\nu) \;\le\; I &&\text{(Park induction)}\\
\text{implies}\quad &[\neg\phi]\cdot\text{lfp } \nu.\,\Phi_{g,C}(\nu) \;\le\; [\neg\phi]\cdot I\\
\text{implies}\quad &\mathrm{pm}[\![C]\!]\,(g) \;\le\; [\neg\phi]\cdot I\;. &&\text{(definition)} \qquad\square
\end{aligned}$$

Example 2. Recall the geometric loop C with initial probability distribution $g = [x = 1 \wedge c = 0]$ from Program 1. Let us now upper-bound $\mathrm{pm}[\![C]\!]\,(g)$ by means of a superinvariant. To this end, consider the measure

$$I(x,c) \;=\; 2^{-(c+1)}\cdot[x = 0] \;+\; 2^{-c}\cdot[x = 1]\;.$$

We have $\Phi_{g,C}(I) \le I$ and thus lfp $\Phi_{g,C} \le I$. Hence, $I(s)$ upper-bounds the expected number of times a state $s \in \mathsf{States}$ is encountered at the loop header when executing C on g. This aligns with our intuition: If $s(x) \notin \{0,1\}$, then s is *never* visited, since we execute the loop on $x = 1$ and x can only ever be set to 0. On the other hand, states satisfying $s(x) \in \{0,1\}$ are visited at most once: after $s(c)$ iterations of incrementing c if $s(x) = 1$, and after one more iteration if $s(x) = 0$. Thus, $I(s)$ upper-bounds the probability of reaching s. By Theorem 5, we now get, as expected,

$$\mathrm{pm}[\![C]\!]\,(g) \;\le\; [x \ne 1]\cdot I \;=\; 2^{-(c+1)}\cdot[x = 0]\;;$$

that is, the probability of terminating in a state s with $s(x) \ne 0$ is 0, and for all states with $s(x) = 0$, the probability of terminating in s is at most $2^{-(s(c)+1)}$.

If I is a superinvariant with finite mass and moreover that mass is the same as the mass of the input measure g, then we can draw an even stronger conclusion:

Theorem 6 (Proof Rule for the Exact Posterior Measure). *Consider a loop $C = \texttt{while}\,(\phi)\,\{C_0\}$ with loop-free body C_0 and an initial measure $g \in \mathcal{M}\,(\mathsf{States})$. Let $I \in \mathcal{M}\,(\mathsf{States})$ be a measure such that all of the following hold:*

1. *I is an occupation superinvariant, i.e., $\Phi_{g,C}(I) \;\le\; I$.*
2. *I has finite mass, i.e., $|I| < \infty$*
3. *$[\neg\phi]\cdot I$ has a mass equal to the mass of g, i.e., $|[\neg\phi]\cdot I| = |g|$.*

Then $[\neg\phi]\cdot I$ is the exact *posterior measure, i.e., $\mathrm{pm}[\![C]\!]\,(g) = [\neg\phi]\cdot I$.*

Proof (sketch). Due to Theorem 4, $|\text{lfp }\Phi_{g,C}|$ is the expected runtime ERT of the loop on input distribution g. Since I is an occupation superinvariant (Condition (1)), we can conclude by Park induction that lfp $\Phi_{g,C} \le I$ and thus also $|\text{lfp }\Phi_{g,C}| \le |I|$. Together with Condition (2), we get that $ERT = |\text{lfp }\Phi_{g,C}| \le |I| < \infty$ and so the expected runtime of the loop is finite. Finite expected runtime implies almost sure termination [30]. Almost sure termination implies that the mass of the input measure g is equal to the mass of the output measure, so $\big|\text{pm}[\![C]\!](g)\big| = |g|$. Now, by Condition (3), we get

$$\big|\text{pm}[\![C]\!](g)\big| = |g| = |[\neg\phi]\cdot I| . \tag{$\dagger\dagger$}$$

By Condition (1) and Theorem 5, we moreover have

$$\text{pm}[\![C]\!](g) \leq [\neg\phi]\cdot I . \tag{$\ddagger\ddagger$}$$

Assume, for contradiction, that there is a state s' such that $\text{pm}[\![C]\!](g)(s') < ([\neg\phi]\cdot I)(s')$. Then,

$$
\begin{aligned}
|[\neg\phi]\cdot I| &= \big|\text{pm}[\![C]\!](g)\big| && \text{(by ($\dagger\dagger$))}\\
&= \text{pm}[\![C]\!](g)(s') + \sum_{s\neq s'}\text{pm}[\![C]\!](g)(s)\\
&< ([\neg\phi]\cdot I)(s') + \sum_{s\neq s'}\text{pm}[\![C]\!](g)(s) && \text{(by assumption above)}\\
&\leq ([\neg\phi]\cdot I)(s') + \sum_{s\neq s'}([\neg\phi]\cdot I)(s) && \text{(by ($\ddagger\ddagger$))}\\
&= |[\neg\phi]\cdot I| . && \text{Contradiction:}\quad |[\neg\phi]\cdot I| < |[\neg\phi]\cdot I| \quad\square
\end{aligned}
$$

Note that an occupation superinvariant that fulfills conditions (1) and (2) for initial distribution $g = \delta_s$ is sufficient to prove PAST on state s by Corollary 1.

Example 3. We continue the analysis of the geometric loop C from Program 1. In Example 2, we established the occupation superinvariant $I = 2^{-(c+1)}\cdot[x=0] + 2^{-c}\cdot[x=1]$ to conclude $\text{pm}[\![C]\!](g) \leq [x\neq 1]\cdot I$. Here, we show that this inequality is actually an equality. We have $|I| = \sum_{k\in\mathbb{N}}2^{-(k+1)} + \sum_{k\in\mathbb{N}}2^{-k} = 3 < \infty$, and $|[x\neq 1]\cdot I| = \sum_{k\in\mathbb{N}}2^{-(k+1)} = 1 = |g|$. By Theorem 6, we now obtain

$$\text{pm}[\![C]\!](g) = [x\neq 1]\cdot I = 2^{-(c+1)}\cdot[x=0] ,$$

and conclude that, for all states $s \in \mathsf{States}$, the probability of terminating in s is *exactly* $2^{-(s(c)+1)}$ if $s(x) = 0$, and 0 otherwise.

6 Invariant Synthesis

In this section, we present an automatic, template-based synthesis technique for occupation invariants (see Definition 10). Template-based probabilistic loop invariant synthesis is common in the literature (e.g., [31, 4]); the novelty here is the use of *generating function templates* representing collections of measures. Given such a template, we can automatically check whether there exists a parameter instantiation that yields a valid occupation invariant. We begin by introducing generating functions and adapting our pm-semantics to operate on this domain.

6.1   Generating Function Semantics

Let $\mathbf{X} = (X_v)_{v \in \mathsf{Vars}}$ be a family of formal variables or *indeterminates*, one per program variable $v \in \mathsf{Vars}$ (in examples, we simply write X, Y instead of X_x, X_y, etc.). Formally, generating functions are (infinite) sequences of values, commonly represented as formal power series. See [55, 37] for detailed expositions.

Definition 11 (Formal Power Series). *Let* R *be a semiring. An* R-*valued formal power series (FPS) in indeterminates* $\mathbf{X}$ *is a function* $\mathfrak{g}: \mathsf{States} \to R$ *denoted* $\mathfrak{g} = \sum_{s \in \mathsf{States}} \mathfrak{g}(s) \cdot \mathbf{X}^s$, *where* $\mathbf{X}^s = \prod_{v \in \mathsf{Vars}} X_v^{s(v)}$. *A polynomial is an FPS* $\mathfrak{g}$ *with* $\mathfrak{g}(s) \neq 0$ *for finitely many* $s \in \mathsf{States}$. *The set of FPSs is denoted by* $R[[\mathbf{X}]]$. *The set of polynomials is denoted by* $R[\mathbf{X}]$.

$R[[\mathbf{X}]]$ and $R[\mathbf{X}]$ are semirings with (pointwise) sum and (Cauchy) product:

$$\mathfrak{g} + \mathfrak{h} := \sum_{s \in \mathsf{States}} (\mathfrak{g}(s) + \mathfrak{h}(s)) \cdot \mathbf{X}^s, \qquad \mathfrak{g} \cdot \mathfrak{h} := \sum_{s \in \mathsf{States}} \left(\sum_{s_1 + s_2 = s} \mathfrak{g}(s_1) \cdot \mathfrak{h}(s_2) \right) \cdot \mathbf{X}^s.$$

If R is a ring, then so are $R[[\mathbf{X}]]$ and $R[\mathbf{X}]$.

We employ FPSs to represent measures on the set of program states as follows:

Definition 12 (Generating Function). *The generating function* GF_μ *of a measure* $\mu \in \mathcal{M}(\mathsf{States})$ *is the FPS* $\mathrm{GF}_\mu := \sum_{s \in \mathsf{States}} \mu(s) \cdot \mathbf{X}^s \in \mathbb{R}_{\geq 0}^\infty[[\mathbf{X}]]$. *Conversely, every FPS* $\mathfrak{g} \in \mathbb{R}_{\geq 0}^\infty[[\mathbf{X}]]$ *defines a measure* $\mu_\mathfrak{g} \in \mathcal{M}(\mathsf{States})$ *with* $\mu_\mathfrak{g}(s) = \mathfrak{g}(s)$ *for* $s \in \mathsf{States}$.

Generating functions as in Definition 12 do not offer much benefit yet; they are merely a different notation for an infinite expression representing a measure. To enable synthesis of occupation invariants represented as generating functions, our key idea is to exploit that a large class of measures admit a *closed form representation* of their generating function; in this paper, we consider only *rational functions* (i.e., fractions of polynomials) as closed forms. For example, the final distribution of the geometric loop running example (Program 1) is

$$\mathrm{GF}_{\mathrm{geom}(1/2)} = \frac{1}{2} + \frac{1}{4}C + \frac{1}{8}C^2 + \dots, \qquad \text{with rational closed form } \frac{1}{2 - C}.$$

Before we explain the details, let us first define a pGCL fragment that preserves measures in rational closed form.

The ReDiP *Fragment of* pGCL. We consider the syntactic fragment of *rectangular discrete probabilistic programs* (ReDiP) of pGCL by [13]. This fragment enables defining a program semantics on generating functions of probability measures which preserves certain closed form representations of the generating functions. We generalize this result to the generating functions from Definition 12.

The syntax of ReDiP is given in Table 2. It includes multiple statements to modify variables: assignment of constants, a decrement operation, and an increment operation. The latter draws a number of i.i.d. samples from a probability distribution over $\mathbb{N}$ and increments the variable's value by the sum of the samples

Table 2: Syntax (left column) and the pm-semantics (right column) of ReDiP programs, where $v, y \in \mathsf{Vars}$, $n \in \mathbb{N}$ and $D \in \mathcal{D}_{=1}(\mathbb{N})$ denotes a probability distribution on $\mathbb{N}$ with $[\![D]\!] \in \mathbb{R}_{\geq 0}[\![T]\!]$ in a fresh formal variable $T \notin \mathbf{X}$.

P	$\mathrm{pm}[\![P]\!]\,(\mathfrak{g})$
$v := n$	$\mathfrak{g}[X_v/1] \cdot X_v^n$
$v{-}{-}$	$(\mathfrak{g} - \mathfrak{g}\!\restriction_{v<1}) \cdot X_v^{-1} + \mathfrak{g}\!\restriction_{v<1}$
$v \mathrel{+}= \mathtt{iid}\,(D, y)$	$\mathfrak{g}[X_y/X_y \cdot [\![D]\!][T/X_v]]$
$\mathtt{if}\,(\,v < n\,)\,\{\,P_1\,\}\,\mathtt{else}\,\{\,P_2\,\}$	$\mathrm{pm}[\![P_1]\!]\,(\mathfrak{g}\!\restriction_{v<n}) + \mathrm{pm}[\![P_2]\!]\,(\mathfrak{g} - \mathfrak{g}\!\restriction_{v<n})$
$P_1\,\mathbin{\mathring{,}}\,P_2$	$\mathrm{pm}[\![P_2]\!]\,\big(\mathrm{pm}[\![P_1]\!]\,(\mathfrak{g})\big)$
$\mathtt{while}\,(\,v < n\,)\,\{\,P_1\,\}$	$\mathfrak{h} - \mathfrak{h}\!\restriction_{v<n},\quad$ where $\mathfrak{h} = \mathrm{lfp}\,\mathfrak{i}.\,\mathfrak{g} + \mathrm{pm}[\![P_1]\!]\,(\mathfrak{i}\!\restriction_{v<n})$

(in plain pGCL, this operation can be expressed by means of a loop; however, in ReDiP it is considered a primitive operation rather than a loop). The number of samples is determined by the value of another program variable in the current state. The language supports branching and loops with rectangular guards of the form $v < n$ with $v \in \mathsf{Vars}$ and $n \in \mathbb{N}$. We can simulate linear expressions on the right hand side of increments (e.g., $x \mathrel{+}= x + 2y + 1$), as well as Boolean combinations of comparisons of variables with constants (e.g., $x = 5 \,\|\, y > 3$) with the loop-free fragment of ReDiP. We also write increments $x \mathrel{+}= E$ as $x := x + E$. See [13] for a detailed exposure of the language.

Definition 13 (ReDiP). *The generating function-based* pm*-semantics of rectangular discrete probabilistic programs (ReDiP) is defined in Table 2, where in the definition of* $\mathrm{pm}[\![P]\!]\colon \mathbb{R}_{\geq 0}^{\infty}[\![\mathbf{X}]\!] \to \mathbb{R}_{\geq 0}^{\infty}[\![\mathbf{X}]\!]$ *we use the following operations:*

- *Substitution: For* $\mathfrak{g}, \mathfrak{h} \in \mathbb{R}_{\geq 0}^{\infty}[\![\mathbf{X}]\!]$ *and* $v \in \mathsf{Vars}$:

$$\mathfrak{g}[X_v/\mathfrak{h}] \;:=\; \sum_{s \in \mathsf{States}} \Bigg(\sum_{\substack{s_1 + s_2 = s \\ s_2(v) = s(v)}} \sum_{k \in \mathbb{N}} \mathfrak{g}(s_1[v \mapsto k]) \cdot \mathfrak{h}^k(s_2) \Bigg) \cdot \mathbf{X}^s \,.$$

- *(Downward) Shifting: For* $\mathfrak{g} \in \mathbb{R}_{\geq 0}^{\infty}[\![\mathbf{X}]\!]$ *and* $v \in \mathsf{Vars}$ *such that* $\mathfrak{g}(s) = 0$ *for all* $s \in \mathsf{States}$ *with* $s(v) = 0$:

$$\mathfrak{g} \cdot X_v^{-1} \;:=\; \sum_{s \in \mathsf{States}} \mathfrak{g}(s[v \mapsto s(v) + 1]) \cdot \mathbf{X}^s \,.$$

- *Formal Derivative: For* $\mathfrak{g} \in \mathbb{R}_{\geq 0}^{\infty}[\![\mathbf{X}]\!]$ *and* $v \in \mathsf{Vars}$:

$$\partial_{X_v}\mathfrak{g} \;:=\; \sum_{s \in \mathsf{States}} (s(v) + 1) \cdot \mathfrak{g}(s[v \mapsto s(v) + 1]) \cdot \mathbf{X}^s \,.$$

– *Restriction: For* $\mathfrak{g} \in \mathbb{R}_{\geq 0}^{\infty}[[\mathbf{X}]]$, $v \in \mathsf{Vars}$, $n \in \mathbb{N}$:

$$\mathfrak{g}\!\restriction_{v<n} \;:=\; \sum_{i=0}^{n-1} \tfrac{1}{i!}(\partial_{X_v}^i \mathfrak{g})[X_v/0] \cdot X_v^i$$

$$and \qquad \mathfrak{g} - \mathfrak{g}\!\restriction_{v<n} \;:=\; \sum_{s \in \mathsf{States}} [\mathfrak{g}(s) \neq \mathfrak{g}\!\restriction_{v<n}(s)]\, \mathfrak{g}(s) \cdot \mathbf{X}^s \;.$$

These operations are all monotonic, with the partial order on $\mathbb{R}_{\geq 0}^{\infty}[[\mathbf{X}]]$ inherited from $\mathcal{M}$ (States). Hence, the least fixed point in Table 2 is well-defined.

Intuitively, updates are performed by extracting the parts of the generating function that are affected by the update through substitution operations. For example, $v := n$ marginalizes w.r.t. X_v (thus effectively setting v to 0 temporarily) and then performs an (upward) shift by n in X_v.

The notation used for the additional operations is suggestive of their intended effect; for example, even though there is no subtraction on $\mathbb{R}_{\geq 0}^{\infty}[[\mathbf{X}]]$, $\mathfrak{g} - \mathfrak{g}\!\restriction_{v<n}$ effectively amounts to what is a subtraction between $\mathfrak{g}$ and $\mathfrak{g}\!\restriction_{v<n}$. The substitution operation corresponds to the intuitive substitution $\mathfrak{g}[X_v/\mathfrak{h}] = \sum_{s \in \mathsf{States}} \mathfrak{g}(s)\mathfrak{h}^{s(v)} \cdot \mathbf{Y}^s$, where $\mathbf{Y}$ contains all formal variables of $\mathbf{X}$ except X_v. Substitution is always well-defined, as every monotone sequence converges in our domain of nonnegative extended reals.

Our semantics is a generalization of [13] from probability generating functions to general generating functions.

Proposition 1. *Given a distribution $\mu \in \mathcal{D}$ (States) and a ReDiP-program P. Then* $\mathrm{GF}_\mu \in \mathbb{R}_{\geq 0}[[\mathbf{X}]]$ *and* $\mathrm{pm}[\![P]\!]$ (GF_μ) *coincides with the ReDiP semantics* $[\![P]\!]$ (GF_μ) *defined in [13, Table 2].*

Proof (sketch). Our definition is structurally identical to the definitions in [13, Table 2], except for the case of loops. Working with (sub)probability generating functions, [13] uses operations on $\mathbb{R}[[\mathbf{X}]]$. (Downward) shifting and formal derivation are defined identically. Similarly for restriction, where $\mathfrak{g} - \mathfrak{g}\!\restriction_{v<n}$ simply uses the subtraction of the ring $\mathbb{R}[[\mathbf{X}]]$. While the substitution operation $\mathfrak{g}[X_v/\mathfrak{h}]$ is not well-defined for all $\mathfrak{g}, \mathfrak{h} \in \mathbb{R}[[\mathbf{X}]]$, it has the same definition and is well-defined for (sub-)probability generating functions $\mathfrak{g}, \mathfrak{h}$, which is sufficient to define the program semantics. Observe that $\mathfrak{g}\!\restriction_{v<1} = \mathfrak{g}[X_v/0]$.

For loops, [13] uses Kozen's higher-order fixed point construction (see Section 4.2) while we use our occupation measure fixed point construction. The equivalence follows just as in Section 4.

Rational Closed Forms. Our goal is to use the algebraic structure of FPSs to obtain finite representations of measures as formal fractions such that we can apply the semantics of ReDiP-programs while preserving the finite representation. We achieve this for measures μ with $\mu(s) \neq \infty$ for all $s \in \mathsf{States}$ by embedding their generating functions into $\mathbb{R}[[\mathbf{X}]]$ and using the set of inverses present therein.

Definition 14 (Rational Closed Form). *For* $\mathfrak{g} \in \mathbb{R}_{\geq 0}[[\mathbf{X}]]$, *a pair of polynomials* $\mathfrak{n}_{\mathfrak{g}}, \mathfrak{d}_{\mathfrak{g}} \in \mathbb{R}[\mathbf{X}]$ *is a* (rational) *closed form of* $\mathfrak{g}$, *written* $\mathfrak{g} = \frac{\mathfrak{n}_{\mathfrak{g}}}{\mathfrak{d}_{\mathfrak{g}}}$, *if* $\mathfrak{d}_{\mathfrak{g}}$ *is invertible in* $\mathbb{R}[[\mathbf{X}]]$ *and* $\mathfrak{g} = \mathfrak{n}_{\mathfrak{g}} \cdot \mathfrak{d}_{\mathfrak{g}}^{-1}$ *in* $\mathbb{R}[[\mathbf{X}]]$.

For example, $1 \cdot X^0 + 2 \cdot X^1 + 4 \cdot X^2 + \cdots = \sum_{i \in \mathbb{N}} 2^i \cdot X^i$ has the rational closed form $\frac{1}{1-2X}$. Excluding ∞ as a coefficient gives closed forms in the ring $\mathbb{R}[[\mathbf{X}]]$. As developed in [13], this allows to define the operations downward shifting, formal derivation and restriction from Definition 13 on the closed forms. The only exception is substitution, as e.g., $(\sum_{i \in \mathbb{N}} 2^i \cdot X^i)[X/1] = \infty \neq -1 = \frac{1}{1-2X}[X/1]$. Substitution is only well-defined on closed forms, if the substitute has no constant term: if $\mathfrak{g} = \frac{\mathfrak{n}_{\mathfrak{g}}}{\mathfrak{d}_{\mathfrak{g}}}$, $\mathfrak{h} = \frac{\mathfrak{n}_{\mathfrak{h}}}{\mathfrak{d}_{\mathfrak{h}}}$ with $\mathfrak{h}(0) = 0$, then $\dfrac{\mathfrak{n}_{\mathfrak{g}}[X_v/\frac{\mathfrak{n}_{\mathfrak{h}}}{\mathfrak{d}_{\mathfrak{h}}}]}{\mathfrak{d}_{\mathfrak{g}}[X_v/\frac{\mathfrak{n}_{\mathfrak{h}}}{\mathfrak{d}_{\mathfrak{h}}}]}$ is a closed form of $\mathfrak{g}[X_v/\mathfrak{h}]$.

With this restriction of operations on closed forms, pm can be computed for loop-free ReDiP programs on closed forms, with two restrictions: for constant assignments $v := n$ it cannot be generally well-defined, e.g., applying $x := 0$ to $\frac{1}{1-X}$ yields ∞ which is not in rational closed form. Secondly, i.i.d. sampling increments $v \mathrel{+}= \mathtt{iid}\,(D, y)$ must be restricted to distributions D with a rational closed form. We call this fragment *closed* ReDiP (clReDiP):

Definition 15 (Closed ReDiP). *A* clReDiP *program is a loop-free* ReDiP *program without constant assignments* $v := n$ *and in which every used probability distribution* D *has a closed form* $[\![D]\!] = \frac{\mathfrak{n}_{[\![D]\!]}}{\mathfrak{d}_{[\![D]\!]}}$.

Corollary 2 ([13]). *Let* $\frac{\mathfrak{n}_{\mathfrak{g}}}{\mathfrak{d}_{\mathfrak{g}}}$ *be a closed form of generating function* $\mathfrak{g} \in \mathbb{R}_{\geq 0}[[\mathbf{X}]]$, *and* P *a* clReDiP *program. Then* $\mathrm{pm}[\![P]\!]\,(\mathfrak{g})$ *has a closed form, obtainable by applying the operations of Table 2 on the closed form.*

Remark 1 (Expressivity of our Language). Even though constant assignments $v := n$ are not allowed in clReDiP, they could be simulated by means of a loop $\mathtt{while}\,(v > 0)\,\{v{-}{-}\}\,\mathring{,}\,x \mathrel{+}= n$. However, the resulting loop may not always admit a rational invariant. Comparing a variable with another variable cannot be simulated in loop-free ReDiP [13], and hence also not in clReDiP. We conjecture that polynomial expressions in guards and assignments cannot be simulated in general either. To our knowledge, the exact class of distribution transformers expressible in loop-free ReDiP and clReDiP remains unknown. We also note that ReDiP *with loops* is Turing-complete despite its syntactic restrictions, as it can simulate two-counter machines.

6.2 Template-based Invariant Synthesis

Consider a ReDiP loop $P = \mathtt{while}\,(v < n)\,\{P_0\}$, with clReDiP body P_0 and initial measure $\mathfrak{g}$ in closed form. We use the generating function pm-semantics on rational closed forms to synthesize occupation invariants for the loop P starting from $\mathfrak{g}$. We will rely on (user-)provided templates to reduce the invariant synthesis problem to a parameter synthesis problem.

Let $\mathcal{T}$ denote a finite set of symbolic template parameters which are distinct from the formal variables $\mathbf{X} = (X_v)_{v \in \mathsf{Vars}}$. Our templates are rational closed forms that contain polynomial expressions $\mathbb{R}[\mathcal{T}]$ instead of only values $\mathbb{R}$ as coefficients. For $\tau\colon \mathcal{T} \to \mathbb{R}$, $I[\tau]$ denotes the instantiation of I where all occurrences of $t \in \mathcal{T}$ have been replaced by $\tau(t)$, provided the result is well-defined. Note that not every parameter valuation yields a valid instantiation, e.g., while instantiating the template $I = p \cdot V + (1 - p) \cdot V^2$ with $\tau = [p \mapsto -1]$ yields a valid FPS $I[\tau] = -1V + 2V^2$ in $\mathbb{R}[[\mathbf{X}]]$, this does not represent a nonnegative measure.

Synthesizing an invariant using a template I becomes a two-step process. First, we apply the loop's characteristic functional $\Phi_{\mathfrak{g},P}$ once on I and get a closed form for $\Phi_{\mathfrak{g},P}(I) = \mathfrak{g} + \mathrm{pm}[\![P_0]\!]\,(I\!\restriction_{v<n})$. By interpreting the parameters $\mathcal{T}$ as fresh program variables, we can directly use the definitions from the previous section. To ensure that I represents a valid invariant, we require it to satisfy the fixed-point equation $\Phi_{\mathfrak{g},P}(I) = I$. Through cross-multiplication of the denominators one obtains an equation between two polynomials. Comparing coefficients results in an equation system imposing constraints on the symbolic parameters $\mathcal{T}$, which can be solved using off-the-shelf computer algebra tools (e.g., rational function arithmetic, Gröbner bases). Second, we verify that an instantiation fulfilling these constraints, results in a generating function of a nonnegative measure.

Theorem 7. *Given* $\mu \in \mathcal{M}$ (States) *with* GF_μ *with a rational closed form,* I *a rational template, and* $\tau\colon \mathcal{T} \to \mathbb{R}$, *such that* $\Phi_{\mathrm{GF}_\mu,P}(I[\tau]) = I[\tau]$. *If* $I[\tau] \in \mathbb{R}^\infty_{\geq 0}[[\mathbf{X}]]$, *then* $\mu_{I[\tau]}$ *is an occupation invariant of* `while` $(v < n)\ \{P_0\}$ *from* μ.

Example 4. We continue the geometric loop example from Example 3 from Program 1. The initial probability distribution $g = [x = 1 \wedge c = 0]$ entering the loop, has generating function $\mathrm{GF}_g = 1 \cdot X^1 C^0 = X$ which is also a closed form. Consider the following rational template I with $\mathcal{T} = \{a_0, a_1, a_2, a_3, b_0, b_1, b_2\}$:

$$I = \frac{a_0 + a_1 \cdot X + a_2 \cdot C + a_3 \cdot X^2}{b_0 + b_1 \cdot X + b_2 \cdot C}.$$

Applying $\Phi_{\mathrm{GF}_g,P}$ of loop $P = $ `while` $(x = 1)\ \{\{x := 0\}\,[\frac{1}{2}]\,\{c := c + 1\}\}$ to I yields:

$$\Phi_{\mathrm{GF}_g,P}(I) = X + \frac{1}{2} \cdot (1 + XC) \cdot \frac{(a_1 b_0 - a_0 b_1) + (a_1 b_2 - a_2 b_1) \cdot C}{(b_0 + b_2 \cdot C)^2}.$$

By solving the equation $\Phi_{\mathrm{GF}_g,P}(I) = I$ symbolically over the rational function template, we obtain the assignment $\tau = [a_0 \mapsto 1, a_1 \mapsto 2, a_2 \mapsto 0, a_3 \mapsto 0, b_0 \mapsto 2, b_1 \mapsto 0, b_2 \mapsto -1]$ fulfilling $\Phi_{\mathrm{GF}_g,P}(I[\tau]) = I[\tau]$. As

$$I[\tau] = \frac{1 + 2 \cdot X}{2 - C} = (1 + 2 \cdot X) \sum_{k \in \mathbb{N}} \frac{1}{2^{k+1}} \cdot C^k = \sum_{k \in \mathbb{N}} \frac{1}{2^{k+1}} \cdot C^k + \sum_{k \in \mathbb{N}} \frac{1}{2^k} \cdot XC^k$$

has only nonnegative coefficients, we conclude that $I[\tau]$ represents an occupation invariant by Theorem 7. Indeed, this is the loop's occupation measure that we obtained in Example 3:

$$\mu_{I[\tau]} = [x = 0] \cdot 2^{-(c+1)} + [x = 1] \cdot 2^{-c}.$$

With Theorem 6 for $\mu_{I[\tau]}$, we conclude

$$\mathrm{pm}[\![C]\!]\,(g) = [x \neq 1] \cdot \mu_{I[\tau]} = [x = 0] \cdot 2^{-(c+1)}.$$

This approach appears particularly effective when the program structure leads to regular recurrence patterns, which can be translated into algebraic equalities over generating functions. Embedding such structure into a template allows analysis of loops on an abstract, intuitive level and leverages automated solvers to delegate the tedious computation of exact coefficients. In more complex cases, additional approximation techniques or domain-specific templates may be required, as demonstrated by the following example.

Example 5. Consider the *Fast Dice Roller* [40] algorithm FDR_N (Program 2) for some fixed integer constant $N > 0$. Let P_N denote the loop body. The loop is initially reached by $\mathfrak{g}_0 := 1 \cdot V^1 C^0 F^0$. For $N > 4$, iterating the loop body yields

$$\mathfrak{g}_1 := \mathrm{pm}[\![P_N]\!]\,(\mathfrak{g}_0 \!\restriction_{f=0}) = \tfrac{1}{2}V^2(C^0 + C^1),$$

$$\mathfrak{g}_2 := \mathrm{pm}[\![P_N]\!]\,(\mathfrak{g}_1 \!\restriction_{f=0})$$
$$= \tfrac{1}{4}V^4(C^0 + C^1 + C^2 + C^3).$$

c is always uniformly distributed between 0 and $v - 1$, as long as $v < N$ [40]. Hence, we expect an invariant to contain terms of the form $a_{N,i} \cdot V^i \sum_{k<i} C^k = a_{N,i} \cdot V^i \frac{1-C^i}{1-C}$ for some $a_{N,i} \in \mathbb{R}_{\geq 0}, i < N$. In an iteration in which v is increased to at least N, the distribution is split into two parts: a terminating part with $c < N$ and f set to 1, and a continuing part where $c \geq N$ and c, v have been reduced by N. For example, for $N = 6$ we have

$$\mathfrak{g}_3 := \mathrm{pm}[\![P_N]\!]\,(\mathfrak{g}_2 \!\restriction_{f=0}) = \frac{1}{8} \cdot FV^8 \frac{1 - C^6}{1 - C} + \frac{1}{8} \cdot V^2 \frac{1 - C^2}{1 - C} .$$

We thus expect an invariant to contain the terms $a_{N,i} \cdot F V^i \frac{1-C^N}{1-C}$ for some $a_{N,i} \in \mathbb{R}_{\geq 0}, i \geq N$. We make the following additional observations: As v is only doubled, or reduced by N if $v \geq N$, v must be congruent to a power of 2 modulo N, and $v < 2N$ always holds between loop iterations. We thus propose the following invariant template:

$$I_N = \sum_{1 \leq i < N \,\wedge\, \exists k:\, i \equiv_N 2^k} a_{N,i} \cdot V^i \frac{1 - C^i}{1 - C} + \sum_{N \leq i < 2N \,\wedge\, \exists k:\, i \equiv_N 2^k} a_{N,i} \cdot F V^i \frac{1 - C^N}{1 - C} .$$

As the detailed calculations in [22, Appendix B] show, $I_N = \mathfrak{g}_0 + \mathrm{pm}[\![P_N]\!]\,(I_N \!\restriction_{f=0})$ has a solution τ_N which yields a nonnegative, finite instantiation with

$$\sum_{N \leq i < 2N \,\wedge\, \exists k:\, i \equiv_N 2^k} \tau_N(a_{N,i}) = \frac{1}{N} .$$

Program 2 The Fast Dice Roller [40] (pGCL version from [5]; $N>0$ constant).

```
⫴ V      /* Initially, v = 1, c = f = 0 */
while (f = 0) {
    v := 2v ⨾
    {c := 2c} [1/2] {c := 2c + 1} ⨾
    if (N ≤ v) {
        if (c < N) {
            f := f + 1
        } else {
            v := v − N ⨾
            c := c − N }}}
```

By Theorem 7, $\mu_{I_N[\tau_N]}$ is an occupation invariant for FDR_N, which we use to bound the program's semantics. We obtain the expected uniform distribution of c between 0 and $N-1$ as an upper bound, after marginalizing out v and f:

$$\mathrm{pm}[\![\mathrm{FDR}_N]\!]\,(\mathfrak{g}_0)\,[V, F/1] \;\leq\; (I_N[\tau_N]\!\restriction_{f>0})[V, F/1]$$

$$= \sum_{N \leq i < 2N \,\wedge\, \exists k:\, i \equiv_N 2^k} \tau_N(a_{N,i}) \cdot \frac{1 - C^N}{1 - C} \;=\; \frac{1}{N} \cdot \frac{1 - C^N}{1 - C}\;.$$

Since $\left|\mu_{I_N[\tau_N]}\right| = 1$ is finite, we conclude that the loop is PAST from $\mu_{\mathfrak{g}_0}$ and thus $\left|\mathrm{pm}[\![\mathrm{FDR}_N]\!]\,(\mathfrak{g}_0)\right| = |\mathfrak{g}_0| = 1$. Hence, by Theorem 6, the uniform distribution upper bound is tight, and we conclude $\mathrm{pm}[\![\mathrm{FDR}_N]\!]\,(\mathfrak{g}_0)\,[V, F/1] = \frac{1}{N} \cdot \frac{1-C^N}{1-C}$.

Nested Loops. To handle nested loops, an invariant has to be found for each nested loops simultaneously, as the measure reaching an inner loop is directly influenced by the measure entering an outer loop. Verification is done starting with the innermost loop, with the resulting measure used to prove the invariant for the next outer loop.

Alternatively, as a pre-processing step, we could rewrite an arbitrary program (automatically) as a loop with a loop-free body (e.g., [48]), assuming such a transformation could be carried out within ReDiP.

7   Implementation and Evaluation

To validate the practical feasibility of our invariant synthesis method for probabilistic loops, we developed a proof-of-concept implementation. The tool realizes the approach presented in Section 6 and enables the validation and, in many cases, the automated synthesis of inductive invariants in rational closed-form.

7.1   Synthesis Overview

Our approach for synthesizing rational function invariants is based on symbolic fixed-point reasoning over probabilistic loops. Given a probabilistic `while`-loop and an initial distribution in rational closed form, we synthesize candidates via a *rational function template heuristic.* Each candidate is interpreted as a symbolic distribution and subjected to a forward semantics step: we compute the effect of one loop iteration under the assumption that the candidate holds inductively. This yields a rational equation between the candidate and the semantic result of one loop iteration, which we *solve symbolically* using either an SMT solver (e.g., Z3) or the computer algebra system SymPy, depending on configuration.

Solutions to the resulting system correspond to instantiations of the symbolic coefficients in the rational candidate. We filter out trivial or invalid solutions, e.g., those that make the denominator identically zero. The remaining candidates are checked using *heuristic positivity tests* to determine whether the resulting generating functions represent valid (i.e., nonnegative) measures. If such a candidate is found, we conclude that it defines a true inductive invariant for the probabilistic loop. If no candidate can be validated, the process fails, signaling that either the heuristic space was insufficient or no rational invariant of the considered form exists.

7.2 Implementation Details

The tool is implemented in Python [53] and supports two symbolic computation backends: the SYMPY [44] library and a custom set of Python bindings to the C++ library GINAC [6]. The latter offers improved performance for rational function manipulations. Backend selection is configurable at runtime.

Initial distributions are specified in terms of generating functions, typically in rational closed form. These generating functions are represented internally as symbolic expressions and manipulated according to the operations required by the fixed-point characterization of inductive invariants. Simplification and algebraic reasoning tasks are delegated to the selected backend.

Beyond the language presented in Section 6 our implementation provides limited support for guards with modulo expressions on univariate generating functions. As in [19], we support expressions of the form $v = c \bmod d$, where $v \in \mathsf{Vars}$ and $c, d \in \mathbb{N}$. This is implemented via a standard method based on Hadamard products; see, e.g., [38, Section 2.4].

Invariant Template Generation. For our benchmark, we explore candidate invariants by systematically generating multivariate rational expressions of increasing structural complexity. Specifically, the heuristic organizes the search by first fixing a total degree bound for the denominator and then enumerating all possible numerator polynomials whose degree does not exceed that of the denominator. For each such degree configuration, it constructs symbolic templates for the numerator and denominator, introducing fresh coefficient parameters for each admissible monomial. The resulting rational expressions are interpreted as generating functions and wrapped into symbolic distribution objects. This breadth-first enumeration strategy ensures that simpler candidates are considered before more complex ones, facilitating an efficient and structured search through the space of rational inductive invariants. Crucially, this enumeration is exhaustive in theory: if a rational function invariant exists, then at some finite degree bound the heuristic will produce a corresponding template that can be instantiated to that invariant.

Positivity Test Heuristics. Determining whether an arbitrary rational function has a nonnegative FPS expansion is an open problem and believed to be decidable [45]. However, to ensure that a candidate rational function indeed represents a valid generating function—that is, a power series with nonnegative coefficients—we apply sufficient heuristics to establish positivity. For the benchmarks, we use heuristics based on structural properties of the rational expression. These decompose the candidate into numerator and denominator. For the numerator polynomial it is verified that it contains only nonnegative coefficients. For the denominator a simple sign condition is checked: the constant term must

Table 3: Verification and Synthesis benchmark results for PRODIGY using the fastest backend (GINAC or SYMPY) for the given benchmark.

Benchmark	Time (s)	Auto/User	Additional Comments
subdist_enter	0.568013	A	
cond_and	0.017394	A	
faulty_decrement	0.120409	A	
geometric	0.026373	A	
geometric_counter	0.124910	A	
modulo_geometric	0.035103	U	$a = 4f, b = 2f, c = f, d = 8f,$ $e = 6f$
thirds_geometric	6.681842	A	Used Z3 to solve
random_walk	0.118271	A	
random_walk_counter	0.106519	U	$a = 1, b = 1, d = -1$
fast_dice_roller	0.155679	U	$w_0 = \frac{1}{3}, w_1 = 0, w_2 = \frac{2}{3}, w_3 = 1,$ $w_4 = \frac{1}{6}, w_5 = 0, w_6 = 0, w_m = 0$
nontermination	Failed	A	Actual invariant is $\infty \cdot X + \frac{1}{2} \cdot X^2$
sequential_loops	Failed	A	Cannot determine pos. of $\frac{2C}{C^2 - 3C + 2} + 1$

be positive, and all other coefficients must be non-positive. If either the function or its negative meets this pattern, the heuristic concludes non-negativity. This test is sound, as it captures the shape of (generalized) geometric distributions and similar rational FPS with guaranteed nonnegative expansions.

7.3   Benchmark Configuration

The evaluation is based on a suite of small to mid-sized benchmark loops containing probabilistic updates, branching, and control-flow structures of varying complexity. Our experiments aim to address the following research questions:

- **Feasibility**: Can non-trivial rational invariants be synthesized in practice?
- **Performance**: How fast are invariants found for the benchmark programs?
- **Coverage**: For which loop patterns does the heuristic succeed or fail?

All benchmarks were executed on an Apple MacBook Pro equipped with an Apple M3 Pro processor and 18GB of RAM, running macOS Sequoia 15.4.1. We report only the execution time of the core synthesis phase, excluding preprocessing steps such as input parsing or output formatting.

7.4   Benchmark Results

Table 3 summarizes the results obtained from running the synthesis tool on each benchmark. Each entry records the fastest time taken to complete the synthesis, whether a valid invariant was computed automatically (**A**) or by a user specified template (**U**), and in the latter case the inferred parameter values.

7.5 Discussion

The results demonstrate that our symbolic synthesis framework is capable of handling a variety of probabilistic loops and is able to synthesize rational inductive invariants efficiently in most cases. Synthesis times are typically below one second. Benchmarks marked as U synthesized invariants given a user specified template solving for specific parameter values, which the tool recovered automatically from the symbolic equation system. We also observed that the choice of backend (GiNaC or SymPy) affects performance but not correctness, with GiNaC generally offering faster simplification for rational expressions.

Failures were rare and typically attributable to the limitations of the heuristic search space or positivity tests. Future work will explore expanding the space of templates and developing more refined positivity checks.

8 Related Work

The main theoretical technique of this paper — reasoning about probabilistic loops with occupation invariants — is inspired by [49]. However, [49] views probabilistic programs semantically as (countably infinite) Markov chains. As a consequence, their definitions and case studies all operate on the level of explicit infinite stochastic matrices. We, on the other hand, define and reason about occupation invariants *directly on the program text*. The latter is essential for our automated verification and synthesis based on generating functions.

In the remainder of the section, we summarize further related work on (1) generating functions, (2) inference of posterior distributions, (3) synthesis of quantitative invariants, and (4) probabilistic model checking.

Generating Functions in Probabilistic Program Analysis and Semantics. The use of generating functions (GFs) in connection with probabilistic programs is a relatively recent trend, whose foundations originate from [33]. Subsequent work implemented and applied this framework to program equivalence [13] and conditioning [34]; see [32] for a comprehensive overview. Independently, [57] amended the method with a basic support for continuous distributions and explored automatic differentiation techniques for exact posterior inference. Recently, [39] introduced a functional language (without unbounded loops/recursion) compiling to GF expressions. Further recent work applies GFs in combination with Banach's fixed-point theorem to derive exact runtime distributions [15], and encodes GFs via weighted automata [19], which appears compatible with our approach as well. However, none of the mentioned papers provides an approach for automatically deriving loop posteriors as closed-form GFs.

Posterior Inference: Approximate vs Guaranteed vs Exact. Algorithmic posterior inference for probabilistic programs has been extensively studied across communities, yielding mature tools such as STAN [10], WebPPL [20], and Pyro [8]. These systems typically rely on sampling-based *approximate* inference without formal guarantees. As shown in [7], some of these methods can yield highly inaccurate results in the presence of unbounded recursion or loops. In the remainder of the discussion, we restrict attention to verification-oriented approaches providing *guaranteed inference*, i.e., mathematically certified results.

Guaranteed inference methods either establish sound *bounds* or compute truly *exact* results. Within the former class, [7, 54] prove upper and lower bounds over a finite interval partition of the posterior domain. These approaches support unbounded loops and recursion, continuous distributions, and general soft conditioning (scoring). For discrete programs, [56] proposes two bounding techniques: one based on loop unrolling with residual masses, and another exploiting so-called *contraction invariants*, a special case of occupation invariants, and eventually geometric distributions. Exact methods include PSI [18], which symbolically represents posterior densities, and DICE [28], which employs weighted model counting for scalable inference in finite-state programs. Both are restricted to statically bounded loops. DICE was later extended with support for unbounded iteration [52]. It seems promising to investigate whether occupation measures could be applied in this setting as well.

Invariant Synthesis for Probabilistic Programs. To our knowledge, this paper is the first to synthesize general occupation invariants for probabilistic loops. Zaiser, Murawski, and Ong [56] recently introduced and synthesized *contraction invariants*, which can be viewed as a special case of occupation invariants. Importantly, in contrast to the latter, contraction invariants are *incomplete*: they cannot certify all valid bounds on the posterior measure. See [22, Appendix D] for a concrete counterexample.

The synthesis of other types of quantitative invariants has been widely explored. We briefly review some representative papers. Early work includes [31], which synthesizes linear *expectation invariants* in the weakest-preexpectation calculus [42] via constraint solving. Such invariants are random variables over program states whose expectation does not decrease across loop iterations; they were later termed *sub-invariants* [29]. Polynomial sub-invariants can be synthesized via templates combined with Positivstellensatz reasoning and semidefinite programming [16]. The dual notion of *super-invariants* has been synthesized using a CEGIS-style approach [4]. Expectation invariants are closely related to probabilistic *martingales* (see, e.g., [24]). The synthesis of explicit martingales and their variants, initiated in [11], has also been studied extensively, often using templates and constraint solving; see [50] for an overview. A widely used variant are *ranking super-martingales* [11], a generalization of ranking functions for probabilistic termination, with several approaches to automatic synthesis [17, 1]. Also in the context of termination proofs, [12] introduces *stochastic invariants*, which are predicates that hold indefinitely with at least a desired probability. [3] initiated the automatic synthesis of *moment-based invariants*, predicates over expectations and higher moments of program variables, via recurrence solving. Yet another, orthogonal notion are *distributional invariants* [25, 2], though we are not aware of any work on their automatic synthesis.

Probabilistic Model Checking. The model checker STORM [26] can compute expected visiting times for *finite* Markov chains [43], which — in principle — could yield occupation invariants for loops with finite state spaces. However, the underlying the numeric techniques do not readily extend to infinite state spaces.

9   Conclusion

We defined the measure transformer semantics of probabilistic loops in terms of the occupation measure — the expected number of visits to each state at the loop header — induced by a given initial distribution. Building on this foundation, we introduced the notion of *occupation superinvariants*, which enable bounding a loop's output distribution and proving PAST. Furthermore, we demonstrated that occupation invariants can be synthesized automatically through a template-based enumeration of generating functions in rational closed form.

Future work includes incorporating additional template enumerations and heuristics for establishing the positivity of generating functions in closed form (e.g., for eventually geometric distributions of [56]), and extending the approach to conditioning, as in [34]. Another promising direction is to extend the closed-form approach to handle ∞-coefficients, thereby broadening the class of supported programs. However, since the extended domain $\mathbb{R}^\infty[[\mathbf{X}]]$ is not a ring, it lacks important algebraic properties required to define and manipulate closed forms. It is unclear, how our invariant synthesis could be generalized to different data types, as it uses generating functions on the discrete non-negative integer domain. We conjecture that most of the theory can also be transferred to the continous setting, likely by switching from (probability) generating functions to moment generating functions or characteristic functions. Finally, it would be interesting to investigate whether occupation measures can be leveraged to compute *stationary distributions* of nonterminating probabilistic loops, analogous to the approach of [43] for finite discrete-time Markov chains.

Acknowledgments

This work was partially supported by the ERC POC Grant *VERIPROB* (grant no. 101158076), by the DFG RTG 2236 *UnRAVeL*, and by the EU's Horizon 2020 research and innovation program under the Marie Skłodowska-Curie grant agreement *MISSION* (grant no. 101008233).

Data Availability Statement

A software artifact containing the implementation and benchmark programs described in Section 7 is publicly available on Zenodo [23].

References

1. Agrawal, S., Chatterjee, K., Novotný, P.: Lexicographic ranking supermartingales: an efficient approach to termination of probabilistic programs. Proc. ACM Program. Lang. **2**(POPL), 34:1–34:32 (2018). https://doi.org/10.1145/3158122
2. Barthe, G., Espitau, T., Gaboardi, M., Grégoire, B., Hsu, J., Strub, P.: An Assertion-Based Program Logic for Probabilistic Programs. In: ESOP. LNCS, vol. 10801, pp. 117–144. Springer, Heidelberg (2018). https://doi.org/10.1007/978-3-319-89884-1_5
3. Bartocci, E., Kovács, L., Stankovic, M.: Automatic Generation of Moment-Based Invariants for Prob-Solvable Loops. In: ATVA. LNCS, vol. 11781, pp. 255–276. Springer, Heidelberg (2019). https://doi.org/10.1007/978-3-030-31784-3_15
4. Batz, K., Chen, M., Junges, S., Kaminski, B.L., Katoen, J., Matheja, C.: Probabilistic Program Verification via Inductive Synthesis of Inductive Invariants. In: TACAS. LNCS, vol. 13994, pp. 410–429. Springer, Heidelberg (2023). https://doi.org/10.1007/978-3-031-30820-8_25
5. Batz, K., Katoen, J., Winkler, T., Zilken, D.: Verifying Sampling Algorithms via Distributional Invariants. CoRR **abs/2509.06410** (2025). https://doi.org/10.48550/ARXIV.2509.06410. arXiv: 2509.06410
6. Bauer, C.W., Frink, A., Kreckel, R.B.: Introduction to the GiNaC Framework for Symbolic Computation within the C++ Programming Language. J. Symb. Comput. **33**(1), 1–12 (2002). https://doi.org/10.1006/jsco.2001.0494. arXiv: cs/0004015 [cs.SC]
7. Beutner, R., Ong, C.L., Zaiser, F.: Guaranteed bounds for posterior inference in universal probabilistic programming. In: PLDI, pp. 536–551. ACM (2022)
8. Bingham, E., Chen, J.P., Jankowiak, M., Obermeyer, F., Pradhan, N., Karaletsos, T., Singh, R., Szerlip, P.A., Horsfall, P., Goodman, N.D.: Pyro: Deep Universal Probabilistic Programming. J. Mach. Learn. Res. **20**, 28:1–28:6 (2019)
9. Bogachev, V.I.: Measure Theory. Springer, Berlin, Heidelberg (2007)
10. Carpenter, B., Gelman, A., Hoffman, M.D., Lee, D., Goodrich, B., Betancourt, M., Brubaker, M., Guo, J., Li, P., Riddell, A.: Stan: A probabilistic programming language. Journal of statistical software **76**, 1–32 (2017)
11. Chakarov, A., Sankaranarayanan, S.: Probabilistic Program Analysis with Martingales. In: CAV. LNCS, vol. 8044, pp. 511–526. Springer, Heidelberg (2013). https://doi.org/10.1007/978-3-642-39799-8_34
12. Chatterjee, K., Novotný, P., Zikelic, D.: Stochastic invariants for probabilistic termination. In: POPL, pp. 145–160. ACM (2017). https://doi.org/10.1145/3009837.3009873
13. Chen, M., Katoen, J., Klinkenberg, L., Winkler, T.: Does a Program Yield the Right Distribution? - Verifying Probabilistic Programs via Generating Functions. In: CAV (1). LNCS, vol. 13371, pp. 79–101. Springer, Heidelberg (2022). https://doi.org/10.1007/978-3-031-13185-1_5
14. Chung, K.L.: Markov Chains. Springer, Berlin, Heidelberg (2012)
15. Collodi, L., Boreale, M., Gregorio, A.P.D.: Towards Algebraic Analysis of Probabilistic Programs. In: ICTCS. CEUR Workshop Proceedings, pp. 147–153. CEUR-WS.org (2025). https://ceur-ws.org/Vol-4039/paper12.pdf
16. Feng, Y., Zhang, L., Jansen, D.N., Zhan, N., Xia, B.: Finding Polynomial Loop Invariants for Probabilistic Programs. In: ATVA. LNCS, vol. 10482, pp. 400–416. Springer, Heidelberg (2017). https://doi.org/10.1007/978-3-319-68167-2_26

17. Fioriti, L.M.F., Hermanns, H.: Probabilistic Termination: Soundness, Completeness, and Compositionality. In: POPL, pp. 489–501. ACM (2015). `https://doi.org/10.1145/2676726.2677001`
18. Gehr, T., Misailovic, S., Vechev, M.T.: PSI: Exact Symbolic Inference for Probabilistic Programs. In: CAV (1). LNCS, vol. 9779, pp. 62–83. Springer, Heidelberg (2016). `https://doi.org/10.1007/978-3-319-41528-4_4`
19. Geißler, D., Winkler, T.: Weighted Automata for Exact Inference in Discrete Probabilistic Programs. In: ICTAC. LNCS, vol. 16237, pp. 261–278. Springer, Heidelberg (2025). `https://doi.org/10.1007/978-3-032-11176-0_16`
20. Goodman, N.D., Stuhlmüller, A.: The Design and Implementation of Probabilistic Programming Languages, `http://dippl.org` (2014). Accessed: 2025-9-30.
21. Goodman, N.D., Tenenbaum, J.B., Contributors, T.P.: Probabilistic Models of Cognition, `http://probmods.org/` (2016). Accessed: 03-05-2025.
22. Haase, D., Batz, K., Gallus, A., Kaminski, B.L., Katoen, J.-P., Klinkenberg, L., Winkler, T.: Generating Functions Meet Occupation Measures: Invariant Synthesis for Probabilistic Loops (Extended Version). (2026). `https://doi.org/10.48550/arXiv.2601.13991`. arXiv: 2601.13991 [cs.PL]
23. Haase, D., Batz, K., Gallus, A., Kaminski, B.L., Katoen, J.-P., Klinkenberg, L., Winkler, T.: *Generating Functions Meet Occupation Measures: Invariant Synthesis for Probabilistic Loops: Artifact*, (2026). `https://doi.org/10.5281/zenodo.18184810`.
24. Hark, M., Kaminski, B.L., Giesl, J., Katoen, J.: Aiming low is harder: induction for lower bounds in probabilistic program verification. Proc. ACM Program. Lang. **4**(POPL), 37:1–37:28 (2020). `https://doi.org/10.1145/3371105`
25. den Hartog, J., de Vink, E.P.: Verifying Probabilistic Programs Using a Hoare Like Logic. Int. J. Found. Comput. Sci. **13**(3), 315–340 (2002). `https://doi.org/10.1142/S012905410200114X`
26. Hensel, C., Junges, S., Katoen, J., Quatmann, T., Volk, M.: The probabilistic model checker Storm. Int. J. Softw. Tools Technol. Transf. **24**(4), 589–610 (2022). `https://doi.org/10.1007/S10009-021-00633-Z`
27. Hoare, C.A.R.: Quicksort. Comput. J. **5**(1), 10–15 (1962). `https://doi.org/10.1093/COMJNL/5.1.10`
28. Holtzen, S., den Broeck, G.V., Millstein, T.D.: Scaling exact inference for discrete probabilistic programs. Proc. ACM Program. Lang. **4**(OOPSLA), 140:1–140:31 (2020). `https://doi.org/10.1145/3428208`
29. Kaminski, B.L.: Advanced weakest precondition calculi for probabilistic programs. PhD thesis, RWTH Aachen University, Germany (2019). `http://publications.rwth-aachen.de/record/755408`.
30. Kaminski, B.L., Katoen, J., Matheja, C., Olmedo, F.: Weakest Precondition Reasoning for Expected Run-Times of Probabilistic Programs. In: ESOP. LNCS, vol. 9632, pp. 364–389. Springer, Heidelberg (2016). `https://doi.org/10.1007/978-3-662-49498-1_15`
31. Katoen, J., McIver, A., Meinicke, L., Morgan, C.C.: Linear-Invariant Generation for Probabilistic Programs: - Automated Support for Proof-Based Methods. In: SAS. LNCS, vol. 6337, pp. 390–406. Springer, Heidelberg (2010). `https://doi.org/10.1007/978-3-642-15769-1_24`
32. Klinkenberg, L.: Analysis of probabilistic programs using generating functions. Dissertation, RWTH Aachen University, Aachen (2025). `https://doi.org/10.18154/RWTH-2025-07571`. `https://publications.rwth-aachen.de/record/1017915`.

33. Klinkenberg, L., Batz, K., Kaminski, B.L., Katoen, J., Moerman, J., Winkler, T.: Generating Functions for Probabilistic Programs. In: LOPSTR. LNCS, vol. 12561, pp. 231–248. Springer, Heidelberg (2020). https://doi.org/10.1007/978-3-030-68446-4_12
34. Klinkenberg, L., Blumenthal, C., Chen, M., Haase, D., Katoen, J.: Exact Bayesian Inference for Loopy Probabilistic Programs using Generating Functions. Proc. ACM Program. Lang. 8(OOPSLA1), 923–953 (2024). https://doi.org/10.1145/3649844
35. Kozen, D.: A Probabilistic PDL. J. Comput. Syst. Sci. 30(2), 162–178 (1985). https://doi.org/10.1016/0022-0000(85)90012-1
36. Kozen, D.: Semantics of Probabilistic Programs. J. Comput. Syst. Sci. 22(3), 328–350 (1981). https://doi.org/10.1016/0022-0000(81)90036-2
37. Kuich, W.: Semirings and Formal Power Series: Their Relevance to Formal Languages and Automata. In: Handbook of Formal Languages, Volume 1: Word, Language, Grammar. Ed. by G. Rozenberg and A. Salomaa, pp. 609–677. Springer (1997). https://doi.org/10.1007/978-3-642-59136-5_9
38. Lando, S.K.: Lectures on generating functions. American Mathematical Soc. (2003)
39. Li, J., Zhang, Y.: Compiling with Generating Functions. Proc. ACM Program. Lang. 9(ICFP) (2025). https://doi.org/10.1145/3747534
40. Lumbroso, J.O.: Optimal Discrete Uniform Generation from Coin Flips, and Applications. CoRR abs/1304.1916 (2013). arXiv: 1304.1916. http://arxiv.org/abs/1304.1916
41. Mahdi Shamsi, S., Pietro Farina, G., Gaboardi, M., Napp, N.: Probabilistic Programming Languages for Modeling Autonomous Systems. In: 2020 IEEE International Conference on Multisensor Fusion and Integration for Intelligent Systems (MFI), pp. 32–39 (2020). https://doi.org/10.1109/MFI49285.2020.9235230
42. McIver, A., Morgan, C.: Abstraction, Refinement and Proof for Probabilistic Systems. Springer (2005)
43. Mertens, H., Katoen, J., Quatmann, T., Winkler, T.: Computing Expected Visiting Times and Stationary Distributions in Markov Chains: Fast and Accurate. J. Autom. Reason. 69(3), 23 (2025). https://doi.org/10.1007/S10817-025-09736-7
44. Meurer, A., Smith, C.P., Paprocki, M., Čertík, O., Kirpichev, S.B., Rocklin, M., Kumar, A., Ivanov, S., Moore, J.K., Singh, S., Rathnayake, T., Vig, S., Granger, B.E., Muller, R.P., Bonazzi, F., Gupta, H., Vats, S., Johansson, F., Pedregosa, F., Curry, M.J., Terrel, A.R., Roučka, Š., Saboo, A., Fernando, I., Kulal, S., Cimrman, R., Scopatz, A.: SymPy: symbolic computing in Python. PeerJ Computer Science 3, e103 (2017). https://doi.org/10.7717/peerj-cs.103
45. Ouaknine, J., Worrell, J.: Positivity Problems for Low-Order Linear Recurrence Sequences. In: SODA, pp. 366–379. SIAM (2014). https://doi.org/10.1137/1.9781611973402.27
46. Park, D.: Fixpoint induction and proofs of program properties. Machine intelligence 5 (1969)
47. Pitman, J.W.: Occupation measures for Markov chains. Advances in Applied Probability 9(1), 69–86 (1977). https://doi.org/10.2307/1425817
48. Rabehaja, T.M., Sanders, J.W.: Refinement Algebra with Explicit Probabilism. In: TASE, pp. 63–70. IEEE Computer Society (2009). https://doi.org/10.1109/TASE.2009.53
49. Sharir, M., Pnueli, A., Hart, S.: Verification of Probabilistic Programs. SIAM J. Comput. 13(2), 292–314 (1984). https://doi.org/10.1137/0213021

50. Takisaka, T., Oyabu, Y., Urabe, N., Hasuo, I.: Ranking and Repulsing Super-martingales for Reachability in Randomized Programs. ACM Trans. Program. Lang. Syst. **43**(2), 5:1–5:46 (2021). https://doi.org/10.1145/3450967
51. Tarski, A.: A lattice-theoretical fixpoint theorem and its applications. Pacific Journal of Mathematics **5**(2), 285–309 (1955). https://doi.org/10.2140/pjm.1955.5.285
52. Torres-Ruiz, M., Piedeleu, R., Silva, A., Zanasi, F.: On Iteration in Discrete Probabilistic Programming. In: FSCD. LIPIcs, 20:1–20:21. Schloss Dagstuhl - Leibniz-Zentrum für Informatik (2024). https://doi.org/10.4230/LIPICS.FSCD.2024.20
53. Van Rossum, G., Drake, F.L.: Python 3 Reference Manual. CreateSpace, Scotts Valley, CA (2009)
54. Wang, P., Yang, T., Fu, H., Li, G., Ong, C.L.: Static Posterior Inference of Bayesian Probabilistic Programming via Polynomial Solving. Proc. ACM Program. Lang. **8**(PLDI), 1361–1386 (2024). https://doi.org/10.1145/3656432
55. Wilf, H.S.: Generatingfunctionology. A K Peters/CRC Press (2005)
56. Zaiser, F., Murawski, A.S., Ong, C.L.: Guaranteed Bounds on Posterior Distributions of Discrete Probabilistic Programs with Loops. Proc. ACM Program. Lang. **9**(POPL), 1104–1135 (2025). https://doi.org/10.1145/3704874
57. Zaiser, F., Murawski, A.S., Ong, C.L.: Exact Bayesian Inference on Discrete Models via Probability Generating Functions: A Probabilistic Programming Approach. In: NeurIPS (2023). http://papers.nips.cc/paper%5C_files/paper/2023/hash/0747af6f877c0cb555fea595f01b0e83-Abstract-Conference.html
58. Zhang, L., Zilberstein, N., Kaminski, B.L., Silva, A.: Quantitative Weakest Hyper Pre: Unifying Correctness and Incorrectness Hyperproperties via Predicate Transformers. Proc. ACM Program. Lang. **8**(OOPSLA2), 817–845 (2024). https://doi.org/10.1145/3689740

A Program Logic for Under-approximating Worst-case Resource Usage

Ziyue Jin and Di Wang[*]

Key Lab of HCST (PKU), MOE; SCS, Peking University, China

`zyjin@stu.pku.edu.cn, wangdi95@pku.edu.cn`

Abstract. Understanding and predicting the worst-case resource usage is crucial for software quality; however, existing methods either over-approximate with potentially loose bounds or under-approximate without asymptotic guarantees. This paper presents a program logic to under-approximate worst-case resource usage, adapting incorrectness logic (IL) to reason quantitatively about resource consumption. We propose quantitative forward and backward under-approximate (QFUA and QBUA) triples, which generalize IL to identify execution paths leading to high resource usage. We also introduce a variant of QBUA that supports reasoning about high-water marks. Our logic is proven sound and complete with respect to a simple IMP-like language, and all meta-theoretical results are mechanized and verified in Rocq. We implement a prototype checker for all three variants of our logic and demonstrate its utility through a few examples and four case studies.

Keywords: Worst-case Resource Bounds · Quantitative Under-approximate Logic · Incorrectness Logic

1 Introduction

Understanding and predicting the worst-case resource usage of programs is a fundamental challenge in computer science. Knowing the bounds of resource usage, whether for memory consumption, CPU cycles, or network bandwidth, is crucial for ensuring system reliability, performance, and security. However, precisely determining these bounds is notoriously difficult. Static methods for analyzing resource usage tend to *over*-approximate worst-case scenarios, resulting in non-tight resource bounds and, consequently, false positives. On the other hand, dynamic methods, such as testing, can typically produce specific inputs of a certain size to induce high resource usage—thus *under*-approximating worst-case scenarios—but do not offer an asymptotic characterization of the worst-case behavior. This paper aims to develop a program logic to under-approximate worst-case resource usage and offer a compositional method for identifying scenarios with high resource usage.

Previous approaches to resource analysis have mainly concentrated on over-approximation methods, including abstract interpretation and constraint-based

---

[*] Corresponding Author

techniques. These techniques aim to compute sound upper bounds on resource usage by taking into account all possible program behaviors. However, they may produce non-tight bounds and typically do not indicate which inputs would result in the worst-case resource usage. Under-approximation techniques, such as fuzzing and dynamic analysis, have been used to identify specific resource-intensive execution paths. However, these techniques lack compositionality and generality for comprehensive resource analysis. Incorrectness logic (IL), which has been successfully applied to bug detection, offers a promising alternative by providing a formal foundation for under-approximate reasoning [21]. Recent work has adapted IL to prove non-termination [26], i.e., a *qualitative* argument about resource usage. However, adapting IL to prove *quantitative* resource bounds has not been explored.

In this paper, we adapt IL to under-approximate worst-case resource usage. The key idea is to use under-approximate triples to reason about the existence of execution paths that lead to high resource usage. Specifically, we introduce a new form of under-approximate triple that captures the relationship between program states and resource consumption. Our approach leverages IL's compositional nature to analyze a program by breaking it down into smaller, manageable components.

One of the main challenges is to formalize resource usage within the IL framework. The original IL triple $\vdash_F [p]\, C\, [ok : q]$—also called a *forward under-approximate* (FUA) triple—denotes that *every* post-state that satisfies q is *reachable* by executing C from *some* pre-state that satisfies p. Raad et al. [26] suggested using *backward under-approximate* (BUA) triples when reasoning about non-termination; that is, $\vdash_B [p]\, C\, [ok : q]$ denotes that from *every* pre-state that satisfies p is possible to *reach some* post-state that satisfies q by executing C. The pre-conditions p and post-conditions q are *qualitative*, i.e., they are Boolean-valued assertions on program states; however, they do not provide a natural way to reason about resource consumption. In our work, we need to extend IL to capture the relationship between program states and resource usage. We adapt the idea of *quantitative Hoare logic* [5,6]: instead of the Boolean *true*, a quantitative assertion returns a natural number that indicates the amount of resource that is required to safely execute the program; at the same time, the Boolean *false* is encoded by ∞. Intuitively, quantitative Hoare logic *refines* classic Hoare logic to reason about both the functionality and the resource usage of a program. In this paper, we devise *quantitative* generalizations of IL: let P and Q be assertions of type $State \to \mathbb{Z} \cup \{-\infty, +\infty\}$; the FUA triple $\vdash_F [P]\, C\, [Q]$ denotes that every post-state with *at least* Q units of resource is reachable by executing C from some pre-state with *at least* P units of resource; and the BUA triple $\vdash_B [P]\, C\, [Q]$ denotes that every pre-state with *at most* P units of resource is possible to reach some post-state with *at most* Q units of resource by executing C. In addition, we adapt Carbonneaux et al. [6]'s approach to separate qualitative assertions and quantitative resource bounds in the FUA/BUA triples, as well as Zhang and Kaminski's approach [30] to calculate quantitative strongest post-conditions, to simplify the reasoning in our prototype implementation and case studies.

Another challenge is to support reasoning about *high-water marks* in our quantitative IL. High-water marks provide a more precise characterization of a program's resource usage when the resource is non-monotone. For example, when reasoning about stack-space bounds, we want to know the highest stack watermark *during* a program's execution. However, an FUA/BUA triple $\vdash_{\mathsf{F}} [P] C [Q]$ only constrains the amount of resource at the pre- and post-states; that is, although the difference between P and Q serves as an under-approximation of the worst-case resource consumption of C, we cannot say that P provides an under-approximation of the high-water mark of executing C. It is worth noting that for quantitative Hoare logic $\vdash \{P\} C \{Q\}$, P is indeed an over-approximation of the high-water mark. In this paper, we devise a variant of the BUA logic to under-approximate high-water marks: the triple $\vdash_{\mathsf{B}}^{\Diamond} [P] C [Q]$ means that every pre-state with at most P units of resource is possible to reach some post-state with at most Q units of resource by executing C, *and the particular execution must make the resource counter non-positive at some point*. In this way, P can serve as an under-approximation of the high-water mark of C because, if we start to execute C with P units of resource, there exists an execution that consumes all the P units at some point. Note that different from quantitative Hoare logic, our quantitative IL allows the quantitative assertions P, Q to take negative values, i.e., they have type $State \rightarrow \mathbb{Z} \cup \{\pm\infty\}$.

In this paper, we focus on the theoretical properties of our quantitative IL for under-approximating worst-case resource usage. We prove that both the FUA and BUA variants are sound and complete with respect to a resource-aware operational semantics for integer IMP programs. To demonstrate the usefulness of our quantitative IL, we implement a prototype checker for our logic that supports arrays via the array theory and present several case studies, including some array-based sorting algorithms. In the future, we plan to automate our logic by integrating with existing tools that target realistic languages, e.g., Pulse [14].

In this paper, we make the following three main contributions.

- We devise a program logic to under-approximate worst-case resource usage of programs. Our logic is a generalization of the incorrectness logic, and we formulate three variants: forward, backward, and backward high-water mark.
- We prove that our program logic (both the forward and the backward variants) is sound and complete with respect to a resource-aware operational semantics, with all proofs mechanized in Rocq.
- We implement a prototype checker for all three variants of our logic and present four case studies to demonstrate the usefulness of it.

2   Overview

We first examine quantitative Hoare logic to introduce the idea of resource-aware program logics (§2.1). Next, we review incorrectness logic and non-termination logic to discuss the concept of under-approximation (§2.2). Finally, we outline our approach to developing quantitative under-approximate logic to reason about worst-case resource usage (§2.3).

2.1 Prior Work: Quantitative Hoare Logic

Our work is not the first to consider developing program logics to derive resource-usage bounds. We take inspiration from the *quantitative Hoare logic* (QHL), which extends classic Hoare logic by incorporating resource consumption into program reasoning [5,6].

The key idea behind QHL is to augment Hoare triples with resource annotations. A *quantitative Hoare triple*, written as $\vdash \{P\}\, C\, \{Q\}$ where P and Q are quantitative assertions of type $State \to \mathbb{N} \cup \{\infty\}$, states that if C is executed in a pre-state with *at least* P units of resource, then after its execution, *at least* Q units of resource will remain. Intuitively, these quantitative assertions can be seen as *potential functions* that map program states to non-negative potentials: the pre-potential P is sufficient to pay for the resource usage of C as well as the post-potential Q. In other words, QHL essentially captures the principle of the *potential method* for amortized complexity analysis [27].

Below are three representative rules of QHL. To explicitly annotate resource consumption, people usually introduce a primitive command tick e that computes e to an integer n and then consumes n units of resource. (If n is negative, this tick command releases $-n$ units of resource.) The rule (QHL:TICK) states that if the pre-potential is at least $P + e$, then it is safe to execute tick e and end with post-potential P. The rule (QHL:SEQ) illustrates the *compositional* nature of QHL: to reason about the resource usage of the sequencing command $C_1; C_2$, one can derive quantitative triples *individually* for C_1 and C_2. The rule (QHL:WHILE) generalizes the invariant-based reasoning of classic Hoare logic, where the predicate $\mathsf{istrue}(B)$ encodes a potential function that returns 0 if B is true and ∞ otherwise.

$$
\text{(QHL:TICK)} \quad \frac{P + e \geq 0}{\vdash \{P + e\}\, \mathsf{tick}\ e\, \{P\}}
$$

$$
\text{(QHL:SEQ)} \quad \frac{\vdash \{P\}\, C_1\, \{R\} \quad \vdash \{R\}\, C_2\, \{Q\}}{\vdash \{P\}\, C_1; C_2\, \{Q\}}
$$

$$
\text{(QHL:WHILE)} \quad \frac{\vdash \{I + \mathsf{istrue}(B)\}\, C\, \{I\}}{\vdash \{I\}\, \mathsf{while}\ B\ \mathsf{do}\ C\, \{I + \mathsf{istrue}(\neg B)\}}
$$

Consider the program while $x < n$ do $(x := x + 1; \mathsf{tick}\ 1)$. Intuitively, the total resource consumption is given by $I := \max(0, n - x)$. Using I as the loop invariant, we can prove the judgement $\vdash \{I\}\, \mathsf{while}\ x < n\ \mathsf{do}\ (x := x + 1; \mathsf{tick}\ 1)\, \{0\}$. By (QHL:WHILE), this amounts to proving $\vdash \{I + \mathsf{istrue}(x < n)\}\, x := x + 1; \mathsf{tick}\ 1\, \{I\}$. If $x \geq n$, then the pre-potential is ∞ and thus the triple is valid; otherwise, we can use (QHL:SEQ) with $\max(0, n - x) + 1$ as the intermediate assertion and conclude by $\max(0, n - (x + 1)) + 1 = \max(0, n - x)$ when $x < n$.

It is worth noting that QHL also supports reasoning about *high-water marks*. In fact, the quantitative triple $\vdash \{P\}\, C\, \{Q\}$ indicates that P is an upper bound (i.e., an over-approximation) of the high-water mark of executing C. Consider the non-terminating program while true do $(\mathsf{tick}\ 1; \mathsf{tick}\ -1)$. We can prove the judgement $\vdash \{1\}\, \mathsf{while}\ \mathsf{true}\ \mathsf{do}\ (\mathsf{tick}\ 1; \mathsf{tick}\ -1)\, \{1\}$, i.e., the high-water mark of the program is upper-bounded by 1. Again, by (QHL:WHILE), this amounts to proving $\vdash \{1\}\, \mathsf{tick}\ 1; \mathsf{tick}\ -1\, \{1\}$. This can be justified by using (QHL:SEQ) with 0 as the intermediate assertion. Note that the triple also indicates that after the program terminates, the resource consumption is upper-bounded by

$1 - 1 = 0$. However, because the program is non-terminating, the triple is indeed an over-approximation in terms of resource consumption.

It is important to note that while QHL focuses on proving sound upper bounds (i.e., over-approximations), the goal of this paper is to establish sound *under-approximations* of resource usage, as we will further elaborate in §2.3.

2.2 Prior Work: Incorrectness Logic and Non-termination Logic

Incorrectness logic (IL), introduced by O'Hearn [21], provides a formal foundation for under-approximate reasoning about program behaviors, particularly for bug detection. Unlike classic Hoare logic, which focuses on proving program correctness by over-approximating program behaviors, IL under-approximates program behaviors to identify specific execution paths that lead to bugs. This makes IL well-suited for detecting errors such as memory safety violations [24], concurrency bugs [25], and non-termination [26], where the goal is to find concrete evidence of incorrect behavior rather than proving the absence of errors.

The key idea behind IL is the use of *forward, under-approximate* (FUA) triples, written as $\vdash_\mathsf{F} [p] \, C \, [\epsilon : q]$, which state that starting from a set of pre-states p, executing program C can lead to a set of post-states under-approximated by q under the exit condition ϵ (e.g., normal termination ok or error er). The under-approximate nature of FUA triples ensures that any bug detected is a true positive, as it corresponds to a concrete execution path that exhibits the error. Below are two rules for under-approximating the behavior of while loops in IL. Different from invariant-based reasoning in classic Hoare logic, IL essentially *unrolls* a loop to examine a subset of execution paths through the loop. The rule (IL:WHILEFALSE) states that if the loop condition B does not hold before entering the loop, the pre-states and post-states coincide because the loop is not entered. The rule (IL:WHILESUBVAR) provides *subvariant*-based reasoning, which generalizes bounded unrolling by asserting that there exists some k satisfying that the loop body C transforms $p(n) \wedge B$ to $p(n+1) \wedge B$ for $n < k$, and that C transforms $p(k) \wedge B$ to $q \wedge \neg B$, i.e., the loop could end after k iterations.

$$(\text{IL:WHILEFALSE})$$
$$\frac{}{\vdash_\mathsf{F} [p \wedge \neg B] \, \mathsf{while} \, B \, \mathsf{do} \, C \, [ok : p \wedge \neg B]}$$

$$(\text{IL:WHILESUBVAR})$$
$$\frac{\forall n < k. \; \vdash_\mathsf{F} [p(n) \wedge B] \, C \, [ok : p(n+1) \wedge B] \qquad \vdash_\mathsf{F} [p(k) \wedge B] \, C \, [\epsilon : q \wedge \neg B]}{\vdash_\mathsf{F} [p(0) \wedge B] \, \mathsf{while} \, B \, \mathsf{do} \, C \, [\epsilon : q \wedge \neg B]}$$

Among the prior extensions of IL, the *under-approximate, non-termination logic* (UNTER) is the most related work because it reasons—qualitatively—about the usage of a particular kind of resource, i.e., time [26]. UNTER introduces divergent triples of the form $\vdash [p] \, C \, [\infty]$, which state that starting from any state in p, the program C has at least one divergent (i.e., non-terminating) execution. A key insight in UNTER is the use of *backward, under-approximate* (BUA) triples, written as $\vdash_\mathsf{B} [p] \, C \, [\epsilon : q]$, which state that starting from a set of pre-states p, executing program C can reach some post-states in q under the exit condition ϵ. Consider the program $x := x - 1$. The FUA judgement

$\vdash_\mathsf{F} [x > 0]\, x := x - 1\, [ok : x > 0]$ is valid, because the precise set of post-states is $x \geq 0$ and $x > 0$ is its subset, i.e., an under-approximation. On the other hand, the BUA judgement $\vdash_\mathsf{B} [x > 0]\, x := x - 1\, [ok : x > 0]$ is *invalid*, because executing from the pre-state $x = 1$ results in $x = 0$, which is not included in the set $x > 0$. UNTER uses BUA triples to reason about the non-termination of loops. For example, the rule (UNTER:WHILE) shown below states that if executing the loop body C keeps the states p and the loop condition B unchanged, we can establish that the loop can diverge. If the rule used FUA triples instead, it would prove the triple $\vdash [x > 0]\, \mathsf{while}\ x > 0\ \mathsf{do}\ x := x - 1\, [\infty]$, which is unsound. Another rule (UNTER:WHILESUBVAR) is similar to (IL:WHILESUBVAR), providing subvariant-based reasoning about divergent loops.

$$(\text{UNTER:WHILE})$$
$$\frac{\vdash_\mathsf{B} [p \wedge B]\, C\, [ok : p \wedge B]}{\vdash [p \wedge B]\ \mathsf{while}\ B\ \mathsf{do}\ C\, [\infty]}$$

$$(\text{UNTER:WHILESUBVAR})$$
$$\frac{\forall n \in \mathbb{N}.\ \vdash_\mathsf{B} [p(n) \wedge B]\, C\, [p(n + 1) \wedge B]}{\vdash [p(0) \wedge B]\ \mathsf{while}\ B\ \mathsf{do}\ C\, [\infty]}$$

2.3 This Work: Quantitative Under-approximate Logic

Our goal is to reason about the *worst-case resource usage* of programs from an *under-approximate* perspective. Indeed, this can in principle be achieved within Incorrectness Logic (IL) by adding a ghost variable that tracks resource consumption. For example, one may introduce a counter *ticks* that is decreased by each tick e command and reason about triples of the form $\vdash_\mathsf{F} [ticks \geq P]\, C\, [ticks \geq Q]$, expressing that there exists an execution of C consuming at least $P - Q$ units of resource. However, such an encoding is less compositional and modular. For instance, from $\vdash_\mathsf{F} [ticks \geq 10]\, C_1\, [ticks \geq 0]$ and $\vdash_\mathsf{F} [ticks \geq 5]\, C_2\, [ticks \geq 0]$ one cannot directly derive a triple for $C_1; C_2$ without re-establishing intermediate assertions such as $\vdash_\mathsf{F} [ticks \geq 15]\, C_1\, [ticks \geq 5]$.

To obtain a more compositional and elegant approach, we draw inspiration from quantitative Hoare Logic and lift incorrectness reasoning itself to the quantitative setting, devising *quantitative under-approximate logic*. Recall that in qualitative under-approximate logic, forward and backward triples capture two complementary reasoning modes: the backward form identifies possible initial states that can lead to certain final states, while the forward form discovers possible final states that can arise from some initial state. Generalizing these two directions to the quantitative setting, we obtain *quantitative, forward/backward, under-approximate* (QFUA/QBUA) triples that reason not only about reachability but also about the amount of resource consumed along executions. Intuitively, QFUA is outcome-oriented, focusing on verifying that certain outputs can arise from executions with high resource usage, whereas QBUA is input-oriented, identifying initial states that can lead to such costly behaviors. Formally:

- A QFUA judgement $\vdash_\mathsf{F} [P]\, C\, [Q]$ states that every post-potential *no less than* Q is reachable by executing C from some pre-potential with *no less than* P. Thus, if we fix the post-potential to Q, the judgement states that there exists an execution path with some pre-potential $P' \geq P$, so that the difference between P and Q serves as an under-approximation of the worst-case cost, which is lower-bounded by the difference between P' and Q.

- A QBUA judgement $\vdash_B [P]\,C\,[Q]$ states that every pre-potential *no greater than* P is possible to reach some post-potential *no greater than* Q by executing C. If we fix the pre-potential to P, the judgement states that there exists an execution path with some post-potential $Q' \leq Q$, so that the difference between P and Q also serves as an under-approximation of the worst-case scenario, which is lower-bounded by the difference between P and Q'.

Different from UNTER [26], where only backward triples are meaningful for non-termination reasoning, we will prove in §3 that both QFUA and QBUA logics are sound and complete for under-approximating worst-case resource usage. In our setting, we allow quantitative assertions to have type $State \to \mathbb{Z} \cup \{\pm\infty\}$.

To illustrate how the forward and backward reasoning modes complement each other, consider the program if $x = 42$ then (tick $2; x := 0$) else tick 1. Suppose we are interested in whether a final state with $x = 0$ can result from an execution that consumes at least 2 units of resource. This can be expressed using a QFUA triple

$$\vdash_F [2] \text{ if } x = 42 \text{ then (tick } 2; x := 0) \text{ else tick } 1 \, [\max(0, [x \neq 0])],$$

where the predicate $[B]$ encodes a potential function that returns $+\infty$ if B is true and $-\infty$ otherwise. It shows that some execution reaching a post-state with $x = 0$ requires at least 2 units of resource, indicating the existence of a high-cost final configuration. On the other hand, if we wish to determine whether there exists an input that causes this high usage, we use a QBUA triple:

$$\vdash_B [\min(2, [x = 42])] \text{ if } x = 42 \text{ then (tick } 2; x := 0) \text{ else tick } 1 \, [0],$$

which states that for any initial state satisfying $x = 42$ and having at most 2 units of resource, it is possible to execute the program and reach a post-state with at most 0 units remaining. This example illustrates the complementary nature of the two logics: QFUA helps confirm that certain costly outcomes are possible, while QBUA helps identify the inputs that lead to them.

Below are some rules to derive the above QFUA and QBUA triples. The (F/B:IfTrue) rules reflect the difference between QFUA and QBUA: the max operator reflects QFUA's "no less than" nature, whereas the min operator reflects QBUA's "no greater than" nature.

(F:Tick)
$$\frac{}{\vdash_F [P]\,\text{tick } e\,[P - e]}$$

(F:IfTrue)
$$\frac{\vdash_F [\max(P, [\neg B])]\,C_1\,[Q]}{\vdash_F [\max(P, [\neg B])]\,\text{if } B \text{ then } C_1 \text{ else } C_2\,[Q]}$$

(B:Tick)
$$\frac{}{\vdash_B [P]\,\text{tick } e\,[P - e]}$$

(B:IfTrue)
$$\frac{\vdash_B [\min(P, [B])]\,C_1\,[Q]}{\vdash_B [\min(P, [B])]\,\text{if } B \text{ then } C_1 \text{ else } C_2\,[Q]}$$

In contrast to the ghost-variable encoding, our logic admits direct composition through the (RELAX) rule, which allows shifting both pre- and post-potentials uniformly without re-verifying the body of the command:

$$(\dagger\text{:RELAX})$$
$$\frac{\vdash_\dagger [P]\,C\,[Q] \qquad F \text{ is invariant under } C}{\vdash_\dagger [P + F]\,C\,[Q + F]}, \quad \text{where } \dagger \in \{\mathsf{F}, \mathsf{B}\}$$

This rule restores the compositionality that is lost in the ghost-variable encoding. For example, recall the non-compositional case discussed at the beginning of this section, where the triples $\vdash_\mathsf{F} [10]\,C_1\,[0]$ and $\vdash_\mathsf{F} [5]\,C_2\,[0]$ could not be directly combined. By applying the (F:RELAX) rule, we can derive $\vdash_\mathsf{F} [15]\,C_1\,[5]$ directly and then combine them via the sequential composition rule to obtain $\vdash_\mathsf{F} [15]\,C_1; C_2\,[0]$, without re-verifying C_1. This demonstrates how our framework supports modular reasoning about resource usage, addressing the compositionality issue mentioned earlier. We will see further examples of such compositional reasoning in §5.

Constructing an equivalent rule for a ghost-variable encoding, however, poses a dilemma. If a ghost-variable rule were designed to only handle pre- and post-conditions of the specific form $ticks \geq \cdots$, it would lack the generality to handle more complex state-resource relationships. Conversely, if the rule were designed to accommodate arbitrary pre- and post-conditions, defining the additive operation $(P + F)$ used in our (RELAX) rule would become non-trivial. Thus, our logics conceptually achieve modularity in a more systematical way.

Recall that a triple in quantitative Hoare logic also provides an over-approximation of the high-water mark for executing a program. However, this is not the case for QFUA or QBUA triples. For example, we can derive the QBUA judgement $\vdash_\mathsf{B} [\min(20, [x > y])]$ if $x > y$ then tick 2 else tick 1 $[18]$, but $\min(20, [x > y])$ is obviously *not* a lower bound of the worst-case high-water mark for executing the conditional command. To support under-approximating high-water marks, we devise a third kind of quantitative under-approximate triples, which we write as $\vdash_\mathsf{B}^\Diamond [P]\,C\,[Q]$ and call QBUA$^\Diamond$ triples[1]. Such a triple is a refinement of $\vdash_\mathsf{B} [P]\,C\,[Q]$; that is, every pre-potential no greater than P is possible to reach some post-potential no greater than Q by executing C, *and during the particular execution, the potential must become non-positive at some point*. We prove in §3 that $\vdash_\mathsf{B}^\Diamond [P]\,C\,[Q]$ indicates that P serves as an under-approximation of the high-water mark for executing C. In addition, the QBUA$^\Diamond$ logic is also complete. Below are the $\Diamond$ versions of the rules shown earlier.

$$(\mathsf{B}^\Diamond\text{:TICK})$$
$$\frac{\min(P, P - e) \leq 0}{\vdash_\mathsf{B}^\Diamond [P]\,\mathsf{tick}\,e\,[P - e]}$$

$$(\mathsf{B}^\Diamond\text{:IFTRUE})$$
$$\frac{\vdash_\mathsf{B}^\Diamond [\min(P, [B])]\,C_1\,[Q]}{\vdash_\mathsf{B}^\Diamond [\min(P, [B])]\,\text{if } B \text{ then } C_1 \text{ else } C_2\,[Q]}$$

In our formulation, the QBUA$^\Diamond$ logic depends on the QBUA logic. For example, there are two possibilities for reasoning about the sequencing command $C_1; C_2$:

---

[1] We discuss why the forward variant QFUA$^\Diamond$ is not developed in §3.3.

$$(\text{BS:Tick})$$
$$\langle \text{tick } e, \sigma, p \rangle \Downarrow^{\min\{p, p - [\![e]\!]\sigma\}} \langle \sigma, p - [\![e]\!]\sigma \rangle$$

$$(\text{BS:Seq})$$
$$\frac{\langle C_1, \sigma, p \rangle \Downarrow^{l_1} \langle \rho, r \rangle \quad \langle C_2, \rho, r \rangle \Downarrow^{l_2} \langle \tau, q \rangle}{\langle C_1; C_2, \sigma, p \rangle \Downarrow^{\min\{l_1, l_2\}} \langle \tau, q \rangle}$$

Fig. 1: Selected Rules for the Big-step Semantics

executing C_1 makes the potential non-positive, or executing C_2 makes the potential non-positive, as shown below.

$$(\text{B}^\Diamond\text{:SeqL})$$
$$\frac{\vdash_\mathsf{B}^\Diamond [P] C_1 [R] \quad \vdash_\mathsf{B} [R] C_2 [Q]}{\vdash_\mathsf{B}^\Diamond [P] C_1; C_2 [Q]}$$

$$(\text{B}^\Diamond\text{:SeqR})$$
$$\frac{\vdash_\mathsf{B} [P] C_1 [R] \quad \vdash_\mathsf{B}^\Diamond [R] C_2 [Q]}{\vdash_\mathsf{B}^\Diamond [P] C_1; C_2 [Q]}$$

3 Technical Details

In this section, we present the formal systems for the QFUA, QBUA, and QBUA$^\Diamond$ logics for under-approximating worst-case resource consumption. §3.1 formulates an IMP-style programming language with integer variables and tick commands. §3.2 describes the QFUA and QBUA logics and proves their soundness and completeness. §3.3 extends QBUA to develop QBUA$^\Diamond$, which aims to under-approximate high-water marks. All metatheoretic results presented in this section have been mechanically verified in Rocq; the full formalization is available in the artifact [12].

3.1 Syntax and Semantics

The language syntax defines resource-aware computation through the grammar:

$$C ::= \mathsf{skip} \mid x := e \mid \mathsf{assume } B \mid \mathsf{tick } e \mid C; C \mid C + C \mid C^* \mid \mathsf{local } x \text{ in } C$$

The basic operations include: skip denoting no-operation, $x := e$ for variable assignments, $\mathsf{assume } B$ constraining execution to paths satisfying boolean condition B, and $\mathsf{tick } e$ modeling resource consumption by deducting the value of arithmetic expression e from an implicit resource counter. Control flow is structured through $C_1; C_2$ for sequencing, $C_1 + C_2$ for non-deterministic choice, and C^* for iterative execution. Variable scoping is managed via $\mathsf{local } x \text{ in } C$. All program variables are integer-valued. Derived control structures are defined as: conditional execution $\mathsf{if } B \text{ then } C_1 \text{ else } C_2 := (\mathsf{assume } B; C_1) + (\mathsf{assume } (\neg B); C_2)$ and looping constructs $\mathsf{while } B \text{ do } C := (\mathsf{assume } B; C)^* ; \mathsf{assume } (\neg B)$.

The big-step semantics formalizes program behavior with explicit resource tracking. The judgment $\langle C, \sigma, p \rangle \Downarrow^l \langle \tau, q \rangle$ states that executing C from initial state $\sigma \in State := Var \to \mathbb{Z}$ with resource $p \in \mathbb{Z}$ terminates in state $\tau \in State$ with residual resource $q \in \mathbb{Z}$, where $l \in \mathbb{Z}$ records the minimal resource level

$$P \curlywedge Q := \lambda\sigma.\min\{P(\sigma), Q(\sigma)\} \qquad P \curlyvee Q := \lambda\sigma.\max\{P(\sigma), Q(\sigma)\}$$

$$\unrhd x.P := \lambda\sigma.\sup_{v}\{P(\sigma[x \mapsto v])\} \qquad \unlhd x.P := \lambda\sigma.\inf_{v}\{P(\sigma[x \mapsto v])\}$$

$$P \preceq Q \quad \text{iff} \quad \forall\sigma.P(\sigma) \le Q(\sigma) \qquad [B] := \lambda\sigma.\begin{cases} +\infty & \text{if } B(\sigma) = \mathsf{true} \\ -\infty & \text{otherwise} \end{cases}$$

Fig. 2: Resource Function Operators

observed during execution. The semantics rules are selectively presented in Fig. 1, with the full set of rules provided in the technical report [13]. We also write $\langle C, \sigma, p\rangle \Downarrow \langle \tau, q\rangle$ to denote $\exists l.\, \langle C, \sigma, p\rangle \Downarrow^{l} \langle \tau, q\rangle$, and $\langle C, \sigma, p\rangle \Downarrow^{\le 0} \langle \tau, q\rangle$ to denote $\exists l \le 0.\, \langle C, \sigma, p\rangle \Downarrow^{l} \langle \tau, q\rangle$.

3.2 Quantitative Under-approximate Logic

We generalize both forward and backward under-approximate logic to quantitative reasoning by extending assertions from Boolean predicates $State \to \{\mathsf{true}, \mathsf{false}\}$ to *resource functions* $State \to \mathbb{Z} \cup \{\pm\infty\}$. These functions map program states to integer-valued resource quantities (with $\pm\infty$ denoting Boolean truth and falsehood). The generalized logics are called *quantitative forward under-approximate* (QFUA) logic and *quantitative backward under-approximate* (QBUA) logic, whose semantics are defined in terms of resource functions.

Definition 1. *The semantics of QFUA and QBUA triples are defined as follows:*

- *QFUA: $\vDash_{\mathsf{F}} [P]\, C\, [Q]$ holds if and only if for all τ and q such that $q \ge Q(\tau)$, there exists a σ and a p such that $p \ge P(\sigma)$ and $\langle C, \sigma, p\rangle \Downarrow \langle \tau, q\rangle$. This implies that for all τ such that $Q(\tau) \in \mathbb{Z}$, there exists an execution of C ending in τ that cost at least $\inf_{\sigma}\{P(\sigma)\} - Q(\tau)$ ticks.*
- *QBUA: $\vDash_{\mathsf{B}} [P]\, C\, [Q]$ holds if and only if for all σ and p such that $p \le P(\sigma)$, there exists a τ and a q such that $q \le Q(\tau)$ and $\langle C, \sigma, p\rangle \Downarrow \langle \tau, q\rangle$. This implies that for all σ such that $P(\sigma) \in \mathbb{Z}$, there exists an execution of C starting from σ that cost at least $P(\sigma) - \sup_{\tau}\{Q(\tau)\}$ ticks.*

To formulate quantitative verification rules, we define operators on resource functions as shown in Fig. 2. The $\curlyvee$ and $\curlywedge$ operators compute pointwise maximum and minimum of two functions respectively, while $\unrhd x.P$ and $\unlhd x.P$—adapted from Batz et al. [3]'s work and Zhang and Kaminski [30]'s work—capture external values over variable assignments. The refinement operator $\preceq$ establishes pointwise ordering between functions, and $[B]$ converts Boolean predicates by mapping truth values to infinite bounds.

Table 1: Correspondence between Boolean and Quantitative Operators

	Boolean	QFUA	QBUA
Conjunction	$P \wedge Q$	$P \curlyvee Q$	$P \curlywedge Q$
Disjunction	$P \vee Q$	$P \curlywedge Q$	$P \curlyvee Q$
Existential	$\exists x.P$	$\llcorner x.P$	$\lrcorner x.P$
Implication	$P \Rightarrow Q$	$P \preceq Q$	$Q \preceq P$
Boolean Predicate	B	$[\neg B]$	$[B]$

These operators extend Boolean logic to integer-valued resource analysis. QFUA and QBUA triples use different interpretations of logical operators due to their opposite inequality directions in their semantics. To illustrate this generalization, consider the case of conjunction: in Boolean logic, $P \wedge Q$ means both predicates must hold. For QFUA triples, this translates to $P \curlyvee Q$, as satisfying both $p \geq P(\sigma)$ and $p \geq Q(\sigma)$ is equivalent to $p \geq \max\{P(\sigma), Q(\sigma)\}$. Conversely, QBUA triples use $P \curlywedge Q$, because $p \leq P(\sigma)$ and $p \leq Q(\sigma)$ is equivalent to $p \leq \min\{P(\sigma), Q(\sigma)\}$. Consider also quantitative existential quantification: in QFUA triples, $p \geq \llcorner x.P(\sigma)$ guarantees $\exists v.\ p \geq P(\sigma[x \mapsto v])$, because the infimum becomes the minimum in discrete domains. The QBUA triples case follows a similar pattern. Similar duality extends to other operators (see Tab. 1). Lastly, the Boolean predicate conversion $[B]$ bridges Boolean and quantitative reasoning. For QFUA triples, $[\neg B]$ assigns $-\infty$ when B is true (because $p \geq -\infty$ always holds), and $+\infty$ otherwise. For QBUA triples, $[B]$ assigns $+\infty$ when B is true (because $p \leq +\infty$ always holds), and $-\infty$ otherwise.

We present the proof rules for QFUA and QBUA triples in Fig. 3. Rules marked with † apply to both QFUA and QBUA triples, while those in blue are specific to QFUA triples, and those in red are specific to QBUA triples. Except for the (†:Tick) and the (†:Relax) rule, all other rules are generalized from the corresponding Boolean cases, with the operators replaced by their quantitative counterparts.

Concretely, the (†:Skip) rule trivially preserves quantitative assertions. The (F:Assign) and (B:Assign) rules for assignment statements are generalized from the standard Floyd assignment rule $\vdash_\dagger [P]\, x\ :=\ e\, [\exists x'.P[x'/x] \wedge x = e[x'/x]]$, which is sound for both QFUA and QBUA triples. The (F:Assume) and (B:Assume) rules for assume statements are generalized from the assume rule $\vdash_\dagger [P \wedge B]\, \mathsf{assume}\ B\, [P \wedge B]$, which filters out states that do not satisfy the predicate B. The (†:Tick) rule models the effect of a tick statement by subtracting the tick cost from the resource function.

The (†:Seq) rule models the sequential composition of two programs, where the postcondition of the first program coincides with the precondition of the second program. The (†:ChoiceL) and (†:ChoiceR) rules approximate non-deterministic choice by considering the behavior of one of the branches. The (†:Loop) rule uses an indexed resource function $P(n)$ as a subvariant to ap-

$$(\dagger\text{:S{\small KIP}}) \qquad \vdash_\dagger [P]\,\mathsf{skip}\,[P]$$

$$(\text{F:A{\small SSIGN}}) \qquad \vdash_\mathsf{F} [P]\,x := e\,[\mathsf{L}\,x'.P[x'/x]\,\curlyvee\,[x \neq e[x'/x]]]$$

$$(\text{B:A{\small SSIGN}}) \qquad \vdash_\mathsf{B} [P]\,x := e\,[\mathsf{2}\,x'.P[x'/x]\,\curlywedge\,[x = e[x'/x]]]$$

$$(\text{F:A{\small SSUME}}) \qquad \vdash_\mathsf{F} [P \curlyvee [\neg B]]\,\mathsf{assume}\,B\,[P \curlyvee [\neg B]]$$

$$(\text{B:A{\small SSUME}}) \qquad \vdash_\mathsf{B} [P \curlywedge [B]]\,\mathsf{assume}\,B\,[P \curlywedge [B]]$$

$$(\dagger\text{:T{\small ICK}}) \qquad \vdash_\dagger [P]\,\mathsf{tick}\,e\,[P - e]$$

$$(\dagger\text{:S{\small EQ}}) \qquad \frac{\vdash_\dagger [P]\,C_1\,[R] \qquad \vdash_\dagger [R]\,C_2\,[Q]}{\vdash_\dagger [P]\,C_1;C_2\,[Q]}$$

$$(\dagger\text{:C{\small HOICE}L}) \qquad \frac{\vdash_\dagger [P]\,C_1\,[Q]}{\vdash_\dagger [P]\,C_1 + C_2\,[Q]}$$

$$(\dagger\text{:C{\small HOICE}R}) \qquad \frac{\vdash_\dagger [P]\,C_2\,[Q]}{\vdash_\dagger [P]\,C_1 + C_2\,[Q]}$$

$$(\dagger\text{:L{\small OOP}}) \qquad \frac{\forall n < k.\ \vdash_\dagger [P(n)]\,C\,[P(n+1)]}{\vdash_\dagger [P(0)]\,C^*\,[P(k)]}$$

$$(\text{F:L{\small OCAL}}) \qquad \frac{\vdash_\mathsf{F} [P]\,C\,[Q]}{\vdash_\mathsf{F} [\mathsf{L}\,x.P]\,\mathsf{local}\,x\,\mathsf{in}\,C\,[\mathsf{L}\,x.Q]}$$

$$(\text{B:L{\small OCAL}}) \qquad \frac{\vdash_\mathsf{B} [P]\,C\,[Q]}{\vdash_\mathsf{B} [\mathsf{2}\,x.P]\,\mathsf{local}\,x\,\mathsf{in}\,C\,[\mathsf{2}\,x.Q]}$$

$$(\text{F:D{\small ISJ}}) \qquad \frac{\forall i \in I.\ \vdash_\mathsf{F} [P_i]\,C\,[Q_i]}{\vdash_\mathsf{F} \left[\bigcurlywedge_{i\in I} P_i\right] C \left[\bigcurlywedge_{i\in I} Q_i\right]}$$

$$(\text{B:D{\small ISJ}}) \qquad \frac{\forall i \in I.\ \vdash_\mathsf{B} [P_i]\,C\,[Q_i]}{\vdash_\mathsf{B} \left[\bigcurlyvee_{i\in I} P_i\right] C \left[\bigcurlyvee_{i\in I} Q_i\right]}$$

$$(\text{F:C{\small ONSTANCY}}) \qquad \frac{\vdash_\mathsf{F} [P]\,C\,[Q] \qquad \mathrm{fv}(B) \cap \mathrm{mod}(C) = \emptyset}{\vdash_\mathsf{F} [P \curlyvee [B]]\,C\,[Q \curlyvee [B]]}$$

$$(\text{B:C{\small ONSTANCY}}) \qquad \frac{\vdash_\mathsf{B} [P]\,C\,[Q] \qquad \mathrm{fv}(B) \cap \mathrm{mod}(C) = \emptyset}{\vdash_\mathsf{B} [P \curlywedge [B]]\,C\,[Q \curlywedge [B]]}$$

$$(\dagger\text{:R{\small ELAX}}) \qquad \frac{\vdash_\dagger [P]\,C\,[Q] \qquad \mathrm{fv}(F) \cap \mathrm{mod}(C) = \emptyset}{\vdash_\dagger [P + F]\,C\,[Q + F]}$$

$$(\dagger\text{:C{\small ONS}}) \qquad \frac{P \preceq P' \qquad \vdash_\dagger [P']\,C\,[Q'] \qquad Q' \preceq Q}{\vdash_\dagger [P]\,C\,[Q]}$$

$$(\dagger\text{:S{\small UBST}}) \qquad \frac{\vdash_\dagger [P]\,C\,[Q] \qquad y \notin \mathrm{fv}(P) \cup \mathrm{fv}(Q) \cup \mathrm{fv}(C)}{\vdash_\dagger [P[y/x]]\,C[y/x]\,[Q[y/x]]}$$

Fig. 3: Proof Rules for QFUA and QBUA Triples

proximate loop behavior: if C transforms $P(n)$ to $P(n+1)$ for all $n < k$, then $P(0)$ can transform to $P(k)$ via C^*. The (F:L{\small OCAL}) and (B:L{\small OCAL}) rules use the L and $\mathsf{2}$ quantifiers, respectively, to erase the effect of local variables, which generalizes the existential quantifier in the Boolean case.

The (F:D{\small ISJ}) and (B:D{\small ISJ}) rules merge multiple triples into a single one by the quantitative corresponding of the disjunction operator. The (F:C{\small ONSTANCY}) and (B:C{\small ONSTANCY}) rule preserves unmodified Boolean constraints — when program C doesn't modify B's free variables, both pre- and post- predicates can be simultaneously conjuncted with B through the quantitative operators. The (†:RELAX) rule allows additive adjustments to resource functions: if F's variables remain unchanged by C, both assertion bounds can be shifted by F through arithmetic addition. The (†:Cons) rule shares identical syntax for both QFUA and QBUA. However, the implication direction is different: QFUA rules allow weakening of preconditions and strengthening of postconditions, while QBUA rules allow the opposite.

We next show that the QBUA and QFUA variants are sound and complete with respect to the corresponding semantics.

Theorem 1 (Soundness of QFUA and QBUA triples). *For all P, Q, C:*

- *If $\vdash_\mathsf{F} [P]\, C\, [Q]$ is derivable, then $\vDash_\mathsf{F} [P]\, C\, [Q]$ holds.*
- *If $\vdash_\mathsf{B} [P]\, C\, [Q]$ is derivable, then $\vDash_\mathsf{B} [P]\, C\, [Q]$ holds.*

Proof. By induction on the derivation of the triple. The detailed proof is provided in the technical report [13].

Theorem 2 (Completeness of QFUA and QBUA triples). *For all P, Q, C such that P and Q are finitely supported:*

- *If $\vDash_\mathsf{F} [P]\, C\, [Q]$ holds, then $\vdash_\mathsf{F} [P]\, C\, [Q]$ is derivable.*
- *If $\vDash_\mathsf{B} [P]\, C\, [Q]$ holds, then $\vdash_\mathsf{B} [P]\, C\, [Q]$ is derivable.*

Proof. By induction on the structure of C. The detailed proof is provided in the technical report [13].

3.3   Under-approximating High-water Marks

To under-approximate the worst-case high-water mark, we refine the QBUA semantics to track minimal resource levels during execution. We introduce QBUA$^\Diamond$ triples, whose semantics are defined as follows.

Definition 2. *A QBUA$^\Diamond$ triple $\vDash_\mathsf{B}^\Diamond [P]\, C\, [Q]$ holds if and only if for all σ and p such that $p \leq P(\sigma)$, there exists a τ and a q such that $q \leq Q(\tau)$ and $\langle C, \sigma, p \rangle \Downarrow^{\leq 0} \langle \tau, q \rangle$. This implies that for all σ such that $P(\sigma) \in \mathbb{Z}$, there exists an execution of C starting from σ that costs at least $P(\sigma) - \sup_\tau \{Q(\tau)\}$ ticks, and has a high-water mark of at least $P(\sigma)$.*

Before presenting the proof rules, we explain why the forward variant is not defined. A natural idea is to refine the QFUA semantics by requiring that the execution must pass through a point where the resource becomes non-positive. Formally, one could define $\vDash_\mathsf{F}^\Diamond [P]\, C\, [Q]$ to mean that for all τ and $q \geq Q(\tau)$, there exists σ and $p \geq P(\sigma)$ such that $\langle C, \sigma, p \rangle \Downarrow^{\leq 0} \langle \tau, q \rangle$. However, this definition leads to unintuitive results. Consider the program $C = \mathsf{tick}\ 10;\mathsf{tick}\ (-5)$. Intuitively, we would expect $\vDash_\mathsf{F}^\Diamond [10]\, C\, [5]$ to hold. But if we take $q = 100 \geq 5$, there is no p such that executing C from p leads to q while the potential ever drops

$$(\text{B}^\Diamond\text{:Skip}) \quad \dfrac{P \preceq 0}{\vdash_\text{B}^\Diamond [P]\,\mathsf{skip}\,[P]}$$

$$(\text{B}^\Diamond\text{:Assign}) \quad \dfrac{P \preceq 0}{\vdash_\text{B}^\Diamond [P]\,x := e\,[\mathsf{S}\,x'.P[x'/x] \curlywedge [x = e[x'/x]]]}$$

$$(\text{B}^\Diamond\text{:Assume}) \quad \dfrac{P \preceq 0}{\vdash_\text{B}^\Diamond [P \curlywedge [B]]\,\mathsf{assume}\,B\,[P \curlywedge [B]]}$$

$$(\text{B}^\Diamond\text{:Tick}) \quad \dfrac{P \curlywedge P - e \preceq 0}{\vdash_\text{B}^\Diamond [P]\,\mathsf{tick}\,e\,[P - e]}$$

$$(\text{B}^\Diamond\text{:SeqL}) \quad \dfrac{\vdash_\text{B}^\Diamond [P]\,C_1\,[R] \qquad \vdash_\text{B} [R]\,C_2\,[Q]}{\vdash_\text{B}^\Diamond [P]\,C_1; C_2\,[Q]}$$

$$(\text{B}^\Diamond\text{:SeqR}) \quad \dfrac{\vdash_\text{B} [P]\,C_1\,[R] \qquad \vdash_\text{B}^\Diamond [R]\,C_2\,[Q]}{\vdash_\text{B}^\Diamond [P]\,C_1; C_2\,[Q]}$$

$$(\text{B}^\Diamond\text{:LoopZero}) \quad \dfrac{P \preceq 0}{\vdash_\text{B}^\Diamond [P]\,C^\star\,[P]}$$

$$(\text{B}^\Diamond\text{:Loop}) \quad \dfrac{\forall n < k.\ \vdash_\text{B} [P(n)]\,C\,[P(n+1)] \qquad \exists m < k.\ \vdash_\text{B}^\Diamond [P(m)]\,C\,[P(m+1)]}{\vdash_\text{B}^\Diamond [P(0)]\,C^\star\,[P(k)]}$$

$$(\text{B}^\Diamond\text{:Disj}) \quad \dfrac{\forall i \in I.\ \vdash_\text{B}^\Diamond [P_i]\,C\,[Q_i]}{\vdash_\text{B}^\Diamond \left[\bigcurlyvee_{i \in I} P_i\right] C \left[\bigcurlyvee_{i \in I} Q_i\right]}$$

$$(\text{B}^\Diamond\text{:Relax}) \quad \dfrac{\vdash_\text{B}^\Diamond [P]\,C\,[Q] \qquad \mathrm{fv}(F) \cap \mathrm{mod}(C) = \emptyset \qquad F \preceq 0}{\vdash_\text{B}^\Diamond [P + F]\,C\,[Q + F]}$$

Fig. 4: Selected Proof Rules for QBUA$^\Diamond$ Triples

to ≤ 0, so the triple fails to hold. This fragility makes the forward definition hard to reason about, whereas the backward formulation (QBUA$^\Diamond$) remains robust and compositional. For this reason, we only develop the backward variant for reasoning about high-water marks.

Selected proof rules for QBUA$^\Diamond$ triples are shown in Fig. 4, which are similar to the QBUA rules but with additional constraints. The full version can be found in the technical report [13]. The (B$^\Diamond$:Skip), (B$^\Diamond$:Assign), and (B$^\Diamond$:Assume) rules assume that the resource function P is non-positive. The (B$^\Diamond$:Tick) rule requires $P \curlywedge P - e \preceq 0$, which ensures that either before or after the tick operation, the resource count is non-positive. For the sequential composition, if an execution of $C_1; C_2$ makes the resource counter non-positive at some point, then the point will occur either during the execution of C_1 or C_2. This is captured by the (B$^\Diamond$:SeqL) and (B$^\Diamond$:SeqR) rules. The loop is similar: if at some point during the execution of $C^\star$ the resource is non-positive, then either $C^\star$ degenerates into a skip and the resource is non-positive from the start, or this point will appear during the execution of C at some step. The former case is captured by the (B$^\Diamond$:LoopZero) rule, while the latter is captured by the subvariant-base (B$^\Diamond$:Loop) rule, with assuming $\exists m < k.\ \vdash_\text{B}^\Diamond [P(m)]\,C\,[P(m+1)]$. The (B$^\Diamond$:Disj) rule is similar to the (B:Disj) rule. Finally, the (B$^\Diamond$:Relax) rule allows only non-positive additive adjustments to resource functions, which ensures that the point of non-positivity resource is preserved.

QBUA$^\Diamond$ is also sound and complete, as shown in the following theorems.

Theorem 3 (Soundness of QBUA$^\Diamond$ triples). *For all P, Q, C, if $\vdash_\mathsf{B}^\Diamond [P] \, C \, [Q]$ is derivable, then $\vDash_\mathsf{B}^\Diamond [P] \, C \, [Q]$ holds.*

Proof. By induction on the derivation of the triple. The detailed proof is provided in the technical report [13].

Theorem 4 (Completeness of QBUA$^\Diamond$ triples). *For all P, Q, C such that P and Q are finitely supported, if $\vDash_\mathsf{B}^\Diamond [P] \, C \, [Q]$ holds, then $\vdash_\mathsf{B}^\Diamond [P] \, C \, [Q]$ is derivable.*

Proof. By induction on the structure of C. The detailed proof is provided in the technical report [13].

4 Implementation

To assess the practicality of our quantitative under-approximate program logic, we implemented a prototype verifier in OCaml targeting a C-style imperative language. The verifier supports semi-automated checking of the three variants of under-approximate logic introduced in this paper: QFUA, QBUA, and QBUA$^\Diamond$. Users provide the preconditions, postconditions, and—when needed—loop sub-variants (and the index m for high-water mark analysis). The verifier then checks the validity of the triple using predicate transformers and SMT solving.

4.1 Quantitative Predicate Transformers

To support the verification of quantitative under-approximate triples, we adopt and adapt Zhang and Kaminski [30]'s quantitative strongest postconditions to define three predicate transformers, each corresponding to one of our three logics: QFUA, QBUA, and QBUA$^\Diamond$. These transformers generalize classical Boolean predicate transformers—such as strongest postconditions and weakest preconditions—by lifting them to operate over resource functions $State \rightarrow \mathbb{Z} \cup \{\pm\infty\}$. For a loop-free program C, all three predicate transformers can be computed compositionally by structural recursion on the syntax of C. The rules for computing the transformers are summarized in Tab. 2. Below we describe each transformer's definition, intuition, and role in verification.

QFUA: Strongest Postcondition. For QFUA triples, which assert that some execution from a sufficiently resourced pre-state leads to a post-state with a certain resource level, we define a quantitative strongest postcondition transformer:

$$\mathrm{sp}\,[\![C]\!]\,(P) := \lambda\tau.\inf\{q : \exists\sigma, p.\, p \geq P(\sigma) \wedge \langle C, \sigma, p\rangle \Downarrow \langle \tau, q\rangle\}.$$

This function maps each post-state τ to the minimum amount of remaining resource q that can result from running C from some pre-state σ with resource at least $P(\sigma)$. Intuitively, $\mathrm{sp}\,[\![C]\!]\,(P)$ gives the lowest postcondition such that the triple $\vdash_\mathsf{F} [P] \, C \, [Q]$ is valid, as long as Q lies above it. To verify a triple $\vdash_\mathsf{F} [P] \, C \, [Q]$, it therefore suffices to compute $\mathrm{sp}\,[\![C]\!]\,(P)$ and check that $Q \succeq \mathrm{sp}\,[\![C]\!]\,(P)$.

QBUA: Weakest Precondition. For QBUA triples, which assert that every pre-state with a bounded resource can lead to some post-state where the remaining resource does not exceed a given bound, we define a quantitative weakest precondition transformer:

$$\mathrm{wp}\,[\![C]\!]\,(Q) := \lambda\sigma.\sup\{p : \exists\tau, q.q \le Q(\tau) \wedge \langle C, \sigma, p\rangle \Downarrow \langle\tau, q\rangle\}.$$

This function maps each pre-state σ to the maximum amount of initial resource p such that there exists some execution of C reaching a post-state τ with remaining resource no greater than $Q(\tau)$. Intuitively, $\mathrm{wp}\,[\![C]\!]\,(Q)$ gives the greatest precondition such that the triple $\vdash_\mathrm{B} [P]\,C\,[Q]$ is valid, as long as P lies above it. To verify a triple $\vdash_\mathrm{B} [P]\,C\,[Q]$, it therefore suffices to compute $\mathrm{wp}\,[\![C]\!]\,(Q)$ and check that $P \preceq \mathrm{wp}\,[\![C]\!]\,(Q)$.

QBUA$^\diamond$: Weakest Precondition with High-water Mark. For QBUA$^\diamond$ triples, which additionally require that the execution passes through a point where the resource drops to zero or below, we define a modified weakest precondition transformer that tracks such high-water behavior:

$$\mathrm{wp}^{\le 0}\,[\![C]\!]\,(Q) := \lambda\sigma.\sup\{p : \exists\tau, q.q \le Q(\tau) \wedge \langle C, \sigma, p\rangle \Downarrow^{\le 0} \langle\tau, q\rangle\}.$$

Compared to the transformer for QBUA, this definition adds the side condition that the execution must deplete the resource to at most zero at some intermediate point. The rest of the structure remains unchanged. This function maps each pre-state σ to the maximum amount of initial resource p such that there exists an execution of C that both reaches a post-state τ bounded by $Q(\tau)$ and passes through a resource level of ≤ 0 during execution. Similarly to the QBUA case, $\mathrm{wp}^{\le 0}\,[\![C]\!]\,(Q)$ gives the greatest precondition such that the triple $\vdash_\mathrm{B}^\diamond [P]\,C\,[Q]$ is valid, as long as P lies above it. And to verify a triple $\vdash_\mathrm{B}^\diamond [P]\,C\,[Q]$, it suffices to compute $\mathrm{wp}^{\le 0}\,[\![C]\!]\,(Q)$ and check that $P \preceq \mathrm{wp}^{\le 0}\,[\![C]\!]\,(Q)$.

4.2   The Verification Framework

To implement the program logic described in the previous sections, we design a verification framework that adapts the theoretical model to a more practical setting. In particular, while our logic formalizes assertions as resource functions of type $State \to \mathbb{Z} \cup \{\pm\infty\}$, our implementation factorizes these into two components: a Boolean specification predicate that identifies admissible program states, and an integer-valued function that represents the required or remaining resource. Furthermore, to support realistic program features, our implementation extends the core language with array operations, treating arrays as total functions and encoding read-over-write semantics via axioms compatible with standard SMT array theories. In the rest of this section, we explain how the predicate transformers introduced earlier are instantiated in this factored setting, how program annotations are provided, and how compositional verification is performed for both loop-free and loop-containing programs.

Table 2: Rules for Computing Quantitative Predicate Transformers

	$\operatorname{sp}[\![C]\!](P)$
skip	P
$x := e$	$\sqcup x'.P[x'/x] \curlyvee [x \ne e[x'/x]]$
assume B	$P \curlyvee [\neg B]$
$C_1; C_2$	$\operatorname{sp}[\![C_2]\!](\operatorname{sp}[\![C_1]\!](P))$
$C_1 + C_2$	$\operatorname{sp}[\![C_1]\!](P) \curlywedge \operatorname{sp}[\![C_2]\!](P)$
local x in C	$\sqcup x.\operatorname{sp}[\![C]\!](P)$

	$\operatorname{wp}[\![C]\!](Q)$	$\operatorname{wp}^{\le 0}[\![C]\!](Q)$
skip	Q	$Q \curlywedge 0$
$x := e$	$Q[e/x]$	$Q[e/x] \curlywedge 0$
assume B	$P \curlywedge [B]$	$P \curlywedge [B] \curlywedge 0$
$C_1; C_2$	$\operatorname{wp}[\![C_1]\!](\operatorname{wp}[\![C_2]\!](Q))$	$\operatorname{wp}^{\le 0}[\![C_1]\!](\operatorname{wp}[\![C_2]\!](Q))$ $\curlywedge \operatorname{wp}[\![C_1]\!](\operatorname{wp}^{\le 0}[\![C_2]\!](Q))$
$C_1 + C_2$	$\operatorname{wp}[\![C_1]\!](Q) \curlyvee \operatorname{wp}[\![C_2]\!](Q)$	$\operatorname{wp}^{\le 0}[\![C_1]\!](Q) \curlyvee \operatorname{wp}^{\le 0}[\![C_2]\!](Q)$
local x in C	$\sqsupseteq x.\operatorname{wp}[\![C]\!](Q)$	$\sqsupseteq x.\operatorname{wp}^{\le 0}[\![C]\!](Q)$

We represent resource functions $P : State \to \mathbb{Z} \cup \{\pm\infty\}$ in a factored form as pairs $[P_S; P_R]$, where $P_S : State \to \{\mathsf{true}, \mathsf{false}\}$ is a logical specification predicate indicating which states are admissible, and $P_R : State \to \mathbb{Z}$ is a numeric function specifying the resource bound. The intention is that the resource constraint P_R applies only when P_S holds. Formally, the pair $[P_S; P_R]$ denotes a resource function whose interpretation depends on the logic. In the case of QFUA, it corresponds to the function $[\neg P_S] \curlyvee P_R$, which evaluates to $+\infty$ on any state not satisfying P_S, and to P_R otherwise. As a result, only states satisfying P_S are allowed, and on those, the available resource must be at least P_R. In contrast, for QBUA and QBUA$^\diamond$ triples, the pair corresponds to $[P_S] \curlywedge P_R$, which evaluates to $-\infty$ outside P_S, again disallowing states that violate the specification, and requires the resource to be at most P_R where P_S holds. With this notation, we provide some derived rules in Fig. 5. The † rule can be used for both QFUA and QBUA triples, while the ‡ rule is valid for all three kinds of triples.

To verify a program against a quantitative triple, our framework requires the user to annotate the program at both the entry and exit points with pre- and post-conditions of the form $[P_S; P_R]$ described above.

For programs without loops, verification is fully automatic. Given the annotated pre- and post-conditions and the desired logic (QFUA, QBUA, or QBUA$^\diamond$), the system performs symbolic predicate transformation and generates the corresponding verification condition. This condition typically takes the form

($\dagger$:Assign')

$$\frac{x \notin \mathrm{fv}(P_R)}{\vdash_\ddagger [P_S | P_R]\, x := e\, [\exists x'.P_S[x'/x] \wedge x = e[x'/x]\, |\, P_R]}$$

($\ddagger$:IfTrue)

$$\frac{\vdash_\ddagger [P_S \wedge B|\, P_R]\, C_1\, [Q_S | Q_R]}{\vdash_\ddagger [P_S | P_R]\, \text{if } B \text{ then } C_1 \text{ else } C_2\, [Q_S | Q_R]}$$

($\dagger$:WhileSubvar)

$$\frac{\forall n < k - 1.\, \vdash_\dagger [P_S(n) \wedge B|\, P_R(n)]\, C\, [P_S(n+1) \wedge B|\, P_R(n+1)] \qquad \vdash_\dagger [P_S(k-1) \wedge B|\, P_R(k-1)]\, C\, [P_S(k) \wedge \neg B|\, P_S(k)]}{\vdash_\dagger [P_S(0) \wedge B|\, P_R(0)]\, \text{while } B \text{ do } C\, [P_S(k) \wedge \neg B|\, P_R(k)]}$$

Fig. 5: Selected Derived Rules

of an implication between symbolic arithmetic expressions over state variables. It is then passed to the Z3 SMT solver [18] to decide validity.

For programs with loops, the user must provide additional annotations. Specifically, the user supplies a variable k that tracks the number of loop iterations on each execution path, and is required to remain unchanged within the loop body and a loop subvariant expressed as a family of assertions $[P_S(n); P_R(n)]$, indexed by the iteration counter n.

For QFUA and QBUA logic, the verifier then checks that for all n such that $0 \leq n < k$, the loop body transforms $[P_S(n); P_R(n)]$ into $[P_S(n+1); P_R(n+1)]$, using the logic-specific predicate transformer. If this inductive check succeeds, the loop is summarized by the precondition $[P_S(0) \wedge 0 \leq k; P_R(0)]$ and the postcondition $[P_S(k) \wedge 0 \leq k; P_R(k)]$, which are used for verifying the continuation of the program.

The QBUA$^\diamond$ logic extends QBUA by requiring that the execution path passes through a point where the resource drops to zero or below. To capture this, the user must additionally provide an index m, indicating the iteration during which this drop is expected to occur. As with k, the value of m must remain unchanged inside the loop. The verifier first checks, as in QBUA, that for all $0 \leq n < k$, the loop body transforms $[P_S(n); P_R(n)]$ into $[P_S(n+1); P_R(n+1)]$. Then, it performs a second check under QBUA$^\diamond$, verifying that the loop body transforms $[P_S(m); P_R(m)]$ into $[P_S(m+1); P_R(m+1)]$ via an execution in which the resource drops to ≤ 0 at some point. Together, these two conditions ensure that the loop behaves correctly both in terms of normal execution and the high-water resource constraint. The loop is again summarized using $[P_S(0) \wedge 0 \leq m < k; P_R(0)]$ and $[P_S(k) \wedge 0 \leq m < k; P_R(k)]$.

Overall, the user supplies structural annotations at key points—preconditions, postconditions, and loop specifications—and the framework handles the rest. Predicate transformation reduces the verification problem to logical and arithmetic conditions, which are then discharged using SMT solving. Our system is fully automatic for straight-line code, and requires only local, bounded annotations for loops to enable modular, compositional verification.

Finally, our verifier supports reasoning over arrays by encoding them as total functions $a : \mathbb{Z} \to \mathbb{Z}$, equipped with two standard operations. The expression $a[e]$ denotes the value stored at index e, while $a\{e \mapsto e'\}$ represents a new array identical to a, except that index e is updated to value e'. These operations satisfy the usual read-over-write axioms:

$$i = k \to (a\{i \mapsto v\})[k] = v \qquad i \neq k \to (a\{i \mapsto v\})[k] = a[k]$$

This abstraction aligns with the standard theory of arrays supported by SMT solvers such as Z3 [18].

5   Case Studies

In this section, we present a total of eight verified programs as our case studies: four small illustrative combinations of pre- and post-conditions for the example from §2.3 and four larger case studies. All the case studies are successfully verified using our prototype implementation, and the corresponding annotated code is provided in the supplementary material.

We begin this section by revisiting the example from §2.3 to demonstrate how our prototype verifier operates concretely on annotated programs. Consider the following simple conditional:

```
1: /* precondition: P_1 = [T : 2] */ /* precondition: P_2 = [x = 42; 2] */
2: if (x == 42) { tick(2); x = 0; } else { tick(1); }
3: /* postcondition: Q_1 = [T; 0] */ /* postcondition: Q_2 = [x = 0; 0] */
```

Let us test the four combinations of these pre- and post-conditions under both QFUA and QBUA. The pair (P_1, Q_1) is not valid under either logic. The pair (P_1, Q_2) is only valid under QFUA, and (P_2, Q_1) is only valid under QBUA. Finally, (P_2, Q_2) is valid under both. These results match the analysis given in §2.3, where we discussed how QFUA and QBUA emphasize output- and input-oriented reasoning, respectively.

5.1   QFUA: Password Validation

This example illustrates the use of QFUA triples to characterize states that can potentially incur high resource consumption. We consider a password validation program where the password is an array of n integers, and the user must input n integers to match it entry-by-entry. Each user input is modeled by a `tick(1)` command, incurring one unit of resource. The program stops early if a mismatch is found, but if the password is fully correct, it consumes n units of input effort. QFUA reasoning allows us to formally express that in any final state where the variable `valid` equals 1, the execution might have consumed up to n units of resource.

```
1: /* precondition: [n ≥ 0; n] */
2: int valid = 1;
3: int i = 0;
```

```
 4: while (i < n && valid == 1)
 5: /* number of iterations: n ;
 6:     subvariant: i_0 ↦ [i == i_0 ∧ valid == 1: n − i_0] */
 7: {
 8:     tick(1);                                        ▷ user input
 9:     int input;
10:     if (input != password[i])
11:         valid = 0;
12:     i = i + 1;
13: }
14: /* postcondition: [n ≥ 0 ∧ valid == 1: 0] */
```

This QFUA-annotated program expresses that reaching a final state where $valid = 1$—i.e., successful password verification—may cost up to n units of input, corresponding to the longest possible execution path. The loop subvariant uses the index i_0 to represent progress through the password, and the quantitative postcondition tracks how many inputs remain to be matched. By computing the strongest postcondition, the verifier confirms that only successful verification can justify the worst-case input cost.

While the same triple holds under QBUA, it does not capture that the high resource usage occurs only when $valid = 1$. In fact, even if we drop this constraint from the postcondition, the QBUA triple remains valid—unlike QFUA, which becomes invalid. This highlights QFUA's expressiveness in specifying output-sensitive resource behavior.

5.2 QBUA: Insertion Sort

This example uses QBUA triples to under-approximate the total number of swaps performed by insertion sort on a worst-case input. Compared to QFUA, QBUA is particularly suitable here because we are interested in identifying initial states (i.e., specific array configurations) that lead to executions incurring high resource usage.

The program below shows the insertion sort algorithm, and it is annotated with loop subvariants and resource assertions. The variable n denotes the length of the array a, and `tick(1)` represents one unit of resource consumption per swap. This annotation expresses that for input arrays sorted in strictly decreasing order, the total number of swaps executed by insertion sort is under-approximated by $n(n-1)/2$, which is tight.

```
 1: /* precondition: [n ≥ 1 ∧ ∀I ∈ [0, n). ∀J ∈ [0, I). a[J] > a[I]: n(n − 1)/2] */
 2: int i = 1;
 3: while (i < n)
 4: /* number of iterations: n − 1;
 5:     subvariant: i_0 ↦ [i = i_0 + 1 ∧ ∀I ∈ [i, n). ∀J ∈ [0, I). a[J] > a[I]: −i_0(i_0 + 1)/2];
 6:     constant prefix: [T: n(n − 1)/2] */
 7: {
 8:     int j = i;
 9:     while (j > 0)
10:     /* number of iterations: i;
11:         subvariant: j_0 ↦ [j = i − j_0 ∧ ∀I ∈ [0, j). a[I] > a[j] ∧ ∀I ∈ [i + 1, n). ∀J ∈ [0, I). a[J] > a[I]: −j_0];
```

```
12:        constant prefix: [i = i_0 + 1:  - i_0(i_0 + 1)/2] */
13:    {
14:        if (a[j - 1] > a[j]) {
15:            tick(1);                                          ▷ swap
16:            int t = a[j];
17:            a[j] = a[j - 1];
18:            a[j - 1] = t;
19:        }
20:        j = j - 1;
21:    }
22:    i = i + 1;
23: }
24: /* postcondition: [n ≥ 1; 0] */
```

To verify this fact, our system introduces index variables i_0 and j_0 to define subvariants that track the outer and inner loop states, respectively. The equalities $i = i_0 + 1$ and $j = i - j_0$ make express the relationship between the program variables i, j and the logical iteration counters i_0, j_0 that parameterize the subvariant families.

The logical part of these assertions captures key ordering properties of the array. In the outer loop, the subvariant $\forall I \in [i, n).\ \forall J \in [0, I).\ a[J] > a[I]$ ensures that the suffix of the array from index i onward remains sorted in strictly decreasing order. This reflects that the portion of the array not yet visited by the outer loop is still in its worst-case configuration. In the inner loop, the subvariant $\forall I \in [0, j).\ a[I] > a[j]$ asserts that the element currently being inserted (at index j) is strictly smaller than all elements to its left, capturing the progress of the inner loop as it "bubbles" the element leftward. In addition, the condition $\forall I \in [i + 1, n).\ \forall J \in [0, I).\ a[J] > a[I]$ preserves the decreasing order in the untouched suffix beyond the current outer loop index, maintaining the worst-case assumption throughout execution.

The numeric part of each subvariant quantifies the resource consumption within the corresponding loop. For the outer loop, this is expressed by the term $-i_0(i_0 + 1)/2$, which tracks the cumulative number of swaps performed after i_0 iterations. For the inner loop, the numeric subvariant $-j_0$ reflects the swaps required for inserting the current element. Together, these expressions describe the local resource evolution of each loop, enabling modular reasoning about their quantitative behavior.

To complete the reasoning for the entire program, each loop is further associated with a constant prefix that remains unchanged during the loop execution but contributes to the overall resource analysis. For the outer loop, the constant prefix is applied after deriving the loop triple, using the (B:RELAX) rule to uniformly shift both the pre- and post-potentials by $n(n - 1)/2$, thereby aligning the result with the precondition of the entire program. For the inner loop, the constant prefix restores the context of the outer loop once the inner loop reasoning is finished: the logical condition $i = i_0 + 1$ through the (B:CONSTANCY) rule, and the resource offset $-i_0(i_0 + 1)/2$ through the (B:RELAX) rule. These constant prefixes involve only variables that remain unchanged by the loop body and thus need not be reasoned about within the loop itself, yet they ensure that the verified subvariants compose correctly into the global quantitative reasoning of the program.

5.3 QBUA: Quicksort with Stack

We also apply QBUA reasoning to analyze the worst-case number of comparisons performed by quicksort. To simplify reasoning, we implement quicksort using an explicit stack to simulate recursion, storing subarray bounds in `lstk` and `rstk`. Instead of actually choosing pivots randomly, we use the command `assume(pivot >= 1 && pivot < r)` to model nondeterministic pivot selection.

Our goal is to verify that when the input array is initially sorted in strictly increasing order, there exists a pivot selection strategy under which quicksort performs at least $n(n-1)/2$ comparisons. This lower bound is tight and corresponds to the degenerate case where each pivot is chosen to be the last element in the subarray. We model each comparison by inserting a `tick(1)` statement before any data movement occurs.

```
 1:  /* precondition: [n ≥ 1 ∧ ∀I ∈ [0, n). ∀J ∈ [0, I). a[J] < a[I]; n(n-1)/2] */
 2:  int top = 0;
 3:  lstk[top] = 0;
 4:  rstk[top] = n;
 5:  top = top + 1;
 6:  while (top > 0)
 7:      /* number of iterations: n;
```

$$
8:\quad \text{subvariant: } t \mapsto
\begin{bmatrix}
\text{if } t < n: & top = 1 \wedge lstk[0] = 0 \wedge rstk[0] = n - t \\
& \wedge \forall I \in [0, n-t). \forall J \in [0, I). a[J] < a[I] \\
\text{else:} & top = 0; \\
& \dfrac{t(2n - t - 1)}{2}
\end{bmatrix}
$$

```
 9:      constant prefix: [n ≥ 1: n(n-1)/2] */
10:  {
11:      top = top - 1;
12:      int l = lstk[top];
13:      int r = rstk[top];
14:      int pivot;
15:      assume(pivot >= 1 && pivot < r);
16:      int i = l;
17:      int j = l;
18:      int k = r;
19:      while (i < r)
20:          /* number of iterations: r - l;
```

$$
21:\quad \text{subvariant: } i_0 \mapsto
\begin{bmatrix}
& pivot = r - 1 \wedge i = l + i_0 \\
\wedge & j = \begin{cases} i & \text{if } i \le pivot \\ i - 1 & \text{otherwise} \end{cases} \wedge k = r \\
\wedge & \forall I \in [l, r). \forall J \in [l, I). a[J] < a[I] \\
\wedge & \forall I \in [l, j). b[I] = \begin{cases} a[I] & \text{if } I < pivot \\ a[I + 1] & \text{otherwise} \end{cases} \\
& \begin{cases} i_0 & \text{if } i \le pivot \\ i_0 - 1 & \text{otherwise} \end{cases}
\end{bmatrix}
$$

```
22:      constant prefix: [top = 0 ∧ l = 0 ∧ r = n - t: - t(2n - t - 1)/2] */
23:      {
24:          if (i != pivot) {
25:              tick(1);                                        ▷ comparison
26:              if (a[i] <= a[pivot]) {
27:                  b[j] = a[i];
28:                  j = j + 1;
```

```
29:            } else {
30:                k = k - 1;
31:                b[k] = a[i];
32:            }
33:        }
34:        i = i + 1;
35:    }
36:    b[j] = a[pivot];
37:    i = l;
38:    while (i < r)
39:        /* number of iterations: r - l;
40:           subvariant: i_0 |-> [i = l + i_0 ∧ ∀I ∈ [l, i). a[I] = b[I]: 0]
41:           constant prefix: [ top = 0 ∧ l = 0 ∧ r = n - t ∧ j = r - 1 ∧ k = r
                                 ∧  ∀I ∈ [l, j). ∀J ∈ [l, I). b[J] < b[I];    ]  */
                                    l(2n - l - 1)/2 - (n - l - 1)
42:    {
43:        a[i] = b[i];
44:        i = i + 1;
45:    }
46:    if (l < j) {
47:        lstk[top] = l;
48:        rstk[top] = j;
49:        top = top + 1;
50:    }
51:    if (j + 1 < r) {
52:        lstk[top] = j + 1;
53:        rstk[top] = r;
54:        top = top + 1;
55:    }
56: }
57: /* postcondition: [n ≥ 1: 0] */
```

To verify this bound, we introduce a subvariant index t to count the number
of partitioning steps performed by the outer loop. The subvariant maintains that
the first $n - t$ elements of the array remain sorted, and that the stack contains
at most one active subarray to process.

In the inner partitioning loop, a second subvariant indexed by i_0 expresses
the progress of scanning through the current subarray $[l, r)$, along with logical
assertions capturing the ordering of values and the correctness of the constructed
temporary array b. The second inner loop copies values from b back into a, while
maintaining that the written prefix is sorted.

The resource subvariants compute the total number of comparisons remaining, and allow us to verify that the number of `tick(1)` operations accumulates
to at least $n(n-1)/2$ along a path where each pivot is selected as the last element
of its subarray.

5.4 QBUA$^\diamond$: Producer-consumer System

We now present an example that uses QBUA$^\diamond$ to verify a lower bound on resource consumption along some execution path—specifically, that the buffer may
reach full capacity, meaning the resource is completely exhausted.

The program models a producer-consumer system with nondeterministic
scheduling. There are initially n production steps and n consumption steps,

and at each iteration, the environment nondeterministically chooses to either produce or consume. This nondeterminism is encoded using a special Boolean variable `demon`, where the conditional `if (demon)` indicates a nondeterministic choice between branches. Each production step adds one item to the buffer and is modeled by `tick(1)`, which consumes one unit of resource—that is, one unit of available buffer space. Each consumption step removes one item and is modeled by `tick(-1)`, which frees up buffer space, increasing the resource.

The variable `buf` tracks the current buffer occupancy, while `p` and `c` represent the number of remaining production and consumption steps, respectively. In this setting, the resource represents the remaining buffer capacity. When the buffer becomes full, the resource value reaches zero. Our goal is to show that, under some execution strategy, the buffer occupancy may reach n at some point— that is, the total resource consumption reaches at least n before the program terminates.

```
 1: /* precondition: [n ≥ 0; n] */
 2: int p = n;
 3: int c = n;
 4: int buf = 0;
 5: while (p + c > 0)
 6: /* number of iterations: 2n;
```

$$
7:\quad \text{subvariant: } i \mapsto \left[\begin{cases} buf = i \wedge p = n - i \wedge c = n & \text{if } i < n \\ buf = 2n - i \wedge p = 0 \wedge c = 2n - i & \text{otherwise} \end{cases} ; \quad \begin{cases} n - i & \text{if } i < n \\ i - n & \text{otherwise} \end{cases} \right] ;
$$

```
 8:     exhaustion point: n */
 9: {
10:     if (demon) {
11:         assume(p > 0);
12:         p = p - 1;
13:         tick(1);                        ▷ addition to buffer
14:         buf = buf + 1;
15:     } else {
16:         assume(buf > 0 && c > 0);
17:         c = c - 1;
18:         tick(-1);                       ▷ removal from buffer
19:         buf = buf - 1;
20:     }
21: }
22: /* postcondition: [n ≥ 0; n] */
```

The subvariant for this loop is indexed by i, representing the total number of steps taken so far. The first n steps correspond to pure production, during which the buffer usage increases and reaches its peak value n at step $i = n$. The remaining n steps simulate pure consumption, reducing the buffer back to zero. In addition to tracking the logical evolution of variables—p decreasing and buf increasing before $i = n$, and c decreasing and buf decreasing afterward—the subvariant also includes an explicit exhaustion point at $i = n$. This marks the iteration at which the resource value (i.e., remaining buffer capacity) reaches zero, indicating the buffer is full.

The QBUA$^\Diamond$ verifier confirms there exists an execution path where the resource value eventually drops to zero—i.e., the buffer becomes full—and that execution can continue to termination without breaking the postcondition.

6 Related Work

Incorrectness Logic Incorrectness logic (IL), introduced by O'Hearn [21], signifies a major shift in program verification by emphasizing *under-approximate* reasoning instead of the *over-approximate* approach employed in classic Hoare logic. The core idea of IL is the use of *forward, under-approximate* (FUA) triples to ensure that any bug detected is a true positive. FUA triples were initially studied by de Vries and Koutavas [28], and they discussed *backward, under-approximate* (BUA) triples as *total* Hoare triples. BUA triples were later studied by Möller et al. [17] and Ascari et al. [1]. As a subroutine of UNTER for under-approximating non-termination, Raad et al. [26] studied the theory of BUA triples and realized them in practice. Le et al. [14] extends IL with separation logic (ISL) to find bugs in heap-manipulating programs. Raad et al. [25] further developed a concurrent variant of ISL to detect concurrency bugs, e.g., races and deadlocks. Zilberstein et al. [31,32] developed Outcome logic (OL) and Outcome separation logic (OSL) as a unified foundation for reasoning about both correctness and incorrectness. Among the aforementioned studies, only UNTER [26] focuses on the resource usage of programs, as it aims to prove non-termination, i.e., a *qualitative* justification for a program's usage of the time resource. Recently, Cousot [8] studies transformational program logics for correctness and incorrectness, including termination and non-termination. In this work, we aim to establish *quantitative* under-approximations of the worst-case resource usage of programs.

Resource-aware Program Logic Haslbeck and Nipkow [11] reviewed three variants of Hoare logic for establishing time bounds. The first one is the quantitative Hoare logic (QHL) [5,6] that we reviewed in §2.1. Note that QHL is not restricted to time bounds; it can also handle general resources like stack bounds. QHL generalizes Boolean assertions by introducing the concept of *potentials* to reason about resource consumption. In QHL, the difference between the pre- and the post-potential provides an upper bound (i.e., an over-approximation) on the resource consumption. Furthermore, because potentials can never be negative, the pre-potential also establishes an upper bound on the high-water mark for executing a program. The second one is a Hoare-like logic to prove big-O-style time bounds, developed by Nielson [19]. Nielson's logic establishes triples of the form $\{p\}\, C\, \{E \Downarrow q\}$, where p and q are Boolean assertions and E is a time bound. The third one is a line of work of incorporating separation logic with potential-like notions such as *time credits* [2,16,23,10]. The high-level idea is to treat resources (or potentials) as a special type of heap fragment, allowing us to use *separating conjunction* to annotate program states with quantitative information, e.g., $\{p * \$3\}\, C\, \{q * \$1\}$ indicates that the pre-state carries 3 units of resources and the post-state carries 1 unit of resources. All the aforementioned logics focus on over-approximating worst-case resource usage (i.e., sound upper bounds) or under-approximating best-case resource usage (i.e., sound lower bounds). In this work, we aim to develop a program logic to under-approximate worst-case resource usage. We could have developed our work based on time credits or similar mechanisms to address the compositionality and modularity issues mentioned in §2.3, but we find it orthogonal to the under-approximation problem we aim to tackle in this paper. In other words, we still need to devise the forward and backward reasoning principles for resource under-approximation, as well as the treatment of high-water marks. Nevertheless, extending our work with time credits within the context of separation logic is an interesting area for our future work, especially in the setting of establishing *asymptotic* bounds [10].

Graded Hoare logic (GHL) [9] augments Hoare logic with a *preordered monoidal analysis* to reason about side-effects, including resource usage, probabilistic behavior, and differential privacy-related properties. Given a preordered monoid $(M, \leq, 1, \cdot)$, GHL proves judgements of the form $\vdash_m \{\phi\} C \{\psi\}$, where $m \in M$ is called the *analysis* of program C and ϕ, ψ are the pre- and post-conditions. For example, one can use the natural-number monoid $(\mathbb{N}, \leq, 0, +)$ to instantiate GHL to reason about resource usage, e.g., $\vdash_0 \{\phi\} \, \mathsf{skip} \, \{\phi\}$ and $\vdash_2 \{\phi\} \, \mathsf{tick} \, 2 \, \{\phi\}$. GHL still follows the methodology of *over-approximating*.

Worst-case Resource Analysis Most existing approaches for identifying reachable worst cases are based on testing, using techniques such as random testing and symbolic execution to generate concrete inputs that can lead to significant resource usage. Recent fuzzing-based methods include KELINCIWCA [20], SLOWFUZZ [22], and resource-usage-aware fuzzing [7]; they are considered blackbox methods as they do not require knowledge of the program's content. On the other hand, symbolic-execution-based methods look into the concrete structures of programs; to name a few, WISE [4], SPF-WCA [15], BADGER [20], and resource-type-guided symbolic execution [29]. All the aforementioned methods can generate concrete inputs, i.e., they provide *concrete* under-approximations of the worst-case resource usage, whereas our quantitative under-approximate logic proves *symbolic* under-approximations.

Data Availability Statement. The artifact accompanying this paper, including the OCaml implementation of the prototype verifier and the mechanized Rocq proofs, is available at Zenodo [12]. The extended version of this paper, which contains detailed pen-and-paper proofs as well as complete semantics and proof rules, is available as a technical report at arXiv [13].

Acknowledgements. This work was sponsored by National Key R&D Program of China, Grant No. 2024YFE0204100.

References

1. Ascari, F., Bruni, R., Gori, R., Logozzo, F.: Sufficient Incorrectness Logic: SIL and Separation SIL (2023), `https://arxiv.org/abs/2310.18156`
2. Atkey, R.: Amortised Resource Analysis with Separation Logic. In: European Symp. on Programming. pp. 85–103. ESOP'10 (2010). `https://doi.org/10.1007/978-3-642-11957-6_6`

3. Batz, K., Kaminski, B.L., Katoen, J.P.: Relatively Complete Verification of Probabilistic Programs: An Expressive Language for Expectation-Based Reasoning. Proc. ACM Program. Lang. **5**(39), 39:1–39:30 (January 2021). https://doi.org/10.1145/3434320

4. Burnim, J., Juvekar, S., Sen, K.: WISE: Automated Test Generation for Worst-Case Complexity. In: Int. Conf. on Softw. Eng. pp. 463–473. ICSE'09 (2009). https://doi.org/10.1109/ICSE.2009.5070545

5. Carbonneaux, Q., Hoffmann, J., Ramananandro, T., Shao, Z.: End-to-End Verification of Stack-Space Bounds for C Programs. In: Prog. Lang. Design and Impl. pp. 270–281. PLDI'14 (2014). https://doi.org/10.1145/2594291.2594301

6. Carbonneaux, Q., Hoffmann, J., Shao, Z.: Compositional Certified Resource Bounds. In: Prog. Lang. Design and Impl. PLDI'15 (2015). https://doi.org/10.1145/2737924.2737955

7. Chen, L., Huang, R., Luo, D., Ma, C., Wei, D., Wang, J.: Estimating Worst-case Resource Usage by Resource-usage-aware Fuzzing. In: Fundamental Approaches to Softw. Eng. pp. 92–101. FASE'22 (2022). https://doi.org/10.1007/978-3-030-99429-7_5

8. Cousot, P.: Calculational Design of [In]Correctness Transformational Program Logics by Abstract Interpretation. Proc. ACM Program. Lang. **8**(7), 175–208 (January 2024). https://doi.org/10.1145/3632849

9. Gaboardi, M., Katsumata, S.y., Orchard, D., Sato, T.: Graded Hoare Logic and its Categorical Semantics. In: European Symp. on Programming. pp. 234–263. ESOP'21 (2021). https://doi.org/10.1007/978-3-030-72019-3_9

10. Gueneau, A.: Mechanized Verification of the Correctness and Asymptotic Complexity of Programs. Ph.D. thesis, Université Paris Cité (2019)

11. Haslbeck, M.P.L., Nipkow, T.: Hoare Logics for Time Bounds: A Study in Meta Theory. In: Tools and Algs. for the Construct. and Anal. of Syst. pp. 155–171. TACAS'18 (2018). https://doi.org/10.1007/978-3-319-89960-2_9

12. Jin, Z., Wang, D.: A Program Logic for Under-approximating Worst-case Resource Usage. Research artifact available on https://doi.org/10.5281/zenodo.18196369 (2026)

13. Jin, Z., Wang, D.: A Program Logic for Under-approximating Worst-case Resource Usage (2026), https://arxiv.org/abs/2502.11091

14. Le, Q.L., Raad, A., Villard, J., Berdine, J., Dreyer, D., O'Hearn, P.W.: Finding Real Bugs in Big Programs with Incorrectness Logic. Proc. ACM Program. Lang. **6**(81), 81:1–81:27 (April 2022). https://doi.org/10.1145/3527325

15. Luckow, K., Kersten, R., Păsăreanu, C.S.: Symbolic Complexity Analysis Using Context-Preserving Histories. In: Int. Conf. on Softw. Testing, Verif. and Validation. pp. 58–68. ICST'17 (2017). https://doi.org/10.1109/ICST.2017.13

16. Mével, G., Jourdan, J.H., Pottier, F.: Time Credits and Time Receipts in Iris. In: European Symp. on Programming. pp. 3–29. ESOP'19 (2019). https://doi.org/10.1007/978-3-030-17184-1_1

17. Möller, B., O'Hearn, P.W., Hoare, C.A.R.: On Algebra of Program Correctness and Incorrectness. In: Relational and Algebraic Methods in Computer Science. pp. 325–343. RAMiCS'21 (2021). https://doi.org/10.1007/978-3-030-88701-8_20

18. de Moura, L., Bjørner, N.: Z3: An Efficient SMT Solver. In: Tools and Algs. for the Construct. and Anal. of Syst. TACAS'08 (2008). https://doi.org/10.1007/978-3-540-78800-3_24

19. Nielson, H.R.: A hoare-like proof system for analysing the computation time of programs. Science of Computer Programming **9**, 107–136 (October 1987). https://doi.org/10.1016/0167-6423(87)90029-3

20. Noller, Y., Kersten, R., Păsăreanu, C.S.: Badger: Complexity Analysis with Fuzzing and Symbolic Execution. In: Int. Symp. on Softw. Testing and Analysis. pp. 322–332. ISSTA'18 (2018). https://doi.org/10.1145/3213846.3213868
21. O'Hearn, P.W.: Incorrectness Logic. Proc. ACM Program. Lang. **4**(10), 10:1–10:32 (December 2019). https://doi.org/10.1145/3371078
22. Petsios, T., Zhao, J., Keromytis, A.D., Jana, S.: SlowFuzz: Automated Domain-Independent Detection of Algorithmic Complexity Vulnerabilities. In: Comp. and Comm. Sec. pp. 2155–2168. CCS'17 (2017). https://doi.org/10.1145/3133956.3134073
23. Pottier, F., Guéneau, A., Jourdan, J.H., Mével, G.: Thunks and Debits in Separation Logic with Time Credits. Proc. ACM Program. Lang. **8**(50), 1482–1508 (January 2024). https://doi.org/10.1145/3632892
24. Raad, A., Berdine, J., Dang, H.H., Dreyer, D., O'Hearn, P.W., Villard, J.: Local Reasoning About the Presence of Bugs: Incorrectness Separation Logic. In: Computer Aided Verif. pp. 225–252. CAV'20 (2020). https://doi.org/10.1007/978-3-030-53291-8_14
25. Raad, A., Berdine, J., Dreyer, D., O'Hearn, P.W.: Concurrent Incorrectness Separation Logic. Proc. ACM Program. Lang. **6**(34), 34:1–34:29 (January 2022). https://doi.org/10.1145/3498695
26. Raad, A., Vanegue, J., O'Hearn, P.W.: Non-termination Proving at Scale. Proc. ACM Program. Lang. **8**(280), 246–274 (October 2024). https://doi.org/10.1145/3689720
27. Tarjan, R.E.: Amortized Computational Complexity. SIAM J. Algebraic Discrete Methods **6** (August 1985). https://doi.org/10.1137/0606031
28. de Vries, E., Koutavas, V.: Reverse Hoare Logic. In: Software Engineering and Formal Methods. pp. 155–171. SEFM'11 (2011). https://doi.org/10.1007/978-3-642-24690-6_12
29. Wang, D., Hoffmann, J.: Type-Guided Worst-Case Input Generation. Proc. ACM Program. Lang. **3**(13) (January 2019). https://doi.org/10.1145/3290326
30. Zhang, L., Kaminski, B.L.: Quantitative Strongest Post: A Calculus for Reasoning about the Flow of Quantitative Information. Proc. ACM Program. Lang. **6**(87), 87:1–87:29 (April 2022). https://doi.org/10.1145/3527331
31. Zilberstein, N., Dreyer, D., Silva, A.: Outcome Logic: A Unifying Foundation for Correctness and Incorrectness Reasoning. Proc. ACM Program. Lang. **7**(93), 522–550 (April 2023). https://doi.org/10.1145/3586045
32. Zilberstein, N., Saliling, A., Silva, A.: Outcome Separation Logic: Local Reasoning for Correctness and Incorrectness with Computational Effects. Proc. ACM Program. Lang. **8**(104), 276–304 (April 2024). https://doi.org/10.1145/3649821

Causal-Broadcast Memory⋆

Amir Karniel and Ori Lahav

Tel Aviv University, Tel Aviv, Israel

Abstract. We investigate the precise consistency guarantees provided by a simple and prominent distributed implementation of shared memory (a.k.a. key-value store) based on the causal broadcast abstraction. We formalize these guarantees within a weak memory model, which we call "causal-broadcast memory" (CBM, for short), and relate it to several established weak memory models. In particular, our study reveals that CBM is strictly stronger than "causal memory" consistency, previously proposed to encapsulate the same distributed implementation. Additionally, we address two core verification challenges for CBM: (i) deciding whether a single abstract execution graph is consistent, which we show is solvable in polynomial time, and (ii) verifying reachability of control states for client programs operating atop causal-broadcast memory, which we prove to be undecidable.

1   Introduction

Consider the following simple reference implementation DistMem of a shared memory in a message-passing distributed system (code shown for process p).

```
method write(x,v)          method read(x)          when Wxv is received
  M_p:=M_p[x ↦ v]            return(M_p(x))         from another process:
  causal_broadcast(Wxv)                               M_p:=M_p[x ↦ v]
  return()
```

In words, each process p maintains a local copy of a location-to-value mapping M_p. When a write of value v to location x is requested at a process p, the mapping is updated locally and then the request is sent over the network to all other processes. To read from location x, each process simply uses its local copy of the mapping. Upon receiving a write request from another process, the update is executed on the local copy.

The broadcast operation is non-blocking: it returns without waiting for the reception of the emitted messages. It is also assumed to maintain *causal consistency*, which means that (1) if some message m_1 is a cause of a later message m_2, then all processes will receive m_1 before m_2; and (2) a message m_1 is a *cause* of message m_2 when the send of m_1 is before the send of m_2 in Lamport's

⋆ This research was supported by the Israel Science Foundation (grant 814/22) and by the European Research Council (ERC) under the European Union's Horizon 2020 research and innovation programme (grant agreement no. 851811).

R. Krebbers (Ed.): ESOP 2026, LNCS 16501, pp. 373–400, 2026.
https://doi.org/10.1007/978-3-032-22720-1_14

Store Buffering (SB) (✓)	Message Passing (MP) (✗)	Coherence (COH) (✓)	Transitive Message Passing (TMP) (✗)	Independent Reads of Independent Writes (IRIW) (✓)
P_1: $\mathtt{Wx1} \to \mathtt{Ry0}$	P_1: $\mathtt{Wx1} \to \mathtt{Wy1}$	P_1: $\mathtt{Wx1} \to \mathtt{Rx2}$	P_1: $\mathtt{Wx1} \to \mathtt{Wy1}$	P_1: $\mathtt{Wx1}$
P_2: $\mathtt{Wy1} \to \mathtt{Rx0}$	P_2: $\mathtt{Ry1} \to \mathtt{Rx0}$	P_2: $\mathtt{Wx2} \to \mathtt{Rx1}$	P_2: $\mathtt{Ry1} \to \mathtt{Wz1}$	P_2: $\mathtt{Wy1}$
			P_3: $\mathtt{Rz1} \to \mathtt{Rx0}$	P_3: $\mathtt{Rx1} \to \mathtt{Ry0}$
Write-Write Synchronization (WWS) (✗)	P_1: $\mathtt{Wx1} \to \mathtt{Wy1} \to \mathtt{Wz1}$			P_4: $\mathtt{Ry1} \to \mathtt{Rx0}$
	P_2: $\mathtt{Wy2} \to \mathtt{Rx0} \to \mathtt{Rz1} \to \mathtt{Ry2}$			

Fig. 1. Examples of behaviors that are possible (✓) or impossible (✗) under DistMem. We assume that the initial value of every location is 0. In each example, every row lists the operations executed by a single process (P_i), in the order in which they occur. Operations are either writes of the form $\mathtt{Wx}v$, denoting a write of value v to location x, or reads of the form $\mathtt{Rx}v$, denoting a read of value v from location x. Message reception is treated as a background activity that is unobservable from the client's point of view and is therefore not depicted in the figure. In SB, $\mathtt{Wx1}$ is received at P_2 only after it performs $\mathtt{Rx0}$, so P_2 reads the initial value of x. Similarly for $\mathtt{Wy1}$. In MP, $\mathtt{Wy1}$ must be received at P_2 before it performs $\mathtt{Ry1}$. Since $\mathtt{Wx1}$ is causally before $\mathtt{Wy1}$, it must be received before it. But then, $\mathtt{Wx1}$ overrides the initial value of x and P_2 cannot read 0 from x. In COH, $\mathtt{Wx1}$ is received at P_2 only after it performs $\mathtt{Wx2}$, so it overrides it and the value of x is 1. Similarly for $\mathtt{Wx2}$. The explanation for TMP is similar to MP. In IRIW, the two messages of P_1 and P_2 are received in different orders in each of the other two processes. This is possible since $\mathtt{Wx1}$ and $\mathtt{Wy1}$ are not causally related. In WWS, P_2 must receive $\mathtt{Wx1}$ after performing $\mathtt{Rx0}$, and must receive $\mathtt{Wz1}$ before performing $\mathtt{Rz1}$. Since $\mathtt{Wx1}$ is causally before $\mathtt{Wy1}$, which is causally before $\mathtt{Wz1}$, $\mathtt{Wy1}$ must be received between the receive of $\mathtt{Wx1}$ and the receive of $\mathtt{Wz1}$—and thus between $\mathtt{Rx0}$ and $\mathtt{Rz1}$. Hence, this receive overrides $\mathtt{Wy2}$ and P_2 cannot read 2 from y.

happens-before [22]—the partial order that (i) contains the sequential program order of each process and (ii) places each message send before its receive.

Concrete manifestations of DistMem have to implement the causal broadcast abstraction. Implementations of causal broadcast were suggested, e.g., in [28,29]. Ahamad et al. [6], who introduced the "causal memory" (CM, for short) consistency model, implement DistMem on top of a point-to-point send/receive network employing outgoing and incoming message queues. Following this seminal work, other scalable real-world implementations, which tolerate process crashes and long partitions between datacenters, were developed (see, e.g., [24]). Researchers have also studied the verification of DistMem implementations in Coq [16,23]. In particular, the abstract operational specification in [23] is equivalent to DistMem.

Several fundamental questions arise about DistMem:

Q1 What consistency guarantees does DistMem provide? Clearly, it is weaker than sequentially consistent memory (SC) [21] (see Fig. 1 for some examples).
Q2 How do these guarantees relate to existing definitions of causally consistent shared memory? In particular, what is the relation to CM from [6]? Can DistMem consistency be specified in common declarative formalisms for weakly consistent memory?

Q3 With the goal of testing implementations of DistMem, how hard is it to check whether a given abstract execution (where message delivery is not exposed) is admitted by DistMem?

Q4 How hard is the verification of (finite-state) shared-memory programs that run on top of DistMem? How does it compare to program verification on top of a centralized (strongly consistent) memory, which is PSPACE-complete [17]?

Our Contribution. This paper addresses these questions. We also identify a subtle gap in previous work on this topic. Concretely, our contributions (in comparison to related work) are as follows:

A1 We propose a novel memory consistency model, called "causal-broadcast memory" (CBM for short). This model precisely captures the observable behaviors of DistMem. Its formulation requires the existence of valid total orders on all operations in the causal past of each process. This definition is obtained as an instance of the definition from [25], which we call CBC for "causal-broadcast consistency". In the same paper, it is related (without proof) to an implementation that lifts an arbitrary sequential transition system to a distributed system by first performing every operation locally and then spreading it over the network by causal broadcast (see Listing 1.1 below). We show that the consistency guarantees provided by this distributed implementation are precisely captured by CBC (see Cor. 1). Then, we prove that queries—operations that do not affect the local state, like reads in a memory system—need not be broadcast (see Cor. 2). As a result, since DistMem is an instance of the more general distributed implementation where queries are not broadcast and CBM is the specialization of CBC for a transition system implementing a memory (a.k.a. key-value store), we obtain the correspondence between CBM and DistMem (see Cor. 3).

A2 We relate CBM to different variants of causal memory consistency that were studied before, all weaker than SC. Our results are summarized in Fig. 2, and we provide examples to demonstrate all "anti-edges" in the figure. In particular, we show that CBM is strictly stronger than CM, which is in contrast to the claim of [25] that argued that DistMem precisely corresponds to CM. Moreover, we establish a data-race-freedom (DRF) guarantee showing that all behaviors allowed by CBM are also admitted by a stronger semantics for programs without write-write races (concurrent writes to the same location). The stronger semantics for this DRF result is "Parallel Snapshot Isolation" (PSI)—a memory model developed in the context of transactional geo-replicated systems, where write-conflicts are all resolved globally [12,30]. Importantly, whether or not a program is write-write-race-free can be checked assuming PSI, which enables client reasoning based solely on the strong semantics. To the best of our knowledge, this is the first result of this kind relating PSI to memory models of causal consistency. Moreover, our DRF guarantee holds for every model between WRA and PSI (see Fig. 2),

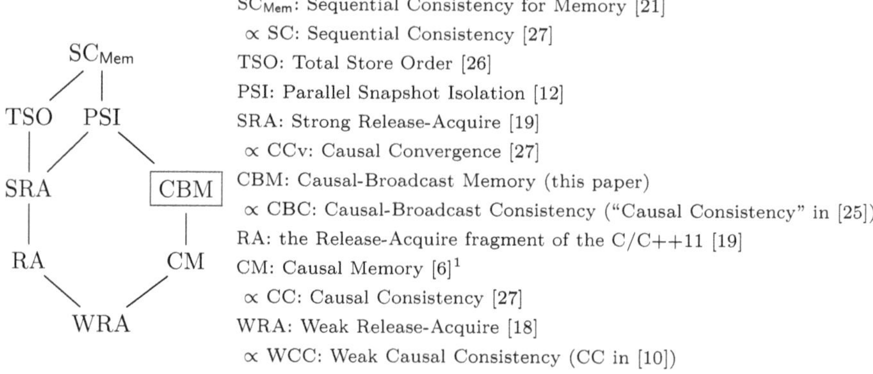

Fig. 2. Models ordered by strength (higher is stronger): Comparison of models is based on consistency of execution graphs (Def. 19), focusing solely on read and write memory accesses (discarding features that exist in some of these models, such as RMWs and transactions consisting of *multiple* accesses). Models following the $\propto$ symbol are corresponding generalizations of shared-memory consistency to general objects (see §7).

and thus it improves the DRF result from [18] that is against SRA, which is strictly weaker than PSI.

A3 We show that testing CBM-consistency of an abstract execution graph can be performed in polynomial time. The input for this problem is a graph whose vertices consist of the performed memory operations, and edges relate vertices by "program order" (the sequential order within each process) and "reads-from" relation (justifying each read action by a write action). Such execution graphs do not track message broadcasts and receives, which makes consistency testing a challenging task. To show a polynomial time complexity, we devise a definition of CBM that avoids existential quantification over total orders altogether. Instead, this definition proposes a computation that adds ordering constraints at each step and guarantees CBM-consistency if the fixpoint of that computation forms an acyclic relation. This result puts CBM together with multiple other models in terms of complexity of consistency testing [31].

A4 We show that client verification on top of CBM is undecidable. More precisely, control-state reachability is undecidable for finite state concurrent programs accessing shared memory that provides CBM. This is in contrast to decidability results for related models, such as TSO [8,3], and SRA and WRA [18] whose corresponding decision problem is decidable (with non-primitive recursive complexity). To establish undecidability, we show how CBM can simulate perfect FIFO channels, and propose a reduction from reachability in finite transition systems that communicate via two such channels, one in each direction. Notably, the undecidability does not follow from

---

[1] The formal relations between CM and CC and between CM and WRA require the assumption that values written to every location are unique (see §7.3 and §7.4).

speculation on the future (CBM forbids load-store reordering), which has been used before to establish undecidability of reachability for weak memory model: for the "Promising" model PS 2.0 [4], for Relaxed Memory Ordering (RMO) [8], and for Power [2]. Moreover, CBM does not employ Read-Modify-Writes (RMWs), which were exploited to show a similar undecidability result under the RA memory model [1].[2]

The rest of this paper is organized as follows. In §2, we present basic notations and definitions. In §3, we formalize the generic distributed implementation, of which DistMem is obtained as an instance. In §4 we define causal-broadcast consistency (CBC) and show that it declaratively characterizes histories generated by the distributed implementation. In §5, we define causal-broadcast memory (CBM), and develop an equivalent definition from which we derive a polynomial-time algorithm for testing consistency. In §6, we show the undecidability of the reachability problem for concurrent programs under DistMem. In §7, we compare CBC and CBM to other consistency criteria and weak memory models, and establish the write-write-race-freedom guarantee against PSI. Concluding remarks are in §8. Related work is discussed throughout the paper. The accompanying technical appendix provides full proofs.

2   Preliminaries

Sequences. For an alphabet Σ, we denote by Σ^* (respectively, Σ^+) the set of all finite sequences (non-empty finite sequences) over Σ. We use ϵ to denote the empty sequence. The length of a sequence s is denoted by $|s|$ (in particular $|\epsilon| = 0$). We often identify a sequence s over Σ with its underlying function from $\{1, \ldots, |s|\}$ to Σ, and write $s(k)$ for the symbol at position $1 \le k \le |s|$ in s. We write $\sigma \in s$ if the symbol σ appears in s, that is if $s(k) = \sigma$ for some $1 \le k \le |s|$. We use "$\cdot$" for the concatenation of sequences. We identify symbols with sequences of length 1, or with their singletons, when needed. Finally, functions in $\Sigma \to \Pi$ are lifted to functions in $\Sigma^* \to \Pi^*$ in the obvious way.

Relations. Given a (binary) relation R, $\mathsf{dom}(R)$ and $\mathsf{codom}(R)$ denote its domain and codomain, and $R^?$, R^+, and R^* denote its reflexive, transitive, and reflexive-transitive closures. The inverse of a relation R is denoted by R^{-1}, and the (left) composition of two relations R_1 and R_2 is denoted by $R_1 \, ; R_2$ (that is, $\langle x, y \rangle \in R_1 ; R_2$ iff there exists z such that $\langle x, z \rangle \in R_1$ and $\langle z, y \rangle \in R_2$). The restriction of a relation R on a set A to a subset $B \subseteq A$ is given by $R|_B = R \cap (B \times B)$. We denote by $[A]$ the identity relation on a set A. In particular, $[A] \, ; R \, ; [B] = R \cap (A \times B)$. When A is finite, we write $[a_1, \ldots, a_n]$ instead of $[\{a_1, \ldots, a_n\}]$. For an acyclic relation R on a finite set A and a subset $B \subseteq A$, we denote by $\mathsf{lin}(R, B)$ the set of all (strict) total orders on B extending $R|_B$. When R is a total order on a set B, we write $\mathsf{seq}(R)$ for the sequence enumerating B following R. This notation is lifted to sets by defining $\mathsf{seq}(\mathcal{R}) \triangleq \{\mathsf{seq}(R) \mid R \in \mathcal{R}\}$.

---

[2] To our knowledge, decidability of reachability under RA *without RMWs* is open.

Listing 1.1. Distributed implementation based on causal broadcast (for process p). We assume a given transducer with set of states Q, initial sate q_0, and transition function $\delta : Q \times O \to D \times Q$, where O is a set of operations and D is a domain of output values. We also assume a set of operations $B \subseteq O$ that is broadcast to other processes. Each process p maintains its local state $q_p \in Q$ (initialized to q_0).

```
method do(o)                    when o is received from another process:
  ⟨d,q_p⟩ := δ(q_p,o)               ⟨_,q_p⟩ := δ(q_p,o)
  if o ∈ B then
    causal_broadcast(o)
  return(d)
```

Labeled Transition Systems. A *labeled transition system* (LTS) is a tuple $A = \langle Q, \Sigma, q_0, T \rangle$, where Q is a set of *states*, Σ is an *alphabet*, $q_0 \in Q$ is the *initial state*, and $T \subseteq Q \times \Sigma \times Q$ is a set of *transitions*. We denote by $A.\mathsf{Q}$, $A.\Sigma$, $A.\mathsf{q_0}$, and $A.\mathsf{T}$ the components of an LTS A. We write $\xrightarrow{}_A$ for the relation $\{\langle q, q' \rangle \mid \langle q, \sigma, q' \rangle \in A.\mathsf{T}\}$ and $\to_A$ for $\bigcup_{\sigma \in \Sigma} \xrightarrow{\sigma}_A$. A state $q \in A.\mathsf{Q}$ is *reachable* in A if $A.\mathsf{q_0} \to_A^* q$. A sequence $\sigma_1,\dots,\sigma_n$ (for $n \geq 0$) is a *trace of A with final state q* if $A.\mathsf{q_0} \xrightarrow{\sigma_1}_A \cdots \xrightarrow{\sigma_n}_A q$. Our LTSs often employ a distinguished label $\varepsilon \in A.\Sigma$, marking *silent* transitions. A sequence $tr \in (A.\Sigma \setminus \{\varepsilon\})^*$ is an *observable trace of A with final state q* if it is obtained from a trace of A with final state q by removing all ε labels. We denote the set of all observable traces of A with final state q by $\mathsf{otraces}(A, q)$, and let $\mathsf{otraces}(A) \triangleq \bigcup_{q \in A.\mathsf{Q}} \mathsf{otraces}(A, q)$.

3   A Distributed Reference Implementation

Listing 1.1 presents a generic distributed implementation. It generalizes DistMem (from §1), and applies to any given transducer S that determines the local behavior and set B of *broadcast operations*. Intuitively, each process maintains its local state, which is a state of the transducer S. To perform an operation o, the process uses S on the current local state to get the next state and the returned value. Then, if $o \in B$, the process broadcasts o to the other processes using the causal broadcast abstraction. Finally, the process returns the value to its caller. In turn, when receiving o from another process, the process updates its local state using the transducer S on the current local state (and dismiss the return value). The parametric set B allows us to capture implementations like DistMem, where some operations (reads for DistMem) are not broadcast.

This section is devoted to formulate the implementation in Listing 1.1 as an LTS, which we denote by $\mathsf{Dist}(S, B)$ (Dist stands for 'distributed'). We start by defining objects, specifications, and transducers (§3.1), and continue by defining *message sequence charts*, used to give the formal meaning to the causal broadcast abstraction (§3.2). Then, the definition of $\mathsf{Dist}(S, B)$ uses the two parts (§3.3).

3.1   Transducers and Objects

$\mathsf{Dist}(S, B)$ applies to a general transducer, which determines the local semantics of the object.

Definition 1. An *object* $\mathcal{O} = \langle O, D \rangle$ consists of a set of *operations* O and a *domain of (output) values* D. We let $\mathsf{Lab}(\mathcal{O}) \triangleq O \times D$ and refer to its elements as *labels*. For $l = \langle o, d \rangle \in \mathsf{Lab}(\mathcal{O})$, the functions op and out retrieve its operation (o) and output value (d). A *specification* for $\mathcal{O}$ is a prefix-closed set $Spec \subseteq \mathsf{Lab}(\mathcal{O})^*$.

Definition 2. A (deterministic) *transducer* for an object $\mathcal{O} = \langle O, D \rangle$ is a tuple $S = \langle Q, q_0, \delta \rangle$, where Q is a set of *states*, $q_0 \in Q$ is the *initial state*, and $\delta : Q \times O \rightarrow D \times Q$ is a *transition function*. We denote by $S.\mathsf{Q}$, $S.\mathsf{q_0}$, and $S.\mathsf{T}$ the components of S. The transition function is lifted to $\delta^* : Q \times O^* \rightarrow Q$ as expected: $\delta(q, \langle \rangle) = q$ and $\delta(q, o \cdot \overline{o}) = \delta(q', \overline{o})$ where $\delta(q, o) = \langle \_, q' \rangle$. The specification (for $\mathcal{O}$) *derived* from S consists of all sequences $\langle o_1, d_1 \rangle, \langle o_2, d_2 \rangle, \ldots, \langle o_n, d_n \rangle$ for which there are states $q_1, q_2, \ldots, q_n$ such that $\delta(q_{i-1}, o_i) = \langle d_i, q_i \rangle$ for $1 \leq i \leq n$.

Specifications derived from transducers have the additional property that all operations are always enabled. That is, for every $s \in Spec$ and $o \in O$, we have $s \cdot \langle o, d \rangle \in Spec$ for some $d \in D$.

The central example used throughout the paper is *memory*:

Example 1. Given a set Loc of *locations*, a set Val of *values*, and a distinguished *initial value* $\mathsf{v_{init}} \in \mathsf{Val}$, the object $\mathsf{Mem} = \langle O_{\mathsf{Mem}}, D_{\mathsf{Mem}} \rangle$ is defined as follows. The set O_{Mem} consists of *write operations* of the form $\mathtt{W}xv$ and *read operations* of the form $\mathtt{R}x$, where $x \in \mathsf{Loc}$ and $v \in \mathsf{Val}$. We use the functions $\mathtt{loc}$ to retrieve the location (x) of an operation and $\mathtt{val}$ to retrieve the value (v) of a write operation. The domain is $D_{\mathsf{Mem}} = \mathsf{Val} \uplus \{\bot\}$ ($\bot$ is used for the output of write operations). The transducer for Mem is given by $S_{\mathsf{Mem}} = \langle Q, q_0, \delta \rangle$, where $Q = \mathsf{Loc} \rightarrow \mathsf{Val}$; $q_0 = \lambda x. \mathsf{v_{init}}$; $\delta(q, \mathtt{W}xv) = \langle \bot, q[x \mapsto v] \rangle$ for all $q \in Q$, $x \in \mathsf{Loc}$, and $v \in \mathsf{Val}$; and $\delta(q, \mathtt{R}x) = \langle q(x), q \rangle$ for all $q \in Q$ and $x \in \mathsf{Loc}$. The derived specification, denoted by $Spec_{\mathsf{Mem}}$, consists of all sequences s satisfying the following:

- If $\langle \mathtt{W}xv, d \rangle \in s$, then $d = \bot$.
- If $s = s_1 \cdot \langle \mathtt{W}xv, \bot \rangle \cdot s_2 \cdot \langle \mathtt{R}x, d \rangle \cdot s_3$ and $\langle \mathtt{W}xv', \bot \rangle \notin s_2$ for every $v' \in \mathsf{Val}$, then $d = v$.
- If $s = s_1 \cdot \langle \mathtt{R}x, d \rangle \cdot s_2$ and $\langle \mathtt{W}xv, \bot \rangle \notin s_1$ for every $v \in \mathsf{Val}$, then $d = \mathsf{v_{init}}$.

In our examples, we assume $\mathsf{Loc} = \{\mathsf{x}, \mathsf{y}, \ldots\}$, $\mathsf{Val} = \mathbb{N}$, and $\mathsf{v_{init}} = 0$. For brevity, we write $\mathtt{W}xv$ for $\langle \mathtt{W}xv, \bot \rangle$ and $\mathtt{R}xv$ for $\langle \mathtt{R}x, v \rangle$.

Below, it is useful to distinguish a particular kind of operations, called "queries":

Definition 3. Let $Spec$ be a specification for object $\mathcal{O} = \langle O, D \rangle$. An operation $o \in O$ is a *query* w.r.t. $Spec$ if the following hold:

- If $s_1 \cdot \langle o, d \rangle \cdot s_2 \in Spec$, then $s_1 \cdot s_2 \in Spec$.
- If $s_1 \cdot s_2 \in Spec$, then $s_1 \cdot \langle o, d \rangle \cdot s_2 \in Spec$ for some $d \in D$.

An operation is an *update* if it is not a query. We denote by Q_{Spec} and U_{Spec} the subsets of O consisting of all queries and updates w.r.t. *Spec*, respectively.

In particular, $\mathsf{Q}_{Spec_{\mathsf{Mem}}}$, the set of queries w.r.t. the memory specification, is the set of read operations, and $\mathsf{U}_{Spec_{\mathsf{Mem}}}$, the set of updates w.r.t. the memory specification, is the set of write operations. Clearly, transitions in a transducer S that do not change the internal state are queries, i.e., if $S.\mathrm{T}(q,o) = \langle \_, q \rangle$ for every $q \in S.\mathsf{Q}$, then o is a query w.r.t. the derived specification.

3.2   Message Sequence Charts

To formalize causal broadcast, we employ *message sequence charts* (which we simply call *charts*). These are directed graphs whose vertices, called *events*, represent actions performed during the run, and edges relate the actions executed in the same process (*"program order"*), as well as the broadcast of each message to its receives (*"propagation relation"*). Charts are used to track the propagation of messages during runs, and make sure that the causal consistency condition holds when messages are received. From here on, we assume a set $\mathsf{Ps} = \{\mathsf{P}_1, \ldots, \mathsf{P}_N\}$ of process identifiers. The formal definitions are given next.

Definition 4. An *event* e for object $\mathcal{O} = \langle O, D \rangle$ is a tuple $\langle p, sn, l \rangle$, where $p \in \mathsf{Ps}$, called the event's *process identifier*, $sn \in \mathbb{N}$, called the event's *serial identifier*, and $l \in \mathsf{Lab}(\mathcal{O}) \cup \{\mathtt{rcv}\}$, called the event's *label*. The functions $\mathtt{proc}$, $\mathtt{sn}$ and $\mathtt{lab}$ return the process identifier (p), serial identifier (sn) and label (l). When $\mathtt{lab}(e) = \mathtt{rcv}$, e is called a *receive event*, and otherwise (i.e., $\mathtt{lab}(e) \in \mathsf{Lab}(\mathcal{O})$), e is called a *do event*. We denote by $\mathsf{Evs}(\mathcal{O})$, Rcv, and $\mathsf{Do}(\mathcal{O})$ the sets of all events for $\mathcal{O}$, all receive events, and all do events for $\mathcal{O}$ (respectively). We lift $\mathtt{op}$ and $\mathtt{out}$ from labels to do events. For $E \subseteq \mathsf{Evs}(\mathcal{O})$, $p \in \mathsf{Ps}$, and $O' \subseteq O$, we let $E|_p \triangleq \{e \in E \mid \mathtt{proc}(e) = p\}$ and $E|_{O'} \triangleq \{e \in E \mid \mathtt{op}(e) \in O'\}$.

Definition 5. A relation po is a *program order* for a set $E \subseteq \mathsf{Evs}(\mathcal{O})$ if $po = \biguplus_{p \in \mathsf{Ps}} po^p$, for some relations po^p, such that each po^p is a strict total order on $E|_p$.

Definition 6. A relation $prop$ is a *propagation relation* for a set $E \subseteq \mathsf{Evs}(\mathcal{O})$ if the following hold:

(1) If $\langle e_1, e_2 \rangle \in prop$, then $e_1, e_2 \in E$.
(2) If $\langle e_1, e_2 \rangle \in prop$, then $e_1 \in \mathsf{Do}(\mathcal{O})$, $e_2 \in \mathsf{Rcv}$, and $\mathtt{proc}(e_1) \neq \mathtt{proc}(e_2)$.
(3) $E \cap \mathsf{Rcv} \subseteq \mathsf{codom}(prop)$.
(4) If $\langle e_1, e \rangle, \langle e_2, e \rangle \in prop$, then $e_1 = e_2$.
(5) If $\langle e, e_1 \rangle, \langle e, e_2 \rangle \in prop$ and $\mathtt{proc}(e_1) = \mathtt{proc}(e_2)$, then $e_1 = e_2$.

For $e_2 \in E \cap \mathsf{Rcv}$, we write $prop^{-1}(e_2)$ to refer to the unique event e_1 with $\langle e_1, e_2 \rangle \in prop$. For a set $E' \subseteq E$, we let $prop^{-1}(E') \triangleq \{prop^{-1}(e) \mid e \in E' \cap \mathsf{Rcv}\}$.

The conditions above ensure that the propagation relation justifies every receive event by a *single* broadcast of a *different* process, and that every broadcast justifies *at most one* receive event of every other process (since a process cannot receive twice the same message). We now have all ingredients to define charts:

Definition 7. A *message sequence chart* (*chart*, for short) for an object $\mathcal{O}$ is a tuple $C = \langle E, po, prop \rangle$, where $E \subseteq \mathsf{Evs}(\mathcal{O})$ is a finite set of events for $\mathcal{O}$, *po* is a program order for E, and *prop* is a propagation relation for E. We denote the components of C by $C.\mathsf{E}$, $C.\mathsf{po}$, and $C.\mathsf{prop}$. For $E' \subseteq \mathsf{Evs}(\mathcal{O})$, we write $C.E'$ for $C.\mathsf{E} \cap E'$ (e.g., $C.\mathsf{Rcv} = C.\mathsf{E} \cap \mathsf{Rcv}$).

Example 2. Consider the following "chart candidates". Events of each process are enumerated from left to right following their po-order and green edges represent the propagation relation:

P_1: Wx1 → Ry0 → rcv P_1: Wx1 → Ry0 → rcv P_1: Wx1 → Ry0 → rcv → rcv

P_2: Wy1 → Rx0 → rcv P_2: Wy1 → Rx0 → rcv P_2: Wy1 → Rx0

The left example describes a valid chart for Mem. The middle one is not a chart since conditions (3) and (4) of Def. 6 are invalidated: some receive receives no messages and another receives more than one. The right example is also not a chart since condition (5) of Def. 6 is invalidated: an event is received more than once by the same process.

An important derived relation in charts is *visibility*, which corresponds to Lamport's *happens-before* [22]—the partial order that (i) contains the sequential program orders and (ii) places each message send before its receive:

Definition 8. The *visibility relation* induced by a chart C (for object $\mathcal{O}$), denoted by $C.\mathtt{vis}$, is given by $C.\mathtt{vis} \triangleq (C.\mathsf{po} \cup C.\mathsf{prop})^+$.

3.3 An Operational Definition of $\mathsf{Dist}(S, B)$

We define $\mathsf{Dist}(S, B)$—the LTS that captures the algorithm in Listing 1.1 using transducer S for object $\mathcal{O} = \langle O, D \rangle$ that only broadcasts operations from a set $B \subseteq O$. DistMem is the instance given by $\mathsf{Dist}(S_{\mathsf{Mem}}, \mathsf{Wr})$, where Wr is the set of write operations. Also, Algorithm 1 from [25] using transducer S and broadcasting all operations is obtained by $\mathsf{Dist}(S, O)$.

The states of $\mathsf{Dist}(S, B)$ are of the form $\langle C, \bar{q} \rangle$, where C is a chart for $\mathcal{O}$ and $\bar{q}$ is a mapping from Ps to $S.\mathsf{Q}$ (the set of states of S). The chart C tracks the generated chart along the run, used to determine what messages can be received at any point, and $\bar{q}$ remembers the local state of each process.

The following notation is useful for the transitions definition:

Notation 1 *The chart obtained from a chart C by adding a do event e, denoted by $\mathsf{Add}(C, e)$, is $\langle E', po', C.\mathsf{prop} \rangle$, where $E' = C.\mathsf{E} \uplus \{e\}$ and $po' = C.\mathsf{po} \cup (C.\mathsf{E}|_{\mathrm{proc}(e)} \times \{e\})$. The chart obtained from a chart C by adding a receive event e receiving from e', denoted by $\mathsf{Add}(C, e, e')$, is $\langle E', po', prop' \rangle$, where E' and po' are as above and $prop' = C.\mathsf{prop} \cup \{\langle e', e \rangle\}$. (We use this notation when $prop'$ satisfies the conditions of Def. 6 for E', so that $\mathsf{Add}(C, e, e')$ is indeed a chart.)*

Definition 9. Let $S = \langle Q, q_0, \delta \rangle$ be a transducer for object $\mathcal{O} = \langle O, D \rangle$, and $B \subseteq O$. $\mathsf{Dist}(S, B)$ is the LTS whose states are tuples $\langle C, \bar{q} \rangle$, where C is a chart for $\mathcal{O}$ and $\bar{q} \in \mathsf{Ps} \to Q$; its alphabet is $(\mathsf{Ps} \times \mathsf{Lab}(\mathcal{O})) \cup \{\varepsilon\}$; its initial state is $\langle C_0, \bar{q}_0 \rangle$, where $C_0 = \langle \emptyset, \emptyset, \emptyset \rangle$ and $\bar{q}_0 = \lambda p.\, q_0$; and its transitions are given by:

$$
\frac{
\begin{array}{c}
\langle d, q' \rangle = \delta(\bar{q}(p), o) \\
\mathsf{proc}(e) = p \qquad \mathsf{lab}(e) = \langle o, d \rangle \\
C' = \mathsf{Add}(C, e)
\end{array}
}{
\langle C, \bar{q} \rangle \xrightarrow{p, \langle o, d \rangle}_{\mathsf{Dist}(S,B)} \langle C', \bar{q}[p \mapsto q'] \rangle
} \text{ DO}
\qquad
\frac{
\begin{array}{c}
e' \in C.\mathsf{Do}(\mathcal{O})|_B \qquad e' \notin \mathsf{dom}(C.\mathsf{prop}^? \,;\, [C.\mathsf{E}|_p]) \\
\mathsf{Do}(\mathcal{O})|_B \cap \mathsf{dom}(C.\mathsf{vis}\,;\,[e']) \subseteq \mathsf{dom}(C.\mathsf{prop}^? \,;\, [C.\mathsf{E}|_p]) \\
\langle \_, q' \rangle = \delta(\bar{q}(p), \mathsf{op}(e')) \\
\mathsf{proc}(e) = p \qquad \mathsf{lab}(e) = \mathsf{rcv} \\
C' = \mathsf{Add}(C, e, e')
\end{array}
}{
\langle C, \bar{q} \rangle \xrightarrow{\varepsilon}_{\mathsf{Dist}(S,B)} \langle C', \bar{q}[p \mapsto q'] \rangle
} \text{ RECEIVE}
$$

In words, when a process p performs $\mathsf{do}(o)$, the output d and the new state q' are calculated using δ according to the current state $\bar{q}(p)$, and the corresponding event is added to the chart C after all previous events of p. In turn, at any point p may receive o from a different process. Then, the new state q' is calculated using δ according to the current state $\bar{q}(p)$, and the corresponding receive event e is added to C after all previous events of p. Also, prop is updated by adding an edge from e' to e, where e' is the broadcast event (whose operation is o). The condition $e' \in C.\mathsf{Do}(\mathcal{O})|_B$ expresses that o belongs to the set of operations that are broadcast. The condition $e' \notin \mathsf{dom}(C.\mathsf{prop}^? \,;\, [C.\mathsf{E}|_p])$ means that the broadcast was executed by a different process, and that the message cannot be received twice by p. The condition $\mathsf{Do}(\mathcal{O})|_B \cap \mathsf{dom}(C.\mathsf{vis}\,;\,[e']) \subseteq \mathsf{dom}(C.\mathsf{prop}^? \,;\, [C.\mathsf{E}|_p])$ captures the fact that the broadcast is causal: all operations that were executed vis-before e' (and should be broadcast according to B) must have already been received by p (or performed by it) before it can receive e'. Note that receive transitions are labeled with ε, since we treat them as *silent*—they are not observable to client programs that use $\mathsf{Dist}(S, B)$.

Example 3. Let C be the following chart for Mem:

$$\mathsf{P}_1: \ \mathsf{Wx1} \twoheadrightarrow \mathsf{Wy1}$$

Let $\bar{q} : \{\mathsf{P}_1, \mathsf{P}_2\} \to S_{\mathsf{Mem}}.\mathsf{Q}$ be the mapping given by: $\bar{q}(\mathsf{P}_1)(x) = \bar{q}(\mathsf{P}_1)(y) = 1$ and $\bar{q}(\mathsf{P}_2)(x) = \bar{q}(\mathsf{P}_2)(y) = 0$. The state $\langle C, \bar{q} \rangle$ is reachable in $\mathsf{DistMem}$, by performing two DO steps (with transition labels $\langle \mathsf{P}_1, \mathsf{Wx1} \rangle$ and $\langle \mathsf{P}_1, \mathsf{Wy1} \rangle$). Now, assume we want P_2 to DO the read operation $\mathsf{Ry1}$ (attempting to get the behavior presented in the MP example in Fig. 1). For the output to be 1, $\bar{q}(\mathsf{P}_2)(y)$ must first be updated using a RECEIVE step in P_2, with the event labeled $\mathsf{Wy1}$ (performed by P_1) as the received event, e'. However, we cannot perform this step from C, since the condition $\mathsf{W} \cap \mathsf{dom}(C.\mathsf{vis}\,;\,[e']) \subseteq \mathsf{dom}(C.\mathsf{prop}^? \,;\, [C.\mathsf{E}|_{\mathsf{P}_2}])$ (where W is the set of write events) does not hold: the event labeled $\mathsf{Wx1}$ is po-before (therefore, vis-before) e', but it has not been received in P_2 yet. P_2 must first RECEIVE the event labeled $\mathsf{Wx1}$, which *is* a valid step. Then it can RECEIVE e', and we can finally perform the desired DO step and obtain the following chart:

$$
\begin{array}{ccc}
\mathsf{P}_1: & \mathsf{Wx1} \twoheadrightarrow & \mathsf{Wy1} \\
& \downarrow & \downarrow \\
\mathsf{P}_2: & \mathsf{rcv} \twoheadrightarrow \mathsf{rcv} \twoheadrightarrow & \mathsf{Ry1}
\end{array}
$$

Note that because of the first RECEIVE step, now $\bar{q}(\mathrm{P}_2)(\mathrm{x}) = 1$, and the operation Rx0 cannot be added to P_2 (without performing more writes first). This explains why the behavior of MP is impossible for DistMem.

4   A Declarative Presentation of $\mathsf{Dist}(S, B)$

We provide a declarative (a.k.a. axiomatic) presentation of $\mathsf{Dist}(S, B)$. Such presentation focuses on which behaviors are allowed by the system, rather than on how they are obtained operationally. The declarative presentation is obtained in two steps. First, we precisely characterize the charts that are generated in runs of $\mathsf{Dist}(S, B)$ (§4.1). Then, we define consistent *histories*, where receive events are hidden (§4.2). Finally, we use this presentation to show that broadcasting queries has no observable effect (§4.3).

4.1   A Characterization of Charts Generated by $\mathsf{Dist}(S, B)$

We identify conditions on C that ensure that it is generated by $\mathsf{Dist}(S, B)$.

Definition 10. A chart C (for object $\mathcal{O}$) is:

1. *generated by* $\mathsf{Dist}(S, B)$ *with final state* $\bar{q}$ if $\langle C, \bar{q} \rangle$ is reachable in $\mathsf{Dist}(S, B)$.
2. *generated by* $\mathsf{Dist}(S, B)$ if C is generated by $\mathsf{Dist}(S, B)$ with some final state.

In short, charts generated by $\mathsf{Dist}(S, B)$: (i) faithfully follow causal broadcast where only operations from B are broadcast; and (ii) respect the local executions of S. First, we encode what "causal broadcast" means:

Definition 11. A chart C for object $\mathcal{O} = \langle O, D \rangle$ is *causal for a set* $B \subseteq O$ if the following hold:

(1) $\mathsf{dom}(C.\mathsf{prop}) \subseteq \mathsf{Do}(\mathcal{O})|_B$.
(2) $C.\mathsf{vis}$ is irreflexive.
(3) $\mathsf{Do}(\mathcal{O})|_B \cap \mathsf{dom}(C.\mathsf{vis}\,;C.\mathsf{prop}\,;[C.\mathsf{E}|_p]) \subseteq \mathsf{dom}(C.\mathsf{prop}^?\,;[C.\mathsf{E}|_p])$ for every $p \in \mathsf{Ps}$.
(4) $C.\mathsf{vis}\,;C.\mathsf{prop}\,;C.\mathsf{po}\,;C.\mathsf{prop}^{-1}$ is irreflexive.

C is called *causal* if it is causal for O (the set of all object operations).

Condition (1) ensures that only the events whose operation is in B are broadcast to other processes. Condition (2) ensures that the visibility relation is a partial order. Condition (3) ensures that if some event e propagates to some process p, then all events in $\mathsf{Do}(\mathcal{O})|_B$ that are visible at e also propagate to p. Condition (4) puts further restrictions on the propagation order requiring the events visible at e to propagate to p before e itself. Taken together, the above conditions formalize the semantics of causal broadcast. In particular, they ensure that if $\langle e_1, e_2 \rangle \in C.\mathsf{vis}|_{\mathsf{Do}(\mathcal{O})|_B}$ and $\langle e_2, r_2 \rangle \in C.\mathsf{prop}$, then either $\langle e_1, r_1 \rangle \in C.\mathsf{prop}$ for some r_1 with $\langle r_1, r_2 \rangle \in C.\mathsf{po}$, or $\langle e_1, r_2 \rangle \in C.\mathsf{po}$. This definition can be seen as an adaptation of *causally-ordered message sequence charts* from [14, Definition 2.4] for broadcasts, instead of point-to-point send, and with the possibility to "block" some operations from being broadcast.

Example 4. Consider the following charts for Mem.

$$P_1: \mathtt{rcv} \to \mathtt{Wx1} \qquad\qquad P_1: \mathtt{Wx1} \to \mathtt{Rx1} \to \mathtt{Wy1} \qquad\qquad P_1: \mathtt{Wx1} \to \mathtt{Wy1}$$
$$P_2: \mathtt{rcv} \to \mathtt{Wy1} \qquad\qquad P_2: \mathtt{rcv} \to \mathtt{rcv} \qquad\qquad\qquad P_2: \mathtt{rcv} \to \mathtt{rcv}$$

The left chart is not causal since condition (2) of Def. 11 is invalidated: we have a $\mathtt{vis}$ cycle. The middle one is not causal since condition (3) is invalidated: the event labeled $\mathtt{Rx1}$ has $\mathtt{vis}\,;\mathtt{prop}$-path to P_2 but not $\mathtt{prop}^?$-path to P_2. However, this chart *is* causal for the set of write operations. The right chart is not causal since condition (4) is invalidated: there is a $\mathtt{vis}$-path from the event labeled $\mathtt{Wx1}$ to the one labeled $\mathtt{Wy1}$, and they both propagate to P_2 but in the opposite order.

Next, we formalize the consistency of a chart w.r.t. the local computation at each process. This is done by requiring that the sequence of events observed at each process matches the derived specification. However, when justifying the outputs in one process, we may "reevaluate" the outputs of events originated at other processes (see Ex. 5 below). This corresponds to the fact that outputs are not broadcast and ignored when invoking S when operations are received.

Definition 12. The *event sequence observed* at a process $p \in \mathsf{Ps}$ in a chart C, denoted by $\mathsf{obs}_p(C)$, is the sequence of do events obtained from $\mathsf{seq}(C.\mathsf{po}|_{\mathsf{Evs}|_p})$ by replacing each receive event e with $C.\mathsf{prop}^{-1}(e)$.

Definition 13. A sequence $s' \in \mathsf{Do}(\mathcal{O})^*$ is a *reevaluation* of a sequence $s \in \mathsf{Do}(\mathcal{O})^*$ if they are identical except possibly for events' outputs (i.e., $|s'| = |s|$ and for every $1 \le k \le |s'|$, $\mathsf{proc}(s'(k)) = \mathsf{proc}(s(k))$, $\mathsf{sn}(s'(k)) = \mathsf{sn}(s(k))$, and $\mathsf{op}(s'(k)) = \mathsf{op}(s(k)))$. A reevaluation s' of s *preserves* a set $E \subseteq \mathsf{Evs}(\mathcal{O})$ if $\mathsf{out}(s'(k)) = \mathsf{out}(s(k))$ whenever $s(k) \in E$. We denote by $\mathsf{reeval}(s, E)$ the set of all reevaluations of s that preserve E.

Definition 14. Let *Spec* be a specification for an object $\mathcal{O}$.

1. A sequence $s \in \mathsf{Do}(\mathcal{O})^*$ *respects Spec* if $\mathtt{lab}(s) \in Spec$.
2. A chart C for $\mathcal{O}$ *respects Spec* if for every $p \in \mathsf{Ps}$, some reevaluation $s \in \mathsf{reeval}(\mathsf{obs}_p(C), \mathsf{Evs}|_p)$ respects *Spec*.

Example 5. Consider the following chart C for Mem:

$$P_1: \mathtt{Wx1} \to \mathtt{rcv} \to \mathtt{rcv} \to \mathtt{Rx2}$$
$$P_2: \mathtt{Rx0} \to \mathtt{Wx2}$$

$\mathtt{lab}(\mathsf{obs}_{P_1}(C))$ is $\langle \mathtt{Wx1}, \mathtt{Rx0}, \mathtt{Wx2}, \mathtt{Rx2} \rangle$. This sequence is *not* in $Spec_{\mathsf{Mem}}$, so $\mathsf{obs}_{P_1}(C)$ does not respect $Spec_{\mathsf{Mem}}$. However, if we change the output of the event labeled $\mathtt{Rx0}$ from 0 to 1, we obtain a reevaluation of $\mathsf{obs}_{P_1}(C)$ that preserves $C.\mathsf{E}|_{P_1}$ (since the process of this read event is P_2) and respects $Spec_{\mathsf{Mem}}$. Also, $\mathsf{obs}_{P_2}(C)$ respects $Spec_{\mathsf{Mem}}$. Therefore, C respects $Spec_{\mathsf{Mem}}$.

With the above definitions we characterize the charts generated by $\mathsf{Dist}(S, B)$:

Theorem 1. *Let S be a transducer for object $\mathcal{O} = \langle O, D \rangle$, Spec be the derived specification, and $B \subseteq O$. A chart C for $\mathcal{O}$ is generated by $\mathsf{Dist}(S, B)$ iff C is causal for B and respects Spec.*

4.2 Causal-Broadcast Consistency

The above characterization is rather concrete, as it tracks message propagation in events. In this section, we provide a more abstract declarative presentation, which is decoupled from the underlying message-passing implementation. Our definition adopts the consistency conditions proposed in [25].

Definition 15. A *history* for object $\mathcal{O}$ is a pair $H = \langle E, po \rangle$, where $E \subseteq \mathsf{Do}(\mathcal{O})$ is a finite set of do events for $\mathcal{O}$ and po is a program order for E. The history *induced by a chart* C *(for $\mathcal{O}$)*, denoted by $\mathsf{H}(C)$, is given by $\mathsf{H}(C) \triangleq \langle C.\mathsf{Do}(\mathcal{O}), po|_{\mathsf{Do}(\mathcal{O})} \rangle$ (i.e., it is obtained from C by removing all receive events and propagation edges). The notations used for charts (e.g., $C.\mathsf{po}$) are also employed for histories (when applicable). We say that a history H is *generated by* $\mathsf{Dist}(S, B)$ if some chart C with $\mathsf{H}(C) = H$ is generated by $\mathsf{Dist}(S, B)$.

Since the propagation relation is abstracted away, consistency of histories cannot refer to the event sequence observed at each process. Instead, the definition uses existential quantification. It requires the existence of a causal order—corresponding to the chart's visibility relation—and a collection of event sequences, one sequence per process to justify its own output values in a way that aligns with the causal order and adheres to the specification.

Definition 16. A relation co is a *causal order* for a history H if it is a partial order on $H.\mathrm{E}$ extending $H.\mathsf{po}$. The *causal past* w.r.t. co of an event $e \in H.\mathrm{E}$, denoted $co^{-1}(e)$, is given by $co^{-1}(e) \triangleq \mathsf{dom}(co^? \, ; [e])$. For a set $E' \subseteq H.\mathrm{E}$, we let $co^{-1}(E') \triangleq \bigcup_{e \in E'} co^{-1}(e)$.

Definition 17. A history H for $\mathcal{O}$ is *causal-broadcast consistent* (CBC, for short) w.r.t. a specification *Spec* for $\mathcal{O}$ if there exist a causal order co for H and a sequence s_p for each $p \in \mathsf{Ps}$ such that:

(1) $s_p \in \mathsf{seq}(\mathsf{lin}(co, co^{-1}(H.\mathrm{E}|_p)))$.
(2) Some $s'_p \in \mathsf{reeval}(s_p, \mathsf{Evs}|_p)$ respects *Spec*.
(3) If $\mathtt{proc}(s_p(j)) = p$, then $\langle s_p(i), s_p(j) \rangle \in co$ for every $1 \leq i < j$.

Condition (1) requires that each s_p totally orders the causal past of p in a way that agrees with co. Condition (2) requires that s_p indeed matches the local computation in process p (in the same way $\mathsf{obs}_p(C)$ does so in a chart C that respects *Spec*). Condition (3) requires that for every $e \in H.\mathrm{E}|_p$, *only* its causal past comes before it in s_p (corresponds to the notion of a "causal past-constrained serialization" from [25]). Note that two events e, e' may be ordered differently by distinct processes, but if $\mathtt{proc}(e') = p$ and e appears before e' in s_p, then condition (3) forces $\langle e, e' \rangle \in co$, which means that all other processes also have to order e before e' (due to condition (1)).

Example 6. Let C be the chart from Ex. 5. $\mathsf{H}(C)$ is CBC w.r.t. $Spec_{\mathsf{Mem}}$: we can take $co = C.\mathtt{vis}|_{\mathsf{Do}(\mathsf{Mem})}$, $s_{\mathsf{P}_1} = \mathsf{obs}_{\mathsf{P}_1}(C)$, and $s_{\mathsf{P}_2} = \mathsf{obs}_{\mathsf{P}_2}(C)$.

The next example shows the effect of condition (3):

Example 7. Consider the following histories:

P_1: $\mathsf{Wx1} \to \mathsf{Ry1} \to \mathsf{Wz1} \to \mathsf{Rx1}$

P_2: $\mathsf{Wx2} \to \mathsf{Wy1} \to \mathsf{Rz1} \to \mathsf{Rx2}$

P_1: $\mathsf{Wx1} \to \mathsf{Wy2}$

P_2: $\mathsf{Wx4} \to \mathsf{Ry2} \to \mathsf{Rx4} \to \mathsf{Wz3}$

P_3: $\mathsf{Rz3} \to \mathsf{Rx1}$

Both histories would be consistent (w.r.t. $Spec_{\mathsf{Mem}}$) without condition (3) in Def. 17. For instance, for the history on the left, we could choose[3] $co = (po \cup \{\langle \mathsf{W}y1, \mathsf{R}y1 \rangle, \langle \mathsf{W}z1, \mathsf{R}z1 \rangle \})^+$, and the following sequences:

$$s_{\mathsf{P}_1} = \langle \mathsf{Wx2}, \mathsf{Wx1}, \mathsf{Wy1}, \mathsf{Ry1}, \mathsf{Wz1}, \mathsf{Rx1} \rangle \quad s_{\mathsf{P}_2} = \langle \mathsf{Wx1}, \mathsf{Wx2}, \mathsf{Wy1}, \mathsf{Ry1}, \mathsf{Wz1}, \mathsf{Rz1}, \mathsf{Rx2} \rangle$$

Note that condition (3) does not hold, e.g., $\mathsf{Wx2}$ is before $\mathsf{Wx1}$ in s_{P_1}, $\mathsf{Wx1}$ belongs to P_1, but $\langle \mathsf{Wx2}, \mathsf{Wx1} \rangle \notin co$. Thus, this choice cannot work for DistMem: if P_1 received the message about $\mathsf{Wx2}$ before its $\mathsf{Wx1}$, then P_2 cannot receive $\mathsf{Wx1}$ before $\mathsf{Wx2}$. In Ex. 11 below, we use an alternative formulation of CBC to demonstrate that these histories are not CBC. Surprisingly, causal memory (CM) [6], the original formulation of causally consistent memory, allows these histories, despite the fact that they are disallowed by DistMem (see also §7.2).

Remark 1. Our definition is meant to allow "broadcast in progress", where some operations in the history have not yet propagated to all processes. In contrast, the definition in [25] requires that $s_p \in \mathsf{seq}(\mathsf{lin}(co, H.\mathsf{E}))$ instead of our condition (1), which means that the whole history appears in the linearization associated with each process, rather than its causal past only. If operations are always enabled in the object specification (i.e., for every $s \in Spec$ and $o \in O$, we have $s \cdot \langle o, d \rangle \in Spec$ for some $d \in D$), then this difference has no impact on the set of consistent histories. (This condition holds for specifications that are derived from transducers, and assumed in [25].) For specifications that do not enable all operations, some histories may be consistent w.r.t. Def. 17 but not w.r.t. the definition of [25]. For example, for $O = \{o_1\}$, $D = \{1\}$, and $Spec = \{\epsilon, \langle \langle o_1, 1 \rangle \rangle \}$, the history in which P_1 and P_2 each performs $\langle o_1, 1 \rangle$ is consistent w.r.t. Def. 17 (take $co = \emptyset$), but it is inconsistent w.r.t. the definition of [25], since no linearization of the whole history satisfies condition (2) above.

Next, we establish the correspondence of CBC to charts that are causal and respect a specification $Spec$, and with Thm. 1, we obtain the correspondence of CBC to $\mathsf{Dist}(S, O)$ (which formalizes the claim in [25, Footnote 2]).

Theorem 2. *If C is a causal chart for an object $\mathcal{O}$ that respects a specification $Spec$ for $\mathcal{O}$, then $\mathsf{H}(C)$ is CBC w.r.t. $Spec$.*

Theorem 3. *If H is a history for an object $\mathcal{O}$ that is CBC w.r.t. a specification $Spec$ for $\mathcal{O}$, then $H = \mathsf{H}(C)$ for some causal chart C that respects $Spec$.*

Corollary 1. *Let S be a transducer for an object $\mathcal{O} = \langle O, D \rangle$ and $Spec$ be the derived specification. A history H for $\mathcal{O}$ is generated by $\mathsf{Dist}(S, O)$ iff H is CBC w.r.t. $Spec$.*

---

[3] For brevity, we identify events with their labels.

4.3 Update-Driven Distributed Implementations

We use the declarative presentation to prove that queries (see Def. 3) do not need to be propagated in $\mathsf{Dist}(S, O)$, in the sense that the observable behaviors of $\mathsf{Dist}(S, O)$ (the histories generated by it) coincide with the ones of $\mathsf{Dist}(S, \mathsf{U}_{Spec})$.

Lemma 1. *For every chart C' (for $\mathcal{O}$) that is causal for U_{Spec} and respects Spec, there exists a causal chart C (for $\mathcal{O}$) that respects Spec such that $C'.E = C.E \setminus codom([\mathsf{Evs}(\mathcal{O})|_{\mathsf{Q}_{Spec}}] ; C.\mathsf{prop})$, $C'.\mathsf{po} = C.\mathsf{po}|_{C'.E}$, and $C'.\mathsf{prop} = [\mathsf{Evs}(\mathcal{O})|_{\mathsf{U}_{Spec}}] ; C.\mathsf{prop}$. In particular, $\mathsf{H}(C) = \mathsf{H}(C')$.*

Lemma 2. *For every causal chart C (for $\mathcal{O}$) that respects Spec, there exists a chart C' (for $\mathcal{O}$) such that: (i) C' is causal for U_{Spec}; (ii) C' respects Spec; and (iii) $C'.E = C.E \setminus codom([\mathsf{Evs}(\mathcal{O})|_{\mathsf{Q}_{Spec}}] ; C.\mathsf{prop})$, $C'.\mathsf{po} = C.\mathsf{po}|_{C'.E}$, and $C'.\mathsf{prop} = [\mathsf{Evs}(\mathcal{O})|_{\mathsf{U}_{Spec}}] ; C.\mathsf{prop}$. In particular, $\mathsf{H}(C) = \mathsf{H}(C')$.*

Example 8. The chart C from Ex. 5 is causal and respects $Spec_{\mathsf{Mem}}$. The following chart C', obtained from C by deleting the propagation of the read event, satisfies properties $(i) - (iii)$ from Lemma 2:

$$P_1:\ \mathsf{Wx1} \to \mathsf{rcv} \to \mathsf{Rx2}$$
$$\uparrow$$
$$P_2:\ \mathsf{Rx0} \to \mathsf{Wx2}$$

Corollary 2. *Let S be a transducer for an object $\mathcal{O}$ and Spec be the derived specification. A history H for $\mathcal{O}$ is generated by $\mathsf{Dist}(S, O)$ iff it is generated by $\mathsf{Dist}(S, \mathsf{U}_{Spec})$.*

In particular, since DistMem is an instance of $\mathsf{Dist}(S, \mathsf{U}_{Spec})$, histories of DistMem coincide with histories that are CBC w.r.t. $Spec_{\mathsf{Mem}}$. As an additional corollary of the above lemmas, we obtain an equivalent definition of CBC consistency that ignores queries of other processes for justifying events of each process (the difference from Def. 17 is highlighted):

Theorem 4. *A history H for $\mathcal{O}$ is CBC w.r.t. a specification Spec for $\mathcal{O}$ iff there exist a causal order co for H and a sequence s_p for every $p \in \mathsf{Ps}$ such that:*

- $s_p \in \mathsf{seq}(\mathsf{lin}(co, co^{-1}(H.E|_p)|_{\mathsf{U}_{Spec}} \cup H.E|_p))$
- *Some $s'_p \in \mathsf{reeval}(s_p, \mathsf{Evs}|_p)$ respects Spec.*
- *If $\mathsf{proc}(s_p(j)) = p$, then $\langle s_p(i), s_p(j) \rangle \in co$ for every $1 \leq i < j$.*

Example 9. In Ex. 6, we showed that the history induced by the chart C from Ex. 5 is CBC w.r.t. $Spec_{\mathsf{Mem}}$. By Thm. 4, the same can be shown by taking s_{P_1} to be $\mathsf{obs}_{P_1}(C)$ without the read event labeled $\mathsf{Rx0}$. Note that this is the same as taking $\mathsf{obs}_{P_1}(C')$, where C' is the chart from Ex. 8.

5 Causal-Broadcast Memory

In this section we use our previous results to derive the declarative consistency guarantees provided by DistMem in the standard formalism of execution graphs used to define weakly consistent memory models (see, e.g., [7,19]).

In the rest of the paper we focus on the memory object. We write Lab, Evs, and Do for Lab(Mem), Evs(Mem), and Do(Mem) (respectively). We lift $\mathtt{loc}$ and $\mathtt{val}$ from operations to labels and events in the obvious way. We call an event e a *write (respectively, read) event* if $\mathtt{op}(e)$ is a write (read) operation. We denote the sets of write events and read events by W and R. For a relation R on events, we let $R|_{\mathsf{loc}} \triangleq R \cap \{\langle e, e'\rangle \mid \mathtt{loc}(e) = \mathtt{loc}(e')\}$. To match other existing formulations, we also include explicit *initialization events* in our graphs. These are events of the form $\langle \bot, 0, \mathtt{W}x\mathsf{v}_{\mathsf{init}}\rangle$ (with $\mathtt{proc}(e) = \bot$), where $\bot$ signifies that the event is not associated with any particular process. We denote by Init the set of all initialization events.

Unlike histories, execution graphs maintain a "reads-from" relation that justifies every read event by a corresponding write event:

Definition 18. A relation rf is a *reads-from relation* for a set $E \subseteq$ Do if the following hold:

- If $\langle w, r\rangle \in rf$, then $w \in$ W and $r \in$ R.
- If $\langle w, r\rangle \in rf$, then $\mathtt{loc}(w) = \mathtt{loc}(r)$ and $\mathtt{val}(w) = \mathtt{out}(r)$.
- If $\langle w_1, r\rangle, \langle w_2, r\rangle \in rf$, then $w_1 = w_2$ (reads have at most one source write).
- $E \cap$ R $\subseteq$ codom(rf) (each read reads from some write).

Definition 19. An *execution graph* is a tuple $G = \langle E, po, rf\rangle$, where:

- $E \subseteq$ Do is a finite set of do events such that Init $\subseteq E$ and $\mathtt{proc}(e) \neq \bot$ for every $e \in E \setminus$ Init.
- $po = po|_{E \setminus \mathsf{Init}} \uplus (\mathsf{Init} \times (E \setminus \mathsf{Init}))$ and $po|_{E \setminus \mathsf{Init}}$ is a program order for $E \setminus$ Init (Def. 5).
- rf is a reads-from relation for E.

We denote the components of G by $G.\mathrm{E}$, $G.\mathrm{po}$, and $G.\mathtt{rf}$. We let $G.\mathrm{po}^p \triangleq G.\mathrm{po}\,;$ $[\mathsf{Evs}|_p]$ and $G.\mathtt{rfe} \triangleq G.\mathtt{rf} \setminus G.\mathrm{po}$ ("external" reads-from). For $E' \subseteq$ Evs, we write $G.E'$ for $G.\mathrm{E} \cap E'$ (e.g., $G.\mathrm{W} = G.\mathrm{E} \cap$ W). The *history induced by* G, denoted by $\mathsf{H}(G)$, is given by $\mathsf{H}(G) \triangleq \langle E \setminus \mathsf{Init}, po|_{E \setminus \mathsf{Init}}\rangle$.

Next, we define the CBM memory model—a variant of CBC that applies to execution graphs and ensures that the justification of reads matches the reads-from relation. We start with a definition that utilizes CBC (Def. 21) and later show more direct equivalent formulations (Thms. 5 and 6).

Definition 20. Let rf be a reads-from relation for a set $E \subseteq$ Do. A sequence $s \in E^*$ *respects* rf if the following hold:

- If e_2 occurs in s and $\langle e_1, e_2\rangle \in [E \setminus \mathsf{Init}]\,;\,rf$, then e_1 occurs before e_2 in s.

- If $s = s_1 \cdot w \cdot s_2 \cdot r \cdot s_3$, $w \in \mathsf{W}$, $r \in \mathsf{R}$, $\mathtt{loc}(w) = \mathtt{loc}(r)$, and no $w' \in \mathsf{W}$ with $\mathtt{loc}(w') = \mathtt{loc}(w)$ occurs in s_2, then $\langle w, r \rangle \in rf$.

Definition 21. An execution graph G is *causal-broadcast memory consistent* (CBM, for short) if there exist a causal order co for $\mathsf{H}(G)$ and a sequence s_p for every $p \in \mathsf{Ps}$ that satisfies the conditions of Thm. 4 for $\mathsf{H}(G)$ and respects $G.\mathtt{rf}$.

Example 10. The requirement s_p respects $G.\mathtt{rf}$ is essential (and without it, Thms. 5 and 6 below would not hold, as well as the relation to WRA given in §7.4). For instance, consider the following execution graph G (Init is elided):

$$\mathsf{P}_1\colon\ \mathtt{Wx1} \xrightarrow{\quad} \mathtt{Wx1} \xrightarrow{\quad} \mathtt{Rx1}$$

with an $\mathtt{rf}$ edge from the first $\mathtt{Wx1}$ to $\mathtt{Rx1}$.

$\mathsf{H}(G)$ is CBC w.r.t. $Spec_{\mathsf{Mem}}$, since $\langle \mathtt{Wx1}, \mathtt{Wx1}, \mathtt{Rx1} \rangle \in Spec_{\mathsf{Mem}}$. However, the corresponding sequence of events does not respect $\mathtt{rf}$ (invalidates the second condition of Def. 20): $\mathtt{Rx1}$ should read from the second write, not the first one. Therefore, G is not CBM. Note that G is not even WRA (see §7.4).

We can establish the following relation:

Lemma 3. *A history H is* CBC *w.r.t.* $Spec_{\mathsf{Mem}}$ *iff* $\langle H.\mathsf{E} \cup \mathsf{Init}, H.\mathsf{po} \cup (\mathsf{Init} \times H.\mathsf{E}), rf \rangle$ *is* CBM *for some reads-from relation* rf *for* $H.\mathsf{E} \cup \mathsf{Init}$.

We conclude (using Cors. 1 and 2) that $\mathsf{DistMem}$ is captured by CBM: the histories generated by $\mathsf{DistMem}$ are precisely the histories induced by CBM graphs.

Corollary 3. *The following hold:*

- *If H is generated by* $\mathsf{DistMem}$, *then $H = \mathsf{H}(G)$ for some* CBM *graph G.*
- *If G is* CBM, *then* $\mathsf{H}(G)$ *is generated by* $\mathsf{DistMem}$.

5.1 Computational Presentation of CBM

We provide an equivalent characterization of CBM that aligns more closely with existing definitions of weak memory models (see §7) and is designed to facilitate efficient consistency checking. The first step is to replace the existential quantification over co and sequences s_p by existential quantification on valid total orders on relevant write events, with one order per process.

Theorem 5. *An execution graph G is* CBM *iff there exist relations $\{wo^p\}_{p \in \mathsf{Ps}}$ such that the following hold for every $p \in \mathsf{Ps}$, where* $wo = \bigcup_{q \in \mathsf{Ps}} wo^q\,;\,[G.\mathsf{E}|_q]$:

(1) wo^p *is a total order on* $\mathsf{Init} \cup dom([\mathsf{W}]\,;\,wo^*\,;\,G.\mathtt{rf}\mathsf{e}^?\,;\,[G.\mathsf{E}|_p])$.
(2) $wo^{p^?}\,;\,G.\mathtt{rf}\mathsf{e}^?\,;\,G.\mathsf{po}^p$ *is irreflexive.*
(3) $wo^p|_{\mathsf{loc}}\,;\,wo^{p^?}\,;\,G.\mathtt{rf}\mathsf{e}^?\,;\,G.\mathsf{po}^p\,;\,G.\mathtt{rf}^{-1}$ *is irreflexive.*
(4) $wo^p\,;\,wo$ *is irreflexive.*

The relations wo^p describe the linearizations s_p restricted to W, and wo represents a "global" write order that all processes agree upon. Condition (2) allows us to extend wo^p with the read events of p to obtain s_p, such that it agrees with po, and every read event is preceded by its rf source. Condition (3) ensures that no write "overrides" the rf source of a read in s_p. Condition (4) ensures that s_p agrees with the order in which other processes place write events before their own write events, which corresponds to the last condition of Thm. 4.

Next, we give an equivalent definition that does not require finding total orders. Instead, it identifies the minimal constraints on $\{wo^p\}_{p\in\mathsf{Ps}}$ and requires that there are no cycles.

Definition 22. The family $\{G.\mathtt{wb}^p\}_{p\in\mathsf{Ps}}$ of *write-before* relations induced by an execution graph G is inductively defined as follows:

$$\frac{\begin{array}{c} w_1, w_2 \in \mathsf{W} \\ \mathtt{proc}(w_2) = p \\ \langle w_1, w_2 \rangle \in G.\mathtt{rfe}^? \,;\, G.\mathtt{po} \end{array}}{\langle w_1, w_2 \rangle \in G.\mathtt{wb}^p} \text{ (B)} \qquad \frac{\begin{array}{c} w_1, w_2 \in \mathsf{W} \qquad \mathtt{loc}(w_1) = \mathtt{loc}(w_2) \\ w_1 \neq w_2 \\ \langle w_1, w_2 \rangle \in G.\mathtt{wb}^{p?} \,;\, G.\mathtt{rfe}^? \,;\, G.\mathtt{po}^p \,;\, G.\mathtt{rf}^{-1} \end{array}}{\langle w_1, w_2 \rangle \in G.\mathtt{wb}^p} \text{ (C)}$$

$$\frac{\begin{array}{c} \mathtt{proc}(w_2) = q \qquad \langle w_1, w_2 \rangle \in G.\mathtt{wb}^q \\ w_2 \in \mathsf{dom}((\cup_{q\in\mathsf{Ps}} G.\mathtt{wb}^q \,;\, [G.\mathsf{E}|_q])^* \,;\, G.\mathtt{rfe}^? \,;\, [G.\mathsf{E}|_p]) \end{array}}{\langle w_1, w_2 \rangle \in G.\mathtt{wb}^p} \text{ (Q)}$$

$$\frac{\langle w_1, w_2 \rangle \in G.\mathtt{wb}^p \qquad \langle w_2, w_3 \rangle \in G.\mathtt{wb}^p}{\langle w_1, w_3 \rangle \in G.\mathtt{wb}^p} \text{ (T)}$$

Definition 22 constructively reflects the requirements of Thm. 5. For example, condition (2) of Thm. 5 is rephrased as "if $\langle w_1, w_2 \rangle \in G.\mathtt{rfe}^? \,;\, G.\mathtt{po}^p$ then $\langle w_1, w_2 \rangle \in wo^p$", as stated in rule (B). The rules specify the basic restrictions that linearizations must obey, and the existence of wo^p boils down to verifying acyclicity of $G.\mathtt{wb}^p$ for each process.

Theorem 6. *An execution graph G is* CBM *iff $G.\mathtt{wb}^p$ is irreflexive for every p.*

Since reaching a fixpoint following Def. 22 and checking acyclicity require polynomial time, we obtain that testing CBM is in PTIME.

The next example applies Thm. 6 to prove that the execution graphs of the histories from Ex. 7 are not CBM. The histories in that example are *differentiated*—every value is written at most once to each location—so the reads-from relation of the execution graph is uniquely determined from the history.

Example 11. Consider the execution graphs that induce the histories in Ex. 7. For the left history, we have $\langle \mathtt{Wx2}, \mathtt{Wy1} \rangle \in G.\mathtt{po}^{\mathsf{P2}}$, and so $\langle \mathtt{Wx2}, \mathtt{Wy1} \rangle \in G.\mathtt{wb}^{\mathsf{P2}}$ by rule (B). Since $\mathtt{proc}(\mathtt{Wy1}) = \mathsf{P2}$, we have $\langle \mathtt{Wx2}, \mathtt{Wy1} \rangle \in G.\mathtt{wb}^{\mathsf{P1}}$ by rule (Q). Now, since $\langle \mathtt{Wy1}, \mathtt{Rx1} \rangle \in G.\mathtt{rfe} \,;\, G.\mathtt{po}^{\mathsf{P1}}$ and $\langle \mathtt{Wx1}, \mathtt{Rx1} \rangle \in G.\mathtt{rf}$, we derive $\langle \mathtt{Wx2}, \mathtt{Wx1} \rangle \in G.\mathtt{wb}^{\mathsf{P1}}$ by rule (C). Since $\mathtt{proc}(\mathtt{Wx1}) = \mathsf{P}_1$, we have $\langle \mathtt{Wx2}, \mathtt{Wx1} \rangle \in G.\mathtt{wb}^{\mathsf{P2}}$ by rule

(Q). However, a symmetric argument for P_2 gives us $\langle \mathtt{Wx1}, \mathtt{Wx2} \rangle \in G.\mathtt{wb}^{P_2}$, which entails a cycle in $G.\mathtt{wb}^{P_2}$.

For the right history, we explain in less details. Using (B) and (Q), $\langle \mathtt{Wx1}, \mathtt{Wy2} \rangle \in G.\mathtt{wb}^{P_2}$. Thus, $\langle \mathtt{Wx1}, \mathtt{Rx4} \rangle \in G.\mathtt{wb}^{P_2};G.\mathtt{rfe};G.\mathtt{po}^{P_2}$, and $\langle \mathtt{Wx1}, \mathtt{Wx4} \rangle \in G.\mathtt{wb}^{P_2}$ follows by rule (C). By rule (Q), $\langle \mathtt{Wx1}, \mathtt{Wx4} \rangle \in G.\mathtt{wb}^{P_3}$. However, by similar arguments we obtain $\langle \mathtt{Wx4}, \mathtt{Wx1} \rangle \in G.\mathtt{wb}^{P_3}$.

Definition 22 and Thm. 6 draw on existing techniques from the study of weak memory models. For example, the *saturation semantics* introduced in [5] for the purpose of efficiently model checking concurrent programs running under the Release-Acquire memory model (RA), uses a similar technique: adding to the execution graph only the edges that must be contained in any modification (a.k.a. coherence) order, and looking for forbidden cycles in the obtained graph. An earlier similar result for RA appears in [20, Appendix B]. A notable difference is that RA uses a single modification order, whereas CBM maintains a separate order per process since processes can disagree on the order of certain writes. We also note that in [15] it is shown that consistency testing *without a given reads-from relation*, under any model between SLOW and SC, is NP-hard. Since CBM is included in this range and this problem is in NP for CBM (using Thm. 6), we deduce the NP-completeness of testing CBM without a given reads-from relation, which puts it together with a variety of other models [13].

6　Control-State Reachability for DistMem

The control-state reachability for DistMem considers a finite-state concurrent program that uses a shared memory implemented by DistMem for communication between processes and asks whether a particular program state can be reached. In this section we precisely define this problem and sketch the undecidability argument (§6.1).

Example 12. Consider the following concurrent program, given in pseudo-code:

$$
\begin{array}{c|c}
\mathtt{x} := 1 & \mathtt{y} := 1 \\
\mathtt{a} := \mathtt{y} & \mathtt{b} := \mathtt{x}
\end{array}
$$

An algorithm solving the reachability problem would have to decide, for example, whether we can have $\mathtt{a} = \mathtt{b} = 0$ after executing this program on top of DistMem. While it cannot happen under sequential consistency (§7.1), it is possible using DistMem. Though it is clear that the reachability problem for SC is decidable and decidability results have been obtained for other memory models [8,3,18], we show this problem is undecidable for DistMem.

The next definitions of a program, linking of a program with a memory system, and control-state reachability are adopted from [18].

Definition 23. A *program* Pr maps each $p \in \mathsf{Ps}$ to a finite LTS $Pr(p)$ over the alphabet $\mathsf{Lab} \cup \{\varepsilon\}$ (ε stands for "silent" actions that do not interact with the memory) representing a top-level parallel composition of sequential programs. A program Pr induces an LTS, which we also denote by Pr: its states are functions, denoted by $\bar{p}$, assigning a state in $Pr(p).\mathsf{Q}$ to every $p \in \mathsf{Ps}$; its alphabet is $(\mathsf{Ps} \times \mathsf{Lab}) \cup \{\varepsilon\}$; its initial state is $\bar{p}_0$ defined by $\bar{p}_0 = \lambda p.\, Pr(p).\mathsf{q}_0$; and its transitions interleave transitions of Pr's components (i.e., if $\bar{p}(p) \xrightarrow{l}_{Pr(p)} q$ for some $l \in \mathsf{Lab}$, then $\bar{p} \xrightarrow{p,l}_{Pr} \bar{p}[p \mapsto q]$; and if $\bar{p}(p) \xrightarrow{\varepsilon}_{Pr(p)} q$, then $\bar{p} \xrightarrow{\varepsilon}_{Pr} \bar{p}[p \mapsto q]$).

Definition 24. The *linking of a program Pr with* $\mathsf{DistMem}$, denoted by $Pr \bowtie \mathsf{DistMem}$, is the LTS whose set of states is $Pr.\mathsf{Q} \times \mathsf{DistMem}.\mathsf{Q}$; its alphabet is $(\mathsf{Ps} \times \mathsf{Lab}) \cup \{\varepsilon\}$; its initial state is $\langle Pr.\mathsf{q}_0, \mathsf{DistMem}.\mathsf{q}_0 \rangle$; and its transitions are:

$$\frac{\bar{p} \xrightarrow{p,l}_{Pr} \bar{p}' \qquad \langle C, \vec{q} \rangle \xrightarrow{p,l}_{\mathsf{DistMem}} \langle C', \vec{q}' \rangle}{\langle \bar{p}, \langle C, \vec{q} \rangle \rangle \xrightarrow{p,l}_{Pr \bowtie \mathsf{DistMem}} \langle \bar{p}', \langle C', \vec{q}' \rangle \rangle}$$

$$\frac{\bar{p} \xrightarrow{\varepsilon}_{Pr} \bar{p}'}{\langle \bar{p}, \langle C, \vec{q} \rangle \rangle \xrightarrow{\varepsilon}_{Pr \bowtie \mathsf{DistMem}} \langle \bar{p}', \langle C, \vec{q} \rangle \rangle} \qquad \frac{\langle C, \vec{q} \rangle \xrightarrow{\varepsilon}_{\mathsf{DistMem}} \langle C', \vec{q}' \rangle}{\langle \bar{p}, \langle C, \vec{q} \rangle \rangle \xrightarrow{\varepsilon}_{Pr \bowtie \mathsf{DistMem}} \langle \bar{p}, \langle C', \vec{q}' \rangle \rangle}$$

The above LTS describes a concurrent client program that uses $\mathsf{DistMem}$ as the shared memory (recall that $\mathsf{DistMem}$ is formally captured by the LTS $\mathsf{Dist}(S_{\mathsf{Mem}}, \mathsf{Wr})$ with states of the form $\langle C, \vec{q} \rangle$; see §3.3). When both Pr and $\mathsf{DistMem}$ step with the same observable label $\langle p, l \rangle$ (p performs a memory operation $\mathsf{op}(l)$ with output $\mathsf{out}(l)$), $Pr \bowtie \mathsf{DistMem}$ steps to the new pair of states. When Pr steps with a silent label (some process performs a silent action), only the Pr component of $Pr \bowtie \mathsf{DistMem}$ steps to the new state. When $\mathsf{DistMem}$ steps with a silent label (some process receives a message), only the $\mathsf{DistMem}$ component of $Pr \bowtie \mathsf{DistMem}$ steps to the new state.

We can now state the reachability problem we study:

Definition 25. A state $\bar{p} \in Pr.\mathsf{Q}$ of a program Pr is *reachable under* $\mathsf{DistMem}$ if $\langle \bar{p}, \langle C, \vec{q} \rangle \rangle$ is reachable in $Pr \bowtie \mathsf{DistMem}$ for some C and $\vec{q}$. The *control-state reachability problem for* $\mathsf{DistMem}$ is the following decision problem:

Input: a program Pr and a state $\bar{p} \in Pr.\mathsf{Q}$.
Output: is $\bar{p}$ reachable under $\mathsf{DistMem}$?

In the undecidability proof, we use an equivalent formulation of reachability under $\mathsf{DistMem}$ that utilizes CBM execution graphs. The connection between a graph and a program trace is established through histories:

Definition 26. The history *induced by a sequence* $tr = \langle \langle p_1, l_1 \rangle, \ldots, \langle p_n, l_n \rangle \rangle \in (\mathsf{Ps} \times \mathsf{Lab})^*$, denoted by $\mathsf{H}(tr)$, is given by:

 - $\mathsf{H}(tr).\mathsf{E} = \{ \langle p_i, i, l_i \rangle \in \mathsf{Evs} \mid 1 \le i \le n \}$
 - $\mathsf{H}(tr).\mathsf{po} = \{ \langle e, e' \rangle \in \mathsf{H}(tr).\mathsf{E} \times \mathsf{H}(tr).\mathsf{E} \mid \mathsf{proc}(e) = \mathsf{proc}(e') \wedge \mathsf{sn}(e) < \mathsf{sn}(e') \}$

Informally, for every $p \in \mathsf{Ps}$, the program order of $\mathsf{H}(tr)$ orders the events performed by p according to the order in which they appear in tr.

Theorem 7. *A state $\bar{p}$ of a program Pr is reachable under* $\mathsf{DistMem}$ *(see Def. 25) iff there exists $tr \in \mathsf{otraces}(Pr, \bar{p})$ such that $\mathsf{H}(tr) = \mathsf{H}(G)$ for some CBM execution graph G.*

6.1 Undecidability Proof Sketch

Given the above definitions, our undecidability result is the following:

Theorem 8. *The control-state reachability problem for* DistMem *is undecidable.*

Our proof reduces from control-state reachability for two finite-state machines communicating via perfect FIFO channels, one in each direction [11].

Definition 27. Let M be a finite set of *messages*, and L and R be two finite-state LTSs with $\{!m, ?m \mid m \in M\} \subseteq L.\Sigma \cap R.\Sigma$. (The labels $!m$ and $?m$ represent a *send* and a *receive* of message m.) The *(two-point) communicating finite state machine* (CFM, for short) $\mathcal{C}$ induced by L and R is defined by:

- The states are tuples of the form $\langle\langle q_\mathsf{L}, q_\mathsf{R}\rangle, w_\mathsf{LR}, w_\mathsf{RL}\rangle$, where $q_\mathsf{L} \in L.\mathsf{Q}$, $q_\mathsf{R} \in R.\mathsf{Q}$, and $w_\mathsf{LR}, w_\mathsf{RL} \in M^*$. Intuitively, w_LR maintains the contents of the channel from L to R, that is, the sequence of messages that were sent from L, in the order in which they were sent, but have not been received yet by R (similarly for w_RL).
- The alphabet is the disjoint union of $L.\Sigma$ and $R.\Sigma$, given by $(\{\mathsf{L}\} \times L.\Sigma) \cup (\{\mathsf{R}\} \times R.\Sigma)$. For brevity, we write, e.g., $\mathsf{L}!m$ for $\langle\mathsf{L}, !m\rangle$.
- The initial state is given by $\langle\langle L.\mathsf{q}_0, R.\mathsf{q}_0\rangle, \epsilon, \epsilon\rangle$.
- $\langle\langle q_\mathsf{L}, q_\mathsf{R}\rangle, w_\mathsf{LR}, w_\mathsf{RL}\rangle \xrightarrow{\sigma}_\mathcal{C} \langle\langle q'_\mathsf{L}, q'_\mathsf{R}\rangle, w'_\mathsf{LR}, w'_\mathsf{RL}\rangle$ if the following hold:
  - If $\sigma \in L.\Sigma$, then $q_\mathsf{L} \xrightarrow{\sigma}_L q'_\mathsf{L}$ and $q_\mathsf{R} = q'_\mathsf{R}$ (similarly if $\sigma \in R.\Sigma$).
  - If $\sigma = \mathsf{L}!m$, then $w'_\mathsf{LR} = w_\mathsf{LR} \cdot m$ and $w'_\mathsf{RL} = w_\mathsf{RL}$ (similarly if $\sigma = \mathsf{R}!m$).
  - If $\sigma = \mathsf{L}?m$, then $w_\mathsf{RL} = m \cdot w'_\mathsf{RL}$ and $w'_\mathsf{LR} = w_\mathsf{LR}$ (similarly if $\sigma = \mathsf{R}?m$).
  - If σ is neither a send nor a receive, then $w'_\mathsf{LR} = w_\mathsf{LR}$ and $w'_\mathsf{RL} = w_\mathsf{RL}$.

A *control state* $\langle q_\mathsf{L}, q_\mathsf{R}\rangle \in L.\mathsf{Q} \times R.\mathsf{Q}$ is *reachable* in $\mathcal{C}$ if $\langle\langle q_\mathsf{L}, q_\mathsf{R}\rangle, w_\mathsf{LR}, w_\mathsf{RL}\rangle$ is reachable in $\mathcal{C}$ for some w_LR and w_RL.

The reduction constructs a concurrent program Pr that simulates runs of $\mathcal{C}$. The program Pr consists of two sequential programs, $Pr(p_\mathsf{L})$ and $Pr(p_\mathsf{R})$, which mimic the transitions of L and R. To simulate the channels, we use memory locations $\mathsf{Loc} = \{\mathsf{l}_0, \mathsf{l}_1, \mathsf{r}_0, \mathsf{r}_1\}$ with values $\mathsf{Val} = M \uplus \{\bot\}$ consisting of messages and a special marker. The marker $\bot$ also serves as the initial value $\mathsf{v}_{\mathsf{init}}$. The locations l_0 and l_1 are used for the channel from L to R, and r_0 and r_1 are for the channel from R to L. The two variables for each channel are used in alternation, inspired by the reduction from PCP in [1], for making sure that the runs of Pr adhere to the perfect FIFO semantics. Concretely, when L sends m, $Pr(p_\mathsf{L})$ alternates between $\mathsf{Wl}_0 m$ and $\mathsf{Wl}_1 m$. (By alternating, we mean using the first for odd-numbered send actions and the second for even-numbered ones.) For receiving a message by R, $Pr(p_\mathsf{R})$ alternates between the sequences of operations $\langle \mathsf{Rl}_0, \mathsf{Wl}_0\bot, \mathsf{Rl}_1\bot\rangle$ and $\langle \mathsf{Rl}_1, \mathsf{Wl}_1\bot, \mathsf{Rl}_0\bot\rangle$. (At the program level, a read of $\bot$ from location x is enforced by reading from x, and moving to a "sink" state if the read value is not $\bot$.) The construction is similar for the symmetric actions.

Now, we can show that $\mathcal{C}$ reaches a control state $\langle q_\mathsf{L}, q_\mathsf{R}\rangle$ iff the constructed program Pr reaches the corresponding state under DistMem. Equivalently, by

Thm. 7, there is an observable trace tr of Pr reaching this state, whose history is induced by a CBM execution graph. To give an example of the main idea in the construction, suppose that L sends messages $\boxed{1}, \ldots, \boxed{5}$ to R in this order, and R receives three messages from the channel. Assume, for the sake of contradiction, that R receives $\boxed{1}$ and $\boxed{2}$, but then skips directly to $\boxed{5}$, violating the perfect FIFO semantics (skipping only $\boxed{3}$ or receiving the same message twice are easier to dismiss). Then, the following history is induced by tr:

$$\mathsf{P_L}: \quad \mathtt{W1}_0\boxed{1} \longrightarrow \mathtt{W1}_1\boxed{2} \longrightarrow \mathtt{W1}_0\boxed{3} \longrightarrow \mathtt{W1}_1\boxed{4} \longrightarrow \mathtt{W1}_0\boxed{5}$$

$$\mathsf{P_R}: \quad \mathtt{R1}_0\boxed{1} \to \mathtt{W1}_0\bot \to \mathtt{R1}_1\bot \longrightarrow \mathtt{R1}_1\boxed{2} \to \mathtt{W1}_1\bot \to \mathtt{R1}_0\bot \longrightarrow \mathtt{R1}_0\boxed{5} \to \mathtt{W1}_0\bot \to \mathtt{R1}_1\bot$$

We show that every execution graph inducing this history is CBM-*inconsistent*. We show it by definition (Def. 21). Indeed, a serialization $s_{\mathsf{P_R}}$ must place $\mathtt{W1}_0\boxed{5}$ before $\mathtt{R1}_0\boxed{5}$, and $\mathtt{W1}_1\boxed{4}$ must be placed before it (to agree with po). To justify the last $\mathtt{R1}_1\bot$, $\mathtt{W1}_1\boxed{4}$ needs to go before $\mathtt{W1}_1\bot$. Similarly, $\mathtt{W1}_0\boxed{3}$ must now be placed before the first $\mathtt{W1}_0\bot$. Finally, $\mathtt{W1}_1\boxed{2}$ has to appear before it, which prevents us from justifying the first $\mathtt{R1}_1\bot$ event.

7   Relation to Other Criteria and Memory Models

We discuss the relation of CBC (Def. 17) and CBM (Def. 21) to other consistency criteria and weak memory models. We deal with two different notions here: CBC refers to the consistency of histories (Def. 15) w.r.t. a general object specification *Spec*, while CBM concerns the consistency of execution graphs (Def. 19) for the standard memory object. Given two consistency criteria, X for histories and Y for execution graphs, we write $Y \propto X$ if a history H satisfies X w.r.t. $Spec_{\mathsf{Mem}}$ iff $\langle H.\mathsf{E} \uplus \mathsf{Init}, H.\mathsf{po} \uplus (\mathsf{Init} \times H.\mathsf{E}), rf \rangle$ satisfies Y for some reads-from relation rf for $H.\mathsf{E} \uplus \mathsf{Init}$. In particular, Lemma 3 says that CBM $\propto$ CBC. Note that $Y \propto X$ implies that $\mathsf{H}(G)$ satisfies X w.r.t. $Spec_{\mathsf{Mem}}$ whenever G satisfies Y. In addition, for consistency criteria X_1 and X_2, we say that X_1 is stronger than X_2, denoted $X_2 \le X_1$, if every history satisfying X_1 w.r.t. a specification $Spec$ also satisfies X_2 w.r.t. $Spec$. Similarly, for memory models Y_1 and Y_2, we say that Y_1 is stronger than Y_2, denoted $Y_2 \le Y_1$, if every execution graph satisfying Y_1 also satisfies Y_2. Strict relations (denoted $<$) are also defined as expected.

7.1   Sequential Consistency [21]

A history H is sequentially consistent (SC, for short) w.r.t. an object specification *Spec* if some $s \in \mathsf{seq}(\mathsf{lin}(H.\mathsf{po}, H.\mathsf{E}))$ respects *Spec*.

The corresponding memory model [7], which we denote by $\mathsf{SC_{Mem}}$, is defined by requiring the existence of a *modification order* mo that totally orders the writes to each location, and requiring that $(G.\mathsf{po} \cup G.\mathtt{rf} \cup mo \cup fr)^+$ is irreflexive, where $fr \triangleq G.\mathtt{rf}^{-1} \, ; mo$. We have $\mathsf{SC_{Mem}} \propto \mathsf{SC}$.

It is easy to show that SC is strictly stronger than all other consistency criteria discussed in this paper, and similarly for SC_{Mem} and all other memory models. SC disallows all examples in Fig. 1.

7.2 Causal Memory [6]

Following the seminal work [6], an execution graph G satisfies "causal memory" (CM, for short) if for every $p \in \text{Ps}$, some $s_p \in \text{seq}(\text{lin}((G.\text{po} \cup G.\text{rf})\ ;^+_{G.\text{E}} \wp\ G.\text{W}))$ respects $Spec_{\text{Mem}}$. To show that CM is achievable in a distributed settings, the same paper proposed a distributed implementation, which is essentially DistMem with the causal broadcast abstraction implemented from lower level primitives. However, our results show that DistMem actually provides CBM, which is strictly stronger than CM. Indeed, the linearizations required in Def. 21 for CBM can be easily extended to include all write events, and these extensions satisfy the conditions of CM. In addition, the histories in Ex. 7, extended with reads-from relations uniquely determined from the read values, are allowed by CM but not by CBM. (For the left history, the sequences given in Ex. 7 for each process, omitting Ry1 from s_{p_2}, satisfy the conditions of CM.)

We note that the original CM definition stated above has a somewhat strange aspect, since it does not require that reads of process p obtain their values in s_p from the write events specified by $G.\text{rf}$. This has no effect for differentiated execution graphs, where $G.\text{rf}$ is uniquely determined from the induced history. All examples above are differentiated (except for Ex. 10), so we do not exploit this quirk in CM's original formulation. In turn, [27, Figure 3(i)] presents a non-differentiated example, where CM is satisfied without respecting rf, that forms another case of CM but not CBM execution graph. For completeness, we also define a version of CM, which we call CM_{rf}, that adds the condition that each s_p respects $G.\text{rf}$ (see Def. 20). Then, again, $\text{CM}_{\text{rf}} \leq \text{CBM}$, and since CM_{rf} and CM coincide for differentiated executions, Ex. 7 again shows strict inclusion.

7.3 Causal Consistency [27]

In [27], Perrin et al. suggested a generalization of CM from memory to general objects. Their definition is as follows:

Definition 28 ([27]). A history H is *causally consistent* (CC, for short) w.r.t. an object specification *Spec* if there exist a causal order co for H and a sequence s_e for every $e \in H.\text{E}$ such that:

- $s_e \in \text{seq}(\text{lin}(co, co^{-1}(e)))$.
- Some $s'_e \in \text{reeval}(s_e, \text{Evs}|_{\text{proc}(e)})$ respects *Spec*.

We have CC < CBC. Indeed, by taking the per-process linearizations required in CBC and restricting them to the causal past of each event, we obtain the sequences required for CC (and moreover, s_{e_1} is a prefix of s_{e_2} when $\langle e_1, e_2 \rangle \in H.\text{po}$). Example 7 again demonstrates strict inclusion for Mem.

We note that CM $\propto$ CC does not hold in general. First, the example in [27, Figure 3(i)] (where CM is satisfied without respecting $\mathtt{rf}$) is an execution graph that satisfies CM, but its induced history does not satisfy CC. Second, even for the $\mathrm{CM}_{\mathtt{rf}}$ refinement discussed above, G is $\mathrm{CM}_{\mathtt{rf}}$ does imply that $\mathsf{H}(G)$ satisfies CC w.r.t. $Spec_{\mathsf{Mem}}$ but we still do not have $\mathrm{CM}_{\mathtt{rf}} \propto$ CC. Nevertheless, if only differentiated histories are considered, then $\mathrm{CM} = \mathrm{CM}_{\mathtt{rf}} \propto$ CC holds.

7.4   Weak Causal Consistency [27] and Weak Release-Acquire [18]

A weakening of CC, called "weak causal consistency" (WCC, for short), is obtained by requiring the reevaluations to preserve one event at a time, rather than all events of each process (replacing the second condition in Def. 28 by requiring that some $s'_e \in \mathsf{reeval}(s_e, \{e\})$ respects $Spec$). In [27] it was shown that WCC < CC. Thus, we also have WCC < CBC.

The corresponding memory model is WRA [18], defined by requiring that $G.\mathtt{hb} \triangleq (G.\mathtt{po} \cup G.\mathtt{rf})^+$ and $G.\mathtt{hb}|_{\mathsf{loc}} ; [\mathsf{W}] ; G.\mathtt{hb} ; G.\mathtt{rf}^{-1}$ are irreflexive. We have WRA $\propto$ WCC, WRA < CBM, WRA < $\mathrm{CM}_{\mathtt{rf}}$, but *not* WRA $\leq$ CM (the example in [27, Figure 3(i)] is CM but not WRA, not even with a different $\mathtt{rf}$).

7.5   Causal Convergence [27] and Strong Release-Acquire [19]

A strengthening of WCC, called "causal convergence" (CCv, for short), ensures eventual consistency—all processes converge to return the same outputs once there are no messages in transit. It is obtained by requiring the sequences justifying each event to agree on a certain "global" order of all events (formally, require that there exists a total "arbitration" order extending the causal order and require that all linearizations s_e agree with this order). CBC is incomparable to CCv (for Mem). Example COH in Fig. 1 is allowed by CBC but not by CCv, whereas WWS is allowed by CCv but not by CBC.

The corresponding memory model is SRA [19], defined by requiring the existence of a *modification order* mo that totally orders the writes to each location, and requiring irreflexivity of $(G.\mathtt{po} \cup G.\mathtt{rf} \cup mo)^+$ and $mo ; G.\mathtt{hb} ; G.\mathtt{rf}^{-1}$ (where $G.\mathtt{hb} \triangleq (G.\mathtt{po} \cup G.\mathtt{rf})^+$). Then, SRA $\propto$ CCv and CBM is incomparable to SRA.

7.6   Release-Acquire [19]

The Release-Acquire memory model (RA) is a well-studied model, obtained as the fragment of the C/C++11 memory model restricted to include only release and acquire atomic accesses [19]. It weakens SRA by requiring that $mo^? ; (G.\mathtt{po} \cup G.\mathtt{rf})^+$ is irreflexive, instead of $(G.\mathtt{po} \cup G.\mathtt{rf} \cup mo)^+$. RA is placed strictly between WRA and SRA, and can be shown to be incomparable to CBM. Again, COH is allowed by CBM but not by RA, and WWS is allowed by RA but not by CBM.

7.7 Total Store Order [26]

Total store order (TSO) is a a widely implemented memory model in multicore architectures, in particular in x86. A formal model is given in [26], and [19] provides an alternative definition, and shows that SRA < TSO. TSO is incomparable to CBM: Again, COH is allowed by CBM but not by TSO, whereas WWS is allowed by TSO but not by CBM.

7.8 Parallel Snapshot Isolation [12]

Parallel snapshot isolation (PSI) [12,30] is a consistency criterion for transactions in a geo-replicated key-value store, which weakens the classical snapshot isolation (SI) [9] to improve efficiency. The restriction of PSI to transactions composed of a single access can be defined by requiring the existence of a *modification order* mo that totally orders the writes to each location such that $(G.\mathsf{po} \cup G.\mathsf{rf} \cup mo)^+$ and $mo \mathbin{;} (G.\mathsf{po} \cup G.\mathsf{rf} \cup mo)^+ \mathbin{;} G.\mathsf{rf}^{-1}$ are irreflexive. With this formulation, and since PSI disallows WWS, it easily follows that SRA < PSI. Moreover, we can also show CBM < PSI (again, COH shows strict inclusion).

Finally, a useful relation between every model stronger than WRA (including CBM) and PSI is stated by the following race-freedom guarantee. To state this guarantee, we define control-state reachability under a general declarative memory model (which generalizes the formulation used in Thm. 7).

Definition 29. A state $\overline{p}$ of Pr is *reachable under a memory model X* if there exists $tr \in \mathsf{otraces}(Pr, \overline{p})$ such that $\mathsf{H}(tr) = \mathsf{H}(G)$ for some X-consistent execution graph G. In this case we also say that G is *generated by Pr*.

Theorem 9. *An execution graph G is* write/write-race free *if for every $w_1, w_2 \in G.\mathsf{W}$ with* $\mathtt{loc}(w_1) = \mathtt{loc}(w_2)$, *we have $w_1 = w_2$, $\langle w_1, w_2 \rangle \in (G.\mathsf{po} \cup G.\mathsf{rf})^+$, or $\langle w_2, w_1 \rangle \in (G.\mathsf{po} \cup G.\mathsf{rf})^+$. Suppose that every* PSI-*consistent execution graph generated by a program Pr is* write/write-race free. *Then, every state of Pr that is reachable under a model stronger than* WRA *is also reachable under* PSI.

This theorem demonstrates that for a broad class of programs the distinctions among WRA, RA, SRA, CM, CBM, and PSI are immaterial. Importantly, users of Thm. 9 can establish the premise of the theorem using PSI, the strongest among these models.

8 Conclusion

DistMem is a classical algorithm that has inspired multiple refinements and verification efforts. In this work, we provide the first rigorous analysis of the guarantees DistMem actually provides. Although DistMem was originally presented to demonstrate that causal memory (CM) can be efficiently implemented in a distributed setting [6], we show that DistMem is captured by our CBM model, which is, in fact, strictly stronger than CM. This observation suggests that CM may be an artifact of an imprecise analysis, and that research on causal memory should instead focus on CBM. We take the first steps in analyzing CBM by studying the complexity of testing consistency and establishing the undecidability of client program verification under DistMem.

More broadly, our work aims to bridge the gap between message-passing distributed systems and weak memory models. Our main contribution is a declarative characterization of a well-known operational message-passing algorithm, along with a comparison to existing memory models and an analysis leveraging techniques from the study of memory models. We hope this work fosters greater communication between these closely related yet largely distinct subfields.

References

1. Abdulla, P.A., Arora, J., Atig, M.F., Krishna, S.: Verification of programs under the release-acquire semantics. In: PLDI. pp. 1117–1132. ACM, New York, NY, USA (2019). https://doi.org/10.1145/3314221.3314649
2. Abdulla, P.A., Atig, M.F., Bouajjani, A., Derevenetc, E., Leonardsson, C., Meyer, R.: On the state reachability problem for concurrent programs under Power. In: NETYS. pp. 47–59. Springer International Publishing, Cham (2021). https://doi.org/10.1007/978-3-030-67087-0_4
3. Abdulla, P.A., Atig, M.F., Bouajjani, A., Ngo, T.P.: A load-buffer semantics for total store ordering. Logical Methods in Computer Science **Volume 14, Issue 1** (Jan 2018). https://doi.org/10.23638/LMCS-14(1:9)2018
4. Abdulla, P.A., Atig, M.F., Godbole, A., Krishna, S., Vafeiadis, V.: The decidability of verification under PS 2.0. In: ESOP. pp. 1–29. Springer International Publishing, Cham (2021). https://doi.org/10.1007/978-3-030-72019-3_1
5. Abdulla, P.A., Atig, M.F., Jonsson, B., Ngo, T.P.: Optimal stateless model checking under the release-acquire semantics. Proc. ACM Program. Lang. **2**(OOPSLA) (Oct 2018). https://doi.org/10.1145/3276505
6. Ahamad, M., Neiger, G., Burns, J.E., Kohli, P., Hutto, P.W.: Causal memory: Definitions, implementation, and programming. Distributed Comput. **9**(1), 37–49 (1995). https://doi.org/10.1007/BF01784241
7. Alglave, J., Maranget, L., Tautschnig, M.: Herding cats: modelling, simulation, testing, and data mining for weak memory. ACM Trans. Program. Lang. Syst. **36**(2), 7:1–7:74 (Jul 2014). https://doi.org/10.1145/2627752
8. Atig, M.F., Bouajjani, A., Burckhardt, S., Musuvathi, M.: On the verification problem for weak memory models. In: POPL. p. 7–18. ACM, New York, NY, USA (2010). https://doi.org/10.1145/1706299.1706303
9. Berenson, H., Bernstein, P., Gray, J., Melton, J., O'Neil, E., O'Neil, P.: A critique of ansi sql isolation levels. In: SIGMOD. p. 1–10. ACM, New York, NY, USA (1995). https://doi.org/10.1145/223784.223785
10. Bouajjani, A., Enea, C., Guerraoui, R., Hamza, J.: On verifying causal consistency. In: POPL. p. 626–638. ACM, New York, NY, USA (2017). https://doi.org/10.1145/3009837.3009888
11. Brand, D., Zafiropulo, P.: On communicating finite-state machines. J. ACM **30**(2), 323–342 (Apr 1983). https://doi.org/10.1145/322374.322380
12. Cerone, A., Bernardi, G., Gotsman, A.: A framework for transactional consistency models with atomic visibility. In: CONCUR. pp. 58–71. Schloss Dagstuhl

    – Leibniz-Zentrum für Informatik, Dagstuhl, Germany (2015). https://doi.org/10.4230/LIPIcs.CONCUR.2015.58

13. Chakraborty, S., Krishna, S.N., Mathur, U., Pavlogiannis, A.: How hard is weak-memory testing? Proc. ACM Program. Lang. **8**(POPL) (Jan 2024). https://doi.org/10.1145/3632908

14. Di Giusto, C., Ferré, D., Laversa, L., Lozes, E.: A partial order view of message-passing communication models. Proc. ACM Program. Lang. **7**(POPL) (Jan 2023). https://doi.org/10.1145/3571248

15. Furbach, F., Meyer, R., Schneider, K., Senftleben, M.: Memory-model-aware testing: A unified complexity analysis. ACM Trans. Embed. Comput. Syst. **14**(4) (Sep 2015). https://doi.org/10.1145/2753761

16. Gondelman, L., Gregersen, S.O., Nieto, A., Timany, A., Birkedal, L.: Distributed causal memory: modular specification and verification in higher-order distributed separation logic. Proc. ACM Program. Lang. **5**(POPL) (Jan 2021). https://doi.org/10.1145/3434323

17. Kozen, D.: Lower bounds for natural proof systems. In: SFCS. p. 254–266. IEEE Computer Society, USA (1977). https://doi.org/10.1109/SFCS.1977.16

18. Lahav, O., Boker, U.: What's decidable about causally consistent shared memory? ACM Trans. Program. Lang. Syst. **44**(2) (Apr 2022). https://doi.org/10.1145/3505273

19. Lahav, O., Giannarakis, N., Vafeiadis, V.: Taming release-acquire consistency. In: POPL. p. 649–662. ACM, New York, NY, USA (2016). https://doi.org/10.1145/2837614.2837643

20. Lahav, O., Vafeiadis, V.: Owicki-gries reasoning for weak memory models. In: ICALP. pp. 311–323. Springer (2015). https://doi.org/10.1007/978-3-662-47666-6_25

21. Lamport, L.: How to make a multiprocessor computer that correctly executes multiprocess programs. IEEE Trans. Comput. **28**(9), 690–691 (Sep 1979). https://doi.org/10.1109/TC.1979.1675439

22. Lamport, L.: Time, clocks, and the ordering of events in a distributed system. Commun. ACM **21**(7), 558–565 (Jul 1978). https://doi.org/10.1145/359545.359563

23. Lesani, M., Bell, C.J., Chlipala, A.: Chapar: certified causally consistent distributed key-value stores. In: POPL. p. 357–370. ACM, New York, NY, USA (2016). https://doi.org/10.1145/2837614.2837622

24. Lloyd, W., Freedman, M.J., Kaminsky, M., Andersen, D.G.: Stronger semantics for low-latency geo-replicated storage. In: NSDI. p. 313–328. USENIX Association, USA (2013), https://dl.acm.org/doi/10.5555/2482626.2482657

25. Mostéfaoui, A., Perrin, M., Raynal, M.: Extending causal consistency to any object defined by a sequential specification. Bull. EATCS **125** (2018), http://eatcs.org/beatcs/index.php/beatcs/article/view/545

26. Owens, S., Sarkar, S., Sewell, P.: A better x86 memory model: x86-TSO. In: TPHOLs. pp. 391–407. Springer, Heidelberg (2009). https://doi.org/10.1007/978-3-642-03359-9_27

27. Perrin, M., Mostefaoui, A., Jard, C.: Causal consistency: beyond memory. In: PPoPP. ACM, New York, NY, USA (2016). https://doi.org/10.1145/2851141.2851170

28. Raynal, M., Schiper, A., Toueg, S.: The causal ordering abstraction and a simple way to implement it. Inf. Process. Lett. **39**(6), 343–350 (Oct 1991). https://doi.org/10.1016/0020-0190(91)90008-6

29. Schiper, A., Eggli, J., Sandoz, A.: A new algorithm to implement causal ordering. vol. 392, pp. 219–232 (09 1989). https://doi.org/10.1007/3-540-51687-5_45

30. Sovran, Y., Power, R., Aguilera, M.K., Li, J.: Transactional storage for geo-replicated systems. In: SOSP. p. 385–400. ACM, New York, NY, USA (2011). https://doi.org/10.1145/2043556.2043592
31. Tunç, H.C., Abdulla, P.A., Chakraborty, S., Krishna, S., Mathur, U., Pavlogiannis, A.: Optimal reads-from consistency checking for C11-style memory models. Proc. ACM Program. Lang. **7**(PLDI) (Jun 2023). https://doi.org/10.1145/3591251

A Category-Theoretic Framework for Dependent Effect Systems

Satoshi Kura[1], Marco Gaboardi[2], Taro Sekiyama[3,4], and Hiroshi Unno[5]

[1] Waseda University, Tokyo, Japan
[2] Boston University, Boston, Massachusetts, USA
[3] National Institute of Informatics, Tokyo, Japan
[4] SOKENDAI, Hayama, Japan
[5] Tohoku University, Sendai, Japan

Abstract. *Graded monads* refine traditional monads using *effect* annotations in order to describe quantitatively the computational effects that a program can generate. They have been successfully applied to a variety of formal systems for reasoning about effectful computations. However, existing categorical frameworks for graded monads do not support effects that may depend on program values, which we call *dependent effects*, thereby limiting their expressiveness. We address this limitation by introducing *indexed graded monads*, a categorical generalization of graded monads inspired by the fibrational "indexed" view and by classical categorical semantics of dependent type theories. We show how indexed graded monads provide semantics for a refinement type system with dependent effects. We also show how this type system can be instantiated with specific choices of parameters to obtain several formal systems for reasoning about specific program properties. These instances include, in particular, cost analysis, probability-bound reasoning, expectation-bound reasoning, and temporal safety verification.

Keywords: effect system · dependent type · refinement type · graded monad · categorical semantics

1 Introduction

Refinement types refine the class of values inhabiting types by means of logical predicates. By using these predicates to quantify over programs' input and output, users can specify and check properties that their programs satisfy, combining in this way programming with program reasoning. Refinement types have found application in a variety of areas including program verification [43, 55, 58, 60], cost analysis [13, 20, 22, 50, 61], probabilistic computations [33], incremental computation [12], security and privacy [7, 9, 36], etc. In several of these applications domains, computations are associated with some notion of *computational effects*, which are often quantitative. For example in cost analysis one usually represents the computational cost, in terms of time, memory space, or other resources, as

© The Author(s) 2026
R. Krebbers (Ed.): ESOP 2026, LNCS 16501, pp. 401–431, 2026.
https://doi.org/10.1007/978-3-032-22720-1_15

an effect produced by the program while computing the result. In differential privacy, random noise is used as a way to protect an individual's data. Aspects of the randomness can be modelled as a quantitative effect: one can represent the privacy loss as an effect that a program produces while computing the result, or one can represent the error incurred because of the noise as an effect produced during the private computation. As a result, most of the works from the application areas we mentioned before use some kind of effect tracking at the type system level, usually either in the form of a type and effect system [38, 40] or in the form of an effect annotated monad [5, 23, 27, 57].

A unifying theory that has emerged in the last decade to reason about quantitative effects is the one based on *graded monads* [27, 54]. Graded monads combines the idea of reasoning explicitly about effects, as in type and effect systems, with the idea of modelling computational effects using monads. Graded monads refine monads using effect annotations which typically are elements of an effect language which forms a preordered monoid. Similarly to ordinary monads, graded monads have strong semantical foundations in category theory. Intuitively, a monad is an endofunctor (on some specific category) satisfying certain compositionality principles, while a graded monad is a functor from the effect language (seen as a category) to the category of endofunctors (on some specific category) satisfying analogous compositionality laws that additionally track the quantitative effect annotations. Several works have explored the use of graded monads for reasoning about effects, e.g. [1, 2, 7, 10, 16–18, 25, 27–29, 35, 37, 42, 46, 47, 51, 52], and some of them have focused on their semantics foundation [10, 16, 18, 27, 28].

Combining two different ways of refinement, namely refinement types and graded monads, is a natural step towards more expressive systems for reasoning about effectful computations, as explored in several works [2, 7, 13, 37, 51]. Most of these works have focused on the practical aspects of this combination. In particular, in order to have precise quantitative information about effects, it is crucial in these systems to allow effects to depend on some of the computation's inputs. For example, in cost analysis it is natural to express the cost of a computation in terms of the size or value of the input data. So, a type system for cost analysis has to be able to express this dependency. Indeed, most of the works combining refinement types and graded monads support this form of dependency. This is usually achieved by allowing the grade to depend on the (refined) typing environment. However, this is not the case for the semantics models of graded monad studied so far. In all these models, grades are defined independently of the typing environment and they cannot express dependences on the input data. One can recover a limited form of dependency at the meta-level, as done for example in [2, 17], but one cannot use these models to interpret effects which can truly depend on the program input as the one used for example in [7, 51].

To overcome this situation, in this paper we focus on the semantics of effects which may depend on the program's input. We call this class of effects *dependent effects*. We consider dependent effects in combination with refinement types and we study their categorical semantics. Traditionally, categorical models of refinement types which allow dependencies on the context (similar to models for dependent types) are based on some form of indexed category. The indexing allows one to express naturally the different dependencies on context that different program components may have. While grading may also be seen as a form of indexing of monads, reason why graded monads are usually considered refinements of monads, it is actually of a semantically different nature from the indexing used to capture the dependency on the context. In order to combine these two forms of indexing in a principled way, we define a new notion of *indexed graded monad* where also effects in the effect language are indexed. Using this notion we build an interpretation for a refinement type system with dependent effects. Soundness in systems with graded monads usually guarantees that the grade is a quantitative bound on the runtime effect of the program. In our model, as we wanted, soundness for indexed graded monads extends these quantitative guarantees also to situations where the runtime effect of the program depends on some input value. In order to help with the design of models for indexed graded monads we provide a construction which build a "naturally chosen" indexed graded monad out of a traditional graded monad. This construction can be used to build a model of dependent effects out of a model for simple effects. We prove the usefulness of indexed graded monads and of our constructions by showing that several existing approaches based on graded monad can be obtained by properly instantiating our framework. These include cost analysis [24], union bound reasoning [8], expectation-bound reasoning [2], and temporal safety verification [44]. In summary, our contributions include:

- We consider a generic refinement type system with dependent effects modelled by indexed graded monads. Different dependent effect systems can be obtained by instantiating it with different axioms.
- We provide categorical semantics for our dependent effect system. Specifically, we formalize the notion of indexed preordered monoids and the notion of indexed graded monads, which are the indexed versions of the usual ones. We prove soundness of our type system with respect to this semantics.
- We provide a construction that builds canonical models of indexed graded monads out of models of traditional graded monads. This allows us to give a semantics to dependent effects starting from the semantics of simple effects.
- We instantiate our framework to capture several examples of dependent effects that have been studied in the literature.

Related work Value-dependent systems for reasoning about certain specific effectful behavior have been broadly studied for a variety of problems. Cost analysis (especially, in terms of time) is one of the actively studied problems, and many value-dependent type and effect systems for bound or amortized analysis have been proposed [11, 21, 22, 30, 45, 50]. Cost analysis can be generalized to linear-time temporal safety verification, which aims to reason about sequences of events, by encoding a cost as a finite number of events to be raised. For linear-time temporal verification, value-dependent effect systems for temporal verification, called *temporal effect systems*, have been studied [44, 53]. As a further generalization,

Gordon [19] studied *effect quantales*, which are an algebraic structure behind effects sensitive to their order, and gave a general value-dependent effect system parameterized by effect quantales. Gordon [19] showed that the proposed effect system can be instantiated to support linear-time temporal safety verification. However, it remains unclear whether effect quantales are expressive enough to address probabilistic reasoning. In contrast, our dependent effect system can accommodate probabilistic reasoning like the union bound logic, thanks to its semantic foundations based on the category theory. Another generic approach to dependent effect systems is the use of Dijkstra monads [56], which enable effective reasoning about effectful higher-order programs through weakest pre-conditions. The reasoning based on Dijkstra monads can address arbitrary monadic effects, but it is left open whether they can also be used for reasoning about probabilistic programs [39].

2   Informal Overview

In this section we will informally introduce our semantic framework. We will use cost analysis as a running example, and defer other example instances of our framework to Section 6.

2.1   Graded Monads

Cost analysis aims at providing upper bounds on the running time, or any other computational resource, of programs. A standard approach to cost analysis is based on the use of a cost monad [13]. This is a monad annotated with a natural number expressing an upper bound on the number of `Tick` (representing one unit of cost) the program execution encounters.

The cost monad can be seen as an instance of a *graded monad*, a concept which emerged in the context of graded algebra [54], and which was related to computational effects in [27]. Given a preordered monoid $\mathcal{M}$, an $\mathcal{M}$-graded monad (T, η, μ) consists of a functor $T : \mathcal{M} \times \mathbb{C} \to \mathbb{C}$ (we often write the first argument $m \in \mathcal{M}$ of T as a subscript, like T_m), a unit $\eta_X : X \to T_1 X$, where 1 is the unit of the monoid $\mathcal{M}$, and a multiplication $\mu_{m_1,m_2,X} : T_{m_1} T_{m_2} X \to T_{m_1 \cdot m_2} X$, where m_1 and m_2 are elements of $\mathcal{M}$ and $\cdot$ is the multiplication of the monoid, satisfying the graded version of the monad laws. When using graded monads to reason about effects, we think about the elements $m \in \mathcal{M}$ as *effects*, and we use them to *grade* the functor T. A graded monad $T_m A$, for some type A, can be seen as a *quantitative refinement* of TA in the sense that it is inhabited by those computations in TA that generate effects upper bounded by m. Here, the preorder on $\mathcal{M}$ expresses the subsumption relation: if $m_1 \leq m_2$, then $T_{m_1} A$ is subsumed by $T_{m_2} A$. In programs, graded monads can be manipulated using the traditional monadic return and let binding typed with the following graded rules.

$$\frac{\Gamma \vdash V : A}{\Gamma \vdash \mathtt{return}\ V : T_1 A} \qquad \frac{\Gamma \vdash M : T_{m_1} A \qquad \Gamma, x : A \vdash N : T_{m_2} B}{\Gamma \vdash \mathtt{let}\ x \leftarrow M\ \mathtt{in}\ N : T_{m_1 \cdot m_2} B}$$

To capture cost analysis we can instantiate the framework of graded monads using the additive monoid $(\mathbb{N}_\infty, 0, +, \leq)$ of extended natural numbers and adding the primitive `Tick` $: T_1$ `unit` which accounts for one unit of cost (notice that the unit of the monoid used in the type of return is now 0). The semantic soundness of the graded monad framework [27] will then guarantee that the type $T_m A$ can be assigned only to computations that generate the number of ticks (i.e., the cost) upper bounded by m. It is worth stressing that it is the semantic soundness of the graded monad framework that justifies the "quantitative refinement" view we informally discussed above.

2.2 Motivation for Dependent Effects

One of the limitations of existing frameworks for graded monads is that they cannot express effects that depend on program values, and so they are limited in their foundational scope. To explain this, let us consider the following example.

$$\texttt{loop\_cost} \quad \coloneqq \quad \mu f\, x.\texttt{if}\ \ x < n\ \ \texttt{then Tick;}\ f(x+1)\ \texttt{else return ()}$$

The function `loop_cost` with simple type `int` $\rightarrow$ `unit` takes an integer x and increments it by 1 until it reaches n. It is easy to see that the cost of this function is $n - x$ if $x < n$ and 0 otherwise. A natural way to express the cost of this function is to allow effects to depend on values in the program. We call such effects *dependent effects*. If we allow dependent effects, the natural typing judgment for the function is

$$n : \texttt{int} \quad \vdash \quad \texttt{loop\_cost} \quad : \quad (x : \texttt{int}) \to T_{\max\{0, n-x\}} \texttt{unit}$$

Here, $\max\{0, n-x\}$ is a dependent effect, which depends on $n : \texttt{int}$ and $x : \texttt{int}$.

Most of existing framework for graded monads cannot express dependent effects because effects are restricted to constant elements of a monoid, which we call *simple effects*. Simple effects limit the expressiveness of these frameworks. If we reason about the example above with simple effects, then a constant $m \in \mathbb{N}_\infty$ must be chosen so that m uniformly bounds the cost of the function `loop_cost` for all $n : \texttt{int}$ and $x : \texttt{int}$. In this case, the only possible choice of m is the trivial upper bound $m = \infty$. So, the best type those framework can give to the function `loop_cost` is the following:

$$n : \texttt{int} \quad \vdash \quad \texttt{loop\_cost} \quad : \quad \texttt{int} \to T_\infty \texttt{unit}$$

This is in sharp contrast with current practice, where systems combining specific instances of graded monads actually also support dependent effects. For example, the cost analyses by [13,22,51], all support dependent effects. Similarly, the privacy analyses by [1,7,37], the incremental computation analysis by [12], the temporal verification by [44] all support dependent effects. Unfortunately, as far as we know, there is no existing semantic framework based on graded monads that can express these dependent effects.

	Simple effect system	Dependent effect system
Type $\Gamma \vdash A$ Term $\Gamma \vdash V : A$	category $\mathbb{C}$ $[\![A]\!]$: object in $\mathbb{C}$ $[\![V]\!]$: morphism in $\mathbb{C}$	indexed category $\{\mathbb{E}_I\}_{I \in \mathbb{B}}$ $[\![A]\!]$: object in $\mathbb{E}_{[\![\Gamma]\!]}$ $[\![V]\!]$: morphism in $\mathbb{E}_{[\![\Gamma]\!]}$
Effect $\Gamma \vdash \mathcal{E}$	monoid $\mathcal{M}$ $[\![\mathcal{E}]\!] \in \mathcal{M}$	indexed monoid $\{\mathrm{M}_I\}_{I \in \mathbb{B}}$ $[\![\mathcal{E}]\!] \in \mathrm{M}_{[\![\Gamma]\!]}$
Computational effect	graded monad $T : \mathcal{M} \times \mathbb{C} \to \mathbb{C}$	indexed graded monad $T = \{T_I : \mathrm{M}_I \times \mathbb{E}_I \to \mathbb{E}_I\}_{I \in \mathbb{B}}$

Fig. 1: Models of simple and dependent effect systems.

2.3 Our Idea: Indexed Graded Monads

To address the limitation we outlined above, we extend the definition of graded monads to allow dependencies on program values. In order to do this, we take inspiration from (1) the categorical semantics of dependent type theory and (2) the 2-category theory point of view.

In dependent type theory, types $\Gamma \vdash A$ are indexed by contexts Γ. Thus, a model of dependent type theory is given by an indexed category $\{\mathbb{E}_{[\![\Gamma]\!]}\}_{\Gamma:\mathrm{ctx}}$ indexed by contexts Γ (Fig. 1, top row). More precisely, if $\mathbb{B}$ is a category for interpreting contexts Γ, then an indexed category $\mathbb{E}_{(-)}$ is a contravariant functor $\mathbb{B}^{\mathrm{op}} \to \mathbf{Cat}$, which is known to be equivalent to a Grothendieck fibration $\mathbb{C} \to \mathbb{B}$. Below, we keep writing an indexed category $\mathbb{E}_{(-)}$ as $\{\mathbb{E}_I\}_{I \in \mathbb{B}}$.

If we take a closer look at the cost analysis example above, we can see that dependent effects also have a similar "indexed" structure. In the example, we have a dependent effect $n : \mathtt{int}, x : \mathtt{int} \vdash \max\{0, n - x\} : \mathbf{Effect}$ (using a well-formedness judgment for effects, formally introduced in Section 3), for which the "index" is given by the context $n : \mathtt{int}, x : \mathtt{int}$. Hence, we can interpret this dependent effect as a function $[\![\max\{0, n - x\}]\!] \in \mathbf{Set}(\mathbb{Z}^2, \mathrm{N}_\infty)$, where $\mathbf{Set}(\mathbb{Z}^2, \mathrm{N}_\infty)$ is the set of functions from $\mathbb{Z}^2$ to the preordered monoid N_∞. Following this intuition, to interpret dependent effects over a preordered monoid $\mathcal{M}$, we can consider families of functions $\{\mathbf{Set}(I, \mathcal{M})\}_{I \in \mathbf{Set}}$. Since $\mathcal{M}$ is a monoid, also each set $\mathbf{Set}(I, \mathcal{M})$ is a monoid, and hence it can be used as a "grade" in the traditional sense. More generally, we have that $\mathbf{Set}(-, \mathcal{M})$ is a contravariant functor $\mathbf{Set}^{\mathrm{op}} \to \mathbf{PreMon}$ from the category $\mathbf{Set}$ of sets to the category $\mathbf{PreMon}$ of preordered monoids. So, generalizing one step further we consider functors $\mathbb{B}^{\mathrm{op}} \to \mathbf{PreMon}$ and we call them *indexed preordered monoid* (Fig. 1, middle row).

Following the same intuition we define *indexed graded monads* as families of graded monads $\{T_I : \mathrm{M}_I \times \mathbb{E}_I \to \mathbb{E}_I\}_{I \in \mathbb{B}}$ whose grading monoids are given by an indexed monoid $\{\mathrm{M}_I\}_{I \in \mathbb{B}}$ (Fig. 1, bottom row). More formally, an indexed graded monad is a contravariant functor from a category $\mathbb{B}$ to the category of graded monads. We can now use indexed graded monads to give semantics to dependent effect systems.

Example 1 (Indexed graded cost monad on the family fibration). Consider the family fibration $\mathrm{fam}_{\mathbf{Set}} : \mathbf{Fam}(\mathbf{Set}) \to \mathbf{Set}$, which is a typical model of dependent type theory. This corresponds to the indexed category given by a family of I-indexed sets: $\{\mathbf{Fam}(\mathbf{Set})_I\}_{I \in \mathbf{Set}} = \{\{X_i\}_{i \in I}\}_{I \in \mathbf{Set}}$. For example, the type $n : \mathtt{nat} \vdash \mathtt{Vec}\ n$ of integer vectors of length n is interpreted as $\{\mathbb{Z}^n\}_{n \in \mathbb{N}}$ in this setting. Now, an indexed graded monad $\{T_I : \mathbf{Set}(I, \mathbb{N}_\infty) \times \mathbf{Fam}(\mathbf{Set})_I \to \mathbf{Fam}(\mathbf{Set})_I\}_{I \in \mathbf{Set}}$ for cost analysis is defined as follows.

$$(T_I)_f\{X_i\}_{i \in I} \quad := \quad \{\ X_i \times \{\ m \in \mathbb{N}_\infty \mid m \leq f(i)\ \}\ \}_{i \in I}$$

This is an indexed graded version of the cost monad $(-) \times \mathbb{N}_\infty$, which captures the situation where the cost is upper bounded by a dependent effect $f : I \to \mathbb{N}_\infty$. $\qquad \Box$

The correspondence shown in Fig. 1 can also be interpreted by the 2-category point of view. It is broadly understood that to pass from simple type theory to dependent type theory one has to go from the 2-category $\mathbf{Cat}$ of categories to the 2-category $\mathbf{ICat}(\mathbb{B})$ of $\mathbb{B}$-indexed categories (or equivalently, to the 2-category $\mathbf{Fib}(\mathbb{B})$ of fibrations over base category $\mathbb{B}$). Now, monoids and graded monads are definable in any 2-category (with finite products). If we define them in $\mathbf{Cat}$, we obtain monoids and graded monads. If we define them in $\mathbf{ICat}(\mathbb{B})$, then we obtain indexed monoids and indexed graded monads.

2.4   From Graded Monads to Indexed Graded Monads

Constructing models for dependent effects as outlined before can be challenging, hence we also provide a method to construct a model for dependent effects out of a model for simple effects. More specifically, we show that given an ordinary graded monad, we can construct an indexed graded monad.

Construction of indexed preordered monoids Suppose we have a preordered monoid $\mathcal{M}$ as a model of simple effects. As we discussed above, a natural model to interpret dependent effects can be the $\mathbf{Set}$-indexed preordered monoid $\{\mathbf{Set}(I, \mathcal{M})\}_{I \in \mathbf{Set}}$. For example, $n : \mathtt{int}, x : \mathtt{int} \vdash \max\{0, n - x\} : \mathbf{Effect}$ can be interpreted as $[\![\max\{0, n - x\}]\!] \in \mathbf{Set}(\mathbb{Z}^2, \mathbb{N}_\infty)$ as we have already discussed above. So, we could try to have a method to construct this interpretation from $\mathbb{N}_\infty$. However, in general, we may have contexts Γ that are refined by predicates. So, we actually need a $\mathbf{Pred}$-indexed preordered monoid where $\mathbf{Pred}$ is the category of predicates and predicate-preserving functions, i.e., an object is a pair $(I, P \subseteq I)$ of a set I and a predicate P on I, and a morphism $(I, P \subseteq I) \to (J, Q \subseteq J)$ is a function $f : I \to J$ such that $f(i) \in Q$ for each $i \in P$. One could try to use the change-of-base construction along the forgetful functor $\mathbf{Pred} \to \mathbf{Set}$, but this does not work because it simply forgets the predicates, and as a result, the subeffecting relation becomes weaker than we expect. For example, the subeffecting relation $x : \{x : \mathtt{int} \mid x \geq 1\} \vDash |x + 1| \leq |2x|$, which compares two effects $|x + 1|$ and $|2x|$ under the assumption $x \geq 1$, should be valid. However, the change-of-base construction does not allow us to take the predicate $x \geq 1$ into account, in which case the subeffecting relation becomes invalid, as $|x + 1| \leq |2x|$ is not true for $x = 0$. To address this issue, our construction instead defines a **Pred**-indexed preordered monoid as follows.

$$\mathbf{Pred} \ni (I, P \subseteq I) \mapsto \big(\mathbf{Set}(I, \mathcal{M}), \leq_P\big) \qquad f \leq_P g \overset{\text{def}}{\iff} \forall i \in P, f(i) \leq g(i)$$

A key point in this definition is that we use the pointwise order on $\mathbf{Set}(I, \mathcal{M})$ restricted to the predicate P instead of the unrestricted pointwise order.

Construction of indexed graded monads We now want to construct an indexed graded monad graded by the **Pred**-indexed preordered monoid above.

Let T be a monad on **Set** that models computational effects. We can build a model of simple effect systems, by using an $\mathcal{M}$-*graded monad lifting* $\dot{T}$ of T along the predicate fibration pred : $\mathbf{Pred} \to \mathbf{Set}$.

$$\dot{T} : \qquad \mathcal{M} \times \mathbf{Pred} \ni (m, (I, Q \subseteq I)) \qquad \mapsto \qquad (TI, \dot{T}_m Q \subseteq TI) \in \mathbf{Pred}$$

As in the case of ordinary monad liftings, the functor pred maps the graded monad structure of $\dot{T}$ to the monad structure of T. This ensures that interpreting computations in the total category **Pred** yields liftings of their interpretations in the base category **Set**, thereby establishing the soundness of the simple effect system.

We would like to extend this construction to indexed graded monads. Since we now consider contexts and types refined by predicates, a context Γ is interpreted as a predicate $[\![\Gamma]\!] = (I, P \subseteq I) \in \mathbf{Pred}$, and a type $\Gamma \vdash A$ is interpreted as a family of predicates $\{(X_i, Q_i \subseteq X_i)\}_{i \in P}$. If we apply $\dot{T}$ index-wise, then a graded monadic type $\Gamma \vdash T_{\mathcal{E}} A$ where $\Gamma \vdash \mathcal{E} : \mathbf{Effect}$ would be interpreted as a family of predicates $\{(TX_i, \dot{T}_{f(i)} Q_i)\}_{i \in P}$ where $[\![\mathcal{E}]\!] = f \in \mathbf{Set}(I, \mathcal{M})$ is the interpretation of the dependent effect $\mathcal{E}$. This intuition brings us to the construction of a **Pred**-indexed graded monad $\dot{T}' = \{\dot{T}'_{(I,P)}\}_{(I,P) \in \mathbf{Pred}}$ (graded by $\mathbf{Set}(-, \mathcal{M})$) from the graded monad lifting $\dot{T}$ (graded by $\mathcal{M}$) as follows.

$$\dot{T}'_{(I,P)} : \quad \big(f : I \to \mathcal{M}, \quad \{(X_i, Q_i \subseteq X_i)\}_{i \in P}\big) \qquad \mapsto \qquad \{(TX_i, \dot{T}_{f(i)} Q_i)\}_{i \in P}$$

We formalize this construction in Section 5, allowing slightly more general predicate fibrations, and use it to provide concrete instances of our type system for cost analysis, union bound reasoning, expectation reasoning, and temporal safety verification in Section 6.

3   A Dependent Effect System with Refinement Types

We consider two layers of type systems. The first layer is a simply typed language based on fine-grain call-by-value (FGCBV) [34]. The language is parameterized by a set of generic effects [49], which allows us to instantiate the language for various applications such as cost analysis and union bound. Then, we define the second layer, a dependent effect system on top of the simply typed FGCBV. This is a novel dependent type system that allows effects to depend on values. Combined with refinement types, the dependent effect system allows us to reason about higher-order functional programs similarly to graded Hoare logics [17]. We explain these type systems using cost analysis and union bound as running examples. We will show other instances later in Section 6.

3.1 Simply Typed Fine-Grain Call-by-Value

In FGCBV, values and computations are syntactically separated as follows.

Definition 2. Let **Op** be a set of effect-free operations and **GenEff** a set of generic effects. *Value terms* V, W and *computation terms* M, N of the fine-grain call-by-value are defined as follows.

$$V, W ::= \quad x \mid \lambda x.M \mid () \mid (V, W) \mid \texttt{inl } V \mid \texttt{inr } V \mid \mu f\, x.M \mid \texttt{op}(V)$$
$$M, N ::= \quad \texttt{return } V \mid \texttt{let } x \leftarrow M \texttt{ in } N \mid \texttt{pm } V \texttt{ to } (x, y) \texttt{ in } M \mid V\, W$$
$$\mid \texttt{gef}(V) \mid \texttt{case } V \texttt{ of } \{\texttt{inl } x \mapsto M, \texttt{inr } y \mapsto N\} \qquad \square$$

Here, a recursive function written as $\mu f\, x.M$ is defined (semantically) as the fixed point of $f \mapsto \lambda x.M$. Effect-free operations (or pure functions) $\texttt{op} \in \mathbf{Op}$ and generic effects $\texttt{gef} \in \mathbf{GenEff}$ can take multiple arguments by using tuples. The language has a simple type system, which we will later extend to a dependent effect system in Section 3.2. Since the typing rules for simple types are standard, we only give the definition of simple types here and omit lengthy typing rules.

Definition 3. Let $\mathbf{Base} = \{\texttt{unit}, \texttt{int}, \texttt{real}, \texttt{nat}, \ldots\}$ be a set of base types. We assume that $\mathbf{Base}$ contains at least the unit type $\texttt{unit}$. *Simple value types* A, B and *simple computation types* C, D are defined as follows.

$$A, B ::= b \mid A \times B \mid A \to C \mid A + B \quad \text{where } b \in \mathbf{Base} \qquad C, D ::= TA \qquad \square$$

Since we have sum types $A + B$, the type $\texttt{bool}$ of boolean values is defined as a shorthand for $\texttt{bool} := \texttt{unit} + \texttt{unit}$, and the if-expression is defined as a shorthand for case analysis on $\texttt{true} := \texttt{inl } ()$ and $\texttt{false} := \texttt{inr } ()$. We say that a value type is a *ground type* if it does not contain arrow types. Specifically, a ground type is in the fragment of simple value types defined by $A, B ::= b \mid A \times B \mid A + B$. We assume that each effect-free operation $\texttt{op} \in \mathbf{Op}$ and each generic effect $\texttt{gef} \in \mathbf{GenEff}$ have a simple type signature $\texttt{op} : A \twoheadrightarrow B$ and $\texttt{gef} : A \twoheadrightarrow B$, respectively, where the input type A and the output type B are ground types.

Example 4 (simple type signatures of effect-free operations). Effect-free operations contain operations such as arithmetic operations, comparison operations, type conversion functions, and constant values for $\texttt{int}$, $\texttt{real}$, and $\texttt{nat}$. For example, the addition operation for integers has the simple type signature $+ : \texttt{int} \times \texttt{int} \twoheadrightarrow \texttt{int}$, and the constant value 0 for integers has the simple type signature $0 : \texttt{unit} \twoheadrightarrow \texttt{int}$. $\qquad \square$

Example 5 (cost analysis). For cost analysis, we use the following generic effect: $\mathbf{GenEff} = \{\texttt{Tick} : \texttt{nat} \twoheadrightarrow \texttt{unit}\}$. Here, we slightly change the type signature of the generic effect $\texttt{Tick}$ from Section 2 so that it takes a natural number n and incurs a cost of n. $\qquad \square$

Example 6 (union bound). For union bound logic, we consider the following generic effect: $\mathbf{GenEff} = \{\texttt{Lap} : \texttt{real} \times \texttt{real} \twoheadrightarrow \texttt{real}\}$. The generic effect

$\mathsf{Lap}(\epsilon, m)$ takes two real numbers as parameters for the Laplace distribution, where ϵ is the scale parameter and m is the location parameter, and returns a real number sampled from the Laplace distribution if $\epsilon > 0$. Here, the probability density function of the Laplace distribution is given by $L_{\epsilon,m}(x) = \frac{1}{2\epsilon}\exp(-\frac{|x-m|}{\epsilon})$. If $\epsilon \leq 0$, then $\mathsf{Lap}(\epsilon, m)$ returns an arbitrary value. $\qquad\square$

Well-typed terms in the simple type system are denoted as $\Gamma \vdash V : A$ and $\Gamma \vdash M : C$ where Γ is a *simple context*, which is defined as a finite list of pairs of variables and simple value types. Typing rules for the simple type system are standard and omitted.

3.2   A Dependent Effect System with Refinement Types

Types We extend simple value/computation types in three ways: (1) by using dependent types, (2) by refining base types with predicates, and (3) by grading computation types with dependent effects. The extension is called *graded refinement value/computation types*. Meta-variables $\dot{A}, \dot{C}$ for these types are written with a dot above them to distinguish them from simple types.

Definition 7. Let **BEff** be a set of *basic effects*, which are symbols that represent dependent effects. *Graded refinement value types* $\dot{A}, \dot{B}$; *graded refinement computation types* $\dot{C}, \dot{D}$; and *dependent-effect terms* $\mathcal{E}$ are defined as follows.

$$\dot{A}, \dot{B} \; := \; \{x : b \mid \phi\} \mid (x : \dot{A}) \times \dot{B} \mid (x : \dot{A}) \to \dot{C} \mid \dot{A} + \dot{B}$$

$$\dot{C}, \dot{D} \; := \quad T_{\mathcal{E}}\dot{A} \qquad\qquad \mathcal{E} \; := \quad 1 \mid \mathcal{E}_1 \cdot \mathcal{E}_2 \mid \mathsf{be}(V) \qquad \text{where } \mathsf{be} \in \mathbf{BEff}$$

Here, ϕ ranges over formulas. We write $\lfloor \dot{A} \rfloor$ and $\lfloor \dot{C} \rfloor$ for the simple types obtained by forgetting predicates and dependent-effect terms. We call them the *underlying type* of $\dot{A}$ and $\dot{C}$. For example, the underlying type of $(x : \{x : \mathtt{int} \mid n \geq x\}) \to T_{n-x}\{u : \mathtt{unit} \mid \mathbf{true}\}$ is $\mathtt{int} \to T\mathtt{unit}$. $\qquad\square$

Dependent Types We consider *dependent pair types* $(x : \dot{A}) \times \dot{B}$ and *dependent function types* $(x : \dot{A}) \to \dot{C}$, in which the type of the second component may depend on x. Note that types are allowed to depend only on value terms, but not on computation terms. This approach to combining dependent types with computational effects follows EMLTT [4], a dependently typed call-by-push-value calculus. When x does not occur in $\dot{B}, \dot{C}$, we often write as $\dot{A} \to \dot{C} = (x : \dot{A}) \to \dot{C}$ and $\dot{A} \times \dot{B} = (x : \dot{A}) \times \dot{B}$.

Refinement Types To specify preconditions and postconditions of programs, we use a type of the form $\{x : b \mid \phi\}$, which we call a *refinement base type*. Intuitively, a value term V has type $\{x : b \mid \phi\}$ if V is of base type b and satisfies the formula ϕ. When the formula ϕ is always true, we write b as a shorthand of $\{x : b \mid \mathbf{true}\}$. *Formulas* ϕ, ψ in refinement base types are constructed from atomic formulas (including **true** and **false**) using boolean connectives $\wedge, \vee, \implies$. Here, an *atomic formula* $\mathsf{a}(V)$ is constructed from a predicate symbol a and a value term V. We assume that the argument type A of each predicate symbol $\mathtt{a} : A \to \mathbf{Fml}$ is a (simple) ground type and do not consider predicate symbols for computation terms. This implies that any value term occurring in a formula does not contain lambda abstractions and recursive functions. On the other hand, it is convenient to extend the syntax of value terms V, W in formulas to include projections (recall that pattern matching is defined as a *computation* term in Definition 2), which allows us to write $(x : \dot{A}) \times (y : \dot{B}) \to \dot{C}$ as a syntactic sugar for $(z : \dot{A} \times \dot{B}) \to \dot{C}[\mathtt{fst}\ z/x, \mathtt{snd}\ z/y]$. Thus, we use *ground value terms* defined below as value terms occurring in formulas.

$$V, W \quad ::= \quad x \mid () \mid (V, W) \mid \mathtt{inl}\ V \mid \mathtt{inr}\ V \mid \mathtt{fst}\ V \mid \mathtt{snd}\ V \mid \mathtt{op}(V) \qquad (1)$$

Note that effect-free operations are allowed here, but generic effects are not. A formula is well-formed and written as $\Gamma \vdash \phi : \mathbf{Fml}$ if any value terms occurring in ϕ is well-typed in Γ and predicate symbols are applied to value terms of appropriate types.

Dependent Effects The main novelty of our dependent effect system is the use of dependent-effect terms $\mathcal{E}$. Intuitively, a dependent-effect term represents an element of a grading monoid that depends on value terms. To convert value terms to dependent-effect terms, we use *basic effects* in $\mathbf{BEff}$. We write $\mathtt{be} : A \to \mathbf{Effect}$ if $\mathtt{be}$ is a basic effect that takes a value term of type A and returns an effect (i.e., an element of a preordered monoid). We assume that the argument type A of each basic effect $\mathtt{be} : A \to \mathbf{Effect}$ is a (simple) ground type. Similarly to formulas, we use ground value terms (1) in dependent-effect terms.

Example 8 (cost analysis). Consider the cost of the following function:

$$M \quad ::= \quad \mu f\ x.\mathtt{if}\ x < n\ \mathtt{then}\ \mathtt{let}\ z \leftarrow \mathtt{Tick}\ 1\ \mathtt{in}\ f(x+1)\ \mathtt{else}\ \mathtt{return}\ ()$$

Here, we consider $(\mathbb{N}, 0, +, \leq)$ as a grading monoid. The program M is a function that takes an integer x and increments it by 1 until it reaches n. It is easy to see that the cost of this function is upper bounded by $\max\{0, n - x\}$. We can express this using our type system as follows:

$$n : \mathtt{int} \quad \vdash \quad M : (x : \mathtt{int}) \to T_{\mathtt{nat2eff}(\max\{0, n-x\})}\mathtt{unit}$$

Here, we use the function $\mathtt{nat2eff} : \mathtt{nat} \to \mathbf{Effect}$ as a basic effect that converts a value term $\max\{0, n - x\} : \mathtt{nat}$ to an effect. $\qquad \square$

Example 9 (simple effect). If a set of basic effects $\mathbf{BEff}$ consists only of a constant effect $\underline{m} : \mathtt{unit} \to \mathbf{Effect}$ for each $m \in \mathcal{M}$ in a grading monoid $\mathcal{M}$, then we obtain a simple effect system. $\qquad \square$

Well-formed Types We define a *graded refinement context* $\dot{\Gamma}$ as a finite list of pairs of variables and graded refinement value types. The *underlying context* $\lfloor \dot{\Gamma} \rfloor$ is a simple context obtained by applying $\lfloor - \rfloor$ to each type in $\dot{\Gamma}$, that is, $\lfloor x_1 : \dot{A}_1, \ldots, x_n : \dot{A}_n \rfloor := x_1 : \lfloor \dot{A}_1 \rfloor, \ldots, x_n : \lfloor \dot{A}_n \rfloor$.

As is common in dependent type systems, we consider judgements for well-formed contexts $\dot{\Gamma} \vdash$ and well-formed types $\dot{\Gamma} \vdash \dot{A}$, $\dot{\Gamma} \vdash \dot{C}$. In addition, we need a judgement for well-formed dependent-effect terms $\dot{\Gamma} \vdash \mathcal{E} : \mathbf{Effect}$. The intuition of well-formedness is that free variables in types and dependent-effect terms are bound in the context $\dot{\Gamma}$. Rules for well-formedness are mostly straightforward. The only rule that requires some attention is the rule for basic effects: for each basic effect $\mathtt{be} : A \to \mathbf{Effect}$, the dependent-effect term $\dot{\Gamma} \vdash \mathtt{be}(V) : \mathbf{Effect}$ is well-formed if $\lfloor \dot{\Gamma} \rfloor \vdash V : A$ is well-typed in the simple type system, and $\dot{\Gamma} \vdash$ is well-formed. One may notice that the predicates in the context $\dot{\Gamma}$ are not used when constructing dependent-effect terms; however, as we will see in Example 11, they play a role in sub-effecting.

Typing Rules for Terms Well-typed value terms and well-typed computation terms are denoted as $\dot{\Gamma} \vdash V : \dot{A}$ and $\dot{\Gamma} \vdash M : \dot{C}$, respectively. Most typing rules are straightforward (Fig. 2). In the rules for function application and generic effects, the argument value term V is substituted for the variable x in dependent-effect terms. For $\mathtt{return}$ and $\mathtt{let}$, we use the monoid structure of effects. The rule for $\mathtt{let}$ does not allow $\mathcal{E}_2$ to depend on x. This restriction stems from the difficulty of combining computational effects with dependent types, as discussed in [48, Section 2.6] and [4]. At first glance, this restriction may appear to be a serious limitation of our dependent effect system. However, even with this restriction, our type system can reason about interesting examples by using refinement types to describe the possible outcomes of computations.

Example 10. Suppose that $f : (n : \mathtt{int}) \to T_n\{m : \mathtt{int} \mid m = 2n\}$ is a function that returns $2n$ at cost n, and consider the cost of the following simple program:

$$x : \mathtt{int} \quad \vdash \quad \mathtt{let}\ y \leftarrow f\ x\ \mathtt{in}\ f\ y \quad : \quad T_{3x}\{m : \mathtt{int} \mid m = 4x\} \tag{2}$$

Here, we omit f from the context for brevity. By the typing rule for function application, the second computation $f\ y$ has the following type:

$$x : \mathtt{int}, \quad y : \{m : \mathtt{int} \mid m = 2x\} \quad \vdash \quad f\ y \quad : \quad T_y\{m : \mathtt{int} \mid m = 2y\}$$

We cannot directly apply the typing rule for $\mathtt{let}$ because the result type contains the variable y, which is bound to the result of the first computation. However, since we know $y = 2x$ from the refinement type, the variable y in the result type of $f\ y$ can be eliminated using the following subtyping relation.

$$T_y\{m : \mathtt{int} \mid m = 2y\} \quad <: \quad T_{2x}\{m : \mathtt{int} \mid m = 4x\}$$

Therefore, our type system can still verify that the cost of the program in (2) is upper bounded by $3x$, which, in this case, coincides with the exact cost. $\quad\square$

This approach may not work in general, as we show in [32, Example 40] for union bound logic, but a better treatment of sequencing is left as future work.

To reason about effect-free operations and generic effects in our dependent effect system, we assume that their *refinement type signatures* are given. An

$$\frac{\dot{\Gamma} \vdash V : (x : \dot{A}) \to T_{\mathcal{E}}\dot{B} \quad \dot{\Gamma} \vdash W : \dot{A}}{\dot{\Gamma} \vdash V\,W : T_{\mathcal{E}[W/x]}\dot{B}[W/x]} \qquad \frac{\dot{\Gamma} \vdash V : \dot{A} \quad \mathtt{gef} : (x : \dot{A}) \overset{\mathcal{E}}{\twoheadrightarrow} \dot{B}}{\dot{\Gamma} \vdash \mathtt{gef}(V) : T_{\mathcal{E}[V/x]}\dot{B}[V/x]}$$

$$\frac{\dot{\Gamma} \vdash V : \dot{A}}{\dot{\Gamma} \vdash \mathtt{return}\ V : T_1\dot{A}} \qquad \frac{\dot{\Gamma} \vdash M : T_{\mathcal{E}_1}\dot{A} \quad \dot{\Gamma} \vdash T_{\mathcal{E}_2}\dot{B} \quad \dot{\Gamma}, x : \dot{A} \vdash N : T_{\mathcal{E}_2}\dot{B}}{\dot{\Gamma} \vdash \mathtt{let}\ x \leftarrow M\ \mathtt{in}\ N : T_{\mathcal{E}_1 \cdot \mathcal{E}_2}\dot{B}}$$

Fig. 2: Selected typing rules. Substitution of a value term V for a variable x is denoted by suffixing $[V/x]$.

effect-free operation has a refinement type signature of the form $\mathtt{op} : (x : \dot{A}) \twoheadrightarrow \dot{B}$ where $\vdash \dot{A}$ and $x : \dot{A} \vdash \dot{B}$ are well-formed, and $\lfloor \dot{A} \rfloor \twoheadrightarrow \lfloor \dot{B} \rfloor$ coincides with the simple type signature of $\mathtt{op}$. For example, the constant 0 has refinement type signature $0 : \mathtt{unit} \twoheadrightarrow \{x : \mathtt{int} \mid x = 0\}$, and the addition operator has $(+) : (x : \mathtt{int}) \times (y : \mathtt{int}) \twoheadrightarrow \{z : \mathtt{int} \mid z = x + y\}$. Similarly, a generic effect has a refinement type signature of the form $\mathtt{gef} : (x : \dot{A}) \overset{\mathcal{E}}{\twoheadrightarrow} \dot{B}$ where $\vdash \dot{A}$, $x : \dot{A} \vdash \dot{B}$, and $x : \dot{A} \vdash \mathcal{E} : \mathbf{Effect}$ are well-formed, and $\lfloor \dot{A} \rfloor \twoheadrightarrow \lfloor \dot{B} \rfloor$ is the simple type signature of $\mathtt{gef}$. For example, the generic effect $\mathtt{Tick}$ for cost analysis (Example 5) has refinement type signature $\mathtt{Tick} : (n : \mathtt{nat}) \overset{n}{\twoheadrightarrow} \mathtt{unit}$, which means that the cost of $\mathtt{Tick}\ n$ is upper bounded by n.

Subtyping Subtyping relation is denoted as $\dot{\Gamma} \vdash \dot{A} <: \dot{B}$ and $\dot{\Gamma} \vdash \dot{C} <: \dot{D}$. Similarly to the consequence rule in Hoare logic, it allows us to derive $\dot{\Gamma} \vdash V : \dot{B}$ from $\dot{\Gamma} \vdash V : \dot{A}$ and $\dot{\Gamma} \vdash \dot{A} <: \dot{B}$. To derive subtyping relations $\dot{\Gamma} \vdash \{x : b \mid \phi\} <: \{x : b \mid \psi\}$ for refinement base types, we use the semantic validity of formulas $\dot{\Gamma}, x : b \vDash \phi \implies \psi$, which means that the formula ϕ implies ψ when all the predicates in $\dot{\Gamma}$ are satisfied. To derive subtyping relations $\dot{\Gamma} \vdash T_{\mathcal{E}_1}\dot{A} <: T_{\mathcal{E}_2}\dot{B}$ for graded refinement computation types (Fig. 3), we use the semantic subeffecting relation $\dot{\Gamma} \vDash \mathcal{E}_1 \leq \mathcal{E}_2$, which means that the dependent-effect term $\mathcal{E}_1$ is less than or equal to $\mathcal{E}_2$ when all the predicates in $\dot{\Gamma}$ are satisfied. We do not provide syntactic derivation rules for these semantic judgements because they are intended to be solved by an external solver, such as an SMT solver [6,14,15], during type checking.

Example 11. For cost analysis, we can derive the following subtyping relation. For notational simplicity, we omit the basic effect $\mathtt{nat2eff} : \mathtt{nat} \to \mathbf{Effect}$ for conversion below.

$$x : \{x : \mathtt{int} \mid x \geq 1\} \quad \vdash \quad T_{|x+1|}\{y : \mathtt{int} \mid y = x\} \quad <: \quad T_{|2x|}\{y : \mathtt{int} \mid y \geq 1\}$$

Here, we need to compare both dependent-effect terms and formulas. For the former, $x : \{x : \mathtt{int} \mid x \geq 1\} \vDash |x + 1| \leq |2x|$ is semantically valid, and for the latter, $x : \{x : \mathtt{int} \mid x \geq 1\}, y : \mathtt{int} \vDash y = x \implies y \geq 1$ is semantically valid. Note that $x \geq 1$ in the context is necessary for the validity. $\square$

$$\frac{\dot{\Gamma} \vdash M : \dot{C} \qquad \dot{\Gamma} \vdash \dot{C} <: \dot{D}}{\dot{\Gamma} \vdash M : \dot{D}} \qquad\qquad \frac{\dot{\Gamma} \vdash \mathcal{E}_1 : \textbf{Effect} \qquad \dot{\Gamma} \vdash \mathcal{E}_2 : \textbf{Effect} \qquad \dot{\Gamma} \vDash \mathcal{E}_1 \leq \mathcal{E}_2 \qquad \dot{\Gamma} \vdash \dot{A} <: \dot{B}}{\dot{\Gamma} \vdash T_{\mathcal{E}_1} \dot{A} <: T_{\mathcal{E}_2} \dot{B}}$$

Fig. 3: Selected rules for subtyping. Here, $\dot{\Gamma} \vDash \mathcal{E}_1 \leq \mathcal{E}_2$ is semantic subeffecting in the refinement context $\dot{\Gamma}$.

4   Preliminaries on Semantics: Stepping Towards Dependent Effect Systems

In this section, we gradually develop categorical semantics starting from the simply typed FGCBV. This development is completed in Section 5 where we introduce the semantics of dependent effects and use it to prove the soundness. We need careful treatment of circularity of definitions when dealing with dependent type systems. However, since we focus on a dependent type system that is a refinement of a simple type system, the situation is slightly simpler than general dependent type systems. The dependency of the definitions of the interpretation is summarized in [32, Fig. 4]. To simplify the presentation, we focus on describing semantics of the recursion-free fragment of FGCBV and leave the details of recursion to [32, Appendix C.2].

4.1   Simply Typed FGCBV

Categorical semantics of simply typed FGCBV (Section 3.1) is given by a bicartesian closed category with a strong monad [34].

Definition 12. A *simple FGCBV model* is a tuple $(\mathbb{C}, T, \llbracket - \rrbracket)$ where $\mathbb{C}$ is a bicartesian closed category, T is a strong monad on $\mathbb{C}$, and $\llbracket - \rrbracket$ is an interpretation of base types, effect-free operations, and generic effects: $\llbracket b \rrbracket \in \mathbb{C}$ for each $b \in \textbf{Base}$, $\llbracket \texttt{op} \rrbracket : \llbracket A \rrbracket \to \llbracket B \rrbracket$ for each $(\texttt{op} : A \to B) \in \textbf{Op}$, and $\llbracket \texttt{gef} \rrbracket : \llbracket A \rrbracket \to T\llbracket B \rrbracket$ for each $(\texttt{gef} : A \to B) \in \textbf{GenEff}$. Here, we implicitly extend the interpretation $\llbracket - \rrbracket$ to ground types A, B by the bicartesian closed structure of $\mathbb{C}$. $\qquad\square$

Given a FGCBV model $(\mathbb{C}, T, \llbracket - \rrbracket)$, we can interpret a well-typed value term $\Gamma \vdash V : A$ as a morphism $\llbracket V \rrbracket : \llbracket \Gamma \rrbracket \to \llbracket A \rrbracket$ in $\mathbb{C}$, and a well-typed computation term $\Gamma \vdash M : TA$ as a morphism $\llbracket M \rrbracket : \llbracket \Gamma \rrbracket \to T\llbracket A \rrbracket$ in $\mathbb{C}$. The concrete definition of the interpretation $\llbracket - \rrbracket$ is standard and can be found in, e.g., [34].

Example 13 (cost analysis). A FGCBV model for cost analysis is given as $(\textbf{Set}, (-) \times \mathbb{N}_\infty, \llbracket - \rrbracket)$. Here, $(-) \times \mathbb{N}_\infty$ is the *cost monad* induced by the additive monoid $(\mathbb{N}_\infty, 0, +)$ of extended natural numbers $\mathbb{N}_\infty = \mathbb{N} \cup \{\infty\}$, and it keeps track of the cost of a program. The generic effect $\texttt{Tick} : \texttt{nat} \to \texttt{unit}$ is interpreted as a function $\llbracket \texttt{Tick} \rrbracket : \mathbb{N} \to 1 \times \mathbb{N}_\infty$ that takes $n \in \mathbb{N}$ and returns the pair $((), n)$ of the unit value $()$ and the cost n. $\qquad\square$

4.2   Semantics of Formulas

Formulas ϕ in refinement types $\{x : b \mid \phi\}$ are interpreted in a preordered fibration with sufficient structure to interpret logical connectives.

Definition 14. Let $(\mathbb{C}, T, [\![-]\!])$ be a simple FGCBV model. A *model of formulas* is a pair $(p, [\![-]\!])$ of (i) a preordered fibration $p : \mathbb{P} \to \mathbb{C}$ that is fibred bicartesian closed and has simple products $\prod : \mathbb{P}_{I \times X} \to \mathbb{P}_I$ satisfying the Beck–Chevalley condition, and (ii) an interpretation $[\![a]\!] \in \mathbb{P}_{[\![A]\!]}$ for each predicate symbol $\mathsf{a} : A \to \mathbf{Fml}$. We often say p is a model of formulas and omit $[\![-]\!]$ when it is clear from the context. $\qquad\square$

Given a model of formulas, a well-formed formula $\Gamma \vdash \phi$ is interpreted as $[\![\phi]\!] \in \mathbb{P}_{[\![\Gamma]\!]}$. The definition of the interpretation $[\![-]\!]$ is straightforward and omitted. In what follows, we mainly focus on the fibration of Ω-valued predicates defined below, which is sufficient for all instances in Section 6. However, our dependent effect system and its semantics are not limited to this fibration.

Example 15. We define the *predicate fibration* $\mathrm{pred}_{\mathbf{Set}} : \mathbf{Pred} \to \mathbf{Set}$ as follows. The total category $\mathbf{Pred}$ is the category of predicates over $\mathbf{Set}$. An object in $\mathbf{Pred}$ is a pair (X, P) where $X \in \mathbf{Set}$ and $P \subseteq X$ is a predicate on X. A morphism from (X, P) to (Y, Q) is a function $f : X \to Y$ that preserves predicates, that is, for any $x \in P$, we have $f(x) \in Q$. The forgetful functor $\mathrm{pred}_{\mathbf{Set}} : \mathbf{Pred} \to \mathbf{Set}$ is defined by $\mathrm{pred}_{\mathbf{Set}}(X, P) = X$ and $\mathrm{pred}_{\mathbf{Set}}(f) = f$. $\qquad\square$

Example 16. We consider a generalization of the predicate fibration (Example 15) to Ω-valued predicates. Let Ω be a complete Heyting algebra. The Ω-*valued predicate fibration* over $\mathbf{Set}$ is defined as follows. The total category $\mathbf{Pred}_\Omega$ is the category of Ω-valued predicates: an object is a pair (X, P) where X is a set and $P : X \to \Omega$ is a function, and a morphism $f : (X, P) \to (Y, Q)$ is a function $f : X \to Y$ such that $P \le Q \circ f$ with respect to the pointwise order on $\mathbf{Set}(X, \Omega)$. Then, the forgetful functor $\mathrm{pred}^\Omega : \mathbf{Pred}_\Omega \to \mathbf{Set}$ is a fibration that is fibred bicartesian closed and has simple products. Note that if $\Omega = \mathbf{2}$ is the two-element Boolean algebra, then this fibration is the same as the predicate fibration in Example 15. $\qquad\square$

Example 17. We can replace the base category $\mathbf{Set}$ in Example 16 with any category $\mathbb{C}$ with terminal object 1 by applying the change-of-base construction along $\mathbb{C}(1, -) : \mathbb{C} \to \mathbf{Set}$. This gives us a fibration $\mathrm{pred}_{\mathbb{C}}^\Omega : \mathbf{Pred}_\Omega(\mathbb{C}) \to \mathbb{C}$ of Ω-valued predicates over $\mathbb{C}$. Specifically, an object in $\mathbf{Pred}_\Omega(\mathbb{C})$ is a tuple (I, P) where $I \in \mathbb{C}$ and $P : \mathbb{C}(1, I) \to \Omega$ is a function. $\qquad\square$

4.3   Dependently Typed FGCBV with Refinement Types

To develop the semantics step by step, we temporarily consider a dependent refinement type system that lies between the simply typed FGCBV (Section 3.1) and the dependent effect system (Section 3.2). Specifically, we consider types defined as follows.

$$\dot{A}, \dot{B} \;:=\; \{x : b \mid \phi\} \mid (x : \dot{A}) \times \dot{B} \mid (x : \dot{A}) \to \dot{C} \mid \dot{A} + \dot{B} \qquad \dot{C}, \dot{D} \;:=\; T\dot{A}$$

We call $\dot{A}$ a *refinement value type* and $\dot{C}$ a *refinement computation type*. The difference from Section 3.2 is that computation types $T\dot{A}$ are not graded by dependent effect terms.

We give the semantics of refinement types based on the construction in [31]. The idea is summarized as follows. Observe that the dependent refinement type system introduced here is a special case of dependently typed FGCBV where types are constructed from $\{x : b \mid \phi\}$, although we do not spell out the definition of *dependently typed FGCBV*. Thus, we necessarily use the semantics of dependent type systems as a basis. Also, simply typed FGCBV (Section 3.1) can be regarded as another special case of dependently typed FGCBV where types are constructed from base types b. Thus, the model of the dependent refinement type system should be given as a "lifting" of the model of simply typed FGCBV. The construction in [31] gives such a lifting from a model of simply typed FGCBV and a model of formulas (Definition 14).

More concretely, dependent type systems are interpreted by a *(split) closed comprehension category* (*SCCompC*) [26, Definition 10.5.3], which is a fibration $p : \mathbb{E} \to \mathbb{B}$ with certain structures. Contexts are interpreted as objects in the base category $\mathbb{B}$; and types and terms are interpreted as objects and morphisms in the fibre category $\mathbb{E}_{[\![\dot{\Gamma}]\!]}$ over the interpretation of the context. In the current setting, we need additional structures: strong fibred (binary) coproducts [26, Exercise 10.5.6] is required to interpret $\dot{A} + \dot{B}$, and a fibred monad (over a fixed base category) is required to interpret computation types $T\dot{A}$ [3, 4]. Given a model of simply typed FGCBV $(\mathbb{C}, T, [\![-]\!])$, the corresponding SCCompC can be constructed as the simple fibration $s_{\mathbb{C}} : s(\mathbb{C}) \to \mathbb{C}$ [26, Definition 1.3.1]. Moreover, a strong monad T on $\mathbb{C}$ bijectively corresponds to a fibred monad $s(T)$ on the simple fibration [26, Exercise 2.6.10]. It can be shown that the interpretation of dependently typed FGCBV in the simple fibration $s_{\mathbb{C}} : s(\mathbb{C}) \to \mathbb{C}$ with a fibred monad $s(T)$ corresponds to the standard interpretation of simply typed FGCBV in a bicartesian closed category $\mathbb{C}$ with a strong monad T.

The construction in [31] combines the simple fibration $s_{\mathbb{C}} : s(\mathbb{C}) \to \mathbb{C}$ with a model of formulas $p : \mathbb{P} \to \mathbb{C}$ and gives us a SCCompC $\{s(\mathbb{C}) \mid \mathbb{P}\} \to \mathbb{P}$ with fibred coproducts. This gives a "lifting" of the simple fibration in the sense that there exists a pair of forgetful functors to the simple fibration (3) that strictly preserves the SCCompC structure and fibred coproducts.

The construction in [31] requires some technical conditions. Since all the instances in Section 6 use Ω-valued predicates (Example 17), which automatically satisfy most of the technical conditions, we only state the construction for Ω-valued predicates here.

$$
\begin{array}{ccc}
\{s(\mathbb{C}) \mid \mathbb{P}\} & \longrightarrow & s(\mathbb{C}) \;\circlearrowright\, s(T) \\
{\scriptstyle \{s_{\mathbb{C}}|p\}}\big\downarrow & & \big\downarrow{\scriptstyle s_{\mathbb{C}}} \\
\mathbb{P} & \xrightarrow{\;\;p\;\;} & \mathbb{C}
\end{array}
\qquad (3)
$$

Proposition 18. *Let $(\mathbb{C}, T, [\![-]\!])$ be a simple FGCBV model and Ω be a complete Heyting algebra such that $\mathrm{pred}_{\mathbb{C}}^{\Omega} : \mathbf{Pred}_{\Omega}(\mathbb{C}) \to \mathbb{C}$ is a model of formulas. If $\mathbb{C}(1, -)$ preserves binary coproducts, then there exists a SCCompC with strong fibred binary coproducts $\{s_{\mathbb{C}} \mid \mathrm{pred}_{\mathbb{C}}^{\Omega}\} : \{s(\mathbb{C}) \mid \mathbf{Pred}_{\Omega}(\mathbb{C})\} \to \mathbf{Pred}_{\Omega}(\mathbb{C})$, which we call the $\mathrm{pred}_{\mathbb{C}}^{\Omega}$-refinement fibration. Moreover, there exists a morphism of fibrations from $\mathrm{pred}_{\mathbb{C}}^{\Omega}$-refinement fibration to the simple fibration $s_{\mathbb{C}} : s(\mathbb{C}) \to \mathbb{C}$ as in (3), which strictly preserves the SCCompC structure and fibred binary coproducts [31].* $\qquad\square$

Consider the situation in Proposition 18 where $\mathbb{P} = \mathbf{Pred}_{\Omega}(\mathbb{C})$. If we have a lifting of the fibred monad $s(T)$ along (3) (i.e., a fibred monad on the refinement fibration such that (3) preserves monad structures), then (well-formed) contexts $\dot{\Gamma}$ and types $\dot{A}, \dot{C}$ are interpreted as $[\![\dot{\Gamma}]\!] \in \mathbb{P}$ and $[\![\dot{\Gamma} \vdash \dot{A}]\!], [\![\dot{\Gamma} \vdash \dot{C}]\!] \in \{s(\mathbb{C}) \mid \mathbb{P}\}_{[\![\dot{\Gamma}]\!]}$, respectively. A bit more concretely, $[\![\dot{\Gamma}]\!] = ([\![\lfloor\dot{\Gamma}\rfloor]\!], P)$ gives a pair of the interpretation of the underlying context $\lfloor\dot{\Gamma}\rfloor$ and an Ω-valued predicate $P : \mathbb{C}(1, [\![\lfloor\dot{\Gamma}\rfloor]\!]) \to \Omega$ on the underlying context; and $[\![\dot{\Gamma} \vdash \dot{A}]\!] = ([\![\dot{\Gamma}]\!], [\![\lfloor\dot{A}\rfloor]\!], Q)$ gives a tuple where $Q : \mathbb{C}(1, [\![\lfloor\dot{\Gamma}\rfloor]\!] \times [\![\lfloor\dot{A}\rfloor]\!]) \to \Omega$ is a predicate on the underlying context $\lfloor\dot{\Gamma}\rfloor$ and the underlying type $\lfloor\dot{A}\rfloor$. If we apply the functor (3) to these interpretations, then predicates are removed, and we obtain the "underlying" or "simple" interpretation $[\![\lfloor\dot{\Gamma}\rfloor]\!] \in \mathbb{C}$ and $([\![\lfloor\dot{\Gamma}\rfloor]\!], [\![\lfloor\dot{A}\rfloor]\!]) \in s(\mathbb{C})$. Subtyping relations $\dot{\Gamma} \vdash \dot{A} <: \dot{B}$ are also interpreted in the refinement fibration as a semantic relation $[\![\dot{\Gamma} \vdash \dot{A}]\!] <: [\![\dot{\Gamma} \vdash \dot{B}]\!]$ defined by $[\![\lfloor\dot{A}\rfloor]\!] = [\![\lfloor\dot{B}\rfloor]\!]$ and $Q \leq Q'$ where $[\![\dot{\Gamma} \vdash \dot{A}]\!] = ([\![\dot{\Gamma}]\!], [\![\lfloor\dot{A}\rfloor]\!], Q)$ and $[\![\dot{\Gamma} \vdash \dot{B}]\!] = ([\![\dot{\Gamma}]\!], [\![\lfloor\dot{B}\rfloor]\!], Q')$. The soundness of the derivation rules for subtyping is straightforward once we define the semantic validity of formulas as follows.

$$\dot{\Gamma} \vDash \phi \quad := \quad [\![\dot{\Gamma}]\!] \leq [\![\phi]\!] \text{ in } \mathbf{Pred}_{\Omega}(\mathbb{C})_{[\![\lfloor\dot{\Gamma}\rfloor]\!]}$$

The interpretation of terms is defined as a lifting of the interpretation of the underlying terms in simply typed FGCBV along (3). Since morphisms in the refinement fibration are morphisms in the simple fibration that preserve predicates, the existence of such a lifting implies the soundness of the refinement type system. Specifically, we have the following. For any well-typed value term $\dot{\Gamma} \vdash V : \dot{A}$, let $[\![V]\!] : [\![\lfloor\dot{\Gamma}\rfloor]\!] \to [\![\lfloor\dot{A}\rfloor]\!]$ be the (underlying) interpretation of the term. Then, $[\![V]\!]$ satisfies $[\![\dot{\Gamma}]\!] \leq [\![\dot{\Gamma}, x : \dot{A}]\!] \circ \mathbb{C}(1, \langle\mathrm{id}, [\![V]\!]\rangle) : \mathbb{C}(1, [\![\lfloor\dot{\Gamma}\rfloor]\!]) \to \Omega$, which means that if the precondition in $\dot{\Gamma}$ holds, then $[\![V]\!]$ satisfies the postcondition in $\dot{A}$. The same holds for computation terms $\dot{\Gamma} \vdash M : \dot{C}$.

5   Graded Monads for Dependent Effect Systems

We introduce indexed graded monads, which are a key concept for the semantics of our dependent effect system. Indexed graded monads have two equivalent presentations in terms of indexed categories and fibrations. In this section, we present indexed graded monads in terms of indexed categories and leave the fibrational presentation to [32, Appendix C.3]. Using indexed graded monads, we provide the soundness theorem for the dependent effect system in Section 3.

5.1   Indexed Preordered Monoids

As we have explained in the introduction (Fig. 1), grading monoids for the dependent effect system should be indexed by contexts. We formalize this idea as $\mathbb{B}$-*indexed preordered monoids*, which is (a specific kind of) a monoidal object in the 2-category $\mathbf{ICat}(\mathbb{B})$ of $\mathbb{B}$-indexed categories. Below, we borrow notations from fibrations and use them for indexed categories: indexed categories are written as $\mathbb{E}_{(-)} : \mathbb{B}^{\mathrm{op}} \to \mathbf{Cat}$, and for any morphism $u : I \to J$, the functor $\mathbb{E}_u : \mathbb{E}_J \to \mathbb{E}_I$ is written as u^* and called the *reindexing functor*.

Definition 19 (indexed preordered monoid). Let $\mathbf{PreMon}$ be the category of preordered monoids, i.e., the category whose objects are preordered sets with a monotone monoid structure and whose morphisms are monotone monoid homomorphisms. For any category $\mathbb{B}$, a $\mathbb{B}$-*indexed preordered monoid* is a functor $\mathbb{M}_{(-)} : \mathbb{B}^{\mathrm{op}} \to \mathbf{PreMon}$. That is, for each $I \in \mathbb{B}$, $\mathbb{M}_I = (\mathbb{M}_I, 1, (\cdot), \leq)$ is a preordered monoid, and for each morphism $u : I \to J$ in $\mathbb{B}$, the reindexing functor $u^* : \mathbb{M}_J \to \mathbb{M}_I$ is a morphism of preordered monoids. $\square$

Example 20 (preordered-monoid-valued functions). For any preordered monoid $\mathcal{M}$, the functor $\mathbf{Set}(-, \mathcal{M}) : \mathbf{Set}^{\mathrm{op}} \to \mathbf{PreMon}$ is a $\mathbf{Set}$-indexed preordered monoid. Concretely, for any set X, the preordered monoid $\mathbf{Set}(X, \mathcal{M})$ is the set of functions from X to $\mathcal{M}$ with pointwise order and pointwise multiplication. For each morphism $f : X \to Y$ in $\mathbf{Set}$, the reindexing $f^* = \mathbf{Set}(f, \mathcal{M}) : \mathbf{Set}(Y, \mathcal{M}) \to \mathbf{Set}(X, \mathcal{M})$ is defined by precomposition with f. $\square$

Example 21 (simple effect). Let $\mathcal{M}$ be a preordered monoid and $\mathbb{B}$ be a category. The constant functor $\Delta\mathcal{M} : \mathbb{B}^{\mathrm{op}} \to \mathbf{PreMon}$ is a $\mathbb{B}$-indexed preordered monoid. This models the *simple effect* where the grading monoid is constant for all contexts. Note that $\Delta\mathcal{M} : \mathbf{Set}^{\mathrm{op}} \to \mathbf{PreMon}$ is an indexed preordered *sub*-monoid of $\mathbf{Set}(-, \mathcal{M})$ in Example 20: $\mathcal{M} \cong \{f : X \to \mathcal{M} \mid f \text{ is constant}\} \subseteq \mathbf{Set}(X, \mathcal{M})$. $\square$

The indexed preordered monoid in Example 20 provides a natural semantics of dependent effect terms if we ignore refinement types. Consider as an example cost analysis where the grading monoid is $\mathcal{M} = (\mathbb{N}_\infty, 0, +)$. Let $n : \mathtt{nat} \vdash \mathtt{nat2eff}(n+1) : \mathbf{Effect}$ be a dependent effect term. Then, the interpretation is given by the composite $[\![\mathtt{nat2eff}]\!] \circ [\![n+1]\!] \in \mathbf{Set}([\![\mathtt{nat}]\!], \mathcal{M})$ of the interpretation of the term $[\![n+1]\!] : \mathbb{N} \to \mathbb{N}$ and the interpretation of the basic effect $[\![\mathtt{nat2eff}]\!] : \mathbb{N} \to \mathcal{M}$.

However, the indexed preordered monoid in Example 20 has a few problems when we consider refinement types. The first problem is the mismatch of the indexing categories. We would like to interpret dependent effect terms $\dot{\Gamma} \vdash \mathcal{E} : \mathbf{Effect}$ as $[\![\mathcal{E}]\!] \in \mathbb{M}_{[\![\dot{\Gamma}]\!]}$. This means that the indexing category of indexed preordered monoids $\mathbb{M}_{(-)}$ must be the category of Ω-valued predicates where $[\![\dot{\Gamma}]\!]$ lives. However, the indexing category in Example 20 is $\mathbf{Set}$. The second problem is about the semantic subeffecting relation. We would like to interpret the semantic subeffecting relation $\dot{\Gamma} \vDash \mathcal{E}_1 \leq \mathcal{E}_2$ as the order relation $[\![\mathcal{E}_1]\!] \leq [\![\mathcal{E}_2]\!]$

in $\mathbb{M}_{[\![\dot{\Gamma}]\!]}$. It should take the predicates in $\dot{\Gamma}$ into account, as we have explained in Example 11. However, the indexed preordered monoid in Example 20 does not provide an appropriate interpretation.

We solve these problems as follows. The first problem can be solved by applying the change-of-base construction along the forgetful functor $\mathbf{Pred}_\Omega(\mathbb{C}) \to \mathbf{Pred}_\Omega \to \mathbf{Set}$ to the indexed preordered monoid in Example 20. In addition, we replace the order relation with the pointwise order restricted by predicates to solve the second problem. This gives the following indexed preordered monoid, which we use for the semantics of dependent effect terms.

Definition 22. Let $\mathcal{M}$ be a preordered monoid. We define a $\mathbf{Pred}_\Omega$-indexed preordered monoid by $(\mathbf{Set} /\!\!/_\Omega \mathcal{M})_{(I,P)} := (\mathbf{Set}(I, \mathcal{M}), 1, (\cdot), \leq_P)$ for $(I, P) \in \mathbf{Pred}_\Omega$ where the unit and the multiplication of $\mathcal{M}$ is extended to $\mathbf{Set}(I, \mathcal{M})$ pointwise, and the order relation $\leq_P$ is defined as follows.

$$f \leq_P g \quad := \quad \forall i \in I, P(i) \neq \bot_\Omega \implies f(i) \leq g(i)$$

Here, $\bot_\Omega \in \Omega$ is the least element. This order relation is a bit ad hoc, but it ensures that the construction in Proposition 26 below gives an indexed graded monad. Note that if $\Omega = \mathbf{2}$ is the two-element Boolean algebra, then we have $f \leq_P g$ if and only if $f(i) \leq g(i)$ for all $i \in P$. We also define a $\mathbf{Pred}_\Omega(\mathbb{C})$-indexed preordered monoid $(\mathbb{C} /\!\!/_\Omega \mathcal{M})_{(-)}$ by the change-of-base along the forgetful functor $\mathbf{Pred}_\Omega(\mathbb{C}) \to \mathbf{Pred}_\Omega$. □

Example 23. Let $\Omega = \mathbf{2}$. Consider the dependent effect term $x : \{x : \texttt{int} \mid x \geq 1\} \vdash |x + 1| : \mathbf{Effect}$ for cost analysis where a grading monoid is given by $\ = (\ , 0, +)$. This dependent effect term can be interpreted as $[\![|x + 1|]\!] = \lambda x.|x + 1| \in (\mathbf{Set} /\!\!/_\mathbf{2} \ )_{(\mathbb{Z}, \{x \in \mathbb{Z} \mid x \geq 1\})}$. The semantic subeffecting relation $x : \{x : \texttt{int} \mid x \geq 1\} \vDash |x + 1| \leq |2x|$ in Example 11 is valid in this setting because $|x + 1| \leq |2x|$ holds for any $x \geq 1$. □

5.2 Indexed Graded Monads

Given an interpretation of $[\![\dot{\Gamma} \vdash \dot{A}]\!] \in \{s(\mathbb{C}) \mid \mathbb{P}\}_{[\![\dot{\Gamma}]\!]}$ and $[\![\dot{\Gamma} \vdash \mathcal{E}]\!] \in \mathbb{M}_{[\![\dot{\Gamma}]\!]}$ where $[\![\dot{\Gamma}]\!] \in \mathbb{P} = \mathbf{Pred}_\Omega(\mathbb{C})$, we would like to interpret a computation type $\dot{\Gamma} \vdash T_\mathcal{E} \dot{A}$ as an object in $\{s(\mathbb{C}) \mid \mathbb{P}\}_{[\![\dot{\Gamma}]\!]}$. For this purpose, we introduce below a novel notion of *indexed graded monads*. Then, an indexed graded monad $T : \mathbb{M}_{[\![\dot{\Gamma}]\!]} \times \{s(\mathbb{C}) \mid \mathbb{P}\}_{[\![\dot{\Gamma}]\!]} \to \{s(\mathbb{C}) \mid \mathbb{P}\}_{[\![\dot{\Gamma}]\!]}$ indexed by $[\![\dot{\Gamma}]\!] \in \mathbb{P}$ naturally gives the interpretation of the computation type $\dot{\Gamma} \vdash T_\mathcal{E} \dot{A}$ as $T_{[\![\dot{\Gamma} \vdash \mathcal{E}]\!]} [\![\dot{\Gamma} \vdash \dot{A}]\!]$.

Definition 24 (indexed graded monad). A -*indexed graded monad* is a functor from ^{op} to the category of graded monads. Concretely, a -indexed graded monad consists of the following data.

- An indexed preordered monoid $\mathbb{M}_{(-)} : \ ^{\mathrm{op}} \to \mathbf{Cat}$. This is the grading indexed preordered monoid of the indexed graded monad. We sometimes say "indexed $\mathbb{M}_{(-)}$-graded monad" to make the grading indexed preordered monoid explicit.

- An indexed category $\mathbb{E}_{(-)} : {}^{\mathrm{op}} \to \mathbf{Cat}$ on which the indexed graded monad is defined.
- For each object $I \in $, an $\mathbb{M}_I$-graded monad (TI, η_I, μ_I) on the category $\mathbb{E}_I$. We often omit the index $I \in $ in (TI, η_I, μ_I) when clear from the context.
- For each morphism $u : I \to J$ in , the pair of reindexing functors $u^* : \mathbb{M}_J \to \mathbb{M}_I$ and $u^* : \mathbb{E}_J \to \mathbb{E}_I$ that is a morphism of graded monads (defined in [32, Definition 47]) from (TJ, η_J, μ_J) to (TI, η_I, μ_I). That is, for any $m, m_1, m_2 \in \mathbb{M}_J$ and $X \in \mathbb{E}_J$, we have $u^* T_m X = T_{u^* m} u^* X$, $u^* \eta_X = \eta_{u^* X}$, and $u^* \mu_{m_1, m_2, X} = \mu_{u^* m_1, u^* m_2, u^* X}$. $\qquad\qquad\square$

Example 25 (indexed graded monad for indexed sets). Indexed sets (or equivalently, the family fibration [26, Definition 1.2.1]) give a typical model of dependent type systems *without* refinement types. We will not use this model for our dependent effect system, but there is a simple example of an indexed graded monad defined on indexed sets. Now, suppose that we have an $\mathcal{M}$-graded monad $T = (T, \eta^T, \mu^T)$ on **Set**. For each $f \in \mathbf{Set}(I, \mathcal{M})$ and $\{X_i\}_{i \in I} \in \mathbf{Fam}(\mathbf{Set})_I$, we define $\hat{T}_f(\{X_i\}_{i \in I}) \in \mathbf{Fam}(\mathbf{Set})_I$ as $\hat{T}_f(\{X_i\}_{i \in I}) := \{T_{f(i)} X_i\}_{i \in I}$. Then, $\hat{T}$ is an indexed $\mathbf{Set}(-, \mathcal{M})$-graded monad. The unit and the multiplication for $\hat{T}$ are defined as expected. Example 1 is an instance of this construction. $\qquad\square$

The following indexed graded monad defined on the refinement fibration $\{s_{\mathbb{C}} \mid \mathrm{pred}_{\mathbb{C}}^{\Omega}\} : \{s(\mathbb{C}) \mid \mathbf{Pred}_\Omega(\mathbb{C})\} \to \mathbf{Pred}_\Omega(\mathbb{C})$ will be used for the semantics of our dependent effect system.

Proposition 26. *Suppose that we have a strong $\mathcal{M}$-graded monad lifting $\ddot{T}$ of a strong monad T along $\mathrm{pred}_{\mathbb{C}}^{\Omega} : \mathbf{Pred}_\Omega(\mathbb{C}) \to \mathbb{C}$. Then, we can construct an indexed $(\mathbb{C} /\!/_\Omega \mathcal{M})_{(-)}$-graded monad $\mathbf{DE}(\ddot{T})$ over the $\mathrm{pred}_{\mathbb{C}}^{\Omega}$-refinement fibration $\{s_{\mathbb{C}} \mid \mathrm{pred}_{\mathbb{C}}^{\Omega}\} : \{s(\mathbb{C}) \mid \mathbf{Pred}_\Omega(\mathbb{C})\} \to \mathbf{Pred}_\Omega(\mathbb{C})$ as follows.*

$$\mathbf{DE}(\ddot{T})_f((I, P), X, Q) \quad := \quad ((I, P), TX, \lambda\langle i, x\rangle. P(i) \wedge (\ddot{T}_{f(i)} Q\langle i, -\rangle)(x))$$

Here, $I, X \in \mathbb{C}$, $P \in \mathbf{Pred}_\Omega(\mathbb{C})_I$, $Q \in \mathbf{Pred}_\Omega(\mathbb{C})_{I \times X}$, $f \in (\mathbb{C} /\!/_\Omega \mathcal{M})_{(I, P)}$, $i \in \mathbb{C}(1, I)$, and $x \in \mathbb{C}(1, TX)$. Moreover, $\mathbf{DE}(\ddot{T})$ is a lifting of the fibred monad $s(T)$ along the morphism (3). $\qquad\square$

Proposition 26 can be viewed as a construction of a model of a *dependent* effect system from that of a *simple* effect system, since a simple effect system is typically modelled by a strong graded monad lifting along a fibration of (some kind of) predicates (e.g., [2]). The models of all instances in Section 6 are obtained by applying this construction to suitable strong graded monad liftings.

5.3   Soundness of the Dependent Effect System

We define models of our dependent effect system defined in Section 3.2 and prove its soundness. The models defined below are specialized for the constructions in Definition 22 and Proposition 26, but it is also possible to define models in a more general setting, as we remark in Remark 29.

Definition 2 7. A *model of the dependent effect system* consists of the following.

- A simple FGCBV model $(\mathbb{C}, T, [\![-]\!]_s)$ (Definition 12). The subscript s indicates that $[\![-]\!]_s$ is the interpretation for the underlying simple type system.
- A complete Heyting algebra Ω and an interpretation $[\![a]\!] \in \mathbf{Pred}_\Omega(\mathbb{C})_{[\![A]\!]}$ for each predicate symbol $\mathtt{a} : A \to \mathbf{Fml}$, which make the Ω-valued predicate fibration $\mathrm{pred}_\mathbb{C}^\Omega : \mathbf{Pred}_\Omega(\mathbb{C}) \to \mathbb{C}$ (Example 17) a model of formulas.
- A preordered monoid $\mathcal{M}$ and an interpretation $[\![\mathtt{be}]\!] \in (\mathbb{C}/\!\!/_\Omega\mathcal{M})_{\top[\![A]\!]}$ for each basic effect symbol $\mathtt{be} : A \to \mathbf{Effect}$, which make the indexed preordered monoid $(\mathbb{C}/\!\!/_\Omega\mathcal{M})_{(-)}$ (Definition 22) a model of dependent effect terms. Here, $\top : \mathbb{C} \to \mathbf{Pred}_\Omega(\mathbb{C})$ is the terminal object functor, which maps $X \in \mathbb{C}$ to the Ω-valued predicate $\top X$ defined by $\top X(x) = \top_\Omega$ for any $x \in \mathbb{C}(1, X)$. In this situation, the semantic subeffecting relation is defined as follows.

$$\dot{\Gamma} \models \mathcal{E}_1 \leq \mathcal{E}_2 \quad := \quad [\![\mathcal{E}_1]\!] \leq [\![\mathcal{E}_2]\!] \text{ in } (\mathbb{C}/\!\!/_\Omega \mathcal{M})_{[\![\dot{\Gamma}]\!]}$$

- A strong $\mathcal{M}$-graded monad lifting $\ddot{T}$ of T along $\mathrm{pred}_\mathbb{C}^\Omega : \mathbf{Pred}_\Omega(\mathbb{C}) \to \mathbb{C}$ (cf. Proposition 26).

These data are required to satisfy the following properties.

Ax 1 For each effect-free operation $\mathtt{op} : (x : \dot{A}) \twoheadrightarrow \dot{B}$ and generic effect $\mathtt{gef} : (x : \dot{A}) \overset{\mathcal{E}}{\twoheadrightarrow} \dot{B}$, the interpretations $[\![\mathtt{op}]\!]_s$ and $[\![\mathtt{gef}]\!]_s$ have the following liftings along $\mathrm{pred}_\mathbb{C}^\Omega : \mathbf{Pred}_\Omega(\mathbb{C}) \to \mathbb{C}$.

$$\langle \mathrm{id}, [\![\mathtt{op}]\!]_s \rangle : [\![x : \dot{A}]\!] \dashrightarrow [\![x : \dot{A}, y : \dot{B}]\!], \quad \langle \mathrm{id}, [\![\mathtt{gef}]\!]_s \rangle : [\![x : \dot{A}]\!] \dashrightarrow [\![x : \dot{A}, y : T_\mathcal{E}\dot{B}]\!]$$

Here, for any Ω-valued predicate X, Y in $\mathbf{Pred}_\Omega(\mathbb{C})$ and a morphism f in $\mathbb{C}$, we write $f : X \dashrightarrow Y$ if there exists a morphism (a lifting) $g : X \to Y$ in $\mathbf{Pred}_\Omega(\mathbb{C})$ such that $\mathrm{pred}_\mathbb{C}^\Omega(g) = f$.

Ax 2 The functor $\mathbb{C}(1, -)$ preserves binary coproducts (cf. Prop. 18). $\square$

Theorem 28 (soundness). *Given a model as in Definition 27, if $\dot{\Gamma} \vdash M : \dot{C}$ is well-typed and recursion-free, then there exists a lifting $\langle \mathrm{id}, [\![M]\!]_s \rangle : [\![\dot{\Gamma}]\!] \dashrightarrow [\![\dot{\Gamma}, x : \dot{C}]\!]$ along $\mathrm{pred}_\mathbb{C}^\Omega : \mathbf{Pred}_\Omega(\mathbb{C}) \to \mathbb{C}$ where x is a fresh variable, and similarly for well-typed value terms $\dot{\Gamma} \vdash V : \dot{A}$.*

Proof. By induction on type derivation. See [32, Theorem 51] for details. $\square$

The above theorem states that if $\dot{\Gamma} \vdash M : \dot{C}$ is well-typed, then for any element $\gamma \in \mathbb{C}(1, [\![\dot{\Gamma}]\!])$, we have $[\![\dot{\Gamma}]\!](\gamma) \leq [\![\dot{\Gamma}, x : \dot{C}]\!](\gamma, [\![M]\!]_s(\gamma))$ with respect to the order relation in Ω. In particular, when $\Omega = \mathbf{2}$, for any γ satisfying the precondition $[\![\dot{\Gamma}]\!]$, the soundness theorem guarantees that the result of the computation $[\![M]\!]_s(\gamma)$ satisfies the postcondition $[\![\dot{\Gamma}, x : \dot{C}]\!](\gamma, -)$.

In Theorem 28, we restrict attention to terms without recursion, purely for simplicity of presentation. Extending the soundness theorem to terms with recursion is relatively straightforward, and we present such an extension in [32, Theorem 79]. The main idea is as follows. We interpret the underlying simple type

Instance		Grading monoid $\mathcal{M}$	Heyting algebra Ω
Cost analysis	Section 6.1	$(\mathbb{N}_\infty, 0, +, \leq)$	$(2, \leq)$
Expectation bound	Section 6.2	$([0,\infty], 0, +, \leq)$	$([0,\infty], \geq)$
Temporal safety	[32, Section 6.3]	$(2^{\Sigma^*}, \{\varepsilon\}, (\cdot), \subseteq)$	$(2, \leq)$
Union bound	[32, Section 6.4]	$([0,\infty), 0, +, \leq)$	$(2, \leq)$

Fig. 4: Instances of graded Hoare logics for simple effects.

system with recursion using ωCPO-enriched models (cf. [32, Definition 70]). By imposing suitable admissibility conditions on graded monads, the construction in Proposition 26 gives a model of the dependent effect system with recursion. In Section 6, we use the soundness theorem with recursion to reason about programs with recursive functions.

Remark 29. Theorem 28 is specialized to models constructed from Proposition 26, since this construction already covers all the instances in Section 6. Nevertheless, the soundness theorem can be stated in a more general setting. We present such a formulation in [32, Theorem 51], using more general predicate fibrations, indexed preordered monoids, and indexed graded monads. Moreover, our semantic framework based on indexed graded monads can be also applied to dependent effect systems *without* refinement types by replacing refinement fibrations with more general SCCompCs. However, we focused on the type system with refinement types in this paper because we aim at refinement-type-based automated verification tools in the future.

6   Instances

We extend several existing simple effect systems (Fig. 4) to dependent effect systems using the results in Section 5. Due to space constraints, we present only two instances: cost analysis and expectation logic. Other instances are presented in the long version [32].

6.1   Cost Analysis

We consider a dependent effect system for cost analysis. Following Fig. 4, we use the complete Heyting algebra $\Omega = \mathbf{2}$ of two-valued boolean algebra to interpret formulas. The grading monoid is given by $\mathcal{M} = \mathbb{N}_\infty = (\mathbb{N}_\infty, 0, +, \leq)$.

Generic Effect We use a generic effect $\mathtt{Tick} : (n : \mathtt{nat}) \xrightarrow{n} \mathtt{unit}$ that takes a natural number n and incurs n units of cost.

Model We define a model of the dependent effect system for cost analysis following Definition 27. We use the simple FGCBV model $(\omega\mathbf{CPO}, (-)_\perp \times \mathbb{N}_\infty, [\![-]\!]_s)$ where the strong monad is given by the composite of the cost monad $(-) \times \mathbb{N}_\infty$

and the lifting monad $(-)_\perp$. We impose a mild additional assumption that the interpretation $[\![b]\!]_s \in \omega\mathbf{CPO}$ of any base type $b \in \mathbf{Base}$ is *discrete*, i.e., the order relation is given by the identity relation $(=)$. Although this assumption is not necessary to interpret simple FGCBV, we need this to soundly interpret recursion in the dependent effect system (see [32, Appendix D.2] for details). As a model of formulas, we use the **2**-valued predicate fibration $\mathrm{pred}_{\omega\mathbf{CPO}}$: $\mathbf{Pred}(\omega\mathbf{CPO}) \to \omega\mathbf{CPO}$ over $\omega\mathbf{CPO}$.

Now, we define a strong $\mathbb{N}_\infty$-graded monad lifting along the predicate fibration $\mathrm{pred}_{\omega\mathbf{CPO}}$. Since the strong monad $(-)_\perp \times \mathbb{N}_\infty$ in the base category is defined as a composite, we define the graded monad lifting as the composite of two graded monad liftings. As a lifting of the cost monad $(-) \times \mathbb{N}_\infty$, we define a strong $\mathbb{N}_\infty$-graded monad lifting $\mathbf{C}$ as follows: for $(X, P) \in \mathbf{Pred}(\omega\mathbf{CPO})$,

$$\mathbf{C}_m(X, P) \quad := \quad (X \times \mathbb{N}_\infty, \{(x, n) \in X \times \mathbb{N}_\infty \mid x \in P \wedge n \le m\}).$$

Here, we implicitly identify $P \subseteq \omega\mathbf{CPO}(1, X)$ with a subset $P \subseteq X$. As for a lifting of the lifting monad $(-)_\perp$, we define a strong (1-graded) monad lifting $\mathbf{Par}$ as $\mathbf{Par}(X, P) := (X_\perp, P \cup \{\perp\})$ for each $(X, P) \in \mathbf{Pred}(\omega\mathbf{CPO})$, which represents partial correctness, since diverging computation $\perp \in X_\perp$ satisfies the predicate $\mathbf{Par}(X, P)$.

Lemma 30. *The composite* $(m, (X, P)) \mapsto \mathbf{C}_m\mathbf{Par}(X, P)$ *is a strong* $\mathbb{N}_\infty$*-graded monad lifting of* $(-)_\perp \times \mathbb{N}_\infty$ *along* $\mathrm{pred}_{\omega\mathbf{CPO}}$: $\mathbf{Pred}(\omega\mathbf{CPO}) \to \omega\mathbf{CPO}$. $\square$

As for the interpretation of basic effects, we define the interpretation of `nat2eff : nat` $\to$ **Effect** as the embedding $i : \mathbb{N} \to \mathbb{N}_\infty$.

Now, we show that the model satisfies the conditions in Definition 27. It is straightforward to show Ax 1. For example, consider the generic effect `Tick` : $(n :$ `nat`$) \overset{n}{\twoheadrightarrow}$ `unit`. The interpretation $[\![$`Tick`$]\!] : \mathbb{N} \to 1_\perp \times \mathbb{N}_\infty$ in the simple FGCBV model has a lifting along the predicate fibration $\mathrm{pred}_{\omega\mathbf{CPO}}$ when paired with the identity: $\langle\mathrm{id}, [\![$`Tick`$]\!]\rangle : \{n \in \mathbb{N} \mid \top\} \overset{\cdot}{\to} \{(n, (r, c)) \in \mathbb{N} \times (1_\perp \times \mathbb{N}_\infty) \mid c \le n\}$. This validates the refinement type signature `Tick` : $(n :$ `nat`$) \overset{n}{\twoheadrightarrow}$ `unit`. Ax 2 is satisfied by $\omega\mathbf{CPO}$ since we have $\omega\mathbf{CPO}(1, X + Y) \cong \omega\mathbf{CPO}(1, X) + \omega\mathbf{CPO}(1, Y)$.

By Theorem 28, we obtain a model of the dependent effect system. By the general soundness theorem, the cost of a well-typed computation term is upper bounded by the dependent effect.

Corollary 31 (soundness of cost analysis). *Suppose that* $\dot{\Gamma} \vdash M : T_\mathcal{E}\dot{A}$ *is well-typed. Let* $\mathrm{cost}(M) := \pi_2 \circ [\![M]\!]_s : [\![\lfloor\dot{\Gamma}\rfloor]\!]_s \to \mathbb{N}_\infty$ *be the cost of* M. *Then,* $\mathrm{cost}(M)$ *is upper bounded by* $\mathcal{E}$ *whenever the predicates in* $\dot{\Gamma}$ *are satisfied.*

$$\forall\gamma \in [\![\lfloor\dot{\Gamma}\rfloor]\!]_s, \quad \gamma \in [\![\dot{\Gamma}]\!] \quad \Longrightarrow \quad \mathrm{cost}(M)(\gamma) \le [\![\mathcal{E}]\!](\gamma)$$

Here, we identify $[\![\mathcal{E}]\!] \in (\omega\mathbf{CPO} /\!/ \mathbb{N}_\infty)_{[\![\dot{\Gamma}]\!]}$ *with a function* $[\![\lfloor\dot{\Gamma}\rfloor]\!]_s \to \mathbb{N}_\infty$. $\square$

Example Program We consider an example program that computes the insertion sort of a list of lists, which is taken from benchmarks for Resource aware ML

```
(* leq : (l1 : list) -> (l2 : list) -> T (min (len l1) (len l2)) bool *)
let rec leq l1 l2 =
  if len l1 = 0 then return true
  else if len l2 = 0 then return false
  else
    let _ = Tick 1 in                    (* cost: 1 *)
    let b = leq (tail l1) (tail l2) in   (* cost: min (len (tail l1)) (len (tail l2)) *)
    return ((head l1) <= (head l2)) && b

(* insert : (x : list) -> (l : list_list) -> T ((len x + 1) * len l) list_list *)
let rec insert x l =
  if len l = 0 then return x :: []
  else
    let _ = Tick 1 in                    (* cost: 1 *)
    let b = leq x (head l) in            (* cost: min (len x) (len (head l)) *)
    if b then return x :: l
    else
      let tl = insert x (tail l) in  (* cost: ((len x + 1) * len (tail l)) *)
      return (head l) :: tl
```

Fig. 5: An example of cost analysis (insertion sort).

[24]. The insertion function is defined in Fig. 5. Here, we use OCaml-style comments to describe the effect (i.e., the cost in this case). We write recursive function definitions using the `let rec` syntax, which is defined by appropriate syntactic sugar. Since the current type system does not explicitly support inductive data types, we include a type of lists of real numbers as a base type denoted as `list`. We assume that basic operations for lists such as $\mathtt{len} : \mathtt{list} \to \mathtt{nat}$, $\mathtt{head} : \mathtt{list} \to \mathtt{real}$, $\mathtt{tail} : \mathtt{list} \to \mathtt{list}$, $[] : \mathtt{list}$, and $(::) : \mathtt{real} \times \mathtt{list} \to \mathtt{list}$ are available as effect-free operations with appropriate refinement type signatures. We also include a base type of lists of lists of real numbers denoted as `list_list` together with basic operations for `list_list`. Then, the functions `leq` and `insert` are typed as $\mathtt{leq} : (l_1 : \mathtt{list}) \times (l_2 : \mathtt{list}) \to T_{\min\{\mathtt{len}\ l_1, \mathtt{len}\ l_2\}} \mathtt{bool}$ and $\mathtt{insert} : (x : \mathtt{list}) \times (l : \mathtt{list\_list}) \to T_{(\mathtt{len}\ x+1) \times \mathtt{len}\ l} \mathtt{list\_list}$, in which the effects depend on the input lists. By the soundness (Corollary 31), it follows that the cost of $\mathtt{insert}\ (x, l)$ is upper bounded by $(\mathtt{len}\ x + 1) \times \mathtt{len}\ l$.

6.2   Expectation Logic

The expectation logic [2, Section 4.2] is a logic for reasoning about expectations of probabilistic programs. This logic is graded by the difference between a given pre-expectation, which is a $[0, \infty]$-valued function, and the weakest pre-expectation, which is the expected value of a given post-expectation. We can instantiate our framework to the expectation logic. One notable difference between the expectation logic and other instances is that the expectation logic interprets predicates as *real-valued predicates* rather than boolean-valued predicates. Formally, we use $\Omega = [0, \infty]^{\mathrm{op}} = ([0, \infty], \geq)$ as a complete Heyting algebra. Note that the order is reversed: the meet operation $x \wedge^{\mathrm{op}} y$ is $\max\{x, y\}$, and the join operation $x \vee^{\mathrm{op}} y$ is $\min\{x, y\}$. Since the expectation logic bounds the difference between $[0, \infty]^{\mathrm{op}}$-valued predicates, we use $\mathcal{M} = ([0, \infty], 0, +, \leq)$ as a grading monoid.

Generic Effects For simplicity, we consider only one generic effect `Bern` that samples a value of type `bool = unit+unit` from the Bernoulli distribution. However, adding other distributions, including continuous distributions, is straightforward. Let A and B be $[0,\infty]^{\mathrm{op}}$-valued predicates and $e \geq 0$. The refinement type signature of `Bern` is given as follows.

$$\texttt{Bern} : (p : \{p{:}\texttt{real} \mid \langle 0 \leq p \leq 1 \rangle \wedge^{\mathrm{op}} C\}) \xrightarrow{e} \{t{:}\texttt{unit} \mid A\} + \{f{:}\texttt{unit} \mid B\}$$
$$\text{where} \quad C = p \cdot A + (1-p) \cdot B - e$$

Here, p is a parameter for the Bernoulli distribution, and $\langle \phi \rangle$ embeds a boolean predicate ϕ into a $[0,\infty]^{\mathrm{op}}$-valued predicate: $\langle \phi \rangle = 0$ if ϕ holds, and $\langle \phi \rangle = \infty$ if ϕ does not hold. Note that $\langle \phi \rangle \wedge^{\mathrm{op}} A$ is equal to A if ϕ holds, and equal to ∞ otherwise. The above type signature means if $0 \leq p \leq 1$, then the difference between the expected value $p \cdot A + (1-p) \cdot B$ and the precondition $C = p \cdot A + (1-p) \cdot B - e$ is upper bounded by e. In the above type signature, A, B, and e are constants, but we may also consider them as *ghost parameters*, which are parameters of a generic effect that are not used in the actual computation but used in the type signature. Using ghost parameters allows us more flexibility in typing, since we can instantiate them with value terms rather than constants.

Model We use the simple FGCBV model $(\omega\mathbf{QBS}, \mathbf{D}(-)_\perp, \llbracket - \rrbracket_s)$ where $\omega\mathbf{QBS}$ is the category of ω-quasi-Borel spaces [59], $\mathbf{D}$ is the probabilistic powerdomain monad on $\omega\mathbf{QBS}$, and $(-)_\perp$ is the lifting monad. We define a strong graded monad lifting of $\mathbf{D}$ along the Ω-valued predicate fibration over $\omega\mathbf{QBS}$ by adapting a $\top\top$-lifting for $\mathbf{QBS}$ used in [2]. Then, we combine it with a lifting of the lifting monad $(-)_\perp$. Details are given in [32, Section D.4]. By Theorem 28, we obtain the soundness of the expectation logic.

Corollary 32 (soundness of expectation logic). *Suppose that $\dot{\Gamma} \vdash M : T_{\mathcal{E}}\{x : b \mid \phi\}$ is well-typed. If $\llbracket \phi \rrbracket(\gamma, -) : \llbracket b \rrbracket_s \to [0, \infty]$ is a morphism in $\omega\mathbf{QBS}$ for each γ, then*

$$\forall \gamma \in \llbracket \lfloor \dot{\Gamma} \rfloor \rrbracket, \quad \llbracket \dot{\Gamma} \rrbracket(\gamma) + \llbracket \mathcal{E} \rrbracket(\gamma) \quad \geq \quad \mathbb{E}_{x \leftarrow \llbracket M \rrbracket_s(\gamma)}[\llbracket \phi \rrbracket(\gamma, x)]$$

Here, we implicitly extend the domain of $\llbracket \phi \rrbracket(\gamma, -)$ by $\llbracket \phi \rrbracket(\gamma, \perp) = 0$. Note that if $\llbracket b \rrbracket_s$ is a measurable space with discrete order, then any measurable function $\llbracket \phi \rrbracket(\gamma, -)$ is a morphism in $\omega\mathbf{QBS}$. $\square$

Example Program We consider a program (Fig. 6) that returns a winner of a duel between two cowboys [41]. We modified the original program so that Cowboy A is given an unfair advantage, which increases the probability of hitting Cowboy B. The advantage is given by a parameter c, which is halved at each round of the duel. If there is no unfair advantage (i.e., $c = 0$), then the "fair" winning probability of Cowboy A is $p_A^{\mathrm{fair}} := a/(a+b-a \cdot b)$ if Cowboy A shoots first, and $p_B^{\mathrm{fair}} := (1-b)a/(a+b-a \cdot b)$ if Cowboy B shoots first. We would like to bound the difference between the fair winning probability and the unfair winning

```
let unfair_cowboy_duel t a b =
  let weight t c = if t then return a + c else return b in
  let rec aux t c =
    let w = weight t c in
    let s = Bern w in           (* bound: t => c * b / (a + b - a * b), not t => 0 *)
    if s then return t
    else aux (not t) (c / 2)   (* bound:     t => 1 / 3 * c * b / (a + b - a * b),
                                          not t => 2 / 3 * c * b / (a + b - a * b) *)
  in aux t ((1 - a) / 3)
```

Fig. 6: The unfair duelling cowboys. Two cowboys A ($t =$ true) and B ($t =$ false) are duelling. Cowboy A hits cowboy B with probability a, and cowboy B hits cowboy A with probability b. However, Cowboy A is given an unfair advantage, which increases the probability by c. The program returns the winner of the duel.

probability. Using our dependent effect system, we can derive the following type for aux, the main loop of the duel.

$$\texttt{aux} : (t{:}\{u{:}\texttt{unit} \mid p_A^{\text{fair}}\} + \{u{:}\texttt{unit} \mid p_B^{\text{fair}}\}) \times (c{:}\{c{:}\texttt{real} \mid \langle 0 \le c \wedge a + c \le 1 \rangle\})$$
$$\to T_{[t]\cdot\frac{4cb}{3(a+b-ab)}+[\neg t]\cdot\frac{2cb}{3(a+b-ab)}}(\{u : \texttt{unit} \mid 1\} + \{u : \texttt{unit} \mid 0\})$$

This type reads as follows. The post-expectation is 1 if Cowboy A wins, and 0 if Cowboy B wins. The pre-expectation for t is the fair winning probability of Cowboy A. The difference between the fair winning probability and the unfair winning probability is bounded by $4/3 \cdot cb/(a+b-ab)$ if Cowboy A shoots first, and $2/3 \cdot cb/(a+b-ab)$ if Cowboy B shoots first. Here, $[-]$ is the Iverson bracket, which is defined as $[t] = 1$ if t is true, and $[t] = 0$ otherwise.

7   Conclusions and Future Work

We have presented a semantic framework for dependent effect systems based on indexed preordered monoids and indexed graded monads, which are generalizations of preordered monoids and graded monads, respectively. We have shown how to construct indexed graded monads from graded monad liftings for simple effect systems and provided several concrete instances. As future work, we would like to apply our semantic framework to relational refinement types for, e.g., differential privacy verification [7] and implement such an effect system. Improving the let rule is another important future work.

Acknowledgments. We would like to thank the anonymous reviewers for their helpful comments and suggestions. This study was supported by JST K Program Grant Number JPMJKP24U2; JST CREST Grant Number JPMJCR21M3; JSPS KAKENHI Grant Number JP25H00446, JP25K21183, JP24H00699, JP23K24820, JP20H05703, JP20H05703. Marco Gaboardi's work was partially supported by the National Science Foundation under Grant No. 2314324.

References

1. Abuah, C., Darais, D., Near, J.P.: Solo: a lightweight static analysis for differential privacy. Proc. ACM Program. Lang. **6**(OOPSLA2), 699–728 (2022). https://doi.org/10.1145/3563313
2. Aguirre, A., Barthe, G., Gaboardi, M., Garg, D., Katsumata, S.y., Sato, T.: Higher-order probabilistic adversarial computations: Categorical semantics and program logics. Proceedings of the ACM on Programming Languages **5**(ICFP), 1–30 (Aug 2021)
3. Ahman, D.: Fibred Computational Effects. Ph.D. thesis, University of Edinburgh (2017)
4. Ahman, D., Ghani, N., Plotkin, G.D.: Dependent Types and Fibred Computational Effects. In: Foundations of Software Science and Computation Structures. Lecture Notes in Computer Science, vol. 9634, pp. 36–54. Springer Berlin Heidelberg, Berlin, Heidelberg (2016)
5. Atkey, R.: Parameterised notions of computation. J. Funct. Program. **19**(3–4), 335–376 (Jul 2009). https://doi.org/10.1017/S095679680900728X
6. Barbosa, H., Barrett, C., Brain, M., Kremer, G., Lachnitt, H., Mann, M., Mohamed, A., Mohamed, M., Niemetz, A., Nötzli, A., Ozdemir, A., Preiner, M., Reynolds, A., Sheng, Y., Tinelli, C., Zohar, Y.: Cvc5: A Versatile and Industrial-Strength SMT Solver. In: Tools and Algorithms for the Construction and Analysis of Systems. Lecture Notes in Computer Science, vol. 13243, pp. 415–442. Springer International Publishing, Cham (2022)
7. Barthe, G., Gaboardi, M., Gallego Arias, E.J., Hsu, J., Roth, A., Strub, P.Y.: Higher-order approximate relational refinement types for mechanism design and differential privacy. In: Proceedings of the 42nd Annual ACM SIGPLAN-SIGACT Symposium on Principles of Programming Languages - POPL '15. pp. 55–68. ACM Press, Mumbai, India (2015)
8. Barthe, G., Gaboardi, M., Grégoire, B., Hsu, J., Strub, P.Y.: A program logic for union bounds. In: 43rd International Colloquium on Automata, Languages, and Programming (ICALP 2016). Leibniz International Proceedings in Informatics (Lipics), vol. 55, pp. 107:1–107:15. Schloss Dagstuhl – Leibniz-Zentrum für Informatik, Dagstuhl, Germany (2016)
9. Bengtson, J., Bhargavan, K., Fournet, C., Gordon, A.D., Maffeis, S.: Refinement types for secure implementations. In: Proceedings of the 21st IEEE Computer Security Foundations Symposium, CSF 2008, Pittsburgh, Pennsylvania, USA, 23-25 June 2008. pp. 17–32. IEEE Computer Society (2008). https://doi.org/10.1109/CSF.2008.27
10. Breuvart, F., McDermott, D., Uustalu, T.: Canonical gradings of monads. In: Master, J., Lewis, M. (eds.) Proceedings Fifth International Conference on Applied Category Theory, ACT 2022, Glasgow, United Kingdom, 18-22 July 2022. EPTCS, vol. 380, pp. 1–21 (2022). https://doi.org/10.4204/EPTCS.380.1
11. Çiçek, E., Barthe, G., Gaboardi, M., Garg, D., Hoffmann, J.: Relational cost analysis. In: Castagna, G., Gordon, A.D. (eds.) Proceedings of the 44th ACM SIGPLAN Symposium on Principles of Programming Languages, POPL 2017, Paris, France, January 18-20, 2017. pp. 316–329. ACM (2017). https://doi.org/10.1145/3009837.3009858
12. Çiçek, E., Garg, D., Acar, U.A.: Refinement types for incremental computational complexity. In: Vitek, J. (ed.) Programming Languages and Systems - 24th European Symposium on Programming, ESOP 2015, Held as Part of the European

Joint Conferences on Theory and Practice of Software, ETAPS 2015, London, UK, April 11-18, 2015. Proceedings. Lecture Notes in Computer Science, vol. 9032, pp. 406–431. Springer (2015). https://doi.org/10.1007/978-3-662-46669-8_17

13. Danielsson, N.A.: Lightweight semiformal time complexity analysis for purely functional data structures. In: Proceedings of the 35th Annual ACM SIGPLAN-SIGACT Symposium on Principles of Programming Languages. p. 133–144. POPL '08, Association for Computing Machinery, New York, NY, USA (2008). https://doi.org/10.1145/1328438.1328457

14. De Moura, L., Bjørner, N.: Z3: An Efficient SMT Solver. In: Tools and Algorithms for the Construction and Analysis of Systems. Lecture Notes in Computer Science, vol. 4963, pp. 337–340. Springer Berlin Heidelberg, Berlin, Heidelberg (2008)

15. Dutertre, B.: Yices 2.2. In: Computer Aided Verification. Lecture Notes in Computer Science, vol. 8559, pp. 737–744. Springer International Publishing, Cham (2014)

16. Fujii, S., Katsumata, S., Melliès, P.: Towards a formal theory of graded monads. In: Jacobs, B., Löding, C. (eds.) Foundations of Software Science and Computation Structures - 19th International Conference, FOSSACS 2016, Held as Part of the European Joint Conferences on Theory and Practice of Software, ETAPS 2016, Eindhoven, The Netherlands, April 2-8, 2016, Proceedings. Lecture Notes in Computer Science, vol. 9634, pp. 513–530. Springer (2016). https://doi.org/10.1007/978-3-662-49630-5_30

17. Gaboardi, M., Katsumata, S.y., Orchard, D., Sato, T.: Graded Hoare Logic and its Categorical Semantics. In: Programming Languages and Systems. Lecture Notes in Computer Science, vol. 12648, pp. 234–263. Springer International Publishing, Cham (2021)

18. Gaboardi, M., Katsumata, S., Orchard, D.A., Breuvart, F., Uustalu, T.: Combining effects and coeffects via grading. In: Garrigue, J., Keller, G., Sumii, E. (eds.) Proceedings of the 21st ACM SIGPLAN International Conference on Functional Programming, ICFP 2016, Nara, Japan, September 18-22, 2016. pp. 476–489. ACM (2016). https://doi.org/10.1145/2951913.2951939

19. Gordon, C.S.: Polymorphic iterable sequential effect systems. ACM Trans. Program. Lang. Syst. **43**(1), 4:1–4:79 (2021). https://doi.org/10.1145/3450272

20. Grobauer, B.: Cost recurrences for dml programs. In: Proceedings of the Sixth ACM SIGPLAN International Conference on Functional Programming. p. 253–264. ICFP '01, Association for Computing Machinery, New York, NY, USA (2001). https://doi.org/10.1145/507635.507666

21. Grodin, H., Niu, Y., Sterling, J., Harper, R.: Decalf: A directed, effectful cost-aware logical framework. Proc. ACM Program. Lang. **8**(POPL), 273–301 (2024). https://doi.org/10.1145/3632852

22. Handley, M.A.T., Vazou, N., Hutton, G.: Liquidate your assets: reasoning about resource usage in liquid haskell. Proc. ACM Program. Lang. **4**(POPL), 24:1–24:27 (2020). https://doi.org/10.1145/3371092

23. Hicks, M., Bierman, G.M., Guts, N., Leijen, D., Swamy, N.: Polymonadic programming. In: Levy, P.B., Krishnaswami, N. (eds.) Proceedings 5th Workshop on Mathematically Structured Functional Programming, MSFP@ETAPS 2014, Grenoble, France, 12 April 2014. EPTCS, vol. 153, pp. 79–99 (2014). https://doi.org/10.4204/EPTCS.153.7

24. Hoffmann, J., Das, A., Weng, S.C.: Towards automatic resource bound analysis for OCaml. In: Proceedings of the 44th ACM SIGPLAN Symposium on Principles of Programming Languages. pp. 359–373. ACM, Paris France (Jan 2017)

25. Ivaskovic, A., Mycroft, A., Orchard, D.: Data-flow analyses as effects and graded monads. In: Ariola, Z.M. (ed.) 5th International Conference on Formal Structures for Computation and Deduction, FSCD 2020, June 29-July 6, 2020, Paris, France (Virtual Conference). LIPIcs, vol. 167, pp. 15:1–15:23. Schloss Dagstuhl - Leibniz-Zentrum für Informatik (2020). https://doi.org/10.4230/LIPICS.FSCD.2020.15

26. Jacobs, B.: Categorical Logic and Type Theory. No. 141 in Studies in Logic and the Foundations of Mathematics, Elsevier, Amsterdam, paperback ed edn. (2001)

27. Katsumata, S.y.: Parametric effect monads and semantics of effect systems. In: Proceedings of the 41st ACM SIGPLAN-SIGACT Symposium on Principles of Programming Languages - POPL '14. pp. 633–645. ACM Press, San Diego, California, USA (2014)

28. Katsumata, S., McDermott, D., Uustalu, T., Wu, N.: Flexible presentations of graded monads. Proc. ACM Program. Lang. 6(ICFP), 902–930 (2022). https://doi.org/10.1145/3547654

29. Kellison, A.E., Hsu, J.: Numerical fuzz: A type system for rounding error analysis. Proc. ACM Program. Lang. 8(PLDI), 1954–1978 (2024). https://doi.org/10.1145/3656456

30. Knoth, T., Wang, D., Reynolds, A., Hoffmann, J., Polikarpova, N.: Liquid resource types. Proc. ACM Program. Lang. 4(ICFP), 106:1–106:29 (2020). https://doi.org/10.1145/3408988

31. Kura, S.: A General Semantic Construction of Dependent Refinement Type Systems, Categorically. In: Foundations of Software Science and Computation Structures. Lecture Notes in Computer Science, vol. 12650, pp. 406–426. Springer International Publishing (2021)

32. Kura, S., Gaboardi, M., Sekiyama, T., Unno, H.: A category-theoretic framework for dependent effect systems (2026), https://arxiv.org/abs/2601.14846

33. Kura, S., Unno, H.: Automated Verification of Higher-Order Probabilistic Programs via a Dependent Refinement Type System. Proceedings of the ACM on Programming Languages 8(ICFP), 973–1002 (Aug 2024)

34. Levy, P.B., Power, J., Thielecke, H.: Modelling environments in call-by-value programming languages. Information and Computation 185(2), 182–210 (Sep 2003)

35. Liell-Cock, J., Staton, S.: Compositional Imprecise Probability: A Solution from Graded Monads and Markov Categories. Proceedings of the ACM on Programming Languages 9(POPL), 1596–1626 (Jan 2025)

36. Liu, J., Kretz, I., Liu, H., Tan, B., Wang, J., Sun, Y., Pearson, L., Miltner, A., Dillig, I., Feng, Y.: Certifying zero-knowledge circuits with refinement types. In: IEEE Symposium on Security and Privacy, SP 2024, San Francisco, CA, USA, May 19-23, 2024. pp. 1741–1759. IEEE (2024). https://doi.org/10.1109/SP54263.2024.00078

37. Lobo-Vesga, E., Russo, A., Gaboardi, M., Cortiñas, C.T.: Sensitivity by parametricity. Proc. ACM Program. Lang. 8(OOPSLA2) (Oct 2024). https://doi.org/10.1145/3689726

38. Lucassen, J.M., Gifford, D.K.: Polymorphic effect systems. In: Ferrante, J., Mager, P. (eds.) Conference Record of the Fifteenth Annual ACM Symposium on Principles of Programming Languages, San Diego, California, USA, January 10-13, 1988. pp. 47–57. ACM Press (1988). https://doi.org/10.1145/73560.73564

39. Maillard, K., Ahman, D., Atkey, R., Martínez, G., Hritcu, C., Rivas, E., Tanter, É.: Dijkstra monads for all. Proc. ACM Program. Lang. 3(ICFP), 104:1–104:29 (2019). https://doi.org/10.1145/3341708

40. Marino, D., Millstein, T.D.: A generic type-and-effect system. In: Kennedy, A., Ahmed, A. (eds.) Proceedings of TLDI'09: 2009 ACM SIGPLAN International Workshop on Types in Languages Design and Implementation, Savannah, GA, USA, January 24, 2009. pp. 39–50. ACM (2009). https://doi.org/10.1145/1481861.1481868
41. McIver, A., Morgan, C.: Abstraction, Refinement and Proof for Probabilistic Systems. Monographs in Computer Science, Springer, New York (2005)
42. Moon, B., III, H.E., Orchard, D.: Graded modal dependent type theory. In: Yoshida, N. (ed.) Programming Languages and Systems - 30th European Symposium on Programming, ESOP 2021, Held as Part of the European Joint Conferences on Theory and Practice of Software, ETAPS 2021, Luxembourg City, Luxembourg, March 27 - April 1, 2021, Proceedings. Lecture Notes in Computer Science, vol. 12648, pp. 462–490. Springer (2021). https://doi.org/10.1007/978-3-030-72019-3_17
43. Mukai, R., Kobayashi, N., Sato, R.: Parameterized recursive refinement types for automated program verification. In: Singh, G., Urban, C. (eds.) Static Analysis - 29th International Symposium, SAS 2022, Auckland, New Zealand, December 5-7, 2022, Proceedings. Lecture Notes in Computer Science, vol. 13790, pp. 397–421. Springer (2022). https://doi.org/10.1007/978-3-031-22308-2_18
44. Nanjo, Y., Unno, H., Koskinen, E., Terauchi, T.: A Fixpoint Logic and Dependent Effects for Temporal Property Verification. In: Proceedings of the 33rd Annual ACM/IEEE Symposium on Logic in Computer Science. pp. 759–768. ACM, Oxford United Kingdom (Jul 2018)
45. Niu, Y., Sterling, J., Grodin, H., Harper, R.: A cost-aware logical framework. Proc. ACM Program. Lang. 6(POPL), 1–31 (2022). https://doi.org/10.1145/3498670
46. Orchard, D., Liepelt, V.B., Eades III, H.: Quantitative program reasoning with graded modal types. Proc. ACM Program. Lang. 3(ICFP) (Jul 2019). https://doi.org/10.1145/3341714
47. Orchard, D.A., Petricek, T.: Embedding effect systems in haskell. In: Swierstra, W. (ed.) Proceedings of the 2014 ACM SIGPLAN symposium on Haskell, Gothenburg, Sweden, September 4-5, 2014. pp. 13–24. ACM (2014). https://doi.org/10.1145/2633357.2633368
48. Pédrot, P.M., Tabareau, N.: The fire triangle: How to mix substitution, dependent elimination, and effects. Proceedings of the ACM on Programming Languages 4(POPL), 1–28 (Jan 2020)
49. Plotkin, G., Power, J.: Algebraic operations and generic effects. Applied Categorical Structures 11(1), 69–94 (2003)
50. Radiček, I., Barthe, G., Gaboardi, M., Garg, D., Zuleger, F.: Monadic refinements for relational cost analysis. Proceedings of the ACM on Programming Languages 2(POPL), 1–32 (Jan 2018)
51. Rajani, V., Gaboardi, M., Garg, D., Hoffmann, J.: A unifying type-theory for higher-order (amortized) cost analysis. Proc. ACM Program. Lang. 5(POPL), 1–28 (2021). https://doi.org/10.1145/3434308
52. Sannier, V., Baillot, P.: Dependent Coeffects for Local Sensitivity Analysis. Proceedings of the ACM on Programming Languages 10(POPL), 806–832 (Jan 2026)
53. Sekiyama, T., Unno, H.: Temporal Verification with Answer-Effect Modification: Dependent Temporal Type-and-Effect System with Delimited Continuations. Proceedings of the ACM on Programming Languages 7(POPL), 2079–2110 (Jan 2023)
54. Smirnov, A.L.: Graded monads and rings of polynomials. Journal of Mathematical Sciences 151(3), 3032–3051 (Jun 2008)

55. Swamy, N., Hritcu, C., Keller, C., Rastogi, A., Delignat-Lavaud, A., Forest, S., Bhargavan, K., Fournet, C., Strub, P., Kohlweiss, M., Zinzindohoue, J.K., Zanella-Béguelin, S.: Dependent types and multi-monadic effects in F. In: Bodík, R., Majumdar, R. (eds.) Proceedings of the 43rd Annual ACM SIGPLAN-SIGACT Symposium on Principles of Programming Languages, POPL 2016, St. Petersburg, FL, USA, January 20 - 22, 2016. pp. 256–270. ACM (2016). https://doi.org/10.1145/2837614.2837655
56. Swamy, N., Weinberger, J., Schlesinger, C., Chen, J., Livshits, B.: Verifying higher-order programs with the dijkstra monad. In: Boehm, H., Flanagan, C. (eds.) ACM SIGPLAN Conference on Programming Language Design and Implementation, PLDI '13, Seattle, WA, USA, June 16-19, 2013. pp. 387–398. ACM (2013). https://doi.org/10.1145/2491956.2491978
57. Tate, R.: The sequential semantics of producer effect systems. In: Proceedings of the 40th Annual ACM SIGPLAN-SIGACT Symposium on Principles of Programming Languages. p. 15–26. POPL '13, Association for Computing Machinery, New York, NY, USA (2013). https://doi.org/10.1145/2429069.2429074
58. Unno, H., Satake, Y., Terauchi, T.: Relatively complete refinement type system for verification of higher-order non-deterministic programs. Proc. ACM Program. Lang. **2**(POPL), 12:1–12:29 (2018). https://doi.org/10.1145/3158100
59. Vákár, M., Kammar, O., Staton, S.: A domain theory for statistical probabilistic programming. Proceedings of the ACM on Programming Languages **3**(POPL), 1–29 (Jan 2019)
60. Vazou, N., Seidel, E.L., Jhala, R.: Liquidhaskell: experience with refinement types in the real world. In: Swierstra, W. (ed.) Proceedings of the 2014 ACM SIGPLAN symposium on Haskell, Gothenburg, Sweden, September 4-5, 2014. pp. 39–51. ACM (2014). https://doi.org/10.1145/2633357.2633366
61. Wang, P., Wang, D., Chlipala, A.: Timl: a functional language for practical complexity analysis with invariants. Proc. ACM Program. Lang. **1**(OOPSLA) (Oct 2017). https://doi.org/10.1145/3133903

Validating Quantum State Preparation Programs

Liyi Li[1], Anshu Sharma[2], Zoukarneini Difaizi Tagba[1],
Sean Frett[1], and Alex Potanin[3]

[1] Iowa State University, USA
`{liyili2,difaizi,fretts}@iastate.edu`
[2] The College of William and Mary, USA
`agsharma@wm.edu`
[3] Australian National University, Australia
`alex.potanin@anu.edu.au`

Abstract. One of the key steps in quantum algorithms is to prepare an initial quantum superposition state with distinct features. These *state preparation* algorithms are essential to the behavior of quantum algorithms, and complicated state preparation algorithms are difficult to program correctly and effectively. We present QSV: a high-assurance framework implemented with the Rocq proof assistant, permitting the development of quantum state preparation programs and validating them to correctly reflect quantum program behaviors. The key is to reduce the program correctness assurance for a program containing a quantum superposition state to that of the program state without superposition. The reduction enables the development of *an effective framework for validating quantum state preparation algorithm implementations on a classical computer* — a problem considered hard and without a clear solution until now. We utilize the QuickChick property-based testing framework to validate state preparation programs. We evaluated the effectiveness of our approach across 5 case studies implemented using QSV; these cases are not simulatable on current quantum simulators.

Keywords: Quantum Computing · Property-based Testing

1 Introduction

Despite recent advances [38,53,51,21,33,50], quantum program developers still lack tools to quickly validate program correctness—testing a program with many test inputs in a short time—and other properties when writing comprehensive programs [22,49]. Testing quantum programs directly on quantum hardware is problematic because running actual quantum computers is expensive, and the probabilistic nature of quantum computing means repeated trials may be necessary to validate correctness, driving up costs further. Ideally, we should ensure that a program satisfies user specifications before running it on the hardware. Unfortunately, such a framework might not exist for validating a quantum program for arbitrary properties since quantum programs are not classically simulatable

R. Krebbers (Ed.): ESOP 2026, LNCS 16501, pp. 432–462, 2026.
https://doi.org/10.1007/978-3-032-22720-1_16

by naive state-vector simulation without an exponential number of classical bits relative to qubits.

A quantum validation framework needs to satisfy three key design goals.

- Programmers can develop a quantum program based on a proper abstraction, with respect to high-level program properties, without worrying too much about low-level gates.
- The framework contains a scalable and effective validator to quickly judge the correctness of a user-defined program, as well as other properties, based on certain types of quantum program patterns.
- The validated program can be compiled into a quantum circuit for execution.

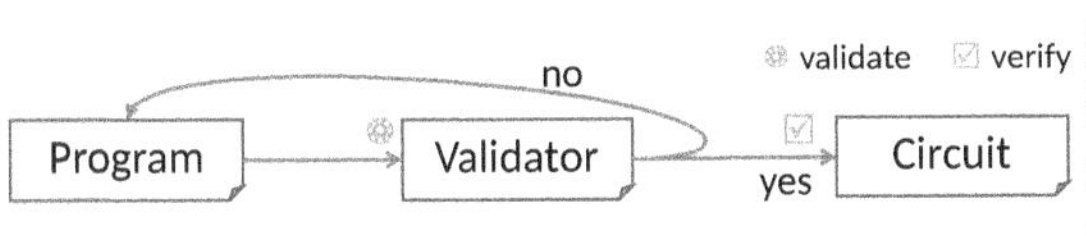

Fig. 1: The QSV Flow

We propose the Quantum State Preparation Program Validation Framework (QSV) (flow in Figure 1), permitting effective validation of state preparation programs. *The limitation is discussed in Section 8.* It includes three components. The first is the language, PQASM, which extends OQASM (Oracle Quantum Assembly Language); the P in PQASM stands for Preparation. To avoid bugs in common libraries [38] and to avoid using operators outside cases they're specific to (sometimes, there is no documentation to tell what cases they allow), we chose to implement our own operators in PQASM. Users can develop their programs in the PQASM language, enabling them to write state-preparation programs at a high level of abstraction. Such programs can be validated by our validator (the second component), based on QuickChick [41] (a Rocq property-based testing facility), and we show several quantum program patterns effectively validated via our framework. Once a program is adequately developed in QSV, users can use our certified circuit compiler to compile it into a quantum circuit that runs on quantum hardware.

Motivating Examples. Below is a simple state preparation subroutine, preparing a superposition of n distinct basis-ket states, appearing in many algorithms [3,37]. It has the following program transition property (a pre-state is transitioned to a post-state connected by $\rightarrow$) with program input of a length m qubit array, initialized as $|0\rangle_m$, and output a superposition of n different basis-ket states, each with basis-vector $|k\rangle_m$.

$$|0\rangle_m \rightarrow \sum_{j=0}^{n-1} \tfrac{1}{\sqrt{n}} |j\rangle_m$$

A state preparation program can be defined as the starting component of a quantum algorithm, typically starting with a length m qubit array, each qubit initialized as zero ($|0\rangle_m$) state, and preparing a superposition state $\sum_j \alpha_j |c_j\rangle_m$ — a linear sum of pairs (basis-kets) of complex amplitude α_j and bitstring (basis-vector) c_j such that $\sum_j |\alpha_j|^2 = 1$ — via a series of quantum operations.

Superposition is a key feature of quantum states, and quantum computers can execute programs with superposition states to query all possible inputs simultaneously, as discussed in Section 2. Many quantum algorithms require a

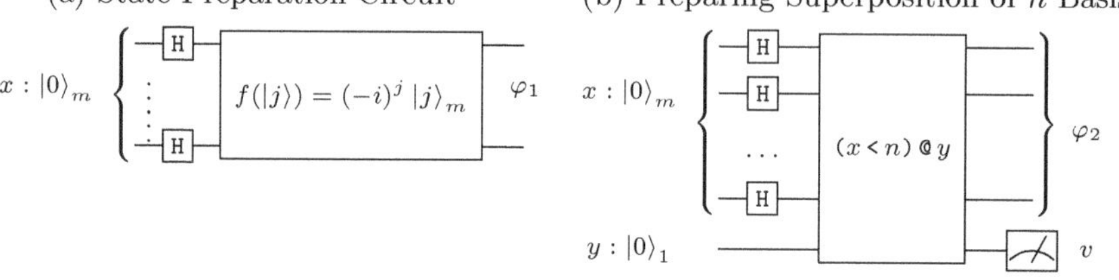

(a) State Preparation Circuit   (b) Preparing Superposition of n Basis-kets

Fig. 2: x has m qubits, and y has 1 qubit; $\varphi_1 = \sum_{j=0}^{2^m-1}(-i)^j |j\rangle_m$. The @ symbol indicates in what qubit the result of an operation is stored. The right is one step in the repeat-until-success program to prepare the superposition state. $\varphi_2 = \frac{1}{\sqrt{n}}\sum_{j=0}^{n}|j\rangle_m$ if $v = 1$; otherwise, $\varphi_2 = \frac{1}{\sqrt{2^m-n}}\sum_{j=n}^{2^m}|j\rangle_m$.

comprehensive design of state preparation components with different superposition structures, e.g., the n basis-ket state in Figure 2b.

A difficulty in developing these programs is that quantum program operations might affect every basis-ket in a superposition that might contain exponentially many basis-ket states, unlike the classical programs, where only a single basis-ket might be affected. In Figure 2a, a function f is applied to every basis-ket in the quantum superposition state after all Hadamard operations were applied. Moreover, many quantum languages are circuit-based [4,14,20,19]. These hinder the quantum program development as writing programs becomes unintuitive.

Figure 2b shows a one-step procedure of the repeat-until-success program implementation for the n basis-ket program. The procedure starts with a series of Hadamard operations to prepare a uniform superposition of 2^m basis-kets as $\frac{1}{\sqrt{2^m}}\sum_{j=0}^{2^m}|j\rangle_m$, and then compares each basis-ket with the number n; such a comparison result is stored in the y qubit. If measuring y results in 1, all the basis-kets $(\alpha_j |j\rangle_m)$, with bitstring numbers $j \geq n$, disappear, while those bitstrings $j < n$ will stay in x's quantum state; thus, the correct state is prepared. Since the measurement result 1 is probabilistic, the repeat-until-success program requires repeating the one-step procedure many times to probabilistically prepare the target state. In writing the program, a key component is the comparator $(x < n)$ @ y, comparing every basis-vector of a quantum array x with n and storing the result in qubit y. Such arithmetic operations have effective implementations [30] and circuit-level optimizations [25,54]. Therefore, QSV abstracts all these quantum arithmetic operations and relieves the pain of writing quantum programs. The QSV compiler compiles and optimizes the arithmetic operations to quantum circuits. Moreover, we also provide types to classify different program patterns for users to write state preparation programs.

Even if we permit high-level abstractions in QSV, validating a program might still be challenging because the number of basis-kets in a quantum state increases exponentially with the number of qubits. E.g., with m qubits, the output state $\sum_{j=0}^{n-1}\frac{1}{\sqrt{n}}|j\rangle_m$ might contain any of 2^m basis-kets and checking them individually might be challenging. In developing our validator, we have two observations on quantum algorithms. First, almost all quantum algorithms start with m Hadamard operations to prepare a uniform superposition having 2^m basis-kets.

These beginning Hadamard operations are simple enough and do not need to be validated, but they provide the source of a superposition state for later program operations to carve on. Second, even though quantum operations are probabilistic, one can "determinize" their behaviors. If we consider the superposition of basis-kets as an array of basis-kets, quantum operations, except measurement, behave similarly to higher-order map functions applying to the quantum state. Measurement behaves similarly to a set selection, selecting a basis-ket element in the array, and the probability of such selection can be computed based on the amplitude value associated with the basis-ket.

QSV classifies beginning Hadamard operations as a special $\mathtt{Had}$ type, to indicate that they are the source of the superposition state. When testing, instead of faithfully representing their operational behavior, QSV adopts a random pick of an individual basis-ket state as a representative, and validates programs based on transitions of the basis-ket. A measurement operation is then determinized and its probability is simply calculated via the amplitude value in the basis-ket.

For example, in dealing with the n basis-ket program above, after applying the Hadamard operations, the program property is turned as the one on the left below, where $\sum_{j=0}^{2^m-1} \frac{1}{\sqrt{2^m}} |j\rangle_m$ being the result of applying m Hadamard operations. The QSV process of determinizing the basis-kets is to select a particular j, which turns the program property to be the right one.

$$\sum_{j=0}^{2^m-1} \frac{1}{\sqrt{2^m}} |j\rangle_m \to \sum_{j=0}^{n-1} \frac{1}{\sqrt{n}} |j\rangle_m \qquad \forall j \in [0, 2^m), \frac{1}{\sqrt{2^m}} |j\rangle_m \to (\frac{1}{\sqrt{n}} |j\rangle_m \wedge j \in [0, n))$$

Essentially, the validation process based on the right property is to assume a single basis-ket $\frac{1}{\sqrt{2^m}} |j\rangle_m$ with a bitstring $j \in [0, 2^m)$, then to validate to see if the output is the bitstring j within range of $[0, n)$ and the associated amplitude being $\frac{1}{\sqrt{n}}$. Via a property-based testing facility, such as QuickChick, by testing the program with enough candidate basis-kets, it will be highly likely that our validator can capture a bug if there is any. After validation, we compile the program to a quantum circuit via our certified compiler.

Contributions and Roadmap. We present QSV, enabling programmers to develop state-preparation programs. Our contributions are as follows, with all Rocq proofs and experiment results available. Limitations are in Section 8.

- We present the syntax, semantics, and type system of PQASM, allowing users to define programs with a type-soundness proof in Rocq (Section 3).
- We develop a property-based testing (PBT) framework for validating programs written in PQASM (Section 4) by showing a general flow of constructing such PBT frameworks for validating quantum programs.
- We certify a compiler from PQASM to SQIR [25] (Section 4.2) to ensure that our PQASM tool correctly reflect quantum program behaviors.
- We evaluate PQASM via a selection of state preparation programs and demonstrate that QSV is capable of validating the programs (Sections 5 and 6), which are hard to verify or validate if the input quibit length is normal (60 qubits per register and up to 361 qubits as the total input qubit size), based on the Qiskit quantum simulator and DDSim [13].

2   Background on Quantum Computing

Quantum Data and Computation. A quantum datum consists of one or more qubits. A single qubit can be represented as a two-dimensional vector $\left(\begin{smallmatrix} z_1 \\ z_2 \end{smallmatrix}\right)$, where z_1 and z_2 are complex amplitudes with $|z_1|^2 + |z_2|^2 = 1$. Using Dirac notation, this is written as $z_1 |0\rangle + z_2 |1\rangle$, with $|0\rangle$ and $|1\rangle$ as the *computational basis-vectors*. When both z_1 and z_2 are non-zero, the qubit is in a superposition of the kets $|0\rangle$ and $|1\rangle$. The value inside the ket is a possible measurement outcome, and the norm square of the scalar factor, e.g., $|z_1|^2$ and $|z_2|^2$, is the probability of the measurement outcome. Multi-qubit data is constructed via the tensor product, e.g., $|0\rangle \otimes |1\rangle = |01\rangle$. However, not all multi-qubit states can be separated into tensor products; some are entangled states, such as the Bell pair $\frac{1}{\sqrt{2}}(|00\rangle + |11\rangle)$.

Quantum computation applies unitary gates to evolve the state of qubits. A gate is represented by a unitary matrix U that acts on the qubit state vector $|\psi\rangle$, producing a new state $U |\psi\rangle$, e.g., the Hadamard gate $\mathtt{H} = \frac{1}{\sqrt{2}}\left(\begin{smallmatrix} 1 & 1 \\ 1 & -1 \end{smallmatrix}\right)$ transforms computational basis states into superpositions: applying $\mathtt{H}$ to $|0\rangle$ yields $|+\rangle = \frac{1}{\sqrt{2}}(|0\rangle + |1\rangle)$, and applying $\mathtt{H}$ to $|1\rangle$ yields $|-\rangle = \frac{1}{\sqrt{2}}(|0\rangle - |1\rangle)$. These operations are composed in quantum circuits for computations, where each wire denotes a qubit and each gate denotes a transformation applied at a specific time.

Measurement collapses the quantum state to a classical outcome with a probability determined by the amplitudes. For instance, measuring $\frac{1}{\sqrt{2}}(|0\rangle + |1\rangle)$ yields $|0\rangle$ or $|1\rangle$, each with probability $\frac{1}{2}$. After measurement, the state irreversibly collapses to the observed basis state, and quantum coherence is lost.

Quantum Oracles. Quantum algorithms manipulate input information encoded in "oracles", which are callable black-box circuits. Quantum oracles are usually quantum-reversible implementations of classical operations, especially arithmetic operations. Their behavior is defined in terms of transitions between single basis-kets. We can infer the global state behavior based on the single basis-ket behavior through the quantum summation formula below. This resembles an array map operation in Figure 2a. OQASM in VQO [30] is a language that permits the definitions of quantum oracles with efficient verification and testing facilities by viewing quantum oracle operations as aggregate operations.

Repeat-Until-Success Quantum Programs. A repeat-until-success program utilizes the probabilistic feature of partial measurement operations. It first sets up a one-step repeat-until-success by linking the desired quantum state with the success measurement of a certain classical value. If such a value is observed after measurement, the desired state is successfully prepared; otherwise, we repeat the one-step procedure. One such example procedure is in Figure 2b to repeat the n basis-ket superposition state. If we measure out $v = 1$, the desired state φ is prepared; otherwise, we repeat the procedure.

No Cloning Theorem indicates there exists no general way of exactly copying a quantum datum [52]. In quantum circuits, it relates to ensuring the reversibility of unitary gate applications. For example, the controlled node and controlled body of a quantum control gate cannot refer to the same qubits, e.g., $\mathtt{CU}\ q\ \iota$ violates the property if q is mentioned in ι. PQASM enforces no cloning by typing.

$$\begin{array}{lll}
\text{Qubit Name } q & \text{Nat } n,m \in \mathbb{N} & \text{Real} \quad r \in \mathbb{R} \\
\text{Complex} \quad z \in \mathbb{C} & \text{Bit} \quad b \in \{0,1\} & \text{Bitstring } c ::= \overline{b} \\
\text{Qubit Basis State } \nu ::= |b\rangle_1 & \qquad | \; |\Delta(r)\rangle & \\
\text{Qubit Records} \quad \theta ::= (\overline{q} \quad , \overline{q} \quad , \overline{q}) & & \\
\text{Type} \quad \tau ::= \mathtt{Had} \mid \mathtt{Nor} \mid \mathtt{Rot} & & \\
\text{Basis Vector} \quad \eta ::= \bigotimes_j \nu_j & & \\
\text{Basis-Ket} \quad \rho ::= z \cdot \eta & & \\
\text{Quantum Data} \quad \varphi ::= \rho \quad | \sum_{b=0}^1 \varphi & & \\
\text{Quantum State} \quad \Phi ::= \theta \to \varphi & &
\end{array}$$

Fig. 3: State syntax. $\overline{S}$: a sequence of S. $|c\rangle_{n+1} \equiv |c[0]\rangle_1 \otimes ... \otimes |c[n]\rangle_1$, as $|c| = n{+}1$.

$$\begin{array}{ll}
\text{Classical Variable } x,y & \text{Boolean Expressions } B \\
\text{Parameters} \quad \alpha ::= \overline{q} \mid n & \\
\text{OQASM Arith Ops } \mu ::= \mathtt{add}(\alpha,\alpha) \mid (n*\alpha)\,\%\,m \mid (\alpha{=}\alpha)\,@\,q \mid (\alpha{<}\alpha)\,@\,q \mid ... & \\
\text{Instruction} \quad \iota ::= \mu \mid \mathtt{Ry}^r q \mid \mathtt{CU}\,q\,\iota \mid \iota\,;\,\iota & \\
\text{Program} \quad e ::= \iota \mid e\,;\,e \mid \mathtt{H}(q) \mid \mathtt{new}(q) \mid \mathtt{let}\,x = \mathcal{M}(\overline{q})\,\mathtt{in}\,e \mid \mathtt{if}\,(B)\,e\,\mathtt{else}\,e &
\end{array}$$

Fig. 4: PQASM syntax.

3 PQASM: A Language for Quantum State Preparations

We designed PQASM to express quantum-state preparation programs at a high-level abstraction. PQASM operations leverage a quantum-state design, with a type system to track the types of different qubits. Such types restrict the kinds of quantum states, facilitating effective validation and analysis of the PQASM program utilizing our quantum state representations. This section presents PQASM states and the language's syntax, semantics, typing, and soundness results. More semantic and typing rules are in the technical report [28] Appx. A.

As a running example, we program the n basis-ket state preparation in Definition 1 (figures in Figure 2b). The repeat-until-success program creates an qubit array $\overline{q}$ consisting of all zeroes and a new qubit q', applies a Hadamard gate to each qubit in $\overline{q}$, uses a comparison operator $(\overline{q} < n)\,@\,q'$ comparing $\overline{q}$ with n and storing the result in q', measures the qubit q', and repeats the process until the measurment result is 1. $\mathtt{H}(\overline{q})$ is a syntactic sugar meaning $\mathtt{H}(\overline{q}[0])\,;\,...\,;\,\mathtt{H}(\overline{q}[m{-}1])$.

Definition 1 (Example Pqasm program P to prepare n superposition states in $\overline{q}$). Qubit array length is at least $\quad g(n) + 1$; q' is a single qubit.

$$P \triangleq \mathtt{new}(\overline{q})\,;\,\mathtt{new}(q')\,;\,\mathtt{H}(\overline{q})\,;\,(\overline{q} < n)\,@\,q'\,;\,\mathtt{let}\,x = \mathcal{M}(q')\,\mathtt{in}\,\mathtt{if}\,(x = 1)\,\{\}\,\mathtt{else}\,P$$

3.1 Pqasm States and Syntax

A PQASM program state Φ is represented based on the grammar in Figure 3, mapping from qubit records θ to a quantum datum φ. A quantum datum is managed as qubit records, each of which is a collection of qubits possibly being entangled, while qubits in different records are guaranteed to have no entanglement. Our quantum data consist of a quantum entanglement state that can be analyzed as two portions: 1) a sequence of sum operators $\sum_{b_1=0}^1 \cdots \sum_{b_n=0}^1$, and 2) a basis-ket ρ, a pair of a complex amplitude z and a tensor product of basis vector η, which is a tensor of single qubit basis states ν. Each sum operator represents the creation of a superposition state via a Hadamard operation H, i.e., the number of sum operators in a state represents the number of Hadamard operations applied to qubits in the state so far. The variable $\rho = z \cdot \eta$ represents a basis-ket of a quantum state. To understand the relation between a basis-ket and a quantum superposition state as a linear sum, one can think of a superposition state as a collection of "quantum choices", and a basis-ket represents a possible choice, i.e., a measurement of a qubit record produces one possible choice, with the amplitude z related to the probability of the choice.

A qubit basis state ν has one of two forms, $|b\rangle_1$ and $|\Delta(r)\rangle$. The former corresponds to the Had and N r types and the latter corresponds to the R t type. The three types of qubit basis states are represented as the three fields in a qubit record, i.e., $(\overline{q}_1, \overline{q}_2, \overline{q}_3)$ has three disjoint qubit sequences. $\overline{q}_1$ is always typed as Had, $\overline{q}_2$ has type N r, and $\overline{q}_3$ has type R t. The Had and N r typed qubits are in the computational basis. The R t typed basis state is different from the other types in terms of *bases*, and it has the form $|\Delta(r)\rangle = $ c s$(r) |0\rangle_1 + $ sin$(r) |1\rangle_1$, which is a basis state in the Y-rotated Hadamard basis. Applying a Ry with the Y-axis angle r to a $|0\rangle_1$ qubit results in $|\Delta(r)\rangle = $ c s$(r) |0\rangle + $ sin$(r) |1\rangle$.

Figure 4 presents PQASM's syntax. A PQASM program e is either an instruction ι, a sequence operation e ; e, applying a Hadamard operation H(q) to a qubit q to create a superposition, creating (**new**(q)) a new blank qubit q, a et binding that measures a sequence of qubits $\overline{q}$ and uses the result x in e, or classical conditional **if** (B) e e se e with classical Boolean guard B. Each et binding assigns a measurement result of qubits $\overline{q}$ to a variable x, representing a binary sequence. We assume H($\overline{q}$) and **new**($\overline{q}$) as syntactic sugars of applying a sequence of Hadamard and new-qubit operations.

The instructions ι correspond to unitary quantum circuit operations, including oracle arithemtic operations (μ) implementable through OQASM operations [30] on a qubit sequence $\overline{q}$ (detailed in the technical report [28] Appx. C), a Y-axis rotation gate Ry$^r q$ that rotates an angle r, a quantum control instruction (CU q ι), and a sequence operation (ι ; ι). Operation CU q ι applies instruction ι *controlled* on qubit q. In this paper, we provide several sample arithmetic oracle operations μ in Figure 4, such as addition (**add**(α, α), adding the first to the second), modular multiplication (($n * \alpha$) % m), quantum equality (($\alpha = \alpha$) @ q), quantum comparison (($\alpha < \alpha$) @ q), etc. Each parameter α is either a group of qubits $\overline{q}$ or a number n. Recall that a basis-ket state of a qubit array $\overline{q}$ is essentially a bitstring with a complex amplitude. A quantum arithmetic operation applies the classical version of the operation to each basis-ket in a quantum superposition state, e.g., ($\overline{q} = n$) @ q compares the bitstring representation of each basis-ket in $\overline{q}$ with the number n and stores the result in q. In a PQASM program containing qubit array $\overline{q}$, x in a et binding binds a local classical value (x's value) with the computational basis measurement result ($\mathcal{M}$) on qubits $\overline{q}$. While the classical variable scope is local, the quantum qubits are immutable and globally scoped, i.e., quantum operations are applied to a global quantum state; each qubit in the state is referred to by quantum qubit names (q) in the program. In PQASM, we express a SKIP operation ({}) via a μ operation having empty qubits, as $\mu \equiv \{\}$ **when** $FV(\mu) = \emptyset$ (FV collects free variables).

$$\begin{aligned}
[\![\mu]\!]\eta &= \eta[\overline{q} \mapsto [\![\mu]\!]\eta(\overline{q})] &&\textbf{where}\ FV(\mu) = \overline{q} \\
[\![\text{Ry}^r q]\!]\eta &= \eta[q \mapsto |\Delta(r)\rangle] &&\textbf{where}\ \eta(q) = |0\rangle_1 \\
[\![\text{Ry}^r q]\!]\eta &= \eta[q \mapsto |\Delta(\tfrac{3\pi}{2} - r)\rangle] &&\textbf{where}\ \eta(q) = |1\rangle_1 \\
[\![\text{Ry}^r q]\!]\eta &= \eta[q \mapsto |\Delta(r + r')\rangle] &&\textbf{where}\ \eta(q) = |\Delta(r')\rangle \\
[\![\text{CU}\ q\ \iota]\!]\eta &= \text{cu}(\eta(q), \iota, \eta) &&\textbf{where}\ \text{cu}(|0\rangle\,1, \iota, \eta) = \eta \quad \text{cu}(|1\rangle\,1, \iota, \eta) = [\![\iota]\!]\eta \\
[\![\iota_1; \iota_2]\!]\eta &= [\![\iota_2]\!]([\![\iota_1]\!]\eta)
\end{aligned}$$

$$\eta[\overline{q} \mapsto \eta'] = \eta[\forall q \in \overline{q}.\ q \mapsto \eta'(q)]$$

Fig. 5: Instruction level PQASM semantics; $\eta(\overline{q})$: the states of the qubits $\overline{q}$ in η.

3.2 Semantics

The PQASM semantics has two levels: instruction and program levels. The former is a partial function $[\![-]\!]$ from an instruction ι and input basis vector state ρ to an output state η', written $[\![\iota]\!]\eta = \eta'$, shown in Figure 5. The *program* level semantics is a labelled transition system $(\Phi, e) \xrightarrow{r} (\Phi', e')$ in Figure 6, stating that the input configuration (Φ, e) is possibly evaluated to an output configuration (Φ', e') with the probability r. It essentially represents a Markov chain, where a program evaluation path is a chain of probabilities that shows the probability of reaching a particular configuration from the initial configuration.

The instruction level semantic rules assume that one can locate the state of a qubit q in η as $\eta(q)$, where we can refer to $\eta[q \mapsto \nu]$ as updating the qubit state ν for the qubit q in η. Recall that a length n basis vector state η is a tuple of n qubit values, modeling the tensor product $\nu_1 \otimes \cdots \otimes \nu_n$. The rules implicitly map each qubit q to a state, e.g., $\eta(q)$ corresponds to some sub-state ν_q, where ν_q locates at the q's position in η. Many of the rules in Figure 5 update a *portion* of a state. We write $\eta[q \mapsto \nu_q]$ to update the state of the qubit of q in η with ν_q, and $\eta[\overline{q} \mapsto \eta']$ to update a range of qubits $\overline{q}$ according to the vector state η', i.e., we update each $q \in \overline{q}$ with the qubit value $\eta'(q)$ and $|\eta'| = |\overline{q}|$. The function cu is a conditional operation depending on the N r/Had typed qubit q.

Figure 6 shows selected program-level semantic rules. Since qubit records in a program state Φ partition the qubit domain, we can think of Φ as a multiset of pairs of qubit records and state values, as in S-MEA, i.e., $\Phi[\theta \mapsto \varphi] \equiv \Phi \uplus \{\theta \mapsto \varphi\}$. Rule S-INS connects the instruction level semantics with the program level by evaluating each basis vector state η through the instruction ι. Rule S-NEW creates a new blank $(|0\rangle_1)$ qubit, which is stored in the record $(\emptyset, q, \emptyset)$, a qubit (q) being created are N r typed. For a N r typed qubit $(\emptyset, q, \emptyset)$, rule S-HAD turns the qubit to be Had typed superposition, as $(q, \emptyset, \emptyset)$. The measurement rule (S-MEA) produces a probability r label, and the value comes from the measurement result. We first rewrite the quantum state to be a linear sum of computational basis-kets $\sum_j r_j |c\rangle_m |c_j\rangle_n + \varphi\langle\overline{q}', c \neq \overline{q}'\rangle$, where every basis-vector $|c\rangle_m$ (or $|c_j\rangle_n$) is a bitstring, and all the sum operators are resolved as a single sum.

Any PQASM state can be written as a sum of computational basis-kets. As the equations shown below, the basis-ket state $|c\rangle_n |\Delta(r)\rangle$ can be rewritten to be a sum of two computational basis-kets as $\text{c s}(r) |c\rangle_n |0\rangle_1 + \text{sin}(r) |c\rangle_n |1\rangle_1$, while

S-INS

$$\frac{b = b_1, ..., b_n \quad \varphi = \sum_{b_1=0}^{1} \cdots \sum_{b_n=0}^{1} z_b \cdot \eta_b \quad [\![\iota]\!](\eta_b) = \eta'_b}{(\Phi[\theta \mapsto \varphi], \iota) \xrightarrow{1} (\Phi[\theta \mapsto \sum_{b_1=0}^{1} \cdots \sum_{b_n=0}^{1} z_b \cdot \eta'_b], \{\})}$$

S-NEW

$$(\Phi, \mathtt{new}(q)) \xrightarrow{1} (\Phi[(\emptyset, q, \emptyset) \mapsto |0\rangle_1], \{\})$$

S-HAD

$$(\Phi[(\emptyset, q, \emptyset) \mapsto |b\rangle_1], \mathtt{H}(q)) \xrightarrow{1} (\Phi[(q, \emptyset, \emptyset) \mapsto \sum_{j=0}^{1} (-1)^{j \cdot b} |j\rangle_m], \{\})$$

S-MEA

$$\frac{\Phi = \Phi' \uplus \{\uparrow \overline{q} \mapsto \sum_j z_j |c\rangle_m |c_j\rangle_n + \phi \langle \overline{q}', c \neq \overline{q}' \rangle\} \qquad r = \sum_j |z_j|^2}{(\Phi, \mathtt{let}\ x = \mathcal{M}(\overline{q})\ \mathtt{in}\ e) \xrightarrow{r} (\Phi' \uplus \{(\uparrow \overline{q})n\overline{q} : \sum_j \frac{z_j}{\sqrt{r}} |c_j\rangle_m\}, e[c/x])}$$

$$\uparrow \overline{q} \triangleq \exists \overline{q}_1, \overline{q}_2, \overline{q}_3 \cdot \uparrow \overline{q} = (\overline{q}_1, \overline{q}_2, \overline{q}_3) \wedge \overline{q} \subseteq \overline{q}_1 \uplus \overline{q}_2 \uplus \overline{q}_3$$

$$(\textstyle\sum_i z_i |c_i\rangle_m |c'_i\rangle_n + \varphi)\langle \overline{q}, b \rangle \triangleq \textstyle\sum_i z_i |c_i\rangle_m |c'_i\rangle_n \quad \mathtt{where} \quad \forall i. |c_i| = |\overline{q}'| = m \wedge [\![b[c_i/\overline{q}']]\!] = \mathtt{true}$$

Fig. 6: Selected program Level PQASM rules.

the two sum operators can be replaced as a single sum operator over length-2 bitstring c, where we replace b_j with $c[0]$ (indexing 0 of c) and b_k with $c[1]$.

$$|c\rangle_n |\Delta(r)\rangle \equiv \cos(r) |c\rangle_n |0\rangle_1 + \sin(r) |c\rangle_n |1\rangle_1 \qquad \textstyle\sum_{b_j=0}^{1} \sum_{b_k=0}^{1} \eta \equiv \sum_{c \in \{0,1\}^2} \eta[c[0]/b_j][c[1]/b_k]$$

3.3 Typing

In PQASM, typing is with respect to a *type environment* Ω, a set of qubit records partitioning qubits into different disjoint union regions, and a *kind environment* Σ, a set tracking local variable scopes. Typing judgments are two leveled, and are written as $\Omega \vdash \iota \triangleright_g \Omega'$ and $\Sigma; \Omega \vdash e \triangleright \Omega'$, which state that instruction ι and program expression e are well-typed under Ω and Σ, and transforms variables' bases as characterized by Ω'. Ω is populated via qubit creation operations ($\mathtt{new}$), while Σ is populated via $\mathtt{let}$ binding. Selected typing rules are in Figure 7.

The instruction level type system is flow-sensitive, where g is the context flag and can be either $\mathtt{M}$ or $\mathtt{C}$, indicating whether the current instruction is inside a controlled operation. The program level type system communicates with the instruction level by assuming a $\mathtt{C}$ mode context flag, shown in rule TUP. We explain the necessity of the context flag below. Each qubit record θ represents an entanglement group, i.e., qubits in the same record might or might not be entangled, while qubits in different records are ensured not to be entangled.

$$(\overline{q_1}, \overline{q_2}, \overline{q_3}) \uplus (\overline{q_4}, \overline{q_5}, \overline{q_6}) \equiv (\overline{q_1} \uplus \overline{q_4}, \overline{q_2} \uplus \overline{q_5}, \overline{q_3} \uplus \overline{q_6})$$
$$(\emptyset, \overline{q_1} \uplus \overline{q_2}, \overline{q_3} \uplus \overline{q_4}) \equiv (\emptyset, \overline{q_1}, \overline{q_3}) \uplus (\emptyset, \overline{q_2}, \overline{q_4})$$

In our type system, we permit ordered equational rewrites among quantum qubit states. Each type environment, mainly the operation $\uplus$, admits associativity, commutativity, and identity equational properties. The $\uplus$ operations in the three fields in a qubit record also admit the three properties. Other than the three equational properties, we admit the above partial order relations, where we

$$\text{R\textsc{y}N} \quad \frac{}{\{(\emptyset,\{q\},\emptyset)\} \uplus \Omega \vdash_c \mathtt{Ry}^r q \rhd \{(\emptyset,\emptyset,\{q\})\} \uplus \Omega}$$

$$\text{M\textsc{u}T} \quad \frac{\overline{q} \subseteq \overline{q_1} \cup \overline{q_2}}{\{(\overline{q_1},\overline{q_2},\overline{q_3})\} \uplus \Omega \vdash_g \mu(\overline{q}) \rhd \{(\overline{q_1},\overline{q_2},\overline{q_3})\} \uplus \Omega}$$

$$\text{R\textsc{y}H} \quad \frac{\mathtt{Rot}(\theta) = \{q\} \uplus \overline{q}}{\{\theta\} \uplus \Omega \vdash_g \mathtt{Ry}^r q \rhd \{\theta\} \uplus \Omega}$$

$$\text{E\textsc{qv}} \quad \frac{\Omega \equiv \Omega' \quad \Omega' \vdash_g e \rhd \Omega''}{\Omega \vdash_g e \rhd \Omega''}$$

$$\text{T\textsc{up}} \quad \frac{\Omega \vdash_c \iota \rhd \Omega'}{\Sigma;\Omega \vdash \iota \rhd \Omega'}$$

$$\text{N\textsc{ew}} \quad \frac{q \notin \Omega}{\Sigma;\Omega \vdash \mathtt{new}(q) \rhd \Omega \uplus \{(\emptyset,q,\emptyset)\}}$$

$$\text{C\textsc{u}N} \quad \frac{\{\mathtt{Nor}(\theta) \downarrow \overline{q}\} \uplus \Omega \vdash_{\mathtt{M}} \iota \rhd \{\mathtt{Nor}(\theta) \downarrow \overline{q}\} \uplus \Omega}{\{\mathtt{Nor}(\theta) \downarrow \{q\} \uplus \overline{q}\} \uplus \Omega \vdash_g \mathtt{CU}\ q\ \iota \rhd \{\mathtt{Nor}(\theta) \downarrow \{q\} \uplus \overline{q}\} \uplus \Omega}$$

$$\text{HT} \quad \frac{}{\Sigma;\Omega \uplus \{(\emptyset,q,\emptyset)\} \vdash \mathtt{H}(q) \rhd \Omega \uplus \{(q,\emptyset,\emptyset)\}}$$

$$\text{C\textsc{u}H} \quad \frac{\{\mathtt{Had}(\theta) \downarrow \overline{q}\} \uplus \Omega \vdash_{\mathtt{M}} \iota \rhd \{\mathtt{Had}(\theta) \downarrow \overline{q}\} \uplus \Omega}{\{\mathtt{Had}(\theta) \downarrow \{q\} \uplus \overline{q}\} \uplus \Omega \vdash_g \mathtt{CU}\ q\ \iota \rhd \{\mathtt{Had}(\theta) \downarrow \{q\} \uplus \overline{q}\} \uplus \Omega}$$

$$\text{M\textsc{ea}} \quad \frac{\overline{q} \subseteq \theta \quad \Sigma \cup \{x\};\Omega \uplus \{\theta n\overline{q}\} \vdash e \rhd \Omega'}{\Sigma;\Omega \uplus \{\theta\} \vdash \mathtt{let}\ x = \mathcal{M}(\overline{q})\ \mathtt{in}\ e \rhd \Omega'}$$

Fig. 7: Selected type rules. $(\overline{q}_1,\overline{q}_2,\overline{q}_3)\backslash\overline{q} \triangleq (\overline{q}_1\backslash\overline{q},\overline{q}_2\backslash\overline{q},\overline{q}_3\backslash\overline{q})$; $\overline{q}_1\backslash\overline{q}$: set subtract.

permit the rewrites from left to right in our type system to permit qubit records merging and splitting. Record merging can always happen, i.e., two qubit entanglement groups can be merged into one. Qubit splitting cannot occur in $\mathtt{Had}$ typed qubits. A qubit record, including a $\mathtt{Had}$ typed qubit, represents a quantum entanglement with qubits not separable, while qubits being $\mathtt{N\ r}$ and $\mathtt{R\ t}$ typed can be split into different records. Rule E\textsc{qv} imposes the equivalence relation to permit the rewrites, only allowing rewrites from left to right, of equivalent qubit records. Note that a type environment determines qubit record scopes in a quantum state φ (Figure 3), i.e., a quantum state should have the same qubit record domain as the type environment at a program point, so the equational rewrite of a type environment might affect the qubit state representation.

Other than the equational rewrites, the type system enforces three properties. First, it enforces that classical and quantum variables are properly scoped. Rule M\textsc{ea} includes the local variable x in Σ. Rule N\textsc{ew} creates a new record $(\emptyset,q,\emptyset)$ in the post-environment, provided that q does not appear in any record in Ω. In rule R\textsc{y}H, the premise $\mathtt{R\ t}(\theta) = \{q\} \uplus \overline{q}$ utilizes $\mathtt{R\ t}$ to finds the $\mathtt{R\ t}$ filed in the record θ and ensures that q is in the field. In rule C\textsc{u}H, the premise $\mathtt{Had}(\theta) \downarrow \{q\} \uplus \overline{q}$ ensures that the controlled position q is in the $\mathtt{Had}$ field in θ. In rule M\textsc{u}T, we ensure that the qubits $\overline{q}$ being applied by the μ operation are $\mathtt{N\ r}$ and $\mathtt{Had}$ typed, through the premise $\overline{q} \subseteq \overline{q_1} \cup \overline{q_2}$.

Second, we ensure that expressions and instructions are well-formed, i.e., any control qubit is distinct from the target(s), which enforces the quantum *no-cloning rule*. In rules C\textsc{u}H and C\textsc{u}N for control operations, when typing the target instruction ι (the upper level), we remove the control qubit q in the records to ensure that q cannot be mentioned in ι. In rule M\textsc{ea}, we also remove the measured qubits $\overline{q}$ from the record θ.

Third, the type system enforces that expressions and instructions leave affected qubits in a proper type ($\mathtt{N\ r}$, $\mathtt{Had}$, and $\mathtt{R\ t}$), representing certain forms of qubit states, mentioned in Figure 3; therefore, one can utilize the procedure mentioned in Section 1 to analyze P\textsc{qasm} programs effectively. The key is to utilize the summation formula to reduce the analysis of a general quantum state to that of a quantum state without entanglement. Specifically, the $\mathtt{Ry}^r q$ opeartion is permitted only if q is of $\mathtt{N\ r}$ type, which is turned to $\mathtt{R\ t}$ type and stays there; μ can be applied to $\mathtt{N\ r}$ typed qubits $\bar{q}$ where $FV(\mu) = \bar{q}$; and a control qubit q in $\mathtt{CU}\ q\ \iota$ can be applied to a $\mathtt{N\ r}$ and $\mathtt{Had}$ typed qubit.

We ensure type restrictions for qubits via pre- and post-type environments. Rule HT permits the generation of $\mathtt{Had}$ type qubits, a.k.a. superposition qubits q, provided that q is of $\mathtt{N\ r}$ type and not entangled with other qubits. Once a Hadamard operation is applied, we turn the qubit types to $\mathtt{Had}$ in the post-type environment, so one cannot apply Hadamard operations again to the qubits. This does not mean that users can only apply Hadamard operations once in PQASM, because combining $\mathtt{X}$ (our oracle operation) and $\mathtt{Ry}$ gates can produce a Hadamard gate. We utilize the type information to locate the first appearance of Hadamard operations, identify them as the source of superposition, and apply treatments for them in our validation testing framework; see Section 4.1.

In Rules CuN and CuH, we ensure that the pre- and post-type environments are the same. In $\mathtt{CU}\ q\ \iota$, if ι contains a $\mathtt{Ry}$ operation, applying to a qubit q, q must already be $\mathtt{R\ t}$ type. Figure 8 provides a programming prototype satisfying this type requirement, where programmers explicitly add a $\mathtt{Ry}$ gate before the controlled $\mathtt{Ry}$ operation to ensure the second qubit is in $\mathtt{R\ t}$ type. The extra $\mathtt{Ry}$ operation can be a 0 rotation, equivalent to a SKIP operation, and can be removed by an optimizer when compiling

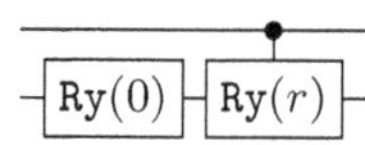

Fig. 8: Ensuring qubits inside a controlled $\mathtt{Ry}$ have the same type.

to quantum circuits. The above qubit type restriction does not depend on the applications of controlled operations. We ensure this by associating the context flags with the instruction level type system. When applying $\mathtt{CU}\ q\ \iota$, rules CuN and CuH turn the context flag to $\mathtt{M}$, indicating that ι lives inside a controlled operation. Rule RyN requires a context flag $\mathtt{C}$, meaning that the rule is valid only if the $\mathtt{Ry}$ operation lives outside any controlled operation. In contrast, rule RyH does not require a specific context flag, which indicates that a $\mathtt{Ry}$ operation inside a controlled node must apply to a qubit already in $\mathtt{R\ t}$ type.

Soundness. We prove type soundness: well-typed PQASM programs are well-defined. The type soundness theorem relies on a well-formed definition of a program e, $FV(e) \subseteq \Sigma$, meaning that all free variables in e are bounded by Σ. We also need the definition of the well-formedness of a PQASM state as follows.

Definition 2 (Well-formed state). A state Φ is *well-formed*, $\Omega \vdash \Phi$, iff:

- For every q such that $\Omega(q) = \mathtt{N\ r}$ or $\Omega(q) = \mathtt{Had}$, $\Phi(q)$ has the form $|b\rangle_1$.
- For every q such that $\Omega(q) = \mathtt{R\ t}$, $\Phi(q)$ has the form $|\Delta(r)\rangle$.

Type soundness is stated as two theorems: type progress and preservation; the proof is by induction on ι and is mechanized in Rocq.

Theorem 1. [PQASM Type Progress] If $\emptyset; \Omega \vdash e \triangleright \Omega'$, $FV(e) \subseteq \emptyset$, and $\Omega \vdash \Phi$, then either $e = \{\}$ or there exists r, e', and Φ', such that $(\Phi, e) \xrightarrow{r} (\Phi', e')$.

Proof. Fully mechanized proofs were done by induction on type rules using Rocq.

Theorem 2. [PQASM Type Preservation] If $\Sigma; \Omega \vdash e \triangleright \Omega'$, $FV(e) \subseteq \Sigma$, $\Omega \vdash \Phi$ and $(\Phi, e) \xrightarrow{r} (\Phi', e')$, then there exists Ω_a, such that $\Sigma; \Omega_a \vdash e' \triangleright \Omega'$ and $\Omega_a \vdash \Phi'$.

Proof. Fully mechanized proofs were done by induction on type rules using Rocq.

4 QSV Applications

This section presents QSV applications, based on PQASM programs, to validate and compile the programs, including QSV's PBT (property-based testing) framework and the translation from PQASM to SQIR and proof of its correctness.

4.1 Effectively Validating State Preparation Programs

The QSV validator is built on PBT to ensure that a PQASM program property is correct by attempting to falsify it using thousands of randomly generated input variables. Case studies of our validator are in Section 5. Below, we show its construction. We leverage the PQASM's state representation and type system, which ensure that states can be represented effectively, to implement a validation framework for PQASM programs using QuickChick [41], a property-based testing (PBT) framework for Rocq in the style of Haskell's QuickCheck [18]. The framework has two main utilities: validating PQASM program correctness properties and experimenting with effective implementations. PQASM measurement operations, due to the randomness inherent in quantum measurement, are difficult to test effectively, even with the assistance of program abstractions. To have an effective validation framework, we restrict the properties that can be questioned to solely focus on the properties related to program correctness.
Implementation. PBT randomly generates inputs using a hand-crafted *generator* and confirms that a property holds for these inputs. We develop a validator, based on the methodology in Section 1, using our effective (symbolic) state representation and carefully selecting the properties to validate for a program.

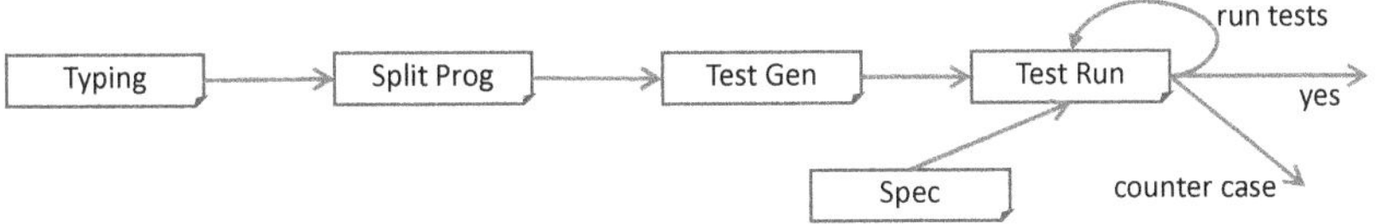

Fig. 9: The Flow of PBT for QSV

Figure 9 shows the flow of the PBT framework. To validate a PQASM program, we first utilize our PQASM type system to generate a type environment Ω for qubits in a program e, i.e., $\emptyset; \emptyset \vdash e \triangleright \Omega$, typing with an empty kind and type environment. Ω partitions all qubits used in e into three sets $(\overline{q_1}, \overline{q_2}, \overline{q_3})$, with $\overline{q_1}$, $\overline{q_2}$, and $\overline{q_3}$ containing all qubits in Had type, N r type, and R t type, respectively. In PQASM, once a qubit is assigned to type Had, it stays in the type. We utilize the property to locate all Had typed qubits in a program e and generate random testing data based on these qubits, i.e., given the set $(\overline{q_1})$ of Had typed qubits in Ω, we generate random boolean values in $\{0, 1\}$ for variables in $\overline{q_1}$.

A program is assumed in the form of $e = \mathtt{new}(\overline{q}) \mathbin{;} \mathtt{H}(\overline{q}) \mathbin{;} e'$ [4], i.e., all the $\mathtt{new}$ and $\mathtt{H}$ operations appear in the front of the program and e' does not contain any such operations. We then split the program by taking the e' part and removing the $\mathtt{new}$ and $\mathtt{H}$ operations, assuming they have already been applied. For some program patterns, such as repeat-until-success programs, we replace recursive process variables in e' with $\{\}$ operations so that we only validate one step of a repeat-until-success. While these programs do not have a fixed termination time, QSV focuses on testing a single loop step, as we are not concerned with executing this program but performing property-based testing on it. One example of programming splitting for Definition 1 is given below; it removes the part $\mathtt{new}(\overline{q}) \mathbin{;} \mathtt{new}(q') \mathbin{;} \mathtt{H}(\overline{q})$ and replacing P with $\{\}$.

$$P' = (\overline{q} < n) \mathbin{@} q' \mathbin{;} \mathtt{let}\ x = \mathcal{M}(q')\ \mathtt{in\ if}\ (x = 1)\ \{\}\ \mathtt{else}\ \{\}$$

The "Test Gen" step in QSV (Figure 9) generates test cases to validate the key component P' above. In Definition 1, after applying the $\mathtt{new}$ and $\mathtt{H}$ operations, the post-state is (Φ, P'), with Φ mapping θ, entanglement groups, to superposition states φ. Each $\mathtt{H}$ operation generates a single qubit uniformly distributed superposition state. However, transitions over a superposition state make it hard to perform effective validation. To resolve this, we treat quantum program operations P' as higher-order map operations and validate the transition correctness based on basis kets, rather than over the whole superposition state.

Generally, given $\theta = (b_0, b_1, ..., b_m, \overline{q_2}, \overline{q_3})$, the superposition state φ could also be written in the Dirac notation of $\sum_j \rho_j$ with $\rho_j = z_j \cdot \eta_j$, as follows.

$$\sum_{b_0=0}^{1} \sum_{b_1=0}^{1} \cdots \sum_{b_m=0}^{1} z(b_0, b_1, ..., b_m) \cdot \eta(b_0, b_1, ..., b_m)$$

Here, b_0, b_1, ..., b_m are qubit variables assumed to have already been manipulated by the initial $\mathtt{H}$ operations. Applying a $\mathtt{H}$ operation to a $\mathtt{N\ r}$ typed qubit $|b_a\rangle_1$ creates a uniformly distributed superposition $\sum_{b=0}^{1} \frac{1}{\sqrt{2}} (-1)^{b \cdot b_a} |b\rangle_1$, so it results in the state form above, with $z(b_0, b_1, ..., b_m)$ and $\eta(b_0, b_1, ..., b_m)$ being an amplitude and asis-vector formula, respectively. We can then select the symbolic basis-ket state $z(b_0, b_1, ..., b_m) \cdot \eta(b_0, b_1, ..., b_m)$ as the representative basis-ket and rewrite φ to be in the form $(\theta \to z \cdot \eta, P')$, with b_0, b_1, ..., b_m acting as random variables. For each variable b_j, we can randomly choose the value $b_j \in \{0, 1\}$ for a particular test instance. For m qubits, we have 2^m different instances depending on the different value selection for the random variables.

For P' above, we view each element in the m-qubit array $\overline{q}$ as a random variable. We generate an initial state $(\theta \to z(\overline{q}[0], ..., \overline{q}[m{-}1]) \cdot \eta(\overline{q}[0], ..., \overline{q}[m{-}1]), P')$ with $\overline{q}[0], ..., \overline{q}[m{-}1]$ being random variables and $\theta = (\overline{q}, q, \emptyset)$. We can then generate test instances for the random variables $\overline{q}[j]$ with $j \in [0, m)$.

As test instances are generated, we can validate the program by running each instance in our PQASM interpreter, based on our program semantics. The interpreter's result is provided as input to a specification checker to validate whether the specification is satisfied. If the checker makes all test instances return $\mathtt{true}$, we validate the program; otherwise, we report a fault. We show below the validation of different program properties.

---

[4] $\mathtt{new}(\overline{q})$ and $\mathtt{H}(\overline{q})$ are syntactic sugar for multiple $\mathtt{new}(q)$ and $\mathtt{H}(q)$ operations.

Validating Correctness. We run a test instance in our interpreter with the initial state, as $(\theta \mapsto z \cdot \eta, P) \longrightarrow^* (\theta' \mapsto z' \cdot \eta', \{\})$, where $\theta \equiv \theta'$. For a user-specified property ψ, a satisfiability check is applied to $\psi(z \cdot \eta, z' \cdot \eta')$ by replacing variables with $z \cdot \eta$ and $z' \cdot \eta'$. Recall the transformation of correctness property in Section 1 for the program in Definition 1, the key is to conduct validation on individual basis-kets rather than the whole quantum state. Such property transformations can be summarized as the transformation from (1) to (3):

(1) $\sum_j z_j \cdot \eta_j \to f(\sum_j z_j \cdot \eta_j)$ (2) $\sum_j z_j \cdot \eta_j \to \sum_k g(z_k \cdot \eta_k) \wedge \phi(k)$ (3) $\forall j. z_j \cdot \eta_j \to g'(z_j \cdot \eta_j) \wedge \phi(j)$

The correctness property should be written in the format of (3). The property (1) describes the program semantics, i.e., f represents the semantic function for a program e. The effects of such a function can always be in the form of a linear sum by moving the sum operator to the front, as in (2): one can always find g such that $f(\sum_j r_j \cdot \eta_j) = \sum_k g(r_k \cdot \eta_k)$. In some cases, we might need to insert the $\phi(k)$ predicate above, constraining index k in the sum operator. Here, both j and k are indices for two different sum operators. Often, the function g can be turned into an equivalent form g' based on the index j. Note that for certain states, there are properties that hold for the state at large but do not imply that they hold for each term. For instance, when k is a bitstring and $\mathbf{n}\ \mathbf{t}(k)$ performs the $\mathbf{n}\ \mathbf{t}$ operator on each value in the bitstring, e.g. $\mathbf{n}\ \mathbf{t}(011) = 100$, if $\sum_i |k_i\rangle = \sum_i |\mathbf{n}\ \mathbf{t}(k_i)\rangle$ that does not imply that $|k_i\rangle = |\mathbf{n}\ \mathbf{t}(k_i)\rangle$.

Once rewriting (1) to (2), we can then transform the formula to (3) without any sum operators, via the axiom of extensionality. Such transformation might come with the index restriction ϕ based on index j, as shown in (3), meaning that we find a representative basis-ket state $r_j \cdot \eta_j$ for the input superposition state and output a basis-ket state $g'(r_j \cdot \eta_j)$, with the index restriction $\phi(j)$.

To validate P' above, we transform the correctness property from the left to the right one below ($\Rightarrow$ is logic implication).

$$x = 1 \Rightarrow \sum_j^{2^m} \tfrac{1}{\sqrt{2^m}} |j\rangle_m |0\rangle_1 \to \sum_j^n \tfrac{1}{\sqrt{n}} |j\rangle_m \qquad \forall j \in [0, 2^m) \,.\, x = 1 \Rightarrow |j\rangle_m |0\rangle_1 \to |j\rangle_m \wedge j < n$$

The right property states that, if the measurement results in 1 ($x = 1$), each basis-ket in the pre-state for $\bar{q}$ and q (values $|j\rangle_m$ and $|0\rangle_1$) results in $\bar{q}$ being the same $|j\rangle_m$ with the restriction $j < n$. In implementing a validation property, the flags m and 1 essentially indicate the length of bitstring pieces, cast into a natural number for comparison. To validate the correctness property against P', we create a length m bitstring for $|j\rangle_m$ and view $j[k]$, for $k \in [0, m)$, being the k-th bit in the bitstring. Recall that P' has an initial basis vector state pattern as $|\bar{q}[0]\rangle_1 \dots |\bar{q}[m{-}1]\rangle_1 |0\rangle_1$. Here, $|0\rangle_1$ is the state for qubit q and $\bar{q}[0], ..., \bar{q}[m{-}1]$ are random variables for qubit array $\bar{q}$. To check the property, we bind each $j[k]$ with $\bar{q}[k]$ for $k \in [0, m)$, and see if the output basis-ket state results in the same $\bar{q}[0], ..., \bar{q}[m{-}1]$. We also check if $\bar{q}$'s natural number representation is less than n, i.e., we turn $\bar{q}[0], ..., \bar{q}[m{-}1]$ to a number and compare it with n.

Validating Other Properties. The above procedure is only useful in validating correctness. There might be other interesting properties, such as probability and effectiveness properties. For example, in validating Definition 1, we might want to ask how likely the qualified state can be prepared, which is hard to validate in general, but it can be effectively sampled out in some cases.

$$x = 1 \Rightarrow \sum_j^{2^m} \frac{1}{\sqrt{2^m}} \, |j\rangle_m \, |0\rangle_1 \to \sum_j^n \frac{1}{\sqrt{n}} \, |j\rangle_m$$

In the property for P' above, the basis-vector number n is related to $\overline{q}$'s qubit number m, as $n \in [0, 2^m)$. We explain how to validate the program's effectiveness, i.e., the probability that the repeat-until-success program produces the correct state. Note that superposition states are always uniformly distributed without any $\mathtt{Ry}$ operations. The success rate of preparing a superposition state in the repeat-until-success scheme is the ratio between the number of desired basis-vector values $(< n)$ and the total number of possible basis-vector values, i.e., different combinations of $\overline{q}[0], ..., \overline{q}[m-1]$. We can validate the effectiveness by dividing the number of different desired basis-vectors and the number of possible values in $\overline{q}$; that is, 2^m. In general, assume that we have a basis-vector expression $e(\overline{q})$ for m qubits $\overline{q}$, a measurement statement $\mathcal{M}(e(\overline{q}))$ storing the result in v, and have a boolean check on v as $B(v)$ defining the good states. By assigning $\{0,1\}^m$ for $\overline{q}$, the probability of having the good states is the division of number of good state values $(B(e(\overline{q})) = \mathtt{true})$ and the possible basis-vector numbers in $e(\overline{q})$ for all possible assignments. Such a property can be validated by sampling. In some complicated cases, the right property might be hard to validate, but one can always use Rocq to verify the effectiveness via the above scheme.

Performance Optimizations. We took several steps to improve validation performance, e.g., we streamlined the representation of states: per the semantics in Figure 5, in a state with n qubits, the amplitude associated with each qubit can be written as $\Delta(\frac{v}{2^n})$ for some natural number v. Qubit values in both bases are thus pairs of natural numbers: the global phase v (in range $[0, 2^n)$) and b (for $|b\rangle_1$) or y (for $|\Delta(\frac{y}{2^n})\rangle$). A PQASM state φ is a map from qubit positions p to qubit values q; in our proofs, this map is implemented as a partial function, but for validation, we use an AVL tree (a kind of self-balancing binary tree) implementation (proved equivalent to the functional map). To avoid excessive stack use, we implemented the PQASM semantics function tail-recursively. To run the tests, QuickChick runs OCaml code that it *extracts* from the Rocq definitions; during extraction, we replace natural numbers and operations thereon with machine integers and operations. Performance results are in Section 5.

4.2   Translation from Pqasm to SQIR

We translate PQASM to SQIR by mapping PQASM virtual qubits to SQIR [25], a quantum circuit language based on Rocq, concrete qubit indices, and expanding PQASM instructions to sequences of SQIR gates. To express the classical components of quantum algorithms, SQIR typically utilizes Rocq program constructs. To define our compiler, we use the SQIR one-step nondeterministic semantics, which includes one-step operational semantics for simple Rocq constructs, such as conditionals and classical sequential operations.

Our translation is expressed as the two-level judgments $\Xi \vdash \iota \gg \epsilon$ and $(n, \Xi, e) \gg (n', \Xi', \chi)$, where ϵ is the output SQIR circuit, and Ξ and Ξ' map a PQASM qubit q to a SQIR concrete qubit index (i.e., offset into a global qubit register), χ is a hybrid program including SQIR quantum circuits and Rocq classical programs, and n and n' are the qubit sizes in the whole system.

$$\textsc{CRy}\qquad \frac{}{\Xi \vdash \mathtt{Ry}^r q \gg (\gamma, \mathtt{Ry}^r(\Xi(q)))}$$

$$\textsc{CCU}\qquad \frac{\Xi \vdash \iota \gg \epsilon \quad \epsilon' = \mathtt{ctrl}(\gamma(q), \epsilon)}{\Xi \vdash \mathtt{CU}\ p\ \iota \gg \epsilon'}$$

$$\textsc{CNew}\qquad \frac{\Xi' = \Xi[\forall q \in \overline{q}\,.\,q \mapsto |\Xi| + \mathtt{ind}(\overline{q}, q)]}{(n, \Xi, \mathtt{new}(\overline{q})) \gg (n + |\overline{q}|, \Xi', \{\})}$$

We show selected rules above; more are in the technical report [28] Appx. C. Rules CRy and CCU are the instruction-level translation rules, which translate a PQASM instruction to a SQIR unitary operation. $\mathtt{Ry}^r q$ has a directly corresponding gate in SQIR. In the $\mathtt{CU}$ translation, the rule assumes that ι's translation does not affect the Ξ position map. This requirement is assured for well-typed programs per rule CU in Figure 7. $\mathtt{ctr}$ generates the controlled version of an arbitrary SQIR program using standard decompositions [37, Chapter 4.3].

Rule CNew is one of the program-level rules, translating a qubit creation operation in PQASM. In SQIR, there is no qubit creation, in the sense that every qubit is assumed to exist in the first place. The translation essentially translates the operation to a SKIP operation in SQIR and increments the qubit heap size in the generated SQIR program.

Below is the translation correctness theorem. The proof utilizes the SQIR nondeterministic semantics, where a qubit measurement produces two possible outcomes with different probabilities associated with them, i.e., this nondeterministic semantics is essentially SQIR's way of describing a Markov-chain procedure. To formally state the correctness property, we relate PQASM superposition states Φ to SQIR states, as $[\![\Phi]\!]^{n'}$, which are vectors of $2^{n'}$ complex numbers. We can utilize Ξ to relate qubits in PQASM with qubit positions in SQIR.

Theorem 3. [Translation Correctness] Suppose $\Sigma; \Omega \vdash e \triangleright \Omega'$ and $(n, \Xi, e) \gg (n', \Xi', \chi)$. Then for $\Omega \vdash \Phi$ and $(\Phi, e) \xrightarrow{r} (\Phi', e')$, we have $([\![\Phi]\!]^{n'}, \chi) \xrightarrow{r} ([\![\Phi']\!]^{n'}, \chi')$ and $(n', \Xi', e') \gg (n'', \Xi'', \chi')$.

Proof. The proof is by induction on the PQASM program e. Most of the proof simply shows the correspondence of operations in e to their translated-to gates ϵ in SQIR, except for **new** and measurement operations, which update the Ξ map.

5 Evaluation: Applicativity via Case Studies

Here, an experimental evaluation of QSV across many programs is conducted to assess how QSV can be used to effectively build and validate useful quantum state preparation programs with different patterns. The efficiency and scalability comparison with other frameworks are in Section 6.

Implementation. We implement QSV in Rocq and utilize QuickChick to create a quantum program validation framework. We also provide a PQASM circuit compiler that translates PQASM programs to OpenQASM via SQIR.

Experimental Setup. We perform our evaluation on an Ubuntu computer, which has 8-core 13-gen i9 Intel processors and 16 GiB DDR5 memory.

We present several case studies here to demonstrate the construction and validation of state preparation programs. We classify *two different program patterns* below and examine their validation strategies. We list the qubit and gate

State Preparation Program	8B Gate #	8B Qubit #	60B Gate #	60B Qubit #
n basis-ket	766	9	5,732	61
Modular Exponentiation	277K	27	3.3M	183
Amplitude Amplification	65	9	481	61
Hamming Weight	9,088	16	170K	120
Distinct Element	16,036	49	120K	361

Fig. 10: Program statistics; a single register with 8 and 60 Qubits (8B/60B); Distinct elements have 5 distinct elements (keys). 'K': thousand, 'M': million.

counts for these programs in Figure 10. The data are collected by compiling our programs to SQIR using the elementary gateset $\{\mathtt{X}, \mathtt{H}, \mathtt{CX}, \mathtt{Rz}\}$. To describe the programs, we define the following repeat operator for repeating a process n times. The function P takes a natural number and outputs a quantum program.

$$Re(P, n) \triangleq \mathtt{if}\ (n = 0)\ \{\}\ \mathtt{else}\ Re(P, n - 1)\ ;\ P(n - 1)$$

Quantum Loop Programs. We first examine the class of programs only involving quantum unitary gates without measurement. Such programs typically contain quantum loops, a repetition of subroutines formed via unitary gates. These programs usually act as a large part of some quantum algorithms. For example, the modular exponentiation state preparation program is the major part of Shor's algorithm, while the amplitude amplification state preparation program is the major part of an upgraded amplitude estimation algorithm [48].
Modular Exponentiation State Preparation. In Shor's algorithm [45], we prepare the the superposition state of modular exponentiation based on two natural numbers c and n with $\gcd(c, n) = 1$, as $\varphi_3 = \frac{1}{\sqrt{2^m}} \sum_j^{2^m} |j\rangle_m |c^j \,\%\, n\rangle_m$.

$$Q(\overline{q_1}, \overline{q_2})(k) \triangleq \mathtt{CU}\ (\overline{q_1}[k])\ (c^{2^k} * \overline{q_2}) \,\%\, n$$
$$P(m) \qquad \triangleq \mathtt{new}(\overline{q_1})\ ;\ \mathtt{new}(\overline{q_2})\ ;\ \mathtt{H}(\overline{q_1})\ ;\ Re(Q(\overline{q_1}, \overline{q_2}), m)$$

The program to prepare the modular exponentiation state is listed above, with the circuit diagram in Figure 11. The program starts with two new length m qubit arrays $\overline{q_1}$ and $\overline{q_2}$, and turns $\overline{q_1}$ to a uniform superposition by m H gates. We then repeat m times a controlled modular multiplication ($\mathtt{CU}\ (\overline{q_1}[k])\ (c^{2^k} * \overline{q_2}) \,\%\, n$) application, controlling on the qubit $\overline{q_1}[k]$ with application to $\overline{q_2}$.

As in Section 4.1, to conduct the the program correctness validation, we cut off the first three operations (**new** and **H** operations) in $P(m)$, producing a program piece $Re(Q(\overline{q_1}, \overline{q_2}), m)$, where $Q(\overline{q_1}, \overline{q_2})$ is a function taking in a number k and outputting a program $\mathtt{CU}\ (\overline{q_1}[k])\ (c^{2^k} * \overline{q_2}) \,\%\, n$. The correctness specification is also transformed without the superposition state description below.

$$\forall j \in [0, 2^m)\,.\ |j\rangle_m |0\rangle_m \rightarrow |j\rangle_m |c^j \,\%\, n\rangle_m$$

Validating the loop program $Re(Q(\overline{q_1}, \overline{q_2}), m)$ essentially executes Q m times. In executing the k-th loop step, we have the following loop invariant.

$$|j\rangle_k |c^j \,\%\, n\rangle_m \rightarrow |j\rangle_{k+1} |c^j \,\%\, n\rangle_m$$

In the pre-state, $|j\rangle_k$ is a length k bitstring while the post-state has $|j\rangle_{k+1}$ being length k+1. To understand the behavior, notice that we have the most significant bit on the right. A k+1 length bitstring $|j\rangle_{k+1}$ can be expressed as a composition over a length k bitstring as $|j\rangle_k |0\rangle_1$ or $|j\rangle_k |1\rangle_1$, with the most

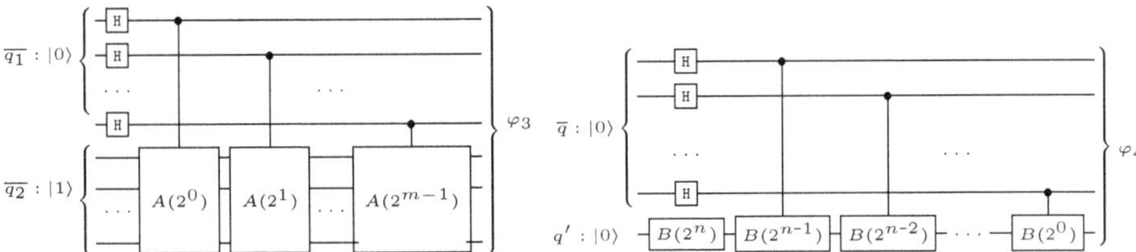

Fig. 11: Modular Exponentiation Circuits; $A(v) = (c^v * \overline{q_2}) \% n$.

Fig. 12: Amplitude amplification state preparation; $B(v) = \text{Ry}(\frac{r}{v})$.

sigificant bit being 0 or 1. For the former case, applying the controlled modular multiplication results in $|j\rangle_k |0\rangle_1 |c^j \% n\rangle_m$, i.e., the $\overline{q_2}$ part of the bitstring remains the same. For the latter case $(|j\rangle_k |1\rangle_1)$, the controlled modular multipliation results in the state $|j\rangle_k |1\rangle_1 |(c^{2^k} * c^j \% n) \% n\rangle_m = |j\rangle_k |1\rangle_1 |c^{j+2^k} \% n\rangle_m$. Both cases can be rewritten to the post-state in the loop invariant above.

To validate the program piece $Re(Q(\overline{q_1}, \overline{q_2}), m)$ against the above specification, we are given a length $2m$ bitstring with $\overline{q_1}$ and $\overline{q_2}$ both being length m, and view $\overline{q_1}$ as a length m array of random variables, and prepare a initial state $|\overline{q_1}[0], ..., \overline{q_1}[m-1]\rangle_m |0\rangle_m$, with random generation of length m binary bitstrings, as test instances, for the variables $\overline{q_1}[0], ..., \overline{q_1}[m-1]$. We then use the mechanism in Section 4.1 to validate the program piece. As we mentioned in Section 1, after we test enough samples of different input basis-ket states by picking different values for random variables, we have a high assurance that the modular exponentiation state preparation program correctly prepares a superposition state.

Note that the program is a deterministic quantum circuit program, so the probability of preparing the superposition state is 100%.

Amplitude Amplification State Preparation Through Ry Gates. In the amplitude amplification algorithm, one needs to prepare a special superposition state [48], as $\varphi_4 = \frac{1}{\sqrt{2^n}} \sum_{j=1}^{2^n} |j\rangle_n |\Delta(\frac{(2j+1)r}{2^n})\rangle$, circuit in Figure 12. Then, the amplitude amplification algorithm utilizes the last qubits $(|\Delta(\frac{(2j+1)r}{2^n})\rangle)$ to amplify the amplitudes of the basis-kets having a particular property with respect to some j. The r value is the upper limit of the possible amplitude value, i.e., we want to carefully select r to ensure $\frac{(2j+1)r}{2^n} \in [0, \frac{\pi}{2})$.

$$Q(\overline{q}, q')(j) \triangleq \text{CU} \; (\overline{q}[j]) \; \text{Ry}^{\frac{r}{2^{n-j}}} q'$$
$$P(n) \quad \triangleq \text{new}(\overline{q}) \; ; \text{new}(q') \; ; \text{H}(\overline{q}) \; ; \text{Ry}^{\frac{r}{2^n}} q' \; ; Re(Q(\overline{q}, q'), n)$$

We implement the program P in PQASM with the input of a qubit array $\overline{q}$ and a single qubit q'. We then apply H gates on $\overline{q}$ and a Y-axis rotation on q'. Eventually, we apply a series of controlled Y-axis rotation operations — controlling on the $\overline{q}[j]$ qubit ($j \in [0, n)$) and applying Ry on q'; each single controlled Y axis roation is handled by the Q process.

Since there is no measurement, the success rate of preparing the amplitude amplification state is theoretically 100%. We mainly test the correctness here.

$$\text{Ry}^{\frac{r}{2^n}} q' \; ; Re(Q(\overline{q}, q'), n) \qquad \forall j \in [0, 2^n) . \; |j\rangle_n |0\rangle_1 \rightarrow |j\rangle_n |\Delta(\frac{(2j+1)r}{2^n})\rangle$$

In doing so, we can adapt the same strategy in the modular exponentiation state preparation, by cutting off $\text{new}(\overline{q}) \; ; \text{new}(q') \; ; \text{H}(\overline{q})$, so we should mainly

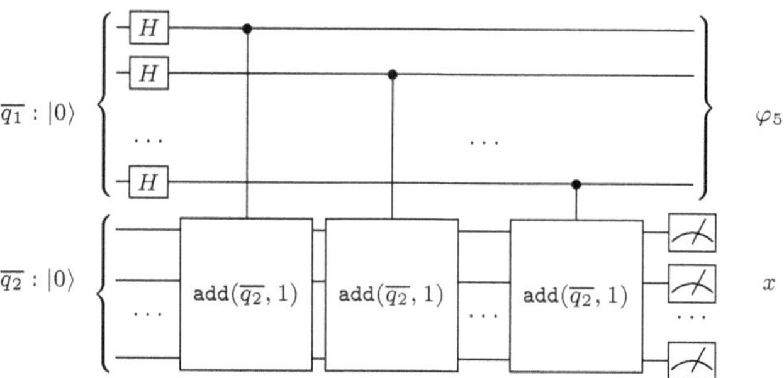

Fig. 13: One-step Hamming weight state preparation (repeat-until-success).

focus on validating the portion shown above on the left. The correctness specification is described above on the right. In validating this portion, we notice that the qubit array $\overline{q}$ is in $\mathtt{Had}$ type, and we generate random variables, with binary values 0 or 1, for every qubit in the array. Through the validation procedure in validating the modular exponentiation program above, we can assure that the result of the program produces the superposition state φ_4.

Repeat-until-success Programs. We then examine the class of repeat-until-success programs, using the strategy in Section 4.1. We show the Hamming weight and the distinct element state preparation program validation below.

Hamming Weights State Preparation. Some algorithms [17] require a k-th Hamming weight superposition state preparation, i.e., we prepare a state $\varphi_5 = \frac{1}{\sqrt{N}} \sum_j^N |c_j\rangle_n$, with the number of 1's bit in c_j is k. Assuming that φ_5 is a length n qubit state, φ_5 has N different basis-kets, with $N = \binom{n}{k}$.

$$Q(\overline{q_1}, \overline{q_2})(j) \triangleq \mathtt{CU}\ (\overline{q_1}[j])\ \mathtt{add}(\overline{q_2}, 1)$$
$$P(n, k) \quad \triangleq \mathtt{new}(\overline{q_1})\ ;\ \mathtt{new}(\overline{q_2})\ ;\ \mathtt{H}(\overline{q_1})\ ;\ Re(Q(\overline{q_1}, \overline{q_2}), n)\ ;\ \mathtt{let}\ x = \mathcal{M}(\overline{q_2})\ \mathtt{in}\ \mathtt{if}\ (x{=}k)\ \{\}\ \mathtt{else}\ P(n, k)$$

The above is a repeat-until-success program of the Hamming weight program, with the circuit in Figure 13 showing a single quantum step in $P(n, k)$. The program starts with two new length n qubit arrays $\overline{q_1}$ and $\overline{q_2}$, and turns $\overline{q_1}$ to a uniform superposition by applying n H gates. We then repeat n times of a controlled addition ($\mathtt{CU}\ (\overline{q_1}[j])\ \mathtt{add}(\overline{q_2}, 1)$) applications. The controlled additions count the number of 1's bits in $\overline{q_1}$ and store the result in $\overline{q_2}$. If the measurement on $\overline{q_2}$ results in k (assigning to x), it means that the φ_5 state of the qubit array $\overline{q_1}$ is a superposition of basis-ket states with the vector having k bits of 1. Otherwise, we repeat the process P with two new qubit arrays $\overline{q_1}$ and $\overline{q_2}$ until the measurement result k appears. Note that $Q(\overline{q_1}, \overline{q_2})$ in Re is a function taking in a natural number argument j and then performing a controlled addition.

$$Re(Q(\overline{q_1}, \overline{q_2}), n)\ ;\ \mathtt{let}\ x = \mathcal{M}(\overline{q_2})\ \mathtt{in}\ \mathtt{if}\ (x = k)\ \{\}\ \mathtt{else}\ \{\}$$
$$\forall j \in [0, 2^n)\ .\ |j\rangle_n |0\rangle_n \to |j\rangle_n \wedge \mathtt{sum}(\mathtt{n2b}(j)) = k$$

To validate the correctness of the Hamming weight program, we shrink the program by removing the **new** and H operations. The program piece and the transformed correctness specification are listed above. We then utilize the procedure in Section 4.1 to perform the validation. Here, we assume that the $\mathtt{Had}$

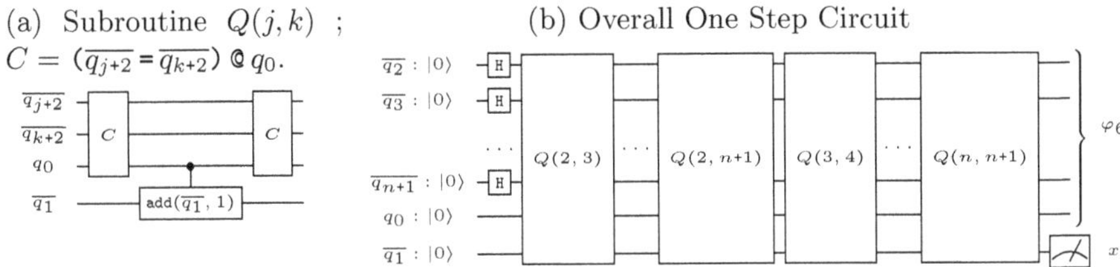

Fig. 14: One step distinct element state preparation.

typed qubits $\overline{q_1}$ are already prepared, and we randomly generate a length n bit-string for the random variables $\overline{q_1}[0], ..., \overline{q_1}[n-1]$. Each random variable, possibly being 0 or 1, represents the basis-bit of a single qubit superposition. We set up the PBT to randomly sample values for the random variables and exclusively test the correctness of the transition behavior of basis-ket states. The key correctness property $(\mathtt{sum}(\mathtt{n2b}(j)) = k)$ for the Hamming weight state is that each output basis-ket of $\overline{q_1}$ should have exactly k bits of 1.

The program efficiency can be easily assessed by counting the number of basis kets in a superposition quantum state. Notice that every superposition state prepared by a simple Hadamard operation produces a uniform superposition, meaning that the likelihood of measuring out any basis-ket vector is equally likely. Thus, we only need to compare the ratio between the number of basis-kets after the Hadamard operations are applied and the basis-ket number in $\overline{q_1}$ after the measurement is applied. The former contains 2^n different basis-kets for n Hadamard operations, and the latter has $\binom{n}{k}$ basis-kets in a k-th Hamming weight state. So, the success rate of a single try in the program is $\binom{n}{k}/2^n$.

Distinct Element State Preparation. Another special superposition state is the one in the element distinctness algorithm. Here, we assume that we are given a graph with n different vertices, and the algorithm begins with a superposition of different combinations of vertices, as shown below.

$$\varphi_6 = \tfrac{1}{\sqrt{n!}} \sum_j \sigma_j(|x_1\rangle |x_2\rangle ... |x_n\rangle)$$

Here, $x_1, x_2, ..., x_n$ are different vertex keys in the graph, σ_j is a permutation of the key list $|x_1\rangle |x_2\rangle ... |x_n\rangle$. There are $n!$ different kinds of permutations, so the uniform amplitude for each basis-ket is $\tfrac{1}{\sqrt{n!}}$. Such a permutation state means we are preparing a superposition of all permutations of the different vertex keys. Such a superposition state is widely used in many algorithms, such as the quantum fingerprinting algorithm [12].

$Q(k)(j) \triangleq (\overline{q_{j+2}} = \overline{q_{k+2}}) @ q_0 ; \mathtt{CU}\ q_0\ (\overline{q_1} + 1) ; (\overline{q_{j+2}} = \overline{q_{k+2}}) @ q_0$

$R(j)(n) \triangleq Re(Q(j), n)$

$H(j) \quad \triangleq \mathtt{H}(\overline{q_{j+2}})$

$T(j) \quad \triangleq \mathtt{new}(\overline{q_{j+1}})$

$P(n) \quad \triangleq \mathtt{new}(q_0) ; Re(T, n+1) ; Re(H, n) ; Re(R(n-1), n) ; \mathtt{let}\ x = \mathcal{M}(\overline{q_1})\ \mathtt{in}\ \mathtt{if}\ (x{=}0)\ \{\}\ \mathtt{else}\ P(n)$

For simplicity, we only implement the above program to prepare a superposition state of distinct elements, i.e., each basis-ket in the superposition state stores n distinct elements (vertex key), each key having a qubit size m. Note that if $n = 2^m$, i.e., we have 2^m different vertices having keys $u \in [0, 2^m)$, then the superposition state represents a superposition of all the permutations. We show a repeat-until-success program for preparing such a state above, with the circuit in Figure 14 showing a single quantum step in $P(n)$. We first initialize a single qubit q_0, and use $T(j)$ to initialize $n + 1$ different qubit arrays, $\overline{q_{j+1}}$, with $j \in [0, n + 1)$, and we assume that $\overline{q_{j+1}}$ is an m length qubit array. We then apply H gates to all qubit arrays $\overline{q_{j+2}}$ ($j \in [0, n)$). q_0 and $\overline{q_1}$ are ancillary qubits.

Essentially, we can view $\overline{q_{j+2}}$ ($j \in [0, n)$) as an n-length array of qubit arrays. The program applies $O(n^2)$ times of Q processes, each of which applies an equivalent check on two elements in the n-length array, i.e., we compare the basis-ket data in q_{j+2} and q_{k+2} ($j, k \in [0, n)$) to see if their content are equal, and store the boolean result in q_0 bit. Then, we also add the result to $\overline{q_1}$ and apply the comparison circuit again to clean up the ancillary qubit q_0, meaning that we restore q_0's state to $|0\rangle$. This procedure describes the circuit in Figure 14a.

After we apply the Q function to any two different elements in the n-length array, we observe that q_0 is back to the $|0\rangle$ state, and $\overline{q_1}$ stores the number of same basis-kets between any two distinct elements in the n-length array. We then measure $\overline{q_1}$ and see if the result is 0. If so, a permutation superposition state is prepared because it means that in all the basis-kets in the prepared superposition, there are no two-qubit array elements $\overline{q_k}$ and $\overline{q_l}$ that have equal key. If not, we repeat the process, and the repeat-until-success program guarantees the creation of the permutation superposition state.

We use the procedure in Section 4.1 to validate the correctness. We create the validating program by removing the **new** and H operations from the original program. The program piece and the transformed specification are listed below.

$$Re(R(n - 1), n) \text{ ; } \mathtt{let}\ x = \mathcal{M}(\overline{q_1})\ \mathtt{in}\ \mathtt{if}\ (x = 0)\ \{\}\ \mathtt{else}\ \{\}$$

$$x = 0 \Rightarrow \forall j, j' \in [0, 2^{n*m}).\ |0\rangle_1\, |0\rangle_n\, |j\rangle_{n*m} \to |0\rangle_1\, |j'\rangle_{n*m} \land \mathtt{dis}(j', m)$$

Here, j and j' represent the values for two qubit arrays, i.e., j represents the bitstring value for composing basis-ket values of all elements in the qubit array $\overline{q_{l+2}}$ ($l \in [0, n)$). The qubit array $\overline{q_{j+2}}$ has $n*m$ qubits, and we slice the basis-vector for the whole qubit array into n different small segments for the qubit ranges $[l*m, l*(m+1)-1)$, each basis-vector segment representing a vertex key. Since we apply Hadamard operations to all of them, it creates a uniform superposition state containing 2^{n*m} different basis-vector states. In the post-state of the specification, the q_0 qubit is still $|0\rangle$. For the qubit arrays $\overline{q_2}, ..., \overline{q_{m+2}}$, if the measurement result is $x = 0$, we result in a superposition state of distinct elements, i.e., any two elements (each element l is a segment of $[l*m, l*(m+1)-1)$) in the qubit array $\overline{q_{j+2}}$ have distinct basis-vectors. We use the predicate $\mathtt{dis}(j', m)$ to indicate that all length m segments in the bitstring $|j\rangle$ are pairwise distinct. Via our PBT framework, we have high assurance that the distinct element state preparation program correctly prepares the superposition state.

The program's efficiency in preparing the superposition state can be easily assessed by counting the number of basis-ket states in the superposition. Notice that every superposition state prepared by a simple Hadamard operation pro-

Program	QSV QCT 8B	QSV QCT 60B	Qiskit Sim 8B	Qiskit Sim 60B	DDSim Sim 60B
n basis-ket	< 1.5	2.4	< 1.5	No	No
Modular Exp.	< 1.5	19.7	No	No	No
Amplitude Amp.	< 1.5	2.1	< 1.5	No	No
Hamming Weight	< 1.5	24.9	< 1.5	No	No
Distinct Element	< 5	336	No	No	No

Fig. 15: Evaluation on different state preparation programs for 8/60 qubit single registers (8B/60B). "QCT" : time (in seconds) for QuickChick to run 10,000 tests. "Sim": time (in seconds) or if Qiskit/DDSim can execute a single test.

duces a uniform superposition, meaning that the likelihood of measuring out any basis state vectors is equally likely. Thus, we only need to compare the ratio between the number of basis-kets right after the Hadamard operations are applied and the basis-ket number in $\overline{q_{j+2}}$. Here, we count the case for $n = 2^m$ where a permutation superposition state is prepared. For $j \in [0, n)$ with $n = 2^m$, after the measurement is applied. The former contains 2^{n*m} different basis-kets for $n*m$ Hadamard operations, and the latter has $n!$ basis-kets in a k-th permutated superposition state. So, the success rate of a single try in the program is $\frac{n!}{2^{n*m}}$.

6 Discussion: Efficiency, Scalability, and Utility

We compare QSV's efficiency and scalability with the state-of-the-art platforms. We show that QSV can effectively validate program properties, providing confidence in program correctness. We also show that QSV *scales* to validate and realize state preparation programs regardless of the size (in terms of qubit number required). We thus justify the QSV's utility in successfully capturing bugs.

Efficiency. We discuss the program development procedure in QSV, compared to other systems such as Qiskit. Discussing the efficiency of a validation framework needs to be put in the context of human efforts for program development, as users mainly care about how to effectively use QSV to develop programs.

The general procedure for developing state preparation programs in QSV is the traditional test-driven program development. We first present the program correctness properties in the superposition state format for different programs, such as the one in Sections 1 and 5. We then start implementing the program using a possible program pattern and see if we can write the correct program based on it, where the PQASM high-level abstraction helps us write programs. For example, in dealing with all the programs in Figure 10, we first try to see if we can write all these programs via the quantum loop program pattern, and rewrite the correctness properties based on the strategy presented in Section 5.

We then run the QSV validator to validate the implemented programs against the properties. After several rounds of corrections, one can typically judge whether the program is implementable. For example, using our validator, we found that implementing the Hamming weight and distinct element programs based on the quantum loop program pattern might be hard. We then switch to other program patterns to implement these programs; e.g., we use the repeat-until-success program pattern to implement the two programs by rewriting their correctness properties to those in Section 5 and successfully find a solution. Our validator can effectively validate a program using our PBT framework, which generates $10,000$ test cases each time. As shown in Figure 15, running $10,000$ randomly generated test cases for all our example programs takes less than 5 seconds for small-size programs (8 qubits) and less than 5.5 minutes for large-size programs (60 qubits). This indicates that a program developer can quickly correct minor bugs when developing their programs.

On the other hand, developing state preparation programs in the state-of-the-art system might be painful, e.g., it is unlikely one can perform test-driven development to implement the programs in Figure 10, mainly because of a lack of proper validation facilities. As we can see in Figure 15, Qiskit might not execute a single test for some small-size (8 qubit) programs, such as distinct-element programs. The modular exponentiation program is executed for some small number settings, but is not executable in general because the Qiskit simulator applies special optimizations to components of Shor's algorithm. Executing a large program (60 qubits) is completely impossible; either the program is too large for IBM's Aer simulator to run at all, and the simulator errors out, or the circuit construction may take hours and still not be done. This indicates the difficulty of developing large-scale programs by conducting small-scale testing in Qiskit, not to mention the need to validate large datasets and coverage. Another key issue is that the high-level abstraction support in the state-of-the-art systems is not well provided. In Qiskit, we can only find quantum addition operations; the other arithmetic and comparison operations are missing. In fact, we implement these operations in Qiskit based on our implementation in QSV.

Scalability. To evaluate the QSV's scalability, we not only compare its execution at small and large sizes with Qiskit but also with another state-of-the-art quantum simulator, DDSim. Here, we attempted to recreate (or find existing implementations of) the aforementioned programs on DDSim and Qiskit. We also performed PBT on our PQASM implementations on systems of various sizes and verified the rigidity of our tests by mutating either the properties or the states and verifying that the tests failed.

As in Figure 15, we have fully validated the five examples in these papers via our PBT framework. As far as we know, these constitute the first validated-correct implementations of the n basis-ket, Hamming weight, and distinct elements programs. All other operations in the figure were validated with Quick-Chick. To ensure these tests were effective, besides our program development procedures above, we also confirmed they could find hand-injected bugs; e.g., we changed the rotation angles in the `Ry` gate in the amplitude amplification state preparation and performed some mutation testing (e.g. replacing some non-skip terms with {} (skip) operations) and confirmed that our PBT could catch the inserted bugs. The tables in Figure 15 give the running times for our validator to validate programs—the times include the cost of compiling the Rocq code and running it with $10,000$ randomly generated inputs via QuickChick. We validated these programs on small (8-qubit) and large (60-qubit) inputs (the numbers relevant to the reported qubit and gate sizes in Figure 10), with all validation completed within 2.5 minutes (most within seconds). For comparison, we translated our programs to SQIR, converted the SQIR programs to OpenQASM 2.0

[20], and then attempted to simulate the resulting circuits on a *single test input* using DDSim [13], a state-of-the-art quantum simulator, and listed the result in the fifth column. Unsurprisingly, the simulation of the 60-bit versions did not complete when running overnight. The third and fourth columns in Figure 15 show the results for executing a *single program run* in Qiskit, and Qiskit executes a few small-size programs (Section 6) and none of the large-size programs. The experiment provided strong assurance of QSV's scalability.

There is a difference in the program execution between DDSim and QSV. The latter abstracts arithmetic operations and assumes they can be handled by the previous VQO [30] framework, whereas DDSim executes the entire circuits generated from a QSV program. To compare the effects, we list the QuickChick testing time (running

Operation	QCT
Addition	2
Comparison	5
Modular Multiplication	794

Fig. 16: Arith OP QC time (60B).

10,000 tests) for the operations used in our state preparation programs in Figure 16; these running time data were provided in VQO. The addition and comparison circuits do not greatly affect the execution of our PQASM programs. Validating modular multiplication circuits might be costly, as our 60-bit modular exponentiation involves 60 modular multiplication operations. However, a typical validation scheme might only validate the correctness of a costly subcomponent once and then use its semantic properties to validate other programs that use it. More importantly, the purpose of the experiment of DDSim/Qiskit executions is to show the state-of-the-art impossibility of executing quantum programs on a classical computer, while our QSV framework can validate quantum programs.

Utility. One of the utilities of a program validation framework is to find bugs or faults in the existing algorithms. During the development of the above programs, we identified several issues in two original algorithms [12,5] that utilize these special superposition states. Both algorithms require preparing a superposition state of distinct elements (or of permutations of distinct elements), but they do not specify how to effectively prepare such a state. To the best of our knowledge, the state preparation program in Section 5 is the first program implementation of the state via the repeat-until-success scheme. As our probability analysis shows, the likelihood of preparing such a state is not very high. This fact might indicate that the quantum algorithms' advantage arguments over classical algorithms in these works are not solid, given the unclear preparation of the initial states. Without our implementations of these state preparation programs, it is impossible to detect these subtle potential faults in these algorithms.

Indeed, in the algorithm [17] that uses the initial Hamming-weight superposition state, the authors recognized the low probability of preparing the initial state via the repeat-until-success scheme and proposed using a specialized gate instead of Hadamard gates to start their repeat-until-success state preparation program. The special gates created a simple superposition state with a different probability distribution, unlike the uniform distribution produced by Hadamard gates. The analysis of these specialized superposition gates with different probability distributions will be included in our future work.

Another utility of using QSV is to judge the implemented programs' correctness and find a more optimized implementation. Other frameworks, such as OpenQASM, do not have property-based testing features.

7   Related Work

This section gives related work beyond the discussion in Section 4.

Quantum Circuit Languages. Prior research has developed circuit-level compilers to compile quantum circuit languages to quantum computers, such as Qiskit [4], t|ket⟩ [14], Staq [8], PyZX [27], Nam *et al.* [36], quilc [43], Cirq [23], ScaffCC [26], and Project Q [47]. In addition, many quantum programming languages have been developed in recent years. Many of these languages (e.g. Quil [43], OpenQASM [20,19], SQIR [25]) describe low-level circuit programs. Higher-level languages may provide library functions for performing common oracle operations (e.g., Q# [35], Scaffold [2,32]) or support compiling from classical programs to quantum circuits (e.g., Quipper [24]), but still leave some important details (like deallocating extra intermediate qubits) to the programmer. There has been some work on type systems to enforce that deallocation happens correctly (e.g., Silq [11]) and on automated insertion of deallocation circuits (e.g., Quipper [24], Unqomp [40]), but while these approaches provide useful automation, they may also lead to inefficiencies in compiled circuits.

Quantum Software Testing and Validation. There have been many approaches developed for validating quantum programs [38,53,51,21,33,50] including the use differential [50] and metamorphic testing [39], and mutation testing [21] and fuzzing [53]. Some key challenges exist for testing quantum programs. First, their input space explodes due to superposition. Second, their results are probabilistic (meaning we need to use statistical measures and/or other approaches to evaluate results). Last, the expected result may be difficult or even impossible to determine. To date, testing approaches have focused on validating small circuit subroutines (i.e., with limited input qubit size) rather than comprehensive quantum programs, and they are all limited to testing in Qiskit, which might not capture all machine limitations.

Methodologies Possibly Used for Validating Quantum Programs. SymQV [10] proposed a method of encoding quantum states and gates as SMT-solvable predicates to perform automated verification. Chen *et al.* [15] and Abdulla *et al.* [1] used tree automata to symbolize quantum gates, instead of quantum states, and utilized tree automata to construct a tree structure for easing automated verification. These works can handle some large programs, but these programs have simple program structures, such as QFT. Mei *et al.* [34] performed quantum stabilizer simulation based on the Gottesman–Knill theorem, which is a small subset of quantum programs and mainly used for error correction programs. Quasimodo [46] is another symbolic execution based on a BDD-like structure to symbolize gates rather than states; their results are similar to the tree automata works [1,15]. QAFNY [31,16] transformed quantum program verification to Dafny for automated verification. These works tried to transform states and gates to perform automated verification, different from QSV, which tries to perform program testing and validation. The methodologies are also different from QSV where they try to symbolize quantum gates and states, while QSV only inserts special treatments in the standard quantum state representations. As a result, QSV can deal with large programs with comprehensive program structures.

Verified Quantum Compilers. Recent work has looked at verified optimization of quantum circuits (e.g., VOQC [25], CertiQ [44]), but the problem of verified *compilation* from high-level languages to quantum circuits has received less attention. The only examples we know of verified compilers for quantum circuits are ReVerC [9], ReQWIRE [42], and Feynman [7] [6]. ReVerC and ReQWIRE support verified translation from a low-level Boolean expression language to circuits consisting of X, CNOT, and CCNOT gates. Feynman verifies the correctness of compiled circuits relative to an input circuit or a path-integral specification of a circuit, while QSV validates whether programs have specified properties before they are compiled to the circuit level. It's feasible that a programmer can use QSV to validate the program and then use Feynman to verify the compiled circuit relative to a circuit or path integral specification of the program. VQO [30] is a certified compilation framework for verifying and compiling quantum arithmetic operations. QSV utilizes VOQC [25] and VQO [30] to compile PQASM programs to quantum circuits.

8   Conclusion and Limitations

We present QSV, a framework for expressing and automatically validating quantum state preparation programs. The core of QSV is a language PQASM, which can express a restricted class of quantum programs that are efficiently testable for certain properties and are useful for implementing state preparation programs. We have verified the translator from PQASM to SQIR and have validated (or randomly tested) many programs written in PQASM. We have used PQASM to implement state preparation programs useful in quantum computation, such as the ones in Figure 10. We hope this work will be the basis for building a quantum validation framework for validating quantum programs on classical computers.

QSV is capable of validating properties of many quantum programs. As mentioned in Section 1, QSV targets validating state preparation programs. For many quantum programs, QSV is able to validate the most significant part of the program. For example, the validated modular multiplication program in Figure 11 is essentially 90% of Shor's algorithm, except for the final inverse QFT gate and measurement.

Our type system specifically locates Hadamard operations, but there are no actual restrictions on Hadamard operations, as users can easily define similar behaviors via our Ry and oracle operations. Via our type system, we identify the beginning Hadamard operations as a general quantum algorithm component to generate superposition sources so that QSV can locate the places to create random inputs for validating programs. We recognize the superposition state generation in many quantum algorithms as the major bottleneck for testing quantum programs; therefore, we utilize types to identify them, with special treatment to transform the superposition states to a simple and testable format.

9   Data-Availability Statement

The Rocq proofs and the experiment in the paper are available on Zenodo: `https://d i. rg/10.5281/zen d .15073729` [29]. The Zenodo artifact can be run in the experimental setting described in its README. There is also a GitHub repository at `https://github.c m/qafny/pqasm`.

References

1. Abdulla, P.A., Chen, Y.G., Chen, Y.F., Holík, L., Lengál, O., Lin, J.A., Lo, F.Y., Tsai, W.L.: Verifying quantum circuits with level-synchronized tree automata (technical report) (2024), `https://arxiv.org/abs/2410.18540`
2. Abhari, A., Faruque, A., Dousti, M.J., Svec, L., Catu, O., Chakrabati, A., Chiang, C.F., Vanderwilt, S., Black, J., Chong, F., Martonosi, M., Suchara, M., Brown, K., Pedram, M., Brun, T.: Scaffold: Quantum Programming Language. Tech. rep., Princeton University (2012)
3. Alagic, G., Moore, C., Russell, A.: Quantum algorithms for simon's problem over general groups (2007), `https://arxiv.org/abs/quant-ph/0603251`
4. Aleksandrowicz, G., Alexander, T., Barkoutsos, P., Bello, L., Ben-Haim, Y., Bucher, D., Cabrera-Hernández, F.J., Carballo-Franquis, J., Chen, A., Chen, C.F., Chow, J.M., Córcoles-Gonzales, A.D., Cross, A.J., Cross, A., Cruz-Benito, J., Culver, C., González, S.D.L.P., Torre, E.D.L., Ding, D., Dumitrescu, E., Duran, I., Eendebak, P., Everitt, M., Sertage, I.F., Frisch, A., Fuhrer, A., Gambetta, J., Gago, B.G., Gomez-Mosquera, J., Greenberg, D., Hamamura, I., Havlicek, V., Hellmers, J., Herok, Ł., Horii, H., Hu, S., Imamichi, T., Itoko, T., Javadi-Abhari, A., Kanazawa, N., Karazeev, A., Krsulich, K., Liu, P., Luh, Y., Maeng, Y., Marques, M., Martín-Fernández, F.J., McClure, D.T., McKay, D., Meesala, S., Mezzacapo, A., Moll, N., Rodríguez, D.M., Nannicini, G., Nation, P., Ollitrault, P., O'Riordan, L.J., Paik, H., Pérez, J., Phan, A., Pistoia, M., Prutyanov, V., Reuter, M., Rice, J., Davila, A.R., Rudy, R.H.P., Ryu, M., Sathaye, N., Schnabel, C., Schoute, E., Setia, K., Shi, Y., Silva, A., Siraichi, Y., Sivarajah, S., Smolin, J.A., Soeken, M., Takahashi, H., Tavernelli, I., Taylor, C., Taylour, P., Trabing, K., Treinish, M., Turner, W., Vogt-Lee, D., Vuillot, C., Wildstrom, J.A., Wilson, J., Winston, E., Wood, C., Wood, S., Wörner, S., Akhalwaya, I.Y., Zoufal, C.: Qiskit: An open-source framework for quantum computing (2019). `https://doi.org/10.5281/zenodo.2562110`
5. Ambainis, A.: Quantum walk algorithm for element distinctness. In: 45th Annual IEEE Symposium on Foundations of Computer Science. pp. 22–31 (2004). `https://doi.org/10.1109/FOCS.2004.54`
6. Amy, M.: Formal Methods in Quantum Circuit Design. Ph.D. thesis, University of Waterloo (2019)
7. Amy, M.: Towards large-scale functional verification of universal quantum circuits. Electronic Proceedings in Theoretical Computer Science **287**, 1–21 (Jan 2019). `https://doi.org/10.4204/eptcs.287.1`, `http://dx.doi.org/10.4204/EPTCS.287.1`
8. Amy, M., Gheorghiu, V.: staq – a full-stack quantum processing toolkit **5**(3), 034016 (Jun 2020). `https://doi.org/10.1088/2058-9565/ab9359`, `https://github.com/softwareQinc/staq`
9. Amy, M., Roetteler, M., Svore, K.M.: Verified Compilation of Space-Efficient Reversible Circuits. In: Majumdar, R., Kunčak, V. (eds.) Computer Aided Verification. pp. 3–21. Springer International Publishing, Cham (2017)

10. Bauer-Marquart, F., Leue, S., Schilling, C.: symqv: Automated symbolic verification of quantum programs. In: Formal Methods: 25th International Symposium, FM 2023, Lübeck, Germany, March 6–10, 2023, Proceedings. p. 181–198. Springer-Verlag, Berlin, Heidelberg (2023). https://doi.org/10.1007/978-3-031-27481-7_12, https://doi.org/10.1007/978-3-031-27481-7_12

11. Bichsel, B., Baader, M., Gehr, T., Vechev, M.: Silq: A High-Level Quantum Language with Safe Uncomputation and Intuitive Semantics. In: Proceedings of the 41st ACM SIGPLAN Conference on Programming Language Design and Implementation. p. 286–300. PLDI 2020, Association for Computing Machinery, New York, NY, USA (2020). https://doi.org/10.1145/3385412.3386007, https://doi.org/10.1145/3385412.3386007

12. Buhrman, H., Cleve, R., Watrous, J., de Wolf, R.: Quantum fingerprinting. Physical Review Letters $87(16)$ (Sep 2001). https://doi.org/10.1103/physrevlett.87.167902, http://dx.doi.org/10.1103/PhysRevLett.87.167902

13. Burgholzer, L., Bauer, H., Wille, R.: Hybrid Schrödinger-Feynman Simulation of Quantum Circuits With Decision Diagrams . In: 2021 IEEE International Conference on Quantum Computing and Engineering (QCE). pp. 199–206. IEEE Computer Society, Los Alamitos, CA, USA (Oct 2021). https://doi.org/10.1109/QCE52317.2021.00037, https://doi.ieeecomputersociety.org/10.1109/QCE52317.2021.00037

14. Cambridge Quantum Computing Ltd: pytket (2019), https://cqcl.github.io/pytket/build/html/index.html

15. Chen, Y.F., Chung, K.M., Lengál, O., Lin, J.A., Tsai, W.L., Yen, D.D.: An automata-based framework for verification and bug hunting in quantum circuits. Proc. ACM Program. Lang. 7(PLDI) (Jun 2023). https://doi.org/10.1145/3591270, https://doi.org/10.1145/3591270

16. Cheng, F., Vangeepuram, S., Allard, H., Jafari, S.M.R., Potanin, A., Li, L.: Embedding quantum program verification into dafny. Proc. ACM Program. Lang. 9(OOPSLA2) (Oct 2025). https://doi.org/10.1145/3763157, https://doi.org/10.1145/3763157

17. Childs, A.M., Farhi, E., Goldstone, J., Gutmann, S.: Finding cliques by quantum adiabatic evolution. Quantum Info. Comput. $2(3)$, 181–191 (Apr 2002)

18. Claessen, K., Hughes, J.: Quickcheck: A lightweight tool for random testing of haskell programs. In: Proceedings of the Fifth ACM SIGPLAN International Conference on Functional Programming. p. 268–279. ICFP '00, Association for Computing Machinery, New York, NY, USA (2000). https://doi.org/10.1145/351240.351266, https://doi.org/10.1145/351240.351266

19. Cross, A., Javadi-Abhari, A., Alexander, T., De Beaudrap, N., Bishop, L.S., Heidel, S., Ryan, C.A., Sivarajah, P., Smolin, J., Gambetta, J.M., Johnson, B.R.: Openqasm 3: A broader and deeper quantum assembly language. ACM Transactions on Quantum Computing $3(3)$ (sep 2022). https://doi.org/10.1145/3505636, https://doi.org/10.1145/3505636

20. Cross, A.W., Bishop, L.S., Smolin, J.A., Gambetta, J.M.: Open quantum assembly language. arXiv e-prints (Jul 2017)

21. Fortunato, D., Campos, J., Abreu, R.: Mutation testing of quantum programs written in qiskit. In: Proceedings of the ACM/IEEE 44th International Conference on Software Engineering: Companion Proceedings. p. 358–359. ICSE '22, Association for Computing Machinery, New York, NY, USA (2022). https://doi.org/10.1145/3510454.3528649, https://doi.org/10.1145/3510454.3528649

22. Gill, S.S., Cetinkaya, O., Marrone, S., Claudino, D., Haunschild, D., Schlote, L., Wu, H., Ottaviani, C., Liu, X., Machupalli, S.P., Kaur, K., Arora, P., Liu, J., Farouk, A., Song, H.H., Uhlig, S., Ramamohanarao, K.: Quantum computing: Vision and challenges (2024), https://arxiv.org/abs/2403.02240
23. Google Quantum AI: Cirq: An Open Source Framework for Programming Quantum Computers (2019), https://quantumai.google/cirq
24. Green, A.S., Lumsdaine, P.L., Ross, N.J., Selinger, P., Valiron, B.: Quipper: A scalable quantum programming language. In: Proceedings of the 34th ACM SIGPLAN Conference on Programming Language Design and Implementation. p. 333–342. PLDI '13, Association for Computing Machinery, New York, NY, USA (2013). https://doi.org/10.1145/2491956.2462177, https://doi-org.proxy-um.researchport.umd.edu/10.1145/2491956.2462177
25. Hietala, K., Rand, R., Li, L., Hung, S.H., Wu, X., Hicks, M.: A verified optimizer for quantum circuits. ACM Trans. Program. Lang. Syst. **45**(3) (Sep 2023). https://doi.org/10.1145/3604630, https://doi.org/10.1145/3604630
26. Javadi-Abhari, A., Patil, S., Kudrow, D., Heckey, J., Lvov, A., Chong, F.T., Martonosi, M.: ScaffCC: Scalable Compilation and Analysis of Quantum Programs. Parallel Computing **45**, 2–17 (Jun 2015). https://doi.org/10.1016/j.parco.2014.12.001
27. Kissinger, A., van de Wetering, J.: PyZX: Large scale automated diagrammatic reasoning. Electronic Proceedings in Theoretical Computer Science **318**, 230–242 (04 2020). https://doi.org/10.4204/EPTCS.318.14
28. Li, L., Sharma, A., Tagba, Z.D., Frett, S., Potanin, A.: Validating quantum state preparation programs (2025), https://arxiv.org/abs/2501.05616
29. Li, L., Sharma, A., Tagba, Z.D., Frett, S., Potanin, A.: Code for Validating Quantum State Preparation (Feb 2026). https://doi.org/10.5281/zenodo.15073729
30. Li, L., Voichick, F., Hietala, K., Peng, Y., Wu, X., Hicks, M.: Verified compilation of quantum oracles. Proc. ACM Program. Lang. **6**(OOPSLA2) (Oct 2022). https://doi.org/10.1145/3563309, https://doi.org/10.1145/3563309
31. Li, L., Zhu, M., Cleaveland, R., Nicolellis, A., Lee, Y., Chang, L., Wu, X.: Qafny: A Quantum-Program Verifier. In: Aldrich, J., Salvaneschi, G. (eds.) 38th European Conference on Object-Oriented Programming (ECOOP 2024). Leibniz International Proceedings in Informatics (LIPIcs), vol. 313, pp. 24:1–24:31. Schloss Dagstuhl – Leibniz-Zentrum für Informatik, Dagstuhl, Germany (2024). https://doi.org/10.4230/LIPIcs.ECOOP.2024.24, https://drops.dagstuhl.de/entities/document/10.4230/LIPIcs.ECOOP.2024.24
32. Litteken, A., Fan, Y.C., Singh, D., Martonosi, M., Chong, F.T.: An updated LLVM-based quantum research compiler with further OpenQASM support. Quantum Science and Technology **5**(3), 034013 (may 2020). https://doi.org/10.1088/2058-9565/ab8c2c, https://doi.org/10.1088/2058-9565/ab8c2c
33. Long, P., Zhao, J.: Testing multi-subroutine quantum programs: From unit testing to integration testing. ACM Trans. Softw. Eng. Methodol. (apr 2024). https://doi.org/10.1145/3656339, https://doi.org/10.1145/3656339, just Accepted
34. Mei, J., Bonsangue, M., Laarman, A.: Simulating quantum circuits by model counting. In: Gurfinkel, A., Ganesh, V. (eds.) Computer Aided Verification. pp. 555–578. Springer Nature Switzerland, Cham (2024)
35. Microsoft: The Q# Programming Language (2017), https://docs.microsoft.com/
36. Nam, Y., Ross, N.J., Su, Y., Childs, A.M., Maslov, D.: Automated optimization of large quantum circuits with continuous parameters. npj Quantum Information

$4(1)$, 23 (May 2018). `https://doi.org/10.1038/s41534-018-0072-4`, `https://doi.org/10.1038/s41534-018-0072-4`

37. Nielsen, M.A., Chuang, I.L.: Quantum Computation and Quantum Information. Cambridge University Press, USA, 10th anniversary edn. (2011)

38. Paltenghi, M., Pradel, M.: Bugs in quantum computing platforms: an empirical study. Proceedings of the ACM on Programming Languages **6**(OOPSLA1), 1–27 (Apr 2022). `https://doi.org/10.1145/3527330`, `http://dx.doi.org/10.1145/3527330`

39. Paltenghi, M., Pradel, M.: Morphq: Metamorphic testing of the qiskit quantum computing platform. In: Proceedings of the 45th International Conference on Software Engineering. p. 2413–2424. ICSE '23, IEEE Press (2023). `https://doi.org/10.1109/ICSE48619.2023.00202`, `https://doi.org/10.1109/ICSE48619.2023.00202`

40. Paradis, A., Bichsel, B., Steffen, S., Vechev, M.: Unqomp: Synthesizing uncomputation in quantum circuits. In: Proceedings of the 42nd ACM SIGPLAN International Conference on Programming Language Design and Implementation. p. 222?236. PLDI 2021, Association for Computing Machinery, New York, NY, USA (2021). `https://doi.org/10.1145/3453483.3454040`, `https://doi.org/10.1145/3453483.3454040`

41. Paraskevopoulou, Z., HriŢcu, C., Dénès, M., Lampropoulos, L., Pierce, B.C.: Foundational property-based testing. In: Urban, C., Zhang, X. (eds.) Interactive Theorem Proving. pp. 325–343. Springer International Publishing, Cham (2015). `https://doi.org/10.1007/978-3-319-22102-1_22`

42. Rand, R., Paykin, J., Lee, D.H., Zdancewic, S.: Reqwire: Reasoning about reversible quantum circuits. In: QPL (2018)

43. Rigetti Computing: The @rigetti optimizing Quil compiler (2019), `https://github.com/rigetti/quilc`

44. Shi, Y., Li, X., Tao, R., Javadi-Abhari, A., Cross, A.W., Chong, F.T., Gu, R.: Contract-based verification of a realistic quantum compiler. arXiv e-prints (Aug 2019)

45. Shor, P.: Algorithms for quantum computation: discrete logarithms and factoring. In: Proceedings 35th Annual Symposium on Foundations of Computer Science. pp. 124–134 (1994). `https://doi.org/10.1109/SFCS.1994.365700`

46. Sistla, M., Chaudhuri, S., Reps, T.: Symbolic quantum simulation with quasimodo. In: Computer Aided Verification: 35th International Conference, CAV 2023, Paris, France, July 17–22, 2023, Proceedings, Part III. p. 213–225. Springer-Verlag, Berlin, Heidelberg (2023). `https://doi.org/10.1007/978-3-031-37709-9_11`, `https://doi.org/10.1007/978-3-031-37709-9_11`

47. Steiger, D.S., Haner, T., Troyer, M.: ProjectQ: an open source software framework for quantum computing. Quantum **2**, 49 (Jan 2018). `https://doi.org/10.22331/q-2018-01-31-49`, `http://dx.doi.org/10.22331/q-2018-01-31-49`

48. Suzuki, Y., Uno, S., Raymond, R., Tanaka, T., Onodera, T., Yamamoto, N.: Amplitude Estimation Without Phase Estimation. Quantum Information Processing **19**(2) (Jan 2020). `https://doi.org/10.1007/s11128-019-2565-2`, `https://doi.org/10.1007/s11128-019-2565-2`

49. Swayne, M.: What Are The Remaining Challenges Of Quantum Computing? (2023), `https://thequantuminsider.com/2023/03/24/quantum-computing-challenges/`

50. Wang, J., Zhang, Q., Xu, G.H., Kim, M.: Qdiff: Differential testing of quantum software stacks. In: 2021 36th IEEE/ACM International Conference on Auto-

mated Software Engineering (ASE). pp. 692–704 (2021). https://doi.org/10. 1109/ASE51524.2021.9678792

51. Wang, X., Arcaini, P., Yue, T., Ali, S.: Quito: a coverage-guided test generator for quantum programs. In: Proceedings of the 36th IEEE/ACM International Conference on Automated Software Engineering. p. 1237–1241. ASE '21, IEEE Press (2022). https://doi.org/10.1109/ASE51524.2021.9678798, https://doi.org/10.1109/ASE51524.2021.9678798

52. Wootters, W.K., Zurek, W.H.: The no-cloning theorem . https://doi.org/10. 1063/pt.grxx.gcmb

53. Xia, C.S., Paltenghi, M., Le Tian, J., Pradel, M., Zhang, L.: Fuzz4all: Universal fuzzing with large language models. In: Proceedings of the IEEE/ACM 46th International Conference on Software Engineering (ICSE) (2024). https://doi.org/10.1145/3597503.3639121, https://doi.org/10.1145/3597503.3639121

54. Xu, M., Li, Z., Padon, O., Lin, S., Pointing, J., Hirth, A., Ma, H., Palsberg, J., Aiken, A., Acar, U.A., Jia, Z.: Quartz: superoptimization of quantum circuits. In: Proceedings of the 43rd ACM SIGPLAN International Conference on Programming Language Design and Implementation. p. 625–640. PLDI 2022, Association for Computing Machinery, New York, NY, USA (2022). https://doi.org/10. 1145/3519939.3523433, https://doi.org/10.1145/3519939.3523433

The Memorist Tale:
Every Thunk Every Cost All At Once

Xing Li[1] , Yao Li[2] , Peter Schachte[1],
and Christine Rizkallah[1] ✉

[1] University of Melbourne, Australia
x.li170@student.unimelb.edu.au, schachte@unimelb.edu.au,
christine.rizkallah@unimelb.edu.au
[2] Portland State University, United States
liyao@pdx.edu

Abstract. Lazy evaluation offers great flexibility by computing only
what is necessary. However, analysing the cost of lazy programs is notoriously challenging, as computation occurs out of order and depends on future demands. Recent work has proposed alternative semantics for modelling lazy evaluation cost that avoid reasoning about program states.
However, existing approaches either rely on nondeterminism or require
complex bidirectional semantics. We present the *Memorist Semantics*,
a novel semantics for analysing the cost of lazy programs by explicitly
tracking the cost and dependencies of every subterm. Our semantics an-
notates components of a term with fine-grained cost and usage information, yielding a deterministic semantics that can be expressed through a
simple monadic interface. We formalize the semantics in Rocq and verify
its soundness with respect to the existing Clairvoyance Semantics. Similar to prior formalized semantics, our semantics is defined for a total,
typed language with built-in structural recursion and without support
for first-class functions. We outline ideas for possible extensions.

Keywords: computation cost · lazy evaluation · operational semantics

1 Introduction

It is challenging to analyse computation cost of functional programs. Functional
programs typically abstract away *how* programs evaluate. However, the computation cost of a program depends partly on the evaluation strategy adopted. The
call-by-need strategy, used by lazy languages such as Haskell, enables expressive
and flexible programming by avoiding unnecessary computation [20]. Unlike call-
by-value which is used by eager languages such as Standard ML, call-by-need
ensures that components of a term are evaluated only when necessary. This allows for elegant program composition and potential efficiency improvements, but
at a cost: analysing the cost of lazy programs is notoriously difficult.

To explain the difference, we consider the following example. Let `truePrefix`
be a function that takes a list of Booleans as input and returns the prefix of

R. Krebbers (Ed.): ESOP 2026, LNCS 16501, pp. 463–492, 2026.
https://doi.org/10.1007/978-3-032-22720-1_17

```
Fixpoint append {A} (xs ys : list A)      Fixpoint truePrefix (xs : list bool)
  : list A :=                               : list bool :=
 match xs with                             match xs with
 | [] => ys                                | [] => []
 | x::xs' =>                               | x::xs' =>
    let zs := append xs' ys                   let zs := truePrefix xs' in
    in x::zs                                  if x then x::zs else []
 end.                                      end.


Definition truePrefixAppend (xs ys : list bool) : list bool :=
  let zs := append xs ys in truePrefix zs.
```

Fig. 1: Rocq definitions of the functions placed in A-normal form

the list that only contains true. The function truePrefixAppend takes two lists of Booleans, concatenates them using append, and applies truePrefix on the resulting list. Figure 1 presents an implementation in Rocq Prover (formerly Coq) [27]. Now consider the program: truePrefixAppend [true;false] [true].

We are interested in the time cost of evaluating this program, which we model by the number of function applications. While Rocq does not prescribe a specific evaluation strategy, we can view this code as a *shallow embedding* of a program in another language. For instance, tools such as hs-to-coq [38, 3] can automatically translate Haskell programs into this form.

Under eager evaluation, truePrefixAppend first fully computes append of the two input lists, evoking 3 calls to append. The result is then passed to truePrefix. Every element is processed, thus evoking 4 calls to truePrefix. Overall, the program evaluates to [true] and incurs a total cost of $3 + 4 + 1 = 8$, with one additional call to the top-level truePrefixAppend.

In comparison, lazy evaluation is demand-driven: computation is performed based on the demand on the output. Figure 2 illustrates how the evaluation proceeds stepwise. If the result is demanded to its weak-head normal form (WHNF), we only need it to compute to true::_ without computing its tail, and can stop at the step marked $(*)$. Only one step of truePrefix and append each is needed. Together with one call to truePrefixAppend, the total computation cost is 3.

With *sharing* in lazy evaluation, if more, *e.g.*, the full list, is demanded from a later computation, we can resume from what was already computed, *i.e.*, true::_. Now we need to compute the tail and fully reduce the result to true::[]. This requires one more step of truePrefix and of append each, making the cost 5 in total. Note that this cost is still smaller than that incurred by eager evaluation, as we never perform computations not necessary for producing the final result, such as computing the recursive call append [] [true].

Challenges. The example shows several challenges in analysing lazy evaluation cost. Firstly, *the cost of lazy evaluation is not local.* Unlike eager evaluation,

$$
\begin{aligned}
&\texttt{truePrefixAppend (t :: f :: []) (t :: [])} \\
&= \checkmark \texttt{let } zs := \texttt{append (t :: f :: []) (t :: []) in truePrefix } zs \\
&= \texttt{let } zs := \checkmark(\texttt{let } z_1 := \texttt{append (f :: []) (t :: []) in t :: } z_1) \texttt{ in truePrefix } zs \\
&= \texttt{let } z_1 := \texttt{append (f :: []) (t :: []) in truePrefix (t :: } z_1) \\
&= \texttt{let } z_1 := \ldots \texttt{ in } \checkmark \texttt{let } w_1 := \texttt{truePrefix } z_1 \texttt{ in t } \leftrightarrow \texttt{ t :: } w_1 \\
&= \texttt{let } z_1 := \ldots \texttt{ in let } w_1 := \texttt{truePrefix } z_1 \texttt{ in t :: } w_1 \qquad\qquad (*) \\[4pt]
&= \texttt{let } z_1 := \checkmark(\texttt{let } z_2 := \texttt{append [] (t :: []) in f :: } z_2) \texttt{ in} \\
&\qquad\qquad \texttt{let } w_1 := \texttt{truePrefix } z_1 \texttt{ in t :: } w_1 \\
&= \texttt{let } z_2 := \texttt{append [] (t :: []) in let } w_1 := \texttt{truePrefix (f :: } z_2) \texttt{ in t :: } w_1 \\
&= \texttt{let } z_2 := \ldots \texttt{ in let } w_1 := \checkmark(\texttt{let } w_2 := \texttt{truePrefix } z_2 \texttt{ in f } \leftrightarrow \texttt{ f :: } w_2) \texttt{ in t :: } w_1 \\
&= \texttt{let } z_2 := \ldots \texttt{ in let } w_1 := (\texttt{let } w_2 := \ldots \texttt{ in []}) \texttt{ in t :: } w_1 \\
&= \texttt{let } z_2 := \ldots \texttt{ in t :: []}
\end{aligned}
$$

Fig. 2: Lazily evaluating the program `truePrefixAppend`. We place a tick ($\checkmark$) immediately after unfolding a step of function application to indicate the incurring of a cost. The notation $e \leftrightarrow xs$ denotes `if` e `then` xs `else []`. We use `t` and `f` as shorthands for `true` and `false`.

cost incurred by a function may not happen at its call site but later inside another function's application. The cost also depends on future demand. For these reasons, it is challenging to analyse individual functions in isolation. Secondly, *evaluation steps of different functions are interleaved.* The evaluation steps of `truePrefix` and `append` in Fig. 2 are an example. Furthermore, *the evaluation is stateful.* To model sharing, an evaluation needs to remember what has been previously computed.

Existing approaches. One can treat lazy programs as stateful programs, reasoning about states using some program logics. One example [35] utilizes the Iris$^\$$ framework [29] and the Iris separation logic [39]. Another approach [8, 15] employs *equational reasoning*, tracking computation cost by, *e.g.*, using a graded monad. Instead of directly dealing with the stateful natural semantics of laziness [24], we can use an *alternative semantics* equivalent in terms of computation cost. Since it only matters *whether*, but not *when*, a computation happens for time cost analysis, one can *localize* lazy cost if the future demand is known. In this vein, the Clairvoyance Semantics [14], encodable in a simple monadic interface [26], simulates future demands via *nondeterminism*. However, nondeterminism makes formal reasoning and testing challenging. In Li *et al.* [26], an additional logic similar to incorrectness logic [33] is proposed for this reason. To avoid nondeterminism, the Demand Semantics [42] employs bidirectional evaluations: a forward one that computes output values from inputs as normal, and a backward one that calculates *the minimal input demand* and computation cost from pure input and *an output demand.* However, this requires a function to be translated into two different versions, which duplicates code, is error-prone and poses new challenges to formal reasoning. We defer a detailed discussion contrasting these approaches to Section 7.

Our key idea. In this paper, we propose the Memorist Semantics, a novel cost semantics for lazy evaluation that tracks both usage and cost of evaluation of terms. The key idea is to run an eager evaluation, while giving every piece of data a unique name and 'memorizing' information used for computing the data. The Memorist Semantics enables analysing computation cost *locally* without considering states, similar to the Clairvoyance and Demand Semantics. Meanwhile, the Memorist Semantics improves on the former by being *deterministic*, and improves on the latter by only employing one semantics and requiring no code duplication, thus combining the best of two worlds.

To achieve this, we address two key challenges. The first is *precise cost attribution* for different components of a term or value. Since lazy evaluation may only require part of a term, we must exclude unnecessary computations from cost calculations. For this, we track the cost of computing each component separately and annotate it with its cost. The second challenge is *accounting for shared computations*. Because lazy evaluation evaluates each component of a term at most once, our semantics must prevent duplicating cost accounting. We achieve this by tracking *usage sets* and using set union for bookkeeping.

Contributions. We make the following contributions:
- We introduce the Memorist Semantics, a deterministic cost semantics for call-by-need that tracks both cost and usage of subexpressions (Section 3).
- We prove that our semantics correctly models the execution cost of a program under call-by-need by relating it to the Clairvoyance Semantics (Section 4).
- We show that our semantics can be encoded using a simple monadic interface via a proof of concept implementation in Rocq (Section 5).
- We formalize our results in Rocq to ensure rigorous proofs.

We describe the intuition behind our semantics in Section 2. We discuss limitations and potential ways to address them in Section 6, including lack of handling of general recursion and formalizing first-class functions. We discuss related work in Section 7 and conclude the paper with future work in Section 8.

2   The Memorist Approach

Imagine a person with a remarkably retentive memory, whom we call a *Memorist*. When evaluating a program, the Memorist does all computations eagerly while memorizing for each computation what other computations ("thunks") it requires and its own computation cost. After evaluating the entire program, the Memorist learns all the thunks used by computing each part of the value and their individual computation cost. If some program demands parts of the value, the Memorist can tell all the thunks that are used in the evaluation up to these parts. A corresponding lazy evaluation would also have to evaluate exactly these thunks. One can thus infer the lazy evaluation cost based on this information.

Thunks and annotations. To realize this approach, we wrap every piece of data inside a *thunk*, and track its usage and cost during evaluations. Thunks here are intended to simulate thunks in lazy evaluation, but they are not encoded as suspended computations. Each Memorist thunk has a unique name to distinguish it from others. We annotate a thunk with a pair of cost and a set of thunk names. The former tracks the cost incurred by evaluating the thunk to its WHNF, *without* the cost incurred by evaluating other thunks. The latter, called a *usage set*, records all thunks whose results are used in that evaluation. We also annotate an output value in the same fashion.

Consider the program `truePrefixAppend [true;false] [true]` from a Memorist's perspective. Since lazy evaluations do not necessarily evaluate every function or constructor argument, we accordingly wrap the input lists and all arguments to the list constructor `::` in thunks. For illustration, we denote a thunked expression x with a thunk name i and an annotation a by $x_{i@a}$. We can then represent the first input list, after being thunked, as

$$\{\!|\, \mathtt{true}_{i_4@a_{i_4}} :: \{\!|\, \mathtt{false}_{i_3@a_{i_3}} :: \mathtt{[]}_{i_1@a_{i_1}} |\!\}_{i_2@a_{i_2}} |\!\}_{i_7@a_{i_7}}$$

and the second as $\{\!|\, \mathtt{true}_{i_6@a_{i_6}} :: \mathtt{[]}_{i_5@a_{i_5}} |\!\}_{i_8@a_{i_8}}$, for some unique names $i_1, \ldots, i_8$ and annotations $a_{i_1}, \ldots, a_{i_8}$. We delay the formal definitions to Section 3.

The Memorist Semantics in action. We evaluate the program eagerly while tracking thunk usage and cost, with detailed steps in Fig. 3. We first compute `append` (Fig. 3a). At each step, we "unthunk" the first argument to access the list inside; *e.g.*, at the first step, we unthunk thunk i_7 wrapping the first argument, and say we *used* i_7. We then recursively apply `append` to the tail of the first input list until we reach the empty list, at which point we unthunk both thunks i_1 and i_8, and return the second input list.

We wrap this result from computing `append` $\mathtt{[]}_{i_1}$ $\{\!|\, \mathtt{true}_{i_6} :: \mathtt{[]}_{i_5} |\!\}_{i_8}$ (bound to z_2) in a new thunk freshly named j_1. The computation incurs one call to `append`; hence, the cost annotation is 1. It uses the thunks i_1 and i_8. Note that the thunks in the usage sets annotated to i_1 and i_8 must all be used if i_1 and i_8 are used. So we include all of them in j_1's usage set annotation. Denoting union of $\{i_1\}$ and i_1's usage set by $s(i_1)$, j_1's usage set annotation is then $s(i_1) \cup s(i_8)$. The rest of the computation proceeds similarly. The final output is also annotated.

Lazy computation cost. With the information in the annotations, we can analyse the cost of `append` with respect to *any demand* on the output. We do so by collecting all thunks used by a demand and aggregating their individual cost. For example, if we demand the output list to its WHNF, we need only to consider the thunk usage in the output annotation, which is $s(i_7)$. Moreover, we are interested in the cost of `append` itself, not in previous computations of its input. We account for this by removing all the thunks existing prior to the evaluation of `append [true;false] [true]` from $s(i_7)$. This gives us the empty set, suggesting no thunked cost to consider. Therefore, we only need to count the cost annotation to the final output. The inferred lazy cost is thus 1, as expected.

$$\text{append } \{\!| t_{i_4 @ a_{i_4}} :: \{\!| f_{i_3 @ a_{i_3}} :: []_{i_1 @ a_{i_1}} |\!\}_{i_2 @ a_{i_2}} |\!\}_{i_7 @ a_{i_7}} \; \{\!| t_{i_6 @ a_{i_6}} :: []_{i_5 @ a_{i_5}} |\!\}_{i_8 @ a_{i_8}}$$
$$= \checkmark \text{let } z_1 := \text{append } \{\!| f_{i_3} :: []_{i_1} |\!\}_{i_2} \; \{\!| t_{i_6} :: []_{i_5} |\!\}_{i_8} \text{ in } t_{i_4} :: \underline{z_1} \qquad\qquad \leadsto i_7$$
$$= \text{let } z_1 := \checkmark (\text{let } z_2 := \text{append } []_{i_1} \; \{\!| t_{i_6} :: []_{i_5} |\!\}_{i_8} \text{ in } f_{i_3} :: \underline{z_2}) \text{ in } t_{i_4} :: \underline{z_1} \qquad \leadsto i_2$$
$$= \text{let } z_1 := (\text{let } z_2 := \checkmark t_{i_6} :: []_{i_5} \text{ in } f_{i_3} :: \underline{z_2}) \text{ in } t_{i_4} :: \underline{z_1} \qquad\qquad \leadsto i_1, i_8$$
$$= \text{let } z_1 := f_{i_3} :: \{\!| t_{i_6} :: []_{i_5} |\!\}_{j_1 @ (1, s(i_1) \cup s(i_8))} \text{ in } t_{i_4} :: \underline{z_1}$$
$$= t_{i_4} :: \{\!| f_{i_3} :: \{\!| t_{i_6} :: []_{i_5} |\!\}_{j_1} |\!\}_{j_2 @ (1, s(i_2))} \qquad @(1, s(i_7))$$

(a) Evaluation steps of append

$$\text{truePrefix } \{\!| t_{i_4} :: \{\!| f_{i_3} :: \{\!| t_{i_6} :: []_{i_5} |\!\}_{j_1} |\!\}_{j_2} |\!\}_{j_3}$$
$$= \checkmark \text{let } w_1 := \text{truePrefix } \{\!| f_{i_3} :: \{\!| t_{i_6} :: []_{i_5} |\!\}_{j_1} |\!\}_{j_2} \text{ in } t_{i_4} \looparrowright t_{i_4} :: \underline{w_1} \qquad \leadsto j_3$$
$$= \text{let } w_1 := \checkmark (\text{let } w_2 := \text{truePrefix } \{\!| t_{i_6} :: []_{i_5} |\!\}_{j_1} \text{ in } f_{i_3} \looparrowright f_{i_3} :: \underline{w_2}) \text{ in} \ldots \qquad \leadsto j_2$$
$$= \text{let } w_1 := (\text{let } w_2 := \checkmark (\text{let } w_3 := \text{truePrefix } []_{i_5} \text{ in } t_{i_6} \looparrowright t_{i_6} :: \underline{w_3}) \text{ in} \ldots) \text{ in} \ldots$$
$$\leadsto j_1$$
$$= \text{let } w_1 := (\text{let } w_2 := (\text{let } w_3 := [] \text{ in } t_{i_6} \looparrowright t_{i_6} :: \underline{w_3}) \text{ in} \ldots) \text{ in} \ldots \qquad \leadsto i_5$$
$$= \text{let } w_1 := (\text{let } w_2 := (t_{i_6} \looparrowright t_{i_6} :: []_{k_1 @ (1, s(i_5))}) \text{ in } f_{i_3} \looparrowright f_{i_3} :: \underline{w_2}) \text{ in} \ldots$$
$$= \text{let } w_1 := (\text{let } w_2 := t_{i_6} :: []_{k_1} \text{ in } f_{i_3} \looparrowright f_{i_3} :: \underline{w_2}) \text{ in } t_{i_4} \looparrowright t_{i_4} :: \underline{w_1} \qquad \leadsto i_6$$
$$= \text{let } w_1 := f_{i_3} \looparrowright f_{i_3} :: \{\!| t_{i_6} :: []_{k_1} |\!\}_{k_2 @ a_{k_2}} \text{ in } t_{i_4} \looparrowright t_{i_4} :: \underline{w_1}$$
$$\text{where } a_{k_2} = (1, s(j_1) \cup s(i_6)) = (1, \{j_1\} \cup s(i_1) \cup s(i_8) \cup s(i_6))$$
$$= \text{let } w_1 := [] \text{ in } t_{i_4} \looparrowright t_{i_4} :: \underline{w_1} \qquad \leadsto i_3$$
$$= t_{i_4} \looparrowright t_{i_4} :: []_{k_3 @ (1, s(j_2) \cup s(i_3))}$$
$$= t_{i_4} :: []_{k_3} \qquad @(1, s(j_3) \cup s(i_4)) \qquad \leadsto j_3, i_4$$

(b) Evaluation steps of truePrefix

$$\text{truePrefixAppend } \{\!| t_{i_4} :: \{\!| f_{i_3} :: []_{i_1} |\!\}_{i_2} |\!\}_{i_7} \; \{\!| t_{i_6} :: []_{i_5} |\!\}_{i_8}$$
$$= \checkmark \text{let } zs := \text{append } \{\!| t_{i_4} :: \{\!| f_{i_3} :: []_{i_1} |\!\}_{i_2} |\!\}_{i_7} \; \{\!| t_{i_6} :: []_{i_5} |\!\}_{i_8} \text{ in truePrefix } \underline{zs}$$
$$= \text{truePrefix } \{\!| t_{i_4} :: \{\!| f_{i_3} :: \{\!| t_{i_6} :: []_{i_5} |\!\}_{j_1} |\!\}_{j_2} |\!\}_{j_3 @ (1, s(i_7))}$$
$$= t_{i_4} :: []_{k_3} \qquad @(1 + 1, s(j_3) \cup s(i_4)) = (2, s(j_3) \cup s(i_4))$$

(c) Evaluation steps of truePrefixAppend

Fig. 3: The Memorist evaluation for the program truePrefixAppend. Annotations are shown once and omitted subsequently. The final output values have their annotations shown next to themselves. We use the same notations and shorthands from Fig. 2. We also denote by $\underline{w_1}$ the thunking of w_1, by $s(i)$ the union of $\{i\}$ and the usage set annotated to i, and by $\leadsto i, j, \ldots$ that thunks named $i, j, \ldots$ are used in the last step proceeding to the expression on the current line.

If we demand the output to the first two elements instead, we must additionally take into account the thunk j_2 wrapping the first cons cell, and the thunks i_4 and i_3 wrapping the first and the second element in the output list. That is, we consider all thunks in the set $s(i_7) \cup s(j_2) \cup s(i_4) \cup s(i_3)$. Only j_2 is created during the computation of append. Thus, we ignore all the other thunks, and add only the cost annotation to j_2 to the output cost annotation. This gives us $1 + 1 = 2$ as the inferred lazy cost. Note that, while we have reasoned about different demand, we need not re-evaluate the entire expression, but only extract and aggregate information based on the demand from the same evaluated result.

Composing lazy cost analysis. A key feature of the Memorist Semantics is that we can analyse cost locally and compose cost analyses. Consider the evaluation of truePrefix and truePrefixAppend. Figure 3b illustrates the evaluation of truePrefix applied to the result of append (wrapped in a thunk named j_3). Its annotation comes from the output annotation of previous computations. The evaluation of truePrefix proceeds similarly as that of append, except it must also examine the list elements, and therefore, use the thunks wrapping the elements. For instance, computing $\text{true}_{i_6} \leadsto \text{true}_{i_6} :: []_{k_1}$ must access the value inside the thunk i_6 to determine which if-branch to take. Hence, the thunk k_2 wrapping this result must include $s(i_6)$ (among others) in its annotation. The similar thing happens with k_3 and the final output. Notice that, if a computation is never necessary, its cost and thunk usage will not be included anywhere in the final result. Indeed, the thunks k_1 (wrapping the empty list) and k_2 (wrapping the third element of the input list) are "thrown away" after encountering false and never needed to compute the final result in a lazy evaluation regardless of demand.

Now consider the top-level program truePrefixAppend in Fig. 3c. The Memorist evaluation of it essentially computes append on the two input lists, thunks the resulting list, and then computes truePrefix. We can collect thunks based on demand as before. If the output list is demanded only to its WHNF, we take only the thunks in the output annotation, which is $s(j_3) \cup s(i_4)$. But all except j_3 already exist in the input environment. The cost is thus the sum of the cost annotations given to the final output and to j_3, which is $2 + 1 = 3$. If the entire output list is demanded, we take also $s(i_4)$ and $s(k_3)$ into account, where the thunk i_4 thunks the first and only element and k_3 wraps the empty tail. With k_3, j_2 and j_3 being the thunks not existing in the input and each having a cost annotation of 1, we infer the total lazy cost to be $2 + 1 + 1 + 1 = 5$.

3   The Memorist Semantics

We consider the following typed total language $\mathcal{L}$ with Booleans, lists, explicit thunks, ticks, and structural recursion on lists. [3]

$$
\begin{array}{lll}
\text{Types} & A, B & ::= \mathsf{bool} \mid \mathsf{list}\, A \mid \mathsf{T}\, A \\
\text{Variables} & x, y & \in \mathrm{Var} \\
\text{Expressions}\ M, N & ::= & x \mid \mathsf{let}\, x = M \,\mathsf{in}\, N \mid \mathsf{true} \mid \mathsf{false} \mid \mathsf{if}\, M_1\, M_2\, M_3 \mid \mathsf{tick}\, M \\
& & \mid\ \mathsf{nil} \mid \mathsf{cons}\, M\, N \mid \mathsf{foldr}\, (\lambda xy.\, M_1)\, M_2\, M_3 \mid \mathsf{lazy}\, M \mid \mathsf{force}\, M
\end{array}
$$

Well-typed terms are given by judgements of the form $\gamma \vdash M : A$. For the typing rules, we refer the readers to [42] where the same language is considered. Thunks are represented with the T type and manipulated explicitly, allowing us to study laziness directly. The lazy construct thunks a computation, and force forces the evaluation of a thunk. The tick construct simulates a computation that incurs a unit cost. The construct foldr is included as a primitive to facilitate structural recursions on lists. We can view the language as an intermediate representation into which an ordinary functional language can be translated.

Memorist Semantics. We define the Memorist Semantics for the language $\mathcal{L}$ formally below. Terms are evaluated into values defined by

$$
v ::= \mathsf{true} \mid \mathsf{false} \mid \mathsf{nil} \mid \mathsf{cons}\, v_1\, v_2 \mid \mathrm{th}_i\, v
$$

A value $\mathrm{th}_i\, v$ of type $\mathsf{T}\, A$, where A is the type of v, represents a thunk and is assigned a unique name $i \in \mathbb{N}$. Following the idea in Section 2, the semantics associates the output value and each thunk with a pair (c, s) of a cost c and a usage set s of names of thunks. Components of an annotation can be extracted via the usual first and second projections on pairs, denoted $\pi_1(\cdot)$ and $\pi_2(\cdot)$ respectively.

An evaluation occurs in an evaluation environment defined as $\Gamma ::= \emptyset \mid \Gamma, x \mapsto v$ that maps variables to values. We also define an *annotation context*, $\mathcal{A} ::= \emptyset \mid \mathcal{A}, i \mapsto \alpha_i$, that maps a thunk name i to its annotation α_i, to track annotations. Keeping track of two separate contexts allows more flexibility in manipulating thunks and analysing their usage and cost.

Formally, the Memorist semantics for well-typed terms in $\mathcal{L}$ is defined by the evaluation judgement $\Gamma; \mathcal{A} \vdash M \Downarrow \mathcal{A}'; \langle v, \alpha \rangle$. It states that the well-typed term M evaluates, under the environment Γ and the annotation context $\mathcal{A}$, to the value v annotated by α with the extended annotation context $\mathcal{A}'$. The judgement is defined by the operational semantic rules in Fig. 4. Evaluation is eager by default, which is easier to reason about than its lazy counterpart. We claim (and prove in Section 4) that the recorded thunk usage captures exactly the thunks needed to be evaluated in a corresponding lazy evaluation, from which we can derive the lazy evaluation cost.

The EMBASIC rule introduces the base cases. The EMVAR rule looks up the variable in the environment for the value it binds to. The rules EMCONS

---

[3] We have also handled pairs in our Rocq formalization; see the accompanying artefact for details. We omit them here for brevity.

$$\text{EMVAR} \quad \frac{\Gamma(x) = v}{\Gamma; \mathcal{A} \vdash x \Downarrow \mathcal{A}; \langle v, \odot \rangle}$$

$$\text{EMLET} \quad \frac{\Gamma; \mathcal{A} \vdash M \Downarrow \mathcal{A}_1; \langle v_1, \alpha_1 \rangle \quad \Gamma, (x \mapsto v_1); \mathcal{A}_1 \vdash N \Downarrow \mathcal{A}_2; \langle v_2, \alpha_2 \rangle}{\Gamma; \mathcal{A} \vdash \text{let } x = M \text{ in } N \Downarrow \mathcal{A}_2; \langle v_2, \alpha_1 \oplus \alpha_2 \rangle}$$

$$\text{EMBASIC} \quad \frac{t \in \{\text{true}, \text{false}, \text{nil}\}}{\Gamma; \mathcal{A} \vdash t \Downarrow \mathcal{A}; \langle t, \odot \rangle}$$

$$\text{EMCONS} \quad \frac{\Gamma; \mathcal{A} \vdash M \Downarrow \mathcal{A}_1; \langle v_1, \alpha_1 \rangle \quad \Gamma; \mathcal{A}_1 \vdash N \Downarrow \mathcal{A}_2; \langle v_2, \alpha_2 \rangle}{\Gamma; \mathcal{A} \vdash \text{cons } M \, N \Downarrow \mathcal{A}_2; \langle \text{cons } v_1 \, v_2, \alpha_1 \oplus \alpha_2 \rangle}$$

$$\text{EMIFTRUE} \quad \frac{\Gamma; \mathcal{A} \vdash M_1 \Downarrow \mathcal{A}_1; \langle \text{true}, \alpha_1 \rangle \quad \Gamma; \mathcal{A}_1 \vdash M_2 \Downarrow \mathcal{A}_2; \langle v, \alpha_2 \rangle}{\Gamma; \mathcal{A} \vdash \text{if } M_1 \, M_2 \, M_3 \Downarrow \mathcal{A}_2; \langle v, \alpha_1 \oplus \alpha_2 \rangle}$$

$$\text{EMIFFALSE} \quad \frac{\Gamma; \mathcal{A} \vdash M_1 \Downarrow \mathcal{A}_1; \langle \text{false}, \alpha_1 \rangle \quad \Gamma; \mathcal{A}_1 \vdash M_3 \Downarrow \mathcal{A}_2; \langle v, \alpha_2 \rangle}{\Gamma; \mathcal{A} \vdash \text{if } M_1 \, M_2 \, M_3 \Downarrow \mathcal{A}_2; \langle v, \alpha_1 \oplus \alpha_2 \rangle}$$

$$\text{EMLAZY} \quad \frac{\Gamma; \mathcal{A} \vdash M \Downarrow \mathcal{A}'; \langle v, \alpha \rangle \quad i \notin \text{dom}(\mathcal{A}')}{\Gamma; \mathcal{A} \vdash \text{lazy } M \Downarrow \mathcal{A}', (i \mapsto \alpha); \langle \text{th}_i \, v, \odot \rangle}$$

$$\text{EMFORCE} \quad \frac{\Gamma; \mathcal{A} \vdash M \Downarrow \mathcal{A}'; \langle \text{th}_i \, v, \alpha \rangle \quad s = \alpha \oplus \{i\} \oplus \pi_2(\mathcal{A}'(i))}{\Gamma; \mathcal{A} \vdash \text{force } M \Downarrow \mathcal{A}'; \langle v, s \rangle}$$

$$\text{EMFOLDRNIL} \quad \frac{\Gamma; \mathcal{A} \vdash M_3 \Downarrow \mathcal{A}_1; \langle \text{nil}, \alpha_1 \rangle \quad \Gamma; \mathcal{A}_1 \vdash M_2 \Downarrow \mathcal{A}_2; \langle v, \alpha_2 \rangle}{\Gamma; \mathcal{A} \vdash \text{foldr } (\lambda xy.M_1) \, M_2 \, M_3 \Downarrow \mathcal{A}_2; \langle v, \alpha_1 \oplus \alpha_2 \rangle}$$

$$\text{EMTICK} \quad \frac{\Gamma; \mathcal{A} \vdash M \Downarrow \mathcal{A}'; \langle v, \alpha \rangle}{\Gamma; \mathcal{A} \vdash \text{tick } M \Downarrow \mathcal{A}'; \langle v, \alpha \oplus 1 \rangle}$$

$$\text{EMFOLDRCONS} \quad \frac{\begin{array}{c} \Gamma; \mathcal{A} \vdash M_3 \Downarrow \mathcal{A}_1; \langle \text{cons } v \, (\text{th}_i \, vs), \alpha_1 \rangle \\ \Gamma; \mathcal{A}_1 \vdash \text{foldr } (\lambda xy.M_1) \, M_2 \, vs \Downarrow \mathcal{A}_2; \langle v_2, \alpha_2 \rangle \quad j \notin \text{dom}(\mathcal{A}_2) \\ x' \neq y' \quad x', y' \notin \text{dom}(\Gamma) \cup \text{FV}(M_1) \cup \text{FV}(M_2) \cup \text{FV}(M_3) \quad s = \alpha_2 \oplus \{i\} \oplus \pi_2(\mathcal{A}_2(i)) \\ \Gamma, (x' \mapsto v), (y' \mapsto \text{th}_j \, v_2); \mathcal{A}_2, (j \mapsto s) \vdash M_1[x', y'/x, y] \Downarrow \mathcal{A}_3; \langle v_3, \alpha_3 \rangle \end{array}}{\Gamma; \mathcal{A} \vdash \text{foldr } (\lambda xy.M_1) \, M_2 \, M_3 \Downarrow \mathcal{A}_3; \langle v_3, \alpha_1 \oplus \alpha_3 \rangle}$$

Fig. 4: The Memorist Semantics. The notation $\text{FV}(M)$ denotes the set of all free variables appearing in M. The empty annotation $(0, \emptyset)$ is denoted $\odot$. The operation $\oplus$ on annotations is defined as $\alpha_1 \oplus \alpha_2 := (\pi_1(\alpha_1) + \pi_1(\alpha_2), \, \pi_2(\alpha_1) \cup \pi_2(\alpha_2))$. We use the shorthand $\alpha \oplus n$ where n is a number to mean $(\pi_1(\alpha) + n, \, \pi_2(\alpha))$ and $\alpha \oplus s$ where s is a set to mean $(\pi_1(\alpha), \, \pi_2(\alpha) \cup s)$.

and EMLET proceed by evaluating the subterms sequentially. The annotations to values of the two sub-evaluations are combined by adding the costs and taking the union of the usage sets. With set union, the semantics can account for potential sharing of thunks. The rules EMIFTRUE and EMIFFALSE evaluates the if-condition and proceeds to evaluate the then- or else-branches accordingly. The rule EMTICK increments the cost count by one.

In EMLAZY, the term M is evaluated to a value v before being wrapped inside a th constructor. The computation cost and thunk usage associated with this evaluation is annotated to the thunked value v. Accordingly, the cost and usage associated with the final result $\text{th}_i \, v$ is empty, as a thunked computation incurs no cost and uses no additional thunks per se.

Thunked cost and usage are taken into effect only when the thunk is needed, forcing the computation to actually take place. Such forcing is explicitly done via the force construct, evaluated according to the EMFORCE rule. While thunks in the usage set annotated to the thunked value (i.e., $\pi_2(\mathcal{A}'(i))$ in the rule) are directly merged into the usage set annotated to the final value, the thunked cost is not added in yet. This avoids duplicating the cost when the same thunk is needed more than once. The total evaluation cost is to be derived afterwards.

The term $\mathrm{foldr}\,(\lambda xy.\,M_1)\,M_2\,M_3$ is evaluated based on whether the list M_3 computes to is empty. If empty, M_2 is evaluated per the rule EMFOLDRNIL. Otherwise, the evaluation follows EMFOLDRCONS which recursively evaluates foldr on the tail of the list and then applies $\lambda xy.\,M_1$ to its head and the thunked result of the recursive call.

Basic properties of annotation contexts. We are only interested in annotation contexts that are *valid* in the following sense. In the following theorem, we denote by $\mathrm{dom}(\cdot)$ and $\mathrm{im}(\cdot)$ the domain and the image of a function, respectively. By "thunks inside v", we mean thunks wrapping the arguments to the outermost and nested constructors of v: *e.g.*, all thunks appearing in the list $\mathrm{cons}\,(\mathrm{th}_i\,\mathrm{true})\,(\mathrm{th}_j\,(\mathrm{th}_k\,\mathrm{nil}))$.

Definition 1 (Valid annotation context). *An annotation context $\mathcal{A}$ is* valid *if for every annotation $\alpha \in \mathrm{im}(\mathcal{A})$, $\pi_2(\alpha) \subseteq \mathrm{dom}(\mathcal{A})$. We say such an $\mathcal{A}$ is* valid *for a value v if for any name i of a thunk inside v, we also have $i \in \mathrm{dom}(\mathcal{A})$. Moreover, $\mathcal{A}$ is* valid *for an environment Γ if $\forall x \in \mathrm{dom}(\Gamma)$, $\mathcal{A}$ is valid for $\Gamma(x)$.*

A Memorist evaluation may extend the annotation context but never modifies the existing annotations. It also preserves the validity of annotation contexts.

Lemma 1 (Evaluation only extends annotation context). *If $\Gamma; \mathcal{A} \vdash M \Downarrow \mathcal{A}'; \langle v, \alpha \rangle$ then $\forall i \in \mathrm{dom}(\mathcal{A}), \mathcal{A}'(i) = \mathcal{A}(i)$.*

Lemma 2 (Evaluation preserves annotation context validity). *If $\Gamma; \mathcal{A} \vdash M \Downarrow \mathcal{A}'; \langle v, \alpha \rangle$ and $\mathcal{A}$ is valid for Γ, then $\mathcal{A}'$ is valid for Γ and v, and $\pi_2(\alpha) \subseteq \mathrm{dom}(\mathcal{A}')$.*

Lazy cost and usage analysis. To derive the complete usage set and cost with respect to a demand, we must consider every thunk inferred to be needed. We have illustrated the basic idea in Section 2, which we express formally here. Consider an evaluation $\Gamma; \mathcal{A} \vdash M \Downarrow \mathcal{A}'; \langle v, (c, s) \rangle$. All thunks recorded in the usage set s annotated to v are needed to lazily evaluate M to v in WHNF. The total lazy cost is then the sum of all annotated costs given to every thunk in s, plus c. To perform such calculations, we define the following operation

$$\mathrm{sumcost}_M(\mathcal{A}, s) := \sum_{i \in s \cap \mathrm{dom}(\mathcal{A})} \pi_1(\mathcal{A}(i))$$

for an annotation context $\mathcal{A}$ and a usage set s. The total lazy cost of the above evaluation can be then expressed as $c + \mathrm{sumcost}_M(\mathcal{A}' \setminus \mathcal{A}, s)$. The set difference

$\mathcal{A}' \setminus \mathcal{A}$ (where $\mathcal{A}$ and $\mathcal{A}'$ are treated as functions, i.e, sets of mappings) excludes thunks already evaluated prior to this evaluation. By so doing, we avoid including the cost incurred by previous computations.

Suppose the above evaluation yields $\mathrm{cons}\,(\mathrm{th}_i\,\mathrm{true})\,(\mathrm{th}_j\,\mathrm{nil})$, annotated with $(c, \{k, m\})$, and subsequent computations demand also the head of the list. We now need to collect also the thunk i and its usage set, $i.e.$, $\{k, m\} \cup \{i\} \cup \pi_2(\mathcal{A}'(i))$. Call this set s'. The cost is then $c + \mathrm{sumcost}_M(\mathcal{A}' \setminus \mathcal{A}, s')$. By collecting names in a set first, we ensure that no thunk can contribute to the cost more than once.

4 Correctness of the Memorist Semantics

We prove the Memorist Semantics is correct by relating it to the Clairvoyance Semantics [14, 26], which is equivalent to the standard call-by-need semantics [24]. The Clairvoyance Semantics nondeterministically chooses to evaluate or skip an expression when first encountered instead of delaying the evaluation until needed.

Reasoning directly about the relationship between the Memorist and the Clairvoyance Semantics is challenging. Instead, we define, as a stepping stone, a variant of the Clairvoyance Semantics where thunks are named and annotated with cost. We prove that this variant is equivalent to the original Clairvoyance Semantics and corresponds to the Memorist Semantics, therefore establishing a correspondence between the original Clairvoyance Semantics and the Memorist Semantics. The proofs presented here have been formalized in Rocq; see the accompanying artefact.

4.1 The Clairvoyance Semantics

Here we present a Clairvoyance Semantics for the language $\mathcal{L}$, adapted directly from the formalization by [42] which is itself based on a monadic variant of the Clairvoyance Semantics due to [26]. Types are interpreted as

$$\llbracket A \rrbracket : \mathrm{Set}$$
$$\llbracket \mathrm{bool} \rrbracket := \{\mathrm{true}, \mathrm{false}\}$$
$$\llbracket \mathrm{list}\,A \rrbracket := \{\mathrm{nil}\} \cup \{\mathrm{cons}\,\hat{v}_1\,\hat{v}_2 \mid \hat{v}_1 \in \llbracket \mathsf{T}\,A \rrbracket, \hat{v}_2 \in \llbracket \mathsf{T}\,(\mathrm{list}\,A) \rrbracket\}$$
$$\llbracket \mathsf{T}\,A \rrbracket := \{\bot\} \cup \{\mathrm{th}\,\hat{v} \mid \hat{v} \in \llbracket A \rrbracket\}$$

The thunk type T is interpreted as a set whose elements are either of the form $\mathrm{th}\,\hat{v}$ representing a thunk evaluated to a value v, or $\bot$ representing skipped computation. The interpretation extends to the type context.

The semantics of evaluating a well-typed term $\gamma \vdash M : A$ is denoted by $\llbracket M \rrbracket : \llbracket \gamma \rrbracket \rightarrow \mathcal{P}(\llbracket A \rrbracket \times \mathbb{N})$ that takes an interpreted environment $\hat{\Gamma} \in \llbracket \gamma \rrbracket$ and produces a set of pairs of values $\hat{v} \in \llbracket A \rrbracket$ and the cost $c \in \mathbb{N}$ incurred by the evaluation. The detailed definition of the semantics can be found in [26, 42]. When evaluating lazy M and foldr which involves creating thunks, the semantics nondeterministically chooses to evaluate a subterm to a value and wrap it in a th

$$\frac{\text{EAVar}}{\tilde{\Gamma}(x) = \tilde{v}}{\tilde{\Gamma}; \mathcal{C} \vdash x \Downarrow^A \mathcal{C}; \langle \tilde{v}, 0 \rangle}$$

$$\frac{\text{EALet}}{\tilde{\Gamma}; \mathcal{C} \vdash M \Downarrow^A \mathcal{C}_1; \langle \tilde{v}_1, c_1 \rangle \quad (\tilde{\Gamma}, x \mapsto \tilde{v}_1); \mathcal{C}_1 \vdash N \Downarrow^A \mathcal{C}_2; \langle \tilde{v}_2, c_2 \rangle}{\tilde{\Gamma}; \mathcal{C} \vdash \text{let } x = M \text{ in } N \Downarrow^A \mathcal{C}_2; \langle \tilde{v}_2, c_1 + c_2 \rangle}$$

$$\frac{\text{EALazy}}{\tilde{\Gamma}; \mathcal{C} \vdash M \Downarrow^A \mathcal{C}'; \langle \tilde{v}, c \rangle \quad i \notin \text{dom}(\mathcal{C}')}{\tilde{\Gamma}; \mathcal{C} \vdash \text{lazy } M \Downarrow^A \mathcal{C}', (i \mapsto c); \langle \text{th}_i \, \tilde{v}, 0 \rangle}$$

$$\frac{\text{EALazySkip}}{\tilde{\Gamma}; \mathcal{C} \vdash \text{lazy } M \Downarrow^A \mathcal{C}; \langle \bot, 0 \rangle}$$

$$\frac{\text{EAForce}}{\tilde{\Gamma}; \mathcal{C} \vdash M \Downarrow^A \mathcal{C}'; \langle \text{th}_i \, \tilde{v}, c \rangle}{\tilde{\Gamma}; \mathcal{C} \vdash \text{force } M \Downarrow^A \mathcal{C}'; \langle \tilde{v}, c \rangle}$$

$$\frac{\text{EAFoldrNil}}{\tilde{\Gamma}; \mathcal{C} \vdash M_3 \Downarrow^A \mathcal{C}_1; \langle \text{nil}, c_1 \rangle \quad \tilde{\Gamma}; \mathcal{C}_1 \vdash M_2 \Downarrow^A \mathcal{C}_2; \langle \tilde{v}, c_2 \rangle}{\tilde{\Gamma}; \mathcal{C} \vdash \text{foldr } (\lambda xy. \, M_1) \, M_2 \, M_3 \Downarrow^A \mathcal{C}_2; \langle \tilde{v}, c_1 + c_2 \rangle}$$

$$\frac{\text{EAFoldrConsSkip}}{\begin{array}{c} \tilde{\Gamma}; \mathcal{C} \vdash M_3 \Downarrow^A \mathcal{C}_1; \langle \text{cons } \tilde{v} \, \tilde{vs}, c_1 \rangle \\ x' \neq y' \quad x', y' \notin \text{dom}(\tilde{\Gamma}) \cup \text{FV}(M_1) \cup \text{FV}(M_2) \cup \text{FV}(M_3) \\ \tilde{\Gamma}, (x' \mapsto \tilde{v}_1), (y' \mapsto \bot); \mathcal{C}_2 \vdash M_1[x', y'/x, y] \Downarrow^A \mathcal{C}_3; \langle \tilde{v}_2, c_3 \rangle \end{array}}{\tilde{\Gamma}; \mathcal{C} \vdash \text{foldr } (\lambda xy. \, M_1) \, M_2 \, M_3 \Downarrow^A \mathcal{C}_3; \langle \tilde{v}_2, c_1 + c_3 \rangle}$$

$$\frac{\text{EAFoldrCons}}{\begin{array}{c} \tilde{\Gamma}; \mathcal{C} \vdash M_3 \Downarrow^A \mathcal{C}_1; \langle \text{cons } \tilde{v} \, (\text{th}_i \, \tilde{vs}), c_1 \rangle \quad \tilde{\Gamma}; \mathcal{C}_1 \vdash \text{foldr } (\lambda xy. \, M_1) \, M_2 \, \tilde{vs} \Downarrow^A \mathcal{C}_2; \langle \tilde{v}_2, c_2 \rangle \\ j \notin \text{dom}(\mathcal{C}_2) \cup \{i\} \quad x' \neq y' \quad x', y' \notin \text{dom}(\tilde{\Gamma}) \cup \text{FV}(M_1) \cup \text{FV}(M_2) \cup \text{FV}(M_3) \\ \tilde{\Gamma}, (x' \mapsto \tilde{v}), (y' \mapsto \text{th}_i \, \tilde{v}_2); \mathcal{C}_2, (j \mapsto c_2) \vdash M_1[x', y'/x, y] \Downarrow^A \mathcal{C}_3; \langle \tilde{v}_3, c_3 \rangle \end{array}}{\tilde{\Gamma}; \mathcal{C} \vdash \text{foldr } (\lambda xy. \, M_1) \, M_2 \, M_3 \Downarrow^A \mathcal{C}_3; \langle \tilde{v}_3, c_1 + c_3 \rangle}$$

Fig. 5: Selected rules of the Annotated Clairvoyance Semantics. $\text{FV}(M)$ denotes the set of free variables in M.

constructor, or to skip the evaluation and produce $\bot$. Forcing a thunk is simply accessing the evaluated value in the thunk. The evaluation of force N fails if the computation of N is skipped. The evaluation cost tracked and output by the semantics varies with the nondeterministic choices made during the evaluation. For a given term and environment, if the output is nonempty, the minimal cost for the same value corresponds to the call-by-need cost.

4.2   A Cost Annotated Variant of the Clairvoyance Semantics

We define a cost-annotated variant of the Clairvoyance Semantics, similar to the Memorist Semantics, except that there are no usage sets. We define values as

$$\tilde{v} ::= \text{true} \mid \text{false} \mid \text{nil} \mid \text{cons } \tilde{v}_1 \, \tilde{v}_2 \mid \text{th}_i \, \tilde{v} \mid \bot$$

Values of the thunk type T now take two forms: an evaluated thunk, $\text{th}_i \, v$, with a unique name $i \in \mathbb{N}$, or a skipped computation $\bot$.

Evaluations occur in an environment $\tilde{\Gamma} ::= \emptyset \mid \tilde{\Gamma}, x \mapsto \tilde{v}$ and a cost annotation context $\mathcal{C} ::= \emptyset \mid \mathcal{C}, i \mapsto c_i$ that maps thunk names to their annotations. The semantics is defined by evaluation judgements of the form $\tilde{\Gamma}; \mathcal{C} \vdash M \Downarrow^A \mathcal{C}'; \langle \tilde{v}, c \rangle$. It states that a well-typed term M is evaluated in an environment $\tilde{\Gamma}$ and a cost annotation context $\mathcal{C}$ to the value $\tilde{v}$ with a cost annotation c and a cost annotation context $\mathcal{C}'$. Most semantic rules are similar to those of the Memorist Semantics sans the tracking of thunk usage with sets. We show some of the rules in Fig. 5. The main difference resides in the evaluation of lazy and foldr, where thunks are created. Under Clairvoyance Semantics, the evaluation non-deterministically evaluates the term (EALAZY and EAFOLDRCONS) or skips it (EALAZYSKIP and EAFOLDRCONSSKIP). Forcing a term by force M only succeeds if M evaluates to an evaluated thunk, and fails otherwise.

Basic properties. An Annotated Clairvoyance evaluation may extend the cost annotation context but never modifies the existing annotations.

Lemma 3 (Evaluation only extends cost annotation context). *If $\tilde{\Gamma}; \mathcal{C} \vdash M \Downarrow^A \mathcal{C}'; \langle \tilde{v}, c \rangle$, then $\forall i \in \mathrm{dom}(\mathcal{C}), \mathcal{C}'(i) = \mathcal{C}(i)$.*

We analogously define validity of cost annotation contexts and show it is preserved by evaluation. We consider only such valid contexts in subsequent proofs.

Definition 2 (Valid cost annotation context). *A cost annotation context $\mathcal{C}$ is valid for a value $\tilde{v}$, if any name i assigned to a thunk nested inside $\tilde{v}$ is in $\mathrm{dom}(\mathcal{C})$. $\mathcal{C}$ is valid for an environment $\tilde{\Gamma}$ if $\forall x \in \mathrm{dom}(\tilde{\Gamma})$, $\mathcal{C}$ is valid for $\tilde{\Gamma}(x)$.*

Lemma 4 (Evaluation preserves cost annotation context validity). *If $\tilde{\Gamma}; \mathcal{C} \vdash M \Downarrow^A \mathcal{C}'; \langle \tilde{v}, c \rangle$ and $\mathcal{C}$ is valid for $\tilde{\Gamma}$, then $\mathcal{C}'$ is valid for $\tilde{\Gamma}$ and for $\tilde{v}$.*

Clairvoyance evaluation cost. The total evaluation cost can be recovered by adding up the cost annotations given to the thunks created during this evaluation, plus the cost annotation given to the output value. We define the following operation to sum over cost annotations from a cost annotation context $\mathcal{C}$:

$$\mathrm{sumcost}_A(\mathcal{C}) := \sum_{i \in \mathrm{dom}(\mathcal{C})} \mathcal{C}(i)$$

For an evaluation $\tilde{\Gamma}; \mathcal{C} \vdash M \Downarrow^A \mathcal{C}'; \langle \tilde{v}, c \rangle$, the cost incurred by the evaluation can be computed by $c + \mathrm{sumcost}_A(\mathcal{C}' \setminus \mathcal{C})$.

Correspondence between the two Clairvoyance Semantics. We define a correspondence between values and between environments of the two semantics.

Definition 3 (Corresponding Clairvoyance values and environments). *Let $\tilde{v}$ and $\hat{v}$ be values of the Annotated and of the monadic Clairvoyance Semantics respectively. They are corresponding values modulo names, denoted $\tilde{v} \sim \hat{v}$, if the rules below apply. The relation extends to environments naturally.*

$$\frac{t \in \{\mathrm{true}, \mathrm{false}, \mathrm{nil}, \bot\}}{t \sim t} \qquad \frac{\tilde{v}_1 \sim \hat{v}_1 \quad \tilde{v}_2 \sim \hat{v}_2}{\mathrm{cons}\ \tilde{v}_1\ \tilde{v}_2 \sim \mathrm{cons}\ \hat{v}_1\ \hat{v}_2} \qquad \frac{\tilde{v} \sim \hat{v}}{\mathrm{th}_i\ \tilde{v} \sim \mathrm{th}\ \hat{v}}$$

If $\tilde{v} \sim \hat{v}$, then $\hat{v}$ can be regarded as abstracting away the name from $\tilde{v}$. Furthermore, a value $\hat{v}$ in the monadic Clairvoyance Semantics corresponds to an infinite set of values $\tilde{v}$ in the Annotated Semantics that are all structurally the same but with different names to thunks, if the values have thunks nested inside.

The theorems below establish the soundness and completeness together with cost equality. We consider the evaluation of a well-typed term $\gamma : M \vdash A$.

Theorem 1 (Soundness of the Annotated Clairvoyance Semantics wrt the monadic Clairvoyance Semantics). *Let $\tilde{\Gamma}; \mathcal{C} \vdash M \Downarrow^A \mathcal{C}'; \langle \tilde{v}, c \rangle$, with the cost annotation context $\mathcal{C}$ valid for $\tilde{\Gamma}$. Then for all $\hat{\Gamma} \in [\![\gamma]\!]$ with $\tilde{\Gamma} \sim \hat{\Gamma}$, there exists $(\hat{v}, c') \in [\![M]\!](\hat{\Gamma})$, such that $\tilde{v} \sim \hat{v}$ and $c + \mathrm{sumcost}_A(\mathcal{C}' \setminus \mathcal{C}) = c'$.*

Theorem 2 (Completeness of the Annotated Clairvoyance Semantics wrt the monadic Clairvoyance Semantics). *Let $\hat{\Gamma} \in [\![\gamma]\!]$ with $\tilde{\Gamma} \sim \hat{\Gamma}$ and let $\mathcal{C}$ be a cost annotation context valid for $\tilde{\Gamma}$. Then for all $(\hat{v}, c) \in [\![M]\!](\hat{\Gamma})$, there is an evaluation $\tilde{\Gamma}; \mathcal{C} \vdash M \Downarrow^A \mathcal{C}'; \langle \tilde{v}, c' \rangle$ with $\tilde{v} \sim \hat{v}$ and $c' + \mathrm{sumcost}_A(\mathcal{C}' \setminus \mathcal{C}) = c$.*

4.3 The Memorist and the Annotated Clairvoyance Semantics

Clairvoyance evaluation can make nondeterministic choices that are more eager than necessary. Thus in principle, to show that the Memorist Semantics corresponds to the lazy semantics, we need to *choose* the right nondeterministic branch of Clairvoyance evaluation for a given demand, which is difficult to do directly. Instead, we take an approach inspired by [42]. We prove that the cost inferred from the Memorist Semantics is no larger than any nondeterministic branch of a corresponding Clairvoyance evaluation, and that there is always a Clairvoyance branch producing the same cost.

However, there is still a problem. The Memorist Semantics provides a summary of all individual pieces of information at the end of evaluation. When a thunk is created, it is not known whether it would be eventually used in the Memorist evaluation, yet it is already evaluated or skipped in a corresponding Clairvoyance evaluation. Therefore, we cannot simply compare the evaluation cost step by step. To address this, we prove first that the thunk usage tracked by the Memorist Semantics correctly captures the lazy behaviour. We show that the inferred thunk usage is *minimal* in that it never gives more thunks than actually evaluated in a corresponding Clairvoyance evaluation, and it is *sufficient* in that there is some corresponding Clairvoyance evaluation evaluating exactly those thunks as inferred. From these we can derive the cost correctness.

Corresponding thunks in Memorist and Annotated Clairvoyance Semantics may have different names. Thus, we define renaming functions of type $\mathcal{N}_A \to \mathcal{N}_M$ mapping Annotated Clairvoyance thunk names $\mathcal{N}_A \subset \mathbb{N}$ to Memorist thunk names $\mathcal{N}_M \subset \mathbb{N}$. Since the Memorist evaluation is always eager, it never evaluates less than the corresponding Clairvoyance evaluation. Hence, thunk renaming functions are always total. We define a notion of validity for renaming functions to ensure that the names in the domains and images are indeed names assigned in the respective evaluation. We also require renaming functions to be injective so that two names, if related under such a function, are uniquely related.

Definition 4 (Validity of renaming functions). *A renaming function $f :$ $\mathcal{N}_A \to \mathcal{N}_M$ is* valid *with respect to some valid annotation context $\mathcal{A}$ and valid cost annotation context $\mathcal{C}$ if f is injective, $\mathrm{dom}(f) = \mathrm{dom}(\mathcal{C})$ and $\mathrm{im}(f) \subseteq \mathrm{dom}(\mathcal{A})$.*

4.4 Functional and Cost Correctness of Memorist Semantics

We define a relation $\tilde{v} \sim_f v$ on an annotated Clairvoyance value $\tilde{v}$ and a Memorist value v, parametrized by a renaming function $f : \mathcal{N}_A \to \mathcal{N}_M$.

Definition 5 (Value-name and environment-name correspondence). *Given a renaming function f as above, the value-name correspondence $\tilde{v} \sim_f v$ is defined inductively by the rules below. The environment-name correspondence $\tilde{\Gamma} \sim_f \Gamma$ for an Annotated Clairvoyance environment $\tilde{\Gamma}$ and a Memorist environment Γ holds if $\mathrm{dom}(\tilde{\Gamma}) = \mathrm{dom}(\Gamma)$ and $\forall x \in \mathrm{dom}(\Gamma), \tilde{\Gamma}(x) \sim_f \Gamma(x)$.*

$$\frac{t \in \{\mathrm{true}, \mathrm{false}, \mathrm{nil}\}}{t \sim_f t} \qquad \frac{\tilde{v}_1 \sim_f v_1 \quad \tilde{v}_2 \sim_f v_2}{\mathrm{cons}\, \tilde{v}_1\, \tilde{v}_2 \sim_f \mathrm{cons}\, v_1\, v_2} \qquad \frac{\tilde{v} \sim_f v \quad f(i) = j}{\mathrm{th}_i\, \tilde{v} \sim_f \mathrm{th}_j\, v} \qquad \frac{i \in \mathcal{N}_M}{\bot \sim_f \mathrm{th}_i\, v}$$

The relation $\sim_f$ describes the partial correspondence on values/environments and names between the two semantics. Given two environments related by $\sim_f$ where f is valid, a Memorist evaluation and an Annotated Clairvoyance evaluation of the same term produce $\sim_f$-related values, and the extended renaming function remains valid. Validity of the renaming functions ensure that each evaluated thunk in the Clairvoyance evaluation corresponds to a unique thunk from the Memorist evaluation. We also define a thunkwise cost correspondence:

Definition 6 (Thunkwise cost correspodence). *Let f be a valid thunk renaming function with respect to an annotation context $\mathcal{A}$ and a cost annotation context $\mathcal{C}$. $\mathcal{A}$ is* thunkwise cost corresponded *with $\mathcal{C}$ under f, denoted $\mathcal{A} \dot{\sim}_f \mathcal{C}$, if $\forall i \in \mathrm{dom}(\mathcal{C}), \mathcal{C}(i) = \pi_1(\mathcal{A}(f(i)))$.*

The theorem below states that, for each thunk evaluated in a Clairvoyance evaluation, there is a corresponding thunk in the Memorist evaluation with equal cost annotation. Intuitively, the cost annotation to a thunk is not associated with evaluating other thunks, and thus must be the same across the two semantics.

Theorem 3 (Functional and cost annotation correctness). *Let $\Gamma; \mathcal{A} \vdash M \Downarrow \mathcal{A}'; \langle v, (c, s) \rangle$ and $\tilde{\Gamma}; \mathcal{C} \vdash M \Downarrow^A \mathcal{C}'; \langle \tilde{v}, c' \rangle$, and f be a valid renaming function wrt $\mathcal{A}$ and $\mathcal{C}$. If $\tilde{\Gamma} \sim_f \Gamma$ and $\mathcal{A} \dot{\sim}_f \mathcal{C}$, then $\tilde{v} \sim_{f'} v$, $c = c'$ and $\mathcal{C}' \dot{\sim}_{f'} \mathcal{A}'$, for some f' extending f and valid wrt $\mathcal{A}'$ and $\mathcal{C}'$.*

Deriving usage from demand. Lazy evaluation is driven by demand which cannot always be determined locally. In Memorist Semantics, we consider such demand via usage sets. As discussed previously, if more than the outermost portion of a value is demanded, we collect all the demanded thunks in the value, along with thunks in the usage sets annotated to them and to the final output.

Since we do not generally know the exact names given to thunks from the outset, we need a way to abstract away from names when representing demand. For the current proof, the partially evaluated values in the monadic Clairvoyance Semantics in Section 4.1 provides a convenient way. We refer to them as *thunk-nameless partial values* below, and relate them with Memorist values as follows.

Definition 7 (Partial evaluatedness). *A thunk-nameless partial value $\hat{v}$ is a partially evaluated version of a Memorist value v of the same type, denoted $\hat{v} \preccurlyeq v$, if the rules below apply. The relation extends naturally to environments.*

$$\frac{t \in \{\text{true}, \text{false}, \text{nil}\}}{t \preccurlyeq t} \qquad \frac{\hat{v}_1 \preccurlyeq v_1 \quad \hat{v}_2 \preccurlyeq v_2}{\text{cons}\,\hat{v}_1\,\hat{v}_2 \preccurlyeq \text{cons}\,v_1\,v_2} \qquad \frac{\hat{v} \preccurlyeq v}{\text{th}\,\hat{v} \preccurlyeq \text{th}_i\,v} \qquad \frac{}{\bot \preccurlyeq \text{th}_i\,v}$$

We use $\hat{v}$ with $\hat{v} \preccurlyeq v$ to represent a demand on a Memorist value v. The following relation characterizes the set of names of all thunks needed given such a demand.

Definition 8 (Usage representation sets). *Given values v and $\hat{v}$ with $\hat{v} \preccurlyeq v$ and a valid annotation context $\mathcal{A}$. $\text{Repr}_{\mathcal{A}}(v, \hat{v}, s)$ if the rules below apply.*

$$\frac{t \in \{\text{true}, \text{false}, \text{nil}\}}{\text{Repr}_{\mathcal{A}}(t, t, \emptyset)} \qquad \frac{\text{Repr}_{\mathcal{A}}(v_1, \hat{v}_1, s_1) \quad \text{Repr}_{\mathcal{A}}(v_2, \hat{v}_2, s_2)}{\text{Repr}_{\mathcal{A}}(\text{cons}\,v_1\,v_2, \text{cons}\,\hat{v}_1\,\hat{v}_2, s_1 \cup s_2)}$$

$$\frac{}{\text{Repr}_{\mathcal{A}}(\text{th}_i\,v, \bot, \emptyset)} \qquad \frac{\text{Repr}_{\mathcal{A}}(v, \hat{v}, s)}{\text{Repr}_{\mathcal{A}}(\text{th}_i\,v, \text{th}\,\hat{v}, \{i\} \cup s \cup \pi_2(\mathcal{A}(i)))}$$

The relation extends to environments: given a Memorist environment Γ and a thunk-nameless partial environment $\hat{\Gamma}$ with $\hat{\Gamma} \preccurlyeq \Gamma$, $\text{Repr}_{\mathcal{A}}(\Gamma, \hat{\Gamma}, s')$ if $s' = \bigcup_{x \in \text{dom}(\Gamma)} \{i \in s_0 \mid \text{Repr}_{\mathcal{A}}(\Gamma(x), \hat{\Gamma}(x), s_0)\}$. Let (c, s_1) be the annotation given to v. We call the set $s \cup s_1$ the usage representation set *for the demand $\hat{v}$ on v.*

Lemma 5. *Let v and $\hat{v}$ be a Memorist value and a thunk-nameless partial value $\hat{v}$ respectively, of the same type. Let $\mathcal{A}$ be a valid annotation context for v. We have $\hat{v} \preccurlyeq v$ if and only if there is a set s of thunk names with $\text{Repr}_{\mathcal{A}}(v, \hat{v}, s)$. The same holds for environments in both directions.*

Usage minimality. We now prove that the usage representation set inferred from the Memorist Semantics is minimal. Specifically, we show that every name in such a usage representation set always corresponds to the name of an evaluated thunk in a corresponding successful Clairvoyance evaluation after renaming.

We can immediately make one observation. If the above minimality holds, then for every Memorist thunk j corresponding to an evaluated Clairvoyance thunk under a thunk renaming function f, its usage set annotation must be included in the image of f, $\text{im}(f)$, that captures all Memorist thunks corresponding to some evaluated Clairvoyance thunks. This is desired; otherwise we would have discovered a Memorist thunk inferred to be needed whereas a successful Clairvoyance evaluation did not evaluate the thunk, failing the minimality.

Definition 9 (Thunkwise usage minimal). *An annotation context $\mathcal{A}$ is thunkwise usage minimal with respect to a cost annotation context $\mathcal{C}$ under a valid thunk renaming function f, denoted $\mathcal{A} \Subset_f \mathcal{C}$, if $\forall i \in \mathrm{dom}(\mathcal{C})$, we have $\pi_2(\mathcal{A}(f(i))) \subseteq \mathrm{im}(f)$.*

The validity of f ensures that $i \in \mathrm{dom}(f)$ and $f(i) \in \mathrm{dom}(\mathcal{A})$. The following lemma states that any two corresponding evaluations of some well-typed term M preserve the thunkwise usage minimality.

Lemma 6 (Thunkwise usage minimality). *Let $\Gamma; \mathcal{A} \vdash M \Downarrow \mathcal{A}'; \langle v, (c, s)\rangle$ and $\tilde{\Gamma}; \mathcal{C} \vdash M \Downarrow^A \mathcal{C}'; \langle \tilde{v}, c'\rangle$. If $\tilde{\Gamma} \sim_f \Gamma$, $\mathcal{A} \dot{\sim}_f \mathcal{C}$ and $\mathcal{A} \Subset_f \mathcal{C}$ for some valid thunk renaming function f, then $\mathcal{A}' \Subset_{f'} \mathcal{C}'$ and $s \subseteq \mathrm{im}(f')$ for a valid f' extending f.*

From here we can establish the desired usage minimality, generalizing to the usage representation set with respect to an arbitrary demand on the output value. The notation $f[\cdot]$ denotes the image of a set under some function f.

Theorem 4 (Usage minimality). *Let $\Gamma; \mathcal{A} \vdash M \Downarrow \mathcal{A}'; \langle v, (c, s)\rangle$ and $\tilde{\Gamma}; \mathcal{C} \vdash M \Downarrow^A \mathcal{C}'; \langle \tilde{v}, c'\rangle$, with $\tilde{\Gamma} \sim_f \Gamma$, $\mathcal{A} \dot{\sim}_f \mathcal{C}$ and $\mathcal{A} \Subset_f \mathcal{C}$ for some valid f. Given any thunk-nameless $\hat{v}$ with $\tilde{v} \sim \hat{v}$ and $\mathrm{Repr}_{\mathcal{A}'}(v, \hat{v}, s')$ for some s', we have $s \cup s' \subseteq f'[\mathrm{dom}(\mathcal{C}')]$ and $(s \cup s') \setminus \mathrm{dom}(\mathcal{A}) \subseteq f'[\mathrm{dom}(\mathcal{C}' \setminus \mathcal{C})]$ for a valid f' extending f.*

The conclusion stated with set difference allows us to exclude thunks that already exist prior to this evaluation. In short, the theorem states that thunks captured by $(s \cup s') \setminus \mathrm{dom}(\mathcal{A})$, i.e., all thunks created during the evaluation and inferred to be needed by the Memorist Semantics, always correspond (under thunk renaming f') to a subset of all thunks evaluated on any successful branch in the corresponding Clairvoyance evaluation as captured by $\mathrm{dom}(\mathcal{C}' \setminus \mathcal{C})$. That is, a corresponding Clairvoyance evaluation can never evaluate fewer thunks.

Usage sufficiency. Usage minimality essentially states that the inferred usage is "not too big". Next, we prove it is "not too small" either: for any Memorist evaluation and some demand, there is a corresponding Annotated Clairvoyance evaluation evaluating exactly what is inferred to be needed by the former.

In general, we cannot assert there is always a successful Clairvoyance evaluation of a well-typed term given an arbitrary environment $\tilde{\Gamma}$: *e.g.*, evaluating $\mathtt{force}\,x$ in an environment $\tilde{\Gamma}$ with $\tilde{\Gamma}(x) = \bot$ can never succeed. To address this, we utilize the usage representation set to characterize a minimal environment. We have shown that every thunk in this set must be evaluated in all corresponding successful Clairvoyance evaluation. It remains a question whether it might be "too minimal" and miss some thunks that should have been evaluated, though it does not matter for now since we only rely on it to set a lower bound on how less evaluated the Clairvoyance environment can be.

Given the union of a usage representation set and the output usage annotation set, if we take the intersection of this union and the domain of the initial annotation context $\mathcal{A}$, the resulting set s should contain all existing thunks inferred to be needed by the evaluation. From s we can construct a partial environment $\hat{\Gamma}$ satisfying $\mathrm{Repr}_{\mathcal{A}}(\Gamma, \hat{\Gamma}, s)$ to use as the "minimal" environment. We then consider any Clairvoyance environment no less evaluated than $\hat{\Gamma}$.

Definition 10 (No less evaluated values and environments). *An Annotated Clairvoyance $\tilde{v}$ is no less evaluated than a thunk-nameless partial value $\hat{v}$ of the same type, denoted $\hat{v} \lesssim \tilde{v}$, if the rules below apply.*

$$\frac{t \in \{\text{true}, \text{false}, \text{nil}\}}{t \lesssim t} \qquad \frac{\hat{v}_1 \lesssim \tilde{v}_1 \quad \hat{v}_2 \lesssim \tilde{v}_2}{\text{cons}\,\hat{v}_1\,\hat{v}_2 \lesssim \text{cons}\,\tilde{v}_1\,\tilde{v}_2} \qquad \frac{\hat{v} \lesssim \tilde{v}}{\text{th}\,\hat{v} \lesssim \text{th}_i\,\tilde{v}} \qquad \frac{}{\bot \lesssim \text{th}_i\,\tilde{v}}$$

The relation extends to environments naturally: let $\tilde{\Gamma}$ and $\hat{\Gamma}$ be an Annotated Clairvoyance environment and a thunk-nameless environment respectively, defined on the same typing context. $\hat{\Gamma} \lesssim \tilde{\Gamma}$ if $\forall x \in \text{dom}(\hat{\Gamma})$, $\hat{\Gamma}(x) \lesssim \tilde{\Gamma}(x)$.

Below we consider a well-typed term $\gamma \vdash M : A$.

Theorem 5 (Usage sufficiency). *Let $\Gamma; \mathcal{A} \vdash M \Downarrow \mathcal{A}'; \langle v, (c, s) \rangle$ with $\mathcal{A}$ valid for Γ. Let $\hat{v} \in [\![A]\!]$ with $\text{Repr}_{\mathcal{A}'}(v, \hat{v}, s')$ for some s'. There is some $\hat{\Gamma} \in [\![\gamma]\!]$ with $\text{Repr}_{\mathcal{A}}(\Gamma, \hat{\Gamma}, (s \cup s') \cap \text{dom}(\mathcal{A}))$, such that for all Annotated Clairvoyance environment $\tilde{\Gamma}$ with $\hat{\Gamma} \lesssim \tilde{\Gamma}$, a valid cost annotation context $\mathcal{C}$ for $\tilde{\Gamma}$ and a valid thunk renaming function f with $\tilde{\Gamma} \sim_f \Gamma$, if $f, \mathcal{A}$ and $\mathcal{C}$ satisfy the assumptions in Theorem 4, then there is some $\tilde{\Gamma}; \mathcal{C} \vdash M \Downarrow^A \mathcal{C}'; \langle \tilde{v}, c' \rangle$ with $\hat{v} \lesssim \tilde{v}$ and $(s \cup s') \setminus \text{dom}(\mathcal{A}) = f'[\text{dom}(\mathcal{C}' \setminus \mathcal{C})]$, for a valid f' extending f.*

The theorem states that, given a Memorist evaluation with some demand, we can always construct a corresponding Clairvoyance evaluation, such that all the thunks in the Memorist evaluation inferred to be needed (as captured by $(s \cup s') \setminus \text{dom}(\mathcal{A})$) coincide with all the thunks evaluated during the corresponding Clairvoyance evaluation (as captured by $\text{dom}(\mathcal{C}' \setminus \mathcal{C})$), after thunk renaming. In other words, there is always a corresponding Clairvoyance evaluation that evaluates exactly as per the inferred usage from the Memorist evaluation.

Together, Theorems 4 and 5 imply that the inferred thunk usage from the Memorist Semantics is minimal but nontrivial. It represents exactly what is evaluated on the laziest branch in a corresponding Clairvoyance evaluation.

4.5   Lazy Cost Correspondence

In the Memorist Semantics, lazy evaluation cost is derived based on the inferred thunk usage and the annotated cost. We have shown that the cost annotations are correct (Theorem 3), and so is the inferred thunk usage (Theorems 4 and 5). Consequently, the derived cost coincides with the evaluation cost of the laziest possible Clairvoyance evaluation. Below consider a well-typed term $\gamma \vdash M : A$.

Theorem 6 (Cost minimality). *Let $\Gamma; \mathcal{A} \vdash M \Downarrow \mathcal{A}'; \langle v, (c, s) \rangle$ and $\tilde{\Gamma}; \mathcal{C} \vdash M \Downarrow^A \mathcal{C}'; \langle \tilde{v}, c' \rangle$, with $\tilde{\Gamma} \sim_f \Gamma$, $\mathcal{A} \dot{\sim}_f \mathcal{C}$ and $\mathcal{A} \Subset_f \mathcal{C}$ for some valid thunk renaming function f. Given any thunk-nameless value $\hat{v}$ with $\tilde{v} \sim \hat{v}$ and $\text{Repr}_{\mathcal{A}'}(v, \hat{v}, s')$ for some s', we have $c + \text{sumcost}_M(\mathcal{A}' \setminus \mathcal{A}, s \cup s') \leq c' + \text{sumcost}_A(\mathcal{C}' \setminus \mathcal{C})$.*

Theorem 7 (Cost existence). *Let $\Gamma; \mathcal{A} \vdash M \Downarrow \mathcal{A}'; \langle v, (c, s) \rangle$ with $\mathcal{A}$ a valid annotation context for Γ. Let $\hat{v} \in [\![A]\!]$ with $\text{Repr}_{\mathcal{A}'}(v, \hat{v}, s')$ for some s'. There is* *some $\hat{\Gamma} \in [\![\gamma]\!]$ with $\mathrm{Repr}_{\mathcal{A}}(\Gamma, \hat{\Gamma}, (s \cup s') \cap \mathrm{dom}(\mathcal{A}))$, such that for all Annotated Clairvoyance environment $\tilde{\Gamma}$ with $\hat{\Gamma} \lesssim \tilde{\Gamma}$, a valid cost annotation context $\mathcal{C}$ for $\tilde{\Gamma}$ and a valid thunk renaming function f with $\tilde{\Gamma} \sim_f \Gamma$, if $f, \mathcal{A}$ and $\mathcal{C}$ satisfy the assumptions in Theorem 4, then there is some $\tilde{\Gamma}; \mathcal{C} \vdash M \Downarrow^A \mathcal{C}'; \langle \tilde{v}, c' \rangle$ with $\hat{v} \lesssim \tilde{v}$, and $c + \mathrm{sumcost}_M(\mathcal{A}' \setminus \mathcal{A}, s \cup s') = c' + \mathrm{sumcost}_A(\mathcal{C}' \setminus \mathcal{C})$.*

The two theorems state that the derived lazy cost from the Memorist evaluation is no larger than the cost incurred by any corresponding Clairvoyance evaluation and equal to the cost by some corresponding Clairvoyance evaluation. Thus, the Memorist Semantics derives the correct lazy evaluation cost.

5   Implementation

We provide a proof of concept implementation of the Memorist Semantics in Rocq. Our implementation uses shallow embedding and encapsulates all the operations over thunks and annotations using a simple monadic interface. We model named thunks using the `Th` type below, and represent an annotation as a pair of a natural number (`nat`) and a finite set of natural numbers (`NatSet`).

```
Record Th (A : Type) : Type := MkTh {name: nat; val: A}.
Definition Annot : Type := nat * NatSet.
```

We implement the Memorist evaluation using a monad `M`, encapsulating the manipulations of thunks and the accumulation of cost:

```
Record Result (A : Type) : Type := MkRes {val: A; annot: Annot; cont: AC}.
Definition M (A : Type) : Type := AC -> Result A.
```

It represents the evaluation of an expression in an annotation context (`AC`), encoded using an association list, to a result (`Result`). The result is a record containing the value (`val`), the output annotation (`annot`), and the final annotation context (`cont`). The monad `M` is essentially a generalized state monad, also known as an *update monad* [1]. All operations over thunks and annotations can be encapsulated using a few combinators of the monad `M`, shown in Fig. 6. Apart from the standard `ret` and `bind`, we also define `lazy` to wrap the value in `M` with a thunk, `forcing` and `force` to unwrap thunks, and `tick` to increment cost. The set of combinators is the same as that of the Clairvoyance Monad [26].

To analyse a program, we can use the operational semantics in Fig. 4 as a recipe to translate a pure program to a monadic program that *reifies* the cost. Let's consider the example in Section 2. We need to encode `lists` first:

```
Inductive ListT (A : Type) : Type :=
  NilT : ListT A | ConsT : Th A -> Th (ListT A) -> ListT A.
```

We show the translations in Fig. 7. The structure of the translated program follows the original one closely. Whenever the value inside a thunk is accessed, the thunk needs to be unwrapped first via forcing (`$!`). We separate the translation of `append` into a top-level `appendM` and an auxiliary `appendM_` (similar for `truePrefix`) so they can pass Rocq's termination checker directly. We put a `tick` at the start

```
Definition ret {A} (x : A) : M A := fun ac => MkRes x (0,emptyset) ac.
Definition bind {A B} (m : M A) (f : A -> M B) : M B := fun ac =>
  let 'MkRes x a1 ac1 := m ac in let 'MkRes y a2 ac2 := (f x) ac1 in
  MkRes y (fst a1 + fst a2, snd a1 ∪ snd a2) ac2.
Notation "x >> y" := (bind x (fun _ => y)).

Definition lazy {A} (m : M A) : M (Th A) := fun ac =>
  let 'MkRes x a ac1 := m ac in
  MkRes (MkTh (nextIdx ac1) x) (0,emptyset) (ext ac1 a).
Notation "'lazyLetM' x := y 'in' z" := (bind (lazy y) (fun x => z)).

Definition collect (i : nat) : M unit := fun ac =>
  MkRes tt (0, mapSu ac i) ac.

Definition forcing {A B} (th : Th A) (f : A -> M B) : M B :=
  match th with MkTh i v => collect i >> f v end.
Notation "f $! x" := (forcing x f).
Definition force {A} (th : Th A) : M A := forcing th ret.

Definition tick : M unit := fun ac => MkRes tt (1,emptyset) ac.
```

Fig. 6: Definitions of the monadic combinators for M, omitting level and associativity declarations for notations. The expression nextIdx ac returns a name not in the domain of the annotation context ac, and ext ac a extends ac by mapping the next new name to an annotation a. The expression mapSu ac i maps a thunk name i to a set containing i and the names in i's usage set annotation under ac.

```
Fixpoint appendM_ {A}                    Fixpoint truePrefixM_ (xs: ListT bool)
  (xs : ListT A) (ys : Th (ListT A))       : M (ListT bool) := tick >>
  : M (ListT A) := tick >>                 match xs with
  match xs with                            | NilT => ret NilT
  | NilT => force ys                       | ConsT y ys =>
  | ConsT x xs' =>                             lazyLetM zs:= truePrefixM_ $! ys
    lazyLetM zs := forcing xs'                 in forcing y (fun y_ =>
      (fun xs_ => appendM_ xs_ ys)               if y_ then ret (ConsT y zs)
    in ret (ConsT x zs)                          else ret NilT)
  end.                                     end.

Definition appendM {A}                   Definition truePrefixM
  (xs ys : Th (ListT A))                    (xs : Th (ListT bool))
  : M (ListT A) :=                          : M (ListT bool) :=
  (fun xs_ => appendM_ xs_ ys) $! xs        truePrefixM_ $! xs.
```

```
Definition truePrefixAppendM (xs ys: Th (ListT bool)) : M (ListT bool) :=
  tick >> lazyLetM zs := appendM xs ys in truePrefixM zs.
```

Fig. 7: Translation of the functions append, truePrefix and truePrefixAppend

of each call to increment cost by one, though not in the top-level `appendM` and `truePrefixM` as they are simply unwrapping the thunks around the arguments.

We are interested in the lazy cost with respect to the length of a list demanded; accordingly, we define the following functions to collect needed thunks.

```
Fixpoint usageL_ (ac : AC) {A} (xs : ListT A) (n : nat) : NatSet :=
  match xs, n with
  | ConsT (MkTh i x) (MkTh j xs'), S n' =>
      mapSu ac i ∪ mapSu ac j ∪ usageL_ ac xs' n'
  | _, _ => emptyset
  end.
Definition usageL {A} (r : Result (ListT A)) (n : nat) : NatSet :=
  usageL_ (cont r) (val r) n.
```

Here n is the number of thunked cons cells demanded in the output list. The notation `mapSu ac i` maps the thunk name i to a set containing i and names of thunks in its usage set annotation. In general, different usage collection functions need to be defined for other datatypes and demands.

The following function captures the lazy cost derivation described in Section 3, where s is the usage representation set collected using *e.g.*, `usageL`. The expression `dom ac` gives the domain of the annotation context ac as a `NatSet`, and `sumcost` sums over the cost annotated to the thunks in the given set.

```
Definition infcost {A} (r : Result A) (s : NatSet) (ac : AC) : nat :=
  sumcost (cont r) (diff (snd (annot r) ∪ s) (dom ac)) + fst (annot r)
```

Now consider the example program, `truePrefixAppend [true;false] [true]`. We can obtain the concrete cost by running the translated program and applying `infcost` to the result. The input may be from some previous computation or from lifting some pure lists. Suppose we have

```
MkTh 4 (ConsT (MkTh 3 true) (MkTh 2 (ConsT (MkTh 1 false) (MkTh 0 NilT))))
MkTh 7 (ConsT (MkTh 6 true) (MkTh 5 NilT))
```

Below we refer to them as tl1 and tl2, and the annotation context at this stage as ac. To infer cost, we apply `infcost` on the result and the usage representation set for some demand. As before, we consider two demands on the same output: one only to WHNF, *i.e.*, 0 cons cells, and the other demanding one more.

```
Compute let r := truePrefixAppendM tl1 tl2 ac in
        let cost0 := infcost r (usageL r 0) ac in
        let cost1 := infcost r (usageL r 1) ac in (cost0, cost1).
```

The above computes to $(3,5)$, *i.e.*, the lazy cost is 3 with respect to the first demand and 5 with respect to the second. Tracking localized cost and usage information along computations enables the derivation of cost via program execution. This stands in contrast to Clairvoyance Monad where we cannot execute programs for cost but only to verify user-provided cost specifications. It also allows the Memorist Semantics to evaluate a program only once for analysing different demands in principle, as suggested by this presentation. In comparison, the Demand Semantics [42] must redo evaluation for each demand. We contemplate that such features may make the Memorist Semantics a suitable basis for developing a framework for testing, enabling more potential applications.

We can also prove specifications of lazy cost for these functions. For now, we focus on mechanically verifying user-provided specifications in Rocq. The first theorem below states that the lazy cost of `appendM` is linear in the length demanded from the output list and at most the size of the first input list, where size is measured using `sizeT` that counts the number of constructors in a list. The second states that the lazy cost of `truePrefixM` is linear in the length demanded from the output. The `ACOk` and `NameOk` premises ensures the existing thunk names and annotations are valid in the sense of Definition 1.

```
Theorem appendM_cost :
  forall ac {A} (txs tys : Th (ListT A)) n (r := appendM txs tys ac),
  ACOk ac -> NameOk txs ac -> NameOk tys ac -> n < sizeT (val r) ->
  infcost r (usageL r n) ac = min (n + 1) (sizeT (Th.val txs)).

Theorem truePrefixM_cost : forall ac txs n (r := truePrefixM txs ac),
  ACOk ac -> NameOk txs ac -> n < sizeT (val r) ->
  infcost r (usageL r n) ac = n + 1.
```

Directly using these theorems, we can prove the following that expresses the lazy cost of `truePrefixAppendM` in terms of that of `appendM` and `truePrefixAppendM`.

```
Theorem truePrefixAppendM_cost :
  forall ac txs tys n d (r := truePrefixAppendM txs tys ac),
  ACOk ac -> NameOk txs ac -> NameOk tys ac -> n < sizeT (val r) ->
  infcost r (usageL r n) ac = min (n+1) (sizeT (Th.val txs)) + (n+1) + 1.
```

Our experience with proving them suggests that more proof engineering improvements can be made in reasoning about usage sets. Nonetheless, our semantics offers the benefit of a simpler and more straightforward process, without the need of verifying two kinds of specifications using additional logic as in Clairvoyance Monad or dual translations for each function as in Demand Semantics.

6   Limitations

We choose to define and mechanize the Memorist Semantics based on the same source language as the Demand Semantics [42], because we are interested in defining a translation from a lazy functional language to Rocq in shallow embeddings. For this reason, we also inherit the same limitations of not covering first-class functions and general recursions.

First-class functions. The current mechanization does not account for first-class functions. This has the benefit of simplicity, since we need not handle closures, but excludes useful constructs like higher-order functions.

To show that the Memorist Semantics works for first-class functions, we additionally developed a pen-and-paper formalization of a heap-based Memorist

Semantics on an untyped λ-calculus similar to the approach of Launchbury [24] and Hackett and Hutton [14]. We demonstrate that the Memorist Semantics does support first-class functions in this version. We provide the pen-and-paper formalization and a proof of correctness in an extended version of this paper.[4]

We leave the mechanization of first-class functions to future work. Due to differences in the languages and the styles of the semantics, we anticipate challenges such as relating variables encoded as de Bruijn indices between the Memorist and Clairvoyance evaluations. The heap-based alternative version would require more explicit handling of index shifting. Moreover, Clairvoyance evaluations may skip let-bindings, potentially resulting in the same variable in the Clairvoyance and Memorist evaluations having different indices. Thus, we need to maintain another relations on indices intertwined with the shifting during proofs. In comparison, it is simpler to maintain thunk-renaming functions in the current mechanization, since Clairvoyance evaluations may only skip thunks in lazy or foldr but not let-bindings, and the thunk names are separate from variables and unchanged during evaluations.

General recursion. Focusing on total programs with structural recursion allows us to keep the semantics simple and shallow-embeddable in Rocq, whose specification language is total, but limits the semantics due to no support of general recursion. In practice, one potential way to simulate general recursion is to limit the number of steps with fuel. When analysing cost, we consider only programs that halt eventually when evaluated lazily, for which there must be fuel that is sufficient. Thus, it may be possible to extend the semantics to handle recursive lets by introducing fuel, allowing us to analyse for infinite data structures and general recursive programs if they compute within some fuel.

7   Related Work

The standard call-by-need semantics. Launchbury's Natural Semantics [24], the standard call-by-need operational semantics, captures demand-drivenness and sharing by storing expressions unevaluated in mutual heaps, evaluating them when needed, and modifying the heaps to memoize the results. However, due to its statefulness, the semantics is difficult to reason about.

Clairvoyance Semantics. The Clairvoyance Semantics [14] instead interprets call-by-need as call-by-value with nondeterministic choices of proceeding or skipping a computation. To adapt it for formally verifying lazy evaluation cost, the Clairvoyance Monad [26] uses a monad to model the nondeterminism and encapsulate cost accumulation, with an option over a *thunk* datatype representing nondeterministic choices. It has a simple interface and avoids the exponential explosion in cost analysis of the underlying semantics. However, it is non-executable, as the embedded programs lead to Rocq propositions as proof obligations. Moreover, an additional logic similar to Incorrectness Logic [33] has to be introduced to reason

---

[4] See `https://doi.org/10.5281/zenodo.18345004`

about nondeterminism. One must provide and prove two kinds of specifications: one for all nondeterministic evaluation branches that succeed in computation, and another for the existence of a more specific branch. In proofs, one often needs to select the correct nondeterministic branch manually. In comparison, the Memorist Semantics is deterministic and executable, and tracks all relevant information alongside the computation, although usage sets can be potentially challenging for formal reasoning in Rocq.

Demand Semantics. The Demand Semantics [42], adapted from [2] to a total and typed setting, is another approach to reason about demand and cost for lazily evaluated programs. It considers two kinds of demand: the externally given demand on the output, and the input demand describing how evaluated the input needs to be per the output demand. The semantics infers the minimum input demand from the output demand, by having a forward evaluation for obtaining fully evaluated output and a backward evaluation to infer the input demand from the output and the demand on it. Like our work, this semantics is deterministic, avoiding the complication of dealing with nondeterminism. However, it essentially has two separate semantics and requires translating a source program into two different versions, which results in code duplication and can be more error-prone. Moreover, the backward inference must always take a specific output demand as input. For the same output from a forward function with a different output demand, the semantics must redo the evaluation. In contrast, the Memorist Semantics tracks all necessary information during evaluation, which does not vary with output demand. Hence, analysis for the same function requires no re-evaluation even when different output demands are specified.

Formally verifying lazy evaluation cost. The monadic framework by [15] analyses computation cost of pure Haskell programs in Liquid Haskell [40], a proof assistant based on extending Haskell with refinement types. Nonstrictness is built into the relevant datatypes in the framework, while users must handle sharing explicitly by inserting a pay construct into code. This approach follows an earlier Agda library by [8] for verifying time cost bounds for lazy functional data structures using amortized analysis techniques from [34], and uses a monadic dependent *thunk* type with information about cost embedded at the type level.

Some recent efforts also focus on formally reasoning about the amortized cost of lazy functional data structures. The Iris$^\$$ framework [29] is used in [35] to verify the banker's queue, the physicist's queue, and the implicit queue in Rocq, via directly reasoning about mutable cells using the Iris separation logic [39]. The Demand Semantics is applied to formally reason about the amortized cost and persistence of the banker's queue and the implicit queue [42]. Proving the amortized cost of simple stacks, binomial heaps, and a variant of finger trees [6] has been done in Liquid Haskell, though in a non-lazy setting without sharing [4].

Analysing resource bounds for call-by-need programs. A strictness analysis based method by [37] mechanically analyses time cost bounds for call-by-need programs and generalizes to higher-order functions by introducing additional structures containing information about function applications and associated cost. A type-based analysis by [22] automatically infers linear cost bounds for call-by-need programs using Automatic Amortized Resource Analysis (AARA) introduced by [19] and employing the notion of prepaying to avoid duplicating shared cost, and extends to univariate polynomial bounds [30] based on the method by [18].

Resource analysis for strict languages. AARA initially deals with linearly-bounded heap space cost of first-order strict functional programs [19], and has been extended (*e.g.,* [18, 21, 17]), implemented in Resource Aware ML [16], and developed into a framework for certified automatic inference of resource bounds for low-level programs [5]. Another line of work analyses time complexity by extracting from programs the recurrence relations for cost [11, 10, 23, 7, 9].

Some recent efforts focus on unifying the analysis of call-by-value and call-by-name languages, though call-by-need is often not supported due to difficulties with modelling laziness. Along this line, the λ-amor framework [36] is a time complexity analysis framework based on amortization and affine types, which monadically simulates call-by-value with call-by-name. The dependently typed logical framework **calf** [32, 31] unifies the two via a call-by-push-value language [25], and has been extended to handle other computational effects by incorporating inequational reasoning into the framework's type theory [12].

On the verification side, the TiML language [41] has built-in support for verifying time complexity bounds of programs using its dependent and refinement types inspired type system, with users providing complexity bound specifications in type annotations. The Rocq library by [28] verifies time complexity by annotating information about cost in a monadic type. Formalizing the big-O notation and extending the Separation Logic, the framework by [13] verifies worst-case time complexity bounds for higher-order imperative programs in Rocq.

8   Conclusion and Future Work

We have presented the Memorist Semantics, a novel cost semantics for call-by-need evaluation that tracks thunk usage and computation cost in a deterministic manner. Our approach improves prior approaches by enabling cost analysis that evaluates independently of demand context, avoids code duplication, and provides fine-grained cost attribution to individual components of a term. Crucially, this semantics enables cost analysis of lazy programs that preserves the deterministic and compositional call-by-value evaluation structure, making it an intuitive practical foundation for further cost-aware program reasoning.

We have presented a proof of concept implementation in Rocq and verified cost of some functions. Apart from addressing the aforementioned limitations, we also plan to apply it on larger case studies, including verifying amortized cost of lazy functional data structures [34]. We would like to optimize the framework for easier use in practice, conduct quantitative experiments and benchmark against related frameworks. By formalizing our model in Rocq, we provide a rigorous basis for developing cost analysis frameworks for real-world lazy functional languages such as Haskell, and pave the way for future work on verifying compiler optimizations, *e.g.,* dead code elimination. In the future, we plan to investigate these applications and the utilization of tools such as `hs-to-coq` [38,3] to automatically translate Haskell code for analysis. Moreover, with an executable semantics, lazy cost can be inferred directly via program execution, and the same program only needs to be evaluated once for analysing various demands. Such features can potentially be helpful in property-based testing, another application area we plan to investigate in the future.

Acknowledgments. The first author is funded by Melbourne Research Scholarship. We thank Katherine Philip and Allison Naaktgeboren for their feedback to a draft of this paper.

Disclosure of Interests. The authors have no competing interests to declare that are relevant to the content of this article.

Data Availability Statement. The Rocq code accompanying this paper is openly available at `https://doi.org/10.5281/zenodo.18168558`.

References

1. Ahman, D., Uustalu, T.: Update monads: Cointerpreting directed containers. In: Matthes, R., Schubert, A. (eds.) 19th International Conference on Types for Proofs and Programs, TYPES 2013, April 22-26, 2013, Toulouse, France. LIPIcs, vol. 26, pp. 1–23. Schloss Dagstuhl - Leibniz-Zentrum für Informatik (2013). https://doi.org/10.4230/LIPICS.TYPES.2013.1, `https://doi.org/10.4230/LIPIcs.TYPES.2013.1`
2. Bjerner, B., Holmström, S.: A composition approach to time analysis of first order lazy functional programs. In: Proceedings of the fourth international conference on Functional programming languages and computer architecture - FPCA '89. pp. 157–165. FPCA '89, ACM Press (1989). https://doi.org/10.1145/99370.99382
3. Breitner, J., Spector-Zabusky, A., Li, Y., Rizkallah, C., Wiegley, J., Cohen, J.M., Weirich, S.: Ready, set, verify! applying `hs-to-coq` to real-world haskell code. J. Funct. Program. **31**, e5 (2021). https://doi.org/10.1017/S0956796820000283, `https://doi.org/10.1017/S0956796820000283`
4. van Brügge, J.: Liquid amortization: Proving amortized complexity with liquidhaskell (functional pearl). In: Vazou, N., Morris, J.G. (eds.) Proceedings of the 17th ACM SIGPLAN International Haskell Symposium, Haskell 2024, Milan, Italy, September 6-7, 2024. pp. 97–108. ACM (2024). https://doi.org/10.1145/3677999.3678282, `https://doi.org/10.1145/3677999.3678282`
5. Carbonneaux, Q., Hoffmann, J., Reps, T.W., Shao, Z.: Automated resource analysis with coq proof objects. In: Majumdar, R., Kuncak, V. (eds.) Computer Aided Verification - 29th International Conference, CAV 2017, Heidelberg, Germany, July 24-28, 2017, Proceedings, Part II. Lecture Notes in Computer Science, vol. 10427, pp. 64–85. Springer (2017). https://doi.org/10.1007/978-3-319-63390-9_4, `https://doi.org/10.1007/978-3-319-63390-9_4`

6. Claessen, K.: Finger trees explained anew, and slightly simplified (functional pearl). In: Schrijvers, T. (ed.) Proceedings of the 13th ACM SIGPLAN International Symposium on Haskell, Haskell@ICFP 2020, Virtual Event, USA, August 7, 2020. pp. 31–38. ACM (2020). https://doi.org/10.1145/3406088.3409026, https://doi.org/10.1145/3406088.3409026

7. Cutler, J.W., Licata, D.R., Danner, N.: Denotational recurrence extraction for amortized analysis. Proc. ACM Program. Lang. **4**(ICFP), 97:1–97:29 (2020). https://doi.org/10.1145/3408979, https://doi.org/10.1145/3408979

8. Danielsson, N.A.: Lightweight semiformal time complexity analysis for purely functional data structures. In: Necula, G.C., Wadler, P. (eds.) Proceedings of the 35th ACM SIGPLAN-SIGACT Symposium on Principles of Programming Languages, POPL 2008, San Francisco, California, USA, January 7-12, 2008. pp. 133–144. ACM (2008). https://doi.org/10.1145/1328438.1328457, https://doi.org/10.1145/1328438.1328457

9. Danner, N., Licata, D.R.: Denotational semantics as a foundation for cost recurrence extraction for functional languages. J. Funct. Program. **32**, e8 (2022). https://doi.org/10.1017/S095679682200003X, https://doi.org/10.1017/S095679682200003X

10. Danner, N., Licata, D.R., Ramyaa: Denotational cost semantics for functional languages with inductive types. In: Fisher, K., Reppy, J.H. (eds.) Proceedings of the 20th ACM SIGPLAN International Conference on Functional Programming, ICFP 2015, Vancouver, BC, Canada, September 1-3, 2015. pp. 140–151. ACM (2015). https://doi.org/10.1145/2784731.2784749, https://doi.org/10.1145/2784731.2784749

11. Danner, N., Paykin, J., Royer, J.S.: A static cost analysis for a higher-order language. In: Might, M., Horn, D.V., Abel, A., Sheard, T. (eds.) Proceedings of the 7th Workshop on Programming languages meets program verification, PLPV 2013, Rome, Italy, January 22, 2013. pp. 25–34. ACM (2013). https://doi.org/10.1145/2428116.2428123, https://doi.org/10.1145/2428116.2428123

12. Grodin, H., Niu, Y., Sterling, J., Harper, R.: Decalf: A directed, effectful cost-aware logical framework. Proc. ACM Program. Lang. **8**(POPL), 273–301 (2024). https://doi.org/10.1145/3632852, https://doi.org/10.1145/3632852

13. Guéneau, A., Charguéraud, A., Pottier, F.: A fistful of dollars: Formalizing asymptotic complexity claims via deductive program verification. In: Ahmed, A. (ed.) Programming Languages and Systems - 27th European Symposium on Programming, ESOP 2018, Held as Part of the European Joint Conferences on Theory and Practice of Software, ETAPS 2018, Thessaloniki, Greece, April 14-20, 2018, Proceedings. Lecture Notes in Computer Science, vol. 10801, pp. 533–560. Springer (2018). https://doi.org/10.1007/978-3-319-89884-1_19, https://doi.org/10.1007/978-3-319-89884-1_19

14. Hackett, J., Hutton, G.: Call-by-need is clairvoyant call-by-value. Proc. ACM Program. Lang. **3**(ICFP), 114:1–114:23 (2019). https://doi.org/10.1145/3341718, https://doi.org/10.1145/3341718

15. Handley, M.A.T., Vazou, N., Hutton, G.: Liquidate your assets: reasoning about resource usage in liquid haskell. Proc. ACM Program. Lang. **4**(POPL), 24:1–24:27 (2020). https://doi.org/10.1145/3371092, https://doi.org/10.1145/3371092

16. Hoffmann, J., Aehlig, K., Hofmann, M.: Resource aware ML. In: Madhusudan, P., Seshia, S.A. (eds.) Computer Aided Verification - 24th International Conference, CAV 2012, Berkeley, CA, USA, July 7-13, 2012

Proceedings. Lecture Notes in Computer Science, vol. 7358, pp. 781–786. Springer (2012). https://doi.org/10.1007/978-3-642-31424-7_64, https://doi.org/10.1007/978-3-642-31424-7_64

17. Hoffmann, J., Das, A., Weng, S.: Towards automatic resource bound analysis for ocaml. In: Castagna, G., Gordon, A.D. (eds.) Proceedings of the 44th ACM SIGPLAN Symposium on Principles of Programming Languages, POPL 2017, Paris, France, January 18-20, 2017. pp. 359–373. ACM (2017). https://doi.org/10.1145/3009837.3009842, https://doi.org/10.1145/3009837.3009842

18. Hoffmann, J., Hofmann, M.: Amortized resource analysis with polynomial potential. In: Gordon, A.D. (ed.) Programming Languages and Systems, 19th European Symposium on Programming, ESOP 2010, Held as Part of the Joint European Conferences on Theory and Practice of Software, ETAPS 2010, Paphos, Cyprus, March 20-28, 2010. Proceedings. Lecture Notes in Computer Science, vol. 6012, pp. 287–306. Springer (2010). https://doi.org/10.1007/978-3-642-11957-6_16, https://doi.org/10.1007/978-3-642-11957-6_16

19. Hofmann, M., Jost, S.: Static prediction of heap space usage for first-order functional programs. In: Aiken, A., Morrisett, G. (eds.) Conference Record of POPL 2003: The 30th SIGPLAN-SIGACT Symposium on Principles of Programming Languages, New Orleans, Louisisana, USA, January 15-17, 2003. pp. 185–197. ACM (2003). https://doi.org/10.1145/604131.604148, https://doi.org/10.1145/604131.604148

20. Hughes, J.: Why functional programming matters. Comput. J. **32**(2), 98–107 (1989). https://doi.org/10.1093/COMJNL/32.2.98, https://doi.org/10.1093/comjnl/32.2.98

21. Jost, S., Hammond, K., Loidl, H., Hofmann, M.: Static determination of quantitative resource usage for higher-order programs. In: Hermenegildo, M.V., Palsberg, J. (eds.) Proceedings of the 37th ACM SIGPLAN-SIGACT Symposium on Principles of Programming Languages, POPL 2010, Madrid, Spain, January 17-23, 2010. pp. 223–236. ACM (2010). https://doi.org/10.1145/1706299.1706327, https://doi.org/10.1145/1706299.1706327

22. Jost, S., Vasconcelos, P.B., Florido, M., Hammond, K.: Type-based cost analysis for lazy functional languages. J. Autom. Reason. **59**(1), 87–120 (2017). https://doi.org/10.1007/S10817-016-9398-9, https://doi.org/10.1007/s10817-016-9398-9

23. Kavvos, G.A., Morehouse, E., Licata, D.R., Danner, N.: Recurrence extraction for functional programs through call-by-push-value. Proc. ACM Program. Lang. **4**(POPL), 15:1–15:31 (2020). https://doi.org/10.1145/3371083, https://doi.org/10.1145/3371083

24. Launchbury, J.: A natural semantics for lazy evaluation. In: Deusen, M.S.V., Lang, B. (eds.) Conference Record of the Twentieth Annual ACM SIGPLAN-SIGACT Symposium on Principles of Programming Languages, Charleston, South Carolina, USA, January 1993. pp. 144–154. ACM Press (1993). https://doi.org/10.1145/158511.158618, https://doi.org/10.1145/158511.158618

25. Levy, P.B.: Call-By-Push-Value: A Functional/Imperative Synthesis, Semantics Structures in Computation, vol. 2. Springer (2004)

26. Li, Y., Xia, L., Weirich, S.: Reasoning about the garden of forking paths. Proc. ACM Program. Lang. **5**(ICFP), 1–28 (2021). https://doi.org/10.1145/3473585, https://doi.org/10.1145/3473585

27. Coq development team: The Coq proof assistant (Sep 2024). https://doi.org/10.5281/zenodo.14542673, https://doi.org/10.5281/zenodo.14542673
28. McCarthy, J.A., Fetscher, B., New, M.S., Feltey, D., Findler, R.B.: A coq library for internal verification of running-times. Sci. Comput. Program. **164**, 49–65 (2018). https://doi.org/10.1016/J.SCICO.2017.05.001, https://doi.org/10.1016/j.scico.2017.05.001
29. Mével, G., Jourdan, J., Pottier, F.: Time credits and time receipts in Iris. In: Caires, L. (ed.) Programming Languages and Systems - 28th European Symposium on Programming, ESOP 2019, Held as Part of the European Joint Conferences on Theory and Practice of Software, ETAPS 2019, Prague, Czech Republic, April 6-11, 2019, Proceedings. Lecture Notes in Computer Science, vol. 11423, pp. 3–29. Springer (2019). https://doi.org/10.1007/978-3-030-17184-1_1, https://doi.org/10.1007/978-3-030-17184-1_1
30. Moreira, S., Vasconcelos, P.B., Florido, M.: Resource analysis for lazy evaluation with polynomial potential. In: Chitil, O. (ed.) IFL 2020: 32nd Symposium on Implementation and Application of Functional Languages, Virtual Event / Canterbury, UK, September 2-4, 2020. pp. 104–114. ACM (2020). https://doi.org/10.1145/3462172.3462196, https://doi.org/10.1145/3462172.3462196
31. Niu, Y., Harper, R.: A metalanguage for cost-aware denotational semantics. In: 38th Annual ACM/IEEE Symposium on Logic in Computer Science, LICS 2023, Boston, MA, USA, June 26-29, 2023. pp. 1–14. IEEE (2023). https://doi.org/10.1109/LICS56636.2023.10175777, https://doi.org/10.1109/LICS56636.2023.10175777
32. Niu, Y., Sterling, J., Grodin, H., Harper, R.: A cost-aware logical framework. Proc. ACM Program. Lang. **6**(POPL), 1–31 (2022). https://doi.org/10.1145/3498670, https://doi.org/10.1145/3498670
33. O'Hearn, P.W.: Incorrectness logic. Proc. ACM Program. Lang. **4**(POPL), 10:1–10:32 (2020). https://doi.org/10.1145/3371078, https://doi.org/10.1145/3371078
34. Okasaki, C.: Purely functional data structures. Cambridge University Press (1999)
35. Pottier, F., Guéneau, A., Jourdan, J.H., Mével, G.: Thunks and debits in separation logic with time credits. Proc. ACM Program. Lang. **8**(POPL) (2024), https://hal.science/hal-04238691/file/main.pdf
36. Rajani, V., Gaboardi, M., Garg, D., Hoffmann, J.: A unifying type-theory for higher-order (amortized) cost analysis. Proc. ACM Program. Lang. **5**(POPL), 1–28 (2021). https://doi.org/10.1145/3434308, https://doi.org/10.1145/3434308
37. Sands, D.: Complexity analysis for a lazy higher-order language. In: Jones, N.D. (ed.) ESOP'90, 3rd European Symposium on Programming, Copenhagen, Denmark, May 15-18, 1990, Proceedings. Lecture Notes in Computer Science, vol. 432, pp. 361–376. Springer (1990). https://doi.org/10.1007/3-540-52592-0_74, https://doi.org/10.1007/3-540-52592-0_74
38. Spector-Zabusky, A., Breitner, J., Rizkallah, C., Weirich, S.: Total Haskell is reasonable Coq. In: Andronick, J., Felty, A.P. (eds.) Proceedings of the 7th ACM SIGPLAN International Conference on Certified Programs and Proofs, CPP 2018, Los Angeles, CA, USA, January 8-9, 2018. pp. 14–27. ACM (2018). https://doi.org/10.1145/3167092, https://doi.org/10.1145/3167092
39. Spies, S., Gäher, L., Tassarotti, J., Jung, R., Krebbers, R., Birkedal, L., Dreyer, D.: Later credits: resourceful reasoning for the later modality. Proc. ACM Program. Lang. **6**(ICFP), 283–311 (2022). https://doi.org/10.1145/3547631, https://doi.org/10.1145/3547631

40. Vazou, N.: Liquid Haskell: Haskell as a Theorem Prover. Ph.D. thesis, University of California, San Diego, USA (2016), http://www.escholarship.org/uc/item/8dm057ws
41. Wang, P., Wang, D., Chlipala, A.: Timl: a functional language for practical complexity analysis with invariants. Proc. ACM Program. Lang. **1**(OOPSLA), 79:1–79:26 (2017). https://doi.org/10.1145/3133903, https://doi.org/10.1145/3133903
42. Xia, L., Israel, L., Kramarz, M., Coltharp, N., Claessen, K., Weirich, S., Li, Y.: Story of your lazy function's life: A bidirectional demand semantics for mechanized cost analysis of lazy programs. Proc. ACM Program. Lang. **8**(ICFP), 30–63 (2024). https://doi.org/10.1145/3674626, https://doi.org/10.1145/3674626

Author Index

A
Adão, Pedro 283
Ambal, Guillaume 42
Ângelo, Pedro 13

B
Baillon, Martin 72
Balik, Patrycja 104
Balzer, Stephanie 135
Batz, Kevin 314
Bouverot-Dupuis, Mathis 166

C
Congard, Sidney 190

D
Derakhshan, Farzaneh 135
Derrick, John 220
Dongol, Brijesh 42
Douence, Rémi 190

E
Edmonds, Chelsea 220
Enea, Constantin 252

F
Forster, Yannick 166
Frett, Sean 432

G
Gaboardi, Marco 401
Gallus, Adrian 314
Gangamreddypalli, Namratha 252
Gonçalves, Rafael 283

H
Haase, Darion 314
Harper, Robert 135

I
Igarashi, Atsushi 13

J
Jędras, Szymon 104
Jin, Ziyue 344
Johnsen, Einar Broch 1

K
Kamburjan, Eduard 1
Kaminski, Benjamin Lucien 314
Karniel, Amir 373
Katoen, Joost-Pieter 314
Klinkenberg, Lutz 314
Kura, Satoshi 401

L
Lahav, Ori 373
Li, Liyi 432
Li, Xing 463
Li, Yao 463

M
Mahboubi, Assia 72
Munch-Maccagnoni, Guillaume 190
Murase, Yuito 13

P
Pédrot, Pierre-Marie 72
Pferscher, Andrea 1
Polesiuk, Piotr 104
Popescu, Andrei 220
Potanin, Alex 432

Q
Qadeer, Shaz 252

R
Raad, Azalea 42
Ramos, Frederico 283
Rizkallah, Christine 463

S
Santos, José Fragoso 283
Schachte, Peter 463

Sekiyama, Taro   401
Sharma, Anshu   432
Stupple, Max   42

T
Tagba, Zoukarneini Difaizi   432
Tapia Tarifa, Silvia Lizeth   1

U
Unno, Hiroshi   401

V
Vasconcelos, Vasco T.   13

W
Wang, Di   344
Winkler, Tobias   314
Wright, Jamie   220

Y
Yao, Yue   135

GPSR Compliance
The European Union's (EU) General Product Safety Regulation (GPSR) is a set
of rules that requires consumer products to be safe and our obligations to
ensure this.

If you have any concerns about our products, you can contact us on

ProductSafety@springernature.com

In case Publisher is established outside the EU, the EU authorized
representative is:

Springer Nature Customer Service Center GmbH
Europaplatz 3
69115 Heidelberg, Germany